8TH EDITION

CRIMINAL BEHAVIOR

A PSYCHOSOCIAL APPROACH

Curt R. Bartol
Anne M. Bartol

PEARSON
Prentice
Hall

Upper Saddle River, New Jersey 07458

Library of Congress Cataloging-in-Publication Data

Bartol, Curt R.
  Criminal behavior : a psychosocial approach / Curt R. Bartol, Anne M. Bartol. — 8th ed.
    p. cm.
  ISBN 0-13-239421-9
  1. Criminal psychology. 2. Criminal behavior—United States. I. Bartol, Anne M. II. Title.
  HV6080.B37 2008
  364.3—dc22

                                                                                    2006101649

Editor-in-Chief: Vernon R. Anthony
Senior Acquisitions Editor: Tim Peyton
Assistant Editor: Mayda Bosco
Editorial Assistant: Jillian Allison
Marketing Manager: Adam Kloza
Production Editor: Patty Donovan,
  Pine Tree Composition
Production Liaison: Barbara Marttine Cappuccio
Managing Editor: Mary Carnis

Manufacturing Manager: Ilene Sanford
Manufacturing Buyer: Cathleen Petersen
Senior Design Coordinator: Miguel Ortiz
Cover Design: Rob Aleman
Cover Image: Paul Anderson, Images.Com/
  Stock-Illustration Source
Formatting and Interior Design: Laserwords Pvt. Ltd
Printer/Binder: Courier Companies

Pearson Education, Ltd., *London*
Pearson Education Australia Pty. Limited, *Sydney*
Pearson Education Singapore, Pte. Ltd.
Pearson Education North Asia Ltd., *Hong Kong*
Pearson Education Canada, Ltd., *Toronto*
Pearson Education de Mexico, S.A. de C.V.
Pearson Education—Japan, *Tokyo*
Pearson Education Malaysia, Pte. Ltd.
Pearson Education, Upper Saddle River, *New Jersey*

10 9 8 7 6 5 4 3 2
ISBN 0-13-239421-9

To Kai, Madeleine, Darya, and Shannon
. . . . the four little ones who have enriched our lives and captured our hearts

CONTENTS

PREFACE   xxi

CHAPTER 1

INTRODUCTION TO CRIMINAL BEHAVIOR   1

Perspectives of Human Nature in Theories of Crime   3

Perspectives in Criminology   5

   Sociological Criminology   5

   Psychological Criminology   6

   Psychiatric Criminology   8

   Psychoanalytic Tradition   9

Defining and Measuring Crime   10

   Uniform Crime Reporting System   11

   UCR Problems   15

   The National Incident-Based Reporting System   16

   Hate Crimes   18

   Self-Report Studies   20

   Drug Abuse Self-Report Surveys   22

   Victimization Surveys   23

Juvenile Delinquency   26

   Legal Definitions of Delinquency   26

   Child Delinquents   27

   Social Definitions of Delinquency   27

   Psychological Definitions   28

The Nature and Extent of Juvenile Offending   28

   Status Offenses   29

   The Serious Delinquent   31

Recap: Defining Crime and Delinquency   33

Key Concepts   35

Review Questions   36

Chapter 2

Developmental Risk Factors   37

Social Risk Factors   38
 Poverty   38
 Peer Rejection and Association with Antisocial Peers   40
 Preschool Experiences   43
 After-School Care   44
 School Failure   45
Parental and Family Risk Factors   45
 Single-Parent Households   45
 Parental Styles and Practices   46
 Parental Monitoring   49
 Influence of Siblings   50
 Parental Psychopathology   50
Psychological Risk Factors   51
 Cognitive and Language Deficiencies   51
 Intelligence and Delinquency   51
 Attention Deficit Hyperactivity Disorder (ADHD)   55
 ADHD and Criminal Behavior   56
 Conduct Disorder   57
Gender Differences in the Development of Delinquency   59
Developmental Theories of Delinquency   60
 Moffitt's Developmental Theory   61
 Coercion Developmental Theory   66
 Other Developmental Theories   68
Summary and Conclusions   68
Key Concepts   71
Review Questions   72

Chapter 3

Origins of Criminal Behavior: Biological Factors   73

Genetics and Antisocial Behavior   74
 Twin Studies   75
 Twin Studies and Criminal Behavior: Recent Research   78
 Adoption Studies   80
Psychophysiological Factors   82

Temperament   83
  Three Things That Define Temperament   84
Environmental Risk Factors   85
  Birth Complications   86
  Nicotine, Alcohol, and Drug Exposure   86
  Brain Development   87
  Neuropsychological Factors   88
Physique and Crime   89
  Body Shape and Crime   91
  Attractiveness   92
  Minor Physical Anomalies   94
  MPAs and Crime   95
Eysenck's Theory of Personality and Crime   96
  Measurement of Eysenck's Theory   97
  Extraversion   98
  Physiological Bases of Extraversion-Introversion   99
  Neuroticism   101
  Neurophysiological Bases of Neuroticism-Stability   102
  Psychoticism   104
  Crime and Conditionability   105
  The Evidence for Eysenck's Theory   108
Summary and Conclusions   110
Key Concepts   112
Review Questions   113

CHAPTER 4

ORIGINS OF CRIMINAL BEHAVIOR: LEARNING AND SITUATIONAL FACTORS   114

Behaviorism   116
  Skinner's Theory of Behavior   116
Social Learning   121
  Expectancy Theory   123
  Imitational Aspects of Social Learning   123
  Differential Association-Reinforcement Theory   125
Frustration-Induced Criminality   128
  The Socialized and Individual Offender   128
  Frustration-Induced Riots   129
  Frustration and Crime   130

Situational Instigators and Regulators of Criminal Behavior   130
  Authority as an Instigator of Criminal Behavior   131
  Deindividuation   134
  Moral Disengagement   137
Summary and Conclusions   138
Key Concepts   140
Review Questions   140

CHAPTER 5

HUMAN AGGRESSION AND VIOLENCE   141

Defining Aggression   143
  Hostile and Instrumental Aggression   144
  Interpretation by Victim   145
Theoretical Perspectives on Aggression   146
  Psychoanalytical/Psychodynamic Viewpoint   146
  Ethological Viewpoints   147
  Frustration-Aggression Hypothesis   149
  Cognitive-Neoassociation Model   151
  Excitation Transfer Theory   152
  Displaced Aggression Theory   152
  Aggressive Driving and Road Rage   153
Social Learning Factors in Aggression and Violence   155
  Modeling   156
  Types of Models   156
  Observation Modeling   157
Cognitive Models of Aggression   158
  Cognitive Scripts Model   159
  Hostile Attribution Bias   159
  Aggressive Behavior: Simple and Easy to Use   161
Overt and Covert Acts of Aggression   162
  Reactive and Proactive Forms of Aggression   164
  Gender Differences in Aggression   165
Environmental Factors   166
  Population Density   166
  Aggression and Ambient Temperature   168
Effects of Media Violence   171
  Contagion Effect   174

The Biology of Aggression   175
    Hormones and Neurotransmitters   176
    Biological Control through Surgery and Drugs   177
Brain Centers and Violence Control   179
    Heredity and the XYY Chromosome   181
    Epilepsy and Violence   183
Summary and Conclusions   183
Key Concepts   185
Review Questions   185

CHAPTER 6
CRIMINAL PSYCHOPATHY   187

    What Is a Psychopath?   188
    An Example of a Psychopath   189
Behavioral Descriptions   190
    Charming and Verbally Fluent   191
    Psychological Testing Differences   192
    Psychopaths are not Mentally Disordered by Traditional Standards   192
    Other Principal Traits   192
The Criminal Psychopath   195
    Prevalence of Criminal Psychopathy   195
    Offending Patterns of Criminal Psychopaths   195
Psychological Measures of Psychopathy   197
    Core Factors of Psychopathy   198
    Recidivism   200
The Female Psychopath   201
Racial/Ethnic Differences   202
Juvenile Psychopathy   203
    Can Juvenile Psychopathy be Identified?   203
    Ethical Considerations   204
    Psychopathic Traits in Juvenile Delinquents   205
    Measures of Juvenile Psychopathy   206
Biological Factors and Psychopathy   206
    Genetic Factors   207
    Neurophysiology and Psychopathy   207
    Central Nervous System Differences   208
    Hemisphere Asymmetry and Deficiency   208

Frontal Neuropsychological Studies   210

Amygdala Dysfunction   211

Stimulation Seeking   212

Optimal Arousal of the Cerebral Cortex   213

Peripheral Nervous System (PNS) Research   216

Autonomic Nervous System Research   217

Childhood of the Psychopath   221

Summary and Conclusions   223

Key Concepts   225

Review Questions   225

CHAPTER 7

CRIME AND MENTAL DISORDERS   226

Defining Mental Illness   228

The DSM-IV   229

Schizophrenic Disorders   231

Delusional Disorders   232

Depressive Disorders   233

Postpartum Depression   233

Antisocial Personality Disorder (APD)   234

Competency and Criminal Responsibility   237

Incompetency to Stand Trial   237

Criminal Responsibility   240

Insanity Standards   243

The M'Naghten Rule   244

The Brawner Rule and the American Law Institute (ALI) Rule   245

The Durham Rule: The Product Test   245

The Insanity Defense Reform Act   246

Guilty but Mentally Ill (GBMI)   247

Unique Defenses   248

Posttraumatic Stress Disorder   248

Pathological Gamblers' Syndrome   251

Dissociative Identity Disorder   252

Amnesia   255

Summary and Conclusions   256

Key Concepts   257

Review Questions   258

CHAPTER 8

MENTAL DISORDERS AND CRIME: DEFENDANTS AND OFFENDERS   259

Mental Disorders and Violence   260
   The MacArthur Research Network   262
   Police and the Mentally Disordered   263
Mentally Disordered Inmates   264
   How Many Prison and Jail Inmates or Probationers Are Mentally Disordered?   264
   What Precisely are the Diagnoses of Mentally Disordered Inmates?   266
Dangerousness and the Assessment of Risk   267
   Risk Assessment   268
   The Tarasoff Case   269
   What Are the Best Predictors of Dangerous Behavior?   273
   Current Risk Assessment Measures   274
The (Non)Mentally Disordered Sex Offender   276
Summary and Conclusions   278
Key Concepts   279
Review Questions   280

CHAPTER 9

HOMICIDE, ASSAULT, AND FAMILY VIOLENCE   281

Definitions   284
   Criminal Homicide   284
   Aggravated Assault   286
Demographics of Homicide   286
   Race/Ethnic Origin   286
   Gender Differences   289
   Age   289
   Socioeconomic Class   290
   Victim-Offender Relationship   290
Weapons Used in Violence   293
   Juvenile Weapon Possession   294
   Weapons and Violence   295
Other Factors   295
   Temporal Factors   295
   Victim Precipitation   296
   Sniper Attacks   296

Demographics of Assault   298
Juvenile Murder   299
    Demographics and Psychological Characteristics of Juvenile Murderers   300
Family Violence   300
    Definitions   301
    Prevalence   301
    Ethnic/Minority Differences   301
    Victims   302
    Brief History of the Modern Era of Family Violence   303
    Incidence, Prevalence, and Demographics of Child Abuse and Neglect   305
    Missing, Abducted, Runaway, and Thrownaway Children   307
    Munchausen Syndrome by Proxy   308
    Shaken Baby Syndrome   309
    Infanticide, Neonaticide, and Filicide   309
    Intimate Partner Abuse: Prevalence, Incidence, and Nature   313
    Same-Sex Domestic Violence   314
    Psychological and Demographic Characteristics of Abusers   314
    Elderly Abuse: Prevalence, Incidence, and Nature   317
    Sibling-to-Sibling Violence   319
    Child-to-Parent Violence   320
    Multiassaultive Families   321
    The Cycle of Violence   321
    The Effects of Family Violence on Children   322
The Nature and Theory of Family Violence   324
    Cessation of Family Violence   326
Summary and Conclusions   328
Key Concepts   329
Review Questions   329

CHAPTER 10

MULTIPLE MURDER   330

Investigative Psychology   331
    Crime Scene Investigative Methods   331
Profiling   334
    Criminal Profiling   336
    Geographical Profiling   339
    The Psychological Autopsy   340
    Racial Profiling   340

Multiple Murderers   342
  Definitions   343
Serial Murderers   344
  Female Serial Killers   345
  The Victimological Perspective in Understanding Serial Killers   346
  Geographical Location of Serial Killing   347
  Ethnic and Racial Characteristics   348
  Juvenile Serial Murderers   348
  Typologies of Serial Murderers   349
Mass Murderers   350
  Classic Mass Murder   350
Product Tampering   351
School Violence   352
  School Shootings   353
Workplace Violence   355
  What Is Workplace Violence?   355
  Examples of Workplace Violence   356
  Who Commits Workplace Violence?   358
Summary and Conclusions   360
Key Concepts   362
Review Questions   362

CHAPTER 11

TERRORISM AND THE PSYCHOLOGY OF VIOLENCE   363

Definitions   364
  Additional Examples   365
  Classification of Terrorism Groups   365
A Terrorist Typology   367
The Psychosocial Context of Terrorism   368
Motives and Justifications   369
Additional Disengagement Practices   370
Psychological Nature of Terrorism   371
Psychological Factors in General Violent Crime   372
  Impulsivity   372
  Overcontrolled and Undercontrolled Offenders   374
  Cognitive Self-Regulation   376
Deindividuation and Crowd Violence   380
Summary and Conclusions   383
Key Concepts   387
Review Questions   387

CHAPTER 12

SEXUAL ASSAULT   388

Who Offends?   389

Legislation on Sex Offenders   390

Rape: Definitions and Statistics   392

　Date Rape   393

　Classification of Rape Offenses   394

　Incidence and Prevalence of Rape   395

Impact on Victims   397

　Psychological Effects on Victims   397

　Situational and Victimization Characteristics   398

Rape Offender Characteristics   399

　Age   400

　Offending History   400

　Demographics   401

　Assumptions about Why Men Rape   401

　Deniers and Admitters   403

　Self-Reported Reasons for Sexual Assault   404

Classification of Rape Patterns   405

　Massachusetts Treatment Center Classification System   405

　The MTC:R3   408

　The Groth Typology   411

Etiology or Causes of Rape   412

　Attitudes toward Rape   413

　Rape Myths   415

Sexual Assault and Pornography   415

Summary and Conclusion   418

Key Concepts   419

Review Questions   419

CHAPTER 13

SEXUAL ASSAULT OF CHILDREN AND YOUTH AND OTHER SEXUAL OFFENSES   421

Incidence and Prevalence of Pedophilia   423

Situational and Victimization Characteristics   424

　Types of Sexual Contact   425

　Psychological Effects of Child Sexual Victimization   426

Offender Characteristics   *426*
Gender of the Offender   *427*
Age   *427*
Attitudes Toward Victims   *428*
Cognitive Functions   *428*
Occupational and Socioeconomic Status   *429*
Interpersonal and Social Skills   *429*
Classification of Child Offender Patterns   430
The MTC:CM3   *432*
The Groth Classification Model   *434*
Juvenile Sex Offenders   435
Female Juvenile Sex Offenders   *436*
Recidivism of Pedophiles   437
Recidivism of Juvenile Sex Offenders   *438*
Theories on Potential Causes   438
Exhibitionism   440
Situational Characteristics   *441*
Offender Characteristics   *442*
Voyeurism and Fetishism   444
Summary and Conclusions   446
Key Concepts   448
Review Questions   448

CHAPTER 14

PROPERTY AND PUBLIC ORDER CRIME   449

Burglary   452
Characteristics of Burglary   *452*
Who Commits Burglary?   *453*
Burglary Cues and Selected Targets   *454*
Burglar Cognitive Processes   *455*
How Far Do Burglars Travel?   *457*
Do They Usually Work Alone?   *457*
Gender Differences in Methods and Patterns   *457*
Use of Alcohol and Other Substances   *458*
What Happens to the Merchandise?   *458*
Motives   *459*
Psychological Impact of Burglary   *460*

Larceny and Motor Vehicle Theft   461
  Motor Vehicle Theft   461
  Carjacking   463
Fraud and Identity Theft   464
Shoplifting   465
  Who Shoplifts?   466
  Motives   468
  Methods of Shoplifting   468
  Types of Shoplifters   469
  Kleptomania: Fact or Fiction?   470
White-Collar and Occupational Crime   471
  Green's Four Categories of Occupational Crime   472
  The Prevalence and Incidence of Occupational Crime   474
  Corporate Crime   475
  Justifications and Neutralizations   476
  Individual Occupational Crime   477
Prostitution   479
  Motives   482
  Sex Trafficking   484
Summary and Conclusions   485
Key Concepts   487
Review Questions   487

Chapter 15

Violent Economic Crime and Crimes of Intimidation   488

Robbery   488
  Bank Robbery   490
  Commercial Robbery   491
  Street Robbery   492
  Professional Robbers   492
  Motives and Cultural Influences   493
Cybercrime   495
Stalking   497
  Categories of Stalking   498
  Cyberstalking   499
Hostage-Taking Offenses   500
  Instrumental and Expressive Hostage Taking   501
  FBI Categories of Hostage Taking   501

Strategies for Dealing with Hostage Takers   *502*

The Stockholm Syndrome   *503*

Some Rules to Follow If Taken Hostage   *504*

Arson   506

Incidence and Prevalence   *506*

Developmental Stages of Firesetting   *507*

Persistent and Repetitive Firesetting   *509*

Motives of Arsonists   *509*

Juvenile Motives   *511*

Female Arsonists   *511*

Pyromania   *512*

Bombings   513

Motives   *514*

Summary and Conclusions   517

Key Concepts   519

Review Questions   519

CHAPTER 16

SUBSTANCE ABUSE, ALCOHOL, AND CRIME   521

Juvenile Drug Use   522

Extent of Juvenile Drug Use   *523*

Who Is Selling to Juveniles?   *524*

Gender Differences in Juvenile Drug Use   *525*

Six Consistent Research Findings on Illict Drug Abuse   526

The Tripartite Conceptual Model   *530*

Major Categories of Drugs   531

Tolerance and Dependence   *532*

The Hallucinogens   534

How Is Marijuana Prepared?   *535*

Cannabis and Crime   *537*

Summary   *538*

Phencyclidine (PCP)   *539*

PCP and Crime   *540*

The Stimulants   540

Amphetamines   *540*

Methamphetamine   *540*

Cocaine and Its Derivatives   *542*

Psychological Effects   *544*

Adverse Physical Effects   545

Stimulants, Cocaine, and Crime   545

Crack Cocaine   546

Crack and Crime   548

Ecstasy (MDMA)   548

Stimulants and Crime   549

Narcotic Drugs   550

Heroin   550

Heroin and Crime   553

Fentanyl   554

Other Narcotic Drugs   554

OxyContin   554

OxyContin and Crime   555

The Club Drugs: Sedative Hypnotic Compounds   555

Ketamine   556

Gamma Hydroxbutyrate (GHB)   556

Rohypnol   558

Alcohol   559

Psychological Effects   560

Alcohol, Crime, and Delinquency   561

Does Substance or Alcohol Abuse Lead Directly to Violence?   563

Inhalants   564

Summary and Conclusions   564

Key Concepts   567

Review Questions   567

Chapter 17

Prevention, Intervention, and Treatment: Juvenile Offenders   568

Treatment and Rehabilitation Strategies   569

Characteristics of Successful Programs   569

They Begin Early   570

They Follow Developmental Principles   570

They Focus on Multiple Settings and Systems   571

They Acknowledge and Respect Cultural Backgrounds   572

They Focus on the Family First   572

A Brief History of Juvenile Justice   573

Juvenile Courts   576

Classification of Prevention and Intervention Programs   578

Primary Prevention   580
   The Enhancement and Development of Resilience   *581*
Selective Prevention   582
   The Fast-Track Experiment   *583*
Treatment Approaches   585
   Traditional Residential Treatment   *587*
   Treatment of Juvenile Sex Offenders   *587*
   Children and Adolescents with Psychopathic Features   *589*
   Treatment of Juveniles Who Kill   *591*
   Nontraditional Residential Treatment   *592*
   Community Treatment: MST with Serious Offenders   *595*
Summary and Conclusions   597
Key Concepts   599
Review Questions   600

CHAPTER 18

CORRECTIONAL PSYCHOLOGY   601

Careers in Correctional Psychology   603
The Correctional System   605
Societal Rationale for Punishment of Offenders   608
Classification and Prediction   610
   Classification Systems   *612*
Psychological Effects of Imprisonment   613
   Psychological Effects of Crowding   *615*
   Psychological Effects of Isolation   *616*
Treatment Strategies   618
   Psychotherapy   *619*
   Treatment of Psychopaths   *624*
   Treatment of Sex Offenders   *625*
Summary and Conclusions   629
Key Concepts   631
Review Questions   631

GLOSSARY   633
CASES CITED   655
REFERENCES   657
AUTHOR INDEX   731
SUBJECT INDEX   749

PREFACE

........................➤

Criminal Behavior: A Psychosocial Approach is a textbook about crime from a psychological perspective. More specifically, this text portrays the criminal offender as embedded in and continually influenced by multiple systems within the psychosocial environment. One focus of this book is that meaningful theory, well-executed research, and skillful application of knowledge to the "crime problem" require an understanding of the many levels of events that influence a person's life course—from the individual to the individual's family, peers, schools, neighborhoods, community, culture, and society as a whole. Like earlier editions, the eighth edition views the criminal offender as existing on a continuum, ranging from the occasional offender who offends at some point during the life course, usually during adolescence, to the serious, repetitive offender who begins his or her criminal career at a very early age. The book reviews the contemporary research, theory, and practice concerning the psychology of crime as comprehensively and accurately as possible. The behavioral, emotional, and cognitive aspects of crime are examined, usually from the perspective of the offender but sometimes the victim as well. *Criminal Behavior* also reviews current research that focuses on the cognitive aspects of criminal offenders, delving into their perceptions, reasoning, beliefs, decision making, and attitudes. The causes, classification, prediction, prevention, intervention, and treatment of delinquency and criminal behavior are also examined.

Many changes were made to reflect rapidly expanding research and theory on the psychology of crime. In recent years, there has been a discernible shift toward a more developmental approach to the understanding, prevention, and treatment of delinquent and criminal behavior. We have made a concerted effort to incorporate this cutting-edge research literature on the development of crime into the text material. We have greatly expanded material on juvenile delinquency and early antisocial behavioral development in young children and preadolescents. Chapter 2 illustrates this shift, and an entirely new chapter on the prevention, intervention, and treatment of the juvenile offender has also been added. Over three-hundred new and up-to-date research citations have been added for further reading and research.

We have made these and other changes with the student in mind. Chapter objectives are now included at the beginning of the chapters, and key concepts and review questions are listed at the end. Key concepts, which are bolded, have been significantly expanded, as has the glossary. Summaries for each chapter have been rewritten to aid review. Many new headings and subheadings have been added to help the reader organize the material. When helpful, summary tables and charts have been included. For illustrative purposes, psychological perspectives, principles, and examples have been linked more strongly to the specific crimes presented later in the book.

The organization and structure of the text has been changed from earlier editions in response to reviewers and students. Although the basic organization of the text continues to run from the broad, theoretical aspects of crime to specific offense categories, some chapters that focus on causes and risk factors now come earlier in the text than in previous editions. For example, the chapter on learning and situational factors has been moved from chapter 5 to chapter 4, and the chapter on human aggression and violence has been moved from chapter 7 to chapter 5. The chapter on the psychopath has been moved to chapter 6. In addition, several of the chapters (on mental disorders, homicide and family violence, sexual offenses, economic and property crime, and treatment) have been split into two chapters to improve readability and to allow a more logical flow of topics. The chapter on drugs and crime (chapter 16) was extensively updated to include ever-changing drug abuse and evolving survey research on that abuse, especially pertaining to juveniles and young adults.

Criminal Behavior is designed to be a core text in undergraduate and graduate courses in criminal behavior, criminology, the psychology of crime, crime and delinquency, and forensic psychology. The material contained in this book has been classroom-tested for over thirty years. The book continues to be heavily research based, although some technical and statistical aspects have been significantly reduced in this new edition. The book's major goal is to encourage an appreciation of the many complex issues surrounding criminal behavior and to avoid oversimplified, prejudicial, dogmatic conclusions about the "crime problem." If, after studying the text with an open mind, the reader puts it down seeking additional information, and if the reader has developed an avid interest in discovering better answers, then this text will have served its purpose well.

Like most books, this one was written with the encouragement, help, and support of various individuals. We know we can always count on the love, support, fun-loving spirit, and wacky humor of our children, Gina and Ian, their respective spouses, Jim and Soraya, and our grandchildren, Kai, Maddie, Darya, and Shannon, to whom this book is dedicated.

On the professional side, we are most grateful to the production staff at Prentice Hall, particularly Assistant Editor Mayda Bosco. Also at Prentice Hall thanks to Managing Editor Mary Carnis, manufacturing manager Ilene Sanford, and Production Liaison Barbara Cappuccio. Patty Donovan of Pine Tree Composition was efficient and responsive, both qualities that are deeply appreciated as authors arrive at the final stages of producing a book. Finally, we wish to thank the book's early reviewers, Professor Ted Sturman, George Washington University; Professor Arnold R. Waggoner, Rose State College; Professor Joseph Dwyer, Webster University; Professor Jay Carlin, Canyon College; and Professor Thomas J. Fagan, Nova Southeastern University. Their thoughtful comments are appreciated and their suggestions have helped us to produce a better book.

Curt R. Bartol
Anne M. Bartol

CHAPTER 1

INTRODUCTION TO CRIMINAL BEHAVIOR

CHAPTER OBJECTIVES

- Define criminal behavior and juvenile delinquency.
- Develop an understanding that such behavior has multiple causes, manifestations, and developmental pathways.
- Identify the different perspectives of human nature that underlie the theoretical development and research of criminal behavior.
- Emphasize that the study of criminal behavior and delinquency, from a psychological perspective, has shifted from a personality focus toward a more cognitive and developmental focus.
- Introduce the reader to the various measurements of criminal and delinquent behavior.

Crime is commonly defined as conduct or failure to act, in violation of the law forbidding or commanding it, and for which a range of possible penalties exist upon conviction. Criminal behavior, then, is behavior in violation of the criminal code. To be convicted of crime, a person must have acted intentionally and without justification or excuse. For example, even an intentional killing may be justified under certain circumstances, as in defense of one's life. Although there is a very narrow range of offenses that do not require criminal intent (called strict liability offenses), the vast majority of crime requires it. Obviously, this legal definition encompasses a great variety of acts, ranging from murder to petty offenses.

Crime intrigues people. Sometimes it attracts us, sometimes it repels us, occasionally it does both at once. It can amuse, as when we hear about capers and practical jokes that presumably do not harm anyone. It can frighten, if we believe that what happened to one victim might happen to us. Crime can also anger, as when a beloved community member is brutally killed, a child is subjected to heinous abuse, or individuals have been deprived of their life savings by fraudulent schemes.

While interest in crime has always been high, understanding why it occurs and what to do about it has always been a problem. Public officials, politicians, "experts," and many people in the general public continue to offer simple and incomplete solutions for obliterating crime: more police officers on the streets, closed-circuit television, street lights, sturdy locks, karate classes, stiff penalties, speedy imprisonment, or capital punishment. As in most areas of human behavior, there is no shortage of experts, but there are few effective solutions.

Our inability to prevent crime is partly because we have trouble understanding criminal behavior and identifying its many causes. Because crime is complex, explanations of crime require complicated, involved answers. Psychological research indicates that most people have limited tolerance for complexity and ambiguity. People apparently want simple, straightforward answers, no matter how complex the issue. Parents become impatient when psychologists answer questions about child rearing by saying, "It depends"—on the situation, on the parents' reactions to it, on any number of possible influences. This preference for simplicity helps to explain the popularity of do-it-yourself, 100-easy-ways-to-a-better-life books. Let it be said from the outset: This is not *Criminal Behavior for Dummies*.

This text presents criminal behavior as a vastly complex, poorly understood phenomenon. Readers looking for simple solutions will either have to reorient their thinking, set the text aside, or read it in dismay. There is no all-encompassing psychological explanation for crime, any more than there is a sociological, anthropological, psychiatric, economic, or historic one. In fact, it is unlikely that sociology, psychology, or any other discipline can formulate basic "truths" about crime without help from other disciplines and well-designed research. Criminology needs all the interdisciplinary help it can get to explain and control criminal behavior. An integration of the data, theories, and general viewpoints of each discipline is crucial. To review accurately and adequately the plethora of studies and theories from each relevant discipline is far beyond the scope of this text, however. Our focus is the *psychological perspective*, although other viewpoints are also described.

The primary aim of this text is to review and integrate recent scholarship and research in the psychology of crime, compare it with traditional approaches, and offer some strategies for the prevention and modification of criminal behavior. We cannot begin to accomplish this task without first calling attention to philosophical questions that underlie any study of human behavior.

PERSPECTIVES OF HUMAN NATURE IN THEORIES OF CRIME

All psychological theories of crime—and many sociological ones as well—have underlying assumptions about or perspectives on human nature. Three major ones can be identified. The **conformity perspective** views humans as creatures of conformity who want to do the "right" thing. To a large extent, this assumption represents the foundation of the humanistic perspectives in psychology. Human beings are basically "good" people trying to live to their fullest potential.

An excellent example of the conformity perspective in criminology is the **strain theory** of Robert K. Merton. Merton's strain theory argues that humans are fundamentally conforming beings who are strongly influenced by the values and attitudes of the society in which they live. In short, most members of a given society desire what the other members of the society desire. The "right" thing, therefore, is what a society or a group within a society says is the "right" thing. American society, according to strain theorists, advocates that the accumulation of wealth or status is all-important and represents the symbols that all members should strive for. Strain theorists contend that humans, being fundamentally conformists, readily buy into these notions. However, access and the means for reaching these well-advertised goals are not equally available to everyone. Some have the education, the social network, personal contacts, and family influence to attain these goals. The socially and economically disadvantaged, however, do not have the opportunities, the education, nor the necessary social network for attaining material wealth and economic or political power. Thus, the strain theory predicts that crime and delinquency occur when there is a perceived discrepancy between the materialistic values and goals cherished and held in high esteem by a society and the availability of the legitimate means for reaching these goals. Under these conditions, a strain between the goals of wealth and power and the means for reaching them develops. Groups and individuals experiencing a high level of this strain are forced to decide whether to violate norms and laws to attain some of this sought-after wealth or power, or give up on the American dream and go through the motions, withdraw, or rebel. In more recent years, strain theorists have emphasized that crimes of the rich and powerful also can be explained by strain theory. Even though these individuals have greater access to the legitimate means of reaching goals, they have a continuing need to accumulate even greater wealth and power and maintain their privileged status in society (Messner & Rosenfeld, 1994).

A second perspective—the **nonconformist perspective**—assumes that human beings are basically undisciplined creatures who, without the constraints of the rules and regulations of a given society, would flout society's conventions and commit crime indiscriminately. This perspective sees humans as fundamentally "unruly" and deviant if allowed to do what they feel like doing. Good illustrations of this perspective are found in biological and neurobiological theories, discussed in chapter 3, and in Travis Hirschi's social control theory which is discussed in several chapters. **Social control theory** contends that crime and delinquency occur when an individual's ties to the conventional order or normative standards are weak or largely nonexistent. In other words, the socialization that normally holds one's basic human nature in check is incomplete or faulty. This position perceives human nature as fundamentally "bad" or "antisocial," an innate tendency that must be *controlled* by society.

The third perspective—the **learning perspective**—sees human beings as born neutral (neither inherently conforming nor unruly). This perspective argues that humans learn virtually all their behavior, beliefs, and tendencies from the social environment. The learning perspective is exemplified most comprehensively by **social learning theory,** to be a main topic in chapter 4, and Edwin H. Sutherland's **differential association theory.** According to differential association theory, criminal behavior is learned, as is all social behavior, through social interactions with other people. It is not the result of emotional disturbance, mental illness, or innate qualities of "goodness" or "badness." Rather, people learn to be criminal as a result of messages they get from others who were also taught to be criminal. Consequently, an excess of "messages" favorable to law violation over unfavorable messages promotes criminal activity. The conventional wisdom that bad company promotes bad behavior, therefore, finds validity in differential association theory.

Another way of looking a human nature is the difference-in-kind and the difference-in-degrees perspective. The difference-in-degrees perspective holds that human beings may be placed along a continuum consisting of all the animals in the known universe. According to this perspective, humans are intimately tied to their animal ancestry in important and significant ways. For example, this perspective might argue that human aggression and violence is a result of innate, biological needs to obtain sufficient food supplies, territory, status, or mates. In many ways, this approach is similar to the nonconformist point of view. Also, the rapidly developing field of evolutionary psychology generally subscribes to this approach. Evolutionary psychology claims that human cognitive and emotional processes have been selected in our evolutionary environment as devices for solving particular adaptive problems faced by the Pleistocene hunter-gatherers (Bereczkei, 2000; Buss & Shackelford, 1997). Evolutionary psychologists stress that Darwinian theory provides ultimate explanations of many types of antisocial behavior (Quinsey, Skilling, Lalumière, & Craig, 2004).

The difference-in-kind perspectives, on the other hand, argues that humans are distinctly different from animals, spiritually, psychologically, and mentally. Noteworthy neurobiologists and pioneer brain researchers such as Sir John Eccles (Eccles & Robinson, 1984), Roger Sperry (1983), and Wilder Penfield (1975) have concluded that humans differ radically in kind from all other animals. According to the difference-in-kind viewpoint, we will understand crime better if we study and build theories based on the human qualities that differ significantly from subhuman features. Consequently, this perspective sees antisocial or criminal behavior as a unique human attribute generated primarily by human cognitive processes.

TABLE 1–1 Perspectives of Human Nature

Perspectives of Behavior	Theory Example	Humans are . . .
Conformity Perspective	Strain Theory (Merton)	Basically good; strongly influenced by the values and attitudes of society
Nonconformist Perspective	Social Control Theory (Hirschi) Biological Theories of Crime	Basically undisciplined; individual's ties to social order are weak; innate tendencies must be controlled by society
Learning Perspective	Differential Association Theory (Sutherland) Social Learning Theory (Rotter, Bandura)	Born neutral; behavior is learned through social interactions with other people

PERSPECTIVES IN CRIMINOLOGY

Criminology is the multidisciplinary study of crime. Many disciplines are involved in the collection of knowledge about criminal action, including psychology, sociology, psychiatry, anthropology, biology, neurology, political science, and economics. Over the years, the study of crime has been dominated by three disciplines—sociology, psychology, and psychiatry—but other disciplines or subdisciplines, such as economics and criminal anthropology (Rafter, 1992), are becoming more actively involved.

Although our main concern in this text is with *psychological principles,* concepts, theory, and research relevant to criminal behavior, considerable attention is placed on the research knowledge of the other disciplines, particularly sociology and psychiatry. Again, criminology needs all the help it can get in its struggle to understand, explain, prevent, and change criminal behavior.

It is not easy to make sharp demarcations between disciplines, since they overlap considerably in focus and practice. For example, what distinguishes a given theory as sociological, psychological, or psychiatric is sometimes simply the stated professional affiliation of its proponent. The reader should also realize that condensing any major discipline into a few pages hardly does it justice. To obtain a more adequate overview, the interested reader should consult texts and articles within those disciplines.

Sociological Criminology

Sociological criminology has a rich tradition in examining the relationships of demographic and group variables to crime. Variables such as age, race, gender, socioeconomic status, interpersonal relationships, and ethnic-cultural affiliation have been shown to have significant relationships with certain categories and patterns of crimes. Sociological criminology, for example, has allowed us to conclude that young African American males from disadvantaged backgrounds are disproportionately overrepresented as both perpetrators and victims of homicide. The many reasons for this overrepresentation are reflected in the various perspectives and research findings that are covered in the book. Sociological criminology also probes the situational or environmental factors that are most conducive to criminal action, such as the time, place, kind of weapons used, and the circumstances surrounding the crime.

A major contribution of sociological criminology, however, is the attention it directs to topics that reflect unequal power distribution in society. This often takes the form of examining how crime is defined and how laws are enforced. It also addresses the underlying social conditions that may encourage criminal behavior, such as inequities in educational and employment opportunities. Conflict theories in sociology are particularly influential in questioning how crime is defined, who is subject to punishment, and in attempting to draw attention to the crimes of the rich and powerful.

Psychological Criminology

Psychology is the science of behavior and mental processes. **Psychological criminology,** then, is the science of the behavior and mental processes of the criminal. While sociological criminology focuses primarily on groups and society as a whole, and how they influence criminal activity, psychological criminology focuses on individual criminal behavior—how it is acquired, evoked, maintained, and modified.

The psychology of crime is really a subdivision of the general field of **forensic psychology,** and forensic psychology itself is one of the forensic sciences. The term *forensic* refers generally to anything pertaining to the law or the courts of justice, and it encompasses both criminal and civil law. In a broad sense, forensic psychology refers to the production and application of psychological knowledge to the civil and criminal justice systems. It includes such areas as police psychology, the psychology of crime and delinquency (the main subject matter of this text), correctional psychology (including institutional and community corrections), psychology and law, victim services, and the delivery and evaluation of intervention and treatment programs for juvenile and adult offenders (Bartol & Bartol, 2004b). Forensic psychology is a rapidly emerging field of both academic study and professional application.

In the psychology of crime, both social and personality influences on criminal behavior are considered, along with the mental processes that mediate that behavior. Personality refers to all the biological influences, psychological traits, and cognitive features of the human being that psychologists have identified as important in the mediation and control of behavior. Recently, psychological criminology has shifted its focus to a more *cognitive* and *developmental* approach to the study of criminal behavior. **Cognitions** refer to the attitudes, beliefs, values, and thoughts that a person holds about the environment, interrelations, human nature, and him- or herself. Beliefs that children must be severely physically disciplined or that victims are not really hurt by burglary are good examples of cognitions that may lead to criminal activity.

A **developmental approach** examines the changes and influences across a person's lifetime that may contribute to the formation of antisocial and criminal behavior, sometimes called "risk factors." Examples are poor nutrition, the loss of a parent, or substandard housing or education. However, the developmental approach also searches for "protective factors," or influences that provide individuals with a buffer against the risk factors. A caring adult mentor and good social skills are examples of protective factors. If we are able to identify those changes and influences that occur across the developmental pathways of life that divert a person from becoming caring, sensitive, and prosocial, as well as those that steer a person away from a life of persistent and serious antisocial behavior, we gain invaluable information about how to prevent and change delinquent and criminal behavior. Consequently, psychological criminology develops, examines, and evaluates strategies and inteventions that have the potential to prevent or reduce criminal behavior.

In the past, psychologists assumed that they could best understand human behavior by searching for stable, consistent personality **dispositions** or **traits** that exerted widely generalized effects on behavior. A trait or disposition is a relatively stable and enduring tendency to behave in a particular way, and it distinguishes one person from another. For example, one person may be extroverted and have a consistent tendency to socialize and meet others, while another may be shy and introverted and demonstrate a tendency to socialize with only very close friends. Trait theories hold that people show consistent behavior across time and place, and that these behaviors characterize personality. Many psychologists studying crime, therefore, assumed they should search for the personality traits or variables underlying criminal behavior. They paid less attention to the person's environment or situation. Presumably, once personality variables were identified, it would be possible to determine and predict which individual was most likely to engage in criminal behavior.

As you will learn, the search for any single personality type of the murderer, rapist, or burglar has not been fruitful. Contemporary psychology today has moved away from a trait approach to a more cognitive-based and developmental approach. Psychologists who provide law enforcement agencies with profiles of the rapist still at large, based *solely on personality variables*, are at best engaging in unvalidated clinical judgment and unsubstantiated hunches. However, psychologists can offer *statistical probability* about some *demographic and behavioral patterns* of certain offenders. For example, they might determine, roughly, that a rapist is *probably* young, white, unemployed, from the area, and so forth. They might also offer possible motives for the attack, based on research findings and accompanied by the necessary warnings that this particular offender may not fit those criteria. This "profile" information, however, is based on the collected knowledge from all sectors of criminology, including psychology, sociology, anthropology, psychiatry, political science, history, and economics.

Thus, while trait psychology standing alone has lost favor, some aspects of this approach have survived, primarily in the profiling endeavor. **Criminal profiling** refers to the process of identifying personality traits, behavioral tendencies, geographic location, and demographic variables of an offender based on characteristics of the crime (Bartol & Bartol, 2004b). To a very large extent, the profiling process is dictated by a database collected on previous offenders who have committed similar offenses. Currently, profiling is at least 90 percent an art based on speculation and only 10 percent science. It should be emphasized early in this text that criminal profiling is not restricted to serial murder or serial sexual assaults, but has considerable value when applied successfully to property crimes, including arson, burglary, shoplifting, and robbery. Criminal profiling is covered in more detail in chapter 10.

Psychiatric Criminology

The terms *psychology* and *psychiatry* are often confused by the lay person and even by professionals and scholars in other disciplines. Many psychiatrists, like psychologists, work in a variety of forensic settings, ranging from providing expert testimony in the courtroom, to offering psychiatric services to correctional facilities and law enforcement agencies. Psychiatrists and psychologists who are closely associated with the law and forensic settings are often referred to as forensic psychiatrists or forensic psychologists.

Psychiatric concepts and theories are often believed to be accepted tenets in the field of psychology. The two professions often see things quite differently and approach explanations of criminal behavior along a different course. Part of this difference is due to the dissimilarity in the education requirements for the two professions. Unlike psychologists, who have earned a PhD (doctor of philosophy), PsyD (doctorate in psychology), or, in some cases, an Ed.D. (doctorate in education), and who often complete specialized training in research and some area of psychology, psychiatrists first earn a medical degree (MD or a DO, doctor of osteopathy) and complete a medical internship, as other physicians do. Then, during a two- or three-year residency program in psychiatry, they receive specific training in psychiatry, often focusing on the diagnosis and treatment of individuals in forensic settings, such as court clinics or mental hospitals with special units for mentally disordered individuals accused of crime. Understandably, this medical training encourages a biochemical and neurological approach to explanations of human behavior, and this is often reflected in the psychiatric theories of criminal behavior.

By contrast, many psychologists receive a one-year internship focusing on clinical training, which is often followed by a one- to three-year postdoctoral focusing on both research and practice. In a majority of cases, the psychologist completes these training steps before practicing professionally. The emphasis of this training is usually far more on the cognitive (thought processes) and learned behavior of human action and less on the biochemical or neurological influences.

Traditionally, psychologists have not been permitted by law to prescribe medication to patients. However, this distinction between the two professions is beginning to disappear. On March 6, 2002, New Mexico became the first state in the United States to allow psychologists to prescribe psychoactive drugs (drugs designed to treat psychological problems). Several other states currently have pending legislation on prescription privileges for psychologists, and it is likely that in the years to come, properly trained psychologists will be able to prescribe psychoactive drugs in nearly all—if not all—the states.

Psychoanalytic Tradition

American psychiatric criminology, or forensic psychiatry, has *traditionally* followed the Freudian, psychoanalytic, or psychodynamic tradition. The father of the psychoanalytical theory of human behavior was the physician-neurologist Sigmund Freud (1856–1939), whose followers are called Freudians. Many contemporary psychoanalysts subscribe to a modified version of the orthodox Freudian position and are therefore called neo-Freudians. Still other psychoanalysts follow the tenets of Alfred Adler and Carl Jung, who broke away from Freud and developed different theories about the human condition.

Collectively, all psychoanalytic positions form the psychodynamic approach, which explains behavior in terms of motives and drives. This perspective views human nature as innately antisocial, similar to the difference-in-degree orientation discussed earlier. That is, humans are biologically driven to get what they want when they want it unless they are held in check by internal (conscience) and external (society) forces. Without an organized society with rules and laws, humans (especially men because of their biology) would aggress, plunder, steal, and even kill at will.

The psychoanalytic position assumes that we must delve into the abysses of human personality to find unconscious determinants of human behavior, including criminal behavior. Consider the following comments by two forensic psychiatrists. "The criminal rarely knows completely the reasons for his conduct" (Abrahamsen, 1952, p. 21). "Every criminal is such by reason of unconscious forces within him" (Roche, 1958, p. 25). Psychoanalytic and psychodynamic theories acknowledge that behavior varies across situations. However, they conclude that there are enduring and generalized underlying dynamic or motivational dispositions that account for this diversity. "Surface" behaviors indirectly signal or symbolize dynamic, underlying attributes. Psychological defenses distort and disguise the "true" meaning of external or observed behaviors. The trained clinician, therefore, must interpret the significance of these external behaviors, since the actor is not aware of their purpose.

The Freudian, psychoanalytic, and psychodynamic positions strongly endorse the view that the prime determinant of human behavior lies within the person and that after the first few years of life the environment plays a very minor role. Consequently, criminal behavior is believed to spring from within, primarily dictated by the biological urges of the unconscious. The environment,

TABLE 1–2 Major Perspectives in Criminology

PERSPECTIVE	INFLUENCE	FOCUS
Sociological Criminology	Sociology	Examines relationships of demographic and group variables to crime; focuses on groups and society as a whole and how they influence criminal activity.
Psychological Criminology	Psychology	Focuses on individual criminal behavior; the science of the behavior and mental processes of the criminal.
Psychiatric Criminology	Psychiatry	The contemporary perspective examines the interplay between psychobiological determinants of behavior and the social environment; traditional perspective looks for the unconscious and biological determinants of criminal behavior.

culture, or society cannot be held responsible for crime rates; biopsychological needs and urges within the individual are the culprits.

It would be unfair, however, to simply classify *contemporary* psychiatric criminology or forensic psychiatry as heavily Freudian or psychoanalytical in perspective. Contemporary **psychiatric criminology** is far more diverse, increasingly research based, and is considerably less steeped in the traditional belief that criminals are acting out their uncontrolled animalistic, unconscious, or biological urges. Therefore, *traditional* psychiatric criminology is distinguished from *contemporary* psychiatric criminology throughout the text. The traditional psychiatric view represents the biological unconscious urges that drive humans; whereas the contemporary psychiatric view of crime represents the diverse and rich knowledge gained through research and clinical experience. Whenever possible, we rely on the more contemporary view of psychiatric criminology in this text.

DEFINING AND MEASURING CRIME

As defined at the beginning of the chapter, *criminal behavior is intentional behavior that violates a criminal code, intentional in that it did not occur accidentally or without justification or excuse.* Since crime encompasses so many types of behavior, should we restrict ourselves to a legal definition and study only those individuals who have been convicted of behaviors legally defined as crime? Or should we include individuals who indulge in antisocial behaviors but have not been detected by the criminal justice system? Perhaps our study should include persons predisposed to be criminal, if such persons can be identified. As a review of criminology textbooks and literature attests, there is no universal agreement as to what group or groups should be targeted for study.

If we abide strictly by the legal definition of crime and base research and discussion only on those people who have committed crimes, do we consider only those who have been convicted and incarcerated or serving a sentence in the community, or do we include those who have "probably" broken the criminal law but have not been convicted? Even by conservative estimates, 16 percent to 18 percent of the total U.S. population has arrest records for nontraffic offenses (U.S. Department of Justice, 1988). While some of these individuals are "truly criminal," an undetermined number of others were arrested but were not truly guilty. Furthermore, how can we include individuals who violate the law but escape detection or those who come to the attention of law enforcement officials but are never arrested?

Trying to study criminal behavior on the basis of incidence presents other problems for social scientists. The incidence of crime is usually measured in one of three ways:

1. Official police reports of reported crime and arrests, such as those tabulated and forwarded to the Federal Bureau of Investigation for publication in its annual national statistical report on crime, the Uniform Crime Reports
2. Self-report studies, whereby members of a sample population are asked what offenses they have committed and how often
3. National or regional victimization studies, which sample a population of households or businesses asking respondents how often they have been victims of specified crimes

Uniform Crime Reporting System

The Federal Bureau of Investigation's (FBI) **Uniform Crime Reporting (UCR)** Program, compiled since 1930, is the most cited source of U.S. crime statistics. The UCR Program publishes an annual document containing accounts of crimes known to police and arrest information received on a voluntary basis from local and state law enforcement agencies throughout the United States. The UCR data are available on the FBI Web site (*www.fbi.gov*). Interestingly, federal law enforcement agencies do not report through the traditional UCR program, although a newly revised reporting system has been implemented that requires federal agencies to report. This new system—called the *National Incident-Based Reporting System*—is described shortly.

The first UCR data were published with fewer than a thousand agencies reporting. The 2002 UCR data collection was based on over seventeen thousand city, county, and state law enforcement agencies, representing about 95 percent of the U.S. population (Federal Bureau of Investigation, 2005). The UCR Program is the only major data source permitting a comparison of national data broken down by age, sex, race, and offense. A *Supplementary Homicide Report* contains data on victim and offender demographics, the offender-victim relationship, the weapon used, and the circumstances surrounding the homicide. Additionally, the FBI provides special reports on hate crimes, campus crimes, and law enforcement officers killed in the line of duty. A special report was also prepared to cover the events of September 11, 2001.

The UCR provides a variety of information relating to crimes that come to the attention of police, including the age, gender, and race of persons arrested, and the city and region where the crime was committed. Prior to 2004, the UCR labeled serious crimes **index crimes or Part I crimes,** and nonserious crimes as **nonindex crimes or Part II crimes.** Index crimes were considered to be "indicators" of the crime problem in the United States. However, this distinction was found to be misleading. For instance, larceny-theft, which includes shoplifting, was categorized as an index crime, whereas fraud and drug offenses were classified as nonindex crimes. Moreover, larceny-theft makes up 59.4 percent of the total reported crime, and the enormous volume of these offenses overshadows more serious but less frequently committed offenses (Federal Bureau of Investigation, 2005). Consequently, since 2004 the term "index crime" has disappeared, but the Part I and Part II designations have remained. Part I crimes are subdivided into violent and property offenses.

Violent crime comprises four offenses: murder and nonnegligent manslaughter, forcible rape, robbery, and aggravated assault. Each of these offenses involves force or the threat of force. Property crime includes burglary, larceny-theft, motor vehicle theft, and arson. The primary objective of the offender in property crime is the taking or destruction of money or property. Arson is included in property crime because it involves the destruction of property, but it may result in the loss of life or serious injury.

For all Part I crimes, the UCR provides information on the crime known to police (reported crime), as well as arrests. Only arrest data are provided for Part II crimes. Thus, in order to appear in the UCR as a Part I crime, a crime must, at a minimum, meet the following requirements:

- Be perceived by the victim or by someone else
- Be defined as a crime by the victim or the observer
- In some way become known to a law enforcement agency as a crime
- Be defined by that law enforcement agency as a crime
- Be accurately recorded by the law enforcement agency
- Be reported to the FBI compilation center

It should be emphasized that the UCR provides crime rate data on the Part I crimes. Part I offenses are the eight violent and property crimes listed above. The crime rate is the percentage of crime known to police per 100,000 populations. For example, in 2004, the murder rate was 5.5, meaning there were 5.5 murders known to police for every 100,000 population. Part II offenses, for which only arrest data are provided, encompass all crimes, except traffic violations, that are not classified as Part I offenses. For example, simple assault, forgery or counterfeiting, fraud, embezzlement, drug abuse violations, vandalism, and illegal gambling qualify as Part II offenses. If a victim reports a simple assault (a Part II crime), that assault would not be included in the *crime rate*. However, the *arrest* of one or more individuals for that simple assault would appear in the UCR.

Crime has decreased significantly in recent years, although the very latest UCR figures show a slight increase in some crimes. When looking at five- and 10-year trends, however, the 2004 total violent crime figure represents a 4.1

TABLE 1–3   Definitions of Part I and Part II Crimes in Uniform Crime Reports

PART I CRIME

Murder and non-negligent manslaughter	The willful (nonnegligent) killing of one human by another.
Forcible rape	The carnal knowledge of a female forcibly and against her will.
Robbery	The taking or attempting to take anything of value from the care, custody, or control of a person or persons by force or threat of force or violence and/or by putting the victim in fear.
Aggravated assault	An unlawful attack by one person on another for the purpose of inflicting severe or aggravated bodily injury. Attempts to inflict are also included.
Burglary	The unlawful entry of a structure to commit a felony or theft.
Larceny-theft	The unlawful taking, carrying, leading, or riding away of property from the possession or constructive possession of another. It includes crimes such as shoplifting, pocket picking, purse snatching, thefts from motor vehicles, and bicycle thefts.
Arson	Any willful or malicious burning or attempt to burn, with or without intent to defraud, a dwelling house, public building, motor vehicle or aircraft, or personal property of another.

COMMON PART II CRIMES

Simple assaults	Assaults and attempted assaults in which no weapon is used and which do not result in serious or aggravated injury to victim.
Forgery and counterfeiting	Making, altering, uttering, or possessing, with intent to defraud, anything false in the semblance of that which is true.
Fraud	Fraudulent conversion and obtaining money or property by false pretenses.
Embezzlement	Misappropriation or misapplication of money entrusted to one's care, custody, or control.
Stolen property	Buying, receiving, and possessing stolen property, including attempts.
Offenses against the family and children	Nonsupport, neglect, desertion, or abuse of family and children.
Drug abuse violations	State and/or local offenses relating to the unlawful possession, sale, use, growing, and manufacture of drugs.
Gambling	Promoting, permitting, or engaging in illegal gambling.
Vandalism	Willful or malicious destruction, injury, disfigurement, or deface-ment of any public or private property, real or personal, without the consent of the owner or persons having custody or control.

Source: Adapted from Federal Bureau of Investigation, 1997.

percent decrease from the 2000 figure and a 24 percent decline from the 1995 level (Federal Bureau of Investigation, 2005). In 2004, the estimated total number of violent offenses known to police was approximately 1.4 million. Remember that these figures do not include Part II violent offenses, however. Property crime *arrests* showed a 1.4 percent increase compared with the 2000 estimate, and a 14.4 percent decrease from the 1995 estimate. Total property crime known to law enforcement was 10.3 million.

FIGURE 1–1   Percentage Distribution of Part I Crimes, 2004

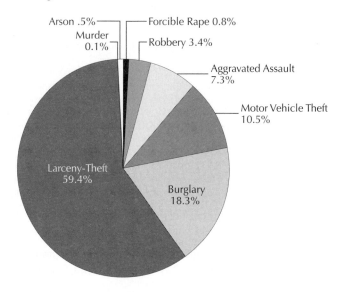

Source: Federal Bureau of Investigation 2005, p. 11.

On a regular yearly basis, if we look at crimes known to police, the property crime of larceny-theft, which usually comprises approximately 60 percent of the Part I crimes, is the most frequently occurring of all Part I crimes (see **Figure 1–1**). The violent crime of murder occurs the least frequently of all Part I crimes, accounting for only 0.1 percent of the total Part I crime.

An estimated monetary value of $16.1 billion in stolen property was reported in 2004 (Federal Bureau of Investigation, 2005). Among individual property crime, the 2004 estimate dollar losses were $3.5 billion for burglary, $5.1 billion for larceny-theft, and $7.6 billion for motor vehicle theft. Approximately one-third of all stolen property is eventually recovered. Property types with the greatest percentage of recoveries are motor vehicles, clothing and furs, livestock, and consumable goods.

The UCR also reports the **clearance rate** of all Part I crimes. An offense is cleared when at least one person is arrested, charged with the commission of the offense, and remanded to the court for prosecution (Federal Bureau of Investigation, 2005). An offense may also be cleared by exceptional means when something happens to an offender outside the control of the reporting law enforcement agency. For example, if a person about to be arrested for rape commits suicide, the crime will likely be cleared. In 2004, 46.3 percent of violent crime in the United States and 16.4 percent of property offenses were cleared by arrest or exceptional means. Usually, murder has the highest clearance rate. In 2004, law enforcement agencies cleared 62.6 percent of murders. See **Table 1–4** for an illustration of clearance rates.

TABLE 1–4   2004 Clearance Rates for Part I Crimes

Violent Crime	**46.3%**
Murder	62.6%
Rape	41.8%
Robbery	26.2%
Aggravated assault	55.6%
Property Crime	**16.5%**
Burglary	12.9%
Larceny-Theft	18.3%
Motor Vehicle Theft	13.0%
Arson	17.1%

Source: Federal Bureau of Investigation, 2005.

UCR Problems

UCR data are not without problems. One of the most frequently mentioned shortcomings is the **hierarchy rule,** which stipulates that when a number of offenses have been committed during a series, only the more serious offense is included in the UCR data. For example, if an offender robs a bank, viciously assaults a bystander, steals a car, and murders the bank security officer, only the murder will appear in the UCR.

The compilation center also relies on the accuracy and compliance of local and state agencies to report crime statistics. The data also do not consider early discretionary decision making by law enforcement officers, such as a decision not to "found" a crime when it is reported by a member of the public or a decision not to arrest an individual. In addition, the Part I category emphasizes street crime to the neglect of the equally serious "white-collar" crime, which includes a wide variety of offenses such as corporate crimes, political, and professional crimes.

Official crime statistics, like those of the UCR Program, are generally believed to underestimate most criminal offenses and are routinely criticized for errors and omissions. The overall number of criminal offenses that go undetected or are unknown by law enforcement agencies, known as the **dark figure,** are difficult to estimate, but data from a victimization survey conducted by the U.S. Census Bureau suggest that out of every 100 offenses committed, 72 are never recorded in the official statistics (Skogan, 1977).

However, Skogan also notes that most unreported violations appear to be minor property offenses rather than more serious crimes. **Figure 1–2,** based on 1980 and 2002 UCR data, shows that arrest rates for serious property crimes peak at around age 17 or 18, just before the age range at which many courts begin prosecuting offenders as adults.

With increasing age, and particularly after age 20, property arrests decline. On the other hand, arrests for violent crime gradually peak and show a gradual decline with age. **Figure 1–2** and **Figure 1–3** show the different trends in arrests for property crimes and violent crimes as the age of the offender increases.

FIGURE 1–2   Property Crime Arrests per 100,000

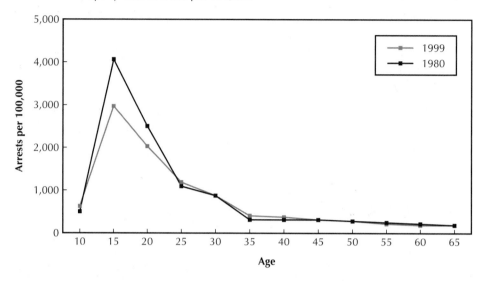

Source: H. N. Snyder 2000a, p. 7.

The figures also compare 1980 with 2002 arrest data for these trends, illustrating the significant decrease in property crimes and slight decrease in violent crimes in 2002.

The National Incident-Based Reporting System

During the late 1970s, the law enforcement community called for the expanded use of the UCR and more detailed information on crime than the statistics offered in the UCR. In response, the UCR reporting system was evaluated under federal contract by ABT Associates of Cambridge, Massachusetts. Recommendations of the research firm are reported in *A Blueprint for the Future of the Uniform Crime Reporting System,* published in 1985. These recommendations formed the basis of the National Incident-Based Reporting System (NIBRS) under the Uniform Federal Crime Reporting Act passed by the U.S. Congress in 1988 (Public Law No. 100-690, 102 Stat. 4181). In this act, Congress required all federal law enforcement agencies, including those agencies within the Department of Defense, to collect and report data to the FBI on two categories of offenses: Group A, which includes 46 serious offense categories, such as arson, assault, homicide, fraud, embezzlement, larceny-theft, and sex offenses; and Group B, which includes 11 less serious offenses, such as passing bad checks, driving under the influence of alcohol, engaging in disorderly conduct, drunkenness, nonviolent family offenses, and liquor law violations (see **Table 1–5** for a list of Group A offenses).

FIGURE 1–3   Violent Crime Arrests per 100,000

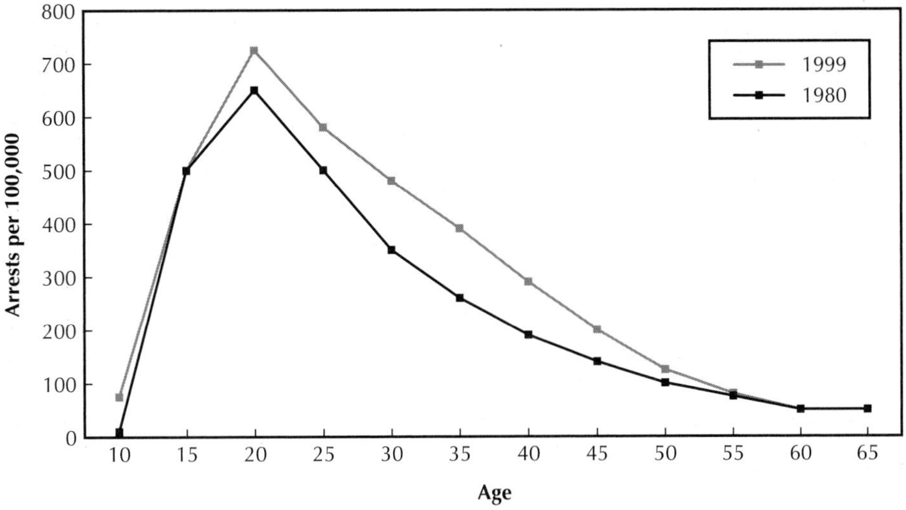

Source: H. N. Snyder 2000a, p. 6.

In the *Group A Incident Report* information, a crime is viewed along with all its aspects. For example, the report of a crime includes information about the victim, weapon, location of the crime, alcohol/drug influence, type of criminal activity, relationship of victim to alleged offender, residence of victims and arrestees (if someone was arrested), and a description of property and its value. Presumably, this added information will become an indispensable tool for law enforcement agencies and researchers because it will provide them with detailed data about when and where specific types of crime take place, what forms they take, and the characteristics of their victims and perpetrators. Like the Part II crimes in the UCR, the crimes in Group B include only information about the arrestee and the circumstances of the arrest.

States were also invited to participate in the project. State and federal agencies participating in the NIBRS use automated systems to report information on Group A and Group B offenses to the FBI on a monthly basis. Ultimately this new approach is intended to be a paperless (electronic) reporting system. However, the new system is expected to take several years to implement completely. Progress has been somewhat slow, but even so data analyses based on Group A crimes are beginning to appear in the criminology literature and are mentioned periodically throughout this text. Eventually, the NIBRS is expected to replace the FBI's traditional UCR that simply provides summary crime statistics.

The anticipated benefits of the NIBRS are primarily through the more precise information it should provide to researchers and investigators about when and where crime takes place, its form, and the characteristics of its victims and

TABLE 1–5   National Incident-Based Reporting System (NIBRS) Group A Offenses

Arson	*Homicide offenses*
Assault offenses	Murder/nonnegligent manslaughter
Aggravated assault	Negligent manslaughter
Simple assault	Justifiable homicide
Intimidation	*Kidnapping/abduction*
Bribery	*Larceny-theft offenses*
Burglary/breaking and entering	Pocket picking
Counterfeiting/forgery	Purse snatching
Destruction/damage/vandalism of property	Shoplifting
Drug/narcotic Offenses	Theft from building
Drug/narcotic violations	Theft from coin-operated machines
Drug/equipment violations	Theft from motor vehicle
Embezzlement	Theft of motor vehicle parts/accessories
Extortion/blackmail	Motor vehicle theft
Fraud offenses	Pornography/obscene materials
False pretenses/swindle/confidence game	*Prostitution offenses*
Credit card/ATM fraud	Prostitution
Impersonation	Assisting or promoting prostitution
Welfare fraud	*Robbery*
Wire fraud	*Sex offenses, forcible*
Gambling offenses	Forcible rape
Betting/wagering	Forcible sodomy
Operating/promoting/assisting gambling	Sexual assault with an object
Gambling equipment violations	Forcible fondling
Sports tampering	*Sex offenses, nonforcible*
	Stolen property offenses
	Weapon law violations

Source: The National Center for the Analysis of Violent Crime, Annual Report, 1992 (Quantico, VA: FBI Academy, 1992), p. 22.

offenders. Another primary objective of NIBRS is to get a better handle on the nature and extent of crimes involving illicit drugs.

Among the additional crime categories now followed by the FBI but not *traditionally* included in the Uniform Crime Reporting System or the NIBRS reports are hate crimes and terrorism. For illustrative purposes we now turn our attention to hate crimes; terrorism and terrorist activities are covered in chapter 11.

Hate Crimes

In 1989, Congress mandated that the FBI collect data on "hate" or bias crimes. Known as the **Hate Crime Statistics Act** (and signed into law by President George Herbert Bush in April 1990), it requires data collection of violent attacks, intimidation, arson, or property damage that are directed at a person or group of persons because of race, religion, sexual orientation, or ethnicity. The FBI defines a hate crime as "a criminal offense committed against a person, property, or society which is motivated, in whole or in part, by the offender's bias against race, religion, disability, sexual orientation, or ethnicity/national origin" (Federal Bureau of Investigation, 2002, p. 59). Note that the federal law does not include hate crimes on the basis of gender.

In September 1994, the Violent Crime Control and Law Enforcement Act amended the Hate Crime Statistics Act to add disabilities, both physical and mental, to the hate crimes category. The disability bias data collection began in January 1997. Also, in 1994, Congress passed the Hate Crimes Sentencing Enhancement Act which provides for longer sentences when the offense is determined to be a hate crime.

The Church Arson Prevention Act, signed into law in 1996, amended the Hate Crime Statistics Act by extending the type of data collected. The alarming increase of arson of churches prompted the passage of the Church Arson Prevention Act. Between October 1991 and May 1996, 110 incidents of church arson were reported to federal authorities, with 33 of them occurring during the early part of 1996. Although the burnings included synagogues, mosques, and church congregations, more than half involved African American places of worship located in the southeastern sections of the United States. In an effort to further extend hate crime statutory provisions, Congress passed the Hate Crime Prevention Act of 1999, which allows more authority for the federal government to investigate and prosecute hate crime offenders who committed their crime because of perceived sexual orientation, gender, or disability of the victim.

In addition to the above federal laws, over 40 states and the District of Columbia have hate or bias crime statutes (Bartol & Bartol, 2004a; Wessler & Moss, 2001). Almost all state jurisdictions that have these laws cover bias based on race, religion, ethnicity, and national origin, but significantly fewer states have statutes that cover bias based on gender, disability, or sexual orientation. Nearly all the state and federal statutes provide an enhancement of penalties once a person has been convicted of a bias or hate crime (Bartol & Bartol, 2004a).

In accordance with the Hate Crime Statistics Act, hate crime data are collected for 11 traditional offense categories and are divided into two major classifications: crimes against persons and crimes against property. Crimes against persons include murder and nonnegligent manslaughter, forcible rape, aggravated assault, simple assault, and intimidation. Crimes against property include robbery, burglary, larceny-theft, motor vehicle theft, arson, and destruction/damage/vandalism of property. The data are submitted to the UCR by city, county, and state law enforcement agencies by various means, such as hard copy, floppy disk, magnetic tape, or electronically.

A victim of a hate crime may be either a person, a business, an institution, or society as a whole. In 2004, nearly two out of every three hate crimes (62.4%) were crimes against persons, with intimidation being the most frequently reported (50.1%) (Federal Bureau of Investigation, 2005). Thirty-seven percent were hate crimes against property, and 0.7 percent were classified as crimes

FIGURE 1–4   Bias-motivated Offenses Percent
Distribution,[1] 2004

[1]Due to rounding, the percentages may not add to 100.

Source: Federal Bureau of Investigation, 2005, p. 65.

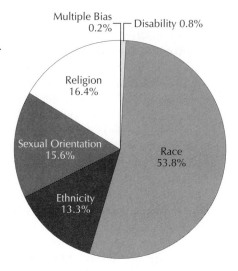

against society. Recent available data (2004) indicate that a majority of hate
crimes are motivated by racial bias (53.8%), followed by ethnic/national origin
bias (13.3%), religious bias (16.4%), sexual orientation bias (15.6%), and disability bias (0.8%) (Federal Bureau of Investigation, 2005). Vandalism was the
most frequent hate crime against property, accounting for 84.4 percent of the
total hate crime against property.

A vivid example of a hate crime occurred in early June 1998 in Jasper, Texas.
James Byrd Jr., a 49-year-old African American, was walking home from a family party when he was offered a ride by three white men, all of them known
white supremacists. The men drove Byrd to a remote dirt road where they severely beat him. Then Byrd was chained to their pickup truck by the ankles
and dragged along the road, tearing his body to pieces. Police found Byrd's
head, neck, right arm, torso, shoes, a wallet, and other personal items scat-
tered along the route. A mile-long blood trail on the road marked the gruesome
scene. Another high-profile hate crime was the 1998 murder of Matthew Shepard, a gay college student who was kidnapped, beaten, tied to a fencepost, and
left to die. Shepard was found and hospitalized in a comatose state and died
shortly thereafter.

Self-Report Studies

Many researchers believe that self-report (SR) studies provide a more accurate
estimate of actual offenses than do UCR statistics, which are based on data provided by law enforcement. In self-report research, people report their own criminal or otherwise antisocial activity to researchers. Although respondents may
inflate or deflate reports of their own criminal activity, proponents of this research strategy maintain that self-report offers a better approximation of criminal activity. In a dated but revealing SR survey (Wallerstein & Wyle, 1947),

1,698 persons were asked to indicate on a list of 49 criminal offenses which, if any, they had committed. The list included felonies and misdemeanors but excluded traffic violations. Of the nearly 1,700 respondents, 91 percent admitted they had committed one or more offenses for which they might have received jail or prison sentences. The average number of offenses for each person was 18. None of the sample had served an actual prison sentence. This study suggests that most people have broken the criminal law at some point in their lives.

In another classic study by Short and Nye (1957), three-thousand high school students, with a guarantee of anonymity, were administered questionnaires about their unlawful actions. Results confirmed the high incidence of unlawful behavior such as was reported by the Wallerstein and Wyle study. Additionally, the study demonstrated that the unlawful conduct was evenly distributed across all socioeconomic classes. Even if the offenses were not serious ones, if these SR studies are representative, violations of the law are common across all levels of society, at least among young people. The Wallerstein and Wyle study did not address the issue of social class.

Most SR investigations focus on delinquency rather than adult offending. When SR studies are done with adults, they are primarily adults who are incarcerated, although there are exceptions. In a study of employee theft, for example, researchers found that about one-third of employees who returned surveys admitted to stealing from their employers (Hollinger, 1986). A self-report survey of income tax evasion found 10 percent of the respondents admitting to cheating on their taxes (Tittle, 1980).

Self-report data are gathered either through interviews (personal or telephone) or questionnaires. In most SR measures, subjects are asked to indicate whether they have engaged in any of the listed illegal activities and, if so, how often. Nettler (1984), in his review of the SR research, concluded the following:

- Almost everyone, by his or her own admission, has violated some criminal law.
- The amount of "hidden crime" (the dark figure) is enormous.
- Most of the infractions are minor.

The last point is an important one because it is the basis for much of the criticism directed at SR studies. Most of the offenses included in a majority of SR questionnaires are relatively minor ones—so minor that they are likely to distort one's impressions of criminal offending unless the content of the questions is known. For example, the questionnaire used by Short and Nye was a 23-item delinquency scale that included such questions as whether one has ever defied his or her parents' authority (to their face). Other items included whether one had ever skipped school without a legitimate excuse; taken little things (worth less than $2); bought or drank beer, wine, or liquor; had sexual relations with persons of the opposite sex or the same sex; run away from home; or gone hunting or fishing without a license. Note that some of the above items (e.g., skipping school and running away) relate to offenses that are against the law only for juveniles, called "status offenses." More "serious" violations listed were engaging in fist fights, gang fights, taking a car for a drive without the owner's (including parents') knowledge, use of narcotic drugs, theft (over $50), and vandalism.

Recent SR studies, responding to the criticisms of earlier investigations, have directed their questions at more serious criminal activities. Still, we must be careful about drawing far-reaching conclusions based on the information from SR research unless the nature of the questions is known, as well as who was asked, why, and how. At this point, however, SR studies do suggest that minor criminal activity is extensive and widespread, at least among youth. Furthermore, SR studies continually show that the number of individuals involved in serious crimes is relatively small, but those few who do engage in serious criminal activity commit a lot of crimes. Moreover, persistent, repetitive offenders do not specialize in any one crime (such as larceny) but show considerable versatility in criminal involvement, committing a wide variety of offenses, violent as well as nonviolent. We discuss this behavioral pattern in more detail in the next chapter.

Drug Abuse Self-Report Surveys

Several nationwide self-report surveys collect data on drug abuse in the United States. The major surveys are the National Household Survey on Drug Abuse (NHSDA), the Monitoring the Future Study (MFS), and the Arrestees Drug Abuse Monitoring Program (ADAM).

NHSDA is an ongoing survey of the noninstitutionalized population of the United States, 12 years old or older. The survey has been conducted by the federal government since 1971, and is the primary source of statistical information on the use of illegal drugs in the United States. It is designed to estimate the rates of drug use, the number of users, and other aspects related to illicit drugs, alcohol, and tobacco products. The survey collects data by administering questionnaires to a representative sample of the population at their places of residence across all 50 states and the District of Columbia. The sample includes residents of households, noninstitutional group quarters (e.g., shelters, rooming houses, dormitories), and civilians living on military bases. Beginning in 1999, the NDSDA interview has been carried out using a computer-assisted interviewing methodology. Computers are used both for personal interviewing conducted by the interviewer and audio computer-assisted self-interviewing. Nationally, nearly 69,000 persons were interviewed in 2001.

The MFS is a nationwide survey of high schoolers in the United States conducted at the Institute for Social Research at the University of Michigan and sponsored by research grants from the National Institute of Drug Abuse. Each year, since 1991, a total of fifty-thousand 8th, 10th, and 12th grade students are surveyed. The MFS also conducts a follow-up survey of each graduating class for a number of years after their initial participation. The mission of the MFS is to predict future trends of drug abuse based on current youth drug use. We describe these surveys and their informative results in more detail in chapter 16.

The ADAM collected data from adult males and females who were arrested in 33 metropolitan areas (or sites) in the United States. In addition, data are collected from male and female juvenile detainees in nine metropolitan areas. The ADAM utilizes both urinalysis and self-report data to identify the level of recent drug use by the arrestees and juvenile detainees. The urinalysis provides a validity check on the openness of the arrestees in providing information about their drug abuse. The urine tests are provided for 11 drugs and self-report information is collected for 15 drugs. The ADAM project offers invaluable insight into drug use of alleged offenders nationwide.

Victimization Surveys

Additional sources of data on criminal offending are victimization surveys. The main source of victimization data on crime is the National Crime Victimization Survey (NCVS), originally called the National Crime Survey (NCS). Workers for the Bureau of the Census interview—in person or by phone—a large national sample of households (approximately 42,000) representing over 76,000 persons over the age of 12. The same households are interviewed every six months for a period of three years, and during each session they are asked about crime they had experienced over the past six months. Crimes committed against children below age 12 are not counted for privacy reasons and because the designers of the survey believe that younger respondents, compared with adults, are not as likely to provide accurate information. Additionally, because young children may be victims of crime within their own households, the topic would be too sensitive to broach. The NCVS provides the largest national forum for victims to describe the impact of crime and characteristics of violent offenders.

The original impetus for the NCVS came from the President's Commission on Law Enforcement and the Administration of Justice in 1966. The commission wanted to supplement the UCR because of the widespread dissatisfaction with and distrust of the accuracy of this source. After considerable experimentation and a variety of pilot projects to test methods and their feasibility, the NCVS (then called the NCS) was fully implemented in July 1973. While the survey has generally been regarded as an effective instrument for measuring crime victimization, the National Academy of Sciences concluded that the survey's methodology and scope could be improved. Consequently, the NCVS has undergone several changes and improvements since it was begun in 1973. The most recent significant changes in the NCVS occurred in 1992 when a redesigned interview method was put into place to improve survey methods and collect previously unreported data. This redesign and other ongoing developments of the NCVS have significantly changed the way in which the survey gathers data and information on victimization. The effects of these methodological changes on data are described in a report published by the Bureau of

Justice Statistics titled *Effects of the Redesign on Victimization Estimates* (BJS Technical Report, April 1997 [NCJ-16438]).

The survey is currently designed to measure the extent to which households and individuals are victims of rape and other sexual assault, robbery, aggravated assault, simple assault, household burglary, motor vehicle theft, and theft. It also provides many details about the victims (such as age, race, sex, marital status, education, income, and whether the victim and the offender were related to each other) and about the crimes themselves. Among other things, the NCVS interviewer wants to know the following:

- Exactly what happened
- When and where the offense occurred
- Whether any injury or loss was suffered
- Whether the crime was reported to the police and if not, why
- The victim's perception of the offender's gender, race, and age

According to the NCVS, residents age 12 or older experienced approximately 23 million crimes during 2002 (Rennison & Rand, 2003). Of that total, 17.5 million (76%) were property crimes (burglary, motor vehicle theft, and household theft), and 5.3 million (23%) were violent crimes (rape or sexual assault, robbery, aggravated assault, and simple assault). Approximately .18 million (1%) were personal thefts (pocket picking and purse snatching).

If we examine the *rates* (victimizations per 1,000 persons age 12 or older), we find that the NCVS data reveals that victimization in 2002 reached the lowest per capita rates in nearly 30 years (Rennison & Rand, 2003). For example, violent victimization rates fell 54 percent in the past 10 years, from 50 to 23 victimizations per 1,000 persons 12 years old and older. The *number* of violent victimizations fell from 10.5 million in 1993 to 5.3 million in 2002. The property crime victimization rate fell 50 percent, from 319 crimes per 1,000 households to 159 per 1,000. In fact, the rate of every major violent and property crime declined from 1993 through 2002. Specifically, rape/sexual assault declined 56 percent, robbery dropped 63 percent, aggravated assault down 64 percent, simple assault down 47 percent, motor vehicle theft dropped 53 percent, household burglary down 52 percent, and property theft down 49 percent.

The NCVS data consistently show demographic differences in victimization rates. Males and blacks are victims of violent crime at rates greater than those of whites and persons of other races (Rennison & Rand, 2003). Persons age 12 to 24 sustained violent victimization at rates higher than individuals of all other ages. The 16 to 19 age group is especially vulnerable. Persons age 16 to 19 experienced overall violence, rape/sexual assault, and assault overall at rates higher than rates for persons in other age categories. Persons in households with an annual income under $7,500 were more likely to be victims of overall violence than members of households with higher incomes. And persons who had never married were victims of violent crime at rates higher than those for married, widowed, or divorced/separated persons.

Relationship patterns are important in understanding victimization also, particularly violent victimization. Females were most often victimized by someone they knew while males were more likely to be victimized by a stranger in 2002 (Rennison & Rand, 2003). More specifically, female victims reported that 40 percent of the offenders were friends or acquaintances, 20 percent were intimates, and 7 percent some other relative. Thirty-one percent of the offenders were strangers. Male victims indicated that 37 percent of the offenders were friends or acquaintances, 3 percent were intimates, and 4 percent were described as some other relative. Strangers committed 56 percent of the violence against males. Robbery was the crime most likely to be committed by a stranger for both male and female victims.

Every year, about 1 million violent crimes are committed against persons by their current or former spouses, boyfriends, or girlfriends (Rennison & Welchans, 2000), a crime designated **intimate partner violence.** Intimate partner violence is committed primarily against women. Women are victims in about 85 percent of reported intimate partner violence; 22 percent of *all* violent crime committed against women is intimate partner violence. Women between the ages of 20 and 24 were most likely to be victimized by an intimate partner (21 per 1,000 women). Black women are subject to intimate partner violence at a rate 35 percent higher than white women and approximately 2.5 times higher than the rate for women of other races. About two-thirds of the victims of intimate partner violence said they were *physically attacked,* and about one-third reported being victims of threats or attempted violence. Approximately one-half of all victims of intimate partner violence (both male and female victims) reported the violence to law enforcement authorities.

The NCVS, similar to all national surveys, has its problems in accurately portraying victimization data. As described earlier in this section, the NCVS samples households and therefore does not usually include the experiences of homeless individuals or those living in institutional settings such as homeless or battered persons' shelters (Rennison & Welchans, 2000). Consequently the extent of intimate partner violence experienced by the homeless or those persons residing in shelters remains largely unknown. For example, a survey conducted by the U.S. Conference of Mayors indicated that intimate partner violence was the primary cause of homelessness for women (U.S. Conference of Mayors, 1998). Another study suggested that as many as 50 percent of homeless women and children became homeless after fleeing abuse (Zorza 1991).

Victimization surveys are considered a good source of information about crime incidents, independent of data collected by law enforcement agencies throughout the country. Often the offending trends reported through NCVS data procedures differ substantially from those found in police data (Ohlin & Tonry, 1989). Although we have focused on the government-conducted NCVS to illustrate victimization data, be aware that independent researchers also survey victims of crime, often with grants from government agencies or private foundations. One noteworthy example is the National Violence Against Women Survey, conducted by the Center for Policy Resesarch (Tjaden, 1997), which included an examination of the extent and nature of stalking in American society.

JUVENILE DELINQUENCY

Juveniles may well be the most maligned age group in our society. Myths abound about their contribution to crime and the extent of damage for which they are responsible. During the last quarter of the twentieth century, it was common to read accounts of skyrocketing juvenile crime, young superpredators in our midst, declining morality in youth, and the woeful state of family life that was seen as a major contributor to juvenile vandalism, drug use, thievery, and violence. To some extent these accounts were supported by statistics, particularly during the 1980s and early 1990s. However, fears were also fueled by atypical illustrations of juvenile crime, such as a particularly heinous account of a murder committed by a juvenile or those associated with a number of school shootings.

Although there is reason to be concerned about juvenile crime, the facts are not quite as alarming as they often appear to be from media accounts. Juvenile crime is troubling, but it is not intractable. Since the mid-1990s, we have seen a decrease in crime committed by youths across most crime categories, including both property and violent crime. Drug use, though, has seen significant increases. Youths charged with drug law violations, for example, increased 169 percent between 1990 and 1999 (National Center for Juvenile Justice, 2003). Juveniles as a group are responsible for a small percentage of arrests compared with adults, although they are arrested disproportionately compared with other age groups. Moreover, the typical juvenile is far more likely to be the victim than the perpetrator of a violent crime. Nevertheless, a significant number of juveniles do victimize one another, drug use persists, and the problem of youth violence has not disappeared. Thus, though we have made strides in understanding the factors leading to these behaviors and developing strategies for prevention and treatment, much work remains to be done.

Legal Definitions of Delinquency

Juvenile delinquency is an imprecise, nebulous, social, clinical, and legal label for a wide variety of law- and norm-violating behavior. At first glance, a simple legal definition seems to suffice: *Delinquency is behavior against the criminal code committed by an individual who has not reached adulthood, as defined by state or federal law.* But the term "delinquency" has numerous definitions and meanings beyond this one-sentence definition. In some states the legal definition also includes status offending, which is not behavior against the criminal code but is behavior prohibited only for juveniles. For example, running away, violating curfew laws, and truancy all qualify as **status offenses.** The most common status offenses in recent years are incorrigibility, followed by running away (Sickmund, 2004). The status offense that has increased substantially in frequency in recent years is underage drinking.

Even age is not a simple issue in the definition of delinquency. Although no state considers anyone above 18 a delinquent, some have provisions for "youthful offenders," who are older, and some use 16 as the cut-off age. At this writing, four states give criminal courts, rather than juvenile courts, automatic jurisdiction over juveniles at age 16, and eight states at age 17. Several other states are considering changes. Furthermore, all states allow juveniles—some as young as age 7—to be tried as adults in criminal courts under certain conditions and for certain offenses. Under federal law, juveniles may be prosecuted under the criminal law at age 15. Increasingly, however, more and more young offenders are moved to adult court in this manner. Under the legal definition of delinquency, the youths transferred to criminal courts are not delinquents.

Many states do not have a legally defined age of criminal responsibility, that is, minimum age of arrest for children (Snyder et al., 2003). The minimum age will also indicate at which point the child may be brought before a juvenile court for delinquency proceedings. When the minimum *is* specified, it varies from age 6 in North Carolina to age 10 in Arkansas, Colorado, Kansas, Pennsylvania, and Wisconsin. Canada stipulates a minimum age of 12. Another interesting and rarely mentioned issue is that of the developmentally disabled individual. The shoplifter or exhibitionist with a mental age of 10 and a chronological age of 33 is not eligible for delinquency status, yet his mental abilities resemble those of children far more than those of adults. On the other hand, an 8-year-old "genius" with a mental age of 25 could presumably not be tried in criminal court simply because of his mental age, though he could be on the basis of the crime he was alleged to have committed.

Child Delinquents

In recent years the term "child delinquent" has come into vogue. **Child delinquents** are juveniles between the ages of 7 and 12, who have committed a delinquent act according to criminal law (Loeber, Farrington, & Petechuk, 2003). Child delinquents often attract the attention of the mass media and public officials, especially after some especially violent incident that involves a very young offender. During the past decade, the number of child delinquents handled by juvenile courts has increased 33 percent, generating some concern in criminal justice circles and society in general. Overall, children younger than age 13 make up about 9 percent of all juvenile arrests (Snyder et al., 2003). According to Loeber, Farrington, and Petechuk (2003), child delinquents are two or three times more likely to become serious, violent, and chronic offenders than adolescents who begin offending in their teens.

Social Definitions of Delinquency

Social and psychological definitions of delinquency may overlap considerably, just as each overlaps with legal definitions. Social delinquency consists of a wide variety of youthful behaviors considered inappropriate, such as aggressive behavior, truancy, petty theft, vandalism, or drug abuse. The behavior may or may not have come to the attention of the police. It is not unusual for "social delinquents" to be referred to community social service agencies or to juvenile courts, but they never legally become delinquents until and unless they are found in a hearing to have committed the crime for which they are charged. For example, a juvenile court intake officer may place a juvenile on "informal probation," giving him a second chance to be supervised in the community rather than formally referred to juvenile court where he faces the possibility of being adjudicated delinquent.

Psychological Definitions

Psychological definitions of delinquency include conduct disorder and antisocial behavior. **Conduct disorder** is a diagnostic term used to represent a group of behaviors characterized by *habitual* misbehavior, such as stealing, setting fires, running away from home, skipping school, destroying property, fighting, being cruel to animals and people, and frequently telling lies. Like the social delinquent, the psychological delinquent may or may not have been arrested for these behaviors. Some of them, in fact, are not even against the criminal law. The term "conduct disorder" is more fully described in the *American Psychiatric Association's Diagnostic and Statistical Manual* (1994, fourth ed.), commonly referred to as the DSM-IV. The DSM-IV—now in a slightly revised edition and referred to as the DSM-IV-R (2000)—divides conduct disorders into two categories, depending on the onset of the misbehaviors. If the misconduct began in childhood (before age 10), it is called *conduct disorder: childhood-onset type.* If the misconduct began in adolescence, it is called *conduct disorder: adolescent-onset type.*

The clinical term **antisocial behavior** is usually reserved for more serious *habitual* misbehavior, especially a behavioral pattern that involves direct and harmful actions against others. It is to be distinguished, however, from the term *antisocial personality disorder,* a diagnostic label reserved primarily for *adults* who displayed conduct disorders as children or adolescents, and continue serious offending well into adulthood. We discuss antisocial personality disorders in more detail in chapter 7.

THE NATURE AND EXTENT OF JUVENILE OFFENDING

Approximately 1.8 to 2.2 million juveniles under age 18 are arrested yearly by law enforcement officers in the United States. Although juvenile crimes have declined in recent years, these statistics still represent an enormous amount of offending by American youth. In 2000, more than 30 million youth were under juvenile court jurisdiction (Puzzanchera et al., 2004). Eight in 10 (80%) of these youth were between the ages of 10 and 15. In 2000, courts with juvenile jurisdiction handled an estimated 1.6 million delinquency cases, and in any day the juvenile courts processed roughly 4,500 cases (Puzzanchera et al., 2004). Nearly two-thirds of the cases involved youths age 15 or younger at the time of referral. Although most juvenile offending is nonviolent in nature, many of the cases involved sex offending or other violent crime.

The nature and extent of delinquent behavior—both what is reported and what is *unreported* to law enforcement agencies—is essentially an unknown area (Krisberg & Schwartz, 1983; Krisberg, 1995), even more so than adult crime. We simply do not have complete data on the national incidence of juvenile delinquency, broadly defined. We do have some statistics collected by law enforcement agencies (e.g., through the UCR reporting system), the courts, and facilities for delinquents, as described earlier. The government regularly publishes reports on juvenile court statistics and on children in custody in both detention and treatment facilities. Nevertheless, as for adult crime, there is a huge dark figure. As Barry Krisberg (1992, p. 2) notes, "Put simply, the amount of crime committed by juveniles is unknown and perhaps unknowable."

Usually, unlawful acts committed by delinquents are placed into five major categories:

1. Unlawful acts against persons
2. Unlawful acts against property
3. Drug offenses
4. Offenses against the public order
5. Status offenses

The first four categories in the list are comparable in definition to crimes committed by adults and are discussed shortly. Before we turn to these criminal acts, it is important to digress briefly on the fifth category, the troubling issue of status offending.

Status Offenses

Status offenses are acts that only juveniles can commit and that can be adjudicated only by a juvenile court. As mentioned earlier, typical status offenses range from misbehavior, such as violations of curfew, running away from home, and truancy, to offenses that are interpreted very subjectively, such as unruliness, unmanageability, or incorrigibility. However, only four status offenses are tabulated by the National Center for Juvenile Justice (2003): running away, truancy, ungovernability (also known as incorrigibility or being beyond the control of one's parents), and underage liquor law violations (e.g., a minor in possession of alcohol, underage drinking). Although a number of other behaviors are often considered status offenses (e.g., curfew violations, tobacco offenses), they are usually not discussed in governmental reports.

The juvenile system has historically supported differential treatment of male and female status offenders. Adolescent girls, for example, have often been detained for incorrigibility or running away from home, when the same behavior

FIGURE 1–5   Proportion of Males and Females in Petitioned Status Offense Cases

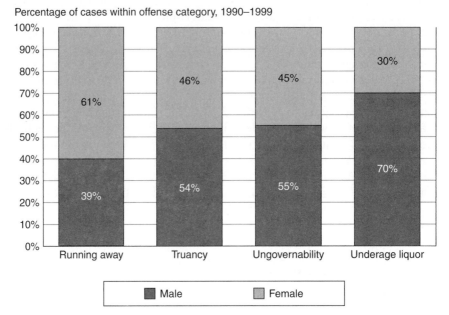

Percentage of cases within offense category, 1990–1999

Note: The proportion of females was greater in petitioned status offense cases than in delinquency cases. Females accounted for 61 percent of petitioned runaway cases. In no other offense category (status or delinquency) was the female share of cases greater than the male share.

Source: National Center for Juvenile Justice 2003, p. 53.

in adolescent boys was ignored or tolerated. Until recently, about three times as many girls were detained for status offenses as boys (U.S. Department of Justice, 1988). In recent years, as a result of suits brought on behalf of juveniles, many courts have put authorities on notice that this discriminatory approach is unwarranted. Even so, recent figures indicate that girls are still more likely than boys to be arrested as runaways (National Center for Juvenile Justice, 2003; Snyder, 2000a) (see **Figure 1–5**).

It has been argued that, because status offenses lend themselves to so much subjectivity, they should be removed from the purview of all state juvenile courts (American Bar Association, 1979). Some states have clearly moved in this direction. On the other hand, while many states do not label status offenders "delinquents," they do allow their detention and/or supervision because they are presumed to be in need of protection either from their own rash behavior or the behavior of others. The statutes allowing this are usually referred to as PINS or CHINS laws (person or child in need of supervision). Under these laws, runaways or incorrigible youngsters are subject to juvenile or family court jurisdiction, often at the instigation of their parents, even though they may not have committed an act comparable to a crime. These statutes also allow these specialized courts to address the needs of neglected and dependent children.

In this text, although status offending and minor delinquent crime are considered, our focus is on violent offending and more serious property offending. We are particularly interested in the developmental trajectories that lead to serious delinquency. In recent years, developmental psychologists have conducted extensive research on this topic, as we note shortly.

The Serious Delinquent

Both self-report studies and official data indicate that only a small percentage of the juvenile population engages in serious delinquent behavior, whether it is defined legally, socially, or psychologically. Nevertheless, those who do commit a variety of antisocial behaviors often escape detection. An early self-report study (Weis & Sederstrom, 1981) indicated that only about 3 percent to 15 percent of serious offenses ever result in "police contact." Likewise, Elliott, Dunford, and Huizinga (1987) suggest that serious, repetitive juvenile offenders escaped detection 86 percent of the time over a five-year period. These figures further suggest that the incidence of offending may be substantially underestimated by official arrest data. In other words, a small percentage of youth are committing a substantial amount of offenses that do not come to the attention of police. Research also suggests that this group of youths—when they do enter the justice system—tend to be high in recidivism, or repeat offending (Bartol & Bartol, 1998). In addition, frequent offenders do not specialize in any one particular kind of offending, such as theft or larceny. Instead, they tend to be involved in a wide variety of offenses, ranging from minor property crimes to highly violent ones. Longitudinal research also indicates that repetitive offenders as a group were unusually troublesome in school, earned poor grades, and had inadequate or poor social skills. Furthermore, these troublesome behaviors often began at an early age, and the more serious the offender, the earlier these childhood patterns appeared. Serious or habitual juvenile offenders rarely restrict their behaviors to one type of offense category.

Public opinion surveys have periodically revealed that many people believe serious youth crime is increasing at a steady and alarming rate (Krisberg, 1992). The most recent juvenile crime figures suggest more optimism, however. Juvenile crime, particularly violent crime, peaked in 1994 and has been decreasing steadily since then. According to the UCR data, between 1994 and 2000, the juvenile arrest rate for violent crime offenses fell 41 percent (Snyder, 2002). In fact, the juvenile violent crime arrest rate in 2000 was the lowest since 1985. In 2002, juveniles were the known offender in 5.4 percent of all homicides and represented 14.8 percent of all those arrested for violent crimes (Federal Bureau of Investigation, 2003). After more than a decade of increases, homicides by juveniles have been steadily decreasing since 1993. Between 1993 and 2000, the juvenile murder arrest rate fell 74 percent, its lowest level since the 1960s (Snyder, 2002).

Between 1994 and 2000, the juvenile property crime arrest rate dropped 37 percent, to its lowest level since the 1960s (Snyder, 2002). "Specifically, juvenile

TABLE 1–6   Juvenile Arrests for Part I Crimes, 2004

OFFENSE CHARGED	TOTAL UNDER AGE 18	TOTAL UNDER AGE 15
Total Part I Crimes	1,120, 971	346,677
Violent Crimes	54,469	17,308
Murder	938	114
Rape	2,960	1,112
Robbery	16,776	4,049
Aggravated Assault	23,291	11,468
Property Crime	296,365	108,255
Burglary	51,819	18,097
Larceny-Theft	127,702	52,198
Motor Vehicle Theft	23,255	5,451
Arson	4,817	2,950

Source: Federal Bureau of Investigation, 2005.

burglary arrest rates declined throughout the 1980s and 1990s, the juvenile larceny-theft arrest rate was at its lowest level in 20 years, and juvenile motor vehicle theft and arson arrest rates were near their 20-year lows" (Snyder, 2002, p. 5). On the other hand, between 1990 and 2000, the juvenile proportion of all arrests for drug abuse violations increased from 8 percent to 13 percent. And juvenile arrests for curfew and loitering violations increased 81 percent between 1991 and 2000. Demographically, 28 percent of curfew arrests in 2000 involved juveniles under age 15 and 31 percent involved females. In addition, 28 percent of arrests for running away from home involved females, and 39 percent involved juveniles under age 15.

How does violent juvenile crime compare with the incidence and rate of property offenses—burglary, larceny-theft, and motor vehicle theft? According to the 2001 UCR data, the four violent categories (murder and voluntary manslaughter, forcible rape, robbery, and aggravated assault) represent slightly over 4 percent of all juvenile arrests. The nonviolent index offenses (larceny-theft, motor vehicle theft, burglary, and arson), represent an additional 22 percent of all juvenile arrests. Thus, approximately three-fourths of all juvenile arrests are for the 21 Part II offenses that include simple assaults, vandalism, drug abuse violations, disorderly conduct, and curfew and loitering violations.

The racial composition of the juvenile population in 2000 was 79 percent white, 16 percent black, 4 percent Asian/Pacific Islander, and 1 percent American Indian (Snyder, 2002). Most Latinos (an ethnic designation and not a race) were classified as white. Black juveniles, however, were overrepresented in arrests for violent crimes, and, to a lesser extent, property crimes. "Of all juvenile arrests for violent crimes, 55% involved white youth, 42% involved black youth, 2% involved Asian youth, and 1% involved American Indian youth. For property crime arrests, the proportions were 69% white youth, 27% black youth, 2% Asian youth, and 1% American Indian youth" (Snyder, 2002, p. 10).

In 2000, 20 percent of the youths arrested were handled by arresting law enforcement agencies themselves, while 71 percent were referred to juvenile court

TABLE 1–7   The Nature and Extent of Juvenile Offending

Unlawful Acts	Definition
Unlawful acts against persons	Violent crimes, similar to those crimes committed by adults, such as aggravated assault, robbery, sexual assault
Unlawful acts against property	Property crimes, similar to those crimes committed by adults, such as burglary, larceny theft, vandalism
Drug offenses	Possession, distribution, and/or manufacture of drugs
Public order offenses	Nuisance crimes against society, such as noise violations
Status offenses	Acts only juveniles can commit, such as violation of curfew, running away, school truancy

(Snyder, 2002). Seven percent were referred directly to criminal court, while approximately 2 percent were referred to either a child welfare agency or some other law enforcement agency. Thus, we see that the proportion of arrests sent to juvenile court has increased somewhat over the past decade, with 64 percent of the juveniles being referred to juvenile court in 1990, compared with the 71 percent referred in 2000. Between 1990 and 1999, the number of delinquency cases processed by juvenile courts nationwide increased by 27 percent (National Center for Juvenile Justice, 2003).

RECAP: DEFINING CRIME AND DELINQUENCY

A major challenge faced by the authors in preparing this book has been striking the balance between antisocial behavior and criminal behavior, or between antisocial individuals and legally defined criminals. Some scholars have argued (e.g., Sellin, 1970; Tappan, 1947)—and the law agrees—that one who engages in undetected criminal activity is not a criminal in the strictest or operational sense, because a criminal is by definition one who has been detected, arrested, and convicted. However, from a psychological point of view, we encounter problems when we limit ourselves to studying persons legally defined as criminals or behavior legally defined as crime. Legal classifications are determined by that which society, at some point in time, considers socially harmful. It may or may not also be considered morally wrong. Therefore, because each society has a different and changing set of values, what may be judged a criminal act in one may not meet the criteria in another, or even in the same society at a later time. Many states in the United States differ significantly in their criminal codes and are continually revising them. Chemical (drug) possession, prostitution, and dissemination of obscene material are examples of activities that generate ever-changing statutes, and if not changing statutes, selective enforcement.

Furthermore, members of every society (and consequently every society's legal system) perceive and process violators of the criminal code with some disparity, so that the offender's background, social status, personality, motivation, sex, age, race, and legal counsel, as well as the circumstances surrounding the offense, may all affect the criminal justice process. It is highly likely that individuals who have been arrested, convicted, and punished represent a distinctly different sample from those who participate in illegal activity but avoid detection, conviction, or punishment.

Approximately one-fifth of those arrested go to trial, according to Sarbin (1979), who describes the legal process of becoming a criminal. First, the agents of social control (usually the police) label the individual as a suspect. Next, the agents may decide that the suspect should be arrested. Third, the arrested party may be charged with a crime, at which point he or she becomes a defendant. Fourth, the defendant may plead guilty or be tried and convicted, at which point he or she becomes an offender (a felon or a misdemeanant, depending on the seriousness of the crime). Finally, the offender may be incarcerated in a correctional facility and be labeled a convict, inmate, prisoner, or criminal. Alternately, the offender may be placed on probation, effectively serving a sentence in the community. At each step in the process, there is a funneling effect that shows that fewer and fewer individuals reach each subsequent step in the criminal justice process. This funneling process is prominently displayed in numerous criminal justice texts to illustrate how the system operates.

One reason is the error and subjectivity that cannot realistically be removed from determinations of guilt or innocence or from determinations of fault in civil cases. Another is the jury decision-making process. In criminal cases, for example, it has been demonstrated that the characteristics of the victim may influence how much punishment is assigned to the offender. Landy and Aronson (1969) report evidence that if the victim is a respectable citizen (i.e., successful and altruistic), the offender will receive a stiffer sentence than if the case involves an "unrespectable" victim (i.e., despicable and dishonest). Jones and Aronson (1973) found that defendants who raped a married woman or virgin were more likely to receive longer sentences than defendants who raped a divorced woman. It has also been found that the more serious a traffic accident the greater the tendency for jurors to believe that the principals involved were at fault (Walster, 1966). Although these were early experiments in social psychology, later studies also confirmed that subjective factors have considerable influence on jury decision making (Bartol & Bartol, 2004a). Such discrepancies in sentencing have led to widespread demands for determinate sentencing, where the punishment is carefully calibrated to the offense and there is less room for discretion on the part of judges or juries.

The aforementioned studies support Lerner's hypothesis (1970, 1980) that people need to believe they live in a just world where the undeserving are appropriately deprived or punished. This **just world hypothesis** predicts, for example, that some victims of rape, assault, or homicide are assumed by many people to have gotten what they deserved or asked for. The implications of this hypothesis in relation to juries' determinations of guilt and decisions as to whether to place a person or probation or sentence the person to prison are obvious.

It is generally acknowledged, therefore, that those individuals sentenced to prison are not representative of the "true" criminal population because many true criminals go undetected and/or unpunished. Furthermore, as we have long suspected but only recently documented with the increasing availability of DNA evidence, convicted persons are not even necessarily true criminals. Yet, with rare exceptions, researchers studying the "criminal mind" use as subjects only those individuals who have reached the final stage of the legal process: inmates in correctional institutions. Consequently, if we discuss only legally determined criminals, we will be neglecting a considerable segment of the population that actually breaks the law. To some extent, we have little choice but to do just that. Because this book is based on research, the kinds and amounts of available empirical data dictate to a great extent what will be covered.

Additionally, if we discuss only behavior that is legally defined as crime, we omit a sizable segment of behavior that is clearly relevant to our concerns. For example, a vast body of psychological research deals with topics like aggression, antisocial behavior, and moral development. Because of their implications for the eventual development of behavior that is legally defined as crime, we will be covering these areas in the text.

The great majority of crime in the United States and other countries is neither serious nor violent. The great majority of offenders are not serious, chronic offenders. Psychological criminology, however, is most concerned about the minority. Therefore, the main focus of the book is the persistent, repetitive *offender*—or the persistent, repetitive antisocial *behavior*—whether detected or undetected by the criminal justice system. In other words, in this text we concentrate on the individual who has frequently committed serious crimes or antisocial acts over an extended period of time (at least several years).

For all of the above reasons, many psychologists and other mental health professionals prefer the term "antisocial behavior" to "crime" or "criminal behavior" to refer to the more serious habitual actions that violate personal rights, laws, and /or widely held social norms. Antisocial behavior includes both the legal designation delinquency and criminal behavior and the actions that violate standards of society but are undetected by law enforcement. Although arrest *may be* a valid indicator of antisocial behavior, it isn't enough. Many antisocial behaviors—probably most—go undetected or escape the attention of law enforcement. Consequently, we use antisocial behavior frequently throughout the text, especially when discussing the development of behavior that has not yet been legally designated delinquent or criminal behavior but is likely to lead to such designation.

 KEY CONCEPTS

Conformity perspective	Traits
Social control theory	Uniform Crime Reporting (UCR)
Social learning history	Index crimes
Criminology	Nonindex crimes
Forensic psychology	Hierarchy rule
Psychiatric criminology	Hate Crime Statistics Act
Developmental approach	Status offenses

Conduct disorder
Just world hypothesis
Nonconformist perspective
Learning perspective
Differential association theory
Sociological criminology
Psychological criminology
Cognitions
Dispositions

Criminal profiling
Part I crime
Part II crime
Clearance rate
Dark figure
Intimate partner violence
Child delinquents
Antisocial behavior

 REVIEW QUESTIONS

1. Briefly explain the difference between psychological criminology and sociological criminology.
2. What are the three perspectives of human nature? Define each briefly.
3. How does the NIBRS differ from the UCR?
4. List the strengths and weaknesses of self-report surveys.
5. What are status offenses and how do they differ from other juvenile offenses?
6. Define child delinquents.
7. In what important ways do the sociological and psychological definitions of juvenile delinquency differ?
8. What is the important difference between the term "juvenile delinquency" and "antisocial behavior"?
9. Compare and contrast the FBI's Uniform Crime Reports and the National Crime Victimization Survey, focusing on (a) how the data are obtained and (b) what type of information is available from each.

CHAPTER 2

DEVELOPMENTAL RISK FACTORS

CHAPTER OBJECTIVES

- Identify social, family, and psychological developmental risk factors that lead to delinquency and crime.
- Demonstrate how early preschool experiences can lead to a life of antisocial behavior.
- Emphasize the overriding influence of peer rejection on child and youth behavior.
- Emphasize the importance of cognitive abilities and skills on delinquency and crime.
- Introduce the major developmental theories on delinquency and crime.

In recent years, the psychological study of juvenile and adult offending has focused on developmental risk factors. The developmental perspective views the life course of all humans as following a pathway (or trajectory) that may be littered with risk factors. Each person follows a different **developmental pathway,** the characteristics of which can be identified at a very early age. Some children follow a pathway leading to serious delinquency and crime, while a majority of children follow a pathway that may lead to minor juvenile offending. For some children there is no offending at all. Along each developmental path, a child may be exposed to a variety of risk factors, and some children are exposed to many more than others. Some experts believe that the more

risks a person is exposed to, the greater the probability that person will participate in antisocial behavior throughout her or his lifetime (Wasserman &
Seracini, 2001). It is important to note that children also may be exposed to
protective factors, characteristics or experiences that are more likely to shield
them from serious antisocial behavior. Warm and caring parents and a high-
quality educational experience are examples. Though we recognize the importance of these factors, the goal here is to pinpoint the origins and causes of
delinquency and criminal behavior, thus the focus is on factors that place individuals at risk for offending.

The risk factors we are most concerned with are individual attributes and
developmental social and family experiences that are believed to increase the
probability that an individual will engage in persistent criminal behavior. Psychological risk factors include but are not limited to inadequate cognitive and
language ability, a troublesome temperament, inadequate self-regulation skills,
and poor interpersonal and social skills. Examples of social risk factors include
poverty and impoverished resources, antisocial peers, peer rejection, and preschool or school experiences. Parental and family risk factors include faulty or
inadequate parenting, sibling influences, and child maltreatment or abuse.

It is important that we learn about these risk factors and how they influence
the developmental pathway, especially during the early stages of development.
Early identification will help improve the effectiveness of prevention and intervention programs designed to eliminate or, at least, reduce delinquent and
criminal behavior. As noted by Terrie Moffitt (2005), we know that certain risk
factors are closely linked to delinquency and criminal behavior, but how or why
they are linked is largely unknown.

SOCIAL RISK FACTORS

Poverty

There is little doubt that poverty has a strong connection to persistent, violent
offending, as measured by official, victimization, and self-report data. Accumulating research evidence strongly indicates that poverty is one of the most
robust predictors of adolescent violence for both males and females (Hammond
& Yung, 1994; Hill et al., 1994; Sampson & Wilson, 1993). However, we must
be extremely careful both in interpreting these data and in making decisions
about how to prevent future offending. Furthermore, it should be emphasized
that this strong connection holds whether we are referring to victims or offenders. Children and youth living under dire economic conditions are more
likely to be victims as well as offenders. Preschool children living in a low-
income family characterized by poor housing and unemployment are especially
at high risk to become delinquent and/or to become victimized (Dodge, 1993a;
Farrington, 1991). Poverty in this context refers to a situation in which the basic
resources to maintain an average standard of living within a specific geographic

region are lacking. This typically includes the absence of sufficient income to meet basic necessities of life.

The exact nature of the relationship between poverty and violence is not well understood. For example, poverty is often accompanied not only by inequities in resources, but also by discrimination, racism, family disruption, unsafe living conditions, joblessness, social isolation, and limited social support systems (Evans, 2004; Hill et al., 1994; Sampson & Lauritsen, 1994). Youth living under poverty conditions are more likely to attend inadequate schools, to drop out of school, to be unemployed, to carry a firearm, to be victimized, and to be a witness to a variety of violent events. Furthermore, having low income affects people differently. For instance, the values of different ethnic and cultural groups provide a cultural context wherein poverty is perceived differently (Guerra et al., 1995). Some subgroups in society may perceive material deprivation as more acceptable if everyone else within that cultural context is in the "same boat."

Poverty influences the family in many ways, not the least of which is the impact on parents' behavior toward children. For instance, the stress caused by poverty in urban settings is believed to diminish parents' capacity for supportive and consistent parenting (Hammond & Yung, 1994). This situation may lead to coercive and highly aggressive methods of child control. Coercive methods of child control are more direct, immediate, and easy to administer. They require less time and energy to administer, compared with parenting that emphasizes sensitivity, interpersonal skills, and patient understanding. It is much "easier" to slap a child than it is to explain and utilize more thoughtful parenting strategies, but the consequences of slapping can be severe. A pattern of slapping or hitting a child to punish or to maintain control promotes a negative self-concept in the child. Furthermore, parenting that utilizes aggressive and violent tactics often provides models and a violent context that can carry the cycle of violence into the next generation. Living in a disadvantaged environment accompanied by physical punishment may also lead to the belief that economic survival and social status depend greatly on being aggressive and violent to others.

Important caveats must be offered in any discussion of serious delinquency and economic status, however. First, the connection between low socioeconomic class and delinquency does not mean that poverty causes or inevitably leads to serious, chronic offending. The great majority of poor children and adults are law-abiding citizens, and children and adults from families of high economic status do engage in serious delinquency and crime. Both self-report and victimization data indicate that sexual assault, serious drug use, theft, and fraud are perpetrated by juveniles and adults across all social classes. Second, in many communities children from the lower socioeconomic class are targeted by law enforcement practices more than are children of the middle and upper classes. They are more likely to be taken into custody by police, referred to juvenile courts, and adjudicated delinquent. Thus they appear in the government statistics that serve as the official measures of crime. Additionally, children of the poor are taken into a system that may itself promote delinquent behavior or adult crime, particularly when they are institutionalized with other offenders. Children of the middle and upper classes, by contrast, are more likely to be handled informally, provided with legal assistance, or placed by their parents in private facilities for the treatment of their problem behavior (Chesney-Lind & Shelden, 1998; Schwartz, 1989).

Peer Rejection and Association with Antisocial Peers

Developmental researchers have continually found that children's peer relations make unique and essential contributions to each child's social and emotional development (Bagwell, 2004; Newcomb, Bukowksi, & Pattee, 1993). During adolescence, there is an increase in susceptibility to peer influence and a decline in susceptibility to parental influence (Mounts, 2002). In addition, numerous investigators have found that peer influence is a strong predictor of adolescent substance use and delinquent behavior (Coie & Miller-Johnson, 2001; Mounts, 2002). Not surprisingly, many members of most societies believe that this connection is obvious. The folk wisdom to "avoid bad companions" has long been the traditional admonishments from parents and other concerned adults. The link between childhood peer *rejection* and antisocial behavior and delinquency is not so obvious, however, and requires a closer examination.

One of the strongest predictors of later involvement in antisocial behavior is early rejection by peers (Dodge, 2003; Parker & Asher, 1987). In elementary school, being liked and accepted by the peer group is a crucial developmental task, generally leading to healthy psychological and social development (Rubin, Bukowski, & Parker, 1998). Social rejection by peers in the elementary school grades, on the other hand, presents a very powerful risk factor for delinquency in adolescence and antisocial behavior throughout the life course (Laird et al., 2001). Research has consistently demonstrated that peer rejection by first grade peers is significantly linked to the development of antisocial behavior by the fourth grade (Cowan & Cowan, 2004; Miller-Johnson et al., 2002). Furthermore, those children who were rejected for at least two or three years by second grade had a 50 percent chance of displaying clinically significant antisocial behavior later in adolescence, in contrast with just a 9 percent chance for those children who managed to avoid early peer rejection (Dodge & Pettit, 2003).

Interestingly, the quality of parent-child and marital relationships seems to play a significant role in whether a child is rejected or not by peers early in his or her life. Research by Cowan and Cowan (2004) demonstrates that "negative qualities in marital- and parent-child relationships in both prekindergarten and kindergarten are risk factors for low social skills, aggressive behavior, and rejection in the early years of elementary school" (p. 173).

Peer-rejected children frequently interact with one another or gravitate to antisocial peers (Laird, Pettit, Dodge, & Bates, 2005). During the adolescent years, involvement with antisocial peers shows a robust and consistent relationship to delinquency, drug use, and a range of other problematic behaviors (Laird et al., 2005). Consequently we would expect that both peer rejection *and* involvement with antisocial peers would be characteristic of those youngsters exhibiting antisocial or delinquent behavior early in their social development.

Why are Some Children Rejected by Their Peers?

Children are often rejected by their peers for a variety of reasons, but aggressive behavior appears to be a prominent reason. Children tend to reject those peers who frequently use forms of physical and verbal aggression as their preferred way of dealing with others. These findings prompted many social scientists to conclude that aggressive children are more likely than nonaggressive children to be rejected by peers. Ongoing research indicates, however, that the relationship may not be that straightforward. First, peers also reject peers who they perceive as shy and socially withdrawn. Second, not all aggressive children are rejected by peers; some are liked, accepted, and sought as friends. In fact research finds that many popular youngsters are often dominant, arrogant, and physically and relationally aggressive (Cillessen & Mayeux, 2004; Rose, Swenson, & Waller, 2004). Thus, if the children are rejected, it is not *always* because they are aggressive.

On the other hand, aggression *combined with* peer rejection does appear to lead to serious antisocial or delinquent behavior. Children who are *both* physically aggressive and socially rejected by their peers have a high probability of becoming serious delinquents during adolescence and violent offenders during early adulthood. Researchers Coie and Miller-Johnson (2001), for example, conclude from their extensive review of the research literature that "those aggressive children who are rejected by peers are at a significantly greater risk for chronic antisocial behavior than those who are not rejected" (p. 201).

Which Children are Prone to Peer Rejection?

An important question still remains: Why are certain aggressive children rejected in the first place? Coie (2004) points out that there are three important differences between peer-rejected boys and nonrejected boys. First, peer-rejected, aggressive boys are more impulsive and have problems sustaining attention and staying on task. Consequently they are more likely to be disruptive of ongoing activities in the classroom or during group play. Second, peer-rejected, aggressive boys are aroused to anger more readily and probably have more difficulty calming down. This emotional rage is more likely to result in physical and verbal attacks on peers, which in turn encourages peers to avoid them altogether. Third, rejected, aggressive youngsters have fewer social and interpersonal skills for making friends and maintaining positive relationships with peers. In addition they probably have acquired fewer social and interpersonal skills because they have had limited opportunities to practice these skills on nonrejected peers.

In summary, peer-rejected children often, though not invariably, are aggressive, but they also tend to be more argumentative, inattentive, and disruptive than others, and generally have poorer social skills. These behaviors are characteristic of attention deficient/hyperactivity disorder (ADHD), to be discussed in more detail later in the chapter under psychological risks. The observation that peer-rejected boys demonstrate inattentive, impulsive, disruptive behavior suggests that ADHD may contribute to some of the peer rejection. A study by Erhardt and Hinshaw (1994) underscores this possibility.

The study involved 25 boys with ADHD and 24 other boys who participated in a summer school program, all of whom did not know one another at the beginning of the program. The boys ranged in ages from 6 to 12 years old. As early as the first day of social interactions between the two groups, the ADHD and comparison boys showed clear differences in social behaviors, with the ADHD youngsters displaying socially noxious and noncompliance-disruptive behaviors. More important, within the first day, the ADHD youngsters were overwhelming rejected by their peers. Other studies have found similar results, with ADHD symptoms and aggression showing a close link to eventual antisocial behavioral patterns (Coie, 2004; Miller-Johnson et al., 2002). Again this topic is discussed in more detail later in the chapter.

Gender Differences in Peer Rejection

It should be noted that, to date, almost all the research and theoretical work examining the effects of peer rejection, aggression, and delinquent behavior has focused on boys. Among girls little is known about the combined effects of aggression and peer rejection. In one of the few studies focusing on girls, Prinstein and La Greca (2004) found that the development of antisocial and delinquent behavior in girls, as in boys, can be predicted by early involvement in aggressive behavior with peers. There is also some evidence to suggest that relationally aggressive girls are more likely than nonaggressive girls to be peer-rejected (Crick, 1995). That is, girls usually use relationship aggression to hurt others and diminish their social status rather than relying on the physical aggression typically used by boys. Prinstein and La Greca discovered—as did Crick—that peer rejection among girls in elementary school increased aggression but also was associated with increased substance abuse and other delinquent behaviors during adolescence. On the other hand, peer acceptance reduced and even eliminated the risk of aggression and other delinquent behaviors later on. More specifically the effects of childhood aggression and antisocial behavior were mollified under conditions of high acceptance by peers.

Gang Influences on Rejected Youth

There are three major perspectives on the influence of peer groups on antisocial and delinquent behavior. One perspective argues that youngsters become delinquent as a direct result of association with deviant peer groups.

According to this view, almost any child is susceptible to the negative influences of participating in a deviant peer group. A second perspective contends that antisocial, peer-rejected youths seek out greater contact with similar peer-rejected and socially unskillful peers. Rejected and antisocial youths seek out other rejected and antisocial youths. A third perspective is somewhat between these two positions. Peer-rejected, antisocial children are drawn to deviant groups with members similar to themselves, and this encourages and amplifies *already existing* antisocial tendencies. Current research evidence is in favor of the third perspective. It appears that childhood peer rejection encourages children to participate in deviant peer groups that then *amplify* tendencies to become more deviant and antisocial. Put another way, deviant group membership or gangs encourage and increase the already existing antisocial patterns in children and adolescents. As noted by Coie (2004), "The impact of deviant peer group influences on the *crystallization of an antisocial developmental trajectory* [emphasis added] has been solidly documented" (p. 257).

Although the bulk of the evidence supports the third perspective of amplification of already existing deviant tendencies, there is some evidence that deviant group membership appears to encourage some nondelinquent children to participate in *minor* delinquent actions. For example, while following the social development of youngsters, ages 11 to 17, Elliott and Menard (1996) discovered that nondelinquent youths were more inclined to engage in minor delinquent activity after joining a deviant peer group than before. And Thornberry, Krohn, Lizotte, and Chard-Wierschem (1993) report that nondelinquent youths who joined gangs were more likely to engage in minor delinquent behavior while gang members but decreased or terminated their delinquent behavior when they left the group.

Temptation Talk

Bagwell (2004) makes the observation that many youths during middle childhood and adolescence engage in what she calls "temptation talk." Temptation talk refers to peer group discussions of potential rule violations and deviant behavior, and it serves as way for boys in particular to explore their thoughts and ideas about rule-breaking behaviors with their friends (Bagwell, 2004). The temptation talk may lead them to join a deviant peer group, even if temporarily. Although it appears both nondelinquents and delinquent youth participate in temptation talk with some regularity, delinquents are more likely to go beyond the talk and actually commit the deviant act.

Preschool Experiences

Over the past 30 years, children have been shifted gradually from home to center-based day care or nursery school. The proportion of mothers participating in the workforce has increased substantially in recent years. Because mothers have traditionally been the primary caretaker, this is a significant change. The percentage of mothers with children under age 6 working outside the home has increased from 12 percent in 1947, to 31 percent in 1975, to 64 percent in 1997 (Tran & Weinraub, 2006). In 2003, more than half of mothers with infants less than 1 year old were in the labor force (Tran & Weinraub, 2006). The most recent data indicate that 63 percent of children under the age of 5 are in some form of day care or nonmaternal (or paternal care) on a regular basis (U.S. Bureau of the Census, 2002).

Today more American children are cared for by paid providers than by relatives (Scarr, 1998). In 1995, there were nearly 21 million children under the age of 5 who were not yet enrolled in school. Of these about 40 percent were cared for regularly by parents, 21 percent by other relatives, 45 percent in child-care centers or family day-care centers, and 4 percent by sitters in the child's home. While there are obviously numerous exceptions, out-of-home child care in the United States is, on average, mediocre. The quality of child care provided by day-care centers is highly variable, in large part due to low wages and high staff turnover in many facilities. Poor quality child care has been reported to put children's development at risk for poorer language, cognitive development, and lower ratings of social and emotional adjustment (Tran & Weinraub, 2006). Unfortunately children from families with single employed mothers and low incomes were more likely to be found in lower quality care (Howes & Olenick, 1986), although there have been some serious attempts to correct this problem.

More encouragingly, low-income children who experience high-quality infant and preschool care show better school achievement and socialized behavior in later years than similar children without child-care experience or with experience in lower quality care. For low-income children, quality child care offers learning opportunities and social and emotional supports that many would not experience at home.

According to Goldstein et al. (2001), day-care teachers worry about aggression in their toddlers more than any other behavioral problem, and they report disruptive behavior as their greatest classroom challenge. These concerns may be important, as aggressive tendencies at 3 years of age predict aggressive behavior later in life (Goldstein et al., 2001). Accumulating evidence indicates that the amount of exposure that a child has to aggressive peers in day care or preschool is predictive of later child aggressive behavior, perhaps because of modeling effects (Dodge & Pettit, 2003).

After-School Care

The quality of after-school care has been closely associated with the development of antisocial behavior (Flannery, Williams, & Vazsonyi, 1999; Posner & Vandell, 1999; Vandell & Posner, 1999). In the 1990s the term "latch-key" children was applied to children who returned from school to an empty house and remained on their own until their parents or guardians finished their own work day. Children who spend fairly large amounts of time in unsupervised after-school self-care in the early elementary grades are at elevated risk for behavior problems in early adolescence (Pettit, Laird, Bates, & Dodge, 1997). Moreover, such children are more likely to spend time in unsupervised activity with peers in early adolescence (Colwell et al., 2001). Antisocial children seek out niches that involve association with antisocial peers and environments with minimal adult supervision (Snyder, Reid, & Patterson, 2003).

School Failure

Early school failure is also linked to antisocial development and delinquency (Dodge & Pettit, 2003). Interestingly, research indicates that retention in kindergarten and in the early school grades has long-term detrimental effects on development, in spite of its immediate academic benefits (Dodge & Pettit, 2003; Holmes, 1989; Sameroff, Peck, & Eccles, 2004). On the other hand, delaying entry into kindergarten does not appear to have the same effects. It is the "staying back" label that prompts retained children to be seen negatively and socially rejected and ridiculed by their peers (Plummer & Graziano, 1987).

In fact, early school failure seems to be more strongly associated with delinquency than low intelligence (Hinshaw, 1992). Some researchers discovered that the odds of severe delinquent behavior in 8-year-old male children who were failing in school were nearly double those of other male children (Loeber, Farrington, Stouthamer-Loeber, & Van Kammen, 1998).

Regardless of race or ethnic background, reading achievement appears to play a prominent role in school failure. In fact, poor reading achievement not only is closely associated with school failure, but also it predicts later arrest and criminal activity in boys (Petras et al., 2004). On the other hand, a high level of reading achievement seems to prevent at-risk youth from engaging in later antisocial behavior. More specifically, a high level of reading achievement brings more acceptance from mainstream peers, greater attachment to school, enhanced job prospects in young adulthood, and better cognitive resources for anticipating the negative consequences of engaging in criminal activity (Petras et al., 2004).

In summary, the most prominent social risk factors that have been identified in the development of criminal behavior include the many disadvantages of living in poverty, peer rejection combined with association with antisocial peers, poor quality child care during the preschool years, and school failure. The more social risk factors a child experiences during his or her early life, the higher the probability a child will follow a developmental pathway toward delinquent and criminal behavior. Parental and family risk factors may play even a more prominent role in the development of antisocial behavior.

PARENTAL AND FAMILY RISK FACTORS

Single-Parent Households

It is estimated that over twelve million American families with children are maintained by only one parent (U.S. Bureau of the Census, 2001). Early studies based on official data found that delinquents were more likely than nondelinquents to come from homes where parents were divorced or separated (Eaton & Polk, 1961; Glueck & Glueck, 1950; Monahan, 1957; Rodman & Grams, 1967). This led to conclusions that the single-parent home—or the "broken home" as it was called—could be blamed for much delinquency and thus could be considered a risk factor. Beginning in the 1970s, when self-report data indicated that delinquent behavior was widespread, criminologists began to question these conclusions. Today, researchers are more likely to examine accompanying factors such as the quality of the parent-child relationship, the family's economic status, and the degree of emotional support provided to the family by other adults, such as extended family members or community agents.

A wide variety of circumstances can lead to a single-parent home. The home may have started that way, as when an unmarried woman gives birth to or adopts a child. Additionally, two-parent homes may be "broken" by a wide variety of circumstances—death, desertion, divorce, or separation. Such separations do not affect all families the same way. Furthermore there is evidence that children from single-parent homes that are relatively conflict free are less likely to be delinquent than children from conflict-ridden "intact" homes (Gove & Crutchfield, 1982). The composition of the home (e.g., grandparents, stepparent, relatives, significant others, or friends) also must be considered. The "nontraditional" family has become a fixture in today's society. Many researchers define family as individuals related by blood or by legal arrangements (i.e., adoptions, legal guardianships, civil unions). Others point out that individuals who live together in long-term committed relationships—either as friends or as sexual partners—and who may be caring for their own or other people's children, are also family.

While the relationship between single-parent homes and delinquency continues to be commonly reported, we are far from explaining it—and it may be pointless to try. If the single-parent home is a risk factor, it is probably influenced by other interacting variables. Rather than concentrating on the *structure* of the family, a focus on the *process* is far more desirable. As Flynn (1983, p. 13) asserts, "One point is indisputably clear in the literature: A stable, secure, and mutually supportive family is exceedingly important in delinquency prevention."

Parental Styles and Practices

Some styles and practices appear to be more likely than others to lead to delinquency, and thus can be called risk factors. **Parental practices** are strategies employed by parents to achieve specific academic, social, or athletic goals across different contexts and situations (Hart et al., 1998). That is, when parents use parenting practices, their focus is on affecting some particular aspect of the child (Mounts, 2002). Giving a child a weekly allowance with the hope of teaching her to manage money is an example of a practice. Reading with children, attending their games, or serving as room parents in school are other examples. Parenting practices have a direct effect on the development of specific child behaviors (from table manners to academic performance) and characteristics (such as acquisition of particular values or high self-esteem).

Parental styles, on the other hand, refer to parent-child interactions characterized by parental attitudes toward the child and the emotional climate of the parent-child relationship (Baumrind, 1991; Mounts, 2002). Non-goal–directed parental behaviors, such as gestures, changes in tone of voice, or the spontaneous expression of emotion, provide examples of parental style. For example, responsive parent-child interactions are described as warm, playful, accepting, and engaging. Studies reveal that a responsive parenting style often leads to social competence, peer acceptance, and less antisocial behavior (Hart et al., 1998).

Three Types of Parental Styles

Diana Baumrind (1991) identified three types of parental styles (1) authoritarian; (2) permissive; and (3) authoritative. Those parents who use an **authoritarian style** try to shape, control, and evaluate the behavior of their children in accordance with some preestablished, absolute standard. The authoritarian household has numerous rules and regulations which must be rigidly observed, often without question or explanation. Authoritarian parents expect their children to be obedient and unquestioningly respectful of authority. These parents are often referred to as "running a tight ship." Deviations and transgressions are met with punitive, forceful measures, which may or may not include physical punishment. The authoritarian parent discourages any verbal exchanges that imply equality between parent and child; the parent is the authority in all important matters, as well as many unimportant ones.

Parents who adopt a **permissive style** display tolerant, nonpunitive, accepting attitudes toward their children's behavior, including expressions of aggressive and sexual impulses. Permissive parents generally avoid asserting authority or imposing social controls or restrictions on the child's behavior. In this type of family, parents see themselves as "resource persons" to be consulted if needed. Permissive parents allow children to set their own time schedule for eating, sleeping, watching television, playing video games, leaving the home, and meeting with friends, and they employ little parental monitoring. They are, in essence, ineffectual in their socializing roles.

In the **authoritative style,** parents try to direct their children's activities in a rational, issue-oriented manner. There are frequent decision-making exchanges and a general spirit of open communication between parents and children. The hallmark of the family led by authoritative parents is reasoned discussion punctuated with social controls. Authoritative parents expect age-related "mature" behavior from the child, and they apply firm, consistent enforcement of family rules and standards. At the same time, they encourage independence and individuality.

Baumrind's types are not without their problems. Many parents, for example, vacillate between permissiveness and authoritativeness, and some vary their

TABLE 2–1   Summary Table of Baumrind's Parental Styles

STYLE	INTEND
Authoritarian	To shape and control child's life
Permissive	No control and extremely few restrictions
Authoritative	To be rational and apply reasonable restrictions

styles according to the age of the child. Authoritative parents may allow their children to set their own eating and sleeping schedules and choose their modes of dress, but may demand extensive input into decisions related to school, careers, or work. Likewise some parents may be generally permissive in style, but suddenly erupt into anger and demand that their children abide by a newly announced rule. Despite its many shortcomings, "Baumrind's conceptualization of parenting style has produced a remarkably consistent picture of the type of parenting conducive to the successful socialization of children into the dominant culture of the United States" (Darling & Steinberg, 1993, p. 487).

Enmeshed and Lax Parental Styles

James Snyder and Gerald Patterson (1987) conclude that two parental styles contribute directly or indirectly to delinquency. They label the two styles "enmeshed" and "lax," and these are very similar to Baumrind's authoritarian and permissive styles. In the **enmeshed style,** parents see an unusually large number of minor behaviors as problematic, and they use ineffective, authoritarian strategies to deal with them. "These parents don't ignore even very trivial excessive behaviors. They issue more and poorer commands, use verbal threats, disapproval, and cajoling more frequently, but fail to consistently and effectively back up these verbal reprimands with nonviolent, nonphysical punishment" (Snyder & Patterson, 1987, p. 221). The ineffective use of coercive punishment sets up a reverberating pattern of family interactions "which elicits, maintains, and exacerbates the aggressive behavior of all family members" (p. 221). When one family member in this coercive interaction acts aversively, other family members react the same way, escalating the exchange. Cathy reacts strongly to her brother's loud music by suddenly screaming to him to turn it off. He screams back at her to "stick it." Cathy bangs violently on his door. He screams louder. The father screams at both, telling them to "shut up" or else. Cathy screams louder and proceeds to kick in her brother's door. She throws a vase at him, just missing. He runs after her, throwing a book. Eventually, the child sometimes "wins" this escalating confrontation when parents "give in" to demands, reinforcing this highly aversive interpersonal strategy. For example, father "orders" her brother to turn the loud music off. Thus parents and children "teach" each other that this harsh tactic works in social interactions, a pattern that soon extends to members outside the family.

Enmeshed parents also sometimes dispense authoritarian, harsh punishment, although it is inconsistent and ineffective. However, they probably do not have the energy to apply punishments to each and every behavior they perceive as problematic. Consequently there are many instances where aversive behavior goes unpunished, such as in the preceding example. This pattern results in an intermittent, inconsistent punishment schedule that, in the long run, does little to discourage antisocial behavior.

The **lax style** employs strategies that are the opposite of the above. According to Snyder and Patterson (1987), lax parents are not sufficiently attuned to what constitutes problematic or antisocial behavior in children. Consequently they allow much of it to slip by, without disciplinary actions. For a variety of reasons, they fail to recognize or accept the fact that their children are involved in deviant, antisocial, or even violent actions. They simply do not believe it is happening, or they convince themselves that there is very little they can do about it.

It appears that overcontrolling parental behaviors—those associated with enmeshed and authoritarian styles—are closely connected to the development of aggression and antisocial behavior in children and adolescents (Blitstein et al., 2005; Ruchkin, 2002). By contrast, an authoritative style has the opposite effect. Blitstein et al. (2005) report evidence that violent behavior and antisocial behavior among girls may be buffered by the presence of a warm, responsive (i.e., authoritative) mother, although the same result was not found for boys. In short, authoritative mothers seem to play a more significant role for the prevention of antisocial behavior in girls than in boys (Hollister-Wagner, Foshee, & Jackson, 2001).

The parental styles most strongly tied to delinquency, though, appear to be Baumrind's permissive and Snyder and Patterson's lax style. The children brought up with these styles often have very low levels of self-reliance and great difficulty controlling their impulses. Permissive parents have long been faulted both for lack of discipline and lack of supervision. They may treat their children as adults, pushing them into adult behaviors or responsibilities far before they are ready and without needed direction from adult authority figures.

Parental Monitoring

Closely related to parental styles and antisocial behavior is the issue of parental supervision or monitoring. **Parental monitoring** "refers to parents' awareness of their child's peer associates, free time activities, and physical whereabouts when outside the home" (Snyder & Patterson, 1987, pp. 225–26). The amount and quality of parental monitoring is influenced by a number of things. For example, divorce, serious financial distress, loss of job, parental psychological disorders, substance abuse, or death may significantly affect family dynamics and parental or caregiver monitoring. Monitoring appears to be especially important from about age 9 to midadolescence, an observation that has received substantial support from several studies (Laird, Pettit, Bates, & Dodge, 2003).

Parental anecdotes often support this as well. As one mother expressed, "I couldn't afford to be a stay-at-home Mom throughout my kids' childhoods, so I chose to do it when my oldest got to middle school. That's when they needed me home the most."

The bulk of the available research also has concluded that the amount and quality of parental monitoring is a strong predictor of antisocial behavior during later childhood and adolescence (Kilgore, Snyder, & Lentz, 2000). Some studies have indicated that poor parental monitoring and supervision increase the risk of delinquency two and a half times over those youth who experienced better supervision (Browning & Loeber, 1999).

Influence of Siblings

Siblings imitate each other, and most often younger children imitate their older siblings rather than the reverse (Garcia et al., 2000). Since siblings generally spend so much time together, it is reasonable to assume that they play a role in shaping the development of aggression and antisocial behavior. This area has not been researched as heavily as other peer influences, but the few studies available indicate that adolescents with high rates of delinquency are also more likely to have siblings with high rates (Coie & Miller-Johnson, 2001). Rowe and Gulley (1992) suggest that older siblings who engage in delinquent behavior reinforce antisocial behavior in younger siblings when there is a close and warm relationship between the youths. If the siblings are not close, the opposite effect may occur. That is, the nonaggressive younger sibling may make it a point not to be like his or her older aggressive or antisocial sibling. In addition, the risk of delinquency is higher when the delinquent sibling is closer in age than those siblings spaced further apart (Rowe, Rodgers, & Meseck-Bushey, 1992).

Parental Psychopathology

Children of parents—especially mothers—who are clinically depressed are at increased risk for a range of socioemotional and behavioral problems, including antisocial behavior, emotion dysregulation, and poor cognitive development (Bennett, Bendersky, & Lewis, 2002; Mazulis, Hyde, & Clark, 2004; Nelson, Hammen, Brennan, & Ullman, 2003). As they grow older, children whose mothers were depressed during their infancy continue to display behavioral problems and often engage in various kinds of criminal behavior. Mothers are singled out because they tend to be the dominant caretakers. However, the risk for developing problem behaviors appears to be magnified if both parents are depressed during early childhood.

Parental alcoholism elevates risk for a variety of negative child outcomes, including behavioral difficulties, antisocial behavior, and subsequent alcoholism (Loukas, Zucker, Fitzgerald, & Krull, 2003; Zucker et al., 2000). Interestingly,

Loukas and her colleagues (2003) found that the presence of paternal alcoholism in the family may be more important than maternal alcoholism in contributing to a son's antisocial behavior and maladjustment.

The aggressive behavior that is demonstrated in domestic violence is clearly a form of parental psychopathology. However, this topic is discussed more fully in chapter 9 under multiassaultive families and family violence. We now turn our attention to psychological risk factors, those that are features of the individual rather than the social context in which he or she is imbedded.

PSYCHOLOGICAL RISK FACTORS

Cognitive and Language Deficiencies

Cognitive and language impairments increase the risk of antisocial behavior, at least in boys (Brownlie et al., 2004). For example, a high percentage of children and adolescents diagnosed and treated for antisocial behavior and conduct disorders demonstrate language impairments (Cohen et al., 1998; Giddan, Milling, & Campbell, 1996). **Language impairment** usually refers to problems expressing or understanding language, and some research has even traced these problems as far back as very early childhood. In an important study of Swedish children, Stattin and Klackenberg-Larson (1993) discovered that poor language development during the second year of life was a significant predictor of adult criminal behavior. Brownlie et al. (2004) also found that boys diagnosed with a language impairment at age 5 were far more likely to exhibit delinquent behavior at age 19 than a group of boys without early indications of a language impairment. This relationship held even when controlling for verbal IQ, demographic, and family variables. Brownlie et al. speculated, though, that the association may be largely due to the negative impact that language impairments have on the child's schooling and academic performance in general. In addition, language impaired children are often rejected by peers and are frequently viewed negatively by their teachers. In essence, language deficiency often makes school a painful and unappealing enterprise, leading to poor or disinterested performance on academic tasks.

Language problems also increase frustration levels in children who have difficulty expressing their points of view, which is so necessary for reasonable resolutions of conflict. This frustration, if not self-regulated, is likely to lead to aggressive and disruptive behavior at home and at school.

Intelligence and Delinquency

For some time, criminologists (and many psychologists) have been eager to label the relationship between intelligence and delinquency and crime as misguided and unsubstantiated. Even to mention the connection may prompt a derisive reaction. As Hirschi and Hindelang (1977, p. 572) wrote some years ago, "Textbooks in crime and delinquency ignore IQ or impatiently explain to the reader that IQ is no longer taken seriously by knowledgeable students simply because no differences worth considering have been revealed by research." Hirschi and Hindelang maintained that these textbooks were misleading, because the delinquency literature consistently reported that delinquents do, as a group, score lower on standard intelligence tests than nondelinquents.

In their 1977 paper, Hirschi and Hindelang hypothesized that an *indirect* causal relationship exists between IQ and delinquency. That is, a low IQ leads to poor performance and negative attitudes toward school, which in turn leads to school failure and ultimately to delinquency. Low IQ does not directly lead to delinquency. A high IQ, on the other hand, leads to good performance and positive attitudes toward school, which in turn leads to the internal acceptance of conventional values and conformity (nondelinquency). The essential point, according to Hirschi and Hindelang, is that the inverse relationship between IQ scores and delinquency continues to be documented by the research.

Why does this relationship exist? To address this question, it is necessary to consider the meaning of IQ and to stress that it is not identical to "intelligence." The term IQ is an abbreviation of the intelligence quotient derived from a numerical score on a so-called "intelligence" test. The term "IQ" originated out of what is now called the **psychometric approach.** The word *psychometric* means "psychological measurement." Traditionally the psychometric approach has searched for unique differences in persons through the use of psychological tests, including intelligence tests, scholastic aptitude tests (e.g., SAT), school achievement tests, personality inventories, and other specific abilities tests. The various tests are used for many purposes, such as selection, diagnosis, and evaluation. The psychometric approach continues to be widely used by practicing psychologists and mental health professionals. However, the term **psychometric intelligence (PI)**—which was preferred by some psychologists (Neisser et al., 1996) in the 1990s—has not caught on. Consequently the traditional term IQ continues to be used with great frequency today.

Satisfactory performance on a vast majority of intelligence tests depends greatly on language acquisition and verbal development. Usually, a person must have considerable experience using and defining words—particularly English words—to do well on most IQ tests. The examinee must be able to make conventional connections and see distinctions between verbal concepts. The examinee must also know the facts that the test designer deems important to know within mainstream culture. At the very least, almost all intelligence tests measure some aspect of academic skills that are taught in school or that predict success in school. A vast majority of psychologists today would agree that IQ scores are strongly influenced by social, educational, and cultural experiences. In short all intelligence tests are culturally biased.

More important, IQ scores and the concept of intelligence should not be confused. The term IQ merely refers to a standardized score from a test. *Intelligence, on the other hand, is a broad, all-encompassing ability that defies any straightforward or simple definition.* It means many things to different people.

Intelligence includes ability ranging from musical talent to logical mathematical skills. The term may also include wisdom, intuition, judgment, and even humor. While delinquents, as a group, do score lower on intelligence *tests,* this observation should not be construed as documenting that delinquents are less intelligent than nondelinquents. For example, Brazilian street children are masters at doing the math required for survival in their street business even though they have failed mathematics in school (Carraher, Carraher, & Schliemann, 1985; Neisser et al., 1996). Likewise institutionalized delinquents often display artistic and verbal skills and a sense of humor that are not tapped by traditional IQ scores.

Nevertheless the relationship between IQ test scores and school performance is strong and consistent. "Wherever it has been studied, children with high scores on tests of intelligence tend to learn more of what is taught in school than their lower-scoring peers" (Neisser et al., 1996, p. 82). Schools help develop certain intellectual skills and attitudes. Quality schools generally have positive effects on IQ. Preschool programs (e.g., Headstart) show significant positive effects on children during their early school years, and recent research shows that these gains do not fade when the program is over, provided there is periodic intervention during the child's middle school years.

IQ and Ethnicity

Average IQ scores do vary among racial and ethnic groups. For example, many studies using different tests and samples typically show African Americans scoring significantly lower than whites (Neisser et al., 1996). Studies show, however, that this IQ gap has been consistently decreasing since 1980 (Nisbett, 2005; Vincent, 1991). Asian Americans and whites, on average, score about the same on IQ tests; Native Americans score slightly lower than other groups on verbal skills, but this slight difference may be the result of chronic middle-ear infections common among Native American children (McShane & Plas, 1984a, 1984b). Latinos, who make up the second largest and fastest-growing minority group in the United States, typically score somewhere between African Americans and whites. It is unclear what these reported differences mean, but there is no evidence to support the view that racial or ethnic differences in psychometric intelligence are due to genetics or biological factors. Although genetics may play a role in *individual* differences in psychometric intelligence, there is little evidence for ethnic *group* differences.

Group differences in IQ are most likely due to a combination of factors, dominated by cultural and social influences. According to Boykin (1986, 1994), for instance, the African American culture is not quite in synchronization with the values and expectations of the American school system. To varying degrees, the black culture "includes an emphasis on such aspects of experience as spirituality, harmony, movement, verve, affect, expressive individualism, communalism, orality, and a socially defined time perspective" (Neisser et al., 1996, p. 95). If schools do not recognize and celebrate these positive aspects, African

American children may feel left out of the mainstream. According to Boykin, black children often find their cultural background in conflict with the culture of the school system, and consequently they become alienated from both the process and products of that educational system. Equally problematic, however, is the fact that many black children attend inner-city schools, where the quality of education and services is below par. It is not surprising, then, that performance on standardized tests would reflect this inequity.

Other factors—such as poor nutrition, inadequate prenatal care, lack of adequate child-care facilities, and inaccessibility to occupational and training opportunities—also play critical but largely unknown roles on intelligence. IQ scores are crude indices of mainstream language skills that are heavily influenced by experience. In general, rich and varied experiences increase IQ scores, and limited experience decreases them (Garbarino & Asp, 1981; Neisser et al., 1996). School experiences, if positive, may increase language skills; if negative, they may stagnate, or even decrease, language skills. IQ scores are also strongly influenced by the type of test used, its content, the many characteristics of testing situations, and the training and skill of the examiner.

Still, even with these many variations, the inverse relationship between IQ scores and the tendency toward delinquency is consistently reported (e.g., Binder, 1988; Quay, 1987; White, Moffitt, & Silva, 1989). As IQ scores go down, the probability of misconduct increases, and vice versa. Children with low IQ scores are at a higher risk for delinquent behavior, and as Anne Crocker and Sheilagh Hodgins (1997, p. 434) write, "To our knowledge, no study has failed to confirm this relation." The relationship is particularly strong for verbal IQ scores (Culberton, Feral, & Gabby, 1989; Kandel et al., 1988). Furthermore, as noted by Crocker and Hodgins (1997), the relationship between low IQ scores and delinquency appears to be independent of socioeconomic status, race, and detection by the police (Lynam, Moffitt, & Stouthamer-Loeber, 1993; Moffitt, 1990b). Moreover, it should be emphasized that this relationship is not specific to delinquency; the relationship is equally robust for adult offenders.

IQ and Adult Offenders

Very low IQ scores, those that indicate mental disability, are of particular concern. Recent estimates indicate that at least 4 percent of the U.S. prison population qualify as being mentally disabled (Ashford, Sales, & Reid, 2001). **Jails** are believed to hold an even higher percentage. Crocker and Hodgins (1997) examined the criminality of mentally deficient men and women in a Swedish birth cohort composed of over fifteen thousand subjects. The subjects were followed from birth to age 30. Subjects who were placed in special classes for the mentally retarded (both at the elementary and high school level) were compared with normal subjects. Subjects considered mentally retarded were more likely to have been convicted for criminal offenses, including violent ones, than normal subjects. Crocker and Hodgins also found that, similar to mentally normal subjects, conduct problems in childhood (before age 12) were predictive of adult antisocial behavior in both mentally deficient male and female groups.

Summary

What does the relationship between IQ scores and delinquency and crime mean exactly? It probably means that delinquents *as a group,* particularly serious delinquents, have had limited experiences in mainstream society, faulty parenting, restricted cognitive and language development, and poor school experiences, but it does not necessarily mean that they are not intelligent. Related to the IQ question is the issue of learning disabilities, a term that is also not synonymous with intelligence. There is considerable empirical evidence that juvenile delinquents have a far greater incidence of learning disabilities than nondelinquents (Brier, 1989; Lombardo & Lombardo, 1991; Scaret & Wilgosh, 1989). While learning disabilities clearly exist, it is believed that they are overdiagnosed or misdiagnosed in many children who then acquire a label that may follow them through the educational system. Like the IQ question, it is very unclear what the relationship between delinquency and learning disability truly means.

Attention Deficit Hyperactivity Disorder (ADHD)

Children are born with a wide range of genetic influences, neurological predispositions, and different temperaments, although the social and physical environments may alter them. These are all biological factors, and some appear to play a major role in the development of crime and delinquency. Chief among them is attention deficient disorder/hyperactivity disorder, commonly abbreviated ADHD.

The term "hyperactive syndrome" (also called minimal brain dysfunction, hyperkinesis, attention deficit disorder, or currently **attention deficit hyperactivity disorder [ADHD]**) includes a variety of behaviors. The central three are (1) inattention (does not seem to listen, or is easily distracted); (2) impulsivity (acts before thinking, shifts quickly from one activity to another); and (3) excessive motor activity (cannot sit still, fidgets, runs about, is talkative and noisy).

ADHD is the leading psychological diagnosis for American children (Cowley, 1993; Staller, 2006). Educators note that ADHD children have difficulty staying on task, remaining cognitively organized, sustaining academic achievement in the school setting, and maintaining control over their behavior. Although the common belief is that one eventually outgrows hyperactivity, the evidence is that the key symptomatic features of hyperactivity persist into adulthood (Klinteberg, Magnusson, & Schalling, 1989; Thorley, 1984). It should be emphasized, however, that many children diagnosed with ADHD grow up to lead highly successful lives, and most do not follow a life course of serious delinquency and crime.

ADHD affects an estimated 3 percent to 5 percent of school age children (Stern, 2001), and occurs more often in boys than girls, usually in a ratio of

5 to 1. Furthermore, ADHD is diagnosed more frequently in children who have a close biological relative with ADHD than in the general population, suggesting there may be a significant biological component involved. Boys with ADHD are at increased risk for engaging in delinquent and antisocial behavior. "As they grow older, children with untreated ADHD . . . may abuse drugs or alcohol, engage in antisocial behavior, and suffer physical injury at higher rates that the general population" (Stern, 2001, p. 1).

ADHD is a puzzling problem, the cause of which is largely unknown. Some scientists contend that ADHD children are born with a biological predisposition toward hyperactivity; others maintain that some children are exposed to environmental factors that damage the nervous system. Rolf Loeber (1990) demonstrates how exposure to toxic substances during the preschool years often retards children's neurological development or otherwise influences it in a negative way, often resulting in symptoms of ADHD. For example, children exposed to low levels of lead toxicity (from paint) are more hyperactive and impulsive, and are easily distracted and frustrated. They also show discernible problems in following simple instructions. The causal factors of ADHD are probably multiple and extremely difficult to identify.

Some researchers observe that ADHD children do not possess effective strategies and cognitive organization with which to deal with the daily demands of school. ADHD children also seem to lack cognitively organized ways for dealing with new knowledge. The core problem appears to center around executive functions, or what can be termed self-regulation skills (Douglas, 2004). **Self-regulation** refers to the ability to control behavior. According to Virginia Douglas (2004), it is not so much "not knowing" as "not doing." Attention, inhibition, and organizing are ways of "doing" or working on cognitive processes. Stimulant drugs, Douglas argues, enable ADHD children to improve on self-regulation processes. These drugs themselves, though, are extremely controversial and are themselves widely believed to be overprescribed.

Although many behaviors have been identified as accompanying ADHD, another overriding theme is that ADHD children are perceived as annoying and aversive to those around them. Although ADHD children are continually seeking and prolonging interpersonal contacts, they eventually manage to irritate and frustrate those people with whom they interact (Henker & Whalen, 1989). They are often rejected by peers, especially if they are perceived as aggressive (Henker & Whalen, 1989). This pattern of peer rejection appears to continue throughout the developmental years (Reid, 1993).

ADHD and Criminal Behavior

Some researchers (e.g., Pffiffner, McBurnett, Rathouz, & Judice, 2005) estimate about one-fourth of all children with ADHD engage in serious antisocial behavior during childhood and adolescence and criminal behavior as adults. Terrie Moffitt (Moffitt, 1993b; Moffitt & Silva, 1988) observes that a very large number of ADHD children self-report delinquent behaviors by early adolescence. She also found that children between the ages of 5 and 7 who demonstrate the characteristics of both ADHD and delinquent behavior not only have special difficulty with social relationships but also have a high probability of consistent serious antisocial behavior into delinquency and beyond (Moffitt, 1990b). Experts generally agree that the most common problem associated with ADHD is delinquency and substance abuse. The data strongly suggest that youth with symptoms of both ADHD and antisocial behavior are at very high risk for developing lengthy and serious criminal careers (Moffitt, 1990; Satterfield, Swanson, Schell, & Lee, 1994). David Farrington (1991), in his well-cited research, also found that violent offenders often have a history of hyperactivity, impulsivity, and attention deficit problems.

Conduct Disorder

ADHD frequently co-occurs with a diagnostic category called "conduct disorders" (Offord, Boyle, & Racine, 1991; Reid, 1993), but the two should be considered separate entities. The term **conduct disorder** (abbreviated CD) represents a cluster of behaviors characterized by persistent misbehavior. Examples of this misbehavior include stealing, fire setting, running away from home, skipping school, destroying property, fighting, frequently telling lies, and cruelty to animals and people. According to the *Diagnostic and Statistical Manual-IV* (DSM-IV), published by the American Psychiatric Association (1994), the central feature of conduct disorder is the *repetitive* and *persistent* pattern of behavior that violates the basic rights of others.

Behavioral indicators of a conduct disorder can be observed in the context of interactions with parents well before school entry (Reid, 1993). For instance children who are aggressive, difficult to manage, and noncompliant in the home at age three often continue to have similar problems when entering school. Furthermore these behaviors show remarkable consistency through adolescence and into adulthood. CD children frequently have significant problems with school assignments, a behavioral pattern that often results in their being mislabeled with a "learning disability." It is important to note that genuinely learning-disabled students are not necessarily conduct disordered, however. In other words, the two designations may overlap, but each is also a distinct categorization. Aggressive CDs are at high risk for strong rejection by their peers (Reid, 1993). This rejection generally lasts throughout the school years and is very difficult to change (Reid, 1993). Children who are consistently socially rejected by peers miss critical opportunities to develop normal interpersonal and social skills. Lacking effective interpersonal skills, these youths are forced to get their needs met through more aggressive means, including threats and intimidation.

The DSM-IV identifies two subtypes of conduct disorders based on the onset of the repetition and persistence of the misbehavior: the *childhood-onset type* and *adolescent-onset type*. According to the DSM-IV, childhood onset type occurs when the pattern begins prior to age ten. The adolescent-onset type, on the other hand, is characterized by the absence of any pattern before age ten. The DSM-IV also notes that if the CD pattern begins before age ten, the prognosis is not good, compared with a more favorable prognosis for a later onset.

There is some recent research suggesting that individual maladjustment and family influences are more highly associated with childhood-onset conduct disorders, whereas ethnic minority status and exposure to deviant peers is more highly associated with adolescent-onset conduct disorders (McCabe, Hough, Wood, & Yeh, 2001). The researchers also found that those children who exhibit childhood-onset conduct disorders are more likely to commit more serious or aggressive offenses than adolescent-onset conduct disorders, although the results were not as strong as the first finding.

Overall, between 2 percent and 6 percent of children and adolescents in the United States show behavioral patterns that may be diagnosed as a conduct disorder (Eddy, 2003). The prevalence in girls ranges from 4 percent to 9.2 percent (Cohen, Cohen, & Brook, 1993; Zoccoulillo, 1993). In addition, CD is the diagnostic label most often placed on youths who appear before the juvenile courts (Lahey et al., 1995). A study by Anna Bardone and her colleagues (Bardone, Moffitt, & Caspi, 1996) found that CD patterns in girls are a strong predictor of a lifetime of problems, including poor interpersonal relations with partners/spouses and peers, criminal activity, early pregnancy without supportive partners, and frequent job loss and firings. Similar to CD boys, CD girls appear destined for a life of interpersonal conflict with the social environment.

TABLE 2–2   Developmental Risk Factors for Delinquency

Social Risk Factors
  Poverty*
  Early peer rejection
  Association with antisocial peers
  Inadequate preschool child care
  Inadequate after-school care
  School failure
Parental and Family Risk Factors
  Single-parent household*
  Permissive or lax parental style
  Minimal parental monitoring
  Parental psychopathology
  Physical and emotional abuse/neglect
  Domestic violence and/or substance abuse
  Antisocial siblings
Psychological Risk Factors
  Cognitive and language deficiencies
  Low IQ scores or psychometric intelligence
  Attention deficit hyperactivity disorder (ADHD)
  Conduct disorder (CD)

*Must be accompanied by other factors in order to be considered strong risk.

GENDER DIFFERENCES IN THE DEVELOPMENT OF DELINQUENCY

As a general rule, boys far outnumber girls in most types of offending, but most particularly in violent offending, suggesting that being male may be a risk factor for delinquency! Victimization data, self-report data, and official data (both police records and court statistics) all support this gender gap. In addition, the reported ratios of males to females for most crimes remained basically the same for decades, apparently regardless of cultural or societal changes. In fact, males were so overrepresented in violent crimes (approximately a 9 to 1 ratio) that some theorists suggested that hormonal and biological factors, including the presence of testosterone in males, were the most logical explanation for these gender differences (Wilson & Herrnstein, 1985).

The most recent data on juvenile arrests suggest, however, that the gender gap may be closing for some offenses. Between 1990 and 1999, arrests of juvenile females generally increased more (or decreased less) than male arrests in most categories (Snyder, 2000a). In 1999, girls accounted for 17 percent of the juvenile arrests for Part 1 violent crimes, which approaches a 6 to 1 male-female ratio; they also accounted for 22 percent of arrests for aggravated assault and 30 percent of arrests for simple assault. The male-female arrest rates were the closest for embezzlement (48% female), prostitution (54%), and runaways (59%). If the gap is closing, factors other than biological ones must account for gender differences.

Research by developmental psychologists has shed considerable light on the gender difference in juvenile offending. There is growing recognition that biology is *not* a significant factor in explaining the gender differences in offending, including violent offending (Adams, 1992; Pepler & Slaby, 1994). Research by Eleanor Maccoby (1986), for example, indicates that girls and boys learn different types of prosocial behavior, with girls being more accommodating than boys. The current work of cognitive psychologists suggests that there may be socialized and cultural differences in the way boys and girls perceive their worlds. Social learning theorists have long held that girls are "socialized" differently from boys, or taught not to be aggressive. Anne Campbell (1993, p. 19) is representative of much of the current thinking when she notes that boys and girls are born with the potential to be equally aggressive, but girls are socialized not to be overtly aggressive, whereas boys are encouraged to be aggressive. The slight change in the ratio of violent offending, coupled with the overall decrease in juvenile violent crime discussed earlier in the chapter, suggests that the socialization of girls and boys is becoming more comparable. On the one hand, girls today are likely receiving the same aggression-supporting messages as boys (e.g., from media), and also have fewer restrictions on their behavior than they have had in the past. On the other hand, both genders are being encouraged to make good decisions and look for socially acceptable ways of channeling aggressive tendencies.

There still remain important differences in the offending of girls and boys, however. Girls are consistently taken into custody by police for status offending (particularly running away and curfew violations) more often than are boys.

Additionally they are arrested more often for shoplifting, despite the fact that boys self-report as much shoplifting behavior. It appears, also, that the value of the items stolen by girls is less than the value of those stolen by boys (Chesney-Lind & Shelden, 1998). Finally the connection between juvenile running away and prostitution is a sobering one. Recent arrest figures indicate that the figures are about equal for girls and boys (54% female, 46% male; Snyder, 2000). Nevertheless girls are believed to be far more likely than boys to run away because of victimization in the home and ultimately to take up prostitution to survive. In fact, a history of violent victimization, in or outside the home, seems to haunt both juvenile and adult female offenders (Acoca & Austin, 1996). According to one study (Acoca & Dedel, 1998), 92 percent of juvenile female offenders reported that they had been subjected to some form of emotional, physical, and/or sexual abuse. Twenty-five percent reported they had been shot or stabbed one or more times.

As many commentators have noted, we know far too little about girls' crime, the reasons it is committed, and the social and developmental factors that precipitate it (Broidy et al., 2003; Chesney-Lind & Shelden, 1998). In the 1990s, the Office of Juvenile Justice and Delinquency Prevention launched a major effort to fund more research and effective prevention programs directed at girls, a population whose needs are too often overlooked by both formal and informal agencies. Additionally, numerous private advocacy agencies are beginning to address their needs and offer supportive community-based programs (Community Research Associates, 1998).

It remains to be seen whether the gender gap in offending will close even more, increase, or remain stable in the years ahead. In addition to psychosocial development, numerous societal factors affect the patterns of offending for both juveniles and adults. These include the economy, community disorganization, the actions of police, the quality of schools, the resources available to courts and to correctional agencies, and the adequacy of health and social services, to name but a few. We can say with a high degree of confidence, though, that cultural and psychosocial factors, rather than biological and genetic factors, play a major role in determining gender differences in offending.

DEVELOPMENTAL THEORIES OF DELINQUENCY

It should be clear by now that a considerable amount of contemporary research has focused on understanding the *developmental processes* leading to aggression, antisocial behavior, and delinquency during the elementary school years and into adolescence. Contemporary research has consistently demonstrated that the offender population consists of various distinct subgroups, each following an identifiable developmental pathway that is associated with different risks and outcomes (Wiesner & Windle, 2004).

Studying the developmental process of individuals requires an examination of the trajectory of that development. A trajectory in this sense refers to the developmental changes a person shows over his or her lifetime. Examining differences in developmental trajectories or pathways of individuals over time adds a deeper understanding of delinquency than focusing on differences among individuals at any one point in time. As noted at the beginning of the chapter, developmental trajectory or pathway reflects the changes in an individual's cognitive, emotional, and social growth as he or she grows into adulthood. Theories that use developmental trajectories as models can identify a sequential chain of events that suggest how antisocial behavior is shaped and sustained (Kazdin, 1989).

Research has led to the striking consensus that children and adolescents follow different developmental pathways in their offending or nonoffending careers. Some children engage in stubborn, defiant, and disobedient behavior at very young ages, progressing to mild and then more severe forms of violence and criminal behavior during adolescence and young adulthood (Dahlberg & Potter, 2001). Some children exhibit cruelty to animals, aggressive behavior toward peers, bullying, and substance abuse at a very early age and continue this antisocial pathway far into adulthood. Other children show very few signs of antisocial behavior at very young ages but during adolescence engage in various forms of delinquent behavior. Still others avoid engaging in any significant antisocial behavior over their lifetimes.

There is good evidence that most serious, persistent delinquency and crime patterns usually begin early and worsen with age. Researchers have noted early childhood differences in impulsiveness, social skills, and feelings for others among those children who become seriously antisocial and those children who stay on a prosocial life course. Contemporary developmental psychologists have begun targeting the development of antisocial behavior even during the preschool years.

Moffitt's Developmental Theory

The major impetus for the developmental perspective as an explanation for delinquency has been the ongoing research by psychologist Terrie Moffitt (1993a, 1993b, 2003) and her colleagues. Originally, her developmental approach identified two developmental paths. On one path, the Moffitt group placed a small group of children who begin a lifelong pattern of delinquency and adult crime at a very early age, probably around age 3 or even younger. Moffitt (1993a, p. 679) observes, "Across the life course, these individuals exhibit changing manifestations of antisocial behavior: biting and hitting at age four, shoplifting and truancy at age ten, selling drugs and stealing cars at age sixteen, robbery and rape at age twenty-two, and fraud and child abuse at age thirty." These individuals, whom Moffitt calls **life-course-persistent (LCP) offenders,** continue their antisocial ways across all kinds of conditions and situations. Moffitt reports that many of these LCP offenders exhibit neurological problems during their childhoods, such as difficult temperaments as infants, ADHD as children, and learning problems during their later school years. Judgment and problem-solving deficiencies are often apparent when the children reach adulthood. LCP offenders generally commit a wide assortment of aggressive and violent crimes over their lifetimes.

LCPs as children miss opportunities to acquire and practice prosocial and interpersonal skills at each stage of development. This is partly because they are rejected and avoided by their childhood peers, and partly because their parents, teachers, and caretakers become frustrated and give up on them (Coie, Belding, & Underwood, 1988; Coie, Dodge, & Kupersmith, 1990; Moffitt, 1993a). According to Moffitt (1993a, p. 684), "If social and academic skills are not mastered in childhood, it is very difficult to later recover from lost opportunities." Furthermore, as noted previously, disadvantaged homes, inadequate schools, and violent neighborhoods are factors that are very likely to exacerbate the ongoing and developing antisocial behavioral pattern.

LCPs are plagued by various psychological and antisocial problems throughout their lifetimes. To paraphrase Jaffee et al. (2005), early onset antisocial behavior appears to be associated with pervasive mental (Moffitt, Caspi, Harrington, & Milne, 2002), physical (Farrington, 1995), economic (Caspi, Wright, Moffitt, & Silva, 1998), and interpersonal (Moffitt et al., 2002) problems across the life span. Wiesner, Kim, and Capaldi (2005) write, "Developmental theories posit that antisocial behavior that onsets early in childhood is likely to lead to a cascade of secondary problems, including academic failure, involvement with deviant peers, substance abuse, depressive symptoms, health risk sexual behavior, and work failure" (p. 252). It appears as though LCPs become entrapped in a deviant lifestyle right out of the developmental gate. They are embedded in a social context that further increases their risk status (van Lier, Vuijk, & Crijen, 2005). Other researchers have consistently reported that a small minority of children (about 10%) follow a high antisocial developmental trajectory (van Lier, Vuijk, & Crijen, 2005). They are almost exclusively males. In addition, the level of antisocial behavior of LCPs seems to diverge from their less antisocial counterparts across time (van Lier, Vuijk, & Crijen, 2005). In other words, LCPs actually increase their offending as they grow older. The reasons for this may be due, at least in part, to their exposure to the learning, practicing, and reinforcement of antisocial behavior through the affiliation with similarly diverging antisocial peers. Basically antisocial youth progressively affiliate with similarly antisocial peers (van Lier, Vuijk, & Crijen, 2005).

The great majority of juvenile offenders are those individuals who follow a second developmental path: They begin offending during their adolescent years and generally stop offending somewhere around their eighteenth birthday. Moffitt labels these youths **adolescent-limited (AL) offenders.** Their developmental histories do not demonstrate the early and persistent antisocial problems that members of the LCP group manifest. However—and this point is important—the frequency, and in some cases, the violence level of offending during the teen years, may be as high as that of the LCP youth. In effect, the teenage offending patterns of the AL and that of the LCP may be highly similar during the adolescent years (Moffitt et al., 1996). "The two types cannot be discriminated on most indicators of antisocial and problem behavior in adolescence; boys on the LCP and AL paths are similar on parent-, self-, and official records of offending, peer delinquency, substance abuse, unsafe sex, and dangerous driving" (Moffitt et al., 1996, p. 400). Accordingly, mental health workers and criminal justice experts could not easily identify the group classification (AL or LCP) simply by examining juvenile arrest records, self-reports, or the information provided by parents during the teen years.

The AL delinquent is most likely, during the teen years, to be involved in offenses that symbolize adult privilege and demonstrate autonomy from parental control. Examples include vandalism, drug and alcohol offenses, theft, and "status" offenses such as running away or truancy. In addition, AL delinquents are likely to engage in crimes that are profitable or rewarding, but they also have the ability to abandon these actions when prosocial styles become more rewarding. For example, the onset of young adulthood brings on opportunities not attainable during the teen years, such as leaving high school for college, obtaining a full-time job, and entering a relationship with a prosocial person. AL delinquents are quick to learn that they have something to lose if they continue offending into adulthood. During childhood, in contrast to the LCP child, the AL youngster has learned to get along with others. It should also be emphasized that "the theory of AL antisocial behavior regards it as an adaptation response to modern teens' social context, not the product of a cumulative history of pathological maldevelopment" (Moffitt & Caspi, 2001, p. 370). They normally have a satisfactory repertoire of academic, social, and interpersonal skills that enable them to "get ahead." Therefore, the developmental histories and personal dispositions of the AL youth allow them the option of exploring new life pathways, an opportunity not usually afforded the LCP youth. In short, Moffitt's theory hypothesizes that most young persons who become adolescence-limited delinquents are able to desist from crime when they age into maturity, turning gradually to a more conventional lifestyle (Moffitt & Caspi, 2001).

However, in a more recent follow-up study, Moffitt, Caspi, Harrington, and Milne (2002) discovered that many ALs, at age 26, were still in trouble. "Although AL men fared better overall than LCP men, they fared poorly relative to the 'unclassified' men, who represented males with no remarkable delinquency history" (Moffitt et al., 2002, p. 199). The researchers found that AL men accounted for twice their share of the property and drug convictions during adulthood, compared with men without a delinquency history. It seemed as though some AL men relied on crime to supplement their incomes. The researchers further state that "the very name 'adolescence-limited' reveals that this much offending by AL men at age 26 was not anticipated by our theory" (p. 200). The researchers, in an effort to explain the discrepancy, speculated that perhaps adulthood in contemporary society may begin after 25 years of age. Therefore, this new developmental stage, called "emerging adulthood," prolongs the crime-promoting conditions of adolescence. "This stage is characterized by roleless floundering, in which young people neither perceive themselves to be adults, nor choose to occupy any adult roles historically favored by people in their twenties (e.g., parenthood, marriage)" (Moffitt et al., 2002, p. 200).

Gender Differences

Moffitt's theory has been developed primarily on the developmental trajectories of males. Do females demonstrate a similar pattern? Moffitt and Caspi (2001) report evidence that the developmental typology fits both genders. However, the LCP pattern of behavior is far more likely to be followed by males than females (approximately 10 males to 1 female), whereas the gender difference is negligible for the AL pattern (approximately 1.5 males to 1 female). These findings are consistent with other studies (Kratzer & Hodgins, 1999; Mazerolle et al., 2000). In other words, the vast majority of female delinquents *appear* to fit the AL pattern. In a study of 820 girls, Coté et al. (2001) found that only 1.4 percent of the girls followed the LCP profile.

According to Moffitt (2003), an ongoing association with delinquent peers appears to be an important factor in the onset of delinquency among adolescent girls. An intimate relationship with a male delinquent is also closely connected to delinquency in adolescent girls (Moffitt, Caspi, Rutter, & Silva, 2001).

Although a majority of the studies have indicated that girls rarely become early onset persistent offenders, a few recent studies suggest that girls may be more vulnerable to early onset of serious antisocial behavior than previously thought. Brennan et al. (2003) found that girls in their sample displayed the same pattern as boys. In the Brennan et al. study, 9 percent of the boys and 7.4 percent of the girls in the high-risk sample were classified as displaying *early onset* persistent aggressive behavior. However, Silverthorn and Frick (1999) maintain that girls tend to engage in serious antisocial behavior for the first time at later ages—and generally in adolescence—than boys. According to Silverthorn and Frick, antisocial behavior in girls is delayed because of such factors as parental and school-based socialization practices that encourage them to restrict their outward aggressive tendencies during middle childhood. However, McCabe, Rodgers, Yeh, and Hough (2004) offer some evidence that a high percentage of antisocial girls began their antisocial behavior before the age of 10. Similar results were reported by Leve and Chamberlain (2004) who found that 23 percent of serious antisocial girls were arrested before age 11, and 71 percent before age 14. These results suggest that a large portion of girls can be considered early onset delinquents and may well follow the same developmental trajectory as early onset boys. These researchers identified parental transitions (separation, divorce, death, incarceration) and biological parental criminality as the strongest predictors of early onset status in girls.

Gorman-Smith and Loeber (2005) report, based on extensive data from the National Youth Survey, that girls tend to follow the same developmental pathways toward antisocial behavior and delinquency as boys. Although fewer girls engage in antisocial or delinquent behavior compared with boys, those that do show similar pathways. In other words, serious antisocial and delinquent involvement in girls showed early onset antisocial patterns similar to boys. However, Gorman-Smith and Loeber did learn that the risk factors for girls may be somewhat different for boys. For example, because girls are more invested in interpersonal relationships than boys, they are more likely to get involved in or be affected by parental conflict and transitions, a finding similar to that reported in the Leve-Chamberlain (2004) study. Peer influences may also be different for boys and girls. Girls may be more likely to be pulled into delinquency through involvement in intimate relationships with delinquent men rather than through involvement with delinquent gangs. Therefore, while the developmental pathways may be similar, the family and peer risk factors may be different for boys and girls.

Coercion Developmental Theory

Similar to Moffitt's theory, Gerald Patterson (1982, 1986) also believes that early starters are at greater risk for more serious criminal offending. However, the major difference is that Patterson places a greater emphasis on the role of parenting rather than focusing on the specific characteristics of the child. The coercion developmental theory contends that poor parental monitoring of child activities, disruptive family transitions (e.g., divorce), and inconsistent parental discipline are major psychosocial contributors to early onset delinquency (Brennan et al., 2003; Patterson, 1982). The theory argues that the key predictor of early onset offending is the family environment in which the child learns to use coercive behaviors, such as temper tantrums and whining, to escape parental discipline and authority.

TABLE 2–3   Summary Table of Comparisons between LCPs and ALs

	LIFE COURSE PERSISTENT (LCP)	ADOLESCENT LIMITED (AL)
Crime or antisocial behavior begins . . .	early (perhaps as early as age three)	later (usually during the early adolescent years)
Criminal behavior . . .	continues throughout the offender's life	usually stops after reaching early adulthood
Types of criminal behaviors	assortment	assortment
Developmental backgrounds . . .	often shows neurological problems, ADHD, conduct problems	usually normal and without neurological problems
Academic skills . . .	usually below average	usually average to above average
Interpersonal and social skills . . .	usually below average	usually average to above average

Coercion theory acknowledges that some children are more likely than other children to elicit inept parenting strategies. For example, a child with an irritable temperament who is constantly whining is more likely to provoke coercive parenting than a pleasant, constantly smiling child. In the coercive cycle, the parent and child each behave in a way that is obnoxious to the other in an attempt to control the other's behavior. As the child's obnoxious behaviors increase in intensity and frequency, the parent eventually acquiesces, unwittingly reinforcing the child's behavior. As the child becomes increasingly irritating, the parent further escalates power assertion techniques and, presumably, the level of hostility displayed toward the child.

Coercion becomes the child's primary interpersonal strategy and thus generalizes to environments outside the home. According to coercive theory, antisocial behavior is seen as progressing from faulty parent-toddler interactions to similar interactions with teachers, peers, and others in the child's environment. The coercion developmental model is largely based on social learning theory. According to the theory, "Developmental trajectories for antisocial behavior are initiated, maintained, and diversified as a result of cumulative daily social experiences with parents, siblings, and peers that are highly aversive, inconsistent, and unsupportive" (Snyder, Reid, & Patterson, 2003, p. 31).

Developmental Trajectories

The theory identifies two developmental trajectories or pathways toward antisocial behavior, each characterized by an orderly sequence of stages (Patterson & Yoerger, 2002). "One trajectory leads to early arrest (prior to age 14) and adult crime and the other to late-onset arrests and desistence from adult crime" (Patterson & Yoerger, 2002, p. 147). However, the theory takes the position that both the early and late-start trajectories represent variations of the same basic processes. That is, social-environmental influences, such as divorce, poverty, and depression, work in combination with inept parenting and deviant peer socialization to produce two different levels of delinquent and antisocial behavior. There are three variables that separate early from late-onset trajectories: (1) the early onset process begins during the preschool years, whereas the late onset begins in midadolescence; (2) the inept parenting is more severe for the early onset compared with the late onset; and (3) the levels of social incompetence are more pronounced for the early as compared with the late-onset delinquency. The inept parenting is often characterized by parents who use ineffective discipline practices and who themselves tend to be antisocial and unemployed, living under low socioeconomic conditions, and plagued by frequent marital transitions and discord.

Because of these differences, early onset delinquents tend to demonstrate limited levels of social skills, more disruptive peer relations, and lower self-esteem. The late-onset delinquents exhibited similar deficiencies, but not to the degree of early onsets. Basically, late-onset delinquents are less antisocial than the early onset delinquents but more antisocial than nondelinquents. Research finds that the likelihood of arrest as a young adult for early onsets is high, whereas the likelihood for late onsets is relatively low (Patterson & Yoerger, 2002). For example, the majority (71%) of late-onset boys desisted becoming involved in adult crime (Patterson & Yoerger, 2002), while 74 percent of early onset offenders are arrested by the time they become young adults (age 21 to 29) (Stattin & Magnusson, 1991).

Gender Differences

According to the coercive development perspective, gender differences in aggression are well in place by age 5 and persist throughout childhood and adolescence (Snyder et al., 2003). These early differences are largely in favor of aggressiveness in boys. The coercive perspective further posits that gender differences in antisocial behavior are the result of the different environmental experiences and reinforcements encountered by boys and girls. Boys and girls evoke different responses from parents, and each gender responds differently to the same parenting conditions. Parents tend to be more coercive toward boys compared with girls, and this difference appears to be more pronounced for highly aggressive boys and girls (Snyder et al., 2003). The coercive development model hypothesizes, therefore, that girls display less antisocial behavior because they are less frequently involved in coercive parent-child interactions.

Peer socialization factors begin to play a significant role as the child moves into preschool and kindergarten. Boys and girls demonstrate a strong preference for interaction with same-gender children beginning at age 3. Boys tend to ignore girls who try to enter their play groups. There are more challenges, noncompliance, and rough-and-tumble play among boys, whereas there tends to be more cooperation, verbal exchange, compliance, and mutual accommodation among girls. Unlike boy groups, there are fewer highly antisocial, same-gender peers with whom younger girls can associate, model, or exchange deviant talk. Consequently, when girls do begin to show antisocial behavior, it most often occurs during the adolescent years, and appears to be somewhat tied to pubescence. During adolescence, the preference for same-gender peers diminishes and a broad array of peer affiliates becomes available, including antisocial ones. This shift in peer associates and reduction of parental monitoring may explain the reciprocal involvement of both men and women in partner-directed violence (Calpaldi, Dishion, Stoolmiller, & Yoerger, 2001; Snyder et al., 2003).

Other Developmental Theories

Other researchers using a developmental perspective have identified more than two trajectories. For example, Loeber and Stouthamer-Loeber (1998) and Chung et al. (2002) were able to identify five developmental pathways. Nagin and Land

(1993), Coté et al. (2001), and Shaw, Gilliom, Ingoldsby, and Nagin (2003) have all found four trajectories that lead to antisocial, delinquent, or criminal behavior. Wiesner and Windle (2004) suggest there may be as many as six different developmental pathways to delinquency and crime. A distinguishing feature of all developmental models is that they identify the different developmental pathways by discovering at what age the serious antisocial behavior began and how severe and persistent the offending becomes as the child grows into adolescence or young adulthood.

SUMMARY AND CONCLUSIONS

In recent years, developmental psychologists have been extremely active in studying the life course of individuals who participate in persistent juvenile and adult offending. They have examined developmental pathways or trajectories that lead to little or no offending, minor juvenile offending that ends around mid to late adolescence, or serious offending into adulthood, among others. Researchers can now point with confidence to a large list of risk factors associated with juvenile delinquency and criminal behavior. No single variable is particularly at fault. In this chapter we began to examine some of the social and psychological risk factors associated with crime and delinquency, including peer and family influences, preschool and school influences, cognitive ability, ADHD, and conduct disorders.

Youth whose families are included in the lower socioeconomic strata of society are disproportionately represented in both arrest and juvenile court statistics. This pattern continues, but not as strongly, in self-report research. Therefore, an adverse economic environment must be considered within the context of the many influences that impinge on young lives. Features often associated with poverty—discrimination, inadequate schools, unsafe living conditions, joblessness, social isolation, and opportunities to learn law-violating behaviors from peers—all play roles in the formation of crime and delinquency.

One risk factor that appears increasingly in the literature on delinquency is early peer rejection, even during the elementary school years. This can occur regardless of a child's socioeconomic status. Children who are rejected by peers are often aggressive, but aggression alone is not the major explanation. Rather, they also tend to be disruptive, impulsive, and/or have few interpersonal skills. Research has demonstrated consistently that antisocial adolescents, particularly those who displayed highly aggressive behavior, experienced significant peer rejection during their childhoods. In girls, substance abuse and other delinquent behaviors in adolescence has been associated with peer rejection in elementary school.

Preschool experiences are also increasingly being recognized as possible risk factors. Poor quality child care places children at risk for poorer language and cognitive development, as well as deficiencies in social skills. Unfortunately, inadequate child care is often associated with low socioeconomic class. On the other hand, high-quality day care has been shown to improve the chances that children from economically deprived families will do well both behaviorally and in school settings.

It is important to stress that delinquency is clearly not limited to youths from the lower class. Self-report data suggest that social class differences become smaller when youths are asked to report their own offending. If poverty and the conditions it generates are not at issue for these youth, we must look to other risk factors, such as parenting styles and practices, the influence of antisocial peers, and the more individual factors such as conduct disorders, ADHD, intelligence, and gender.

Among the parental and family risk factors discussed in the chapter are single-parent households, which have too often been blamed for antisocial behavior of children. We stressed process variables rather than structure variables were more likely risk factors. For example, researchers have found associations between certain parental styles and antisocial behavior in children. Styles are typically identified as authoritarian, permissive, or authoritative (Baumrind, 1991) or as enmeshed or lax (Snyder & Patterson, 1987). Although many parents may well vary their styles across situations and as children get older, in general one style dominates. The permissive and lax styles—characterized by little or no control over the children and extremely few restrictions—are highly correlated with delinquent behavior. In similar fashion, parental monitoring or supervision of the child's activities, particularly from the ages of 9 to midadolescence, is crucial to the development of prosocial behavior.

We covered psychological risk factors—those that are unique to the child—as factors on the road to delinquency. Low IQ scores have consistently been associated with delinquency, not necessarily directly but more likely because children with low scores do not do well in school, and school failure is also commonly associated with antisocial behavior. We stressed, though, that a low score on an "intelligence" test does not mean that a child is not intelligent. In addition, we know not only that many delinquents are intelligent despite scoring below normal on IQ tests but also that other delinquents score high on IQ tests. Therefore the IQ-delinquency connection must be expressed very cautiously.

Children with ADHD are at some risk of antisocial behavior both as juveniles and adults. This disorder apparently affects 3 percent to 5 percent of school-aged children, though in some communities the percentages are even higher, leading to questions about misdiagnoses. ADHD appears to be a disorder affecting social relationships; the children have difficulty staying on task, they get easily distracted, are impulsive, display excessive motor activity, and are annoying to others. These features often lead to peer rejection. Although ADHD is routinely treated with medication, this in itself is a controversial issue. Untreated, however, ADHD children are at risk for delinquency and substance abuse.

Conduct disorder is somewhat of a catch-all category that is characterized by persistent misbehavior, including stealing, running away, fighting, telling lies, and cruelty. Signs of conduct disorder may occur as early as age 3; when children reach school age, they are often mislabeled with a "learning disability" or with ADHD, but the three are distinct categories. Not surprisingly, conduct disorder is also associated with peer rejection.

We discussed differences in the developmental pathways of girls and boys and noted that many questions remain about gender differences in offending. However, although some researchers strongly disagree, it is likely that socialization rather than biology is the most significant factor in the observed differences. This is not to say that biology plays no part, rather that socialization overrides it. Girls do seem to learn more prosocial behavior than boys, which may explain their lower rates of aggressive behavior. Increases in violent offending suggest that girls may be receiving the same violence messages from the environment. Nevertheless nonviolent offenses still comprise the greatest portion of both female and male offenses. In later chapters we highlight other juvenile offenses, including drug use and sex offending.

We ended the chapter with a discussion of the major developmental theories advanced in recent years, beginning with Terrie Moffitt's widely cited and heavily researched approach to life-course-persistent (LCP) and adolescent-limited (AL) offenders. The great majority of juvenile offenders belong in the second category, beginning their offending just before or during adolescence and stopping around their 18th birthday. Interestingly the offending patterns of these ALs can be highly similar to those of LCPs during these years. Contemporary research, including research by Moffitt herself, suggests that there may be more than these two developmental tracks, however. We discussed gender differences in this theory, noting that some research suggests that—while there are fewer girls than boys in each category—the pathways themselves are similar. However, family and peer risk factors may be different.

Coercion-development theory, formulated by Gerald Patterson and his colleagues, also sees two developmental tracks: early and late onset. They contend that parenting tactics and strategies are the crucial factor in the early initiation of antisocial behavior.

The research on developmental pathways represents the most contemporary approach to explaining delinquency. As noted earlier, there are likely multiple developmental paths rather than the two originally proposed. Regardless of the number of paths, however, it is likely that theories emphasizing cognitive processes (e.g., beliefs, values, and thoughts) are favored in contemporary psychological explanations of crime and delinquency. Beliefs, values, images of oneself, and philosophies are the primary guides to behavior. Most people try to live according to their internal standards and respond to others according to their perspectives of human nature. If one's family, friends, models, and heroes perceive life a certain way, it is likely that one will do the same. In most instances, delinquency seems to be an expression of the values the juvenile has either adopted or is testing as a result of being exposed to them through models in the environment.

We will learn later in the text that only a *minority* of highly aggressive and violent offenders began their criminal careers during adulthood; most displayed overt aggressive tendencies during childhood. This is why the developmental approach is so important. Typically, even from the preschool years, highly aggressive or violent individuals have been found to show habits of thought that reflect lower levels of social problem-solving skills and higher endorsement of beliefs that support the use of violence. Thus programs that attempt to teach effective, alternative conflict-resolution strategies show promise.

The evidence is clear that prevention and intervention must begin early. Such early intervention is especially critical for children growing up in inner-city neighborhoods where risk factors for delinquency are more prevalent. When children reach school age, though, it is important to direct prevention at all children rather than to isolate certain groups. Research strongly indicates that intervention becomes more difficult and encounters more intransigent behavior patterns from teenagers who exhibit antisocial behavior from an early age. The life-course-persistent offender who enters adolescence fully engaged in delinquent or antisocial behavior is usually highly resistant to change. The adolescence-limited offender, on the other hand, is far more likely to be responsive to intervention and treatment strategies during the teen years. Adolescence-limited offenders are also more likely to show spontaneous recovery from their delinquency patterns as they embark on a more responsible "adult" life course. The fact that there are multiple developmental paths rather than just two makes the task of intervention a bit more complex.

 ## KEY CONCEPTS

Developmental pathways	Temptation talk
Parental practices	Parental styles
Authoritative style	Permissive style
Authoritarian style	Enmeshed style
Lax style	Parental monitoring
Language impairment	Psychometric approach
Psychometric intelligence	Attention deficit hyperactivity
ADHD	disorder
Conduct disorder	Self-regulation
LCP	Life-course-persistent offenders
AL	Adolescent-limited offenders

▶ REVIEW QUESTIONS

1. Name and explain briefly any six risk factors for delinquency.
2. Describe the features of ADHD that create problems for the child who has this disorder.
3. Explain the difference between ADHD and conduct disorder.
4. In what ways may preschool experiences influence a life of delinquency and crime?
5. Summarize and explain Terrie Moffit's developmental theory of delinquency, and explain how it has been modified by other researchers in recent years.
6. In what important ways does coercion development theory differ from Moffitt's developmental theory?

CHAPTER 3

ORIGINS
OF CRIMINAL BEHAVIOR:
BIOLOGICAL FACTORS

CHAPTER OBJECTIVES

- Explore the genetic and biological aspects of criminal behavior.
- Provide an overview of twin and adoption studies on the development of crime.
- Identify environmental risk factors that play a role in the psychobiological aspects of criminal behavior.
- Explore the relationship between body physical attributes and crime.
- Present in some detail Eysenck's theory of crime as an interactionist perspective.

Many—perhaps most—contemporary criminologists would agree with the following statement: "Genetics may play a role in criminality, but it is only an insignificant one. There is little doubt that environment, as well as individual or group values, are important determinants and causes of criminal behavior." Poverty, greed, desire for power, the glorification of violence, high unemployment, poor education, faulty parenting, and group values that deviate from society's norms are often considered the major culprits in producing crime. Heredity-based physiological components have been traditionally scoffed at, and their possible role as causal agents in criminality is often dismissed.

Why so? Perhaps because accepting heredity or biological factors as causal factors in criminal behavior imply that criminal acts are unavoidable, inevitable consequences of the "bad seed," "bad blood," or "mark of Cain." Heredity is destiny. Little can be done to prevent the ill-fated person from becoming a criminal. Most behavioral scientists today—and many social scientists—recognize, however, that behavioral traits result from an *interaction* of hereditary and environmental factors. We no longer ask whether behavior is strictly due to heredity or environment; we agree that both are involved in a complex way. However, researchers usually focus on one or the other for intensive study. In this chapter, we discuss the work of psychologists who study heredity and biopsychology as factors in the genesis of criminal behavior.

Biopsychologists (psychologists who study the biological aspects of behavior) try to determine which genetic and neurophysiological variables play a part in criminal behavior, how important they are, and what can be done to modify them. In recent years, molecular biology has focused on specific genes as foundations for certain patterns of behavior. Further, "a central precept of molecular biology is that all the information needed to construct a mammalian body, whether human or mouse, is contained in the approximately 100,000 genes of mammalian DNA and that a set of master genes activates the DNA necessary to produce the appropriate proteins for development and behavior" (Cacioppo, Berntson, Sheridan, & McClintock, 2000, p. 833).

Biopsychologists do not believe that genetic or neurophysiological components are the sole or even primary causal agents of human behavior. Most would say that understanding the social environment is as important as understanding the biological one. In the words of one group of biopsychologists, "—The social world, as well as the organization and operation of the brain, shapes and modulates genetic and biological processes, and accordingly, knowledge of biological and social domains is necessary to develop comprehensive theories in either domain" (Cacioppo et al., 2000, p. 833). In this chapter, we concentrate on the biological relationships to criminal behavior, while, at the same time, continually appreciating the enormous influence of the social environment on the neurological and biological processes. More than 100 studies have addressed the question of genetic influences on antisocial behavior (Moffitt, 2005). Although we cannot examine these investigations in detail here, we present a summary of their findings.

The chapter first explores the genetic aspects of crime, including findings from twin and adoption studies and physical aspects such as body shape and attractiveness, and then moves on to one of the major theories and research areas in the psychology of crime, Eysenck's theory of personality. The theory is covered in detail because it offers a compelling view of how personality, biological factors, and the social environment work together in developing criminal behavioral patterns.

GENETICS AND ANTISOCIAL BEHAVIOR

According to Adrian Raine (2002), a prominent biopsychologist, "There is now clear evidence from twin studies, adoption studies, twins reared apart, and molecular genetic studies to support the notion that there are genetic influences on antisocial and aggressive behavior" (p. 312). The more challenging issues,

Raine notes, are determining if and how genetic processes interact with environmental factors in predisposing individuals to antisocial and violent behavior. So far, twin studies provide more support for the heritability of antisocial behavior than adoption studies. Nevertheless, both twin and adoption studies have the potential of providing a more convincing case for the relative influence of genetic and environmental factors.

Twin Studies

One way to determine the role of genetics in criminality is to compare the incidence and type of delinquency or criminal convictions among identical (monozygotic) and fraternal (dizygotic) twins. **Dizygotic twins** (also called **fraternal twins**) develop from two different fertilized eggs and are no more genetically alike than nontwin siblings. **Monozygotic twins** (or **identical twins**) develop from a single egg; they are always the same sex and share the same genes. Presumably, then, if genes are determinative, identical twins should display highly similar behavior. Because MZ twins share 100 percent of their genes, it can be inferred that a child's genetic risk for antisocial behavior is high if his or her cotwin shows antisocial behavior and low if the MZ cotwin does not.

However, to complicate matters a bit, approximately two-thirds of monozygotic twins are monochorionic (share the same chorion), and one-third of the monozygotic pair is dichornionic (two different chorions) (Rhee & Waldman, 2002). The chorion is the outer membrane enclosing the embryo. Therefore, some identical twins develop in slightly different prenatal environments, which may contribute to some individual differences that may emerge as the twins develop into maturity. In fact, several studies have found that monochorionic, monozygotic twins are more similar in personality and cognitive ability than dichorionic, monozygotic twins (Rhee & Waldman, 2002). Theoretically, however, by comparing fraternal twins and identical twins, researchers should be able to identify the relative contributions of genes compared with environmental factors in the development of personality, cognitive ability, and behavior in general.

Shared and Nonshared Environments

Two important concepts need to be recognized before a good understanding of twin studies can be achieved: **shared environments** and **nonshared environments.** Shared or common environments include prenatal and life experiences affecting both twins in the same way. For example, twins raised by the same biological parents share a common hereditary and home environment. Shared environments in this sense are apt to promote high trait or behavioral similarity between twin pairs, especially for identical twins. Nonshared environments, on the other hand, include living experiences that are different for each twin, such as being raised in a different home environment. Therefore, in order to determine the relative influence of genes on behavior, compared with the environment, shared and nonshared aspects must be considered.

Twin research indicates that, for a variety of traits, the magnitude of genetic and nonshared environmental influences increases as a person gets older, whereas the magnitude of shared environmental influences decreases (Loehlin, 1992; Plomin, 1986; Rhee & Waldman, 2002). That is, as the child begins to spend more time outside the family circle, especially when he or she becomes a young adult, the influence of the shared environment (family) tends to wane, whereas the influence of genetics and nonshared environments (e.g., peers) becomes more discernible. Rhee and Waldman (2002) describe a longitudinal study by Matheny (1989) which revealed that the temperaments (e.g., emotional tone, fearfulness, approach or avoidance toward others) became more similar for identical pairs than for fraternal pairs as they grew older. Thus we might expect that developmental age of the subjects in any twin study may play an important role in determining the influences of genetics compared with the environment. We return to this point shortly.

Some investigators suggest that identical twins are so physically alike that they probably elicit similar social responses from their environment (shared environment), more so than fraternal twins. In this sense, they are more likely to develop similar personalities. There may be merit to this viewpoint, but research does not yet support it. Rather, some research has found that identical twins reared apart are more alike in some personality attributes than are identical twins reared in the same home environment (Canter, 1973; Shields, 1962). When reared together, identical twins may make a conscious effort to accentuate their individual identities, whereas when reared apart they may have less need to be different.

Concordance

Concordance, a key concept in twin study research, is the genetics term for the degree to which related pairs of subjects both show a particular behavior or condition. It is usually expressed in percentages. Assume that we want to determine the concordance of intelligence among 20 pairs of identical twins and 20 pairs of fraternals. If we find that 10 pairs of the identical twins have approximately the same IQ score, but only five pairs of the fraternals obtain the same score, our concordance is 50 percent for identicals and 25 percent for fraternals. The concordance for identicals would be twice that of fraternals, suggesting that hereditary factors play an important role in intelligence. If, however, the two concordances were about the same, we would conclude that genetics is irrelevant, at least as represented in our sample and measured by our methods.

Numerous early twin studies using this concordance method have indicated that heredity may be a powerful determinant of intelligence, schizophrenia, depressions, neurotic disorders, alcoholism, and criminal behavior

(Claridge, 1973; Hetherington & Parke, 1975; McClearn & DeFries, 1973; Rosenthal, 1970, 1971). The first such study relative to criminality was reported by the Munich physician Johannes Lange (1929) in his book *Crime as Destiny* (Christiansen, 1977; Rosenthal, 1971). The title reflects Lange's conviction that criminal conduct is a predetermined fate dictated by heredity. He found a criminality concordance of 77 percent for 13 pairs of adult identical twins and only 12 percent for 17 pairs of adult fraternal twins. Auguste Marcel Legras (1932) then found a 100 percent criminal concordance for five pairs of identicals. Note that both of these studies used small samples. Subsequent studies, using more sophisticated designs and methods of twin identification and sampling, continued to find a substantially higher criminal concordance for identical twins when compared with fraternals. The levels were not as high as those reported by either Lange or Legras, however. **Table 3–1** summarizes relevant investigations of criminal concordance. Although these tabulated investigations differed in method and definitions of criminality, the combined concordance levels demonstrate that, where criminal behavior is concerned, identical twins seem better matched than fraternal twins.

Hans Eysenck reviewed other twin studies, found similar concordances, and concluded, "Thus concordance is found over four times as frequently in identicals as in fraternals, a finding which seems to put beyond any doubt that heredity plays an extremely important part in the genesis of criminal behaviour" (Eysenck, 1973, p. 167). Rosenthal, however, injects a word of caution,

TABLE 3–1 Summary of Twin-Criminality Studies showing Pairs and Concordance Rates

	Identical Twins			Fraternal Twins		
RESEARCHERS	NO. OF PAIRS	PAIRS CONCORDANT	PERCENTAGE	NO. OF PAIRS	PAIRS CONCORDANT	PERCENTAGE
Lange (1929)	13	10	77	17	2	12
Legras (1932)	4	4	100	5	0	0
Rosanoff (1934)	37	25	68	60	6	10
Kranz (1936)	31	20	65	43	20	53
Stumpfl (1936)	18	11	61	19	7	37
Borgstrom (1939)	4	3	75	5	2	40
Rosanoff et al. (1941)	45	35	78	27	6	18
Yoshimasu (1961)	28	17	61	18	2	11
Yoshimasu (1965)	28	14	50	26	0	0
Hayashi (1967)	15	11	73	5	3	60
Dalgaard & Kringlen (1976)	31	8	26	54	8	15
Christiansen (1977)						
Males	71	25	35	120	15	13
Females	14	2	21	27	2	8
Total	339	185	55	426	73	17

stressing the many pitfalls of the concordance twin method and the ramifications of using different legal definitions of criminality. Nevertheless, he allows, "—It is clearly not possible to rule out the potential fact that genetic factors may indeed be the primary source of the higher concordance rate in MZ (identical) as compared to DZ (fraternal) twins" (Rosenthal, 1975, p. 10).

Eysenck further complicates the issue by suggesting that twin studies may actually have deflated the true concordance rate, since it is likely that identical twins were often confused with fraternal twins, especially in the earlier studies. If the twins are of the same sex, it is difficult to distinguish identicals from fraternals from appearance alone. Today, blood type, fingerprints (which are highly similar but not identical), and various genetically determined serum proteins allow differentiation. Since these methods were not available to earlier investigators, Eysenck contends that mix-ups may have confounded the results. However, the concordance rates may just as easily have been inflated as deflated.

As Table 3–1 shows, twin studies have not invariably found high criminal concordance rates in favor of identical twins. One study by Dalgaard and Kringlen (1976) found no significant difference between identicals and fraternals. The Dalgaard-Kringlen sample included all the registered male twins born in Norway between 1921 and 1930. However, 32 percent of the sample was deleted from the analysis for various reasons, which might have affected the results. Also, the label "criminal" was applied to traffic violations, military offenses, and treason during World War II, as well as to all actions against the penal code. This was a broader definition than was used in most twin studies. The late Karl O. Christiansen, who devoted much of his research work to twin studies, could not explain the lack of significant differences reported by Dalgaard and Kringlen. He advocated an additional study to determine whether "some special conditions exist in Norway that would dampen the expression of genetic factors—" (Christiansen, 1977, p. 82).

Overall, despite procedural and definitional problems and except for the Dalgaard-Kringlen data, the studies examining concordance rates among twins have consistently indicated higher concordance for identical twins. More recent research, however, indicates that these higher concordance rates may hold only for adult nonviolent offending and not for juvenile offending (Blackburn, 1993). In a careful review of the literature, Adrian Raine (1993, p. 79) concludes, "Summary statistics from 13 twin analyses show that 51.5% of MZ twins are concordant for crime compared to 20.6% for DZ twins, indicating substantial evidence for genetic influences on crime."

Twin Studies and Criminal Behavior: Recent Research

The twin data clearly suggest that it might be wise to consider heredity a significant component in criminality. However, it should also be emphasized that the research cited above favors the heritability of nonviolent crime, but not violent crime (Dodge & Pettit, 2003; Raine, 1993). Most of early concordance research either did not define criminal behavior clearly, or utilized nonviolent criminal behavior largely to the exclusion of violent criminal behavior. In addition, "Although specific genes . . . may have special relevance for the development of conduct problems, the genetic base for most problem behaviors likely reflects combinations of genes that are expressed in different ways at different points of life" (Dodge & Pettit, 2003, p. 351). Thus some combination of genes does appear to render certain children at risk for developing delinquent or antisocial behavior, but environmental factors play prominent roles in the formation of that behavior also (Dodge & Pettit, 2003; Rhee & Waldman, 2002).

In a more recent study, Jaffee and her colleagues (2005) used monozygotic (MZ) and dizygotic (DZ) twin pairs to study the interplay between genetic and environmental risks on the development of antisocial behavior in a representative sample of over one thousand twin pairs of British 5-year-olds and their families. The Jaffee researchers ascertained the children's antisocial behavior through parent and teacher interviews. The environmental risk factor in the study was the amount of maltreatment the child reportedly received from parents, because research shows that early maltreatment often leads to antisocial behavior (Lansford et al., 2002). Not surprisingly, Jaffee et al. (2005) discovered that the effect of maltreatment on the risk to develop antisocial behavior was strongest among those at higher genetic risk. In other words, those children with a genetic predisposition to become troublesome and antisocial were especially likely to be that way if they were mistreated. These findings and the findings of many other studies support the general consensus that environmental changes turn genetic influences on and off during the developmental years, and that biological factors and environmental influences do interact (Raine, 2002). In fact there is emerging evidence that suggests the social environmental (e.g., parenting) can affect people who are at genetic risk more strongly than previously appreciated (Moffitt, 2005).

These environmental influences seem to wane somewhat as a person moves into adulthood, however. For example, there is emerging evidence that the magnitude of familial or parental influences on aggressive behavior decreases with increasing age, and genetic factors increasingly play a prominent role in the stability of aggression and antisocial behavior across the life span (Rhee & Waldman, 2002; van Beijsterveldt, Bartels, Hudziak, & Boomsma, 2003). This effect seems to be particularly strong in males. Female aggressive behavior, on the other hand, seems to be more strongly affected by the family environment (van Beijsterveldt et al., 2003). In other words, family influences appear to be more powerful in the inhibition of antisocial behavior in girls than in boys, particularly as the girls approach adolescence and early adulthood.

In a longitudinal study of 1,226 twin pairs, Tuvblad, Eley, and Lichtenstein (2005) used a well-researched behavioral scale to measure parental-reported aggression in children ages 8 and 9, and asked the same group of children to report their own delinquent behavior eight years later. The researchers used both monozygotic and dizygotic twins in their effort to disentangle genetic factors from environmental factors. They found that genetic factors played an important role in the early onset of aggressive behavior in children, but appeared to play a less important role in the development of delinquent be-havior as reported by male adolescents. A similar finding was reported by Tay-lor, Iacono, and McGue (2000) who found that genetics played a more prominent role in early onset delinquency (life-course-persistent offenders) whereas the social environment (e.g., delinquent peers) was more influential in late-onset delinquency (adolescent-limited offenders). The subjects in the study were all boys. Surprisingly, genetics appeared to play a much more prominent role in development of *both* aggressive behavior and delinquency in girls in the Tuvbald et al. (2005) study. These results appear to be in contrast to the study of Rhee and Waldman (2002), who concluded that the magnitude of genetic and environmental influences on antisocial behavior is equal for both genders. It is clear from these two contrasting studies that further research on the rela-tive influence of genes on gender differences in antisocial behavior is warranted.

Adoption Studies

Another method used to identify crucial variables in the interaction between heredity and environment is the adoption study, which helps identify environ-ments most conducive to criminality. There have been exceedingly few such in-vestigations, however, and those few have been fraught with methodological problems.

One of the first adoption studies was carried out in Denmark by Schulsinger (1972), who explored the incidence of psychopathy in the biological relatives of adopted adults. Schulsinger compared 57 adopted adults whom he diagnosed psychopathic to a control group of 57 nonpsychopathic adopted adults. The two groups were matched for sex, age, social class, and age of transfer to the adopting family. The study's direct implications for criminal behavior are ques-tionable, because Schulsinger defined psychopathy by his own loose criteria. In-dividuals who were impulse-ridden and who exhibited acting-out behavior qualified. As we will see in Chapter 6, these descriptions do not necessarily con-note either psychopathy or criminality.

Schulsinger found that 3.9 percent of the biological relatives of psycho-pathic adoptees could also be classified as psychopathic, whereas only 1.4 per-cent of the control group's biological relatives could. The results just failed to reach statistical significance, indicating that we should be very cautious about accepting their implications. It is interesting, though, that psychopathy—even given its loose definition—was about two and a half times greater in the fam-ily backgrounds of acting-out adoptees.

Crowe (1974) conducted a better-designed study, a follow-up of 52 persons relinquished for early adoption by female offenders. Ninety percent of the bio-logical mothers were felons at the time of the adoptive placement, the most common offenses being forgery and passing bad checks. Twenty-five of the adoptees were female, and all were white. Another 52 adoptees with no evi-dence of criminal family background were selected as a control group and matched for sex, race, and age at the time of adoption.

For the follow-up phase of the study, Crowe selected 37 index and 37 control subjects who had by then reached age 18. (Index subjects in research are those subjects who are of major concern.) Seven of the index adoptees had arrest records: As adults, all seven had at least one conviction, four had multiple arrests, two had multiple convictions, and three were felons. Of the 37 matching controls, two had adult arrest records and only one of these had been convicted. Each subject's personality was diagnosed by three clinicians based on test results and data gathered in an interview; no family background was included. The clinicians made their diagnoses independently of one another and without knowing the subject's group. Six of the adoptees born of female offenders were labeled "antisocial personality"; one control group subject was labeled "probable antisocial personality."

Crowe found a positive correlation between the tendency of the index group to be antisocial and two other variables: the child's age at the time of adoptive placement, and the length of time the child had spent in temporary care (orphanages and foster homes) prior to that placement. The older the child of an offender upon adoptive placement and the longer the temporary placement, the more likely the child would grow up antisocial. The control group members were not affected by these conditions. This suggests either that the two adoptee groups responded differently to similar environmental conditions or that the adoption agency placed the offspring of female offenders in less desirable homes—and there was no indication that this selective placement had occurred.

Hutchings and Mednick (1975) also conducted a study examining the effects of genetics and environment. They reasoned that if there is a genetic basis for criminality, then there should be a significant relationship between the criminal tendencies of biological parents and those of their children who were adopted by someone else. In 1971, using Copenhagen adoption files, Hutchings and Mednick identified 1,145 male adoptees, who were by then 30 to 44 years old. They were matched with an equal number of nonadoptee controls on sex, age, occupational status of fathers, and residence. The researchers learned that 185 adoptees (16.2%) had criminal records, compared with 105 nonadoptees (8.9%). A check on the biological fathers of the adoptees revealed that they were nearly three times more likely to be involved in criminal activity than were either the adoptees' adoptive fathers or the fathers of the nonadopted controls. Furthermore, there was a significant relationship between the criminality of the sons and that of the fathers. Where the biological father had a criminal record and the adoptive father had none, a significant number of adoptees still became criminal (22%), but where the biological father had no record and the adoptive father had a criminal record, the number of adoptees who pursued criminal activities was lower (11.5%). If both the biological and adoptive fathers were criminal, the chances were much greater that the adoptee would also be criminal than if only one man was criminal. Hutchings and Mednick concluded that genetic factors continue to exert strong influences in the tendency toward criminality, even though environmental factors also play important roles.

One serious limitation to the Hutchings-Mednick data, as well as to any adoption study, is that agencies often try to match the adopted child with the adoptive family on the basis of the child's biological and sometimes socioeconomic background as well. The Crowe study involving the children of offenders found no evidence of this, but the Danish agency used in the Hutchings-Mednick investigation confirmed that this was done. To their credit, the researchers not only recognized this problem, but also admonished that extrapolations to American society should be made cautiously, since Danish society is more homogeneous in cultural values and race.

The most comprehensive adoption study to date was conducted by Mednick, Gabrielli, and Hutchings (1984, 1987). These researchers compared the court convictions of 14,427 adoptees (adopted between the years 1927 and 1947) in a small European country with conviction records of their biological and adoptive parents. The study showed a significant relationship between the conviction history of the adoptees (for both males and females) and their biological parents. Specifically, if either biological parent had been convicted of a crime, the risk of criminality in the adoptee (the biological child) increased significantly. This relationship was especially strong for male adoptees who were chronic or persistent offenders. As we might expect, chronic offenders accounted for a disproportionate share of the total offending for the entire cohort. Interestingly there was no evidence that the type of crime committed by the biological parent had any relation to the type of crime committed by the biological child. Both the biological parent and biological child tended to engage in crime but selected different kinds of crime. There was also no indication that the adopted children knew about the criminality of their biological parents. The researchers concluded that some factor transmitted by criminal parents increased the probability that their children would engage in criminal behavior. Elsewhere, Gabrielli and Mednick (1983, p. 63) commented, "It is reasonable . . . to conclude that some people inherit biological characteristics which permit them to be antisocial more readily than others."

In summary, twin and adoption studies suggest that genetic components may contribute moderately to a tendency to become criminal, especially pertaining to nonviolent crime, but they have also found that environment is highly important (Raine, 2002). According to biopsychologists, the available data so far indicate that some people may be born with a biological predisposition to behavior that runs counter to social values and norms, but environmental factors may either inhibit or facilitate it. Genes may not influence criminal behavior directly, but genes may act to influence people's susceptibility or resistance to environmental risk factors.

PSYCHOPHYSIOLOGICAL FACTORS

Psychophysiology is the study of the dynamic interactions between behavior and the autonomic nervous system. The autonomic nervous system is the subdivision of the peripheral nervous system that regulates involuntary functions, such as heartbeat, blood pressure, breathing, and digestion, and is closely connected to the genetic makeup of the individual. Heart rates (cardiovascular activity) and electrical conductance in the skin (electrodermal activity) are the usual measures of psychophysiological investigations examining the relationship between antisocial behavior and autonomic activity. Autonomic arousal theory of crime hypothesizes that persistent, chronic offenders compared with those with no or little offending history, will exhibit low levels of autonomic arousal across a wide variety of situations and conditions. Presumably, low levels of arousal predispose a person to crime because it produces some degree of fearlessness, and also because it encourages antisocial stimulation (excitement) seeking (Raine, 2002). That is, persistent offenders experience little anxiety and fear, and are not troubled about getting caught and punished. Furthermore, they find certain aspects of crime exciting and challenging. On the other hand, high levels of autonomic arousal, in light of the amount of fear and anxiety involved, encourage childhood socialization because of fear of disapproval.

Some studies reveal that antisocial boys and criminal psychopaths do appear to have lower levels of physiological arousal (as measured by electrodermal and cardiovascular activity) than their non-antisocial counterparts (Brennan, Mednick, & Raine, 1997; Raine, 2002; Raine, Venables, & Williams, 1995, 1996). We cover this in more detail when we discuss the psychopath in chapter 6.

TEMPERAMENT

A child's **temperament**—defined as a "natural" mood disposition determined largely by genetics and biological influences—may offer important clues about criminal behavior. How we approach and interact with our social environment influences how that environment will interact with us. This is true even of infants and very young children. Parents, teachers, physicians, and caretakers know very well that infants and young children differ in activity, emotionality, and general sensitivity to stimuli. A smiling, relaxed, socially interactive child is apt to initiate and maintain a different social response than a fussy, tense, and withdrawn one. A consistently ill-tempered child—assuming the ill temper cannot be attributed to physical discomfort such as hunger or pain—may become so frustrating to his parents that they feel overwhelmed and helpless in dealing with him. The parents' resulting irritability may feed into the behavior of the child in a reciprocal fashion, producing a serious disruption in the parent-child relationship. Frustration may progress into physical or emotional abuse or neglect by the parent(s). In essence, parents (or caregivers) and the child are active agents, who, by continuous transactions, cocreate their emerging relationship (Kochanska, Friesenborg, Lange, & Martel, 2004). The overwhelming consensus among experts is that parental responsiveness, nurturance, and warmth have emerged as critical core determinants of the early parent-child relationship (Kochanska et al., 2004).

It is suggested here that temperament increases or decreases the *probability* of antisocial behavior, not that it determines directly whether an individual will or will not engage in antisocial behavior. That is, the concurrence of these temperaments and certain kinds of family environments may lead to delinquent or criminal outcomes. Studies have continually discovered significant *links* between children's "difficult" temperament and the occurrence of persistent antisocial behavior (e.g., Bates, Pettit, Dodge, & Ridge, 1998; Rubin, Burgess, Dwyer, & Hastings, 2003; Shaw, Owens, Giovannelli, & Winslow, 2001).

Three Things That Define Temperament

As it is currently used in the research and scholarly literature, "temperament" is assumed to: (1) have a constitutional or biological basis; (2) appear in infancy and continue throughout life; and (3) be influenced by the environment (Bates, 2000). Most developmental experts today believe that temperament has biological underpinnings that are best identified at birth (Bates, Pettit, Dodge, & Ridge, 1998; Dodge & Pettit, 2003; Lahey & Waldman, 2003). Else-Quest, Hyde, Goldsmith, and Van Hulle (2006) write, "Temperament reflects biologically based emotional and behavioral consistencies that appear early in life and predict—often in conjunction with other factors—patterns and outcomes in numerous other domains such as psychopathology and personality" (p. 33). Most of the contemporary research on temperament, therefore, focuses on the infant, because the connection between temperament and behavior seems uncomplicated at this stage and becomes more complex as the child matures and interacts with the psychosocial environment.

Most developmental experts agree that activity and emotionality are two of the behaviors that are strong indicators of temperament. Activity, the most widely studied, refers to gross motor movement across a variety of settings and times, such as the movement of arms and legs, squirming, crawling, or walking. Emotionality refers to such features as irritability, sensitivity, soothability, and general intensity of emotional reactions. Self-regulation (a technical term for controlling impulsivity) is another behavior which is often included in descriptions of temperament. Self-regulation refers to the extent that a child controls his or her own behavior, independent of the control of others and the social environment. Highly impulsive and unmanageable children (poor self-regulators) move into (and often against) their environments at a higher pace and more aggressively than less impulsive children. Recent research (see Olson et al., 2005) has shown a strong connection between poor self-regulation and antisocial behavior across different social situations.

Failure to acknowledge these dispositional or temperamental variables may leave researchers and practitioners with an incomplete picture of the development of antisocial behavior, especially in cases of individuals who demonstrate a persistent pattern of violent or serious offending. Else-Quest et al. (2006) report that girls temperamentally seem better able than boys to manage and regulate their attention and inhibit their impulses (self-regulation). Henry, Caspi,

Moffitt, and Silva (1996) found that children considered temperamentally explosive and lacking in self-control were more likely to become violent adolescents compared with their more temperamentally stable peers. However, although temperament is present at birth, it must be emphasized that its manifestations can be modified by the social environment, especially by parents and significant caregivers. Difficult temperaments can be challenging, but a nurturing and warm caregiver environment in which rules are firmly laid out and appropriate self-regulation is encouraged can prevent, change, or eliminate antisocial behavior in children (Moffitt, 2005b).

Likewise the temperament of parents must also be considered as a possible component in the development of the criminal behavior. Moffitt (1993) suggests that parents and their offspring often resemble each other in temperament and personality. An irritable, temperamental child may have a high probability of being born to highly irritable, temperamental parents. Thus parents of difficult children often lack the necessary psychological and emotional resources to cope effectively with a difficult child.

In the next section, we will take a closer look at those environmental factors that may facilitate or inhibit antisocial tendencies. These factors include prenatal influences, postnatal diseases, and inadequate nutrition and medical care.

ENVIRONMENTAL RISK FACTORS

In addition to genetic factors, in utero experiences may also play a role in the predisposition toward criminal behavior. During pregnancy the fetus is exposed to various influences that may adversely affect development, leading to potential risks for serious antisocial behaviors later in life. Exposure to a toxic or diseased prenatal environment is one example. "Fetuses exposed to opiates or methadone are at heightened risk for conduct problems 10 to 13 years later, as are fetuses exposed to alcohol, marijuana, and cigarette by-products during pregnancy" (Dodge & Pettit, 2003, p. 351). Also, before and after birth, lead poisoning found in old paint can lead to long-term conduct problems in adolescence and young adulthood (Dodge & Pettit, 2003). It should be noted that during the years 1999 to 2002, approximately 2 percent of children ages 1 to 5 had blood-lead levels above 10 micrograms per deciliter (Federal Interagency Forum on Child and Family Statistics, 2005). Children ages 1 to 5 are particularly affected because of frequent hand-to-mouth behavior. Although 10 micrograms per deciliter is considered elevated according to federal safety standards, significant and troubling behavioral and health effects have been shown to occur at lower levels (Federal Interagency Forum on Child and Family Statistics, 2005). Childhood exposure to chips or dust from lead-based paint has been shown to contribute to learning and cognitive development problems, which increases the risk for antisocial and delinquent behavior. Fortunately, since the 1970s lead exposure has declined primarily because of the removal of lead from gasoline and the drastic reduction in the use of lead-based paint.

However, even today, many children have blood-lead levels at or above 5µg/dl, and these children are predominantly in homes with incomes below poverty level (Dietrich et al., 2001; Needleman et al., 2002). Some racial and ethnic groups may be particularly susceptible (e.g., African American children, 19%; Mexican-American children, 7%). Bone-lead levels have been shown to be closely related to antisocial behavior in adolescents (Dietrich et al., 2001; Needleman et al., 2002).

Birth Complications

Birth complications are also associated with violent and persistent offending, but usually the relationship is most significant when *combined* with other psychosocial risks. The most common psychosocial risks are maternal separation, maternal rejection, marital discord, parental mental health problems, and paternal absence. For example, Raine, Brennan, and Mednick (1997) followed the criminal offending history of over four thousand Danish babies to age 34. Birth complications, when combined with early maternal rejection, predicted careers of violent crime. Interestingly, the relationship did not hold for *nonviolent* criminal careers, such as burglary, theft, shoplifting, and drug distribution. Another study (Neugebauer, Hoek, & Susser, 1999) found that maternal malnutrition during pregnancy in combination with adverse caregiving conditions may also be closely linked to violent behavior in the offspring.

The relationship between birth or pregnancy complications and a disadvantaged familial environment found in the Denmark study has also been replicated in four other countries (Sweden, Finland, Canada, and the United States) (Raine, 2002). It should be emphasized that birth or pregnancy complications by themselves are not be enough to trigger violent crime and serious antisocial behavior. The relationship seems to require the presence of negative environmental circumstances and heightened psychosocial risks in general. For example, one study (Arseneault, Tremblay, Boulerice, & Saucier, 2002) discovered that obstetrical complications (preeclampsia, chronic fetal hypoxia, placenta problems, umbilical cord prolapse, and induced labor) increased the risk of being violent at both 6 and 17 years of age among boys who grew up in highly adverse familial environments (early maternal rejection or a disadvantaged familial environment).

Birth and pregnancy complications in combination with a faulty psychosocial environment are most likely to have a negative impact on children's abilities to learn to self-regulate their behavior. Neurological deficits (such as brain damage) due to birth and pregnancy problems—if not modified and buffered by a stable home environment—are apt to lead to antisocial behaviors characterized by poor impulse or self-control and limited verbal ability because the child lacks the patience to develop socially appropriate verbal skills.

Nicotine, Alcohol, and Drug Exposure

There is substantial literature on the effects of prenatal exposure to drugs on child development. However, the prenatal effects of substance and alcohol abuse on antisocial behavioral development have received relatively little attention.

A few studies have examined these effects, however. According to Raine (2002, p. 317), "The effects of fetal exposure to alcohol in increasing risk for conduct disorders is well known, but recently a spate of studies has established beyond reasonable doubt a significant link between smoking during pregnancy and later conduct disorder and violent offending." The evidence for the relationship between maternal smoking during pregnancy and antisocial behavior in her children is quite strong for boys, but weak for girls (Wakschlag & Hans, 2002). One study (Brennan, Grekin, & Mednick, 1999), using a birth cohort of 4,169 males, found a strong connection between adult violent offending and smoking by their mothers during their pregnancy. On average, the mothers smoked 20 cigarettes a day. This relationship was especially strong (increasing by fivefold) when the offspring were exposed to both nicotine and birth complications. In another study that used a large sample from the general population of Finland, Räsänen et al. (1999) found that, compared with the sons of mothers who did not smoke, the sons of mothers who smoked during pregnancy had more than a twofold risk of having committed a violent crime or having repeatedly committed crimes. This finding held even when other biopsychological risk factors were controlled. The available evidence suggests that smoking during pregnancy may contribute to brain deficits that have been frequently found in adult offenders (Raine, 2002).

Maternal substance abuse during pregnancy does show a link to substance abuse by their offspring during adolescence, but it is difficult to determine whether this link is due to a shared genetic predisposition between parent and child, the child modeling the parents' behavior, or the in utero effects of the substances themselves (Allen, Lewinsohn, & Seeley, 1998). Identifying the differential effects of maternal substance abuse of specific drugs is also daunting because the drug-abusing mother rarely uses a drug in isolation. That is, abusers usually use multiple substances. Nonetheless, there is some strong evidence to suggest that prenatal cocaine use by mothers adversely affects emotional and attention regulation in infants and preschool aged children (Mayes, 1999). This finding is significant because cocaine or crack continued to be used by some pregnant women at least into the 1990s. For example, in some inner-city populations, nearly 50 percent of women giving birth reported or tested positive for cocaine use at the time of delivery (Mayes, 1999).

Brain Development

Neurological and brain dysfunction due to faulty brain development is clearly linked to serious and violent antisocial behavior (Ishikawa & Raine, 2004). The link is especially strong if the brain dysfunction is located in the frontal lobe, which comprises about one-third of the front part of the human brain. Organized thought, planning, and self-regulation are located in this area. After their careful review of the research literature, Ishikawa and Raine (2004) concluded that "in all likelihood . . . both prefrontal cortices play a role in the onset and persistence of antisocial behavior" (p. 290).

The quality of the prenatal environment is clearly important in brain development. The brain is highly vulnerable to intrinsic hazards (cell development gone wrong) and to external insults resulting from viral infection, drug or alcohol exposure, malnutrition, or other teratogens. Nutritional adequacy is crucial on prenatal and postnatal influence on brain development because of the growing brain's reliance on folic acid, iron, vitamins, and other nutrients. Malnutrition is a biological hazard to which the developing infant brain is especially vulnerable. Other hazards include fetal exposure to maternal viruses like HIV and rubella, illicit drugs such as cocaine and heroin, maternal alcohol ingestion, exposure to environmental toxins (e.g., DDI, lead, mercury, and PCB) and other teratogens. The vulnerability of the developing brain to many of these hazards continues throughout the early years after birth.

Brain Plasticity

After birth, early experiences are crucial in shaping the cultivation and pruning of neural synapses that underlie the functional capabilities of the developing brain (Thompson & Nelson, 2001). Recent studies of humans and other species have made it clear that the developing brain is profoundly responsive to experience (Nelson & Bloom, 1997). Both structure and function are affected by experience, a phenomenon known as **plasticity.**

Among the most important of these early experiences is nurturant, sensitive care. Although there are few relevant human neuroscience data, parents and caregivers are encouraged to talk and sing to, play with, and sensitively nurture young children because of how these contingent sensory experiences provide stimulation for the brain (Thompson & Nelson, 2001). On the other hand, when caregivers are unable to provide these multisensory stimulations, brain development is likely to be delayed, either temporarily or permanently depending on the timing and quality of the intervention.

The first three years of life are significant in the prevention of antisocial behavior and persistent, serious criminal behavior throughout life, but other developmental periods are also important. Research demonstrates that the brain retains its capacity to grow throughout life (Thompson & Nelson, 2001). Brain development can be facilitated not only during the first three years, but also at other developmental stages. This point suggests that early deprivation and harm can be treated and modified during later years, even in adults.

Neuropsychological Factors

Neuropsychological deficits, especially those associated with executive function problems (e.g., problems associated with self-regulation and planning), are reasonably well-established risk factors for antisocial behavior in children, adolescents, and adults (Raine, 2002). Moffitt (1993) has argued that neuropsychological deficits in combination with certain family risk factors are often found in persistent, serious, violent offenders. Liu, Raine, Venables, and Mednick (2004) report from their investigations that malnutrition at age 3 predisposes a child to neurocognitive deficits, which in turn predispose a child to persistent antisocial behaviors throughout childhood and adolescence. The authors believe that early malnutrition negatively affects brain growth and development and that the brain impairments may promote antisocial and violent behavior by affecting cognitive executive functions. Morgan and Lilienfeld (2000) concluded after an extensive review of the research literature that there is a robust and statistically significant relationship between antisocial behavior and executive function deficits. However, the relationship between executive function and neuropsychological deficits was far from clear and will require far more research for any firm conclusions to be made on this topic.

PHYSIQUE AND CRIME

Theorists have linked physical characteristics with personality ever since Hippocrates outlined a typology of physiques and tried to relate them to personality. He also introduced the concept of humors, or body fluids, which presumably influenced personality (Hall & Lindzey, 1970). More pertinent to our discussion of crime is the theory of William H. Sheldon (Sheldon & Stevens, 1942; Sheldon, Hartl, & McDermott, 1949), who developed a similar but superior classification of body type in the United States and related physique to delinquency. Sheldon's method is called **somatotyping.** After extensively collecting and documenting physical measurements, Sheldon found he could delineate three basic body builds: the endomorphic (fat and soft), ectomorphic (thin and fragile), and mesomorphic (muscular and hard) (see Figure 3–1 on page 90). The reader with some background in embryology will recognize that the terms refer to layers of the embryo. The endodermal embryonic layer develops primarily into the digestive viscera, and thus individuals who are plump (endomorphs) are tied to the digestive system. The mesodermal layer of the embryo develops into muscle; therefore, the tough, muscular body, well equipped for strenuous activity, is labeled the mesomorph. The ectodermal layer is developmentally responsible for the nervous system. The ectomorph has a large brain and central nervous system compared with the rest of his or her body, which is usually tall and thin.

We should emphasize that Sheldon avoided making sharp distinctions between body types or somatotypes. People were scored on the basis of three 7-point scales corresponding to the three somatotypes, with a 7 indicating that they were exclusively that body type. This was a rare occurrence, however. For example, a "pure" mesomorph would have a somatotype of 1-7-1, with the ones denoting that he or she was devoid of that particular body build. A 3-2-5 person would be primarily ectomorphic (5), but have some features of endomorphs (3) and mesomorphs (2). The average body build would be assigned a 4-4-4 index, indicating constitutional balance (see **Figure 3–1**).

FIGURE 3–1   Sheldon's Somatotypes in Relation to Physique and Temperament

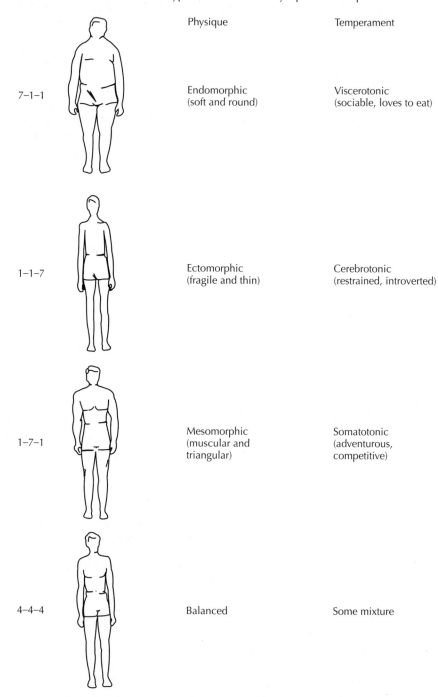

	Physique	Temperament
7–1–1	Endomorphic (soft and round)	Viscerotonic (sociable, loves to eat)
1–1–7	Ectomorphic (fragile and thin)	Cerebrotonic (restrained, introverted)
1–7–1	Mesomorphic (muscular and triangular)	Somatotonic (adventurous, competitive)
4–4–4	Balanced	Some mixture

Sheldon found a strong connection between personality (or temperament) and **somatotypes.** In other words, he linked certain personality types with certain body types. One personality loves comfort, food, affection, and people. This type is usually even tempered and easy to get along with. Sheldon labeled this disposition *viscerotonia,* and, as you might have guessed, he connected it closely to the basic endomorph. A second personality type ordinarily needs vigorous physical activity, risk taking, and adventure. A person with this temperament, according to Sheldon, is more likely to be indifferent to pain and is aggressive, callous, even ruthless in relationships with others. This cluster of personality traits was called somatotonia and was linked with the mesomorph. *Cerebrotonia* labels the person who is inhibited, reserved, self-conscious, and afraid of people; it correlates highly with the ectomorphic body build.

Body Shape and Crime

Sheldon began to test his theory in 1939 by exploring the relationship between delinquency and physique. His first study involved nearly four hundred boys in a residential rehabilitation home. Biographical sketches—family background, medical history, mental and educational performance, and delinquent behavior—were collected for each boy, and they were all assigned somatotype ratings. Sheldon studied his delinquents for eight years, comparing them to a group of male college students. He found that the college men generally clustered around the "average" somatotype of 4-4-4. Delinquents, on the other hand, tended to be heavily mesomorphic, but there were also signs of endomorphy. Ectomorphs were rare in the delinquent group. On the basis of his study, Sheldon concluded that there were definite somatotypic and temperamental differences between delinquent and nondelinquent males.

Subsequent investigations (primarily on males) provided additional, although not very strong, support for Sheldon's findings. Glueck and Glueck (1950, 1956) found that mesomorphs were proportionately overrepresented in the delinquent population (60%, with 30% endomorphs). In general, their findings established that delinquent boys were larger and stronger than nondelinquent boys. In another study, Cortes and Gatti (1972) reported that delinquent subjects (one hundred boys adjudicated delinquent by the courts) were much more mesomorphic than nondelinquents (one hundred male high school seniors). Fifty-seven percent of their delinquent group could be easily classified as mesomorphic compared with 19 percent of the nondelinquents. These percentages roughly correspond to those cited by Glueck and Glueck (1950) in their study of five hundred youths. Hartl, Monnelly, and Elderkin (1982) claim that, in their 30-year follow-up of Sheldon's original group, the relationship between mesomorphs and antisocial behavior still holds.

More sophisticated research yielded different results. McCandless, Persons, and Roberts (1972) found physique unrelated to either self-reported delinquency or the seriousness of the criminal offenses. Wadsworth (1979), using data from the British National Survey, reported that delinquents, especially those who committed serious offenses, were generally smaller in stature and appeared to reach puberty later than their nondelinquent peers. While no somatotyping was done, the results suggest that the delinquents were not mesomorphs, since mesomorphs reportedly reach puberty before the other body types (Rutter & Giller, 1984). Finally, in their longitudinal study of working-class boys in London, West and Farrington (1973) reported little association between delinquency and either height-weight ratios or physical strength.

Wilson and Herrnstein (1985, p. 90), in their influential but controversial book *Crime and Human Nature,* concluded that the evidence on the relationship between physique and crime "leaves no doubt that constitutional traits correlate with criminal behavior." Some of the evidence does suggest a relationship between body build and crime, but there is also a significant amount of evidence that indicates that there may be no relationship. Thus, the research is equivocal and far from conclusive. While it may make logical sense to argue that the mesomorph's physique, because it is so muscular and strong, is well suited for involvement in aggressive or antisocial acts, much more sophisticated and well-executed research needs to be conducted before we can get a better understanding of the physique-crime connection. In a recent study, Sampson and Laub (1997) found evidence that mesomorphy is a poor predictor of adult arrests for any crime, including violence. Thus, while mesomorphy seems related to official delinquency, it does not seem related to criminal offending during adulthood.

Attractiveness

Some researchers have studied physical features, such as facial characteristics, and related them to body build, criminal activity, or treatment by the criminal justice system. Some have argued that physical features, such as spacing of the eyes, the shape of forehead, body stature and shape, are related to honesty, intelligence, and even criminal conduct. Others contend that facial and general physical attractiveness are also related to temperament and certain enduring personality traits. But it is not clear whether the physical attributes directly influence the development of personality characteristics, whether they elicit responses from the social environment that encourage the development of certain personality characteristics, or whether there is some complicated interaction between the physical characteristics and the environment.

One of the most robust findings in the research literature is that physical attractiveness presents a significant advantage for both children and adults across a wide range of situations and experiences (Langlois et al., 2000). For example, attractive children and adults are *judged* more positively than unattractive children and adults, even by those who know them well; attractive children and adults are *treated* more positively than unattractive children and adults, even by those who know them well; and attractive children and adults exhibit more positive behaviors and traits than unattractive children and adults (Langlois et al., 2000). In general, attractive individuals are more successful, have better social skills, and are more mentally healthy than unattractive persons

(Langlois et al., 2000). And these observations hold for both genders. It is reasonable to suppose, therefore, that attractiveness may show some connection to criminal behavior. The connection is not necessarily always as suggested above, however. Attractive individuals sometimes use their attractiveness to facilitate the perpetration of crimes, such as fraud or rape.

Attractiveness and Crime

Unfortunately the amount of research devoted to the attractiveness-crime connection is very sparse and limited methodologically. Cavior and Howard (1973), concentrating on facial features, found that both black and white delinquents were rated significantly less attractive than nondelinquents. Moreover, correctional personnel often comment that inmates, as a group, have "uglier" faces than the general population, but very little research has been directed at verifying these observations.

Facial unattractiveness, promoting rejection by peers and unfavorable treatment from the social environment, may play a role in the development of crime and/or increase the probability of being adjudicated delinquent by the courts. Research has found that attractive children are favored by adults and other children. In fact, attractive children are less negatively evaluated than less attractive children, even when they have committed identical antisocial acts (Dion, 1972; Dion, Berscheid, & Walster, 1972). In one study using a simulated jury, good-looking defendants were treated more gently and were considered less dangerous than a comparable group of unattractive defendants (Sigall & Ostrove, 1978).

The thesis that physical unattractiveness might have something to do with criminal behavior has been applied to rehabilitation. In the mid-1970s, corrective surgery was offered to inmates with facial deformities at Rikers Island as part of a pilot project testing the value of plastic surgery as a rehabilitative measure (Kurtzberg et al., 1978). The surgery was to be performed just prior to prison release. After extensive medical and psychological screening, 425 inmates were divided into four groups. Depending on his group, the inmate would receive either surgery, counseling, both, or neither (the control group).

The results, though complex, showed some support for the benefits of a new image. The offenders who seemed to benefit most from the intervention were nonaddicts who received surgery; they were substantially less likely to engage in crime during a one-year follow-up period than a comparable group of offenders who received no surgery. Interestingly the group that received counseling alone committed more detected crime during the follow-up period than even the group that had neither counseling nor surgery. Although the study's results are not clear-cut, they do suggest that physical improvements also improve prisoner self-image and the likelihood of acceptance by others. Possibly the individual with the improved appearance has less need to defend or prove his or her worth through crime or to react aggressively to slights or challenges. And, possibly, the slights and challenges are fewer in number.

Based on a nationwide survey, Thompson (1990) estimated that 5,000 to 6,000 inmates in the United States undergo some type of cosmetic or reconstructive surgery each year. Thompson, in his review of the research literature, found that six of the nine studies examining recidivism rates after cosmetic or reconstructive surgery concluded that reoffending was significantly reduced following the surgical treatment. However, since there are a number of methodological problems in all these studies, other interpretations and conclusions of the data are possible. It is also unclear whether corrective surgery reduces recidivism over the long haul or merely delays a return to prison. It is important to note, though, that in many cases such surgery is medically necessary and is a part of the health care to which inmates are constitutionally entitled—it is not simply undertaken as an elective procedure to make the inmate "look better."

In a more recent study, Zebrowitz and colleagues (Zebrowitz, Andreoletti, et al., 1998) examined the influence of "babyfaceness" on the behavioral patterns and personalities of boys, including their involvement in delinquency and adult crime. As the researchers noted, most people believe that baby-faced individuals are likely to have childlike traits—such as submissiveness, dependency—and are more likely to be warm, affectionate, honest, weak, and naïve than their non–baby-faced peers. Although this baby-faced stereotype has been well documented, the *accuracy* of the stereotype is another matter. In one study, Zebrowitz, Collins, and Dutta (1998) reported that, in contradiction to the stereotype, middle-class, baby-faced adolescent boys were far more assertive and hostile than their mature-faced peers. In a second study, Zebrowitz, Andreoletti et al. (1998) discovered that baby-faced boys from lower social economic families were more likely to be delinquent and commit significantly more crimes than their mature-faced peers, refuting the stereotype of baby-faced boys as warm, submissive, and physically weak. Delinquency and crime data were compiled from the criminal history data of each delinquent from birth to age 17. The researchers also found that baby-faced boys from higher social economic backgrounds tended to confirm the traditional stereotype, showing less likelihood of being delinquent than their mature-faced peers. The researchers hypothesized that the effect of a baby face on the lower social economic class boys may reflect a desire to promote the reputation that one is tough, a characteristic highly valued among their peers. In other words, the boys may have compensated for the expectation that they would be unassertive, dependent, and weak by behaving contrary to these undesirable expectations.

Minor Physical Anomalies

During the past three decades, there has been renewed interest in **minor physical anomalies (MPAs),** which are unusual but often barely noticeable physical features. MPAs have been associated with disorders of pregnancy and are thought to be a marker for problems in fetal neural development during the first three months of pregnancy (Raine, 2002). While the specific origin of MPAs is not fully understood, some experts believe that they may be indirect signs of abnormal brain development and later behavioral problems (Brennan et al., 1997; Mednick & Kandel, 1988).

MPAs are typically not noticed by people who have them or by others. They are discernible only to trained observers and usually do not significantly interfere with attractiveness. Examples of MPAs in children include asymmetrical ears, soft and pliable ears, curved fifth finger, ocular hypertelorism (widely spaced eyes), multiple hair whorls, webbed toes, and a furrowed tongue. MPAs seem to be related to some temperamental, neurological, and behavioral attributes in children. It should be emphasized that it is the total number of MPAs rather than any specific physical anomaly that seems to be most closely connected to antisocial behavior or violence.

MPAs and Crime

At least six studies have discovered an association between increased MPAs and increased antisocial behavior in children (Raine, 1993, 2002). For example, Pine, Shaffer, Schonfeld, and Davies (1997) note that high numbers of MPAs have been found in boys demonstrating conduct disorders. In a study conducted by Mednick and Kandel (1988), an experienced pediatrician assessed MPA in 129 boys age 12; the researchers then followed the boys' development until they were 21 years old. The researchers discovered that MPAs were related to violent offending, but only if the boys were from unstable, nonintact homes. In other words, the presence of MPAs increased the likelihood that a boy from an unstable home would become violent. Boys from stable homes with high MPAs did not show the relationship. In addition, Mednick and Kandel did not find an MPA relationship for nonviolent or property crimes, only violent crimes. In another study, Brennan, Mednick, and Kandel (1993) found that subjects who had delivery complications at birth and a high number of MPAs were more likely to be adult violent offenders than individuals who had only one of these conditions, or neither of them. These findings underscore the importance of considering the interactions of the psychosocial environment and biological factors in any explanations of antisocial behavior involving biological factors.

Not all studies have reported the frequently observed interactions between the psychosocial environment and MPAs, however. Arsenault et al. (2000) discovered that adolescent boys with higher counts of MPAs evaluated at age 14 were likely to be violent at age 17, independent of the psychosocial environment. It is intriguing that the MPAs most closely associated with violence were anomalies of the mouth, such as a high steepled palate, rough spots, or furrowed tongue. Anomalies of the mouth, the authors point out, have been found in individuals with neurological deficits and may be associated with neurological problems that increase the risk for violent delinquency. The critical period for the development of anomalies of the mouth and certain neurological structures begins at the ninth week of gestation. "It is then plausible," Arseneault et al. write, "that insults occurring at specific periods during gestation increase the risks for the development of violent delinquency as a result of atypical brain development" (p. 921). Unlike previous studies (e.g., Brennan, Mednick, & Kandel 1993; Mednick & Kandel, 1988), however, the interaction between MPAs and family adversity as a predictor of violence was not found.

EYSENCK'S THEORY OF PERSONALITY AND CRIME

We will spend some time on the late Hans J. Eysenck's theory of crime in this section not only because it has been one of the most influential psychological perspectives on crime today (Cale, 2006), but also because it exemplifies many of the principles and issues discussed in this chapter, especially how genetic and biological factors play an important role in the understanding of criminal behavior. The reader is encouraged to take his measure of personality, the *Eysenck Personality Questionnaire—Revised,* which takes only about 15 minutes to complete, and which is helpful in understanding the theory.

Eysenck (1977, 1996; Eysenck & Gudjonsson, 1989) proposed that criminal behavior is the result of an **interaction** between certain environmental conditions and features of the nervous system. Eysenck believed that a comprehensive theory of criminality must allow for an examination of the neurophysiological makeup and the unique socialization history of each individual. Theories that argue that crime is caused by social conditions such as poverty, poor education, or unemployment are as misleading as theories that rely exclusively on hereditary and biological explanations. Crime cannot be understood in terms of heredity alone, but it can also not be understood in terms of environment alone (Eysenck, 1973, p. 171). Eysenck also suggested that different combinations of environmental, neurobiological, and personality factors give rise to different types of crime (Eysenck & Eysenck, 1970). This position implies that different personalities are more susceptible to certain crimes than others, an issue we will return to shortly.

Unlike most contemporary theories of crime, Eysenck's theory places heavy emphasis on genetic predispositions toward antisocial and criminal conduct. Eysenck (1996, p. 146) asserted "genetic causes play an important part in antisocial and criminal behaviour. This simple fact is no longer in doubt." It is important to note at the outset that he was not suggesting that individuals are born criminal, but rather that some people are born with nervous system characteristics that are significantly different from the general population and that affect their ability to conform to social expectancies and rules. "It is not crime itself or criminality that is innate; it is certain peculiarities of the central and autonomic nervous system that react with the environment, with upbringing, and many other environment factors to increase the probability that a given person would act in a certain antisocial manner" (Eysenck & Gudjonsson, 1989, p. 7). Eysenck isolated features of the central and autonomic nervous systems to account for a substantial portion of the differences found in personality in general. The way each individual's nervous system functions may be as unique as his or her personality characteristics. Carrying this one step further, we could posit that some nervous systems are more likely to engage in criminal activity because of their reactivity, sensitivity, and excitability.

Based on a series of empirical studies and statistical analyses, Eysenck argued that there are four higher order factors of personality—one higher order factor for ability called "g" (general intelligence), and three higher order factors for temperament, called **extraversion, neuroticism,** and **psychoticism.** Eysenck believed that the ability factor is an important factor in the cause of criminality, but is less important than the temperament factors. He wrote, "We may conclude that intelligence is a factor in the causation of criminality but that its contribution is probably smaller than one might have thought at first" (Eysenck & Gudjonsson, 1989, p. 50).

Most of the research on crime and personality has focused on extraversion and neuroticism, which are essentially the core concepts of Eysenckian theory. Eysenck did not identify psychoticism until he found a need to account for behaviors not fully explained by extraversion or neuroticism.

Eysenck visualized each of the three temperament or personality factors on a continuum, with the neuroticism and extraversion lines at right angles and intersecting. Psychoticism is on a separate continuum. Most people fall in the intermediate or midpoint area of each, and people are rarely at either extreme. (See **Figure 3–2.** Most people fall within the square.) The extraversion dimension runs from the extreme pole extraversion to the extreme pole introversion, with the middle range called **ambiversion.** Thus, depending on where a person falls on this dimension, that person may be an extravert, introvert, or ambivert. The neuroticism continuum runs from the polar ends of neuroticism to stability, with no middle label. Psychoticism runs from tough-mindedness (high psychoticism) to tender-mindedness (low psychoticism), also with no label for the middle majority. The extraversion dimension is believed to reflect basic functions of the central nervous system (CNS), which consists of the brain and spinal cord, while neuroticism represents functions of the peripheral nervous system (nerve pathways outside the central nervous system). As yet, neither Eysenck nor other researchers have postulated a nervous system mechanism for psychoticism.

Measurement of Eysenck's Theory

Eysenck developed several self-report questionnaires to measure these personality variables, the best-known being the British Maudsley Personality Inventory (MPI) and its American editions, the Eysenck Personality Inventory (EPI) and the Eysenck Personality Questionnaire (EPQ). More recently, the Eysenck Personality Questionnaire-Revised (EPQ-R) has been published. The questionnaires have stimulated extensive research to explore both their validity and Eysenck's concept of personality. Overall, worldwide research has supported the general theory, but when it is applied to criminality, the support is a bit

FIGURE 3–2   Illustration of Eysenck's Personality Dimensions for Neuroticism and Extraversion

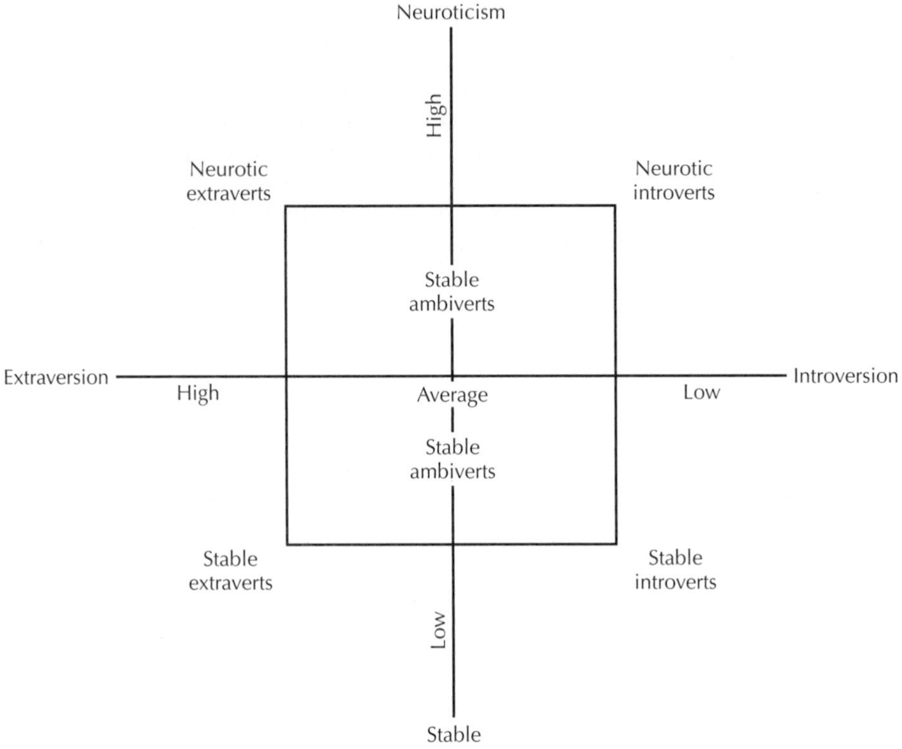

more mixed. We will review some of this research later in this chapter, after examining more closely the basic concepts behind each dimension.

Extraversion

Behavioral Characteristics and Incidence

Usually, two out of every three people will score in the "average" range on the extraversion dimension, thus disqualifying them from studies based on extraversion and introversion. Roughly 16 percent of the population are extraverts, and another 16 percent introverts, and the remainder (68%) are ambiverts.

According to Eysenck, the typical extravert is sociable, impulsive, optimistic, and has high needs for excitement and for a varied, changing environment. Extraverts tend to lose their temper quickly, become aggressive easily, and be unreliable. They like to have people around, enjoy parties, and are usually very talkative. The typical introvert, on the other hand, is reserved, quiet, and cautious. He or she keeps feelings under close control and generally tries to avoid excitement, change, and most social activities. Introverts tend to be reliable and unaggressive and to place great value on ethical standards (Eysenck & Rachman, 1965). Ambiverts exhibit some features of both extraversion and introversion, but not to the same degree or consistency as extraverts and introverts.

Think of the extraversion dimension as a continuum representing a progressive need for stimulation, which can be defined as the impact stimuli have on areas of the brain. The impact is analogous to the taste of food. Some people have a relatively consistent tendency to prefer spicy, hot foods (e.g., Szechuan cuisine) that have more impact on their taste centers, while others more often choose bland foods (e.g., macaroni and cheese) because they do not desire the high taste impact. Some people prefer and actively seek out more stimulation or stimulus impact from other areas of their lives as well—they like rousing music, perpetual bustle, psychedelic drugs. Eysenck maintained that people at the extraversion end of the dimension require high levels of stimulation from their environment because of their biological makeup.

If you conceptualize the dimension this way, you may find that the popular term "extrovert" (note the spelling) takes on added meaning. Extroverts are sociable creatures who like to be around people and to be immersed in activity because of the stimulation this provides them. It is important to note, though, that our everyday usage of the nouns *extrovert* and *introvert* are not identical to Eysenck's polar classifications.

Because extraverts have higher needs for excitement and stimulation to break the daily boredom, they are also most likely to run counter to the law. They tend to be impulsive, fun-loving, thrill-seeking people who are willing to take chances and stick their necks out. They enjoy pranks and practical jokes, and find challenge in opportunities to do the unconventional or even to engage in antisocial behavior. In an interesting study involving Brazilian offenders, Labato (2000) found that extraverts are more likely to use dramatic, powerful firearms when committing crime, whereas introverts have a strong tendency to use less dramatic weapons, such as knives. Some features of the extraverted nervous system not only encourage stimulation seeking but also inhibit the acquisition and internalization of society's rules, as we will see shortly.

Physiological Bases of Extraversion-Introversion

Eysenck (1967) hypothesized that people differ along the extraversion-introversion axis because of genetic differences in certain mechanisms in their central nervous system, particularly the tiny but complex network of neurons located in the central part of the brain stem called the reticular activating system (RAS) (see **Figure 3–3** on page 100). The RAS, which we discuss in detail in chapter 4, is believed to act as a sentinel that awakens and keeps alert the portion of the brain called the cerebral cortex. All higher level functions, like thinking, memory, and decision making, occur in the cerebral cortex (French, 1957). The RAS arouses the cerebral cortex and keeps it alert to incoming stimuli. Nerve pathways communicating information to the cerebral cortex branch off into collateral pathways traveling to the RAS. In effect, these collaterals "tell" the RAS to alert the brain to incoming information.

Figure 3–3   Location of the Reticular Activating System (RAS) Relative to Other Brain Structures

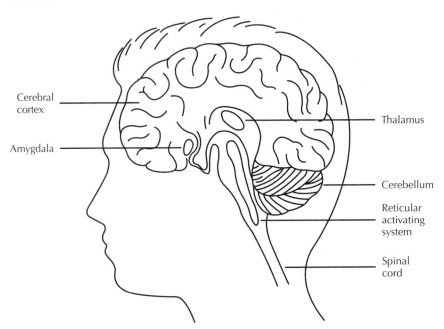

Cerebral cortex

Amygdala

Thalamus

Cerebellum

Reticular activating system

Spinal cord

Eysenck postulated that both extraverts and introverts inherit an RAS that handles cortical arousal in a unique way, differently from the RAS of the general population. The extravert's RAS does not seem to generate cortical excitation or arousal effectively. In fact, it appears to reduce the impact of stimulation and the arousal properties of stimuli before they can reach the cortex. The introvert, on the other hand, apparently has inherited an RAS that amplifies stimulation input, keeping cortical arousal at relatively high levels. So we have the extravert, who is cortically underaroused, seeking additional stimulation to achieve an optimally aroused cortex, and the introvert, who is cortically overaroused, trying to avoid stimulation. The ambivert, who obtains an intermediate level of arousal, is generally content with moderate amounts of stimulation.

In chapter 6, we also discuss the concept of optimal level of stimulation or cortical arousal. One motivation behind human behavior is the desire to achieve a just-right level of stimulation and cortical arousal. Too much stimulation becomes aversive and even painful, while too little results in boredom and eventual sleep. It is assumed that the extravert, because of the dampening effect of the RAS, needs higher levels of stimulation to maintain that just-right or optimal level of cortical arousal. The introvert, because of the amplifying effect of the RAS, desires relatively lower levels of stimulation. This explains the typical extravert's attraction to spicy foods, loud music, and vividly colored objects, and the introvert's preference for bland foods, soft music, and cool or dark-colored objects.

The extravert's stimulation needs are well documented (see Eysenck, 1967, 1981). As mentioned previously, the greater tendency of extraverts to seek sensation is presumably more likely to put them in conflict with the law. Eysenck suggested that most people involved in criminal activity are cortically under-aroused and have a strong drive to obtain stimulation or sensation from their environment. They are thus drawn to risk taking, joy riding, and illegal activities that have high stimulation value.

Before leaving the section on extraversion, let's digress for a moment on the effects of alcohol on cortical arousal. Alcohol is a general central nervous system depressant. It lowers cortical arousal to the point that one may pass out or fall asleep. The extravert without alcohol is already "half in the bag," and with alcohol he or she is even less alert. For introverts, however, alcohol has the effect of lowering a normally high cortical arousal to a point where they become more extraverted, behaviorally and physiologically. Thus, the usually quiet, reserved person may become boisterous or perform a soft shoe routine on the coffee table after a few drinks. The drunk introvert now has an extraverted arousal level and seeks more stimulation.

Eysenck supposed that the active, aroused cortex is a better inhibitor of activity than the poorly aroused one. Therefore, high cortical arousal leads to inhibition, while low cortical arousal allows subcortical regions of the central nervous system to function without restraint. Alcohol lowers the alertness of the cortex, which presumably lessens its censorship over the primitive, subcortical regions of the nervous system. This facilitates inappropriate, antisocial behaviors usually held in check by the cortex. Thus, according to the Eysenckian perspective, under the influence of alcohol, introverts will do things they normally would not do. On the other hand, even relatively small quantities of alcohol influence the extravert, who already functions at a low level of cortical arousal, toward even more uninhibited behavior. The correlation between alcohol and crime is a strong one and is discussed in greater detail in chapter 16.

By now you should have a basic understanding of one of Eysenck's personality dimensions. We will now move on to consider the second dimension, which is equally important.

Neuroticism

Like extraversion, neuroticism is a significant variable in the relationship between personality and crime. Sometimes called emotionality, this dimension reflects an innate biological predisposition to react physiologically to stressful events. Basically neuroticism deals with the intensity of emotional reactions. It is believed to occur in the general population in the same frequencies as extraversion, with 16 percent of the population falling above and below one standard deviation from the mean.

A person high on the neuroticism scale reacts intensely and lastingly to stress. In fact, even under low-stress conditions, the person is likely to be moody, touchy, sensitive to slights, and anxious, and likely to complain of various physical ailments such as headaches, backaches, and digestive problems. He or she tends to overreact to stress and has difficulty returning to a normal, calm state. People high in emotionality also have a strong propensity to develop neurotic features such as phobias and obsessions. Their opposites, persons at the other end of the continuum, display emotionally stable, calm, and even-tempered behavior. They tend to keep their wits about them under stress and intense excitement and to select appropriate reactions to emergencies. Researchers testing Eysenckian theory refer to high emotionality individuals as neurotics and their counter opposites as stables.

Neurophysiological Bases of Neuroticism-Stability

Whereas the extraversion-introversion dimension is linked to the central nervous system, the neuroticism-stability continuum relates to the autonomic nervous system, which can be divided into the sympathetic and parasympathetic nervous systems (see **Figure 3–4** on page 103). The *sympathetic system* activates the body for emergencies by increasing heart rate, respiration flow, blood flow, pupil dilation, and perspiration. The *parasympathetic system* counterbalances the sympathetic; it brings the body back to its normal arousal state. According to Eysenck, differences in emotionality are due to variances in the sensitivity of these subdivisions, which are both under the control of the so-called visceral brain or limbic system. In addition to a complicated array of neuronal circuitry, the *limbic system* includes the neurological structures known as the hippocampus, amygdala, cingulum, and hypothalamus. The hypothalamus appears to exert the greatest amount of control over the autonomic nervous system and thus represents the central mechanism in emotionality.

Neurotics are believed to have unusually sensitive limbic systems, so they achieve emotionality quickly, and for longer periods of time. Theoretically it may be that their sympathetic system is activated quickly while their parasympathetic system is slow in counterbalancing this. Stables, low in emotionality, may possess an underactive sympathetic system and an overactive parasympathetic system.

Although autonomic activation appears to produce a generalized arousal state in everyone, there is good reason to believe that each person reacts to the stress in unique ways. Some of us tense the muscles in our neck, forehead, or back; others breathe more heavily; for others, the heart pumps faster. This tendency for response specificity may account for the various forms of neurotic behaviors displayed by humans reacting to stress. Some complain of headaches, others of digestive problems or backaches. (Obviously, we are not suggesting that all backache sufferers are neurotics.)

Eysenck assumed that the person high on emotionality is more likely to engage in criminal activity than the person low on that dimension. He based this assumption on the consistent research finding that emotionality can serve as a drive, pushing an individual to resort to habitual ways of behaving. Under high emotionality (high drive), a person is more vulnerable to his or her habits—

FIGURE 3–4   Illustration of the Sympathetic and Parasympathetic Subdivision of the Autonomic Nervous System

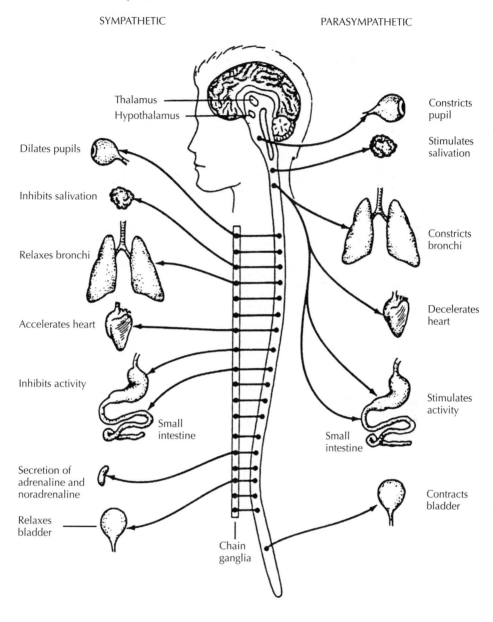

good or bad. Thus, if the individual has acquired antisocial habits, he or she will be more driven to commit them under high drive than low drive conditions. Neuroticism, therefore, encourages whatever mindless or habitual behaviors the person has acquired. Furthermore, because habits are usually not as well ingrained in the young as they are in the old, we would expect neuroticism to be an important factor with respect to adult criminals, less so with adolescents, and least so with young children (Eysenck, 1983).

The two dimensions we have looked at thus far are usually combined in classifying an individual's personality. That is, based on Eysenck's personality inventories, a person will be a neurotic introvert, a stable extravert, a neurotic ambivert, and so forth. If we accept Eysenck's views up to this point, we should agree that the neurotic extravert is the most likely of the possible personality types to be involved in criminal behavior.

Psychoticism

No neurophysiological mechanism has been established to explain the characteristics of psychoticism, Eysenck's most recently formulated dimension. Eysenck (1996) does suggest, however, high levels of the male hormone testosterone combined with low levels of the enzyme monoamine oxidase and the neurotransmitter serotonin may play a significant role in the formation of psychoticism. A neurotransmitter is a chemical that carries information from one neuron to another across the space between neurons called the synaptic cleft.

Psychoticism seems to be highly similar to primary psychopathy, which we discuss in chapter 6. Behaviorally, psychoticism is characterized by cold cruelty, social insensitivity, unemotionality, disregard for danger, troublesome behavior, dislike of others, and an attraction to the unusual. "Psychotics" are hostile toward others and enjoy duping or ridiculing them. It is important that we distinguish between Eysenck's psychotics and persons who are psychotic in the clinical sense of being out of touch with reality. Although this latter label is losing favor among clinicians, it appears frequently enough in literature to warrant making the distinction. Psychosis as a classification of mental disorder and abnormality is dealt with in chapter 7.

TABLE 3–2   Summary Table of Eysenck's Theory

PERSONALITY TRAIT	NEUROBIOLOGICAL INFLUENCE	HIGH SCORES	LOW SCORES
Extraversion	RAS, CNS	Stimulation seeking	Stimulation avoidance
Neuroticism	Autonomic NS	Nervous, unstable	Stable, calm
Psychoticism	Excessive androgen	Tough minded	Tender minded

Eysenck's psychoticism dimension has not received the research attention that extraversion and neuroticism have. However, he hypothesizes that, like extraversion and neuroticism, psychoticism will prove to be a striking characteristic of the criminal population. He suggests that psychoticism will be especially prominent in hard-core, habitual offenders convicted of crimes of violence (Eysenck, 1983). Furthermore, unlike neuroticism, it apparently is important at all stages of development, from childhood through adolescence to adulthood.

Thus far we have only defined Eysenck's dimensions, and, in the case of neuroticism and extraversion, we have isolated the physiological mechanisms that control them. None of this explains, however, why neurotics, extraverts, and psychotics are more likely to be criminal. The reason has to do with some very basic psychological principles to which we now turn our attention.

Crime and Conditionability

A basic premise of this text is that criminal behavior is learned. Traditionally, psychologists have delineated three major types of learning: **classical** or **Pavlovian conditioning, instrumental** or **operant conditioning,** and social learning. It is important now to examine these processes more carefully if we are to approach an understanding of why some people engage in crime.

The reader with a background in introductory psychology will recall Ivan Pavlov's famous experiments with dogs who learned to salivate at the sound of a bell. Pavlov discovered that pairing a neutral stimulus (in this case a bell) with a significant stimulus (e.g., food) would result in the dogs' eventually learning to associate the sound of the bell with that of food. How do we know the dogs learned to make that association? Because they salivated at the mere sound of the bell, a response they usually reserved for food. The process of learning to respond to a formerly neutral stimulus (bell) that has been paired with another stimulus that already elicits a response (salivation) is basically *classical* or *Pavlovian conditioning.* In classical conditioning, animals (or persons) have no control over the situation, even over what happens to themselves. The animal is "forced" to take the consequences. The bell will ring, and food will appear shortly afterward, regardless of what the animal does. In anticipation, and without any effort on its part, the animal salivates. This learning occurs not because of any reward or gain, but merely because of the association between the bell and the food.

In *instrumental learning* (or operant conditioning), the process is quite different. The learner must do something to the environment in order to obtain a reward or, in some cases, to avoid punishment. Instrumental learning is based on learning the consequences of behaving a certain way: If you do something, there is some probability that a certain rewarding event (or at least an avoidance of punishment) will occur. A child may learn, for example, that one parent will give her a piece of candy to quell a temper tantrum; the other parent will not yield. The child will eventually learn to use temper tantrums when Dad's around, but not to use them in front of Mom (or vice versa).

One important aspect of instrumental learning should be stressed: There must be a goal driving the animal or person to operate on the environment. That is, the individual must have a purpose or expectation for his or her behavior, and must expect a reward for the response. A reward or reinforcement is the event that increases the likelihood of a response. Classical conditioning, by contrast, results from an association between stimuli and takes place without reward.

Social learning is more complex than either classical conditioning or instrumental learning, because it involves learning from watching others and organizing social experiences in the brain. Since Eysenck did not deal directly with social learning principles, we reserve this topic for chapter 4.

Eysenck (1977) turns the question of criminal behavior around from the usual, "Why do people become criminal?" to "Why don't more people engage in criminal behavior?" To answer this with the adage, "Crime doesn't pay" is nonsense, since there is evidence that for much of the criminal population, crime does pay. After all, one of the chief motivators of behavior may be the desire to gain reward and pleasure (referred to as hedonism). "It would seem . . . that a person may, with a fair degree of safety, indulge in a career of crime without having to fear the consequences very much" (Eysenck, 1964, p. 102). According to Eysenck, those detected, convicted, and incarcerated often represent that portion of the criminal population who are of lower intelligence, poorly taught, unable to afford an influential attorney, or simply unlucky. So, if instrumental learning is a major factor, there should be substantially more crime, because people would be more often than not rewarded for operating criminally on their environment. Moreover, when punishment does occur, it is so long in coming that it cannot reasonably be considered a deterrent. Eysenck suggests, in fact, that delayed and sometimes arbitrary punishment may actually encourage criminal activity.

To explain why more people do not become criminal, Eysenck contends that classical conditioning has a stronger effect on most people than instrumental learning. That is, most people behave themselves because they have been classically conditioned during childhood about the rules of society. That guiding light, superego, conscience, or whatever it is that makes us feel uncomfortable before, during, and after a socially and morally disapproved act is, according to Eysenck, a *conditioned reflex*. In a traditional family environment, children may be verbally reprimanded or physically punished for behavior that is against the social mores. Immediately after engaging in a socially or morally frowned-upon act, say, punching a friend, a child finds that punishment quickly follows.

Let's return to Pavlov's dog experiments for a moment, and substitute the food with painful shock. Immediately following the sound of the bell, the dog receives a severe electrical shock (punishment) through the grids in the floor of the cage. After a number of trials (bell followed by shock) the dog, rather than salivating at the bell, begins to shake in fear. The animal has been classically conditioned to fear the sound of the bell, even when shock no longer follows it. The dog now associates shock with the bell rather than food.

Eysenck asserts that basically the same sequence occurs in childhood—inappropriate behavior followed by reprimand. For example, child punches another child, mother reprimands. Following a few repetitions of this sequence, the thought of punching stimulates fear of the consequences. In essence, "by punishing antisocial behavior numerous times, parents, teachers, and others concerned with the upbringing of the child, including his or her peers, perform the role of the Pavlovian experimenter" (Eysenck, 1983, p. 60). The child associates punching with punishment, and this bonding between the behavior and the aversive consequences should deter him or her from performing the act. Moreover, the closer the individual comes to performing the act, the stronger the association (fear) becomes.

Most people, Eysenck believes, do not participate in criminal activity (he prefers the term antisocial behavior) because after a series of trials they have made strong connections between deviant behavior and aversive consequences. On the other hand, those persons who have not made adequate connections, either because of poor conditionability (e.g., extraverts) or because the opportunity to do so was not presented (socialization), are more likely to display deviant or criminal behavior. According to Eysenck, these people do not anticipate aversive events strongly enough to be deterred, since the association has not been sufficiently developed.

Pavlov observed that dogs differ widely in their conditionability to the sound of a bell and theorized that these differences come from properties of their nervous systems. Eysenck also made this observation, commenting that "German Shepherds are very law abiding: They are easily conditioned and are well known to animal fanciers and shepherds for this property. Basenjis, however, are natural psychopaths, difficult or almost impossible to condition, disobedient and antisocial" (Eysenck, 1983, p. 61). Eysenck advanced the same observation concerning humans: Extraverts condition less readily than introverts due to biological differences in their nervous systems. Introverts condition better and therefore are less likely to engage in behavior contrary to society's laws and mores.

The principles of conditioning have been firmly established in the field of psychology as a valid explanation for many forms of behavior. The conditioning process appears to be a powerful force in the socialization of children, particularly in the suppressing of undesirable behaviors. There is every reason to believe that it may be a critical process in determining who becomes involved in deviant or criminal behavior. However, there is also evidence that conditioning can serve as an instigator of such behavior. As we will see in later chapters, the association between pleasurable events and specific behavior is also an extremely powerful motivator of criminal activity.

According to Eysenck, the conditioned conscience has two effects on behavior: It may prevent us from indulging in forbidden activities, or it may make us feel guilty after we commit them. The conditioned conscience inhibits us from engaging in antisocial activities by its association with prior adverse consequences. In addition, once we have committed the act we tend to feel uncomfortable about our transgressions. Eysenck (1983) supposed the difference rests in the timing of the aversive consequences. Reprimanding a child before or during an act would produce different effects than reprimanding a child after the act. The former situation would result in feelings of discomfort before the act (or while committing it), whereas the latter would produce discomfort (guilt) after the act.

What part does neuroticism or emotionality play? As noted earlier, Eysenck predicted that neuroticism functions as a drive strongly encouraging the performance of behavior previously acquired during childhood. That is, neuroticism amplifies existing habits in a person's repertoire of responses. If a neurotic extravert has not been properly conditioned to avoid stealing and has engaged in frequent, successful stealing in the past, neuroticism will function as a strong force or drive toward the old habit—stealing. In other words, behavior (inappropriate or appropriate) equals prior conditioning or learned habits times (intensified by) emotionality.

According to Eysenck (1983, p. 65), "The general growth in permissiveness in homes, schools, and courts has led to a significant reduction in the number of conditioning contingencies to which children are exposed. It would follow as a direct consequence that they would grow up with a much weaker conscience, and consequently that many more children would be led to engage in criminal and antisocial activities." In essence, Eysenck is asserting that increases in crime may be traced directly to conditions within the home or schools that are not conducive to the development of a conditioned conscience toward avoiding antisocial conduct.

The Evidence for Eysenck's Theory

Now that we have scrutinized Eysenck's theory of criminality, the relevant question becomes, "Can we find research to support it?" Eysenck's theory of criminality predicts that criminals, as a group, will demonstrate lower levels of cortical arousal (high extraversion), higher levels of autonomic (sympathetic) arousal (high neuroticism), and be more tough-minded (high psychoticism). In short, he postulates that criminals will score high on the E, N, and P scales of the Eysenck Personality Questionnaire (EPQ-R), and that these dimensions are more than merely correlated with crime; they are causally related to it. It should also be mentioned that the EPQ-R also contains a Lie (L) scale, which measures trying to look "too good" or as Eysenck called it "faking good." He also believed that the scale measures a stable personality dimension of a person's response to social expectations. Low L scores indicate that the respondent is indifferent to social expectations and is not well socialized (Kemp & Center, 2003). Consequently we may hypothesize that those persons prone to be criminal will not only score high on E, N, and P scales, but also demonstrate a low L-scale score as well.

Overall, recent research strongly supports Eysenck's position that people likely to commit delinquent and criminal behavior will score high on the P scale (Cale, 2006; Center, Jackson, & Kemp, 2005; Heaven, Newbury, & Wilson, 2004;

Kemp & Center, 2003; Levine & Jackson, 2004; van Dam, Janssens, & De Bruyn, 2005; Walker & Gudjonsson, 2006). This is to be expected since high scorers are generally described as cold, hostile, aggressive, and insensitive to the needs of others. Heaven et al. (2004) report that the P-scale is effective in identifying those adolescents likely to commit delinquent offenses of all kinds, but it appears to be effective in identifying only serious offending in young adults. More specifically the P-scale predicted those involved in sex crimes and crimes of violence, but it was not predictive of nonviolent crimes, such as crimes of theft, vandalism, and other economic or property offenses.

Neuroticism has generally shown a significant relationship with offending, although not as strong as the P-scale (Cale, 2006). The N-scale does well in predicting serious crimes (Kemp & Center, 2003) and is somewhat successful in predicting recidivism (van Dam, Janssens, & De Bruyn, 2005). We might expect the N scale to do better at predicting recidivism since Eysenck hypothesized that high N scorers tend to be driven to continue their habitual behaviors and be unusually impulsive.

The power of the E-scale is more in question, as several studies have found only a weak connection to offending (Cale, 2006; Center, Jackson, and Kemp 2005; Kemp & Center, 2003). However, Eysenck (1987) pointed out that incarcerated persons cannot properly answer the social activity questions which are part of the E-scale (see van Dam, Janssens, & De Bruyn, 2005, p. 16). Eysenck recognized this early in his formulation of his theory, when he commented (1971, p. 289) that "not all crimes are likely to be equally highly correlated with extraversion, and some types of criminals, such as the recidivist 'old lag,' lacking entirely in the social skills needed to make a success of living outside an institution, may in fact show introverted tendencies." Therefore, we might suspect that low E-scales of offenders might be due in part to the effects of incarceration. Furthermore, many murderers and sex offenders do show strong introverted behavior, as we shall see later in the book. Thus researchers must make distinctions between the various types of offenders when using the E-scale in their studies. In addition scores on the E-scale, compared with the P- and N-scales, are more strongly influenced by such factors as age and gender of the respondent; the scale may be measuring more than one dimension of personality, such as sociability, needs for stimulation, and impulsiveness.

Low L scores do show some ability to identify respondents likely to be involved in delinquency and crime, especially women (Walker & Gudjonsson, 2006). However, most research projects have failed to include the L-scale in their analysis, so conclusions about its power to predict criminal tendencies is difficult to assess.

Although Eysenck's theory is in a state of flux, we have given it a considerable amount of attention here for three reasons. First, the theory is one of the few comprehensive statements about the role of genetics in antisocial behavior, as stated at the beginning of this section. We still have much to learn from this attempt, and perhaps some modifications will strengthen its explanatory potential. Second, Eysenck's theory recognizes the interaction of the environment—specifically via classical conditioning—with characteristics of the nervous system. Of particular importance is the attention Eysenck gives to individual differences in the nervous system as a biological basis for personality in general (Nebylitsyn & Gray, 1972). Criminology cannot afford to discount the existence of biological factors in antisocial behavior, even if these factors account for the behavior of only a small percentage of the population. At this point, however, it appears that Eysenck's emphasis on classical conditioning as a primary explanation of criminality and his tendency to ignore other forms of learning and mediational (cognitive) processes may be the theory's most damaging weaknesses. In addition, Gordon Trasler (1987) notes that even the concept of conditionability is fraught with difficulties and encourages much debate among contemporary psychologists. There is even considerable debate about what the term means, and the empirical evidence examining the concept remains elusive and conflicting. Finally, Eysenck's theory is unique because it represents one of the few attempts by a psychologist to formulate a general, universal theory of criminal behavior.

SUMMARY AND CONCLUSIONS

Realizing that crime, like all human behavior, results from an interaction among heredity, neurophysiology, and the environment, we have in this chapter looked at the research on the genetic and biological makeup of persons who become criminal. The biopsychological approaches of today are far more sophisticated compared with very early efforts to link biology with criminal behavior. Contemporary researchers assert that, while some people may be predisposed toward aggressive behavior or behavior that indicates a need for stimulation, socialization or medication can keep inappropriate expressions of those behaviors in check. However, many other criminologists, including some from a psychological orientation, resist any notion of biological or genetic predispositions.

The genetic factor has been explored in twin and adoption studies. To date, there have been over 100 of these studies of antisocial behavior (Rhee & Waldman, 2002). Yet, it is difficult to draw firm conclusions concerning the magnitude of genetic and environmental influences on antisocial behavior on the basis of current research. Some empirical studies, however, have found a high concordance rate between identical twins engaged in crime, lending some credence to genetic predisposition. These studies have shown that even when separated at birth, identical twins tend to be similar in their pursuit of criminal careers. However, researchers continually have difficulty separating the social environment (shared or nonshared) from the nature-nurture equation, and it is becoming increasing clear that the social and biological approaches to understanding human behavior are complementary rather than antagonistic (Cacioppo et al., 2000).There have been relatively few adoption studies conducted, primarily because of the inaccessibility of records. Researchers in this area who say their research supports the genetic viewpoint admonish that the social environment can either stimulate or inhibit any inborn tendency toward criminality.

Considerable research has explored temperament, a mood disposition determined largely by genetics and biological influences, and its relationship with antisocial or criminal behavior. Temperament appears in infancy and continues throughout one's life. An irritable baby, according to these researchers, is a challenge to parents or caretakers who may become highly frustrated dealing with him. Likewise, a child who is impulsive is a poor self-regulator who often comes into conflict with the environment. On the other hand, nurturing and warm caretakers can override the effects of such difficult temperaments.

We discussed a number of environmental factors that can significantly affect brain development, which has been linked to serious and violent antisocial behavior. The frontal lobe of the human brain is the location for organized thought, planning, and self-regulation. Such factors as pregnancy and birth complications, exposure to toxic substances (including nicotine, alcohol, and drugs), and malnutrition all can be detrimental to healthy brain development.

Less sophisticated (and older) research on physique and crime and attractiveness and crime also illustrate the biopsychological approach. Classic work by William H. Sheldon (Sheldon & Stevens, 1942) and later Glueck and Glueck (1950, 1956) established some connection between the physique, personality, and temperament of juvenile delinquents and their antisocial behavior. Mesomorphic individuals (muscular, adventurous) were most likely to be aggressive and callous in relationships with others and, therefore, antisocial. Endomorphs (round, passive individuals) and ectomorphs (thin, nervous folk) were less likely to be, though each body type was represented in delinquent samples. With respect to attractiveness, many studies in social psychology have shown that people judged unattractive are treated more negatively by others and are less mentally healthy. However, very few criminologists today consider either physique or attractiveness good predictors of antisocial behavior.

Interestingly, contemporary researchers have studied minor physical anomalies (MPAs) in children as indicators of abnormal brain development and, subsequently, behavioral problems. MPAs are typically noticeable only to trained observers and include such features as multiple hair whorls or asymmetrical ears. Some research has found that boys with high numbers of MPAs also demonstrated conduct problems and violent offending. On the other hand, other research found the violence only if the boy was also from an unstable home. It should be emphasized that the abnormality itself is not seen as the culprit; rather it is seen as a sign that some fetal injury, again early in the pregnancy, contributes to atypical brain development.

We covered Eysenck's theory, highlighting distinctions between extraverts and introverts in some detail. Eysenck proposed an interaction theory of crime, seeing it as the result of environmental conditions (primarily classical conditioning) working on inherited features of the nervous system. The essence of Eysenckian theory is that individuals with certain types of nervous systems (introverts) condition better, or learn the mores of society much more readily than individuals with other types (extraverts and ambiverts). In other words, introverts link transgressions with disapproval much sooner than others do. Some people would say introverts have a stronger conscience and experience more fear prior to their transgressions and more guilt after committing them. However, as we note in chapters 12 and 13, this quick associative or conditioning ability also means that introverts are more likely to acquire sexually deviant behavior.

Eysenck hypothesized that neuroticism or emotionality intensifies existing habits, which in some cases may be antisocial ones. Individuals with high emotionality may be more driven toward antisocial habits than individuals with low emotionality. Psychoticism, a dimension that has received less research attention, appears to correlate with features of the psychopath and frequent offenders.

It is obvious that the Eysenckian position needs revision and refinement. As it now stands, the theory has flaws that could be damaging to its construct validity. One glaring weakness is its reliance on classical conditioning to the exclusion of mediational (cognitive) factors and social learning. Despite these problems, Eysenck's work represents a broad, testable theory of criminality that continues to stimulate research. More important for our purposes, the theory integrates nicely the biopsychological perspective with the social environmental perspective in the formation of antisocial behavior.

We emphasize that most studies in this area focus on violent crime or aggressive antisocial behavior. A considerable body of contemporary research explores the relationship between "violence and the brain." However, assigning a major role in the causation of such behavior to diverse neurological deficits and nervous system functioning is unwarranted. While biopsychology and neurophysiological factors may play some role in the formation of criminal behavior—specifically by affecting brain development—it is far more likely that violent and nonviolent antisocial behavior develops as a result of a series of complicated interactions with significant others in the social environment.

 ## KEY CONCEPTS

Biopsychologists	Dizygotic twins
Fraternal twins	Monozygotic twins
Identical twins	Shared environments
Nonshared environments	Concordance
Psychophysiology	Temperament
Plasticity	Somatotyping
Minor physical anomalies	MPAs
Interaction	Extraversion
Neuroticism	Psychoticism
Ambiversion	Classical conditioning
Pavlovian conditioning	Instrumental learning
Operant conditioning	Social learning

REVIEW QUESTIONS

1. Briefly describe Eysenck's theory of criminality.
2. Briefly describe Sheldon's somatotyping and the three basic body builds.
3. Summarize the findings of adoption studies on the interaction between heredity and environment.
4. Define the following concepts: concordance, RAS, minor physical anomaly.
5. What aspects of the Eysenck's theory of criminality are supported by the research and what aspects are not? In general, how strong is the support?
6. What is meant by the term "shared environment" and why is it important in genetic research on crime?
7. Explain how temperament plays a role in the development of antisocial behavior.

CHAPTER 4

ORIGINS OF CRIMINAL BEHAVIOR: LEARNING AND SITUATIONAL FACTORS

CHAPTER OBJECTIVES

- Present learning and cognitive factors as one of the key elements in the development of delinquent and criminal behavior.
- Review the historical background of behaviorism and its contributions to understanding human learning of delinquent and criminal behavior.
- Learn the fundamentals of operant conditioning and learning.
- Learn the fundamental principles of social learning and its contributions of understanding antisocial behavior.
- Introduce frustration-induced crime.
- Learn about the power of the social situation in instigating criminal actions.

People do not come into situations empty-headed. They have an infinite store of living experiences and an extensive repertoire of strategies for reacting to events. Up to this point, we have not highlighted these strategies, concentrating instead on various individual, family, and social risk factors during the development of criminal behavior.

As we learned in chapter 3, genetic and biological factors appear to account in part for individual differences in susceptibility to classical conditioning. Since the capacity to be conditioned strongly affects fear of reprisal, it contributes to the inhibition of socially undesirable criminal behavior. However, the classical conditioning perspective presumes that the human being is an automaton; that is, humans act in a monotonous routine manner without active intelligence.

Pair a neutral stimulus with a closely following painful event, and the alert, intact robot will eventually, and automatically, connect the stimulus with the pain. This sequence is probably a very powerful factor in many behaviors, but certainly not in all or even most. Conditioning is only one of several factors involved in the acquisition (or avoidance) of criminal behavior.

In order to understand criminal behavior in some depth, it is crucial that we regard all individuals—whether or not they violate the rules of society—as *active* problem solvers who perceive, process, interpret, and respond uniquely to their environments. For the moment, consider unlawful behavior as subjectively adaptable rather than deviant. In this sense, unlawful conduct or antisocial behavior is a response pattern that a person has found to be effective, or thinks will be effective, in certain circumstances.

Violent crimes like aggravated assault and homicide are sometimes called "irrational," "uncontrollable," "explosive," or "motiveless," and therefore are believed to resist or defy analysis (e.g., President's Commission on Law Enforcement and Administration of Justice, 1967). By the early twenty-first century, it had become chillingly clear to the public that some violence, specifically that violence associated with terrorism, was carefully controlled and motivated. Later in this text we will find that different types of violence can be placed into different theoretical frameworks. The decision to act violently may be a quick one, but the violent behavior—including but not limited to terrorist acts—is usually not irrational or uncontrollable. If we consider individual violence, such as a domestic assault, we can say that some people have poor self-regulation skills, but most individuals can be taught to control their behavior, regardless of their excuses. Furthermore, it is almost impossible to determine what is rational or irrational unless we examine the psychological processes of the offender.

Engaging in criminal behavior might be one person's way of adapting or surviving under physically, socially, financially, or psychologically dire conditions. Even behavior that can be attributed to a severe mental disorder may be adaptive, though it may not be legally culpable. Another person might decide that violence is necessary to defend honor, protect self, or reach a personal goal. In either case, the person is choosing what he or she believes is the best alternative for that particular situation (although real choice may be illusory in the case of the person who is severely mentally disordered). It is not, of course, necessarily the alternative that others would choose, nor what society condones. Besides susceptibility to classical conditioning, what accounts for the difference? In a very general sense, learning—both operant (or instrumental) and social learning—is an extremely important component in the equation. In the following pages we will expand the concept of conditioning to include these two distinct forms of learning, which play a major role in the acquisition and maintenance of criminal behavior. Later we will introduce situational factors that appear to affect the learning process. Since each of these topics springs from the school of psychological thought called behaviorism, we will begin our discussion there.

BEHAVIORISM

Behaviorism officially began in 1913 with the publication of a landmark paper by John B. Watson (1878–1958), "Psychology as the Behaviorist Views It." The paper, which appeared in the journal *Psychological Review,* is considered the first definitive statement on behaviorism, and Watson is thus acknowledged as the school's founder. However, Watson was by no means the first to discuss the basic elements of behaviorism. Its roots can be traced back at least to Aristotle (Diserens, 1925). Watson's behaviorism represents a recurring phase in the cyclical history of psychology. A psychology of consciousness or mind is followed by a psychology of action and behavior (behaviorism), from which a psychology of mind and consciousness reemerges. Today psychology is immersed once again in a psychology of mind, especially cognitive processes. **Cognitive processes** are those internal mental processes that enable humans to imagine, to gain knowledge, to reason, and to evaluate information. For the moment, let's return to Watsonian behaviorism, which has heavily influenced psychological interpretations of criminal behavior.

Watson frequently declared that psychology was the science of behavior. He believed that psychologists should eliminate the "mind" and all of its related vague concepts from scientific consideration because they could not be observed or measured. He was convinced that the fundamental goal of psychology was to understand, predict, and control human behavior, and that only a rigidly scientific approach could accomplish this.

Greatly influenced by Ivan Pavlov's famous research on classical conditioning, Watson thought that psychology should focus exclusively on the interplay between stimulus and response. A **stimulus** is a person, object, or event that elicits behavior. A response is the elicited behavior. Watson was convinced that all behavior—both animal and human—was controlled by the external environment in a way similar to that described by Pavlov in his initial study—stimulus produces response (sometimes called S-R psychology). Therefore, for Watson, classical (or Pavlovian) conditioning was the key to understanding, predicting, and controlling behavior, and its practical applicability was unlimited.

The chief spokesperson for behaviorism for several decades was B. F. Skinner (1904–1990), who was the most influential psychologist in the United States in the twentieth century. The Skinnerian perspective especially dominated the application of behavior modification or behavior therapy in the correctional system and in many institutions for the mentally handicapped or disturbed. Some contemporary theories on criminal behavior (e.g., Akers, 1985) try to integrate Skinnerian behaviorism with sociological perspectives. It is worthwhile, therefore, to spend some time sketching the Skinnerian approach to human behavior in general before assessing its impact on the study of criminal behavior.

Skinner's Theory of Behavior

Like Watson, Skinner believed that the primary goal of psychology is the prediction and control of behavior. And like Watson, he believed that environmental or external stimuli are the primary—if not the sole—determinants of all behavior, both human and animal. The environmental stimuli become **independent variables** and the behaviors they elicit the **dependent variables.** In the behavioral sciences, a **variable** is any entity (or behavior) that can be measured. A behavior (or response) is called "dependent" because it is under the control of (or dependent on) one or more independent variables. The consistent relationships between independent and dependent variables (stimulus and response) are scientific laws. Thus, according to Skinner, the aim of behavioristic psychology is to uncover these laws, making possible the prediction and control of human behavior, including criminal behavior.

Unlike Watson, Skinner did not deny the existence and sometimes usefulness of private mental events or cognitive processes. He emphasized, however, that these stimuli are not needed by a *science* of behavior, since the products of mental activity can be explained in ways that do not require allusion to unobserved mental states. Specifically, mental activity can be explained by observing what a person does, and it is what a person does that counts. Watson, remember, insisted that consciousness and mind simply do not exist. Thought, to Watson, was little more than tiny movements of the speech apparatus. To Skinner, thought and cognitive processes existed, but studying them is unlikely to lead to the "hard" science of behavior. Consequently, in order to understand and modify criminal behavior, the thoughts, values, decisions, and intentions of a criminal mind are irrelevant. According to Skinner, to understand the development of delinquency and criminal behavior we must focus on environmental stimuli, observable behavior, and rewards.

Behaviorism as a Method of Science

At this point we must emphasize the need to distinguish between behaviorism as a *perspective on human nature* and a *method of science.* As a method of science, behaviorism posits that knowledge about human behavior can be best advanced if scientists use referents that have a physical basis and can be *publicly observed* by others. Since private events that happen inside our heads cannot be seen by others, they cannot be subjected to the rules of science. According to Skinner, behavioral science data must be comparable to be verified or disconfirmed. Otherwise psychology would remain a philosophical exercise steeped in armchair speculation and untestable opinions. Self-proclaimed experts could continue to assert that shoplifting is an addiction, just like alcoholism, without being taken to task about the validity of their statements. Only a well-executed, systematic study in which the terms *shoplifting* and *addiction* are clearly spelled out and rigorously tested will advance our knowledge about the accuracy of the shoplifting-addiction connection. Therefore, every psychological experiment, every sentence written into a psychological report, should be anchored to something that we can all observe, or that is testable by another professional. Rather than merely saying that someone is anxious or angry, we must identify the precise behaviors that prompt us to make these interpretations. This offers a basis for others, including the person being observed, to agree or disagree with us.

Behaviorism as a Perspective of Human Nature

Concerning behaviorism as a perspective of human nature, Skinner—and a majority of psychologists with a strong behavioristic leaning—embraced the view that humans differ only in degree from their animal ancestry. The behavior of humans follows the same basic natural laws as that of all animals. Like Darwin, Skinner saw no radical differences between humans and animals. Even human language and conceptual thinking are nondistinctive. Verbal behavior "is a very special kind of behavior, but there is nothing by way of processes involved that would distinguish it from non-verbal behavior and hence [verbal behavior] would not distinguish man from the [other] animals" (Skinner, 1964, p. 156). To Skinner, therefore, research on subhumans such as monkeys, rats, and pigeons has great value; if carefully done, it will reveal lawful relationships between all organisms and their environments.

By recognizing how behaviorism views human nature, we are better able to understand the basic framework behaviorism employs in studying and explaining criminal behavior. It also helps us understand the fundamental recommendations advocated by this perspective for reducing or changing criminal behavior, such as might be found in the management policy of certain correctional facilities.

Clearly, Skinner was also a strong situationist. **Situationism** refers to the belief that all behavior is at the mercy of stimuli in the environment, and individuals have virtually no control or self-determination. Independent thinking and free will are myths. Animals and humans alike react, like complicated robots, to their environments. The environmental stimuli and the range of reactions are complex and infinite, but with careful research, this complexity is not unmanageable. Complex human behavior can be broken down into more simple behavior, a procedure sometimes referred to as **reductionism.** In other words, complicated behavior can be best understood by examining the simplest stimulus-response chains of behavior. This point brings us to the issue of operant conditioning.

Operant Learning

Skinner accepted the basic tenets of classical conditioning, but asserted that we need an additional type of conditioning to account more fully for all forms of behavior. Ivan Pavlov conducted a series of experiments on classical conditioning with hungry dogs during the turn of the twentieth century. The dogs did not operate on their environments to receive rewards; the event (food) occurred regardless of what they did. Skinner called this "responding conditioning" and contrasted it to a situation in which a subject does something that affects the situation. In other words, subjects behave in such a way that reinforcement is forthcoming. To uncover this operant conditioning principle, Skinner established an association between *behavior* and its *consequences*. He trained pigeons (apparently less troublesome and less expensive than dogs) to peck at keys or push levers for food. The pecking or pushing are operations on the environment. **Operant conditioning,** then, is learning to either make or withhold a particular response because of its consequences. Operant conditioning (or operant learning) is a fundamental learning process that is acquired (or eliminated) by the consequences that follow the behavior. For example, a temper tantrum by a toddler at the check-out counter when she wants some candy from the nearby shelves may prompt the parent to give in and provide the child with the candy. Next time at the same or similar check-out aisle, the temper-tantrum strategy will be tried again since it worked the first time. The child has learned the consequences of timely temper tantrums.

The learning that comes about through operant conditioning was described before Skinner's time, but he is credited with drawing contemporary attention to it. In the early nineteenth century, for example, the philosopher Jeremy Bentham observed that human conduct was controlled by the seeking of pleasure and the avoidance of pain. In essence, this is what is meant by operant learning. It assumes that people do things solely to receive rewards and avoid punishment. The rewards may be physical (e.g., material goods, money), psychological (e.g., feelings of importance or control over one's fate), or social (e.g., improved status, acceptance).

Reinforcement

Skinner called rewards **reinforcement,** defining that term as anything that increases the probability of future responding. Furthermore, reinforcement may be either positive or negative. In **positive reinforcement,** we *gain* something we desire as a consequence of certain behavior. We spend hours practicing a difficult piece on the keyboard or perfecting a ski jump and are rewarded by praise from listeners or a gold medal in the Olympics. In **negative reinforcement,** we *avoid* an unpleasant event or stimulus as a consequence of certain behavior. For example, if as a child you were able to avoid the unpleasantness of certain school days by feigning illness, your malingering was negatively reinforced. Therefore, you were more likely to engage in it again at a future date, under similar circumstances—high school dress-up day, class discussion day in a difficult college course, or the day the district supervisor was scheduled to visit the office. Thus, both positive and negative reinforcement can increase the likelihood of future behavior.

Punishment and Extinction

Negative reinforcement is to be distinguished from punishment and extinction. In **punishment,** an organism receives noxious or painful stimuli as consequences of behavior, such as being slapped or hit for "being bad." In **extinction,** a person or animal receives neither reinforcement nor punishment. Skinner argued that punishment is a less effective way to eliminate behavior, because it merely suppresses it temporarily. At a later time, under the right conditions, the response is very likely to reoccur. Extinction is far more effective, because once the organism learns that a behavior brings no reinforcement, the behavior will be dropped from the repertoire of possible responses for that set of circumstances.

According to Nietzel (1979), C. R. Jeffrey (1965) was one of the first criminologists to suggest that criminal behavior was learned according to principles of Skinnerian operant conditioning. Shortly afterward, Burgess and Akers (1966) agreed with this, and further hypothesized that criminal behavior was both acquired and maintained through operant conditioning. But, as Nietzel points out, most of the direct evidence for this claim comes from experiments with animals. Evidence that the same occurs in humans is scarce and replete with possible alternate interpretations. Nevertheless, neither Jeffrey nor Burgess and Akers relied exclusively on Skinnerian theory. Rather they combined sociologist Edwin Sutherland's principles of social learning with operant conditioning, particularly the reinforcement aspect, to suggest explanations for criminal behavior (Williams & McShane, 2004). We will return to Sutherland's theory shortly.

Operant Learning and Crime

The premise that operant conditioning is the basis for the origin of criminal behavior is deceptively simple: Criminal behavior is learned and strengthened because of the reinforcements it brings. According to Skinner, human beings are born neutral—neither good nor bad. Culture, society, and the environment shape behavior. Therefore, behavior will be labeled good, bad, or indifferent, as society chooses. What is judged "good" behavior in one society or culture may be labeled "bad" in another. Members of one group in a society may believe that it is "bad" for a child to masturbate or to pretend that a block of wood is a toy truck and "good" to hit the child to stop these behaviors. To others, the behavior of the adults who hit the child is "bad." Depending on the severity of the punishment, it may also be aggravated assault.

Skinner was convinced that searches for individual dispositions or personalities that lead to criminal conduct are fruitless, because people are ultimately determined by the environment in which they live. He does not completely discount the role of genetics in the formation of behavior, but he sees it as a very minor one; the dominant player is operant conditioning. According to Skinner and his followers, if we wish to eliminate crime, we must change society through behavioral engineering based on a *scientific* conception of humans. Having agreed on rules and regulations (having defined what behaviors constitute antisocial or criminal offenses), we must design a society in which members learn very early that positive reinforcement will not occur if they transgress against these rules and regulations, but will occur if they abide by them.

This is a tall order, since the reinforcements for antisocial behavior are already occurring, are not always obvious, and may actually be highly complex.

Property crimes such as shoplifting and burglary, or violent crimes such as robbery, appear to be motivated in many cases by a desire for physical rewards. However, they may also be prompted by a desire for social and psychological reinforcements, such as increased status among peers, self-esteem, feelings of competence, or simply for the thrill of it. It is a safe bet that much criminal behavior is undertaken for reinforcement purposes, positive or negative. The problem then becomes, how do we identify those reinforcements and how do we prevent them from happening, or at least minimize their value?

Contemporary psychology still embraces a behavioristic orientation toward the *scientific* study of behavior, but has grown very cool toward the Skinnerian perspective of human nature. All behaviorists are not Skinnerians. Many (if not most) find Skinner's brand of behaviorism too limiting (e.g., Bandura, 1983, 1986). While they agree that a stimulus can elicit a reflexive response (classical conditioning) and that a behavior produces consequences that influence subsequent responding (operant conditioning), they are also convinced that additional factors must be introduced to explain human behavior. **Cognitive learning** is also extremely important, for example. Cognitive learning involves the formation of concepts, schemas, theories, attitudes, beliefs, and other mental or abstract versions of the world. Cognitive psychologists, for example, would argue that mental processes are as crucial—if not more so—in understanding criminal action as behavior itself.

This brings us to the topic of mental states and cognitive processes, which Skinner urged all behavioral scientists to shun. In recent years, many psychologists have been examining the roles played by self-reinforcement, anticipatory reinforcement, vicarious reinforcement, and all the symbolic processes that occur within the human brain. To avoid confusion, we must now begin to distinguish Skinnerian behaviorism from other forms, including social behaviorism (social learning) and differential association-reinforcement.

Social Learning

Early learning theorists worked in the laboratory, using animals as their primary subjects. Pavlov's, Watson's, and Skinner's theories, for example, were based on careful, painstaking observations and experiments with animals. The learning principles gleaned from their work were generalized to a wide variety of human behaviors. In many cases, this was a valid process. Few psychologists would dispute the contention that the concept of reinforcement is one of the most soundly established principles in psychology today.

However, behaviorists also suggested that, since all human behavior is learned, it can also be changed, using the same principles by which it was acquired. This generated a plethora of behavior therapies or behavior modification techniques. Use learning principles to establish conditions that change or maintain targeted behaviors and voilà! therapeutic success! The apparent simplicity of the procedures and methods was especially appealing to many clinicians and other professionals working in the criminal justice system, and behavior modification packages sometimes guaranteed to modify criminal behavior were rushed to correctional institutions, including facilities for juveniles. Prisoners (and juveniles) would be rewarded for good behavior with such incentives as cigarettes, canteen privileges, or an extra shower.

But oversimplification is dangerous when we deal with human complexity. Human beings do respond to reinforcement and punishment, and behavior therapy based on learning principles can change certain elements of behavior. Moreover, humans can be classically conditioned, although there are individual differences in their susceptibility. When we lose sight of the person and overemphasize the environmental or external determinants of behavior, however, we may be overlooking a critical level of explanation. Remember that human beings are, in large part, active problem solvers who perceive, encode, interpret, and make decisions on the basis of what the environment has to offer. Thus, internal factors, as well as external ones, may play significant roles in behavior. This is the essence of **social learning theory,** which suggests that to understand criminal behavior we must examine perceptions, thoughts, expectancies, competencies, and values. Each person has his or her own version of the world and lives by that version.

To explain human behavior, social learning theorists place great emphasis on cognitive processes, which are the internal processes we commonly call thinking and remembering. Classical and operant conditioning ignore what transpires between the time the organism perceives a stimulus and the time it responds or reacts. Skinnerian behaviorists claim, "If we can account for the facts by using observable behavior, why worry about the labyrinths of internal processes?" Social behaviorists, however, counter that this perspective offers an incomplete picture of human behavior.

The term *social learning* reflects the theory's strong assumption that we learn primarily by observing and listening to people around us—the social environment. In fact, social learning theorists believe that the social environment is the most important factor in the *acquisition* of most human behavior. Humans are basically social creatures. These theorists do accept the necessity of reinforcement for the *maintenance* of behavior, however. Criminal behavior, for example, may initially be acquired through association and through observation, but whether or not it is maintained will depend primarily upon reinforcement (operant conditioning). For example, if a boy sees someone he admires (i.e., a role model) successfully pilfering from the local sporting goods store, the boy may try some pilfering of his own. Whether he continues that behavior, however, will depend on the personal reinforcement or value it assumes. If no reinforcement is forthcoming (he fails to pocket a baseball because someone else walked into the store, or he finds that the gym shorts he stole do not fit), then the behavior will probably drop out of his response repertoire (extinction). If the behavior brings aversive results (punishment), this will inhibit or suppress future similar behavior.

Several clusters of psychologists are enrolled in the social learning school of thought. Additionally the discipline of sociology has its own social learning school. We will focus first on the work of two prominent representatives, psychologists Julian Rotter and Albert Bandura, since they seem to have the most to offer to the study of criminal behavior from the social learning perspective.

Expectancy Theory

Julian Rotter is best known for drawing attention to the importance of expectations (cognitions) about the consequences (outcomes) of behavior, including the reinforcement that will be gained from it. In other words, before doing anything, we ask, "What has happened to me before in this situation, and what will I gain this time?" According to Rotter, whether a specific pattern of behavior occurs will depend on our expectancies and how much we value the outcomes. To predict whether someone will behave a certain way, we must estimate that person's expectancies and the importance he or she places on the rewards gained by the behavior. Often the person will develop "generalized expectancies" that are stable and consistent across relatively similar situations (Mischel, 1976). **Expectancy theory,** therefore, argues that a person's performance level is based on that person's *expectation* that behaving in a particular way will lead to a given outcome.

The hypothesis that people enter situations with generalized expectancies about the outcomes of their behavior is an important one for students of crime. Applying Rotter's theory to criminal behavior, we would say that when people engage in unlawful conduct, they *expect* to gain something in the form of status, power, security, affection, material goods, or living conditions. The violent person, for example, may elect to behave that way in the belief that something will be gained; the serial murderer might believe that God has sent him on a mission to eliminate all "loose" women; the woman who poisons an abusive husband looks for an improvement in her life situation. Simply to label a violent person impulsive, crazy, or lacking in ego control fails to include other essential ingredients in the act. Although self-regulation and moral development are involved, people who act unlawfully perceive and interpret the situation and select what they consider to be the most effective behavior under the circumstances. Usually, when people act violently, they do so because that approach has been used successfully in the past (at least they believe it has been successful). Less frequently they have simply observed someone else gain by employing a violent approach, and they try it for themselves. This brings us to Bandura's imitational model of social learning.

Imitational Aspects of Social Learning

An individual may acquire ways of doing something simply by watching others do it; direct reinforcement is not necessary. Bandura (1973b) introduced this idea, which he called **observational learning** or **modeling,** to the social learning process. Bandura contends that much of our behavior is initially acquired by watching others, who are called models. **Models** are those significant persons in the social environment that provide cues for how to do something. For example, a child may learn how to shoot a gun by imitating television or video characters. He or she then rehearses and fine-tunes this behavioral pattern by practicing with toy guns. The behavior is likely to be maintained if peers also play with guns and reinforce one another for doing so. Even if the children have not pulled the triggers on real guns, they have acquired a close approximation of shooting someone by observing others do it. It is likely that just about every adult and older child in the United States knows how to shoot a gun, even if they have never actually done so: "You aim and pull the trigger." Of course, shooting safely and accurately is much more complicated, but the rudimentary know-how has been acquired through **imitational learning** (also called modeling or observational learning). The behavioral pattern exists in our repertoires, even if we have never received direct reinforcement for acquiring it.

According to Bandura, the more significant and respected the models, the greater their impact on our behavior. Relevant models include parents, teachers, siblings, friends, and peers, as well as symbolic models like literary characters or television, video, or movie personages. Rock stars and athletes are modeled by many young people, which is one reason we are exposed to so many public figures touting everything from cosmetics to a drug-free life to beer. Interestingly, the commercial and public service advertisements often miss the point. In observational learning, it is not so much what the model says as what the model does that is effective. If sports stars actually avoided the use of drugs in their daily lives, their messages to youth might be more effective. Conversely the messages that young people do get from sports and entertainment figures encourage, rather than discourage, criminal behavior. Media accounts of stars allegedly engaging in domestic violence, rape, child molestation, assault, tax evasion, illegal gambling, drug abuse, and the use of steroids or other muscle enhancing drugs suggest that such behavior is normative and acceptable rather than to be avoided.

The observed behavior of the model is also more likely to be imitated if the observer sees the model receive a reward, such as fame plus millions of dollars per year. It is less likely to be imitated if the model is punished. Thus, according to social learning principles, convictions of sports and entertainment figures charged with the crimes mentioned above would suggest that the behaviors will not be imitated. On the other hand, if they serve little or no time and write a widely purchased book about their experiences, an observer might not perceive this as a punishment. Bandura believes—much like Rotter—that once a person decides to use a newly acquired behavior, whether he or she performs or maintains it will depend on the situation and the expectancies for potential gain. This potential gain may come from outside (the praise of others, financial gain) or it may come from within (self-reinforcement for a job the individual perceives as well done).

Much of Bandura's research was directed at the learning of aggressive and violent behavior. We will be returning to his theory, therefore, in chapter 5 on aggression and violence. At this point, however, be aware that a substantial body of experimental findings gives impressive support to his theory. In a classic study, preschool children who watched a film of an adult assaulting an inflated plastic rubber doll were significantly more likely to imitate that behavior than were a comparable group who viewed more passive behavior (Bandura & Huston, 1961; Bandura, Ross, & Ross, 1963). Many studies employing variations of this basic procedure report similar results, strengthening the hypothesis that observing aggression leads to hostility in both children and adults (Walters & Grusec, 1977). In recent years, this research has been extended to viewing media violence and playing violent video games (Dodge & Pettit, 2003). While the research in these areas is not totally conclusive, the growing evidence is that people who observe aggressive acts not only imitate the observed behavior but also become generally more hostile and aggressive themselves (Bryant & Zillman, 2002; Huesmann, Moise-Titus, Podolski, & Eron, 2003).

To some extent, social learning, as it is discussed by Rotter and Bandura, humanizes the Skinnerian viewpoint, since it provides clues about what transpires inside the human brain (or mind). It draws our attention to the cognitive aspects of behavior, while classical and operant conditioning focus exclusively on the environment. Social learning theorists use environment in the social sense, which includes the internal as well as the external environment. Skinnerians prefer to limit relevant stimuli to external surroundings.

Differential Association-Reinforcement Theory

Ronald Akers (1977, 1985; Burgess & Akers, 1966) proposed a social learning theory of deviance that tries to integrate the core ingredients of Skinnerian behaviorism, the social learning theory as outlined by Bandura, and the differential association theory of criminologist Edwin H. Sutherland (1947). Akers called his theory **differential association-reinforcement (DAR).** Briefly, the theory states that people learn to commit deviant acts through interpersonal interactions with their social environment.

To understand DAR theory, we must grasp Sutherland's differential association theory, which dominated the field of sociological criminology for over four decades. It was first set forth in the third edition (1939) of Sutherland's *Principles of Criminology* and restated in 1947. Although Sutherland died in 1950, the theory was left intact in Donald R. Cressey's subsequent revisions of the original text (Sutherland & Cressey, 1978; Sutherland, Cressey, & Luckenbill, 1992).

Sutherland believed that criminal or deviant behavior is learned the same way that all behavior is learned. The crucial factors are with whom a person associates, for how long, how frequently, how personally meaningful the associations, and how early they occur in the person's development. According to Sutherland, in our intimate personal groups we all learn definitions, or normative meanings (messages or values), favorable or unfavorable to law violation.

A person becomes delinquent or criminal "because of an excess of definitions favorable to violation of law over definitions unfavorable to violation of law. This is the principle of differential association" (Sutherland & Cressey, 1974, pp. 80–81).

Note that criminal behavior does not invariably develop out of association or contacts with "bad companions" or a criminal element. The messages, not the contacts themselves, are crucial. Furthermore, in order for the person to be influenced toward delinquent behavior, the deviant messages or values from the "bad companions" must outweigh conventional ones. Therefore, Sutherland also believed that criminal behavior may develop even if association with criminal groups is minimal. For example, law-abiding groups—such as parents—may communicate subtly or bluntly that it is all right to cheat, or that everyone is basically dishonest. This is an extremely important point that will be reiterated when we discuss moral disengagement later in the chapter. Nevertheless contemporary reviews of differential association theory emphasize that the associations with deviant peer groups have a major effect on illegal behavior (Williams & McShane, 2004). As we noted in chapter 2, what is not known is which comes first: the behavior or the associations (Williams & McShane, 2004).

Sutherland's theory is probably popular among social scientists because, as one writer put it, "it attempts a logical, systematic formulation of the chain of interrelations that makes crime reasonable and understandable as normal, learned behavior without having to resort to assumptions of biological or psychological deviance" (Vold, 1958, p. 192). However, the theory is also ambiguous; because of this feature it did not at first draw much empirical research (see Gibbons, 1977, pp. 221–28). How are a person's contacts to be measured and weighed? Also, as Cressey (Sutherland & Cressey, 1974) admits, the theory does not specify what kinds of learning are important (e.g., operant, classical, modeling). Neither does it adequately consider individual differences in the learning process. Among some sociologists, however, differential association theory remains popular and continues to attract research interest (Williams & McShane, 2004).

Akers (1985) tries to correct some of the problems with differential association theory by reformulating it to dovetail with Skinnerian and social learning principles. He proposes that most deviant behavior is learned according to principles outlined in Skinner's operant conditioning, with classical conditioning playing a secondary role. Furthermore, the strength of deviant behavior is a direct function of the amount, frequency, and probability of reinforcement the individual has experienced by performing that behavior in the past. The reinforcement may be positive or negative, in the Skinnerian meanings of the terms.

Crucial to the Akers position is the role played by *social* and *nonsocial reinforcement,* the former being the more important. "Most of the learning relevant to deviant behavior is the result of social interactions or exchanges in which the words, responses, presence, and behavior of other persons make reinforcers available, and provide the setting for reinforcement" (Akers, 1985, p. 45). It is also important to note that most of these social reinforcements are symbolic and verbal rewards for participating or for agreeing with group norms and expectations. For example, doing something in accordance with group or subcultural norms is rewarded with "Way to go," "Great job," "Good going," a pat on the back, or a friendly grin. Nonsocial reinforcement refers primarily to physiological factors or material acquisition that may be relevant for some crimes, such as drug-related offenses or burglary.

Deviant or antisocial behavior, then, is most likely to develop as a result of social reinforcements given by significant others, usually within one's peer group. The group first adopts its own *normative definitions* about what conduct is good or bad, right or wrong, justified or unjustified. These normative definitions become internal, cognitive guides to what is appropriate and will most likely be reinforced by the group. In this sense, normative definitions operate as **discriminative stimuli**—social signals transmitted by subcultural or peer groups to indicate whether certain kinds of behavior will be rewarded or punished within a particular social context.

According to Akers, two classes of discriminative stimuli operate in promoting deviant behavior. First, positive discriminative stimuli are the signals (verbal or nonverbal) that communicate that certain behaviors are encouraged by the subgroup. Not surprisingly, they follow the principle of positive reinforcement: The individual engaging in them gains social rewards from the group. The second type of social cue, *neutralizing* or *justifying discriminative stimuli,* neutralizes the warnings communicated by society at large that certain behaviors are inappropriate or unlawful. According to Akers, they "make the behavior, which others condemn and which the person himself may initially define as bad, seem all right, justified, excusable, necessary, the lesser of two evils, or not 'really' deviant after all" (Akers, 1977, p. 521). Statements like "Everyone has a price," "I can't help myself," "Everyone else does it," or "She deserved it" reflect the influence of neutralizing stimuli.

The more people define their behavior as positive or at least justified, the more likely they are to engage in it. If deviant activity (as defined by society at large) has been reinforced more than conforming behavior (also defined by society), and if it has been justified, it is likely that deviant behavior will be maintained. In essence our behavior is guided by the norms we have internalized and for which we expect to be continually socially reinforced by significant others.

Akers accepts the validity of Bandura's modeling as a necessary factor in the initial acquisition of deviant behavior. But its continuation will depend greatly on the frequency and personal significance of *social reinforcement,* which comes from association with others.

Akers's social learning theory has received its share of criticism. Some scholars consider it circular and difficult to follow: Behavior occurs because it is reinforced, but it is reinforced because it occurs. Kornhauser (1978) asserted that there was no empirical support for the theory. During the 1980s and 1990s, though, Akers himself—along with research colleagues—published a number of studies supportive of his theory, particularly as it related to drug use (e.g., Akers

& Cochran, 1985; Akers & Lee, 1996; Krohn, Akers, Radosevich, & Lanza-Kaduce, 1982). Like Sutherland's differential association theory, Akers's approach retains respectability within sociological criminology.

FRUSTRATION-INDUCED CRIMINALITY

Several learning investigators (e.g., Amsel, 1958; Brown & Farber, 1951) have noted that when organisms—including humans—are prevented from responding in a way that had previously produced rewards, their behavior often becomes more energetic and vigorous. Animals bite, scratch, snarl, and become irritable; humans may snarl and become irritable and rambunctious (and may also bite and scratch). Researchers assume that these aroused responses result from an aversive internal state of arousal that they call **frustration.**

Thus, when behavior directed at a specific goal is blocked, arousal increases, and the individual experiences a drive to reduce it. Behavior is energized, but more significantly the responses that lead to a reduction in the arousal may be strengthened or reinforced. This suggests that people who employ violence to reduce frustration will, under extreme frustration, become more vigorous than usual, possibly even resorting to murder and other violent actions. It also suggests that violent behavior directed at reducing frustration will be reinforced, since it reduces unpleasant arousal by altering the precipitating event or stimuli.

The Socialized and Individual Offender

Leonard Berkowitz (1962) conducted numerous studies relating frustration to criminality. He divided criminal personalities into two main classifications: the **socialized** and the **individual offender.** You have already met socialized offenders. We have discussed them throughout this chapter as products of learning, conditioning, and modeling. They offend because they have learned to, or are expected to, as a result of their interactions with the social environment. The individual offender, by contrast, is the product of a long, possibly intense series of frustrations resulting from unmet needs. According to Berkowitz, both modeling and frustration are involved in the development of criminal behavior, but one set of life experiences favors a particular criminal style. "Most lawbreakers may have been exposed to some combination of frustrations and aggressively antisocial models, with the thwartings being particularly important in the development of 'individual' offenders and the antisocial models being more influential in the formulation of the 'socialized' criminals" (Berkowitz, 1962, p. 303).

Berkowitz adds an important dimension to frustration, suggesting that it is particularly intense if an individual has high expectancy of reaching a goal (Berkowitz, 1969). People who anticipate reaching a goal, and who feel they have some personal control over their lives, are more likely to react strongly to interference than those who feel hopeless. In the first case, delay or blockage may generate intense anger and even a violent response, if the frustrated individual believes that type of response will eliminate the interference. The power of frustration may well have been what Maslow (1954) was referring to when he stated that crime and delinquency represent a legitimate revolt against exploitation, injustice, and unfairness. The frustration hypothesis also fits neatly into theories offered by radical or conflict criminologists. Individuals who feel suppressed by the power elite and feel they have a right to reap society's benefits may well experience intense frustration at continuing domination.

Frustration-Induced Riots

The frustration-induced theory helps to explain the behavior of looters during unexpected events like floods, fires, urban riots, or electrical blackouts. For example, between April 30 and May 3, 1993, businesses in Los Angeles were burned and looted largely but not only by African Americans who were frustrated by a jury's acquittal of four white LA police officers in the March 1991 beating of African American motorist Rodney G. King. Fifty-eight people were killed in the four days of rioting, and damage was estimated to be at least $1 billion. People of all ages and racial or ethnic backgrounds were stealing everything from food and alcohol to firearms and stereos. The rioting triggered smaller uprisings in several other cities, including San Francisco, Atlanta, Seattle, Las Vegas, and Miami. Authorities concluded that the riots were brought on by frustrations with economic, social, and political inequalities found in many sectors of American society, including the court system. The Los Angeles riot was similar to the August 1965 uprising of the Watts section of LA, when 34 were killed and one thousand were injured. The riot was prompted by deeply felt frustrations with the same perceived inequalities in American society. Since 1980, there have been at least five major city riots in the United States, mostly started in the wake of reports of police violence and perceived inequities.

Following Hurricane Katrina in 2005, there were many reports of property crime and some violence. Many commentators noted that this was a reflection of the frustration residents of New Orleans and other communities felt at the failure on the part of federal and state agencies to provide a quick, humane, and efficient response to this natural disaster.

The frustration-induced theory also would suggest that individuals who commit larceny under these situations have materialistic goals (e.g., their fair share of middle-class goods) that they have not yet attained. Society blocked the goals, and the individuals became impatient and frustrated. When the opportunity to loot arises, they are there to take it. Demographic profiles of the 2,706 adults arrested and charged with looting during the New York City blackout of 1977 support this theory. The defendants had stronger community ties and higher incomes than the average defendant in the criminal justice system (*New York Times*, August 14, 1977). Only about 10 percent were on welfare; approximately half were gainfully employed. Sixty-five percent of those arrested were

African American and 30 percent were Hispanic. These data indicate that these defendants were, in general, eager to eliminate further delays in meeting their expectancy for a better life.

Frustration and Crime

Berkowitz hypothesizes that the more intense and frequent the thwartings or frustrations in a person's life, the more susceptible and sensitive the person is to subsequent frustration. Thus the individual who frequently strikes out at society in unlawful or deviant ways may have encountered numerous severe frustrations, especially during early development, but has not given up hope. In support of this argument, Berkowitz cites the research findings on delinquency (e.g., Bandura & Walters, 1959; Glueck & Glueck, 1950; McCord, McCord, & Zola, 1959), revealing that delinquent children, compared with nondelinquents, have been considerably more deprived and frustrated during their lifetime.

Berkowitz also suggests that parental neglect or failure to meet the child's needs for dependency and affection are internal, frustrating circumstances that germinate distrust of all others within the social environment. This generalized distrust is carried into the streets and school, and the youngster may exhibit a "chip on the shoulder." The frustration of not having dependency needs met prevents the child from establishing emotional attachments to other people. The individual may thus become resentful, angry, and hostile toward other people in general. Current psychological approaches to delinquency would not disagree, but would place far less blame on the parent. They are more likely to recognize the restrictions that parents face as a result of social problems like racism and economic inequality. In addition contemporary psychologists recognize the influences of other social systems in the juvenile's life, including peers and the educational system.

SITUATIONAL INSTIGATORS AND REGULATORS OF CRIMINAL BEHAVIOR

Most contemporary theories and research support the view that human behavior results from a mutual interaction between personality and situational variables. However, several behavioral and social scientists (e.g., Alison, Bennett, Ormerod, & Mokros, 2002; Gibbons, 1977; Mischel, 1990) complain that much crime research and theory neglects situational variables in favor of dispositional factors. They contend that criminality in many cases may simply reflect being in the wrong place at the wrong time with the wrong people. For example, Gibbons comments, "In many cases, criminality may be a response to nothing more temporal than the provocations and attractions bound up in the immediate circumstances out of which deviant acts arise" (Gibbons, 1977, p. 229). Skinner, of course, exemplifies the position that behavior is controlled by environmental contingencies and events.

Haney (1983) discusses **fundamental attribution error,** which refers to a common human tendency to discount the influence of the situation and explain behavior by referring to the personality of the actor instead. Fundamental attribution error is a concept that applies to making attributions about others, not ourselves. For example, when correctional counselors were asked why inmates had committed the crimes that put them in prison, the counselors attributed the causes almost exclusively to dispositional or personality factors (such as laziness, or meanness) rather than to environmental factors, such as upbringing, poverty, or social factors (Saulnier & Perlman, 1981). The inmates, on the other hand, said that factors they believed landed them in prison were largely external in nature, such as poverty, poor employment opportunities, and physical and sexual abuse. When it comes to ourselves, we engage in **self-serving biases,** in which we tend to attribute good things about ourselves to dispositional factors, and bad things to events and forces outside ourselves. For example, when we do well on an exam, we tend to attribute the cause to our intelligence and study habits. On the other hand, when we do poorly, we tend to attribute the cause to a poorly designed or unfair exam.

Haney believes that personality or internal states account very little for how we act. He contends that the important determining influence is the situation in which we find ourselves. In essence, Haney is arguing that, given the appropriate circumstances, anyone might engage in culpable criminal behavior—that we all have our price.

Situations are rarely static. Our behavior influences them to some extent, and they in turn influence our behavior. This reciprocal interaction between person and environment is one reason students of crime are beginning to pay more attention to victimology—victims often influence the course of criminal actions, particularly violent ones. **Victimology** is the scientific study of the causes, circumstances, individual characteristics, and social context of becoming a victim of a crime. Although victimologists are very careful not to blame victims for the crimes perpetrated against them, they do note that certain actions can facilitate, precipitate, and sometimes even provoke others to commit crime (Karmen 2001). At this point we will turn our attention to two situational factors that seem to play a particularly important role in antisocial behavior, obedience to authority, and deindividuation.

Authority as an Instigator of Criminal Behavior

Sometimes people behave a certain way because someone with power told them they must, even though the actions do not "set right" with their own principles. Kelman and Hamilton (1989) refer to this phenomenon as **crimes of obedience.** "A crime of obedience is an act performed in response to orders from authority that is considered illegal or immoral by the larger community" (Kelman & Hamilton, 1989, p. 46). The classic example of the influence of authority is the military order to kill indiscriminately or to commit some other atrocity, such as Lieutenant William Calley's carrying out the massacre of villagers at

My Lai in the Vietnam War. An example of crimes of obedience in a political/bureaucratic context is the Watergate scandal, when, on June 17, 1972, a group of men under the auspices of the White House burglarized and tried to "bug" the Democratic National Headquarters in the Watergate apartment complex. Crimes of obedience appear to be widespread in the corporate world, an issue we deal with in more detail in chapter 11.

In an attempt to delineate some of the variables involved in obedience to authority, Stanley Milgram (1977) designed a series of experiments, using as subjects persons who volunteered (for money) in response to a newspaper ad. The experiments, which eventually received intensive public scrutiny and are now cited in nearly every introductory psychology textbook, studied the amount of electrical shock people were willing to administer to others when ordered to do so by an apparent authority figure.

The subjects were adult males, ages 20 to 50, who represented a cross section of the socioeconomic classes. They were told that the researchers were studying the effects of punishment on memory. The experiment required a "teacher" and a "victim." Unknown to the volunteers, the victim was part of the experiment, a confederate who had been trained to act in a certain manner as part of the experimental design. In a rigged coin toss, the naive subject (the volunteer) always became the teacher and the confederate the victim. The victim-learner was taken to an adjacent room and strapped into an "electric chair" in the presence of the "naive" teacher.

Next the teacher was led back to a room where he saw a simulated shock generator—a frightening apparatus with thirty toggle switches presumably capable of delivering thirty levels of electric shock to the learner in the adjacent room. Each level was marked in volts ranging from 15 to 450 and accompanied by a switch. In addition, labels indicated "slight shock," "danger: severe shock," and beyond, to an "XXX" level. Each time the learner gave an incorrect answer to a learning task, the teacher was instructed to administer a stronger level of shock. The victim, who did not of course receive any shock at all, purposefully gave incorrect answers; he had also been trained to scream in agony, plead with the subject to stop, and pound on the wall when the higher levels of shock were administered.

Milgram wanted to discover how far people would go under the orders of an apparent authority figure (the experimenter). He may have found more than he bargained for. Almost two-thirds of the subjects obeyed the experimenter and administered the maximum shock levels. In subsequent experiments, using similar experimental conditions but different subjects (including both males and females), Milgram continued to find similar results. Interestingly, when Milgram originally asked mental health experts to predict the outcome of this experiment, the majority of them thought that only a pathological few would obey the experimenter's commands to incrementally increase the shock to dangerous levels (Tsang, 2002). The experts apparently discounted the enormous pressures that the experiment placed on subjects and committed the fundamental attribution error, assuming that "the obedient person who obeys evil commands is sadistic and ill" (Tsang, 2002, p. 27).

Many of Milgram's subjects, while obeying the experimenter's instructions, demonstrated considerable tension and discomfort. Some stuttered, bit their lips, twisted their hands, laughed nervously, sweated profusely, or dug their fingernails into their flesh, especially after the victim began pounding the wall in protest (Milgram, 1963). After the experiment some reported that they wanted to stop punishing the victim but continued to do so because the experimenter would not let them stop. Milgram (1977, p. 118) concluded, "The individual, upon entering the laboratory, becomes integrated into a situation that carries its own momentum."

In subsequent studies, Milgram modified the procedure to include women and to determine more precisely what conditions inhibited or promoted this extreme obedience. For example, he varied the psychological and physical distance between the subject and the victim. To increase the psychological distance between the two, Milgram eliminated the cries of the victim that had been programmed into the original experiment. In another experiment, to minimize the physical and psychological distance between them, the subject sat next to the victim.

In general, Milgram found that the subjects obeyed the experimenter less as physical, visual, and auditory contact with the victim increased. However, the nearer the *experimenter* got to the "teacher," the more likely the teacher was to obey. Milgram found no evidence of significant personality or gender differences in the studies as far as shocking behavior was concerned, but he did find that female teachers were more distressed about their task than their male counterparts.

The psychological and physical distance variable suggests some interesting implications. If we were to analogize between Milgram's studies and violent actions, we would expect that the more impersonal the weapon or situation (psychological and physical distance) the greater the likelihood for destruction and serious violence. Certainly, killing someone with a firearm at a distance versus killing someone point-blank are two different tasks. And both methods differ from choking someone to death with one's bare hands. It would appear that the firearm offers a more impersonal and possibly easier way to eliminate someone, and thus is more likely to lead to violent behavior. Admittedly, this suggestion makes some quantum jumps from a psychological experiment in an artificial setting, but it is a point worth considering when we discuss the relationship between weapons and violence in chapter 9.

In assessing the profound influence of commands from an authority figure, we should also pay close attention to the reactions of the subjects in Milgram's study. Individual differences were noted in the way the subjects reacted to the situation, but not in their actual willingness to shock. Although some subjects refused to continue with the experiment when they believed that they were hurting the victim, most (about 65%) administered the full range of shock levels. Most also displayed anxiety and conflict.

Milgram noted a curious dissociation between word and action. Many subjects said they could not go on, but nevertheless they did. Some justified their action by concluding that the experimenter would not permit any harm to come to the victim. "He must know what he is doing." Other subjects expressed different interpretations and expectancies, such as the belief that the scientific knowledge gained in the experiment justified the method. It is interesting to note that people who have not undergone the ordeal are quite convinced that they would be members of the defiant group who refused to deliver the extreme levels of shock. Later studies conducted both in the United States and abroad confirmed Milgram's findings, however (Penrod, 1983).

Milgram hypothesized that the subject's obedient behavior could be explained by a shift in the perceived role played by the subject. He referred to this shift in role as an "agentic state" where "a person sees himself as an agent for carrying out another wishes" (Milgram, 1974, p. 133). In other words, the subject believes he is no longer acting on his own accord but for another authorized agent. Tsang (2002, p. 28) notes that Bandura (1999) also theorizes "that many individuals in an obedient situation have a shift in attention from their responsibility as moral agents to their duty as obedient subordinates." Similar points of view have been expressed by Kelman and Hamilton (1989) and Blumenthal (1999).

Milgram suggested that our culture may not provide adequate models for disobedience to authority. Likewise, Kelman and Hamilton (1989) argued that it was important for schools to provide *all* children with opportunities to develop leadership skills and encourage them to be critical thinkers and to question authority in an effective manner. Milgram admonished (1977, p. 120) that his studies raise the possibility that human nature or, more specifically, the kind of character produced in American democratic society, cannot be counted on to insulate its citizens from brutality and inhumane treatment at the direction of malevolent authority. A substantial proportion of people do what they are told to do, irrespective of the context of the act and without limitations of conscience, so long as they perceive that the command comes from a legitimate authority.

Milgram's theory may account to some extent for immoral or despicable acts committed under the influence of authority. Moreover, Milgram, convinced that situational factors normally override individual factors, would probably find personality or the morality of the individual fundamentally irrelevant in the explanation of the behavior. Other theorists, however, would argue that it is precisely personality or moral development that account for resistance to authority. Kelman and Hamilton (1989) would argue that the behavior in high authority situations most likely is a result of an interaction between personality characteristics and the roles played. Philip Zimbardo (1970, 1973; Haney & Zimbardo, 1998), on the other hand, believes he has demonstrated the overwhelming power of roles in the famous Stanford Prison Experiment and more broadly in his concept of deindividuation, to which we now turn our attention.

Deindividuation

Deindividuation theory is based on the classic crowd theory of Gustave Le Bon. The theory, formulated in Le Bon's book *The Crowd: A Study of the Popular Mind* (1885/1995) was introduced into mainstream social psychology by Festinger,

Pepitone, and Newcomb in 1952 (Postmes & Spears, 1998). Deindividuation, according to Festinger, Pepitone, and Newcomb (1952), refers to the observation that in crowds or groups, many people lose their sense of individuality and remove self-imposed controls and internalized moral restraints over behavior. Thus, "deindividuation was closely associated with the feeling of not being scrutinized or accountable when submerged in the group" (Postmes & Spears, 1998, p. 240). Philip Zimbardo (1970) extended and further developed deindividuation theory in a number of well-known research projects. For Zimbardo, deindividuation involved feelings of reduced self-observation, and he sought to identify the things that could induce that state (Postmes & Spears, 1998).

Deindividuation, Zimbardo hypothesized, usually follows a complex chain of events. First, the presence of many other persons encourages feelings of anonymity. Then the individual feels he or she loses identity and becomes part of the group. Under these conditions he or she can no longer be singled out and held responsible for behavior. Apparently this feeling then generates a "loss of self-awareness, reduced concern over evaluations from others, and a narrowed focus of attention" (Baron & Byrne, 1977, pp. 581–82). When combined, these processes lower restraints against antisocial criminal behavior and appear to be basic ingredients in mass violence. However, they also may be at work in nonviolent offenses, such as looting.

In one early experiment, Zimbardo (1970) purchased two used cars, left one abandoned on a street in Manhattan, New York, and the other on a street in Palo Alto, California (about 55,000 population in the late 1960s). Zimbardo's deindividuation hypothesis predicted that, due to the large population of New York, people would more likely lose their identity and feel less responsible for their actions. Consequently, New Yorkers would be more likely to loot the abandoned vehicle. This is exactly what happened. Within 26 hours, the New York car was stripped of battery, radiator, air cleaner, radio antenna, windshield wipers, side chrome, all four hubcaps, a set of jumper cables, a can of car wax, a gas can, and the only tire worth taking. Interestingly the looting was not done by delinquents or members of a criminal subculture; all the looters were well-dressed, middle-class whites. On several occasions the looting was done by entire families: children and parents together in a family enterprise.

On the other hand, the car in Palo Alto was untouched during the seven days it was left abandoned. At one point during a rainstorm, a passerby actually lowered the hood to prevent the motor from getting wet. Why such a dramatic difference?

Zimbardo suggests that the anonymity of the New York residents worked in combination with situational cues, implying that they could get by without repercussions. Zimbardo's hypothesis contends that in high population areas, who cares what you are doing as long as you are not bothering others or damaging a concerned party's property? Passersby in New York even stopped and chatted with the looters. In Palo Alto, people could be more easily identified. Moreover, a person engaging in this kind of behavior would expect to be the target of social disapproval or gossip.

Deindividuation is a commonly used concept to explain various expressions of collective behavior such as violent crowds, mindless hooligans, and the lynch mob, as well as social atrocities such as genocide (Postmes & Spears, 1998). As we saw from the car experiment, deindividuation is not necessarily associated with crowds. Nor is a massive population required. The effect may be achieved by a disguise, a mask, or a uniform also worn by others, or it may be achieved by darkness (Zimbardo, 1970). Research data suggest that people may be more abusive, aggressive, and violent when their identity is hidden. This phenomenon *might* explain why, throughout history, war paints, masks, and costumes have been donned by warriors preparing for battle (Watson, 1973). Even contemporary soldiers, guerrillas, and military advisors are deindividuated by their uniforms. Deindividuation also helps explain the apparent ease with which members of groups such as the Ku Klux Klan regressed from being apparently respectable citizens by day to violent, hooded terrorizers by night. Again, however, it is too simplistic to assume that no dispositional or other factors are at work.

The disguise aspect of deindividuation was vividly illustrated in another sobering Zimbardo experiment (1973) known as the Stanford Prison Experiment. Zimbardo and his colleagues simulated a prison environment in the basement of the psychology building at Stanford University, with physical and psychological trappings supposedly representative of an actual prison: bars, prison uniforms, identification numbers, uniformed guards, and other features that encouraged identity slippage. (The facility actually represented a jail more than a prison. Furthermore, as critics of the experiment have noted, the simulation lacked authenticity in a number of ways, including the sacklike uniforms and stocking caps worn by the "prisoners" and the mirrored sunglasses worn by "guards" [Johnson, 1996]. Corrections officers in real prisons and jails also undergo training and are not given the unlimited power that Zimbardo placed in the hands of his experimental subjects.)

Student volunteers were screened through clinical interviews and psychological tests to ensure that they were emotionally stable and mature. According to Zimbardo, the subjects finally selected were "normal," intelligent college students from middle-class homes throughout the United States and Canada. They were paid $15 a day for participating.

The experiment required two roles, guard and prisoner, which were assigned by random coin toss. The randomization assured that there were no significant differences between the two groups. The "prisoners" were unexpectedly "arrested" and brought to the simulated prison in a police car. There they were handcuffed, searched, fingerprinted, booked, stripped, "deloused," given a number, and issued a prison uniform. Each prisoner was then placed in a six-by-nine-foot cell with two other inmates.

The guards wore standard uniforms and mirrored sunglasses to encourage deindividuation, but as noted, they were not representative of the attire worn by "real" correctional officers. In addition, they carried symbols of power: a night stick (which many "real" officers do not carry), keys to the cells, whistles, and handcuffs. Before the prisoners could do even routine things (e.g., write a letter, smoke a cigarette), they had to obtain permission. Guards drew up their own formal rules for maintaining law and order in the prison (16 rules in all) and were free to improvise new ones.

> Within six days, both guards and prisoners had completely absorbed their roles:
>
> Three prisoners had to be released during the first four days because of hysterical crying, confusion in thinking, and severe depression. Many others begged to be paroled, willing to forfeit the money they had earned for participating in the experiment.
>
> About a third of the guards abused their power and were brutal and demeaning. Other subjects did their jobs as tough but fair correctional guards, but none of these supported the prisoners by urging the brutal guards to ease off. The realism of the prison was apparently striking. "The consultant for our prison . . . an ex-convict with sixteen years of imprisonment in California's jails, would get so depressed and furious each time he visited our prison, because of its psychological similarity to his experiences, that he would have to leave" (Zimbardo, 1973, p. 164).

The situation became such that Zimbardo decided to terminate the experiment during the sixth day, instead of proceeding through the planned two weeks. The experiment prompted him to conclude, "Many people, perhaps the majority, can be made to do almost anything when put into psychologically compelling situations—regardless of their morals, ethics, values, attitudes, beliefs, or personal convictions" (1973, p. 164). Much the same conclusion had been reached by Milgram with respect to the influence of authority figures. Although the Stanford Prison Experiment underscores the crucial importance of situational variables in determining behavior, there were still significant individual differences in the way the subjects responded to the conditions. For example, only one-third of the guards became brutally enthralled with their power. Rather than making far-reaching conclusions on the basis of how a total of twenty-one subjects (both guards and prisoners) responded, it would be much more fruitful to give some attention to individual variables. For example, it would have been helpful to examine the values, expectancies, competencies, and moral development of the participants, in combination with the situational factors. What developmental factors most likely predisposed individuals to act the way they did, and exactly how did they perceive the situation? What did they expect to gain by their behavior? We return to the deindividuation issue when we discuss mass violence in chapter 10 and offer other perspectives of what happens to people caught up in the excitement of the crowd.

Moral Disengagement

Bandura (1990, 1991) has proposed a theory of **moral disengagement** to explain why people do immoral or heinous acts against their own moral judgment when ordered to do so by some higher authority or under high social pressure. According to Bandura, individuals, through social learning, internalize moral principles that bring self-worth when they are maintained and self-condemnation when they are violated. Consequently it is not simply the power of the situation that determines a person's actions. Additionally people's moral principles and the ease with which they can become detached from them strongly influence the extent to which they will follow immoral or illegal orders. Bandura further supposes that before a person can engage in behaviors that violate their moral principles, he or she has to *disengage* his or her own moral sanctions to avoid self-condemnation. Specifically, "effective moral disengagement . . . frees one from the restraints of self-censure experience as anticipative guilt from detrimental conduct" (Bandura et al., 2001, p. 125). For example, Bandura, Barbaranelli, Caprara, and Pastorelli (1996) found that delinquents used various methods of moral disengagement, relying most heavily on moral justification and dehumanization of victims. The delinquents could justify certain antisocial behavior by relying on habitual and various forms of moral disengagement from the social standards of conduct. Dehumanization refers to the process of maintaining beliefs that strip people of human qualities or invests them with demonic or bestial qualities (Bandura et al., 2001). "The victims are then seen as subhuman, without the same feelings or hopes as the perpetrators, and thus one can rationalize that normal moral principles do not apply" (Tsang, 2002, p. 41). Dehumanization is covered in more detail in chapter 11.

In a more recent study, Bandura and associates (Bandura et al., 2001) discovered that male adolescents, compared with female adolescents, were "more prone to disengage moral self-sanctions from detrimental conduct, were quicker to rouse themselves to anger through hostile rumination, and were less prosocially oriented" (p. 131). These results, the researchers conclude, lend support to the influence of social learning as a major determinant of the frequently reported gender differences in detrimental or immoral conduct. "Girls are substantially more consoling, sharing, helpful, and affectionately demonstrative" (Bandura et al., 2001, p. 131). Boys, on the other hand, tend to be far less likely to engage peers in discussions of their negative feelings and hostility toward others. Bandura's studies underscore the importance of considering the situation *and* the personal attributes of the person in understanding why people do what they do.

SUMMARY AND CONCLUSIONS

This chapter has led us away from the biologically oriented approaches of chapter 3 to the perspective that all behavior, including antisocial behavior, is learned as a result of interactions with the environment—after, not before birth. According to the theories discussed in this chapter, people are not born with a predisposition to violence or deficient conditionability; rather they become that way as a result of social experiences. Furthermore, criminal behavior, again like all behavior, is an individual's way of adapting to his or her environment.

We have reviewed Skinnerian behaviorism, a theory based on the psychology of J. B. Watson and Ivan Pavlov. Together, Skinnerian, Watsonian, and Pavlovian psychology provided the field with some of its most fundamental concepts, such as classical conditioning, operant conditioning, reinforcement, punishment, and extinction. Today most behaviorists may applaud the basic premise that stimuli elicit responses (classical conditioning), and behavior produces consequences that influence subsequent responses (operant conditioning). However, they also believe other factors must be introduced to explain human behavior. Thus social learning theorists have focused on cognitions, attitudes, beliefs, and other mental processes that must be taken into consideration.

We covered the expectancy theory of Rotter, the observational learning theory of Bandura, and the social learning theories of Sutherland and Akers to illustrate these mental processes. Sutherland, a sociologist with antipathy toward psychology, probably would not want to be included in this group, but his is still a learning theory. Berkowitz's frustration theory, and Zimbardo's concept of deindividuation were also discussed. Each of these emphasizes to varying degrees the importance of learning in the development *and maintenance* of criminal behavior. Most of them also outline the external reinforcements involved in this maintenance, or alternately, its cessation. People who engage in persistent antisocial behavior get tangible rewards, as well as social and psychological ones. Collectively, external reinforcements that bring us material, social, or psychological gain are called positive reinforcements. Behaviors that enable us to avoid unpleasant circumstances are negatively reinforced.

Also included in the regulation of behavior is vicarious reinforcement, which consists of both observed reward and observed punishment. When we observe others (models) receiving rewards or punishments for certain behavior, we tend to alter our behavior correspondingly. Models are extremely important in the acquisition and regulation of criminal behavior. They are reference points for what we should and can do in a particular set of circumstances. Therefore, models may act as inhibitors or facilitators of behavior. People internalize the actions and philosophies of significant models, thereby making them part of their own behavioral repertoire and cognitive structure. Research in recent years has focused extensively on the models available in the media, violent video games, and Internet sites. There is growing evidence that some individuals who observe aggressive acts to a great degree themselves become more violent and aggressive.

In addition to models, situational factors can be important contributors to criminal behavior. To some theorists, frustration plays a significant role in violent criminality. When children are frustrated at not having their needs met by parents or caretakers, for example, this promotes distrust of other adults and prevents the forming of emotional attachments. Individuals who strike out at society have encountered severe frustration, according to this approach.

We also discussed the influence of authority figures and the environmental factors involved in the process of deindividuation. People sometimes engage in illegal or violent conduct because they are told or ordered to do so, as Milgram's classic shocking experiment demonstrated. There are many anecdotal illustrations as well in the military, in law enforcement, and in places of business. Some psychologists have searched for individual differences that might predict the extent to which a person will or will not obey an order perceived to be immoral or illegal, such as differences in personality or moral development. On the other hand, others point to the powerful influence of roles, illustrated by Zimbardo's Stanford experiment. In still other instances, one's personal sense of identity appears to be lost in the excitement of the crowd. Under these deindividualized conditions, people—again not all—may do things they normally would not do.

KEY CONCEPTS

Behaviorism	Cognitive processes
Stimulus	Independent variable
Dependant variable	Variables
Situationism	Reductionism
Operant conditioning	Reinforcement
Positive reinforcement	Negative reinforcement
Punishment	Extinction
Cognitive learning	Social learning theory
Expectancy theory	Observational learning
Modeling	Models
Imitational learning	Differential association-
DAR	reinforcement
Frustration	Discriminative stimuli
Individual offender	Socialized offender
Self-serving biases	Fundamental attribution error
Crimes of obedience	Victimology
Moral disengagement	Deindividuation

REVIEW QUESTIONS

1. Describe the process of operant conditioning and give an example of how criminal behavior is acquired.
2. Explain the difference between differential association theory and differential association-reinforcement theory.
3. Explain the concept of deindividuation and illustrate by describing any one experiment in social psychology.
4. What is "frustration-induced criminality"? Provide an illustration.
5. Briefly explain Bandura's theory of moral disengagement.
6. Compare and contrast the behaviorism promoted by B. F. Skinner with the modern behaviorism promoted by Bandura.
7. Describe and discuss the situational factors that can influence criminal behavior. In addition to those mentioned in this chapter, what others might be identified?
8. What is meant by crimes of obedience? Give examples.
9. Give an example of fundamental attribution error not mentioned in the book.

CHAPTER 5

HUMAN AGGRESSION AND VIOLENCE

CHAPTER OBJECTIVES

- Explore the vast array of problems in defining and identifying aggressive behavior.
- Review the major theories on the development of aggression and violence.
- Emphasize the importance of cognitive processes in aggressive behavior.
- Explore the interactions of biology and cognitive processes in aggressive behavior and violence.
- Outline the important key concepts in understanding aggression and violence, such as hostile attribution bias, weapons effect, contagion effect.
- Illustrate common occurrence of aggression with a discussion of road rage and aggressive driving.
- Review the effects of electronic and other media on aggression and violence.

There is ample evidence of the long history of human involvement in aggression and violence. The 5,600 years of recorded human history, for example, include 14,600 wars, a rate of more than 2.6 per year (Baron, 1983; Montagu, 1976). Today we are under the constant threat of violent terrorism, such as illustrated by the attack on the Twin Towers in New York and the Pentagon in Washington in 2001, or the attacks on public transportation systems in Spain and England in 2005 and India in 2006. Some writers argue that aggression has been instrumental in helping people survive. Through centuries of experience, humans learned that aggressive behavior enabled them to obtain material goods, land, and treasures; to protect property and family; and to gain prestige, status, and power. Although some might wonder whether the human species could have survived had it not used aggression, others are quick to point out that both historically and in the present, aggressive behavior is at the root of numerous social and individual problems.

Aggression—a psychological concept that we will define shortly—warrants an entire chapter because it is the basic ingredient in violent crime. By studying aggression, psychologists have made substantial contributions to society's efforts to understand both violent and nonviolent crime, as well as violent behavior that may not necessarily be defined as crime (e.g., legitimate uses of force). Is human aggression instinctive, biological, learned, or some combination of these characteristics? If it results from an innate, biological mechanism, the methods designed to control, reduce, or eliminate aggressive behavior will differ significantly from methods used if aggression is learned.

Perspectives of human nature emerge very clearly from the scholarly and research literature on aggression. Some writers and researchers believe that aggressive behavior is basically biological and genetic in origin, a strong residue of our evolutionary past. This physiological, genetic contention is accompanied by compelling evidence that explanations of human aggressive behavior may be found in the animal kingdom from which it originated. On the other hand, researchers who subscribe to the learning viewpoint believe that, while some species of animals may be genetically programmed to behave aggressively, human beings learn to be aggressive from the social environment. The learning position also offers cogent evidence to support its theory. Other researchers remain on a theoretical fence, accepting and rejecting some aspects of each argument. Research does indicate, however, that the level of aggressive behavior demonstrated by an 8-year-old appears to remain largely unchanged well into adulthood for many children, regardless of gender (Kokko & Pulkkinen, 2005).

If aggression and violence represent a built-in, genetically programmed aspect of human nature, we may be forced, as Baron (1983) suggests, toward a pessimistic conclusion. At best we can only hope to hold our natural, aggressive urges and drives temporarily in check. Furthermore, we should design the environment and society in such a way as to discourage violence, including administering immediate and aversive consequences (punishment) when it is displayed. Even better—and setting aside ethical or legal considerations for the moment—we might consider psychosurgery, electrode implants, and drug control—all effective methods for the reduction, if not the elimination, of violence.

If, on the other hand, we believe that aggression is learned and is influenced by a wide range of situational, social, and environmental variables, we can be more optimistic. Aggression is not an inevitable aspect of human life. Once we understand what factors play major roles in its acquisition and maintenance, we will be able to change human behavior by manipulating these factors. There are, of course, both positive and negative aspects of human aggression. Many individuals who play in competitive sports, hunt for sport, serve in the military, and work for law enforcement engage in socially permissible forms of aggression that may be necessary or that enhance their quality of life. The focus in this chapter is on the negative aspects, or the forms of aggression that are not socially permissible.

By most accounts, animal aggression reflects the biological programming carried in the genes to ensure the survival of the species. Humans, with their enormously complex and sophisticated brain (cerebral cortex), rely heavily on thought, associations, beliefs, and learning; these become primary determinants of behavior. Theorists differ over the degree to which genetic programming contributes to human behavior. Thus, are people aggressive and violent because their animal instincts continue to promote this particular behavior? And, if the evolutionary aggressive drives still reside within the subcortical structures of the brain (below the cortex in the "old" brain), as some writers tell us they do, are they modifiable? If not, how can we best prevent people from attacking and killing one another? On the other hand, a difference-in-kind perspective suggests that genetic predispositions, or biological precursors of aggression, have a minimal influence on human behavior, if they have any influence at all. After defining aggression, we will return to these different points of view.

DEFINING AGGRESSION

The task of defining human aggression is surprisingly difficult, as many social psychologists have discovered. Forcibly jabbing someone in the midsection is certainly defining it by example—or is it? Now what about jabbing someone more softly, in jest? Would everyone consider football and boxing aggressive behaviors? If someone pointedly ignores a question, is that an example of aggression? What if someone spreads malicious gossip? If a burglar breaks into your home and you reach for your trusty but rusty rifle, aim it at the intruder, and pull the trigger, is yours an act of aggression? Is it any less so if the rifle does not fire? If someone sits passively on a doorstep and blocks your entry, is this aggression?

Some social psychologists define aggression as the intent and attempt to harm another individual, physically or socially, or, in some cases, to destroy an object. This definition seems adequate for many situations, but it has several limitations. Refusing to speak does not fit well, since it is not an active attempt to harm someone, nor is the person blocking entry trying to injure anyone. Most psychologists place these two behaviors in a special category of aggressive responses and call them **passive-aggressive behaviors,** since they are generally interpreted as aggressive in intent, although the behavior is passive and indirect.

As fascinating as passive-aggressive behavior may be, it is generally irrelevant when we discuss crime, since the aggression we are concerned about is the type that manifests itself directly in violent or antisocial behavior. We might stretch the point by suggesting that the doorstep sitter is trespassing, in which case he or she might be charged with a criminal offense. Likewise there are other situations in which passive-aggressive behavior could lead to various

TABLE 5–1 Varieties of Human Aggression

	Active		Passive	
	DIRECT	INDIRECT	DIRECT	INDIRECT
Physical	Punching, Hitting	Practical joke, Booby trap	Obstructing passage	Refusing to perform a necessary task
Verbal	Insulting the victim	Malicious gossip	Refusing to speak	Refusing consent

Source: Adapted from Buss 1971.

types of crime. Refusing to file income tax because one is intensely dissatisfied with the current administration is one example. In general, however, the aggressive behavior we wish to focus on in this chapter is not of the passive-aggressive kind.

In an effort to conceptualize the many varieties of human aggression, Buss (1971) tried to classify them based on the apparent motivation of the aggressor (see **Table 5–1**). You may easily find exceptions and overlapping categories in the Buss scheme, but that emphasizes how difficult it is to compartmentalize human aggressive behavior. It also epitomizes the many definitional dilemmas that hamper social psychologists studying aggression.

Hostile and Instrumental Aggression

Before finally settling on a satisfactory definition of aggression (and we will get there), it may be useful to recognize two types, **hostile** (or **expressive**) and **instrumental aggression,** a distinction first made by Feshbach (1964). They are distinguished by their goals, or the rewards they offer the perpetrator. Hostile (or expressive) aggression, which we are most concerned with in this chapter, occurs in response to anger-inducing conditions, such as real or perceived insults, physical attacks, or one's own failures. The aggressor's goal is to make a victim suffer. Most criminal homicides, rapes, and other violent crimes directed at harming the victim are precipitated by hostile aggression. The behavior is characterized by the intense and disorganizing emotion of anger, with anger defined as an arousal state elicited by certain stimuli, particularly those evoking attack or frustration. Angry at the economic system that deprived him of a job, a sniper may open fire on passing motorists and feel satisfaction at having lashed out "successfully" at society.

Instrumental aggression begins with competition or the desire for some object or status possessed by another person—jewelry, money, territory. The perpetrator tries to obtain the desired object regardless of the cost. Instrumental aggression is usually a factor in robbery, burglary, larceny, and various white-collar crimes. The perpetrator's obvious goal in a robbery is to obtain items of value. Usually there is no intent to harm anyone. However, if someone or something interferes with the perpetrator's objective, he or she may feel forced to harm the victim or risk losing the desired goal. In that sense, a robbery may lead to murder, but the aggression represented is still instrumental. Instrumental aggression is also usually a feature of calculated murder committed by a hired, impersonal killer. Although psychologists make the distinction between hostile and instrumental aggression, the law does not, insofar as responsibility for the crime is concerned. However, certain factors associated with hostile aggression (e.g., if the crime is committed in a particularly heinous fashion) can affect the criminal sentence. On the other hand, a contract killer's instrumental aggression may also bring a longer sentence if information about prior offenses comes to light at sentencing.

It should be mentioned, however, that some scholars (e.g., Bushman & Anderson, 2001) find fault with a strict hostile-instrumental dichotomy. Bushman and Anderson point out that this two-category division fails to take into account that many aggressive acts have multiple motives. Furthermore, they say, aggressive acts can be better understood if they are placed somewhere along a continuum that runs from controlled aggression at one pole to automatic (impulsive or thoughtless) aggression at the other pole. Bushman and Anderson believe that, although the dichotomy was useful during the early stages of theory development, it is time to move to a more cognitive approach to understanding the various types of aggressive behavior. This is discussed more fully in the section on the cognitive models of aggression later in the chapter.

Interpretation by Victim

As Bandura (1973a) noted, most definitions of aggression imply that aggression revolves around the behaviors and intentions residing within the perpetrator (or performer). Going a step further, he suggests that an adequate definition of aggression must consider both the "injurious behavior" of the perpetrator and the "social judgment" of the victim. Thus, a soft poke in the belly may qualify as aggression if it is both done derisively and the recipient interprets it that way. A textbook on criminal behavior, however, must focus on aggression as manifested in conduct, not as it is perceived by a victim; it is the actions of the perpetrator that are critical. For our purposes, therefore, we define aggression as *behavior perpetrated or attempted with the intention of harming another individual physically or psychologically (as opposed to socially) or to destroy an object.* The psychological harm would cover aggressive actions that do not involve physical force but are still criminally accountable, such as intimidation, threats, or stalking. This definition encompasses all the behaviors described in Buss's typology. Note, however, that aggressive behavior will not *always* qualify as criminal. A law enforcement officer using *reasonable* force against a criminal suspect is displaying aggressive behavior, but it is not criminal. A hunter shooting a turkey (in season) falls into the same category.

Furthermore we define violence as *destructive physical aggression intentionally directed at harming other persons or things.* Violence may be methodical or random, sustained or fleeting, intensive or uncontrolled. It always harms or destroys the recipient or is intended to do so (Daniels & Gilula, 1970). Therefore all violent behavior is aggressive behavior, but not all aggressive behavior is violent. Spreading malicious, false information about someone or stalking are cases in point. Both are aggressive, one is also criminal in most jurisdictions, but neither is violent.

THEORETICAL PERSPECTIVES ON AGGRESSION

Behavioral and social scientists have debated for over a half century whether humans are born aggressive and naturally violent, or born relatively free of aggressive tendencies. Several theories have been developed that try to provide some answers to the debate. A **theory** is an integrated set of principles that describes, predicts, and explains some phenomena. It also guides research. The aggression debate, part of a wider controversy about the respective merits of nature and nurture, touches every school of thought in human behavior. According to the first perspective, humans are programmed aggressive to defend themselves, family, and territory from intruders. According to the second, humans become violent by acquiring aggressive models and actions from society. In this section, the topics will move from the instinctive and biological perspectives to the more learning-based perspectives.

Psychoanalytical/Psychodynamic Viewpoint

Psychodynamic theorists assume that humans, by their very nature, will always be prone to aggressive impulses and hence are likely to commit violent acts if these impulses are not appropriately managed or held in check. Sigmund Freud, the father of psychoanalysis and a physician by training, was convinced that human beings are susceptible from birth to a buildup of aggressive energy, which must be dissipated or drained off before it reaches dangerous levels. This is known as the **psychodynamic** or **hydraulic model** since it bears a close resemblance to pressure build-up in a container. If excessive pressure accumulates in the container—the human psyche—an explosion is likely to occur, as demonstrated by tirades that may involve violence. According to the traditional Freudian perspective, people who have tirades are blowing off the excess steam of aggressive energy.

Freud suggested that violence in all of its forms is a manifestation of this aggressive energy discharge. Internal energy accumulates to dangerous levels when people have not discharged it appropriately through a process called catharsis, one of the most important concepts in psychoanalytic psychotherapy. Catharsis may be accomplished by actual behavior (e.g., playing football) or may occur vicariously (watching football). The Freudian-psychodynamic position predicts that children who participate in or avidly watch school sports will ultimately be less aggressive than children who do not. Freudian psychody-namic followers also maintain that people who engage in violent crime (par-ticularly hostile aggression) have not had sufficient opportunity to "blow off steam" and keep their aggressive energies at manageable levels.

According to the psychoanalytical viewpoint, if violent crime is to be con-trolled, the human animal must be provided with multiple but appropriate channels for catharsis (e.g., adequate recreational facilities). In this way, chil-dren and adults presumably learn to dissipate aggression in socially approved, appropriate ways. Psychotherapy is one such channel, encouraging catharsis under the guidance of a therapist.

Ethological Viewpoints

Ethology is the study of animal behavior in relation to the animal's natural habitat, and it compares that behavior to human behavior. In the mid-1960s, a number of ethologists published books and articles about aggression that in-terested and appealed to the general public. Three especially popular books were Konrad Lorenz's *On Aggression* (1966), Robert Ardrey's *The Territorial Im-perative* (1966), and Desmond Morris's *The Naked Ape* (1967). Before his death, Lorenz was the chief spokesperson for a theoretical formulation of ethology as it relates to aggression.

A Nobel laureate in biology, Lorenz believed that aggression is an inherited instinct of both humans and animals. One of its main purposes is to enable the animal—and the human being—to defend "staked out" territory, a territory that ensures sufficient food, water, and space to roam and reproduce. If this space is violated, Lorenz argued, the instinctive or genetically programmed re-sponse is to attack, or at least to increase aggressive behavior toward the in-truder, thus preventing further territory violation. The tendency to attack space violators is referred to as **territoriality.** Lorenz believed it is an innate propen-sity developed through the lengthy, complex process of evolution. This innate aggressive behavior among members of the same animal species (intraspecific aggression) prevents overcrowding and ensures the best and most powerful mates for the young.

The more deadly the animals' evolutionarily developed weaponry (e.g., fangs, claws, size, and strength), the more intense the innate inhibitions against engaging in physical combat with members of its own species. This innately programmed inhibition is a form of insurance for species survival, Lorenz be-lieved, since constant intraspecific physical combat would eventually extin-guish the species. Intraspecies aggression is accomplished, therefore, not by actual combat but by complicated displays of force and superiority, such as a show of teeth, size, or color array. These displays are referred to as **ritualized aggression.** Through an intricate communication system not yet understood by scientists, the animals transmit signals, after which the more powerful, domi-nant animal generally wins out. The losing animal demonstrates defeat by var-ious appeasement behaviors, such as rolling over on its back (characteristic of puppies), lowering its tail or head, and emitting cries of defeat. The weaker animal then leaves the territory of the dominant one.

What does all of this have to do with human aggression? Lorenz and other ethologists believe that it is important to understand animal aggression before we try to understand human aggression, since humans are part of the animal world and probably follow many of its basic principles. In other words ethologists subscribe to the **difference-in-degree** Darwinian perspective, discussed briefly in chapter 1. Efran and Cheyne (1974), for example, observed after studying invasion of personal space among humans that "human society may operate through mechanisms which are less uniquely human than is currently fashionable to suggest" (p. 225).

Lorenz raises another issue that, if valid, is more significant to criminal behavior, however. He maintained that human beings have outdistanced the evolutionary process of inhibiting aggression. Instead of developing natural weapons and the species-preserving function of ritualized aggression, humans have developed technological weaponry. Thus he and many other ethologists believe they can provide at least a partial answer to why human beings wantonly maim and kill members of their own species: They have not developed the ability to engage in the species-preserving behavior of ritualized aggression. Instead, through superior learning ability, they have developed the capacity to annihilate.

The ethological position is intriguing, but it has not been supported by human aggression research (Bandura, 1983; Montagu, 1973; Zillmann, 1983). Zoologists, biologists, and psychologists have tried with little success to apply the Lorenzian tenets to humans. One problem is that the ethological position relies on a strong analogy between animals and humans. Lorenz argued, for example, that the Greylag goose is remarkably similar to the human species (Berkowitz, 1973). However, the human brain makes us remarkably unlike the Greylag goose and considerably less likely to rely on instinct for determining behavior. Research has yet to delineate any instinctive or invariant genetically programmed behavior determinant in humans. Furthermore, "the capacity to exercise control over one's own thought processes, motivation, and action is a distinctively human characteristic" (Bandura, 1989, p. 1175).

Ethologists also fail to acknowledge and interpret the vast body of existing scientific research that has tested their position and found it wanting. This curious response—or nonresponse—undermines the validity of their whole presentation. Some critics have referred to ethological theorizing as "scientific-sounding misinformation" (Leach, 1973). To date, therefore, there is little evidence to justify portraying humans as *innately* dangerous and brutal or as controlled by instinct. Some contemporary theories do adopt a biological perspective on violence, however, as we discuss later in the chapter.

The ethological perspective has evolved into what is referred to today as **evolutionary psychology.** Evolutionary psychology is the study of the evolution of behavior using the principles of natural selection. It argues that human evolutionary history provides the fundamental framework for understanding human cognition and behavior. An important point to remember here is that evolutionary psychology does not see aggression as pathology, but something that is normal, especially for men (Spallone, 1998).

Frustration-Aggression Hypothesis

Around the time of Freud's death in 1939, a group of psychologists at Yale University proposed that aggression is a direct result of frustration (Dollard et al., 1939). According to John Dollard and his colleagues, people who are frustrated, thwarted, annoyed, or threatened will behave aggressively, since aggression is a natural, almost automatic response to frustrating circumstances. Moreover, people who exhibit aggressive behavior are frustrated, thwarted, annoyed, or threatened. "Aggression is always a consequence of frustration" (Dollard et al., 1939, p. 1).

Because of its simplicity and important implications, the **frustration-aggression hypothesis** drew much research, along with much criticism. Psychologists found it difficult not only to decide what frustration was, but also to determine how it could be measured accurately. Researchers also learned that aggression was a much more complex phenomenon than Dollard and his associates had postulated. Frustration does not always lead to aggression, and aggressive behavior does not always signify "frustration." Experiments indicated that people respond to frustration and anger differently. Some do indeed respond with aggression, but others display a wide variety of responses.

Led by Leonard Berkowitz (1962, 1969, 1973), whose general views on some of the causes of criminality were presented in chapter 4, researchers began to propose a revised, contemporary version of the frustration-aggression hypothesis. According to Berkowitz, frustration increases the probability that an individual will become angry and soon act aggressively. In short frustration facilitates the performance of aggressive behavior. The behavior may be overt (physical or verbal) or implicit (wishing someone dead). Anger, however, is not the only emotion that potentially leads to aggression. Aversive conditions, such as pain, or pleasant states, such as sexual arousal, may also lead to aggressive behavior (Berkowitz, 1973). We will return to this subject shortly.

As we learned in chapter 4, an important component of the revised frustration-aggression hypothesis is the concept of anticipated goals or expectations. When a behavior directed at a specific goal is thwarted, frustration is likely to result. Thus the person must have been expecting or anticipating the attainment of a goal or achievement. Mere deprivation of goods will not necessarily lead to frustration. People who are living under deprived conditions may not be frustrated unless they actually expect something better. "Poverty-stricken groups who have never dreamed of having automobiles, washing machines, or new homes are not frustrated because they have been deprived of these things; they are frustrated only after they have begun to hope" (Berkowitz, 1969, p. 15).

Aggression, Berkowitz says, is only one possible response to frustration. The individual may learn others, like withdrawal, doing nothing, or trying to alter the situation by getting out of the situation completely or by compromising. With this approach Berkowitz not only emphasizes the importance of learning but also stresses the role of individual differences in response to frustrating circumstances.

The revised frustration-aggression hypothesis, therefore, suggests the following steps: (1) the person is blocked from obtaining an expected goal; (2) frustration results, generating anger; and (3) anger *predisposes* or readies the person to behave aggressively. Whether the person actually engages in aggressive actions will depend in part on his or her learning history, interpretation of the event, and individual way of responding to frustration. It will also depend, however, on the presence of aggression-eliciting stimuli in the environment.

Weapons Effect

Berkowitz notes that the presence of aggressive stimuli in the external environment (or internal environment represented by thoughts) increases the probability of aggressive responses. A weapon is a good example of such a stimulus. Most people in our society associate firearms with aggression. Berkowitz (1983) likens the firearm to a conditioned stimulus in that the weapon conjures aggressive associations, facilitating overt aggression. A gun, even when not used, is more likely to generate aggressive action than is a neutral object. "The mere sight of the weapon might elicit ideas, images, and expressive reactions that had been linked with aggression in the past." (Berkowitz, 1983, p. 124).

In one experiment designed to test this hypothesis (Berkowitz & LePage, 1967), angry male subjects were more likely to engage in aggressive action in the presence of a gun than a comparable group of angry subjects in the presence of a badminton racket. This suggests that a visible weapon (such as a law enforcement officer might carry) may actually facilitate, rather than inhibit, a violent response in some people.

The Berkowitz-LePage finding generated much controversy as to whether weapons actually do provoke aggressive behavior. A number of studies tried to replicate the finding, but failed to find evidence of a **weapons effect** (Penrod, 1983). Some researchers believed that many of the subjects used in some of the studies "saw through" the purpose of the study, a research flaw called demand characteristics. However, a comprehensive review of the research literature found strong evidence that the weapons effect does—in fact—exist (Carlson, Marcus-Newhall, & Miller, 1990). Carlson et al. concluded, "Aggression-related cues present in experimental settings act to increase aggressive responding. This cue effect occurs more strongly when subjects have been negatively aroused before their exposure to aggression-facilitating cues" (p. 632). The weapons effect has also been found in other countries, including Belgium, Croatia, Italy, and Sweden (Berkowitz, 1994).

It should be mentioned that the aggression-eliciting stimuli need not be aggressive or violent in appearance (i.e., a gun, knife, or bomb) but can be seemingly neutral stimuli. That is, the stimuli need only be associated with aversive events or have a decidedly unpleasant meaning to an individual to intensify aggressive reactions. Even some types of music may facilitate or encourage aggressive behavior (Rogers & Ketcher, 1979).

Berkowitz (1989) emphasized two important components to the frustration-aggression equation. Aggressive behavior will be generated (1) to the extent that a person perceives the mistreatment as intentional and (2) to the degree that the frustration experienced is aversive. According to Berkowitz, people become angry and aggressive at being kept from reaching a desired goal if they think someone had intentionally blocked them from achieving that goal or deliberately and wrongly tried to hurt them. "They are much more likely to become openly aggressive at someone's blocking their goal attainment if they believe their frustrater had deliberately and unjustifiably attempted to keep them from reaching their goal than if they think the thwarting had not been intentional or had not been directed at them personally" (Berkowitz, 1989, p. 68). Thus self-restraint comes into play when people think they have not been deliberately mistreated or that the blocking of the goal was legitimate. On the other hand, people become angry and aggressive when they perceive that they have been treated unfairly or were personally attacked.

Berkowitz also postulates that thwartings or frustrations generate a negative affect, which refers to an emotional state people typically seek to lessen or eliminate. Furthermore, an unexpected interference is more apt to provoke an aggressive reaction than is an anticipated barrier to goal attainment, because the former is usually much more unpleasant. That is, it has more negative affect.

Cognitive-Neoassociation Model

In his reformulation of the frustration-aggression hypothesis, Berkowitz has emphasized the importance of cognitive factors. Currently it is called the **cognitive-neoassociation model.** It operates in the following manner. During the earlier stages, an aversive event produces a negative affect (discomfort). This negative affect may be due to physical pain or psychological discomfort. Physical pain as an aversive circumstance is clear, but psychological discomfort needs further elaboration. Being verbally insulted is a good example. While there is no physical pain, personal insults or demeaning comments engender anger, depression, or sadness in just about everyone—all negative affects. Unpleasant feelings or negative affects presumably then give rise, almost automatically, to a variety of feelings, thoughts, and memories that are associated with flight (fear) and fight (anger) tendencies. During this early stage, mediating cognitive processes have little influence beyond the immediate appraisal that the situation is aversive. Some people may act quickly on the basis of these initial emotions without further deliberation or forethought, sometimes engaging in violence. During the later stages, however, cognitive appraisal may go into operation and substantially influence the subsequent emotional reactions and experiences after the initial, automatic responses. These cognitions mediate and evaluate a proper course of action. During the later stages, roused people make causal attributions about the unpleasant experience, think about the nature of their feelings, and perhaps try to control their feelings and actions.

Berkowitz emphasizes that any unpleasant feeling or arousal can evoke aggressive, even violent responses. A depressed person can murder his or her family, or a thwarted teenager may violently lash out at authority.

Excitation Transfer Theory

Zillmann (1988) has proposed a theory to explain how physiological arousal can generalize from one situation to another. Called **excitation transfer theory,** it is based on the assumption that physiological arousal, however produced, dissipates slowly over time. For example, a person who receives some anger-producing criticism at work is likely to have some residual arousal from that criticism when he or she arrives home later that evening. Encountering some annoying event at home, the person is apt to "fly off the handle" and overreact to the minor home incident. Consequently, the combination of preexisting arousal, plus anger generated by the irritation at home, may increase the likelihood of aggression. The transfer of arousal from one situation to another is most likely to occur if the person is unaware that he or she is still carrying some arousal from a previous situation to a new, unrelated one.

Displaced Aggression Theory

Closely related to the excitation transfer theory is **displaced aggression theory,** especially the recent model proposed by Bushman, Anderson, Miller, and their colleagues (Anderson & Bushman, 2002; Bushman, et al., 2005: Miller, Pedersen, Earleywine, & Pollack, 2003). According to Bushman et al. (2005), "Aggression is *displaced* when the target is innocent of any wrongdoing but is simply in the wrong place at the wrong time" (p. 969). Displaced aggression can occur when an individual cannot aggress against a source of provocation, such as a boss at work, but feels less constrained about being aggressive toward an innocent, nonprovoking, or mildly provoking individual (or pet). The displaced aggression is probably more likely to be directed at a person (or pet) who emits a mildly annoying act—the cat that tips over the water dish, for example. Bushman et al. refer to this phenomenon as *triggered displaced aggression.* "Following an initial provocation, the target commits a minor provocation, the triggering event, which in turn prompts an aggressive response" (p. 970). The "displaced" aggressive response is normally far in excess of what might be expected to be directed at the minor provocation but probably is in proportion to the perceived severity of the initial provocation. One may believe the boss deserves a good kick for not appreciating one's hard work on a project; since one can't kick the boss, the cat bears the brunt of the anger.

Bushman et al. (2005) take the model one step further by working into the equation the concept of rumination. **Rumination** refers to self-focused attention toward one's thoughts and feelings. In other words, the person keeps thinking about the incident long after it is over. More importantly, ruminative thought can harbor and maintain angry feelings over a period of time, far removed from the initial provocation. It is, according to Bushman et al., the ruminative thoughts that can promote subsequent aggression against someone who is mildly annoying but not highly deserving of an aggressive attack.

Aggressive Driving and Road Rage

Aggressive driving and road rage illustrate the previous displaced aggression-arousal theory very well. Before we proceed, however, it is important to note that although aggressive driving and road rage are sometimes used interchangeably, many experts consider them distinct phenomena (Asbridge, Smart, & Mann, 2006). **Road rage,** a term coined by the media in the late 1980s (Roberts & Indermaur, 2005), is defined as an incident in which an angry, impatient, or aroused motorist *intentionally* injures or kills, or tries to injure or kill, another motorist, passenger, or pedestrian, in response to a traffic dispute, altercation, or grievance (Joint, 1995; Mizell, 1995). The provocation may be real or imaged. It is also considered road rage when an aroused, upset motorist drives his or her vehicle into a building or other structure or property (Mizell, 1995). Additional examples include chasing another vehicle, driving straight at another vehicle when angered, extreme tailgating, and trying to edge another car off the road (Galovksi & Blanchard, 2004).

Aggressive driving, on the other hand, is usually considered less serious. Generally aggressive driving is the result of a motorist becoming impatient or frustrated, and it is often not the direct result of the behavior of another motorist. In other words aggressive driving is often the result of the triggered displaced aggression discussed in the previous section. The aggressive driver was already angry at someone or something and "takes out" this anger on the road. Common examples of aggressive driving include tailgating, cutting in and out of lanes, excessive speed, illegal passing, horn blowing, flashing headlights, refusing to yield right of way, slow driving with intent of blocking other vehicles, and running red lights. In contrast, road rage is most often the result of interpreting the actions of other motorists as personal affronts which require retaliating to vindicate one's self esteem (Neighbors, Vietor, & Knee, 2002). Aggressive driving, on the other hand, is most often caused by traffic congestion, travel impedance, and time urgency (Neighbors, Vietor, & Knee, 2002). Both aggressive driving and road rage are particularly problematic in the United States, but they appear to be growing worldwide problems (Asbridge, Smart, & Mann, 2006; Junger, West, & Timman, 2001: Krahé, 2005). It is estimated that an average of over 1,500 men, women, and children are injured or killed each year in the United States as a direct result of aggressive driving or road rage, and this is increasing at a rate of about 7 percent per year (Yu, Evans, & Perfetti, 2004).

An interesting survey of drivers in 20 major U.S. cities was conducted by Prince Market Research for Auto Vantage, an automobile membership club offering travel services (Associated Press, 2006). Two thousand adult drivers who regularly commuted within each city were asked to rate the amount of road rage and "rude" driving in their metropolitan area. The survey found that Miami drivers reported the most incidents of road rage and rude driving during 2006. Phoenix was second in the road rage and rude driving, followed by New York City, Los Angeles, and Boston. Nashville and Minneapolis reported the fewest incidents. The drivers were also asked what driving behavior most incites road rage in themselves. Thirty-nine percent said being "cut off," 30 percent said tailgating, and 23 percent reported slow driving. There were no significant gender differences in the survey.

Who Are the Road Ragers?

A growing number of studies reveal that the majority of road ragers are young males (ages 18 to 35) who have criminal and violent histories, psychiatric problems, and drug or alcohol problems (Asbridge, Smart, & Mann, 2006; Mizell, 1995; Smart, Asbridge, Mann, & Adlaf, 2003). For example, Galovski and Blanchard (2002) report that nearly half of the motorists referred by a traffic court to a program specifically designed for highly aggressive drivers (mostly road ragers) had one of more convictions for driving under the influence of alcohol. In reference to the relationship between criminal history and aggressive driving, Junger, West, & Timman, (2001) examined the criminal histories of a random sample of 1,531 persons involved in traffic accidents in the Netherlands. The researchers discovered that those motorists involved in traffic accidents due to risky or highly aggressive driving (according to the police) were far more likely to have a police record for violent crime, vandalism, property crime, and similar traffic accidents in the past. However, aggressive drivers and road ragers come from all walks of life, across a variety of socioeconomic levels and occupations. Celebrities are not immune. "In California, Oscar winner Jack Nicholson believed that a driver of a Mercedes-Benz cut him off in traffic. The [then] 57-year-old actor grabbed a golf club, stepped out of his car at a red light, and repeatedly struck the windshield and roof of the Mercedes" (Mizell, 1995, p. 5).

Weapons Used

The weapons most commonly used by road ragers are firearms (37%) and the vehicle itself (35%). In fact, some research suggests that having a gun in the car is linked to high levels of aggressive behavior behind the wheel (Miller, Hennenway, & Solop, 2002). Other weapons used are tire irons, jack handles, baseball bats, hurled projectiles, defensive sprays, fists, and feet. Mizell (1995, p. 8) writes, "While the event that sparks the incident may be trivial, in every case there exists some reservoir of anger, hostility, or frustration that is released by the triggering incident." In one case, a man was attacked by fellow motorists because he could not turn off the antitheft alarm on his rented jeep. Surprisingly, it is not unusual for angry drivers to use their motor vehicles to attack law enforcement personnel and vehicles.

Precipitating Factors in Road Rage

Domestic violence or domestic disputes are very common factors in both aggressive driving and road rage, when upset spouses and intimate partners vent their anger on the highway. Under these conditions, the gender differences in aggressive driving are not as great as might be expected. In one survey, 54 percent of the women admitted to aggressive driving behavior compared with 64 percent of men (Joint, 1995). In that survey, respondents reported that aggressive tailgating (62%) was the most common form of aggressive driving, followed by headlight flashing (59%), obscene gestures (48%), deliberately obstructing other vehicles (21%), and verbal abuse (16%).

However, the immediate, precipitating causes of road rage are largely minor misunderstandings that are perceived and interpreted by the other drivers as aggressive, aversive, or directed personally at them. It also appears that a major factor in the road rage reaction is frustration, followed by emotional arousal that detaches the angry driver from his or her usual cognitive control of appropriate behavior. In many instances, the road rager is already primed for aggressive or violent action due to an incident that happened before reaching the highway (Connell, 1996). A quarrel with a loved one, some difficulty on the job, problems making financial ends meet, or any number of previous events can contribute to the arousal factor. The stimulus that sets off the aggression, as Berkowitz might argue in his cognitive-neoassociation model, is the annoying behavior of another driver. The available weapon is the motor vehicle. Thus, the necessary components of a negative affect and the appropriate stimuli are in place for aggression to occur. Obviously not all drivers in these circumstances react with rage. In the following section we focus more on the factors that might distinguish one person's reactions from another's.

SOCIAL LEARNING FACTORS IN AGGRESSION AND VIOLENCE

Why do some people behave aggressively when intensely frustrated, while others change their tactics, withdraw, or seem not to be affected? One major factor may be past learning experiences. The human being, as we noted in chapter 4, is very adept at learning and maintaining behavior patterns that have worked in the past, even if they only worked occasionally. This learning process begins in early childhood. Children develop many behaviors merely by watching their parents and significant others in their environment, a process we have called modeling or observational learning. A child's behavior pattern, therefore, is often acquired through the modeling or imitation of other people, real and imagined, in the child's environment (Bandura, 1973a). In fact, available research reveals that the conditions most conducive to the learning of aggression are those in which the child (1) has many opportunities to observe aggression, (2) is reinforced for his or her own aggression, or (3) is often the object of aggression (Huesmann, 1988).

Suppose Harris's father returns home feeling harried after a hot and humid day during which he accomplished nothing (frustration). He finds an official-looking letter from the IRS in the mailbox. He opens it, perhaps muttering mild obscenities under his breath, and finds that the IRS apparently suspects he has shortchanged the U.S. government by several hundred dollars, although he knows he has not (more frustration). He is invited for an audit (even more frustration). In response, he slams his fist on the table, exclaims "Damn it!" or some colorful variation, and kicks the nearest chair (just enough not to damage his toe, since he has learned the painful consequences from past similar episodes). Unknown to father, Harris has observed this whole scenario. Several hours later, when his block tower crumbles, little Harris pounds his fist, kicks the living room chair, and curses, "Damn it!"

Modeling

When a child's imitative behavior is reinforced or rewarded by praise and encouragement from significant models, the probability that the behavior will occur in the future is increased. There is evidence that American parents (consciously or inadvertently) encourage or reinforce aggressive behavior in their children, particularly in their sons. For example, Harris's behavior might have been reinforced if Dad or Mom drew attention to it—"Isn't that cute?"—or if they laughed. In a future episode, the kicking behavior might be directed at the family cat. Furthermore, while kicking chairs and towers (or even the family cat, in the minds of some readers) may seem relatively mild, the same behavior becomes very sobering if the parent's anger is taken out on a family member, as too many Harrises in our society have observed. Others are "merely" expected or encouraged to be hard-hitting linebackers and to hold their own against neighborhood bullies, providing they are approximately the same size. They learn that the child who aggresses successfully against others is often rewarded by status, prestige, and the most attractive toys or material goods.

Types of Models

Bandura (1983) identifies three major types of models: family members, members of one's subculture, and symbolic models provided by the mass media. As we noted in chapter 2, family members, particularly parents, can be very powerful models up until early adolescence. Beginning in early adolescence, peer models are likely to dominate. Not surprisingly, the highest incidence of aggression is found in communities and groups in which aggressive models abound and fighting prowess is regarded as a valued attribute (Bandura, 1983; Short, 1968; Wolfgang & Ferracuti, 1967).

The mass media, including television, movies, magazines, newspapers, and books, provide abundant symbolic models. Video games and the Internet have vastly expanded this collection. Television pervades the life of the growing child, even the very young one, and offers hundreds of potentially powerful aggressive and violent models in a variety of formats, ranging from Saturday morning cartoon film festivals to triple-X-rated cable movies. The effects these models have on children is a highly debated issue, and one we cover later in this chapter.

Since parents are powerful models, we would expect aggressive or antisocial parents to have aggressive or antisocial children. In an old but classic study, Sears, Maccoby, and Levin (1957) interviewed four hundred mothers of kindergarten children about their disciplinary techniques, their attitudes about children's aggressiveness, and the children's expressions of aggression toward peers, siblings, and parents. One of the major findings was that physical punishment by parents was related to aggressiveness in the children. This was especially true when physical discipline was supplemented by high permissiveness toward aggression. In support of this finding, some researchers found that preschoolers played more aggressively when they were watched by a permissive adult than when no adult was visible (Siegel & Kohn, 1959).

Bandura (1973a) argues persuasively that aggressive behavior can be most productively understood and modified if we give attention to the learning principles like those alluded to earlier. As psychologists learn more about human behavior, many are beginning to agree with him.

Social learning theory hypothesizes that the rudiments of aggressive behavior are initially acquired through observing aggressive models or on the basis of direct experience; aggression is then gradually refined and maintained by reinforcement. Therefore, people may have an aggressive behavioral pattern, but may rarely express it if it has no functional value or is not condoned by significant others in their social environment. The social learning system acknowledges that biological structures can set limits on the types of aggressive responses that can be learned, and that genetic endowment influences the rate at which learning progresses (Bandura, 1973a). Biology does not program the individual to specific aggressive behavior, however. These behaviors are learned by observation, either deliberately or inadvertently; they become refined through reinforced practice.

Observation Modeling

In addition, mere exposure to aggressive models does not guarantee that the observer will try to engage in similar aggressive action at a later date. First, a variety of conditions may prevent observational learning from even taking place. Individuals differ widely in their ability to learn from observation. Some people may fail to notice the essential features of the model's behavior or may have a poor symbolic or visual memory. Alternately, they may not wish to imitate the model. Bandura suggests also that one important component of observational learning may be the motivation to rehearse what has been observed. He notes that a mass murderer, for example, may get an idea from descriptive accounts of another mass killing. The incident remains prominent in his mind long after it has been forgotten by others. He continues to think about the crime and to rehearse the brutal scenario mentally until, under appropriate conditions, it serves as a script for his own murderous actions.

Another restriction on observational learning is what happens to the observed model. If the model is reprimanded or punished either during or immediately after an aggressive episode, this will probably inhibit the observer's behavior. The "bad guy" should not get away with violence, if we are to discourage antisocial behavior via the entertainment media.

If aggressive behavior is to be maintained, it needs periodic reinforcement. According to social learning theory, aggression is maintained by instrumental learning. In the initial stage of learning, observation is important, but in the later stages, reinforcement is essential. The reinforcement may be positive, as when the individual gains material or social rewards, or it may be negative, if it allows the individual to alter or avoid aversive conditions. If aggressive behavior brings rewards in either of these ways, the person is likely to continue it. Research has consistently discovered that aggressive children anticipate more positive outcomes and fewer negative outcomes following their aggressive acts (Hubbard et al., 2001). "When compared with average peers, aggressive children are more likely to believe that aggression will produce tangible rewards, reduce aversive treatment by others, make themselves and peers feel good, increase self-esteem, and help to avoid a negative image" (Hubbard et al., 2001, p. 268).

A youngster subjected to unmerciful harassment or bullying because of his unusual name or where he lives may be able to stop the teasing with his fists. The reinforcement he gets from his newly found aggressive behavior is negative, but it is still rewarding. Aggression can also allow the individual to feel in control of a situation if things have not been going his or her way. A more extreme example is when a student who is constantly bullied by peers decides to put a stop to the aversive circumstances by using a firearm on all those he (or she) perceives as participants. The psychological reinforcement offered by feeling in control is an extremely powerful component in any human behavior, especially aggressive or violent behavior.

COGNITIVE MODELS OF AGGRESSION

Recent cognitive models for learning aggression have hypothesized that, while observational learning is important in the process, the individual's cognitive capacities and information processing strategies are equally important. Two major cognitive models have emerged in recent years. One that has been proposed by Rowell Huesmann (1997) is a hypothesis called the **cognitive scripts**

model. The other model has been developed by Kenneth Dodge and his colleagues (Dodge, 1986; Dodge & Coie, 1987), and is called the **hostile attribution model.**

Cognitive Scripts Model

According to Rowell Huesmann (1988), social behavior in general, and aggressive behavior in particular, are controlled largely by **cognitive scripts** learned and memorized through daily experiences. "A script suggests what events are to happen in the environment, how the person should behave in response to these events, and what the likely outcome of those behaviors would be" (Huesmann, 1988, p. 15). Scripts may be learned by direct experience or by observing significant others (Bushman & Anderson, 2001). Once learned, the script is usually followed. Each script is different and unique to each person, but once established they become resistant to change and may persist into adulthood. For a script to become established, it must be rehearsed from time to time. With practice the script will not only become encoded and maintained in memory, but also it will be more easily retrieved and utilized when the individual faces a problem. Furthermore, the individual's "evaluation of the 'appropriateness' of a script plays an important role in determining which scripts are stored in memory, in determining which scripts are retrieved and utilized, and which scripts continue to be utilized" (Huesmann, 1988, p. 19). The evaluation process includes the confidence that one has in predicting outcomes of the script, the extent to which an individual judges himself or herself capable of executing the script, and the extent to which the script is seen as congruent with the person's self-regulating internal standards. Scripts that are inconsistent or violate one's internalized standards are unlikely to be stored or utilized. An individual with poorly integrated internal standards against aggression, or who is convinced that aggressive behavior is a way of life, is more likely to incorporate aggressive scripts for behavior. Importantly, the aggressive child is apt to instigate aggressive reactions from others, confirming his or her beliefs about the aggressiveness of human nature in a circular, perpetuating fashion.

Hostile Attribution Bias

Kenneth Dodge and his colleagues discovered that highly aggressive youth often have a **hostile attribution bias.** That is, youth prone toward violence are more likely to interpret ambiguous actions as hostile and threatening than are their less aggressive counterparts (Dodge, 1993b). For example, a foot casually and innocently positioned near a school desk may be interpreted as a deliberate attempt to trip. As Dill, Anderson, Anderson, and Deuser (1997, p. 275) put it, people described as having hostile attribution bias "tend to view the world through blood-red tinted glasses." Children with a hostile attribution bias are twice as likely as average children to see aggressive actions from others where there is none (Hubbard et al., 2001). In addition, the bias is present in both boys and girls (Vitale, Newman, Serin, & Bolt, 2005).

Research consistently indicates that violent youth "typically define social problems in hostile ways, adopt hostile goals, and seek few additional facts, generate few alternative solutions, anticipate few consequences for aggression, and give higher priority to their aggressive solutions" (Eron & Slaby, 1994, p. 10). Similarly, Serin and Preston (2001, p. 259) conclude, "Aggressive juvenile offenders have been found to be deficient in social problem-solving skills and to espouse many beliefs supporting aggression. Specifically, they tend to define problems in hostile ways, adopt hostile goals, seek less confirmatory information, generate fewer alternative solutions, anticipate fewer consequences for aggressive solutions, and choose less effective solutions."

Research indicates that this hostile attribution bias begins to develop during the preschool years and seems to be a stable attribute that is still present into adulthood (Dodge et al., 2002; Nigg & Huang-Pollock, 2003). Dodge (1993b) reports that when children were followed from elementary school to middle school, a child's tendency to attribute hostile intentions to others showed a significant relationship between peer rejection during elementary school and increased aggression during middle school. Coie (2004) asserts, "The fact that rejected, aggressive males show persistently higher tendencies toward hostile attribution biases, as well as other social cognitive deficits related to aggression, fits with their pattern of higher involvement in violent delinquent acts in adolescence and their tendency to persist in violent behavior into the early adult years" (p. 255).

There is further research to suggest that some children are especially primed to develop hostile expectations of peers because of earlier exposure to family abuse and maltreatment (Dodge, Bates, & Pettit, 1990; Hubbard et al., 2001). Studies have revealed that children exposed to maltreatment early in their lives become "hypervigilant toward hostile social cues, perceptually ready to perceive hostility in others' intentions, and quick to generate aggressive retaliatory responses to even mild provocations" (Dodge, 2001, p. 65). In addition peer rejected children with hostile attribution bias are frequently targets of physical assault by others, prompting them to be more suspicious of the motives of others (Coie & Miller-Johnson, 2001). These children appear to be especially quick at developing hostile attribution biases against a wide range of peers, including new acquaintances. "These children come to have a generalized set of social cognitions that dispose them to draw hostile inferences from the behavior of new peer acquaintances more quickly than their peers do" (Hubbard et al., 2001, p. 277). Some other children, although prone to hostile attribution bias, tend to be specific in who they identify as hostile, probably due to certain behavioral patterns or interests they find threatening.

Ronald Blackburn (1998) also reports research evidence that suggests that persistent lawbreaking by adults represents attempts to master a social environment perceived as hostile and threatening. Blackburn hypothesizes that highly criminal offenders approach the world with a well-developed hostile-dominance interpersonal style. That is, rather than be simply a reflection of deficits in conscience or self-control, frequent criminal behavior may represent an ongoing attempt to control and dominate others in the social environment. According to Blackman, chronic criminality can be understood as "an attempt to maintain status or mastery of a social environment from which they feel alienated" (1998, p. 174). The well-rehearsed cognitive script of persistent, life-long offenders, therefore, is to dominate—often in a hostile manner—social environments they perceive as hostile.

Blackburn's observations have been recently supported by research by Vitale, Neumann, Serin, and Bolt (2005) who investigated the amount of hostile attribution in 150 incarcerated males. The researchers discovered that psychopaths were significantly more likely to exhibit hostile attribute bias than nonpsychopaths in a variety of situations. The study also supported the hypothesis that there may be different antisocial pathways associated with hostile attributions. That is, hostile attribution bias was also prevalent in those prisoners who held negative thoughts about themselves, other people, and the world in general.

Aggressive Behavior: Simple and Easy to Use

Aggression is a simple, direct way of solving immediate conflicts. If something is not going your way, approaching the social environment in a threatening, hostile manner is the most direct way (not necessarily the most effective in the long run) of confronting your tormentors. On the other hand, prosocial solutions and alternative nonaggressive scripts are less direct and more complex than aggressive solutions. In essence, they are more difficult to apply. Theoretically, the more cognitively "simple" individual would be more inclined to pursue simplistic and direct solutions to problems. In addition, because prosocial solutions are more complicated and more difficult to apply, they also require effective social skills. However, the development of effective social skills takes time, and those skills will have a spotty reinforcement history until perfected. Aggressive behavior, on the other hand, often receives immediate reinforcement for the aggressor, and therefore is more likely to be retained in one's arsenal of strategies for immediate solutions of conflictual situations.

After a 22-year longitudinal study, Eron and Huesmann (1984) concluded that diminished intellectual competence and poor social skills have an early effect in increasing the likelihood that a child will adopt characteristically more aggressive styles of behavior to conflict resolution. For example, research has repeatedly documented the fact that juveniles who are serious sexual offenders have significant deficits in social competence, such as inadequate social skills, poor peer relationships, and social isolation from peers (Righthand & Welch, 2001). Further, the evidence indicates that this aggressive style will persist across situations and time and become a preferred style throughout adulthood. But the relationship is not simply one-way, with limited intellectual competence and inadequate skills causing aggressive behavior. Rather it appears to be interactive. Aggressive behavior may interfere with positive social interactions with teachers and peers for intellectual and social advancement, perpetuating a chain of mutually influencing events: aggressive behavior influencing the social environment, and the social environment, in turn, influencing aggressive behavior.

Dolf Zillmann (1988) proposes a similar idea to the cognitive script theory, but, like Berkowitz, emphasizes the importance of physiological arousal and its interaction with cognitions. Zillmann agrees with Hebb (1955, p. 249) that arousal "is an energizer, but not a guide, an engine but not a steering gear." Cognition provides the steering and direction to the energizing effects of anger, fear, or frustration. A long-standing observation in the study of animal and human aggression is that when the organism recognizes or perceives a threat to its welfare and well-being, it can either fight or flee. Following this "recognition of endangerment," physiological arousal quickly sets in, preparing the organism for fight or flight. The "recognition of endangerment," Zillmann reminds us, can be immediate, and the response can be reflexlike. What happens then is also highly dependent on cognition, especially in humans. Very likely this is when cognitive scripts come in.

If the arousal is moderate, the individual with skills and well-integrated standards of prosocial values will probably pursue nonaggressive scripts, even though the person may have been angry or threatened at first. However, very *high* levels of arousal interfere with the complex cognitive processes that mediate our consideration of our internal codes of conduct, as well as our ability to assess the intentions of others and the mitigating circumstances around the incident (Zillmann, 1988). Think of a very stressful or frightening situation that has happened to you, and how difficult it was to think clearly. Or think of a time when you became extremely angry and said or did things you wish you hadn't. At high levels of arousal, our cognitions seem to become narrower and more restricted, almost incapacitated at times. Generally under these high states of arousal, we resort to strongly established habits to guide and dominate our behavior. In essence we become "impulsive" and largely unthinking, and cognitions that mediate the diminution of hostile or even violent actions are substantially reduced. However, *if we have practiced or rehearsed nonviolent or nonaggressive behaviors as solutions*, these cognitive scripts are likely to be the habits we resort to under high stress, fear, and high arousal.

OVERT AND COVERT ACTS OF AGGRESSION

Rolf Loeber and Magda Stouthamer-Loeber (1998) recommend that researchers on aggression and violence be mindful of two types of aggressive actions: overt and covert. According to Loeber and Stouthamer-Loeber, the two forms of aggression are different in (1) behavior patterns, (2) emotions, (3) cognitions, and (4) development. Behaviorally, overt aggression usually involves direct confrontation with victims and the administration of physical harm or threats of physical harm. Covert aggression, on the other hand, does not involve direct confrontation but relies on concealment, dishonesty, or sneaky behavior. It is similar to the passive-aggressive behavior discussed earlier in the chapter. In many instances, overt aggression decreases with age, while covert aggression increases with age (Loeber, Lahey, & Thomas, 1991; Stanger, Achenbach, & Verhulst, 1997). However, children who exhibit serious forms of overt aggression (violence) tend to increase their violence as they get older, and often commit both violent and property crimes as adults (Loeber & Stouthamer-Loeber, 1998).

Emotionally, anger is usually an important ingredient in most overt acts of aggression, while more neutral emotions are characteristic of covert actions. Violent actions are usually accompanied by high levels of arousal brought on by anger. Covert actions, on the other hand, tend to be less emotional in nature, such as fraud, theft, embezzlement, burglary, and other white collar or property offenses. (See Table 5–2 on page 164.)

Covert and overt aggression can also be distinguished on the basis of the cognitions that accompany them. As we explained in this chapter, violent persons (covert aggression) tend to have cognitive deficiencies that make it difficult for them to come up with nonaggressive solutions to interpersonal conflicts and disputes. Covert aggressors also have hostile attributional biases that contribute to violence-prone cognitive processing. On the other hand, people who use covert aggression as a preferred strategy do not demonstrate the degree of cognitive deficiencies in solving their interpersonal problems, nor do they manifest a hostile attributional bias. "Instead, it is postulated that most covert acts are facilitated by specific cognitive capabilities, such as planfulness (i.e., casing situations prior to theft), preoccupations with consumables and property, and lying to escape detection" (Loeber & Stouthamer-Loeber, 1998, p. 250). Occupationally related crimes, for instance, such as theft of company property, the misuse of information, or software piracy, are often committed with planning and forethought. Crime committed through the use of computers, called **cybercrime,** is also a good example of covert actions of aggression, and is discussed more fully in chapter 15.

Developmentally, overt aggression generally begins early, especially in boys, as seen, for example, in the case of life-course-persistent offenders. However, Loeber and Stouthamer-Loeber suggest that development of overt aggressive behavior does not necessarily parallel the development of covert actions. Instead, "some children have never been socialized by their parents to be honest and to respect the property of others. This is common among neglectful parents or parents who hold an indistinct or a weak moral stance in these respects" (1998, p. 251). The formation of honesty and respect for the property of others is instilled by parents' teaching and the prosocial models they offer their children. Some covert actions, especially lying, can also evolve as a well-learned strategy that serves to minimize the chances of detection and punishment by adults.

It should be emphasized that not all overt aggressors who engage in violence start early. As Loeber and Stouthamer-Loeber note, "It is necessary to account for the emergence of violence in individuals during adulthood who do not have a history of aggression earlier in their lives" (1998, p. 246). These *late-onset types* represent a minority of adult violent offenders, but the hypothesis does

TABLE 5–2   Overt and Covert Aggressive Actions

AGGRESSION	BEHAVIOR PATTERNS	EMOTIONS	COGNITIONS	DEVELOPMENT
Overt	Direct confrontation with victims; generally decreases with age	Anger, high level of arousal and violence	Lacks social for coming up with nonaggressive solutions	Aggression begins early, especially in boys
Covert	Concealment, dishonesty, sneaky behavior, increases with age	Less emotion; crimes such as fraud, larceny, and theft	Relies on cognitive capabilities, such as planfulness, deceitfulness	Can evolve as well-learned strategy to escape punishment

suggest that not all highly aggressive and violent individuals manifested aggression in childhood.

Reactive and Proactive Forms of Aggression

Kenneth Dodge and his colleagues (Dodge et al., 1997) have suggested that another way of classifying aggression in children (and adults) is to make a distinction between reactive aggression and proactive aggression. **Reactive aggression** includes anger expressions, temper tantrums, and vengeful hostility, and more generally "hot-blooded" aggressive acts. **Proactive aggression,** on the other hand, includes bullying, domination, teasing, name-calling, and coercive acts—in other words, more "cold-blooded" aggressive actions. Reactive aggression appears to be a reaction to frustration and is associated with a lack of control due to high states of arousal. In general, reactive aggressive is a hostile act displayed in response to a perceived threat or provocation. Proactive aggression, by contrast, is less emotional, and more driven by expectations of rewards. "Proactive aggression is unprovoked, deliberate, goal-directed behavior used to influence or coerce a peer" (Hubbard et al., 2001, p. 269). Reactive aggression has its theoretical roots in the frustration-aggression model proposed by Berkowitz (1989) discussed earlier. The theoretical roots of proactive aggression are found in social learning theory which, as we learned previously, states that aggression is acquired behavior that is controlled and maintained by reinforcement. It is highly similar to the concept of instrumental aggression. Reliable observations of these two forms of aggression have been found in children (as young as 3 to 6 years of age) through teacher ratings, peer ratings, clinical psychiatric records, and direct observations of peer interactions by researchers (Dodge & Coie, 1987; Dodge et al., 1997; Poulin & Boivin, 2000).

Reactively aggressive children, compared with proactively aggressive children, display greater problems in social and psychological adjustment (Dodge et al., 1997). Psychological adjustment problems include a lack of emotional control when angry accompanied by sleep disorders, depressive symptoms, and personality disorders. On average, these problems emerged around age 4 to 5. In addition reactive aggression is related to the tendency to overattribute hostile intent to peers in ambiguous provocation situations (hostile attribution bias) (Hubbard et al., 2001). That is, when a reactive aggressive child interprets a peer's behavior as intentionally harmful or aggressive, he is far more likely to respond with angry retaliation or even violence.

Dodge (1991) proposed that reactive and proactive aggression originate from different social experiences and develop independently. According to Dodge, reactive aggression develops in reaction to a harsh, threatening and unpredictable environment or abusive or cold parenting (Vitaro, Brendgen, & Barker, 2006). Proactive aggression, on the other hand, develops as a result of exposure to aggressive role models who value the use of aggression to resolve conflict or advance personal interests (Vitaro et al., 2006). However, Vitaro et al. are quick to point out that proactive and reactive aggression may not only be fostered by different social environments but may also be influenced by differences in temperamental and genetic factors. That is, reactive aggression appears to be associated with a temperamental disposition toward anxiety, angry reactivity, emotional impulsiveness, and inattention. Proactive aggression appears to be less affected by temperament and is more based on beliefs that aggressive behavior will bring rewards and positive outcomes. Furthermore, preliminary research results suggest that reactive aggression develops earlier in the lifespan than proactive aggression, and the two types of aggression seem to follow different developmental trajectories (Vitaro & Brendgen, 2005).

Gender Differences in Aggression

While boys engage in more overt aggression and direct confrontation as they grow up, it is not clear if boys are generally more aggressive than girls. It is clear that *physical* aggression is more prevalent among males than females and that this consistent finding holds across hundreds of studies and across nations (Archer, 2004; Campbell, 2006), but what about other forms of aggression?

The current work of cognitive psychologists suggests that there may be socialized differences in the way girls and boys construct their worlds. Social learning theorists have long held that girls are "socialized" differently than boys, or taught not to be overtly aggressive. Anne Campbell (1993, p. 19) argues that "boys are not simply more aggressive than girls; they are aggressive in a different way." Other researchers concur with this observation (Hawkins, Pepler, & Craig, 2001; Lumley, McNeil, Herschell, & Bahl, 2002, Wood, Cowan, & Baker, 2002). According to Campbell, boys and girls are born with the potential to be equally aggressive, but girls are socialized not to be overtly aggressive, whereas boys are encouraged to be overtly aggressive "to defend" themselves.

Research supports the observation that boys and girls are equally physically aggressive toward their peers when they are toddlers, but that this pattern soon changes as they get older and enter their elementary school years (Xie, Farmer, & Cairns, 2003). Loeber and Stouthamer-Loeber (1998, p. 253) conclude from their review of the research that "in general, gender differences in aggression, as expressed by frustration and rage, are not documented in infancy." They note that only in the preschool period (3 to 5 years of age) do observable gender differences begin to emerge, with boys displaying more overt aggression than girls. Overt aggression becomes especially prominent in boys from elementary school age onward. Boys are taught to be tough, not to cry, to take on the bullies and physically defend themselves. However, many researchers report that girls are more likely to engage in relationship or interpersonal forms of aggression rather than the physical forms of pushing and hitting (Casey-Cannon, Hayward, & Gowen, 2001; Crick & Zahn-Waxler, 2003; Prinstein, Boergers, & Vernberg, 2001). For example, researchers (Björkqvist, Lagerspetz, & Kaukianinen, 1992; Cairns et al., 1989) find that girls and women tend to use more covert, indirect, and verbal forms of aggression, such as character defamation and ostracism. Other researchers report that girls are far more likely to employ *relational aggression*, such as abandoning one friend in favor of another, spreading malicious gossip, or ridiculing another's physical traits (e.g., their attractiveness, weight, or general demeanor) (Crick, 1995; Crick & Grotpeter, 1995; Crick & Zahn-Waxler, 2003; Garside & Klimes-Dougan, 2002; Loeber & Stouthamer-Loeber, 1998).

In conclusion, there is growing recognition that gender differences in aggression are not simply due to biology, but are primarily due to cultural and socialization processes that promote different kinds of aggression. Environmental cues are also important in cognitive scripts and in the aggressive strategies individuals employ for various situations. Which script or strategy an individual employs is dependent on which environmental cues are present.

ENVIRONMENTAL FACTORS

Population Density

Closely related to the ethological point of view (discussed earlier in the chapter) is one that sees aggression as a result of population density or overcrowded conditions. In areas of high population concentration, personal space is constantly violated. In urban areas, crowded mass transit systems and apartment complexes teeming with people infringe on personal space and territory. Might this overcrowding be a principal factor in crimes of violence and perhaps in personal property offenses?

Over 40 years ago, John B. Calhoun (1961, 1962) conducted a series of provocative studies using domestic rats, and suggested analogies between the rats and humans. He first allowed groups of rats to propagate freely in a limited physical space with adequate quantities of rat chow and water. Eventually, the rat colonies became overpopulated to such an extent that the rodents demonstrated abnormal behaviors.

Normally, male rats find one or more mates, build a nest, and, together with their mates, produce and raise offspring. Although they roam freely, they rarely show interest in another nest. In Calhoun's crowded conditions, however, the males either no longer cared about building a nest or could not defend it from bands of marauding male rats. The marauders entered the nests, attacked the females, and tore up the surroundings. Females were so harassed by these marauders that they lost interest in caring for the young. The marauding rats were those who could not build nests of their own because of lack of space. They developed a lifestyle that revolved around attacking other males and females, physically and sexually.

Calhoun also discovered a group of "juvenile delinquents"—male and female rats without nests who were usually too weak to defend or find a mate. These young rats would gather in large clusters and spend their days milling around the floor of the cage, sometimes fighting, sometimes sleeping, sometimes harassing other rats in the vicinity. Rather quickly the rat society deteriorated, and the population declined. Calhoun's studies have been replicated by other researchers using other animals, with generally similar results.

Can we analogize from rats to humans? Obviously we must do so only very cautiously. The research concerning the effects of crowding on human behavior is far from clear-cut, and at present there is no evidence of a relationship between overcrowding and *crime* among humans. However, some work suggests a link between overcrowding and *aggression*.

Some investigators have exposed people to crowded conditions combined with various room temperatures (Griffith & Veitch, 1971). In general, as population density and temperature increased so did subjects' negative feelings toward one another. Other investigations (Freedman, Levy, Buchanan, & Price, 1972) found gender differences in response to overcrowding. Males in same-gender, overcrowded groups were more aggressive and hostile than males in same gender, uncrowded groups. The reverse was true for females. In mixed groups, the gender differences did not occur. This evidence could suggest that men are uncomfortable and hostile in crowded same-gender conditions, while women tend to become more affable and friendly. However, the data also lend themselves to other interpretations. Mueller (1983), for instance, finds that the Freedman data indicate that men in the low-density condition were actually less competitive and aggressive, and only slightly more punitive than women. The issue of gender differences in aggressive behavior as a function of crowding or density is far from resolved.

Freedman (1975) conducted a number of correlational studies in various geographic areas throughout the United States and found no relationship between population density and crimes of violence like murder, rape, and aggravated assault. When populations were matched for socioeconomic class and other relevant variables, crimes of violence actually decreased in proportion to the population as density increased. Freedman attributed this finding to the large number of potential witnesses in high-density areas.

Population density studies, therefore, do not clearly support a relationship between overcrowding and aggression (Harries, 1980; Kirmeyer, 1978; Mueller, 1983). While density may play a significant role in engendering aggressive behavior in animals, in the human population the situation is far more complicated. Overall the available evidence at this point does not support the view that a city's or a neighborhood's density has a significant influence on crime.

Aggression and Ambient Temperature

The idea that hot temperatures promote aggression and violence has been around for centuries. Even the classic works of the theater, such as Shakespeare's *Romeo and Juliet* and *The Merchant of Venice,* allude to the relationship (Anderson, 1989). Anderson notes that our language is replete with imagery that illustrates this linkage, such as "tempers flare," "hot under the collar," "hot headed," "hot temper," "heated debate," and we do a "slow burn" when angered. Today we wonder about the long-term effect of global warming on world violence. In addition the temperature-aggression relationship appears to exist across a variety of settings. Even on the baseball field, heat and hostility seem to go together. For example, in major league baseball, significantly more batters are hit by a pitch when the temperature reaches 89 degrees Fahrenheit and above (Reifman, Larrick, & Fein, 1991).

The nature of the temperature-aggression relationship is unclear and the subject of considerable scholarly debate. As temperature increases, violence increases. Or does it? This heat-of-the-night assumption was proposed as a partial explanation for riots and civil disturbances during the late 1960s and early 1970s (Baron, 1977). Later, research spearheaded by Robert Baron (Baron & Bell, 1975; Baron & Lawton, 1972; Baron & Ransberger, 1978; Bell & Baron, 1977) found empirical support for a relationship between ambient temperature and aggression. The relationship seems highly complex, however. According to Baron (1972), extremely low and high temperatures tend to inhibit aggression, while intermediate levels tend to be associated with it. Baron suggests that when the temperature becomes very unpleasant (too hot or too cold), the person's major concern is to do something self-protective, such as getting a cold drink or donning thermal clothing. In other words the individual is attempting, as Berkowitz (1989) suggests, to escape aversive circumstances (negative reinforcement). Slightly lower levels of discomfort tend to enhance the likelihood of aggression in some people, however. Picture yourself on an uncomfortably hot, but not excessively humid, summer day in a large, crowded city. Baron would maintain that your discomfort, compounded by unpleasant odors and other environmental variables, may induce irritability; in potential aggressors, it may produce hostility.

Baron's proposal suggests that collective or individual violence may be prominent at uncomfortable intermediate temperatures, rather than at extremely hot or bitterly cold ones. In an attempt to test this hypothesis, Cohn and Rotton (1997) plotted the relationship between ambient temperature and assault and discovered an inverted U-shaped curve, with assaults peaking at around 75 degrees Fahrenheit. Their data were based on the assault rate received by the Minneapolis Police Department in 1987 and 1988 and the outside temperature at the time of the assault. However, Bushman, Wang, and Anderson (2005a, 2005b), in their reanalysis of the Cohn-Rotton data, concluded that the U-shaped curve reportedly found may be misleading because it fails to take into account the time of the day. Essentially, Bushman, Wang, and Anderson argue that both the time of the day and assaults are strongly associated with temperature, but in the opposite directions. "Assaults are highest in the late evening and early morning hours when temperatures are coolest, whereas temperatures are highest in the afternoon hours" (2005b, p. 74). Consequently, since data across the globe indicate that assaults and violence most likely occur during the evenings and very early morning hours when the temperatures are low (compared with the daytime hours), aggression and assault rates would be expected to be low at high temperatures and high at lower temperatures. Therefore, the observed relationship would also be a function of time of day rather than simply recorded temperature levels. In this sense, many of the time-of-day effect on assaults is likely due to the different types of activities and places in which people typically engage at different times of the day. Bushman, Wang, and Anderson (2005a) do not discount the inverted U-shape hypotheses predicting that aggression and violent crime might decrease when temperatures are very hot, but they believe that the Minneapolis data do not provide a sufficient test of this hypothesis.

Earlier research by Anderson and Anderson (1984) failed to yield the predicted curvilinear (inverted U-shaped) relationship. They found that the number of daily violent crimes increased directly as a function of temperature in two different cities. As temperature increased, violent crime increased in a *linear* (straight-line) fashion. Further study (Anderson, 1987; Anderson, Bushman, & Groom, 1997) discovered that overall violent crime in the United States was more prevalent in the hotter summer months, as well as in the hotter years. The study also revealed that hotter cities have higher violent crime rates than the cooler cities. These relationships also exhibited a linear function rather than a curvilinear one. (See **Figure 5–1** on page 170.) At this point the jury is still out on whether the temperature-aggression relationship is best illustrated as an inverted U-shape or a straight line, although the weight of the current evidence is slightly favoring the former.

There are several other environmental or situational factors that might be associated with hot weather, such as air pollution, humidity, and offensive odors. With reference to air pollution, for example, some studies indicate that individuals exposed to cigarette smoke are more aggressive than individuals in clean-air conditions (Jones & Bogat, 1978). Some people are even more aggressive when someone is simply smoking (inappropriately) around them (Zillmann, Baron, & Tamborini, 1981), even if the air is not heavily infiltrated with smoke. Other investigators (e.g., Rotton, 1983) report that malodorous pollution also encourages hostile aggressive behavior. There is also some evidence to suggest that loud, unpredictable, or complex noises may influence aggressive tendencies. For example, Konečni (1975) found that angry subjects exposed to loud or complex noise became more aggressive than angry subjects exposed to soft and simple noise. Apparently, the additional arousal instigated by the noise adds to the arousal effects of anger already felt by the subject. This increase in arousal level presumably facilitates aggressive behavior.

Some investigators have found that a combination of high temperature and air pollution is highly related to family disturbance and violent behavior (Rotton & Frey, 1985). Kenrick and MacFarland (1986) also found a strong linear

FIGURE 5–1   Hypothesized Curvilinear Relationship between Aggression and Temperature

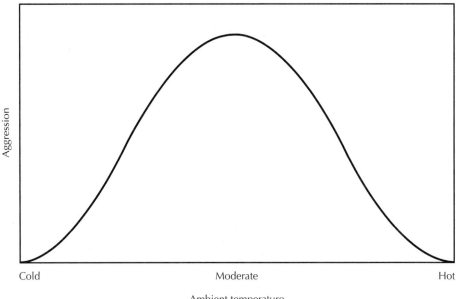

relationship between horn honking and ambient temperature, at least up to 106 degrees Fahrenheit. The researchers designed a field study in which a car (a 1980 Datsun 200SX) was purposely stalled during a green light at an intersection in the metropolitan Phoenix area. Phoenix, of course, is a city where daily temperatures in excess of 90 degrees are quite common. Results indicated that horn honking was directly linked to the temperature-humidity index. That is, the frequency of horn honking increased as temperature increased (especially when the humidity was also high). The relationship was particularly strong for those honkers who had their windows down (presumably they did not have an air conditioner on or did not have one). In addition to frequency of horn honking, the amount of time spent leaning on the horn also increased as a function of the temperature-humidity index, often accompanied by verbal and nonverbal signals of hostility. The researchers also observed that the highest levels of horn honking were from young male drivers.

Available data also indicate that hotter regions of the world yield more violence, such as murder, rape, assaults, riots, and spouse abuse. In reviewing the research literature on the relationship between violence and temperature in various contexts, Anderson (1989) concludes that there is little doubt of a strong connection between high temperature and violent crime. Simon Field (1992, p. 340) writes the following:

> Apart from the criminological universals of age and gender, it would be difficult to find any other factor which is so consistently correlated with violent crime. Under the circumstances the issue receives little attention in the main-

stream criminological literature. This is perhaps because the idea that high temperatures induce criminal behaviour is redolent of an outdated environmental determinism, and therefore sits very uneasily with modern sociological theory. Whatever the reasons, the evidence is so compelling that the issue must be addressed.

However, though the relationship seems to be a strong one, it, as we mentioned previously, is also likely to be a very complex one. For example, people may be more inclined to drink alcoholic beverages during high temperatures. Therefore, alcohol may be playing a very critical role in the incidence of violence rather than strictly the ambient temperature itself. Field (1992) also suggests that the violence-temperature connection may be due to the increased availability of victims who try to beat the heat by getting outside their homes and doing things besides their usual daily activities—such as going to amusement parks.

Field (1992) extended the hypothesis of the violence-temperature relationship by examining the crime-temperature relationship, including property crime (burglary, theft, robbery, and criminal damage). Although robbery is usually considered a violent crime—because it involves force or the threat of force—it may justifiably also be considered less violent than murder, rape, or assault. In his study, Field looked at temperature and crime statistics in England and Wales over a 40-year period, with particular emphasis on the very complete monthly data between 1977 and 1987. In addition to temperature, he included rainfall and sunshine in his analysis, since rain is often believed to be the police officer's friend by keeping potential victims and offenders off the street. The results showed a consistent and strong statistical relationship between temperature and crime of most types, but no relationship between crime and rainfall or sunshine. Specifically, high temperatures corresponded to high crime rates, regardless of the type of crime. Field (1992, p. 347) concludes, "These findings represent compelling evidence that prevailing temperatures affect the level of most types of crimes in England and Wales." Furthermore, Field contends, "The findings cannot generally be explained by the hypothesis that temperature causes aggression, for this would not explain the findings concerning property crime" (p. 348). Therefore, the linear hypothesis propounded by Anderson and others—inasmuch as it is limited to violent crime—is inadequate to explain the findings, suggesting a far more complex relationship than originally supposed. Perhaps temperature affects violence directly, and affects other types of crime indirectly by influencing social behavior. That is, temperature affects property crime by influencing routine activities. In hot weather, for example, the family may be more inclined to go to the beach, leaving their home more susceptible to burglary and themselves more vulnerable to robbery and theft.

EFFECTS OF MEDIA VIOLENCE

American youth are growing up in a media-saturated environment (Gentile and Walsh, 2002). Surveys estimate that the average American youth between the ages 2 and 18 spends nearly 6 hours per day with electronic media (e.g., television, music, computers, movies, and video games) and 44 minutes per day with print media (Gentile & Walsh, 2002). Although television still dominates the electronic media (averaging around 25 hours per week), video games are becoming increasingly popular.

Violence is a common theme in the movie, TV, and video game media. Some surveys estimate that the average American child sees more than 100,000 violent episodes and some 20,000 murders on television before reaching adolescence (Myers, 1996). Other studies estimate there are four scenes of violence portrayed on network television to every one scene expressing affection. A three-year study (1994–1997) by four universities on violence on American television revealed that 90 percent of movies shown on television include violence (National Cable Television Association, 1998). Violence was found most frequently on subscription television (85% on premium cable and 59% on basic cable), while the lowest incidence of violence (18%) was found on Public Broadcasting stations (PBS). Across three years of the study, nearly 40 percent of the violent incidents on television were initiated by "good" characters who are likely perceived as attractive role models. In 67 percent of the programs, violence was portrayed within a humorous context. In general, the study found that most media violence is glamorized and that the long-term negative consequences of violent behavior are rarely depicted. Nearly three-quarters of violent scenes contain no remorse, criticism, punishment, or emotional reactions from the perpetrators. Overall the survey found that the percentage of programs on television that contain some violence remained unchanged over the three-year period of study.

It is clear that video games have become one of the favorite activities of youth in America. The average American child between the ages of 2 and 17 plays video games for over 7 hours per week (Gentile & Walsh, 2002). In addition, there are age and gender differences in video playing time. Adolescent girls play video games for an average of 5 hours per week, whereas boys average 13 hours a week (Gentile, Lynch, Linder, & Walsh, 2004). The most popular game category is fantasy violence and other human violence games (Anderson & Dill, 2000; Funk & Buchman, 1996). Dietz (1998) examined 33 popular Sega and Nintendo games and discovered that nearly 80 percent of the games were violent in nature. Dietz also found that 21 percent of the violent games depicted violence toward women.

To date the overwhelming bulk of the research reveals that portrayals of television, movie, and video games violence have a significant effect on the frequency and type of aggressive and violent behavior expressed. Over the past 45 years, research has consistently demonstrated that media violence viewing is one of the strongest factors contributing to the development of aggression and violence in children, adolescents, and adults (Huesmann, Moise-Titus, Podolski, & Eron, 2003). Moreover, media violence appears to influence children more strongly than adults, as they seem to be more susceptible to its long-term effects. Interestingly, the Huesmann et al. (2003) study discovered that violent films and TV programs that have the most deleterious effects on children are not always the ones that adults perceive as the most violent. Research suggests that violent scenes in which children can identify with the perpetrator of the violence, and those in which the perpetrator gets rewarded for the violence have the greatest impact on children. It is not necessarily the level of violence per se.

Lately the effects of violent video or electronic games on the development of aggressive behavior have received considerable scrutiny. The influence of violent video games on youth violence became a serious topic for study after a series of school shootings by avid players of such games occurred during the late 1990s and early 2000. In April 1999, public concern was especially strong after 13 persons were murdered and 23 were wounded during a shooting spree by two students at Columbine (Colorado) High School. The two assailants were considered social outcasts and seemed preoccupied with the violence presented in the media, music, and video games. Reports indicated that the two were especially fascinated by the bloody video game *Doom,* one of the earliest and most successful of all electronic games.

The impact of violent electronic games is not restricted to the U.S. It occurs in other countries also (Anderson, 2004). For example, Krahé and Möller (2004) describe an incident that occurred in Germany in April 2002, in which 17 people were killed in a shooting spree by an expelled student who had spent much of his time playing violent electronic games.

Similar to violent film and TV programs, recent research consistently has demonstrated that heavy exposure to violent video games is significantly linked to increases in aggressive behavior, aggressive thoughts, aggressive feelings, and decreases in helping behavior (Anderson 2004; Anderson & Bushman, 2001; Dill & Dill, 1998). Before proceeding it is important to distinguish between short-term and long-term effects of violent media on aggressive behavior. Long-term effects occur as a result of learning and storing violent and aggressive material into the thought process. Young children are especially open to new learning, and these early experiences often have a greater impact during the early development years than learning events that occur during adulthood. To this effect, Huesmann, Moise-Titus, Podolski, and Eron (2003) write, "In recent theorizing, long-term relations have been ascribed mainly to acquisition through observation learning of three social-cognitive structures: schemas about a hostile world, scripts for social problem solving that focus on aggression, and normative beliefs that aggression is acceptable" (p. 201). Over time and with frequent exposure to aggressive behavior, children develop beliefs (schemas) that the world is basically a hostile place, that aggression is an acceptable social behavior, and that the best way to solve conflicts and to get things is to be aggressive. These aspects may actually become part of the personality over the long run. Research by Krahé and Möller (2004) supports these hypotheses. They found that adolescents were more likely to endorse beliefs condoning aggression and developed a tendency toward hostile attribution biases of ambiguous cues as a function of exposure to violent electronic games. Another study (i.e., Funk, Baldacci, Pasold, & Baumgardner, 2004) has demonstrated that high exposure to violent electronic games is associated with lower levels of empathy and more positive attitudes toward violent behavior in general. This study also indicated that violent video games may have greater impact than other forms of violent entertainment media.

Huesmann and his colleagues (2003) report strong long-term effects of media violence observed in early childhood that carries over into adulthood. They conclude:

> Overall, these results suggest that both males and females from all social strata and all levels of initial aggressiveness are placed at increased risk for the development of adult aggressive and violent behavior when they view a high and steady diet of violent TV shows in early childhood. (p. 128)

Furthermore, aggressive children tend to enjoy and continually seek out aggressive behavior. Huesmann et al. (2003) contend that aggressive children feel happier and more justified in their aggressive behavior if they believe they are not alone in their aggression.

Contagion Effect

Even news reports of violence may have a **contagion effect** or **copycat effect,** a tendency in some people to model or copy an activity portrayed in the entertainment or news media. Contagion effect is said to occur when action depicted in the media is assessed by certain individuals as a good idea and then mimicked. An ingenious bank robbery, dramatized on television, might be imitated. The contagion effect is not simply restricted to media portrayals, however. For example, a study by Joiner (1994) illustrates how depression in a college classmate may be contagious. A classmate who is depressed can lower the mood of friends, family, and others who associate with the depressed person and try to help.

A tragic illustration of the copycat effect can be found in a series of school shootings, discussed briefly above, that began in 1997. In October of that year, a 16-year-old, having just stabbed his mother to death, arrived at the high school in Pearl, Mississippi, and began randomly shooting his classmates, killing two and wounding seven. Less than two months later, a 14-year-old boy opened fire on a group of fellow high school students participating in a prayer circle in West Paducah, Kentucky. He killed two schoolmates and wounded five others. The West Paducah incident received worldwide media coverage for several weeks, accompanied by extensive stories about the shooter. A few months later, on March 24, 1998, two boys, ages 13 and 11, armed with seven handguns and three rifles, opened fire on their classmates as they gathered on the school playground in Jonesboro, Arkansas, killing four very young girls and their teacher and wounding 10 others. Of the 15 killed or wounded, only one was male, indicating that the young shooters were aiming specifically at girls.

After Jonesboro and exactly one month later, came Edinboro, Pennsylvania, where a 14-year-old male student began shooting during a school dance, killing a teacher. This incident was followed by another shooting less than a month later in Fayetteville, Tennessee, resulting in the death of a student. A week later, a 15-year-old male in Springfield, Oregon, walked into the high school cafeteria and began randomly shooting at fellow students, firing 50 rounds from a .22-caliber semiautomatic rifle in less than a minute. As he stopped to reload, the young shooter was tackled and disarmed by a varsity wrestler. During that one minute, however, he managed to kill two classmates and wounded 22 others. He had also shot both his parents prior to leaving for school. Less than two weeks later, on June 15, 1998, a 14-year-old student, armed with a .32-caliber semi-automatic handgun, opened fire in the hallway of a high school as students took final exams, wounding a basketball coach and a volunteer aide. All of these young shooters had an inordinate interest in guns, had troubled backgrounds, knew the details of the previous school shootings, and had a strong fascination with violence presented through the media. And as mentioned earlier, on April 20, 1999, two teenagers, Eric Harris and Dylan Klebold, in Littleton, Colorado, entered Columbine High School and killed 13 people and injured dozens of others before taking their own lives. Exposure to media-portrayed violence does not, of course, automatically promote aggression. Some individuals are affected more than others. Children from low-income families are apparently more influenced by media violence than middle-class children (Eisenhower, 1969); it is not clear whether this reflects exposure to the violence itself or other factors as well. It is clear that no one causal factor alone accounts for more than a small proportion of variance of individual differences in aggressive behavior (Bartholow, Sestir, & Davis, 2005; Huesmann, 1998). Researchers have found evidence that positive parental models are likely to override violent models on television (Goldstein, 1975; Huesmann et al., 2003). Moreover television violence seems to have substantially less effect on families in which the parents do not rely on aggressive behavior for solving problems (Wright et al., 2001).

In summary, hundreds of research articles conclude that *heavy* exposure to violent media is one of the most significant causes of violence in American society (American Psychological Association, 2003a). The evidence is especially strong on the effects of violent electronic games where the participant learns aggressive schema and practices new aggression-related cognitive scripts that become more and more accessible for use when real-life conflict situations arise (Anderson & Dill, 2000).

THE BIOLOGY OF AGGRESSION

There is growing consensus in popular culture that, by understanding genes and the biological determinants of behavior, it is possible to understand all of life, including human nature and aggression (Lickliter & Honeycutt, 2003). Much of the scientific community that deals with human behavior is not so convinced. Considerable evidence does exist for a strong relationship between aggression and biological and genetic factors in nonhuman animals, and it has been known for some time that animals of many species can be bred for aggressiveness. The evidence for the relationship between genetics or biology and aggression *in humans* is far less compelling, however. Part of the problem in disentangling the relationship is that human behavior is strongly influenced by thoughts, values, schemas, and scripts acquired from the social environment, beginning at a very early age.

As we learned in chapters 2 and 3, research in developmental psychology, for example, has continually shown that human development and behavior is a result of a constant and complex interplay between biology and experience. This conclusion is hardly new or unique. The question is not so much whether biology and genes *cause* behavior or whether there is an *interaction* between the environment and biology. Rather, the question is, Do genes and other biological influences *predispose* some individuals to engage in aggressive behavior? Let's look at the evidence.

A common finding is that many if not most children exhibit high levels of physical aggression in preschool or kindergarten, but in most cases they typically show significant reductions of these behaviors during the early school years due to the effects of socialization and parenting (Bongers et al., 2003; Séguin, et al., 2004). Another common finding, however, is that certain brain and biochemical abnormalities appear to *predispose* some children to exhibit higher levels of aggression than exhibited by their peers, and if these abnormalities are not neutralized by socialization and competent parenting, many of these children grow up to follow a life path characterized by high levels of aggression and violence. Youngsters who follow an early onset of persistent antisocial behavior often exhibit biological/neurological abnormalities, while late onset offending appears to be more influenced by social factors (Moffitt, Lynam, & Silva, 1994; Rutter, 1997; Rutter, Giller, & Hagell, 1998).

Hormones and Neurotransmitters

Neurotransmitters are chemicals, manufactured in the brain, that are intimately involved in biochemical activity and transmission of messages in the nervous system. Recent research suggests that the neurotransmitter **serotonin** may play the most significant role in aggression and violence (Coscina, 1997; Lesch & Merschdorf, 2000; Loeber & Stouthamer-Loeber, 1998; Moffitt et al., 1997). Specifically, many individuals who act aggressively toward others or commit violent suicide may have abnormally low levels of serotonin (Bear, Connors, & Paradiso, 1996; de Boer & Koolhaas, 2005; Rosenzweig, Leiman, & Breedlove, 1999; Stanley et al., 2000). There is also some evidence that levels of serotonin may explain to some extent the differences in physical aggression between men and women (Verona et al., 2006).

Much of the research on the relationship between serotonin and aggression has focused on animals rather than humans. In one study, for example, the serotonin concentrations of aggressive rhesus monkeys was lower than normally found in the species (Higley et al., 1992), and in another study, tame silver foxes and laboratory rats appeared to have higher levels of serotonin than their wild, more aggressive counterparts (Pihl & Peterson, 1993; Popova, Voitenko, Kulikov, & Augustinovich, 1991).

In humans, Pihl and Peterson (1993, p. 114) assert, "Reduced brain serotonin function is associated with heightened vulnerability to depression, increased risk of violent suicide, propensity to exhibit aggressive or impulsive behavior, and susceptibility to alcohol abuse both among persons with psychiatric disorders and among the general public." For example, Mann, Arango, and Underwood (1990)—in their review of the literature—found that decreased levels of serotonin were prevalent among suicide victims. Serotonin does seem to play a significant role in some forms of depression, as can be seen by the relative success of the antidepressant drugs Prozac and Zoloft, which keep concentrations of serotonin high in various parts of the brain. Some additional preliminary but inconclusive findings suggest that humans who become violent with alcohol (Virkkunen & Linnoila, 1993), and children who torture animals (Kruesi, 1979; Kruesi et al., 1990), appear to be abnormally low in concentrations of serotonin. Other research suggests that low levels of brain serotonin encourage impulsive forms of aggressive or violent behavior (Kruesi & Jacobsen, 1997).

If certain neurotransmitters are implicated in aggressive behavior, it is not too far-fetched to consider drug regimens for control, similar to the antilibidinal drugs discussed above. Neurotransmitters are strongly affected by drugs. However, since neurotransmitters are the basic chemicals for all behavior, any modification of their levels in the nervous system is likely to affect a large range of behavior and emotions, not only the behavior that researchers are seeking to control. Therefore, although the considerable potential of drugs in controlling and reducing aggression cannot be overlooked, their peripheral effects must be considered.

Some researchers believe that the differential hormonal effects may partly explain why males overwhelmingly display higher levels of aggression and commit more violent crimes than do females. Some studies report that high testosterone levels in males may be associated with violent crimes, such as murder (Dabbs, Carr, Frady, & Riad, 1995; Dabbs, Riad, & Chance, 2001). Despite the progress in the last few years, the link between hormones and violence remains extremely unclear and unsubstantiated (Ramirez, 2003). We underscore, however, that learning and social expectations and cognitions play an extremely powerful role in any statistics that indicate gender or age differences in criminal behavior.

Biological Control through Surgery and Drugs

Another controversial issue relating to the biology of aggression is the treatment of violent offenders. Although treatment in the broad sense can mean psychotherapy, in the narrow sense it takes on a medical connotation. Those who advocate such treatment believe violent individuals should be administered drugs to dull their senses or overcome the effects of presumably overactive aggression hormones. More drastically, they may be submitted to psychosurgery or castration. The former procedure modifies aggressive centers in the brain; the latter excises the testicles, which contain testosterone, or demolishes their functioning through chemicals.

It is fairly well documented that castration lessens the tendency for animals to be aggressive. In rare instances, castration of prisoners convicted of sex crimes may have significantly reduced their aggressive episodes (Hawke, 1950; Le Maire, 1956). It may surprise you to learn that compulsory castration was legal in the United States until as late as the 1960s. For example, over 370 "voluntary" bilateral orchidectomies (excision of both testes) were performed on mentally disordered sex offenders in San Diego as a "judicial mandate" (Reiss, 1977).

Today, this literal castration for purposes of reducing sexual aggression is no longer an option. Rather, some individuals volunteer or request to be treated with drugs that mimic the chemical composition and action of sexual hormones. For example, medroxyprogesterone (Depo-Provera), which is chemically similar to the female hormone progesterone, is apparently highly effective in lowering testosterone levels (Day & Berney, 2001; Moyer, 1976). Lowered levels of the aggression-inducing male hormone testosterone presumably lessen the male drive to engage in sexual activity. Depo-Provera, the reasoning goes, will inhibit the excessive and impulsive sexual and aggressive behaviors of sex offenders. There is some evidence to support this assumption. Blumer and Migeon (1973), for example, found that ingestion of high levels of Depo-Provera successfully reduced sexual arousal and the need to engage in sexual "deviations."

Medroxyprogesterone and similar antilibidinal drugs (also called antiandrogen drugs) continue to be used by many clinicians as a supplement to psychotherapy for adults with deviant sexual behaviors. Because there is a risk that they will affect bone and testicular maturation, they are not recommended for males under 18 (Day & Berney, 2001). In some cases, antilibinal drugs are used as an initial, short-term measure until other treatment options are investigated. In other cases, they are offered on an "as needed" basis, such as when the person is under very high stress. However, these drugs may be used as the *principal* therapeutic intervention "in patients who have failed to respond to other treatment approaches and who continue to pose serious problems to their own well being and the safety of others" (Day & Berney, 2001, p. 209).

Recent work in the neuropsychological sciences has provided additional information about aggressive behavior. We must emphasize that about 95 percent of what is now known about the brain has been learned in the past 10 to 15 years (Comer, 2004). Advances in technology and instrument sophistication have allowed neuropsychologists to study the potential influence of molecular components, especially substances known as *neurotransmitters*, in facilitating and inhibiting aggression. Neurotransmitters are biochemicals directly involved in the transmission of neural impulses. Without them communication within the mammalian nervous system would be impossible. Researchers have learned that some of these neurotransmitters—namely, norepinephrine, acetylcholine, and serotonin—may significantly influence the cortical and subcortical mechanisms responsible for aggression and violence. No single neurotransmitter solely excites or inhibits aggression, however.

BRAIN CENTERS AND VIOLENCE CONTROL

Some neurophysiologists concentrate their research on trying to identify aggression centers in the brain. Presumably, if the part of the brain that controls or facilitates aggressive or violent behavior could be located, it might be manipulated. The research to date indicates that if an aggression center exists, it is most likely in the general area of the brain stem known as the *limbic system*, which consists of a diverse group of complicated brain structures and circuitry. Specifically, a small, almond-shaped group of nerve cells in the stem called the *amygdala*, another structure called the *hypothalamus*, and a portion of the brain itself called the *temporal lobe* have been the focus of scientific research. To date, however, we know too little about how our brain works, and we do not know where behavioral centers are located (Chorover, 1980).

Until drugs to help control behavior became widely available, researchers examining the relationship between aggression and brain centers often used *stereotaxic* procedures, which they believed had great potential for the control of hostile aggression. By drilling a small hole in the skull, researchers were able to penetrate the brain with small insulated wire electrodes for electrical stimulation. They also sometimes inserted minute glass hollow tubes (cannulae) to allow them to chemically stimulate specific sites in the brain and stem. The needle electrode, once properly implanted, could be permanently attached to the skull with screw fittings, allowing a small segment of the electrode to protrude from the skull for the attachment of wires or to receive radio transmission from a distance. This procedure of wireless communication was known as *telemetry*. The external part of the electrode was small enough so that it could be covered with hair and thus not be noticeable. The individual felt no pain from the procedure.

Small electric currents could then be passed through the electrodes to the brain site, stimulating the brain structure (or destroying it, if necessary, with direct current or high-frequency alternating current). In this way, aggressive and violent behavior could be stimulated or inhibited, depending on whether the site had an excitatory (facilitating) or inhibitory effect on aggressive behavior. If the researcher applied low frequency alternating current to an area with a facilitating function, the individual would probably behave aggressively; conversely, when current was applied to an inhibitory area, the person would be mild-mannered.

Violence also could be controlled by producing permanent alterations of brain tissue (lesions) by surgical, electrical (direct current), or chemical means (collectively called psychosurgery). Lesions in the temporal lobe of the brain were performed on several prisoners in California (Valenstein, 1973). The Japanese neurosurgeon Hirataro Narabayashi claimed success with amygdala operations on a diversity of patients plagued by aggressive, uncontrollable, destructive, and violent behavior. He reported that about 68 percent of his patients showed a significant decline in aggressive, violent behavior (Valenstein, 1973).

It should be noted that surgery such as that described above is not commonplace today. Psychosurgical procedures are highly refined and are considered primarily experimental. They are used only as a last resort in very severe cases of some mental illnesses (Comer, 2004). However, as a result of the aforementioned research, it is now possible for scientists to implant electrodes into a specific region of the human brain and monitor brain-wave patterns by computer, even when the individual is some distance away from the laboratory. When a brain-wave configuration known to be associated with violent behavior in that particular individual occurs, the computer activates an electrical stimulation to the brain site.

What are the social implications of such scientific practices? To what extent are they justified? In other words, just because we "can," does this mean that we "should?" Some investigators assert that we should control the antisocial elements in our society by any perfected biochemical, electrical, or surgical means necessary. In the early 1970s, the then-president of the American Psychological Association, Kenneth B. Clark, urged his colleagues to make full use of these breakthroughs in biological research, which he referred to as **psychotechnology.** Assuming that no individual would choose to be a criminal if he or she were "not impelled by some forms of internal, biochemical, or external, social forces—or some combination of both" (1971, p. 1056), Clark made the following comment:

> The implications of an effective psychotechnology for the control of criminal behavior and the amelioration of the moral insensitivities which produce reactive criminality in others are clear. It would seem, therefore, that there would be moral and rational justification for the use of compulsive criminals as pretest subjects in seeking precise forms of intervention and moral control of human behavior.

Clark also suggested that world leaders be required to submit themselves to perfected forms of psychotechnological and biochemical intervention so that their potentially aggressive, hostile impulses could be controlled. This would be justified, since it would prevent the mass destruction of civilization.

Since Clark's widely quoted address, few psychologists have called for similar drastic interventions, although biochemical intervention and surgical techniques on the human brain (psychosurgery) are increasingly sophisticated. The medical, legal, moral, and ethical ramifications if Clark's proposals were to be carried out on a large scale would be overwhelming, and the questions posed would be unanswerable. Who would decide which technique should be used on whom? Which individuals would be required to submit to psychosurgery, and which would be encouraged to? What are the constitutional rights of the subjects? Although some courts have already begun to answer some of these questions with respect to institutionalized individuals, there remain numerous unsettled issues that are not within the scope of this text.

Furthermore, biological alleviation of aggressive behavior would undoubtedly affect socially desirable behaviors as well. There is evidence to suggest that aspects of a person's emotional, cognitive, and intellectual functioning may be significantly affected by biological manipulation of the brain. Neuronal networks in the central nervous system do not function in physiological isolation. It is estimated that the brain contains between 100 and 200 billion brain cells (neurons) whose interconnecting pathways form the most complex intercommunication network in the known universe. Each nerve cell or neuron may play some role in behavior. Scientists talk about areas or structures in the brain that may account for some type of behavior, but they know that each of these areas contains numerous neurons and supportive cells that contribute to a variety of functions. Thus, surgical, electrical, or chemical intervention to affect aggression may also incidentally affect other behaviors that need not and should not be changed.

Heredity and the XYY Chromosome

Some early investigators believed that criminal behavior and predispositions to be violent were a result of heredity. The most prominent proponent of this view was Lombroso, who was convinced that a criminal "type" could be identified by specific physical characteristics, such as an unsymmetrical head and jaw, a low forehead, protruding ears, and bushy, connected eyebrows.

Later, mid-twentieth century inquiries on the relationship between genetics and criminality focused on the so-called XYY chromosomal syndrome. The impetus for this research was a study by Jacobs and his associates (1965), who reported that the presence of an extra Y chromosome in the male is significantly associated with the triad of tall stature, mental retardation, and an unusually high level of aggressive behavior. After the Jacobs study was released, some investigators hypothesized that the XYY chromosomal anomaly was closely related to violent criminal activity in males.

Chromosomes are chains of genetic material known as DNA that contain hereditary instructions for the growth and production of every living cell in the organism. Within each chromosome there are numerous genes; in fact, each cell contains between 30,000 and 40,000 genes (Andreasen, 2001). Chromosomes and their genes control physical traits such as eye and hair color and height, and they may have substantial influence on many psychological predispositions and temperaments. For example, chromosomes may account for a predisposition to depression. Each cell in the human body normally possesses 46 chromosomes, or 23 pairs. One pair in each cell is responsible for sex determination and sex characteristics. One member of the pair is always an X, but the other member may be either an X or a Y, depending on the sex of the individual. They are named after their appearance under a microscope. Each cell of the normal woman has two X chromosomes, while each cell of the normal man has an X and a Y. In rare instances, however, a genetic anomaly occurs in males in that two Y chromosomes pair with a single X—hence the phenomenon XYY. Rather than the usual 46 chromosomes, the individual has 47.

The principal characteristics associated with the presence of an extra Y chromosome include unusual height, episodes of violent aggression, and borderline intelligence—although there are many exceptions. Severe acne or scars from acne are also a characteristic.

A number of infamous murderers apparently had the XYY abnormality. One was Robert Peter Tait, who was convicted of beating to death a 77-year-old woman in Australia (Fox, 1971). The XYY characteristic was discovered after his trial but did not delay his execution. The XYY genotype was first used as a basis for criminal defense in 1968, at the trial of Daniel Hugon in Paris. Hugon was charged with the brutal murder of an elderly prostitute. Although convicted, he received only seven years imprisonment. It is not certain that the court considered the XYY abnormality a mitigating factor in determining his sentence, however (Fox, 1971). In the United States, criminal defendants have not used the defense successfully. "Big Bad John" (Sean) Farley, a 6-foot, 8-inch, 240-pound individual who murdered and mutilated a Queens, New York, woman in 1969, was convicted in spite of his plea of insanity due to chromosomal imbalance. Finally, Richard Speck, who murdered eight student nurses, possessed some of the physical features associated with the XYY chromosome. After his conviction, researchers examined his chromosomal structure. Although there was considerable confusion at the time the results were released, it has been concluded that Speck's genetic structure does not include the abnormality.

Although XYY has not been used as a criminal defense, there is some empirical support for its relationship with crime. So far, however, there is little evidence that violence and XYY go hand in hand. After an extensive review of the world literature, Jarvik, Klodin, and Matsuyama (1973) concluded that the presence of the XYY configuration in the general population averages between 0.11 percent and 0.14 percent; among mental patients it is significantly higher, averaging between 0.13 percent and 0.20 percent. However, in criminal populations, Jarvik found that XYY occurred in 1.9 percent of the cases. Jarvik's research combined information from 26 studies, including 5,066 criminal subjects. The 1.9 percent figure for the presence of the XYY chromosome, however, constitutes a very small percentage of the total prison population and seems to represent very little of the violence in our society. In another study, XYY prisoners were found to have fewer assault incidents than comparable groups of "normal" XY prisoners (Price & Whatmore, 1967). A great majority of the XYY crimes were against property.

Contemporary researchers have not pursued the extra-Y theory, because this particular chromosome does not appear to be a powerful explanatory factor for human violence. However, there is widespread recognition that—as a general principle—the numerous genes contained within a person's chromosomes influence not only one's physical characteristics but perhaps even one's behavior (Comer, 2004). Thus, there may be genetic *susceptibilities* to mood disorders, including severe depression, schizophrenia, and other mental disorders. As we discuss in chapter 6, some of these disorders have been associated with various crimes. In 2000, an extensive *Human Genome Project* designed to map all of the genes in the human body was completed. Results from that project are expected to contribute significantly to the understanding of human disorders, both medical and psychological (Comer, 2004).

Epilepsy and Violence

Between 1889 and 1970, there were only 15 court cases in the United States in which epilepsy had been used as a defense against charges of murder, homicide, manslaughter, or disorderly conduct (Delgado-Escueta, Mattson, & King, 1981). However, during the 1970s medical researchers implied that there was a causal relationship between temporal lobe epilepsy and violence (Goldstein, 1974; Pincus, 1980). This implied relationship resulted in a rash of diminished responsibility or insanity defenses for violent acts beginning in 1977. Presumably, the person plagued with this disorder is prone to uncontrollable periods of violence and destruction. However, available research fails to support any relationship between violence and epilepsy in general or violence and psychomotor epilepsy (Blumer, 1976; Valenstein, 1973).

Although angry, irritable behavior between seizures is commonly reported in individuals with chronic temporal lobe seizures, they rarely inflict physical harm (Blumer, 1976). In rare cases, some violence may occur in the confusional state that takes place immediately after an epileptic seizure, if the individual is provoked. During this brief rage attack, the person appears to lose control and may even destroy some furniture or strike a family member. Rarely is there actual physical injury, and rarely are criminal charges brought. Furthermore, it is not clear whether aggression occurs because of the seizure itself, because of associated brain damage that often accompanies psychomotor seizure activity, or is independent of the seizure itself (Herzberg & Fenwick, 1988). Available evidence (e.g., Wong, Lumsden, Fenton, & Fenwick, 1994) indicates that if violence does occur during the seizure episode, the violent behavior is probably due to a long-standing response pattern of the individual and is not directly related to the seizure itself.

 SUMMARY AND CONCLUSIONS

In this chapter we reviewed the major psychological perspectives on aggression and violence. Answers to what can be done about aggression and violent crime rest ultimately on one's perspective of human nature. If one believes that aggression is innate and part of our evolutionary heritage, a position held by mainstream psychoanalytic and ethological thought, then the conclusion must be that aggression is part of life, and that little can be done to alter this basic ingredient of human nature. Clues for reducing aggression are found in the behavior demonstrated throughout the animal kingdom. If, on the other hand, one believes that human aggression is acquired, then the key becomes principles of human learning and thought, and hope that one can change this acquired behavior for the betterment of humankind. The distinction between the innate and learning viewpoints has been somewhat oversimplified, but most contemporary theories on aggression fall within one or the other camp. At this point, the learning perspective has garnered considerably more empirical support than the innate perspective. Cognitive factors are especially important in explanations of human aggression.

Complicating the above, though, is the increasing amount of research being done in the biological sciences, most particularly relating to the brain and to human genetics. As noted in the chapter, 95 percent of everything we know about the human brain has been learned within the last 15 years. Researchers are acquiring extensive information about the contribution of genes to physical characteristics and susceptibility to medical problems. Many believe that they will eventually link genes to a variety of behavioral problems and mental disorders as well. It is crucial to keep in mind, though, that although some genes may *predispose* individuals to certain disorders that may lead to violence or other antisocial behavior, genes do not *determine* behavior.

Furthermore, as more research data are published, even the *learning* perspective becomes increasingly complex, and additional factors must be considered. For one thing, physiological arousal certainly plays a major role in aggressive and violent behavior, as suggested by Berkowitz (1989). High levels of arousal seem to *facilitate* (again, not cause) aggressive behavior in certain situations. Extremely high arousal seems to interfere with our sense of self-awareness and internal control, rendering us more susceptible to environmental cues and to mindless or habitual behaviors. In this sense, under very high arousal, we may not stop to consider the consequences of our violent behavior. The discussion of road rage and aggressive driving in the chapter illustrates this very well.

The different types of aggressive behavior were also emphasized in this chapter. Overt and covert forms of aggression must be considered in any discussion of crime. Overt aggressors are more likely to be involved in both violent and serious property-economic crimes, whereas covert aggressors are more prone to be involved in property offenses, particularly occupational crime. And although the conventional wisdom has been that boys are more likely to commit highly aggressive crimes, the evidence suggests that girls may be equally involved in aggressive behavior of a different kind. Gender differences in aggressive behavior are believed to be mainly due to socialization factors.

Situational and neurophysiological factors also contribute significantly to aggressive behavior. Aggressive stimuli, including weapons, crowds, pollution, temperature, smells, and central nervous system pathology all must be entertained as possible contributors. Social learning theorists also note that the media and the models they provide substantially affect our attitudes, values, and overall impressions about violence as well as our behavior. There are both anecdotal and some research evidence of contagion and copycat effects. Attitudes, beliefs, and thoughts refer to the cognitive processes that are beginning to emerge as contenders for a leading role in the psychological explanation of criminal behavior. Operant and classical conditioning remain important, but they do not adequately address the many intricacies of criminal behavior.

We end the chapter with a concise summary statement by Rowell Huesmann who, after reviewing the research literature, concludes, "No one causal factor by itself explains more than a small portion of individual differences in aggressiveness" (1997, p. 70). He hastens to add, however, that "early learning and socialization play a key role in the development of habitual aggression" (1997, p. 70).

 KEY CONCEPTS

Passive aggressive behavior	Hostile aggression
Expressive aggression	Instrumental aggression
Theory	Psychodynamic model
Hydraulic model	Territoriality
Ritualized aggression	Difference-in-degrees
Evolutionary psychology	Weapons effect
Frustration-aggression hypothesis	Rumination
Cognitive-neoassociation model	Excitation transfer theory
Displaced aggression theory	Road rage
Aggressive driving	Cognitive scripts model
Hostile attribution bias	Reactive aggression
Proactive aggression	Contagion effect
Copycat effect	Neurotransmitters
Serotonin	Psychotechnology

REVIEW QUESTIONS

1. What physiological factors have been associated with aggression?
2. What accounts for gender differences in aggression? Cite relevant research findings.
3. Briefly describe the various environmental factors that influence aggression.
4. Define cognitive scripts and how they may be applied in quick action violence.
5. Define weapons effect and how it may account for some of the violence in today's society.
6. Define hostile attribution bias and how it might explain chronic aggression in young children.

7. Explain the difference between each of the following: overt and covert acts of aggression, cognitive scripts model and hostile attribution model, and reactive and proactive aggression.
8. What is the relationship between violence and (a) the XYY chromosome and (b) epilepsy?
9. Discuss the various theoretical perspectives on aggression, including the research in support of or refuting these perspectives.
10. Review the research presented in this chapter on the effects of the mass media on violence.

CHAPTER 6

CRIMINAL PSYCHOPATHY

- Present a special type of violent offender (the psychopath) who is different emotionally, cognitively, and behaviorally from other offenders.
- Review the various measures of psychopathy.
- Examine the neurobiological aspects of psychopathy.
- Review the evidence for juvenile psychopathy.
- Identify the ethical dilemmas that juvenile psychopathy presents.

Psychopathy has become one of the central focuses of research in psychology, particularly forensic psychology with its concentration on adult criminal behavior. Most recently, *juvenile* psychopathy has become the subject of considerable interest and debate, with a number of researchers questioning its validity and implications. As we will see in the chapter, the psychopath is not identical to the person with an antisocial personality disorder, but some researchers and clinicians continue to confuse the two terms (Gacono et al., 2001). Because psychopathy is such an important topic in criminal psychology, we devote an entire chapter to describing the research and clinical characteristics of this interesting behavior.

WHAT IS A PSYCHOPATH?

The term "psychopath" is currently used to describe a person who demonstrates a discernible cluster of psychological, interpersonal, and neurophysiological features that distinguish him or her from the general population. Psychologist Robert Hare (1993), one of the world's leading experts on psychopathy, describes psychopaths as "social predators who charm, manipulate, and ruthlessly plow their way through life, leaving a broad trail of broken hearts, shattered expectations, and empty wallets. Completely lacking in conscience and empathy, they selfishly take what they want and do as they please, violating social norms and expectations without the slightest sense of guilt or regret" (p. xi).

Hare (1970) proposed a useful scheme to outline three categories of psychopaths: the primary, the secondary or neurotic, and the dyssocial. Only the **primary psychopath** is a "true" psychopath. The primary or "true" psychopath has certain identifiable psychological, emotional, cognitive, and biological differences that distinguish him or her from the general or criminal population. We discuss these differences in some detail throughout the chapter. The other two categories meld a heterogeneous group of antisocial individuals who comprise a large segment of the criminal population. **Secondary psychopaths** commit antisocial or violent acts because of severe emotional problems or inner conflicts. They are sometimes called acting-out neurotics, neurotic delinquents, symptomatic psychopaths, or simply emotionally disturbed offenders. The popular entertainment media often refer to these persons as "psychopathic killers," or utilize some other attention-getting terminology designed to conjure a bloodthirsty disturbed person indiscriminately killing all those whom he meets. The third group, **dyssocial psychopaths,** display aggressive, antisocial behavior they have *learned* from their subculture, like their gangs or families. In both cases, the label "psychopath" is misleading, because the behaviors and backgrounds have little if any similarity to those of primary psychopaths. Yet both secondary and dyssocial psychopaths are often incorrectly called psychopaths because of their high recidivism rates.

The term **antisocial personality disorder (APD)** is used by psychiatrists and many clinical psychologists to describe "a pervasive pattern of disregard for, and violation of, the rights of others that begins in childhood or early adolescence and continues into adulthood" (American Psychiatric Association, 1994, p. 645). Antisocial personalities (ASPs) are further described as those persons who "fail to conform to social norms with respect to lawful behaviors. They may repeatedly perform acts that are grounds for arrest, such as destroying property, harassing others, stealing or pursuing illegal occupations" (American Psychiatric Association, 1994, p. 646). As we noted, the descriptions of the psychiatric term "antisocial personality disorder" follow very closely the descriptions of the psychological term "psychopathy." However, the definition of APD is more narrow than primary psychopathy because it restricts its definition to behavioral indicators. Hare's definition of primary psychopathy also includes both emotional and cognitive aspects. Nevertheless, with each new publication of the American Psychiatric Association's *Diagnostic and Statistical Manual of Mental Disorders,* the characteristics used to describe the antisocial personality (ASP) are increasingly similar to Hare's primary psychopathy in behavioral terms. It is easy to understand why clinicians often confuse the terms.

This text adopts Hare's scheme, considering "primary psychopath" an empirically and clinically useful designation. It is distinguished from secondary or neurotic psychopaths in its behavioral, cognitive, and neurophysiological features. From this point on, when we refer to the psychopath, we mean the primary psychopath. He or she is unique: neither neurotic, psychotic, nor emotionally disturbed, as commonly believed and portrayed by the entertainment media. Primary psychopaths are usually not volcanically explosive, violent, or extremely destructive. They are more apt to be outgoing, charming, and verbally proficient. They may be criminals—in fact, in general they run in perpetual opposition to the law—but many are not. The term **criminal psychopath** will be used to identify those primary psychopaths who engage in repetitive antisocial or criminal behavior.

An Example of a Psychopath

The late Ferdinand Waldo Demara Jr., the "Great Impostor," who forged documents and tried dozens of occupations without stopping to obtain a high school education, is a good example of a primary psychopath. A brief description of some of his exploits may help put the psychopath in perspective. (See Critchton, 1959, for a more complete version.)

Demara frequently came into contact with the law, primarily because he persisted in adopting fake identities. He once obtained the credentials of a Dr. French, who held a Harvard PhD in psychology. Demara was in the U.S. Navy at the time, awaiting a commission on the basis of other forged documents, but when he realized he was in danger of exposure via a routine security check, he decided he would prefer the Dr. French identity. He dramatized a successful suicide by leaving his clothing on the end of a pier with a note stating that "this is the only way out." Navy officials accepted his "death," and Demara became Dr. French. With his impressive credentials in hand, he obtained a dean of philosophy position in a Canadian college, successfully taught a variety of psychology courses, and assumed administrative responsibilities.

He developed a friendship with a physician, Joseph Cyr, and learned the basics of medicine from their long conversations. He eventually borrowed and duplicated Cyr's vital documents—birth, baptism, and confirmation certificates, school records, medical license—and obtained a commission in the Royal Canadian Navy as Dr. Cyr. He read extensively to nurture his growing knowledge of medicine.

During the Korean War, Demara/Cyr was assigned to a destroyer headed for the combat zone. The ship met a small Korean junk carrying many seriously wounded men, who were brought on board for emergency medical care. Three men were in such critical condition that only emergency surgery could save their lives. Although Demara had never seen an operation performed, he hurriedly reviewed his textbooks. With unskilled hands, he operated through the night. By dawn, he had not only saved the lives of the three men, but had also successfully treated 16 others.

Demara/Cyr's deeds were broadcast over the ship's radio and disseminated, along with his photo, by the press. The real Dr. Cyr, shocked to see Demara's visage over his own respected name, immediately exposed him. Demara was discharged from the Canadian Navy which, to save itself from additional embarrassment, allowed him to leave without prosecution. Demara's biography represents an example of a psychopath who did not engage in serious or lifelong violent crime.

Many psychopaths do commit violent crimes, though, some of them heinous and brutal. Neville Heath—charming, handsome, and intelligent—brutally and sadistically murdered two young English women (Critchley, 1951; Hill, 1960). Like Demara, Heath had an extraordinary career, much of it in the armed forces. Unlike Demara, his brushes with the law were serious and occasionally ended in imprisonment. He was commissioned and dishonorably discharged on three separate occasions, once each in the British Royal Air Force, the Royal Armed Service Corps, and the South African Air Force. He flew in a fighter squadron in the RAF until he was court-martialed for car theft at age 19. He then committed a series of thefts and burglaries and was sentenced to Borstal Prison. Pardoned in 1939, he joined the Royal Armed Service Corps but was dismissed for forgery. On his way home to England, he jumped ship and eventually managed to obtain a commission in the South African Air Force until his past caught up with him. When not in trouble, Heath was regarded as a daring, confident, and highly charming officer—and a rake. After the third court-martial, he developed a taste for sadistic murder.

You may be able to identify other examples of psychopaths at their worst. The notorious Charles Manson, who in the 1960s exhibited an uncanny ability to attract a devout cluster of unresisting followers, is one probable example. The fictional Hannibal Lechter, whose sadistic offenses and deadly charm have captivated screen audiences, is another.

Throughout the remainder of this chapter, we examine in more detail the behavioral patterns, the cognitive processes, the interpersonal features, the neuropsychological characteristics, and the general background of the psychopath.

BEHAVIORAL DESCRIPTIONS

One pioneering authority on the behavioral characteristics of the psychopath was Hervey Cleckley, a well-known psychiatrist from Augusta, Georgia, who died in 1984 at the age of 79. A large part of Cleckley's professional recognition came as a result of the nonfiction book, *The Three Faces of Eve,* which he coauthored with Corbett Thigpen. The book, which is about the phenomenon of "multiple personality," was made into a very popular 1957 movie with the same title. However, his major professional contribution to the field of psychiatry can

TABLE 6–1   Psychopathic Behaviors Identified by Hare and Cleckly

HARE PCL CHECKLIST	CLECKLEY'S PRIMARY PSYCHOPATH DESCRIPTION
Glibness/superficial charm	Superficial charm and good intelligence
Grandiose sense of self-worth	Pathological egocentricity
Pathological lying	Untruthfulness and insincerity
Cunning/manipulative	Manipulative
Lack of remorse or guilt	Lack of remorse or guilt
Shallow affect	General poverty of affective reactions
Callous, lack of empathy	Unreponsivenss in interpersonal relationships
Failure to accept responsibility for actions	Unreliability
Promiscuous sexual behavior	Impersonal sex life
Lack of realistic, long-term goals	Failure to follow any life plan
Poor behavioral controls	Impulsive
High need for stimulation/prone to boredom	Inadequately motivated antisocial behavior
Irresponsibility	Poor judgment
	Absence of delusions
	Absence of anxiety
	Bizarre behavior after drinking alcohol

be found in his often-quoted text, *The Mask of Sanity* (first published in 1941). The book describes in clear and empirically useful terms the major behaviors demonstrated by the full-fledged or primary psychopath, as distinct from the other psychopathic types referred to previously. Cleckley was able to identify 16 characteristics he felt described the typical psychopath (see **Table 6–1**).

Charming and Verbally Fluent

Superficial charm and average to above-average intelligence are two of the psychopath's main features, according to Cleckley, and they are both especially apparent during initial contacts. Many psychopaths usually impress others as friendly, outgoing, likable, and alert. They often appear well educated and knowledgeable, and they display many interests. They are verbally skillful and can talk themselves out of trouble. In fact, their vocabulary is often so extensive that they can talk at length about anything (Hare, 1991). However, systematic study of their conversation reveals that they often jump "from one topic to another and that much of their speech is empty of real substance, tending to be filled with stock phrases, repetitions of the same ideas, word approximations, abstract terms and jargon used in a superficial or inappropriate fashion, logically inconsistent statements and phrases, and half-formed sentences" (Hare, 1991, p. 57). As Hare (1996, p. 46) notes, "In some respects, it is as if psychopaths lack a central organizer to plan and keep track of what they think and say." However, since psychopaths are so charming and manipulative, these language shortcomings are not readily apparent.

Psychological Testing Differences

Psychometric studies (studies that use standard psychological tests as measures) indicate that psychopaths usually score higher on intelligence tests than the general population (Hare, 1970, 1996), particularly on individually administered tests. In fact, Hare wryly comments, the psychopaths who were the sample for his studies were probably the least intelligent of their ilk, since they were not quite bright enough to avoid being convicted for their offenses. (Hare has conducted much of his research on imprisoned psychopaths.) Recent research (e.g., Ishikawa et al., 2001) has found that a useful dichotomy of psychopathy may be to divide them into "successful" psychopaths (those who have committed crimes but avoided arrest and conviction for offenses) and "unsuccessful" psychopaths (those who have been convicted and imprisoned). We return to this dichotomy later in the chapter.

Psychopaths Are Not Mentally Disordered by Traditional Standards

Psychopaths usually do not exhibit mental disorders, either mild or severe. Most lack any symptoms of excessive worry and anxiety, psychotic thinking, delusions, severe depressions, or hallucinations. Even under high pressure conditions they remain cool and calm, as did Ian Fleming's fictitious James Bond, probably a prime example. Feasibly, the doomed psychopath might enjoy a steak dinner (*au poivre*) with gusto just before being executed. The infamous multiple murderer Herman W. Mudget, alias H. H. Holmes, retired at his normal hour the evening before his execution, fell asleep easily, slept soundly, and woke up completely refreshed. "I never slept better in my life," he told his cell guard. He ordered and ate a substantial breakfast an hour before he was scheduled to be hanged. Until the moment of death, he remained remarkably calm and amiable, displaying no signs of depression or fear (Franke, 1975).

Not everyone agrees with the view that psychopaths do not suffer from some mental disorder. Some clinicians argue that psychopathy and schizophrenia are part of the same spectrum of disorders (Hare 1996). Some forensic clinicians maintain that they occasionally see a mentally disordered offender who qualifies as both a psychopath and a schizophrenic (Hare, 1996). There is some evidence to suggest that it is not uncommon to find psychopaths who seem mentally disordered in maximum security psychiatric units for highly violent or dangerous patients.

Other Principal Traits

Other principal traits of the psychopath are selfishness and an inability to love or give affection to others. According to Cleckley, egocentricity is *always* present in the psychopath and is essentially unmodifiable. The psychopath's inability to feel genuine, meaningful affection for another is absolute. Psychopaths may be likable, but they are seldom able to keep close friends, and they have great difficulty understanding love in others. They may be highly skillful at pretending deep affection, and they may effectively mimic appropriate emotions, but true loyalty, warmth, and compassion are foreign to them. Psychopaths are distinguished by flat emotional reaction and affect. And since psychopaths have so little need to receive or give love, psychopaths, as a group, have relatively little contact with their families, and many change their residences frequently (Hare, 1991). In addition they do not usually respond to acts of kindness. They show capacity only for superficial appreciation. Paradoxically they may do small favors and appear considerate. One prototype mowed the lawn for his elderly neighbor and slipped her some schnapps when she was ill—the next morning he stole her car.

Psychopaths have a remarkable disregard for truth and are often called "pathological liars." They seem to have no internalized moral or ethical sense and cannot understand the purpose of being honest, especially if dishonesty will bring some personal gain. They have a cunning ability to appear straightforward, honest, and sincere, but their claims to sincerity are without substance.

Psychopaths are unreliable, irresponsible, and unpredictable, regardless of the importance of the occasion or the consequences of their impulsive actions. Impulsivity appears to be a central or cardinal feature of psychopathy (Hart & Dempster, 1997). This pattern of impulsive actions is cyclical, however. Psychopaths may, for months on end, be responsible citizens, faithful spouses, and reliable employees. They may experience great successes, be promoted, and gain honors, as did Demara and Heath. Skillfully as they have attained these socially desirable goals, they have an uncanny knack of suddenly unraveling their lives. They become irresponsible, and may pass bad checks, sabotage the company computer, go on a drunken spree, or steal the boss's car. They also tend to have a "bad temper" that flares quickly into an argument and attack. Psychopaths may later say they are sorry and plead for another chance—and most will probably get it. Invariably, if the psychopath is a young adult, the irresponsible behavior will return.

Even small amounts of alcohol prompt most psychopaths to become vulgar, domineering, loud, and boisterous and to engage in practical jokes and pranks. Cleckley noted that they choose pranks that have no appeal for most individuals, and that seem bizarre, inappropriate, and cruel. They lack genuine humor and, not surprisingly, the ability to laugh at themselves.

Although often above average in intelligence, psychopaths appear incapable of learning to avoid failure and situations that are potentially damaging to themselves. Some theorists suggest that the self-destructive, self-defeating deeds and attitudes reflect a need to be punished to mitigate the guilt they subconsciously experience, or more simply, that they are driven by a masochistic purpose. Evidence refuting these explanations is offered later in this chapter.

When a psychopath drifts into criminal activity, impulsivity will usually prevent him or her from performing like a professional criminal. Psychopaths are more likely to participate in capers and hastily planned frolics, or in spontaneous, serious crimes for immediate satisfaction. The professional criminal has purpose and a plan of action; the psychopath is impulsive and lacks long-range goals.

A cardinal fault of psychopaths is their absolute lack of remorse or guilt for anything they do, regardless of the severity or immorality of their actions and irrespective of their traumatic effects on others. Since they do not anticipate personal consequences, psychopaths may engage in destructive or antisocial behavior—such as forgery, theft, rape, brawls, and fraud—by taking absurd risks and for insignificant personal gain. When caught, they express no genuine remorse. They may readily admit culpability and take considerable pleasure in the shock these admissions produce in others. Whether they have bashed in someone's head, ruined a car, or tortured a child, psychopaths may well remark they did it "for the hell of it."

Psychopaths have little capacity to see themselves as others perceive them. Instead of accepting the facts that would normally lead to insight, they project and externalize blame onto the community and family for their misfortunes. Interestingly, educated psychopaths have been known to speak fluently about the psychopathic personality, quoting the literature extensively and discussing research findings, but they cannot look into their own troublesome antics or mount a reasonable attack on their actions. They articulate their regrets for having done something, but the words are devoid of emotional meaning, a characteristic Cleckley calls **semantic aphasia.** Johns and Quay (1962) remarked that psychopaths "know the words but not the music." Similarly, Grant (1977) notes that the psychopath knows only the book meaning of words, not the living meaning. Hare (1996, p. 45) concludes, "In short, psychopaths appear to be semantically and affectively shallow individuals."

Another important behavioral characteristic of psychopaths noted by Blair et al. (2006) is their *excessive* use of instrumental aggression. Instrumental aggression, as discussed in the chapter on aggression, is purposeful and goal-directed aggression used to achieve a specific goal, such as the possessions of another person.

Finally, an important behavioral distinction underlying much of Cleckley's description is what Quay (1965) refers to as the psychopath's profound and pathological stimulation seeking. According to Quay, the actions of the psychopath are motivated by an excessive *neuropsychological* need for thrills and excitement. It is not unusual to see psychopaths drawn to such interests as race car driving, skydiving, and motorcycle stunts. We will examine this alleged need for stimulation in the pages to follow.

In recent years, it has become useful for research purposes to focus on psychopaths who repeatedly commit crimes, collectively called criminal psychopaths. Concentrating on psychopaths who are violent or chronic offenders provides invaluable information about their backgrounds, learning history, and behavioral patterns. Such research also might offer key strategies for how to deal and potentially treat this challenging group of individuals.

THE CRIMINAL PSYCHOPATH

Probably no topic has caught the attention of forensic psychologists interested in the development of habitual criminal behavior more in recent years then the topic of criminal psychopathy. Again we must emphasize that many psychopaths have no history of serious antisocial behavior and that persistent, serious offenders are not necessarily psychopaths. For our purposes here the term "criminal psychopath" will be reserved for those psychopaths who demonstrate a wide range of *persistent* and *serious* antisocial behavior. As a group they tend to be "dominant, manipulative individuals characterized by an impulsive, risk-taking and antisocial lifestyle, who obtain their greatest thrill from diverse sexual gratification and target diverse victims over time" (Porter et al., 2000, p. 220).

As further noted by Stephen Porter and his colleagues (2000, p. 227): "Given its relation to crime and violence, psychopathy is arguably one of the most important psychological constructs in the criminal justice system."

Prevalence of Criminal Psychopathy

Overall, Robert Hare (1998) estimates that the prevalence of psychopaths in the general population is about 1 percent, whereas in the adult prison population, estimates range from 15 percent to 25 percent. Some researchers (e.g., Simourd & Hoge, 2000) wonder, however, whether these estimates are not somewhat inflated. Simourd and Hoge (2000) report only 11 percent of their inmate population could be identified as criminal psychopaths. The inmates used in the Simourd-Hoge study were not simply inmates in a medium security correctional facility. All 321 were serving a current sentence for violent offending, more than half of them had been convicted of a previous violent offense, and almost all of them had extensive criminal careers. Therefore, percentage estimates of criminal psychopathy within any given population should be tempered by the type of facility, as well as the cultural, ethnic, and age mix of the targeted population. Interestingly the American Psychiatric Association (1994) estimates that the overall prevalence of *antisocial personality disorder* (APD) in the community at large is about 3 percent in males and about 1 percent in females. In clinical samples (those receiving therapy for various disorders), the prevalence estimates vary between 3 percent and 30 percent, depending on the characteristics of the sample surveyed. Keep in mind, though, that APD is *not* identical to psychopathy.

Offending Patterns of Criminal Psychopaths

Criminal psychopaths are believed responsible for a disproportionate amount of crime in society, and they are considered to be the most violent and persistent offenders (Forth & Burke, 1998; Hart & Hare, 1997; Newman, Schmitt,

& Voss, 1997; Saltaris, 2002). Gretton et al. (2001, p. 428) point out that criminal psychopaths generally "lack a normal sense of ethics and morality, live by their own rules, are prone to use cold-blooded, instrumental intimidation and violence to satisfy their wants and needs, and generally are contemptuous of social norms and the rights of others." Hare (1996, p. 38) posits, "The ease with which psychopaths engage in . . . dispassionate violence has very real significance for society in general and for law enforcement personnel in particular." Hare refers to a report by the Federal Bureau of Investigation (1992) that found that nearly half of the law enforcement officers who died in the line of duty were killed by individuals who closely matched the personality profile of the psychopath. Moreover, the unlawful acts of psychopathic sex offenders are likely to be more violent, brutal, unconventional, and sadistic than those of other sex offenders (Hare, Clark, Grann, & Thornton, 2000; Porter, Birt, & Boer, 2001; Woodworth & Porter, 2002). Psychopathic sex offenders appear to be more motivated by thrill seeking and excitement rather than simply sexual arousal (Porter et al., 2003). Psychopaths as a group also appear to be significantly more sadistic than violent nonpsychopaths (Holt, Meloy, & Stack, 1999), and commit more diverse and severe forms of sexual homicides (Firestone et al., 1998; Porter et al., 2003). Porter and his colleagues (2003) found that in a sample of the male offenders incarcerated in two Canadian federal prisons for homicide, nearly half could be classified as sexual homicide offenders. (In order to be classified as a sexual homicide, there had to be physical evidence of sexual activity with the victim before, during, or after the homicide.)

Murderers described as excessively sadistic and brutal tend to have many psychopathic features (Hare et al., 2000; Stone, 1998). Serial murderers who exhibit psychopathic features are especially sadistic and brutal in their murders. Collectively the research suggests that psychopaths may be more likely than other offenders to derive pleasure from both the nonsexual and sexual suffering of others (Porter et al., 2003).

Many of the murders and serious assaults committed by nonpsychopaths occurred during domestic disputes or extreme emotional arousal. This pattern of violence is rarely observed for criminal psychopaths (Hare, Hart, & Harpur, 1991; Williamson, Hare, & Wong, 1987). Criminal psychopaths frequently engage in violence as a form of revenge or retribution, or during a bout of drinking. Many of the attacks of nonpsychopaths are toward women they know well, whereas many of the attacks of criminal psychopaths are directed toward men who are strangers. Hare et al. (1991, p. 395) observe that the violence committed by criminal psychopaths was callous and cold-blooded "without the affective coloring that accompanied the violence of nonpsychopaths." Research also indicates that rapists who have psychopathic characteristics are more likely to have "nonsexual" motivations for their crimes, such as anger, vindictiveness, sadism, and opportunism (Hart & Dempster, 1997).

PSYCHOLOGICAL MEASURES OF PSYCHOPATHY

Currently, the most popular instrument for measuring criminal psychopathy is the 22-item **Psychopathy Checklist (PCL)** (Hare, 1980) and its 20-item revision (**PCL-R**) (Hare, 1991). The PCL-R has been published in a second edition, which includes new information on its applicability in forensic and research settings. The second edition also has been expanded for use with offenders in other countries, and includes updated normative and validation data on male and female offenders. A 12-item short-form version has also been developed, called the **Psychopathy Checklist: Screening Version (PCL:SV)** (Hart, Cox, & Hare, 1995; Hart, Hare, & Forth, 1993). Other additions are the **Psychopathy Checklist: Youth Version (PCL:YV)** and the **P-Scan: Research Version.** The PCL:YV is beginning to be researched more extensively and is covered in more detail in the section on juvenile psychopathy. The P-Scan is a screening instrument that serves as *rough* screen for psychopathic features and as a source of working hypotheses to deal with managing suspects, offenders, or clients. It is designed for use in law enforcement, probation, corrections, civil and forensic facilities, and other areas in which it would be useful to have some information about the possible presence of psychopathic features in a particular person. Of course the P-Scan needs much more research before it can be used as a valid instrument in practice. All five checklists are conceptually and—with the exception of the P-Scan—psychometrically similar.

The PCL scales are largely based on Cleckley's (1976) conception of psychopathy, but are specifically designed to identify psychopaths in male prison, forensic, or psychiatric populations. Since the PCL-R is currently the most frequently used instrument for both research and clinical application, it will be the center of attention for the remainder of this section.

The PCL-R assesses the affective (emotional), interpersonal, behavioral, and social deviance facets of criminal psychopathy from various sources, including self-reports, behavioral observations, and collateral sources, such as parents, family members, friends, and arrest and court records which can help to establish the credibility of self-reports (Hare, Hart, & Harpur 1991; Hare, 1996). In addition item ratings from the PCL-R, for instance, require some integration of information across multiple domains, including behavior at work or school; behavior toward family, friends, and sexual partners; and criminal behavior (Kosson et al., 2002). Typically, highly trained examiners use all this information to score each item on a 0 to 2 scale, depending on the extent to which an individual has the disposition described by each item on the checklist (0 = consistently absent; 1 = inconsistent; 2 = consistently present). Scoring is, however, quite complex and requires substantial time, extensive training, and access to a considerable amount of background information on the individual. A score of 30 or above usually qualifies a person as a primary psychopath (Hare, 1996). In some research and clinical settings, cut-off scores ranging from 25 to 33 are often used (Simourd & Hoge, 2000). Hare (1991) recommends that persons with scores between 21 and 29 be classified as "middle" subjects who show many of the features of psychopathy but do not fit all the criteria. Scores below 21 are considered "nonpsychopaths."

So far the research has strongly supported the reliability and validity of the PCL-R for distinguishing criminal psychopaths from criminal nonpsychopaths, and for helping correctional and forensic psychologists involved in risk assessments of offenders (Hare, 1996; Hare, Forth, & Stachan, 1992). In addition the instrument provides researchers and mental health professionals with a universal measurement for the assessment of psychopathy that facilitates international and cross-cultural communication concerning theory, research, and eventual clinical practice (Hare et al., 2000). Currently the PCL-R is increasingly being used as a clinical instrument for the diagnosis of psychopathy across the globe, although it appears to be most powerful in identifying psychopathy among North American white males (Hare, Clark, Grann, & Thornton, 2000). Interestingly, Scott Lilienfeld and his colleagues (Lilienfeld et al., 1999) have developed a psychopathy scale for chimpanzees, called the Chimpanzee Psychopathy Measure (CPM). Preliminary data indicate that the scale appears to be a reliable measure of psychopathic-like behavior in chimpanzees. According to the researchers, the psychopathic behavior of chimps include excessive displays of sexual activity, daring behaviors, teasing, silent bluff displays, and temper tantrums. These data underscore the potential neuropsychological basis for psychopathy in humans.

Core Factors of Psychopathy

From the research on the PCL-R, it has become clear that psychopathy is multidimensional in nature. One statistical procedure designed to find different dimensions or factors in test data is **factor analysis.** When expert ratings of psychopathy on the PCL-R were submitted to a factor analysis, at least two behavioral dimensions or factors emerged (Hare, 1991; Harpur, Hakstian, & Hare, 1988; Hart, Hare, & Forth, 1993). Some researchers note that more have been identified.

The Two Factor Position

In the two factor scheme, **Factor 1** reflects the interpersonal and emotional components of the disorder and consists of items measuring remorselessness, callousness, and selfish use and manipulation of others. The typical psychopath feels no compunctions about using others strictly to meet his or her own needs. **Factor 2** is most closely associated with a socially deviant lifestyle, as characterized by poor planning, impulsiveness, an excessive need for stimulation, proneness to boredom, and a lack of realistic goals. Some researchers have found that Factor 1 appears to be associated with planned predatory violence, while factor 2 appears to be related to spontaneous and impulsive violence (Hart & Dempster, 1997). Factor 1 is also linked to resistance and inability to profit from psychotherapy and treatment programs (Seto & Barbaree, 1999). Factor 2 appears related to socioeconomic status, educational attainment, and cultural/ethnic background, whereas Factor 1 may be more connected to biopsychological influences (Cooke & Michie, 1997). Research also suggests that Factor 1 *may* be a more powerful indicator of psychopathy than Factor 2 (Cooke, Michie, Hart, & Hare, 1999). In addition, while it is quite clear that Factor 1 does a better job of identifying psychopathy in general, there is some evidence that Factor 2 does a better job of predicting general recidivism and violent recidivism (Walters, 2003).

The Three Factor Position

Psychopathic behavior may be too diverse to be captured in only two dimensions. With increasing sophistication of statistical methods (e.g., confirmatory factor analysis, model-based cluster analysis), contemporary research indicates that there may be at least three core behavioral or personality dimensions that best describe psychopathy (Cooke & Michie, 2001; Cooke, Michie, Hart, & Clark, 2004; Vitacco, Neumann, & Jackson, 2005). In an influential paper, Cooke and Michie (2001) challenged the traditional two-factor explanation of psychopathy, and recommended that psychopathy be divided into the following core dimensions:

1. An arrogant and deceptive interpersonal style, which includes a grandiose sense of self-worth, glibness, superficial charm, lying, conning, manipulation, and deceitfulness. (This dimension is also referred to as impression management.)
2. Deficient affective or emotional experience characterized by low remorse, low guilt, a weak conscience, the absence of anxiety, fearlessness, callousness, little empathy, and a failure to accept responsibility for one's actions.
3. An impulsive and irresponsible behavioral style, including failure to think before acting, a lack of long-term goals, stimulation seeking, unsatisfactory work habits, and a parasitic lifestyle (living off others, including spouses, intimate partners, friends, and parents).

The Four Dimensions Position

Some researchers (e.g., Hare, 2003; Salekin et al., 2006; Vitacco, Neumann, & Jackson, 2005) have asserted that, in addition to disturbances in interpersonal, affective, and behavioral functioning, the definition of psychopathy should also include a fourth dimension: antisocial behavior. This argument is based on the finding that individuals manifesting psychopathic traits often exhibit violence and a large collection of other antisocial behavioral patterns. Consequently the argument contends that researchers and clinicians are missing a critical ingredient in the understanding and definition of the psychopath if measures of antisocial behavior are left out of the equation. It is also argued that much of the predictive power of psychopathy is enhanced if we take into consideration past criminal behavior (Salekin et al., 2006).

Recidivism

Research studies report that the recidivism rate of psychopaths is very high. **Recidivism** refers to the tendency to return to criminal offending. In other words, psychopaths commit crimes again and again, regardless of the measures used to stop or rehabilitate them. According to Porter et al. (2000), research suggests psychopaths reoffend faster, violate parole sooner, and perhaps commit more institutional violence than nonpsychopaths. In one study (Serin, Peters, & Barbaree, 1990), the number of failures of male offenders released on unescorted temporary absence programs (furloughs) was examined. The failure rate for psychopaths was 37.5 percent, while none of the nonpsychopaths failed. The failure rate during parole was also examined. While 7 percent of nonpsychopaths violated parole conditions, 33 percent of the psychopaths violated their conditions. In another study (Serin & Amos, 1995), 299 male offenders were followed for up to eight years after their release from a federal prison. Sixty-five percent of the psychopaths were convicted of another crime within three years, compared to a reconviction rate of 25 percent for nonpsychopaths. Quinsey, Rice, and Harris (1995) found that within six years of release from prison, more than 80 percent of the psychopaths convicted as sex offenders had violently recidivated, compared with a 20 percent recidivism rate for nonpsychopathic sex offenders. Richards, Casey, and Lucente (2003) found the PCL-R and the PCL:SVA measures of persistent offending history, in conjunction with high scores on the PCL-R, are probably two of the most powerful predictors of violent recidivism available anywhere. In fact, the PCL-R is a strong predictor of recidivism even when the offender's criminal history is not known to the examiner (Hemphill & Hare, 2004; Hemphill, Hare, & Wong, 1998).

High recidivism rates are also characteristic of psychopathic adolescent male offenders. Shortly, though, we will discuss the controversy over whether juvenile psychopathy even exists. According to Gretton et al. (2001), these offenders are more likely than other adolescent offenders to escape from custody, violate the conditions of probation, and commit nonviolent and violent offenses over a five-year follow-up period. The high recidivism rates among adult and juvenile offenders have prompted some researchers to conclude that there is "nothing the behavioral sciences can offer for treating those with psychopathy" (Gacono et al., 1997, p. 119). This is partly because psychopaths tend to "be unmotivated to alter their problematic behavior and often lack insight into the nature and extent of their psychopathology" (Skeem, Edens, & Colwell, 2003, p. 26).

THE FEMALE PSYCHOPATH

Very little research has been conducted so far on psychopathy in women, including female offenders. Overall, research suggests that there are far fewer female than male psychopaths, both in the general population and among persons convicted of crime. Based on PCL-R data, Salekin, Rogers, and Sewell (1997) reported that the prevalence rate of psychopathy for female offenders in a jail setting was 15.5 percent, compared with the 25 percent to 30 percent prevalence rate estimated for male offenders. In another study, Salekin, Rogers, Ustad, and Sewell (1998) found, using a PCL-R cutoff score of 29, that 12.9 percent of their sample of 78 female inmates qualified as psychopaths. In a more recent investigation involving 528 adult women incarcerated in Wisconsin, Vitale, Smith, Brinkley, and Newman (2002) report that 9 percent of their participants could be classified as psychopaths, using the recommended cutoff score of 30 on the PCL-R.

Because the known psychopathic population is dominated by men, little research has been directed at the women, although both Hare and Cleckley included female psychopaths in some of their work. However, Hare's PCL and PCL-R have been developed almost exclusively on male criminal psychopaths. Some preliminary studies using the PCL-R suggest that female criminal psychopaths may demonstrate different behavioral patterns than male criminal psychopaths (Hare, 1991; Vitale et al., in press). Although the data are far from conclusive, female psychopaths, compared with male psychopaths, appear to demonstrate a lack of realistic long-terms goals and show a greater tendency to be sexually promiscuous (Salekin, Rogers, & Sewell, 1997). In addition, they may not express the same emotional processing abnormalities as male psychopaths (Sutton, Vitale, & Newman, 2002).

There is also evidence that female psychopaths are less aggressive and violent than male psychopaths (Mulder, Wells, Joyce, & Bushnell, 1994) and may begin their offending careers later than males psychopaths (Hart & Hare, 1997). Female psychopaths may also recidivate less often than male psychopaths (Salekin, Rogers, Ustad, & Sewell, 1998). In fact, the evidence suggests that psychopathic female inmates may have recidivism rates that are no different than the recidivism rates reported for nonpsychopathic female inmates (Salekin et al., 1998).

In an early study, Robins (1966) found that female psychopaths followed the same behavioral patterns as male psychopaths, except that they were more frequently involved in sexual misconduct. In her sample, 79 percent of the females displayed abnormally high sexual activity and "excessive" interest in sexual matters. This finding is common in other female psychopath research.

However, in the absence of other behavioral descriptors, it suggests that the psychopath label associated with some of these studies may have been attached indiscriminately to women who were believed to engage inappropriately in sexual activity.

In summary, earlier research on possible gender differences in psychopathy was complicated by a tendency to equate sexual activity in women with abnormal stimulation-seeking behavior. When "excessive" or "aberrant" sexual activity is separated from other behaviors, female psychopaths appear to have characteristics largely similar to their male counterparts.

The more recent research utilizing the PCL-R shows considerable promise in identifying gender differences in psychopathy. Salekin, Rogers, and Sewell (1997) have found evidence for at least two broad categories of female psychopaths. One category appears to be characterized by a lack of empathy or guilt, interpersonal deception, sensation seeking, and proneness to boredom. The other group appears to be characterized by early behavioral problems, promiscuous sexual behavior, and adult antisocial (not violent) behavior. In recent years, we have seen a renewed interest in studying the female psychopath. It appears, therefore, that further investigations into gender differences of core factors may result in a more refined description of both male and female psychopaths.

RACIAL/ETHNIC DIFFERENCES

Kosson, Smith, and Newman (1990) noticed that most measures of psychopathy have been developed using white inmates as subjects. In their research they found that psychopathy, as measured by Hare's PCL, does exist in African American male inmates in a pattern that resembles white male inmates. However, Kosson et al. found one important difference. The African American criminal psychopaths tended to be less impulsive than white criminal psychopaths. This finding raises some questions as to whether the PCL is entirely appropriate to use with African American inmates. On the other hand, Jennifer Vitale et al. (2002) found no significant racial differences in the scores and distributions of female psychopaths. More specifically, Vitale et al. report that 10 percent of the 248 incarcerated Caucasian women who participated in their study reached the cutoff scores of 30 or higher on the PCL-R compared with 9 percent of the 280 incarcerated African American women who had similar scores.

A meta-analysis by Jennifer Skeem, John Edens, and Lori Colwell (2003) supports the conclusion that the differences between blacks and whites are minimal. Questions remain, however, as to the potential differences among other minority or disadvantaged groups.

Some researchers have raised the intriguing and serious issue of whether the stigmatizing diagnosis of psychopathy is likely to be used in a biased manner among minority or disadvantaged groups (Edens, Petrila, & Buffington-Vollum, 2001; Skeem, Edens, & Colwell, 2003; Skeem, Edens, Sanford, & Colwell, in press). In essence the consequence of being diagnosed a psychopath is becoming more serious (Skeem, Edens, Sanford, & Colwell, in press). As pointed out by Skeem et al. (2003), Canada and the United Kingdom use the diagnosis of psychopathy to support indeterminate detention for certain classes of offenders. Furthermore, "there is evidence that psychopathy increasingly is being used as an aggravating factor in the sentencing phase of U.S. death penalty cases, where it has been argued that the presence of these personality traits renders a defendant a 'continuing threat to society' " (Skeem et al., 2003, p. 17). Edens, Petrila, and Buffinton-Vollum (2001) suggest that perhaps the PCL-R should be excluded from capital sentencing until more solid research on its ability to predict future dangerousness in minority and disadvantaged individuals is established.

JUVENILE PSYCHOPATHY

As we have seen, one of the serious shortcomings of the extensive research conducted on psychopathy is that it has focused almost exclusively on white, adult males (Frick, Bodin, & Barry, 2000). Consequently research on juvenile (adolescent and child) psychopathy is limited, but it is rapidly growing. There is substantial evidence that male criminal psychopaths begin their offending patterns at a very early age (Rutter, 2005). However, attempts to apply the label "psychopathy" to juvenile populations "raise several conceptual, methodological, and practical concerns related to clinical/forensic practice and juvenile/criminal justice policy" (Edens, Skeem, Cruise, & Cauffman, 2001, p. 54). Some debate has focused on whether psychopathy can or should be applied to juveniles at all. Can features of adult psychopathy be found in children and adolescents in the first place? Others are concerned that—even if psychopathy can be identified in adolescents—the label may have too many negative connotations. More specifically the label implies that the prognosis for treatment is poor, a high rate of offending and recidivism can be expected, and the intrinsic and biological basis of the disorder means little can be done outside of biological interventions. This encourages those working in the juvenile justice system to give up on the juveniles so labeled. A third debate contends that psychopathy assessments of youths must achieve a high level of confidence before they can be employed in the criminal justice system (Seagrave & Grisso, 2002).

Can Juvenile Psychopathy be Identified?

Another major problem of identifying juvenile psychopaths is that psychopathy—if it exists in this age group—may be very difficult to measure reliably because of the transient and constantly changing developmental patterns across the life span. Many clinicians and researchers have resisted any trend to search for psychopathy in juveniles, noting that features of the adult psychopath simply represent normal adolescent development. In other words adolescents often appear callous and narcissistic, sometimes to hide their own fear and anxiety. They are often impulsive and engage in sensation-seeking behaviors, and many are not particularly good at long-range planning. In reality these and other psychopathic-like characteristics represent either a passing phase in the difficult transition to adulthood and/or the adolescent's "cover" to make him or herself appear noncaring. For other children, psychopathic-like characteristics might be indicative of physical or sexual abuse. Children in abusive homes often demonstrate an abnormally restricted range of emotions that are similar to the emotional characteristics of psychopathy. Actually, these symptoms are the child's way of coping with a very stressful home environment (Seagrave & Grisso, 2002). Furthermore, "Some adolescent behavior may . . . appear psychopathic by way of poor anger control, lack of goals, and poor judgment, but is actually influenced by parallel developmental tasks encountered by most adolescents" (Seagrave & Grisso, 2002, p. 229). Going against the rules is part of many adolescents' attempts to gain autonomy from adult dominance, such as found in adolescent-limited offending.

Nevertheless, certain problem characteristics in children and adolescents—for example, conduct problems, hyperactivity, impulsivity, and attention difficulties—resemble features of the adult psychopath and suggest that the term juvenile psychopath may have some validity. On the other hand, these characteristics may simply represent disorders such as conduct disorder (CD) or oppositional defiant disorder (ODD) that are distinct from psychopathy. As Cruise, Colwell, Lyons, and Baker (2003) have emphasized, to be useful the construct of juvenile psychopathy must be distinguished from other diagnoses. We return to this point shortly.

Ethical Considerations

On the whole, though, there is considerable concern about misuse of labels suggesting psychopathy by juvenile justice professionals, including judges, youth detention workers, and treatment providers. Because of the widespread assertion that psychopaths are highly resistant to treatment, an adolescent "psychopath" accused of a crime—or even a youth demonstrating psychopathic characteristics—is more likely to be transferred to the adult court system rather than kept in the juvenile system. In the latter, treatment is more likely to be available once the youth has been adjudicated delinquent. Until very recently, a 16- or 17-year-old juvenile labeled a psychopath also was more likely to be sentenced to death in some states (Edens, Guy, & Fernandez, 2003). However, in 2005 the U.S. Supreme Court ruled that juveniles who committed their crimes at these ages could not be sentenced to death (*Roper v. Simmons*). The court had previously set 16 as the minimum age at which juveniles were eligible for the death penalty (*Thompson v. Oklahoma*, 1989). Nevertheless, juveniles who are tried in criminal courts continue to be subjected to punitive criminal sanctions, including life sentences.

Even when juveniles are kept in the juvenile system and placed in treatment centers, though, the label "psychopath" can become a self-fulfilling prophecy with treatment providers who may be unlikely to expend considerable effort on a seemingly hopeless case. However, supporters of the construct of juvenile psychopathy argue that treatment providers should have that information at their disposal, both to make management decisions regarding custody and programming and to fashion the type of treatment that could be effective. Researchers are beginning to identify such treatment (e.g., Spain, Douglas, Poythress, & Epstein, 2004), as we discuss later in the chapter. In essence, if there is a distinct difference between psychopathic youth and nonpsychopathic youth, supporters claim it is critical that knowledge of this difference be communicated to those who work most closely with them. Supporters also believe there is wisdom in targeting for early intervention a subgroup of adolescents who otherwise might become career criminals (Skeem & Cauffman, 2003). This presumes, of course, that youth are correctly identified, which leads to the issue of reliability and validity.

Psychopathic assessments of youths must achieve a high level of confidence before they can be used in the criminal justice system, where individuals face dire consequences (Seagrave & Grisso, 2002). For example, if an assessment instrument is designed to measure juvenile psychopathy, then there must be considerable research to demonstrate that it, in fact, does measure what it says it measures. A majority of experts (e.g., Salekin, 2002; Seagrave & Grisso, 2002) maintain that, with reference to "juvenile psychopathy," we are not near that point yet.

Even so, over the past 15 years, knowledge regarding the theoretical and empirical applicability of juvenile "psychopathy" has expanded at a fast pace (Salekin et al., 2005). The research has demonstrated that the diagnostic label is linked to conduct disorder (Forth & Burke, 1998; Frick, 1998; Lynam, 1998) and higher levels of delinquency and police contacts (Corrado, Vincent, Hart, & Cohen, 2004; Falkenbach, Poythress, & Heide, 2003; Murrie et al., 2004; Salekin et al., 2003). Only about 25 percent of juveniles with conduct disorders show psychopathic tendencies (Blair et al., 2006). Forth and Burke (1998) report that children and adolescents with psychopathic traits differ from other antisocial youngsters in terms of the age of onset of their behavior problems, the number of violent acts committed, the seriousness of their offenses, and their recidivism rates. Consequently it appears that those youth who demonstrate psychopathic characteristics also seem to be heavily involved in antisocial behavior, at least hinting that the psychopathic label may have some validity.

Psychopathic Traits in Juvenile Delinquents

A number of researchers have reported finding the traits associated with psychopathy in children and adolescents, particularly juvenile delinquents. In a study examining the prevalence rate of psychopathic tendencies in children, Skilling, Quinsey, and Craig (2001) found that 4.3 percent of a sample of over one thousand boys in grades 4 to 8 could be classified as psychopathic on every measure employed in the study. Dåderman and Kristiansson (2003) found that 59 percent of their sample of violent juvenile offenders qualified as psychopaths. Similarly, Brandt, Kennedy, Patrick, and Curtain (1997), using a sample of incarcerated adolescents with persistent violent offending histories, reported that they could identify 37 percent of the sample as psychopathic. By contrast, Campbell, Porter, and Santor (2004) found that only 9 percent of their sample of incarcerated adolescent offenders could be classified as psychopaths. These authors note, though, that the juveniles they studied were primarily nonviolent in nature, with only 15 percent having a history of violent offending It is clear, therefore, that the sample used in a study, as well as the measuring instrument itself, will strongly influence the number of identifiable psychopathic traits within a given group of adolescents.

Measures of Juvenile Psychopathy

It is not surprising that the avid interest in psychopathy, including juvenile psychopathy, would lead to the development of a variety of instruments designed to measure it, or at least psychopathic characteristics. Several instruments for measuring juvenile psychopathy have been developed in recent years, including the *Psychopathy Screening Device* or the PSD (Frick & Hare, 2001; Frick, O'Brien, Wootton, & McBurnett, 1994), the *Childhood Psychopathy Scale* or the CPS (Lynam, 1997), the *Youth Psychopathic traits Inventory* or YPI (Andershed, Kerr, Stattin, & Levander, 2002), and the *Psychopathy Checklist: Youth Version* or the PCL:YV (Forth, Kosson, & Hare, 2003). Although originally developed as research instruments rather than for diagnosis purposes in clinics or for the courts, they are rapidly becoming available to forensic clinical examiners for use in their private practice and their consulting work with the courts and the juvenile justice system. As Seagrave and Grisso (2002) pointed out, "It is not overstated to imagine that juvenile psychopathy measures will become one of the most frequently used instruments in forensic assessments of delinquency cases of any kind within a few years after they are made generally available to forensic clinical examiners" (p. 220).

All the measures have some difficulty because juvenile psychopaths are unlikely to give accurate or honest self-reports about their emotions, thoughts, or behavior. The PCL:YV relies on an interview that has some specific questions to ask, plus collateral and other written data. Because of the interview and collateral data requirement, the PCL:YV requires extensive training to administer and is time consuming. In addition the PCL:YV is more research-based and measures all three dimensions of psychopathy. In contrast the PCS and the YPI rely heavily on self-reports, while the APSD and CPS are designed to obtain information from teachers, parents, and the child or adolescent him or herself.

There have been several attempts to compare these measures of juvenile psychopathy in terms of their validity and reliability (Farrington, 2005a). Preliminary research so far indicates that they do not have much in common, but considerably more research needs to be done before conclusions can be drawn.

BIOLOGICAL FACTORS AND PSYCHOPATHY

There is a widespread belief among the general public that psychopathic tendencies are caused exclusively by social factors, such as abuse and poor upbringing. However, researchers have implicated a variety of biological factors as well. Contemporary research favors the view that psychopathic behavior results from a complex interaction between neuropsychological and learning or socialization factors.

Genetic Factors

There is emerging evidence that genetics may play a role in the development of psychopathy (Blonigen, Carlson, Krueger, & Patrick, 2003; Blonigen et al., 2005; Viding, Blair, Moffitt, & Plomin, 2005). For example, some evidence suggests that temperament linked to low arousal and fear responses is associated with psychopathy (Frick & Morris, 2004). A temperament of this nature may disrupt the formation of guilt, conscience, or concern about punishment.

The overall influence of genetics on psychopathy is not large, but it seems large enough to draw the increasing attention of developmental and genetic researchers, especially those investigators interested in twin studies. Blair et al. (2006) believe that genetic contributions may play a significant role in the emotional dysfunction frequently found in psychopaths. That is, heredity may contribute significantly to the underarousal and low emotional responsiveness of psychopaths. However, at this point in our knowledge we appear to be a long way off from a genetic account of psychopathy.

Neurophysiology and Psychopathy

Although the research on psychopaths in recent years has focused on the psychometric characteristics of psychopaths, the current trend in psychopathy research is the investigation of neuropsychological factors involved in determining their behavior (Vien & Beech, 2006). Neuropsychological indicators (called **markers**) have been repeatedly found in psychopaths, as reflected in electrodermal (skin conductance) measures, cardiovascular, and other nervous system indices (Fishbein, 2001; Morgan & Lilienfeld, 2000). It is important, therefore, to become familiar with additional neuropsychological vocabulary and basic structures of the nervous system, some of which appeared in chapter 3. The concepts presented here will also lay the foundation for topics in later chapters (e.g., chapters 12 and 13 on sexual offenses, and chapter 16 on drugs) as well.

Basic Neurophysiological Concepts and Terminology

The human nervous system can be divided into two major parts, either on the basis of structure or function. The structural division—the way it is arranged physically—is perhaps the clearest distinction. The central nervous system (CNS) and the peripheral nervous system (PNS) are the two principal parts. The CNS comprises the brain and spinal cord, and the PNS comprises all nerve cells (called neurons) and nerve pathways located outside the CNS (see **Table 6–2**). In other words, those nerves that leave the spinal cord and brain stem

TABLE 6–2   Divisions of the Human Nervous System

I. Central nervous system (CNS)
   A. Brain
   B. Spinal cord
II. Peripheral nervous system (PNS)
   A. Skeletal nervous system (communicates with voluntary muscles)
   B. Autonomic nervous system
      1. Parasympathetic nervous system (relaxes and deactivates after emergencies)
      2. Sympathetic nervous system (activates for emergencies)

and travel to specific sites in the body belong to the peripheral (outside) nervous system. This includes all the nerves connecting the muscles, skin, heart, glands, and senses to the CNS.

The basic function of the PNS is to bring all the outside information to the CNS, where it is processed. Once the CNS has processed information, it relays the interpretation back to the PNS if action is necessary. When you place your finger on a hot object, the PNS relays this raw data (it is not yet pain) to the CNS, which interprets the datum as the sensation of pain, and in return, relays a command to the PNS to withdraw the finger. The PNS cannot interpret; it only transmits information to the CNS and carries communications back. In the following pages, we will consider the significance of each of these systems to the diagnosis of psychopathy.

Central Nervous System Differences

Structurally, the CNS consists of the brain and spinal cord. Interpretation, thoughts, memories, and images all occur in the cerebral cortex (the highest center of the brain). It is the processing center for stimulation and sensations received from the outside world and the body via the PNS. The cerebral cortex, which is the outer surface of the human brain, contains more than 100 billion nerve cells (called neurons) (Hockenbury & Hockenbury, 2004; *Scientific American*, 1999). Each neuron has a complicated communication link to numerous other neurons, creating an extremely complex and poorly understood communications network. Although the physical structures of the brain do not directly concern us, the electrical circuitry and arousal properties of the cortex are relevant in understanding the neuropsychological characteristics of the psychopath.

Hemisphere Asymmetry and Deficiency

The human brain can be divided anatomically into two cerebral hemispheres—a right and a left. These two cerebral hemispheres seem to coexist in some sort of reciprocally balancing relationship in cortical functioning and information processing. For most individuals, the right hemisphere specializes in nonverbal functions, whereas the left specializes in verbal or language functions. Furthermore the left hemisphere processes information in an analytical, sequential fashion. Language, for example, requires sequential cognition, and the left seems to be the best equipped for this operation. The right hemisphere, on the other hand, seems to process information holistically and more globally. For example, the right is involved in the recognition of faces, a complicated process requiring the processing of information all at once or simultaneously. Thus the right and left hemispheres are two functionally differentiated information processing systems.

In addition to information processing, research is now finding that these two cerebral hemispheres also make different contributions to human emotions (Jacobs & Snyder, 1996; Tomarken, Davidson, Wheeler, & Doss, 1992). The right hemisphere appears to be particularly important in the understanding and communication of emotion (Kosson et al., 2002; Wheeler, Davidson, & Tomarken, 1993). The left seems to be closely tied to self-inhibiting processes, in contrast to the right which appears to be more spontaneous and impulsive (Tucker, 1981). Furthermore the two hemispheres must have a balance of contribution from each for normal judgment and appropriate self-control (Tucker, 1981), and self- regulation of emotion (Tomarken et al., 1992). These control and judgment processes are especially prevalent in the frontal lobes (front sections of the brain).

Hare (Hare, 1998; Hare & Connolly, 1987; Hare & McPherson, 1984) hypothesizes that criminal psychopaths manifest an abnormal or unusual balance between the two hemispheres, both in language processing and in emotional or arousal states, which he calls **hemisphere asymmetry.** Hare notes that criminal psychopaths are often strikingly inconsistent with their verbalized thoughts, feelings, and intentions. Criminal psychopaths seem to be highly peculiar in the organization of certain perceptual and cognitive processes. Their left hemisphere seems, in some ways, deficient in linguistic processing because they do not rely on the verbal sequential operations to the extent that a majority of individuals do. Hare (1998) also hypothesizes that as the language task increased in complexity, nonpsychopathic persons relied more and more on the left hemisphere to process the information, while psychopaths rely more on the right hemisphere. Recent research supports this hypothesis (Lorenz & Newman, 2002).

There is also some research indicating that psychopaths are less accurate than nonpsychopaths at reading emotional expressions portrayed by faces. More specifically, psychopaths appear to be less accurate than nonpsychopaths in facial emotional recognition under conditions designed to promote reliance on left-hemisphere processing (Kosson et al., 2002). These data are in support of the *left-hemisphere activation hypothesis* (Kosson, 1998), which states that psychopaths exhibit deficits on a variety of tasks that require activation of the left hemisphere.

Since language plays a very important role in the self-regulation of behavior, one of the contributing factors in the extremely impulsive, episodic behavior of psychopaths may reside in some deficiency in their use of internal language. This characteristic was pointed out some time ago by Flor-Henry (Flor-Henry, 1973; Flor-Henry & Yeudall, 1973), who was convinced that psychopathy is closely linked to left-hemispheric language dysfunction. There has been some research to suggest that the right hemisphere of psychopaths may be deficient as well (Herpertz & Sass, 2000). Research by Day and Wong (1996) and Silberman and Weingartner (1986), for example, suggest that many psychopaths have impairments in the right hemisphere that prevents them from experiencing emotions as strongly as the normal population. Other researchers have found evidence that psychopaths exhibit an **emotional paradox.** "That is, psychopaths demonstrate normal appraisal of emotional cues and situations in the abstract (i.e., verbal discussion), but they are deficient in using emotional cues to guide their judgments and behavior in the process of living" (Lorenz & Newman, 2002, p. 91). In other words, psychopaths seem to be able to talk about emotional cues but lack the ability to use them effectively in the real world. This deficiency seems to be due to processing problems located in the left hemisphere (Bernstein, Newman, Wallace, & Luh, 2000; Lorenz & Newman, 2002).

Nachshon (Nachshon, 1983; Nachshon & Denno, 1987) points out that many studies have found that a disproportionate percentage of violent, repetitive offenders have left hemispheric dysfunction. Researchers in Germany had found similar results (Pillmann et al., 1999). Moreover, several researchers have argued that left-handedness may be an indicator of left hemispheric dysfunction and have predicted that left-handedness will be overrepresented in the criminal or psychopathic population. Fitzhugh (1973) reported that about one-third of a group of juvenile delinquents were left-handed, while Andrew (1978) found that about one out of five adult male offenders preferred their left hand. However, in a later study, Andrew (1980) reported that the left handers seemed to be less violent than right-handed offenders. On the other hand, Nachshon and Denno (1987), in their investigation of 1,066 black male children—whose mothers participated in the Philadelphia Collaborative Perinatal Project—found that nonoffenders (based on official statistics) showed a significantly higher incidence of left-handedness than offenders. Thus the research results are far from conclusive. Researchers have used different samples, have not been very definitive about their sample composition, and have used a variety of procedures and methods in obtaining and analyzing the data. Much more needs to be done before we can entertain any conclusions about left versus right preferences or left versus right hemispheric functioning in criminal or psychopathic populations.

Frontal Neuropsychological Studies

Some studies suggest that psychopaths may also suffer from frontal lobe problems or dysfunctions (Kiehl, 2006; Morgan & Lilienfeld, 2000; Sellbom & Verona, in press). The frontal lobe refers to that section of the cerebral cortex we commonly call the forehead. The frontal lobes (there are two) are believed to be responsible for the "higher level" cognitive functions of abstraction, decision making, cognitive flexibility, foresight, the regulation of impulses, and the control of appropriate behavior (Ishikawa et al., 2001). In other words, the frontal lobes perform the "executive functions" of the human brain. **Executive functions** refer to higher order mental abilities involved in goal directed behavior. Executive functions include organizing behavior, memory, inhibition processes, and planning strategies. Research has been consistent in demonstrating that prefrontal damage results in poor decision making, reduced autonomic functioning, and a psychopathic-like personality (Yang et al., 2005).

Gorenstein (1982) and Newman, Patterson, and Kosson (1987) report findings that indicate psychopaths may have defects in frontal lobe processing. On the other hand, research by Hare (1984), Hoffman, Hall, and Bartsch (1987), and Sutker and Allain (1983) failed to support the frontal lobe hypothesis. These equivocal results prompted Ishikawa et al. (2001, p. 423) to assert, "Clearly, research on the frontal dysfunction hypothesis in psychopaths is far from conclusive. However, a recent meta-analysis of the extant research on the topic by Morgan and Lilienfeld (2000) *suggests* that psychopaths, as a group, do show executive function deficits, which may result in faulty impulse control, judgment, and planning under certain conditions.

Cathy Widom (Widom, 1978; Widom & Newman, 1985) points out that the mixed research results may stem from differences in the population of psychopaths being tested. Specifically, Widom (1978) found that psychopaths recruited from newspaper advertisements did not demonstrate the same level of frontal lobe deficits as incarcerated psychopaths. Widom speculated that "successful psychopaths" (community-based psychopaths who escaped conviction of their offenses and who answered the ad) probably had better functioning frontal lobes for controlling their behavior than the "unsuccessful" institutionalized psychopaths. Consistent with Widom's results, Ishikawa et al. (2001) discovered that successful psychopaths do not show the same psychophysiological or neuropsychological deficits as unsuccessful psychopaths. Overall, the researchers found that successful psychopaths exhibited stronger and better organized executive functions than either the unsuccessful psychopaths or the controls used in the study. Interestingly the *unsuccessful* psychopaths did show most of the neuropsychological characteristics reported in the previous studies conducted over the past 30 years.

At this point, the evidence suggests that the frontal lobes may play an important role in explaining some of the observed behavioral differences between psychopaths and nonpsychopaths. Furthermore, frontal lobe dysfunction may not be simply limited to psychopaths but may be a feature that is characteristic of many other types of offenders (Raine, 1993).

Amygdala Dysfunction

Psychopaths clearly demonstrate some problems in emotional processing. The frontal lobe is most often associated with this observation, as we have seen. Some researchers are beginning to believe that another neurological structure responsible for this dysfunction may be the amygdala (Kiehl, 2006). The amygdala is an almond-shaped cluster of neurons in the brain responsible for emotions such as fear, anger, and disgust. The amygdala is also involved in learning and short-term memory, especially in those learning situations involving high emotions.

Kiehl et al. (2001) found that psychopaths exhibited lower amygdala activity during an emotional processing task when compared with criminal non-psychopaths and noncriminal controls. Similar findings were reported by Müller et al. (2003). With further research, the relationship between amygdala and learning might emerge as a highly significant factor in understanding the emotional behavior of the psychopath.

Stimulation Seeking

Herbert Quay (1965) suggested that much of the psychopath's behavior represents an extreme form of stimulation seeking. He hypothesized that psychopaths do not receive the full impact of sensations from the environment and thus are always craving more. Therefore, in order to get the optimal amount of stimulation necessary to keep the underaroused cerebral cortex satisfied, they must engage more frequently in various forms of excitement than the normal person.

Several early studies have supported Quay's hypothesis. For example, Wiesen (1965) found that psychopaths worked harder for visual (colored lights) and auditory (music on a radio) stimulation than did a group of nonpsychopaths. In a second experiment that provided continued bombardment of lights and music, Wiesen also demonstrated that nonpsychopaths worked harder than psychopaths to obtain three seconds of silence and relative darkness.

Skrzpek (1969) delineated psychopaths and "neurotic delinquents" on the basis of a behavior rating list for psychopathy and neuroticism developed by Quay (1964). He found that conditions that increased "cortical arousal" (e.g., where the subject was required to make difficult auditory discriminations) decreased preference for visual complexity in both the psychopathic and neurotic groups, but was most pronounced in the latter. On the other hand, a brief period of stimulus deprivation (presumably low cortical arousal) increased preference for complexity in both groups, but a significantly greater increase was shown by the psychopaths.

In an attempt to test Quay's hypothesis that deficient responsivity of the nervous system might account for pathological stimulation seeking, Whitehill, DeMyer-Gapin, and Scott (1976) conducted an experiment using 103 boring slides of "concrete facades of a modern college campus building." As subjects, the researchers used 55 institutionalized "disturbed" preadolescent boys. The professional staff at the institution rated eight boys psychopathic (antisocial) and eight neurotic. A group of seven "normal" noninstitutionalized adolescent boys, matched with the index subjects for age, were used as controls. The average age was 11.5 years. Results showed that the psychopathic and normal boys looked at the slides significantly less than the neurotic group. More important, the psychopathic preadolescents showed a significant decrease in viewing time earlier than the other groups, suggesting that they became bored more quickly than the other groups. Whitehall concluded that the data support the pathological stimulation-seeking hypothesis and favored a physiological ingredient in the formulation of psychopathy. In another project, Orris (1969) found that, compared with nonpsychopaths, psychopathic boys performed more poorly on a boring task requiring continuous attention and that they engaged more in boredom-relieving activities like singing or talking to themselves.

Optimal Arousal of the Cerebral Cortex

A number of theorists have postulated (e.g., Berlyne, 1960; Hebb, 1955; Fiske & Maddi, 1961) that organisms seek to maintain preferred or optimal levels of stimulation, with stimulation referring to the amount of sensation and/or information processed by the cortex. In effect, their theories argue for an inverted U-shaped function, with intermediate levels of stimulation most preferred and the extremes least preferred (see **Figure 6–1**). Insufficient amounts of stimulation lead to boredom, which can be reduced by an increase in stimulation-seeking behavior. On the other hand, exceptionally high levels of stimulation are also aversive and may promote behavior designed to avoid stimulation in an effort to bring the stimulus input to a more pleasurable level.

Cortical arousal appears to have a direct relationship with the amount of stimulation received by the cortex. Low stimulation produces a relatively low

FIGURE 6–1   Optimal Levels of Stimulation for Ambiverts, Introverts, and Extraverts

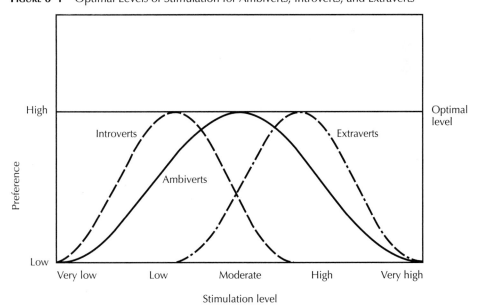

Note: Introverts reach their optimal level sooner than ambiverts or extraverts do.

level of cortical arousal, whereas high levels of stimulation initiate high cortical arousal. To fall asleep we must lower the cortex's arousal level by minimizing external and internal stimulation (noises, lights, thoughts). If we do not wish to fall asleep, but our cortical arousal is low (e.g., during a boring lecture), we seek excitement to increase the arousal level. On the other hand, if stimulation becomes excessive, such as via a blaring radio or the pandemonium of rush hour traffic, we are distressed if unable to control the stimulus input. Some psychologists argue that much behavior can be explained as an attempt by the person to maintain optimal or just-right levels of stimulation—levels that are the most comfortable and pleasurable to the individual.

It is generally agreed that there are individual differences in the quality and quantity of stimulation necessary for each person to reach the optimum level of stimulation. Some of this individual difference may be attributed to certain physiological structures, particularly those found in the brain stem. Eysenck (1967), you will recall, hypothesized that personality differences are largely due to differential needs for stimulation, which are dictated by functional properties of the reticular formation.

The reticular formation can be conveniently divided into several anatomical areas. Chief among these is the reticular activating system (RAS), a tiny but complex nerve network located in the central portion of the brain stem. The RAS underlies our attentiveness to the world and acts as a sentinel that activates the cortex and keeps it alert. Sensory signals or inputs from all parts of the body must travel through the brain stem on their way to the processing center, the cortex. Inside the brain stem, they branch into two major pathways. One major pathway goes through a relay station known as the thalamus; the other travels through the RAS which, in turn, alerts the cortex to incoming information being routed through the thalamic pathway. The RAS-generated arousal is nonspecific in that it energizes the entire cortex and not any specific area. Therefore, any particular stimulation or sensation, from the outside world or from inside the body, has both a coded message (which travels through the thalamus) and a nonspecific arousing effect (which travels through the RAS).

The RAS can also decrease cortical arousal. If certain incoming stimuli are no longer significant or relevant, the cortex "tells" the RAS to filter out that particular group of stimuli. That process is called adaptation or **habituation.** Therefore, repetitive and insignificant stimuli are prevented by the RAS from unnecessarily bombarding the cortex with meaningless detail.

Contemporary research and theory suggests that the psychopath has a pathological need for excitement and thrills because of some deficiency in or excessive habituation property of the RAS. We emphasize the word "suggest" because, while the research seems consistent in demonstrating that psychopaths appear to have a strong need for stimulation, research has not clearly identified what neurophysiological mechanisms are involved. However, mainstream theory concerning the neurophysiological processes is as follows. The RAS either does not activate the cortex sufficiently to receive the full impact of the incoming information, or else it adapts too quickly, thereby shutting down the cortex's activation before it receives complete information. Either way, the psychopath is unable to reach optimal arousal levels with the same amount of stimulation that normals find adequately arousing. So, the psychopath engages in behaviors that society refers to as thrill-seeking, chancy, antisocial, or inappropriate in order to reach satisfying optimal cortical arousal.

The general concept of arousal has been used interchangeably with cortical arousal throughout this chapter. In discussing psychopathy, many investigators refer to other forms of arousal, like autonomic (anxiety) or behavior arousal. Basically, these terms mean the same thing. Many states of activation or arousal involve overlapping systems (Korman, 1974). Thus, although there may be slightly different processes and mechanisms involved in different states of arousal, all must involve the heightened arousal levels of the cortex.

In an interesting experiment, Chesno and Kilmann (1975) tested the arousal hypothesis of psychopathy by manipulating stimulation variables (aversive white noise and shock) and personality variables (psychopaths, neurotics, and normals). Ninety male offenders incarcerated in a maximum security penitentiary were selected for the experiment by various criteria. Psychopaths were classified according to Cleckley's criteria. The procedure involved an avoidance learning task, with electric shock being administered for certain incorrect choices by the subject. During the avoidance learning task, each subject received either 35, 65, or 95 decibels of white noise through earphones. (White noise is an auditory stimulus that sounds like a hissing radiator.)

If the arousal hypothesis is correct, the underaroused psychopath under low levels of stimulation should require some form of increased stimulation. Since errors in avoidance learning led to electric shock, psychopaths would be most likely to commit errors and benefit by the stimulation provided by the electric shock. Accordingly, as external stimulation increases (higher levels of white noise), the psychopath should have a decreased need for stimulation and, therefore, should learn to avoid the shock more effectively. The results of the study supported the hypothesis. Psychopaths made significantly more avoidance errors than the other groups as the stimulation decreased, which suggests that they prefer punishment to boredom. The finding may explain the well-known inability of psychopaths to benefit from punishment in situations low in stimulation, like prisons or even classrooms. It might even be that imprisoned psychopaths would "learn better" if the conditions under which they were incarcerated were more stimulating.

Therefore, psychopaths apparently do not learn to avoid aversive circumstances because of underarousal. However, if their arousal is increased, their avoidance learning should correspondingly increase. Furthermore, there is evidence that if incentives (e.g., money or other rewards) are used, avoidance learning in psychopaths also increases. In summarizing the research on this topic, Newman and his colleagues (Newman, 1987; Newman & Kosson, 1986; Newman, Patterson, Howland, & Nichols, 1990) have studied how rewards or incentives change the avoidance learning patterns of psychopaths. Their research suggests that, with adequate incentives, psychopaths become highly motivated to learn certain tasks and requirements. In fact, psychopaths under incentive conditions may learn better than nonpsychopaths. Raine (1993,

p. 228) writes, "Psychopaths do indeed learn poorly when the reinforcer is physical or social punishment, but they do appear to learn well when (1) their arousal is increased, or (2) they are sufficiently motivated by financial incentives."

Peripheral Nervous System (PNS) Research

The PNS is subdivided into a *skeletal division*, comprising the motor nerves that innervate the skeletal muscles involved in body movement, and an autonomic division, which controls heart rate, gland secretion, and smooth muscle activity. Smooth muscles are those muscles found in the blood vessels and gastrointestinal system; they look smooth under a microscope in comparison to the skeletal muscles, which look striped or textured.

The autonomic segment of the PNS is extremely relevant to our discussion of the psychopath, because here, too, research has consistently uncovered a significant difference between the psychopath's and the general population's reactivity or responsiveness to stimuli. The autonomic division is especially important, because it activates emotional behavior and responsivity to stress and tension. It can be subdivided into the *sympathetic* and *parasympathetic systems* (see **Figure 3–4** on page 103).

The sympathetic system is responsible for activating or arousing the individual for fight or flight before (or during) fearful or emergency situations. As you will recall, the psychopath displays a James Bond-like coolness, even in stressful situations. We might explain this in one of two ways. Either the sympathetic nervous system does not react sufficiently to stressful stimuli, or the parasympathetic system springs into action in the psychopath more rapidly than in nonpsychopaths. There is research support for both of these positions.

Before discussing in more detail the psychopath's autonomic nervous system, we should note the principles and techniques of measuring autonomic activity. Emotional arousal, which is largely under the control of the autonomic nervous system, can be measured by monitoring the system's activity, such as heart rate, blood pressure or volume, and respiration rate. The most commonly used physiological indicator of emotional arousal, however, is *skin conductance response* (SCR), also known as the *galvanic skin response* (GSR). Since SCR is the label most advocated by contemporary researchers (Lykken & Venables, 1971), it will be used throughout this chapter.

SCR is simply a measure of the resistance of the skin to conducting electrical current. Although a number of factors in the skin influence its resistance, perspiration seems to play a major role. Perspiration corresponds very closely to changes in emotional states and has, therefore, been found to be a highly sensitive indicator of even slight changes in the autonomic nervous system. Other things being equal, as emotional arousal increases, perspiration rate increases proportionately. Small changes in perspiration can be picked up and amplified by recording devices, known as polygraphs or physiographs. An increase in perspiration lowers skin resistance to electrical conductance. In other words, skin conductance increases as emotional arousal (anxiety, fear, and so on) increases.

We noted earlier that psychopaths lack the capacity to respond emotionally to stressful or fearful situations. Essentially they give the impression of being anxiety-free, carefree, and cool, and they display a devil-may-care attitude. We would expect, therefore, that compared with the normal population, the psychopath has a comparatively underactive, underaroused autonomic nervous system. What has the research literature revealed? Consistently, investigators have reported low SC arousal in psychopaths (Fishbein, 2001). "Deficits in measures of SC arousal are believed to be associated with low autonomic arousal levels which are, in turn, related to low emotionality, poor conditionability, lack of empathy and remorse, and ability to lie easily" (Fishbein, 2001, p. 51). There is also some evidence that juvenile psychopaths show low SC arousal levels (Fung et al., 2005).We now turn our attention to the division of the nervous system most responsible for SC arousal.

Autonomic Nervous System Research

In a pioneering study, Lykken (1957) hypothesized that since anxiety reduction is an essential ingredient in learning to avoid painful or stressful situations, and since the psychopath is presumed to be anxiety free, then the psychopath should have special difficulty learning to avoid unpleasant things. Recall that two characteristic features of psychopaths are their inability to learn from unpleasant experiences and their very high recidivism. Lykken carefully delineated his research groups according to Cleckley's criteria. His psychopaths (both males and females) were drawn from several penal institutions in Minnesota and were classified as either primary or neurotic psychopaths. College students comprised a third group of normals.

Lykken designed an electronic maze that subjects were expected to learn as well as possible in twenty trials. There were 20 choice points in the maze, each with four alternatives, with only one being the correct choice. Although three alternatives were incorrect, only one of these would give the subject a rather painful electric shock. Lykken was primarily interested in discovering how quickly subjects learned to avoid the shock, a process called **avoidance learning.** He reasoned that avoidance learning would be rewarded by the reduction of anxiety on encountering the correct choice point, but since psychopaths are presumably deficient in anxiety, their performance should be significantly worse than that of normals. The hypothesis was supported.

Prior to the maze portion of the experiment, Lykken measured the skin conductance changes of each subject while he or she tried to sit quietly for 30 to 40 minutes. During this time, the subjects would periodically hear a buzzer and occasionally receive a slight, brief electric shock several seconds after the buzzer. Eventually, the buzzer became associated with the shock. In normal individuals the sound of the buzzer itself produced an anxiety response in anticipation of the electric shock (classical conditioning) and was reflected by a substantial increase in SCR. Psychopaths, however, were considerably less responsive to this stress. Furthermore, psychopaths were incapable of learning to avoid the painful electric shocks, while the normals learned significantly better.

Lykken's data indicate that psychopaths do in fact have an underresponsive autonomic nervous system and, as a result, do not learn to avoid aversive situations as well as most other people. More recent research continues to support these findings (Gottman, 2001; Ogloff & Wong, 1990). Does this provide at least a partial explanation for why psychopaths continue to get into trouble with the law, despite the threat of imprisonment?

Schachter and Latané (1964) followed up on Lykken's work by using similar apparatus and basic procedures, with the exception of one major revision. Each subject was run through the maze twice, once with an injection of a harmless saline solution, once with an injection of adrenaline, a hormone that stimulates physiological arousal. Subjects were prisoners selected on the basis of two criteria: how closely they approximated Cleckley's primary psychopath and how incorrigible they were, as measured by the number of offenses and time in prison. Prisoners high on both criteria were psychopaths; prisoners relatively low were nonpsychopaths.

Injections of adrenaline dramatically improved the performance of the psychopath in the avoidance learning task. In fact, with adrenaline injections, the psychopaths learned to avoid shocks more quickly than did normal prisoners with similar injections. On the other hand, when psychopaths had saline injections, they were as deficient in avoidance learning as Lykken's psychopaths.

Since anxiety is presumed to be a major deterrent to antisocial impulses, the manipulation of arousal or anxiety states by drugs may suggest policy implications for the effective treatment of convicted psychopaths. Specific drugs apparently have the potential to increase the emotional level of psychopaths to a point equivalent to the level of the general population.

Subsequent research by Hare (1965a, 1965b) found that primary psychopaths have significantly lower skin conductance while resting than do nonpsychopaths. Other researchers have reported similar results (Herpertz & Sass, 2000; Lorber, 2004). In a major study, Hare (1968) divided 51 inmates at the British Columbia Penitentiary into three groups—primary psychopaths, secondary psychopaths, and nonpsychopaths—and studied them under various conditions, while constantly monitoring their autonomic functioning. The experimental conditions also permitted the observation of a complex physiological response known as the *orienting response* (OR).

The OR is a nonspecific, highly complicated cortical and sensory response to strange, unexpected changes in the environment. The response may take the form of a turning of the head, a dilation of the eye, or a decrease in heart rate. It is made in an effort to determine what the change is. Pavlov referred to the OR as the "what-is-it" reflex. It is an automatic, reflexive accompaniment to any perceptible change, and it can be measured by various physiological indices. The OR produces, among other things, an increase in the analytical powers of the senses and the cortex.

Hare found that not only did psychopaths exhibit very little autonomic activity (skin conductance and heart rate), but also that they gave smaller ORs than did nonpsychopaths. His data suggest that psychopaths are less sensitive and alert to their environment, particularly to new and unusual events.

Hare later reported intriguing data relating to the heart or cardiac activity of the psychopath. The aforementioned conclusions were based on skin conductance data. When cardiovascular variables are considered, however, some apparent anomalies appear. While skin conductance is consistently low, cardiac activity (heart rate) in the psychopath is often as high as that found in the nonpsychopathic population (Hare & Quinn, 1971). Hare comments, "The psychopaths appeared to be poor electrodermal [skin conductance] conditioners but good cardiovascular ones" (Hare, 1976, p. 135). That is, although psychopaths do not learn to react to stimuli as measured by skin variables, it appears that they learn to react autonomically as well as nonpsychopaths when the heart rate is measured. Hare suggests that the psychopath might be more adaptive to stress when "psychophysiological defense mechanisms" are brought into play, thereby reducing the impact of stressful stimuli.

Hare and his colleagues designed experiments in which the heart rate could be monitored throughout the experimental session. In one experiment a tone preceded an electric shock by about 10 seconds (Hare & Craigen, 1974). In anticipation of the shock, psychopaths exhibited a rapid acceleration of heartbeat, followed by a rapid deceleration of heart rate immediately before the onset of the noxious stimulus (a "normal" reaction is a gradual but steady increase in heart rate until the shock). However, their skin conductance remained significantly lower than that of nonpsychopaths. Therefore, psychopaths appear to be superior conditioners when cardiac activity is measured, indicating that they do indeed either learn or inherit autonomic adaptability to noxious stimuli. Hare suggests that this accelerative heart response is adaptive and helps the psychopath tune out or modulate the emotional impact of noxious stimuli. This, he speculates, may be the reason that skin conductance responses are relatively low in the psychopath.

Lykken (1955) also conducted experiments testing the performance of psychopaths on polygraph equipment. If psychopaths are generally underaroused, we would expect that lie detectors would be unable to differentiate their deceptive from their truthful responses, since polygraphs rely on physiological reactivity to questions. Also, psychopaths should have no trouble being deceptive, since they are typically adept at manipulating and deceiving others. Lykken's research confirmed these expectancies. Psychopaths emitted similar skin conductance responses, regardless of whether they were lying or telling the truth. Nonpsychopaths displayed significant differences in reactivity; their lie ratios, reflected by skin conductance, were larger than those of psychopaths. Because of the artificial atmosphere of the laboratory compared with real-life situations, particularly stressful ones, Lykken admonished against uncritical acceptance of his findings until further testing.

Few studies have since directly examined the relationship between psychopathy and lie detection. However, Raskin and Hare (1978) did reexamine the Lykken study, using more sophisticated equipment and better standardization for lie detection. Using 24 psychopathic prisoners and 24 nonpsychopathic prisoners, they found that both groups were equally easily detected at lying about a situation involving a $20 mock theft. This contradictory finding underscores the fact that fine-tuning is still needed if we are to understand the neurophysiological characteristics of the psychopath.

There is evidence, for example, that sufficiently aroused or motivated psychopaths will give physiological responses to interesting events that equal the responses of nonpsychopaths (Hare, 1968). On the other hand, when it comes to highly stressful, serious occasions, psychopaths appear to have incomparable skill at attenuating guilt or aversive reactions (Lykken, 1978). The simulated crime scene in the Raskin-Hare experiment was not only relatively unstressful; it may also have been regarded by the psychopath as an interesting "game." The acid test for the lie detection hypothesis will rest with carefully designed experiments under real-life, highly stressful situations. The present data do not justify firm conclusions. Christopher Patrick and his colleagues (Patrick, Bradley, & Lang, 1993) conducted a study designed to test in what ways the startle reflex action in psychopaths differs from that of the normal population. An example of a startle response is the eye blink reflex in response to a puff of air. These researchers note that psychophysiological research on the psychopath has relied almost exclusively on skin conductance and cardiovascular measures. The researchers found that criminal psychopaths (measured by Hare's PCL-R) exhibited much lower startle responses under aversive conditions than nonpsychopaths. Their findings confirm previous research showing that criminal psychopaths give smaller autonomic responses under aversive conditions than do other nonpsychopathic offenders. Hare (1993, 1996) postulates that psychopaths suffer from a general "hypoemotionality." That is, it appears that psychopaths fail to experience the full impact of any kind of emotion—positive or negative. Psychopaths may be born with this hypoemotionality and that may account for their lack of remorse throughout their lifetimes.

In summary, the research reviewed thus far allows us to make four tentative conclusions about the autonomic functioning of the psychopath. First, psychopaths appear to be both autonomically and cortically underaroused, both under rest conditions and under some specific stress conditions. They are much more physiologically "drowsy" than nonpsychopaths. Second, because they lack the necessary emotional equipment, psychopaths appear to be deficient in avoidance learning, which might account partially for their very high recidivism rates. Third, some data suggest that if emotional arousal can be induced, such as by adrenaline, psychopaths can learn from past experiences and avoid normally painful or aversive situations, such as prison, embarrassment, or social censure. And fourth, with adequate incentives, such as monetary rewards, psychopaths can learn from past experiences and avoid aversive consequences as well as anyone.

Adrian Raine, in his excellent review of the relevant research, finds that many of these psychophysiological indicators discussed for psychopaths may be characteristic of repetitive, violent offenders in general. In fact, in reference to resting heart rate levels in *noninstitutionalized offenders,* he concludes, "This is probably the best replicated and most robust biological finding on antisocial behavior reported to date" (1993, p. 190).

We noted earlier that psychopaths are often profoundly affected by alcohol, even in small amounts. Alcohol is a general CNS depressant, decreasing arousal levels in the nervous system. Research indicates that underaroused psychopaths are already half asleep and "half in the bag"; alcohol has the general effect of "bagging" them completely. Therefore, we would expect not only that the psychopath would get intoxicated more rapidly than the nonpsychopath of comparable weight, but also would probably pass out sooner. We would also expect the psychopath to have few sleep difficulties. Steven Smith and Joseph Newman (1990) found that a higher percentage of criminal psychopaths have been polydrug users when compared with criminal nonpsychopaths. In addition, criminal psychopaths were particularly heavy alcohol abusers, and alcohol may have played a very significant role in prompting their extensive antisocial behavior.

Recent research has shown that adult psychopaths usually exhibit significant antisocial behavior in their childhoods (Seagrave & Grisso, 2002). It is reasonable, therefore, to expect researchers to begin searching the developmental trajectory of psychopathy in order to identify tomorrow's psychopaths. The next section examines what we currently know about the childhood of the psychopath. In light of our earlier discussion of juvenile psychopathy, though, we must be careful not to assume that adult psychopaths were necessarily psychopathic as juveniles.

CHILDHOOD OF THE PSYCHOPATH

We have discussed the behavioral descriptions and biopsychological components of psychopaths. Now, how did they get that way? Criminal behavior and other behavior problems are often assumed to be rooted in the home, usually in homes with conflict, inadequate discipline, or poor models. From our discussion of the biopsychological components of psychopaths, however, it is obvious that the answer is not that simple. Psychopathy seems to be a result of a highly complex interaction of biopsychological, social, and learning factors.

Cleckley (1976) was not convinced that any common precursors exist in the family backgrounds of psychopaths, even though relatively homogeneous classifications of psychopathy do exist. However, even if we accept that neurophysiological factors may be causal factors in the development of psychopathy, this does not mean they are hereditary. In fact, there is little evidence to support a *strong* genetic influence on psychopathy so far. It is possible, though, that psychopaths are born with a biological predisposition to develop the disorder, independent of any genetic factors. In line with the Eysenckian view, it could be that psychopaths have a nervous system that interferes with rapid conditioning and association between transgression and punishment. Because of this defect, the psychopath fails to anticipate punishment and, hence, feels no guilt (no conscience). As an alternative to the defect argument, it is possible that certain aspects of the psychopath's nervous system simply have not matured. Another possibility is that genetics, toxicity (e.g., lead paint) in utero, birth difficulties, temperament, and other early developmental factors may affect certain processes in the nervous system, rendering some children vulnerable to develop conduct problems and psychopathic characteristics. These early contexts are especially prevalent for disadvantaged children. In addition, it should be emphasized that social factors play a major role in affecting these predispositions. "For example, a problematic temperamental predisposition at 6 months of age *and* low socioeconomic status at birth *and* early life experiences of physical abuse *and* peer rejection in early elementary school combine to predict clinically significant conduct-problem outcomes . . . in adolescence" (Dodge & Pettit, 2003, p. 354). Basically, persistent and serious offending that emerges early in life is driven partially by heritable influences that are strengthened or weakened during childhood and adolescence by parenting and other environmental factors (Tengström et al., 2004).

Many researchers believe that psychopathy begins in childhood and continues throughout adulthood (Farrington, 2005b; Forth & Burke, 1998; Lynam, 1998), which has led to the intense interest in juvenile psychopathy. According to the research, the childhood of the psychopath is littered with signals that something is amiss. Marshall and Cooke (1999) found that, compared with nonpsychopaths, psychopaths were more likely to have experienced family difficulties such as parental neglect, abuse, or even antipathy and indifference. They were also more likely to have experienced negative school experiences. Poor parental monitoring and discipline have also been identified in the backgrounds of psychopaths (Tolan, Gorman-Smith, & Henry, 2003). Lynam (1998) reports that children with symptoms of hyperactivity, impulsivity, and attention problems *and* conduct problems closely resemble psychopathic adults. We hasten to add, however, that while it may appear that all psychopaths have experienced all or some of these problems as children, this is not to say that children with similar problems are necessarily fledgling psychopaths.

"Few researchers have tried to investigate early childhood risk factors that might predict, influence, or cause psychopathy" (Farrington, 2005a, p. 493). And very few researchers have conducted prospective longitudinal investigations of those risk factors (Farrington, 2005a). Some retrospective studies (Koivisto & Haapasalo, 1996; Patrick, Zempolich, & Levenston, 1997) and some longitudinal studies (Lang, af Klinteberg, & Alm, 2002; Weiler & Widom, 1996) have found that PCL-R scores appear to be related to early childhood abuse. In one prospective longitudinal study of 400 London boys, ages 8 to 10 years, it was found that physical neglect, poor parental supervision, a disrupted family, large family size, a convicted parent, a depressed mother, and poverty predicted psychopathy scores at age 48 (Farrington, 2005b).

A fruitful avenue for exploring the childhood of the psychopath would be close examination of the life-course-persistent (LCP) offender described by developmental theorists. Developmental theory postulates that LCP offenders manifest antisocial behaviors across all kinds of conditions and situations in their childhoods. Neurologically, LCPs demonstrate a variety of minor neuropsychological disorders, such as difficult temperaments as infants, attention deficit disorders or hyperactivity as children, and learning problems as adolescents. Socially, LCPs are rejected by peers during their preteen years and are annoying to adults. Emotionally, these children display virtually no empathy or concern for others, show very little bonding to family, and often are sadistic and manipulative. They are highly impulsive and lack insight. A careful reading of LCPs developmental histories often shows a striking resemblance to the symptomology of criminal psychopaths.

SUMMARY AND CONCLUSIONS

The primary psychopath should be distinguished from people who may be classified as psychotic, neurotic, or emotionally disturbed. The primary psychopath should also be distinguished from the sociopath, who is similar in many ways. However, the term sociopath usually refers to a person who *habitually* violates the law and who does not seem to learn from past experience. Another common term—antisocial personality disorder—also is distinct from psychopath, even though these two terms are often confused by clinicians and researchers. This is understandable, because the diagnostic category "antisocial personality disorder" as defined in the latest editions of the DSM, has many parallels to Robert Hare's concept of criminal psychopathy.

The psychopath as discussed here may or may not run afoul of the law. In addition, psychopaths demonstrate a variety of behavioral and neurophysiological characteristics that differentiate them from other groups of individuals. In this text we are of course most interested in the psychopath who does run afoul of the law, particularly by way of persistent and/or violent offending. Hare has proposed the term *criminal psychopath* to describe this individual. In this sense, the criminal psychopath, the sociopath, and the person with antisocial personality disorder are very similar in their offending patterns.

Psychopaths most often function in society as charming, daring, witty, intelligent individuals, high on charisma but low on emotional reaction and affect. They appear to lack moral standards or the ability to manifest genuine sensitivity toward others. If criminals, they become the despair of law enforcement officials because their crimes appear to be without discernible or rational motives. Even worse, they show no remorse or ability to be rehabilitated.

We reviewed much of the neurophysiological research suggesting that the psychopath is different from the rest of the population on a number of physiological measures. The psychopath seems to be underaroused, both autonomically and cortically, a finding that may account for his or her difficulty in learning the rules of society. However, there is some evidence to suggest that with adequate incentives psychopaths may learn societal expectations very well. Recalling our discussion of Eysenck's theory in chapter 3, it is clear that the psychopath would be a stable extravert with high psychoticism. The psychopath, like the extravert, apparently is not aroused enough to profit as easily from the classical conditioning that perhaps sets most of us on the straight and narrow path in childhood. If, in addition to this physiological lack, the psychopath's family situation leaves him or her without appropriate models, then he or she is doubly cursed.

Many psychopaths also apparently have abnormal brain-wave patterns, mostly of a slow-wave childlike variety, which suggests that their nervous system is immature, at least until middle age. There are indications of more than the usual amounts of positive spikes, which are brain-wave bursts that correlate with aggressive episodes and impulsivity. Research has failed to discover, however, whether these abnormalities engender psychopathic behavior or vice versa. There is also little evidence to support a strong hereditary influence, although we should not overlook the possibility that psychopaths may be born with a biological predisposition to the disorder.

Studies on the childhood of psychopaths strongly suggest that they may have been ADHD as children, causing chaos for parents and teachers. It would be folly to maintain, though, that the ADHD child of today is the psychopath of tomorrow. Perhaps because they are physiologically underaroused, psychopaths do not respond as well to admonishments, threats, or actual punishment as do their nonpsychopathic peers. They do not learn society's expectations and the rules of right and wrong, possibly because anxiety-inducing disciplinary procedures are not that anxiety-producing for them. In many respects, the criminal psychopath follows a developmental path highly similar to the life-course-persistent offender described by developmental theory, outlined in chapter 2.

There are still numerous gaps in our knowledge of the psychopath, one being in the area of gender differences. Research on female psychopaths is scant. Some research suggests that behavioral characteristics for females are generally similar to those of male psychopaths, with slightly more emphasis among females on sexual acting-out behavior. This probably reflects a cultural bias, however, since women have been traditionally chastised more than men for behavior deemed inappropriate according to sexual mores. However, research on female criminal psychopaths using Hare's PCL-R implies that their behavioral patterns may be somewhat different than those of male criminal psychopaths.

A highly controversial area relating to psychopathy is the measurement and existence of juvenile psychopathy. Some researchers are very actively involved in developing scales to assess this construct and in comparing features of juvenile and adult psychopaths. Other researchers prefer to focus on psychopathic "characteristics" in juveniles that may or may not mean they are themselves psychopathic. Many juveniles, for example, are impulsive, seek stimulation, and appear to be noncaring; these features are often part of the normal turmoil of adolescent development. While it is worthwhile to study these characteristics, we must not rush to judgment and assume they are indicative of psychopathy. Others are even more cautious, suggesting that the concept itself simply is not valid when applied to juveniles. However, representatives of each of the above groups have expressed concern that juvenile psychopathy will be misdiagnosed, condemning juveniles to a label that is frequently associated with defeat: Psychopaths do not feel remorse, therefore cannot be helped.

Contemporary research on psychopathy is robust and shows few signs of abating. By now it is quite clear that Hare's primary psychopath—as measured by the PCL—has many unique features and that it may involve more than the two factors originally identified. At the least we can say that psychopathy includes a distinctive cognitive and emotional style, physiological indicators, and perhaps a childhood marked by parental deficiency and conduct problems.

These features combine to render the psychopath highly resistant to treatment. This is particularly frustrating to clinicians working with criminal psychopaths, many of whom know how to play the clinical games that will make it appear that they have changed their behavior.

KEY CONCEPTS

Primary psychopath	Antisocial personality disorder
Dyssocial psychopath	Criminal psychopath
APD	PCL
Psychopathy Check List	Psychopathy Checklist: Youth
PCL-R	Version
PCL:YV	P-Scan: Research Version
Factor analysis	Psychopath Factor 1
Psychopath Factor 2	Recidivism
Markers	Hemisphere asymmetry
Emotional paradox	Executive functions
Habituation	Avoidance learning
Secondary psychopath	

REVIEW QUESTIONS

1. Briefly describe the core behavioral characteristics of the criminal psychopath.
2. What differences have been found between male and female psychopaths?
3. Name and describe briefly five instruments used to measure psychopathy.
4. Define each of the following as proposed by Hare: primary psychopath, secondary psychopath, dyssocial psychopath, and criminal psychopath.
5. What has been learned about (a) recidivism and (b) treatment of the criminal psychopath?
6. Identify some of the ethical problems that may following labeling a child a "psychopath."
7. Define executive functions.
8. Describe some of the differences between the three core factors of psychopathy that have been identified through factor analysis.
9. How is the psychopath different from the nonpsychopath on psychophysiology? Thoroughly discuss all relevant features.
10. Describe the differences between psychopathy and antisocial personality disorder.

CHAPTER 7

CRIME AND MENTAL DISORDERS

CHAPTER OBJECTIVES

- Define mental disorders.
- Learn some of the relevant terms and concepts used in the mental health field.
- Provide an overview of the DSM-IV and the diagnoses that are most relevant to criminal behavior.
- Define and review issues relating to competency to stand trial.
- Review the insanity defense rules and standards.
- Discuss special defenses sometimes raised to absolve defendants of criminal responsibility.

On June 20, 2001, Andrea Yates called 911 seeking help. When the police arrived, she confessed that she had drowned her five children, ages 6 months to 7 years, in a bathtub because she had been a bad mother who hopelessly damaged them. Police found the bodies of four of the children who were found lying on a double bed, clothed and soaking wet. The body of the fifth child, Noah, age 7, was found still floating facedown in the bathtub. Police also noticed wet footprints that indicated that one of the children had escaped the bathtub before she caught him again.

According to Yates's defense, she believed she was possessed by Satan, that the mark of the devil was hidden under her hair, and the only way to be rid of Satan was to be executed. Furthermore, her children would suffer in hell because she represented evil. To save her children from hell, she thought it was critical that they die now so that they could go to heaven, and she would be executed for their deaths, as Satan demanded.

Yates's defense lawyers used a psychotic episode of postpartum depression as the basis for an insanity defense to get her into a psychiatric facility. Under Texas law, for the defense to succeed it had to be established that Yates could not distinguish right from wrong at the time of the crime, a common requirement for establishing insanity across the country. However, other aspects of the Texas law are among the most restrictive in the nation, and despite the fact that she had attempted suicide twice and had been hospitalized four times for psychiatric care, establishing insanity was going to be an uphill battle (Roche, 2006). Experts testified that she was mentally disordered but whether she knew what she was doing at the time of crime was an open question for the jury. Apparently, the jury believed she did know what she was doing; on March 12, 2002, Yates was found guilty of murder for drowning three of her children. The charges did not include the deaths of two of her sons, Paul, age 3, and Luke, age 2.

The Texas 1st Court of Appeals, however, ruled that the convictions be overturned because expert testimony of a famous forensic psychiatrist, Park Dietz, was false. The jury seemed to rely heavily on the persuasive testimony of Dietz, who testified during the trial that Yates may have been influenced by an episode of the television program *Law and Order,* in which a woman suffering from postpartum depression drowned her children in a bathtub and was found insane. During their appeal, Yates' lawyers documented that such an episode was never aired, thus doing irreparable damage to the psychiatric testimony. At this writing, lawyers are preparing for a new trial, though Yates remains confined under psychiatric care following the court's decision.

The Yates case created a national debate over the legal standards for mental disorders. In this and the next chapter, we discuss many of the points and issues brought up by the Yates case, including the various standards for the insanity defense.

It is a popular misconception that brutal, violent, and apparently senseless crimes are usually committed by people who are mentally ill or "sick." Someone who walks into a business establishment and randomly shoots its customers and employees must be mentally ill. Likewise, someone who sexually assaults, tortures, and kills a 4-year-old child has to be sick. How else could these people do this? An alternate explanation focuses on the subhuman perspective: If not sick, they are less than human. Closely related is the view that these individuals are basically evil. Although these latter approaches are gaining ground, perhaps reflecting public impatience with perceived insanity loopholes in the law, there is still wide public subscription to a presumption of mental illness, particularly in the case of outrageous, inexplicable crimes.

The media have been instrumental in developing the connection between mental disorder and crime, particularly serious violent crime. Along with greed and revenge, mental illness is a basic motivation for criminality in the vast majority of crimes on television and other entertainment media (Surette, 1999).

John Monahan (1992) cites an early survey (Gerbner, Gross, Morgan, & Signorielli, 1981) showing that on prime-time American television, 73 percent of all individuals characterized as mentally disordered also displayed some violent behavior. In a later analysis (Shain & Phillips, 1991), 86 percent of all print stories dealing with former mental patients focused on the violence of the patients, especially if the topics dealt with serial or mass murder.

The tendency to make the connection between crime and mental disorder is not new, nor is it limited to the media. Throughout the history of civilization, there has been a strong tendency to forge this link (Monahan, 1981). Most societies and their legal systems have been confused about and often frightened by mental disorder. In fact, the first mental hospital in the American colonies was established after Benjamin Franklin argued forcefully that the mentally ill were prone to violence and should be confined, involuntarily if need be, to protect society (Monahan & Geis, 1976).

Those who subscribe to the view that the mentally disordered are a threat assume that these individuals do not play by the rules of society, are unpredictable, and cannot control their own actions. Since they are apt to do anything at any given time, these "crazy people" are potentially dangerous. It should be emphasized, however, that the perception that mental disorder inevitably or even frequently leads to violence is not universal. Surveys suggest that only about one-quarter of the U.S. adult population strongly subscribe to such a view (Monahan, 1992). This more realistic appraisal is at least partly due to the efforts of advocates for the mentally ill, who have waged and supported public information campaigns aimed at disseminating truth and alleviating fear. However, while most people may not believe the mentally ill as a group are dangerous, many do believe that senseless or incomprehensible violent acts are the work of someone who must be "crazy" or "sick." Thus, to some members of the public, mentally ill people are dangerous; to others, people who commit bizarre crimes are mentally ill. Still others would subscribe to both views. For the present, we will set aside the issue of who is and is not dangerous but will revisit it in the following chapter.

DEFINING MENTAL ILLNESS

Mental illness is a disorder (some say a disease) of the mind that is judged by experts to interfere substantially with a person's ability to cope with life on a daily basis. It presumably deprives the person of freedom of choice, but it is important to note that there are degrees to this deprivation. In other words, even a seriously disordered individual has some decision making ability. Mental illness is manifested in behavior that deviates notably from normal conduct. However, the word *illness* encourages us to look for etiology, symptoms, and cures and to rely heavily on the medical profession both to diagnose and to treat. It also encourages us to excuse the behavior of persons plagued with the "sickness." The term **mental disorder,** however, need not imply that a person is sick, to be pitied, or even necessarily less responsible for his or her actions. Therefore, although *mental illness* is still used in the psychological, psychiatric, and legal literature, as well as in both civil and criminal law, we prefer the less restrictive *mental disorder.*

Another term that must be distinguished is **mental retardation,** professionally known as **developmental disability.** This is a cognitive deficiency—measured by "IQ tests"—that cannot be cured. However, many mentally retarded individuals can be provided training and support services to lead productive and independent lives. Even so, mentally retarded individuals are sometimes charged with primarily minor offenses that result in arrests, being detained in jail, and serving time. Dual diagnoses of mental retardation and substance abuse have been observed in a significant number of these individuals (Day & Berney, 2001). Misperceptions about the mentally retarded are perhaps not as strong as misperceptions about the mentally disordered, but they represent a population whose needs may go unrecognized by the criminal justice system. Thus, while the chapter focuses primarily on issues related to the mentally disordered, we will also give attention to unique problems faced by the developmentally disabled.

Mental disorders are manifested in a variety of behaviors, ranging in severity from dangerous, harmful acts to conduct that is essentially innocuous. Morse (1978) prefers the term "crazy behavior," which he characterizes as behavior that is obviously strange and unusual *and cannot be logically explained.* The person who walks onto the hotel elevator at the lobby level and faces the rear, staring blankly at the elevator's rear wall, while others are facing the front, is exhibiting strange behavior. However, if the elevator subsequently opens at the "back" door, there is a logical explanation: the person is a hotel guest or employee who is familiar with the elevator's setup. In the absence of such an explanation, the behavior becomes disconcerting to the other passengers and, if only mildly, "crazy." In this instance, some clinicians—again in the absence of a logical explanation—might see the behavior as symptomatic of an anxiety disorder or a dissociative disorder, depending on other aspects of the individual's behavior. However, the behavior, as described above, is not dangerous. On the other hand, a person who walks into a hotel lobby in a highly agitated state, brandishing a knife, and stating that hotel employees were all trained by Satan and must die for their sins is exhibiting both "crazy" and dangerous behavior. There is obviously a crucial distinction between the above scenarios.

The DSM-IV

The concept of mental disorder, therefore, connotes a very wide range of bizarre, dramatic, harmful, or mildly unusual behaviors whose classifications are published in the **Diagnostic and Statistical Manual of Mental Disorders (DSM).** Compiled by committees appointed by the American Psychiatric Association, the DSM—now in its fourth edition (DSM-IV)—is the guidebook for clinicians seeking to define and diagnose specific mental disorders. It is used by virtually every mental health professional in the United States to guide diagnosis and to justify third-party reimbursement for treatment. A slightly revised version of the DSM-IV called the DSM-IV-TR (TR stands for "text revision") was published in 2000 and is the most recent edition available. A fifth edition of the DSM is expected to be released in approximately 2008.

The current version lists approximately 400 mental disorders (Comer, 2004). Interestingly approximately half of the people in the United States will qualify for a DSM diagnosis at some point in their lifetimes (Comer, 2004). Diagnoses based on the DSM also are provided to courts in a wide range of forensic settings, including evaluations of competence to stand trial, mental state at the time of an offense, sentencing, and assessments of harm suffered by both victims of crime and plaintiffs in civil suits.

The DSM is reviewed and revised periodically to conform to the contemporary, mainstream thinking of psychiatrists and other mental health professionals. According to a recent edition (DSM-IV 1994, p. xxi), a mental disorder

> is conceptualized as a clinically significant behavioral or psychological syndrome or pattern that occurs in an individual and that is associated with present distress (e.g., a painful symptom) or disability (i.e., impairment in one or more important areas of functioning) or with a significantly increased risk of suffering death, pain, disability, or an important loss of freedom. In addition, this syndrome or pattern must not be merely an expectable and culturally sanctioned response to a particular event, for example, the death of a loved one. Whatever its original cause, it must currently be considered a manifestation of a behavioral, psychological, or biological dysfunction in the individual.

As noted by Wakefield (1992), there are two basic principles that guide the DSM-IV definition for mental disorder. *First,* the mental condition must have negative consequences for the person. That is, the person must be experiencing some pain, distress, discomfort, or disability. The *second* principle rests on the assumption that a mental disorder is a dysfunction of some internal process within the person—that is, for some reason, something is wrong. This principle differentiates the disorder from the normal or expected internal processes that result from a trauma or tragedy of daily living, such as the loss of a loved one.

We now turn to the specific disorders identified in the DSM that are most likely to be associated with criminal conduct. It must be stressed, however, that (1) persons with these disorders are not "crime prone" and (2) even if an individual is diagnosed with these disorders, he or she still can be held responsible for criminal conduct.

For the present, the four categories of mental disorders most relevant are (1) schizophrenic disorders, (2) paranoid disorders, (3) mood disorders (serious depression), and (4) the personality disorder called "antisocial personality disorder." Note that the first two fall into what was previously called the "psychotic" category. The third was considered in that psychotic category only if serious enough, such as bipolar depression. The fourth is a separate category under the general label "personality disorders." These four disorders are relevant because they are most likely to be associated with violent, serious criminal, or antisocial behavior and are most often cited to support an insanity defense to criminal charges. We review each of these disorders and then assess their relevance to criminal behavior. However, toward the end of the chapter, we discuss less common disorders that, when cited in courts, attract considerable media attention.

Schizophrenic Disorders

Schizophrenia is the mental disorder that people most often associate with "crazy behavior," since it frequently manifests itself in highly bizarre actions. It is a mental disorder that continues to be extremely complex and poorly understood (Andreasen & Carpenter, 1993). The disorder generally begins early in life, often leads to social and economic impairment, and leaves traces on its victims for the rest of their lives (Andreasen & Carpenter, 1993). Behavioral manifestations of schizophrenia are varied, but there are some common characteristics.

Severe breakdowns in thought patterns, emotions, and perceptions are common. Spells of extreme social withdrawal from others are also typical. The thoughts and cognitive functioning of the person with schizophrenia become disorganized and fail to correspond to reality, and his or her speech will reflect this. The most common example is a loosening of associations, in which ideas shift between totally unrelated and only obliquely related subjects. Thought becomes fragmented and bizarre, and **delusions**—false beliefs about the world—are common. An example of a delusion is *believing* some alien from another universe is listening in on your cell phone conversations and ultimately plotting against you.

The person with schizophrenia is typically inappropriate in emotion or affect (e.g., indiscriminate giggling or crying), or reflects emotional flatness, where very little—if any—emotional reaction is exhibited. The voice is monotonous, the face immobile and expressionless. The major disturbances in perception are various forms of **hallucinations,** which involve sensing or perceiving things or events that others do not sense or perceive. The most common hallucinations are auditory, with the individual hearing voices or sounds that no one else in the vicinity hears.

The DSM-IV outlines five characteristic symptoms of schizophrenia, at least two of which must be manifested before a diagnosis can be entertained: (1) delusions, (2) hallucinations, (3) disorganized speech, (4) grossly disorganized behavior, and (5) inappropriate affect. Furthermore, the social interactions, self-care, and/or occupational life of the individual must show signs of being markedly below the level achieved prior to the onset. In addition, there must be continuous signs of the disturbance for at least six months.

The DSM-IV also recognizes five subtypes of schizophrenia: (1) disorganized, (2) catatonic, (3) paranoid, (4) undifferentiated, and (5) residual. Following is a brief summary of the essential features of each subtype:

1. *Disorganized type:* Inappropriate affect (flat, incongruous, or silly emotional responses) and marked incoherence and disorganization in thought patterns. Associated features include grimaces, strange mannerisms, complaints of nonexistent physical ailments, extreme social withdrawal, and other oddities of behavior.

2. *Catatonic type:* Severe disturbances in muscular and voluntary movement. Extended periods of mutism are common. Parrotlike and senseless repetition of a word or phrase just spoken by another person is also common. Prominent grimacing is another frequent characteristic. The catatonic may assume a bizarre posture for long periods of time (usually several hours) and then fly into an overactive, agitated state of screaming and throwing things.

3. *Paranoid type:* Characterized by delusions and hallucinations (usually auditory hallucinations). A person with paranoid schizophrenia may be convinced that the world is inhabited by extraterrestrials who are plotting to take over the world. Another may hear voices commanding him to rid the world of red-haired individuals. Of all the schizophrenic types, the paranoid is the most frequently represented in criminal behavior.

4. *Undifferentiated type:* This type shows psychotic symptoms that cannot be classified into any of the foregoing categories. People with this type display active psychotic features, such as hallucinations, delusions, incoherent speech, or confused and disorganized behavior, but do not meet the specifications of the other types.

5. *Residual type:* These individuals have had at least one episode of schizophrenia, and there is evidence that some of the symptoms are continuing. For example, the person may still display blunted emotions or illogical thinking, but no other symptoms.

The DSM-IV identifies a sixth category, *schizophreniform disorder,* a behavioral pattern that shows at least two indicators of delusions, hallucinations, disorganized speech, grossly disorganized behavior, and emotional inappropriateness. It is a temporary disorder and underscores the difficulty in classifying schizophrenic disorders in general. In order to qualify for schizophreniform disorder, the symptoms must persist for at least one month but less than six months. If the symptoms continue more than six months, the clinician is encouraged to classify the disorder into one of the five longer-lasting types.

Delusional Disorders

The **delusional disorders** (also called **paranoid disorders**) are characterized by the presence of one or more *nonbizarre* delusions that persist for at least one month. The judgment of whether the delusion's systems are bizarre or nonbizarre is especially important in deciding between a delusional disorder and schizophrenia. In delusional disorder, the delusions are reasonably believable and not completely far-fetched. An example of a nonbizarre delusion is the belief that a neighbor is spying and attempting to poison one's dog, when there is no evidence to that effect. Even so, neighbors sometimes spy and sometimes do try to poison dogs. A bizarre delusion—more characteristic of schizophrenia—

is the belief that the neighbor has disguised herself as a mosquito and is hovering outside one's window.

Delusional disorders often accompany other disorders like schizophrenia, organic mental disorder, paranoid personality disorder, and depressions. However, the essential feature of all delusional disorders is the delusional system, which most often includes persecutory beliefs about being spied on, cheated, conspired against, followed, drugged, maliciously maligned, harassed, or obstructed. Generally, anger, resentment, and sometimes violence accompany these false persecutory beliefs. Suspiciousness, either generalized or directed at one or more persons, is also common. The DSM-IV (1994) recognizes seven different types of delusional disorders, but the persecutory type is the one most closely associated with criminal conduct, especially violent criminal conduct. Thus the individual who believes he is being followed by someone intending to do him harm may try to kill or otherwise harm his "persecutor."

Depressive Disorders

The disorders described in this section have a variety of names and diagnostic labels, such as affective disorders, mood disorders, and bipolar depressive disorders. The most common label is **major depressive disorder.** The symptoms include an *extremely* depressed state that lasts for at least two weeks and is accompanied by a generalized slowing down of mental and physical activity, gloom, despair, feelings of worthlessness, and perhaps frequent thoughts of suicide. Everyone has up and down periods, but these mood changes are extreme and the depression is deep and usually long-lasting. Persons with major depression describe themselves as down, discouraged, and hopeless. A less common form of depression is bipolar depression in which there are both periods of depression and periods of excessive euphoria called *mania*.

The role of depression in the development of criminal behavior is just beginning to be explored. Preliminary data indicate that depression may be strongly associated with delinquency, especially in teenage girls (Kovacs, 1996; Obiedallah & Earls, 1999; Teplin, 2000). Depression seems to render teenagers—both boys and girls—indifferent to their own personal safety and the consequences of their actions. They just don't care what happens to them, which may increase the likelihood of gravitating toward delinquency. When depressed, people lose interest in life and the activities going on around them, isolating them further from social life and school or work.

Depression also very likely plays a significant role in mass murders, workplace violence, and "suicide-by-cop" incidents in which a person sets up a situation wherein police are essentially forced to shoot. These incidents are discussed in greater detail in chapter 9.

Postpartum Depression

We begin this section with a return to the Andrea Yates case presented at the beginning of the chapter. The case, you will recall, involved postpartum depression and whether she knew what she was doing at the time she drowned her children.

Traditionally, mothers who kill their children are viewed by the legal system as either "evil" or suffering from a severe mental disorder. Often, the mental disorder diagnosed by the clinical experts is postpartum depression, a depressive disorder believed to be brought on by childbirth. It is important, though, to realize that experts recognize that there are three categories of mental reactions that may occur after childbirth: postpartum blues, postpartum depression, and postpartum psychosis (Dobson & Sales, 2000).

The most common is **postpartum blues,** which features crying spells, irritability, anxiety, confusion, and rapid mood changes. It is not unusual, and approximately 50 percent to 80 percent of women display some minor characteristics of postpartum blues between one and five days after delivery (Durand & Barlow, 2000). The symptoms may last for a few hours to a few days and are clearly linked to childbirth. It is generally considered unusual to have the symptoms last more than two weeks. There is very little evidence that postpartum blues leads to the murder of the newborn by the mother (Dobson & Sales, 2000).

The second category, **postpartum depression,** occurs during the weeks and months following childbirth. The symptoms include depression, loss of appetite, sleep disturbances, fatigue, thoughts of suicide, loss of interest in life's activities, and disinterest in the newborn child. The mother often feels guilty about her disinterest when she should be happy about the new arrival. Postpartum depression affects 7 percent to 17 percent of childbearing women in North America (Dobson & Sales, 2000).

Experts believe that postpartum depression is not directly linked to childbirth but is more a form of clinical depression that is present before childbirth. This form of depression seems to be a recurring mood disorder across the life cycle of the woman. Although there have been some cases in which women killed their children while depressed, the research finds that it is not common after childbirth.

The third category of mental disorders associated with the postpartum period is **postpartum psychosis.** It is regarded as a severe mental disorder that is rare, occurring in one out of every one thousand women following delivery. Usually the symptoms are highly similar to the symptoms of serious bipolar depression and are believed to be directly linked to childbirth (Dobson & Sales, 2000). Sometimes the psychosis is severe enough to encourage the mother's attempted or successful suicide, together with the murder of the infant and other children (Kendall & Hammen, 1995). Which of the three descriptions would most likely follow the Andrea Yates case?

Antisocial Personality Disorder (APD)

The DSM-III and the DSM-III-R criteria for the **antisocial personality disorder** have been among the most frequently criticized because of their vagueness and lack of empirical anchoring (Widiger et al., 1991). The DSM-IV and

DSM-IV-TR, however, have tried to address these problems by incorporating into the criteria more empirically based attributes. As mentioned in chapter 6, many of the new criteria closely follow the Robert Hare definition of the criminal psychopath.

The essential feature of a person with an antisocial personality disorder (APD) is a history of continuous behavior in which the rights of others are violated. The individual must be at least 18 years of age and must have a history of some symptoms of conduct disorder before age 15. Recall that a diagnosis of **conduct disorder** is reserved for children and adolescents. Before a person can be diagnosed with APD, a pervasive pattern of disregard for and the violation of the rights of others must be indicated by at least three of the following behavioral patterns:

1. Failure to conform to social norms or the criminal law, as reflected by frequent performance of acts that are grounds for arrests
2. Irritability and unusual aggressiveness, as indicated by repeated physical fights or assaults
3. Consistent irresponsibility, as reflected in a poor work history or failure to honor financial obligations
4. Impulsivity or a failure to plan ahead (characteristic at all ages)
5. Deceitfulness, as reflected in frequent lying, use of aliases, or conning others for personal profit or pleasure
6. Reckless disregard for the safety of others or self
7. Lack of remorse or guilt for wrongdoings, as indicated by indifference to or rationalization of having hurt, mistreated, or stolen from another

Additional symptoms, as outlined in the DSM-IV, include stealing, fighting, truancy, and resisting authority—typical childhood symptoms. Antisocial personalities lack empathy and tend to be callous, cynical, and contemptuous of the feelings, rights, and sufferings of others. Furthermore they frequently exhibit precocious and aggressive sexual behavior, excessive drinking, and the use of illicit drugs. There is a markedly impaired capacity to maintain lasting, close, warm, and responsible relationships with family, friends, or sexual partners.

On average, ASPs fail to become independent, self-supporting adults. They spend most of their lives in institutions (usually correctional facilities) or remain highly dependent on their families. Other accompanying features include restlessness, an inability to tolerate boredom, and a belief that the world is hostile. ASPs often complain of tension and depression, but they do not usually meet the criteria for a diagnosis of depression. They are often impulsive and unable to plan ahead, and show deficits in executive functioning.

Antisocial personality disorder occurs more frequently in males than in females. It is estimated that about 3 percent of the American male population and about 1 percent of the American female population fall into this category (DSM-IV). Furthermore, the disorder is more common in lower-socioeconomic populations, partly because it is connected with impaired earning capacity and partly because of the greater likelihood of being raised in an economically disadvantaged, dysfunctional household with limited adequate role models and resources. Lastly, the DSM-IV concludes that the disorder runs in families, possibly due to a genetic link that predisposes the child to antisocial behavioral patterns. Other perspectives would emphasize that family members share the disorder—not because of a genetic link—but because they also share the economic and social background that facilitates it.

Research dating from the 1970s has indicated that ASP is a common diagnosis of criminal defendants and offenders. In an early study, Henn and his colleagues conducted an extensive series of investigations on all defendants referred by a St. Louis, Missouri, court for psychiatric assessment over a 10-year period (Henn, Herjanic, & Vanderpearl, 1976a). Focusing on a sample of 1,195 defendants accused of a variety of crimes and referred for psychiatric assessment, Henn and colleagues learned that the most frequent diagnosis was personality disorder, accounting for nearly 40 percent of all the diagnoses. Two-thirds of those classified as personality disorders were specifically designated antisocial personality. The second most frequent diagnosis was schizophrenia (which also included those labeled probable schizophrenia), comprising 17 percent of the total. The other diagnostic labels were evenly distributed and of low frequency.

Henn et al. also found frequent references to alcoholism, primarily as a secondary diagnosis, in the diagnostic reports. Alcoholism cut across all diagnostic categories, with the notable exception of schizophrenia, where only a few cases were reported. The combination of alcoholism and drug addiction as a secondary diagnosis was common in persons labeled antisocial personality. These findings support those reported by Guze (1976), who found the diagnosis of alcoholism prevalent among offenders with a diagnosis of antisocial personality disorders.

The pervasiveness of this diagnosis continues today. APD is very frequently offered as a diagnosis in criminal courts and in corrections, sometimes serving as a catch-all category. Researchers have noted that when courts press for a diagnosis, many clinicians will oblige by concluding that an individual qualifies for APD (Melton et al., 1997). In correctional facilities, rates of inmates considered APD range from 30 percent to 50 percent, and it is not unusual to find the diagnosis in over 50 percent of the correctional population (Gacono et al., 2001). APD is such a common diagnosis applied to persons both accused of and convicted of criminal offenses that some jurisdictions specifically exclude it from the list of mental disorders that can support an insanity defense.

The validity of the antisocial personality disorder as a meaningful concept has been debated. Blackburn (1988) contends that there is no single type of abnormal personality that is prone to chronic rule violation. Furthermore, he believes the diagnostic label "antisocial personality disorder" remains a mythical entity that fails to be meaningful for theory development, research, clinical communication, or prediction. Such a concept is little more than a moral judgment masquerading as a clinical diagnosis. Given the lack of demonstrable scientific evidence of clinical utility of the concept, it should be discarded

(Blackburn, 1988, p. 511). Others have observed that there remains widespread confusion about the distinction between APD and psychopathy, with many clinicians viewing them as synonymous (Gacono et al., 2001). As we noted earlier, the DSM-IV now describes APD in such a way that it is virtually indistinguishable from Hare's concept of psychopathy, described in chapter 6.

COMPETENCY AND CRIMINAL RESPONSIBILITY

The above psychiatric diagnoses are often those that come into play when decisions must be made as to whether defendants who are mentally disordered are competent to stand trial or, if competent, are culpable enough to be held responsible for the crimes that occurred. In this section we review these two very important legal constructs.

Incompetency to Stand Trial

Some persons charged with a crime are considered so intellectually and/or psychologically impaired that—were they to be tried—they would be present in body but not in mind. The U.S. Supreme Court has determined that the trial of such an individual violates the Constitution. Specifically, defendants are competent to stand trial if they have "sufficient present ability to consult with their lawyer with a reasonable degree of rational understanding . . . and a rational as well as factual understanding of the proceedings." (*Dusky v. United States*, 1960, p. 402). To protect the rights of the individual and to preserve the dignity of the court process, the law states that a person who is incompetent must not be tried.

The competency issue does not relate only to the actual trial, however. In fact, some scholars now prefer to use the term "**adjudicative competence**" rather than competence to stand trial (e.g., Bonnie & Grisso, 2000; Mumley, Tillbrook, & Grisso, 2003; Nicholson & Norwood, 2000). The former term relates to the ability to participate in a wide variety of court proceedings and court-related activities, including plea bargaining, preliminary hearings, and other pretrial hearings related to one's case. It also encompasses two distinct concepts: (1) the competence to proceed (which implies understanding the purpose of the proceedings and being able to help one's attorney) and (2) decisional competence (which implies the ability to comprehend the significance of various decisions to be made) (Mumley et al., 2003). If a criminal defendant is found incompetent to stand trial, the court has essentially determined that he or she cannot understand the process that is occurring or effectively participate in it.

The competency issue can be raised at any time during the actual proceedings. For example, a defendant may be competent up to and into the beginning phases of his trial; during a long and protracted trial he may become incompetent. A defendant also may be competent before and during trial, but may be ruled incompetent at the time of sentencing.

Evaluations for **competency to stand trial** represent the most common referral for criminally related forensic assessments (Cruise & Rogers, 1998).

Most typically, defendants referred for competency evaluation have a history of psychiatric care or institutionalization or exhibited signs of mental disorder at arrest or while detained in jail. Data indicate that approximately 25,000 criminal defendants nationwide, or about one in 15, are evaluated each year by state and federal courts for their competency to stand trial (Cruise & Rogers, 1998; Nicholson & Kugler, 1991). About four out of every five of these evaluated defendants are found competent (Grisso, 1986; Nicholson & Kugler, 1991; Roesch, Zapf, Golding, & Skeem, 1999).

Interestingly, mental health clinicians have been criticized extensively in the literature for the poor quality of their assessments, even sometimes confusing competence with criminal responsibility (Skeem & Golding, 1998). In recent years, the quality of the assessments has improved, though examiners are still faulted for not making sufficient use of the competence assessment tools developed by researchers or providing adequate explanations to judges in their reports (Nicholson & Norwood, 2000).

It is important to emphasize the distinction between **incompetence to stand trial (IST)** and insanity, the legal concept to be discussed below. Although they may be related, the two concepts are distinct and should be assessed separately—although this is not always done. Criminal responsibility, which is at the core of the insanity defense, and competency to stand trial refer to a defendant's mental state/capacity at *two different points in time*. If a defendant pleads not guilty by reason of insanity, the law asks, "What was the defendant's state of mind at the time the offense was committed?" In competency considerations, the question becomes, "What is the defendant's state of mind at the present time, or at the time of the pretrial proceedings or trial?" An individual who was seriously mentally disordered at the time of an offense and whose criminal responsibility is questionable may have enough mental stability by the time of the trial to be competent to stand trial. On the other hand, a person may be of sound mind during the unlawful act, but may later become disordered or disoriented and be determined incompetent to stand trial.

If found incompetent to stand trial—a decision that must be made by the presiding judge—the defendant is typically sent to a mental institution, or less frequently, to an outpatient therapeutic program, until rendered competent. For those defendants who are restored to competency, some research suggests that the average time needed for restoration is about three months (Hoge et al., 1996). In a survey of mental health program directors across the United States, Miller (2003) found that outpatient treatment to restore competency was rare. Outpatient *evaluations* of competency were on the increase, however.

Until the 1970s, the typical procedure for evaluating competency required that defendants be confined within a maximum security institution for a lengthy psychiatric-psychological evaluation (usually 60 to 90 days). Following evaluation, the defendant was granted a hearing on the matter of competency. If the court found the defendant unable to understand the charges or the judicial proceedings, or to help counsel in his or her defense, then the defendant would automatically be committed to a secure hospital for an indefinite period of time—until competent. Theoretically, this indefinite time period could extend—and sometimes did—into a lifetime of involuntary commitment.

In 1972, in *Jackson v. Indiana*, the Supreme Court declared that such an indefinite confinement violated the Constitution. While the court allowed the confinement, it specified that if no progress was made toward competence, the individual must be released or must be recommitted under civil, not criminal statutes. Today, individuals found IST with little likelihood of being restored to competency often have their cases dismissed. However, in many jurisdictions, the prosecutor still retains the option of reinstituting charges if the person regains competency at some later time.

In recent years, ISTs have asserted additional constitutional rights in connection with their status, including the right to the "least restrictive or drastic alternative," specifically the right to be treated in a community setting rather than in an institution. As noted earlier, though, recent research suggests that community treatment is not the typical approach (Miller, 2003). In addition, because treatment is often offered in the form of psychoactive drugs, some defendants ruled IST have argued that they should not be forced to take these drugs. Psychoactive drugs are "those drugs that exert their primary effect on the brain, thus altering mood or behavior, or that are used in the treatment of mental disorders" (Julien, 1992, p. xii). Although these drugs have been improved considerably over the past few decades, many have side effects—including in some cases debilitating side effects—and are resisted by many patients.

In a recent Supreme Court ruling on this matter (*Sell v. United States*, 2003), the court ruled that, in a case that did not involve violence, courts must be wary of ordering such medication against a defendant's will. Sell, a former dentist charged with insurance fraud, had been found incompetent and was hospitalized for treatment. He had a history of mental disorder and had prior hospitalizations, during which he had received psychoactive drugs. Psychiatrists again prescribed psychoactive drugs in an effort to render him competent to stand trial, but Sell refused to take them. Both a trial judge and a federal court of appeals ruled against him, but the U.S. Supreme Court did not agree. The court noted that the trial court had not adequately weighed the advantages and disadvantages of the drugs, and it sent the case back to the court to do just that. However, for serious, violent crimes, where the government has a strong interest in bringing a defendant to trial, the court has been less sympathetic to the defendant, refusing to hear an appeal of an order for involuntary medication (*United States v. Weston*, cert. denied). Rusty Weston is the individual charged with the lethal shooting of two Capitol police officers in 1998 and the non-lethal shooting of two other individuals. In light of the nature of the crimes, Weston's long history of serious mental illness, and the government's strong interest in bringing him to trial, courts have ruled in favor of the involuntary medication. Even so, the lower court in Weston's case had given careful consideration to the advantages and disadvantages of ordering the medication.

Research on persons found IST indicates that they are highly similar in background characteristics. Most have limited social and occupational skills and a history of prior criminal charges and psychiatric hospitalizations (Williams & Miller, 1981). Compared with the general population, ISTs are disproportionately unmarried, African American, and poorly educated (less than ninth grade education) (Steadman, 1979). More recent research has continued to support these earlier findings (Nicholson & Kugler, 1991; Roesch, Zapf, Golding, & Skeem, 1999). However, these differences do not hold when we compare persons referred for evaluations and ultimately found competent to those referred and ultimately found incompetent. Competent and incompetent defendants do not differ significantly on demographic variables such as race, gender, or marital status (Nicholson & Kugler 1991; Riley, 1998; Rosenfeld & Ritchie, 1998). They do differ, not surprisingly, on clinical variables. Thus, persons found incompetent are more likely to be diagnosed with a psychotic disorder or organic mental disorder (Warren, Rosenfeld, Fitch, & Hawk, 1997) or schizophrenia and affective disorders (Hoge, et al., 1997).

The offense charged seems to play some part in the ultimate competency decision, but the research in this area is quite mixed. A meta-analysis by Nicholson and Kugler (1991) indicated that individuals adjudicated IST are much more likely than other criminal defendants to be charged with violent offenses. However, Warren et al. (1997) found that public order offenses were more likely to yield a finding of incompetence than were serious charges like homicide or sex offenses. Rosenfeld and Ritchie (1998) found that misdemeanor defendants were more likely to be found incompetent than felony defendants. Mumley, Tillbrook, and Grisso (2003) surmise that these differences may be due to the clinical diagnosis; in other words, persons with more severe diagnoses may be charged with the less serious offenses. IST defendants are often diagnosed psychotic or with other serious mental disorders. Nicholson and Kugler (1991, p. 364) conclude, "Defendants who manifested disorientation and impaired memory, poor judgment, thought and communication disturbances, hallucinations, delusions, and bizarre, unmanageable behavior were considered unfit to proceed to trial more often than defendants who did not exhibit such symptoms."

In recent years, far more attention has been given to the issue of mentally retarded individuals and adjudicative competence. As Mumley et al. (2003, p. 343) noted, "Unlike psychotic defendants, persons with mental retardation often do not show obvious signs of poor understanding or reasoning, so that attorneys may be less capable of identifying those who are in need of AC (adjudicative competence) evaluation." Consequently, we have little information on the extent to which mentally retarded defendants are referred for competency evaluation, and virtually no information on the proportion of IST defendants who are mentally retarded. However, researchers are developing instruments and guidelines for the assessment of competence in mentally retarded individuals (e.g., Coles, Freitas, & Tweed, 1996; Smith & Hudson, 1995).

Criminal Responsibility

Given the widespread publicity associated with the insanity defense, most people are probably far more aware of defendants found **not guilty by reason of**

insanity (NGRI) than those found incompetent to stand trial. Insanity is a legal term, not a psychiatric or psychological one; for our purposes, it should be used only in the context of a criminal offense. Insanity refers to a person's *state of mind at the time an offense was committed.* When an individual is found not guilty by reason of insanity, a judge or jury have determined that he or she was so mentally disordered at the time of the crime that the person should not be held responsible. The law assumes that mental disorder *can* rob an individual of free will or the ability to make appropriate choices. Note that insanity should not be *equated* with mental disorder, even serious mental disorder. That is, a mentally disordered person can still be found responsible for committing a criminal offense. Likewise, an individual who is mentally retarded can still be held criminally responsible.

Insanity defenses, especially if they are successful, receive extensive media coverage and commentary. When John Hinckley, charged with an attempt on the life of President Reagan, was found NGRI by a federal jury, there was widespread public indignation accompanied by numerous demands for repeal of the insanity defense in both federal and state law. Since the Hinckley acquittal by reason of insanity in June 1982, at least 34 states have made some kind of alteration to their insanity statutes (Steadman et al., 1993). Moreover, in response to the public outcry against the Hinckley acquittal, the U.S. Congress passed the *Insanity Defense Act of 1984,* which is discussed below. Virtually all these legal changes made it more difficult for defendants who wished to plead not guilty by reason of insanity. Incidentally, to this day Hinckley remains hospitalized, although he has been allowed to visit his parents' home for brief visits.

It is important to note that the number of insanity defenses raised in the United States is believed very small compared with the total number of criminal cases. Furthermore, despite the outcry after the Hinckley verdict, insanity defenses are rarely successful. Unfortunately there are no *systematic, nationwide* data on how often the insanity defense is actually used (McGinley & Paswark, 1989). County, state, and federal levels of government rarely share information about these issues (Steadman et al., 1993). Steadman and his colleagues write, "County level information on insanity pleas, for example, is rarely, if ever, aggregated to the state level, meaning almost nothing is known about the earliest stages of the insanity defense process" (1993, p. 3). However, there are some very good estimates based on studies conducted by independent and governmental researchers. These researchers estimate that insanity defenses are used in only 1 percent of all U.S. felony criminal cases (Callahan, Steadman, McGreevy, & Robbins, 1991; Golding, Skeem, Roesch, & Zapf, 1999).

How Successful Is the Insanity Defense?

Data on acquittals suggest that the defense is typically not successful. In an eight-state study of 9,000 defendants who pleaded not guilty by reason of insanity, Callahan et al. (1991) found a 22 percent to 25 percent success rate. Other studies have reported wide statewide differences, with a high of 44 percent in Colorado and a low of 2 percent in Wyoming (McGinley & Paswark,

1989). Cirincione and Jacobs (1999) found a mean of only 33.4 insanity acquittals per year across 35 states over the period 1974–1995. More important, acquittals seem to be closely tied to the diagnosis placed on the defendant and, to some extent, on the crime charged (Cochrane, Grisso, & Frederick, 2001; Warren, Rosenfeld, Fitch, & Hawk, 1997). Cochrane et al. found that federal defendants with diagnoses of psychotic disorders, affective disorders, and mental retardation had higher rates of acquittal than those diagnosed with other disorders. Personality disorders were negatively correlated with a finding of insanity. Recall that many states specifically exclude antisocial personality disorder as a mental disorder to support an insanity defense. Warren et al. (1997) found that defendants charged with violent crimes against others had the highest acquittal rates, while sex offenders significantly are more likely to be *convicted*. Nevertheless, the research literature strongly indicates that the clinical diagnosis, more than the offense, seems to be the critical factor. This also explains the low acquittal of sex offenders, because these offenders are often not considered by clinicians to be mentally disordered.

In the United States, acquittals are far more difficult to obtain from juries (jury trials) than from judges (bench trials), a pattern that underscores the pervasive negative attitude the American public has toward the insanity defense. For example, in their eight-state study, Callahan, Steadman, McGreevy, and Robbins (1991) found that only 7 percent of the acquittals were handed down by juries. In another study, Boehnert (1989) found that 96 percent of defendants found not guilty by reason of insanity had gone before a judge. Thus it seems wise for defendants who plan to use the insanity defense to have a bench trial (where the judge decides) rather than a jury trial. On the other hand, recent research suggests that, if jurors are informed of the consequences of an NGRI verdict—specifically that the defendant will likely be hospitalized for treatment—they may be more likely to acquit the defendant (Wheatman & Shaffer, 2001).

Callahan et al. (1991) found that successful NGRI defendants, compared with unsuccessful defendants, tended to be older, female, better educated, and single. They also had a history of prior hospitalization and were considered extremely disturbed. Furthermore, 15 percent of the acquitted defendants had not themselves raised the insanity defense, indicating that they were so disordered that an insanity verdict was essentially imposed on them. The tragic case of Andrea Yates, the Texas woman who drowned her children in a bathtub in 2001, is inconsistent with several of the above criteria, however. Yates had some college education and a history of serious mental disorder, including postpartum psychosis and hospitalization. Despite evidence of disorder—which even the prosecutor acknowledged—Yates was convicted and sent to prison, although as noted above her conviction has been overturned.

When Is the Insanity Defense Most Often Used?

Defense attorneys generally do not recommend that their clients plead not guilty by reason of insanity unless they are charged with a serious offense and the evidence against them is overwhelming. Nevertheless, it is a mistake to think that defendants charged with misdemeanor offenses do not raise this defense; it is sometimes used to obtain treatment for mentally disordered individuals who might not otherwise be eligible for institutionalization. However, when the possible penalty is capital punishment or life imprisonment without parole, an insanity defense becomes more palatable to the defense. In many jurisdictions, however, insanity acquittees are immediately confined to a mental institution, where they are kept for as long as needed to produce substantial improvement in their condition. In fact, research shows that persons found NGRI on average spend at least as much time in mental institutions or treatment facilities as they would have spent in prison if convicted (Golding, Skeem, Roesch, & Zapf, 1999). Moreover the individual can be required to bear the burden of proving that he or she is no longer mentally ill. John Hinckley is a case in point. Hospitalized since his acquittal in 1981, Hinckley has argued that his mental illness is now in remission. He has been allowed out of the institution for supervised day trips and visits, and he recently convinced a court to allow him to go to his parents' home for unsupervised, overnight visits. Eventually Hinckley will almost assuredly seek total release from the institution.

When that happens, the ultimate determination of whether he remains mentally ill will be a critical factor. In 1992, the U.S. Supreme Court placed some limits on the hospital confinement of persons found not guilty by reason of insanity. In *Foucha v. Louisiana*, the court ruled that they may not be held in psychiatric facilities once they are no longer mentally disordered, even if it could be argued that they are dangerous. Foucha had been hospitalized for four years. While a committee of mental health practitioners found his mental illness to be in remission, they could not certify that he was no longer dangerous. Nevertheless, a divided Supreme Court (5–4) ruled that, if no longer mentally ill, he should be discharged. Critics of the *Foucha* decision maintain that the court did not sufficiently recognize the recurring quality of serious mental disorders. While they may go into remission, persons suffering from them are not necessarily cured (Golding et al., 1999). On the other hand, it is difficult to justify holding an individual who is not disordered on the premise that at some point in the future his or her disorder is likely to reappear. In many jurisdictions, such individuals are now released conditionally or on community treatment orders. This allows mental health authorities to monitor their progress and assure that they are taking the medication that presumably keeps them stabilized and their mental disorder in remission.

Thus far we have discussed the consequences of a finding of not guilty by reason of insanity. In the following section, we cover a variety of standards that courts use to decide whether a person was insane.

INSANITY STANDARDS

The insanity defense has been recognized in English courts for over 700 years (Simon, 1983). Since the American legal system is derived from British law, American courts have generally recognized it as well. Standards or tests to determine insanity vary widely among the states, but they usually center around one of three broad models: the M'Naghten Rule, the Brawner Rule, or the Durham Rule. Moreover, all the insanity standards are fundamentally based on two criteria: **irrationality** and **compulsion** (Morse, 1986). If it can be established that a person was not in control of his or her mental processes (was thinking irrationally) and/or was not in control of his or her behavior (was driven by compulsion) at the time of the offense, then there are grounds for absolving that person of some or all responsibility for the offense. Jurisdictions, however, differ in the extent they accept both these criteria. That is, some jurisdictions accept both criteria, while others will accept only the irrationality component.

The M'Naghten Rule

The **M'Naghten Rule** has been around in some form since at least the nineteenth century. The current rule was formulated in 1843, after Daniel M'Naghten, a Scottish woodcutter, was acquitted of killing a man he believed to be the prime minister. M'Naghten thought he was being persecuted by the Tories and their leader, Prime Minister Sir Robert Peel. He fired a shot into a carriage transporting Peel's secretary, Edward Drumond, thinking Peel himself was in the carriage. There was no question that M'Naghten had committed the act, but the court believed he was so mentally deranged that it would be inhumane to convict him. Applying a "wild beast" test in use at the time, the court concluded it was clear he was not in control of his faculties. He was committed to the Broadmoor Mental Institution, where he remained until his death 22 years later. It was widely believed that M'Naghten "knew" his actions were wrong and that he should have been convicted. Therefore the law was changed to prevent a similar "miscarriage of justice" in the future. Thus the rule that bears M'Naghten's name is not the rule under which he was tried.

In 1851, the M'Naghten Rule was adopted in the federal and most state courts in the United States. It is deceptively simple, and therein lies its popularity. It states that a person is not responsible for a criminal act if, "at the time of committing the act, the party accused was labouring under such a defect of reason, from disease of the mind, as not to know the nature and quality of the act he was doing; or if he did know it . . . he did not know he was doing what was wrong" (*M'Naghten*, 1843, p. 718). Essentially, the rule states that if a person, because of some mental disease, did not know right from wrong at the time of an unlawful act, or did not know that what he or she was doing was wrong, that person cannot be held responsible for his or her actions.

Thus, the M'Naghten Rule, sometimes referred to as the **right and wrong test,** emphasizes the *cognitive elements* of (1) being aware and knowing what one was doing at the time of the illegal act; or (2) knowing or realizing right from wrong in the moral sense. The rule recognizes no degree of incapacity. You are either responsible for the action or you are not. There are no in-betweens.

Some states supplement M'Naghten with an irresistible impulse test, which has similarities to the "wild beast" test applied in the original M'Naghten case.

The irresistible impulse test recognizes or assumes that people may realize the wrongfulness of their conduct, be aware of what is right or wrong in a particular set of circumstances, but still be powerless to do right in the face of overwhelming pressures from uncontrollable impulses. In other words there are conditions under which people presumably cannot help themselves. The M'Naghten Rule alone would not cover those circumstances, since it requires that the person did not know right from wrong.

The Brawner Rule and the American Law Institute Rule

The **Brawner Rule,** which is largely based on an insanity rule suggested by the Model Penal Code (MPC), is another rule for determining insanity. The MPC was proposed in 1962 by a group of legal scholars associated with the American Law Institute (ALI). The Code was drafted to serve as a model for legislatures seeking to modernize and rationalize their criminal statutes. According to the Brawner Rule, "A person is not responsible for criminal conduct if at the time of such conduct as a result of mental disease or *defect* [italics added], he lacks substantial capacity either to appreciate the criminality [wrongfulness] of his conduct or to conform his conduct to the requirements of the law" (*United States v. Brawner,* 1972, p. 973). It must be demonstrated that the disease or mental defect *substantially* and directly (1) influenced the defendant's mental or emotional processes, or (2) impaired his or her ability to control behavior. The Brawner Rule, unlike M'Naghten, recognizes *partial* responsibility for criminal conduct, as well as the possibility of an irresistible impulse beyond one's control. It also excludes from the definition of mental disease or defect any repeated criminal or otherwise antisocial conduct, an exclusion we referred to earlier in the chapter. This provision (called the **caveat paragraph**) was intended to disallow the insanity defense for criminal psychopaths who persistently violate social mores and often the law. Thus, psychopaths and persons with antisocial personality disorders cannot claim that their abnormal condition is a mental disorder, disease, or defect, even if they have been diagnosed APD.

The Durham Rule: The Product Test

The **Durham Rule** was created in 1954 in *Durham v. United States* by the same court that later rejected it in favor of the Brawner Rule. Monte Durham, a 26-year-old resident of the District of Columbia, had a long history of mental disorder and petty theft. His crime of the moment was burglary, but he was acquitted because his unlawful act was considered to be "the product of a mental disease or mental defect" (*Durham v. United States,* 1954, p. 874). While the M'Naghten Rule focuses on knowing right from wrong (the mental element in a crime), Durham assumes that one cannot be held responsible if an unlawful action is the product of mental disease or defect.

There is nothing in the Durham Rule that relates directly to the person's mental judgment. If the person has a disease or defect, lack of culpability is easily assumed. The rule was later clarified in *Carter v. United States* (1957), which held that mental illness must not merely have entered into the production of the act, it must have played a necessary role.

Many states were attracted to the apparent simplicity of the Durham Rule, since it seemed more straightforward and comprehensible to juries. However, it soon became apparent that definitions of "mental illness" are vague and subjective, a situation that fostered the widespread discretionary power of psychiatry and considerable misuse of mental health experts during trial. Moreover, virtually any defendant could be excused, once mental disease or defect had been established, and the Durham Rule quickly lost its popularity.

Until the 1980s, most jurisdictions adopted one of the above rules, with varying degrees of satisfaction. However, the well-publicized Hinckley acquittal sparked a public outcry for the elimination of the insanity defense and prompted legislative bodies and many professional organizations to reexamine it. The American Bar Association and the American Psychiatric Association, for example, proposed new, more restrictive standards (Steadman et al., 1993). Nearly 100 different reforms in 34 jurisdictions occurred soon after Hinckley's acquittal, the most active insanity reform period in American history. In most instances these reforms reflected a return to the M'Naghten Rule in a modified, more restrictive form (Steadman et al., 1993). Five states—Montana, Idaho, Utah, Nevada, and Kansas—have abolished the insanity defense altogether. Other changes include (1) placing on defendants the burden of proving they were insane (where in the past prosecutors had been required to prove they were not insane); (2) restricting the role of clinical testimony; and (3) requiring persons found NGRI to prove they were no longer mentally ill before being released from a mental institution. Many of these changes were modeled after the federal law discussed below.

The Insanity Defense Reform Act

Amid public clamors to abolish the insanity defense completely after the Hinckley acquittal, Congress passed the **Insanity Defense Reform Act of 1984,** which kept the defense in the federal law but modified it in important ways. Rita Simon and David Aaronson (1988, p. 47) assert, "The Hinckley verdict was unquestionably the decisive influence on congressional modifications to the insanity defense." Essentially, Congress made it more difficult for persons using the insanity defense in federal courts to be acquitted. The Insanity Reform Act changed the Brawner/ALI Rule—the rule that has been most consistently adhered to in all federal circuits (except the Fifth Circuit) since its adoption during the early 1970s—to one patterned more along the lines of the M'Naghten Rule. Specifically, a defendant cannot be held responsible if "at the time of the commission of the acts constituting the offense, the defendant, as a result of a severe mental disease or defect, was unable to appreciate the nature and quality or the wrongfulness of his acts. Mental disease or defect does not otherwise constitute a defense" (18 U.S.C., sec 20[a] [1984]).

In addition, the new federal standard changed the Brawner/ALI Rule in three principal ways (Simon & Aaronson, 1988). First, the act abolished the irresistible impulse test (commonly called the **volitional prong**) of the Brawner/ALI Rule. The inability to control one's actions because of mental defect was no longer acceptable as an excusing condition. Second, the act modified the "cognitive" requirement by replacing the phrase "lacks substantial capacity . . . to appreciate" with "unable to appreciate." The intention was to tighten the requirement to a total lack of ability to appreciate that what they did was wrong (Simon & Aaronson, 1988). Third, under the new law, the mental disease or defect must be severe, to emphasize that certain behavioral disorders (especially personality disorders) do not qualify as a defense. It should be noted that the federal law also bars mental health clinicians from expressing an opinion as to whether the defendant was insane. Clinicians may testify, report on the findings of their evaluations, and provide a diagnosis, but they may not express an ultimate opinion. This is to emphasize that insanity is a legal determination that must be made by the court.

Guilty but Mentally Ill

Also in response to disenchantment with the insanity defense, some states have introduced a new verdict alternative, **Guilty but Mentally Ill (GBMI).** Michigan was the first to adopt this alternative in 1975, and by 1992 eleven other states had followed Michigan's lead. The GBMI option is intended as an alternative to, not a substitute for, the NGRI verdict. Although states differ in the

TABLE 7–1 Standards for Criminal Responsibility

Standard	Year First Used	Description
M'Naghten Rule	1843	It must be clearly proved that at the time of committing the act, the party accused was laboring under such a defect of reason, from disease of the mind, as not to know the nature and quality of the act he was doing, or if he did know it, that he did not know he was doing what was wrong.
Durham Rule	1954	An accused is not criminally responsible if the unlawful act was the product of mental disease or mental defect.
Brawner/ALI Rule	1972	A person is not responsible for criminal conduct if at the time of such conduct as a result of mental disease or defect he lacks substantial capacity to either appreciate the criminality [wrongfulness] of his conduct or to conform his conduct to the requirements of the law.
Insanity Defense Reform Act	1984	A person charged with a criminal offense should be found not guilty by reason of insanity if it is shown that, as a result of mental disease or mental retardation, he was unable to appreciate the wrongfulness of his conduct at the time of his offense.
Guilty but Mentally Ill	1975	Holds the defendant blameworthy for the offense, but recognizes the presence of a mental disorder.

standards and procedures associated with the GBMI verdict, the major intention of the option was to reduce the number of insanity acquittals, hold the defendant blameworthy, but still recognize the presence of a mental disorder. Thus it allows the court to render a "middle-ground" verdict in the case of allegedly mentally disordered defendants. The verdict allows juries, for example, to reconcile their belief that a defendant who commits a crime should be held responsible with the belief that he or she also needs help.

Research on the GBMI laws indicates that the intended purposes may not have been accomplished. In Michigan, for example, insanity acquittals have remained stable while guilty verdicts have generally declined (Smith & Hall, 1982). The same findings have been reported in other states that have adopted the GBMI option (McGinley & Paswark, 1989). Furthermore, defendants found GBMI have received longer sentences and had longer confinements than "sane" defendants found guilty of similar charges (Callahan, McGreevy, Cirincione, & Steadman, 1992; Steadman et al., 1993). In addition, research indicates that those individuals found GBMI are no more likely to receive psychotherapy or rehabilitative services than other mentally disordered defendants in the prison system (Morse, 1985; Slobogin, 1985). Thus the promise of treatment that is implicit in the statutes remains unfulfilled. Interestingly, there is also evidence that defendants charged with a serious violent crime often elect the GBMI alternative as part of the plea bargaining process. Defense attorneys may be more willing to accept this option than go to trial and risk their client's life (Steadman et al., 1993). Considering the research strongly suggesting that GBMI statutes do not accomplish what was intended, virtually all of the scholarly writing on this issue has questioned the wisdom and efficacy of these laws (Cohen, 2000).

UNIQUE DEFENSES

Earlier in the chapter we discussed some of the psychiatric diagnoses that are most likely to accompany a decision that a defendant is incompetent to stand trial or used to bolster an insanity defense. In this section we discuss additional disorders or diagnoses that are less common but still cited by defense lawyers, either to absolve defendants completely or to support a claim of diminished capacity or responsibility.

Posttraumatic Stress Disorder

According to the DSM-IV, **posttraumatic stress disorder (PTSD)** is "the development of characteristic symptoms following exposure to extreme traumatic stress or involving direct personal experience of an event that involves actual or threatened death or serious injury, or other threat to one's physical integrity; or witnessing an event that involves death, injury, or threat to the physical integrity of another person; or learning about unexpected or violent death, serious harm, or threat of death or injury experienced by a family member or other close associate" (p. 424). The precipitating event would be substantially distressing to almost anyone, and it is "usually experienced with intense fear, terror, and help-lessness" (p. 424).

PTSD was formally recognized as a distinct disorder in the 1980 edition of the DSM-III following efforts by veterans' groups to have mental health professionals recognize a "post-Vietnam syndrome" that led to a variety of disabling symptoms (Appelbaum et al.). Since being formally recognized, PTSD has been broadly applied to war veterans, survivors of the Holocaust, survivors of major disasters—such as the events of September 11, 2001—and victims and survivors of rape, child abuse, spousal abuse, and sexual harassment. PTSD falls under the broader category of "dissociative disorders" in the DSM-IV-R. Dissociative disorders are marked by major changes in memory not due to physical causes (Comer, 2004). Other examples of these disorders are certain forms of amnesia, fugues, and dissociative identity disorder.

Surveys estimate that between 1 percent and 2 percent of all Americans suffer from PTSD (Sutker, Uddo-Crane, & Allain, 1991). One study estimated that PTSD affected 31 percent of all male and 27 percent of all female Vietnam veterans (Kulka et al., 1991).

The symptoms of PTSD include "flashbacks," recurrent dreams or nightmares, or painful, intrusive memories of the traumatic event. A diminished responsiveness, a don't-care attitude, or psychological "numbing" to the external world are common, particularly during the weeks following the event. On the other hand, some research indicates that the symptoms of PTSD may not emerge until considerable time has elapsed, six months to a year or more. In fact, the DSM-IV-TR distinguishes among acute (symptoms last less than three months), chronic (symptoms last longer than three months), and delayed onset PTSD (when at least six months have passed since the traumatic event). Feelings of alienation or detachment from the social environment are also characteristic, a pattern that leads to difficulty in developing close, meaningful relationships with others. Other symptoms include sleep problems, being easily startled, considerable difficulty concentrating or remembering, and extreme avoidance of anything that reminds them of the event. Even anniversaries of the trauma are often enough to precipitate symptoms. Individuals with a diagnosis of PTSD tend to be moody, depressed, and difficult to be around or work with. They often move from job to job, relationship to relationship.

PTSD has been used to support a defense of NGRI, in both violent and nonviolent cases (Monahan & Walker, 1990, 1994). For example, PTSD has been used as an excusing condition for drug trafficking (e.g., *United States v. Krutschewski*, 1981). Evidence to date, however, shows that—while courts are willing to admit evidence of PTSD—using it to support an insanity defense is no more successful than using other mental disorders (Appelbaum et al., 1993). Moreover, PTSD defendants, as a rule, do not follow the stereotypic images portrayed by the media as "tortured but essentially upstanding veterans, who at some point, become overwhelmed by their symptoms, 'snap,' and commit a violent crime" (Appelbaum et al., 1993, p. 233). Specifically the research evidence reveals that defendants who use PTSD to support an insanity defense have been in as much trouble and involvement with the criminal justice system as other defendants who use the insanity defense (Appelbaum et al., 1993).

When the PTSD defense has been successful, it usually results in a finding of *diminished responsibility,* rather than the complete absolution of responsibility (NGRI) for the defendant. PTSD has also been cited in plea bargaining and in presentence reports (Monahan & Walker, 1990). That is, prosecutors may be more willing to accept a guilty plea to a reduced charge, and judges more willing to impose a lighter sentence, if evidence of PTSD exists. Appelbaum and colleagues (1993) also found that, in cases involving veterans, PTSD was frequently used as evidence for diminished responsibility in assigning cases to pretrial diversion, in plea bargaining, and in sentencing.

The primary legal argument used by the defense is that the defendant was in a PTSD dissociated state when he committed the act. A **dissociated state** refers to symptoms where the individual feels detached from themselves and their surroundings and basically loses some contact with reality. While in that state, a person typically does not remember what he or she has experienced or even his or her own identity. In *State v. Felde* (1982), the defendant—a Vietnam veteran who shot a police officer—"claimed that he was in a dissociative state and that he believed that he had been captured by the North Vietnamese at the time he shot the officer" (McCord, 1987, p. 65). In *Miller v. State* (1983), the defendant, charged with a prison escape, argued that he thought he was still in Vietnam and his only intention was to get back to the United States.

PTSD has been used to excuse or mitigate criminal responsibility in cases involving battered women who maintain that they have **battered woman syndrome,** sometimes considered a variant of PTSD (Appelbaum et al., 1993). This is a controversial area for at least two major reasons. First, there is not universal agreement in the psychological literature that there exists a battered woman syndrome. Second, advocates for battered women resist the implication that they have a mental disorder or that they are "insane." When PTSD is used, a battered woman may claim that the abuse was so extensive and brutal that, in a dissociative state brought about by the disorder, she killed the abuser. In this case she is more likely to claim "temporary insanity" than "insanity," in the hope that acquittal will not be followed by commitment to a mental institution. However, PTSD in battered woman also may be used to support a claim of self-defense rather than insanity, though courts have not been sympathetic to this approach (Slobogin, 1999). When used in this way, the defendant focuses on other symptoms of PTSD—for example, heightened fear, anxiety, depression—rather than on the dissociative state. In a different context, evidence that an alleged rape victim shows the symptoms of PTSD has been accepted in some courts as proof that the victim has indeed been raped (Appelbaum et al. 1993). Likewise, PTSD has been used in civil suits involving emotional or physical personal injury, such as sexual harassment suits or civil suits against former abusers.

While courts are increasingly accepting PTSD evidence, some legal scholars and researchers remain skeptical. They believe that objective assessment of PTSD lacks solid validity, and the diagnosis depends almost exclusively on self-report. Consequently critics argue that there is considerable opportunity for faking the disorder, especially if the individual rehearses and practices the symptoms. Appelbaum et al. (1993, p. 230) conclude that the problem of PTSD in the courts as an excusing condition is "particularly acute with something as new, as 'unverifiable,' as potentially useful, and as politically charged as PTSD."

Pathological Gamblers' Syndrome

The syndrome of **compulsive gambling** began with psychoanalytic case studies during the early part of the twentieth century (Cunnien, 1985). Compulsive gamblers, the early case studies concluded, are neurotics with an insatiable, unconscious desire to lose what was gained (Cunnien, 1985). The DSM-IV describes pathological gambling as the inability to resist impulses to gamble, despite the dire consequences to family, interpersonal relationships, and daily living. "The essential feature of Pathological Gambling is persistent and recurrent maladaptive gambling behavior that disrupts personal, family, or vocational pursuits" (DSM-IV, p. 615). It is a progressive and eventually overwhelming urge to engage in gambling behavior. The disorder may afflict as many as 1 percent to 3 percent of the adult population, and is more common among males than females (DSM-IV-TR). In a survey of 1,200 residents of Ontario, Insight Canada Research (1998) found that about 8 percent of Ontarians could be classified as "problem gamblers," while 0.9 percent are probable pathological gamblers. Pathological gambling usually begins during adolescence in males, and later in life in females (DSM-IV-TR). Pathological gamblers are often overconfident, very energetic, and easily bored, but sometimes exhibit stress, anxiety, and depression during their losing streaks.

The distinguishing characteristic of pathological gambling from "normal" or social gambling is its "addictive" nature. Addicted gamblers are believed to be unable to walk away from a gamble and are tense and restless if gambling is denied them.

Pathological gambling became fully recognized in the DSM-III in 1980 as a serious mental disorder, and since that time the disorder has been used by defendants as an excuse for a variety of illegal activities. The crimes with which defendants have been charged are not gambling offenses, but rather crimes committed for monetary gain. The defendants contended that money was necessary in order to support their pathological gambling habit (McCord, 1987). For example, in *United States v. Gillis* (1985), the defendant, who was charged with interstate transportation of stolen vehicles and forged securities, argued that he engaged in these illegal activities to support his gambling habit. The following are additional examples where similar defenses were used: *United States v. Davis* (1984), where the defendant was charged with forging and converting government checks payable to deceased relatives; *United States v. Gould* (1984), where the defendant was charged with bank robbery; and *United States v. Lewellyn* (1985), where the defendant was charged with embezzlement, making a false statement, and mail fraud.

In general, defendants using this defense have been unsuccessful, because they have been unable to demonstrate a connection between "the syndrome and the inability of the defendant to resist the impulse to commit crimes in order to support the gambling urge" (McCord, 1987, p. 67). However, it should be noted that the pathological gambling defense has been occasionally successful, as seen in *State v. Lafferty* (1984) in a case involving embezzlement, and in *State v. Campanaro* (1980) in a case involving forgery.

Cunnien (1985, p. 89) writes, "There are . . . no available data to suggest whether pathological gambling and attendant criminal behavior are uncontrollable or merely uncontrolled." He further concludes, "It remains unproven that impulses to gamble are uncontrollable" (p. 98).

Dissociative Identity Disorder

The essential feature of **dissociative identity disorder** (formerly called **multiple personality disorder (MPD))** is "the existence within the person of two or more distinct personalities or personality states that recurrently take control of behavior" (DSM-IV, p. 484). Furthermore, "each personality state may be experienced as if it has a distinct personal history, self-image, and identity, including a separate name" (DSM-IV, p. 484). Periodically, at least two personalities take full control of the individual's behavior. The change or transition from one personality to another is often very sudden (seconds to minutes), and is generally triggered by stress or some relevant environmental stimuli. Often hypnosis can also bring about this shift into another personality.

According to the DSM-IV, each of the personalities may be aware of some or all the other personalities in varying degrees. There may be as many as a hundred different identities. The disorder occurs about three to nine times more frequently in females than in males. Persons who experience DID are highly suggestible and impressionable, and can be readily hypnotized either by themselves or others. Reported cases of what was then called MPD have historically been extremely rare. However, between 1980 and 1989 the number of cases diagnosed in the United States rose dramatically, from two hundered to six thousand (Slovenko, 1989). Part of this increase is due to the American Psychiatric Association officially recognizing the disorder in the DSM-III.

There is a good deal of controversy surrounding the existence and prevalence of DID, which in recent years has gained more status among clinicians, while researchers are far more skeptical. The concept of individuals having "multiple personalities" or "alter egos" that control their lives is fascinating to many but remains scientifically questionable. While this phenomenon may exist in a very minute segment of the mentally disordered population, it is also highly susceptible to being overdiagnosed.

On occasion, MPD has been used successfully as an excusing condition for criminal responsibility. In *State v. Rodrigues* (1984), a defendant accused of three counts of sodomy and one count of rape of young girls was acquitted on the basis of MPD. In *State v. Milligan* (1978), Billy Milligan claimed he had 24 separate personalities and was found NGRI in criminal charges of raping three women. In general, however, MPD has not been a successful defense (Slovenko, 1989). One of the more well-known cases in which the MPD defense was tried involved serial killer Kenneth Bianchi, known as the Hillside Strangler. The Hillside Strangler was given wide publicity because of the brutality and sadistic quality of his murders. The victims were young, attractive women who were raped and strangled, and whose nude bodies were conspicuously displayed on the hillsides in the Los Angeles area. The Hillside Strangler was responsible for at least a dozen murders during a one-year period (1977–1978).

Much of the following material was acquired from an article written by Martin T. Orne, David F. Dinges, and Emily Carota Orne (1984), and the interested reader is encouraged to study that paper. Throughout his adult life, Bianchi's most consistent career aspiration was to become a police officer, and he even attended a junior college program in police science. Although he repeatedly applied for positions at various police departments, he was not successful at landing a job. However, he did obtain employment as a security guard.

Overall, Bianchi was unable to sustain a successful career pattern, holding at least 12 different jobs during the nine-year period following high school. His background was a series of lies, scams, and illegal activities, ranging from the use of stolen credit cards to the pimping of juvenile prostitutes. During his last year in Los Angeles, Bianchi masqueraded as a psychologist, complete with an office and answering service. He obtained false diplomas and credentials by placing a classified ad in the *Los Angeles Times,* offering a position to a recently graduated psychologist. He requested that the applicants send not only résumés, but also their official university transcripts. From the hundreds of applications he received, he obtained enough information to forge a transcript and diploma with his name on them.

At age 19, Bianchi married a high school girlfriend, but the marriage lasted less than eight months. At age 26, he began to live with a woman in a common-law relationship; she bore him a son. After the birth of his son, his common-law wife moved to Bellingham, Washington, where Bianchi joined her three months later. In Bellingham, he obtained a job as a supervisor for a private security agency. Bianchi, however, was arrested on January 11, 1979, for the murders of two women in Washington—murders that followed a pattern similar to the Hillside Strangler in California.

Despite considerable evidence against him, Bianchi insisted that he was innocent. Eventually, he maintained under hypnosis that his alter personality "Steve" had done the killings. Since Steve did the killings, Ken Bianchi argued he should not be held responsible and pleaded NGRI under the State of Washington's M'Naghten Rule. The court appointed a team of experts to determine if Bianchi really was suffering MPD. The court (*State v. Bianchi*, 1979) posited that if the experts could agree, the insanity defense might prevail. The team of experts, however, after careful examination of his past and present behavior, found no basis for Bianchi's claim of MPD. Although Bianchi knew the "textbook version" of MPD (probably knowledge gained during the time he impersonated a psychologist), he was less than convincing on the more subtle aspects of the disorder recognized by the experts. The team concluded that Bianchi was a psychopath. Bianchi then quickly changed his plea to guilty in order to avoid the death penalty.

There is considerable debate among practitioners and scholars as to whether the syndrome MPD/DID actually exists, and it is sometimes referred to as the "UFO of psychiatry" (Ondrovik & Hamilton, 1991). In some instances, it may be **iatrogenic**—that is, unintentionally caused by clinicians or practitioners themselves (Comer, 1992). This means that practitioners who firmly believe in and are perceptually sensitive to DID look for and interpret a variety of behaviors as symptoms of the disorder. Clinicians are now told that the symptoms of DID are very subtle and that the average length of time it takes for the disorder to be diagnosed is seven years (Gelinas, 1993). In effect, the practitioner may develop the syndrome in the patient, and the patient, in turn, learns to believe that he or she is afflicted with it. It has also been argued that implicit and explicit suggestions during hypnosis can shape segments of self into the appearance of MPD (Orne et al., 1984). Regardless of whether the syndrome is iatrogenic or whether it is possible for several personalities to "possess" a physical body, an important point must be made. The syndrome is *often subjectively real* to the patient, and the person who allegedly experiences it often plays each of the roles well and convincingly. Martin Orne and his colleagues (Orne et al., 1984, p. 120) observe, "So striking are the behavioral differences between personalities that the assertion is often made that one would need to have the dramatic skills of Sarah Bernhardt or Sir Laurence Olivier, along with a detailed knowledge of psychiatry, to effectively simulate such radically different persons."

Everyone to some degree hosts a number of subpersonalities (Slovenko, 1989). One aspect of our subpersonalities is our moods: One day we may be cool and withdrawn, and the next day, warm and sociable. The situation also makes a big difference. For example, each person is different when at home with parents than when spending time with friends. At home, parents might treat you like the immature 16-year-old they remember, and you find yourself assuming that role quickly and easily. The old conflicts and squabbles with your parents return, just as they did years ago. It is possible that these changes in moods, together with the fact that some clinics "look hard" for MPD/DID and some patients are happy to oblige, all contribute to the increased prevalence of this disorder.

In summary, the validity of DID as a viable entity is very much open to debate by both the mental health and legal professions. Supporters of the concept maintain that diagnostic procedures among clinicians are more accurate today than in the past, and clinicians have at their disposal specific diagnostic tests to detect the disorder (Comer, 2004). At present, though, there is very little solid evidence that the syndrome, as a bona fide mental disorder in which one personality completely controls the other(s), actually exists, except possibly in very rare situations. Nevertheless, it is not unusual to be in a roomful of clinicians who seem firmly convinced that DID is a significant problem encountered in their practices and one that mental health practitioners still fail to diagnose. According to this perspective, treatment is a highly complex and multistage process. It involves allowing the alter egos to emerge and enabling the client to confront them. Eventually, the "alters" are left behind, a process that can be very frightening to the client. As one therapist commented, after a long period of treatment, the client had successfully confronted her problems and was ready to move on to a normal life. However, she was concerned about how she would handle financial matters, because "Ruth"—one of her alters—was the one who had always balanced the checkbook.

Amnesia

Amnesia refers to complete or partial memory loss of an event, series of events, or some segment of life's experiences, either due to physical trauma, neuro-physiological disturbance, or psychological factors. According to the DSM-IV, "Individuals with an amnestic disorder are impaired in their ability to learn new information or are unable to recall previously learned information or past events" (p. 156). Amnesia is not simply forgetting a name, a date, or an incident, but is reserved for severely impaired ability to remember past material (retrograde amnesia) or to acquire and retain new material (anterograde amnesia).

Some researchers have identified a classification of amnesia called **limited amnesia,** which is "a pathological inability to remember a specific episode, or small number of episodes, from the recent past" (Schacter, 1986b, p. 48). Limited amnesia may be caused by emotional shock, alcohol or drug intoxication, or a blow to the head. Therefore, limited amnesia is not ongoing, nor does it involve extensive memory loss. Rather the loss is temporary and restricted to a specific event or incident.

In general the courts have not been receptive to amnesia as a valid condition in either the insanity defense, or as a condition that promotes incompetence to stand trial (Rubinsky & Brandt, 1986). Paull (1993) notes that there have been cases in at least 20 states and five federal circuit courts where the court has held that amnesia per se does not render a defendant incompetent. One reason for this judicial "hard line" approach to amnesia is the suspicion that the defendant may be faking the memory loss. It is easy for people to simply say they cannot remember committing the crime, and it is difficult for psychologists to determine whether a person can or cannot remember. In recent years, though, psychologists have been able to fine-tune a number of instruments designed to measure malingering—or faking—of various symptoms, including symptoms of amnesia (Rogers, 1997). Additionally, some psychologists believe that amnesia can be evaluated with recognition tests that are tailored to the information that the client claims not to know (Frederick, 2000).

Amnesia associated with alcoholic intoxication presents a favorite excuse for reprehensible behavior, and is the most commonly invoked excusing condition in criminal cases. "When I drink I go blank about some things" is the usual line. It is intriguing to note that 30 percent to 65 percent of persons convicted of criminal homicide claim they cannot remember the crime, usually because of alcoholic intoxication at the time of the offense (Schachter 1986b). A similar pattern exists for other violent crimes (e.g., rape) as well.

However, the courts have not been very sympathetic to defendants who rely on excuses based on alcohol or other drug intoxication. This is because the courts hold the person blameworthy since he or she should have known, at the outset, the risks involved in drinking alcohol or taking drugs. Thus, attempts to use amnesia in this way have met with strong judicial resistance. For example, one court held that "insanity is the incapacity to discriminate between right and wrong while amnesia is simply the inability to remember" (Rubinsky & Brandt, 1986, p. 30). Therefore amnesia per se fails to qualify as a mental disorder that robs a person of the ability to distinguish between right and wrong.

 ## SUMMARY AND CONCLUSIONS

In this chapter we began to focus on the relationship between mentally disordered individuals and crime. In order to understand this relationship we must go beyond labels, which do not explain why someone behaves in a certain way. Furthermore, labels are assigned by the mental health profession and, along with the definitions, sometimes change with each edition of the DSM, the standard diagnostic manual used by most clinicians. Since the 1980s, however, the DSM has remained relatively stable.

Mental illness (or mental disorder) is a disorder or disease of the mind that interferes substantially with a person's ability to cope with life on a daily basis. Although it deprives someone of freedom of choice, this deprivation is rarely total. As noted in the chapter, even severely disordered individuals can have some decision-making ability. Mental illness should be distinguished from retardation or developmental disability. The former can be treated, cured, or held in remission; the latter cannot, although developmentally disabled individuals can be taught to perform many tasks and supported in their desires to be self-sufficient.

We reviewed diagnostic categories that are most often associated with criminal behavior. For example, persons accused of crime may introduce these diagnoses to support an insanity defense. The main categories discussed were schizophrenic disorders, with particular emphasis on the paranoid type that is most frequently represented in criminal behavior; delusional disorders, with emphasis on the persecutory type; depressive disorders, which may play a major role in delinquency, mass murders, and workplace violence, among others; postpartum depression, with emphasis on the very rare postpartum psychosis that can result in serious crime; and antisocial personality disorder, which most courts today do not accept in support of an insanity defense. The juvenile equivalent of APD is conduct disorder, and it is a very frequent diagnosis of adolescents held in detention and treatment facilities. In the following chapter, we will note that several of these diagnoses also are relevant when police deal with the mentally disordered or when inmates in correctional facilities are treated for mental illness. We will also discuss the issue of whether individuals with these diagnoses are rightfully considered dangerous.

The chapter also reviewed the legal constructs of competency and insanity. Criminal defendants are found incompetent if they are so disordered that they cannot understand the proceedings or help their attorneys in their own defense. Adjudicative competence is relevant to a wide range of proceedings, including a variety of pretrial hearings and the trial itself as well as the sentencing stage. Basically the law says that an incompetent defendant is not present; therefore, before proceeding with prosecution, he or she must be rendered competent. As we noted the common approach with incompetent defendants is to hospitalize them for treatment until they attain competency; alternately the case against them is dismissed. A major issue today relating to incompetent defendants is the extent to which they can be medicated against their will. Courts have generally ruled that, when the government has a strong interest in bringing the defendant to trial—such as in a very serious crime—medication will be allowed.

Although it is the competency issue that affects the greatest number of defendants, it is the insanity issue that most intrigues the public. The truly insane individual is not responsible for his or her crime. Successful insanity defenses are very rare, but even when they occur they are no bargain. Persons found not guilty by reason of insanity are typically institutionalized, very often for longer periods of time than they would have served in prison. We reviewed the various standards for establishing insanity, including the M'Naghten (right/wrong) Rule, the ALI/Brawner Rule, and the Durham Rule (product test). Since the 1980s, largely as a result of the acquittal of John Hinckley, many states and the federal government have passed more restrictive insanity statutes, making it even more difficult for defendants to be absolved of criminal responsibility. Some states also have adopted a "guilty but mentally ill" verdict form, which allows a judge or jury to find a defendant guilty, but also acknowledges that he or she needs treatment. Research indicates, though, that the treatment implied is rarely provided in correctional facilities.

We ended the chapter with a review of intriguing "special defenses" that are sometimes raised in criminal cases, either to absolve a defendant completely or to support a defense of diminished capacity: PTSD, pathological gamblers' syndrome, dissociative identity disorder (DID; formerly called multiple personality disorder), and amnesia. Although still very rare in criminal courts, the numbers of diagnosed individuals in the general population, particularly with reference to PTSD and DID, are increasing. Numerous veterans are returning from the Middle East and being diagnosed with PTSD, for example, and DID can sarcastically be called the diagnosis of the decade. We might speculate that these could be on the increase in criminal courts as well.

 ## KEY CONCEPTS

Mental illness	Postpartum blues
Mental retardation	Antisocial personality disorder
Schizophrenia	Conduct disorder
Diagnostic and Statistical Manual of Mental Disorders	Competency to stand trial
	IST
Delusional disorders	Not guilty by reason of insanity
Major depressive disorder	Compulsion

Right and wrong test
Caveat paragraph
Insanity Defense Reform Act
  of 1984
Guilty but mentally ill
Posttraumatic stress disorder
Dissociative disorder
Compulsive gambling
MPD
Amnesia
Mental disorder
Developmental disability
Delusions
DSM
Hallucinations
Paranoid disorders
Postpartum depression

Postpartum psychosis
APD
Adjudicative competence
Incompetent to stand trial
NGRI
Irrationality
M'Naghten rule
Brawner rule
Durham rule
Volitional prong
GBMI
PTSD
Battered woman syndrome
Multiple personality disorder
iatrogenic
Limited amnesia

REVIEW QUESTIONS

1. Briefly describe four legal standards for insanity and their requirements.
2. Describe the essential features of antisocial personality disorder.
3. Identify and include symptoms of the four diagnostic categories most relevant to criminal behavior.
4. What are guilty but mentally ill statutes? Why do many legal scholars oppose them?
5. Describe the three types of postpartum depressions and which one is most likely to be involved in suicide/murder by the mother.
6. Give an example of iatrogenic effects in counseling or psychotherapy.
7. Why does the text prefer the term "mental disorder" over "mental illness"?
8. Describe fully and evaluate any three of the unique defenses discussed in the chapter.
9. Thoroughly explain the difference between incompetence to stand trial (or adjudicative incompetence) and insanity. Include in your answer what researchers have learned about the individuals who receive those legal designations.
10. Which mental disorder is most likely to be involved in violent behavior?

CHAPTER 8
·······················▶

MENTAL DISORDERS AND CRIME: DEFENDANTS AND OFFENDERS

CHAPTER OBJECTIVES

- Review the research on whether the mentally disordered are more violent than the non-mentally disordered population.
- Examine issues relating to police and the mentally disordered.
- Examine issues relating to the mentally ill in jails and prisons.
- Evaluate the research on risk assessment and the prediction of dangerousness.
- Discuss legal issues relating to the mentally disordered sex offender.

While the mental disorders described in the previous chapter may be associated with a variety of criminal offenses, it is the crimes of violence that are most disturbing. The depressed individual may embezzle funds in an effort to obtain a way out of his dire economic situation. The individual with a delusional disorder may break into a building to seek shelter from those who persecute him. The person with an antisocial personality disorder may perpetrate a series of economic scams on unsuspecting victims. Publicity is most likely to accompany criminal behavior when it is violent, however, and the public is most fearful of these offenses, despite the fact that we are far more likely to be victims of economic crimes than violent crimes. And as we learned in the previous chapter, the mere presence of a mental illness does not guarantee that a defendant will be found incompetent to stand trial or absolved of criminal responsibility. In some jurisdictions this is even more true when defendants are accused of violent crimes than when they are accused of property offenses.

259

As a group, individuals who are mentally ill are no more likely to commit crimes than those who are not. Nevertheless they do appear with some regularity on police blotters, in jails, in prisons, and on probation and parole caseloads. As a matter of fact, the prevalence of mental disorders is more than three times higher in the criminal justice population than in the general population (Skeem, Emke-Francis, & Louden 2006). Part of this is due to a decrease in the availability of inpatient care for mental health problems.

Long-term inpatient care or hospitalization of the mentally disordered has largely disappeared, particularly in public institutions. While these institutions still exist, they are generally intended for short-term crisis care and treat patients with drugs rather than psychotherapy. They typically do not hold most patients for more than three to six months, although there are exceptions. (One is the sexually violent predator, who is discussed later in the chapter.) Although the mentally disordered may be discharged from these institutions with orders to continue taking medication, they are often not well supervised. Consequently the mentally disordered have become a more visible presence within the community. When problems arise, it is often the responsibility of law enforcement officials to handle the situation.

In the 1980s, it was widely acknowledged that jails—and sometimes prisons—were becoming repositories for individuals who could no longer be kept in mental institutions for lengthy periods (Teplin, 1984). This trend has not abated significantly, although some communities try to address the problem by offering more support services. The presence of mentally disordered individuals in the criminal justice system does not mean that they are dangerous and at high risk of committing serious crimes. Rather, they are often without shelter, may be disruptive, and may commit minor offenses, such as trespassing, drug possession, or petty theft. Periodically, though, we do hear of a person with a history of mental illness who kills a stranger on the street, or one who brutally beats an acquaintance. The question then asked is, "Are the mentally disordered more violent than those who are not disordered?"

MENTAL DISORDERS AND VIOLENCE

Early research literature consistently supported the position that mentally disordered individuals—even the severely mentally disordered—are no more likely to commit serious crimes against others than the general population (Brodsky, 1973, 1977; Henn, Herjanic, & Vanderpearl, 1976a; Monahan, 1981; Rabkin, 1979). However, more recent research (Brennan, Mednick, & Hodgins, 2000; Klassen & O'Connor, 1988, 1990; Monahan, 1992) finds that this cannot be said of a certain subset of the mentally disordered population. Specifically, male mentally disordered patients, *who have a history of at least one violent incident,* have a high probability of being violent within a year after release from the hospital. In fact evidence is beginning to accumulate that individuals with schizophrenia are at increased risk for violent offending and even at higher risk to commit murder (Naudts & Hodgins, 2005). In addition, when offenders with schizophrenia do commit murder, they most often kill relatives, and many are exhibiting hallucinations and delusions at the time of the offense (Häkkänen & Laajasalo, 2006).

We cannot emphasize enough that a majority of people with mental disorders do *not* commit serious or violent offenses. For example, only 11.3 percent of the men and 2.3 percent of the women who developed schizophrenia committed violent offenses (Tengström et al., 2004). In addition those individuals with schizophrenia who commit violent crime constitute a very heterogeneous group. "Some display a history of antisocial behavior from a very early age; others begin engaging in antisocial behavior around the time of schizophrenia onsets; others commit only 1 violent attack in their lives, while others behave aggressively only when acutely psychotic" (Naudts & Hodgins, 2005, p. 1).

Recent research also finds that offenders with schizophrenia who have high scores on the Psychopathy Checklist List-Revised (PCL-R) are usually convicted for more violent offenses than those with low scores on the PCL-R (Tengström et al., 2004). The results suggest that PCL-R scores offer the strongest predictor of violent and chronic offending histories. Tengström et al. (2004) write, "These results indicated that among offenders with schizophrenia, as among non-mentally ill offenders, high PCL-R ratings are associated with more severe histories of offending and violence" (p. 385).

The Tengström et al., 2004 study underscores the fact that males who develop schizophrenia *and* exhibit antisocial behavior at an *early* age often demonstrate persistent and versatile patterns of criminal offending. Essentially, early onset offenders with schizophrenia show a pattern very similar to life-course-persistent offenders (LCP), discussed in chapter 2.

In addition, there is further evidence that men who have both schizophrenia and a substance abuse problem are at an increased risk of violent offending. For instance, Räsänen et al. (1998) report evidence that male schizophrenics with alcohol abuse problems are 25 times more likely to commit violent crimes than males with no mental disorders and no alcohol problems. Follow-up studies of patients with schizophrenia and substance abuse problems have frequently found them to be at risk of committing violent offenses (Appelbaum, Robbins, & Monahan, 2000; Tengström et al., 2004).

John Monahan (1992) stresses two things about the research showing a connection between mental disorders and violence. First, the relationship refers only to people *currently* experiencing a *serious* mental disorder. People who have experienced a serious mental disorder in the past and are not showing symptoms currently are unlikely to engage in violent behavior. Second, it is still a fact that a great majority (over 90%) of the currently mentally disordered are not violent. Media portrayals of common psychotic killers driven berserk by bloodthirsty delusions are sensational, frightening, and perhaps entertaining, but in reality the phenomenon is rare. Finally, it must be emphasized not only that the mental disorder–violence link relates to the seriously mentally disordered (e.g., schizophrenics), but also that the relationship is also stronger for individuals who have a history of violent behavior.

Furthermore, it is possible, as some clinicians believe, that the more bizarre violent offenses are committed by the mentally disordered, particularly those categorized as schizophrenic or paranoid. Moreover, the more extreme violence of schizophrenics is typically directed toward family members or acquaintances, and bizarre self-mutilation is more likely than mutilatory murders (Blackburn, 1993). However, Ronald Blackburn (1993, p. 274) admonishes, "Although there appears to be an increased risk in schizophrenia, particularly in paranoid schizophrenia, it must be reiterated that only a small minority of patients in this category are violent, and that the disorder itself is rarely sufficient to account for violent acts in instances where they occur."

Individuals experiencing affective (mood) psychoses are less likely to be violent. When affective psychoses are associated with violence they are usually manifested in women within the context of extended suicide, in which the offender kills herself as well as others in the environment, including her immediate family (Blackburn, 1993). However, as is noted in chapter 10, mass murders in public settings are often committed by men who feel hopeless and also have the signs of affective psychoses. In most cases mass murderers plan to die or commit suicide at the site of their crime.

The MacArthur Research Network

Some of the best known research on the potential violence of the mentally disordered has been conducted by the MacArthur Research Network (Monahan et al., 2001; Steadman et al., 1998). Researchers followed over one thousand patients discharged from civil psychiatric hospitals in an effort to determine the extent to which they demonstrated aggressive behavior over a one-year period. The patients also had been measured on a wide range of "risk factors"—134 in all—while they were hospitalized. These included such factors as violent fantasies, history of abuse as a child, frequency of parents fighting with each other, and number of negative and positive persons in the social network, to name but a few. The data allowed the MacArthur researchers to develop a risk assessment instrument, The Multiple Iterative Classification Tree (ICT), which they believe can help clinicians identify low, average, and high-risk individuals. It is worth noting that about half of the discharged patients in this study were in the low-risk group, while the remaining patients were about evenly divided between average and high-risk groups. However, no single risk factor was a significant predictor of violence. As Monahan et al. (2001, p. 142) stated, "The propensity for violence is the result of the accumulation of risk factors, no one of which is either necessary or sufficient for a person to behave aggressively toward others."

In sum, then, the research on the mentally disordered and violence allows us to conclude the following:

- Past mental disorder alone, even serious mental disorder, is not necessarily a good predictor of violence.

- The mental disorder most closely associated with violent and serious offenses is schizophrenia.
- Persons with schizophrenia who commit violent crimes consist of a very heterogeneous group.
- Males who have developed schizophrenia and who score high on the PCL-R have an increased risk of being violent.
- Males who develop schizophrenia *and* exhibit antisocial behavior at an *early* age often demonstrate persistent and versatile patterns of criminal offending.
- Violence is associated with *current* serious mental disorder, particularly when a history of violent behavior is also present.
- While researchers have developed some instruments to assess the likelihood that a person will engage in violence, no one factor serves as strong predictor; violent behavior seems to be a result of an accumulation of risk factors, unique to each individual.

Police and the Mentally Disordered

During the last quarter of the twentieth century, researchers focused a good deal of attention on interactions between law enforcement officials and the mentally disordered. An early literature review of the criminal behavior of discharged mental patients is instructive (Rabkin, 1979). Rabkin found that a significant number of studies documented a higher arrest rate for discharged mental patients than for the general population, especially for assaultive behavior. Rabkin suggested two explanations for the disproportionate arrest rates. First, a small subset of patients who had criminal records prior to hospital admission continued their antisocial ways soon after discharge from the mental institution. These habitual offenders significantly inflated the arrest rates for all mental patients. In fact, those discharged patients *without* prior criminal records were substantially below the arrest rates for the general population. Second, most criminal offenses after discharge were committed by individuals who had been diagnosed with alcoholism, substance addiction, or antisocial personality disorder (APD), all of which appear consistently in the research. Alcoholism and substance addiction are in the fringe areas of traditional diagnoses because they do not represent what are considered serious or typical mental disorders. With respect to APD, it was often used when clinicians could find no other way to label a person acting antisocially. When these three categories were omitted, Rabkin found that the arrest rates among the discharged patients, *without a criminal history,* were comparable to those reported in the general population. "When patients with arrest histories, primary diagnoses of substance abuse, and personality disorders are considered separately, the remainder of the patient group appears to be considerably less dangerous than are those members of the general public who are not mentally ill" (Rabkin, 1979, p. 26).

Research has also documented that police may be more apt to arrest the mentally disordered (Teplin, 1984). Trained graduate students in psychology observed 1,382 police-citizen encounters (involving 2,555 citizens) and evaluated the mental status of the citizens according to specific criteria (a symptom checklist that listed the major characteristics of severe mental disorders). The police determined that 506 citizens qualified as suspects, and they arrested 148. The graduate students classified 30 of the 506 suspects and 14 of the 148 suspects arrested as exhibiting definite symptoms of mental disorders. Therefore, the police arrested 20 percent more individuals with symptoms than without symptoms. Considering that many disordered individuals tend to have annoying symptoms, such as verbal abuse, belligerence, and disrespect, the slightly higher probability of arrest is hardly surprising. To some extent, police also may have taken some of these individuals into custody in order to provide them with shelter. However, police officers failed to recognize the behavior as representing a mental disorder in a large number of cases, believing the individuals were simply being disrespectful and asking for trouble.

In the 20-plus years since Teplin's now-classic study, significant changes have occurred nationwide relative to law enforcement's handling of mentally disordered individuals. First, police academies are more likely to offer some training in both recognizing and dealing with mental disorders (Fields, 2006). In some communities police have taken the initiative to appoint specially trained liaison officers to work with the disordered (Smith, 2002). Second, communities across the nation are establishing specialized courts—mental health courts—that provide diversionary options to jailing and prosecuting the mentally disordered—and the mentally retarded—who are charged with nonviolent offenses, or even minor violent crimes, such as simple assault. Rather than being held in jail, they are offered shelter and treatment or training services. Mental health courts are of recent origin and need continuing evaluation before we can conclude that they are effective. However, they offer a promising alternative to the short-term cycles of arrest, jail, court, release, and rearrest that characterize the lives of some mentally disordered individuals.

MENTALLY DISORDERED INMATES

Mental disorders in those incarcerated in prison and jail are sometimes cited as evidence of a link between crime and abnormal behavior. Both the prevalence and the nature of disorder among these populations are difficult to determine, however, because statistics and descriptions vary widely. Furthermore, some data are based on the inmates' own self-report, while other data are based on clinical findings.

How Many Prison and Jail Inmates or Probationers Are Mentally Disordered?

A Bureau of Justice Statistics survey (Ditton, 1999) estimated that 283,000 mentally disordered offenders were incarcerated in U.S. prisons and jails in 1998. In that survey, 16 percent of all state prison and local jail inmates and 7 percent

TABLE 8–1   Mental Health Status of Inmates and Probationers

	STATE PRISON INMATES, 1997	FEDERAL PRISON INMATES, 1997	JAIL INMATES 1996	PROBATIONERS 1995
Identified as mentally disordered	16.2%	7.4%	16.3%	16.0%
Reported a mental or emotional condition	10.1	4.8	10.5	13.8
Admitted overnight to a mental hospital or treatment program	10.7	4.7	10.2	8.2

Source: Ditton, 1999.

of federal prisoners reported that they had a mental disorder or had had an overnight stay in a mental hospital or treatment program (see **Tables 8–1** and **8–2**). In addition, over 75 percent of mentally disordered inmates have been sentenced to time in prison or jail at least once prior to their current sentence, suggesting that mentally disordered offenders who do offend demonstrate a high recidivism rate (Ditton, 1999).

Other researchers have reported that 10 percent to 15 percent of persons in jails and federal and state prisons have *severe* mental disorders (Lamb, Weinberger, & Gross, 2004). It is difficult to determine to what extent these data include antisocial personality disorders; it is estimated that 40 percent to 80 percent of inmates carry that diagnosis (Steffan & Morgan, 2005). Nevertheless both researchers and mental health professionals working with jail and prison inmates report significant increases in *serious* mental health problems (Ashford, Sales, & Reid, 2001).

Some research reveals that the rates of serious mental disorders among prison inmates vary widely, ranging from 5 percent to 16 percent psychotic

TABLE 8–2   Inmates and Probationers Identified as Mentally Disordered, by Gender, Race/Hispanic Origin, and Age

OFFENDER CHARACTERISTICS	Percent Identified as Mentally Disordered			
	STATE INMATES	FEDERAL INMATES	JAIL INMATES	PROBATIONERS
Gender				
Male	15.8%	7.0%	16.6%	14.7%
Female	23.6	12.5	22.7	21.7
Race/Hispanic Origin				
White	22.6%	11.8%	21.7%	19.6%
Black	13.5	5.6	13.7	10.4
Hispanic	11.0	4.1	11.1	9.0

Source: Ditton, 1999.

(Teplin, 1990). Among a sample of adult male jail detainees in Cook County (Chicago), Teplin (1990) found 9.5 percent had experienced a severe mental disorder (schizophrenia, mania, or major depression) at some point in their life, compared with 4.4 percent of males in the U.S. general population. Robins and Regier (1991) found that 6.7 percent of prisoners had suffered from schizophrenia at some point in their lives, compared with 1.4 percent of the U.S. population. In the New York correctional system, it was estimated that about 8 percent of the inmates had "severe" mental disorders and another 16 percent had "significant" mental disorders (Steadman, Fabisiak, Dvoskin, & Holobean, 1987). However, it is unclear whether the mental disorders were present prior to incarceration, or developed as a result of being incarcerated. In addition, it is often not clear from the research what percent of the disordered have been diagnosed with APD, the catch-all category we discussed earlier.

In the 1970s and 1980s, it was not unusual for mentally disordered individuals—particularly those serving time in prison rather than jails—to be transferred to secure units of civil mental hospitals. As the number of disordered inmates increased, prison systems across the United States began to open treatment facilities within the prison system. Depending on the jurisdiction, then, a seriously mentally disordered inmate might be treated in a separate mental health wing of the prison, transferred to a prison facility specifically designated for the mentally disordered, or transferred to a civil mental institution. It is also possible that the offender might not receive any treatment, because the extent of his disorder is not recognized or, more soberingly, not acknowledged.

Young offenders—including juveniles—may be more likely than adults to be diagnosed with mental disorder. Linda Teplin (2000) found that two-thirds of juveniles in a sample of more than 1,800 youths held in Chicago's Cook County Juvenile Temporary Detention Center tested positive for at least one drug, and two-thirds were diagnosed with at least one mental disorder. A considerable portion of the mental disorders in these juveniles consisted of major depressions, especially among female juveniles. The Teplin study, known as the Northwestern Juvenile Project, strongly suggests that many mentally disordered juveniles are also abusing drugs and alcohol quite extensively at the time of their arrest.

It is obvious that jail and prison conditions, as well as conditions in juvenile facilities, can have deleterious effects on mental states. Therefore, an individual may become mentally disordered after being institutionalized, which may be reflected in these statistics. We assess more fully the potential deleterious effects of imprisonment in chapter 17. However, considerable evidence indicates that many inmates or prisoners were showing signs of mental disorders prior to incarceration (Bureau of Justice Assistance, 2000).

What Precisely Are the Diagnoses of Mentally Disordered Inmates?

It remains difficult to determine, however, the precise clinical diagnoses associated with these mental disorders. Many could have been diagnosed with antisocial personality disorder. Second, some data were collected by asking the inmates themselves about their mental conditions. (See Table 8–1). Third, the reliability of psychiatric diagnoses, even in the general population, is often in doubt. Finally, we do not know whether the mental disorders reported are the result of being in prison or jail, or whether the individual entered the system with the existing disorder. Regardless, however, if the disorder exists it is a problem.

The subgroup of individuals who are transferred to civil mental institutions may be declining with the availability of secure treatment facilities within the prison setting. Because states differ greatly in the treatment and transfer options they provide for mentally disordered prisoners, it is difficult to distinguish a general pattern in either the disorders or the circumstances surrounding the transfers. However, in 1980, the U.S. Supreme Court ruled that the transfer of an inmate to a mental health hospital requires, at a minimum, an administrative hearing to determine whether such transfer is appropriate (*Vitek v. Jones,* 1980). An inmate is entitled to challenge that transfer, and to have legal assistance for that purpose. The Supreme Court recognized the special nature of confinement in a mental health facility and the stigma that often accompanies a commitment (Churgin, 1983). Furthermore, transfer to a mental institution not only entails forced treatment of almost any variety, but also may substantially reduce chances for parole, since parole boards may be reluctant to release into the community a prisoner who was recently in a mental hospital setting. Nevertheless, researchers have observed that transfers to civil mental institutions—or to prison mental hospitals—are not often challenged, despite the due process protections afforded to these inmates by the *Vitek* case (Cohen, 1998). Cohen adds that inmates are less likely to resist a transfer than to face delays in getting timely admission to a hospital setting when it is needed.

In summary it is very clear that prisons and jails today are facing increasing numbers of mentally disordered inmates whose problems will escalate if not sufficiently treated. In chapter 17 we discuss approaches to the treatment of these offenders.

DANGEROUSNESS AND THE ASSESSMENT OF RISK

Up to this point in this and the previous chapter we have covered a range of situations involving mentally disordered individuals, criminal courts, police, and prisons and jails. In many—but not all—of those situations, the courts and other agents of the criminal justice system were concerned about whether the disordered individual was also a danger to society.

The concept of **dangerousness** pervades much of the criminal law and appears in civil law as well. Defining dangerous behavior is a challenge faced by legislatures, courts, and clinicians. All states and all courts recognize that behavior that is likely to result in *physical harm* is dangerous. They begin to differ when behaviors that lead to property damage or psychological injury are involved. One example of psychological injury is the effect on victims of stalking, who may be continually shadowed, photographed, contacted by phone or e-mail, and otherwise harassed. Some courts have ruled that this type of behavior can cause irreparable emotional damage. They conclude that a threat of "psychological trauma is . . . as much a menace to the health or safety of others as is possible physical injury" (Developments in the Law, 1974, p. 1237). This form of psychological damage has prompted many state legislatures to pass "stalking laws" that state that persons who continually follow and otherwise harass other individuals are dangerous and can be charged with a criminal offense.

It is fair to say, though, that dangerousness is used primarily in conjunction with violent behavior. Defendants charged with violent crimes are sometimes denied bail because they are judged dangerous, violent offenders are sentenced to long prison terms to prevent them from committing more crime, and some are sentenced to death because it is feared they will commit more violence. Decisions on whether to parole prisoners convicted of violent crimes are largely based on whether they are dangerous.

Risk Assessment

Implicit in the above decisions is the belief that it is possible to predict an individual's violent behavior. Although some clinicians believe they can do so with a high degree of confidence, most are far more modest about this ability. Since the 1990s, the research and professional literature have increasingly preferred the term "risk assessment" rather than prediction of dangerousness. **Risk assessment** suggests that clinicians and researchers are more proficient at *assessing the probability* that a given individual—or group of individuals—will engage in harmful behavior than they are at outrightly predicting that someone will be violent. We will return to this change in terminology shortly.

Controversy over the ability to predict has been longstanding. Not surprisingly, it has often been fueled by highly publicized incidents. In August 1966, Charles Whitman, a University of Texas student majoring in architectural engineering, murdered his wife and his mother. Shortly thereafter, he carried his personal arsenal in a footlocker to the observation deck of the 307-foot-tall University Tower, where he loaded a number of high-powered, scope-equipped rifles and began randomly shooting at people near the observation deck and on the ground far below. Whitman managed to shoot 44 victims, killing 14, before a police officer and a citizen climbed to the tower and ended the tragedy by shooting Whitman himself.

An investigation revealed that the 25-year-old Whitman had consulted a psychiatrist five months before the incident, and, during a two-hour interview, had described "overwhelming violent impulses" and great fear of his inability to control them. He had also revealed a compelling need to "go up on the tower with a deer rifle and start shooting people." Whitman did not return for further consultation after the initial two-hour session. Nevertheless, when the news of his contact with a psychiatrist was disseminated, there was public outcry and many questions about why he was not treated, confined, or referred to the proper authorities. Similar questions were raised when the public learned that James Huberty, who killed 22 fast-food restaurant patrons in the summer of 1984, had also had contact with a mental health clinic. In Huberty's case, social workers had apparently tried without success to return his telephone calls.

The Tarasoff Case

In another highly publicized case, an outpatient at a University of California–Berkeley clinic revealed to his psychiatrist his fantasies about harming, or perhaps even killing, a woman whom he had met at a dance. The psychologist, who learned from one of his patient's friends that he planned to purchase a gun, became increasingly concerned. When the patient discontinued therapy, clinic officials wrote to the police requesting their help in getting the individual committed to a mental institution. Police investigated the case, interviewed the patient, warned him to stay away from the woman, but did not pursue the commitment, apparently because California's new civil commitment law was difficult to interpret. Two months later, Prosenjit Poddar—the patient—killed Tatiana Tarasoff by stabbing her, though he was carrying his newly purchased gun. He was charged with first-degree murder. Tarasoff's family sued the university clinic, claiming the psychologist had been negligent in not warning the young woman or the family of the danger.

The *Tarasoff* case, undoubtedly familiar to all clinicians, addressed very directly the question of what duty therapists owe to third parties in warning them of possible harmful behavior from their clients. The California Supreme Court first ruled that when a therapist determines that a patient is a serious danger to another person, the therapist has a **duty to warn** that individual (*Tarasoff v. Regents,* 1974). Two years later (*Tarasoff v. Regents,* 1976), the Court redefined the role as a **duty to protect.** That is, the therapist need not directly warn the individual, but he or she should take some steps to protect the individual from harm. Following the California court's decisions, courts in many other states issued similar decisions, but others rejected the doctrine. In the 1980s, the doctrine was widely applied, but in the 1990s the doctrine was rejected altogether or severely limited in many states (Felthous, 2001). Whether or not there exists a statutory duty to warn/protect, many practitioners have interpreted the "spirit" of *Tarasoff* as a standard of practice, believing that the clinician has a professional obligation to take some steps to protect an identifiable potential victim (e.g., Litwack & Shlesinger, 1999).

Courts that have adopted duty to warn/protect rules apparently believe that mental health professionals can predict with considerable accuracy who is or will be dangerous and who will not. The law has been relying on predictions of dangerousness for a long time, dating at least as far back as the sixteenth century (Morris & Miller, 1985). Yet researchers and clinicians have long struggled both to define dangerousness and to predict its occurrence. After the *Tarasoff* case, dangerousness generated more controversy than even the insanity defense (Simon & Cockerham, 1977).

When courts consider this question, they often turn to the psychiatric and psychological professions. However, as noted, many in these professions have resisted the notion that dangerousness could be predicted. Instead, they maintain that, at best, they can offer probabilities based on known factors relating to the individual, often based on data obtained from large groups. (Recall our earlier discussion of the MacArthur Risk Assessment Study with civilly committed psychiatric patients.) Thus, increasingly, the psychological literature has avoided the term prediction of dangerousness and has replaced it with risk assessment. Regardless of the terminology, it is clear that some attempt at assessing/predicting the likelihood that an individual will commit violence is warranted.

There is little doubt that a person who has been violent in the past and indicates by word or deed that he or she plans to do serious harm to others is dangerous. Someone who has committed a series of murders, mutilations, or rapes, and who attests to planning to do more of the same, is certainly—by anyone's definition—a dangerous individual. If a person has no history of violence and threatens harm, however, the situation becomes more problematic. Likewise, if a person has been violent in the distant past but has shown no recent signs of violent behavior, the situation is again problematic. In these contexts, clinicians have difficulty reaching a consensus on who is dangerous and who is not. This is why current thinking favors surveying a list of "risk factors" in attempt to determine the likelihood that aggressive behavior will occur. Risk assessment is perhaps the most complicated and controversial issue in the entire field of forensic psychology (Borum, 1996). Many researchers and scholars (e.g., Steadman et al., 1993) consider it one of the most important issues in both criminal and civil matters worldwide. A variety of instruments are available for clinicians engaging in the risk assessment enterprise. Additionally, during a clinical interview, mental health practitioners are often advised to be attuned to background factors. Before reviewing some of these instruments, it is wise to consider conceptual issues relating to prediction.

Until very recently, the psychological research literature consistently concluded that clinicians are unable to specify the type or severity of harm an individual may cause, or to predict with great accuracy the probability of harm even occurring. That early literature can best be summarized in the words of Alan Stone (1975, p. 33), who wrote,

> It can be stated flatly on the basis of my own review of the published material on the prediction of dangerous acts that neither objective actuarial tables nor psychiatric intuition, diagnosis, and psychological testing can claim predictive success when dealing with the traditional population of mental hospitals. The predictive success appropriate to a legal decision can be described in three levels of increasing certainty: Preponderance of the evidence, 51% successful; clear and convincing proof, 75% successful; beyond a reasonable doubt, at least 90% successful.

Stone asserted that mental health professionals have failed to predict dangerous behavior by even the lowest criterion, a *preponderance of the evidence.* Likewise, Cocozza and Steadman (1976)—referring to the involuntary civil commitment of mentally disordered individuals—asserted that "any attempt to commit an individual solely on the basis of dangerousness would be futile if psychiatric testimony were subjected to any of these three standards of proof" (p. 1101). They added that the psychological research has demonstrated "clear and convincing evidence of the inability of psychiatrists or anyone else to predict dangerousness accurately" (p. 1099).

The early research on prediction also demonstrated that clinicians had a strong tendency to overpredict dangerousness, a pattern that held for criminal offenders as well as mentally disordered patients (Monahan, 1981, 1984). At a minimum, the most sophisticated predictive methods yield 60 percent to 70 percent false positives (people who were predicted to be dangerous but did not engage in harmful behavior) (Kozol, Boucher, & Garofalo, 1972; Rubin, 1972; Wenk, Robison, & Smith, 1972). In a ten-year follow-up investigation of 592 convicted male offenders, mostly sex offenders (Kozol, Boucher, & Garofalo, 1972), two of every three persons predicted dangerous were false positives, even after extensive background data and results of independent clinical exams by psychiatrists had been made available to those doing the predicting. Moreover, because of some flaws in the design of the study, the odds for accurate prediction were very much in the researchers' favor (Dix, 1980; Monahan, 1976; Steadman, 1976).

In the 1970s, classic studies that followed individuals after their release from mental institutions also documented the limitations of prediction. Steadman (1976) followed patients who were released from New York hospitals after a landmark U.S. Supreme Court case, *Baxstrom v. Herold* (1966). These "Baxstrom patients" had first been convicted of crimes and had then been transferred to civil mental institutions without hearings shortly before their prison sentences expired. On average they had spent eight years in confinement beyond their prison sentence. The Baxstrom patients were predominantly nonwhite, lower socioeconomic class, middle-aged males. Although a vast majority had arrest records and many had previous convictions, only 58 percent had been convicted of violent crimes (Steadman, 1976). On the average the patients had been institutionalized continuously for 14 years. In its *Baxstrom* decision, the Supreme Court noted that—like other individuals committed to civil mental institutions—the prisoners had a right to a hearing to determine whether they were mentally disordered and dangerous. As a result, many were released, often against the advice of clinicians who predicted that they were dangerous.

The Baxstrom patients were considered some of New York's most dangerous mental patients, but follow-up reports found that predicted dangerousness had been grossly overstated (false positives) (Monahan, 1976). Steadman and Cocozza (1974) followed up 85 Baxstrom patients and discovered that 20 percent were rearrested, but only 7 percent were convicted, usually for minor violations such as vagrancy and public intoxication. An examination of both in-hospital and community behaviors revealed that only 20 percent of the "extremely dangerous" patients were assaultive toward others during the four-year follow-up period (Steadman, 1976). A prominent variable predicting whether Baxstrom patients demonstrated assaultive behavior was age: The younger the patient, the more likely he or she was to engage in assaultive behavior. Even using the Legal Dangerousness Scale (Cocozza & Steadman, 1976), a measure of four criminal background characteristics, there were two false positives for every three patients predicted to be violent, again underscoring the inaccuracy of clinical prediction.

In a similar research project, Thornberry and Jacoby (1979) followed up a group of mentally disordered offenders in Pennsylvania who were transferred from criminal to civil mental hospitals in that state. These patients had notable past histories of mental problems and criminal offenses. Forty-three percent had been hospitalized in the past, and 90 percent were diagnosed psychotic on current admission. Over 80 percent had prior arrest records, 64 percent had previously served jail and prison sentences, and 39 percent had committed five or more offenses in the past. Until a court ordered their reevaluation (*Dixon v. Attorney General of the Commonwealth of Pennsylvania*, 1971), the patients had been institutionalized indefinitely on the basis of presumed dangerousness.

Thornberry and Jacoby (1979) found that, after their court-ordered transfer to civil and less secure mental hospitals, only 19 percent were involved in some kind of violence within the hospital setting. Two-thirds of the patients were discharged from the civil hospitals within nine months of the transfer. During a four-year follow-up, about 24 percent were arrested, and only one-quarter of these arrests were for violent offenses. Overall, the incidence of false positives—in which clinicians had predicted harmful or violent behavior that did not occur—was 67 percent, or two out of every three predictions.

Although we have focused on the above classic studies, it is important to emphasize that other research in the 1970s also supported these findings (e.g., Kozol, Boucher, & Garofalo, 1972; Rubin, 1972; Wenk, Robison & Smith, 1972). Reviews of the literature led scholars to conclude that, in the area of dangerousness prediction with respect to the mentally disordered, **false positives** outnumbered **true positives** by a margin of two to one (Monahan, 1988; Wettstein, 1984).

The ratio of false to true positives deserves some attention. False positive is a descriptor we use for persons who are labeled dangerous (positive), but who do not engage in harmful behavior during a specific period of time after release from custody (false). True positives are persons predicted to be dangerous (positive) who do engage in subsequent harmful behavior (true). (See **Table 8–3.**) For example, assume a team of mental health professionals concludes that ten persons are dangerous. If, during a two-year period following release, six do engage in harmful behavior, we have a 60 percent rate of true positives and a 40 percent rate of false positives. On the other hand, the team may predict that ten people will not engage in violent behavior (negatives). If some of them do, they are called **false negatives. True negatives** are those who are predicted not to engage in harmful behavior within a certain period of time and who do not.

TABLE 8–3   Four Possible Outcomes of Prediction

	Criterion Behavior	
PREDICTION	DID	DID NOT
Will	True positive	False positive
Will not	False negative	True negative

Thus, if the team predicts that 7 out of 10 people will not engage in harmful behavior, and 5 of the 10 do not, the team was wrong in two cases. We therefore have a ratio of 20 percent false negatives to 50 percent true negatives.

In many ways it is clearly advantageous for mental health professionals to predict more positives than negatives, especially if there is some question about whether a person is dangerous. The *Tarasoff* decision also encourages this trend. Clinicians who fail to warn and protect the community by not detecting persons who eventually commit violent or harmful acts will likely pay a higher social and professional price than clinicians who overpredict dangerousness.

It is quite clear that clinicians tend to overpredict dangerous behavior, under the premise that it is better to be safe than sorry. It is also quite clear that predictions of dangerousness, in general, are inaccurate. Even though researchers have made impressive strides in developing risk assessment instruments, prediction remains a tenuous enterprise. What accounts for this?

First, the behavior being predicted, violence, occurs relatively infrequently in the daily lives of even the most frequent offender. Therefore, the prediction of an infrequent behavior is akin to finding a needle in a haystack of behaviors. Violent behavior happens (or is reported) so infrequently that if you say it will happen, the odds are already against you. Second, while human behavior is generally consistent across time (temporal consistency), it is often inconsistent across situations (trans-situational consistency). More specifically, people tend to act the same way during their lifetimes, if the situations eliciting this behavior are basically the same. However, if the situations are different, as is so characteristic of life, people are unlikely to act the same way. As noted earlier, for example, most of us act differently with our parents than we do with our friends, or we act one way with members of the same sex, but another way with members of the opposite sex. Thus mental health professionals would be substantially more accurate if they could be certain that the social environment remained the same. In reality the social environment is always changing, rendering the predictions based on one situation inapposite for another.

What Are the Best Predictors of Dangerous Behavior?

Overall, the best predictor of future behavior is *past behavior*, but even past behavior will not necessarily be repeated. The best predictor of criminal behavior is a history of criminal behavior, and past violence will suggest a probability of future violence. A history of criminal behavior is the best predictor of criminal recidivism regardless of whether the offender is mentally disordered or normal (Bonta, Law, & Hanson, 1998). But again, people change. Furthermore, the more frequently the behavior has occurred in a variety of situations, the more accurate will be the predictions. Someone who frequently manifests violence across many different situations will be far easier to predict than a person who is only occasionally violent in some situations.

Since the 1990s, researchers have made considerable strides in the ability to identify more factors that are associated with violence. In addition to criminal history, recent research strongly indicates that other predictors of criminal recidivism include some combination of age, juvenile delinquency, and substance abuse (Andrews & Bonta, 1994; Bonta, Law, & Hanson, 1998; Gendreau, Little, & Goggin, 1996). However, researchers have also warned that risk factors are unique for each individual, and that no one factor will necessarily predict violence in any one individual. We now turn to the types of clinical measures that have been offered to help clinicians assess the likelihood that a person will engage in harmful behavior toward others.

Current Risk Assessment Measures

Many of the *risk assessment instruments* have been developed by Canadian psychologists. These instruments generally require a clinician or assessor to evaluate an individual based on information in certain areas of background and behavioral patterns. The first of these instruments was the Dangerous Behavior Rating Scheme (DBRS) developed by Christopher Webster and Robert Menzies (1993). The scale underwent considerable research development but became a disappointment when it failed to predict dangerousness and violence to a satisfactory level. A second, more promising attempt is the Violence Risk Assessment Guide (VRAG) developed by Grant Harris, Marnie Rice, and colleagues (Webster et al., 1994). The VRAG is based on data from 618 men with prior histories of significant violence who were initially confined at the Oak Ridge Division of the Penetanguishene Mental Health Center in Ontario, Canada. Oak Ridge is a maximum security facility providing assessment and treatment for persons referred from the courts, correctional services, and other provincial psychiatric hospitals (Webster et al., 1994). Twelve variables believed to predict future violence make up the VRAG. The variables include separation of parents by age 16 or younger, schizophrenia, elementary school maladjustment, alcohol abuse history, and symptoms of psychopathy. The 618 violent men in the project were followed for 10 years. Overall, 31 percent of the subjects committed another violent offense, usually within seven years after release (Rice, 1997). The best predictor of violent recidivism was the score of the psychopathy scale (i.e., PCL-R). "It alone predicted better than any combination of other criminal history variables" (Rice, 1997, p. 415). On the other hand, the presence of a mental disorder did not predict violence. Based on preliminary research, Rice concludes, "Our work and that of others on the prediction of violence has shown that long-term criminal violence can be predicted with a considerable degree of accuracy among men who have already been apprehended for a violent criminal offense" (p. 418).

Another promising instrument for evaluating risk is the Historical/Clinical/Risk Management (HCR-20) scale developed by Christopher Webster and his colleagues (Webster, Douglas, Eaves, & Hart, 1997). The HCR bases its predictive power on three major areas: past or historical factors, clinical or current factors, and risk management factors. The HCR contains 10 historical items, 5 clinical items, and 5 risk management items, for a total of 20 items. The historical items include "previous violence," which, as we have learned, is one of the strongest predictors of future violence. Another historical or "H" item is "young age at first violent incident" (Webster et al., 1997, p. 267). In other words, the younger the person at the time of the first violent incident, the greater the likelihood that a violent pattern will persist into the future. "Early maladjustment" at home, at school, or in the community is another predictive H item. Other H items in the HCR-20 are relationship instability, employment problems, substance use problems, and major mental illness (particularly psychotic or mood disorders). Clinical or "C" items include lack of insight, negative attitudes (antisocial, hostile, angry), and "active symptoms of major mental illness" (Webster et al., 1997, p. 263). Active symptoms of serious mental illness that include delusional systems characterized by sadistic fantasies and homicidal and suicidal ideation are especially related to violence prediction. Risk management or "R" variables are related to the future circumstances of the individuals they are evaluating—that is, whether the person being evaluated is likely to have adequate housing, meals, daily activities, and finances. Research suggests that individuals without these basics are at higher risk for violence than those who have these needs managed and taken care of. Examples of R items are lack of personal support, noncompliance with remediation attempts, feasibility of future plans, and stress. The researchers of the HCR-20 find that the historical (H) items are the strongest for predicting future violent behavior (Webster et al., 1997), and C items are second strongest (Borum, 1996). The HCR-20 is still relatively new and will need ongoing research before it receives widespread acceptance as a valid risk-assessment instrument.

The MacArthur Network research project discussed in the previous chapter (Steadman et al., 1998) represents still another example of efforts to develop a risk assessment measure. The project involves acute psychiatric patients discharged from mental institutions in three locations (Pittsburgh, Pennsylvania; Worcester, Massachusetts; and Kansas City, Missouri). The goals of the project were threefold: (1) to improve the validity of clinical risk assessment, (2) to improve the effectiveness of clinical risk management, and (3) to provide useful information for reforming mental health policy. The project resulted in the development of the Multiple Iterative Classification Tree, a means of assessing the likelihood that a mentally disordered individual will engage in future aggressive behavior. Among the many factors considered are episodes of violent behavior, violent fantasies, persons in one's positive social network, and substance abuse. Like other researchers, Steadman et al. (1998) emphasize that no one factor can predict that violence will occur.

It should also be emphasized that risk assessment instruments, such as those already described, are not invariably supported in the clinical literature. Many mental health practitioners are suspicious of measures that rely on actuarial data or that were developed on specific populations, such as incarcerated violent offenders or persons held in civil mental hospitals. Some scholars have noted that risk assessment instruments may ignore factors that are specific to the case at hand (Heilbrun et al., 2002), or that clinicians often adjust the scores to incorporate their own clinical impressions (Doren, 2002). Heilbrun et al. acknowledge the value of risk assessment instruments, but they also urge clinicians not to undermine the role of clinical judgment. In essence, one should supplement the other, because neither approach, standing alone, is likely to produce consistent, valid results.

THE (NON)MENTALLY DISORDERED SEX OFFENDER

Throughout this chapter we have discussed mentally disordered defendants and offenders as a group, without focusing on the specific crimes they commit. It is clear that, in assessing risk, we are most concerned about violent crimes, but this encompasses a range of offenses, from simple assaults to murder. In recent years, fueled by media accounts, the public has been particularly concerned about the crimes of the sexual offender, sometimes referred to as the sexual predator, who is believed to be particularly dangerous. Because until relatively recently sexual predators were considered to be mentally disordered, we discuss them in this chapter rather than later in the book when sex offenses are highlighted.

Historically the **mentally disordered sex offender (MDSO)** was the individual either charged with or convicted of a sexual offense and involuntarily committed to a civil mental institution on the basis of his mental disorder and presumed dangerousness to society. Today the great majority of these offenders are committed under **sexually violent predator** laws, and they do not necessarily require a finding of a diagnosable mental disorder. In some jurisdictions, "mental abnormality" (a vaguer term) will suffice. This is a critically important point to make, because *many if not most mental health professionals do not consider sex offenders mentally disordered.*

MDSO statutes first appeared on the scene during the early part of the twentieth century, and were then called "sexual psychopath" laws. The term psychopath was not really appropriate for a vast majority of these individuals, whose crimes ranged from minor to very serious acts. In most cases, the legislative intention was to provide special dispositional procedures for persons who exhibit a tendency to commit sex offenses, but each state developed its own set of procedures and definitions. Either explicitly or implicitly, the statutes depicted the sexual "psychopath" as a mentally disordered individual who was particularly dangerous to children, women, or both.

Sexual psychopath statutes were challenged in the 1960s and 1970s on a number of constitutional grounds, but particularly because they were vague and overbroad and placed individuals in mental institutions without evidence of their dangerousness. In the late 1980s and 1990s, however, these statutes were resurrected in various forms, most notably sexually violent predator legislation. That is, the term *sexual predator* or *sexually violent predator* is used in place of the outdated "sexual psychopath" terminology. For example, in 1990, the state of Washington enacted the **Sexually Violent Predator Act (SVPA)** that provides for special commitment facilities and allows for a possible lifetime commitment for sexual predators with a mental or personality disorder (Cohen, 1998). Other states quickly followed suit. In Iowa the law authorizes involuntary civil commitment for an indefinite period of time for those mentally unstable sex offenders who are a threat to strike again. The law requires that sex offenders be evaluated near the end of their prison terms. If they are determined to be sexual predators, they are confined indefinitely in a high-security treatment facility until no longer a threat to society. Approximately 16 states have passed similar statutes, including Kansas, Washington, Arizona, California, and New York. LaFond (2003) estimates that as many as 2,209 individuals may be held under these laws. In the late 1990s, the U.S. Supreme Court gave its approval to these statutes as long as the state could document (1) a history of sexually violent conduct; (2) a current mental disorder *or abnormality;* (3) a risk of future sexually violent conduct; (4) a connection between the disorder and the conduct; and (5) some inability to control behavior (*Kansas v. Hendricks,* 1997; *Kansas v. Crane,* 2002).

The terms *sexually violent predator* or *sexual predator* are used purposely to avoid the traditional requirements that both mental disorder and dangerousness must be established before an individual can be committed involuntarily to a civil mental institution (Cohen, 1998). Additionally the state wishes to be able to confine the individual for long periods, even after serving a prison term and without proof of a recent overt act (Cohen, 1998). Lawmakers reasoned that predators, by their very nature, are dangerous to society and must be kept out of circulation as long as possible. We stress again that the statutes do not necessarily require a finding of mental disorder; in some, "abnormality" is sufficient. Because clinicians recognize that many sexual offenders are not mentally disordered (Janus & Walbeck, 2000), this allows their confinement even if their behavior does not meet the standard for a diagnosable mental illness. The Supreme Court has emphasized, though, that *present* dangerousness must be *established* (it can not merely be presumed) (*Kansas v. Crane,* 2002). In other words, if you want to confine a sexual predator to a mental institution, you must prove that—at this time—he is highly likely to harm one or more individuals if not confined.

While it is understandable that the public wishes to be protected from dangerous sex offenders, both the earlier statutes and their latest incarnations have a number of flaws. The early sexual psychopath laws often attempted to intercept sexual psychopaths before they had been convicted of a crime (Morris, 1982). They were also based on the false premise that sexual offenders start with minor sexual offenses (e.g., indecent exposure, voyeurism) and move on to serious crimes of violence, like rape. While some do, most do not. The sexual predator laws of today require a conviction, but in some of these statutes the crime can range from relatively minor acts to serious offenses—again seeming to assume that the offender will move from minor to more serious acts. The early laws illustrated "a legislative capacity to conceal excessive punitiveness behind a veil of psychiatric treatment. At base lies the false assumption of a connection between sexual offenses and mental illness" (Morris, 1982, p. 136). Critics of the latest statutes argue that here, too, little has changed. Research has found that many sex offenders do not suffer from mental disorder (Janus & Walbek, 2000), yet the statutes imply that they do. Thus, individuals continue to be committed under the guise that they will receive treatment. In reality, treatment is believed to be sporadic and ineffective (Janus, 2000). Like the GBMI statutes discussed in the previous chapter, the sexually violent predator statutes appear to be a questionable response to a highly disturbing problem. One better solution to the problem, according to clinical psychologists and psychiatrists, is to offer meaningful treatment in prisons or in the community for those individuals who have been convicted of sexual offenses. We discuss some of these treatment strategies in chapter 17.

 ## SUMMARY AND CONCLUSIONS

In this chapter we learned that individuals with mental disorders as a group are no more likely than the general population to commit crimes, including violent crimes. If we include the category antisocial personality disorder, the catch-all diagnostic category discussed in chapter 7, the likelihood of committing crime increases somewhat. In addition recent research documents that the subgroup of *currently* mentally disordered male patients, particularly with schizophrenic diagnoses, and who have a *history of violence*, do demonstrate far more violence than nondisordered members in the general population. According to Monahan (1996), this relationship is especially significant if a current mental disorder is accompanied by three symptoms: (1) feeling that others wish to do one harm; (2) feeling that one's mind is dominated by forces beyond one's control; and (3) feeling that others' thoughts are being put into one's head.

Although the mentally disordered as a group are no more likely to commit crime, they do appear frequently in the criminal justice system, whether on police blotters, in court, or in correctional populations. By all indications, the percentages of mentally disordered in jails and prisons is increasing significantly. Much of this is due to a decrease in the use of public mental institutions. Hospitalization of the mentally disordered is typically now much shorter, and a lack of community living options has placed many mentally disordered on the streets, where they may be involved in minor offenses. The mentally disordered also often have co-occurring problems such as substance abuse, which makes them vulnerable to arrest under drug laws and public inebriation statutes.

The visibility of the mentally disordered, as well as publicity given to the occasional sensational case in which a severely disordered individual kills a stranger, has led to questions about dangerousness and our ability to predict it. When the criminal justice system deals with a defendant charged with a violent crime or an offender convicted of one, whether or not the individual is disordered, the system wants to know if he or she is dangerous. For many years, mental health practitioners tried to answer this question with very little success. Traditionally, clinicians overestimated the potential violence of this population, engendering debate about the proper criteria for assessing dangerousness. How many persons were forcefully confined, on the basis of dangerousness, without justification?

Recently this enterprise has shifted to "risk assessment." Rather than trying to predict whether someone is dangerous and will commit a violent act, the clinician is now more likely to identify risk factors that may make it *more likely* that he or she will do so. Various risk assessment instruments have been developed and tested for this purpose. Among them are the HCL-20, the Iterative Classification Tree, and the VRAG. Examples of risk factors include heavy use of alcohol, history of violence, and high scores on the PCL-R, to name but a few. Thus the prediction of dangerousness has been transformed to an assessment of the probability that violence will occur in the future. Again, although we have discussed this topic in the chapter on the mentally disordered, readers should be aware that risk assessments are conducted on many nondisordered offenders. Overall, the best predictor available is past behavior. Those who were violent in the past, compared with those without such a history, are more likely to offend in the future. Nevertheless, it is important to emphasize that no one factor—even past violence—is a foolproof predictor of future violence.

We ended the chapter with a discussion of the sexual predator, both because this individual is usually considered dangerous and because sexual predators were formerly considered mentally disordered. Today clinicians do not consider most sexual offenders mentally disordered. Nevertheless many states now have sexually violent predator laws that allow them to be committed to mental institutions following their prison terms. Critics of these statutes believe that mental disorder in these individuals is often wrongfully diagnosed and that the statutes are used to punish offenders beyond their legal sentence. Furthermore, even if these predators *are* mentally disordered, they do not necessarily receive the treatment that the statutes imply.

 ## KEY CONCEPTS

Risk assessment	*Tarasoff*
Duty to warn	Duty to protect
Sexually violent predator	Dangerousness
True positive	False positive
True negative	False negative
Mentally disordered sex offender	MDSO
Sexually Violent Predator Act	

REVIEW QUESTIONS

1. What is meant by a "duty to warn" and a "duty to protect"? And to whom does it pertain?
2. What are the conditions under which mentally disordered people may become violent or seriously criminal?
3. Define dangerousness.
4. What is the best predictor of violent behavior?
5. Which mental disorder is most closely associated with violent and serious criminal behavior. Why do you think this is so?
6. How accurate are mental health workers and clinicians in predicting dangerousness?

CHAPTER 9

HOMICIDE, ASSAULT, AND FAMILY VIOLENCE

CHAPTER OBJECTIVES

• Define criminal homicide, negligent manslaughter, and aggravated assault.
• Review the demographics of homicide victims and offenders.
• Emphasize that criminal homicide is rare compared with other violent offenses.
• Review what we know about juvenile murderers and their victims.
• Present the research on family violence, its dynamics, and its causes.

If the news and entertainment media are reasonably decent barometers of human interest, homicidal violence must be one of Western civilization's most fascinating subjects and, along with sex, the most marketable. Usually, the more bizarre, senseless, or heinous the murder, the more extensive press coverage it receives, followed shortly thereafter by books, television specials, and movies. Unusual mass murders, serial murders, and so-called motiveless killings are especially popular. On a national level criminal homicide consistently accounts for only about 1 percent or 2 percent of all violent crimes reported in the FBI's UCR.

A total of 16,137 such homicides were reported in 2004 (Federal Bureau of Investigation, 2005). In the same year an estimated 1.37 million violent offenses were reported to law enforcement agencies. The rate for violent crime was 465.5 offenses per 100,000 inhabitants, a rate that is similar to the data reported the past five years. If we consider its percentage distribution among all violent

Figure 9–1   Violent Crime Distribution in the United States, 2004

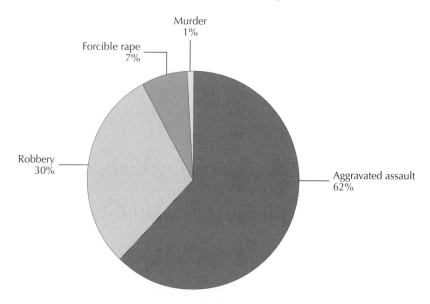

Source: Federal Bureau of Investigation, 2005.

crimes, murder represents only 1.2 percent of the total. (See **Figure 9–1**). Furthermore, a vast majority of these criminal homicides offer very little mystery or intrigue. In many cases, they involve angry friends, spouses, or acquaintances killing friends, spouses, or acquaintances. During 2004, for example, the relationship between the victims and perpetrators was known in 44.1 percent of all of the homicides. Within those known relationships, 29.8 percent of the victims were related to their killer, and 70.2 percent were acquainted with them. This does not make them less serious. It is simply a reminder that homicidal attacks of strangers are not common.

The disproportionate amount of attention paid to criminal homicides may be explained in a variety of ways. Obviously this is a highly serious crime, with death being the ultimate victimization. However, another reason for the attention may be related to our fascination with the mysterious and the macabre. We crave science fiction, tales of terror, even haunted houses. Perhaps we need a certain amount of excitement and arousal to prevent our lives from becoming too mundane and boring. Psychologists have long known that novelty produces arousal and excitement and breaks monotony (Berlyne, 1960). This human need for stimulation and excitement—which is greater in some people (extraverts) than others (introverts), as we learned in chapter 3—may partly explain the appeal of roller coasters, skydiving, race car driving, bungee jumping, and gambling. Extraverts also may enjoy films featuring vampires, werewolves, and heavy violence—or these vicarious pleasures might be enjoyed by ambiverts or introverts not wishing to seek out this type of excitement directly. In any case, tales of murder, fictional or not, add zest to life. For the family that has been touched by murder, however, this vicarious response on the part of others must be difficult to understand and to accept.

The marketability of murder might also be explained by curiosity or exploratory behavior, which is very closely related to excitement and arousal. One purpose of curiosity is to allow organisms to adjust to their environments (Butler, 1954). An individual or an organism explores a new situation to satisfy this curiosity—which is theorized to be a physiological drive state—and in the process of discovering information, adapts to the new situation. Curiosity about murder might help us prepare for the possibility that a similar event might happen to us. Reading about bizarre, seemingly irrational homicides might help us to identify danger signals. Information about the incident gives clues about who murders, who gets murdered, and under what circumstances. To some extent we can take preventive measures, even though there is no guarantee that such measures will keep us safe. Furthermore, families and close friends of murder victims would say that nothing can prepare someone for the devastation that is experienced when a loved one is murdered.

The above reactions to depictions of violence—experienced vicariously—may be regarded as adaptive or functional. Extensive exposure to violence also has a dysfunctional side, however. Specifically, it may immunize us from the horror of violence. Many social commentators have advanced cogent arguments that Western civilization has become conditioned or jaded to cruelty and inhumane behavior and that people are desensitized to human suffering. In addition, the constant attention that the news media and politicians give to violence also makes it seem more widespread and frequent than it really is. This phenomenon is called the **availability heuristic** by social psychologists. Heuristics refer to cognitive shortcuts that people use to make quick inferences about their world. When the news media continually show graphic and frightening accounts of violence, people are likely to incorporate these vivid details into cognitive shorthand and have them readily available for future reference. When they think of violence at a later time, they remember the most frequently seen and horrific accounts, increasing their fear of violent crime and exaggerating its incidence in their minds.

To speculate about why we are attracted to accounts of murder and violence, or to wonder about the effects of repeated exposure, may not seem to address the main focus of this chapter, which is the violent offender. Speculation becomes relevant, however, when we shift the focus to the individual who is part of a society that seems to have an inordinate need to seek out stimulation or to know details of crimes. When that individual is insensitive to suffering and begins to create his or her own excitement by torturing and murdering, we have a social problem. Psychology, as we will see in this chapter, can offer some suggestions for understanding and solving this problem.

After defining our terms, we examine situational and dispositional factors that occur consistently in homicide and aggravated assault, beginning with statistical data on their incidence and prevalence and their demographic correlates. Thus far in the text, theoretical issues and potential causes of crime have been introduced with minimum application to specific offenses. Beginning here and throughout the remainder of the book, we interweave the research and concepts previously outlined with specific categories of criminal behavior. Thus in this chapter we focus on family violence.

DEFINITIONS

Criminologists generally study aggravated assault and homicide together, primarily because they view many aggravated assaults as failed homicide attempts (Doerner, 1988; Doerner and Speir, 1986). Dunn (1976) challenges this practice. He notes that the aggravated assault rate is at least 20 times that of homicide. "Given this disparity in rates, it is difficult to imagine that even one-quarter of all aggravated assaults were attempted homicides or would have been homicides except for the intervention of medical care" (Dunn, 1976, p. 10). Therefore, it may be unwarranted to consider aggravated assault as being in the same league as homicide; the two may differ in important variables, including the motives of the perpetrator. A purist, therefore, would try to maintain an aggravated assault–homicide distinction. And, of course, the distinctions are maintained in crime statistics, as well as in criminal law.

For our purposes, it is neither realistic nor desirable to maintain a definitive assault-homicide distinction. Not realistic, since much of the relevant research on offender *characteristics* collapses the categories into one, under the rationale that people who kill usually (but not invariably) have a history of assaultive behavior. It is not desirable, since, from a psychological point of view, the two types of behavior are comparable. Often, the type of weapon used determines the final outcome. The high-powered bullet, as an obvious example, is in most cases far more lethal than the knife. A stabbing or even a beating may represent behavior similar to that displayed in homicide with a small firearm. In law, the distinctions between murder and aggravated assault are crucial; in psychology, they are less so. The individual is displaying highly aggressive behavior in either situation. For this chapter, combining the discussion of homicide and aggravated assault as one form of violent behavior makes sense, although the statistics section will separate them briefly. In later chapters we discuss other forms of violent behavior, including rape, armed robbery, and arson.

Criminal Homicide

Criminal homicide is causing the death of another person without legal justification or excuse. Legally, it is usually divided into two categories: **murder** and **nonnegligent manslaughter.** The term murder is reserved for the "unlawful killing of one human being by another with malice aforethought, either expressed or implied" (Black, 1990, p. 1019). "Malice aforethought" refers to premeditation, or the mental state of a person who thinks ahead, plans, and voluntarily causes the death of another, without legal excuse or justification. However, "premeditation" can occur in a very short period of time (even a minute); it does not require weeks of planning. In most states murder is divided into two degrees, a statutory provision that allows courts to impose a more severe penalty for some murders than others. Some states even specify three degrees of murder. The degree system was once a useful and meaningful method of distinguishing between murder that was punishable by death and that which was not (Gardner, 1985). In more recent times, the distinctions between the degrees have been more blurred. Usually, murder of the first degree is a homicide that was committed with particularly vicious, willful, deliberate, and premeditated intent. Murder of the second degree is characterized by the intentional and unlawful killing of another but without the type of malice and premeditation required for first-degree murder. Examples of second-degree murder include "crimes of passion" such as an enraged father who strangles the drunken driver who just killed his son. Although there was no premeditation, the angry father still wanted to kill him. Many states that do not distinguish between degrees of murder would call this an example of nonnegligent manslaughter.

The Uniform Crime Reports include both murder and nonnegligent manslaughter under the rubric criminal homicide for reporting purposes. Deaths of others that occur as a result of negligence (negligent manslaughter) are not included. The essential difference between murder and nonnegligent manslaughter is that malice aforethought must be present for murder, whereas it must be absent for nonnegligent manslaughter.

Negligent manslaughter is killing another as a result of recklessness or culpable negligence. Although there is no intent to kill, the law says you should have known that your actions could result in the death of another person. For example, a man who recklessly waves a gun around in jest, and the gun discharges and kills someone, is still responsible for that person's death. A driver who turns to look at her passenger, crosses the center lane, and hits an oncoming car, killing its occupant, displayed negligent (not reckless) behavior, but would still be responsible for the death. What the above two individuals have in common is that they did not intend to kill anyone. Both situations would illustrate negligent manslaughter, as opposed to the nonnegligent manslaughter covered along with murder in the UCR statistics. Nonnegligent manslaughter refers to an action that is more than negligent or reckless, but less than premeditated. It typically occurs in a highly aroused emotional state.

The person charged with murder (first or second degree) or with nonnegligent manslaughter intended that his victim die. In the case of nonnegligent manslaughter, the original intent may not have been to kill the victim. However, the person became so agitated and emotionally upset in a particular situation that he or she lost partial control of his or her self-regulatory system. A man who chokes a woman to death during rough sex would be an example. In some states, nonnegligent manslaughter would be similar to second degree murder.

In line with UCR classifications, we combine both murder and nonnegligent manslaughter under the general term homicide in this chapter. We are not concerned with suicides, accidental deaths, negligent manslaughter, or justifiable homicide (e.g., the justifiable killing of a person by a law enforcement officer in the line of duty). In other words, from a psychological point of view, these are not illustrative of the aggressive behavior we are concerned about in a book about criminal behavior.

Aggravated Assault

Assault is the intentional inflicting of bodily injury on another person, or the attempt to inflict such injury. It becomes **aggravated assault** when the intention is to inflict serious bodily injury. Aggravated assault is often accompanied by the use of a deadly or dangerous weapon. Simple assault is the unlawful, intentional inflicting of less than serious bodily injury without a deadly or dangerous weapon, or the attempt to inflict such bodily injury, again without a deadly or dangerous weapon. However, even one's fists can become a deadly weapon; thus, if a victim is seriously assaulted in a fistfight, the perpetrator will likely be charged with aggravated assault.

DEMOGRAPHICS OF HOMICIDE

Researchers have found that a variety of demographic factors are strongly associated, or correlated, with criminal homicide. These factors may be characteristics of the offenders or the victims. We must emphasize, though, that the factors reported in the literature often refer to *arrests* for murder or nonnegligent manslaughter. Although the minimum standard for an arrest is probable cause that the individual committed a crime or is about to commit a crime, arrests do not necessarily result in conviction, or a finding of guilt. This is an important caveat whenever we consider the official police data which are cited in numerous research studies. As we discuss the demographics of homicide, readers should keep in mind the distinctions between arrests, convictions, and victimizations.

Race/Ethnic Origin

One of the most consistent findings reported in the criminology literature is that African Americans in the United States are involved in criminal homicide—both as offenders and victims—at a rate that significantly exceeds their numbers in the general population. Although African Americans make up about 13 percent of the U.S. population, they accounted for approximately 37 percent of all arrests for violent crimes in 2004 (Federal Bureau of Investigation, 2005). Blacks represented 47 percent of those arrested for murder and one-third of the persons arrested for aggravated assault (Federal Bureau of Investigation, 2005). Of persons under the sentence of death in 2001, 44 percent were black and 54 percent were white (Bureau of Justice Statistics, 2003c). Both male and female incarceration rates also reflect this disproportion, although incarceration does not necessarily relate to violent offenses. For example, approximately 40 percent of all prisoners have been convicted of drug-related offenses. Black males comprised, on average, about 25 percent of inmates in local jails, federal prisons, and state correctional facilities during 2005 (Harrison & Beck, 2006). Black female incarceration rates reveal similar racial and ethnic disparities. The incarceration rate for black females is nearly 2.5 times higher than the rate for Hispanic/Latino females, and four times higher than the rate for white females (Harrison & Beck, 2006).

This pattern has been observed now for many decades. Wolfgang (1958, 1961) studied 588 homicides reported in Philadelphia from 1948 to 1952 and found that about 73 percent of those arrested and 75 percent of the victims were black. Furthermore, in 94 percent of all the reported cases, blacks killed blacks or whites killed whites, indicating that most homicide is *intraracial*. Intraracial means that offenders commit crime against members of their own race, whereas interracial means that offenders commit crime against members of a different race. More recent data from 2002 continue to show this trend: 92 percent of the black victims were allegedly slain by black offenders, whereas 85 percent of the white murder victims were allegedly killed by white assailants (Federal Bureau of Investigation, 2003). Nationwide, black males have a 1 in 40 chance of becoming a homicide victim during their lifetime (Federal Bureau of Investigation, 2003). White males, on the other hand, have a 1 in 280 chance. Black females have a 1 in 199 chance of becoming a homicide victim, while white females have a 1 in 794 chance. (See **Table 9–1** on page 288 for 2004 data.)

The disproportionate representation of African Americans in the arrest and conviction data for violence probably reflect social inequities, such as lack of employment or educational opportunities, racial oppression in its many forms, discriminatory treatment at the hands of the criminal justice system, and law enforcement practices in inner-city areas where many African Americans reside. There is no evidence to suggest that a racial biological or neuropsychological predisposition plays a role in the consistently reported differences in violence rates over the years.

Latinos/Hispanics are now projected to become the largest ethnic minority group in the United States within the next decade. The Latino/Hispanic population now equals the African American population and is growing (Martinez, 2002). Latinos/Hispanics constitute about 12.5 percent of the U.S. population and account for about 12 percent of the arrests for violent crimes. Furthermore, only about 1 percent of those arrested for homicide are Latinos or Hispanics. However, Latinos/Hispanics make up about 27 percent of the federal prison population and 17 percent of state prison population (Bureau of Justice Statistics, 2003c). In addition, 12 percent of the inmates under a sentence of death in 2001 were Latino/Hispanic (Bureau of Justice Statistics, 2003). Overall, though research indicates that the Latino/Hispanic violence victimization rate falls below the rates found for black and white populations, including the *economically disadvantaged* segments of the U.S. population (Martinez, 2002; Reidel, 2003).

TABLE 9–1   Murder Victims by Race and Gender, 2004

RACE	TOTAL	MALE	FEMALE	UNKNOWN
Total	**14,121**	**10,990**	**3,099**	**32**
White	6,929	5,031	1,898	2
Black	6,632	5,562	1,067	3
Other race	365	269	95	1
Unknown	195	128	41	26

Source: Federal Bureau of Investigation, 2005, p. 16.

Persons of Latino/Hispanic origin experience about 11 percent of all violent crime against persons age 12 or older in the United States, mostly in the form of simple assault (Bureau of Justice Statistics, 2002). Most of the victims received only minor injury from the assault. Martinez argues that the relatively low violence rates are partly due to the fact that Latinos generally have high rates of participation in the labor force and also have close and highly supportive connections to the local community and extended family.

American Indians and Alaska Natives account for 1.5 percent of the U.S. population and represent 1.3 percent of the total arrests reported in 2002 (Federal Bureau of Investigation, 2003). Similarly, they accounted for 1.1 percent of the arrests for murder and 1.1 percent of the total violent crime in 2002. On the other hand, the rate of violent *victimization* of American Indians appears to be well above that of other U.S. racial or ethnic subgroups and is more than twice as high as the national average (Greenfeld & Smith, 1999). In fact, American Indians experience aggravated assault and simple assault at the highest rates of any racial or ethnic group in the United States (Rennison, 2002). Moreover, American Indians are more likely than other races to experience violence at the hands of someone of a different race (interracial violence) (Chaiken, 1999).

Asians account for 4.2 percent of the U.S. population, and Pacific Islanders another 0.3 percent. Although available research is limited, the UCR data indicate that Asian Americans/Pacific Islanders are arrested in numbers that fall significantly below their representation in the general population, both in overall arrests (1.1%) and arrests for violent crime (1.2%) and, specifically, murder (1.2%) (Federal Bureau of Investigation, 2003, 2005). Asian Americans experience the lowest victimization rates of violence of any racial or ethnic group in the United States (Rennison, 2002).

Although much more research needs to be done on the relationship between racial/ethnic minorities and crime, using rigid categories such as black, Latino/Hispanic, Asian, Native Americans, and white represents an oversimplification of the multiethnic and multicultural mixtures across the nation. Cultures and subcultures are highly complex and multidimensional, and meaningful research on the ethnic/minority differences in violence requires a knowledgeable awareness of and sensitivity to this complexity.

Gender Differences

The relationship between homicide and gender is also robust. Wolfgang (1958) reported that 82 percent of the alleged murderers and 76 percent of the victims in his Philadelphia sample were male. Specifically, the homicide offender rate per 100,000 inhabitants was 41.7 for African American males, 9.3 for African American females, 3.4 for white males, and only 0.4 for white females. Notice how the race factor emerges strongly in combination with the gender factor. That is, the group displaying by far the highest incidence of homicide is that of African American males. **Table 9–2** shows murder victims by race and gender in 2004. The 2004 data also indicated that 91 percent of black murder victims were apparently killed by black offenders and 84 percent of white murder victims by white offenders (Federal Bureau of Investigation, 2005).

UCR data consistently reveal that the annual arrest rates for murder run about 90 percent male, 10 percent female (Federal Bureau of Investigation, 2003, 2005). In 2004, 82 percent of all arrests for violent crime offenses were male (Federal Bureau of Investigation, 2005). (In addition to murder, nonnegligent manslaughter, and aggravated assault, other violent offenses include rape, robbery, and simple assault). In 2002, males also accounted for about 77 percent of the murder *victims* (Federal Bureau of Investigation, 2003). It should be noted, however, that there are substantial situational and victim differences between murders attributed to males and to females, a topic that reappears in chapters 10 and 11.

Age

With monotonous regularity, national statistics from all sources continue to underscore the fact that about half of all those arrested for violent crime are between the ages of 20 and 29. In 2004, individuals under age 25 made up 44 percent of all violent crime arrestees and comprised 50 percent of all those arrested for murder or nonnegligent manslaughter. (Federal Bureau of Investigation, 2005). By far the highest rate of offending occurs among young black males, aged 18 to 22 (Federal Bureau of Investigation, 2003).

TABLE 9–2   Murder Victim/Offender Relationship by Race, 2004

RACE OF VICTIM	Race of Offenders			
	WHITE	BLACK	OTHER	UNKNOWN
White victims	3,727	522	37	45
Black victims	3,067	2,784	7	48
Other race victims	177	42	110	2
Unknown race	68	34	15	1

Source: Federal Bureau of Investigation, 2005, p. 18.

The young are also the victims. For example, in 2002, persons age 12 to 24 sustained violent victimization at rates higher than individuals of all other ages combined (Bureau of Justice Statistics, 2003b). Of all murder victims, 50 percent were under 30 years of age (Federal Bureau of Investigation, 2003).

Socioeconomic Class

Criminologists have long assumed that crime, especially violent crime, is found primarily among the lower socioeconomic class (e.g., Chamlin & Cochrane, 2005: Lahey & Waldman, 2003; Nielsen, Martinez, & Rosenfeld, 2005). Some time ago, research and commentary by Tittle (Tittle, 1983; Tittle & Villemez, 1977) challenged both the theory and empirical research based on class distinctions in criminal activity. Tittle argued that criminologists have established their theories and conducted their research on the basis of unfounded assumptions about the lower class. After reviewing 35 self-report studies, Tittle and Villemez (1977) asserted that the supposed link between social class and crime was a myth.

Other criminologists at that time believed that a rejection of the relationship was premature. Braithwaite (1981) reviewed over 100 studies and disagreed with Tittle's conclusions, finding considerable support for the view that individuals in the lower class commit more crime than those in other classes. Elliott, Ageton, and Huizinga (1980), after analyzing data from their self-report youth survey, emphasized the importance of distinguishing between serious crime against persons and property and nonserious offenses. They noted that lower-class youth are proportionately more involved in serious crimes than other youth.

Criminologists today readily acknowledge a relationship between crime and low socioeconomic status, but they caution against misinterpreting this information. There is little doubt of a relationship between socioeconomic position in society and those adult crimes that tend to come to the attention of police and to appear in official crime statistics, including the violent crimes that are the subject of this chapter. However, we know that violence within families or between intimates and acquaintances, when perpetrated by persons of higher economic status, does not always come to the attention of police. Thus, the official statistics are at least somewhat misleading. Furthermore, as we learned in chapter 2, the relationship between crime and poverty is complex, involving a myriad of factors, including limits on educational and employment opportunities. Finally, persons of high socioeconomic status commit varieties of crime whose enforcement and prosecution are often not considered a high priority in our society.

Victim-Offender Relationship

Research has consistently indicated that offenders and victims of homicide often know one another. Early studies found that in at least two-thirds of all homicides the offender and the victim knew one another well (Bullock, 1955; Driver, 1961; Hepburn & Voss, 1970; Svalastoga, 1956; Wolfgang, 1958; Wong & Singer, 1973).

In the Wolfgang data, the victim and offender were strangers in only about 14 percent of the cases. In a Chicago investigation, Hepburn and Voss (1970) reported a slightly higher victim-offender unfamiliarity figure, 19 percent.

Recent UCR data (Federal Bureau of Investigation, 2005) show that nearly half the murder victims in 2004 were either related to the offender (13%) or acquainted with the offender (30%). Strangers were murder offenders in 13 percent of the cases. The relationships were unknown for the remaining 44 percent (see **Figure 9–2**). The 2004 data also revealed that 33 percent of female victims were killed by their husbands or boyfriends, and 2.7 percent of the male victims were killed by their wives or girlfriends (Federal Bureau of Investigation, 2005).

FIGURE 9–2 Murder by Relationship[1]
Percent Distribution.[2] Volume by Known Relationship, 2004

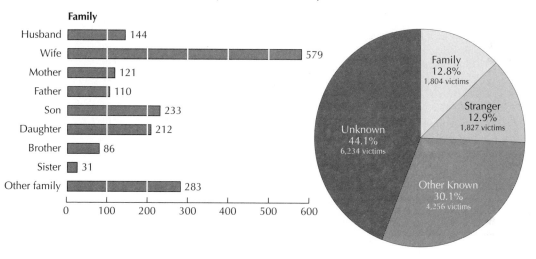

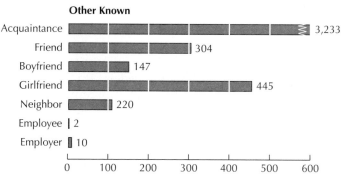

1 Relationship is that of victim to offender.

2 Due to rounding, the percentages may not add up to 100.0

Note: Figures are based on 14,121 murder victims for whom Supplementary Homicide Report Data were received.

Source: Federal Bureau of Investigation, 2005, p. 21.

TABLE 9–3   Murder Circumstances by Gender, 2004

CIRCUMSTANCES	TOTAL MURDER VICTIMS	MALE	FEMALE	UNKNOWN
Total	**14,121**	**10,990**	**3,099**	**32**
Felony type total	2,089	1,718	370	1
Rape	36	0	36	0
Robbery	988	874	113	1
Burglary	77	52	25	0
Larceny-theft	14	12	2	0
Motor vehicle theft	38	33	5	0
Arson	28	12	16	0
Prostitution	9	3	6	0
Other sex offenses	14	8	6	0
Narcotic drug laws	554	505	49	0
Gambling	7	6	1	0
Other—not specified	324	213	111	0
Suspected felony-type	117	93	22	0
Other than felony-type total	6,972	5,227	1,739	6
Romantic triangle	97	76	21	0
Child killed by babysitter	17	7	10	0
Brawl due to influence of alcohol	139	120	19	0
Brawl due to influence of narcotics	98	83	14	1
Argument over money or property	218	190	28	0
Other arguments	3,758	2,761	995	2
Gangland killings	95	90	5	0
Juvenile gang killings	804	776	28	0
Institutional killings	17	17	0	0
Sniper attack	1	1	0	0
Other—not specified	1,728	1,106	619	3
Unknown	4,943	3,950	968	25

Source: Federal Bureau of Investigation, 2005, p. 23.

The 2002 data indicate that 28 percent of the murders resulted from arguments, and 16.5 percent were committed in the process of committing felonies such as forcible rape, robbery, arson, or drug trafficking (Federal Bureau of Investigation, 2003). Twenty-three percent involved other types of circumstances—some also involving felonies—such as brawls, sniper attackers, or juvenile and gang killers. (See **Table 9–3.**)

Men are victimized by violent strangers at an annual rate more than double that of women (Federal Bureau of Investigation, 2005). The chance of becoming the victim of a violent crime perpetrated by a stranger increases with age for women but remains about the same across all ages for men (U.S. Department of Justice, 1989b).

While the homicide offender and his or her victims frequently have similar demographic characteristics, this observation holds primarily for family and acquaintance homicide. When it comes to stranger homicide, there is a tendency for the offender to be younger and of a different race than the victim.

Weapons Used in Violence

Guns and knives (or other cutting instruments) are the two preferred instruments for inflicting death, but this preference is somewhat influenced by gender, race, geography, and other parameters (see **Table 9–4**). For example, in Philadelphia, stabbing was the most common lethal method during the early 1950s (Wolfgang, 1958). In Chicago during the 1960s and early 1970s, shooting was preferred (Block, 1977; Hepburn & Voss, 1970). Later, firearm-related homicides in Chicago increased almost threefold (Block, 1977). However, death inflicted by other weapons increased only slightly.

Nationwide data indicate that firearms were used in over 70 percent of all homicides committed between 1993 and 2004 (Federal Bureau of Investigation, 2003, 2005; Zawitz & Strom, 2000), while knives or cutting instruments were used in less than 13 percent of the homicides (Federal Bureau of Investigation, 2003). Approximately 80 percent of firearm homicides are committed with handguns, 6 percent with shotguns, 5 percent with rifles, and 7 percent with unspecified firearms. Furthermore, in 1998, 400 police officers were injured in firearm assaults, and 58 police officers were killed while responding to a crime (Zawitz & Strom, 2000).

In 1994, 44 million Americans owned 192 million firearms, 65 million of which were handguns (Cook & Ludwig, 1997), and an additional 12.5 million firearms were purchased between March 1994 and November 1998 (Bureau of Justice Statistics, 1999). Although there are enough firearms to provide every American adult with one, only 25 percent of the adults actually own guns. In the U.S. population, approximately 12 percent of Hispanic/Latino households own a firearm compared with 14 percent of black households (Nielsen, Martinez, & Rosenfeld, 2005). Approximately 40 percent of white households own a firearm. Most gun owners, specifically 74 percent, possess two or more. Interestingly, gun ownership is highest among middle-aged, college-educated people of rural

Table 9–4   Weapons Used by Male and Female Murderers, 1998

Weapon Used	Murderer (%)	
	Female	Male
Handgun	42%	51%
Other firearm	11	16
Knife	31	18
Blunt object	4	6
Other	12	9

Source: Greenfeld, 1999, p. 4.

small-town America (Cook & Ludwig, 1997). About 14 million adults (approximately one-third of gun owners) carry firearms for protection. Two-thirds of those who carried guns kept them in their vehicles, while the others sometimes carried them on their person. Young black males are far more likely to carry a firearm than other groups (Nielsen, Martinez, & Rosenfeld, 2005). Although it is often pointed out that many individuals own guns for sport, these same individuals typically consider protection a secondary purpose for gun ownership.

Juvenile Weapon Possession

According to the 2004 UCR data, 24 percent of the total arrests for carrying or possessing a firearm were juveniles, and 9 percent of the total arrestees were under age 15. Males, compared with females, were four times more likely to report carrying a weapon. The weapons most often carried were knives or razors (55%), followed by clubs (24%), and firearms (21%). In a national survey of more than 16,000 students in grades 9–12, 18 percent said they had carried a weapon outside the home in the previous 30-day period (Lizotte & Sheppard, 2001). The percentages were higher (22%) for youths living in inner-city high schools. A more recent survey (PRIDE, 2003) reported that approximately 2 percent of middle-school youths (grades 6 to 8) carried a gun to school on a regular basis during 2002–2003. Available data (e.g., Decker, Pennel, & Caldwell, 1997) suggest that more than two-thirds of juveniles who carry weapons said they do so primarily for self-protection.

Gun ownership by gang members appears to be a standard feature of many youth gangs (Lizotte & Sheppard, 2001). Gun ownership by juveniles is also related to a wide range of antisocial behaviors, including gun-related crimes, gang membership, and drug selling (Lizotte & Sheppard, 2001). For example, the amount of serious violent crime these juveniles committed during periods of carrying a gun was more than five times the amount they committed while not carrying a gun.

The Violent Crime Control and Law Enforcement Act of 1974 made it a federal offense for any person to sell or transfer a handgun to a person under age 18; it is also a crime for a juvenile to possess ammunition of a handgun. Yet, there are multiple ways for juveniles to obtain firearms, and they report being able to do so with ease. Some juveniles (about 28%) ask others, such as older siblings or friends, to buy guns for them (Braga & Kennedy, 2001). About 11 percent of juveniles buy them from a gun shop or pawnshop. Theft is also an important source of firearms for juveniles. It is estimated that about 500,000 guns are stolen each year, mostly from residences (Braga & Kennedy, 2001). It is further estimated that about 70 percent of the firearms used by offenders are obtained through theft (Wright & Rossi, 1994). As pointed out by Braga and Kennedy (2001), juveniles obtain guns through corrupt licensed dealers, unregulated dealers, gun shows, organized gun rings and fences, and criminal firearms trafficking.

Weapons and Violence

About every 14 minutes someone in America dies from a gunshot wound. About half of those deaths are suicides, about 44 percent are homicides, and 4 percent are unintentional shootings (*Washington Post,* October 12, 1993; Zawitz & Strom, 2000). Moreover, considerable research, including a study in the *New England Journal of Medicine* (*Washington Post,* October 12, 1993), contradicts the common view that having a gun protects people from violence. The study reported that households with guns are three times more likely to experience the death of a household member than gunless households. Research such as the above suggests that, while guns do not *cause* violent crime, accessibility of guns facilitates it. Hepburn and Hemenway (2004) found that where there are higher levels of gun ownership, homicides are substantially higher. Of course, where homicides are higher, families may be more likely to own guns for protection, but the evidence stills strongly points toward the availability of firearms as the major reason for the higher homicide rates.

In Chapter 5 we discussed the **weapons effect,** where the mere sight of an aggressive stimulus can influence behavior. Because weapons are associated with violence, the visible presence of a handgun, a club, or a knife automatically brings violence-related thoughts (cognitions) to mind. The classic study of Berkowitz and LePage (1967) was among the first experiments to provide evidence of a strong link between aggressive thoughts engendered by the presence of a weapon and subsequent aggressive behavior. Hepburn and Hemenway's discovery that a high number of available weapons within a neighborhood promote more aggression in a vicious circle of violence may be partially due to the widespread presence of aggressive stimuli.

OTHER FACTORS

Several other factors associated with violent crime are reported consistently in the research. They relate to temperatures and seasons, actions of victims, and the presence of alcohol and other drugs.

Temporal Factors

Homicides are equally distributed across the 12 months of the year, although there is a slight increase during some holidays (December and January) and the summer months. The holidays are the time many family gatherings and celebrations take place, and also when interpersonal tensions and alcohol consumption can be at their highest levels. Weekends, especially the hours between 8 P.M. Saturday and 2 A.M. Sunday, are clearly when homicides most often occur (Block, 1977; Hepburn & Voss, 1970; Wolfgang, 1958).

Victim Precipitation

In his classic study of homicide, Wolfgang (1958) found that about 26 percent of the cases were victim-precipitated: The victim contributed in a significant way to his or her own demise by taking the first step toward violence. Hepburn and Voss (1970) found that about 38 percent of Chicago homicides seemed provoked by the victim. Studies do suggest that offender motives for killing are often based on minor altercations and domestic quarrels in which both parties were actively aggressive. Recall the phenomenon of escalation presented in the previous chapter, where we noted that some people tend to retaliate in kind to insults or blows. Moreover, verbal quarrels very often escalate to physical altercations. Separated from the context in which they took place, the precipitating factors of violent behavior are often pitifully trivial. It should be noted, though, that Wolfgang did not consider verbal taunts or insults a form of victim precipitation; rather, the victim had to actively make the first physically violent move. In that sense, "pure" victim-precipitated homicide, as defined by Wolfgang, may qualify as self-defense on the part of the individual who committed the homicide. We should emphasize, also, that official statistics, such as those represented in the UCR, do not make inferences about the victim's possible role in the offense.

Wolfgang reported that in nearly two-thirds of the cases, either the victim, the offender, or both had been drinking immediately prior to the slaying. This continually emerges as a factor associated with homicide. In 2002 a very small number of homicides (153) were *the result of* a brawl due to the influence of alcohol (Federal Bureau of Investigation, 2003). However, we have no way of knowing from the official statistics how much alcohol was *a factor* in the other homicides. (The noteworthy relationship between alcohol and other drugs and violence are discussed in detail in chapter 12.)

Sniper Attacks

On November 25, 2003, Gail Knisley, while heading to a doctor's appointment, was killed on Ohio Interstate 270 by a sniper. Throughout the year, at least 13 other reports documented shots fired at vehicles along the same highway which surrounds Cleveland. One shot broke a window at an elementary school. The reports began in May. The shots had been fired at different times of the day, piercing cars, trucks, vans, and horse trailers, shattering windows and flattening tires (McCarthy, 2003). Investigators believe that all 14 incidents were related, or caused by the same person or persons. Although the sniper attacks did not continue, neither have the cases been solved.

Perhaps the most frightening sniper attacks in modern times took place over a 23-day period in October 2002. Ten persons, chosen at random, were killed by sniper fire, the first six killed within the first 27 hours of the incident. The attacks took place in and around the Washington, D.C., area. The two alleged snipers, 42-year-old Army veteran John Allen Muhammad and his teenage sidekick, 17-year-old Lee Boyd Malvo, were arrested on October 24, 2002, while sitting in their 1990 Chevrolet Caprice. The beat-up Caprice had been modified to enable the snipers to crawl into the vehicle's trunk from the backseat and shoot a high-powered rifle (a Bushmaster XM-15, a semiautomatic version of the M-16) through a hole sawed just above the license plate. In total, the two men were accused of shooting 19 people, killing 13, and wounding 6, in Alabama, Georgia, Louisiana, Maryland, Virginia, and Washington, D.C., in an attempt to extort $10 million from the government.

Muhammad was convicted of two counts of capital murder on November 17, 2003, after a Virginia jury deliberated for six and one-half hours. A week later, a seven-woman, five-man panel sentenced him to death. He was the first person ever charged and sentenced under Virginia's new post–September 11, 2001, terrorism law. The law outlaws attempts to intimidate the civilian population at large, or to influence the conduct or activities of the government through intimidation.

Muhammad was an ex-U.S. soldier who served in the Gulf War and who was an award-winning expert marksman. He was trained as a mechanic, truck driver, and metal worker. He is the father of four children, had been married at least twice, and was involved in bitter custody battles for his children. At least on one occasion, he was accused of abducting the children. Malvo and his mother left Jamaica when he was about 14-years-old and moved to the island of Antigua, and then to Fort Myers, Florida. Muhammad and Malvo were very close, with Muhammad referring to the teenager as his son. Malvo, tried separately, advanced an insanity defense, arguing that he was brainwashed by Muhammad and was thus not responsible for the crimes. He was also convicted in December 2003, but a jury recommended that he be sentenced to life imprisonment without parole rather than given a death sentence. Malvo has since testified when Muhammad was prosecuted for additional sniper killings.

The Washington sniper attacks apparently prompted the FBI to study other sniper incidents between 1982 and 2001 (Federal Bureau of Investigation, 2003). Much of the material in the remainder of this section pertains to that study. During this 20-year interval, there were an estimated 327 incidents of sniper attacks in which a total of 379 victims were killed. Although the numbers seem large, research demonstrates that sniper attacks are unique circumstances that occur infrequently. More specifically, of the total 364,648 homicides that occurred during the 20-year period, only 0.1 percent were caused by sniper fire.

Nearly 80 percent of the victims of sniper attacks were males. Although the victims included all age ranges, 14 percent were under the age of 18. In about nine out of the 10 cases, the victim and the sniper were either strangers and/or the relationship was unknown. A breakdown of the data by race indicated that 52.5 percent of the victims were white, 44.1 percent were black, and the remaining 3.4 percent were other races. A handgun was the weapon of choice in two-thirds (63.6%) of the incidents; a rifle or shotgun was used in the remainder. Nearly half of the sniper attacks took place in the Western regions of the country.

In a vast majority of cases (96.9%), the sniper was male, usually between the ages of 18 and 24. Female offenders cut across all age groups with no particular age group emerging as the most prevalent. The youngest female sniper identified was 13, and the oldest fell into the 30- to 34-year-old age group. The youngest male sniper identified was in the 10- to 12-year-old age group. In 54.5 percent of known cases, the offender was white, and 43.7 percent of the time the offender was black. The remainder of the offenders were either American Indian/Alaskan Natives or Asian/Pacific Islanders. Other than demographic data, the psychological characteristics of criminal snipers are largely unknown.

DEMOGRAPHICS OF ASSAULT

Assault has not drawn nearly the amount of research, publication, or popular interest that homicide has. And yet, aggravated assault is the most common type of Part 1 violent crime, accounting for approximately 63 percent of all Part I violent crimes reported to police in 2004 (Federal Bureau of Investigation, 2005; see Figure 9–1). On the average, approximately 850,000 to one million incidents of aggravated assault and over 600,000 of simple assault are reported annually. It should be noted that for 11 consecutive years the estimated number of aggravated assaults in the United States has declined (Federal Bureau of Investigation, 2005). In 2004, there were 291 reported victims of aggravated assault for every 100,000 people in the United States. This rate was 10 percent lower than in 2000 and 30.4 percent lower than in 1995 (Federal Bureau of Investigation, 2005). The frequency of aggravated assaults has been consistently higher during summer months. During 2004, personal weapons (i.e., hands, fists, feet) were used in 26.6 percent of the aggravated assaults, firearms were used in 19.3 percent, and knives and cutting instruments in 18.6 percent of the cases.

Blacks make up about one-third of those arrested for assault, aggravated or simple, a number disproportionate to their representation in the population. Like the disproportionate involvement in homicide, however, we must be careful in the interpretation of these statistics. Similar to the statistics for homicides, assaults are overwhelmingly intraracial (Federal Bureau of Investigation, 2005). Nationwide in 2004, law enforcement agencies cleared 55.6 percent of the reported aggravated assaults.

The victim and offender know one another or are relatives in at least 50 percent of the reported assault cases (Federal Bureau of Investigation, 2003, 2005; U.S. Department of Justice, 1988, 1989b). As might be expected, the lethal firearm is significantly less often employed in assault than in homicide. In 2002, personal weapons, such as hands, fists, and feet, were used in 27.7 percent of reported aggravated assaults (Federal Bureau of Investigation, 2003). In addition, firearms were used in 19 percent of aggravated assaults, and knives or cutting instruments were used in 17.8 percent. Blunt instruments or other dangerous instruments were used in 35.4 percent of the reported aggravated assaults.

Twelve percent of the aggravated assaults in 2004 were committed by juveniles; assault is the most common violent crime committed by juveniles. In addition, males outnumber females 7 to 1 in total arrests for assault. Among the 15.4 million college students in 1995, about 1.5 million experienced a violent crime (Greenfeld, 1998). Aggravated assault is the most common form of violent crime reported on college campus, representing 28 percent of the total, followed by robbery (12%) and forcible rape (9%) (Seymour, 2000). About 87 percent of the violent crimes sustained by college students occurred off-campus. About one-third of the violent incidents experienced by college students involved alcohol. It should be noted that official college campus statistics, such as those reported by the FBI (2003), are gathered as a result of the Student Right-to-Know and Campus Security Act of 1990, which required that all institutions receiving federal aid report their crime statistics to the public. However, these official campus crime statistics are notoriously limited in value. Campus crime is often underreported, and colleges and universities are also allowed to take in-house measures to deal with some incidences (including date rape and assault) rather than have them result in arrests (Karmen, 2001).

JUVENILE MURDER

The 2004 UCR data reveal that 89 percent of the offenders arrested for murder were adults and 11 percent were juveniles (Federal Bureau of Investigation, 2005). A breakdown of the overall data by gender showed that 90.1 percent of the offenders were male and 9.9 percent were female. Two percent of all murders were allegedly perpetrated by juveniles under age 15. Girls accounted for about one in five of the alleged assailants. From 1985 through 2000, the juvenile courts handled 1,700 juvenile murders, but the number of cases has steadily decreased since 1996 (Puzzanchera et al., 2004). To some extent this reflects nationwide trends to transfer juveniles charged with serious crimes to criminal courts rather than process them in the juvenile system.

Nonetheless, regardless of the courts in which they are processed, the number of juveniles age 15 or younger who murder is relatively small (Snyder, 2001). Between 1980 and 1997, about 2 percent (or 600 cases) of murders involved *child* delinquents (ages 7 to 12), and the annual rate of these homicides is relatively stable, averaging about 30 homicides per year (Loeber, Farrington, & Petechuk, 2003). Nearly all of the homicides committed by children (94 percent) involved a single victim, mostly male (70%). More than half (58%) of the murder victims of child delinquents were juveniles under age 18 and more than a third (38%) of the victims were under age 13 (Snyder, 2001). Rarely was the victim a parent. The killing of a parent by a juvenile is often precipitated by child maltreatment, especially psychological abuse and neglect (Heide, 1993). More than half (54%) of the victims of child delinquents were killed with firearms. Gun play is often a contributing factor when children kill other children (Goetting, 1993). Sexual homicides by child offenders are very uncommon (Myers & Blashfield, 1997).

Demographics and Psychological Characteristics of Juvenile Murderers

In recent years, researchers have conducted studies with small samples of juvenile murderers in order to obtain more detailed information both about the crimes and about the backgrounds of the offenders. A study by Myers and Scott (1998) examined 18 male juvenile murderers between the ages of 14 and 17 who met the criteria for conduct disorder at the time of their crimes. Thirty-three percent of the offenders were white, and 67 percent were black. Their homicides were committed either in relation to criminal activities (72%) or during interpersonal conflict (28%). The victims were male in eight cases (45%) and females in 10 cases (55%). Half of the victims were strangers, whereas the other half were acquaintances (39%) or family members (11%).

The results revealed that 16 of the 18 (89%) juvenile murderers had histories of one or more psychotic episodes (especially paranoid ideation), and other forms of mental disorders. These results were remarkably similar to the prevalence rate in others studies examining the psychological characteristics of juvenile murderers (e.g., Lewis et al., 1985; Lewis et al., 1988).

Juvenile murderers—and those juveniles who commit violent crimes in general—tend to have a history of severe educational difficulties compared with nonviolent juveniles (Heckel & Shumaker, 2001). Myers, Scott, Burgess, and Burgess (1995) report that within their sample of 25 juvenile murderers, 76 percent demonstrated a learning disability, and 86 percent had failed at least one grade. Significant language handicaps appear to be the most prominent learning problems among juvenile murderers (Heckel & Shumaker, 2001; Myers & Mutch, 1992).

Many juvenile murderers also appear to have a variety of neurological abnormalities (Heckel & Shumaker, 2001), similar to what has been reported in the medical histories of life course persistent offenders. Myers and his colleagues (e.g., Myers, 1994; Myers & Mutch, 1992; Myers, Scott, Burgess, & Burgess, 1995) have continually noted the high incidence of conduct disorders in his samples of juvenile murderers, ranging from 84 percent to 88 percent. ADHD has also been identified with juvenile murderers with some regularity (Heckel & Shumaker, 2001).

FAMILY VIOLENCE

The passage of the Violence against Women Act of 1994 (Public Law 103-322, Title IV) represented a substantial change in the nation's efforts to identify, control, and prevent crimes of domestic violence. "The Act explicitly recognizes that domestic violence is a serious crime that harms not only its immediate victims, but also their families, children, and the larger community" (Campbell, 1996, p. 2). The *Violence against Women Act of 2000* (often referred to as VAWA-2) expanded research and services to victims nationwide and focused on the role of courts in combating violence against women through training, education, and technical assistance for judges and other court personnel (Roberts, 2002).

Definitions

Family violence (also called domestic violence, intimate partner violence, or spouse abuse) refers to any assault, intimidation, battery, sexual assault, sexual battery, or any criminal offense resulting in personal injury or death of one family or household member by another who is or was residing in the same single-dwelling unit (Wallace & Seymour, 2001). The term "battering" is often used in a slightly more specific fashion to describe *physical violence* in intimate relationships, either during a dating relationship, marriage or partnership, or separation and divorce. Moreover, family violence "is an ongoing, debilitating experience of physical, psychological, and/or sexual abuse in the home, associated with increased isolation from the outside world and limited personal freedom and accessibility to resources" (Wallace & Seymour, 2001, p. 4). At the heart of family violence is usually the perpetrator's misuse of power, control, and authority (American Psychological Association, 2003a).

Prevalence

About one of every five murders and nonnegligent manslaughters in the United States—in which the victim-offender relationship is known—involves a family member killing another family member, with a majority (about 50%) involving spouse killing spouse (Federal Bureau of Investigation, 2005). Similar statistics have also been reported in Canada (Silverman & Mukhergee, 1987). Homicide within the family accounts for 45 percent of all murders in England and Wales (d'Orban & O'Connor, 1989; Home Office, 1986). A neglected area of research in family violence is homicide followed by suicide, in which a family member kills other family members and then kills himself or herself. One reason for the neglect is that homicide-suicides are relatively rare, accounting for less than 2 percent of all homicides. Research has consistently shown, however, that a high proportion of homicide-suicides (usually well over 50%) involve spouses, especially ex-spouses.

Ethnic/Minority Differences

Research on the incidence of family violence among various races and ethnic/minority groups has been largely neglected. Although indications are that family violence is substantially underreported at all levels of society, this is especially true for families outside the majority culture (American Psychological Association, 2003a). Based on what is known, however, violence within the African American family is similar to that within white families, except that it occurs at higher rates. "As is the case for all types of homicide, African Americans are victimized by lethal violence at the hands of family members at rates that are many times higher than those for other racial groups in the United States" (Mercy & Salzman, 1989). Exceedingly few studies document the prevalence of domestic violence against Latinas (Santiago, 2002), Asian women (Lee, 2002), or other ethnic minorities in general (Roberts, 2002). Very few existing studies on the prevalence of domestic or family violence make reference to race or ethnicity.

Victims

In 1995, approximately 19 percent of all arrests made for aggravated assaults and 68 percent for simple assault involved family members (U.S. Department of Justice, 2000b). Children under 12 comprised 5 percent of victims of family aggravated assault and 4 percent of the victims of family simple assault. Infants (under 1 year old) are the most vulnerable victims of family violence. **Figure 9–3** shows the nature of offenses that occurred against infants during the years 2001 to 2003. Most often, the offense committed against infant victims is simple assault, and the second most common is aggravated assault (Federal Bureau of Investigation, 2005). **Figure 9–4** shows the age of victims who were also present at the time of infant victimizations. Although infants make up the majority of victims, sometimes additional victims of other ages are present at the infant's victimization, demonstrating the multiple aspects of family violence. Infants are rarely the solitary victim in family violence.

Self-report victimization studies also suggest that at least 20 percent of simple or aggravated assaults involve family members (U.S. Department of Justice, 1989b). Although these official statistics are woefully incomplete, they still underscore the considerable magnitude of family violence.

FIGURE 9–3   Offenses Related to Infant Victims

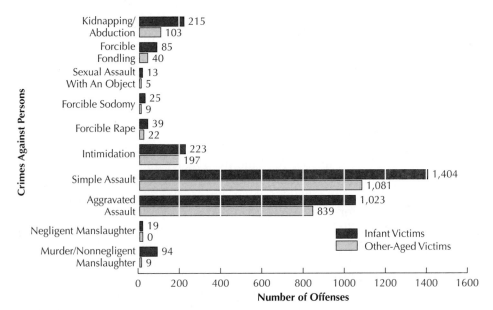

Source: Federal Bureau of Investigation, 2005, p. 359.

FIGURE 9–4   Age of Victims Present at Infant Victimizations

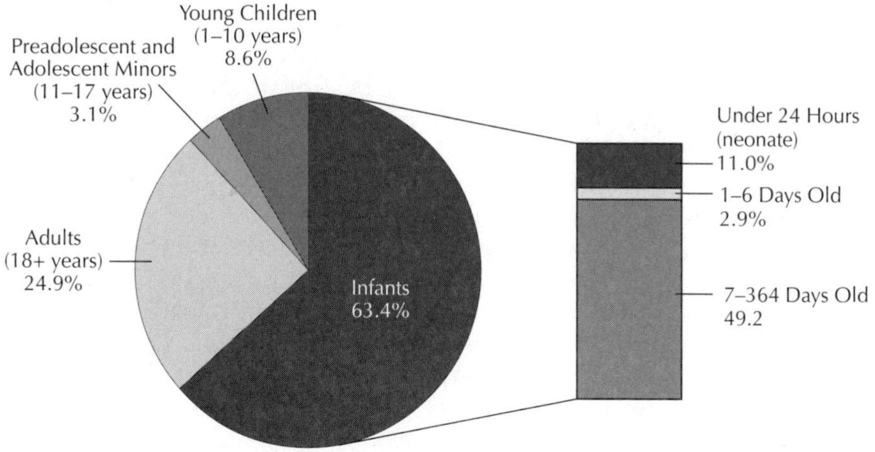

Source: Federal Bureau of Investigation, 2005, p. 360.

   Some variant of family violence has probably existed for as long as individuals grouped together as families, both nuclear and extended. However, with the notable exception of intrafamilial homicide, domestic or family violence has not traditionally been regarded as serious crime or worthy of criminal prosecution in this country. State governments and the courts have long claimed that family relationships require or deserve special immunity, including the views that parents have a right to discipline children physically, that a husband possesses the right to have sexual access to his wife, or that nagging women or disobedient children often provoke and deserve the beatings they receive (Pleck, 1989). This view has been energetically challenged in recent years by various interest groups attempting not only to acquaint the public with the problem but also to activate lawmakers and the criminal justice system toward more stringent legal and social sanctions.

Brief History of the Modern Era of Family Violence

The modern era of family violence interest and research began in 1962 when a Denver pediatrician (C. Henry Kempe) and four of his medical colleagues published a paper in the *Journal of the American Medical Association* titled "The Battered Child Syndrome" (Kempe, et al., 1962). The paper documented evidence of repeated multiple bone fractures of children suspected of being abused, and the article gradually became instrumental in the "rediscovery" of serious child abuse. The article was certainly not the sole precipitating factor in prompting the reexamination of child abuse. During the 1960s a very large and influential child welfare movement, bent on drawing public and professional attention to the plight of abused and neglected children, was also taking hold.

In the early 1970s the women's movement was highly influential in the rediscovery of wife beating, and shortly thereafter drew attention to marital rape. What began as a women's rights issue soon picked up support as a law-and-order issue (Pleck, 1989). The women's movement spawned legislation to increase or establish penalties for wife beating, to strengthen civil remedies, and to make it easier for women victims to file criminal charges against their assailants (Pleck, 1989). During the 1980s several other types of family violence, from sibling violence to filial abuse of the elderly, have been acknowledged and empirically investigated. Thus, family violence includes spouse or partner abuse, child abuse, sibling violence, abuse of the elderly, and child-to-parent violence. Currently, child abuse research is the most advanced, sophisticated, and extensive in the field of family violence (Finkelhor & Lewis, 1988). The problem of child abuse has also been the most widely publicized. Nationwide polls in 1976 revealed that only 10 percent of the general population considered child abuse a serious problem. In 1983, however, over 90 percent of the population considered it a serious problem (Wolfe, 1985).

However, despite the current interest and public concern about family violence, we still know very little about it. Systematic study of family violence is new and often poorly designed. Even definitions, terms, and concepts in the field are excessively broad, ambiguous, and applied inconsistently, jeopardizing the comparability, generalizability, and reliability of the research findings (Weis, 1989). For example, it is unclear what behaviors should be included under the rubric family violence. Should verbal threats, shouting, slapping, aggressive gestures, intimidation, or spanking be included as examples of violence? Or only the more serious, physical forms of violence such as punching, stabbing, striking, shooting, and burning? Surveys conducted during the 1960s and 1970s indicated that between 84 percent and 97 percent of all parents used physical punishment at some time to discipline their children (Gelles, 1982). Surely we cannot conclude that 90 percent of the American parents were abusive during that era. Rather, this high incidence of corporal punishment was due to the widespread and firmly held tradition that a spanking now and then did the child some good. Although that tradition is currently shifting toward less or no corporal punishment, there still remains considerable controversy as to whether parental spankings and slaps constitute abuse.

It is also unclear how the term violence differs from abuse, maltreatment, neglect, and emotional and social deprivation. As noted by Gelles (1982), the battered child syndrome quickly gave way to the terms child abuse, child neglect, and child maltreatment. Child abuse, once restricted by Kempe and his associates to physical violence, has become increasingly broad, encompassing an extensive range of behaviors and misbehaviors by parents and caretakers. Furthermore, it also remains unclear what relatives or intimates should be included in family violence. Should lovers, intimate friends, common-law spouses, distant relatives, ex-spouses, or separated spouses also be included? Therefore, a troubling aspect of family violence research is that terms are defined differently and often unclearly, and an assortment of family members are included in the sample, making reliable comparisons between studies difficult and valid conclusions nearly impossible to come by. In addition, each study collects data from a variety of sources and often uses substantially different procedures and methodology to tabulate and analyze the data.

For our purposes, research on family violence will be divided into four major questions: (1) How much family violence is there? (2) What are the common characteristics (or correlates) of the offenders and victims? (3) Is family violence fundamentally different from other kinds of violence (such as street violence)? (4) What are the causes of family violence? We will explore the research in these four areas, keeping in mind the critical problems in definition, sampling, and methodology just described. It should be pointed out that intrafamilial sexual abuse, although mentioned in the following sections, is discussed in greater detail in chapter 9.

Incidence, Prevalence, and Demographics of Child Abuse and Neglect

Estimates of the prevalence and incidence of family violence differ widely. The term incidence in this section will refer to the total number of cases (frequency) per year. Prevalence will refer to the proportion or ratio of the population involved, such as the number of children experiencing abuse per 1,000 children in the general population.

In the United States, about 1 in 7 children (138 per 1,000) are maltreated at some during their childhood (Finkelhor, Ormrod, Turner, & Hamky, 2005). Maltreatment refers to all forms of abuse and/or neglect, and can be divided into five types: physical abuse, sexual abuse, emotional abuse, neglect, and family abduction (see **Table 9–5**). Finkelhor and his associates, in a national survey of over two thousand children, discovered that emotional abuse (name calling or denigration by an adult) was the most frequent of the five types. Boys and girls experienced similar rates for maltreatment with the exception of sexual abuse. Girls are four times more likely to be sexually abused.

The prevalence of this victimization is approximately 12 per 1,000 children, a rate that has been relatively consistent over the past decade. The data also indicate that child protective services received approximately 2,672,000 reports of *possible* maltreatment in 2001 (U.S. Department of Health and Human Services, 2003). According to the U.S. Department of Health and Human Services (2003), approximately two-thirds (63%) of all victims were neglected, and about one out of five children (19%) experienced physical abuse. Approximately 10 percent were sexually abused, and another 8 percent were emotionally abused. There is a high probability that emotional abuse is substantially underreported. Over one-quarter of the victims were victims of more than one type of maltreatment. Definitions for each of these terms are found in **Table 9–5** on page 306.

The highest victimization rates were for the 0 to 3 age group, and rates declined as age increased. Child abuse/neglect perpetrators, defined as persons

Table 9–5   Definitions of Child Abuse and Neglect

Type of Abuse	Definition
Physical Abuse	Occurs when a parent willfully injures, causes injury, or allows a child to be injured, tortured, or maimed out of cruelty or excessive punishment.
Emotional Abuse	Chronic pattern of behavior in which the child is belittled, denied love to promote specific behavior, or subjected to extreme and inappropriate punishment.
Emotional Neglect	Failure to provide a child with appropriate support, attention, and affection.
Sexual Abuse	Exploitation of a child or adolescent for another person's sexual and control gratification.
Child Neglect	Chronic failure of a parent or caretaker to provide a child with basic needs such as food, clothing, shelter, medical care, educational opportunity, protection, and supervision.
Missing and Exploited	Kidnapping a child from a custodial parent, child abduction by strangers, or child sexual exploitation for child pornography, child prostitution.

Source: Adapted from Whitcomb, 2001.

who have maltreated a child while in a caretaking relationship to the child, were mostly female (three-fifths). More than four-fifths (87.1%) of the victims were maltreated by one or both parents. The most common pattern of maltreatment was a child neglected by a female parent with no other perpetrators identified (44.7%). In cases involving sexual abuse, more than half (55.5%) of the victims were abused by known male adults.

Boys and girls are about equally neglected, physically, or emotionally abused, but, as mentioned earlier, girls are four times more likely to be sexually abused. In 2001, an estimated 1,300 children died of abuse and neglect, a rate of approximately 1.81 deaths per 100,000 children in the general population (U.S. Department of Health and Human Services, 2003). This child fatality figure due to maltreatment is very probably an underestimation, however. The figure is probably closer to 2,000 or more. Determining the actual number of children who die each year from maltreatment is exceedingly difficult. Child fatalities due to maltreatment are probably underreported because *some* deaths labeled as accidents, or sudden infant death syndrome (SIDS), might be attributed to child maltreatment if more comprehensive investigations were conducted.

Interestingly, research has found that pet abuse and child abuse commonly occur together in dysfunctional families (Arkow, 1998). Adults who are cruel and inhumane to children (and their spouses) are often cruel and inhumane to the family pet(s) as well. Abusers often threaten to harm or actually kill a pet to frighten a child into secrecy or to punish the child or to keep the spouse from reporting the abuse to authorities. In one study, more than half of the women at a shelter reported that their pets had been harmed or killed by their partner, and they delayed coming to the shelter for fear of harm to their pets (Ascione, 1997).

Missing, Abducted, Runaway, and Thrownaway Children

Each year, thousands of children run away, are abducted, or are thrown away. A thrownaway youth refers to one whom a parent or caretaker "throws" out of the home. A vast majority of children who run away do so to escape neglect or abuse from their current home or living arrangement. Most of the nationwide data on these children are reported in the NISMART Bulletins. NISMART is an acronym for the National Incidence Studies of Missing, Abducted, Runaway, and Thownaway Children, a large nationwide survey of households, juvenile residential facilities, and law enforcement agencies conducted by the Office of Juvenile Justice and Delinquency Prevention. NISMART consists of several studies designed to estimate the size and nature of the missing children problem in the United States. The more recent study, the NISMART-2, covers 1997–1999. Much of the information in this section comes from that report (U.S. Department of Justice, 2002a).

In 1999, an estimated 1,682,900 youth had a runaway or thrownaway episode (U.S. Department of Justice, 2002a). In most instances (71%), the runaway/thrownaway youth could have been endangered during the episode by virtue of such "street" factors as substance dependency, use of hard drugs, sexual or physical abuse, and their presence in places where criminal activity is prevalent.

Child abduction is another form of child abuse. In many instances, child abduction by a noncustodial parent from the custodial parent takes place. However, an undetermined number of child abductions are done by a parent who wants to protect the child or children from abuse by the other parent. Even a custodial parent may, in these circumstances, "abduct" the child, if the two parents share joint custody. An estimated 203,900 children were victims of family abduction in 1999, and nearly half were younger than 6 years of age (U.S. Department of Justice, 2002a).

Abduction of children by nonfamily members—every parent's nightmare—is less frequent. In this type of abduction, a nonfamily perpetrator takes a child by use of physical force or threat of bodily harm or detains the child for a substantial period of time (at least one hour) in an isolated place without lawful authority or parental permission. Nonfamily abduction also may occur when a child younger than 15 is taken or detained or voluntarily accompanies a nonfamily person who conceals the child's whereabouts, demands a ransom, or expresses the intention to keep the child permanently. Approximately 58,200 children were abducted by nonfamily perpetrators in 1999.

Although abduction by a stranger is uncommon, when it occurs the child's chance for survival is significantly lowered (Whitcomb, 2001), and sexual motivations appear to be major factor. In 1999, there were 115 stereotypical kidnappings, defined as abductions perpetrated by a stranger or slight acquaintance and involving a child who was transported 50 or more miles, detained overnight, held for ransom or with intent to keep the child permanently (U.S. Department of Justice, 2002a). In 40 percent of the stereotypical abductions, the child was killed, and in another 4 percent, the child was not recovered (U.S. Department of Justice, 2002a). Nearly half of all child victims of stereotypical kidnappings were sexually assaulted by the perpetrator, and about one-third required medical attention for injuries (U.S. Department of Justice, 2002a). In addition, over two-thirds of the victims of stereotypical kidnapping are female.

One out of five nonfamily abductions (21%) and almost half the victims of stereotypical kidnappings (48%) were abducted by multiple perpetrators (U.S. Department of Justice, 2002b). About half of the offenders of nonfamily abductions and one-third of the abductors in stereotypical kidnappings are in their twenties. Most of the abductions took place in the streets, parks, wooded areas, and other public areas, but rarely from the home, backyard, or school environments. Most children were taken into vehicles (45%) or to the offender's home (28%). Ransom is rarely demanded by the perpetrator(s) (less than 5% of all nonfamily or stereotypical abductions).

Munchausen Syndrome by Proxy

An unusual but serious type of child abuse is called **Munchausen syndrome by proxy (MSBP).** This is a form of child abuse in which the parent (usually the mother), or parents, *consistently* and *chronically* bring a child in for medical attention with symptoms falsified or directly induced by the parent or parents (Murray, 1997). Munchausen syndrome by itself is the chronic and relentless pursuit of medical treatment for combinations of symptoms that are either falsely reported or that are the results of consciously self-inflicted injury. In its proxy form, MSBP, another person, usually a child, is the victim. MSBP cases are found in homes of all socioeconomic levels (Pearl, 1995), and the victims are most often children between infancy and 8 years of age (Jones et al., 1986). Both male and female children may be victims. In most cases (about 98% of the time), the mothers are the offending parent, while the father is often unaware of what is happening. There does not seem to be a gender preference for the victim, as both male and female children are represented in equal numbers.

Very often the offending mother is very knowledgeable about medical issues, has a fascination with medical details, has her own medical history of fabricated illnesses, and may be a health professional herself. In addition, the mother will be unusually attentive to the child and will be reluctant to leave the child's side during medical examination or treatment. Another important symptom of MSBP is the child's series of reoccurring medical conditions that either do not respond to treatment or follow an unusual course that is persistent, puzzling, and unexplained. Another MSBP symptom is a series of physical or laboratory findings that are highly unusual, discrepant with medical history, or physically or clinically impossible. In extreme cases, the parent may initiate starvation in the child, nearly suffocate the child, inflict vaginal/rectal injuries in order to produce bleeding, add fat to stool collection to produce a lab abnormality, put her blood into child's urine sample before lab testing, or even inject contaminated material intravenously into the child's bloodstream (Murray, 1997; Pearl, 1995). The extreme forms of abuse certainly can lead to serious injury or even death. Unfortunately, the prevalence or incidence of MSBP is unknown at this time, probably partly due to the difficulty of identifying actual illnesses as opposed to the fabricated ones.

In some instances, the family pet may be the victim of MSBP, with the pet owner consistently taking the pet to the veterinarian for a variety of vague or fake symptoms. The pet owner often is trying to get sympathy and attention through the pet's misfortune.

Shaken Baby Syndrome

Another form of child abuse is **shaken baby syndrome (SBS),** in which a parent or caretaker, usually in anger, shakes a baby so hard that serious head injury results. Although there are no accurate statistics regarding the frequency of this form of abuse, there is consensus that head trauma is the leading killer of abused children (over 50%) and that shaking is involved in many of these cases (Duhaime, Christian, Rorke, & Zimmerman, 1998; Showers, 1999; Smithey, 1998). Ellis and Lord (2001) estimate that 10 percent to 12 percent of all deaths due to abuse and neglect are attributable to SBS (see also National Information Support and Referral Service, 1998). In addition, available research suggests that 70 percent to 80 percent of the perpetrators of SBS are male, and most of the time they are the parent of the child (Child Abuse Prevention Center, 1998; Ellis & Lord, 2001). Both male and female babies appear to be equally victimized. And, of course, not all baby victims of SBS die, but many suffer significant brain damage, such as cerebral palsy, blindness, deafness, seizures, learning disabilities, and coma.

Available research indicates that childhood abuse and neglect in general increase the odds of future delinquency and adult criminality by 40 percent. More specifically, being abused or neglected as a child increases the likelihood of arrest as a juvenile by over 50 percent, as an adult by 38 percent, and for a violent crime by 38 percent (Widom, 1992). More recent research by Widom (2000) confirms these data further. She states (2000, p. 5), "The odds of arrest for a juvenile offense were 1.9 times higher among abused and neglected individuals than among controls; for crime committed as adult, the odds were 1.6 times higher." In addition, psychological and emotional problems were prevalent among the abused and neglected sample. Specifically, the abused and neglected individuals were significantly more likely than the controls (a comparison group who had not experienced abuse or neglect) to have attempted suicide and to have met the criteria for antisocial personality disorder.

Infanticide, Neonaticide, and Filicide

In this section, the focus is on that form of child homicide that occurs when a person intentionally kills a child or infant, and *intends that the death occur.* That is, the homicide is not accidental or the incidental result of abuse or neglect. Although the term **infanticide** literally means the killing of an *infant,* it has become synonymous with the killing of a child by a parent. Some forms of infanticide can be traced back to ancient societies, including ancient Greece,

Rome, China, India, and Europe. "In some instances, it took place as part of socially sanctioned religious sacrifice, was meant to dispose of physically defective infants, was a way to dispose of female infants when males were preferred, or was a form of population control (Smithey, 2002, p. 888).

An estimated 1,200 to 1,500 children are intentionally killed each year by a parent or other person, representing about 12 percent to 15 percent of the total homicides in the United States (Emery and Laumann-Billings 1998). There were 69 children under the age of 18 murdered in Canada, comprising 12 percent of the total homicides in that country in 2001 (Au Coin 2003b). In the United States and Canada, about two-thirds of murdered children are killed by family members, mostly parents. Child homicide is not randomly distributed, but occurs with greater frequency across the globe in areas characterized by poverty, limited opportunity, and urbanization. A majority of child homicides across the globe are the result of parents killing their own child. Interestingly, the United States ranks fifth in homicides of infants under one year of age (with a rate of 5.4 per 100,000 live births) among 18 developed countries (Smithey, 2002).

Infants aged 12 months or younger have the highest homicide victimization rate of any single group in Australia, England and Wales, Canada, and the United States (Brookman and Nolan 2006). In England and Wales, for instance, children younger than 1 year old are at least twice as likely to be a victim of homicide as any other age group (Brookman and Nolan, 2006). They are, in most cases, killed by a biological parent.

In Canada, between 1974 and 2001, children under age 6 were more likely to have been killed as a result of strangulation or a beating than by other methods (Au Coin, 2003b). In England and Wales, two-thirds of the infants are killed as a result of suffocation or nonspecific methods such as shaking (shaken baby syndrome) and physical abuse (Brookman and Nolan, 2006). Older Canadian children, on the other hand, were more likely to be killed by a firearm, with 32 percent of victims aged 6–8 years and over 50 percent of victims 15–17 years of age dying of gunshot wounds (Au Coin, 2003b).

Several decades ago, Resnick (1970) recommended that the killing of one's children be divided into two separate categories, **neonaticide,** which refers to the killing of the newborn within the first 24 hours after birth, and **filicide,** which refers to the killing of a child older than 24 hours. Resnick's research indicated that neonaticide was more likely to represent an attempt to dispose of a problem, while filicide was more likely a reflection of parental depression or feelings of being overwhelmed. This distinction has now largely disappeared from the literature, but social concerns about neonaticide continue. An increasing number of jurisdictions, for example, now have laws that bar the prosecution of parents who leave newborns or infants in "safe harbors" such as hospitals, churches, or synagogues. The assumption is that if the parents have no such safe harbor, they might not sufficiently care for the infants or, worse, take the drastic step of ending their lives.

Newborns, infants, and children ages 1 to 4 are more vulnerable to homicide than are children ages 5 to 9 (Reiss & Roth, 1993). The number and rates of homicides of children under age 5 increased during the years 1976 to 1995, but have declined since 1996. Of all children under 5 murdered from 1976 to 1999, 31 percent were killed by fathers, 30 percent by mothers, 23 percent by male acquaintances, 6 percent by other relatives, and 3 percent by strangers (Bureau of Justice Statistics, 2001a). Of those children killed by someone other than their parents, 82 percent were killed by males. Most of the children killed were male.

While it appears that men and women are equally likely to be responsible for infanticide, both research and the law tend to view these perpetrators differently. Furthermore, there is more research conducted on women who kill their children than on men who do so. Traditionally, women who kill their children have been viewed by the legal system and the mental health profession as suffering from severe emotional problems, rendering them either insane (the legal system) or psychotic (the mental health profession). Men who kill their children are more likely to be viewed as evil (Wilczynski 1997). Nevertheless, women also have been viewed in that way.

Ania Wilczynski (1991, 1997), who conducted research in England and Wales, pointed out that if the woman wasn't "crazy," then the woman was obviously morally flawed, calloused, or noncaringly cold. These women are thus viewed as either "mad" or "bad." Mothers, after all, are supposed to act in a loving, warm, selfless, and protective fashion toward their children (Wilczynski, 1991). Any deviation from this stereotype promotes a conclusion that the women are either mentally ill and need to be treated with sympathy, or, alternatively, fundamentally wicked or callous, and therefore need to be punished harshly. Interestingly, in 1938 England passed the Infanticide Act, based primarily on the assumption that a mother who kills her infant is probably mentally disturbed and psychotic. Today, the courts of England continue to convict on the grounds of "infanticide"—that is, the mother killed her child while mentally ill. Rarely is there conviction of murder or manslaughter. In short the overwhelming perception of the criminal justice system in England (and perhaps throughout North America) is that women who kill their children are "mad" and "abnormal," whereas men who kill their children are perceived as "bad" and "normal" (Wilczynski, 1997).

Wilczynski (1991) studied 22 prosecuted cases of maternal infant-killings (in which a mother killed her child under the age of 12 months) in England and Wales between 1971 and 1989. In 14 of the cases, the women were seen as emotionally disturbed. They were seen as "essentially good women and mothers, for whom something had gone tragically wrong" (Wilczynski, 1991, p. 74).

Similarly following the mental health tradition, Resnick (1969, 1970) concluded that two-thirds of the mothers who commit filicide are psychotic, compared with only 17 percent of the women in the neonaticide group. As noted, Resnick found that a vast majority of the filicide group suffered from serious depression, while very few women in the neonaticide group exhibited this feature. Furthermore, suicide attempts accompany one-third of the filicides, but rarely accompany neonaticide.

More recent research sheds additional light on maternal murder of their young. In a cross-national comparison of British and Canadian filicidal women by McKee and Shea (1998), the data suggested that women who were charged with murdering their children usually suffered from a diagnosable mental disorder and were contending with many stressful events in their lives at the time of the murder. In another study, results showed that women suffering from a diagnosed mental disorder were more likely to use a weapon to murder their children than filicidal women not suffering from an apparent mental disorder (Lewis, Baranoski, Buchanan, & Benedek, 1998). The Lewis et al. study found that guns were used 13 percent of the time and knives 12 percent of the time.

Coramae Richey Mann (1993) investigated the patterns and characteristics of maternal filicide in six major U.S. cities (Chicago, Houston, Atlanta, Los Angeles, New York, and Baltimore) between 1979 and 1983. Although the data set for the study consisted of 296 cleared (or solved) homicide cases in which the offender was female, Mann restricted her research sample to 25 maternal filicides of preschool children (ages birth to 5 years). Because of the small sample size, any far-reaching conclusions must be viewed cautiously.

Mann found that 40 percent of the women who killed their preschool children had arrest records. One offender had 15 misdemeanor arrests, while another had six felony arrests. Twenty-five percent had arrest records for violent crime. Moreover, 12 of the 25 filicide offenders had recorded child abuse histories where court or social service intervention had taken place. Most of the victims were killed in the bathroom (30%), or the bedroom (26%), usually on Sunday morning. Manual methods were used in 80 percent of the cases—hands or feet (52%), suffocation or strangulation (16%), or drowning (12%). The killing of older children (ages 4 or 5) tended to be more brutal.

Although the most frequent victim was an African American female infant under the age of 2, Mann cautions that her sample was too small to advance any firm conclusions about racial patterns. Mann also emphasizes that location is a critical variable when examining the racial/ethnic factor in filicide. Large metropolitan cities, for example, are far more likely to have a minority population than more affluent, suburban areas. While a majority of the offenders were initially charged with murder, only 19 percent were convicted of that charge. Forty percent of the women who killed their preschool children were sent to prison, most often on a conviction of manslaughter, and another 36 percent received a probation sentence. The remaining six cases were either not processed, dismissed, or received special treatment from the court, and their dispositions were sealed. A determination of a mental disorder of the offenders was apparently rare.

In a more recent summary of the data, Dobson and Sales (2000) conclude, "There is certainly little evidence that women who kill their infant within the first 24 hours of birth are seriously mentally ill, and furthermore, many women who kill their infant after the first 24 hours do not exhibit symptomatology that meets the requirements for diminished capacity or insanity" (p. 1109). However, they also concluded that the potential role of psychosis in *some* women should not be underestimated in filicide. In some instances of filicide, such as observed by Resnick, some mothers are psychotic or otherwise seriously mentally disordered. This is one reason that the ongoing Andrea Yates case, discussed at the beginning of chapter 7, is so intriguing to observers. Yates's supporters insist that there was a very clear pattern of severe mental illness that offers an explanation for the tragic circumstances surrounding the death of her children.

In sum, although researchers have expended considerable energy studying infanticide committed by mothers, there is little consensus on the explanation for this behavior. Earlier studies suggested it must be the result of serious mental disorder, but recent research has questioned this conclusion. In addition, although men and women kill their children in almost equal proportion, researchers have not focused on studying the behavior in men to the extent they have studied the phenomenon in women.

Intimate Partner Abuse: Prevalence, Incidence, and Nature

The National Family Violence Survey of 1995–1996 estimated that the prevalence of women battering in the United States ranged from 6 to 8.7 million annually (Roberts, 2002). It is further estimated that one in three murders every year are intimate partner homicides (Roberts, 2002). According to estimates from the National Crime Victimization Survey (NCVS), there were 691,710 nonfatal violent victimizations committed by current or former spouses, boyfriends, or girlfriends of the victims during 2001 (Rennison, 2003). Eighty-five percent of victimizations by intimate partners were against women. Overall, **intimate partner violence** comprised 20 percent of violent crime against women in 2001. In 2002, 32.1 percent of female murder victims were slain by their husbands, ex-husbands, or boyfriends, compared with 2.7 percent of the male murder victims who were killed by their wives, ex-wives, or girlfriends (Federal Bureau of Investigation, 2003).

Battered Woman Syndrome

The term **battered woman syndrome** was coined and developed by Lenore Walker (1979), a psychologist who specializes in domestic abuse. Walker has identified a cluster of behavioral and emotional features that, she believes, are often shared by women who have been physically and psychologically abused over a period of time by the dominant male figure in their lives. Feelings of low self-esteem, depression, and helplessness are among the important components that frequently accompany the syndrome.

Research on domestic violence finds that a great majority of battered women either remain in lifelong abusive relationships, leave the relationship, or are killed by their abusers. Very rarely do battering relationships get better. A small minority of abused women kill their abusers. Although evidence for the battered woman syndrome is being admitted into the trials of women who do kill their abusers (Schuller & Vidmar, 1992), it is rarely successful in bringing about an acquittal (Browne, 1987; Ewing, 1990).

Currently, there is considerable debate concerning the reliability, validity, and usefulness of the diagnosis "battered woman syndrome" (Bartol & Bartol, 2004b). One of the major problems with the concept is the tendency for mental health and law professionals to regard it as a *single* entity representing some kind of mental or behavioral disorder displayed by all women who experience a severe abusive relationship. In addition, some theorists prefer to view the psychological effects of battering as a form of the posttraumatic stress disorder (PTSD) discussed in chapter 6, rather than as a separate syndrome.

However, battered women demonstrate a wide range of behavioral patterns that often reflect survival skills and adaptation to serious, life-threatening situations rather than a psychological disorder. Many women simply do not exhibit discernible clusters of psychological maladjustment, depression, and helplessness as portrayed by the battered women syndrome or by PTSD, even though they may have experienced high degrees of coercion, domination, and abuse during a lengthy relationship (Stark, 2002). Some victims, regardless of the abuse, may not demonstrate any signs of a syndrome or mental health problems at all.

Same-Sex Domestic Violence

In recent years, the nature and extent of same-sex partnerships has received increased attention. Some researchers (Potoczniak, Mourot, Crosbie-Burnett, & Potoczniak, 2003) have discovered some strong similarities in the research literature comparing the violence cycles and stages of abuse between same-sex domestic violence (SSDV) and opposite-sex domestic violence (OSDV). For example, similar to OSDV perpetrators, SSDV perpetrators are extremely controlling, threatened by outside influences, are highly selfish, and blame their partners for the abuse. In addition, the SSDV victims show many of the same behavioral and thought characteristics of OSDV victims.

Turrell (2000) examined SSDV among lesbians, gay women, and gay men. In the survey female participants were able to choose between the designation lesbian and gay women. Turrell found a physical abuse prevalence rate of 44 percent for gay men, 58 percent for gay women, and 55 percent for lesbians in a past or present relationship. With increased attention relating to issues involving civil unions and same-sex marriages across the nation in recent years, it is obvious that a better understanding and skillful research attention to SSDV are important, especially pertaining to providing adequate domestic violence and psychological services to the victims and in the training of competent criminal justice personnel in handling the incidents.

Psychological and Demographic Characteristics of Abusers

As the section on battered woman syndrome indicates, most of the research on psychological characteristics in domestic violence has focused on the characteristics of the person being abused, particularly the woman in heterosexual relationships. It has been a traditional belief in some quarters that these battered women allow themselves to be battered (Frieze & Browne, 1989). Others have argued that victims of spouse abuse are masochistic, consciously and unconsciously precipitating the violence to which they are subjected (Megargee, 1982). Still others have depicted battered wives as lacking self-esteem, being highly passive and dependent on their husbands, and willing to place greater value on maintaining the marriage above their safety (Megargee, 1982).

Some researchers, though, have preferred to focus on the characteristics of the abusers. Abusive husbands, for example, have been depicted as extremely possessive and unreasonably jealous men who treat their wives like property coveted by other men. This depiction led to other assumptions about the inadequacy, incompetence, and low self-esteem of these abusive husbands who saw threats to their masculinity everywhere. Christine Rasche (1993) examined 155 "mate" homicides in Florida that occurred between 1980 and 1986. She was able to identify several motives for these intimate homicides, with possessiveness the most prominent. The list of motives and related percentages was as follows:

- Possessiveness (48.9%)
- Self-defense (15.5%)
- Abuse by victim (2.6%)
- Feelings arising out of arguments (20.7%)
- Other motives (9.7%)
- Unknown (7.7%)

Alcohol abuse is also often seen as part of the clinical picture. Similarly, men who abuse their children were seen as incompetent, immature individuals, overwhelmed and frustrated by the responsibilities of parenting. The violence of both the abusive husband and the abusive father was seen as irrational and expressive, precipitated by frustration and extreme anger. Some professionals have suggested that street violence is generally rational and instrumental, whereas family violence is predominately irrational and expressive (see Hotaling & Straus, 1989; Megargee, 1982).

The empirical evidence for these depictions is meager, equivocal, and confusing and no more persuasive than the depictions of battered women as passive and lacking in self-confidence. Some studies find some support for these correlates; others provide no support. Despite several attempts at psychological typologies for wife and child abusers (Megargee, 1982), there does not seem to be any evidence for typical psychological profiles for either the abusers or the abused. However, recent research results look promising for a typology that might help in the prevention, intervention, and treatment of abusers. In an extensive review of the research literature, Holtzworth-Munroe and Stuart (1994) identified three primary types of male spouse batterers: Type 1 batterers who abuse family members only. Type 2 batterers who abuse family members because of emotional problems, and Type 3 batterers who are generally violent toward both family members and persons outside the family. Type 1 abusers are the most common, tend to be less aggressive than the other two, and also tend to be more remorseful for their actions. They are generally inadequate, passive men who are dependent on others. Type 2 batterers tend to be depressed, inadequate individuals who are emotionally volatile and who display indicators of personality disorders and psychopathology. Type 3 batterers are individuals who are antisocial, criminally prone, and violent across situations. They are more likely to abuse alcohol and are generally more belligerent toward almost everyone. They are also most likely to be involved in serious violence toward a spouse.

The search for demographic variables has been equally mixed and inconclusive (Hotaling & Straus, 1989; Weis, 1989). Wife and child abuse appears to cut across socioeconomic, religious, and ethnic lines. Even current research on gender does not reveal clear trends for women or men as assaulters of spouse, child, or parent.

The abuse of alcohol and drugs seems to play a role as an exacerbater, *but not as a cause,* of the family violence. Abusive men with severe alcohol or drug problems are apt to abuse their partners both when drunk and when sober. However, abusive husbands who drink heavily are violent more frequently, and inflict more serious injuries on their partners than do abusive men who do not have a history of alcohol or drug problems (Frieze & Browne, 1989). A similar pattern also holds for men who abuse their children. Many use alcohol as an excusing agent that allows them to escape some culpability for their antisocial or violent actions, as well as to avoid the full impact of legal sanctions. Babcock, Waltz, Jacobson, and Gottman (1993), in some very promising research, examined the interactions of marital power, interpersonal strategies, and communication skills as predictors of marital violence. They reasoned that husbands who are unable to effect their intentions through negotiation or general communication skills are more likely to resort to physical aggression—pushing, slapping, beating—to achieve their intentions. This is especially the case if the wives are more verbally competent, more educated, or have better jobs than their husbands. For example, previous research suggests that women with jobs that are higher in status than their husband's jobs experience more life-threatening violence than wives who were occupationally similar to their husbands (Hornung, McCullough, & Sugimoto, 1981). Frustrated with some combination of power discrepancy between him and his wife, the husband's only effective expressive retort may be physical aggression. Moreover, husbands who battered their wives were more likely to be in relationships where their demands were met with their wives' withdrawal (e.g., defensiveness, passive inaction, "stonewalling," or the "silent treatment"). The researchers interpreted the withdrawal pattern as one of power (the individual has resources the other partner wants), whereas the demanding role represented a weak position (the individual wants something the other partner has). This research emphasizes the importance of studying the reciprocal interaction of a relationship if we are to understand family violence more fully.

Elderly Abuse: Prevalence, Incidence, and Nature

It is estimated that approximately 2.5 million older Americans are victims of abuse each year (National Center on Elder Abuse, 1999). Elder abuse is characterized by the infliction of physical, emotional, or psychological harm on the older adult, usually defined as age 65 or older (Marshall, Benton, & Brazier, 2000). "The general concept involved in the numerous definitions of 'elder abuse' is that the victim is injured, neglected, or exploited because of vulnerabilities associated with age, such as impaired physical or mental capacities" (Klaus, 2000, p. 13).

Neglect in this instance is "the refusal or failure to fulfill any part of a person's obligation or duties to an elder" (Seymour, 2001, p. 4). More specific elder abuse definitions include "the refusal or failure to provide an elderly person with such life necessities as food, water, clothing, shelter, personal hygiene, medicine, comfort, personal safety, and other essentials included in the responsibility or agreement with an elder" (Seymour, 2001, p. 4). Abandonment may also be included in the definition of neglect, and is characterized by such things as the desertion of an elder at a hospital, a nursing facility, or other similar institution, or desertion of an elder at a public location. (See **Table 9–6**.)

The elderly appear to be maltreated in much the same way that children are maltreated—with one notable exception: financial exploitation (Pagelow, 1989). The likeliest candidates for elder abuse appear to be white women between the ages of 75 and 85, middle to lower class, Protestant, and suffering from some form of physical or mental impairment (Pagelow, 1989). Only 5 percent of the elderly are placed in institutions or rest homes, although 85 percent of them have at least one chronic illness (Hudson, 1986). Most elderly are living at home or in the homes of relatives. Abusive caretakers tend to lack resources, feel trapped, and may be abusing drugs or alcohol.

Spouses constitute the second-largest abuser category. Male caretakers are more likely to abuse the elderly physically, while female caretakers are prone to abuse them psychologically or neglect them. However, both men and women are equally likely to exploit them financially. The most common abuse is a

TABLE 9–6   Estimated Incidence of Specific Types of Elder Abuse, 1996

Type of Abuse	Estimated Percentage
Neglect	58.50
Physical Abuse	15.70
Financial Exploitation	12.30
Emotional Abuse	7.30
Sexual Abuse	0.04
Other Types	5.10
Unknown	0.06

Source: National Center on Elder Abuse, 1999.

combination of psychological abuse and neglect (Pagelow, 1989). About 20 percent of elder abuse cases are physical, and 45 percent involve neglect (Marshall, Benton, & Brazier, 2000).

Although there are similarities between the various types of family abuse, elder mistreatment is a more complex phenomenon that encompasses both aspects of interpersonal violence and the aging process (Wolf, 1992). That is, elder abuse and neglect are often a result of long-standing troubled family dynamics and interpersonal processes that have been highly charged when the dependency relationship is altered, either because of illness or financial needs.

Estimates of the proportion of elderly persons (persons 65 or older) who are abused range from 4 percent to 10 percent, but it is difficult to make confident estimates because of a lack of reliable statistics (Klaus, 2000; Pagelow, 1989; Pillemer & Suitor, 1988). The first-ever National Elder Abuse Incidence Study, conducted by the National Center on Elder Abuse (1999), estimated that during 1996, at least one-half million older persons in domestic settings were abused and/or neglected, or experienced self-neglect, and that for every reported incidence of elder abuse, neglect, or self-neglect, approximately five go unreported (Seymour, 2001). The same report found that female elders are abused at a higher rate than males, even after accounting for their larger numbers in the aging population. And two-thirds of the perpetrators of elder abuse are adult children or spouses. While there is no one single causal factor to fully explain why family members abuse their seniors, some explanations have focused on caregiver stress and dependency issues (either the caregiver's or the senior's) (Au Coin, 2003a).

Pillemer and Finkelhor (1988) focused on the Boston metropolitan area and found that 3 percent of the elderly suffered from one of three kinds of abuse: physical abuse, chronic verbal abuse, or neglect. Based on their findings, the researchers extrapolated that about one million elderly persons are similarly abused throughout the United States. A Canadian survey (Podnieks, Pillemer, and Nicolson, 1990) reported that about 4 percent of the elderly population living in private homes in Canada was subjected to abuse and neglect.

The violent crime committed against persons age 65 or older is most likely to be simple assault (Klaus, 2000). Nevertheless, there is ample evidence that they are also victims of more serious violent crimes. Recent statistics from two countries are illustrative. In Canada, 6 percent of the total homicide victims were older Canadians (65 or older), with a family member being responsible for over half of the cases (Au Coin, 2003a). The same statistic (6.4%) was reported in the United States for older Americans (Federal Bureau of Investigation, 2003). The term **eldercide** is usually reserved for the murder of a person age 65 or older. In Canada, when the incident involved a family member, a majority of older women were killed by a spouse or ex-spouse (53%), whereas older men were most often killed by an adult son (43%) (Au Coin, 2003a). The data are similar for American senior citizens (Klaus, 2000). In Canada, the most common cause of death for older victims of family related homicides was beating (29%) and shooting (28%), followed by stabbing (23%) (Au Coin, 2003a). Although a similar family breakdown is not currently available in the U.S. data, the most common causes of death for all older victims were firearms (45%), followed by stabbing (20%), blunt objects (14%), and beatings with fists or feet (13%) (Federal Bureau of Investigation, 2003).

Sibling-to-Sibling Violence

Violence between siblings is believed to be the most common form of intimate violence within families, but surprisingly little is known about it (Gelles, 1997; Wallace, 1996). The violence and abuse a child or adolescent receives from a sibling is often overlooked and trivialized (Simonelli, Mullis, & Rohde, 2005). Sibling conflicts are generally seen as a normal part of growing up (Underwood & Patch, 1999). Mothers and fathers display a great tendency to deny the seriousness of the aggressive outburst of siblings or their children—including violence toward themselves—in order to perpetuate a "myth of family harmony" (Harbin & Madden, 1979). Yet in many cases, sibling conflict and violence involves punching, choking, beating up, threatening to use a weapon, and actually using a weapon. In addition, sibling violence appears to be linked to violence in dating relationships, family violence in adulthood, and nonfamily adult violence in general (Hoffman, Kiecolt, & Edwards, 2005). More severe forms of child-to-family violence involve murder, and have specific terms, such as **siblicide** (sibling killing sibling), **patricide** (killing one's father), **matricide** (killing one's mother), **sororicide** (killing one's sister), **fratricide** (killing one's brother), and **parricide** (killing one or more of one's parents).

Nearly 30 years ago, Steinmetz (1981) reported that two-thirds of the adolescent siblings in the family sample she studied—a sample characterized by family violence—used physical violence to resolve conflict. These findings have been recently supported by Hoffman, Kiecolt, & Edwards (2005) who found 70 percent of the adolescents in their sample (students) had committed at least one violent act against their closest-age sibling during their senior year of high school. Families having only sons consistently experience more sibling violence than do families with only daughters (Hoffman et al., 2005). Hoffman et al. (2005) found that males perpetrated more violent acts against their brothers than against sisters or sisters against their siblings. In 2002, 72 percent of murders by siblings involved a brother killing a brother, and 14 percent involved a brother killing a sister (Durose et al., 2005). An additional 14 percent of siblicides involved a sister killing a brother or sister. Among the 671 intrafamilial murders reported in 2002, 18 percent (or 119 murders) involved a sibling victim (Durose et al. 2005).

Victims of the more extreme forms of sibling violence tend to be younger siblings. For example, Fehrenbach, Smith, Monastersky, and Deisher (1986) reported that over 40 percent of victims of adolescent sexual assault were younger siblings. Available data also suggest that 85 percent of siblicide offenders and 73 percent of siblicide victims are male (Dawson & Langan, 1994). Approximately one out of every 100 homicides in the United States is a siblicide (Federal

Bureau of Investigation, 2005; Underwood & Patch, 1999). In their analysis, Underwood and Patch (1999) reported that the most common circumstance of sibling homicide was some type of argument between the perpetrator and the victim. Interestingly, the same study uncovered very few incidents involving Asian Americans or Pacific Islanders in their data set. African Americans, on the other hand, were overrepresented in the data. In addition, firearms predominated as the weapon of choice in siblicides.

Child-to-Parent Violence

Child-to-parent violence and abuse has also become an important topic. In one early study (Gelles, 1982), approximately four adolescents (ages 15 to 17) in 100 were reported to kick, bite, punch, hit with an object, beat up, threaten, or use a gun or knife against a parent. Almost one-third of restraining orders issues in Massachusetts were requested by parents against their adolescent children (Pagani et al., 2004). In a study using a nationally representative sample of American children, Ullman and Straus (2003) concluded that 10% of the adolescents (ages 10 to 17) participated in child-to-parent violence during the previous 12 months. Sixty percent of these youths had witnessed violence between their parents. In one longitudinal study involving 2,524 Canadian adolescents, Pagani et al. (2003) affirmed that 13 percent of the teenagers engaged in physical aggression toward their mothers, ranging from pushing and shoving, punching or kicking, throwing objects, to using a weapon.

In 2004, 3 percent of murder victims were killed by their children (Federal Bureau of Investigation, 2005). The killing of parents, termed **parricide,** is most often committed by sons by a ratio of about three to one over daughters (Federal Bureau of Investigation, 2005; Lubenow, 1983; Pagelow, 1989). Mothers are killed (**matricide**) far more often than fathers (**patricide**) by both adolescents and adult sons and daughters. Female parricide is exceptionally rare in all countries of the world (d'Orban & O'Connor, 1989). When daughters kill a parent or parents, they often secure the help of a male friend or sibling. In Britain, boys most often kill a parent (or parents) with explosive violence in response to prolonged provocation and parental brutality and abuse (d'Orban & O'Connor, 1989). Heide (1993) identifies three types of youth parricide: (1) the severely abused child, (2) the severely mentally ill child, and (3) the dangerously antisocial child. The complex dynamics of families in which parricides occur often include multiassaultive family patterns, easy access to firearms, alcohol and drug abuse, and the youthful offender's strong feelings of helplessness in coping with the stresses at home. Sometimes the adolescent murderer, as well as other family members, feels a sense of relief that the parent(s) is (are) dead.

Although males predominant in the more extreme forms of juvenile violence toward parents, the gender differences disappear at more moderate levels of violence (Pagani et al., 2004). In addition, the risk of violence toward parents gradually increases during adolescence, peaking at age 15 and diminishing thereafter (Pagani et al., 2004). This pattern corresponds to the peak age of adolescent violence toward nonrelated individuals noted by Loeber and Stouthamer-Loeber (1998). Most violent incidents between child and parents are associated with conflicts about home responsibilities, money, and privilege (Pagani et al., 2004). Children and adolescents who displayed early and chronic forms of aggression and antisocial behavior are most likely to be aggressive toward parents (Pagani et al., 2004). "As adolescents, those described as chronically aggressive by their (annually) different primary school teachers were (9 and 4) times at greater risk of engaging in verbal and physical aggression (respectively) toward their mothers in comparison to their persistently nonaggressive peers" (Pagani et al., 2004, p. 534). In fact, violent predispositions during childhood, measured by teachers, are among the best predictors of later violence toward mothers. "Indeed," Pagani et al. (2004) concluded in their study, "teacher-rated disruptiveness during early childhood predicted the risk of engaging in physical aggression toward mothers during adolescence" (p. 220).

Multiassaultive Families

Some families, referred to as **multiassaultive families,** are characterized by continual cycles of intrafamilial physical aggression and violence. Siblings hit each other, spouses hit each other, parents hit the children, and the older children hit the parents. According to the available data, at least 7 percent of all intact families may be considered multiassaultive (Hotaling & Straus, 1989).

Research supports the notion that assault is a generalized pattern in interpersonal relations that crosses settings and is used across targets beyond the immediate family (Hotaling & Straus, 1989). Men in families in which children and wives are assaulted are five times more likely to have also assaulted a nonfamily person than are men in nonassaultive families. A similar pattern holds for women from multiassaultive families, although the relationship is not as strong. Sibling violence is particularly high in families in which child assault and spouse assault are present, with boys displaying significantly more assaultive behavior (Hotaling & Straus, 1989). Moreover, children from multiassaultive families have an inordinately high rate of assault against nonfamily members (Hotaling & Straus, 1989). These children are also more likely to be involved in property crime, to have adjustment difficulties in school, and to be involved with police (Hotaling & Straus, 1989). It should be carefully noted that it is extremely difficult to tell what is causing what in this complicated web of interrelated variables. Nevertheless, it is quite clear that multiassaultive family members are violent and antisocial across a variety of settings, toward both family members and society in general, and may demonstrate this behavioral pattern throughout most of their lifetimes.

The Cycle of Violence

For some time, the scholarly and popular literature has concluded that both abusive parents and abusive spouses have themselves been the victims of family violence during their childhoods (Megargee, 1982). Some research suggests that highly violent offenders may have been subjected to more severe and frequent physical and psychological abuse and punitive parenting during their childhoods than other offenders (Hämäläinen & Haapasalo, 1996). Individuals grow up to be abusive because they were abused themselves, a belief referred to as the **cycle-of-violence** hypothesis.

According to social learning theory, those who receive harsh discipline learn that physical violence can be used to change the behaviors of others (Schwartz, Hage, Bush, & Burns, 2006). **Coercion theory** proposed by Patterson (1982) and discussed in chapter 2 also posits that coercive and punitive tactics in parenting increase the likelihood of later aggressive behavior and potential domestic violence. Theories that view domestic violence as a tactic for gaining power and control in relationships are highly consistent with coercion theory. As noted by Schwartz et al. (2006), "Men involved in intimate violence have been found to have demand and/or withdraw patterns of communication with their partners and perceive themselves as lacking power in their relationships" (p. 212). Consequently, abusing spouses and other family members is one way, in the abuser's eyes, of gaining and maintaining control over those in their immediate social environment. There is also accumulating evidence that males who experience parental neglect during their childhoods are more likely to engage in dating violence, a behavior that is a precursor to spousal abuse (Chapple, 2003; Simons, Lin, & Gordon, 1998).

Nevertheless, violence does not necessarily beget violence. The cycle of violence and the presumed overall consequences of abuse and neglect do not take into account the resilience of human beings, which rules out any simple cause-and-effect relationship between maltreatment and future violent behavior (Garbarino, 1989). In many cases, rather than finding that abusive parenting is the logical consequence of being victimized as children, the opposite sequence is likely to take place. Realizing and sensitive to the enormous psychological and social costs of family violence, many victims of child abuse may be even less likely than their nonabused peers to commit aggressive acts as adults within their families. Garbarino (1989, p. 222), for example, writes, "Many victims of child abuse, probably most, survive it and avoid repeating the pattern in their own child rearing." Nevertheless, the effects of family violence in general on children are devastating, as we see in the following section.

The Effects of Family Violence on Children

Domestic violence is recognized as a serious problem in our society today, but how such violence affects the children who are exposed to it did not appear in the research literature until the 1980s. Children who are exposed to violence between adults in their homes have often been referred to as the "silent," "forgotten," and "unintended" victims of domestic violence. These children were initially referred to as simply "witnesses" or "observers," but recent research literature has discovered that some are not only directly involved victims themselves but also suffer some troubling consequences.

Children experience domestic violence through a bewildering array of events. Most often, children see or hear the violence, but they experience the violence in many other ways, too. Direct involvement, such as trying to intervene or calling 911, is one example (Edleson, 1999). Additional examples include taking the child hostage to force the mother's return, using a child as a physical weapon against the victim, forcing the child to watch the violence, forcing the child to participate in the abuse, and using the child as a spy or questioning the child about the mother's activities (Ganley & Schechter, 1996).

Experiencing the aftermath of the violence may be equally traumatic for children (Edleson, 1999). Examples include the child seeing the mother with physical injuries and possibly in need of medical help, observing maternal emotions (such as anxiety, depression, stress), and having the mother move to a shelter for battered women to escape further abuse. The aftermath can also include a father alternating between physical violence and loving care, as well as police intervention that could result in the removal of the father from the home. In some instances, removal of the children from the home by child welfare agencies is also a terrifying possibility.

The number of children exposed to domestic violence in the United States each year is largely unknown. Straus (1991, p. 98) estimates that "at least a third of Americans have witnessed violence between their parents, and most have endured repeated instances." This estimation is based on Straus and Gelles's (1990) national survey that discovered that the 30 percent of parents who admitted domestic violence existed in their home also reported that their children had witnessed at least one violent incident during the length of the marriage.

Research has also found that 13 percent to 27 percent of adults recall witnessing physical violence during their childhood years between their parents (Forrstrom-Cohen & Rosenbaum, 1985). Police arrest data from five U.S. cities revealed that children were directly involved in adult domestic violence incidents about 27 percent of the time (Fantuzzo et al., 1997). Fantuzzo et al. also found that younger children were disproportionately represented in households where domestic violence occurred. Another study (Silvern et al., 1995) found that exposure to domestic violence may be even higher in some populations. Silvern and colleagues found that 118 (41.1%) of the 287 college women and 85 (32.2%) of the 263 college men surveyed had witnessed abuse by one parent against the other.

Explanations about how domestic violence affects a child must include an assortment of already existing risk factors. The child's age, the nature and severity of the violence, socioeconomic status, and parental substance abuse all must be entered into the equation.

The child's behavioral and emotional functioning is the area that has received the most attention from researchers. Overall, these studies report the consistent finding that children exposed to domestic violence exhibit many behavioral and emotional problems when compared with other children. For instance, studies using the Child Behavior Checklist (Achenbach and Edelbrock,

1983) and similar measures have found that children who are exposed to domestic violence display more aggressive and antisocial behaviors as well as fearful and inhibited behaviors (Fantuzzo et al., 1991; Hughes, 1988; Hughes, Parkinson, & Vargo, 1989), and show lower social competence and interpersonal skills than other children (Adamson & Thompson, 1998; Fantuzzo et al., 1991; Hughes, 1988). More aggressive and antisocial behaviors are often referred to as "externalized" behaviors, while fearful and inhibited behaviors are referred to as "internalized" behaviors (Carlson, 1991; Edleson, 1999; Stagg, Wills, & Howell, 1989).

Domestic violence has also been shown to have dramatic negative effects on children's emotional health and overall adjustment. Both boys and girls in families with spousal violence demonstrate far more depression and aggression (McClosky, Figueredo, & Koss, 1995; Wolfe, Jaffe, Wilson, & Zak, 1985), and lower self-esteem (Hughes & Barad, 1983) compared with other children. In addition, children who are exposed to violence between parents are more likely to show anxiety, depression, trauma symptoms, and temperamental problems (Hughes, 1988; Maker, Kemmelmeier, & Peterson, 1998).

Another consequence of experiencing violence within the home is the overall effects it has on the child's immediate and long-term cognitive functioning and attitudes about how to deal with violence and conflict resolution in their own lives. Many researchers conclude that children's exposure to adult domestic violence may generate attitudes justifying their own use of violence to solve problems and deal with frustrations. For example, Spaccarelli, Coatsworth, and Bowden's (1995) study found support for such an association by showing that, among a sample of 213 adolescent boys incarcerated for violent crimes, those boys who had experienced family violence were more likely to subscribe to the viewpoint that "acting aggressively enhances one's reputation or self-image" (p. 173). And Carlson (1991) reports that in a sample of 101 adolescents, boys who witnessed domestic violence were significantly more likely to approve of violence than were girls who had witnessed domestic violence.

In conclusion, the empirical evidence reveals that children's exposure to domestic violence is a serious and widespread problem. Such violence affects children indirectly through its effect on the parenting relationship, as well as directly affecting children's behavioral, emotional, cognitive, psychological, and social adjustment.

THE NATURE AND THEORY OF FAMILY VIOLENCE

Once violence has occurred in a relationship, it tends to be repeated (Frieze & Browne, 1989). Over time, violence, if not adequately sanctioned, may also become more severe and more frequent. Furthermore, being violently victimized by an intimate over an extended period of time may result in emotional reactions and psychological scars decidedly different from those incurred by victims of violent crime by strangers.

As noted earlier, some clinicians and writers have suggested that family violence is fundamentally different from general (or street) violence and thus should be examined separately (Megargee, 1982). Physical violence against children and spouses are "special" cases of violence that require family based theories to explain them. Wife abusers are psychologically distressed, and their violence is irrational. As also mentioned earlier, child abusers are depicted as incompetent and immature, unable to cope with the responsibilities of parenting and holding unrealistic expectations of children. Similarly, child abusers are extremely emotional and irrational in their assaults. Street offenders, on the other hand, presumably use violence in a deliberate, rational way to gain things, such as material goods, status, or other social reinforcements. General violent offenders utilize violence for a purpose, whereas family violent offenders are lashing out in anger and without discernible purpose.

Empirical evidence for differences between criminal violence in the streets and family violence is weak and equivocal, with most of the studies being unsystematic or seriously flawed methodologically (Hotaling & Straus, 1989). The evidence we have so far, however, strongly suggests that the etiology or cause of violent behavior may be very similar, whether it is used against a family member or a nonfamily member. Violent people tend to be violent generally, both within and outside the family context. They are aggressive and assaultive toward a large variety of targets and across a wide array of settings.

The development of theory requires well-designed and executed research. Without theoretical testing through sound research, speculations and free-floating explanations abound with no empirical anchoring. This describes what is happening in the field of family violence. Gelles and Straus (1979), for example, were able to identify 15 different theories attempting to explain family violence. Weis (1989, p. 123) observes that "the field is, with few exceptions, characterized by descriptive work, with little hypothesis testing, causal modeling, or attempts to construct and test integrated theories of the different types of family violence."

The systematic study of family violence, however, is a new undertaking. Thus, it suffers from a constellation of uncoordinated research and a matrix of poorly integrated theory, as all new sciences do. Furthermore, the family is a difficult social situation to study. It is a complex social system consisting of many roles, and it is a private social group in which interactions and behaviors are invisible to outsiders. Social interactions are more intense, emotional, and consequential than other interactions (Weis, 1989). In addition, family influences do not flow in one direction; they are apt to be multidirectional, a process called reciprocal influence (Bartol & Bartol, 1998). For example, while the parents affect the development of the child, the child also affects the development and psychological growth of the parents, including their marital relationship, relationships with friends, and even the level of job satisfaction. Reciprocal influence implies that the social environment influences the individual, and the individual, in turn, has an impact on the social environment. Therefore, theories that are sensitive to the reciprocal interactionism of family dynamics are the best candidates to advance our knowledge about family violence.

Cessation of Family Violence

Although theories of family violence are underdeveloped, the effectiveness of various procedures or strategies to reduce family violence can still be tested. Unfortunately, there have been very few systematic evaluations of the effectiveness of particular strategies in combating family violence (Elliott, 1989).

One of the more influential investigations examining the effectiveness of police responses to spouse abuse was the Minnesota Domestic Violence Experiment (Sherman & Berk, 1984). The police officers participating in this project handled marital conflict one of three ways: arrest, separating the parties, or advising (or mediating) the parties. Follow-up of the effectiveness of these approaches over a six-month period indicated that arrest of the suspected abuser was the most effective police response for reducing misdemeanor family assaults. However, the study had serious design problems that undermine both its external validity and internal validity. Subsequent research in other cities failed to replicate the results of the study (Buzawa & Buzawa, 1996). Moreover, there is some evidence that the impact of an arrest wears off over a relatively short period of time (8 to 12 months), and the assaults return to their original level (Elliott, 1989).

The effectiveness of the legal sanctions of prosecution, conviction, and sentencing in deterring subsequent family violence is questionable. There are also many unanswered questions about the effectiveness of community services and care for family violence victims (Saunders & Azar, 1989). Nevertheless, approaches that combine arrest with supportive services for the victims and monitoring if the abuser remains in the community offer some hope for decreasing the violence.

Much of the contemporary work and commentary has been directed at reducing wife abuse or male abuse of female intimate partners. Fagan (1989) hypothesizes that a large segment of the rewards and support men receive for abusing women derives from a long-standing cultural stereotype that men must be dominant and show women who is boss. One very "masculine" way of achieving and maintaining this expected dominance is through physical aggression and, if necessary, some violence. Some of the reinforcement comes from the satisfaction of maintaining this physical dominance and the positive social status that accompanies domination over women, particularly wives, advocated by one's peer group and subculture. Accordingly, men subscribing to this subculture socialize together, drink together, and participate in male-oriented recreation activities, generally excluding their wives from these activities. This male subculture provides a social milieu that supports and encourages traditional male dominance in male-female relationships, even if it requires violence now and then. Frequent contacts with this exclusive male subculture by the husband, combined with increasing social isolation of the wife, are particularly associated with the more severe forms of wife abuse (Bowker, 1983; Fagan, 1989). Presumably, the more deeply immersed into this subculture a man is, the more likely he is to batter his wife.

To what extent some women also support this male-dominating tradition is largely unknown, but knowledge about the degree to which women explicitly or implicitly favor this belief system may be extremely important in a deeper understanding of the dynamics of the relationship. This is not to imply that a subculture that supports male domination in a marriage necessarily advocates violence in carrying out this dominance, but research does suggest that many wife batterers manage to isolate their families socially while receiving considerable encouragement and support for physical aggression from their social network of friends.

An effective way of breaking the wife- or female partner–abuse cycle, therefore, is to change the abuser's attitudinal system and social network of friends who support or at least condone physical male domination of family relationships. Obviously, this strategy will not be easy to apply in many abusive behavioral patterns. Abusers have had a lifelong learning experience in developing belief systems, and probably have had considerable reinforcement history for their aggressive actions toward women from their subculture. "Leaving the subculture is not unlike leaving the world of the addict or the alcoholic" (Fagan, 1989, p. 408).

Initiating motivation to change a behavioral pattern of abuse often requires establishing a series of situations where the psychological costs for the abuse outweigh its psychological benefits. Legal sanctions may be one way, but many batterers realize that these sanctions are normally weak and without teeth. However, serious attempts by the criminal justice system to put some bite into these legal sanctions (such as arrests, criminal charges, and conviction) may begin to prove effective over the long haul, provided that they are accompanied by community support systems for the woman. It is important to note that it is unlikely that any one arrest or single event will promote a wish to change. It is more likely that a series of aversive and costly events, such as strong legal sanctions, combined with social sanctions from the community (public disclosure, visits by social agencies) and emotional sanctions from the victim (reporting the abuse to authorities, leaving the home, separating, threatening divorce) will wear the abuser down to a point at which he makes a decision to change his behavioral patterns.

However, the more severe and protracted the violence is, the more difficult it may be to stop, despite formal external interventions—legal or otherwise (Fagan, 1989). Legal and social sanctions for spouse abuse may work for less chronic and severe situations. However, legal sanctions, regardless of the nature and strength of the sanction, may not only be ineffective for the more serious cases, but could possibly lead to escalation in violence. Therefore, social, legal, and emotional sanctions may be more effective with individuals who do not have an extensive history of repetitive and serious violence. One of the most sobering research findings in recent years has been the discovery that a woman's life is in the greatest danger from an abusive partner within the first six months of leaving that partner.

As we shall see in chapter 10, it is one thing to get a person to decide to stop acting a certain way. It is quite another for an individual to continue to avoid that behavior. Research clearly demonstrates that the maintenance of positive behavior is far more difficult to achieve than stopping the negative behavior.

........➤ **SUMMARY AND CONCLUSIONS**

In this chapter, we began to narrow our focus to consider specific offenses. Previous chapters were broader, in that they dealt with general theoretical orientations to crime. Here, we reviewed the major sociological data on violence and summarized empirical and clinical research on family violence.

Sociological and official data indicate that homicides are rare compared with the total incidence of violent crime. In the United States, violent crime is often committed by young males living in environments that implicitly or explicitly advocate violence for the resolution of conflict. Guns (especially handguns) are commonly used in the crime. Certain minority groups are overrepresented in violent crime statistics, but there are a number of explanations for this that have nothing to do with racial or ethnically based individual factors. Statistics indicate also that, when the relationship of victim and offender is known, the homicide victim and the offender are usually family members, friends, or acquaintances. The relationship is known in between half to two-thirds of the offenses. While assaults are far more common than homicide, the same sociological features appear, particularly for aggravated assault.

Considering the rapidly expanding research on the topic, family violence undoubtedly deserves a chapter of its own. Family violence is a broad subject that encompasses child abuse, spouse or partner abuse, elder abuse, sibling abuse, and child-to-parent abuse. Some researchers also include intimate partner abuse that occurs when the victim and perpetrator occupy separate households. Abuse comes in many forms, including physical, psychological, or sexual abuse. Family violence is found across ethnic, racial, and socioeconomic classes. Women are disproportionately subject to spousal violence and the dire economic situations that may lead to both victimization and victimizing. Children are particularly vulnerable targets for family violence and maltreatment, enduring physical maltreatment, sexual exploitation, medical and emotional neglect, and psychological trauma—all of which are usually lifelong in their consequences. In this chapter we focused not only on "typical" forms of child abuse, but also on statistics and research relating to shaken baby syndrome, Munchausen syndrome by proxy, and infanticide. For the child who survives abuse, the psychological consequences can nevertheless be devastating. Though he or she does not necessarily become an abuser, perpetuating the cycle of abuse, emotional scars relating to one's self-concept and the ability to trust others are often very deep and long lasting.

In addition to the obvious physical injuries and deaths that result, family violence is often cited in research and clinical studies as contributing to other individual, family, and societal problems. Most of all, family violence and maltreatment highlight the importance of considering a victimological approach for the complete understanding of violent crime, and underscore the fact that the family is far from being a safe haven for many. Factors such as family instability and violence have been consistently found to be prevalent among juveniles who engage in sexually abusive and violent behavior (Righthand & Welch, 2001).

Many studies conclude that abused children have trouble recognizing appropriate emotions in others, have less empathy for others, and have difficulty taking another person's perspective (Knight & Prentky, 1993). It is very likely that many of the LCP offenders discussed elsewhere in the text spring from families characterized by abuse, violence, and neglect.

 ## KEY CONCEPTS

Availability heuristic	Criminal homicide
Murder	Nonnegligent manslaughter
Negligent manslaughter	Assault
Aggravated assault	Weapons effect
Munchausen syndrome-by-proxy	Shaken baby syndrome
Infanticide	Neonaticide
Filicide	Intimate partner violence
Battered woman syndrome	Eldercide
Siblicide	Patricide
Matricide	Fraticide
Sororicide	Parricide
Multiassaultive family	Cycle-of-violence hypothesis
Coercion theory	

 ## REVIEW QUESTIONS

1. Briefly describe any four factors that are associated with homicide.
2. What is the availability heuristic? How might it account for our perception of violence?
3. What are the psychological effects of (a) child abuse and (b) other domestic violence on children?
4. Define "battered woman syndrome" and briefly state the controversy associated with it.
5. Define each of the following: neonaticide, infanticide, filicide, eldercide, homicide.
6. Define "weapons effect" and how it might contribute to violence in our society.
7. Define the cycle-of-violence hypothesis.
8. Explain how juvenile homicide is different from adult homicide.
10. Compare and contrast shaken baby syndrome and Munchausen syndrome-by-proxy as specific forms of child abuse.
10. Discuss eldercide as a form of family violence, including its prevalence, perpetrators, and etiology.

CHAPTER 10

MULTIPLE MURDER

CHAPTER OBJECTIVES

- Define and review research on investigative psychology and profiling.
- Evaluate the validity of various types of profiling, including psychological autopsies.
- Summarize what is known about serial killers and their victims.
- Summarize what is known about mass murderers and their victims.
- Discuss crime that can lead to multiple murder, including product tampering and school and workplace violence.
- Review the research on workplace violence and its potential causes.

This chapter takes a more detailed look at criminal homicide, including several psychology-related investigative methods commonly used to identify offenders. We will revisit criminal homicide, but focus more on serial murder, mass murder, product-tampering homicide, and the violence at schools and the workplace that ends in death. Terrorism, which often involves multiple killings, will be covered in some detail in the next chapter. Although the homicides covered in this chapter are relatively rare, the social and emotional impact they have on a community—and on a society as a whole—is considerable. The fear and terror they engender can alter the lifestyles of thousands. Moreover, they draw extensive media coverage; some of it is accurate, but much of it lacks a solid understanding of the psychosocial aspects involved in the crime. Therefore, it is important that we give some attention to what we know—and do not know—about these well-publicized offenses. Finally, we end the chapter by discussing some of the current psychological theories and research that try to explain contemporary violence.

INVESTIGATIVE PSYCHOLOGY

Before discussing the various categories of multiple murder, it is important that we consider contemporary research on psychology's efforts to shed some light on this phenomenon. In recent years, considerable public attention has been given to topics like profiling and investigative psychology. Readers are undoubtedly familiar with popular movies and television shows (e.g., *Silence of the Lambs, Criminal Minds*) that feature these activities. Although the various types of profiling are not restricted to the serious crimes that are the subject of this chapter, they often focus on those serious, and sometimes sensational, crimes.

Investigative psychology, a term coined by David Canter, the director of the Centre for Investigative Psychology at the University of Liverpool in England, refers to the application of psychological research and principles to the investigation of criminal behavior. Investigative psychology tries to answer three fundamental questions that are crucial in criminal investigations (Canter & Alison, 2000, p. 3):

1. What are the important behavioral features of the crime that may help identify and successfully prosecute the perpetrator?
2. What inferences can be made about the characteristics of the offender that may help identify him or her?
3. Are there any other crimes that are likely to have been committed by the same person?

Although these questions are central to the investigative psychology—as well as to the profiling—which is discussed shortly, to what extent are investigative methods able to answer these questions accurately and on a regular basis? Let's examine the research evidence.

Crime Scene Investigative Methods

According to John Douglas and Corinne Munn (1992a), three important features of offender behavior may be evident at the scene of a crime: (1) the modus operandi, (2) the personation or signature, and (3) staging. **Modus operandi** (the **MO**) refers to the actions and procedures an offender engages in to commit a crime successfully. It is a behavioral pattern that the offender learns as he or she gains experience in committing the offense. Since the offender generally changes the MO until he or she learns which method is most effective, investigators may make a serious error if they place too much significance on the MO when linking crimes, however (Douglas & Munn, 1992c).

Anything that goes beyond what is necessary to commit the crime is called the **personation** or the **signature.** For example, a serial offender may demonstrate a repetitive, almost ritualistic behavior from crime to crime, an unusual pattern that is not necessary to commit the offense. The signature may involve certain items that are left or removed from the scene, or other symbolic patterns, such as writings on the wall. If the victim is murdered, the signature may include unusual body positions or mutilations. In very rare instances, the signature may involve a "DNA torch," where the offender pours gasoline over the genital areas of the victim and sets the victim and the structure or motor vehicle on fire in an effort to destroy any evidence of sexual assault. A signature may also involve the repetitive acts of domination, manipulation, and control used by a serial rapist (Douglas & Munn, 1992b). The signature is often thought to be related to the unique cognitive processes of the offender and, in this sense, may be more important to an investigator than the MO.

Staging refers to the intentional alteration of a crime scene prior to the arrival of the police, and it is sometimes done by someone other than the perpetrator. As Douglas and Munn (1992a) note, staging is usually done for one of two reasons: either to redirect the investigation away from the most logical suspect, or to protect the victim or the victim's family. Staging is frequently done by someone who has an association or relationship with the victim. For example, staging done by the family with the intent to protect the victim may be seen in autoerotic fatalities. **Autoeroticism,** a term coined by Havelock Ellis, refers to self-arousal and self-gratification of sexual desire without a partner. Holmes and Holmes identify four types of autoeroticism besides simple masturbation. The most common appears to be autoerotic hanging. The second type is aquaeroticism, the third is chemical eroticism, and the fourth type is self-suffocation. Aquaeroticism refers to the use of water to induce near-drowning experiences for sexual enhancement. Chemical eroticism refers to the practice of using chemical substances (such as Freon) to induce states of erotic asphyxiation. Self-suffocation refers to the behavioral pattern where the person will "deliberately attempt to suffocate to the point of almost losing consciousness" (Holmes & Holmes, 2002, p. 176). All four types are based on a deficiency of oxygen that presumably enhances sexual stimulation, and they are usually accompanied by masturbation. Ronald Holmes (1991) notes that there is even a national organization for erotic asphyxiates called the Olenspiegel Society.

In some instances, the method of autoeroticism may result in the death of the victim, such as self-strangulation or hanging. Douglas and Munn (1992a) assert that in about one-third of autoerotic fatalities the victim is nude, and in about another one-third the victim is clothed in a costume, such as a male in female clothing. Under these conditions, friends or family members may alter the scene to make the victim more "presentable" to the authorities. In some instances, they may even stage a criminal homicide.

In some instances, an offender may engage in **undoing,** a behavioral pattern found at the scene in which the offender tries to psychologically "undo" the murder. For example, the offender may wash and dress the victim, or place the body on a bed, gently placing the head on a pillow and covering the body with blankets. This pattern typically occurs in offenders who become especially distraught about the death of the victim. Very often, the offender has a close association with the victim. In other cases, an offender may try to dehumanize the victim by engaging in actions that obscure the identity of the victim, such as excessive facial battery. Other offenders may employ more subtle acts of dehumanization, such as covering the victim's face with some material or object, or placing the victim facedown. Note that the difference between undoing and staging is the reason behind the action; in staging, the offender or someone else is trying to alter the crime scene in order to divert suspicion. In the classic case, the offender wipes fingerprints from a weapon and positions it close to the body in such a way that a death looks like a suicide.

Crime scenes and offenders are also classified as organized, disorganized, or mixed (see **Tables 10–1** and **10–2**). An **organized crime scene** indicates planning and premeditation on the part of the offender. The crime scene shows signs that the offender maintained control of himself and the victim. Often, the victim is moved from the abduction area to another secluded area, and perhaps the body is moved to still another area. Furthermore, the offender in an organized crime usually selects his victims according to some personal criteria. The infamous serial killer Ted Bundy, for example, selected young, attractive women who were similar in appearance. He was also successful in the abduction of these young women from highly visible areas, such as beaches, campuses, and ski lodges, indicating considerable planning and premeditation (Douglas, Ressler, Burgess, & Hartman, 1986).

TABLE 10–1   Profile Characteristics of Organized and Disorganized Murderers as Classified by the FBI

ORGANIZED	DISORGANIZED
Average to above-average intelligence	Below average intelligence
Socially competent	Socially inadequate
Skilled work preferred	Unskilled work
High birth order status	Low birth order status
Father's work stable	Father's work unstable
Sexually competent	Sexually incompetent
Inconsistent childhood discipline	Harsh discipline as a child
Controlled mood during crime	Anxious mood during crime
Use of alcohol with crime	Minimal use of alcohol
Precipitating situational stress	Minimal situational stress
Living with partner	Living alone
Mobility (car in good condition)	Lives/works near crime scene
Follows crime in news media	Minimal interest in news media
May change job or leave town	Significant behavior change

Source: Federal Bureau of Investigation, 1985, p. 19.

TABLE 10–2   Crime Scene Differences between Organized and Disorganized Murderers
as Classified by the FBI

ORGANIZED	DISORGANIZED
Planned offense	Spontaneous offense
Victim a targeted stranger	Victim/location known
Personalizes victim	Depersonalizes victim
Controlled conversation	Minimal conversation
Crime scene reflects control	Crime scene random and sloppy
Demands submissive victim	Sudden violence to victim
Restraints used	Minimal use of restraints
Aggressive acts prior to death	Sexual acts after death
Body hidden	Body left in view
Weapon/evidence absent	Weapon/evidence often present
Transports victim or body	Body left at death scene

Source: Federal Bureau of Investigation, 1985, p. 19.

A **disorganized crime scene** demonstrates that the offender very probably committed the crime without premeditation or planning. The crime scene indicators suggest the individual acted on impulse or in rage, or under extreme excitement. The disorganized offender obtains his victim by chance, often without specific criteria in mind. For example, Herbert Mullin of Santa Cruz, California, killed 14 people of varying types (e.g., an elderly man, a young girl, and a priest) over a four-month period (Douglas, Ressler, Burgess, & Hartman, 1986). Generally, the victim's body is found at the scene of the crime. The **mixed crime scene** has ingredients of both organized and disorganized crime aspects. For example, a crime may have begun as carefully planned, but deteriorated into a disorganized crime when things did not go as planned.

Although the organized-disorganized classification system seems intuitively logical, it appears to have limited usefulness (Kocsis, Cooksey, & Irwin, 2002). It is probably more realistic to assume that crime scenes fall along a continuum, with the organized description at one pole and the disorganized description at the other pole (Bartol & Bartol, 2004b).

PROFILING

The term "profiling" is used to describe the gathering of various kinds of information about a person or persons. For clarity of presentation, we divide the term into five somewhat overlapping categories: (1) psychological profiling, (2) criminal profiling; (3) geographical profiling; (4) equivocal death analysis; and (5) racial profiling. For our purposes, **psychological profiling** will be reserved for the psychological description of a person or persons *in general,* criminal or noncriminal. It was first used by the Office of Strategic Services (OSS) during World War II, primarily to profile enemy leaders and their proclivities (Ault & Reese, 1980). It included their preferred strategies and ways of thinking. After the war, profiling was largely shelved until the FBI started using it again during the early 1970s. Essentially, psychological profiling has its basic scientific roots in psychological testing or psychometrics.

It is important to note that psychological profiling is not necessarily designed to describe criminal tendencies, but refers to a broad behavioral realm of tendencies, foibles, faults, likes and dislikes, interests, strengths, and so on. Football coaches, business leaders, political leaders, attorneys, and other professionals often prefer to have some idea or psychological sketch about the psychological characteristics of their opponents or adversaries. Consequently, we will not discuss the general category of psychological profiling to any great extent in this text but will focus on those methods that are directly related to crime.

Criminal profiling is the process of identifying personality traits, behavioral patterns, geographic habits, and demographic features of an offender based on characteristics of the crime. It can be considered a skill or an activity that is a part of the investigative psychology described earlier. Therefore, while investigative psychology is the broad application of psychological research and principles to solving crimes, profiling is the narrower activity that focuses on the traits, features, and habits of the offender. Some researchers (e.g., Knight, Warren, Reboussin, & Soley, 1998) have introduced the term "crime scene analysis," or the more technical term "criminal investigative analysis," to describe the practice of developing offender descriptions based on the analysis of the crime scene. However, we prefer to use the more straightforward label "criminal profiling."

Geographical profiling is a method of identifying the area of probable residence or the probable area of the next crime of an unknown offender based on the location of and the spatial relationships among various crime sites (Guerette, 2002). Geographical profiling, therefore, can help in any criminal investigation of an unknown offender by locating the approximate area in which he or she lives, or by narrowing the surveillance and stakeouts to places where the next crime by the offender is most likely to occur. This type of profiling basically tries to identify the geographical territory the offender knows well, feels most comfortable in, and prefers to find or take victims in (Rossmo, 1997). Although a *criminal* profile hypothesizes about the demographic, motivational, and psychological features of the crime and offender, a geographic profile focuses on the location of the crime and how it relates to the residence and/or base of operations of the offender. Geographical profiling is useful not only in the search for serial violent offenders but also in the search for property offenders, such as serial burglars.

Equivocal death analysis, also called **reconstructive psychological evaluation,** is the reconstruction of the emotional life, behavioral patterns, and cognitive features of a deceased person. In this sense, it is a postmortem psychological analysis and therefore is frequently referred to simply as a **psychological autopsy** (Brent, 1989; Ebert, 1987; Selkin, 1987). Most often, equivocal death analysis or the psychological autopsy is done to determine whether the death was a suicide, and if it was a suicide, the reasons why the person did it.

The psychological autopsy differs from criminal profiling in two important ways: (1) The profile is constructed on a dead person, and (2) the identity of the person is already known. **Racial profiling** is defined as "police-initiated action that relies on the race, ethnicity, or national origin rather than the behavior of an individual or information that leads the police to a particular individual who has been identified as being, or having been, engaged in criminal activity" (Ramirez, McDevitt, & Farrell, 2000, p. 3).

Because the last four forms of profiling are relevant to criminal behavior issues, we will now cover each in some detail in the remainder of this section.

Criminal Profiling

It is clear that descriptions or profiles of the general characteristics of a person on the basis of a limited amount of information were used long before the OSS or the FBI employed such methods (Canter & Alison, 2000). Criminal profiling can be traced back to Jack the Ripper, the serial killer who brutally murdered five prostitutes in separate incidents in London's East End in 1888. Although the case was never solved, the chief forensic pathologist, Dr. George Baxter Phillips, attempted to help police investigators by inferring personality characteristics based on the nature of the wounds inflicted on the victims (Turvey, 2002). That is, he noticed that the wounds were inflicted with considerable skill and knowledge, suggesting that the killer had a sophisticated knowledge of human anatomy. "In particular, he was referring to the postmortem removal of some of Annie Chapman's organs, and what he felt was the cleanliness and preciseness of the incisions involved" (Turvey, 2002, p. 10). Interestingly, the fictional detective Sherlock Holmes, first created by Sir Arthur Conan Doyle in 1887, consistently employed a form of criminal profiling in his intriguing search for the offender. Since then, virtually every detective or mystery novel has the main characters engaging in criminal profiling.

The FBI began using criminal profiling when it was introduced by special agent Howard Tegen in 1970 (Turvey, 2002). He taught the first criminal profiling course at the FBI National Academy, called Applied Criminology, and later constructed his first actual profile as an FBI agent in Amarillo, Texas (Turvey, 2002). In 1972, the new FBI Academy was opened and Special Agent Jack Kirsch developed the FBI's Behavioral Science Unit. The Unit was a major contributor to criminal profiling during the 1970s and 1980s. Currently, the Unit operates under the direction of the National Center for the Analysis of Violent Crime (NCAVC) at the FBI Academy in Quantico, Virginia.

Criminal profiling "is best viewed as a strategy enabling law enforcement to narrow the field of options and generate educated guesses about the perpetrator" (Douglas, Burgess, Burgess, & Ressler, 1992, p. 21). Other researchers write that a criminal profile "focuses attention on individuals with personality traits that parallel traits of others who have committed similar offenses" (Pinizzotto & Finkel, 1990, p. 215). In short, criminal profiling is an attempt to identify demographic variables, geographical location, and behavioral patterns of an offender based on characteristics of previous offenders who have committed similar offenses.

Pinizzotto and Finkel (1990) conclude from their research that criminal profiling requires a complex number of tasks that involve a "multilevel series of attributions, correlations, and predictions" (p. 230). Much profiling is guesswork based on hunches and anecdotal information accumulated through years of experience, and it is full of error and misinterpretation. Currently, profiling is probably at least 90 percent an art and speculation and only 10 percent science, probably in its most sophisticated form. Professional profilers continually provide predictions of some demographic variables (e.g., white male, age 25 to 35), but rarely do they provide accurate information on psychological variables of the offender. Furthermore, very rarely does profiling provide the specific identity of the offender, nor is it intended to. Criminal profiling basically tries to narrow the field of investigation to a manageable number of potential suspects (Douglas, Ressler, Burgess, & Hartman, 1986). Broadly, criminal profiling suggests the kind of person who might have committed the crime under investigation, but it is highly unlikely to pinpoint an individual's exact identity.

A profile report normally includes the gender, age, marital status, education level, and some broad identification of the occupation of the offender. There is also some prediction or estimation as to whether the offender will strike again, whether he or she likely has a police record, and what types of victims are at risk. In some instances, the profiler will try to identify possible motivational factors for the crime as well as the offender's personality traits.

Experienced profilers assert that profiling of *serial* offenders is most successful when the offender demonstrates some form of psychopathology at the crime scene, such as sadistic torture, evisceration, postmortem slashings and cuttings, and other mutilations (Pinizzotto, 1984). The reasoning behind this conclusion is that such individuals are likely mentally disordered, and mentally disordered individuals show consistency in behavior from situation to situation. Whether mentally disordered persons truly are more consistent in their behavioral patterns than those who are not mentally disordered remains an open question, however. It is likely that some are, and some are not.

Profiling appears to be particularly useful in serial sexual offenses, such as serial rape and serial sexual homicides (Pinizzotto & Finkel, 1990). This is because we have a more extensive research base on sexual offending than we do on homicide. Furthermore, profiling is largely ineffective at this time in the identification of offenders involved in fraud, burglary, robbery, political crimes, theft, and drug-induced crime because of the limited research base, although significant gains in these areas have been made in recent years.

Computer-based models of offender profiles developed from extensive statistical data collected on similar offenses hold considerable promise. To date, however, there is very little research on the utility, reliability, and validity of criminal profiling in general. And the FBI agrees with this assessment. "At present, there have been no systematic efforts to validate these profile-derived classifications" (Douglas et al., 1992, p. 22). There has been very little published research on the utility, reliability, and validity of criminal profiling in general (Alison, Smith, & Morgan, 2003; Woodworth & Porter, 2001).

Pinizzotto and Finkel (1990) did try to assess the accuracy of profiling in a study involving four trained FBI experts, six trained police detectives, six experienced detectives without training, six clinical psychologists naive about criminal profiling, and six untrained undergraduate students. The results, in general, were not strongly supportive of profile accuracy. Trained experts were somewhat more accurate in profiling the sexual offender, but were not much better than the untrained groups in profiling the homicide offender. The researchers also tried to identify any qualitative differences in the way experts and nonexperts processed the information provided. Overall, the results showed that experts did not process the material any differently than the nonexperts. This finding suggests that the cognitive methods and strategies used by expert profilers are not discernibly different from the way nonexperts process the available information about the crime. The artificiality of the experiment and the quality of information given the groups may have been influential factors in this observation, however. What the researchers did find is that some trained profilers were more interested and skillful in certain areas than other profilers. Some profilers, for example, were good at gaining information from the medical reports, whereas others were better at gaining clues from the crime scene photos. This finding indicates that group profiling by a team of trained experts may be more effective than utilizing one single profiler. Canter and Alison (2000) also assert that it is a misconception that there are some special sets of skills and knowledge for profiling available only to those who have worked with criminals or those who have considerable experience in police investigations. Researchers and thoughtful practitioners can also make significant advances and discoveries in criminal profiling.

In recent years, criminal profiling has caught the attention of the general public through popular films (e.g., *Silence of the Lambs*), and extensively watched TV series (e.g., *CSI: Crime Scene Investigation, CSI: Miami, Crossing Jordan, Criminal Minds, Autopsy*). However, despite the media portrayals of highly successful and probing profilers employing sophisticated techniques and thoughtful strategies for identifying the offender, reality is far more sobering. Contemporary researchers on profiling (Alison, Bennell, Omerod, & Mokros, 2002; Alison & Canter, 1999) point out that there are two basic flaws in modern-day profiling. One flaw is the assumption that human behavior is consistent across a variety of different situations. The other flaw is the assumption that offense style or evidence gathered at the crime scene is directly related to specific personality characteristics. Psychology has consistently found that behavior varies according to situations or the social context, especially if the social contexts are significantly different. Moreover, there is little empirical data that link crime scene characteristics to personality or other psychological features of the offender.

The above points underscore the fact that many professional profilers are prone to rely on outdated personality theory and psychological principles, and are basically unfamiliar with the current research literature on profiling and human behavior in general. Some believe that profiling is best done on "gut feelings" and "instinct" based on many years of experience of crime scene investigations. However, the potential usefulness of criminal profiling is too critical to be relegated to the entertainment media and questionable applications by law enforcement. It is important, therefore, that we learn how reliable and valid the various profiling methods currently utilized are, and how they can be improved to allow meaningful application in forensic settings.

In summary, much serious research needs to be done on profiling accuracy, usefulness, and processing before any tentative conclusions can be advanced in the area. Raymond Knight and his colleagues (Knight, Warren, Reboussin, & Soley, 1998) have made a solid step in that direction by conducting an empirical study based on crime scene information across a wide variety of incidents. Contrary to popular perceptions, criminal profiling is not and should not be restricted to serial murder and serial sexual assaults. It has considerable potential value when applied competently to crimes such as arson, burglary, shoplifting, and robbery. However, because the research is still in its infancy, the effectiveness of profiling to these areas has yet to be demonstrated.

Geographical Profiling

In 1995, D. Kim Rossmo completed a doctoral dissertation on the method of geographical profiling that has emerged as a promising tool for serial offender identification. He also developed a computer program called "Criminal Geographic Targeting," or CGT, which is designed to analyze the geographical or spatial characteristics of an offender's crimes. The CGT generates a three-dimensional map that assigns statistical probabilities to various areas that seem to fall into the offender's territory. The three-dimensional map is then placed over a street or topographical map where the crimes have occurred. The program considers known movement patterns, possible comfort zones, and victim searching patterns of the offender. Ultimately, the objective of the program is to pinpoint the location of the offender's residence and/or base of operations.

Rossmo identifies four hunting patterns serial offenders use in their search for victims: (1) hunter, (2) poacher, (3) troller, and (4) trapper. Rossmo (1997) writes, "Hunters are those criminals who specifically set out from their residence to look for victims, searching through the areas in their awareness space that they believe contain suitable targets" (p. 167). The hunters are geographically stable in that their crimes usually occur near the offender's residence or neighborhood. Poachers are more transient, traveling some distance from their neighborhood in their search for suitable victims. The troller, on the other hand, does not specifically search for victims but depends on random encounters during the course of other activities. The trapper creates situations (traps) to entice victims to come to him.

Although geographical profiling was originally designed to help investigations of murder, rape, and arson, it is now being used for serial bombings, bank robbery, and child abductions (Guerette, 2002). Geographical profiling still has a way to go before it establishes its predictive validity across a variety of serial offenses. Most of the available research has been conducted by Rossmo himself. To his credit, however, Rossmo warns that the method is essentially an investigative tool that does not necessarily solve crimes, but should help in identifying appropriate areas for surveillance, patrol saturation, stakeouts, and monitoring.

The Psychological Autopsy

The psychological autopsy was first used to help medical officials determine the cause of deaths that were classified as ambiguous, uncertain, or equivocal (Shneidman, 1994). Today, the psychological autopsy is usually done to determine what may have been in the mind of the deceased person leading up to and at the time of death—particularly if the death appears to be a suicide (La Fon, 2002).

La Fon (2002) notes that there are two basic types of psychological autopsies used in modern practice: (1) suicide psychological autopsy (SPA) and (2) equivocal death psychological autopsy (EDPA). The objective of the SPA is to identify and understand the psychosocial factors that contributed to the suicide. The purpose of the EPDA, on the other hand, is to determine the *reasons* (i.e., suicide or otherwise) for the death. In most cases, the EPDA is done for insurance claim purposes. Although some insurance policies compensate beneficiaries if death is determined to be the result of a suicide, many policies do not. In that case, it is important for life insurance companies to have a ruling on the *manner* of death before payment claims are honored.

The reliability and validity of the psychological autopsy, however, has yet to be demonstrated and remains open to debate (Poythress, Otto, Darkes, & Starr, 1993). Poythress et al. write, "persons who conduct reconstructive psychological evaluations should not assert categorical conclusions about the precise mental state or actions suspected of the actor at the time of his or her demise. The conclusions and inferences drawn in psychological reconstructions are, at best, informed speculations or theoretical formulations and should be labeled as such" (1993, p. 12). Selkin (1994) further notes that clear, definitive procedures for carrying out the psychological autopsy have yet to be developed and that investigators still have a long way to go before standardized methods for conducting the psychological autopsy are established.

Racial Profiling

In the late 1990s, racial profiling became a serious and troubling issue for the country. **Racial profiling** is defined as "police-initiated action that relies on the race, ethnicity, or national origin rather than the behavior of an individual or information that leads the police to a particular individual who has been identified as being, or having been, engaged in criminal activity" (Ramirez,

McDevitt, & Farrell, 2000). Apparent incidents of racial profiling were experienced so commonly by people of color that they began to label the phenomenon "driving while black" or "driving while brown" (commonly abbreviated DWB), as a play on the legally accepted term DWI (driving while intoxicated or impaired). A Gallup Poll released in 1999 revealed that 72 percent of black men between the ages of 18 and 34 who had been stopped by police believed that police stopped them because of their race. Research supports this belief, as we will see below. By contrast, only 6 percent of white men believed their race played a role in being pulled over by the police. More specifically, members of communities of color say they are being stopped for minor traffic violations, such as underinflated tires, failure to signal properly before switching lanes, vehicle equipment failure, or speeding less than 10 miles above the speed limit. Another common complaint is that police often stop people of color traveling through predominately white neighborhoods because the officers believe that people of color do not belong in the area and consequently suspect them of engaging in criminal activity.

A large segment of racial profiling is based on beliefs by law enforcement that many minorities are involved in drug trafficking or carrying contraband, such as illegal weapons. However, the available data suggest that this assumption is unjustified. One of the first cases involving the empirical evidence of racial profiling in a court hearing was *Wilkins v. Maryland State Police* (cited in Harris, 1999). *Wilkins* was a class-action lawsuit against the Maryland State Police (MSP) on behalf of Robert L. Wilkins, an African American attorney who was stopped, detained, and searched by the MSP for no apparent reason (Harris, 1999). With the assistance of Dr. John Lambert, a psychology professor at Temple University, the American Civil Liberties Union (ACLU) conducted a survey on traffic violations on Maryland highway I-95. The survey revealed that 74.7 percent of the 5,354 speeders stopped by the MSP were white and 17.5% were African American. However, "between January 1995 and September 1996, the Maryland State Police reported searching 823 motorists on I-95, north of Baltimore. Of these, 600, or 72.9% were black. Six hundred and sixty-one, or 80.3%, were black, Hispanic, or other racial minorities. Only 19.7% of those searched in this corridor were white" (Harris, 1999, p. 23). Based on his analysis of these data, Lambert concluded the following:

> The evidence examined in this study reveals dramatic and highly statistically significant disparities between the percentage of black Interstate 95 motorists legitimately subject to stop by Maryland State Police and the percentage of black motorists detained and searched by MSP troopers on this roadway. While no one can know the motivations of each individual trooper in conducting a traffic stop, the statistics presented herein, representing a broad and detailed sample of highly appropriate data, show without question a racially discriminatory impact on blacks and other minority motorists from state police behavior along I-95. (Harris, 1999, p. 24)

The "war on drugs" during the 1970s and 1980s appears to be the major impetus for developing the "drug courier profile." In 1985, when the war on drugs was intensifying, the Florida Department of Highway Safety and Motor Vehicles issued guidelines for law enforcement on how to identify drug couriers. The guidelines encouraged officers to be suspicious of rental cars, drivers who are scrupulously obeying traffic laws, drivers wearing lots of gold, drivers whose status does not "fit" the vehicle, and drivers who represent *"ethnic groups associated with the drug trade."* The unsubstantiated conclusion of various agencies at that time was that African Americans and Latinos were the principal participants in the exploding drug trade business. In 1986, a racially biased drug courier profile was introduced by the Drug Enforcement Administration (DEA) to various law enforcement agencies across the nation. The profile was used extensively in their training methods for officers in "Operation Pipeline" (Harris, 1999). In 1999, a preliminary survey by the San Diego Police Department found that Latino and African American drivers were far more likely to be stopped and searched than other drivers (Dvorak, 2000). Several studies in New Jersey and New York report similar results (Ramirez, McDevitt, & Farrell, 2000). In recent years, lawsuits alleging racial profiling by law enforcement agencies have been brought on behalf of minority motorists in Pennsylvania, Florida, Illinois, and Maryland. In 1996, a New Jersey Superior Court judge threw out 19 drug possession cases, concluding that state troopers patrolling the New Jersey Turnpike had improperly singled out and stopped black motorists. Over a dozen states have passed laws against racial profiling, many of them requiring antibias training and the gathering of statistics on every driver who is stopped (Lewin, 2001), and many states are considering similar laws (Dvorak, 2000). The catastrophic events of September 11, 2001, have led to new forms of racial profiling, as well as ethnic and religious profiling.

International data indicate that racial profiling is not restricted to the United States. A 1998 study by the British Government's Home Office investigated the racial and ethnic demographics of the stop-and-search patterns of police agencies in England and Wales. The study found that blacks were 7.5 times more likely to be stopped and searched, and four times more likely to be arrested than whites (Ramirez, McDevitt, & Farrell, 2000). According to 1999 census data, Britain is 93 percent white and 7 percent ethnic minority.

In conclusion, empirical research, anecdotal evidence, and survey data confirm the existence of racial and ethnic profiling as a social problem. It occurs despite the fact that there is no evidence to support a valid profile based strictly on race or ethnicity. Even if there were—and again, there is not—a profile model that revolves around these factors as critical components violates or infringes on civil rights. With the above backdrop, we now turn to specific offenses that are often the focus of the profiling and investigative efforts described.

MULTIPLE MURDERERS

One of the most frightening and perhaps incomprehensible types of homicide is the random killing of groups of people, either in one episode or individually over a period of time. Although multiple murders are still rare occurrences, when they do happen they cannot escape attention, and they remain etched in the public consciousness. The slaughter of 21 patrons at a McDonald's restaurant in San Ysidro, California, in July 1984, by James Oliver Huberty is a case in point. Another is the mass murder of 22 patrons at Luby's Cafeteria in Killeen, Texas, on October 16, 1991. Many people still recall the planned, separate murders of 33 young men and boys whose bodies were found in the cellar of the suburban Chicago home of John Wayne Gacy during the late 1970s. During the early 1990s, Jeffrey Dahmer lured at least 17 boys and young men into his home in Milwaukee, where he drugged, killed, and dismembered them. The public was shocked to learn the details of how Dahmer ate the victims' flesh and had sex with the corpses. Other notorious multiple murderers include David Berkowitz, known as the infamous Son of Sam; Kenneth Bianci, the Hillside Strangler; Albert DeSalvo, the Boston Strangler; the Green River Killer, Gary Ridgeway; the nursing-care killer, Donald Harvey; and Theodore Bundy.

In England, we have had Jack the Ripper in earlier times, and, more recently, Peter Sutcliffe, the Yorkshire Ripper who killed 13 women in the red-light districts of Northern England. Dennis Nilsen became England's first serial killer to prey on homosexuals, committing at least 15 known murders (Jenkins, 1988).

Definitions

Serial murder is usually reserved for incidents in which an individual (or individuals) kills a number of individuals (usually a minimum of three) over time. The time interval—sometimes referred to as the cooling-off period—may be days or weeks, but more likely months or years. The cooling-off period is the main difference between serial murders and other multiple murders (Douglas, Ressler, Burgess, & Hartman, 1986). The murders are premeditated and planned, and the offender usually selects specific victims. **Spree murder** normally refers to the killing of three or more individuals without any cooling-off period, usually at two or more locations. A bank robber who kills some individuals within the bank, flees with hostages, and kills a number of people while in flight during a statewide chase would be an example of a spree murderer. **Mass murder** involves killing three or more persons at a single location with no cooling-off period between murders.

The FBI identifies two types of mass murder: classic and family (Douglas et al., 1986). An example of a **classic mass murder** is when an individual barricades himself or herself inside a public building, such as a fast-food restaurant, randomly killing the patrons and any other individual he or she has contact with. The shootings of patrons at the McDonald's restaurant and Luby's cafeteria, mentioned earlier, are examples. Another example is Sylvia Seegrist (nicknamed "Ms. Rambo" because of her military-style clothing), who began shooting people at a Pennsylvania mall in October 1985, killing three and wounding seven (Douglas et al., 1986). A **family mass murder** is when at least three family members are killed (usually by another family member). Very often, the perpetrator kills himself or herself, an incident that is classified as a mass murder/suicide.

SERIAL MURDERERS

Serial murders *seem* to be on the increase in the United States and England. In the United States during the 1950s and 1960s, there were only two cases of an individual killing 10 or more victims over a period of time. Since 1970, however, there have been at least 40 known individuals who qualify as serial murderers (Jenkins, 1988). The U.S. Department of Justice estimated that there were about 35 serial murderers active at any given point in the United States during the 1970s and 1980s (Jenkins, 1988). Realistically, though, there are no accurate data on the prevalence and number of serial murderers active at any one time in the United States or internationally (Brantley & Kosky, 2005). In addition, it remains debatable whether serial murders are on the increase or whether the dramatic improvement in communication and computer networks among law enforcement agencies and the news media may account—at least in part—for the statistical increments in the crime. Prior to 1970, information exchange between agencies was difficult and primitive by today's standards. Therefore, serial murderers who moved from one geographic location to another (which they commonly do) probably went undetected.

Jenkins (1988) noted that victims of serial murderers tend to be young women, especially active prostitutes. Today, the primary victims of serial killers tend to be children of both sexes (ages 8 to 16). In response to the increase in child victims, then FBI Director Louis Freeh created a specialized unit to focus on investigation of child abduction and murder. The unit is called the "Child Abduction and Serial Killer Unit." In addition, the Missing and Exploited Children's Task Force (MECTF) was created by Congress in the 1994 Omnibus Crime Bill to assist in investigating the most difficult cases of missing and exploited children. Both the Child Abduction and Serial Killer Unit and the MECTF work closely with the National Center for Missing and Exploited Children. In 1987, the Office of Juvenile Justice and Delinquency Prevention (OJJDP) conducted six studies in an effort to determine the incidence of abducted children by non-family members. This research was discussed in chapter 9.

In his study of serial killers in England, Jenkins (1988) found that—unlike the typical violent individual who demonstrates a propensity for violence at an early age—serial murderers generally begin their careers of repetitive homicide at a relatively late age. He concluded that most started their careers between the ages of 24 and 40. Interestingly, the median age of arrested serial murderers in Jenkins's sample was 36. Arrests typically occurred about four years after they began killing. While the serial murderers had extensive police records, the records reflected a series of petty theft, embezzlement, and forgery, rather than a history of violence (Jenkins, 1988). Surprisingly, they also did not have extensive juvenile records. Jenkins concluded that the English cases did not provide any early indicators or predictors of eventual murderous behavior. When British serial murderers committed their first murder, about half were married, had a stable family life, and had usually lived in the same house for many years. A majority had stable jobs, and, disconcertingly, a good number had been former police officers or security guards.

Holmes and DeBurger (1988) have analyzed the characteristics of serial killers in the United States. In general, the patterns and characteristics of the British sample correspond closely to the American. However, while the British serial murderers generally stayed in the same neighborhood, many of their American counterparts preferred to move around the country, committing murders in a number of states and jurisdictions. Holmes and DeBurger also noted that serial murder predominately involves white males killing white females. There are exceptions, of course. Jeffrey Dahmer, a 31-year-old white male, killed at least nine African American males in 1991, and apparently killed many more over a 10-year period. Victims, both in the British and American samples, tended to be strangers or individuals whom the killer met only briefly before, a pattern that makes it particularly difficult for law enforcement agencies to identify the assailant. Moreover, the motive for the killing is usually aberrant and extremely difficult for those who seek the murderer's arrest to understand.

Serial murderers kill about four people per year, an average that seems to be characteristic of both British and American offenders. However, the evidence does not support any notion that they kill on the basis of some compulsion or irresistible urge. Rather, the murder appears to be more a result of opportunity and the random availability of a suitable victim.

It is a mistake, therefore, to assume that serial murderers are seriously mentally disordered according to traditional clinical standards. Some are, but most are not. Although their cognitive processing and values may be considered extremely aberrant when it comes to sensitivity and concern for other human beings, a vast majority of serial killers fail to qualify as seriously mentally disordered in the traditional diagnostic categories of mental disorders discussed in chapters 7 and 8. Serial killers have developed versions of the world that facilitate repetitive murder, often in a brutal, demeaning, and cold-blooded manner. They are especially drawn to committing murders that attract media interest, send spine-chilling fear into the community, and are incomprehensible to the public. The motives of many serial killers appear to be based on psychological rewards of control, domination, media attention, and personal excitement rather than identifiable material gain. Their actions are predictably planned, organized, and purposeful.

Female Serial Killers

Although relatively rare, there have been at least three dozen female serial murderers in U.S. history. Hickey (1991) identified 34 documented female serial murderers, with 82 percent of them acting after 1900. Moreover, there are some discernible differences between female and male serial murderers. For example, only about one-third of the female offenders killed strangers, in contrast to males who almost exclusively killed strangers (Holmes, Hickey, & Holmes, 1991). Most victims of female serial killers are husbands, former husbands, or suitors. For example, Belle Gunness murdered an estimated 14 to 49 husbands or suitors in La Porte, Indiana (Holmes et al., 1991). Nannie Doss killed a combination of 11 husbands and family members in Tulsa, Oklahoma.

Traditionally, female serial killers murder primarily for material or monetary gain, such as insurance benefits, will allocations, trusts, and estates. Furthermore, the method of killing is through poisons (usually cyanide) or overdoses of pills. Approximately half of the female serial killers had a male accomplice. Some women murdered because of involvements in cults or with a male serial murderer. A good example of cult involvement is the female following of the Charles Manson family. An example of involvement with a male serial murderer is Charlene Gallego, the common-law wife of serial killer Gerald Gallego (Holmes et al., 1991). Charlene Gallego helped Gerald Gallego select, abduct, and murder at least 10 individuals.

Over the past two decades, several female health care workers who have killed patients have been identified, although males—including a physician—have also been identified. A female health worker may have been responsible for the deaths of 28 patients at two hospitals in the Hague, Netherlands. Her victims were either children or elderly patients, and her method of killing involved injections of various substances. She was arrested in December 2001 and was later convicted of four counts of first-degree murder and three counts of attempted murder.

The motivations of female health care workers serial killings are variable: recognition, attention, revenge, power, and control (Brantley & Kosky, 2005). Some of these health care workers admitted that the killers relieved tension, stress, and frustration (Linedecker & Burt, 1990). Some also maintained that they killed to put the patients out of their misery and that these were essentially mercy killings.

The Victimological Perspective in Understanding Serial Killers

Jenkins (1993) contends that the current popular image of the serial murderer—a white male who kills for sexual motives—may be an inaccurate one. He argues that lack of a **victimological perspective** encourages confusion and distorted information. He suggests that our current knowledge about serial murderers is strongly influenced by two factors: availability of the victims and the attitudes of law enforcement agencies toward those victims. Rather than strictly focusing on individual and personality attributes of the offender, he believes we should also examine the *social opportunity* to kill. In other words, what we know about serial murder may be strongly influenced by the nature and type of the potential victims.

To illustrate, Jenkins (1993) provides the case of Calvin Jackson, who was arrested in 1974 for murder committed in a New York apartment building. Actually, Jackson was a serial murderer, but none of his victims led the police to suspect a serial killer. Jackson's killings took place in a single-occupancy hotel where the guests were poor, socially isolated, largely forgotten, and mostly elderly. Time after time, the police were called to the hotel to deal with cases of death or injury due to alcohol, drugs, or old age. When foul play was suspected, the police never considered it the work of a serial murderer, because the victims did not fit the stereotypic profile. Since there was no evidence of grotesque sexual abuse of the victim (the victim stereotype), there was little reason for the police to entertain the possibility of a serial murderer. Other serial murderers may set up situations where murders resemble drug-related homicides. Therefore, our current knowledge of serial murderers may be restricted to a certain category of offender.

An examination of the victim selection of known serial murderers will reveal that killers prefer the group of people offering easy access, transience, and a tendency to disappear without seeming to cause much alarm or concern. Victims are often prostitutes, especially streetwalkers, street runaways, young male drifters, and itinerant farm workers. Young women in or near a university or college campus or the elderly and solitary poor appear to be the groups next preferred. The strongest determining factor in victim selection for both groups seems to be easy availability of potential victims. Rarely do known serial murderers break in and kill middle-class strangers in their homes, for example, despite media portrayals. It should be pointed out, however, that although serial killers begin their murderous careers by selecting highly vulnerable victims, they may, as their killings continue, gain substantially more confidence in their ability to abduct more "challenging" victims. Fortunately, very few serial killers become this successful before they are arrested.

Jenkins (1993) further suggests that dramatic increases in serial murder are directly related to dramatic increases in potential victims, such as severe downturns in the economy or deinstitutionalization of mental patients that result in putting more vulnerable people on the streets.

Geographical Location of Serial Killing

Interestingly, 31 of the 52 known cases of serial murderers in the United States since 1971 have occurred in the western states, especially California (Jenkins, 1993). Only four have occurred in the northeastern states. The reason for this geographical distribution remains largely a mystery, although the answer probably lies in some combination of lifestyles, economic conditions, and the availability of potential victims.

Most serial killers have specific preferences for the location of their killings. They tend to select victims near their current residence or place of work. Hickey (1997) estimates that 14 percent of serial killers use their homes or workplaces as the preferred location, whereas another 52 percent commit their murders in the same general location or region, such as the same neighborhood or city. This tendency suggests that geographical profiling may be an invaluable aid in the identification of serial killers.

Perhaps an effective method for reducing serial murder is to identify and protect specific high-risk groups and regions and to take whatever social measures are needed to reduce their vulnerability. Focusing on the offender through criminal profiling and other investigative measures is usually of limited usefulness because most serial killers are apprehended by a mixture of fortuitous events and carelessness by the offender. In the meantime, community leaders and authorities should concentrate on reducing the availability of potential victims.

Ethnic and Racial Characteristics

The widespread belief that only whites are serial killers and blacks and other minorities never commit this type of crime is basically a myth (Walsh, 2005). Walsh found that approximately 21.8 percent of the serial killers in the United States have been black, and was able to document 90 black serial killers during the post–World War II era. Research on Latino and other minority serial killers is virtually nonexistent.

The number of victims black killers admitted killing does not differ significantly from white serial killers either. Jake Bird, for instance, was verified to have killed 44 victims, just 4 victims short of the white killer Gary Ridgeway's (the Green River Killer) record setting 48. And some are equally chilling. Walsh (2005) describes the methods of black serial killer Maury Travis when he writes, "Travis had a secret torture chamber in his basement, where police found bondage equipment, videotapes of his rape and torture sessions, and clippings relating to police investigations of his murder victims (mostly prostitutes and crack addicts). Travis hanged himself in jail after confessing to 17 murders" (p. 274).

We may have assumed that serial killings are perpetrated almost exclusively by whites because of how serial murder is identified and investigated. For example, law enforcement agencies may be less prone to investigate African American victims as casualties of serial murderers if they are found in a rundown apartment complex located in a poverty-stricken, crime-infested neighborhood. Under these circumstances, law enforcement officials are more likely to conclude that the victim is simply another fatality in the long stream of never-ending violence found in parts of inner cities. This point was made by Jenkins (1993) in the previous section.

Also, as Walsh (2005) has observed, the media tend to cover the sensational serial killings by whites but fail to cover in any detail those offenses committed by blacks and other minorities. "The extensive media coverage of Bundy, Gacy, and Berkowitz cases have made these killers almost household names, but African Americans such as Watts, Johnson, Francois, and Wallace are practically unknown, despite having operated within the same general time framework (1980s and 1990s)" (Walsh, 2005, p. 274). Similar disparity in media coverage of other crimes has occurred. In many communities it is not unusual to see extensive coverage of the disappearance or murder of a white child and very little attention given to a similar tragedy involving a black victim.

Juvenile Serial Murderers

Serial murder by children and adolescents is an exceedingly rare phenomenon, and scientific information is extremely sparse. According to Myers (2004), most serial murders by juveniles are prompted by sexual desires. The sexual element of the crime may be overt or symbolic. Myers (2002) studied 16 juveniles who committed a sexual homicide and noted some common characteristics. All 16 had a history of serious school problems, and a majority (94%) came from families who were considered dysfunctional and abusive. Eighty-eight percent of the families were evaluated as violent. Most of the offenders (88%) exhibited a history of serious interpersonal violence and criminal offenses, and displayed the behaviors typical of juvenile psychopaths.

Typologies of Serial Murderers

Efforts to classify any offenders into categories, or typologies, must be made with caution because many individuals do not fit neatly into these divisions. In addition, typologies based on behavior are problematic because behavior is not always consistent from situation to situation. Nevertheless, typologies can be useful in organizing an array of behavioral patterns that would otherwise be confusing—but they need to be subjected to empirical verification.

Holmes and DeBurger (1988) make a gallant attempt to classify serial murderers into a typology based on motive and have accumulated some research evidence in support. They identify four major types: (1) visionary, (2) mission-oriented, (3) hedonistic, and (4) power/control oriented. The *visionary type* is driven by voices or visions that demand that a particular group of people be destroyed, such as prostitutes, homosexuals, or derelicts. The visionary killer often operates on the basis of a "directive from God." In many instances, this type qualifies as psychotic or crazy, which is atypical because serial killers—as we learned—are not usually mentally disordered. He (or she) is probably the most difficult to understand for investigators and the public alike. The crime scene is usually chaotic and has an abundance of physical evidence, often including fingerprints and the murder weapon (Holmes & Holmes, 1998).

The *mission-oriented type* determines that there is a particular group of people who are undesirable and who must be destroyed or eliminated. The undesirables may be prostitutes, gays or lesbians, "street people," or members of a particular religious, racial, or minority group. This killer demonstrates no discernible mental disorder. He sees no visions, hears no voices, and functions on a day-to-day basis without exhibiting notable psychologically aberrant behavior.

The *hedonistic type* strives for pleasure and thrill seeking, and feels that people are objects to use for one's own enjoyment. Reportedly, the hedonistic killer gains considerable pleasure from the murder event itself. According to Holmes and Holmes (1998), hedonistic killers may be divided into three subtypes based on the primary motive for the murder: lust, thrill, or comfort. The lust killer's primary motive is sexual gratification. The thrill killer is primarily motivated to induce pain or a terrified reaction from the victim. The pain and terror created, in combination with the process of murder itself, are highly stimulating and exciting for the killer. The primary motive for the comfort killer is to acquire activities (business or financial interests) or objects (money or assets) that provide a comfortable and luxurious lifestyle.

The *power/control type* strives to get satisfaction by having complete life-or-death control over the victim. Sexual components may or may not be present, but the primary motive is the extreme power and control over the helpless victim. These killers also tend to seek specific victims who appear especially vulnerable and easy to victimize.

Despite the extensive media coverage and several interesting books on the subject in recent years, there have been very few well-designed, empirically based studies on serial murderers during the past 10 to 15 years. Much of the available information has been gathered through anecdotal, interview, or case-study methods, which, while informative and interesting, fail to provide a systematic and functionally useful data base for predicting and identifying these offenders.

MASS MURDERERS

Surprisingly little research has been directed at mass murderers, especially in comparison to the attention directed at serial murderers. Perhaps this is because mass murder, while frightening, is not as intriguing or mysterious as serial murder. Furthermore, mass murder happens quickly and unpredictably without warning—then the killing is usually over. It is often clear who the offender is, and his or her life is usually ended on the spot. Serial murderers, on the other hand, occur over a period of weeks, months, or years.

Classic Mass Murder

Mass murderers tend to be frustrated, angry people who feel helpless about their lives. They are usually between the ages of 35 and 45, and they are convinced there is little chance that things will get better for them. Their personal lives have been a failure by their standards, and they have often suffered some tragic or serious loss, such as a loss of meaningful employment. George Hennard, for example, the 35-year-old who drove his Ford Ranger pickup into the plate glass window of Luby's Cafeteria in Killeen, Texas, and proceeded to shoot to death 22 patrons, had lost his cherished job as a merchant marine.

In addition, mass murders are usually carefully planned, sometimes over very long periods of time. For example, on November 2, 1991, Gang Lu, a former graduate student at the University of Iowa, sought six specific professors he felt kept him from getting a $1,000 award for his doctoral dissertation. He managed to kill five of the six within 10 minutes before taking his own life. Lu had written five separate letters to people detailing his plans prior to the murder. Likewise, Hennard had apparently planned his onslaught for many months, even studying video documentaries of previous mass murders.

Moreover, the targets selected by mass murderers are either symbolic of their discontent (such as their workplace) or are likely to contain individuals they hate or blame for their misfortunes. George Hennard, for example, had a lifelong hatred of women, and he knew that Luby's Cafeteria during lunch would be filled with them. Hennard moved from victim to victim, frequently selecting women, and methodically shot each victim in the head at close range as he shouted "bitch." Fourteen of the 22 deaths that day were women. Marc Lepine walked calmly through the University of Montreal engineering school (Ecole Polytechnique) with a semiautomatic rifle in search of women to kill. In one classroom he shouted, "I want to kill women!" and as he proceeded to shoot them he shouted, "You're all a bunch of feminists!" He killed 14 women that day and wounded 13 more people (four of them men) before he took his own life. In his pocket was a three-page suicide note in which he complained that feminists had always ruined his life. James Oliver Huberty, the McDonald's killer, selected a fast-food restaurant in a Hispanic community (San Ysidro) because he apparently disliked Hispanics and children.

Mass murderers often take a very active interest in guns, especially semiautomatics that maximize the number of deaths in a short period of time. In large measure, the availability of high-powered semiautomatic or automatic weaponry accounts for the increasingly large death toll in recent mass murders. Moreover, mass murderers usually plan to die at the scene, either by committing suicide or by being shot down by law enforcement.

Also, mass murderers are often socially isolated and withdrawn people who are without a strong social network of friends or supports. Their isolation is probably due to some combination of an active dislike of people interacting with their inadequate interpersonal and social skills. The mass murder is their chance to get even, to dominate others, to take control, to call the shots, and to gain recognition.

The remainder of the chapter addresses some specific offenses that have been or possess the strong possibility of becoming mass murder. Product tampering, school violence, and workplace violence do not necessarily result in death, of course, but when they do the deaths may be multiple. These crimes have drawn extensive media coverage, and some research interest, in recent years.

Product Tampering

Product tampering is the sabotaging of a commercial product, usually for commercial gain. It becomes **product tampering homicide** when the sabotaging is so serious that it results in the death of one or more individuals. Because the product is typically used by many persons before the tampering is discovered, this crime has the potential of resulting in multiple such deaths. Between 1982 and 1986, there were 12 confirmed deaths directly due to product tampering (Lance, 1988). Thus, this form of homicide is very rare. The offender usually expects financial gain either through litigation on behalf of the victim (wrongful death), through extortion, or through business operations (Douglas, Burgess, Burgess, & Ressler, 1992). The business operation strategy refers to attempts to damage a competing business by tampering with its products.

The method most commonly employed in product-tampering homicide is to place cyanide within the product, either before (if the offense involves extortion or business operations) or after purchase (in cases claiming wrongful death). Cyanide is often the poison of choice because of its potency (an ounce can kill 250 people) and its availability (Douglas et al., 1992).

Fortunately, although there are numerous threats to tamper, very few are actually carried out. Nearly two-thirds of the threats are directed at retail stores, and the products threatened are usually well-known national brands (Lance, 1988). News of product tampering sometimes prompts a contagion effect (also known as copycat effect), in which many people either copy or falsely report the offense. For example, when a baby food company was accused by an individual of having glass in its baby food, more than six hundred complaints of glass particles were immediately received across the country. A vast majority of the complaints were false claims by consumers seeking monetary reward by claiming that glass in the products had caused them some injury. One individual was arrested for deliberately feeding shards of glass to his retarded son in an attempt to obtain money from the baby food company.

SCHOOL VIOLENCE

The topic of school violence took on a more chilling urgency in the later 1990s when a rash of school shootings made headlines. As discussed briefly in chapter 2, the most infamous case was the mass murder of 12 students and one teacher at Columbine High School in Littleton, Colorado, in April 1999. The two teenage boys who did the shootings committed suicide during the incident. Twenty more students were injured. Although there had been a number of school shootings prior to Columbine (there were at least 10 school shootings between 1996 and 1999), the Columbine shooting prompted a great deal of alarm and concern nationwide. In addition, the media and some experts were quick to make gross generalizations about the school violence problem.

However, even prior to these violent incidents, anecdotal and media accounts of children being victimized at school by other children prompted researchers to study the issue to document the magnitude of the problem. In 1974, the U.S. Congress funded a three-year study to evaluate the nature and extent of crime, violence, and disruption in the nation's schools. The U.S Department of Education National Institute of Education, which conducted the study, released its findings in 1977, and Safe School Study (National Center of Education Statistics, 2005) remains the most comprehensive study available.

The 2005 National Center for Education Statistics report indicated the following:

- Between 1995 and 2001, the percentage of students who reported being victims of crime at school decreased from 10 percent to 6 percent.
- Victims of theft decreased from 7 percent to 4 percent.
- Victims of violence decreased from 3 percent to 2 percent.

The report also indicates that there was no detectable increase or decease over time in:

- The percentage of students threatened or injured with a weapon
- The percentage of teachers physically threatened or injured with a weapon
- Marijuana use, alcohol use, and drug distribution at school

In the 2002–3 school year, an estimated 54.2 million students in prekindergarten through grade 12 were enrolled in about 125,000 U.S. elementary or secondary schools (National Center for Education Statistics, 2005). In 2003, violent crimes occurred at a rate of 6 per 1,000 in that student population. Students were more likely to be victims of serious violence or homicide away from school, occurring at a rate of 12 crimes per 1,000 students away from school. For example, in each school year from 1992 to 2002, youths ages 5 to 19 were over 70 times more likely to be murdered away from school than at school. Still, national statistics indicate that about one out of 10 students in secondary schools fear that they will be attacked or harmed while at school (Verlinden, Hersen, & Thomas, 2000).

School Shootings

Although school shootings are understandably frightening and are of deep concern, statistically they are rare. Between 1992 and 2002, the number of homicides of school-aged youth at school declined from 33 to 14. In addition, violent crime rates in the nation's public and private schools in 2003 remained unchanged and continued at about half those recorded in 1992 (Bureau of Justice Statistics, 2005).

O'Toole (2000, p. 4) lists the usual wrong or unverified impressions of school shooters often promoted by the news media. Among these myths are the following:

- School violence is an epidemic.
- All school shooters are alike.
- The school shooter is always a loner.
- School shootings are exclusively motivated by revenge.
- Easy access to weapons is the most significant factor.
- Unusual or aberrant behaviors, interests, or hobbies are hallmarks of the student destined to become violent.

Investigations of school shooters have consistently found that the two characteristics that emerge are peer rejection and social rejection. The Columbine High School shooter, Dylan Klebold, wrote in his diary how lonely he was without friends and was especially tortured by his failures with girls (Meadows,

2006). The other shooter, Eric Harris, wrote in his diary how everyone continually made fun of him. A vast majority of shooters have poor social and coping skills and felt picked on or persecuted (Verlinden, Hersen, & Thomas, 2000). They expressed anger about being teased or ridiculed and vowed revenge against particular individuals or groups. Moreover, as a group "they lacked social support and prosocial relationships that might have served as protective factors" (Verlinden et al., 2000, p. 44). Cruelty to animals was prominent in the backgrounds of at least half of the shooters (Verlinden et al., 2000). Their backgrounds also revealed a keen interest in guns and other weaponry, and they often had easy access to firearms (see **Table 10–3**). Most of these assailants expected to be killed or planned suicide during or immediately after the attacks. All the attacks seemed to be carefully planned and thought out beforehand.

In virtually all school shootings, investigators discovered that the violent intentions of the assailants were repeatedly made clear to others, particularly peers, often including the time and place. Documents show that the Columbine school shooters repeatedly dropped hints at school about their murderous intentions (Meadows, 2006). However, peers rarely reported these threats to the authorities. The reasons for this behavior are not well understood, but fear seems to play a major role. A survey by the Safe School Coalition of Washington State (1999) (cited in Verlinden et al., 2000) revealed that fear of not being believed, fear of retribution, or fear for what might happen to the youth threatening the school violence were the most frequently reported concerns of peers. Verlinden et al. (2000) concluded that the risk for school violence is high when there are multiple warning signs and risk factors. "The more signs there are and the greater the opportunity, motivation, and access to weapons, the greater the possibility that the child may commit a violent act" (Verlinden et al., 2000, p. 47).

In a national study of school violence, Gottfredson, Gottfredson, Payne, and Gottfredson (2005) report that schools in which students find the rules fair and in which discipline is managed consistently experience less violence and disorder. This is regardless of the type of school and community. They also found that schools characterized by high teacher morale, focus, strong leadership,

TABLE 10–3   School Homicides, 1994–1999

TYPE OF WEAPON	NUMBER	PERCENT
Total	172	100%
Firearm	119	69
Handgun	89	52
Rifle	18	11
Unknown	12	7
Sharp Object	31	18
Beating	12	7
Strangulation	5	3
Other	5	3

Source: Perkins, 2003, p. 11.

and high teacher involvement are protected from school crime and violence. Their conclusions: The school climate makes a significance difference in reducing the overall crime, disorder, and violence that occur within the school building.

WORKPLACE VIOLENCE

What Is Workplace Violence?

Many terms and behaviors have been subsumed under the rubric of workplace violence. In the public mind, workplace violence usually means a worker killing his or her coworkers or supervisors. Commentators, researchers, and experts, on the other hand, have used workplace violence to refer to a wide range of aggressive actions, such as gossip, assaults, sexual assaults, robberies, murders. For our purpose, it is worthwhile to distinguish between workplace aggression and workplace violence. **Workplace aggression** is "a general term encompassing all forms of behavior by which individuals attempt to harm others at work or their organizations" (Neuman & Baron, 1998, p. 393). Workplace aggression may range from subtle and hidden actions to active confrontations or direct destruction of property (Hepwoth & Towler, 2004). **Workplace violence,** on the other hand, refers to incidents in which the offender intends to cause *serious* physical or bodily harm to an individual or individuals within an organization or to the organization itself.

Data collected by the Bureau of Labor Statistics (2004) indicate that an average of 900 people are murdered at work each year, making it the third leading cause of occupational death in the United States (see **Table 10–4**). In 2003, 14 percent of workplace fatalities were due to assaults and violent acts. Although the impression derived from media reports over the past two decades

TABLE 10–4   Average Annual Workplace Homicide, by Victim-Offender Association, 1993–1999

ASSOCIATION OF OFFENDER TO VICTIM	NUMBER	AVERAGE ANNUAL NUMBER	PERCENT OF TOTAL
Worker association	6,316	899	100%
Stranger	5,274	753	84
Work associate	721	103	11
Coworker, former coworker	469	67	7
Customer, client	252	36	4
Intimate	194	28	3
Husband	122	17	2
Wife	3	—	—
Boyfriend	72	10	1
Other relative	38	5	1
Other acquaintance	65	9	1

Source: Critical Incident Response Group, 2001, p. 42.

is that workplace violence is expanding, it must be emphasized that a large majority of workplace homicides do *not* involve murder between coworkers or supervisors *within* an organization but occur in robberies and related crimes by people *outside* the organization (Neuman & Baron, 1998). That is, young convenience store clerks or fast-food restaurant workers are often the victims of robbery and other forms of violence while working.

The following statistics, compiled in an overview by Gregorie (2000), show how dangerous the workplace can be:

- Each year, about 2 million Americans are victimized while working.
- Approximately 900 workplace homicides occur annually.
- Guns are the primary weapon used in 82 percent of workplace homicides, followed by knives and physical force.
- About one of every six violent crimes experienced by U.S. residents occurs in the workplace.
- Boyfriends and husbands, both current and former, commit more than 13,000 acts of violence against women in the workplace every year.
- The National Institute for Occupational Safety and Health reports that murder is the leading cause of death for women at work.

Examples of Workplace Violence

Gregorie (2000, pp. 2–3) further outlines four types of offenders who commit violence at the workplace, in an effort that is very useful for understanding this phenomenon. The classification system or typology was first identified by the California Division of Occupational Safety and Health in *Guidelines for Workplace Security* (1995). The four types of offenders are:

- *Type I.* This offender has no legitimate relationship to the workplace or the victim and usually enters the workplace to commit a criminal action such as a robbery or theft. Common victims of Type I offenders are small, late-night retail establishments, including convenience stores and restaurants, and taxi drivers. This type of workplace violence also includes terrorist and hate crimes such as the World Trade Center and Alfred P. Murrah Federal Building bombings, as well as abortion clinic attacks.
- *Type II.* This offender is the recipient of some service provided by the victim or workplace and may be either a current or former client, patient, or customer.
- *Type III.* This offender has an employment-related involvement with the workplace. The act of violence is usually committed by a current or former employee, supervisor, or manager who has a dispute with another employee of the workplace. This type of workplace violence offender is usually referred to as the "disgruntled employee" and is often

someone who has been fired, demoted, or lost benefits. When death results from the violence, if the victim or victims were of higher authority than the perpetrator, the crime may be called **authority homicide.**

* *Type IV.* This offender has an indirect involvement with the workplace because of a relationship with an employee. The offender may be a current or former spouse or partner, someone who was in a dating relationship with the employee, or a relative or friend. This type of violence follows the employee into the workplace from the outside.

The first of these categories, depicting violence by someone not connected to workplace, accounts for the vast majority of violence and homicides, perhaps as high as 80 percent of the total (Critical Incident Response Group, 2001). The motive is usually robbery, and in many cases the offender or offenders are carrying a gun or other weapon, greatly increasing the likelihood that the victim (most often, the victims) will be killed or seriously wounded. For example, in May 2000, two men entered a Wendy's in Flushing, New York, with the intent to rob the fast-food restaurant. They left with $2,400 in cash after shooting seven employees. Five of the employees died, and two others were seriously wounded. Convenience store clerks, taxi drivers, security guards, and proprietors of "mom-and-pop" stores are also vulnerable to this type of workplace violence.

Workers who exchange cash with customers as part of the job, work late night hours, and work alone are at greatest risk for type I workplace violence. In California, for example, the majority (60%) of workplace homicides involved a person entering a small, night-retail establishment, such as a liquor store, gas station, or convenience food store, to commit a robbery (Southerland, Collins, & Scarborough, 1997).

Type II workplace violence usually involves health care workers, police officers, counselors, schoolteachers, college professors, social workers, and mental health workers. An example of Type II workplace violence is provided by the University of Iowa Injury Prevention Research Center (2001, p. 7).

> Rhonda Bedow, a nurse who works in a state-operated psychiatric facility in Buffalo, NY, was attacked by an angry patient who had a history of threatening behavior, particularly against female staff. He slammed Bedow's head down onto a counter after learning that he had missed the chance to go outside with a group of other patients. Bedow suffered a concussion, a bilaterally dislocated jaw, an eye injury, and permanent scarring on her face from the assault.

In the 1970s and 1980s, a number of social workers were assaulted—and sometimes killed—by individuals who were furious because their children were removed from the family home or because they lost custody based on social worker recommendations. These tragedies prompted many state agencies to erect barricades between clients and the workers and, in many cases, to hire private security officers to screen those entering the offices.

Type III probably is regarded by the media as the most sensational and receives a bulk of its coverage. As noted by the Critical Incident Response Group

(2001, p. 11), "mass murders in the workplace by unstable employees have become media-intensive events." An example of type III violence occurred on August 20, 1986, when a part-time letter carrier, facing possible dismissal after a troubled work history, walked into the Edmond, Oklahoma, post office where he worked and shot 14 people to death before killing himself. In the previous three years, four postal employees were slain by present or former coworkers in separate shootings in South Carolina, Alabama, and Georgia (Critical Incident Response Group, 2001). Similar mass murders in the workplace by emotionally disturbed employees have drawn considerable media scrutiny and—because they initially came to attention with the post office crimes—the term "going postal" was introduced into the American lexicon. The Critical Incident Response Group (2001) has identified a number of additional examples, including four state lottery executives killed in Connecticut by a lottery accountant (1998), seven coworkers killed by a Xerox technician in Honolulu (1999), seven murdered by a software engineer at the Edgewater Technology Company in Massachusetts (2000), four killed by a 66-year-old former forklift driver in Chicago (2001), three killed by an insurance executive at Empire Blue Cross and Blue Shield in New York City (2002), three murdered by a plant worker at a manufacturing plant in Missouri (2003), and six killed by a plant worker at Lockheed-Martin aircraft plant in Mississippi (2003). The Chicago, New York, Mississippi, and Connecticut shooters killed themselves during the incident. The Honolulu and Massachusetts shooters went to trial, both raised the insanity defense, but both were convicted.

Type IV workplace violence represents a spillover of domestic violence or intimate partner violence into the workplace, and usually women are the victims. As noted earlier, homicide is the leading cause of workplace death for women, accounting for 41 percent of all female worker fatalities (Kelleher, 1997). A good example of Type IV workplace violence is provided by the University of Iowa Injury Prevention Research Center (2001, p. 11):

> Pamela Henry, an employee of Protocall, an answering service in San Antonio, had decided in the summer of 1997 to move out of the area. The abusive behavior of her ex-boyfriend, Charles Lee White, had spilled over from her home to her workplace, where he appeared one day in July and assaulted her. She obtained and then withdrew a protective order against White, citing her plans to leave the country. On October 17, 1997, White again appeared at Protocall. This time he opened fire with a rifle, killing Henry and another female employee before killing himself.

Who Commits Workplace Violence?

According to the FBI (Southerland, Collins, & Scarborough, 1997), the workplace homicide offender whose motivation is not robbery is often a disgruntled employee (Type III) who believes the job is (or was) his life, is a loner, has few friends, and lacks a support system. The target of the attack may be a person or persons (usually innocent) working within a building or structure or for an organization that symbolizes the authority (Douglas, Burgess, Burgess, & Ressler, 1992). However, it should be emphasized that there is no precise "profile" or litmus test that will provide clear signs that an employee will become violent. Rather, it is important for employees and employers to remain alert to unstable or problematic behavior that, in combination with threatening behavior, could result in violence (see **Table 10–5**).

A vast majority of type III victims are killed (often randomly) by disgruntled employees who were fired or felt mistreated by the company or agency. It seems that a particular autocratic work environment, such as found in large, impersonal bureaucratic organizations, can be a problem. However, as the examples provided by the Critical Incident Response Group (2001) indicate, no workplace seems immune. As we discussed previously, when an employee feels frustrated and angry, he or she may be more likely to strike out, and this could occur even in a benevolent work environment.

Similar to mass murderers in general, offenders who commit authority homicide—where a figure in authority, such as a supervisor, is killed—tend to be white males who have few social supports, are socially isolated, and who blame others (externalize) for their problems and misfortune. They are often seriously depressed. Very often the offender expects to die at the scene, either at his own hands or by the police. Authority offenders also tend to be preoccupied with weapons, accumulating a number of them over a period of time with eventual revenge or "occupational martyrdom" in mind. The weapons are often of maximum lethality, such as automatic assault weapons (e.g., AK-47) (Douglas et al., 1992). In most instances, the offender is middle-aged (over 30 and under 60) (Kelleher, 1997). There is also evidence that workplace offenders tend to have a history of violent behavior, alcohol or drug abuse, and will vocalize, or otherwise act out, their violent intentions prior to the authority homicide (Kelleher, 1997).

TABLE 10–5 Identifying Problematic Behaviors in Coworkers Which Might Lead to Violence

- Increasing belligerence
- Ominous specific threats
- Hypersensitivity to criticism
- Recent acquisition/fascination with weapons
- Apparent obsession with a supervisor or coworker or employee grievance
- Preoccupation with violent themes
- Interest in recently publicized violent events
- Outbursts of anger
- Extreme disorganization
- Noticeable changes in behavior
- Homicidal/suicidal comments or threats

Source: Critical Incident Response Group, 2001, pp. 21–22.

···➤ ● SUMMARY AND CONCLUSIONS

In this chapter we have taken a closer look at types of homicides that are relatively rare but have significant impact on large numbers of victims, both directly
and indirectly. Multiple murders can be divided into three main categories: serial, spree, and mass killings, with the latter divided into classic and family mass
murders. We focused on the classic form here. The deaths that occur as a result
of terrorism, a distinct form of mass murder, are discussed in chapter 11.

The crimes that are covered here are often investigated by police with the
help of criminal profilers or investigative psychologists, terms that are often
used interchangeably. Investigative psychology is actually a broader term referring to the application of psychological research and principles to the investigation of criminal behavior. It typically includes crime scene investigative
methods, such as reviewing features of the modus operandi, the personation or
signature, and staging. Criminal profiling focuses more on the offender, identifying personality traits, behavioral patterns, demographic features, and sometimes geographical habits.

Criminal profiling is a strategy widely used in law enforcement, particularly for multiple murders or sex crimes. In serial murders, for example, profiling is helpful particularly if the offender demonstrates some psychopathology,
such as a specific method of torture. However, it may also be very useful for nonviolent crimes, such as burglaries or arsons. Profiling is a very complex enterprise and, unfortunately, is often based on hunches or anecdotal information.
Rarely does a profile provide the specific identity of an offender, but it is not intended to. As Douglas, Ressler, Burgess, & Hartman, (1986) noted, profiling
tries to narrow the field to a manageable number of suspects.

The form of multiple murder that most terrorizes a community is the serial
killing, particularly because it may appear that anyone can be a potential victim. Serial killers generally choose their victims for their specific characteristics, however. For example, victims may be women in their twenties, transients,
preadolescent and adolescent boys, prostitutes, or, in the case of the rare female serial killers, husbands or suitors. Research indicates that the great majority of serial killers are males; however, prior assumptions that they were
invariably white males may be unwarranted. They are rarely juveniles.

Attempts have been made to place serial murderers into typologies, the
most useful being the four-category typology of Holmes and DeBurger (1988).
They have identified the visionary, mission-oriented, hedonistic, and
power/control oriented murderers. We discussed features of each of these
groups. It is important to emphasize, though, that very few well-designed
and empirically based studies of serial murders have been conducted. Virtually all available information is based on anecdotal reports, interviews, and
case studies.

Mass murderers have received even less research attention. In its classic
form, one or more individuals enter a scene and open fire on a group of peo-

ple, such as in a restaurant, a place of worship, or a place of work. This form of mass murder is usually carefully planned, and the victims are often symbols of the murderer's discontent (e.g., the workplace or a group of women). Alternately, the group of victims includes one or more individuals whom the killer hates or blames for his misfortunes. Mass murderers are typically socially isolated and withdrawn and have inadequate interpersonal and social skills.

We discussed unique crimes that have the potential of becoming mass murders: product tampering and school and workplace violence. Although serious product tampering is rare, when it does occur it strikes terror in consumers because the lethal product may be used by many people before it is discovered. Cyanide has been the weapon of choice because of its potency and availability. Offenders usually seek financial gain, revenge, or want to damage a competing business.

School violence is a widespread problem in the educational system, although it rarely ends in death. In the 1990s, however, an inordinate number of school shootings were reported, the most noteworthy being the Columbine incident in Littleton, Colorado in 1999. Investigations of school shootings consistently find that peer rejection and social rejection in general were factors contributing to the eruption of violence. Cruelty to animals appeared in the background of at least half of the shooters, and fascination with guns and other weaponry was almost always present. Virtually all had communicated their intentions to other students, sometimes in very specific terms.

Recent data indicate some decline in violent incidents in schools, but we must view these statistics cautiously because school districts are often motivated to underreport them. On the other hand, the percentage of students and teachers threatened or injured with weapons neither increased nor decreased. Although children are far more likely to be victimized in their homes or away from school than in the school itself, any amount of violence or threats of violence is unacceptable.

The chapter ended with coverage of workplace violence, another phenomenon that may or may not end in mass murder. By all indications, however, both assaults and deaths due to assaults or other violent acts are increasing. Nevertheless, a large majority are caused by individuals coming into the workplace from the outside, not by workers themselves. Offenders are divided into four categories: those having no connection to the workplace, those who have received some service provided by the organization, those who currently or formerly worked there, and those who have some relationship with one or more employees. Again, the vast majority of violence is perpetrated by the first category. Most psychological research has focused on the third type, the disgruntled employee who kills supervisors and/or fellow workers. These individuals are not only angry but also usually socially isolated and seriously depressed. Typically, they expect or plan to die at the scene.

KEY CONCEPTS

Investigative psychology
MO
Signature
Autoeroticism
Organized crime scene
Mixed crime scene
Criminal profiling
Equivocal death analysis
Reconstructive psychological
  evaluation
Serial murder
Classic mass murder
Victimological perspective
Workplace aggression

Authority homicide
Modus operandi
Personation
Staging
Undoing
Disorganized crime scene
Psychological profiling
Geographical profiling
Psychological autopsy
Racial profiling
Spree murder
Family mass murder
Product tampering homicide
Workplace violence

 REVIEW QUESTIONS

1. Briefly describe the difference between an organized and disorganized crime scene. Discuss the profile characteristics of each.

2. Identify and discuss the motives of the four types of serial murders according to Holmes and DeBurger. What information about serial killers is provided by Fox and Levin?

3. Define geographical profiling, and identify in what ways it is useful to law enforcement.

4. Why is the victimology perspective important in understanding serial murder?

5. Define staging, and give examples of when it is most likely to occur.

6. Define investigative psychology.

7. Define racial profiling, and identify the situations it is most likely to occur.

8. What is the difference between workplace aggression and workplace violence?

9. What are the psychological characteristics of mass murderers, according to the available research?

10. School shootings are most likely to be committed by what kind of student?

CHAPTER 11

TERRORISM AND THE PSYCHOLOGY OF VIOLENCE

CHAPTER OBJECTIVES

- Examine the many definitions of terrorism.
- Evaluate the motives of terrorists.
- Identify the social contexts that spawn and promote terrorism.
- Introduce two typologies of terrorism in order to emphasize the multidimensional features of persons who engage in it.
- Explore the psychological factors that play major roles in precipitating violence and murder.

An entire nation and much of the world were stunned by the destruction of life and property on September 11, 2001, when two airliners were intentionally flown into the World Trade Center in New York City, a third airliner was flown into the Pentagon in the nation's capital, and a fourth crashed into a field in Somerset County, Pennsylvania. The plane that crashed in Pennsylvania was believed to be heading for the White House, but passengers on board took over the plane, preventing it from remaining on its original course. At the World Trade Center, 2,823 were killed (including five children under the age of 5); at the Pentagon, 184 lives were lost; and all 40 passengers died in the Pennsylvania crash. Nineteen terrorists (all under the age of 35) were directly involved in the airline hijacking (10 at the World Trade Center, 5 at the Pentagon, and 4 in Pennsylvania) (Federal Bureau of Investigation, 2002). The al-Qaeda terrorist group was believed to be responsible.

The United States, in response to the tragedy, decided to launch strong military forces into Afghanistan in an effort to weed out al-Qaeda cells in that country. Soon thereafter the U.S. launched another military attack into Iraq, again in apparent pursuit of al-Qaeda-sponsored organizations, though critics have argued forcefully that this was unjustified. Furthermore, many people believe that these military responses are rarely successful in preventing future attacks because they do not address the root conditions that spawn terrorism (Marsella, 2004). Instead, "there must be a response to prevent its emergence and its growth and development as an appealing option" (Marsella, 2004, p. 34). Furthermore, "terrorism may be contained but never defeated as long as there are real or perceived threats or injustices that foster widespread hatred and revenge. There may be small and large military successes, but eventually there must be coming to grips with the strengths and weaknesses of the human psyche and the cultural milieu in which it is fostered" (Moghaddam & Marsella, 2004b, p. 4).

DEFINITIONS

Terrorism is defined in the Code of Federal Regulations as "the unlawful use of force or violence against persons or property to intimidate or coerce a government, the civilian population, or any segment thereof, in furtherance of political or social objectives." Terrorism may be either domestic or international, depending on the origin, base, and objectives of the terrorist organization (U.S. Department of Justice, 2000a). Domestic terrorism refers to groups or an individual based and operating entirely within the United States or Puerto Rico without foreign direction. International terrorism refers to violent acts or acts dangerous to human life that are a violation of the criminal laws of the United States or any state and under the direction of a foreign government, group, organization, or person. Although terrorist activities are widespread and affect people throughout the world, the most vivid example of international terrorism and the one most covered by the media is that represented by the events that occurred on September 11, 2001.

Sternberg (2003) defines terrorism simply "as the systematic use of terror, especially as a means of coercion" (p. 299). Hallett (2004) defines the term as a theatrical crime against person or property in which only symbolic or psychological satisfaction to the perpetrators is gained. A quick scan of the literature reveals there are multiple definitions of terrorism. Moreover, trying to reach a comprehensive definition is complicated by the maxim, "One person's terrorist is another person's freedom fighter" (Marsella, 2004, p. 15).

Despite the vast and sometime overwhelming array of definitions, Marsella (2004) finds some common ground in all of them. "Terrorism is broadly viewed as (a) the use of force or violence (b) by individuals or groups (c) that is directed toward civilian populations (d) and intended to instill fear (e) as a means of coercing individuals or groups to change their political and social positions" (p. 16). However, he further notes that any comprehensive definition of terrorism also requires thoughtful consideration of the psychosocial context, motives, and consequences of the act.

Additional Examples

A well-known example of domestic terrorism in the United States occurred on April 17, 1995. A truck bomb destroyed the Alfred P. Murrah Federal Building in Oklahoma City, killing 167 (19 were children) and injuring 684 persons. Timothy McVeigh, a U.S. citizen and former soldier, was convicted and eventually executed for this crime. His coconspirator, Terry Nichols, pled guilty to avoid the federal death penalty but remains at risk of being tried and sentenced to death in Oklahoma state courts. The Oklahoma City attack remains the deadliest *domestic* terrorist incident ever committed on U.S. soil. Further illustrations of domestic terrorism include the actions of the so-called "Army of God," whose members claimed responsibility for bombings of abortion clinics and an alternative lifestyle nightclub in Atlanta.

Most international terrorism is aimed at U.S. property or citizens located in a foreign country. Examples of international terrorism include groups in Columbia who target American interests and who have kidnapped seven U.S. citizens and have carried out multiple bombings against oil pipelines used by American companies (U.S. Department of Justice, 2000). Another example involves the American embassies in Nairobi, Kenya, and Dares Salaam, Tanzania, where in August 1998 both embassies were bombed almost simultaneously. The truck bombings killed 224, including 12 American citizens, and injured over 4,500 located in or near the embassies.

Classification of Terrorism Groups

The number of victims killed or injured by terrorists differs widely from year to year. In addition to the domestic and international classifications, there are several other ways to classify terrorism. The FBI classifies terrorists according to political leanings. For example, *right-wing terrorists* are extremist groups that generally adhere to an antigovernment or racist ideology and often engage in a variety of hate crimes and violence. Recent stimuli that have encouraged right-wing militia groups or individuals to become active include gun-control legislation, the United Nations' involvement in international affairs, and clashes between dissidents and law enforcement. Examples include the Unabomber, who sent mail bombs to individuals involved with technology, killing three and seriously injuring 23 over a 17-year period. The intention of the Unabomber was to stop the Industrial Revolution and technological progress in American society. Another example of right-wing extremists was the bombing of the Alfred P. Murrah Federal Building in Oklahoma City, referred to previously.

Another FBI classification relates to **radical environmental groups,** such as the Earth Liberation Front (ELF). The ELF organization received particular attention during the late 1990s by destroying homes, earth-moving equipment, powerlines, computer systems, and buildings that they believed damaged the earth's ecology. In its own words, the organization's primary mission is to "speed up the collapse of industry, to scare the rich, and to undermine the foundations of the state." **Special interest extremists,** particularly violent antiabortion activists, continue to be a problem in the United States.

During the past several decades, **nuclear/biological/chemical** (abbreviated NBC) forms of terrorism have become prominent. The thought of being exposed to an invisible or undetectable agent can be more frightening to the general public than the prospect of physical injury or death caused by conventional weapons. The use of sarin, a deadly nerve agent, in the subway system of Tokyo, Japan, in 1995 provides a horrifying example. The attacks were carried out by the doomsday cult Aum Shinrikyo (Supreme Truth Sect) and resulted in the deaths of 11 people and injuries to more than five thousand. It is estimated that about 375 pounds of sarin is enough to kill over fifty thousand persons. The threat of NBC is more realistic today because terrorists are able to take advantage of the greater availability of information and weapons technology.

Bioterrorism involves the use of bacteria, viruses, germs, and other agents such as anthrax, bubonic plague, and smallpox (Marsella, 2004). A recent example of domestic bioterrorism is represented by the anthrax attacks that occurred in the United States less than a month after 9/11. The bioterrorist(s) sent the anthrax by letter to various persons in the eastern sections of the United States, including the Washington offices of Senators Patrick Leahy and Tom Daschle, and the New York office of former CBS anchor Dan Rather. Anthrax is an acute infectious disease caused by the spore-forming bacterium *Bacillus anthracis.* Although anthrax is most commonly found in hoofed mammals, it can also infect humans. Symptoms of the disease vary depending on how the disease was contracted, but they usually occur within seven days after exposure. The serious forms of human anthrax are inhalation anthrax, cutaneous (skin) anthrax, and intestinal (ingestion) anthrax. Inhalation (pulmonary) anthrax starts with inhalation of anthrax spores and has a mortality rate of around 95 percent, even with treatment. Cutaneous anthrax starts with the spore colonizing the skin through an abrasion, cut, or wound. The mortality rate of the cutaneous anthrax ranges from 20 percent to 25 percent without treatment, and is less than 1 percent with treatment. Intestinal anthrax, by far the worst, is usually transmitted through eating contaminated meat. It has a mortality rate of 95 percent, even when treated.

The bioterrorist or bioterrorists (at this writing the author of the anthrax letters is unknown and the case is still under investigation) sent letters containing both inhalation and cutaneous anthrax to the victims. The anthrax spores were mixed with a light powder in the folds of the letters. The first known case of the anthrax letter attack killed a photo editor of a tabloid in Boca Raton, Florida, in October 2001. In total, the bioterrorist letters resulted in at least five deaths due to inhalation anthrax infections; another eight cases of nonfatal cutaneous anthrax infections were reported during 2001. Bioterrorism, if delivered under the right conditions and by using a highly infectious biological agent, could be devastating.

Other forms of terrorism include nuclear terrorism, such as the use of nuclear bombs or dirty bombs that make use of radioactive material, and chemical terrorism, such as the use of sarin gas that occurred with the Aum Shinriyko cult in Japan (Marsella, 2004). Terrorism is an area of obvious concern today, and this section has only provided a brief overview of the statistical and informational aspects of the crime.

A TERRORIST TYPOLOGY

Ditzler (2004) describes a terrorist typology promulgated by the U.S. Army Command and General Staff College (Terrorism Research Center, 1997). The typology also incorporates some of the research conducted at RAND (Hoffman, 1993). The typology identifies three motivational categories: (1) the rationally motivated terrorist, (2) the psychologically motivated terrorist, and (3) the culturally motivated terrorist.

The *rationally motivated terrorists* are those who consider the goals of the organization and the possible consequences of their actions. They develop well-defined and theoretically achievable goals that may involve political, social, economic, or other specific objectives. In many cases, rationally motivated terrorists try to avoid loss of life but focus instead on destroying infrastructures, buildings, and other symbolic structures to get their message across.

Psychologically motivated terrorists are driven by "a profound sense of failure or inadequacy for which the perpetrator may seek redress through revenge" (Ditzler, 2004, p. 202). The attraction to terrorism is usually based on the psychological benefits of group affiliation and collective identity. They are especially drawn to terrorist groups that have a charismatic leader. One variation of the psychologically motivated terrorist, though, is the lone wolf operation, "for whom the validation of the self is not derived through group affiliation, but through the sense of power, mastery, and autonomy that attends to the ability to make unilateral decisions" (Ditzler, 2004, p. 203). The classic example of this type of terrorist is Theodore Kaczynksi, known as the Unabomber. Often, lone wolf terrorists have strong feelings of social alienation, anger, and extreme antigovernment ideology. In most instances, they view themselves as victims of the "system."

The culturally motivated terrorist is driven by fear of irreparable damage to their way of living, national heritage, or culture done by an organization, foreign country, or powerful factions. Most often, religion is the aspect that generates the fervor or passion in the group. National or cultural groups that are largely governed or socially defined by a particular system of faith are often constantly vigilant for forces that may eradicate their religious way of life or cultural identity. Ditzler gives the example of Afghanistan under the Taliban, where "Islam provided not only a system of religious faith as understood in the West, but the entire system of civil and criminal law, political organization, and social behavior" (2004, p. 203). Under such conditions a perceived threat to the faith would be cause for alarm and a threat to the group's existence. However, as we know from the millions of law-abiding and peaceful Islamics, most members of the religious group do not respond to threats to their way of life with acts of terrorism. One of the most troubling outcomes of the events of September 11 was the widespread and unjustified distrust of people of Islamic faiths. It is important, therefore, that we examine the psychosocial context in which terrorism of all kinds develops.

THE PSYCHOSOCIAL CONTEXT OF TERRORISM

The psychosocial context refers to those social and psychological circumstances that encourage certain behaviors to develop and expand. The psychosocial context is a cognitively constructed world that is sustained through the socialization process associated with each culture. Culture in this sense may be as broad as an entire country or as narrow as a small group of individuals. Thus, there is psychosocial context relevant to both the entire society and to the subcultural components of that society.

Ervin Staub (2004) postulates that certain cultural characteristics are conducive to the emergence of terrorist groups One characteristic is what he calls *cultural devaluation,* a process that occurs when a group or culture is selected by another group or culture as a scapegoat or an ideological enemy. "It might consist of beliefs that the other is lazy, or of limited intelligence, or manipulative, or morally bad, or a dangerous enemy that intends to destroy society or one's own group" (Staub, 2004, p. 158). The United States itself is often seen this way. Many groups and individuals see the United States as being indifferent to the world's suffering and insensitive to global cultural diversity and local identity (Marsella, 2004). Many are convinced that this indifference contributes to the political suppression of the poor and the disadvantaged on a global basis (Marsella, 2004). In addition, some believe American culture is a real and tangible threat to cultural identities, religious affiliation, and ways of life (Marsella, 2004).

It is also worth noting that in the United States persons associated with racial, ethnic, or religious groups often believe the "dominant" values of American society are inconsistent with the values of their own subgroups. The vast majority of these individuals either accepts this discrepancy or works within the system to change the dominant views. However, some individuals may take a terrorist approach. Thus, although Staub (2004) discusses *terrorist groups,* the principle of cultural devaluation can also apply to individuals or groups who engage in terroristlike activities but who are not usually considered terrorists. Persons who in the 1980s and 1990s firebombed women's health clinics where abortions were provided are a case in point.

A second characteristic noted by Staub involves perceptions of *inequality, relative deprivation,* and *injustice.* Disadvantaged, powerless, and shunned peoples are sometimes more likely to join violent or terrorist groups, not only to get some of their basic needs met, but also to gain a sense of identity and community that the terrorist group offers. Staub (2001) calls such situations *difficult life conditions* characterized by hunger, sickness, no sense of community, and lack of shelter for oneself and one's family. "People with few material resources, having little to lose, are prime candidates for joining extremist organizations that promise better living conditions as soon as the haves are removed from power" (Wagner & Long, 2004, p. 211). Not only is there promise of better physical living conditions but also promise of feeling a sense of belonging. Taylor and Louis (2004) make a similar point when they argue that, in addition to disadvantaged economic and political factors, the need for psychological identity draws some individuals into terrorist groups. They assert, "What makes terrorist groups particularly attractive is their simplistic worldview that offers recruits a clear collective identity" (p. 184). To this end, terrorist groups also fill a necessary psychological void. Some individuals, however, may also join because they "have moral principles that lead them to identify with those who are affected by difficult conditions or are unjustly treated" (Staub, 2004, p. 159).

A third characteristic is that many—perhaps most—terrorist groups have a strong hierarchy, sometimes with leaders who are described as all-powerful, convincing, and charismatic. Staub calls this psychosocial characteristic a *strong respect for authority.* Some persons who join simply wish to relinquish their unfulfilled selves and submit themselves to power leaders and chain-of-command organizations. They feel most comfortable in hierarchical social structures organized for some challenging or exciting mission. Overall, these real or perceived conditions are apt to be productive areas for terrorist recruitment when promises of a better life beckon.

MOTIVES AND JUSTIFICATIONS

Clearly, there is no single motive for engaging in terrorism. The motives are multiple and complex, ranging from revenge and anger, to paradise, status, respect, and life everlasting (Marsella, 2004). "The roots of terrorism are complex and reside in historical, political, economic, social and psychological factors. Of all of these, psychosocial factors have been among the least studied and the least understood, but arguably the most important" (Moghaddam & Marsella, 2004a, p. xi). A solid understanding of international terrorism is best achieved by careful consideration of the multicultural perspectives and psychological dynamics in which they are embedded.

Bandura (2004) skillfully takes the explanation for motives of terrorism into the cognitive realm. He posits that terrorists justify their horrific acts through **cognitive restructuring,** a psychological process that involves moral justifications, euphemistic language, and advantageous comparisons.

Moral justification enables people to engage in reprehensible conduct by telling themselves that their actions are socially worthy and have an ultimate moral and good purpose. Bandura writes,

> The conversion of socialized people into dedicated fighters is achieved not by altering their personality structures, aggressive drives, or moral standards. Rather, it is accomplished by cognitively redefining the morality of killing, so that it can be done free from self-censuring restraints. Through moral sanction

of violent means, people see themselves as fighting ruthless oppressors who have an unquenchable appetite for conquest or as protecting their cherished values and way of life, preserving world peace, saving humanity from subjugation to an evil ideology, and honoring their country's international commitments. (2004, p. 124)

The second cognitive restructuring process of **euphemistic language** is based on the well-known research finding that language shapes thought patterns on which people base many of their actions. People behave more cruelly when their conduct is given a sanitized or neutral label. Consequently, they use terms such as "waste" people rather than kill them or "collateral damage" to designate civilians who are killed in bombings. Among the colorful metaphors and euphemisms offered by Bandura to emphasize his point are bombing missions referred to as "serving the target," and bombs themselves called "vertically deployed anti-personal devices."

The third cognitive restructuring process is **advantageous comparison,** where terrorists are convinced that their way of life and fundamental cultural values are superior to those they attack. Advantageous comparison is further advanced when the terrorists are told and come to believe that the enemy engages in widespread cruelties and inhumane treatment of the people the terrorists represent. The United States, for example, is seen by many people in Arab countries as blameworthy for their problems because of a variety of U.S. policies and practices (Staub, 2004), thus providing a fertile atmosphere for terrorist recruitment. Advantageous comparison methods draw heavily on history to justify violence. For example, terrorist leaders will indoctrinate their people about the many oppressive policies and tyrannical tactics their targeted organization or country has employed on them in the past. Many people believe, for example, that the United States has historically and consistently supported repressive governments in the Arab world and elsewhere.

ADDITIONAL DISENGAGEMENT PRACTICES

Bandura also states that other disengagement practices are also at play in developing motivations, such as dehumanization, displacement of responsibility, and diffusion of responsibility. **Dehumanization** is based on the premise that mistreating or randomly killing *humanized* or known persons significantly increases the risks of self-condemnation. It is easier to mistreat (and kill) strangers who are divested of human qualities. "Once dehumanized, they are no longer viewed as persons with feelings, hopes, and concerns but as subhuman forms" (Bandura, 2004, p. 136). Now they can justifiably be called "savages," "gooks," "degenerates," "monsters," "the unwashed masses," "evil cowards," and so on.

In displacement of responsibility, terrorists may view their actions as stemming from the dictates of authorities and leaders rather than from their own personal responsibility, similar to the **crimes of obedience** discussed in chapter 5. Consequently, they avoid self-condemning reactions because they are not personally responsible for their conduct; they are only following orders, perhaps even from their god. Some serial killers (e.g., "Son of Sam") have used similar justifications for their actions. Diffusion of responsibility is similar to the concept of **deindividuation,** also discussed in chapter 5. Terrorism often requires the services of many people in the organization, all pulling together to achieve some ultimate purpose. Bandura points out that each person in the organization often performs relatively small, fragmentary jobs that, taken individually, seem harmless, and out of the limelight. The collective sense of identity that results allows members of the group to participate in being part of horrific or heinous actions that individually they may resist doing themselves.

PSYCHOLOGICAL NATURE OF TERRORISM

The nature of terrorism is basically psychological; its aim is to create crippling fears and psychological debilitation in a civilian population (Levant, 2002). Ditzler (2004, p. 189) writes. "Terrorist acts are defined to a large degree by their impact, and especially their psychological effects." Without a doubt, "the September 11 attack had achieved its purpose: to create a global psychological state of fear, uncertainty, and terror" (Marsella, 2004, p. 39). Given the psychological nature of terrorism, it is clear that psychology has an important role to play in understanding it, counteracting it, and treating its traumatizing effects (Levant, Barbanel, & DeLeon, 2004). Not until September 11, however, did psychologists demonstrate more than a passing interest in investigating, studying, and writing about terrorism (Marsella, 2004). Since then, there has been an enormous increase in books, articles, and commentary on the psychological foundations of modern-day terrorism by psychologists, psychiatrists, and other mental health professionals.

   After the attacks of September 11, 44 percent of the adults in a national survey said they experienced significant amount of stress, and 90 percent said they had some degree of stress following the attack (Schuster et al., 2001). However, it has also been shown that ethnic background, gender, and age influence the psychological reactions to terrorism (Walker & Chestnut, 2003). Many participants in the Walker-Chestnut survey thought that the United States has been overly involved in the affairs of other countries and that those countries are now retaliating. In addition, participants felt that the United States has developed a false sense of security in believing terrorist groups would not retaliate for the policies the United States has used on other countries and cultural groups.

   Although psychologists or other mental health professionals provide psychological services to those persons adversely affected by terrorism, it is equally important to try to prevent it. One important point that was made in the beginning of this chapter bears repeating. "The overwhelming majority of evidence indicates that responding to violence with violence only provokes further violence" (Wagner & Long, 2004, p. 215). Aggressive military action is rarely the solution, unless it is in response to an imminent, documented threat to a country and its inhabitants. International terrorism is unlikely to be reduced until the root causes of the violence are addressed and corrected. "These causes often include real or imagined injustice in meeting basic human needs for coping with difficult life conditions, insecurity, lack of self-determination, and disrespect for one's social identity" (Wagner & Long, 2004, p. 219).

In the above section, we focused almost exclusively on international terrorism, with a few allusions to domestic terrorism on the part of individuals or small groups. Nevertheless, the psychological principles outlined can apply to domestic terrorism as well. Both historically and in modern times we can point to chilling examples of such terrorism, including some activities of the Ku Klux Klan, neo-Nazi groups, radical environmentalists, and radical "right-to-life" members and groups. Virtually all of the concepts we have discussed—for example, cognitive reconstructing, strong hierarchical organization, perceptions of relative deprivation, diffusion of responsibility, and dehumanizing—may be applied to domestic, as well as to international, terrorism.

PSYCHOLOGICAL FACTORS IN GENERAL VIOLENT CRIME

Earlier in the text, specifically in chapter 5, we focused on aggression as a psychological state. Recall that we discussed the difficulties in defining aggression, its many manifestations, the fact that it can be active or passive, and the etiology of aggression, including some of its physiological components. Although all violent crime involves aggressive behavior, not all aggressive behavior is criminal. In this section, we review psychological factors that, in addition to aggression, are often believed to accompany violent crime and sometimes to precipitate it. As we will see, though, these beliefs are not necessarily justified.

Impulsivity

Violent crime is often seen as resulting from the impulsive, spur-of-the-moment, and unpredictable acts of enraged individuals. The person who savagely assaults and sometimes kills is thought to be operating on impulse, slashing out at a victim without much forethought or planned strategy. In most cases, "impulsive violence" is a result of faulty or inadequate self-regulation compounded by a simplistic belief of how to accomplish goals. This point of view, of course, partly supports the argument for gun control. If the gun were not available, the perpetrator would not have wounded or killed the victim—at least not as easily. We have also seen that with the significant increase in the technology and availability of rapid fire and automatic weapons, the number of innocent people killed by mass murderers has increased dramatically in the past 10 years. The technology and availability of weapons, however, is only part of the story.

Some theorists believe that certain personalities or dispositions are more likely to react violently under certain circumstances than others. In *Violent Men*, Hans Toch (1969) theorizes that most violent episodes can be traced to well-learned, systematic strategies of violence that some people have found effective in dealing with conflictual, interpersonal relationships. Thus, violence is not simply the act of a person acting on impulse; it is the act of one who has habitual response patterns of reacting violently in particular situations. It is Toch's impression that, if we examine the history of violent persons, we will discover surprising consistency in their approaches to interpersonal relationships. They learned, probably in childhood, that violence works for them. They used violent responses effectively to obtain positive and negative reinforcement. They got what they wanted or avoided unpleasant situations by being violent.

Toch posits that humiliating affronts and threats to reputation and status are major contributing factors to violence. A blow to the self-esteem of the person who has few skills for resolving disputes and conflicts (such as verbal or other cognitive skills) may precipitate violence. This is especially true if the person's subculture advocates that disputes be settled through physical aggression and violence.

In a similar vein, Berkowitz hypothesized that people sometimes react violently, not because they anticipate pleasure or displeasure from their actions, but because "situational stimuli have evoked the response (they) are predisposed or set to make in that setting" (Berkowitz, 1970, p. 140). That is, individuals have been conditioned—specifically, classically conditioned—to react violently by prior experiences in similar situations. In some instances, according to Berkowitz, powerful environmental stimuli essentially produce impulsive behavior. Under these conditions, one's "thinking" becomes highly simplified, responding "mindlessly" to stimuli in a well-learned manner. Thus, some people "fall into" a rage, striking out in an impulsive and automatic response to unpleasant feelings brought on by aversive or noxious stimuli. Aversive or noxious stimuli can be anything from a face one "doesn't like" to physical abuse by another. Nevertheless, the individual is not likely to strike out unless he or she has been in a rage in past situations.

A similar view was expressed by Zillmann (1979, 1983), who believed that cognitive or thinking processes are greatly impaired at extreme levels of emotional arousal. Under high excitement, such as anger, behavior normally controlled by thought becomes controlled by mindless habits. Therefore, at very high levels of emotional upset, hostile or aggressive behaviors are likely to become "impulsive," a term Zillmann associates with **habit strength.** That is, the behaviors have been so well learned that they appear quickly and without thought on the part of the individual. They seem to be "mindless" actions. Impulsive behavior, then, is not unusual, out-of-character behavior; it reflects habitual responses that might be rejected by the individual under low arousal or normal conditions.

Toch, Berkowitz, and Zillmann all suggest that when experiencing powerful emotional reactions, many people become incapable of considering the consequences of their violent actions. High arousal inhibits cognitive processing to the point that they may not think before acting. The environment and the relevant external stimuli take control over the internal mediation processes that have been weakened by extremely high levels of arousal. Of course, while these "arousal" perspectives explain the most frequent and common violent incidences found in a majority of societies, many serial and mass murderers, as we learned in chapter 10, are more thoughtful and calculating in their killings. These multicide offenders tend to fantasize, dream, and cognitively rehearse their violence before actually participating in it.

Overcontrolled and Undercontrolled Offenders

One of the most heuristic explanations of violence was advanced by Edwin Megargee (1966), who identified two distinct personalities in the highly assaultive population: the undercontrolled and the chronically overcontrolled aggressive types. The **undercontrolled personality** has few inhibitions against aggressive behavior and frequently engages in violence when frustrated or provoked. Aggression is a behavioral pattern that becomes the habitual response when the person is upset or angry.

By contrast, the chronically **overcontrolled personality** has well-established inhibitions against aggressive behavior and rigidly adheres to them, even in the face of provocation. This person has learned (or been conditioned) about the consequences (real, imagined, or implied) of engaging in violence. The overcontrolled individual is the socialized, or perhaps oversocialized, person who readily associates violations of social mores and regulations dictated by others with potentially punishing consequences. Even more than others, he or she will often say, "If I violate the rules, I will be punished." Recalling Eysenck's dichotomy, we might posit that the introvert is much like the overcontrolled personality, while the extravert exhibits many features of the undercontrolled.

According to Megargee, however, there may come a time when frustration and provocation overwhelm the overcontrolled person. If this happens, he or she may strike out violently, perhaps even exceeding the violence exhibited by the undercontrolled person. The undercontrolled-overcontrolled typology, therefore, suggests that the more brutal and unexpected slayings are often performed by usually inhibited, restricted individuals. It also seems that numerous family mass murders are committed by overcontrolled family members. Thus, neighbors, friends, and relatives are shocked by a homicide committed by a "nice, quiet, well-mannered boy." The following excerpt from a news story is over 25 years old, but it is still representative of a seemingly unexplainable crime committed by someone who may have been overcontrolled.

> A 16-year-old choir boy described as a "hell of a nice kid" was arraigned here Thursday as funeral services were held for three girls he is accused of stabbing to death.
>
> The girls' bodies were found Monday, face down in a stream in deep woods about a quarter of a mile from their homes.
>
> The state medical examiner said two of the girls were stabbed 40 times each and the third eight times. The death weapon was believed to be a hunting knife. (Tom Stuckey, Associated Press release, October 14, 1977)

In an empirical test of Megargee's hypothesis, Blackburn (1968) divided a group of violent offenders into extreme assaultives and moderate assaultives.

Extreme assaultives were defined as those convicted of murder, manslaughter, or attempted murder. *Moderate assaultives* included persons who had wounded with intent to cause serious bodily harm, or who had maliciously wounded or assaulted. On the basis of personality measures, extreme assaultives were significantly more introverted, conforming, and overcontrolled and less hostile than moderate assaultives. Moreover, their extreme aggressive behaviors had occurred only after prolonged or repeated provocation (real or imagined).

In another study (Tupin, Mahar, & Smith, 1973), convicted murderers with a history of violent offenses were found to have a much higher incidence of hyperactivity, fighting, temper tantrums, and other extraverted features during childhood than a comparable group of murderers without previous criminal records of violence. These "sudden murderers"—those without a previous record—were also found in other clinical studies to be introverted and plagued by feelings of inadequacy, loneliness, and frustration (e.g., Blackburn, Weiss, & Lamberti, 1960; Weiss, Lamberti, & Blackburn, 1960). These are all features of the overcontrolled personality type.

Lee, Zimbardo, and Bertholf (1977) reported a limited but pertinent study using a small group of 19 murderers. Ten were classified as "sudden murderers" because their background reflected no other criminal offenses, while nine were regarded as habitual offenders with prior arrests for violent acts. The Stanford Shyness Survey and Minnesota Multiphasic Personality Inventory (MMPI) were administered to both groups. Eight of the ten sudden murderers indicated they were "shy" on the Stanford Scale, compared with only one of the nine habitual offenders. According to MMPI results, the sudden murderer group tended to be significantly more overcontrolled and passive than the habitual offender group, who tended to be more undercontrolled and assertive. These results combined with other observations suggested to the researchers that people who are overcontrolled are capable of more extreme violence when "inner restraints" break down than are individuals who hold their behavior under looser controls.

At present, there is some evidence to suggest that violent offenders may differ along a continuum of undercontrolled-overcontrolled, with most at the polar ends of the continuum. We could further hypothesize that undercontrolled violent offenders will be the habitual criminals. Overcontrolled offenders, who usually do not have criminal records, are more likely to engage in one quick, highly violent or murderous episode.

There is also some evidence, however, that indicates that undercontrols and overcontrols are found in the nonviolent populations about as often as found in violent populations (Henderson, 1983). This finding implies that the Megargee schema may not offer as much help in explaining the various types of violence as originally expected. Furthermore, the over- and undercontrolled dimension does not fully account for the role of situational parameters. For example, persons who are passive and unassertive are more likely to experience intense frustrations and to find themselves in many situations where they feel threatened, insecure, and powerless. The Lee-Zimbardo-Bertholf group (1977) tried to relate this lack of social and verbal skills to the sudden murderer, who is typically a shy individual without the necessary interpersonal skills to assert himself in social situations. Obviously, however, most shy people do not become sudden murderers.

When people lack the skills and strategies to modify at least some of their social situations, feelings of helplessness usually result. These feelings are in turn likely to provoke one of two response patterns: approach (attack) or avoidance (withdrawal). The withdrawal response, as theorized by Martin Seligman (1975), is often called *reactive depression* or **learned helplessness.** The person feels there is nothing that can be done about his or her predicament, so why bother? This response pattern is vividly illustrated by powerless people living under dire poverty conditions, who perceive that they have little opportunity for change—a life without hope.

On the other hand, an alternative response is to attack, to lash out in desperation, especially if a person believes this response pattern will be effective in improving his or her circumstances. The sudden murderers, who have been passive and pushed around all their lives, may be resorting to one final attempt to change what is happening to them. Their homicidal violence may be a desperate response to gain immediate control over their lives, without consideration for the future consequences of their act. An interesting question might be posed at this point: Which is more adaptive under seemingly hopeless conditions, remaining depressed and hopeless, committing suicide, or doing something violent in a desperate attempt to change things?

Cognitive Self-Regulation

Research by social learning and cognitive theorists suggests that one's **self-regulatory mechanisms** may be extremely important factors in explaining violent behavior. In fact, considerable research indicates that treatment approaches that improve the self-regulatory systems of violent people hold the greatest promise for reducing violence (Serin & Preston, 2001). According to social learning theory (e.g., Bandura, 1983) and social cognition theory (Bandura, 1986, 1989), we are able to exercise considerable cognitive control over our behavior. Cognitive capacity enables us to transcend the present and think about the future as well as the past, even in the absence of immediate environmental cues. This conceptual thinking ability lets us guide our own behavior by thinking about its possible outcomes. However, circumstances sometimes weaken cognitive control and facilitate impulsive actions. Under certain conditions, therefore, our actions are directed more by external stimuli than by cognitive self-regulatory mechanisms.

The self-regulatory process presumes the development and refinement of cognitive structures and concepts, which is learning. As we stated earlier, the world as we know it is based on our cognitive structures, which are nonspecific but organized representations of prior experiences. Some people possess more structures than others, and some deviate from what the social mainstream regards as "accurate" structures of the world and human nature. People with many sophisticated structures can evaluate behavior in more complex ways than can people with few, crude structures. For example, someone with a large storehouse of sophisticated concepts would be less inclined to label a murderer simply as "sick" or "an animal," but see the individual as a complex of different beliefs and motives.

Under normal circumstances, we perceive, interpret, compare, and act on the basis of these structures, which we will refer to as personal standards. If we do not like what we are doing, we can change our behavior, justify it, or try to stop thinking about it. We can also reward and punish ourselves for our conduct. Self-punishment is expressed as guilt or remorse following actions we consider foreign to our standards. In most instances, however, we prefer self-reinforcement to punishment; therefore, we behave in ways that correspond to our cognitive structures. We anticipate the feelings of guilt we will experience for alien actions, and thus we restrain ourselves. "Anticipatory self-condemning reactions for violating personal standards ordinarily serve as self-deterrents against reprehensible acts" (Bandura, 1983, p. 30). Therefore, each of us develops personal standards or codes of conduct that are maintained by self-reinforcement or self-punishment, as well as by external reinforcement and punishment.

Our standards may be built around simplistic beliefs that "there is a sucker in every crowd," or "people are basically mean and brutal," or "the surest route to success is to take care of number one." People who have adopted the "me first" or "it's all about me" approach, and who are convinced that rigorous competition and aggression are the best strategies for achieving success, may find that aggression—even violent behavior—is a source of self-reinforcement and pride (Toch, 1977). In the extreme, "number one" individuals lack self-reprimands for aggression and harmful conduct. Their personal standards about human nature are a built-in justification for their cruel acts.

Standards are not confined to individuals, but may be characteristic of entire cultures and societies. Some cultures, subcultures, or groups try to develop ethical and moral standards of conduct in their members. We might ask at this point to what extent American society cultivates nonviolent behavior.

Relating all of this specifically to aggression and violence, we can see that personal and group standards dictate much of our behavior. If one's philosophy is that "life is cheap," and if insensitive conduct is the norm, violence can become a way of life. Some people, therefore, are cruel and violent not necessarily to receive reward from the external environment, but because violence reflects their internal standard and implicit theory of human nature. Others, perhaps the majority, have adopted standards and have built cognitive structures that do not condone hurtful or reprehensible conduct.

To some extent, we have oversimplified the self-regulatory mechanisms theory in an effort to introduce some of its concepts. Self-regulation does not invariably operate across all situations. Otherwise, how do we explain destructive and reprehensible conduct perpetrated by apparently decent, moral people over the centuries in the name of religious principles and righteous ideologies? What, if anything, justifies deliberate, planned large-scale violence such as bombing, or war? What about terrorism in the name of some higher principle? How do we explain mob violence, in which seemingly good people appear to be swept along by their emotions or by the crowd? Why don't self-regulatory mechanisms operate then, when they are so needed?

Social learning theory explains some of this by hypothesizing that under certain circumstances self-regulatory processes become *disengaged* from conduct. "In the social learning analysis, moral people perform culpable acts through processes that disengage evaluative self-reactions for such conduct" (Bandura, 1983, p. 31). This disengagement may be what takes place in impulsive violence. As described by Berkowitz (1983) and Zillmann (1983), high levels of emotional arousal take our attention away from our internal mechanisms of control. When we become extremely angry, for example, we often say and do things we later regret. We feel upset, remorseful, and guilty, and we wish we could take back our words and actions. If we had carefully considered and evaluated the consequences of our behavior, we would probably have acted differently. But under the heat of emotion, our self-regulatory system, with all its standards and values, was held in abeyance. As we get older, however, we generally learn from experience to pay closer attention to our internal control mechanisms, and we engage in fewer impulsive outbursts. This "mellowing" feature may partly account for the lower rates of impulsive violence as age increases.

Treatment approaches that focus on arousal reduction techniques, interpersonal skills acquisition, and correcting faulty cognitive reasoning are most likely to be effective in reducing violent behavior (Serin & Preston, 2001). Research has consistently demonstrated that violent offenders (both juvenile and adult) have a dominant collection of irrational beliefs, hostile attribution biases, and usually uncontrolled anger. A prominent example of irrational beliefs found in rapists is the belief that women want to be raped.

Regardless of our personal standards against violence or doing harm to others, therefore, we all may occasionally engage in harmful or even violent conduct. When this happens, we use several approaches to convince ourselves of the "rightness" of our actions. We may feel, for example, that under certain conditions some people need to be taught a lesson. An errant child may be hit; an experimental subject may be shocked; a murderer may be executed in the service of justice. The problematic logic of these explanations becomes evident when they are turned about and used to justify actions of which most people disapprove. As we saw in the section on terrorism, terrorists justify their acts of violence under the premise that they are accomplishing a greater good, like freeing a society from tyrannical rule. Ideally, then, we should very narrowly define conditions under which physical aggression and violence might be justified (e.g., to save another human life). Interestingly, this debate is now occurring over the treatment of detainees in military facilities, such as Guantanamo Bay. Few American citizens would now deny that the United States has tortured detainees, if torture is defined as applying physical or psychological pain in a systematic fashion to extract information. Some believe these tactics are justified in order to accomplish the greater good of preventing terrorist attacks, while others believe they violate human rights and are never justified. A middle position is that a national debate is needed to define specifically which tactics can be used and under what conditions.

We may also neutralize our internal standards to some extent by concluding, "Others are doing it, many of them much more than I am," or "Most people cheat on their income tax returns; it's part of the game." Certainly, this perspective is relevant to participants engaged in corporate or white-collar crime, a topic we return to in chapter 11. In addition, as we saw in the chapter on juvenile delinquency, some groups neutralize their criminal conduct by removing from it the onus of "badness." In fact, engaging in the "bad" conduct may increase one's status within the group.

Another way in which we may downplay our internal standards, especially those against violence, is by convincing ourselves that some individuals are less than human, more animal-like than most. As we learned earlier in the chapter, we may **dehumanize** people who commit terribly cruel and heinous murders, in effect seeing them as closer to animals than most other people. Some people justify capital punishment on the basis that some criminals are subhuman. Dehumanization helps explain the numerous lynchings of African Americans in U.S. history and the treatment of the Jews in Nazi Germany. In war, we dehumanize the enemy by using derogatory epithets. Like justifying the "rightness" of violence, however, dehumanization also works from both perspectives. Thus, the mass or serial murderer and the individual who continually engages in assaultive behavior, as we have seen, view victims as objects divested of humanity. The offender feels little remorse for any suffering inflicted and does not worry about anticipatory self-punishment. On the other hand, it becomes more difficult to behave cruelly toward others as they become personalized and humanized. In other words, if an assailant becomes acquainted with a potential victim, there is less likelihood that he or she will be cruel. This would seem especially true of crimes in which killing the victim is not the primary goal.

Finally, we may also disengage our personal standards from our conduct when we are told to do something reprehensible by a legitimate authority. Again as we learned in the terrorism section, when someone who possesses legitimate power commands us to do something, we are, in a sense, relieved of personal responsibility for the conduct, even if the conduct is alien to our personal standards. This concept is called **displacement of responsibility** by Bandura (2004), **strong respect for authority** by Staub (2004), or **obedience to authority** by Milgram (1974).

In sum, the self-regulatory system we develop is not invariant or automatic, but dynamic and subject to certain experiences and circumstances. Moreover, many events are ambiguous and do not fit readily into our existing cognitive templates. Under these conditions, we are more likely to seek clues from outside sources. Nevertheless, the value of the self-regulatory system is its tendency to guide our behavior toward what we believe is the right thing to do in a particular situation. The more we believe in our internal standards, the less prone we will be to rely on outside sources, even under stress or pressure situations. This suggests that the best internal standards are those we have developed ourselves, rather than those imposed or advocated by an external group, which we embrace only for convenience or for appearances.

Interestingly, some research suggests that women are more likely to see aggression as a breakdown of self-regulatory mechanisms than are men (Campbell, Muncer, & Coyle, 1992). To women, aggressive behavior "represents a personal failure to adhere to standards of behaviour which they (and others) set for themselves, and consequently they view it negatively" (Campbell et al., 1992, p. 98). Conversely, men are more likely to see aggression as a means of imposing control and dominance over others and, therefore, regard aggressive behavior as more positive.

Fortunately, most people have developed an internal standard that to wantonly harm another person is wrong. Therefore, the reason that a vast majority of people do not engage in violent behavior is not simply because of a classically conditioned reflex. Rather, it is most likely because they have adopted a belief system that subscribes to the view that it is wrong to harm another human being, at least without just cause. Of course, the human tendency to justify one's behavior—the just-cause argument—is often inseparable from the most heinous violence in human history. We justify large-scale organized violence (wars), claiming we must protect ourselves, family, and way of life from the brutal (less than human) enemy.

The next section focuses on mob behavior and what happens to the self-regulatory mechanisms of normally gentle people caught up in a madding crowd. The crowd, it seems, often robs the individual of his or her identity and, consequently, his or her usual reliance on personal standards of conduct. Some of the most violent behavior is exhibited, not by single individuals, but by excited groups, especially large ones. Physical assaults that occur in the midst of riots or demonstrations, vigilante-instigated lynchings or beatings, gang rapes, and public stonings all illustrate this mob violence.

DEINDIVIDUATION AND CROWD VIOLENCE

The powerful effects of crowds on individual behavior has interested social scientists since the early 1900s. Crowd influence is usually studied under the rubric *collective behavior,* which includes riots, gang rapes, panics, lynchings, demonstrations, and revolutions. For our purposes, we are concerned with collective behavior only as it affects the instigation and maintenance of violence.

One of the first theorists of collective behavior was Gustave LeBon, whose 1896 book *The Crowd* is regarded as the classic study of groups. Because his views were colored by the French Revolution, LeBon did not take kindly to individual behavior swayed by the crowd. Humans in a crowd are like a herd of animals, he said, easily swayed or spooked. LeBon believed that those who normally are nonviolent and law abiding are capable of the kind of violence, intolerance, and general cruelty found in the most primitive savages. The person enmeshed in the mob loses sensibility and the ability to reason, and forfeits his or her own mind to the crowd. The collective mind is dangerously brutal and destructive to people and property. According to LeBon, even educated people become simpleminded and irrational under its influence. Essentially, LeBon claimed, each person comes under the control of the reflexive "spinal cord" rather than the cerebral cortex.

Most of us have seen dramatizations of a "berserk" mob clamoring for the destruction of some political, social, or physical institution or for swift "justice" for an individual or group. Descriptions of mob actions often liken them to brush fires that grow in intensity and are quickly out of control. However, since true mob actions are naturally occurring and spontaneous events, it is difficult to place them under the scrutiny of scientific, systematic investigation. The processes involved in mob action are still not well understood. Some social psychologists (e.g., Diener, 1980; Zimbardo, 1970) have attempted laboratory studies of mob or group violence, generally by approximating conditions that might bring out aggression and positing that, if allowed to continue, the aggression would likely result in violence. Obviously, they must stop far short of actual violence, so whether it would have occurred remains speculative. The procedure of trying to mimic an event under laboratory conditions is called a **simulation.**

Zimbardo (1970) believed that deindividuation accounts for much of the tendency of otherwise "tame" individuals to engage in antisocial, violent behavior. Recall from chapter 5 that deindividuation includes a reduction in feelings of personal distinctiveness, identifiability, and personal responsibility. Furthermore, in a crowd the threshold of normally restrained behavior is lowered. In other words, people feel anonymous, less responsible for their behavior, and less inhibited. According to Zimbardo, these conditions encourage the antisocial behavior associated with selfishness, greed, hostility, lust, cruelty, and destruction.

In one widely cited experiment, Zimbardo manipulated two variables, feelings of anonymity and features about the victim. He randomly assigned female college students to deindividuation and "identifiable" groups. Subjects in the deindividuation group wore shapeless white lab coats and hoods over their heads and worked in dimly lit conditions. The experimenters avoided using their names. By contrast, participants in the identifiable groups felt anything but anonymous. They wore large name tags, were greeted by name, worked under fully illuminated conditions, and wore their own clothes with no added lab coats or hoods.

Subjects were told the project was set up to study empathy. The real purpose, of course, was to study the relationship between deindividuation and aggression. Each subject listened to a five-minute recorded interview between her future "victim" and the experimenter. Some victims were portrayed as warm, sincere, honest persons, while others were obnoxious, self-centered, conceited, and critical. After each interview, the subjects were allowed to administer shock to the interviewees they had heard on tape. They were allowed to observe the reactions of their victims by way of a one-way mirror. Aggressive behavior of the subjects was measured by the length of time a painful electrical shock was administered. "Victims"—who actually received no shock—were trained to writhe, twist, and grimace.

Recall now that Zimbardo was manipulating two variables, anonymity (loss of personal identity) and features of the victim (environmental stimuli). Thus, some subjects were hooded, others were well-identified. Some victims were pleasant and likable, others were obnoxious. Zimbardo reasoned that members of the deindividuation group would administer shocks of longer duration because of the diffusion of responsibility and loss of personal identity. He also hypothesized that victim features would be irrelevant, because the heightened arousal experienced under deindividuation would interfere with the ability to discriminate between the victims. Put another way, the excitement and resulting arousal engendered by shocking someone without the threat of any repercussions would prevent discernment of the target (the person receiving the shock).

One additional hypothesis was tested. Zimbardo predicted that subjects in the deindividuation group would administer longer shocks as the experiment progressed. He believed the act of administering shock without responsibility would be exciting and reinforcing for its own sake (what he called "affective proprioceptive feedback"). Zimbardo predicted that members of the deindividuation group would increase the duration of shock administered to the victim as the experiment progressed. In brief, the person finds that doing the antisocial behavior feels "so good" each time she does it that the behavior builds on itself in intensity (vigor) and frequency.

Results of the experiment supported all three hypotheses. The deindividuation group shocked victims twice as long as the identifiable group. The deindividuation group also administered the same levels of shock, regardless of the victim's personality features. And, finally, this group shocked for longer periods as the experiment progressed. "Under conditions specified as deindividuating, these sweet, normally mild-mannered college girls shocked another girl almost every time they had an opportunity to do so, sometimes for as long as they were allowed, and it did not matter whether or not that fellow student was a nice girl who didn't deserve to be hurt," Zimbardo concluded (1970, p. 170).

Essentially, Zimbardo argued that deindividuated aggression is not controlled by the social environment; it is unresponsive to both the situation and the state or characteristics of the victim. That is, the high arousal generated by the excitement of a crowd reduces both (1) a person's private self-awareness and (2) his or her ability to discriminate among external stimuli, such as victim characteristics. The participant is no longer guided by self-regulatory mechanisms and is "blind" to such stimuli as the victim's distress or discomfort. The aggressor loses individuality to the collective mind of the crowd; he or she neither feels compassion nor considers the circumstances. The victim may plead, beg, cry, or scream, but these stimuli will have little effect on the crowd behavior. Even a prestigious and powerful authority figure may be unable to stop the violence once self-identity is obliterated by the furor of the crowd.

Zimbardo's research design, like that of Milgram, has been criticized extensively for its questionable use of subject deception and shock (albeit simulated) and its focus on the negative aspects of human behavior. In a sense, these types of experiments constitute a form of psychological entrapment. Would people really act this way if not prompted by an experimenter? In the wake of such experiments, the National Institute of Mental Health, the American Psychological Association, and other organizations have adopted ethical guidelines that are applied to the funding and approval of research. Experiments like Zimbardo's, therefore, are unlikely to be replicated. Nevertheless, their possible implications cannot be ignored.

Diener (1980) disagrees with the tenets of Zimbardo's deindividuation theory, postulating that deindividuated behavior is responsive to situational or victim characteristics. He believes that a person's normal self-regulatory behavior is reduced by the unusual and exciting activity of the crowd and that this reduced private self-awareness creates an internal state of deindividuation. Since the individual has trouble retrieving his or her standards of appropriate conduct, he or she becomes more responsive to environmental cues (Prentice-Dunn & Rogers, 1982, 1983). In crowds, people do report a strong loss of individual identity, an overwhelming tendency to concentrate on the moment rather than the future, and substantially altered thinking and emotion (Prentice-Dunn & Rogers, 1983). They become less aware of thoughts, moods, bodily states, and other internal processes. Think of the athlete caught up in the excitement of the game, who continues to play while seriously injured. After the game the athlete might exclaim about a fractured arm, "It didn't feel that serious!"

According to Diener, because deindividuated individuals do not pay attention to their internal processes, including their self-regulatory capabilities, they depend more on environmental cues for behavioral direction. Thus, when aggressive and violent cues are present, they are far more likely than usual to engage in violence. It is Diener's contention that if the victim of a mob action could, in some way, be "humanized," the crowd might stop its brutality. In other words, perpetrators' attention should be directed toward the victim rather than the violence being displayed by other actors. Diener also believes that participants in a mob action can be made to pay closer attention to their internal regulation norms. His hypothesis deserves to be tested by further research. Of course, whether the cries and pleas of the victim during an attack actually could alter the crowd behavior is a question unlikely to be answered by laboratory research. Furthermore, because the theories of Zimbardo and Diener are based on laboratory studies, we cannot conclude that they generalize to actual situations. They do, however, suggest possible explanations for violent mob behavior.

 ## SUMMARY AND CONCLUSIONS

In the latter part of the twentieth century, the typical textbook in criminology paid scant attention to the topic of terrorism. The events of September 11, 2001, drastically changed that. Although terrorist activities had been occurring, both in the United States and worldwide, long before the attacks on the World Trade Center and the Pentagon, that date marked a radical shift in public attention and fear, law enforcement activity, and psychological interest. By definition, terrorism involves the unlawful use of force or violence, so by definition, terrorist activities are criminal.

We covered in this chapter the FBI's classifications of terrorist *groups*—according to their political leanings—and psychology's classifications of terrorist *motivations*. The groups include the right-wing terrorists, the radical environmental, the special interest extremists, and the nuclear/biological/chemical group. Note that these categories best characterize domestic terrorism; while the Al-Qaeda terrorists would probably be classified in the right-wing group, they are far different in organization, skills, and motivations from Timothy McVeigh or Theodore Kaczynski. Classifications of psychological motives are better able to capture terrorism in all its facets, despite the fact that we discussed only three *categories:* rationally motivated, psychologically motivated, and culturally motivated terrorists.

The chapter also covered the psychosocial context of terrorism, specifically those social and psychological characteristics of a society or a group that are conducive to the emergence of terrorist groups. When a society or a group devalues another, the devalued other can be seen as a scapegoat or an ideological enemy and thus can become the target of terrorist attacks. Abortion providers became the targets of terrorist attacks because their activities were seen as morally bad. Symbols of power in the United States—the Trade Center and the Pentagon—were attacked by al-Qaeda because the United States was seen as a dangerous enemy. Perceptions of inequity, relative deprivation, or injustice are also conducive to the emergence of terrorist groups. While most individuals and groups with these perceptions do not terrorize others, those who do terrorize often harbor those perceptions. Finally, the hierarchical command structure evident in many terrorist groups suggests that strong belief in authority and respect of a charismatic leader may facilitate terrorist activity, when the group is already predisposed to that type of action.

While there is no single motive for terrorism, most terrorist acts, because of their horrifying nature, involve some cognitive restructuring. As Bandura has observed, individuals who engage in terrorism justify their actions in a variety of ways. These include using techniques of moral justification, whereby they convince themselves that their actions are socially worthy and have an ultimate moral purpose—the ends justify the means. Terrorists also use euphemistic language and advantageous comparison to restructure their cognitions; thus their own actions are seen as harmless compared with the actions of the targets of their activities. Finally, terrorists may dehumanize their targets and lose their own identities—and their individual responsibility—by deindividuating. It is the collective not the individual identity that is responsible.

We ended the chapter with a focus on psychological explanations of violence as an aggressive activity. While all violence is aggressive, not all aggression is violence. The psychological perspective suggests several issues that surround common violence, including the violence that results in loss of life. We must be careful not to assume that these features are present in all violent offenders, however.

For many who engage in violent actions, the self-regulatory mechanism is flawed, particularly under states of high emotional arousal. Violence is most often committed while the participants are under these very high levels of emotional arousal, particularly anger. High arousal seems to reduce the ability to attend to internal standards of conduct and general self-awareness. Furthermore, high arousal seems to make people feel less responsible for their actions; they often claim, "I don't know what came over me," or "I couldn't help it." In short, high arousal renders people more susceptible to "mindless" behaviors and places them under the influence of external stimuli or events. Another enemy of self-regulation is deindividuation, which is displayed in aggressive behavior carried out in crowds (e.g., mob violence) or in small group situations. In such a context, self-regulatory mechanisms may break down.

Self-regulatory mechanisms develop through socialization and personal beliefs about what is right or appropriate, wrong or inappropriate. Under normal conditions, they control behavior by providing cognitive templates for what is proper behavior for a specific situation. The effect of arousal on these self-regulatory mechanisms appears especially important in explaining street or domestic violence, in which the violence is spontaneous, highly charged, and often used as a way of settling personal conflicts.

Individual construct systems are highly similar to the self-regulation process, but refer in this context to the human ability to justify or neutralize conduct, no matter how reprehensible. Self-regulation refers to behavioral control; the construct system enables a person to perform an act and deal with it later. Human beings, with their intricate cognitive equipment, have an uncanny knack for neutralizing, disregarding, minimizing, rationalizing, and misjudging their deeds. We have an enormous capacity for disengaging our beliefs and our internal standards from our actions, and we can do this both before and after they are completed.

Bandura (1983) lists six common disengagement practices we use for dealing with our own reprehensible, antisocial conduct. It is instructive to examine each of these strategies, although we only alluded to them in the chapter. These practices, though, serve as a good summary of much of what we have covered here.

First, people do not ordinarily engage in antisocial conduct until they have justified to themselves the rightness or morality of their actions. Reprehensible acts can be made honorable through cognitive restructuring. Thus, a distressed father, convinced that he must save his family from the evil of the world, kills his children, his wife, and then himself. In essence he reconstructed his construct system to fit what he believed was the right thing to do under the circumstances. Another example is that of a moral young man who believes killing is wrong and who voluntarily goes to war to protect his country. At first, these two actions may seem to have nothing in common. However, they both represent cognitive restructuring.

A second disengagement practice—related to the first—is that of people convincing themselves that their violent acts are really trivial and not all that bad compared with what others have done. In war we convince ourselves that the atrocities committed by the enemy are far worse than anything we do. The concept of advantageous comparison, discussed with reference to cognitive reconstructing by terrorists, is similar. A rapist might convince himself that rape is not really that serious, since no "real" physical harm comes to the victim.

A third strategy involves the power of language. One of the costs of human intellectual ability is the considerable power of words; they allow us to justify our actions with relative ease. We use euphemisms to neutralize reprehensible behavior. For example, intelligence manuals use words like neutralize and terminate instead of assassinate and kill. The euphemisms carry less onus and cause less disruption to moral beliefs. In the chapter on juvenile delinquency, we noted that youth subcultures employ various euphemisms to neutralize their antisocial acts.

A fourth strategy—one most commonly found in group violence—is the diffusion of responsibility. Statements that best typify this practice include "I was just following orders," "I was just following the crowd," and "The executive board decided that it was in the best interest of the economy (and the company) to continue production, despite some risk to the health of others." These assertions have the effect of displacing responsibility for one's actions to others, or to forces outside oneself.

A fifth strategy is to not even think about the consequences of one's actions. Here, people convince themselves that the consequences are not important. Alternately, they manage to detach themselves from the aftermath of violent actions. For example, the bombardier or the person who pushes the button that will release lethal chemicals onto a civilian population is not only following orders (diffusion of responsibility) but also is probably not allowing himself to think about the tragedy that will result.

Finally, the sixth practice is to dehumanize the victim. "She was loose and got what she deserved." "He was scum." The enemies are labeled "gooks" or something akin to vicious animals. Dehumanization removes all the human, dignifying qualities from the victim or intended victim. As Bandura (1983, p. 32) points out: "Many conditions of contemporary life are conducive to dehumanization. Bureaucratization, automation, urbanization, and high social mobility lead people to relate to each other in anonymous, impersonal ways." These impersonal, dehumanizing aspects of life facilitate violence and make living with it possible.

KEY CONCEPTS

Radical environmental groups
Bioterrorism
Moral justification
Advantageous comparison
Crime of obedience
Habit strength
Overcontrolled personality
Self-regulatory mechanisms
Displacement of responsibility
Obedience to authority

Special interest extremists
Cognitive restructuring
Euphemistic language
Dehumanization
Deindividuation
Undercontrolled personality
Learned helplessness
Dehumanize
Strong respect for authority
Simulation

REVIEW QUESTIONS

1. Based on your reading of the chapter, what factor is the most important in influencing young people to become terrorists?
2. Define moral justification and how it may play a part in terrorist acts.
3. Define cognitive restructuring, with particular emphasis on how advantageous comparisons play an important role in the development of terrorism.
4. Summarize Megargee's theory of violence.
5. Identify and discuss the psychological factors that have been associated with general violent crime.
6. Define euphemistic language, and identify how it is linked to terrorism and other acts of violence.
7. Define dehumanization and how it enters into brutal, demeaning acts of violence.

CHAPTER 12

SEXUAL ASSAULT

CHAPTER OBJECTIVES

- Define rape and its many legal complexities.
- Examine the psychological effects of rape on victims.
- Briefly review the legislation on sex offending.
- Describe in detail the Massachusetts Treatment Center's classification system of rapists to highlight the heterogeneity of rape offenders.
- Describe the Groth typology of rape offenders.
- Identify attitudes toward rape and the extent of rape myths in society.
- Evaluate the effects of pornography on sex offending.

Sexual behavior in many societies is a subject fraught with moral codes, taboos, norm expectations, religious injunctions, myths, and unscientific conclusions. In the United States, the daring venture of Albert Kinsey and his colleagues in publishing the scientific evidence they had gathered at the Institute for Sexual Research dispelled numerous myths and corrected fallacies about sex. Many still linger, however, especially with reference to the sex offender, for whom society has little tolerance. Moreover, society often does not distinguish between types of sex offenses. "Degenerates" who expose themselves to passersby or watch unsuspecting women undressing are as likely to be feared or to attract disgust and anger as are rapists and child molesters. Often, the community clamors for the strict and speedy prosecution of the offender, who is considered a deranged or evil person (or animal) driven by some inner sinister force, and from whom citizens must be protected.

Sexual offenders are frequently viewed as a homogeneous class of individuals. Research shows, however, that they vary widely in the frequency and type of sexual activity they engage in, and they differ in personal attributes such as age, background, personality, race, religion, beliefs, attitudes, and interpersonal skills (Knight, Rosenberg, & Schneider, 1985). *There is no single profile that encompasses a majority of sex offenders.* The features of their crimes also differ markedly among offenders, including time and place, the gender and age of the victim, the degree of planning the offense, and the amount of violence used or intended (Knight, Rosenberg, & Schneider, 1985). In addition, sex offenders often commit a variety of crime beyond sexual offenses. In fact, there is considerable evidence to show that adult sexual offenders are more likely to be convicted for nonsexual offenses than they are for sexual offenses, both before and after a conviction for a sexual offense (Smallbone & Wortley, 2004).

WHO OFFENDS?

Surprisingly, adolescent males commit 20 percent to 30 percent of all rapes and 30 percent to 50 percent of all child molestations (Becker & Johnson, 2001). What is also surprising is that 70 percent of these adolescent sex offenders come from two-parent homes, most attend school and achieve average grades, and very few suffer from major mental disorders (Becker & Johnson, 2001). Researchers also have begun to focus on sexual offending by girls, a subject that until recently was virtually ignored (Becker & Johnson, 2001). There is also considerable evidence that prepubescent children—both boys and girls—may commit sexual offenses at a rate much higher than commonly supposed. Several studies have reported sexual aggression in children as young as 3 or 4 years of age (Araji, 1997), although their aggressive actions do not qualify as crimes because children at these ages cannot form the necessary criminal intent. In addition, a surprisingly large number of preadolescent girls are reported to be sexually aggressive toward other children, and these girls often engage in behaviors that are just as aggressive as boys' behaviors (Araji, 1997). Victims of preadolescent offenders are generally very young (averaging between ages 4 and 7), most often are female (when the offender is a male), and typically are siblings, friends, or acquaintances (Righthand & Welch, 2001).

The causes of sexual offending are neither simple nor straightforward. As the knowledge from systematic study accumulates, it is clear that this behavior is influenced by multiple, interactive factors. Past learning experiences, cognitive expectations and beliefs, conditioning, environmental stimuli, and reinforcement contingencies (both rewards and punishments) are all involved. In this chapter we review the major research findings on potential causal factors involved in rape, particularly rape of adults. In the following chapter, chapter 13, we discuss in detail sexual assaults of children, as well as additional sexual offenses.

Some studies (e.g., Revitch & Schlesinger, 1988) reveal that many sex offenders are not prone to violence or physical cruelty, but rather are timid, shy, and socially inhibited. While this may be correct for a large segment of pedophiles—those who offend against children—it is not for rapists, whose attacks often have strong aggressive features. In fact, their sexual aggression can be divided into at least two major categories: instrumental and expressive. **Instrumental sexual aggression** is when the sexual offender uses just enough coercion to gain compliance from his victim. In **expressive sexual aggression,** the offender's primary aim is to harm the victim physically as well as psychologically. In some cases the expressive aggression is "eroticized" in that the offender becomes sexually aroused in the presence of physical or psychological brutality.

Regardless of the sex offender's characteristics, motivations, and method of attack or coercion, the social and psychological costs to victims and their families are immeasurable and often devastating. A survey of 3,132 households in the Los Angeles Epidemiologic Catchment Area (ECA) study illustrates this very well. Researchers found that over 13 percent of the individuals interviewed had been victims of sexual assault at least once in their lifetimes (Burnam et al., 1988; Siegel et al., 1987; Sorenson et al., 1987). Two-thirds of the sexually assaulted subjects reported two or more assaults. Moreover, lifetime sexual assault was more frequently reported by women (16.7%) than men (9.4%). In a sobering finding, 13 percent of the victims were first assaulted between the ages of 6 and 10, 19 percent between 11 and 15, 34 percent between 16 and 20, and 15 percent between 21 and 25. The experience of being sexually assaulted was associated with substantially higher risks for later onset of serious, self-destructive depression, substance abuse, numerous fears and inhibiting anxieties, and a variety of major interpersonal problems. Overall, the ECA project found that both male and female victims of sexual assault are two to four times more likely than nonvictims to develop serious psychological problems.

LEGISLATION ON SEX OFFENDERS

Before proceeding into the chapter, it is important to understand that several pieces of landmark legislation have been enacted during the past decade that strongly influence how the federal and state governments view sex offenders. National data suggest that there are approximately 234,000 sex offenders under the care, custody, or control of correction agencies on any given day (Chaiken, 1998b). We caution, though, that the term sex offender ranges from rapists to exhibitionists. Although not all sex offenders are violent, in recent years highly publicized, brutally violent attacks were perpetrated by convicted-but-released sex offenders on young, vulnerable victims. These incidents had an enormous influence on state and federal legislation designed to prevent similar offenses. Much of the recent legislation on sex offenders is derived from the comprehensive Violent Crime Control and Law Enforcement Act of 1994, legislation that formed the basis for the U.S. Department of Justice's strategy for dealing with violent offenders. For our purposes here, we will briefly describe three laws that are most relevant to the topics in this chapter.

During the past two decades, the U.S. Congress passed three laws that collectively require states to strengthen the procedures they use to keep track of sex offenders or risk the loss of federal funding. The laws were (1) The Jacob Wetterling Crimes against Children and Sexually Violent Offender Registration Act (enacted in 1994), (2) the federal version of Megan's Law (enacted in 1996), and (3) the Pam Lychner Sexual Offender Tracking and Identification Act (also enacted in 1996). All three statutes require states to establish registration programs so that local law enforcement and community officials will know the whereabouts of sex offenders released into their jurisdiction, and enforce notification programs so the public can be warned about sex offenders living in the community (Chaiken, 1998b).

The Jacob Wetterling Act encourages states to require convicted child molesters and sexually violent offenders to notify law enforcement of their whereabouts for 10 years after they are released from prison, parole, or community supervision. The required notification time may be longer if the offender is considered a "sexually violent predator," or one whose crimes were especially heinous. The act encourages states to adopt registration systems for convicted child molesters and other persons convicted of sexually violent crimes. The act was named in honor of 11-year-old Jacob Wetterling of St. Joseph, Minnesota, who was abducted at gunpoint by a masked man in 1989. The young boy was never found.

The second type of legislation, known as Megan's Law, requires states to release registration information to the public *when it is necessary for public safety,* a requirement often referred to as "mandatory community notification." While the Wetterling Act does not require that communities be notified of the release of sex offenders, Megan's Law specifies that local communities be so notified, although the extent of notification varies according to the offender's level of dangerousness. For example, in the case of Level 3 offenders, officials must notify the community at large; in the case of Level 2 offenders, only certain agencies (e.g., schools, day care centers) must be notified; in the case of Level 1 offenders, a passive notification process is in effect. That is, members of the community are told if they ask. Megan's Law was named after 7-year-old Megan Kanka of Hamilton Square, New Jersey, who in 1994 was assaulted, raped, and murdered by a twice-convicted pedophile living across the street.

The Lychner Act amended the Violent Crime Control and Law Enforcement Act of 1994 to require the FBI to establish a national offender database and to handle sex offender registration and notification in states unable to maintain "minimally sufficient" programs on their own. Basically, the Lychner Act establishes more stringent registration requirements for sex offenders living within the community. Under the act, offenders considered the most dangerous to public safety will be required to register for life wherever they go. The Lychner Act was named for a Houston real estate agent named Pam Lychner. A twice-convicted felon, waiting for her, brutally assaulted Lychner when she went to show a vacant house. Her life was saved when her husband arrived on the scene and interrupted the attack. Tragically, Pam Lychner and her two daughters were later killed in the explosion of TWA Flight 800 off the coast of Long Island, New York, in July 1996.

Although Congress determined that states must have registration and notification laws on the books if they wished to continue to receive federal funds, it was left to the states to determine precisely how these laws would be crafted. Most state laws are modeled on the above federal statutes, with some modifications. In 2002, the U.S. Supreme Court upheld provisions of the registration laws in two states, Alaska and Connecticut, making it highly likely that registration and community notification will continue far into the foreseeable future. Information about sex offenders has now become so widely available that it is commonly on the Internet. In some communities, cable stations carry pictures of offenders along with some details of their crimes, including the ages of their victims.

As part of the Violent Crime Control and Law Enforcement Act of 1994, Congress also passed the Violence against Women Act (VAWA), which takes a comprehensive approach to domestic violence and sexual assault through a broad array of legal reforms. This law launched the first major federal effort to address violence against women. One of the many things the VAWA does is to extend the rape shield law to protect victims from abusive inquiries regarding their private sexual conduct. Two additional federal initiatives expanded the scope of the Violent Crime Control and Law Enforcement Act of 1994. One of the initiatives makes it illegal for a U.S. citizen or permanent resident to travel in interstate or foreign commerce with the intent to engage in sexual acts with a minor that are prohibited under federal law in the United States. This law is often referred to as the "child sex tourism" offense. The second initiative, enacted in 1996, is known as the Child Pornography Prevention Act. The act stipulates that it is illegal to purchase or download any computer-generated depiction of a child engaged in sexually explicit conduct.

RAPE: DEFINITIONS AND STATISTICS

Definitions of rape vary widely from state to state; in many states the term *sexual assault* has replaced *rape* in the criminal statutes. According to the U.S. Department of Justice, rape is "unlawful sexual intercourse with a female, by force or without legal or factual consent" (U.S. Department of Justice, 1988, p. 2). The UCR defines rape somewhat differently, distinguishing forcible from statutory rape or rape by fraud. **Forcible rape** is "the carnal knowledge of a female forcibly and against her will" (Federal Bureau of Investigation, 2005, p. 27). It includes assaults and attempts to commit rape by force or threat of force. **Statutory rape** without force and other sex offenses are excluded. Statutory rape is the carnal knowledge of a girl (a female under statutory age), with or without her consent. The limitation of the previous definitions is that they are restricted to female victims. In other words, *male* rape victims are not included in the UCR tabulations. Statutory rape pertains exclusively to consensual intercourse, as opposed to other types of sexual contact (Langan, Schmitt, & Durose, 2003).

The critical factor for statutory rape is the age of the victim, an arbitrary legal cutoff point below which a girl is believed not to have the maturity to consent to intercourse or understand the consequences. Age limits vary from state to state, but most set the limit at 16 or 18. Thus, if an adult male engages in sexual relations with a minor female, he may be convicted of statutory rape.

Rape by fraud is having sexual relations with a consenting adult female under fraudulent conditions. Among the most frequently cited examples is that of the psychotherapist who has sexual intercourse with a patient under the guise of offering treatment.

Many in the general population (including the victims themselves) do not define sexual attacks as rape unless the assailant is a stranger. Thus, if the victim is sexually assaulted by a husband or a boyfriend, she may not report the incident. Criminal justice officials, as well as the general public, often feel that marital or date rapes are unimportant because they are believed to happen so rarely, compared with stranger rape, or to be less psychologically traumatic to the victim. Criminal prosecutors, for example, admit they are reluctant to prosecute marital or date rape cases because of concerns that juries will not believe that a woman could be raped by a husband or male friend (Kilpatrick, Best, Saunders, & Veronen, 1988). However, in a survey of the general population conducted by Kilpatrick and colleagues (1988), subjects who had been raped identified their husbands as assailants in 24 percent of the cases and male friends in 17 percent of the cases. These data suggest that over 40 percent of the rapes were committed by husbands or dates, a significant and frequently overlooked statistic in the tabulation of rape.

Date Rape

Date rapes (sometimes called acquaintance rapes) may be far more common than generally realized, perhaps as high as 60 percent of all rapes. Some recent data suggest that up to one-third of young adults between the ages of 16 and 24 have reported being involved in at least one abusive dating incident (Lingren, 2001). **Date rape,** a term coined in 1984, refers specifically to a sexual assault that occurs within the context of a dating relationship. In a survey conducted by Frintner and Rubinson (1993) of 925 college women, over one-fourth of the respondents had experienced sexual assault or attempted sexual assault. Nearly 83 percent of the college women who had been sexually assaulted said the attacker had been someone they knew and that most of these incidents had happened during their freshman year.

Date rape has many risk factors because the male often feels he is "entitled to payback" since he probably initiated the date, paid all or most the expenses, and drove his vehicle. Under these conditions, the woman often blames herself for the attack and, as noted earlier, is blamed by others for somehow arousing her date. In addition, sexual assault by a date or acquaintance may be more traumatizing than assault by a stranger because of the implicit trust involved.

Another traumatizing aspect of date rape refers to a phenomenon pointed out by Karmen (1996). Karmen distinguishes a common belief in society between a "real rape" and a date rape. In real rapes, the presumption is that the woman is clearly raped if she is ambushed as an unsuspecting victim by a blitz attack by a complete stranger. It is more convincing if the attacker is armed and leaps out of the darkness to surprise his prey. The rape is even more real if the victim suffers some physical injury. A date rape, on the other hand, is often not considered a real rape since it occurred on an arranged date with someone she knew and agreed to go out with. We return to the topic of date rape in chapter 16 when "date rape drugs" are discussed.

Classification of Rape Offenses

The classification and study of rape offenses are hampered by the fact that jurisdictions vary widely in their definitions of rape, often disagreeing with the Department of Justice or UCR guidelines. In the mid-1970s, the National Institute of Law Enforcement and Criminal Justice funded extensive surveys of law enforcement agencies that illustrate these differences (Chappell, 1977a, 1977b). Most agencies reported that vaginal penetration was the minimum criterion for an alleged offense to qualify as rape. Over half of the law enforcement agencies surveyed also required evidence of both penetration and force, while another third required evidence of penetration, force, a weapon, and/or resistance by the victim. As might be expected, the average number of rapes reported by the latter agencies was significantly lower than the average number reported by other law enforcement agencies accepting less-demanding criteria.

Prosecutors require more stringent evidence than law enforcement agencies before accepting an incident as a probable rape. Most of the 150 prosecutors polled in the Chappell survey set four threshold criteria for filing a complaint of forcible rape: (1) evidence of penetration, (2) lack of victim consent, (3) threat of force, and (4) female gender of the victim. It is intriguing to note, however, that 92 percent of the prosecutors sampled did not have formal guidelines for filing a charge of forcible rape. Therefore, their survey responses were more likely to reflect their own judgments about the minimum threshold requirements for initiating action against an alleged offender.

Although some agencies follow the UCR guidelines for classifying rape, many adopt different classification systems. About one-third have more stringent requirements, one-fifth less stringent. Some jurisdictions distinguish between attempted rape and forcible rape. Many, especially the larger ones, include different degrees of forcible rape (e.g., first and second degree). In addition, the term sexual assault is now increasingly being used, either to replace rape or in addition to it.

In cases involving multiple offenses (e.g., rape plus burglary, homicide, or robbery), the offense considered the more "serious" takes precedence and is more likely to be tabulated in the offense statistics, while the "lesser" crime committed at the same time is not recorded. For instance, since homicide is considered to be a more serious crime than forcible rape, homicide-rapes traditionally are tabulated under homicide and not under rape. This is the procedure used under the UCR "hierarchy rule" that was discussed in chapter 1. With the new incident-based reporting system also discussed in that chapter, accurate statistics are more likely to be gathered. At present, because of the wide variations in defining rape and sexual assault as well as procedures for collecting data, we must view statistical comparisons and information pertaining to the "average" rape very cautiously.

Incidence and Prevalence of Rape

From all indications, the United States has the highest incidence of rape in the world. An estimated 94,635 forcible rapes were reported to law enforcement agencies nationwide in 2004 (Federal Bureau of Investigation, 2005). This rate represents 6 percent of the total violent crime reported. As mentioned in the previous section, the UCR's definition recognizes only women and girls as victims of rape. Available data suggest that about 10 percent of the rapes in this country do not conform to the UCR definition (Chaiken, 1998a). Specifically, it is estimated that in about 9 percent of the reported rapes, the victim was male. And in another 1 percent, both the offender and the victim were female. In 2004, an estimated 64.4 of every 100,000 females (women and girls 12 and over) were reported victims of forcible rape (Federal Bureau of Investigation, 2005). Rapes by force accounted for 91 percent of the total rapes reported in 2004, with the remaining 9 percent being attempts to commit forcible rape. Forcible rape had a national clearance rate of 41.8 percent during 2004 (Federal Bureau of Investigation, 2005).

Of course we must recognize that the actual rape rate is greatly underestimated, partly because of some of the problems listed in the previous section, and partly because of the ordeal women must go through just to report the incident. Victimization studies offer a revealing contrast to the official rates. The National Crime Victimization Survey finds that about two-thirds of the rape and sexual assaults committed in the United States go unreported (Ringel, 1997). Russell (1983) selected at random and interviewed 930 women living in the San Francisco area. She learned that 175 of them (19%) reported at least one completed extramarital rape, and 284 (13%) reported at least one attempted extramarital rape. Fifty percent of those reporting these incidents said they had been raped or attacked more than once, and only 8 percent said they had reported any rape incident to law enforcement authorities. An early study by Hindelang and his associates (Hindelang, Dunn, Sutton, & Aumick, 1976), designed to gather victimization rates on randomly selected households, found that only about one out of every four forcible or attempted rapes were reported to law enforcement agencies. Another early study of hitchhike rape estimated that over two-thirds went unreported (Nelson & Amir, 1975). Based on a national sample of college students from 32 U.S. colleges and universities, Koss and her colleagues (Koss, Gidycz, & Wisniewski, 1987) discovered that about 28 percent of the college women had been victims of rape or attempted rape (as defined by the UCR). More startling, however, was the finding that virtually none of the incidents were reported to the police and thus were not recorded in official crime statistics. Based on their data, Koss and her colleagues estimated that the victimization rate for women was 3,800 per 100,000, a rate drastically different from the official rates of 65 to 75 per 100,000.

Additional victimization data indicate that there is approximately a one in five chance that a woman will be raped at some time during her lifetime (Furby, Weinrott, & Blackshaw, 1989). If we include *attempted* rape, the odds may be three to one (Russell & Howell, 1983). As mentioned previously, a surprising number of women are sexually victimized while on a date. Approximately 22 percent of college women surveyed indicated they had been subjected to a forced sexual encounter (e.g., fondling, oral sex, or intercourse) by a date at some point in their lives (Dull & Giacopassi, 1987; Yegidis, 1986). Rapaport and Burkhart (1984) found that 15 percent of a sample of college men acknowledged that they had obtained sexual intercourse against their dates' will. Koss, Gidycz, and Wisniewski (1987) report that about 8 percent of their sample of nearly three thousand college men admitted raping or attempting to rape their dates.

For several years, data suggested that rape reporting by victims was on the increase. Chappell (1977a) found that rates of reported rape more than doubled over a 10-year period, and others noted that the numbers continued to increase steadily until 1991. However, between 1992 and 2001, the reporting of forcible rape in the United States has decreased steadily. (In 2002, there was a *slight* increase [4.7%] from the previous year.) For example, the rate per 100,000 women decreased 19.4 percent from 1993 to 2002, decreasing from a rate of 80.4 per 100,000 in 1993 to 64.8 per 100,000 in 2002 (Federal Bureau of Investigation, 2003). Adult arrests for forcible rape in 2002 declined 25.9 percent, and juvenile arrests decreased 26.5 percent when compared with arrests in 1993. It is too early to tell exactly why the rate has decreased for more than 10 years.

The increase in reporting until 1992 may be attributed to many factors. For example, it may reflect (1) a higher level of community awareness about rape and other sexual assault, (2) the influence of the women's movement, (3) increased training and sensitivity of law enforcement officers, and (4) the gradual revision of statutes and procedures that make the gathering of legal evidence less stressful for the victim. In Chappell's national survey of 150 prosecutors' offices (Chappell, 1977b), 61 percent of the respondents believed that the increased reporting of rape at that time reflected a change in public attitude toward crime. Another third of the prosecutors felt that the increase was a result of the heightened sensitivity of the criminal justice system. It is interesting to note, however, that a vast majority of the prosecutors felt that the increased rape rate also reflected to some extent a "general pattern of increased violence" in America.

IMPACT ON VICTIMS

It is often said that rape victims are victimized twice, once by the perpetrator and again by the criminal justice system during the investigation of the crime and, if a suspect is arrested, during the prosecution phase. Victims also may be victimized by media scrutiny and by a public that may question whether the incident happened or denigrate the victims and attribute some blame to them. In the infamous case involving Duke University Lacrosse players, a case which at this writing has yet to go to trial, supporters of the accused men gave numerous media interviews in which they reminded listeners and viewers that the woman they were charged with assaulting was, after all, "a stripper."

Many women who have been raped prefer the term survivor to victim because of its more positive connotation. To be a rape survivor suggests that one is in control and that the rapist, the criminal justice system, and the public have not succeeded at totally demolishing one's self-concept.

Psychological Effects on Victims

The psychological effects on the rape victim, both during and after the assault, are often severe and incalculable. As noted, she is frequently victimized at least twice, by the assailant and by the criminal justice process. Upon reporting the assault, she is expected to recall and describe personally stressful and humiliating events in vivid detail for law enforcement personnel who are often men. Today, increasingly more police departments take steps to ease the victim's ordeal. These include having victim advocates present, having women officers available, and/or providing rape sensitivity training for both male and female officers. In addition to the interview with representatives of law enforcement, the victim is required to undergo a medical examination to establish physical evidence of penetration and use of physical force.

If the victim is able to withstand these stressful conditions, which are sometimes exacerbated by negative reactions from parents, husband, friends, and even by threats from the assailant, she must then prepare for the courtroom, where her privacy is invaded and her credibility may be attacked. Rape trials are usually covered extensively by the press, although most news organizations do not reveal the victim's name or photograph her. Her reputation, however, is especially vulnerable. Ninety-two percent of the prosecutors surveyed by Chappell (1977b) asserted that victim credibility was one of the most important elements in convincing juries to convict for forcible rape. Therefore, the defense has often concentrated on the victim's prior sexual history to destroy her credibility. The strategy of disparaging the victim in this way has come under attack in recent years, and many states have revised their evidentiary rules in an attempt to limit the use of a victim's sexual history. Virtually all states have enacted "rape shield" laws that restrict, to varying degrees, the admissibility of the victim's sexual history into the courtroom (Kilpatrick, Whalley, & Edmunds, 2000). In 1993, Congress extended the federal rape shield law to civil proceedings, ruling that a plaintiff's sexual behavior is only admissible if the defendant can show that the evidence it provides to the court outweighs any prejudicial effect on the plaintiff (Fitzgerald, 2003). In addition, victim assistants, whose function it is to offer support, give direct services, and advocate for victims, have been instrumental in easing the victim's burden. It should be emphasized, however, that rape shield laws do not always provide the protection for which they were designed (Ross & Bachar, 2002). Rape shield laws vary from state to state (Kinports, 2002). Consequently, many victims are surprised and dismayed when they are asked questions about their social and sexual histories during adjudication, which they believed would not happen (Ross & Bachar, 2002).

Although criminal justice agencies are beginning to be more sensitive to the stressful ordeal a victim must go through, the costs are still high. If the woman reports the sexual assault to the police, it means she must devote many hours to the process of the investigation and the subsequent court proceedings (Kilpatrick, Whalley, & Edmunds, 2002; Ross & Bachar, 2002). She must bear the costs of missed days of work, child care, medical expenses for the physical and psychological trauma, and transportation. She may feel a need to change lifestyles, move, and install expensive security systems and locks. Sleeplessness, anxiety, and depression must also be factored into the cost equation. We discuss these issues in more detail shortly.

Situational and Victimization Characteristics

Rape is primarily a crime against youth. The National Women's Study (Tjaden & Thoennes, 1998b) report the following statistical data concerning the age of victims:

- 29% of all forcible rapes occurred when the victim was less than 11 years old.
- 32% occurred when the victim was between the ages of 11 and 17.
- 22% occurred between the ages of 18 and 24.
- 7% occurred between the ages of 25 and 29.
- 6% occurred when the victim was older than 29 years old.

The use of alcohol and other disinhibiting substances is common in rapists. The substance abuse is apparent both in the personal history of the rapist and at the time of the offense. Anywhere between 42 percent and 90 percent of convicted rapists admit they were under the influence of a disinhibiting substance at the time of the sexual assault, and between 58 percent and 90 percent exhibit a history of substance abuse (Marques & Nelson, 1989; Pithers, Beal, Armstrong, & Petty, 1989).

Kilpatrick, Whalley, and Edmunds (2000, p. 12) report cogent evidence that most of the rapists are intimate partners, and not strangers. They list the following victimization information on adult women gathered from the National Women's Survey:

- 24.4% of the rapists were strangers.
- 21.9% were husbands or ex-husbands.
- 19.5% were boyfriends or ex-boyfriends.
- 9.8% were relatives.
- 14.6% were other nonrelatives, such as friends or neighbors.

Women's fears about being physically harmed in rape are not unfounded. While weapons, especially firearms and knives, are used in only about 25 percent of the reported assaults (U.S. Department of Justice, 1988), about one-fourth of all rape victims sustain injury serious enough to warrant medical attention or hospitalization. *Severe physical injury,* however, is relatively rare, with about 5 percent receiving serious, lasting injury (Williams & Holmes, 1981). Another 39 percent receive minor injuries, and 23 percent receive a variety of cuts and bruises (Williams & Holmes, 1981). Further study suggests that women receive more physical and psychological trauma from sexual assault by husbands than by strangers (Kilpatrick, Best, Saunders, & Veronen, 1988). Furthermore, the psychological damage is apparently longer lasting and more damaging, resulting in serious depression, extensive fears, and problems of sexual adjustment.

Victim surveys also indicate that the most commonly used methods of force during date rapes are verbal persuasion, alcohol, or drugs. While weapons are rarely used, physical overpowering (similar to a wrestling match) is commonly reported (Kanin, 1984). Furthermore, data suggest that date rapes occur most frequently in the male's apartment or room, with the next likely location being the female's apartment or room. Very few occur in a car or outside. About 7 percent of rape/sexual assault involved multiple offenders who were strangers to the victim (Greenfeld, 1997).

Rapists often expect more than vaginal intercourse. In approximately 25 percent of the rapes Chappell studied (1977a), the assailant also demanded oral sexual acts; in about 10 percent, he demanded both oral and anal sexual acts; in about 6 percent, anal sexual acts only; and in 4 percent, other sexual actions. An earlier study (Amir, 1971) reported similar patterns.

RAPE OFFENDER CHARACTERISTICS

What kind of a person rapes? How did he get that way? Why does he do it? Can the "rapist personality" be easily identified? Are rapists mentally disordered? In this section, we should keep in mind that many studies addressing these questions are based on information obtained from convicted offenders located in

prisons, forensic evaluation clinics, or secure psychiatric facilities—a very biased sample, since less than 3 percent of reported rapes in the United States result in a conviction (Battelle Law and Justice Study Committee, 1977).

Age

The most consistent demographic finding is that rapists tend to be young. According to UCR data for 2004, 45.8 percent of those *arrested* were under age 25,
and 16.7 percent were actually under age 18 (Federal Bureau of Investigation,
2005). Six percent of the total arrests for forcible rape and 11 percent of the
total arrests for other sex offenders were under age 15. The percentage of juvenile arrests for rape has largely been the same for years. The UCR data, however,
represent an underestimation. As reported earlier, some studies indicate that at
least 30 percent of the rapes in the United State are committed by juveniles
(Cellini, 1995). In a survey of high school students, nearly half (48%) of the females reported experiencing sexual aggression, and one-third (34%) of the males
admitted committing this type of offending (Maxwell, Robinson, & Post, 2003).

Offending History

Another consistent finding is that many men accused of and convicted of rape
have been in perpetual conflict with society, long before the current rape offense. Juvenile sex offenders (JSO), for example, who rape and sexually assault
frequently, engage in a wide range of other criminal and antisocial but nonsexual behaviors. They tend to shoplift, steal, engage in firesetting, bully and intimidate, display cruelty to animals, and physically assault others. In one study,
for example, more than half of violent juvenile sex offenders were abnormally
cruel to animals, including their own pets (Tingle et al., 1986). In addition, JSOs
who rape are more likely to commit the sexual offense along with a co-offender,
commit a nonsexual offense in conjunction with the sexual assault, and have a
previous arrest record (Hunter, Figueredo, Malamuth, & Becker, 2003). Most can
be regarded as life-course-persistent or chronic juvenile offenders. In a follow-
up study of 3,115 convicted rapists released from prison in 1994, 1.3% were arrested for a new sex crime six months after release (Langan, Schmitt, & Durose,
2003). By the end of a three-year follow-up, 5 percent of the rapists were arrested
for a new sex crime. However, 46 percent were arrested within three years after
release for another crime.

In a sample of 114 convicted rapists studied by Scully and Marolla (1984),
12 percent had a previous conviction for rape or attempted rape, 39 percent
had previous convictions for burglary and robbery, 29 percent for abduction, 25
percent for sodomy, and 11 percent for first- or second-degree murder. Overall,
82 percent had a prior criminal record, but only 23 percent had been convicted
of sexual offenses.

Demographics

Some recent demographic data can be found in a comprehensive study of sex offenders assessed at the Ohio Department of Rehabilitation and Correction (ODRC) (Black & Pettway, 2001). The ODRC data involved 437 sex offenders. The study found that many rapists (49%) were unemployed or had a history of seasonal or unstable employment. Interestingly, a greater proportion of child and teen molesters, compared with rapists, had stable employment prior to their arrest (56% and 53%, respectively). Further, nearly two-thirds of the rapists had never been married, whereas a majority of the child molesters were married (66%).

In a follow-up study of 3,115 rapists released from prison in 1994, 1.3 percent of the rapists were rearrested for a new sex crime within six months of release (Langan, Schmitt, & Durose, 2003). At the end of three years after release, 5 percent of the rapists were rearrested for a new sex crime. Nearly half, however, were rearrested after three years for another crime (sexual or nonsexual) after release. These data clearly indicate that rapists have a low recidivism rate for *sexual* offenses but a very high rate for offenses *in general*.

Assumptions about Why Men Rape

Traditionally, the rapist has been considered by many clinicians the victim of "uncontrollable urges" (Edwards, 1983) or the recipient of a "disordered personality" (Scully & Marolla, 1984). Psychiatric criminology has, for a long time, dominated the popular literature on the sexual offender and continues to have substantial impact on the thinking of Western civilization. As Scully and Marolla (1985) observe, the psychiatric literature, as well as the general public, have traditionally attributed four fundamental causes for rape behavior. They are (1) uncontrollable impulses or urges, (2) mental illness or disease, (3) momentary loss of control precipitated by unusual circumstances, and (4) victim instigation. (See **Table 12–1** at page 403.) Further, Scully and Marolla assert that each of these statements attribute the cause of the rape behavior to parameters outside of the rapist himself, often to the victim. In other words, the traditional psychiatric literature has consistently attributed the causal factors of sexual deviations to circumstances beyond the offender's direct or immediate control. Empirical research has not supported these assumptions, however. After discussing each in brief, we will outline what researchers have been finding.

Uncontrollable or **irresistible impulse attribution** refers to a psychological state wherein the normal restraints of self-control are substantially reduced or virtually eliminated by an overwhelming sex drive. The major argument from this perspective maintains that high levels of sexual deprivation may cause a bubbling over of an innate, natural sex drive of such intensity that the individual loses control of his behavior and consequently can no longer help himself. Driven by this powerful, biological force his only release is immediate sexual gratification. Symons (1979), for example, writes that men's sexual impulses are part of human nature and that men innately seek "no-cost, impersonal copulations."

Mental illness or **disease attribution** contends that rape—and most other sexual deviations—is symptomatic of some deep-seated sickness or mental aberration. All sexual offenders are basically "sick" and in need of help. Inherent in this perspective is the conviction that sexually deviant behaviors are similar in causation and represent a single type of psychopathology, usually some form of character disorder (Lanyon, 1986). According to Lanyon (p. 176), this belief "tends to be the view held by the judicial system, by social service agencies, and by the general public." And as Scully and Marolla (1985) point out, "belief that rapists are or must be sick is amazingly persistent" (p. 298). Also related to this perspective is the contention that many rapists are actually latent homosexuals who sexually assault a female to prove their masculinity to themselves and others.

An interesting development within the disease model perspective is the contention that sexual offending represents an addiction (e.g., Carnes, 1983). This sexual-addiction approach is persuasive and appealing because sex offending has some obvious and compelling similarities to other forms of addiction, such as alcoholism, overeating, gambling, shoplifting, and drug abuse. Interestingly, the approach relies heavily on the same treatment strategies advocated by Alcoholics Anonymous (AA) and emphasizes the "twelve steps to recovery." Consequently, various self-help groups have appeared, such as Sex and Love Addicts Anonymous, Sexaholics Anonymous, Sexual Addicts Anonymous, and Sexual Abuse Anonymous. The basic text for Sex and Love Addicts Anonymous (Augustine Fellowship, 1986), for example, states that one's need for a close relationship with another "could be debased by addiction into a compulsive search for sex and romance, or obsessional entrapment in relationships characterized by personal neediness and hyperdependency—in patterns that could forever prevent really meeting the underlying need for authentic experience of self and other" (p. viii). These groups and approaches should not be confused with Relapse Prevention (RP), a treatment regimen that shows considerable promise in the reduction of sexual offending. We discuss this form of treatment near the end of this chapter.

A third popular belief, **drug attribution,** argues that one can momentarily lose control of one's urges in certain circumstances, such as through the use of drugs or alcohol. Alcohol, for example, is believed to remove social and moral constraints, leaving some men at the mercy of their sexual appetites. This desire simply becomes overwhelming, causing some men to attack the most convenient victim. In one study, two-thirds of the men who raped their dates attributed their assaults to excessive drinking (Kanin, 1984). They claimed the date rape was caused by their own inebriation together with a loss of judgment due to high levels of sexual excitement. One-fifth were convinced that there was no way the attack would have occurred had they been sober.

The fourth perspective, **victim attribution,** contends that the victim has, in some way, led the perpetrator into temptation. Rape, according to this view, is a sexual act that is promoted unconsciously by the female. "Nice girls don't get raped," or at least they don't "let it get out of hand." Hitchhike rape, for example, is, according to this view, probably victim-precipitated rape. Because of their unconscious desires, women unwittingly cooperate with the rapist by making themselves available to him in various ways. In the Kanin (1984, p. 96) date rape study, two-thirds of the men said that "although it was probably rape in the legal sense, the fault for the incident resided with the female because of her sexual conduct." According to these males, the sexual demeanor of their victims literally absolved them of guilt so that we are now confronted with something akin to justifiable rape, an analogue to justifiable homicide. Several major surveys conducted on a wide section of the American population strongly suggest that many people continue to believe a victim is at least partially responsible for her rape and that only certain "girls" get raped (Lottes, 1988).

Deniers and Admitters

As noted earlier, empirical study has not supported the validity of these four fundamental assumptions; it does, however, support their persistence. In other words, people continue to believe that rape is caused by drugs, precipitated by the victim, or is the product of mental illness or the offender's uncontrollable urges or addiction. These misconceptions are held by offenders as well as others. Scully and Marolla (1984) interviewed 114 convicted rapists to obtain information about their perceptions, motivations, and afterthoughts and found that most could be divided into two major groups, "admitters" and "deniers." **Admitters** essentially corroborated the story told by police and victims. They are those sex offenders willing to take responsibility for this behavior. Deniers' versions differed significantly from those of police and victims. The researchers identified 47 admitters and 32 deniers. Apparently, the remainder could not be classified into either category.

Deniers justified their rape behavior primarily by making the victim blameworthy. Five themes ran through these justifications: (1) women are seductresses, (2) women mean yes when they say no, (3) most women eventually relax and really enjoy it, (4) nice girls don't get raped, and (5) the act was a minor wrongdoing, since the victims were not physically hurt. Thirty-one percent of the deniers said the victim was the aggressor; a seductress who lured

TABLE 12–1   The Four Fundamental Assumptions about Why Men Rape

THE ATTRIBUTION	THE DESCRIPTION
Irresistible impulse	The normal restraints of self-control and self-regulation are overwhelmed by an excessive sex drive.
Mental illness or disease	Sexual deviations are caused by mental disorders or disease.
Drug and alcohol	Offender loses control of his impulses when under the influence.
Victim	Victim was seductive and at fault.

them, unsuspecting, into sexual action. About 22 percent said the victim had not resisted enough or that her no had really meant yes. As one offender put it, despite some struggle, "deep down inside I think she felt it was a fantasy come true." Most of the deniers justified their behavior by claiming not only that the victim was willing, but also that she enjoyed herself, in some cases to an immense degree. Most of the deniers (69%) were also convinced that "nice girls don't get raped." Their victims, they said, had dressed seductively, were hitchhiking, or were generally known to be "loose."

The belief that bad things happen to bad people and good things happen to good people is called by psychologists the **just world hypothesis** (Lerner, 1980), mentioned in chapter 1. It is the simplistic belief that one gets what one deserves and deserves what one gets. Just-worlders—people who are most apt to adopt this hypothesis—believe that victims of misfortune or crime deserve their fate. Deniers noted that their victims should not have been in the bar alone, should not have been hitchhiking, or should have worn a bra. The deniers, in this sense, were just-worlders.

Self-Reported Reasons for Sexual Assault

A majority of the deniers said that their actions were not reprehensible since they believed they had not physically harmed the victim. Many felt that, although their behavior was not completely proper, it should not have been considered a serious criminal offense, despite the fact that they had threatened their victims with lethal weapons.

Admitters, in contrast to deniers, regarded their behavior as morally wrong and as a serious, harmful attack on their victims. However, most of them tried to diminish their own culpability by asserting that they could not help themselves or were compelled by forces outside their control. Three themes ran through the admitters' justifications: (1) the use of alcohol and drugs, (2) emotional problems, and (3) a "nice guy" self-image. Over three-fourths said they had been under the influence of alcohol or drugs at the time of the attack and that the substance had influenced their judgment and behavior. They were convinced that the ingested substance had, in effect, reduced their awareness as well as their self-control. Normally, they said, they would not have engaged in such a disgusting act.

Forty percent of the admitters said they believed emotional problems were at the root of their rape behavior, and 33 percent specifically cited an unhappy, unstable childhood, or a marital-domestic situation. Furthermore, 80 percent of the admitters described an upsetting problem or anger-inducing event that occurred prior to the attack. Consistently, Scully and Marolla (1984) found that these men described themselves as being in a rage because of an incident involving a woman with whom they believed they were in love. By contrast, only about 20 percent of the deniers described such problems.

Most of the admitters described themselves as "nice guys," who under normal circumstances would never dream of doing such a violent thing to a woman.

In other words, their actions during that violent episode did not represent their true selves. Many expressed regret and sorrow for their victim and apologized to the researchers. We will return to these justifications and excuses later in this chapter.

CLASSIFICATION OF RAPE PATTERNS

Since such a wide variety of sexual offenders are involved in rape, some interesting attempts have been made to categorize rapists according to their behavioral patterns. Researchers at the Massachusetts (Bridgewater) Treatment Center (Cohen, Seghorn, & Calmas, 1969; Cohen, Garafalo, Boucher, & Seghorn, 1971; Knight & Prentky, 1987; Prentky & Knight, 1986) recognized that rape involves both sexual and aggressive features and tried to formulate a behavioral classification system that takes these elements into consideration.

Before we proceed, however, it is important to remind readers that classification systems are permeated with numerous problems and drawbacks. One obvious problem is that individuals do not fit neatly into a category. Furthermore, there may not be many who do. As astutely noted by Gibbons (1988), classification systems or typologies generally consist "of criminological foundations that assume that real life persons can be found in significant numbers who resemble the descriptions of offenders in the various typologies that have been put forth . . . researchers have often failed to uncover many point-for-point real-life cases of these hypothesized types of offenders" (p. 9). However, as we have noted earlier in the book, typologies or classification systems are valuable in organizing an otherwise confusing array of behaviors. They are also useful in correctional facilities for risk management, such as deciding where to place an inmate, or in treatment programming, such as deciding what particular treatment modality might be most beneficial for an inmate. It should be stressed, however, that rape is not a unified behavior pattern but rather is a complicated, often poorly understood, individualized behavior that appears to be precipitated by a variety of internal and external stimuli.

Massachusetts Treatment Center Classification System

The Massachusetts Treatment Center (MTC) originally identified four major categories of rapists: (1) displaced aggression, (2) compensatory, (3) sexual aggressive, and (4) impulsive rapists. **Displaced aggression rapists** (also called in other classification systems **displaced anger** or **anger-retaliation rapists**) are primarily violent and aggressive in their attack, displaying minimum or total absence of sexual feeling. These men use the act of rape to harm, humiliate, and degrade the woman. The victim is brutally assaulted and subjected to sadistic acts like biting, cutting, or tearing. In most instances, the victim is a complete stranger who happens to be the best available object or stimulus for the violence, although she may possess characteristics that attract the assailant's attention. The assault is not sexually arousing for the displaced aggression rapist, and he often demands oral manipulation or masturbation from the victim to become tumescent. Available evidence suggests that resisting this type of rapist only makes him more violent.

According to Knight and Prentky (1987), an offender must demonstrate the following characteristics during the attack in order to be assigned to the displaced aggression category:

1. The presence of a high degree of nonsexualized aggression or rage expressed either through verbal and/or physical assault that clearly exceed what is necessary to force compliance of the victim.
2. Clear evidence, in verbalization or behavior, of the intent to demean, degrade, or humiliate the victim.
3. No evidence that the aggressive behavior is eroticized or that sexual pleasure is derived from the injurious acts.
4. The injurious acts are not focused on parts of the body that have sexual significance.

Although many of these rapists are married, they are usually ambivalent toward the women in their lives (Cohen, Garafalo, Boucher, & Seghorn, 1971), and their relationships with women are often characterized by frequent irritation and periodic violence. They perceive women as being hostile, demanding, and unfaithful. In addition, they often select as their targets for sexual assault women whom they consider active, assertive, and independent. The occupational history of these assailants is stable and often shows some level of success. Usually, the work is "masculine," such as truck driving, carpentry, construction, or mechanics. The attack typically follows an incident that has upset or angered the rapist, particularly about women and their behavior. The term *displaced aggression* is derived from the fact that the victim rarely has played any direct role in generating the aggression and arousal. This offender often attributes his offense to "uncontrollable impulses."

Compared with other rapists, the childhood of the displaced aggression offender is often chaotic and unstable. Many were physically and emotionally neglected. A large number were adopted or placed in foster homes. About 80 percent were brought up in single-parent homes.

Compensatory rapists rape in response to an intense sexual arousal initiated by stimuli in the environment, often quite specific stimuli. This type of rapist is sometimes referred to in the clinical and research literature as the "power-reassurance," "sexual aim," "ego dystonic," or "true" sex offender. Aggression is not a significant feature here; the basic motivation is a desire to prove sexual prowess and adequacy. In their day-to-day lives, compensatory rapists tend to be extremely passive, withdrawn, and socially inept. They live in a world of fantasy that centers on images of eagerly yielding victims who will submit to pleasurable intercourse and find the rapist's performance so outstanding that they will plead for a return engagement. The compensatory rapist's fantasies or personal versions of the world may so distort his view of the victim that he may seek further contact with her, even if she strongly resisted the sexual assault.

Although his victim is usually a stranger, the compensatory rapist has probably seen her frequently, watched her, or followed her. Specific stimuli associated with her probably excite him. For example, he may be drawn to college women but may feel the attraction would not be mutual if he approached them via a socially accepted route. He cannot face the prospect of rejection. However, if he can prove his sexual prowess, the victim will appreciate his value. If the victim vigorously resists the compensatory rapist, he is likely to flee; if she submits passively, he will rape without much force or violence. This sexually aroused passive assailant will often ejaculate spontaneously, even on mere physical contact with the victim. In general, he does not demonstrate other kinds of antisocial behavior.

The compensatory rapist is often described by others as a quiet, shy, submissive, lonely nice man. Although he is a reliable worker, his withdrawn, introverted behavior, lack of self-esteem, and low levels of need for achievement usually preclude academic, occupational, or social success. His rapes—or attempts at rape—are efforts to compensate for his sense of inadequacy, hence the category to which he is assigned. More recent research by Knight and Prentky (1987) questions the incompetence issue. They found that, compared with the other rapist types, the compensatory rapist evidenced the best heterosexual adaptation and achieved the highest employment skill level. If this finding is replicated, the very term *compensatory rapist* would become misleading.

The **sexual aggressive** or **sadistic rapist** is the one in whom sexual and aggressive features seem to coexist at equal or near equal levels. In order for him to experience sexual arousal, it must be associated with violence and pain, which excite him. He rapes, therefore, because of the combination of violence and sexual features in the act. He is convinced that women enjoy being forcefully raped and being dominated and controlled by men. This, he believes, is part of woman's nature. Anger and aggression are not always present during the early stages of the assault, which may actually begin as a seduction. In this sense, the sexual aggressive rapist considers the victim's resistance and struggle a game, a form of protesting too much; what she really wants is to be sexually assaulted and raped. This belief appears deeply ingrained and widely accepted in many Western societies (Edwards, 1983). Consider the following remarks made by a Scottish attorney general: "M.P.s would do well to remember that rape involves an activity which was normal . . . it was part of the business of men and women that they hunted and were hunted and said 'yes' and 'no' and meant the opposite" (Edwards, 1983, p. 114).

Sexual aggressive offenders are often married, but because they display little commitment or loyalty, they also often have a history of multiple marriages, separations, and divorces. They also may be frequently involved in domestic violence. In fact, their backgrounds include antisocial behaviors beginning during adolescence or before and ranging from truancy to rape-murder. They have been severe management problems in school. Throughout their childhood, adolescence, and adulthood, they exhibit poor behavior controls and a low frustration tolerance. Their childhoods are characterized by physical abuse and neglect.

In the extreme, these rapists engage in sexual sadism much like the displaced aggression rapists: Their victims may be viciously violated, beaten, and even killed. The difference between the two types is that the sexual aggressive rapist derives intense sexual satisfaction from aggression, pain, and violence. In order to qualify for assignment to this category, the offender needs to demonstrate (1) a level of aggression or violence that clearly exceeds what is necessary to force compliance of the victim and (2) the explicit, unambiguous evidence that aggression is sexually exciting to him.

A fourth type of rapist, the **impulsive** or **exploitative rapist,** demonstrates neither strong sexual nor aggressive features, but engages in spontaneous rape when the opportunity presents itself. The rape is usually carried out in the context of another crime, such as robbery or burglary. The victims simply happen to be available, and they are sexually assaulted with minimum extra-rape violence or sexual feeling. Generally, this offender has a long history of criminal offenses other than rape. In order to be assigned to this group, the offender must show (1) callous indifference to the welfare and comfort of victim and (2) the presence of no more force than is necessary to gain the compliance of the victim.

The MTC:R3

The Massachusetts Treatment Classification scheme offers a rough framework for conceptualizing and simplifying the behaviors and motives involved in rape. However, it needs refinement and reconstruction, a process the group has been pursuing for a number of years (e.g., Knight & Prentky, 1990). After a series of analyses and further development, the new Massachusetts Treatment Classification scheme (called the MTC:R3) finds that rape offenders can now be classified into *four* major types and *nine* subtypes. Although the basic four offender types are still in the equation, the researchers have also discovered there are subtle differences within the original four types. The researchers decided that four primary motivations for rape could improve the MTC significantly: *opportunity, pervasive anger, sexual gratification,* and *vindictiveness* (Knight, Warren, Reboussin, & Soley, 1998). Knight and his colleagues (Knight et al., 1998) concluded that these four motivations appeared to describe enduring behavioral patterns that distinguished most rapists. The opportunistic types (types 1 and 2) are similar to the fourth type of rapist described earlier. Their sexual assaults appear to be impulsive, predatory acts as a result of being in a situation where the opportunity for the sexual attack arises, and they are not primarily driven by sexual fantasy or explicit anger at women. However, analysis of offender data showed that the opportunistic type can be subdivided on the basis of their social competence (see **Figure 12–1**). Type 1 offenders are higher in social com-

FIGURE 12–1   Breakdown of Four Categorizations of Rapist Type into Nine Rapist Subtypes from the MTC:R3

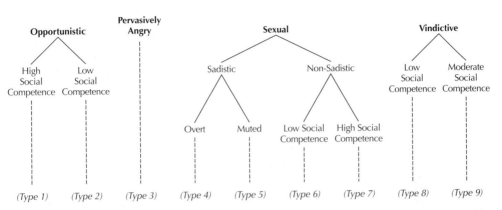

Source: R. A. Knight et al., *Criminal Justice and Behavior,* Vol. 25, p. 57, fig. 2. Copyright © 1998 by Sage Publications, Inc. Reprinted by permission of Sage Publications, Inc.

petence and first exhibited their impulsive sexual tendencies in adulthood. Type 2 offenders, on the other hand, are lower in social competence and first demonstrated their impulsive sexual actions during adolescence.

The **pervasive anger type** (type 3) is similar to displaced aggression rapists but with the difference that his generalized anger pervades all areas of his life. Their pervasive anger is not simply directed at women but at everyone. Consequently, they often have a long history of antisocial, violent behavior of all kinds, and they tend to inflict high levels of physical injury on their victims, especially their rape victims. In many ways they manifest behaviors similar to the life-course-persistent offender. Sexual motivations and preoccupation characterized four types of rapists in the newly developed MTC classification scheme (types 4, 5, 6, and 7; see **Figure 12–2**). The sadistic rapists (types 4 and 5) are subdivided into overt and muted types "on the basis of whether their sexual-aggressive fantasies are directly expressed in violent attacks or are only fantasized" (Knight et al., 1998, p. 58). The non-sadistic sexual rapists (types 6 and 7) are subdivided on the basis of their social competence.

The new MTC:R3 also includes vindictive offender types (types 8 and 9), characterized by anger directed exclusively at women. These types are highly similar to the displaced aggressive type described in the original MTC. "The sexual assaults of these men are distinguished by behaviors that are explicitly intended to harm the woman physically, as well as to degrade and humiliate her" (Knight et al., 1998, p. 58). Similar to the opportunistic and non-sadistic rapists,

the vindictive types can be subdivided into high social competence and low social competence people.

Knight et al. (1998) postulate that these nine rape-offender classifications
can help substantially in providing additional clues in crime-scene investigations. With refinement and continuing research, the MTC:R3 should ultimately
enable investigators to identify "type" based on parameters gathered at the
crime scene. The MTC:R3 also underscores the multiple strategies and cognitive beliefs possessed by rapists and discourages dogmatic proclamations about
why rape occurs. The MTC:R3 increases the understanding of the etiology of
sexual offending and helps mental health professions predict recidivism.

A frequently asked question is, To what extent should a woman fight back
or resist the attack? The MTC rape categories suggest alternative strategies to
women who may wonder to what extent they should resist a rapist. In an interesting study, Sarah Ullman and Raymond Knight (1993) examined the police
reports and court testimonies of 274 women who were either raped or avoided
rape by violent stranger rapists. They found that forceful resistance (fighting,
screaming, fleeing, or pushing the offender) was more effective for avoiding
rape than nonresistance. This strategy was especially effective in dangerous situations in which the offender had a weapon. However, although the victim
avoided being raped or sexually assaulted, she often received more physical injury when the offender had a weapon, even if the weapon was not used. Nonresistance strategies were largely ineffective in avoiding rape or physical injury.
In fact, victims who used nonresistant strategies—such as pleading, crying, or
reasoning with the offender—were more likely to be sexually and physically assaulted than women who strongly resisted. Pleading, crying, or reasoning seem
to encourage the offender even further. One thing to keep in mind is that the
Ullman-Knight study focused on violent, stranger offenders who were committed as sexually dangerous to the MTC. Whether the same results would occur
when examining another type of offender, such as date or acquaintance rape,
is unclear. Moreover, the MTC rape categories make it fairly clear that compensatory rapists and impulsive rapists—and possibly many sexual aggressive
rapists—will be deterred by a victim who struggles. However, the displaced aggression rapists are apt to respond with more violence as the victim resists.

In their comprehensive review of the research, Rosenbaum, Lurigio, and
Davis (1998) identify four basic strategies of resistance to rape: (1) forceful
physical resistance, (2) forceful verbal resistance, (3) nonforceful physical resistance, and (4) nonforceful verbal resistance. Forceful physical resistance involves hitting, kicking, biting, using fingernails, or a weapon. Research suggests
that using this method of resistance generally helps reduce the probability of
severe sexual abuse or rape completion, but it also increases the risk that the
victim will be attacked and physically injured. Forceful verbal resistance includes screaming, calling for help, or threatening the attacker. While this strategy reduces the probability of a rape completion, the degree of physical injury
inflicted on the victim is unclear from the research evidence. The third strategy,
nonforceful physical resistance, includes trying to flee the scene, pushing the

attacker away, or shielding oneself. This type of resistance reduces the probability of rape completion but has little or no effect on the amount of injury received by the victim. Nonforceful verbal resistance, such as pleading, crying, or trying to reason with the attacker, generally leads to an increased probability of rape completion, and has no effect in reducing physical injury. Overall, it appears that some type of forceful resistance is most effective in reducing a violent sexual attack and completion of a rape.

The Groth Typology

Groth (1979) has developed a typology with many similarities to the MTC scheme. The Groth proposal is based on the presumed motivations and aims that underlie almost all rapes. Rape is seen as a "pseudo-sexual act" in which sex serves merely as a vehicle for the primary motivations of power and aggression. Groth—rather dogmatically—asserts, "Rape is never the result simply of sexual arousal that has no other opportunity for gratification. . . . Rape is always a symptom of some psychological dysfunction, either temporary and transient or chronic and repetitive" (p. 5). Later, he states, "Rape is always and foremost an aggressive act" (p. 12). Consequently, Groth divides rape behavior into three major categories: anger rape, power rape, and sadistic rape.

In **anger rape,** the offender uses more force than necessary for compliance and engages in a variety of sexual acts that are particularly degrading or humiliating to the woman (such as sodomy, fellatio, or even urinating on her). He also expresses his contempt for the victim through abusive and profane language. Thus, for the anger rapist, rape is an act of conscious anger and rage toward women, and he expresses his fury physically and verbally. Sex is actually dirty, offensive, and disgusting to him, and this is why he uses it to defile and degrade the victim. Very often his attacks are prompted by some previous conflict or humiliation by some significant woman (often a wife, a boss, or a mother). The assault is characterized by considerable physical brutality.

In **power rape,** the assailant seeks to establish power and control over his victim. Thus, the amount of force and threat used depends on the degree of submission shown by the victim. "I told her to undress and when she refused I struck her across the face to show her I meant business" (Groth, 1979, p. 26). His goal is sexual conquest, and he will try to overcome any resistance. Sexual intercourse is his way of asserting identity, authority, potency, mastery, and domination rather than strictly sexual gratification. Often the victim is kidnapped or held captive in some fashion, and she may be subjected to repeated assaults over an extended period of time. The sexual assault is sometimes disappointing to the power rapist because it fails to live up to his frequent fantasies of rape. "Everything was pleasurable in the fantasy, and there was acceptance, whereas in the reality of the situation, it wasn't pleasurable, and the girl was scared, not turned on to me" (Groth, 1979, p. 27).

The third pattern of rape, **sadistic rape,** includes both sexual and aggressive components. In other words, aggression is eroticized. The sadistic rapist experiences sexual arousal and excitement in the victim's maltreatment, torment, distress, helplessness, and suffering. The assault usually involves bondage and torture, and he directs considerable abuse and injury on various areas of the victim's body. Prostitutes, women he considers promiscuous, or women representing symbols of something he wants to punish or destroy often incur the wrath of the sadistic rapist. The victim may be stalked, abducted, abused, and sometimes murdered.

Groth (1979) reports that over half of the offenders evaluated or treated by his agency (Connecticut Sex Offender Program) were power rapists, 40 percent were anger rapists, and only 5 percent were sadistic rapists. The similarities between Groth's scheme and the MTC typology are multiple. The anger rapist is similar to the displaced aggression rapist, the sadistic rapist is similar to the sexual aggressive rapist, and the power rapist shows many commonalities with the compensatory rapist.

ETIOLOGY OR CAUSES OF RAPE

Generally speaking, sexual socialization and social learning play a crucial role in the rapist's perceptions of what the rape accomplishes and what is "masculine." It is important to realize that sexual socialization (or sexual training) is rarely acquired entirely from home or school; much of it comes from peers, friends, the entertainment media, and experimentation. Most of us, even as children, were fed misconceptions, taboos, and strategies for dealing with the opposite sex. Males often learn it is "manly" to take the sexual initiative and to persist, even against resistance. Details of a sexual conquest, related to buddies, represent the badge of masculinity and self-worth. On the other hand, if attempts to conquer turn into a comedy of errors, they are seen as personal failure and sexual inadequacy. In addition, some people (both men and women) believe that a woman cannot be raped unless she wants to be. Others learn that women want to be dominated and controlled and that successful lovers demonstrate the "I'm-the-boss" syndrome. It is interesting to note in this context that some victims actually receive marriage proposals from their assailants (Russell, 1975). Other rapists ask their victims to evaluate their performance during or after the act.

Some researchers have proposed an **immaturity hypothesis** to account for a large portion of the rape. Goldstein (1977) found that a sample of convicted sex offenders (who were mostly rapists) continued in adulthood to derive most of their sexual pleasure from fantasizing sexual stimuli they had derived from the media or from their own imagination. Average males (controls), by contrast, drew much of their sexual pleasure from real-life sexual encounters. Goldstein also discovered that many rapists have pervasive and obsessive preoccupations with sexual matters, to the point where the sexual preoccupation permeates their lives, and where normally nonerotic material becomes vividly incorporated into sexual fantasies.

Goldstein found that rapists, compared with the average male, relied substantially more on masturbation during adulthood, and that this was frequently accompanied by erotic material derived from the entertainment media. Furthermore, *all types* of sexual offenders had on the average *fewer* contacts with erotica during their formative years than did most other males. In addition, sexual curiosity was often repressed because of a punitive parental approach to matters sexual. Together, these factors provide a conducive setting for sexual misconceptions and ignorance.

Attitudes toward Rape

Undoubtedly a major explanatory factor for many rapes is the attitudes about women and rape itself held by the perpetrators. Some researchers go so far as to say that these attitudes also are held by many individuals in the general population. Koss and Dinero (1988) conducted a well-designed survey of approximately three thousand male students at 32 U.S. colleges and universities. Students were asked questions about the extent of verbal coercion and physical force they had used to become sexually intimate with women without their consent. They were also questioned about attitudes and habits. The results indicated that highly sexually aggressive men expressed greater hostility toward women, frequently used alcohol, frequently viewed violent and degrading pornography (in contrast to Goldstein's finding), and were closely involved with peer groups that reinforce highly sexualized and dominating views of women. In addition, the more sexually aggressive the student, the more likely he was to believe that force and coercion are legitimate ways to gain compliance in sexual relationships. The researchers concluded, "In short, the results provided support for a developmental sequence for sexual aggression in which early experiences and psychological characteristics establish conditions for sexual violence" (p. 144).

In summary, most rapists seem to subscribe to attitudes and ideology that encourage men to be dominant, controlling, and powerful, whereas women are expected to be submissive, permissive, and compliant. Such an orientation seems to have a particularly strong disinhibitory effect on sexually aggressive men, encouraging them to interpret the ambiguous behavior of females as come-ons, to believe that women are not really offended by coercive sexual behaviors, and to perceive rape victims as desiring and deriving gratification from being sexually assaulted (Lipton, McDonel, & McFall, 1987).

Additional evidence of rapists' deviant attitudes and beliefs comes from physiological research. Abel and his associates (Abel, Barlow, Blanchard, & Guild, 1977; Abel, Becker, Blanchard, & Djenderedjian, 1978) have found that rapists show high and nearly equal sexual arousal to audiotaped portrayals of both rape and consenting sexual acts. The degree of sexual arousal was indicated by the subject's penile tumescence, which is measured by a device called a plethysmograph. Male nonrapists, on the other hand, show significantly less penile tumescence to rape depictions. In fact, convicted rapists became highly aroused by rape depictions in which the victim experiences abhorrence and pain rather than sexual pleasure. Encouraged by these findings, Abel developed a physiological measure called the "rape index." The index is arrived at by dividing the average percentage of full penile erection to rape stimuli by the average percentage of full penile erection to consenting sexual stimuli. Avery-Clark and Laws (1984) have developed a similar indicator for pedophiles called the *Dangerous Child Abuser Index*. Today, many investigators use this measure in the diagnosis and treatment of rapists, as well as child molesters. Generally, research suggests that rapists tend to have a higher rape index than nonrapists. The overall accuracy of the penile plethysmograph and its sensitivity to extraneous factors and faking remain very much in question, however.

Abel and his group also discovered that some rapists became highly sexually aroused even to scenes of *nonsexual aggression,* such as a man beating a woman with his fists. Thus, it appears that some men strongly associate aggression and violence toward women with sexual arousal, a pattern very similar to that of the sexual aggressive rapist described earlier. In fact, in rapists the intensity of this deviant arousal has been found to be positively related to the number of rapes committed and the degree of injury inflicted on victims (Abel et al., 1978). Some rapists apparently find scenes that show women being beaten exciting and pleasurable. In addition, male spouse abusers may, in part, be motivated by such arousal. On the other hand, a majority of men (70%) in the general population find the presence of aggression inhibiting to sexual arousal (Malamuth, Check, & Briere, 1986). Interestingly, men in the general population who are sexually aroused by force also are more accepting of an ideology that justifies male aggression against and dominance over women. These men also admit that they would probably rape if the opportunity were presented.

The role played by fantasy and imagination in the development of sexually aggressive behavior is becoming an increasingly important topic (Laws & Marshall, 1990). Self-reports by sexual offenders find that frequent imagery and fantasy of sexually aggressive scenes is extremely important in motivating and guiding overt sexual aggression. Aggressive fantasies are particularly exciting to men convicted of rape (Abel et al., 1977). Interestingly, in an SR survey of 114 college men conducted by Greendlinger and Byrne (1987), over one-third indicated they fantasize about aggressively raping a woman, and 54 percent fantasize about "forcing a woman to have sex."

Related to the role played by fantasy in the development of sexual deviance is the role played by masturbation. The intrinsically physiological pleasure and arousal generated by masturbation can serve as a strong bonding agent, particularly if paired repeatedly with some fantasized object or person. Also, it is important to realize that there are two powerfully reinforcing processes in masturbatory activity: sexual arousal and the reduction of that arousal at orgasm. Fantasized or actual behaviors that are sexually arousing and that result in sexual satisfaction (i.e., orgasm) are likely to increase in strength and frequency. This process is known as "masturbatory conditioning" (Marshall & Barbaree, 1988). On the basis of clinical studies (e.g., George & Marlatt, 1989; Groth, 1979; Marshall, 1988), it appears that masturbatory conditioning may play an integral part in the development of both normal and deviant sexual behavior.

In sum, the evidence to date indicates overwhelmingly that rapists learn to be rapists and that much of the teaching is done by equally naive peers, parents, significant social models, and the entertainment media. Rape springs from a culture, characterized by violence, that communicates a dominant ideology that degrades women and justifies coercive sexuality. Fortunately, most males eventually acquire a close approximation of sexual sophistication and some understanding of the needs of others. Many rapists, however, seem to remain sexually and, in some ways socially, immature.

Rape Myths

Rape myths have received considerable research attention during the past three decades. **Rape myths** are "attitudes and beliefs that are generally false but widely and persistently held, and that serve to deny and justify male sexual aggression against women" (Lonsway & Fitzgerald, 1994, p. 134). They stem from the traditional view of masculinity that men should be strong, assertive, sexually dominant, and heterosexual (Davies, 2002). Rape myths essentially are the false beliefs that women must be dominated and coerced into sexual activity.

Rape myths and misogynistic (hatred of women) attitudes appear to play a major role in sexual assault. Many—but not all—rapists and violently sexually aggressive men tend to hold them. Research indicates that men who subscribe to rape myths are hostile toward women in general (Forbes, Adams-Curtis, & White, 2004). Furthermore, attitudes that promote the denigration of women may be widespread. There is distressing evidence that rapists may reflect the explicit and implicit beliefs held by many others. For example, in one study 35 percent of male college students on several different campuses felt there was some likelihood that they would rape if they could be sure of getting away with it (Malamuth, 1981). In another study, 60 percent of a group of 352 male undergraduates indicated there was some likelihood they would rape or force a female to perform a sexual act against her will if given the opportunity (Briere, Malamuth, & Ceniti, 1981).

Malamuth (1989) cautions, however, that one should not conclude that subjects who indicate they would sexually force a woman are necessarily "potential rapists." The scale used in his research, Attraction to Sexual Aggression (ASA), is designed to measure the belief that actually engaging in sexual aggression would be an arousing, attractive experience. Whether they would act on that belief is dictated by a myriad of factors across a wide spectrum of influences, including the degree of motivation to commit the act, the internal and external inhibitions present, and the opportunity to commit the act.

Sexual Assault and Pornography

The relationship between rape and pornography is shrouded with confusion and surrounded by debate. Two presidential commissions established to study the effect of pornography on crime and human behavior reached opposite conclusions. The first and most comprehensive, established in 1967, was directed not to issue recommendations unless the effects were clearcut. Because of the complexity it uncovered, the commission could not conclude whether explicit sexual material contributed significantly to sex crimes, prompting then-President Richard M. Nixon to remark that the commission was "morally bankrupt." Many have used this conclusion to support their contention that pornography is not harmful. The second National Commission on Obscenity and Pornography, which issued a report in 1984, recommended widespread restrictions of pornographic material. This commission has been extensively criticized for its lack of scientific objectivity.

Part of the problem is determining exactly what is meant by pornography. Seto, Maric, and Barbaree (2001) offer some help. First, there is the distinction between erotica and pornography. Erotica refers to "sexually explicit material that depicts adult men and women consensually involved in pleasurable, non-violent, nondegrading, sexual interactions" (Seto et al., 2001, p. 37). Pornography may be described as depictions of sexual contact where one of the participants is portrayed as powerless or nonconsenting, or is little more than an object for the pleasure of the other participant or participants. Pornography may be further described as either physically violent or degrading and humiliating to one of the participants, usually the woman. Both forms of the pornography portray sexual interactions as impersonal and without affection or consideration of the actors as individuals.

Overall, Seto et al. (2001) were able to conclude from their critical review of the research literature that there is little support for a direct causal link between pornography use and sexual aggression. However, some research evidence has suggested that under *certain* conditions pornography facilitates aggressive, sexual behavior toward women. Studies by Donnerstein (1983) and Malamuth (Malamuth & Check, 1981; Malamuth, Haber, & Feshbach, 1980; Malamuth, Heim, & Feshbach, 1980) indicate, for example, that a general statement that pornography does not negatively influence people needs several qualifiers. In a series of ongoing experiments, Donnerstein found evidence that three factors influence the relationship between erotica and human aggression: (1) the level of arousal elicited by pornographic films, (2) the level of aggressive content, and (3) the reactions of the victims portrayed in these films and photographs. Donnerstein and others (e.g., Meyer, 1972; Zillman, 1971) angered male subjects in a variety of ways, then found that pornography shown to these aroused subjects significantly increased their aggressive behavior toward others. Because of their arousing properties, the pornographic stimuli apparently may promote aggression under certain conditions. This finding accords with Berkowitz's theory (discussed in chapter 5) on the relationship between arousal and aggression. Anything—sexual or not—that increases the arousal level of an already aroused subject will increase aggressive behavior in situations where aggression is the dominant behavior. The increased arousal may also draw the subject away from his own internal control or self-regulatory mechanisms, thereby allowing him to be less concerned about the consequences of his behavior. Furthermore, pornography investigations reveal that if the subject was angered by a woman, he would be even more aggressive toward other women after being exposed to the erotic film. These findings corroborate the frequent clinical observation that prior to a rape many rapists had been angered, upset, humiliated, or insulted, often by a woman (e.g., Groth, 1979).

Extremely violent stimuli, both pornographic and nonpornographic, can also facilitate aggression toward women, even in nonangered males, under certain conditions. The level of violence in the film appears significant. Portrayals of women being assaulted, even nonsexually, can increase subsequent aggressive behavior by men toward women, even when the males are not angry. Therefore, highly aggressive and violent acts depicted in the media may facilitate the rape act for some males. Since many rapists regard their act as a direct aggressive attack on women, seeing films where women are physically abused may encourage and support their own violent inclinations. Seto et al. (2001) make the point, though, that individuals who are already predisposed to sexually offend are the most likely to demonstrate the strongest effects of pornographic materials on their sexual and aggressive behavior. Men who are not predisposed toward aggressive sexual behavior are unlikely to be affected by pornographic materials.

The reactions of the victims portrayed in films also seem crucial. Films or photographs that depict the female victim enjoying rape (common in pornography) encourage acceptance of the rape myth and promote violence against women (Allen, Emmers, Gebhart, & Giery, 2001; Malamuth & Check, 1981). In fact, Allen and his colleagues (1995) found that as the level of coercion depicted in the pornographic material goes up so does the acceptance of the rape myth. If, on the other hand, the victim finds the rape both painful and abhorrent (negative aggressive pornography), male observers are disinclined to act aggressively. However, several qualifiers must be attached to this finding. If the male observer is already angered (aroused), seeing the victim suffer may make him more aggressive, since any arousal increase in an already aroused subject will increase subsequent aggressive behavior. The specific content of the film becomes irrelevant, as long as it meets the minimum criterion of being somehow arousing. On the other hand, males who are not upset or aroused before seeing a female victim suffer are less likely to aggress against women.

For some individuals, however, due to their conditioning history, pain cues are reinforcing if they are repeatedly associated with sexual gratification. Precisely how they react to various pornographic portrayals is unclear, but it seems reasonable to suggest that they would find depictions of pain both highly arousing and supportive of their belief that pain and sexual gratification go together. They might also conclude that the pain-pleasure relationship is inherently characteristic of everyone's sexual gratification and that women really enjoy being "roughed up."

The relationship between violent pornography and sexual aggression remains complex and troubling. Although sexually arousing nonviolent pornography should be available in a free society and arguably has social value, violent pornography has no redeeming value. Its harmful effects, however, are difficult to document except as they relate to a subgroup of individuals. If all violent pornography were eradicated today, sex crimes would likely decrease. The same argument could be made to support confiscation of handguns and rifles, or random, unannounced drug testing of the citizenry. The extent to which a society should be asked to barter freedom in exchange for security remains a topic about which reasonable people consistently disagree.

SUMMARY AND CONCLUSION

The very serious crime of rape is widely believed to be the most underreported crime. When we consider the psychological toll it takes on its victims—or rape survivors—it is not surprising that the vast majority of rapes never come to the attention of police. We noted early in the chapter that many researchers, as well as statutes, now use the term sexual assault, which can encompass both penetration and a variety of behaviors that fall short of that ultimate violation.

Rape, as well as other violent sexual offenses, is committed for a variety of reasons by a variety of offenders. A major motivation appears to be to harm, derogate, or embarrass the victim. In some situations, the rapist may interpret his behavior as harmless, believing that his victims enjoy being "roughed up." Nevertheless, the effect is invariably the opposite. The psychological and social damages to the victim are incalculable.

We reviewed statistics on rape and sexual assault, as well as available demographic information about offenders and victims. Sexual assaults by husbands, dates, and intimate friends are more frequent than commonly supposed. Most rapists are young and often show a history of rape and other violent actions. Traditionally, both rape and other sexual assaults have been considered almost exclusively a male enterprise. In the 1990s, researchers began to question this assumption. Although it is still a fact that men and boys commit the great majority of sexual offenses, we can no longer ignore the reality that women and girls also commit them. Because most theory building and typologies have been developed on males, we have used the male pronoun to refer to offenders throughout the chapter.

Several attempts at typologies or classification systems of sex offenders have been made, the most notable being those developed by the Massachusetts Treatment Center and Nicholas Groth. Of the two, the MTC classification system is the most widely used and has been the one most submitted to empirical research.

Rape and other sexual behavior appear to be due, in part, to the type of socialization experiences the offender has had. He has constructed, from information received from a variety of sources and models, a belief and value system that encourages and justifies the aggressive behavior. Furthermore, most rapists have attitudes and an ideology that encourage men to be dominant, controlling, and powerful, while expecting women to be submissive, permissive, and compliant. This attitudinal pattern may be much more prevalent in society in both men and women than commonly realized.

We also learned that under very high levels of arousal, any consideration of the rightness of a sexual assaulter's behavior or its consequences may be obliterated. As we saw with reference to homicide and assault, high levels of arousal reduce attention to private self-awareness and personal standards of appropriate conduct. Under high levels of excitement, some normally law-abiding persons may become rapists, or at least use the high excitement as a justification for their rape behavior. Of course, some people possess a value system that justifies rape or the resolution of interpersonal conflict through violence, regardless of their arousal level.

We ended the chapter with a brief discussion of the role of pornography in facilitating aggressive sexual behavior. In a free society, pornographic material obviously cannot be banned (although restrictions can be and are placed on the pornography that exploits children). Considering the appeal of pornography, it is clear that there is no direct causal link to rape or other sexual assault. However, research does indicate that individuals who are predisposed to commit such assault often use pornography as a stimulus. Furthermore, *violent* pornography has been shown to increase violent tendencies even in some males who were not otherwise predisposed. Thus, the effect of violent pornography on aggressive behavior is troubling.

KEY CONCEPTS

Instrumental sexual aggression	Expressive sexual aggression
Forcible rape	Statutory rape
Rape by fraud	Date rape
Uncontrollable impulse attribution	Irresistible impulse attribution
Mental illness attribution	Drug attribution
Victim attribution	Deniers
Admitters	Just world hypothesis
Displaced aggression rapist	Anger-retaliation rapist
Displaced anger rapist	Compensatory rapist
Sexual aggressive rapist	Sadistic rapist
Impulsive rapist	Exploitative rapist
Pervasive rapist	Anger rape
Power rape	Sadistic rape
Immaturity hypothesis	Rape myths

REVIEW QUESTIONS

1. Briefly describe the actions taken in the past decade by the U.S. Congress to protect victims from sexual offenders.
2. Describe the five common attributions used by rapists to justify their sexual behavior.
3. What precisely is date rape, and what is the estimated incidence?
4. What is the just world hypothesis, and how might it enter into sexual assault?
5. Define and provide examples of rape myths.

6. How did Groth classify rapists? Be sure to describe all of his classifications.
7. The MTC rape classification system is empirically based, and the Groth typology is clinically based. What is meant by these terms?
8. What are the known offender characteristics of rapists?
9. Does pornography play a crucial role in sex crimes against women and children? Briefly support your answer with reference to research findings.
10. Contrast the Massachusetts Treatment Center's original classification of rapists with its most recently revised version.

CHAPTER 13

SEXUAL ASSAULT OF CHILDREN AND YOUTH AND OTHER SEXUAL OFFENSES

CHAPTER OBJECTIVES

- Define pedophilia and related concepts.
- Outline the demographic and other characteristics of child molesters.
- Review the research literature on classifications systems of child molesters.
- Summarize what is known about the recidivism rates of adult and juvenile child molesters.
- Discuss the sexual deviations of exhibitionism, voyeurism, and fetishism.

Pedophilia (from the Greek word for child lover) is the clinical term for the more commonly used terms child molestation and child sexual abuse. **Pedophile** refers to term for the offender himself, or in rare cases, herself. Pedophilia is defined in a variety of ways. The DSM-IV (1994) defines it as a condition in which, "over a period of at least 6 months, recurrent, intense sexually arousing fantasies, sexual urges, or behaviors involving sexual activity with a prepubescent child or children (generally age 13 years or younger) occur" (p. 528). The DSM-IV further specifies that some pedophiles are sexually attracted only to children (the exclusive type), whereas others are sexually attracted to both children and adults (nonexclusive type).

According to Finkelhor and Araji (1986), pedophilia is a male adult's conscious sexual interest in prepubertal children. One of two behaviors signifies that interest. Either the adult has had some sexual contact with a child (touched the child or had the child touch him with the purpose of arousing him sexually), or the adult has masturbated to sexual fantasies involving children. The last definition recognizes that a male adult may have very strong sexual interest in children and be blocked only by circumstances from acting on it more directly. Occasionally, researchers extend the definition to include ages 13 through 15, but most literature reserves the term **hebephilia** for sexual contact by adult males with young adolescents. However, the distinction between hebephilia and pedophilia does not appear to be clinically meaningful as a distinct, diagnostic category (Blanchard et al., 2001).

Traditionally, most definitions of pedophilia were restricted to sexual contact between an adult and child who are not closely related. Sexual contact with immature family members by individuals from outside the family is called **extrafamilial child molestation.** Sexual acts between members of a family when at least one participant is a minor has traditionally been labeled incest or **intrafamilial** (within the family) **child molestation** and is most commonly perpetrated by men who molest their sexually immature daughters or stepdaughters (Rice & Harris, 2002).

Some mental health professionals argue that pedophilia and child molestation should refer to two different things, with the former limited to fantasies or sexual attraction to children and the latter referring to the act itself (Bartol & Bartol, 2004b). Other professionals prefer the all-encompassing term **paraphilia.** The essential features of paraphilia "are recurrent sexually arousing fantasies, sexual urges, or behaviors generally involving 1) nonhuman objects, 2) the suffering or humiliation of oneself for one's partner, or 3) children or other nonconsenting persons, that occur over a period of at least 6 months" (American Psychiatric Association, 1994, p. 522). In this chapter, however, we will continue to use the term pedophilia, which for our purposes includes ille-

TABLE 13–1   Summary Table of Terms Used in Research on Child Molestation

TERM	DEFINITION
Extrafamilial child molestation	Sexual contact with a minor child by someone *outside* the immediate family.
Intrafamilial child molestation	Sexual contact with a minor child by someone *within* the immediate family.
Pedophilia	For some researchers and clinicians, the term refers to strong sexual *attraction* toward children. Others use the term to refer to sexual *contact* with children. In this text, it will refer to the latter.
Pedophile	Someone with strong sexual attraction toward children, or someone who has frequent sexual contacts with children.
Child molester	Largely accepted term for someone who has sexual contact or sexually abuses a minor child. In this text, it will be used interchangeably with pedophile.
Hebephilia	Sexual contact by adult males with young adolescents.
Paraphilia	Sexual disorders in which sexual arousal occur almost exclusively in the presence of inappropriate objects or individuals.

gal sexual actions on children, ranging from sexual touching to penetration. Later in the chapter, though, we will cover activities that better fall under the term paraphilia.

INCIDENCE AND PREVALENCE OF PEDOPHILIA

As with sexual offenses in general, a caveat pertaining to the statistics is necessary. Data on pedophilia are difficult to obtain, since there are no central or national objective recording systems for tabulating sexual offenses against children. Sex crimes as a group have the lowest rates of reporting of all crimes (Terry & Tallon, 2004). Most estimates of the distribution of pedophiles in the general population are derived from arrest or prison data. However, offenders may be arrested and prosecuted under a variety of statutes and for a variety of offenses, including child rape, aggravated assault, sodomy, incest, indecent exposure, or lewd and lascivious behavior. Furthermore, although the UCR lists sex offenses, it does not differentiate pedophilia from the mixture of other possible sexual offenses.

From a national survey of about 1,200 American males (Finkelhor & Lewis, 1988), it is estimated that between 5 percent and 10 percent of the male population has engaged or will engage in child sexual abuse at some time in their lives. It is important to note, however, that this figure may include a one-time incident that—although still to be condemned—may not represent the offender's usual behavior and would not qualify him as a pedophile for purposes of this chapter. However, these data indicate that children are sexually victimized at levels that far exceed those reported for adults (see Finkelhor & Dziuba-Leatherman, 1994).

Prison data also give us an indication of the extent of the problem. Two-thirds of all prisoners in state prisons convicted of rape or sexual assault had committed their crime against a child, and in most cases the victim was female (Greenfeld, 1996). Approximately 60 percent of those convicted of child molestation had attacked victims less than 13 years old.

Nationwide tabulations of the number of victims are equally difficult to obtain. For example, the National Crime Victimization Survey only collects data from victims *older than age 12*, thus neglecting the victimization of young children. However, a variety of retrospective surveys of the general population indicate that from a quarter to a third of all females and a tenth or more of all males have indicated that they were molested during childhood (Finkelhor & Lewis, 1988; Peters, Wyatt, & Finkelhor, 1986). Moreover, only 35 percent of the children who are sexually victimized report it to anyone (Finkelhor, 1979). Russell (1984) found that in her survey sample only 2 percent of all incestuous abuse cases and 6 percent of all cases of extrafamilial abuse of girls under 18 had ever been reported to the police. In a nationally representative sample of 2,030 children ages 2 to 17 years, Finkelhor and his associates (2005) discovered that one in 12 children or youth had experienced a sexual victimization *during the year of the survey*. Sexual assaults were substantially more common against girls than boys. The survey also found that the great majority of sexual victim-izations were perpetrated by acquaintances.

The National Incident-Based Reporting System (NIBRS), as described in chapter 1, has the potential to provide better information on the prevalence of sexual assaults on young children. Using NIBRS data between 1991 and 1996, Snyder (2006) found that 34 percent of the victims of sexual assault reported to law enforcement were under age 12. Most disturbing was the finding that one of every seven victims of sexual assault (14% of the victims) was under age six.

Russell (1984) surveyed 930 randomly selected female residents of San Fran-cisco during 1978. The purpose of the project was to obtain an estimate of the incidence and prevalence of rape and other forms of sexual assault, including the amount of sexual abuse respondents experienced as children. Twelve percent of the women said they had been sexually abused by a relative before the age of 14. Twenty-nine percent reported at least one experience of sexual abuse by a nonrelative before reaching the age of 14. Overall, 28 percent of the 930 women reported at least one incident of sexual abuse before reaching the age of 14.

The reports of perpetrators themselves indicate that numerous children are affected. Abel and his colleagues (Abel, Becker, Murphy, & Flanagan, 1981) re-ported that incarcerated homosexual pedophiles had, on the average, 31 victims, while heterosexual pedophiles had an average of 62 victims. A Dutch study (Bernard, 1975) reported that at least half of its respondents claimed sexual contacts with at least 10 or more children. Fourteen percent of the sample—which included both arrested and nonarrested pedophiles—admitted to sexual contacts with more than 50, and 6 percent to contacts with between 100 and 300 children. Fifty-six percent of this sample indicated they had one or more "reg-ular" sexual contacts with children. Fully 90 percent asserted that they did not want to stop their pedophilial activities.

In a meta-analysis of studies examining victim prevalence, Bolen and Scan-napieco (1999) found that 13 percent of male children had been sexually abused, and 30 percent to 40 percent of female children had been sexually abused dur-ing childhood. Both rape and molestation that did not meet the criteria for rape are included in these statistics. In summary, the amount of sexual abuse and violence against children in the United States is staggering. To what extent it is a major problem worldwide is unknown.

Situational and Victimization Characteristics

The offender, or pedophile, is almost always male, but the victim may be of either gender. As noted earlier, however, research is beginning to focus more on the sexual offending of women (Becker & Johnson, 2001; Ellis, 1998). Al-though the predominant view remains that men far outnumber women as per-petrators, there is growing recognition that women are not immune to committing this type of crime. We will discuss this topic again below.

Heterosexual pedophilia—male adult with female child—appears to be the more common type, with available data indicating that three-quarters of pedophiles choose female victims exclusively (Langevin, 1983; Lanyon, 1986). Homosexual pedophilia—male adult preference for male child—appears to be substantially less frequent (about 20% to 23% of the reported cases). A small minority of pedophiles choose their victims from both sexes. The behavior of the pedophile or child molester is usually limited to caressing the child's body, fondling the child's genitals, and/or inducing the child to manipulate his or her genitals. Heterosexual penetration is apparently involved in only a small proportion of the total number of offenses.

The offender and the victim know one another in most instances, often very well (McCaghy, 1967; Schultz, 1975; Virkkunen, 1975). Many victims were actively seeking natural affection from their offenders, as a child seeks to be hugged or cuddled. Some victims feel kindly and lovingly toward the offender, who sometimes interprets this behavior as "seductive." Clinical observations suggest that pedophiles, as a group, tend to have positive feelings toward their victims, generally perceive them as being willing participants, and frequently victimize children living in their immediate households (Miner, Day, & Nafpaktitis, 1989). It is not uncommon for the sexual behavior between the offender and victim to have gone on for a sustained period of time.

Types of Sexual Contact

The form of the sexual contact seems to depend on three factors: the degree to which the offender had previous nonsexual interactions with children, the nature of the relationship between the child and the offender, and the age of each. Offenders who have had limited interaction with children are more likely to perform or expect genital-genital and oral-genital contact, rather than to indulge only in caressing or fondling. Furthermore, the more familiar the offender and the victim are with one another, the greater the tendency for genital-genital or oral-genital contact.

There is some disagreement about the extent to which child molesters harm the child physically or use physical force. According to most research, pedophiles do not usually use overt physical coercion. McCaghy (1967) found no evidence of any kind of coercion, verbal or physical, in three-fourths of the child molestation cases he examined. Research by Groth and his colleagues (Groth, Hobson, & Gary, 1982) supports these findings. Lanyon (1986), summarizing the research, concluded that violence is involved in about 10 percent to 15 percent of child sexual abuse cases. However, Hall, Proctor, and Nelson (1988) report that 28 percent of a sample of convicted pedophiles (122 nonpsychotic patients of a state mental hospital) were officially identified as having used physical force or the threat of force beyond what was necessary to gain the victim's compliance. Marshall and Christie (1981) found that in a sample of 41 pedophiles incarcerated in Canadian federal penitentiaries, 29 had used physical force. In an earlier study of 150 pedophiles, Christie, Marshall, and Lanthier (1979) had reported that 58 percent used excessive force in their attack, and 42 percent of the child victims had sustained notable injuries. The researchers suggested that the offenders in their sample were highly sexually aroused by physical violence, significantly more so than other nonaggressive sex offenders. The reported differences in the use of violence and force by pedophiles appears to be explained by the sample used. Studies reporting a high incidence of violence or aggression focus on incarcerated, relatively hard-core offenders, while those reporting little or no violence sampled less-criminal or nonincarcerated pedophiles, generally those on probation.

Groth, Hobson, and Gary (1982) recommend that the few offenders using violence or force and causing physical harm to the child should be labeled "child rapists." On the other hand, those offenders only using psychological pressures should be considered child molesters or pedophiles. Although Groth's suggestion has merit, researchers in this area have used pedophile or child molester as umbrella terms to cover all child sexual abusers.

Psychological Effects of Child Sexual Victimization

Research offers strong support for the assumption that sexual abuse in childhood (both violent and nonviolent) produces long-term psychological problems in many children (Briere, 1988). Reports of depression, guilt, feelings of inferiority, substance abuse, suicide ideation, anxiety, chronic tension, sleep problems, and fears and phobias are common. Depression is the symptom most commonly reported among adults who were molested as children. The extent of psychological damage to the child produced by sexual abuse is dependent on several factors. Groth (1978) contends that the greatest trauma occurs in children who have been victims for long periods of time, are victimized by a closely related person (such as a father or stepfather), when the victimization involves penetration, and when it is accompanied by aggression. In their careful review of the research literature on pedophilia, Browne and Finkelhor (1986) concluded that (1) younger children appear to be somewhat more vulnerable to trauma than older children, (2) the closer the relationship between offender and victim the greater the trauma, and (3) the greater the force used the greater the trauma. They also maintained, however, that there is no conclusive support for the contention that the longer and more frequent the abuse the greater the trauma. Nor is there any clear evidence that traumas are related to the type of sexual abuse (e.g., intercourse, fondling, fellatio, cunnilingus). This suggests that "mild" abuse may be as traumatizing as intercourse, especially if the victim is young and closely related to the offender. The Browne and Finkelhor review also suggests that, for some unexplained reason, victims of child sexual abuse are more likely than nonvictims to be sexually assaulted again as adults.

Offender Characteristics

Many aggressive pedophiles demonstrate a large number of similarities with rapists and the prison population in general (Knight, Rosenberg, & Schneider, 1985). The most notable commonalities are the following: (1) They have problems with alcohol, (2) they have a high rate of high school failure and dropout,

(3) they tend to have unstable work histories in unskilled occupations, and (4) they tend to come from the low socioeconomic class. Alcohol abuse is frequently a problem in sex offenders. While about one-third to one-half of convicted rapists have serious problems with alcohol, about one-quarter to one-third of convicted pedophiles have such problems (Knight, Rosenberg, & Schneider, 1985).

Prentky, Knight, and Lee (1997) conclude from their extensive research on the subject that the classification and diagnosis of child molesters are complicated by a high degree of variability among individuals in reference to personal characteristics, life experiences, criminal histories, and reasons or motivations for offending. Essentially, there is no single "profile" that accurately describes all child molesters. With this caveat in mind, we proceed with some commonly observed characteristics of many of the pedophiles.

Gender of the Offender

Pedophilia is primarily committed by males, but it is not exclusively a male offense. The National Center on Child Abuse and Neglect (2000) reported that 46 percent of the abusive sexual experiences encountered by children included a female perpetrator. This figure is misleading, however, in that it includes any female caretaker who "permitted acts of sexual abuse to occur" (Russell & Finkelhor, 1984). In other words, leaving the child with a boyfriend as a babysitter who in turn molests the child would be considered sexual abuse by the mother. The mother who fails to report her suspicions that her husband is sexually abusing her daughter may also be included in the statistic. If only those women who actually *committed* child sexual abuse are included, the percentage of female offenders drops to 13 percent in the case of female victims and 24 percent in the case of males (Russell & Finkelhor, 1984). According to more recent data reported by Kaplan and Green (1995), between 4 percent and 25 percent of victims of child sexual abuse stated their abusers were female. Becker, Hall, and Stinson (2001) report that the available evidence to date suggests that female sex offenders (pedophiles) are more prone to abuse female children than male children.

Nevertheless, because sexual abuse of children by females is so little explored, we will concentrate in the remainder of this chapter on what is known about male pedophiles. It should be noted, as well, that almost all theories and typologies have been developed on male offenders.

Age

Although there is considerable age variability, it is well documented that pedophiles tend to be older, on average, than rapists (Hanson, 2001). While about 75 percent of convicted rapists are under 30, about 75 percent of convicted child molesters are over that age (Henn, Herjanic, & Vanderpearl, 1976b). Groth (1978), however, notes that all the child molesters he and colleagues have worked with had committed their first child molestation offense before age 40.

Over 80 percent were first offenders by age 30, and about 5 percent had committed their first sexual assault before they reached adolescence. However, despite the statistical finding that child molesters tend to be older than most other sexual offenders, there seems to be a pattern of victim preference as a function of age. Older pedophiles (over 50) seek out immature children (age 10 or younger); younger pedophiles (under age 40) prefer girls between the ages of 12 and 15 (Revitch & Weiss, 1962). The latter offenders are technically classified as hebephiles.

Attitudes toward Victims

Perhaps because of the extremely negative attitude society displays toward child molesters, pedophiles almost always resist taking full responsibility for their offenses (McCaghy, 1967). They are motivated to disguise their thoughts and feelings about their sexual beliefs and attraction toward children. Many claim that they went blank, were too intoxicated to know what they were doing, could not help themselves, or did not know what came over them. They show a strong preference to attribute the cause of their behavior to external forces or motivating factors largely beyond their personal control.

Self-control emerges as a critical variable in cognitions of pedophiles. As outlined by Hanson (2001), low self-control refers to the tendency to respond impulsively to temptation, have little consideration of the consequences, and engage in high-risk behaviors. However, pedophiles appear to have significantly better self-control than rapists (Hanson, 2001), leading to the conclusion that the argument that pedophiles claim their behavior is outside of their control may have very little validity.

Cognitive Functions

In an important study, Cantor et al. (2005) found that adult males who commit sexual offenses score significantly lower in IQ measures than adult males who commit nonsexual offenses. However, IQ differences between sexual and nonsexual offenders do not occur uniformly across sexual offender subtypes. That is, offenders who commit rape against *adults* did not differ in IQ from the nonsexual offenders. Overall, the results revealed that the younger the victim, the lower the intelligence of the offender. Consequently, the observed difference in intelligence for sexual offenders and nonsexual offenders appears to be largely due to the scores of child molesters. In fact, the IQ scores of pedophiles were, on average, two-thirds of one standard deviation below the population mean. Cantor et al. (2005) admonish that the results do not indicate that low IQ scores *cause* pedophilia, only that something may have happened during early childhood to limit their cognitive functioning.

Lower levels of intellectual functioning in pedophiles are associated with a stronger sexual attraction for male children and a greater interest in younger children compared to pedophiles with higher levels of intelligence (Blanchard et al., 1999). Lower intelligence may limit the individual from appreciating the nature of the sexual assault or its long-term consequences.

Occupational and Socioeconomic Status

About two-thirds of those arrested and convicted for child molestation offenses come from the unskilled or semiskilled occupational groups (Gebhard, Gagnon, Pomeroy, & Christenson, 1965; McCaghy, 1967). However, other occupational groups may handle the incident quite differently to prevent additional trauma for the victim and social embarrassment for their families during the legal investigation and process. In the 1980s, the media were filled with accounts of the alarming increase in child sex abuse rates. These same accounts note that it knows no economic or social barriers: Child offenders exist in all levels of society and among all occupational groups.

Interpersonal and Social Skills

Prentky, Knight and Lee (1997) assert that the more an offender's sexual preference is limited to children, the less socially competent the offender tends to be. In this context, social competence refers to the offender's social and sexual relationships with adults. Several studies (e.g., Marshall, Barbaree, & Fernandez, 1995; Marshall & Mazzucco, 1995; Prentky, Knight, & Lee, 1997) have revealed that, on average, pedophiles are inadequate socially, lack interpersonal skills, are unassertive, and have poor self-esteem. (See **Table 13–2** for a comparison of pedophile and rapist characteristics.)

　　Similar to other sexual offenders, the classification, diagnosis, and assessment of pedophiles are complicated by a high degree of variability among individuals in reference to personal characteristics, life experiences, criminal histories, and motives for offending (Prentky et al., 1997). "There is no single 'profile' that accurately describes or accounts for all child molesters" (Prentky et al., 1997, p. v). The best way to highlight the complex nature of pedophilia

TABLE 13–2　General Comparisons between Pedophiles and Rapists on Important Variables

COMMON CHARACTERISTIC*	PEDOPHILE	RAPISTS
Cognitive functioning	below average	average
Interpersonal skills	below average	average
Education level	low	average
Employment	unstable	stable
Age	older	younger
Self-control	average	low
Sexual recidivism	unknown, but likely high for a small group	low
Offending history	largely restricted to pedophilia	variable and extensive
Alcohol use	frequent problem	less of a problem

* This table is intended to provide only the typical findings from the available research. It should be emphasized, however, that there are many individual exceptions to these comparisons.

is through a discussion of two-well known classification systems or typologies. Like the rape typologies described in the previous chapter, they were developed by the Massachusetts Research Center and by Groth, with the former being more research based and the latter more clinically based. In addition, like the rapist typologies discussed in the previous chapter, they have been formulated primarily on information gathered on male offenders.

CLASSIFICATION OF CHILD OFFENDER PATTERNS

The Massachusetts Treatment Center (MTC) (Cohen, Seghorn, & Calmas, 1969; Knight, 1988; Knight, Rosenberg, & Schneider, 1985) has been developing a widely cited typology of pedophile behavioral patterns. Four major pedophil-iac patterns have been identified: (1) the fixated type, (2) the regressed type, (3) the exploitative type, and (4) the aggressive or sadistic type.

The **fixated** (or **immature**) **pedophile** demonstrates a long-standing, ex-clusive preference for children as both sexual and social companions. He has never been able to develop a mature relationship with his adult peers, male or female, and he is considered socially immature, passive, timid, and dependent by most people who know him. He feels most comfortable relating to children, whom he seeks out as companions. Sexual contact usually occurs only after the adult and child have become well acquainted. Fixated pedophiles rarely marry, and their social background lacks much evidence of dating peers or even any sustained, long-term friendship with an adult (outside of relatives). This pedophile wishes to touch, fondle, caress, and taste the child. He rarely expects genital intercourse, and very rarely does he use physical force or aggression.

The fixated pedophile generally has average intelligence. His work history is steady, although it is often work that is below his ability. His social skills are adequate for day-to-day functioning. Probably most troubling about the fixated or immature pedophile is that he is not concerned or disturbed about his ex-clusive preference for children as companions, nor can he see why others are concerned. Therefore, he is difficult to treat and is most likely to recidivate.

The **regressed pedophile** had a fairly normal adolescence and good peer relationships and heterosexual experiences, but later developed feelings of mas-culine inadequacy and self-doubt. Problems in the individual's occupational, social, and sexual lives followed. The regressed child offender's background commonly includes alcohol abuse, divorce, and a poor employment record. Each pedophilial act is usually precipitated by a significant jolt to the offender's sexual adequacy, either by female or male peers. For example, the pedophile may perceive other males as being more successful with women after a female acquaintance rejects him in favor of a male coworker. Unlike the immature child offender, the regressed child offender usually prefers victims who are strangers and who live outside his neighborhood. The victims are nearly always female. Unlike the fixated pedophile, he seeks genital sex with his victim. Be-cause he feels remorseful and expresses disbelief after that act, clinicians usu-ally find him a good prospect for rehabilitation. As long as stressful events are kept to a minimum and he learns to cope adequately with those he does have, he is unlikely to reoffend.

The **exploitative pedophile** seeks children primarily to satisfy his sexual needs. He exploits the child's weaknesses any way he can, and tries various kinds of strategies and tricks to get him or her to comply. He is usually unknown to the child and commonly tries to get the child isolated from others and his familiar surroundings. If necessary, he will use aggression and physical force to get the child to comply with his wishes. The exploitative offender does not care about the emotional or physical well-being of the child, but only sees the victim as a sexual object.

The exploitative offender exhibits a long history of criminal or antisocial conduct. His relationships with peers are unpredictable and stormy. He is unpleasant to be around and is often avoided by others who know him. He tends to be highly impulsive, irritable, and moody. His markedly defective interpersonal skills may be the principal reason that he chooses children as victims (Knight, Rosenberg, & Schneider, 1985). Clinicians find him difficult to treat, as his deficiencies extend to all phases of his daily life.

The **aggressive** (or **sadistic**) **pedophile** is drawn to children for both sexual and aggressive reasons. Pedophiles in this group are apt to have a long history of antisocial behavior and poor adaptation to their environments. Most prefer victims of the same sex (homosexual pedophilia). Since the primary aim is to obtain stimulation without consideration for the victim, this group often assaults the child viciously and sadistically. The more harm and pain inflicted, the more this offender becomes sexually excited. Aggressive or sadistic pedophiles are most often responsible for child abductions and murders. Clinicians find this type not only dangerous to children, but also among the most difficult to treat. Fortunately, this type is rare. Although rare, this is the type frequently portrayed in the media and is most associated with the image of the child molester.

An example of an aggressive child molester was Albert Fish (1870–1936), whose background is discussed by Nash (1975). Fish, called the "Moon Maniac," admitted sexually molesting more than 400 children over a span of 20 years. In addition, he confessed to six child murders and made vague reference to numerous others. He was eventually convicted of murdering a 12-year-old girl and was electrocuted in 1936. A more contemporary example might well be John Wayne Gacy Jr., who sadistically murdered 33 teenage boys and young men and buried their bodies in the cellar of his suburban Chicago home.

Fish thought the conditions of his childhood led to a "perverted" life of crime. He was abandoned at an early age and placed in an orphanage, where he first witnessed and experienced brutal acts of sadism. Fish was quoted as saying, "Misery leads to crime. I saw so many boys whipped it ruined my mind." He apparently began his career of child molesting in earnest when his wife deserted him for another man. This suggests that, like regressed offenders, aggressive offenders may begin their crimes in response to precipitating events involving rejection and feelings of sexual inadequacy.

The above are two quite distant examples of the individuals who committed a multitude of heinous acts over periods of time. Both were subjected to sensational media coverage, but the more typical cases that receive less attention are no less troubling. Persons familiar with court and social service records (e.g., lawyers, social workers, juvenile justice professionals) offer chilling information about the behaviors engaged in by pedophiles and the effects on their victims.

The MTC:CM3

Like the Massachusetts Treatment Center classification scheme for rapists, the MTC classification system of child molesters has also undergone some refinement in recent years. In an effort to depict more accurately the complexity involved in classifying pedophiles, the MTC:CM3 (referring to Massachusetts Treatment Center: Child Molester, Version 3) includes tentative changes to the original scheme described earlier. Specifically, three significant changes are recommended: (1) Divide the regressed and fixated types into three separate factors—degree of fixation on children, the level of social competence achieved, and the amount of contact an offender has with children; (2) incorporate into the scheme a new narcissistic offender type; and (3) partition the violence of the sexual assault into physical injury and sadistic components (Knight, 1989).

The researchers discovered that, although the regressed or fixated pedophile classification is a valid one, it was also more complicated than originally supposed. Researchers found that the regression or fixated (immature) classification could be further subdivided into the molester's style of offending, his interpersonal relationships with children, the intensity of the offender's interest, and the level of social competence achieved by the offender. For example, offenders could be classified according to their level of fixation and social competence. Level of fixation refers to the strength of an offender's sexual interest in children (Knight, Carter, & Prentky, 1989). For example, to what extent are children the major focus of the offender's thought and attention? If children are the central focus of the offender's sexual and interpersonal fantasies and thoughts for more than six months, then the offender qualifies for high fixation. Social competence refers to the degree to which the offender can participate effectively in daily living. An offender would have high social competence if he has demonstrated at least two of the following behaviors: (1) has had a single job lasting three or more years, (2) has had a sexual relationship with an adult for at least one year, (3) has assumed responsibility in parenting a child for three or more years, (4) has been an active member in an adult-oriented organization (e.g., church group, business group) for one or more years, or (5) has had a social friendship with an adult for at least one year. The dimensions of fixation and social competence result in four types of child molesters: high fixation, low social competence (type 0); high fixation, high social competence (type 1); low fixation, low social competence (type 2); and low fixation, high social competence (type 3). The regressed type was dropped in MTC:CM3 in favor of the term "low fixation."

FIGURE 13–1   Flow Diagram of the Decision Process for Classifying Child Molesters on Axis I and Axis II of the MTC:CM3

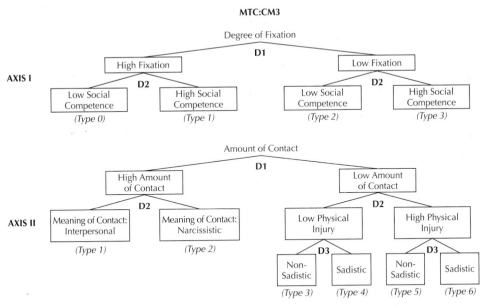

Source: R. A. Knight et al., *Journal of Interpersonal Violence*, Vol. 4, p. 8, fig. 1. Copyright © 1989 by Sage Publications, Inc. Reprinted by permission of Sage Publications, Inc.

Research further revealed that pedophiles can also be distinguished on the basis of how much daily contact with children they seek (see **Figure 13–1**). A high contact offender demonstrates regular contact with children in both sexual and nonsexual contexts (Knight et al., 1989). Offenders of high contact often become involved in an occupation or recreation that brings them in considerable contact with children, such as bus drivers, schoolteachers, Boy Scout leaders, or Little League coaches. Research data revealed there are two kinds of offenders who seek more extensive involvement with children beyond their sexual offenses. The first high-contact type, the *interpersonal offender* (type 1), seeks the extensive company of children for both social and sexual needs. He sees the child as an appropriate companion in a relationship, and believes the friendship is mutually satisfying. The second type, the *narcissistic offender* (type 2), solicits the company of children only to increase his opportunities for sexual experiences. Like exploitative offenders, these offenders typically molest children they do not know and their sexual acts with children are typically genitally oriented (Knight, 1989). Furthermore, there is little or no concern about the needs, comfort, or welfare of the child (Knight et al., 1989).

Another group of pedophiles are low-contact seekers. Low-contact offenders' only contacts with children are in the context of sexual assault. Low-contact offenders are classified according to the amount of physical injury they administer to their victims. Two types of low-contact seekers tend to administer very little physical injury to their victims: the exploitative type and the muted sadistic type. Low injury refers to the absence of physical injury to victim and the presence of such acts as pushing, shoving, slapping, holding, or verbal threats. None of the acts of low injury results in a lasting injury (e.g., cuts, bruises, contusions). The *exploitative, nonsadistic offender* (type 3) uses no more aggression or violence than is necessary to secure victim compliance. Furthermore, the assault does not reveal evidence that sadistic actions engender sexual arousal in the offender. The *muted* or *symbolic sadistic offender* (type 4) engages in a variety of distressing, painful, and threatening acts, none of which causes significant physical injury to the child.

Finally, the MTC:CM3 classifies two offenders who have often administered a high amount of physical injury to their victims: the aggressive offender and the sadistic offender. High injury is characterized by hitting, punching, choking, sodomy, or forcing the child to ingest urine or feces (Knight et al., 1989). The *aggressive, nonsadistic offender* (type 5) is similar to the aggressive pedophile described earlier except that sadism is not a primary aim of the assault. This offender is extremely angry about all things in his life and is generally violent toward people in his life, including children. The *sadistic offender* (type 6) obtains sexual pleasure from the pain, fear, and physical harm he inflicts on the child.

The newly developed MTC:CM3 helps identify offender type based on crime scene information and perhaps presents a more refined classification system of child molester types. However, research beyond the MTC population is needed before investigators feel comfortable about adopting this promising scheme.

The Groth Classification Model

In a classification system similar to that of the Massachusetts Treatment Center, Groth (1978; Groth & Burgess, 1977) classifies child offenders on the basis of the longevity of the behavioral patterns and the offender's psychological aims. If the sexual preference for children has existed persistently since adolescence, he is classified as an *immature* or *fixated child offender.* Like the MTC classification system, the fixated child offender has been sexually attracted primarily or exclusively to significantly younger people throughout his life, regardless of what other sexual experiences he has had. Groth believes that this fixation is due to an arresting of psychological maturation, resulting from unresolved formative issues that persist and underlie subsequent development. On the other hand, if the offender has managed to develop some normalcy in his relationships with adults, but resorts to child offending when stressed or after suffering a devastating blow to his self-esteem, he is called a *regressed* child offender.

Based on his clinical research, Groth has also subdivided child offenders according to their intentions or psychological aims. He identifies two basic categories: (1) sex pressure offenders and (2) sex force offenders. In sex pressure offenses, the offender's typical modus operandi is to entice children into sexual behavior through persuasion or cajolement, or to entrap them by placing them in a situation in which they feel indebted or obligated. A child may feel he owes something to the person who taught him to swim or bought him a bike. The sex force offense, on the other hand, is characterized by threat of harm and/or the use of physical force in the commission of the offense. The offender either intimidates the child—by exploiting the child's relative helplessness, naiveté, and awe of adults—or attacks and physically overpowers his victim.

Groth finds he can further subdivide the sex force group into the *exploitative type,* in which the threat of force is used to overcome victim resistance, or the *sadistic type,* who derives great pleasure in hurting the child. The exploitative type typically employs verbal threats, restraint, manipulation, intimidation, and physical strength to overcome any resistance on the part of the child. His intent is not necessarily to hurt the child but to obtain compliance. The sadistic type, which fortunately is rare, eroticizes physical aggression and pain. He uses more force than is necessary to overpower the victim and may commit a so-called lust murder. Therefore, the physical and psychological abuse and/or degradation of the child is necessary for him to experience sexual excitement and gratification. Often, the child is beaten, choked, tortured, and violently sexually abused.

Certainly the Groth typology has strong commonalities with the MTC typology. The immature and the regressed child offenders display features of the sex pressure offender, and the aggressive child offender shows strong similarities to the sex force offender. It may be more appropriate at the present time to classify the child offender according to the degree of coercion or force he uses rather than according to personality features. The first method focuses on offender behavior, a criterion that is more objective and clearcut. The second focuses on "understanding" the behavior by assuming a variety of personality constructs. We have too little information about child offenders at this point to do that with total confidence.

JUVENILE SEX OFFENDERS

We discuss the topic of juvenile sex offending in this chapter because almost all such offending is perpetrated against individuals the age of the juvenile or younger. Therefore, almost all qualifies as crimes against children. In addition, the research on juvenile sex offending typically divides it into the two major categories of rape and molestation, with the first involving penetration and the second a variety of activities, including fondling and oral manipulation. We caution, though, that these categories are not always maintained in the research.

As much as 30 percent to 50 percent of child molestation offenses (known and unknown) may be committed by adolescents (Cellini, 1995). Van Wijk et al. (2005) discovered that juvenile child molesters represent a very different group compared with juvenile rapists. These researchers found that juvenile child molesters demonstrate significantly more social isolation because of poorly developed social skills and very limited interactions with peers. This and other research indicates that those youngsters who molest children (individuals at least four or five years younger in age than the perpetrator) were introverted and rejected by peers from an early age. The majority of their victims (more than 60%) are younger than 12, and two-thirds of these young victims are younger than age 6 (Veneziano & Veneziano, 2002). Ryan et al. (1996) found that 63% of the victims of juvenile molesters were younger than age 9. Adolescent rapists, on the other hand, are more likely to select victims their own age or older (Veneziano & Veneziano, 2002). A study investigating incest cases reported that sibling offenders are more likely to have molested younger children than are non-sibling offenders (Worling, 1995).

Juvenile molesters are far more likely than juvenile rapists to have been sexually abused themselves in early childhood (Prentky, Harris, Frizzell, & Righthand, 2000). Juveniles who sexually offend against children display lower self-efficacy and self-esteem, and higher levels of depression, anxiety, and pessimism than found for other juveniles (Hunter & Figueredo, 1999; Hunter, Figueredo, Malamuth, & Becker, 2003). They view themselves as socially inadequate and anticipate peer ridicule and rejection (Hunter et al., 2003). They also show greater deficits in psychosocial functioning than other juvenile sex offenders, are less aggressive, and are more likely to offend against victims to whom they are related (Hunter et al., 2003).

Female Juvenile Sex Offenders

According to the latest UCR statistics, juvenile females accounted for only 5.5 percent of all juveniles arrested for sex offenses (excluding forcible rape and prostitution) (Federal Bureau of Investigation, 2005). However, the prevalence of juvenile female sexual offending is probably underreported. When female juveniles sexually offend, the victim is usually a child younger than themselves by five years or more. In addition, research on girls who have committed sex offenses has been sparse. Existing investigations have been limited to small sample sizes and other methodological shortcomings (Becker, Hall, & Stinson, 2001; Righthand & Welch, 2001). In addition, most of the research on female sex offending has focused on adult female offenders (Bumby & Bumby, 1997).

Fehrenbach and Monastersky (1988) found that most adolescent girls who sexually victimized young children did so while doing child care or babysitting. The victims of the 28 female sex offenders they studied were 12 years old or younger. They were mostly acquaintances (57%), followed by siblings (29%) and other relatives (14%). Mathews, Hunter, and Vuz (1997) provided data on 67 female adolescent sex offenders who ranged in age from 11 to 18. More than 90 percent of their victims were acquaintances or relatives. Each of the above two studies also found that a high percentage of the abusers (50% and 77.65%, respectively) themselves had a history of being sexually abused. These findings suggest that female juveniles who sexually offend are far more likely to have been sexually abused themselves than male juvenile sex offenders. Similarly, Bumby and Bumby (1997) found that adolescent female sex offenders tend to be depressed, have a poor self-concept, have a suicide ideation, and have most often been sexually abused during childhood.

RECIDIVISM OF PEDOPHILES

If pedophilia is learned, we would expect a fairly high incidence of recidivism. Like the national recidivism rates for most offenses, however, pedophile recidivism rates are difficult to confirm. Moreover, the second time around, the pedophile is undoubtedly more careful about detection.

Hanson (2001) examined the recidivism rates of over 4,500 sexual offenders from diverse settings (Canada, United States, and the United Kingdom). The data revealed a 19 percent sexual recidivism rate for extrafamilial pedophiles, compared with a sexual recidivism rate of 17 percent for rapists during an average follow-up time of five years. These figures seem low compared with the findings of other researchers. For example, in a follow-up investigation of 4,295 child molesters released from prison in 1994, Langan, Schmitt, and Durose (2003) found that 39 percent were rearrested within three years after release. However, this figure represents rearrest for any type of offense, not just sexual offenses. If we examine rearrest data for sex crime against a child, only 3.3 percent of the child molesters were rearrested within the three-year follow-up. Thus, Langan's rates are actually lower than those of Hanson. However, in a dated California study by Frisbie (1965), recidivism rates over a five-year period were reported to be 18.2 percent for heterosexual pedophiles and 34.5 percent for homosexual pedophiles.

Other types of data, including research on treatment dropout, suggest that recidivism is a significant problem. Abel and colleagues (Abel et al., 1988) report that of the 192 nonincarcerated child offenders who voluntarily participated in a treatment program, the men most likely to drop out of treatment were those with a history of considerable and varied pedophilic behavior. That is, 70 percent of the frequent child offenders who demonstrated no age preference (child or adolescent) or gender preference (male or female) dropped out of treatment, usually early in the process. The treatment program consisted of 30 group sessions of 90 minutes given weekly and directed at decreasing deviant arousal, developing cognitive restructuring of distorted sexual attitudes and beliefs, and increasing subjects' social competence with adults. Interestingly, those subjects who managed to complete the program, and who had varied child offending behaviors and multiple victims, were the ones who were most likely to recidivate within one year after treatment. This should not suggest that treatment is ineffective, however. We return to this issue in chapter 17, when a variety of treatment options are discussed.

Further indications of recidivism rates of child offenders can be garnered from the 13-year outpatient treatment program described by Marshall and Barbaree (1988). This Canadian project offered psychological treatment of deviant sexual behavior on a voluntary basis to a variety of sexual offenders. Forty percent of the child offenders refused treatment. The project had access to official records (charges and convictions) throughout North America, as well as to information from "unofficial" files of local police departments and Children's Aid Societies in the towns where the offenders lived. Thirty-two percent of the untreated child offenders reoffended, compared with 14 percent of the treated offenders (a somewhat more optimistic appraisal of the effectiveness of treatment). The average follow-up period for both groups was approximately 3.5 years. Of the 26 men who recidivated, only 11 were identified "officially" (charges and convictions), whereas the remainder were identified through the "unofficial" information. Even so, the unofficial measures of recidivism were still collected by public agencies, leaving us to wonder how high the "true" unofficial recidivism rates for child offenders really are.

Recidivism of Juvenile Sex Offenders

Some investigators (Alexander, 1999; Hunter & Becker, 1999) have reported that juvenile sex offenders are significantly less likely to reoffend than adult offenders. In general, studies have reported that the juvenile offender recidivism rate for sex offenses ranges between 2 percent and 14 percent (Reitzel, 2003; Rubinstein, Yeager, Goodstein, & Lewis, 1993; Sipe, Jensen, & Everett, 1998; Waite et al., 2005). Alexander (1999) found an overall sexual recidivism rate (based on rearrest) of 7 percent, with juvenile rapists having the highest sexual reoffending rate of all juvenile sex offenders. There is also considerable evidence that juvenile sex offenders who are highly impulsive and demonstrate poor self-regulation are far more likely to reoffend than those juvenile sex offenders who are evaluated as less impulsive (Waite et al., 2005).

If juveniles do indeed reoffend less than adult sex offenders, this may be due to a variety of factors, including the aging out process and the availability of effective treatment. As we will note later in the book, extensive attention has been given to sex offender treatment in juvenile facilities, as well as in community placements. It is possible—though still speculative—that this attention is bearing fruit. As juveniles get older and move out of their living situations, they also are more likely to develop sexual relationships with persons within their own age group. Thus they neither need nor have the same opportunity for contact with younger children.

THEORIES ON POTENTIAL CAUSES

Most explanations of pedophilia focus on a single factor as the principal cause of sexual and social preferences for children by adults. One clinical hypothesis, for example, suggests that pedophiles select children as sex objects because they are haunted by feelings of masculine and sexual inadequacy in adult relationships (e.g., Groth, Hobson, & Gary, 1982). They are terrified of being ridiculed in their sexual and social behavior by the adult world. In the world of the child, they can be safely curious, awkward, and inexperienced. This observation might help explain why pedophiles rarely engage in intercourse with adults. Although this inadequacy hypothesis appears to have some validity, it fails to explain the full range and diversity of pedophilic behavior.

Finkelhor and Araji (1986) find four basic explanations for pedophilia in the research and clinical literature: emotional congruence, sexual arousal, blockage, and disinhibition theories. (See **Table 13–3**.) The most common is the *emotional congruence theories*. These theories try to explain why a person would think that relating sexually to a child is emotionally gratifying and congruent with their needs. They convey the idea of a fit between the adult's emotional needs and the child's characteristics. Most congruence theories are psychoanalytic in origin and focus on "arrested psychological development." According to this perspective, pedophiles see themselves as children with childish emotional needs and dependency, and consequently they feel most comfortable with children. A similar version focuses on the low self-esteem and loss of efficacy pedophiles experience in their daily lives. Relating to a child is congruent, because the inadequate adult finally feels powerful, omnipotent, and in control of a relationship. In short, relating to a child provides a sense of mastery and control in their lives.

The second group of theories, the *sexual arousal theories*, try to explain why pedophiles become sexually aroused by certain characteristics of children. Sexual arousal is typically measured by penile tumescence to the presence of children or to sexual fantasies of children. This perspective contends that pedophiles become sexually aroused to stimuli (features of children) that, for a variety of reasons, do not generate sexual arousal in normal males. One set of theories within this group posits that it is a common childhood experience to engage in sexual play with playmates. For the pedophile, the childhood sexual play may have been particularly vivid, rewarding, stimulating, and even possibly the most sexually exciting experience he has ever had. Adult sexual play, by comparison, was less arousing, satisfying, or rewarding, perhaps even nonexistent. The pedophile's shyness, for example, may have precluded adult sexual contacts. Under these conditions, he probably took the most available sexual avenue, masturbation. The powerful reinforcing role of masturbatory behavior (masturbatory conditioning) has been demonstrated in clinical studies of most sexual offenses (Marshall, 1988). During masturbation, the pedophile's fantasies may focus on the satisfying sexual experiences he had during childhood. Repetitive masturbatory activity, therefore, reinforces the immature level of sexual behavior associated with childhood. Whereas masturbation of itself may be a normal outlet for sexual tension, for the pedophile it becomes an act that reinforces his attraction to children. Continual association between the pleasurable masturbatory activities and fantasies about childhood sexual experiences results in a strong bond between sexual arousal and children. Eventually, the children become sexual stimuli capable of arousing high levels of sexual excitation.

Another version of the sexual arousal perspective links traumatic sexual victimization to pedophilic behavior. Many researchers have found unusually high amounts of childhood sexual victimization in the background of pedophiles (Bard, et al., 1987). It is unclear, however, how sexual trauma, which is aversive, becomes conditioned or associated with the presumed sexual pleasures of pedophilia.

TABLE 13–3   Summary Table of Four Theoretical Explanations for Pedophilia

THEORY	BASIC PREMISE
Emotional congruence	Pedophiles see themselves as children with childish emotional needs and interests, and therefore feel most comfortable with children.
Sexual arousal	Pedophiles become unusually sexually aroused to stimuli not typical of the usual male.
Blockage	Pedophilia is the result of unattainable sexual and emotional gratification with adults, usually because of inadequate interpersonal and social skills. Feel more comfortable socially and sexually with children.
Disinhibition	Pedophilia is the result of poor self-regulation or self-control.

Blockage theories assume that pedophilia is the result of blockage of normal sexual and emotional gratification from adult relationships. Frustrated in his quest for normal channels of sexual gratification, the offender seeks the company of children. Blockage theories emphasize the unassertive, timid, inadequate, and awkward personalities of the pedophile, arguing that these social deficiencies make it nearly impossible for him to develop normal social and sexual relationships with adult women. When the marital relationship breaks down, for example, the pedophile may turn to his daughter as a substitute.

The fourth set of explanations focus on the loss of self-control and personal constraints on behavior. *Disinhibition theories* outline a variety of circumstances that presumably propel the offender to his deeds. Poor impulse control, excessive use of alcohol and drugs, and an assortment of stressors could all lead him over the brink to his favorite deviant sexual practices. As mentioned earlier, many pedophiles refuse to take blame, but attribute the cause of their pedophilic behavior to forces outside themselves. "I couldn't help myself" or "I don't know what came over me" are frequent pleas.

Which theoretical perspective has the inside track for the explanation of pedophilia? By themselves none can account for the multiple causes and the full range of learning experiences, beliefs, motivations, and attitudes of pedophiles.

For the remainder of the chapter, we discuss a variety of other sexual activities that are far milder in their consequences and their effect on victims. Nevertheless, they are prohibited by the criminal law and thus qualify for consideration in this text. As will become clear, many of the same psychological principles discussed above as well as in chapter 12 are relevant here.

EXHIBITIONISM

Exhibitionism is the deliberate exposure of the genitals to another person to achieve sexual gratification. Several authors have reported that in some parts of the world exhibitionism—often called indecent exposure—is the most frequent sexual offense known to the police (e.g., Coleman, 1976; Wincze, 1977). In Canada and the United States, exhibitionism—sometimes encompassed under the general class of lewd and lascivious behaviors in the legal system—accounts for about one-third of all sex crimes (Evans, 1970; Rooth, 1974), and in the United Kingdom it accounts for one-fourth (Feldman, 1977). While exhibitionism, along with other relatively mild offenses such as voyeurism and frottage, make up a substantial number of officially recorded sex offenses, persons convicted of these offenses are rarely incarcerated (Rice, Harris, & Quinsey, 2001). Bancroft (1976) estimates that exhibitionism is the second most common sexual deviation treated at mental health facilities in England.

Rooth (1973, 1974) argued that the practice of exposing oneself is primarily a Western phenomenon. In India, extensive surveys failed to uncover a single case (Rooth, 1974). In Japan, the incidence for one year was 59 convicted cases, compared with 2,767 in England and Wales during the same year. Rooth (1973) also suggested that exhibitionism is rare in Latin America and Third World countries.

To what extent exhibitionism is exclusively a Western phenomenon remains open to debate. Much depends on the culture and police discretion in each country. In Latin American countries, for example, it is a common sight to see men and women openly urinating in public (Rhoads & Borjes, 1981). If a society reacts so casually to nudity or exposure of sexual organs, exhibitionism will lose its shock value. In an effort to determine comparable rates of exhibitionism, Rhoads and Borjes asked working women in both the United States and Guatemala how often men had exposed themselves to them in public. The survey indicated no difference in number of incidences, but the official records of the two countries were drastically different. This may reflect reluctance on the part of the Guatemalan women to report exhibitionism, since officers are likely to ridicule the victims.

Exhibitionists are almost always males who delight in surprising and shocking their audiences. They differ from "strippers"—both male and female—in that the former expose themselves for economic gain rather than sexual gratification. In addition, of course, persons watching strippers do so deliberately, openly, and voluntarily. Exhibitionists sometimes masturbate during the exposure, but most prefer to do so in private, immediately following their exposure.

Situational Characteristics

If the offender is not particularly brazen, he may habitually hide behind the curtain of a window in his home when school lets out and, as young girls walk by, tap on the window, quickly expose himself, and make a fast retreat behind the curtain. This is risky, however, since his identity is easily traceable. Another favorite procedure is to use a car, drive slowly by a girl or woman, open the car door, show himself, and quickly drive away. The bolder exhibitionist is often the "street flasher" who opens his coat to a selected victim, makes certain the impression registers, and then runs or walks away.

Favorite locations for exposure vary, but most exhibitionists prefer public places like parks, theaters, stores, or relatively uncrowded streets. An early

Toronto study (Mohr, Turner, & Jerry, 1964) reported that 74 percent of a sample studied preferred open places, and most displayed themselves from a parked car. The remainder of the sample generally preferred their own homes, often exhibiting themselves through windows or doorways.

The overwhelming majority of exhibitionists prefer strangers for victims, and they rarely expose more than once to the same victim. Although the preferred victim is usually female, an exhibitionist will occasionally expose himself to adult males and male children. Exhibitionists who prefer adult women will usually expose to them individually, while those who prefer children will generally expose to small groups of two or three (Evans, 1970; Mohr, Turner, & Jerry, 1964). Most adult female victims are in their late teens or early twenties, supporting the theory that most exhibitionists deliberately select their victims on the basis of specific stimuli. For example, an exhibitionist may have a definite preference for exhibiting to young girls between the ages of 9 and 11 who look "naive." Another may search for a pretty face, dark hair, shapely legs, or various other physical features. Exhibitionists also tend to be consistent in the setting and time of day they choose for exposure. In fact, many are so predictable that, once the incident is reported, they are easily detected and arrested.

Offender Characteristics

Most exhibitionists begin their behavior at puberty, with a peak period occurring between ages 15 and 30 (Evans, 1970). Contrary to popular belief, onset after age 30 is extremely rare, except in men with mental impairment due to organic brain damage or senility. Compared with the general population, exhibitionists usually have at least average intelligence, educational levels, and vocational interests (Blair & Lanyon, 1981). The majority also appear to have a reliable work record (Mohr, Turner, & Jerry, 1964).

Psychosis or other mental disorders are found no more frequently in exhibitionists than in the general population (Blair & Lanyon, 1981). However, exhibitionists show an above average incidence of previous sexual offenses other than exhibitionism, including voyeurism and even attempted rape. In the main, however, exhibitionists neither assault their audience physically nor desire sexual intercourse with them. It is highly probable that if victims expressed interest in sexual activity, most exhibitionists would be frightened and confused and would flee. In most cases, the primary motive behind the exhibitionism is the sexual excitation (reinforcement) the offender receives from shocking, surprising, or mildly frightening his victims. These reactions generate considerable sexual arousal. Later, he will probably masturbate to that image. On the other hand, if his exposure fails to engender the anticipated fright or surprise, and produces instead a disinterested, noncommittal facial expression, the offender is disappointed and suffers some loss of self-esteem.

Although many exhibitionists are married, most are considered socially and sexually inadequate both by themselves and by those around them. Many are introverted, shy, socially reserved individuals who feel uncomfortable in most social situations. Generally, they are described as unassertive, self-effacing, timid, and passive. A majority of exhibitionists feel the urge to expose following a blow to their fragile self-esteem, which prompts heightened feelings of inadequacy and stress.

Therefore, like other sexual offenses, exhibitionism is a learned behavioral pattern reinforced by sexual arousal and the subsequent tension reduction achieved through masturbation. Many exhibitionists indicate that their behavior was initially acquired through some preadolescent sex play or by chance. For example, the history of most exhibitionists includes a vivid memory of a young girl expressing amazement or fear at their penis, viewed either accidentally or during sexual play. Characteristically, this attention was sexually exciting to the male, and he masturbated to the imagery of the incident. This not uncommon incident by itself is usually not sufficient to establish exhibitionism. However, a repeated pairing of the memory of the event with the sexual arousal derived from masturbation may lead to a proclivity for exhibitionism in individuals who lack sufficient self-control or self-regulatory mechanisms. That is, pleasurable, repetitive masturbatory activities in the presence of this mental imagery strongly encourage eventual exposure of the penis to victims who are perceived as similar to the initial observer. If the first, real-life exposure is sexually arousing, a strongly reinforcing chain of events is established. Each time the exhibitionist exposes and receives this sequence of rewards, the behavior pattern becomes that much more firmly entrenched.

During subsequent periods of stress and inadequacy, exposure becomes an increasingly effective way of dealing with uncomfortable emotions, especially when preferred victims are available. Therefore, because exhibitionism is a learned response, it continues to be repetitive and resistant to extinction. Furthermore, exhibitionists may expose themselves many thousands of times without complaints from victims. Irate adults do not report an incidence of exhibitionism unless the victim was their offspring. Even then they may not report in order to protect the child from having to describe the incident to police.

It is important to note that exhibitionists, in contrast to many pedophiles, often express a desire to change their behavior. Although they may expose themselves numerous times, once detected they are more likely to seek therapeutic help. Moreover, it is not uncommon for an exhibitionist to seek professional help prior to being arrested for his behavior. Reviewing the literature on treatment for sex offenders, Rice, Harris, & Quinsey (2001) note that motivated exhibitionists have been helped by pharmacological or other treatments designed to reduce sexual arousal together with attention to other factors that might facilitate their offending, such as depression or lack of employment. Day and Berney (2001) note that antiandrogen drugs have been shown to be effective in cases of exhibitionism, pedophilia, and fetishism in mentally retarded individuals. There is no evidence that these individuals are any more likely than others to engage in these activities, however.

VOYEURISM AND FETISHISM

Voyeurism, also known as scoptophilia or inspectionalism, is the tendency to gain sexual excitement and gratification from observing unsuspecting others naked, undressing, or engaging in sexual activity. The term **fetishism** refers specifically to a sexual attraction to inanimate objects rather than to people. It is distinct from **partialism,** which is an exaggerated sexual interest in some part of the human anatomy not usually associated with sexual arousal, such as the knee. The individual with a fetish may become sexually aroused at the sight of boots, handbags, stockings, panties, fur, or even tailpipes on motor vehicles. The fetish object may be kissed, fondled, tasted, smelled, or just looked at.

Both voyeurism and fetishism are little more than minor sexual offenses, since they usually do not seriously harm the community. They are, of course, egregious violations of other people's privacy, because "victims" are being observed without their knowledge or their possessions are appropriated for "deviant" purposes. The voyeur or the fetishist runs afoul of the law when he harasses, trespasses, burglarizes, damages property, or steals objects.

Recall that the voyeur is sometimes an exhibitionist, and vice versa. However, the voyeur is even less likely than the exhibitionist to become involved in serious forms of antisocial behavior, such as rape or other forms of violence. He does not harm his victims physically, and, like the exhibitionist, he is often described as a passive, shy, introverted, submissive, and harmless person. Clinical studies reveal that he suffers from strong heterosexual anxieties and immaturity.

One observation made in a dated but widely cited study by the Queen's Bench Foundation (1978) demands attention. About 10 percent of the convicted rapists interviewed for that study stated that they had watched their victim through a window before attacking her. The authors suggested that, in light of this finding, some "peeping Toms" should be watched for possible rape tendencies. However, some distinguishing aspects about voyeurism should be noted. All but one offender had intentions of raping before observing. The one rapist who said that he did not intend to rape when he watched his victim admitted that he did intend to "have sex" with her. In addition, all but one of these offenders had weapons in their possession at the time of their arrest (knives, guns, meat fork), even though they ordinarily did not carry them. Also, forceful entry into the victim's apartment was the common approach, and the victim was often raped with extreme violence.

These rapists, therefore, probably had little in common with the typical voyeur. Their intention from the outset was to attack the victim violently. They apparently watched the victim to determine her habits, whether anyone else was at home, and the best way to get into her residence. In other words, they were stalking their victims. The typical voyeur gets his satisfaction from watching, imagining, and eventually masturbating, with no intention of having sexual contact, forced or otherwise, with the victim.

Voyeurism, like other forms of sexual deviation, is a learned behavior. Although each individual has a unique approach to viewing, many voyeurs report the preadolescent experience of becoming sexually aroused while watching an unsuspecting woman undress. A common theme running through clinical studies is that the mental imagery of that scene is later coupled with sexual arousal, again perhaps satisfied through masturbation. Eventually, this conditioning produces a desire to observe different, realistic sexual scenes. Keep in mind that an important component of the sexual excitement experienced by the voyeur is his victim's unawareness of his presence. Erotic films or pornography, by themselves, are not likely to serve his purpose.

In contrast to voyeurism, fetishism is pursued in the privacy of one's home, without interference. It is primarily a male phenomenon. A fetish refers to the use of nonliving objects as a repeatedly and strongly preferred method of achieving sexual excitement. The fetish object is most often a woman's wearing apparel, such as undergarments, shoes, boots, or stockings. The person with a fetish typically masturbates while rubbing, holding, or smelling the fetish object or may ask the sexual partner to wear the object during their sexual encounters (DSM-IV, 1994, p. 526). Through classical conditioning, virtually any object may assume sexual significance. Gosselin and Wilson (1984) describe a study of a man who was strongly attracted to safety pins. From the age of 8, he had experienced extreme sexual pleasure from gazing at these shiny objects in the privacy of his bathroom. "When he was 23 his wife observed the complete sequence, which began with him staring at the safety pin for about a minute. This was followed by a glassy-eyed appearance, vocal humming noises, sucking movements of the lips and total immobility for another minute or two" (Gosselin & Wilson, 1984, p. 104).

As mentioned previously, most fetish objects are those worn by a woman, such as undergarments, shoes, boots, or hosiery. Chalkley and Powell (1983) found that underwear, stockings, and other types of lingerie were most popular for British fetish collectors. Next most common were rubber and certain rubber articles such as Mackintoshes, tubes, dolls, and paraphernalia for giving enemas.

In an excellent, if controversial, demonstration of fetish conditioning, Rachman (1966) showed male subjects a slide of a pair of women's black boots, followed immediately by slides of attractive, naked women (sexual arousal). After a number of such trials, the subjects became sexually excited, as measured by penile circumference, in response to the boots slide itself. There were also indications that the subjects not only became aroused by the particular boots, but also by slides of other boots and shoes as well.

Fetishism merits attention here primarily because the person with a strong attachment to an object might commit larceny or burglary to get it. Fetish objects, particularly if they are items of apparel, are not typically purchased in retail outlets. They must belong to, or have been used by, someone else. Therefore, one of the major avenues for obtaining fetishes is to steal, and, since clothes dryers are more in vogue in modern society than clotheslines, the fetishist's traditional method of stealing from the backyard clothesline has been replaced by more daring techniques. Chalkley and Powell (1983), in their British sample of 48 cases of fetishism, found that 38 percent experienced considerable excitement and sexual arousal even in the act of stealing the fetish. In this sense, it is conceivable that an indeterminant number of unexplained burglaries (when minor things are taken but more valuable items remain untouched) are a result of an impatient quest for fetishes! Some fetish burglars find sexual excitement just being in someone's house without his or her knowledge and presence. It is also not unusual for the fetish burglar to take valuable objects along with his fetish, however, either to throw off suspicion or to offer a face-saving "reasonable" explanation for the burglary if he is apprehended. In one serious fetish case described by Hazelwood and Burgess (1987), the offender admitted committing over five thousand burglaries primarily to obtain panties to satisfy his fetish. He also estimated that he stole valuables in about one-half of these burglaries.

SUMMARY AND CONCLUSIONS

Following upon the chapter on serious sexual assaults of adults, the present chapter has focused upon sexual offenses against children. We used the term pedophilia to characterize these offenses but noted that the legal terms include but are not limited to child molestation, child sexual assault, and child rape. Individuals are not arrested and charged with pedophilia; this is a clinical term that covers a range of sexually related offenses against children. However, the term pedophile is now commonly used by the public and in media accounts.

Sexual assaults against children—covering a range of offenses—are disturbingly too common, although accurate statistics are difficult to obtain. Much of our information is derived not only from arrest and conviction data but also from the reports of adults who say they were victimized as children and from the perpetrators themselves. Arrest data indicate that 34 percent of all victims of sexual assault reported to law enforcement in the early 1990s were under age 12. In a related finding, some research indicates that approximately two-thirds of convicted rapists in state prisons committed their crimes against children. By their own accounts, offenders admit to molesting not one but many children, sometimes over a period of years. Other research suggests that from a quarter to a third of all women and one-tenth of men say they were sexually abused during childhood. As we discussed in the chapter, the long-term psychological effects of this victimization are often, if not typically, devastating.

We reviewed a variety of offender characteristics, including both demographic and psychological features. Aggressive pedophiles—not all are—show similarities to men who rape adults, including problems with alcohol, high school failure rates, unstable work history, and low socioeconomic status. Pedophiles as a group tend to be older than rapists, although the great majority apparently commits the first offense before age 30. Although increasingly more attention is being given to female pedophiles, pedophilia is still predominantly a male phenomenon.

The cognitive skills of pedophiles are typically lower than those of the general population. They often lack social skills and adequate self-control mechanisms. They rarely take responsibility for their offenses, preferring to attribute their behavior to external forces beyond their control. Although there have been successful treatment programs for pedophiles, program dropout rates are often high. However, many clinicians maintain that pedophiles are far easier to treat than rapists, a topic we return to in chapter 17.

The Massachusetts Treatment Center has developed a classification system for the behavioral patterns of pedophiles. This system has undergone some revision to further specify some of its categories and to incorporate crime scene information. We reviewed the MTC system in some detail, focusing on the MTC:CM3, the latest version. A similar but less elaborate classification system proposed by Groth was also covered. Of the two, the MTC classification system is the most widely used and has been the one most submitted to empirical research.

We discussed some of the available research on juvenile sex offending, which is clearly a major challenge to the juvenile justice system. Distinctions are often made in the literature between juvenile molesters and juvenile rapists. For example, molesters almost invariably choose children younger than they are as victims, while rapists choose victims of about the same age or older. Molesters are also more likely than rapists to have been victims of child sexual abuse and to view themselves as socially inadequate. The topic of female juvenile sex offending is increasingly making an appearance in the literature. These offenders typically have been abused themselves and often commit their abuses while babysitting or otherwise caring for children.

Recidivism of both adult and juvenile child sex abusers was covered. There is a bit more reason for optimism with reference to the young offenders, either because they received effective treatment or because their life situations changed and they no longer perceived a need to victimize children. Adult offenders, though, seem to recidivate at rates ranging from about 10 percent to 45 percent, depending on the study and the time period covered. It is always difficult to measure recidivism, however, and probably not wise to read too much into these statistics, although they cannot be ignored. From a psychological point of view, the critical factor is to discover why these offenses are occurring and reduce their future occurrence.

A variety of explanatory theories were covered, but it is clear that no one theory or no one factor would account for the behavior of all offenders. We cannot say, for example, that all pedophiles engage in their actions because they are haunted by feelings of sexual inadequacy with adults. Theories have been placed in one of four major groups: the emotional congruence, the sexual arousal, the blockage, and the disinhibition theories. While pedophilia appears to be motivated by both sexual desire and an expectation of sexual adequacy that would not occur in sexual congress with another adult, it is engaged in for a variety of reasons by a variety of offenders.

Thus, there is no such thing as a common "molester profile." Each has his own construct system and beliefs about his behavior and motivations. Some offenders, for whatever reason, are vicious and violent; others are passive, relatively meek people who enjoy the companionship of children. It appears from the research that many if not most pedophiles are the latter. They apparently see themselves as sexually and interpersonally inept adults who feel more comfortable interacting with children.

We also gave some attention to the minor sexual offenses of exhibitionism, voyeurism, and fetishes. Classical conditioning, particularly masturbatory conditioning, appears to play a crucial role in the development of these sexual deviations, as it does with pedophilia. Sexual arousal repeatedly linked with objects and persons seems especially important.

Treatment of sexual offenses can be successful if the offender's motivation to change is evident. Successful treatment strategies must not only focus on the cessation of the antisocial sexual conduct, but also on maintenance of prosocial behaviors as well. Thus, continual monitoring or supervision should be a part of the treatment regimen. Nevertheless, reviews of the literature on sex offender treatment are not encouraging, particularly for the more serious and violent sexual offenses. The "milder" offenses such as exhibitionism are more likely to yield positive treatment results if the offender is motivated and if a treatment strategy focused on individualized needs is adopted.

KEY CONCEPTS

Pedophilia	Pedophile
Hebephilia	Extrafamilial child molester
Intrafamilial child molester	Paraphilia
Immature pedophile	Regressed pedophile
Exploitative pedophile	Aggressive pedophile
Sadistic pedophile	Exhibitionism
Voyeurism	Fetishism
Partialism	

REVIEW QUESTIONS

1. Define partialism and paraphilia.
2. What are the major differences between extrafamilial pedophiles and intrafamilial pedophiles?
3. What type of property crime(s) may be involved in the acquisition of fetishes?
4. List four demographic characteristics of pedophiles.
5. Summarize the research on the recidivism of pedophiles.
6. Does voyeurism lead to sexual assaults? Explain.
7. Outline the pedophile typologies of the MTC and the Groth system. Which is better supported by the research literature?
8. List some of the justifications that pedophiles use for their sexual behavior.
9. What does the research literature conclude about juvenile sex offenders?
10. In what major way does a fixed pedophile differ from a regressed pedophile?

CHAPTER 14

PROPERTY AND PUBLIC ORDER CRIME

CHAPTER OBJECTIVES

- Provide an overview of property crimes.
- Sketch burglary, including property cues, motives, demographics, and cognitive processes of burglars.
- Discuss the psychological effects of burglary on victims.
- Examine motor vehicle theft, including carjacking and the motives and decision making of offenders.
- Present the many aspects of shoplifting, including the psychological factors.
- Summarize white-collar and occupational crime.
- Review briefly prostitution and sexual trafficking issues.

This chapter deals with a wide variety of criminal activity that at first glance would appear to have little in common. However, for the most part, the offenses in this chapter are radically different from the criminal behavior we have discussed up to this point. What they all have in common is a lack of physical aggression—or violence—in the perpetration of the act itself, although in some cases, for example carjacking, sexual trafficking, and prostitution, violence may be a by-product. The crimes discussed here also will implicate different psychological concepts from those thus far covered. Whereas we have spent considerable time on learning, classical conditioning, self-esteem, frustration, and of course aggression in the previous chapters, we will see a de-emphasis on these concepts in this chapter, despite the fact that they may still be relevant.

On the other hand, we will place more emphasis on such concepts as self-reinforcement, expectations, justifications, and motivations.

Property crimes generally involve the illegal acquisition of money and material goods, or the illegal destruction of property for financial gain. According to the UCR, the four major property crimes (all Part 1) are larceny, burglary, arson, and motor vehicle theft. Of the four, arson is the most complex to categorize because it is not always committed for profit. For this reason, it is not included in the property crime rate reported to the public along with the violent crime rate.

Although property crimes do not typically involve physical aggression, they are similar to the violent offenses discussed in earlier chapters in one important psychological aspect. Most of them involve a dehumanization of the victim, albeit in a different sense from the dehumanization that often occurs in violence. **Dehumanization** occurs when a person or group of persons sees and treats certain individuals as objects, rather than as human beings. When a person is not responding to the human qualities of other people, it becomes much more possible to act inhumanely toward them. Therefore, offenders find it easier to see their victims as objects rather than as people. In most economic or property crimes (such as larceny and burglary), the offenders avoid confronting their victims directly. Therefore, they do not directly observe or experience the economic, social, and psychological discomfort of their victims. In the victim's absence, internal values and social constraints are less effective, allowing the offender to repress, deny, or justify the crime more easily. As Gresham Sykes (1956) puts it, the individual's internal sentiments are more easily neutralized by the physical absence of the victim. The offender does not have to think of the effects his or her actions have on the victim, because the offender does not know the victim as a human being, only as a target.

Crimes against the public order are actions against public or moral decency, or other conduct that is interpreted as a threat to the orderly operations of a given society. Examples include prostitution, gambling, vagrancy, disorderly conduct, public drunkenness, and drug use. Often, these violations are called "victimless crimes" because of the difficulty of pinpointing an identifiable victim.

We decided to include robbery in this chapter as well, not because it is strictly a property crime (it isn't), but because robbers have more in common with the crimes discussed in this and the next chapter than with those discussed up to this point. Robbery is classified as a violent crime against persons in the UCR because it involves the threat or the use of force. A robber points a gun at a store clerk and orders her to empty the cash drawer. Two young robbers accost a third youngster on the street and, at knifepoint, forcefully remove his new boots and leather jacket. Physical aggression is clearly implicated in these actions, but it is of a different nature from the aggression of the assaulter, the rapist, or the murderer. As we will note, though, a substantial proportion of robberies do amount to physical harm to the victim. Nevertheless, the psychological principles involved in robbery are closer to those involved in burglary and other economic crimes.

TABLE 14–1 Part I Property Crimes, 2004

OFFENSE	NUMBER OF OFFENSES	PERCENT OF PART I PROPERTY
Total property	10,328,255	100.0%
Larceny-theft	6,947,685	67.3
Burglary	2,143,456	20.8
Motor vehicle theft	1,237,114	12.0
Arson	63,215	0.6

Source: Federal Bureau of Investigation, 2005.

Table 14–1 gives a percentage breakdown of the UCR Part I property crimes for 2004. As you can see, larceny-theft accounted for two-thirds of the property crime, followed by burglary at a little over one-fifth of the property offenses. In 2004, law enforcement reported an estimated 10.3 million property crimes (Federal Bureau of Investigation, 2005). The 2004 property crime rate was estimated to be 3,517 property crimes per 100,000 inhabitants, and has declined 14.4 percent from the 1995 rate. The additional statistical facts are as follows:

• In 2004, larceny-theft made up 67.3 percent of the total property crimes.
• Burglary comprised 20.7 percent of the total *property* crimes.
• Motor vehicle theft, 11.9 percent.
• The overall clearance rate for property crime in 2004 was 16.4 percent.
• Robbery comprised 29.3 percent of the total *violent* crime rate.
• The overall clearance rate for robbery was 26.2 percent.

In addition to the crimes specified above, the chapter will also cover "white-collar" offenses and discuss the difficulty defining that concept. Specific crimes like fraud and embezzlement will be discussed.

Obviously, most people engage in economic and property crime for the money, or for other tangible rewards that meet biological, psychological, or social needs. Sykes (1956) notes, however, that this does not tell us why some people commit economic crime under certain social conditions, while others do not. Explanations based strictly on economic necessity and the satisfaction of basic human needs do not go far enough. Sykes proposes the concept of **relative deprivation** as one additional factor. To assess the economic want associated with economic crime, we should consider not what the person has or is making in personal income, but rather how great the discrepancy is between what he or she has and what he or she would like to have. Specifically, relative deprivation is the psychological distance between what people perceive they have now and what they feel they can realistically attain. In another sense, relative deprivation refers to a pervasive sense of injustice that develops between the "haves" and "have nots."

From a psychological perspective, economic crimes cannot be simply explained by biological needs, material wants, or even in terms of relative deprivation. Powerful cognitive motivators must also be considered. These cognitive factors are in the form of outcome expectations and the capacity to predict and appreciate future consequences of one's behavior. Furthermore, the cognitive forces may be relatively independent of external reinforcements like tangible rewards or even social and status rewards. Self-reinforcements, including self-rewards and self-punishments, may represent a major motivating factor in many property crimes. That is, the offender may receive pleasure and self-satisfaction in the completion of a crime and from doing it well.

Cognitive factors are also extremely important in another sense: They allow the offender to justify his or her behavior. A strong theme of this chapter is the tendency of economic offenders to minimize, distort, or deny misconduct or reprehensible behavior. The aforementioned psychological separation from the victim helps them to do this. We expand on these psychological issues of motivation and justification throughout the following pages.

BURGLARY

Burglary is the unlawful entry of a structure, with or without force, with intent to commit a felony or theft. The FBI classifies burglary into three categories: (1) forcible entry, (2) unlawful entry where no force is used, and (3) attempted forcible entry. Approximately 2.14 million burglaries occurred in the United States during 2004 (Federal Bureau of Investigation, 2005). Nationwide, the residential burglary rate is 29.6 per 1,000 inhabitants (Catalano, 2005). The victimization rate of burglary has fallen nearly 50 percent since 1993. The National Crime Victimization Survey (NCVS) reports that about 3.4 million residential burglaries occurred in 2004 (Catalano, 2005). A major reason for the discrepancy between burglary data reported in the UCR and that found in the NCVS is that not all residential burglaries are reported to the police, even though they are mentioned on victimization surveys. As we noted in chapter 1, this occurs with many other offenses as well, because most crime does not come to the attention of police.

Characteristics of Burglary

About 32.4 percent of burglaries did not involve forced entry in 2004 (Federal Bureau of Investigation, 2005). That is, the offenders entered through an unlatched window or unlocked door or used a key "hidden" in an obvious place, such as under a doormat. Another 6.2 percent of the 2004 burglaries were *attempts* at forcible entry.

Consistently, year after year, about two-thirds of all reported burglaries involve residential property, while the remaining one-third involves commercial establishments. To be considered residential burglary, the structure entered need not be the house itself. Illegal entry of a garage, shed, or other structure on the premises also constitutes a residential burglary. Burglaries of residences occur more frequently during the daytime (65.2% in 2004), whereas burglaries of businesses and nonresidential property mostly occur at night (58% in 2004). In 2004, the overall loss due to burglary was estimated to be $3.3 billion, with the average dollar loss per burglary of residences averaging $1,607 (Federal Bureau of Investigation, 2005). The clearance rate for burglary in 2004 was 12.9 percent.

Burglaries are more likely to occur during the warmer months, especially July and August, apparently because people are more likely to be outdoors or away on vacation and are more likely to leave doors and windows open, making their residences vulnerable. A study by Langer and Miranksy (1983) reveals that a large segment of the population does not take responsibility for burglary prevention. Approximately half of the New York City residents questioned admitted they did not lock all their doors when away from home, even if they had been burglarized before. Interestingly, while 66 percent believed that burglary could be prevented, 61 percent of these subjects did not use all their locks. They believed that it was the responsibility of others (e.g., the police, the landlord, the building superintendent) to guard the premises, rather than their own personal responsibility. We must be very careful not to blame victims for *any* criminal offenses, however. It is one thing to alert people and make them aware of steps they can take to protect themselves from crime; it is quite another to fault them for not taking the steps. In the above study, those who thought their neighborhoods were unsafe and burglary-prone were less likely to use locks than those who considered their neighborhoods safe and less burglary-prone. Possibly, people in burglary prone areas are convinced that if someone decides to burglarize their homes there is not much they can do about it, locks or no locks. Another factor, though, is that good locks cost money. If one lives on a tight budget, buying a lock may be seen as a low priority.

Who Commits Burglary?

Like other criminal offenses, burglary seems to be primarily a crime committed by the young; 60 percent of those arrested in 2004 were under 25, with the average age being about 22 (Federal Bureau of Investigation, 2005). Twenty-five percent were under 18. To some extent, this arrest ratio may reflect the lack of sophistication of younger burglars who, because of their inexperience, are more likely to be detected. However, researchers have noted that, with increasing age, some burglars find they are not as nimble and athletic as they once were. Crawling through small open windows and climbing fences take their toll, and these strenuous activities become more burdensome with age. Thus, many older burglars turn to shoplifting (Cromwell, Olson, & Avary, 1991). Shoplifting is considerably easier, less risky, and more cost efficient. Shoplifted items are more easily converted to cash and are more profitable than items gained through burglary, because they are new, untraceable, and have their price tags attached. Furthermore, the criminal penalties are significantly less for shoplifting than they are for burglary.

Burglary is largely a male enterprise, with only 14 percent of those arrested being women in 2004. Although 70.8 percent of those arrested in 2004 were white, minorities (30 percent are black) are overrepresented in proportion to their numbers in the general population (Federal Bureau of Investigation, 2005).

As noted earlier, about two of every three burglaries are residential, and burglary of residences usually occurs during the daytime and on weekdays. Commercial establishments are usually burglarized late at night and on weekends (Cromwell et al., 1991; Pope, 1977b). This is not surprising, since burglary is a passive crime; the offender selects times and places that will minimize the possibility of an encounter with victims. Almost all experienced burglars (well over 90%) assert they will not even enter a residence when the occupants are believed to be at home (Cromwell et al., 1991). Homes occupied during the day most commonly are occupied by a parent providing child care or by retired individuals. However, burglars know that occupants develop predictable patterns regarding the use of discretionary time for the purposes of shopping, errands, or visiting friends or relatives. Individuals who work outside the home during weekdays also show similar patterns on weekends. Generally, the prime time for these errands and visits tends to be between 10:00 and 11:00 A.M., and from 1:00 to 3:00 P.M. (Cromwell et al., 1991). Parents also usually develop predictable patterns of taking children back and forth to school, nursery programs, and recreational activities.

Of all crimes, burglary offers the greatest probability of success with the least amount of risk. Not only is it a crime without victim contact and probability of identification, but also it does not require weapons. Furthermore, the penalties usually are less severe than those for robbery, a violent crime that involves confronting a victim by force or the threat of force. Juvenile offenders are more likely than their older counterparts to burglarize during the daytime hours (Pope, 1977c). In fact, a prime time for many juvenile burglaries is at the end of the school day, often between 3:00 and 6:00 P.M.

Burglary Cues and Selected Targets

The identification of situational cues is especially important in successful burglary. Nee and Taylor (1988) found that there are at least four broad categories of relevant cues used by experienced residential burglars. They are as follows:

1. *Occupancy cues,* such as letters or newspapers visible in mailbox, motor vehicles present, windows, blinds, and curtains shut or open
2. *Wealth cues,* such as the appearance of the house, the neighborhood, the quality of the landscaping, the make(s) of car(s) driven, and visible furnishings
3. *Layout cues,* such as how easy it would be to gain access to the house or building, as well as escape
4. *Security cues,* such as alarm systems, window locks, and dead bolt locks

Taylor and Nee (1988) designed a study that tested the possible differences in identifying these cues between burglars and home owners. The burglars consisted of a group of 15 experienced burglars serving time in Cork Prison in Ireland, and the home owners consisted of 15 Irish home owners. Each subject was requested to explore a simulated environment made up of slides and maps of five different houses. The researchers found that burglars were better able to discern security provisions and were more concerned about escaping successfully from the scene than were home owners. Most surprising, however, was the high amount of agreement between burglars and home owners on which houses were most vulnerable to burglary.

Burglar Cognitive Processes

Bennett and Wright (1984) conducted an extensive three-year project on convicted burglars confined in various prisons throughout southern England. The researchers' primary interest was to learn the decision-making processes and perceptions of the residential burglars at the time of the crime. The principal method of data collection in the study was semistructured interviews with the burglars themselves. Although a majority of the burglars had committed a variety of other economic crimes, almost all of them considered burglary their main criminal activity. Therefore, most of them probably qualify as professionals rather than amateurs.

Bennett and Wright discovered that almost all the burglaries were planned. Very few were the result of spur-of-the-moment decisions, nor were there any constant or irrepressible urges to burglarize. More than likely, though, those burglaries that appeared to be impulsive or opportunity-driven are probably the result of well-learned cognitive scripts, as described in chapter 5. **Cognitive scripts,** as you recall, are mental images and plans of how one will act and react in certain situations. The more one rehearses these scripts, behaviorally and mentally, the more habitual they become under similar conditions.

The two main aspects that went into the planning of burglars in the Bennett and Wright investigation were the situational cues of surveillability and occupancy. Surveillability cues were related to the amount of cover or openness around the house, whether it was overlooked by neighboring houses, the availability of access to the rear, and the presence or proximity of neighbors. Occupancy cues were similar to the ones reported by Nee and Taylor, such as a car in the driveway, lights on in the house, the presence of mail, whether the walks were shoveled or the lawn was cut, and so forth. Experienced burglars said that "occupancy proxies" were the major deterrents in attempts to burglarize. Specifically, burglar alarms and dogs were extremely important in the prevention of burglary. This was also a consistent finding of Cromwell and colleagues (1991). In fact, Cromwell and colleagues found that the dog does not have to be a large one. Any dog will do, since a large one poses a physical threat, and the small dog will be noisy. Cats do not seem to qualify.

Cromwell and his associates also found that dead bolts caused burglars considerable difficulty in entry, even though some of the experienced burglars claimed such locks would not be any problem. However, Cromwell and colleagues not only obtained self-report data from experienced burglars, but also had them demonstrate their claims. Security locks and dead bolts caused all kinds of trouble, even for highly experienced burglars—even though they said prior to the demonstration these locks would not be a deterrent. Much of the research on burglary, on the other hand, finds that increased police patrols and other such strategies have very little influence on decisions to burglarize, or on its success rate. This is primarily because the patrols cannot last indefinitely, and police cannot be everywhere at once. However, curious neighbors—those always peeking out their windows or finding yard chores to do when there is different activity next door—do tend to be strong deterrents for burglars. This observation is supported by both experienced burglars and crime statistics.

Research data suggest that, although burglary is a "planned" behavior, burglars identify a large number of potential targets, and then select the most vulnerable. Cromwell and his colleagues caution, however, that although much of the research on burglary suggests that a high percentage of burglars make carefully planned, highly rational decisions based on a detailed evaluation of environmental cues, the crime seems to be more of finding the right opportunity from an array of potential targets. Burglary is not generally an impulsive crime, but it isn't usually planned to precise detail either.

The Cromwell and colleagues study found that many burglars engage in what they referred to as **rational reconstruction.** That is, "Our findings indicate that burglars interviewed in prison or those recalling crimes from the past, either consciously or unconsciously, may engage in rational reconstruction— a reinterpretation of past behavior through which the actor recasts activities in a manner consistent with 'what should have been,' rather than 'what was'" (Cromwell et al., 1991, p. 42). Thus, self-report data from burglars may indicate that there was considerable planning involved in the burglary, whereas the crime was actually one of opportunity. In other words, they tended to reconstruct their behavior in a manner that made rational sense to them.

The Cromwell project not only gathered data from self-reports, but also had the experienced burglars simulate their burglaries. Moreover, the research team went on "ride-alongs" during which the burglars described their previous burglaries or described how they would burglarize a residence they perceived as vulnerable. Thus, the researchers were able to identify some of the disparities between what the professional burglars told them and what they actually did before, during, and after the real burglary. These findings suggest that research based exclusively on self-report data may be incomplete or suspect.

Cromwell and his colleagues (1991) also found in their systematic study of experienced burglars that one of the most popular entry methods was through sliding glass patio doors. Burglars said that these doors are easily popped out of their sliding tracks by hand or with aid of a crowbar or screwdriver. Entry is therefore quick and noiseless. Another common method is to remove, cut, or gently break a windowpane and crawl through the open window. A skillful burglar will carefully remove the pane, crawl through, and then replace the pane in a professional manner. Other commonly preferred methods for residential burglary include forcing the rear door open with a pry tool or kicking it down, or opening the garage door and forcing open the door between the garage and the house.

How Far Do Burglars Travel?

National research data on arrested burglars in the United States indicate that a large proportion commit the offense near their own residence. This seems especially true for juvenile offenders (Pope, 1977a). The Santa Clara Criminal Justice Pilot Program (1972) found that over one-half of the apprehended offenders traveled no more than a mile from their own home to commit the offenses. In a study of serial burglars who operated in a small town in southern England, Barker (2000) found that these offenders tended to live surprisingly close to the areas they burglarized. She discovered, however, that the mean home-to-offense distance increased during the later stages of burglary. For example, the average home-to-first-offense distance was 2.16 kilometers, the average distance from home to the middle offense in the series was 3.57 kilometers, and the average distance from home to the last offense in the series was 5.52 kilometers. It is difficult to generalize from these data, however, because apprehended burglars are presumably less skillful and thus more detectable than burglars who succeed. It is possible that successful burglars operate farther away from home. Eskridge (1983) found that those who burglarized commercial establishments were more willing to travel much greater distances.

Do They Usually Work Alone?

Over half of the apprehended burglars worked with an accomplice (Chimbos, 1973; Pope, 1977a). Eskridge (1983), who conducted a survey of crime in Lincoln, Nebraska, reports that nearly two-thirds of the identified burglars worked in groups of two or more. On a national level, groups of two or more are responsible for just under half (42%) of all burglary incidents. National data also suggest that very few burglars work with more than three accomplices. Younger offenders and females are more likely to use accomplices than older males (Pope, 1977a). However, this pattern also depends to some extent on the sophistication of the offender. Experienced, competent offenders who realize the formidable challenge presented by protection instruments (alarms or safes) may also be more likely to take on assistants (Shover, 1972).

Gender Differences in Methods and Patterns

In their study of male *and* female burglars, Decker, Wright, Redfern, and Smith (1993) found that the offending patterns of female burglars were very similar to those of males. One major exception was that male burglars often stole cars, whereas the female burglars did not. Decker and his colleagues found that they could divide the female burglars into two major groups: accomplices and partners. Accomplices committed the burglary because of their subservience to others—usually men—during their burglaries. Partners, on the other hand, participated as equals in the commission of burglary. Although some of the females co-offended with males, they did not take orders from them.

As for other criminal offenses, the best predictor of burglary is an offender's record. In a California analysis, 80 percent of the offenders studied had a prior arrest record (Pope, 1977c). Of these, 58 percent had a prior burglary arrest, and 47 percent had prior drug arrests, usually selling. Males were far more likely to have a previous criminal record than females.

Use of Alcohol and Other Substances

Although a well-known Santa Clara 1972 project concluded that burglars are rarely under the influence of alcohol and other drugs at the time of their crime, the more recent data reported by the Cromwell and associates (1991) study indicates this is not so. Ninety-three percent of the professional burglars studied by the Cromwell group said they "fixed" or "got high" before entering a residence. These experienced, professional burglars admitted they needed to lower their anxiety levels and reduce their fear prior to the burglary. The vast majority of these burglars reported moderate amounts of alcohol or drugs simply made them better burglars, because these substances increased their alertness, vigilance, and improved their nerve to stay in the residences long enough to search for and locate a variety of items to steal. Female burglars do the same thing (Decker et al., 1993). Specifically, the calming effects of drugs and alcohol enabled them to focus more on environmental cues related to risk, as well as valuable items hidden in the house that they normally would not find. Psychologically, this observation makes sense because high levels of arousal do narrow one's attention span and reduce one's focus on environmental cues under certain pressure situations (Easterbrook, 1959). Also, the Cromwell study found that heroin-using burglars tend to be more rational, more professional, and less likely to be arrested than burglars using cocaine or speed (or more generally, stimulants). Moreover, the heroin user was able to exercise considerable control over the amount of the drug used for maximum proficiency in burglarizing.

What Happens to the Merchandise?

Amateur burglars usually take money or personal items that they need, whereas the professional takes items with excellent resale value, such as stereos, cameras, television sets, jewelry, and furs (Vetter & Silverman, 1978). The professional usually has access to a **fence,** whereas the amateur rarely has that kind of contact. A fence, an integral component in the professional burglary cycle, is a person who knowingly buys stolen merchandise for the purpose of resale. Professional burglars also have individually distinctive methods and not infrequently leave their mark (their signature) to goad the investigators they have foiled. Many professional burglars prefer retail stores over residential homes.

The Cromwell and associates (1991) research raises serious questions about the extent to which professional fences are used today, however. In their investigation of experienced burglars operating in an urban Texas metropolitan area of 250,000, they found considerable diversity in the channels through which stolen property was distributed. Some burglars sold their stolen property to pawnshops, others to friends and acquaintances, and still others traded their property for drugs. Some resold the merchandise to legitimate businesses or strangers. The researchers, therefore, suggest that today the "professional fence may have been displaced by a more diverse and readily accessed market for stolen property" (p. 73). Stolen property today, for example, is often disposed of via Internet sites.

Motives

As you might expect, the motives for burglary are varied, but the primary factor for professionals is undoubtedly monetary gain. When performed competently, burglary is a lucrative business with low risks and with monetary rewards far surpassing those the burglar might earn in the "straight" world. David (1974) learned that a husband and wife team he interviewed made, on the average, $400 to $500 a day; a solitary offender in his sample made about $500 per week. These figures will obviously be much higher in today's market. Many professionals also conceive of their behavior as a challenging skill to be continually developed and refined. Some even said they get a "rush" of excitement during the planning and commission of the crime, especially if they are good at it (Cromwell et al., 1991). In this sense, burglary is highly adaptive and represents an instrumental behavior supported by strong reinforcement. For many burglars, however, a simple conclusion that they participate in their crimes as their sole profession or lucrative business may be unwarranted. A vast majority of burglary is committed to supplement the offender's incomes and to improve their quality of life (Rengert & Wasilchick, 1985). The income gained from burglary enables the offender to buy drugs, alcohol, expensive goods, and, more broadly, to be able "to party." Alternatively, it may be used, like the profits from other economic crimes, to finance a college education. Subsistence needs are often met through other sources of income, such as a regular job.

Some burglars may burglarize the same place again, or even repeatedly, in a pattern called **repeat burglary.** Burglars that participate in repeat burglary do it because of the efficiency in time, planning, and risk involved (Farrell, Phillips, & Pease, 1995). Residential locations are especially vulnerable because residents rarely change the layout or make entry more difficult after a burglary. In other words, the burglar knows the layout of the target well, was successful the first time, and may even have seen valuables the first time around that prompted a return visit.

Shover (1972) discusses some of the outstanding features of the competent professional burglar, whom he calls the **good burglar.** This burglar demonstrates technical skill, maintains a good reputation for personal integrity among colleagues in the criminal subculture, gets most of his income from burglary, and has been at least relatively successful at the crime. A good reputation means that the burglar is closemouthed, stands up to police, and is sympathetic to the criminal way of life.

The professional burglar, then, is primarily motivated by money but also by self-satisfaction and accomplishment. When self-satisfaction and self-reinforcement are conditioned on certain accomplishments, people are motivated to expend the effort needed to attain the desired goal, perhaps even independently of monetary gain. Walsh (1980), for example, has emphasized the expressive and psychological components of burglary. He posits that, for some burglars, the challenge of the crime is far more rewarding than the material reward. Based on interviews with victims and offenders, Walsh identifies three kinds of **expressive burglars:** (1) *the feral threat,* (2) *the riddlesmith,* and (3) *the dominator.* The feral burglar engages in destructive, malicious vandalism during the break-in by spilling things, breaking glass, smashing objects, and urinating and defecating in various areas throughout the house. The riddlesmith, on the other hand, tries to demonstrate his or her technical skill to the victims and investigators by setting up puzzles, mysteries, and booby traps throughout the house. The riddlesmith is inventive in the way he or she causes damage, and messages may be left on walls, floors, and mirrors. The dominator enjoys threatening or frightening victims, and therefore breaks into homes that are occupied. All three of these expressive burglars are interested in communicating to burglarized victims through a particular style or MO. Thus, a burglar who takes great pride in developing ingenious techniques and stumping police is even more likely to continue his illegal conduct. While external reinforcements (tangible rewards) are important, internal reinforcement may be a very powerful motivating and regulating factor.

Psychological Impact of Burglary

Merry and Hansent point out that, for all of us, the home is a sanctuary: "It is a special place that is central to our daily lives, a place that is at the beginning and end of most of our journeys; it is chosen and personalized" (2000, p. 36). The manner in which homes are decorated and arranged and the objects within them represent important aspects of our lives and personalities. When our homes are burglarized, therefore, it is an invasion of our intimate space and an attack on our identity, physically and symbolically. Some victims describe burglary as a rape of their home, especially when the burglar has disturbed personal photographs, letters, and diaries, leaving the feeling of having been violated or at least "touched" by the intruder (Merry & Hansent, 2000). The distress levels experienced by victims are often more pronounced when the invasion extends to private areas, such as bedrooms, closets, chests-of-drawers, bathrooms, and desks. The invasion also endangers the victims' sense of control and threatens their ability to protect their own personal territory. Many victims, after being burglarized, install security systems such as video cameras, increase and improve the locks, buy dogs, or even move to new homes. Overall, the psychological trauma caused by a burglary can be substantial for many victims, and its effects may continue for many years.

Very often the burglar's actions are intended to produce some response from the victim. In other words, some burglars specifically tailor their styles (or signatures) to convey messages to victims and investigators, hoping to induce some strong emotional reactions from the victims. The emotional reactions of burglarized victims often run the gamut from anger and depression to fear and anxiety (Brown & Harris, 1989). In addition, the individual style utilized by the offender probably reflects something about his character and personality. According to Merry and Hansent (2000), this aspect is referred to as the interpersonal dimension of the crime. It is suggested, therefore, that the victim's feelings of fear and vulnerability are psychological losses that are translated into gains for the offender. In this sense, the burglar gains materially and psychologically from the crime. The interpersonal aspects of the burglary (i.e., the style used by the burglar) are areas that provide considerable potential for burglary profiling in future research.

LARCENY AND MOTOR VEHICLE THEFT

McCaghy (1980) refers to the larceny-theft category as a "garbage can" because it is heterogeneous and hard to classify. Larceny-theft is defined as the "unlawful taking, carrying, leading, or riding away of property from the possession or constructive possession of another" (Federal Bureau of Investigation, 1997, p. 43). It differs from burglary in that it does not involve unlawful entry. Larceny includes pickpocketing, purse snatching, shoplifting (which is discussed in a separate section), stealing from vending machines or from motor vehicles, and theft of property left outdoors (bicycles, pedigreed dogs, lawn mowers), and so on. The larceny-theft offenses in the United States during 2004 accounted for 59.4 percent of the Part 1 total and 67.3 percent of the property crime total (Federal Bureau of Investigation, 2005). Table 14–1 (on page 451) includes a percentage distribution of the more common types of theft. The clearance rate for larceny-theft was 18.3 percent in 2004, nationwide. **Figure 14–1** shows the percent distribution of the various crimes that make up larceny-theft.

The 2004 larceny-theft rate in the United States was 2365.9 per 100,000 people (Federal Bureau of Investigation, 2005). Five- and 10-year trends showed the rate declined 4.5 percent from the 2000 rate and 22.3 percent from the 1995 rate (Federal Bureau of Investigation, 2005). Thefts of motor vehicle parts, accessories, and things left in cars made up the largest portion of reported larcenies (36%) in 2004, followed by shoplifting (14.5%). The average value of property stolen in 2004 was $727.

Motor Vehicle Theft

Motor vehicle theft is defined as the theft or attempted theft of a motor vehicle, including the stealing of automobiles, trucks, buses, motorcycles, motor scooters, and snowmobiles (Federal Bureau of Investigation, 1997). The taking of a

FIGURE 14–1   Larceny-Theft, Percent Distribution, 2004

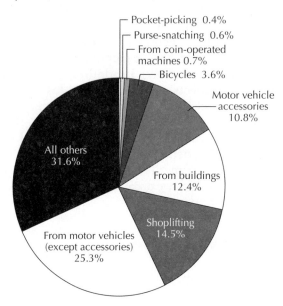

Source: Federal Bureau of Investigation, 2005, p. 52.

motor vehicle for temporary use by persons having lawful access is excluded from the definition (Federal Bureau of Investigation, 2005). An estimated total of 1.24 million thefts of motor vehicles occurred in the United States during 2004 (Federal Bureau of Investigation, 2005). The 2004 national motor vehicle theft rate was about 421.3 per 100,000 people, and represents a 16 percent decrease since 1995. Auto theft accounts for approximately 12 percent of all property crimes reported to the police in the United States, and 13 percent of all property crimes reported to the police in England and Wales (Copes & Cherbonneau, 2006). Clearance rate for motor vehicle theft in 2004 was 13 percent.

Of the estimated 105,746 arrests for motor vehicle theft in 2004, males accounted for 83.5 percent of those arrested. Persons in the under-18 age group were involved in 26.5 percent of the motor vehicle thefts cleared nationally in 2004.

Motor vehicle manufacturers have developed effective and highly sophisticated ways of preventing theft in recent years, making it increasingly difficult for thieves to steal the vehicle by traditional means. Offenders have adapted to these changes by seeking out more effective ways of obtaining keys for the vehicles (Copes & Cherbonneau, 2006). Consequently, there has been a growth in the prevalence of auto theft involving keys (Copes & Cherbonneau, 2006). In addition, obtaining keys minimizes damage done to the vehicle, which will ultimately increase its resale value. Some offenders go to great lengths to steal, find, or manipulate the keys from owners. Others are becoming skillful at manufacturing matching keys themselves.

Carjacking

Carjacking is the completed or attempted theft in which a motor vehicle is taken by force or threat of force (Klaus, 1999). It differs from other motor vehicle theft in that it involves the use of force or threat of force on the occupants of the vehicle. On average 34,000 carjacking incidents occur each year in the United States (Klaus, 2004). Approximately a dozen homicides are associated with these carjackings each year; in other words, the driver or a passenger is killed. In about three-fourths of carjackings, the occupants face an armed offender or offenders (Klaus, 2004). In most instances, the carjacker uses a firearm. Victimization surveys indicate that the victim resisted the carjacker in two-thirds of the incidents, which resulted in about 9 percent of the victims receiving serious injury (e.g., gunshot or knife wounds, broken bones, or internal injuries).

Men tend to be more victimized than women, blacks more than whites, and Hispanics more than non-Hispanics (Klaus, 2004). Carjackings are highly concentrated in particular areas and at particular times. They are highest in urban areas. They occur in parking lots and garages (24%), or in an open area, such as on the street or near public transportation (bus, subway, train station, or airport) (44%). They most often occur at night. Males committed 93 percent of the carjackings, while groups involving both males and females committed 3 percent. Women committed about 3 percent of the incidents.

Although the offense is violent, it appears to contain some elements of short-term planning and decision making and often is directed more at the object (the vehicle) than the person (Jacobs, Topalli, & Wright, 2003). Jacobs and his colleagues interviewed 28 active carjackers recruited from the streets of St. Louis, Missouri. "Active carjackers were defined as individuals who had committed two or more carjackings in the previous year" (2003, p. 675). In this study, all active carjackers were black and three were women. The interviews were semistructured and informal, allowing offenders to speak freely in their own words.

The researchers discovered that the active carjackers remain in permanent state of "alert opportunism" and ready to commit the offense if the chance came their way. Many had gotten away with carjackings in the past, and therefore believed they would succeed when the need for quick cash or quick transportation arose again. In other words, most have developed well-learned cognitive scripts for how to proceed with their offense. Moreover, each had a preference for the vehicle they sought (gold-spoked wheels, a high-performance engine, or a booming sound system). These features bring a good price on the streets. In some cases, a driver would become a victim because the carjacker interpreted him as demonstrating disrespect. Punishing the driver added an incentive to the incentive of obtaining quick cash. Thus, the carjacking became a way to punish drivers who dare to "floss their little stuff by cruising through their neighborhoods in a disrespectful way" (Jacobs et al., 2003, p. 682). For example, "flossing" might include turning the sound system up loud in the neighborhood to mark the driver's presence.

Larceny and motor vehicle theft are common and widespread offenses, but research reporting specifically on these areas is rarely available. To some extent, the motivating factors that apply to burglary apply here as well. On the other hand, larceny and motor vehicle theft is more likely to be committed by the nonprofessional and the desperate.

FRAUD AND IDENTITY THEFT

Crimes of fraud involve deception used for the purpose of obtaining illegal financial gain. They often involve the misrepresentation of facts and the deliberate intent to deceive with the promise of goods, services, or other benefits that either do not exist or that were never intended to be provided (Deem & Murray, 2000). Examples of fraud include identity theft, elder financial abuse, counterfeiting, mail fraud, bank fraud, and various corporate or organizational wrongdoings. Over the last two decades, fraud has increased in awareness with such high-profile corporate cases as the savings and loan debacle of the 1980s and the massive Enron and Tyco cases of the early 2000s.

Identity theft occurs when one individual or a group of individuals misappropriate another person's personal identification information, such as name, social security number, date of birth, mother's maiden name, and uses the information to take over existing credit card or bank accounts, apply for a mortgage or car loan, make large purchases, or apply for insurance (Deem & Murray, 2000). In many instances, unsuspecting victims have no idea that anything is amiss until they receive phone calls from creditors or have difficulty applying for a job, loan, or mortgage. According to available data, the amount of loss due to identity theft has increased dramatically over the past 10 years, rising to over $745 million in 1997 (Deem & Murray, 2000).

In 2004, 3 percent of the households in the United States (3.6 million) were victimized by identity theft (Baum, 2006). Credit care theft is the most common type of identity theft. In most cases, persons discover the theft by noticing unfamiliar charges on accounts, or they are contacted by a credit card bureau (see **Table 14–2**). The average amount of money lost in identity theft in 2004 was $1,290 (Baum, 2006).

The increase in this type of fraud is due partly to the development of new technologies associated with the Internet and telecommunications. At this stage, research on the demographics, motives, or tactics of the perpetrators is virtually nonexistent. Ironically, considering the fact that the thief assumes someone else's identity, it is likely that dehumanization or denial of the victim is involved. The perpetrator does not have to see what the victim looks like, experience the victim's stress, or know anything about the victim's life, with the exception of financial data. Though we know little about the offenders, we do know that the emotional impact of identity theft—and fraud in general—on victims is substantial and should not be underestimated. In addition to having strong feelings of being victimized, feelings emerge that one should blame oneself, can no longer trust one's own ability to handle financial matters, or can no

TABLE 14–2   Identity Theft in American Households, 2004

DID HOUSEHOLDS DISCOVER IDENTITY THEFT IN PREVIOUS 6 MONTHS?	NUMBER OF HOUSEHOLDS	PERCENT OF HOUSEHOLDS	PERCENT OF VICTIMIZED HOUSEHOLDS
Yes	3,589,100	3.1%	100.0%
Unauthorized use of existing credit cards	1,736,700	1.5	48.4
Other existing accounts (such as a checking account)	896,500	0.8	25.0
Misuse of personal information (to obtain new accounts or loans)	538,700	0.5	15.0
Multiple types of theft during the same episode	417,100	0.4	11.8
No	111,773,400	96.7%	NA
Don't know	251,800	0.2%	NA

Source: Baum, 2006, p. 1.

longer trust people. This is accompanied by the long drawn-out process of repairing one's credit rating and, as in the case of other victimizations, one's emotional well-being.

SHOPLIFTING

Shoplifting, a form of larceny-theft, is a frequent and costly type of crime. Although shoplifting comprised about 14.5 percent of all arrests for larceny-theft in 2004 (see Figure 14–1), it is obviously underreported by a large margin. The National Retail Federation and surveys by the Security Research Project at the University of Florida in Gainesville estimate the total monetary loss due to shoplifting in the United States to be roughly $10.15 billion (Coleman, 2000). This figure represents a 14 percent increase from 1997 to 2000. Interestingly, total losses from employee theft jumped 34 percent, to $12.85 billion, during that same time period.

Based on self-report data, as many as 60 percent of American consumers have shoplifted at least once in their lives, and 30 percent to 40 percent of adolescents admit that they shoplift repeatedly (Krasnovsky & Lane, 1998). These data are surprising in light of the rapid improvement in security measures designed to discourage and prevent the crime. For example, most sizeable retail establishments have private security officers on the premises. Furthermore, cameras now are ubiquitous in large retail stores, hidden in clocks, smoke alarms, and pushbars on fire-exit doors (Adler, 2002).

Comprehensive data on all other economic crimes are difficult to obtain, but data acquisition for shoplifting offenses is especially difficult, since store personnel exercise wide discretion in reporting offenses. Hindelang (1974) found that whether charges were filed depended on the retail value of the stolen object, what was stolen, and the manner in which it was taken, rather than demographic and personality characteristics of the shoplifter. Specifically, the offender's race did not seem to matter, nor whether the offender was male or female, poor or middle class. What determined referral for arrest was whether the item was expensive, had resale value, or was stolen in a professional, skillful manner. Later research by Davis, Lundman, and Martinez (1991) found that shoplifters are more likely to be arrested not only when they take expensive items, but also when they resist being apprehended, have no local address, and/or live in poor neighborhoods. In England, on the other hand, store managers consider the age of the shoplifter as well as the value of the stolen item (Farrington & Burrows, 1993). The British study found that, generally, store managers did not report to the police the very young (under age 17) or very old (over 60), the mentally impaired, or those shoplifters in an advanced stage of pregnancy, unless they were caught repeatedly. In a series of observational studies (also in England) by Abigail Buckle and David Farrington (1984), random samples of customers were followed by trained observers as they shopped. Approximately one in 50 was observed to steal. The amount of shoplifting, however, differed dramatically from store to store. Shoplifting characteristics in supermarkets are likely to differ significantly from those exhibited in retail department stores or hardware stores. Buckle and Farrington (1994) conducted a replication of the 1984 study. Again, trained observers randomly followed approximately 500 customers in a small department store located in another city. The proportion of customers who shoplifted was between 1 percent and 2 percent, and a majority was male. Most of the shoplifters also purchased goods as they checked out of the store, probably to allay suspicion. In general, the items stolen were small, low-cost items. In contrast to the original study where there was a preponderance of older shoplifters (age 55 or over), Buckle and Farrington found that most of the shoplifters were young (age 25 or less). These studies underscore the warning that estimations concerning the incidence of shoplifting must be placed within a situational, cultural, and historical context. Furthermore, apprehension statistics may tell us more about the store security personnel practices and biases than about the shoplifting population (Klemke, 1992). In fact, it is not uncommon for security personnel to claim that they have developed a "sixth sense" for picking out likely suspects. This "sixth sense" is, in some cases, a bias or stereotype against certain segments of the population more than any all-encompassing, accurate skill.

Who Shoplifts?

Roughly 40 percent of all apprehended shoplifters are adolescents (Cox, Cox, & Moschis, 1990). An analysis of one million juvenile court records across nearly two thousand jurisdictions reveals that shoplifting is the most common juvenile court referral for youths under age 15 (Kelly, Kennedy, & Homant, 2003). Shoplifting appears to decline, however, both in number of offenses and the number of those engaging in this behavior, as offenders mature and move into early adulthood (Krasnovsky & Lane, 1998: Osgood, O'Mailey, Bachman, & Johnstone, 1989). Klemke (1992) conducted one of the first major studies on adolescent shoplifting. He collected self-report data from students in four small town high schools in the Pacific Northwest during the late 1970s. Klemke (1992) discovered that approximately three-fourths of the frequent shoplifters began shoplifting before the age of 10, but then stopped soon after their eighteenth birthday. Interestingly, data from college bookstores indicate that first-year students are more likely to be apprehended for shoplifting than other college students (Klemke, 1992). Readers undoubtedly can think of a variety of explanations for this, ranging from the high minded ("Upper class students love their college more and are more committed to the college community") to the cynical ("Upper class students don't go near the bookstore any more").

It has been assumed that shoplifting is committed primarily by adolescent girls and women. Among the explanations offered for women's greater involvement in shoplifting, the most common is that women have greater opportunity to steal small items from merchants than do men. As Gibbens (1981) also noted, women are more likely to be in stores where detectives are stationed. As men join the ranks of frequent shoppers, however, their shoplifting rates are beginning to increase, and the gap between men and women is narrowing (Moore, 1984). In an extensive review of the available research, Baumer and Rosenbaum (1984) concluded that gender ratio appears to be about 50–50. Farrington and Burrows (1993) report a similar gender ratio in England. Although women apparently shoplifted more than men in the past, more men than women were actually convicted (Smart, 1976).

Baumer and Rosenbaum outline some of the psychological characteristics and behavioral patterns of shoplifters. They note that such things as extreme nervousness, aimless walking up and down the aisles, looking around frequently, glancing up from the merchandise frequently, and leaving the store and returning a number of times are some of the indicators that suggest shoplifting.

In spite of its traditional prominence in economic crime, shoplifting has received little psychological research attention. The most heavily quoted source on the subject, Mary Owen Cameron's *The Booster and the Snitch: Department Store Shoplifting* (1964), reported data accumulated in the 1940s and early 1950s. Cameron divided her shoplifters into two groups: Commercial shoplifters were "**boosters,**" and amateur pilferers were "**snitches.**" All of her data were subsequently explained with reference to this dichotomy. The boosters were professionals, accepted members of the criminal subculture. They stole for substantial financial gain by choosing items from preselected locations. Boosters used a wide range of techniques such as "booster boxes," packages designed for concealing items inserted through hidden slots or hinged openings, or "stalls," containers with hidden compartments (large handbags, coats with hidden pockets). Snitches, on the other hand, were "respectable" persons who rarely had criminal records. They did not consider themselves thieves, and the idea that they might actually be arrested and prosecuted rarely crossed their minds. Very often, once apprehended, they claimed they stole the item on impulse and did not know what came over them.

Some social science research has focused on elderly shoplifters. Feinberg (1984) found that shoplifting was neither a female-dominated offense nor undertaken for subsistence purposes. Elderly shoplifters, he notes, are neither indigent, lonely, nor victims of poor memory. He attributes their criminal offenses to changes in status that separate the elderly from mainstream society. Often, they must reevaluate their past values and try out different selves and meanings. To what extent Feinberg's research may be generalized to other age groups remains an open question.

Motives

The motives behind commercial shoplifting may be clearer than those behind the amateur type. Whereas boosters take merchandise of value, snitches tend to take inexpensive items they can use. Some research has noted that male snitches prefer items of more value, such as stereo equipment, records, and jewelry. Women snitches seem to take clothing, cosmetics, and food. The boosters shoplift for the money; the snitches for more obscure reasons.

Theories concerning the intentions of snitches range from economic ones, like attempts to stretch the family budget (Cameron, 1964), to emotional ones, like attempts to satisfy needs centering around matrimonial stress, loneliness, and depression (Russell, 1973). In recent years, some have even concluded that most shoplifting is an addiction, much like gambling and alcoholism. The notion of shoplifting as a means of alleviating unmet needs or addiction is weak and poorly documented, however. The behavior gains attention, but it also becomes aversive. On the other hand, the contention that shoplifting has primarily an economic motivation seems oversimplified. Shoplifting is pursued by different people for different reasons.

Methods of Shoplifting

Males tend to favor concealing stolen merchandise in pockets or clothing, while females generally prefer purses or shopping bags. The method of concealment, however, depends considerably on the merchandise, the gender of the offender, and the type of store. In clothing stores, shoplifters would more likely attempt to walk out wearing the clothing after leaving the fitting room, for example. Men prefer to hide items beneath their clothing in supermarkets, while pockets are preferred in drug and discount stores. Women tend to prefer purses for concealment in supermarkets or grocery stores, and packages and bags in drug and discount stores. Two things that draw the attention of store security personnel are broken arm casts (some are false) and large shopping bags obtained from a prior visit. In addition, women with babies in strollers or in backpacks often report that they are carefully watched by store personnel even though there is no documentation that these women are any more likely to steal than other customers.

The item most commonly stolen in supermarkets or grocery stores is meat, while in drug stores clothing tends to be more common, followed by health and beauty aids. A common trick for some shoplifters in a supermarket is to do a lot of "grazing" while shopping. That is, the shopper openly eats, drinks (commonly soda), or "tastes" while shopping, especially in the fruit section, and fails to pay for the items while checking out. Many individuals who do this do not consider it shoplifting, however, and many stores would not report this type of behavior without first speaking with the individual. Klemke (1992) notes that some shoplifters prefer to conceal the items, while others do not. Some walk nonchalantly out the door with the item(s) as though nothing is amiss.

Types of Shoplifters

Moore (1984), studying three hundred convicted shoplifters referred for presentence investigation, identified five patterns of offending. Although no shoplifters were considered professional to the degree of Cameron's booster category (the professionals may have escaped detection), 11.7 percent were semiprofessional, reporting shoplifting behavior at least once a week. Their "take" amounted to approximately $1,250 a year (a significant amount in the early 1980s).

The most frequent type of shoplifter in Moore's study was the "amateur" (56.4%) who stole small personal items when the opportunity arose. The methods used by amateurs were less sophisticated than those of the semiprofessionals, and unlike the semiprofessionals, the amateurs admitted that their behavior was morally wrong or illegal. Both types of shoplifting were premeditated, habitual, and directed toward financial gain. Persons in the amateur category were more likely to exhibit mild personality disorders or to be plagued by psychosocial stressors associated with interpersonal problems, such as family disruption.

Approximately 17 percent of Moore's offender population was impaired by mental or emotional problems. However, very few individuals (1.7%) had severe mental or emotional problems that directly "compelled" them to shoplift. The persons in this latter category were called "episodic" offenders.

Fifteen percent of the sample were "impulse" shoplifters, and another 15 percent were "occasional" offenders. Impulse shoplifters typically had seen an item that they desired but were unable to afford. They had picked it up and pocketed it or carried it around the store, often in a daze, trying to decide whether to steal it. It is likely that walking around the store in this fashion alerted store personnel. Eventually they tried to walk out but were detected. Later, they could not recall at what point they had made the decision to shoplift. Occasional offenders were less impulsive, but more likely to steal for excitement or a dare. Both impulse and occasional offenders were extremely embarrassed when detected, pleaded with officials to give them another chance, and were considered unlikely to shoplift again.

Although Moore found no significant gender differences in overall shoplifting, 68 percent of the teenage offenders were male, whereas 56.5 percent of the adult offenders were female. Moore also found interesting differences between male and female adult offenders with respect to psychological stress. More women reported being under great stress in their lives than did men (28.9% of the women compared with 13.5% of the men). However, this difference may also be due to the greater reluctance of men to report stress or other emotional problems in general. Mental disorders, found in only a small percentage of the total shoplifter population, appeared twice as often in women as in men. There were no gender differences in the incidence of milder mental disorders, however. Substance abuse, on the other hand, was more common among men than women (52% to 26%).

Kleptomania: Fact or Fiction?

One thing does appear clear. Clinicians and researchers have been unable to substantiate evidence of **kleptomania,** the *irresistible* impulse to steal unneeded objects. Some have even questioned its very existence as a behavior pattern. According to the DSM-IV, the kleptomaniac "experiences a rising subjective sense of tension before the theft and feels pleasure, gratification, or relief when committing the theft" (p. 612). A strong argument against kleptomania is that shoplifters display exceedingly low recidivism rates. Once apprehended, the amateur rarely shoplifts again (Cameron, 1964; Russell, 1973). If kleptomania were an important ingredient, we would expect the individual to steal repeatedly as the tension increases.

Lloyd Klemke (1992) suggests that kleptomania is a psychiatric label intended to ease the guilt of affluent women caught stealing during the turn of the twentieth century. Merchants, Klemke points out, did not want to antagonize their affluent clientele. Furthermore, affluent families wanted to keep their moral reputations untarnished and keep their women at home. Nor did the courts want to convict "respectable ladies" as common criminals. Thus, kleptomania (the Greek word for "stealing madness," a term presumably coined by Esquirol in 1838) legitimized the actions of the merchants and the courts to dismiss or acquit the "afflicted" woman and excuse her from being held personally responsible for her actions.

If kleptomania does exist, it seems to be a rare phenomenon. For example, in a recent study conducted by Sarasalo, Bergman, and Toth (1997), 50 shoplifters (29 males, 21 females) were interviewed immediately after being caught red-handed in central Stockholm, Sweden. None of the persons interviewed fulfilled the DSM-IV criteria for kleptomania. Sarasalo et al., however, did find that many of the shoplifters reported a "thrill" and challenge in connection with the crime.

Much of the literature on the causes of kleptomania focuses on its relationship to anxiety, depression, or sexual disturbances (Goldman, 1991; Sarasalo, Bergman, & Toth, 1996). Citing sexual disturbances as a cause for kleptomania is primarily based in the psychoanalytic tradition. But as Marcus Goldman (1991, p. 990) notes, "there are no modern data available to refute or confirm these earlier psychoanalytic findings."

Overall, much of the recent research has found depression to be a common symptom of people who engage in "nonsensical shoplifting" (Lamontagne, Boyer, Hetu, & Lacerte-Lamontagne, 2000), a term with many similarities to kleptomania but without the compulsion aspect. Yates (1986) claims that 80 percent of those who engaged in nonsensical shoplifting were depressed. McElroy and colleagues (McElroy et al., 1991) found that all 20 patients they studied who engaged in nonsensical shoplifting met the DSM-III-R criteria for a lifetime diagnosis of a major mood (depression) disorder. In addition, many of these patients said they engaged in nonsensical shoplifting far more often when they were depressed. It seems that some depressed people may engage in nonsensical shoplifting as a stimulating, exciting activity that moves them away from feelings of helplessness. In fact, Goldman (1991) finds that depressive states are often reported throughout the literature as precursors to many kinds of theft that are not related to profit.

For some unexplained reason, women seem to engage in nonsensical shoplifting more often than men. According to Marcus Goldman (1991, p. 994), "It would appear that the average person suffering from kleptomania is a 35-year-old married woman who has been apprehended for the theft of objects she could easily afford and does not need." However, statistics on nonsensical shopping are unavailable. Any statement concerning gender differences in either kleptomania or nonsensical shoplifting should be made very cautiously.

Shoplifting can be controlled to some extent by the use of electronic article surveillance (EAS) or ink tags (Eck, 2000). EAS involves attaching electronic tags on merchandise that only store clerks can remove at the time of payment. Failure to remove the tag sets off an alarm at the door as the customer leaves the store. Ink tags deface the merchandise if it is removed from the store without paying, thereby destroying the value of the stolen goods (Eck, 2000). Eck, in his review of the research literature, reports that EAS measures can reduce shoplifting from 32 percent to 80 percent, and are found to be more effective than either security guards or store redesign (see Bamfield, 1994; DiLonardo, 1996; Farrington et al., 1993 for more detail on relevant studies). Ink tags as an effective prevention of shoplifting have been less studied than EAS, but appear to be equally promising.

WHITE-COLLAR AND OCCUPATIONAL CRIME

The term **white-collar crime** was coined by Edwin H. Sutherland in his presidential address to the American Sociological Society in 1939. In his speech, Sutherland urged his fellow sociologists to pay attention to the law-violating behavior of businesses, particularly large corporations. He had uncovered these violations by reviewing government files on 70 large American corporations and had learned that breaking rules was commonplace. In 1949, Sutherland published his now classic book, *White-Collar Crime*, in which he detailed his findings without naming the corporations. A later edition of the book (Sutherland, 1983) did include the names.

Following Sutherland's lead, a considerable amount of pioneering research was done on white-collar crime between 1939 and 1963 (Geis, 1988). This was followed by a decade of inactivity. Since 1975, there has been a revival of interest in studying the area, although criminological literature gives far less attention to white-collar crime than to other forms of criminal behavior. The highly publicized individual and corporate scandals of recent years, like the Enron debacle, have only served to illustrate that this attention is needed.

According to Sutherland, "white-collar crime may be defined approximately as a crime committed by a person of respectability and high social status in the course of his occupation" (1949, p. 9). Although Sutherland used the word "crime," he did not intend it strictly in the legal sense. He recognized that numerous laws and regulations violated by persons of high social status carried civil rather than criminal sanctions, and he wanted these violations to be condemned. In fact, this was a critical factor to Sutherland, who saw a double standard phenomenon at work. The law-violating behavior of the poor carried criminal penalties; the law-violating behavior of the rich often did not. This was so despite the fact that "[t]he financial cost of white-collar crime is probably several times as great as the financial cost of all the crimes which are customarily regarded as 'the crime problem' " (Sutherland, 1949, p. 12).

Although Sutherland's call to study white-collar crime was heeded, his working definition produced numerous problems for subsequent criminologists. Some, most notably Paul Tappan (1947), argued that white-collar "crime" could not really be crime unless it violated the criminal law. The terms "respectability" and "high social status" were considered vague. Over the past four decades, researchers have tried to improve on Sutherland's definition. Marshall Clinard and Richard Quinney (1980) preferred to dichotomize the concept into (1) occupational crime, committed by an individual for his or her own profit, and (2) corporate crime, committed by the corporation through its agents. This dichotomy is probably the most commonly used by criminologists today. Horning (1970) proposed a threefold division to distinguish the various behaviors that might be at issue. He reserved *white-collar crime* for acts committed by salaried employees in which their place of employment is either the victim or the locale for the commission of an illegal act from which they personally benefit. Embezzlement would be a good example of this. *Corporate crime* refers to illegal acts by employees in the course of their employment that primarily benefit the company or corporation. Illegal dumping of hazardous wastes is an example. *Blue-collar crime* refers to the whole array of illegal acts committed by non-salaried workers against their place of employment. Thefts of machinery, tools, or paper are examples.

Green's Four Categories of Occupational Crime

Gary Green (1997) has made significant contributions to clarifying the definitional dilemmas associated with the term white-collar crime by proposing the concept of **occupational crime.** Unfortunately, Green's approach has not been widely adopted. To Green, occupational crime encompasses all of the behaviors previously subsumed under white-collar crime, blue-collar crime, and their variants. Occupational crime is "any act punishable by law that is committed through opportunity created in the course of an occupation that is legal" (Green, 1997, p. 15). Green then subdivides occupational crime into four categories: (1) organizational (which includes corporate crime), (2) professional, (3) state-authority, and (4) individual (see **Table 14–3**).

In **organizational occupational crime,** a legal entity such as a company, corporation, firm, or foundation profits by the law-violating behavior. An example would be the chief financial officer of a company falsifying the company's tax records with the tacit approval of its board of directors. Other examples are antitrust violations, overcharging the government for products or services, violations of Occupational Safety and Health Administration (OSHA) standards, and bribery of public officials. **Professional occupational crime** includes illegal behavior by persons such as lawyers, physicians, psychologists, and teachers committed through their occupation. A physician's Medicaid fraud or a lawyer's suborning the perjury of a client are illustrations.

State-authority occupational crime encompasses the wide range of law violation by persons imbued with legal authority; the individual who commits state-authority occupational crime is essentially violating the public trust. Bribe taking by a public official, police brutality, and the torture of detainees in violation of the Geneva Convention are illustrative. Finally, Green uses the category **individual occupational crime** to cover all violations not included under one of the previously discussed categories. The employee who steals equipment from his employer and the person who deliberately underreports income to the IRS are covered in this category.

As evident from the earlier examples, the concept of occupational crime proposed by Green covers a wide variety of offenses, not all of which are economic in nature and not all of which are committed by persons of high social status. A therapist who sexually assaults a patient and a correctional officer who uses excessive force against an inmate are both committing violent occupational crimes, one in the professional and one in the state authority category. Neither the therapist's nor the correctional officer's behavior would qualify as white-collar crime in its classic sense. Some criminologists also have contended that certain corporate crimes should qualify as violent crimes, however. James Coleman

TABLE 14–3   Summary of Green's Occupational Crime Typology

CATEGORY	DESCRIPTION
Organizational	Law-violating behavior promoted by the corporation or agency.
Professional	Law-violating behavior committed as a result of being in a profession that offers the opportunity for crime.
State-authority	Law-violating behavior by those in government.
Individual	Law-violating behavior committed by an individual working for a company or organization, but committed for his or her own advancement or financial gain

(1998), for example, cites unsafe working conditions, illegal disposal of toxic waste, and the manufacture of unsafe products as examples of violent crime.

Green argues convincingly that his four-part division allows us to move away from the conceptual quagmire of "white-collar crime" and study a significant amount of workplace-facilitated illegal behavior in a logical, ordered manner. Although the term **white-collar crime** continues to be widely used, perhaps in deference to Sutherland's contributions to criminology, Green's approach offers an appealing alternative. As noted, however, the approach that seems to be preferred in the criminological literature is the "white-collar" dichotomy proposed by Clinard and Quinney, occupational and corporate crime.

The Prevalence and Incidence of Occupational Crime

Regardless of which term is used, the extent of occupationally linked illegal behavior is extremely difficult to measure. The standard methods of measuring crime discussed in chapter 1 rarely apply. The typical UCR report, for example, does not tell us whether a reported crime or an arrest was related to the perpetrator's occupation. Fraud can be committed by a bank executive, a college student, a Fortune 500 Corporation, or a recipient of welfare benefits. Even when uncovered, the violations we have been discussing are often not reported to law enforcement and recorded in official data. Rather than publicize a theft by an employee, for example, a business might prefer to demand restitution, dismiss the employee, or force a resignation. It does not benefit the company's public image to file a criminal complaint.

When an organization is itself the violator, civil suits are often preferred to criminal charges. The plaintiff in a civil suit is more likely to get some form of restitution, in the form of damages, than the victim in a criminal case. In addition, the government regulatory process is widely acknowledged to be inefficient in preventing, uncovering, and punishing violators. When it comes to the professions, law violation is often shielded from the public, because society authorizes them to police themselves by means of standards, codes of ethics, and licensing.

Nevertheless, some attempts have been made to collect data on "white-collar" offenses, particularly those committed by individuals (Clinard & Quinney's "occupational crime" category). The National White Collar Crime Center (NW3C), a nonprofit organization based in Richmond, Virginia, collects information, publishes a newsletter, and sponsors training sessions and conferences devoted to this issue. In 2003, together with another group—the Coalition for the Prevention of Economic Crime (CPEC)—the NW3C sponsored its seventh annual Economic Crime Summit (*The Informant*, 2003). Topics that have recently come to the attention of the NW3C are Internet gambling, Internet fraud, online child pornography, insurance crime, and identity theft. Information is available at *www.nw3c.org*. It should be noted, though, that none of the offenses mentioned above are offenses committed by the businesses; rather they are committed by individuals. The business or its consumers may be the victims; they are not the offenders.

Without settling the difficult definitional morass associated with "white-collar crime," we will nevertheless proceed to discuss in more detail one example of this serious crime problem, specifically, crime committed by corporations and their agents. Sutherland, you will recall, focused on corporations in his original research. Following that discussion, we will consider crimes at the opposite end of the continuum, wherein individual employees victimize their employers. Although not necessarily white-collar crimes, these latter behaviors qualify as individual occupational crimes according to Green's approach.

Corporate Crime

For purposes of the criminal law, a corporation is a person; that is, a corporation can be charged, tried, sentenced, and punished. Nevertheless, individuals within that organization are making decisions that render the corporate behavior a crime. Therefore, in discussing explanations for corporate crime, we will focus on the behavior of persons, despite the fact that the organizational culture as well as the economic structure of society may facilitate and reward the illegal behavior.

Corporate crime refers to any criminal offense committed by a corporation. It covers offenses ranging from price fixing to failure to recall a product known to have a serious defect that could potentially cause physical harm. The offenses are so varied, in fact, that most criminologists subdivide the crimes into more manageable categories. Thus, we hear of crimes against consumers, crimes against the environment, institutional corruption, and fiduciary fraud (Rosoff, Pontell, & Tillman, 1998); fraud and deception, manipulating the marketplace, violating civil liberties, and—as noted earlier—violent white-collar crimes (Coleman, 1998); crimes of fraud, offenses against public administration, and regulatory offenses (Albanese, 1995); and false and misleading advertising, defrauding the government, antitrust crimes, manufacture and sale of unsafe consumer products, unfair labor practices, unsafe working conditions, crimes against the environment, and political bribe giving (Green, 1997).

The estimated costs of these corporate offenses—both financial and from a human-suffering standpoint—are staggering. However, up-to-date, reliable, or accurate statistics are nearly impossible to find. Although the available research is very dated, the financial cost of corporate crime has been estimated to be between $20 and $40 billion a year (Kramer, 1984). Most scholars in this area would consider that a very conservative estimate at that time and even more so today. Kramer (1984) estimated that over 100,000 deaths a year could be attributed to occupationally related diseases, most caused by the knowing and willful violation of occupational health and safety standards by businesses and industries. Annually, 20 million serious injuries are associated with unsafe and defective consumer products, unsafe foods and drugs, and defective autos, tires, or appliances. About 110,000 of these injuries result in permanent disability, and 30,000 result in death (Schrager & Short, 1978). Obviously, not all of these accidents, injuries, and deaths are due to corporate neglect or illegal action, but the data suggest that many are (Hochstedler, 1984). Reiman (1995) has estimated that a conservative total of 90,105 Americans die every year as a result of occupational hazard and disease. Although some would argue that these deaths are not necessarily attributable to corporate malfeasance, others would say that corporations should be held responsible for the harms suffered by their workers.

Public attention to corporate crime has focused primarily on the economic crimes that have been highly publicized. These include a variety of practices that constitute fraud, including but not limited to price-fixing, false advertising, deceptive pricing, and securities fraud. Environmental and health-related crimes such as those already discussed have also attracted considerable public attention, however. In the 1990s both the tobacco and the asbestos industry were barraged with lawsuits brought on behalf of individuals who had either died or been seriously harmed by exposure to these hazardous products.

Explanations for corporate criminality often focus on the criminogenic or crime-producing nature of the business environment; that is, in order to survive, law breaking is essential. Conklin (1977), for example, argued that law breaking in American business was normative and that executives often believe that some dishonesty or deceit has to be tolerated in the best interest of the company. In response to comments such as these, corporations proclaim that they have entered an era of social responsibility and that the extent of corporate malfeasance is exaggerated. Business schools note that business ethics courses are a requirement in virtually all programs. Gilbert Geis (1997), however, a prominent scholar in the area of white-collar crime, chastises business schools for using "lulling terms, especially 'ethics,' to camouflage what essentially are considerations of criminal behavior" (Geis, p. xii).

Justifications and Neutralizations

You may recall that in chapter 5, we referred to strategies people use to neutralize some of their violent conduct and separate it from their personal codes. The strategies, proposed by Bandura (1978), are worth repeating here. Although they operate with reference to a wide range of reprehensible conduct, they are particularly relevant to the discussion of corporate crime. The strategies may be used individually or in combination.

One set of neutralizing strategies operates at the level of behavior. What is culpable is made honorable through moral justifications and euphemistic jargon. In other words, a normally reprehensible act becomes personally and socially acceptable when it is associated with beneficial or moral ends. "We did it in the best interest of the company, the employees and their families, and the country." Similarly, corporate decision makers may regard the laws they are violating as unfair, unjust, or simply not in keeping with good business practices.

Cressey (1953) called such justifications "vocabularies of adjustment." Conklin (1977) asserted that vocabularies of adjustment may play an even more crucial role in corporate crime than in juvenile delinquency, where they are frequently encountered.

A second set of neutralizing or dissociative strategies obscures or distorts the relationship between actions and their effects. In this group of strategies, people do not see themselves as personally responsible or accountable for their actions. They may disregard or deny the consequences of their actions—"It simply didn't happen the way the press reported it." Alternately, they may displace responsibility to the victim—"Consumers often don't use the appliance properly"—or diffuse the responsibility among the decision-making group—"After careful deliberation the board decided this would be the right decision."

A third set of strategies addresses the effects of the action on the recipients. Here, the dignifying qualities of the victims are removed. "Most consumers are greedy and stupid." "Third World countries are overcrowded anyway." We saw this strategy in action earlier in this text, when aggressors regarded their victims as less than human. This dehumanizing approach also seems to be a hallmark of prejudice and scapegoating. However, we also saw the strategy used in a slightly different way property and economic crimes, like burglary and identity theft, where the perpetrator does not have to confront the "personhood" or humanity of the victim.

In sum, through cognitive restructuring supported by corporate norms, decision makers can justify and rationalize behavior that appears reprehensible to outsiders. The restructuring process prevents the manager or executive from labeling himself or herself "criminal." In fact, in some corporations, the extent to which the norms and justifying mechanisms are embraced may well determine how far up the corporate ladder one climbs.

Individual Occupational Crime

When illegal behavior is pursued for the direct benefit of the individual, and the individual is neither a professional nor someone with state authority, Green refers to it as individual occupational crime. In the Clinard-Quinney white-collar crime dichotomy referred to at the beginning of this section, the behavior would simply be "occupational" crime, distinguished from "corporate" crime. In this largely solitary pursuit, the offender is guided primarily by his or her own personal justifications and reasoning. An embezzler, for example, is operating outside organizational norms, although he may justify the behavior in much the same way as the corporate criminal may. The dissociation strategies identified by Bandura apply here as well. In other words, an embezzler may convince himself that the activity really is not a crime, since he is merely borrowing the money temporarily and will put it to good use. Later, he will reimburse the company (secretly, of course).

One common type of illegal behavior in which the workplace is the victim is employee theft, which is an enormous drain on American business. One estimate has it costing business and industry $5 to $10 billion a year (Clark &

Hollinger, 1983). In a survey of employees from 47 retail, manufacturing, and service organizations, one-third admitted stealing company property (Clark & Hollinger, 1983). The property included merchandise, supplies, tools, and equipment. In addition, almost two-thirds of the employees surveyed reported other types of misconduct, such as sick leave abuse, drug or alcohol use on the job, long lunch and coffee breaks, slow and sloppy workmanship, and falsifying time sheets. Collectively, these are counterproductive behaviors. They do not involve actual removal of material goods from the organization, but they do reduce production and services.

Modern versions of employee theft involve the Internet and electronic payments. For example, the NW3C reports that some employees are taking advantage of the Automated Clearinghouse (ACH) network to make personal purchases via the telephone or web, using the company's corporate checking account numbers that the employees obtain, often from their own paychecks. Telephone or Internet merchants often accept the account number without verifying the account ownership. Thus, "some companies remain unaware of the fraudulent entries against their accounts for many months, leading to extended problems in regaining their funds" (*The Informant*, 2003, p. 14). Other examples of theft and fraud via use of electronic transactions abound.

Explanations for employee theft and counterproductive behaviors are multiple, but most cluster around the themes of age, dissatisfaction, and one's normative group at the workplace. The highest levels of theft and counterproductive behaviors are reported by younger, unmarried male employees (age 16 to mid-20s). Apparently, these younger employees do not feel any commitment or loyalty to the organization, probably because they do not expect to spend their lives in that situation. Many are college and high school students working only until they graduate. High levels of theft and counterproductive behaviors are also found among employees expressing dissatisfaction with some aspect of their employment, especially with their immediate supervisor. Another component of job dissatisfaction is the workers' perception of the company's attitude toward them. If the workers perceive the organization as caring little about them, job dissatisfaction and the concomitant theft and counterproductive behaviors tend to follow. In these situations, the individuals typically know that what they are doing is "wrong," and if caught they will admit their guilt and hope for a light sentence. Interestingly, financial restitution may involve more than they actually stole. A woman who admitted to ACH debit fraud made unauthorized transactions of $6,661.08 but was sentenced to 24 months probation and restitution of $8,126.56 (*The Informant*, 2003).

While age and job dissatisfaction are highly correlated with theft and counterproductive behavior, normative support offers a viable explanation. Normative support refers to the standards, perceptions, and values the work group has established for itself, with or without the organization's implicit (or explicit) approval. In short, normative support refers to group norms. For example, the group may consider pilfered material a supplement to one's hourly wages, a fringe benefit. Vocabularies of adjustment are frequently employed. "It goes with the job." "The company expects you to take a little on the side." Another example is the work group verbally neutralizing the societal and organizational prohibitions against theft. "Everyone does it." "No one cares if we take a few things." "This is not really stealing." Sieh (1987) found that garment workers took "only what was owed them" and rarely stole items of substantial value.

Whether the group considers it acceptable to take something and where it decides a line should be drawn ("You can help yourself to ballpoint pens, but staplers are hands off"), depends on many variables. For example, the size of the organization is likely to be a factor. Smigel (1970) found that when workers were "forced" (in a questionnaire) to select an organization they would be most inclined to victimize, they first chose large businesses, then government, and lastly, small businesses. They considered large corporations and big government impersonal bureaucratic giants able to absorb losses more easily than smaller organizations.

Regardless of the explanation, employee theft seems to require some subjective justification on the part of the worker. He or she often does not perceive his or her conduct as illegal or even unethical, either because the behavior is in line with group norms, in line with internal standards, or both. From the group's or worker's perspective, the theft or the counterproductive behavior either are expected or they adjust the imbalances inherent in working for the company. It is interesting to note that employee theft diminishes when an organization clarifies for the workforce precisely what constitutes misconduct and what is expected (Clark & Hollinger, 1983). This approach, combined with working conditions that convince employees their organization cares about them, seems to be the most effective in reducing employee theft and counterproductive behavior. Furthermore, improvement in the work environment functions both ways; the worker is also expected to demonstrate loyalty and commitment to the organization, setting up appropriate models for new workers. But loyalty to a company may go too far, as when it represents a higher obligation than commitment to law and ethics. Individual blind loyalty often leads to corporate crime.

PROSTITUTION

One nonviolent economic crime that has long received attention in the psychological literature is prostitution, often regarded as a victimless crime. Prostitution—essentially sex for sale—is illegal in all states except Nevada. Nevada does, however, prohibit prostitution in counties in the state that exceed 200,000 in population (Miller, 1991). People may be arrested for both soliciting and providing sex, but by far the majority of arrests are for the latter. In the popular literature, prostitution is blamed for decreases in neighborhood property values, increases in drug abuse and violent crime, and deterioration of the American family. Some commentators note that prostitutes (especially female prostitutes) are more often victims than offenders, and more than one author suggests that the criminal justice system shares the role of victimizer with pimps and persons who patronize prostitutes (James, 1978). Of particular concern to many observers is juvenile prostitution. On the other hand, some social scientists and social commentators suggest that adult prostitution is a lucrative career, and it has even been suggested that prostitutes be recruited to assist in the treatment of some sexual problems (Adler, 1975).

Cogent arguments have been advanced in favor of the legalization or decriminalization of adult prostitution. Traditionally, it has been treated as primarily a female crime, with women comprising the great majority of the arrests. In the past, female prostitutes accounted for approximately one-third of the female jail and prison population (James, 1978), whereas male prostitutes were rarely incarcerated. Today, the arrest figures are more closely parallel, with women accounting for approximately two-thirds of all arrests for prostitution and commercial vice (Federal Bureau of Investigation, 2003). The arrest figures do not distinguish between soliciting and providing services, however. Conservative estimates suggest that prostitution is the primary source of personal income for at least one million women and girls in the United States (Miller, 1991); no similar estimates are available for male prostitutes. In addition, there are virtually no reliable statistics on the extent to which people procure the illegal services of prostitutes.

Prostitution is relevant to this text because it is a "deviant behavior" that lends itself well to psychological examination. Our purpose in discussing prostitution is not to consider its moral and policy implications, but to focus on the sociological and psychological myths and misconceptions that surround it and to review the available psychological research. That research focuses almost exclusively on the person providing the service, particularly female prostitutes, rather than on the person who obtains it. Consequently, the discussion herein does the same. It should be emphasized, though, that—if prostitution is to remain a crime—researchers should give equal attention to both parties in the transaction. A parallel might be drawn to illegal drug use, where the reverse phenomenon occurs. That is, researchers in psychology are far more likely to study the substance abuser than the seller or distributor. Both are committing a criminal offense.

We will not, however, address the exploitation of juveniles of both sexes for prostitution purposes, a phenomenon quickly gaining the attention of social science researchers. Miller (1991) argues that prostitution is a form of sexual exploitation and a form of sexual coercion for all women, because they are compelled or forced (usually by men), physically and psychologically, to engage in a sexual act.

Prostitution is defined as the offering, agreement to offer, or provision of sexual relations in return for tangible rewards or special favors. Increasingly more jurisdictions are adding solicitation of services to their criminal statutes and thereby render illegal the behavior of the "john" as well as the prostitute. Prostitution may involve either a heterosexual or homosexual pairing, or it may involve group behavior. Although it most commonly refers to the procurement of sexual intercourse with a woman by a man, a variety of sexual activities may be involved.

It is impossible to estimate the number of commercial prostitutes in the United States, since police agencies interpret the criminality of the behavior very subjectively and arbitrarily. Arrests are often dependent on social and political pressures. It is generally recognized that prostitutes are harassed and detained, with or without formal arrest, and for purposes other than the idealized goal of eliminating the practice. Primary clientele of both female and male prostitutes are believed to be white, middle-class men between the ages of 30 and 60 (Haft, 1976; Jolin, 1994).

Theorists and researchers have traditionally offered biased, subjective generalizations, all about the female prostitute. They have alternately called her feeble-minded, emotionally disturbed, a latent or manifest homosexual, oversexed, sexually deprived, a primitive creature, or an individual rigidly fixated at her oedipal (or Electra) stage of psychosexual development. From all indications, none of these labels adequately describes the prostitute. Women who become prostitutes appear to come from many different walks of life, possess varied educational and family backgrounds, demonstrate a wide range of personality types, and express a great variety of motives for involvement in prostitution. Although research on male prostitutes is less available, there is no reason to believe that the same could not be said of them.

Several researchers have brought attention to a system of class structure among female prostitutes. At the lower end of the continuum are the "streetwalkers" who work the streets; at the uppermost level are "call girls," who cater to a select clientele and who are rarely arrested. In recent years, a new category has been documented, which is apparently lower in status than the streetwalker. This is the "lot lizard," a prostitute who works truck stops and highway rest areas (Luxenburg, 2000). (The offensiveness of this term is testimony to the dehumanization so often associated with prostitution.) The call girl is usually more sophisticated and educated than the streetwalker, and is more often protected from the physical brutality and humiliation women at the lower levels of prostitution hierarchy encounter (D'Emilio & Freedman, 1988). In between are a variety of categories, which may include stag party workers, escorts, masseuses, conventioneers, bar girls, brothel girls, circuit travelers (who move around in groups to labor camps or lumber camps), and rap booth girls (who occupy glassed-in booths for customer viewing). Coleman (1976) found that, as we go up the social class structure, the women are increasingly physically attractive, intelligent, well educated, and sophisticated. Adler (1975) pointed out that the contemporary prostitute is, in many instances, socially and culturally indistinguishable from women in general.

It was generally believed that many prostitutes, especially at the lower status levels, came from lower- or lower-middle-class homes, but even this is now in question. James (1978) noted that a full 64 percent of her sample of streetwalkers reported their childhood family's income as middle or upper class. There seems little doubt, however, that most prostitutes come from conflictual families, where patterns of alienation from a single parent or from both parents are discernible. Many prostitutes also report negative sexual experiences in the home during preadolescence or adolescence. In an oft-cited study, 41 percent of 136 prostitutes reported incestuous experiences, usually with their fathers (James, 1976). Forty-seven percent reported they had been raped, and 17 percent had been raped more than once, most before reaching the age of 16. Studies of juvenile prostitutes lend support to these findings. Silberman (cited in Bracey, 1982) interviewed over 200 juvenile prostitutes and reported that 61 percent had been sexually molested by a member of their household. Bracey (1982) found that 50 percent of juvenile prostitutes in her sample reported forcible sexual advances by older men before they reached puberty.

Contrary to popular assumption, a majority of prostitutes do not appear to be lured into the activity by organized crime, brutal pimps, under false pretenses, or to support drug habits. Recruitment by pimps, madames, or organized crime appears to have been a factor for only about 20 percent of the prostitute population. Nevertheless, rather than "choosing prostitution," they appear to have been precipitated into it by negative effects in their lives, such as the loss of someone close to them or a series of economic setbacks (Luxenburg, 2000). However, juvenile girls, particularly runaways, are more likely to have been recruited. "American society has defined as desirable young, physically perfect women, and girls on the streets, who have little else of value to trade, are encouraged to use this 'resource' " (Chesney-Lind & Shelden, 1998, p. 116). While we do not discuss juvenile prostitution in detail here, it is important to stress that this is a major social problem. According to Chesney-Lind & Shelden (1998), figures have varied widely in the surveys taken, ranging from 600,000 prostitutes under age 16 to close to one million.

The assumption of heavy drug use among adult prostitutes also appears questionable. James (1978) suggests that the prostitutes apprehended by police (and who thus end up in the criminal statistics) tend to be the "hypes"—the addicts working as prostitutes to support a drug habit. They "form a special, lower class in the hierarchy of the 'fast life' " (James, 1978, p. 306). Inciardi (1980) surveyed 149 female heroin users and found a high incidence of prostitution (about one-third) among them. However, he did not find evidence for a strong causal link. The women who committed crimes to support their drug habits were much more likely to choose economic offenses, like larceny or fraud, rather than prostitution.

Motives

What motivates people to engage in prostitution? An obvious, although oversimplistic answer, is money. It is important to distinguish between financial necessity and financial comfort, however. James (1976) found that only 8.4 percent of her sample started prostitution out of economic necessity, but 56.5 percent did out of a desire for money and material goods. They saw prostitution as a lucrative business that offered material rewards they otherwise might not have attained. Social rewards like parties, dancing, and expensive dining were also a factor.

The James study and others like it have dispelled several alleged motives for entering into prostitution. Early research included numerous studies that portrayed prostitutes as narcissistic, frigid, hating men, fearful of lesbianism, or having an unresolved sexual attachment to their fathers (Electra complex) (Gibbens, 1957; Greenwald, 1958). Virtually none of these assumptions was verified by later research. For example, James (1976) found that only 1 percent of her sample demonstrated hostility toward men.

The Freudian theory that prostitution is a result of early sexual love for the opposite-sex parent and subsequent sexual partners are insufficient surrogates also seems weak. According to this theory, the bulk of sexual energy and attraction is directed to the initial love object; later partners are unsatisfactory. Therefore, the sexually promiscuous person endlessly but subconsciously searches for the treasured first love object, the father (or in the case of male prostitutes, the mother). The Freudian perspective sees prostitution as individual psychopathology rather than a social phenomenon. Since a consistent finding in the research literature is that more than half of all prostitutes did not have an available father figure in the home, it is questionable whether they would develop unconscious, imagined incestuous relationships. Because of the dearth of information on backgrounds of male prostitutes, we cannot draw conclusions. However, it is highly unlikely that male prostitutes are subconsciously searching for their treasured first love object, their mother.

As the above should indicate, a continual focus on "explaining" the behavior of women while ignoring the behavior of men who either solicit sex or who offer it may seem unwarranted. Prostitution has traditionally been considered a crime that women commit, a judgment that reflects long-standing assumptions about the respective roles of women and men. The theories should have been applied to male as well as female prostitutes, but there was little if any recognition that male prostitution existed. On the other hand, it could be argued that—because female prostitutes are more likely than male prostitutes to be abused and victimized—the attention placed on them is warranted. Furthermore, numerous questions could be raised about the individuals who patronize prostitutes, if society is to consider this a criminal act.

To conclude that anyone goes into prostitution and remains there for financial gain is premature, and it oversimplifies human behavior. Why do not more individuals opt for that life style? Furthermore, although material gains may provide an initial incentive, it is widely recognized that most female prostitutes—with the possible exception of independent, high-class "call girls"—do not directly profit much from their work, given the obligatory payoffs to pimps, police, hotel clerks, and taxi drivers. Male prostitutes are likely at a greater advantage, however, because they are less likely to be dependent on the protection offered by pimps.

Human behavior represents an infinite array of learned responses, and prostitution as a complex behavior should be no exception. It is frequently observed that most prostitutes find out about prostitution through friends and get started through their efforts and encouragement (James, 1978). These personal contacts provide significant models and opportunities for imitative learning. In addition, the sex-for-sale behaviors offer greater reward possibilities (money, excitement, adventure) than a previous life predicament. For some, prostitution offers a more positive and potentially exciting alternative than the home situation. In the case of the female prostitute, the relationship with a pimp who often serves as husband, boyfriend, father, lover, agent, and protector (James, 1976) may be considerably more rewarding than the relationship with family.

Once these expectations and potentially rewarding behaviors are acquired, continued involvement depends partly on the actual rewards obtained. Do the positives of prostitution outweigh the negatives? Even given "good money" and an ideal situation in which the prostitute is relatively independent, few personalities would seem suited for long-term prostitution. To be habitually used solely as a sexual object would appear to require, among other things, a learned method of detachment and the availability of other sources of self-esteem.

Prostitution appears to be an emotionally stressful and psychologically draining occupation. James found that at least 50 percent of her sample listed emotional stress, worry about physical harm at the hands of a customer, or low self-esteem as major disadvantages. Another 20 percent listed the stress of worrying about venereal disease, reactions of family and society, personal vulnerability, and feelings of helplessness as primary disadvantages. Contemporary prostitutes have added the HIV to the long list of dangers they already face.

Sex Trafficking

In recent years, much attention has focused away from prostitution as it has traditionally been regarded and toward a related topic, **human trafficking.** In some literature it is referred to as forced prostitution (Cook, 2000). Human trafficking has become a highly lucrative criminal market in the United States (Finckenauer & Schrock, 2000). According to some experts (e.g., Schauer & Wheaton, 2006), the United States ranks as the world's second largest destination country (after Germany) for women and children trafficked for purposes of sexual exploitation in the sex industry. The "commodities" involved in this illicit worldwide trade are women, children, and men, and the criminal activity is usually sex-related and is committed for long-term exploitation for high profits. Examples include women who agree to come to this country as waitresses or dancers, but then are forced into prostitution until they are able to pay off the debt incurred through a smuggling fee. In some Third World countries, parents "sell" their children to traffickers who take them to other parts of the world, including the United States, and profit from their sexual exploitation. Violence, intimidation, and brutality are particularly common with trafficking victims brought in for the sex industry. "Women who are forced into prostitution are often forcibly trafficked between brothels, cities, and countries in what has become the modern slave trade. They experience rape, sexual assault and harassment, physical injury, drug addiction, depression, chronic pain, and serious health problems, including constant exposure to AIDS" (Cook, 2000, p. 212).

Human trafficking often involves a variety of additional illicit activities, including fraud, extortion, racketeering, money laundering, bribery of public officials, drug use, document forgery, and gambling (Finckenauer & Schrock, 2000; Richard, 1999).

Arguments for the decriminalization or legalization of prostitution are often appealing, particularly if one believes that the present laws are selectively enforced against women, or that prostitution is essentially a victimless crime. However, such decriminalization or legalization approaches must find an alternative way to address the exploitation of juveniles and the many abuses that occur as a result of human trafficking.

 ## SUMMARY AND CONCLUSIONS

At first glance, the offenses discussed in this chapter appear to represent a hodgepodge of unrelated crimes, ranging from petty larceny to human sexual trafficking. What they have in common is that they are distinct from the crimes discussed to this point, and, although there are exceptions, they are essentially committed for economic reasons. Their primary distinguishing feature from murder, assault, terrorist activities, and the sexual offenses discussed thus far is a lack of physical aggression or violence against persons. The crimes discussed in this chapter are not, by definition, violent acts. Nevertheless, there may be incidental violence—such as often occurs in prostitution or sex trafficking—or indirect violence—such as would occur when people die as a result of a corporation's negligence.

The property offenses of burglary, larceny/theft, and motor vehicle theft make up the greatest proportion of the nation's Part I crime rate in any given year. Put another way, they are reported far more frequently than are violent crimes. We discussed the official and victimization statistics on these crimes, as well as the effects on their victims. We have little information on the characteristics of offenders, however, with the exception of burglars who appear to be more willing than other offenders to share their secrets with researchers. In a number of studies, burglars have described how they choose victims, what tactics they use to gain access to targets, which targets they avoid and why. Professional burglars seem to carefully plan their offenses and do not seem to consider themselves "real criminals."

Likewise, individuals who shoplift do not seem to consider this behavior unnormative. Self-report data indicate that a great majority of juveniles have shoplifted at least once; surprisingly, large numbers of adults also admit to this behavior at some point during their adult lives. There is no research evidence that kleptomania—a supposed compulsion to steal—actually exists to the extent that it would explain a significant proportion of shoplifting. While some individuals undoubtedly shoplift to gain attention, get recognition, or embarrass their family, it seems that most do so to obtain goods, go along with peers, or—in the case of some juveniles—on a dare. Furthermore, although there is some suggestion that depressed individuals may engage in "nonsensical shoplifting," the evidence that this is characteristic of large numbers of people is not persuasive.

In the discussion of motor vehicle theft we included a section on carjacking, a crime that is of relatively recent origin. We covered information about the behavioral attributes or the motives of carjackers obtained from studies based on interviews with the offenders themselves. Carjackers seem motivated primarily by a need for quick money, a quick ride, or a quick thrill. Some, however, apparently wish to punish the victim of the carjacking for riding through their neighborhood in a disrespectful manner.

We covered the area of white-collar crime and the difficulties in defining this concept. We adopted Green's four-part typology to discuss varieties of crimes committed by individuals in the course of their legal occupations. Not all would be considered in the traditional concept of white collar crime, but all are criminal offenses worthy of consideration. A display of excessive force by a police officer may be considered an aggravated assault, but the police officer's status as a person in authority suggests an additional element that should be taken into consideration in any attempt to understand this behavior. Likewise, a medical doctor's sexual assault of a female patient is still a rape, but the violations of trust and professional ethics add a dimension that render it different, from a psychological perspective, from a date rape or a stranger assault. Not worse, but different.

The traditional type of white collar crime is the crime committed by corporations, businesses, or organizations or by individuals within those entities. We noted that one of the best explanations for this behavior lies in neutralizing techniques, in which individuals and groups convince themselves that their behavior was not really criminal or that no one was hurt, among other justifications. However, corporate crime is rarely studied by criminal psychologists, psychiatrists, or criminal justice researchers, beyond the gathering of data available from court records or government regulatory agencies. Burglars and rapists get interviewed and participate in studies. Corporate criminals are more likely to write their own books than to cooperate with professionals seeking some insight into their actions.

We ended the chapter by shifting to prostitution, included here because of its economic nature. Prostitution, often considered a victimless crime, is accompanied by many myths, most directed at the female prostitute. She has alternately been considered emotionally upset, evil, frigid, oversexed, unloved, abused, and intellectually limited. Prostitutes, who are both male and female, represent a very wide range of individuals who, similar to other offenders throughout this book, defy rigid classification. To say their motives are chiefly economic may be oversimplifying, particularly for those at all but the highest levels of the status ladder. Prostitutes, like other offenders, likely gain something by their behavior. However, it makes little sense to focus on the prostitute without also studying the individuals who use their services, and this is rarely done.

Although criminologists pay attention to prostitution primarily because the behavior is a crime, most are far more concerned about juvenile prostitution, which implies exploitation of the young, and sex trafficking, which is apparently increasing. Much of sex trafficking is international, with individuals brought in from other countries with the promise of a better life. The United States ranks in the top three countries as a destination for individuals coming into the country in this way. However, an unknown number of U.S. citizens, primarily homeless juveniles, are also persuaded to participate. Following their recruitment or their arrival in the country, their participation in the sex trade is often accompanied by economic exploitation and physical and sexual assault.

 KEY CONCEPTS

Dehumanization	Relative deprivation
Burglary	Rational reconstruction
Fence	Good burglar
Cognitive scripts	Crimes against the public order
Expressive burglars	Repeat burglary
Carjacking	Identity theft
Kleptomania	Boosters
Snitches	White-collar crime
Prostitution	Human trafficking
Occupational crime	Organized occupational crime
Professional occupational crime	State-authority occupational crime
Individual occupational crime	Corporate crime

REVIEW QUESTIONS

1. Define larceny and burglary. How are they different from each other?
2. Briefly describe Green's occupational crime typology. Give an example of each.
3. What is meant by rational reconstruction and how it explains some forms of criminal behavior.
4. Define expressive burglars and describe each type of burglary associated with the term.
5. Define kleptomania and describe the empirical support for the phenomenon.
6. Give some examples of crimes against the public order.
7. Choose any two crimes covered in this chapter, and discuss them from the perspective of the psychological effects on their victims.
8. Choose any two crimes discussed in this chapter, and describe how cognitive scripts may explain the apparent "impulsive" criminal behavior associated with each crime.
9. How extensive is identity theft? And give some examples of how it is accomplished.
10. How might relative deprivation account for some forms of burglary?

CHAPTER 15

VIOLENT ECONOMIC CRIME AND CRIMES OF INTIMIDATION

CHAPTER OBJECTIVES

- Detail sketch of robbery and the reasons behind the offense.
- Briefly look at cybercrime and cyberstalking.
- Examine the literature on stalking.
- Outline hostage-taking offenses and their characteristics.
- Carefully summarize the literature on arson, with particular emphasis on juvenile firesetting.
- Examine the psychological motives attached to serial arsons and bombings.

This chapter focuses primarily on the violent economic crimes of robbery and arson. While the UCR program considers only robbery a violent crime, we approach each as violent because there is moderate to high level of serious injury or death to the victims, or at least the threat or possibility of such injury. The chapter is also concerned with crimes of intimidation, such as stalking, cyberstalking, and cybercrime. Crimes of intimidation are intended to frighten, threaten, embarrass, or harass the victim or victims. Finally, hostage taking is an offense with elements of both violence and extreme intimidation. It has the strong potential of resulting in the deaths of the participants.

ROBBERY

Robbery "is taking or attempting to take anything of value from the care, custody, or control of a person or persons by force or violence and/or by putting the victim in fear" (Federal Bureau of Investigation, 2003, p. 303). The major distinctions between robbery and other economic crimes are the direct contact between the offender and the victim and the threat or use of force. The offender threatens bodily harm if the victim resists or impedes the offender's progress; usually, but not invariably, this threat is backed up by a clearly visible lethal weapon, such as a firearm or a knife.

There were 401,326 robberies reported in 2004, reflecting a national robbery rate of 136.7 per 100,000 people (Federal Bureau of Investigation, 2005). These figures represent about a 5.7 percent drop from 2000 and a 38.1 percent drop from 1995. Interestingly, strong-arm tactics through the use of hands, feet, or fists was the "weapon" used most often in the commission of robberies during 2004 in the United States (41.1%), closely followed by firearms (40.6%).

Strong-arm robbery (without a weapon) is more likely to result in injury to the victim than is robbery with a firearm or knife. Presumably, victims are less fearful (and thus more daring) when confronted by an unarmed individual. In the absence of a gun or other weapon, the victim's resistance to losing valuable personal property is stronger, and he or she is more apt to try to resist or fight off the perpetrator. The tendency to resist, therefore, may partly account for the higher rates of victim injury in these no-weapon situations. On the other hand, the offender is likely to feel more confident, powerful, and in control of the incident when he or she has a weapon. Because of this increase in confidence, the offender is less likely to be anxious and disorganized in response patterns, and thus is better able to think clearly and evaluate the consequences of actions.

The average loss per robbery in 2004 was $1,308. Individuals lost an average $923 from robberies on streets and highways. Average dollar losses were highest for banks during 2004, which lost $4,221 per offense, a significant decrease from previous years.

The national clearance rate for robbery in 2004 was 25.3 percent (Federal Bureau of Investigation, 2005), meaning that about one in four reported robberies were solved by the arrest of at least one individual. Like many other crimes, it is primarily an offense committed by young adults (under the age of 25), who accounted for 61.4 percent of arrestees. The majority of the arrestees (approximately 90%) were males.

Robbery accounts for only about 4 percent of all arrests for economic crimes (but 35% of the violent crimes). However, because of its potential physical harm to victims, it is among the crimes most feared by the American population (Garofalo, 1977). This is especially the case for street robbery, which has an edge of desperation to it (Wright, Brookman, & Bennett, 2006). It involves a high probability of physical harm from a stranger, and it can happen to anyone. (More than half of the robberies occur on streets and highways [see Table 15–1]). One in three victims are injured in robbery (also called stickup, holdup, mugging), and one in 10 so seriously that he or she requires medical attention (U.S. Department of Justice, 1988). Furthermore, robbery offenders are more likely to use weapons than other violent offenders, although as noted earlier a

TABLE 15–1   Robbery Location, Percent Distribution, 2004

LOCATION	PERCENT
Street/highway	42.8%
Commercial house	14.7
Gas or service station	2.7
Convenience store	6.1
Residence	13.8
Bank	2.4
Miscellaneous	17.4

Source: Federal Bureau of Investigation, 2005.

surprising number use strong arm tactics. Yet, despite its dangerousness, robbery is among the least-studied criminal offenses.

One reason for the lack of research interest on the psychology of robbery is that the crime seems so obvious and straightforward: People rob to obtain money. The process is quick, and the potential returns are lucrative. Compared with burglary, however, the risks are great and the penalties substantial. Much of this may be true but, as we have seen, human behavior should not be oversimplified. The motives of offenders may be extremely varied. People behave a certain way because they have convinced themselves that is what works best for them.

Bank Robbery

"A bank robbery is indicated when the crime is robbery and the location is a financial institution" (Federal Bureau of Investigation, 2003). It accounts for 2.4 percent of all robbery in the United States (Federal Bureau of Investigation, 2003). Although robbery in general had a clearance of rate of only 25 percent in 2001, the clearance rate for bank robbery approaches 60 percent. Only murder has a higher clearance rate.

According to data collected from the Bank Crime Statistics (BCS), collected by the Violent Crimes/Fugitive Unit of the FBI, the average amount of money netted from a bank robbery from 1996 through 2000 was $8,000 (Federal Bureau of Investigation, 2003). Although clearance rates may be high, the amount of money eventually recovered is quite small, averaging about 20 percent of the total amount taken during the robbery. Bank robbery incidents are most likely to occur on Fridays. Historically, Friday has been payday for much of the nation, requiring large amounts of cash to be delivered to the various branch banks. Fridays continue to be the favorite day, even with the reduction of branch bank offices in recent years and the substantial increase in electronic banking. The time period during which most bank robberies occur is between 9:00 and 11:00 A.M.

Also according to BCS, 32 percent of bank robberies involve the use of a firearm, and about 2 percent of those involve actual shooting (Federal Bureau of Investigation, 2003). Most (80%) bank robberies are carried out by a single offender. A vast majority of all bank robbers are males (95%), and most are between the ages of 18 and 29.

The great majority of bank robbers (80%) are amateurs who have *not* been convicted of a bank crime in the past (Federal Bureau of Investigation, 2003). An amateur tends to rob a bank on the spur of the moment without much planning, and primarily to fulfill some need, such as to pay for drugs, alcohol, or some status-enhancing goods. Therefore, bank robberies usually do not involve the meticulously planned caper carried out by a group of highly experienced criminals often portrayed by the media. A professional, according to the BCS database is a bank robber with a prior criminal record, no matter how unsuccessful he or she has been at bank robbing in the past.

Commercial Robbery

Approximately 15 percent of all robberies take place in commercial establishments, compared with 14 percent for residences. Convenience stores appear to be favorite commercial sites of robbery, with an estimated 16,000 to 20,000 robbed per year in the United States. Approximately 6.1 percent of all robberies take place in convenience stores, followed by gas or service stations (2.7%) (Federal Bureau of Investigation, 2005). An average of $653 per robbery was taken at convenience stores during 2004 (Federal Bureau of Investigation, 2005). Most convenience stores have no robberies, but a few have many robberies (Eck, 2000). One of the debates concerning prevention of convenience store robbery is whether two or more clerks in the store, rather than one, reduce the robbery attempts. So far, the evidence is unclear, but the two-clerk experiment does not appear to discourage robberies as much as anticipated (Eck, 2000). Cameras and silent alarms do not seem to reduce convenience store robberies, but some preliminary evidence suggests that the installation of interactive CCTV (allowing communication between store personnel and security personnel watching a monitor in a remote location) may be effective in reducing store robberies by nearly one-third (Eck, 2000).

Although convenience stores have traditionally been the favorite robbery sites, America's fast-food restaurants are now becoming the most preferred target. Many restaurant robberies occur at fast-food restaurants because they are open late, staffed by teenagers, full of cash, and conveniently near a highway. In describing the vulnerability of fast-food restaurants to armed robbery, Schlosser (2001, p. 84) writes, "A couple of sixteen-year-old crew members and a twenty-year-old manager are often the only people locking up a restaurant, long after midnight." About two-thirds of the robberies at fast-food restaurants involve current or former employees, and frequently the on-duty manager suffers much of the anger and violence administered during the robbery. In 1998, more fast-food restaurant workers were murdered on the job in the United States than police officers (Schlosser, 2001).

The leading fast-food chains have tried to reduce robbery by spending millions on new security measures, including video cameras, panic buttons, drop-safes, burglar alarms, and additional lighting (Schlosser, 2001). But even the most secure restaurant remains highly vulnerable to robbery.

Street Robbery

Overall, the greatest proportion of robberies in the United States in 2004 (42.8%) occurred on streets and highways (Federal Bureau of Investigation, 2005). Street robbery is most common in urban areas, particularly in cities over 250,000 in population. In 2004, 52 percent of the robberies in large American cities occurred on the streets, while in cities with populations under 10,000, only 23.8 percent of the robberies occurred on the streets or highways (Federal Bureau of Investigation, 2005).

Compared with bank and commercial robbery, street robbery has received very little research attention. Unlike bank and commercial robbery, however, street robbery tends to more based on opportunity than planning. Street robbery is driven by the culture on the streets, and follows many of the characteristics of carjacking discussed in the previous chapter. Street robbers remain in a state of "alert opportunism," where the motivation to offend is always present. They are in perpetual need of money to buy status-enhancing goods, drugs, and alcohol. When an opportunity to rob occurs, there is little or no time for contemplation; otherwise the opportunity is lost forever. Still, street robbers are most likely to follow well-rehearsed cognitive scripts that have been developed and practiced through offending activities. Even though little contemplation is used when opportunity knocks, their methods and targets have developed through experimentation and tinkering of their own personal approaches or scripts. We will discuss in more detail the motivations of street robbers and situational dynamics that stimulate their criminal activity later in the section.

Professional Robbers

Assessing skilled robbery, Peter Letkemann (1973) offers pertinent remarks about the successful robber's confidence and victim "management." Comparing the robber with the burglar, he notes that burglars do not have to be concerned with people, but professional robbers must be able to maintain control and handle their victims at all times. Bank robbers, for example, assert that the keys to a successful heist are confidence and the ability to control people under highly stressful conditions. Confidence, they believe, is reflected in the robber's tone of voice and general behavior. High levels of self-confidence are crucial if robbers are to maintain control of the situation. Successful robbers also note that the posture and physical location of the victims are deliberately designed to enhance the offender's control over them.

According to Letkemann, professional robbers often express dismay over media treatment of robbery. For example television and movies generally downplay the seriousness of bank robbery; the offenders therefore must work harder to convince their victims that they mean business. The entertainment media also encourage some victims to be heroes; robbers consider heroes irrational and extremely dangerous.

Motives and Cultural Influences

Some researchers view robbery as a rational choice driven primarily by the need for money and a desire to minimize the risk of detection. Other researchers believe street robbery represents a cultural pursuit in which the money and risks take second place to the psychological and social rewards toward the offender's lifestyle (Wright, Brookman, & Bennett, 2006).

In a revealing study, Richard Wright and Scott Decker (1997) interviewed 86 individuals who were actively engaged in armed robbery on a regular basis in St. Louis. None of the robbers interviewed were incarcerated or otherwise under supervision of the criminal justice system (e.g., under arrest, on probation, or on parole). Most studies of armed robbery feature interviews with prisoners who either admit engaging in the offense or have been convicted for robbery.

Wright and Decker focused on determining what factors influenced the robbers as to when, how, and whom to rob. The researchers were also interested in the offenders' thoughts and actions during the commission of the crime. In addition to interviewing, the researchers took 10 of the robbers to the site of a recent holdup for which they had not been apprehended and asked them to reconstruct the crime. The sample was overwhelmingly black, poor, male, and uneducated. Although all age groups were represented, a majority were between 18 and 29. Most of the offenders had committed numerous robberies in their lifetimes—so many in fact that they found it impossible to specify the exact number. Despite the very high number of armed robberies they said they had committed, 60 percent of the sample had never been convicted of armed robbery. Almost all the sample (96%) reported committing many other offenses, particularly theft, burglary, assault, and drug selling. A majority (85%) typically did their robbery on the street, while 12 percent preferred to rob commercial establishments (e.g., pawnshops, jewelry stores, liquor stores).

Wright and Decker found that a vast majority of the offenders did not plan the armed robbery. "The reality for many offenders is that crime commission has become so routinized that it emerges almost naturally in the course of their daily lives, often occurring without substantial planning or deliberation" (Wright & Decker, 1997, p. 30). The researchers discovered that, with few exceptions, the decision to rob was strongly influenced by a pressing need for cash to support their hedonistic, carefree lifestyle. The robbers in this sample were deeply enmeshed in the street culture where immediate gratification reigned supreme. Many robbers spent their take with reckless abandon without much thought to financial obligations or commitments. The offenders chose armed robbery as a lifestyle because it provides quick cash as the need arises. Armed robbery offered immediate cash compared with the delays inherent in disposing of hot merchandise acquired through burglary, shoplifting, and motor vehicle theft.

Although the need for cash was the overwhelming reason for armed robbery, a secondary gain expressed by some robbers was the control they held over their frightened victims, unless their victims were themselves lawbreakers. In addition, many offenders preferred to rob white victims because they usually complied with their demands and did not offer much resistance, particularly white women. According to many of these offenders, black victims were more likely to resist and fight back. Also, many robbers in this sample reported that whites were more likely to carry credit cards and checkbooks rather than cash; the opposite was true for blacks. However, when whites did carry cash, the amounts were substantial.

One of the favorite targets of the street robbers in this sample were individuals who themselves were involved in lawbreaking, especially drug sellers and wealthy drug users. Drug dealers carry considerable amounts of cash as a result of their illegal activities. Of course, the risks are higher when targeting dealers because they are more likely to be armed, more likely to resist, and are sometimes connected to a powerful drug organization. Wealthy drug users tend to be white persons who come into a neighborhood looking to buy drugs with considerable cash. They can be easily victimized, and like other lawbreakers, they are unlikely to report the robbery to the police.

In a more focused examination of street robbery, Wright et al. (2006) discovered that American and United Kingdom **street culture** seem to be a very powerful social force in the commission of these crimes. "American street culture subsumes a number of powerful conduct norms, including, but not limited to, the hedonistic pursuit of sensory stimulation, disdain for conventional living, lack of future orientation and persistent eschewal of responsibility" (Wright et al., 2006, p. 2). The image you present is paramount and one of the few sources of status available to most offenders. The same social impetus is present in the United Kingdom street culture. As noted by Katz (1988), while the obvious reason for street robbery is money, the reasons for needing the money are far more revealing.

According to Wright et al. (2006), street robbery accomplishes five things, depending on the needs of the offender:

- Generates quick cash that could be spend quickly and used easily to finance gambling, drug use, and heavy drinking.
- Allows purchasing nonessential, status-enhancing items (such as clothing or jewelry) to improve standing in the street culture.
- Creates excitement and dominance over victims who are overpowered.
- Prompts anger and eagerness to start a fight in those offenders already prone toward fighting and violence.
- Achieves a certain measure of informal justice, such as debt collecting or revenge.

One of the major findings of the Wright and Decker (1997) and Wright et al. (2006) projects is that there is little psychological mystery behind the motives of armed robbery: These offenders need cash now to support their impulsive, hedonistic lifestyle, and robbery provides the best route to that cash. Some also enjoy dominating their victims and frightening them, seek the "buzz" they receive from the offense, or come across as not to be messed with in the street culture, but these motives are only secondary to cash acquisition. An important point must be emphasized, however. Even though many street robberies appear to be impulsive and hold to the philosophy "strike while the iron is hot," it is highly likely the offender is following his or her favorite **cognitive script,** developed and perfected over a series of similar street crimes. Furthermore, the script has been formulated most probably through a combination of observation (social learning) and participation with a payoff (instrumental learning). When opportunity knocks, their offending cognitive script immediately comes into play. The script contains information that guides the offending behavior (Ward & Hudson, 2000). "These scripts can be enacted without conscious intention and with minimal awareness of the overall goal" (Ward & Hudson, 2000, p. 197).

CYBERCRIME

Cybercrime—a term that was hardly heard of a decade ago—refers to any illegal act that involves a computer system. It is therefore also called computer crime. The main types of cybercrime are unauthorized access to computers (hacking), mischief to data (virus generation), theft of communications, copyright violations of computer software, and transmission of pornographic material, including child pornography (see Table 15–2). In 2003, persons allegedly associated with the Gambino organized crime family were arrested and charged with a $230 million Internet fraud scheme that involved money laundering and a credit card scam perpetrated against individuals who visited a pornographic Web site (*The Informant*, 2003). To cite a slightly less ambitious illustration:

> Four high school students, age 14 to 16, hacked into a Bay Area Internet server and then used stolen credit card numbers to go on a giant shopping spree at an on-line auction house. They ordered $200,000 worth of computers, then had United Parcel Service deliver the equipment to vacant homes in San Carlos, where they would pick up the packages after school. (Power, 2000, p. 7)

Another popular cybercrime today is illegal gambling on the Internet. "Since the mid-1990s, Internet gambling operators have established approximately 1,800 e-gaming Web sites in locations outside the U.S., and global revenues from Internet gaming in 2003 are projected to be $5 billion" (*The Informant*, 2003, p. 23). Not all online gambling is illegal, however. Criminal violations occur when it is conducted from or to a location that prohibits or regulates gambling activities. Authorities stress that a major concern of Internet gambling is its tie to organized crime and to terrorist groups.

TABLE 15–2   Cybercrime Type Detected by American Businesses, 2001

TYPE OF INCIDENT	PERCENT
Theft	
Embezzlement	2.8%
Fraud	6.1
Theft of proprietary information	4.3
Computer Attack	
Denial of service	18.0
Vandalism or sabotage	13.4
Computer virus	45.8
Other	9.6

Source: Rantala, 2004.

Cyberstalking is a serious form of cybercrime that will grow in scope and complexity as more people take advantage of the Internet and other telecommunications technologies. A cyberstalker is able to send repeated, threatening, or harassing messages by the simple push of a button, whereas more sophisticated cyberstalkers can use programs to send messages at regular or random intervals without being physically present at the computer terminal (U.S. Department of Justice, 1999). The anonymity leaves stalkers at an advantageous position for avoiding detection.

A relatively new phenomenon is **cyberbullying,** defined as "sending or posting harmful or cruel text or images using the Internet or other digital communication devices" (Li, 2006, p. 158). Even more than those who bully face to face, those who bully online can be daring, vicious, and threatening because they can remain anonymous. Cyberbullying has become a worldwide problem among students. In Britain, one in four youths between the ages of 11 and 19 said they had been cyberbullied in 2002 (Li, 2006). A similar statistic is found among Canadian youth (Li, 2006).

The extent of computer crimes is expanding rapidly and the economic impact of those crimes that involve money is staggering (Carter & Katz, 1996). The British Banking Association reports that the world loss to computer fraud alone is approximately $8 billion each year (Carter & Katz, 1996). Software piracy is estimated to cost American software companies around $7.5 billion annually.

In May 1999, the Clinton administration established a new national initiative to address the problem in Internet fraud. The initiative encouraged the FBI to join forces with the NW3C to establish the Internet Fraud Complaint Center for strategic information about and analysis of Internet fraud schemes.

The fastest-growing computer-related crime is theft, and the most commonly stolen commodity is information such as new product plans, new product descriptions, research, marketing plans, and prospective customer lists (Carter & Katz, 1996). Since the theft of intellectual property often has no tangible value, the offender does not as readily perceive it as being wrong.

In response to the dramatic increase in computer crimes, the U.S. Congress passed the *Federal Computer Fraud and Abuse Act of 1984,* which was amended and expanded in the *Computer Abuse Amendments Act of 1994.* Computer crime is a serious problem that will continue to draw considerable attention from law enforcement agencies across the globe. In 1997, eight of the world's industrial nations joined forces to fight computer crime, particularly security intrusions and telecommunications fraud. Research focusing on the psychological characteristics of cybercrime is just beginning.

STALKING

Stalking is defined as "a course of conduct directed at a specific person that involves repeated physical or visual proximity, nonconsensual communication, or verbal, written, or implied threats sufficient to cause fear in a reasonable person" (Tjaden, 1997, p. 2). Systematic information on stalking in the United States is limited, despite the attention it receives from the media and state and federal legislatures (Tjaden, 1997). Most of the previous research has focused on the stalking of famous persons, entertainment personalities, or politicians, known as "celebrity stalking." However, a substantial increase in the stalking of noncelebrities over the past decade has generated numerous media accounts of stalking victims and the passage of antistalking laws in all 50 states and the District of Columbia (Tjaden & Thoennes, 1998a). Legal definitions of stalking vary widely from state to state. While most states define it as the willful, malicious, and repeated following and harassing of another person, some include such activities as lying-in-wait, surveillance, nonconsensual communication, telephone harassment, and vandalism (Tjaden & Thoennes, 1998a). Some states specify that at least two stalking events must occur before the conduct can be considered illegal.

California became the first state to enact antistalking legislation in 1990. The impetus for this legislation was not the stalking/homicide of television actress Rebecca Schaeffer as commonly believed, but had its roots in domestic violence (Lemon, 1994). A California municipal court judge initiated the development and passage of the anti-stalking law following his frustration over existing laws that failed to protect four Orange County women who were killed in different incidents despite the issuance of restraining orders against their assailants. Since 1990, stalking statutes have spread rapidly to all states.

In an attempt to fill in the large gap in our knowledge about stalking, the Center for Policy Research conducted a comprehensive victimization survey of eight thousand women and eight thousand men 18 years of age or older on issues relating to violence (Tjaden & Thoennes, 1997). The survey revealed that 8 percent of women and 2 percent of men reported they had been stalked at some point in their lives (Tjaden, 1997). Overall, the survey indicated that approximately 1.4 million Americans are victims of stalkers every year, a surprisingly large number. In most cases, the stalking lasted less than one year, but some people were stalked for over five years. It is estimated that one out of every 12 women and one out of every 45 men in the United States has been stalked during his or her lifetime (Tjaden & Thoennes, 1998a).

The survey found that the motives of most stalkers were to control, intimidate, or frighten their victims. This observation was made by both male and female victims. Eighty-seven percent of the time the stalker was male, and 80 percent of the time the victim was female. In most stalking incidents, the victims (particularly women) knew their stalker. About half of the female victims were stalked by current or former marital or cohabiting partners, and a majority of these women (80%) had been physically assaulted by that partner either during the relationship, during the stalking episode, or during both. In about one-third of the cases, stalkers vandalized the victim's property, and about 10 percent of the time the stalker killed or threatened to kill the victim's pet. In nearly half the cases, the stalker made overt threats to the victim. The survey dispels the myth that most stalkers are psychotic or delusional. Only 7 percent of the victims perceived their stalkers as "crazy" or abusers of drugs or alcohol.

Half of all victims reported the stalking to the police, and about one-quarter of the female victims obtained a restraining order. Not surprisingly, 70 percent of all restraining orders were violated by the assailant. About one-quarter of victims in cases where a restraining order was violated pursued prosecution. When prosecution was pursued, most cases resulted in conviction of the stalker and well over half received jail time. Although most of the stalking stopped within two years, the emotional and social effects of being stalked continued for many victims long after the incident. About one-third of the stalking victims sought psychological treatment because of the emotional and social trauma that resulted from the stalking episodes.

Meloy (1998) asserts that stalkers rarely cause serious physical injury to their victims, threaten them with weapons, or use weapons. Even so, the psychological trauma is often substantial. In a survey of 145 stalking victims (120 females, 25 males), Doris Hall (1998) reports that the experience of being stalked for months or even years is akin to psychological terrorism. A majority of the victims said their entire lives changed as a result of being stalked. "Many move or quit jobs, some change their names, others have gone underground, leaving friends and family in order to escape the terror" (Hall, 1998, p. 134). Some change their physical appearance or wear disguises. Others become exceedingly suspicious of the motives of others, often leading lonely and isolated lives. Many victims constantly worry that the stalker will find them, and that the entire experience will start all over again.

Categories of Stalking

Researchers have identified four very broad categories of stalking: (1) simple obsession stalking, (2) love obsession stalking, (3) erotomania stalking, and (4) vengeance stalking (Beatty, 2001). **Simple obsession stalking** accounts for the majority of stalking (about 60%), and often represents extensions of previous patterns of domestic violence and psychological abuse. The stalker in these case scenarios usually seeks power and control after a failed relationship with the victim. Simple obsession stalking is perhaps the most dangerous to the victim, since it is often motivated by the stalker's conclusion that "If I can't have you, nobody will." In **love obsession stalking,** the stalker and victim are casual acquaintances or complete strangers. Stalkers in this category are characterized by low self-esteem and tend to select victims they perceive to have certain qualities they believe will raise their self-esteem. Essentially they seek a love relationship with the object of their obsession, contrary to the wishes of their victim. For example, John Hinckley was convinced he would win the heart of actor Jodi Foster by shooting President Ronald Reagan.

Erotomania stalking is considered delusional, and the stalker is often plagued by serious mental disorders. This type of stalker usually targets public figures or celebrities in their misguided attempts to gain self-esteem and status for themselves. For example, talk show host David Letterman was stalked over a number of years by a woman who believed she was his wife. The woman frequently trespassed on Letterman's property, hid in his home, and even stole his car to go grocery shopping. Tragically, the delusional woman eventually took her own life. Fortunately, erotomania stalking appears to be relatively rare, and normally the stalker is not violent. **Vengeance stalkers** are quite different from the other three because they do not seek a personal relationship with their targets (Beatty, 2001). Instead, vengeance stalkers try to elicit a particular response or change of behavior from the victims. For example, the stalker who wishes to torment those responsible for a perceived injustice or violation of their rights might follow the "guilty parties" day and night until he is fairly compensated.

What terminates stalking? Some stalkers stop their activity toward the current victim when they find a new "love" interest. About 18 percent of the victims in the Center for Policy Research Survey indicated the stalking stopped when their assailant got a new spouse, partner, or boyfriend/girlfriend. Informal law enforcement interventions also seem to help. Fifteen percent said the stalking ceased when the assailant received a warning from the police. More formal interventions such as arrest, conviction, or restraining orders do not appear to be very effective. When it comes to persistent, frightening stalking that creates risks to personal safety, the survey suggests that the most effective method may be to relocate as far away from the offender as possible with no information of whereabouts provided to the offender.

Cyberstalking

A form of stalking that has emerged in recent years is **cyberstalking,** the use of the Internet or other forms of online communications to threaten or engage in unwanted advances toward another. Although online harassment and threats may take many forms, cyberstalking is in many ways similar to off-line stalking. In most instances the stalkers wish to establish relationships with the victims, and are often males seeking females. In many cases, the cyberstalker and the victim had a prior relationship, and the cyberstalking begins when the victim attempts to break off the relationship (U.S. Department of Justice, 1999).

Ultimately, much cyberstalking is designed to control the victim, usually through threats and harassment.

"Because e-mail is used daily by what some experts say are as many as 35 million people, and it is estimated that there are approximately 200,000 stalkers in the United States, the Internet is a perfect forum with which to terrorize their victims" (Jenson, 1996, p. 1). "Chat rooms," e-mail, and instant messaging have provided far-reaching and unregulated opportunities for cyberstalkers to harass unsuspecting victims, especially women. In addition, there is an enormous amount of personal information available through the Internet, and a cyberstalker can easily and quickly locate private information about a target. Unfortunately, victims of cyberstalking cannot be adequately protected due to the lack of enforceable laws to prosecute and deter this behavior (Jenson, 1996). And there are substantial obstacles to using criminal and civil law to thwart the persistent cyberstalker, bringing into question whether it is possible to regulate this type of behavior at all. Most stalking laws require that the perpetrator make a credible threat of violence against the victim (U.S. Department of Justice, 1999).

Meloy (1998) points out that the Internet provides a means of stalking that lacks the usual social constraints. "Only written words are used, and other avenues of sensory perception are eliminated; one cannot see, hear, touch, smell, or emotionally sense the other person" (Meloy, 1998, p. 11). The lack of face-to-face interaction with their victims and the overall anonymity encourages some individuals who would not ordinarily behave in such a fashion to act out their fantasies. An example of cyberstalking is provided by Jenson (1996), who describes a South Carolina woman who had been stalked by an unknown cyberstalker for several years via e-mail. Not only had the stalker threatened her life, but he also threatened to rape her daughter. The stalker also posted the woman's home address on e-mail for 35 million people to see.

The Internet does provide an extremely inviting avenue for cyberstalkers, which may have substantial ramifications in the future. To date, however, very little systematic research has been conducted to examine the prevalence and incidence of cyberstalking, the personal characteristics of cyberstalkers, effective deterrents to cyberstalking, or even the psychological consequences of being cyberstalked.

The National Center for Victims of Crime (NCVC, 2000) has several recommendations for victims of cyberstalking. Its Web site (listed in the References section) also has suggestions on how to handle cyberstalking.

HOSTAGE-TAKING OFFENSES

The hostage taker holds victims against their will and uses them to obtain material gain or personal advantage. Typically, this offender threatens to take the lives of the victims if certain demands are not met within a specified time period. Included in the broad hostage-taking category are abductions and kidnappings, skyjackings, and some acts of terrorism. Recall that we gave considerable attention in chapter 11 to acts of international and domestic terrorism. In this chapter, the topic is discussed only as it relates specifically to hostage-taking.

Instrumental and Expressive Hostage Taking

Miron and Goldstein (1978) divide hostage-taking offenses into two major categories based on the offender's primary motivation: **instrumental** and **expressive hostage taking.** In instrumental hostage taking, the offender's goal is recognizable—material gain. An example is kidnapping a child and holding him or her for ransom. The goal in expressive hostage taking is psychological: The offender wants to become significant and to take control over his or her own fate. Expressive offenders generally feel that they have little control over events in their lives. They want to become important, and they believe the media coverage accompanying their hostage taking will help them to achieve this goal. To the observer, the conduct of the expressive offender often seems senseless and even suicidal. A skyjacker who demands that a pilot fly an aircraft full of passengers from one continent to another, for no apparent reason, is an example. Hostage-taking offenses sometimes begin as instrumental acts but develop into expressive ones. An offender who initially kidnaps someone for material gain may find that his demands are unrealistic and not likely to be met; in this case the person may decide to play out the scenario for the attention, significance, and control it affords. Sometimes both instrumental and expressive motives are clearly involved from the beginning. That is, the offender expects both material and psychological gain from the abduction.

FBI Categories of Hostage Taking

Since the 1970s, the FBI has classified hostage takers into four broad categories: terrorists, prisoners, criminals, and the mentally disordered (Fuselier & Noesner, 1990). Research suggests that over 50 percent of all hostage-taking incidents are perpetrated by mentally disordered individuals (Borum & Strentz, 1993), thus representing the largest category. Research also indicates that the average terrorist hostage taker is not as sophisticated as commonly believed (Fuselier & Noesner, 1990). Training for his or her terrorist activity is marginal or nonexistent. Terrorist hostage takers are usually young males from deprived socioeconomic backgrounds with little formal education. Moreover, they are very willing to kill innocent victims, and therefore they are considered more dangerous than the more sophisticated hostage taker. However, "negotiation strategies and tactics for terrorist incidents are identical to those that would be used during any hostage or barricade incident, regardless of the political or religious backgrounds of the subjects" (Fuselier & Noesner, 1990, p. 10).

Criminal and prisoner hostage taking situations have similar features. Both are likely to be instrumental in nature. In the process of committing a bank robbery, for example, the robber may take a hostage as a human shield to assist in the getaway. Likewise, during a prison riot or escape attempt, inmates may take corrections officers or staff as hostages to help earn their way to freedom or aid in their negotiations with prison officials. Such incidents are extremely rare, and the hostages are not usually harmed, but there are exceptions. A riot in the brutal New Mexico Penitentiary in 1980 was extremely violent, and seven of the 12 officers who were taken as hostages were seriously physically injured (Johnson, 1996). However, in the Attica uprising of 1971, prisoners in New York's Attica facility held a number of officers hostage but did not harm them (Wicker, 1976).

Strategies for Dealing with Hostage Takers

Experienced negotiators suggest strategies for dealing with hostage takers or barricaded individuals (see Table 15–3). A **barricade situation** is one in which an individual has fortified or barricaded himself or herself in a building or residence, and threatens violence, either to himself or to others. First, that person should be denied the excitement and stimulation he or she hopes to initiate; this requires that a potentially chaotic situation be handled as calmly as possible, with minimum media attention. This is difficult to accomplish, because hostage taking incidents are extremely media worthy. As noted in chapter 5, very high levels of arousal tend to promote disorganized response patterns and reduce internal thought processes. Under high excitement and chaos, the offender is more likely to revert to "mindless" behavior, which may include violence. The most dangerous phase in most hostage or barricade situations is the first 15 to 45 minutes (Noesner & Dolan, 1992). Therefore, the first officers on the scene should hold their positions until additional resources, including the

TABLE 15–3   Guidelines for Negotiation

Stabilize and contain the situation.
Take your time when negotiating.
Allow the subject to speak: It is more important to be a good listener than a good talker.
Don't offer the subject anything.
Avoid directing frequent attention to the victims; do not call them hostages.
Be as honest as possible; avoid tricks.
Never dismiss any request as trivial.
Never say "no."
Never set a deadline; try not to accept a deadline.
Do not make alternate suggestions.
Do not introduce outsiders (nonlaw enforcement) into the negotiation process.
Do not allow any exchange of hostages; especially do not exchange a negotiator for a hostage.

Source: Fuselier & Noesner, 1990, p. 10.

negotiation team, arrive at the scene. If possible, the officers who are first on the scene should try to engage the hostage taker in conversation, emphasizing that they wish no harm to the individual. Experienced negotiators believe that conversation distracts the offender from violence and generally calms the situation, especially if the negotiator maintains a calm and steady demeanor.

Second, offenders must be allowed to feel that they are in some control of the situation. Helplessness and powerlessness may have prompted the offense in the first place. If the captors do not feel they have attained any control, they may take steps to prove the opposite, such as shooting one of the hostages.

Third, in hostage or barricade situations time is usually a strong ally. Once the early stages of a crisis have passed and some stability and calm have been achieved, the passage of time plays a positive role. Time has several effects. After the initial high-arousal state, the body winds down and eventually the offender begins to feel tired, sluggish, and depressed. Under these conditions the event takes on aversive properties for the hostage taker, and the offender is likely to begin to wish the situation were over. Time also promotes, in the hostage taker, some thought processes and greater reliance on internal standards of conduct. If the offender has incorporated some values of society, he or she may begin to appreciate the ramifications of his or her behavior. However, the hostage taker may also begin to construct justifications. Either process, however, may enable the offender to accede more easily to police requests. Experienced negotiators strongly recommend that the negotiator act as spokesperson for the authorities and a conduit of information, emphasizing to the hostage taker that things will take time. Consequently, the negotiator should not be a decision maker or in command. Otherwise, if the hostage taker is under the impression that the negotiator (or anyone in the immediate environment) has the power and decision-making authority, he or she will believe that decisions should be made quickly and directly. Under these conditions, any delay generates frustration in the captor and further increases arousal.

Time also affects the relationship with the hostage. According to social psychological research, the more familiar one is with an object or person, the more one tends to become attracted to it (e.g., Freedman, Sears, & Carlsmith, 1978). In many hostage situations, the more the victim and captor get to know one another, the more they begin to accept one another. Furthermore, if the hostage was a stranger to the captor, the hostage takes on human qualities with the passage of time.

The Stockholm Syndrome

The attraction between victim and captor is called the **Stockholm syndrome,** after a hostage-taking incident in Sweden in 1973 that resulted in marriage between a female hostage and one of her abductors. Police negotiators have noted that on occasion the hostage will side with the captor in working out demands. Although this may simply reflect a wish to end the terrifying ordeal as quickly as possible, it may also signify some attraction to the abductor. When hostages act this way, experts sometimes maintain that they have been brainwashed. An alternate explanation is that they have become attracted to their captors and temporarily identified with their values and goals. In general, though, the Stockholm syndrome is a rare occurrence. According to the FBI's Hostage/Barricade System (HOBAS), a national database that contains data from over 1,200 reported federal, state, and local hostage situations, 92 percent of the victims of such incidents showed no aspect of the Stockholm syndrome (Fuselier, 1999).

How can a hostage-taking incident, which by its very nature is stressful, generate attraction? We have already noted that mere familiarity can increase attraction to an object or person. There is evidence, also, that unpleasant emotion may intensify attraction (Middlebrook, 1974). Research by Schachter (1971) suggests that when people are physiologically aroused, they may have difficulty labeling the arousal with the appropriate emotion, because several conflicting emotional labels may be available. It does not seem to matter whether the arousal derives from negative or from positive circumstances. For example, sexual deprivation may lead to physiological arousal, which may be labeled love. The same process may operate in a highly charged hostage-taking incident, where familiarity combined with very high arousal leads to mutual attraction. If the victim or kidnapper is deindividualized by a hood or a mask, the incident is much less likely to develop into attraction. Also, ideals and purpose may override any tendency to humanize and be attracted to the victims.

Some researchers have suggested that three things must be present before the Stockholm syndrome can take place (Fuselier, 1999). First, the hostage taker and victim must be together for a significant length of time. Second, the hostage must be in direct social contact during the incident. For example, physical separation of the hostages (such as complete isolation in a separate room) from the hostage taker will likely prevent development of the effect. Third, the hostage taker must treat the hostages kindly. Although the first two conditions make sense, the third, in light of the general effects of arousal just discussed, may not be necessary.

Some Rules to Follow If Taken Hostage

Thomas Strentz (1987) outlines some rules to follow should you personally ever be taken hostage, especially if you plan to travel abroad with some regularity. His suggestions are based on the psychological reactions of those hostages who survive (survivors) compared with those who do not (succumbers). **Survivors,** Strentz notes, are those "who returned to a meaningful existence with strong self-esteem, and who went on to live healthy and productive lives with little evidence of long-term depression, nightmares, or serious stress-induced illness" (p. 4). Although survivors do not ever forget the hostage experience, the experience does not prevent them from living relatively normal lives. **Succumbers,** on the other hand, are those who either did not live through the ordeal, or upon release or rescue have considerable difficulty dealing with the emotional trauma caused by the ordeal. They have great trouble getting on with their lives.

Strentz emphasizes, as we did earlier, that the most dangerous phase of any hostage situation is the moment of the abduction and the early minutes thereafter. Arousal levels are extremely high for the abductors and the hostages. Unpredictable and unforeseen things can happen. Strentz asserts that, without exception, any form of resistance is extremely dangerous and should not be tried. He recommends playing the subordinate role immediately. Furthermore, throughout the entire abduction, maintaining a positive mental attitude that things will be all right in the end is absolutely essential. Feelings of hopelessness, abandonment, and isolation can lead to serious depression. On the other hand, a mature, controlled, and stable appearance—even if you are terrified— also helps settle the hostage taker(s). Anything that calms the situation increases survival for everyone. Furthermore, hostile feelings toward your captors must be masked as best they can, again to keep the situation calm. Do not get into arguments with captors about politics, religion, social issues, or anything else. Strentz refers to the opposite strategy as the **London syndrome,** a behavioral pattern demonstrated by the Iranian press secretary, Abbas Lavasani, during a six-day hostage situation in the Iranian Embassy in London. Lavasani refused to compromise his dedication to his cause, constantly and stubbornly proclaiming his beliefs, and seemingly intent on martyrdom. Despite the pleas of his fellow hostages for silence, he kept arguing and was eventually killed by his captors.

Your chances of survival improve greatly if you try to blend in with your fellow captives. The individual who stands out in the crowd "by crying, by being overly polite and helpful, or by doing more than the abductors require, is immediately setting himself or herself up as an easy mark to be exploited" (p. 6). If you are more comfortable in the leadership role, be prepared to take the brunt of the abuse from the captors, and you may be killed as an example to the rest of the hostages. Individuals who have experienced a hostage-taking episode say that being able to fantasize during the many empty hours is one of the critical factors in dealing with the situation. Some imagine travel to various places or dream what they plan to do after the episode. Also, trying to keep a normal routine as much as possible will relieve stress. Exercise, personal hygiene, writing letters, or keeping logs—if these things are possible—are examples. This is especially recommended for people who have a strong need to control the situation. Finally, Strentz recommends that no matter what the circumstances, you should never blame yourself or ruminate about what you should have done to avoid the abduction. Accept your status, and follow the patterns described here. Survival will be greatly enhanced if you do.

In sum, the psychological research on hostage taking focuses more on the effects of the incident on the hostage than on the characteristics of the individual committing the crime. Strategies are offered both to the hostage, for surviving the incident, and to negotiators, for dealing with the hostage taker effectively in order to prevent escalation and to end the crisis.

ARSON

Arson is defined "as any willful or malicious burning or attempt to burn, with or without intent to defraud, a dwelling house, public building, motor vehicle or aircraft, personal property of another" (Federal Bureau of Investigation, 2005, p. 53). According to the UCR guidelines, only fires that law enforcement investigation determined to have been willfully or maliciously set may be classified as arson. Agencies participating in the UCR program do not report fires of suspicious or unknown origin.

Incidence and Prevalence

In 2004, complete information was collected for a total of 63, 215 arson fires in the United States. Nearly 43 percent of those fires were set by juveniles (Federal Bureau of Investigation, 2005). Of those, the majority (76.3%) involved community or public buildings such as churches, jails, or schools. In Australia, approximately 20 percent of the arson fires are known to be set by children and adolescents (Lambie, McCardle, & Coleman, 2002). Most of the known arsonists are young males. Some studies have found that between 75 percent and 85 percent of all firesetting is done by males, with increasing percentages of females in the 13- to 17-year old group (Federal Bureau of Investigation, 2003; Stadolnik, 2000).

In a typical year in the United States, fires set by children and youth claim the lives of approximately three hundred individuals and destroy more than $300 million worth of property (Putnam & Kirkpatrick, 2005). Children are often the victim of these fires, accounting for 85 percent of the lives lost in the United States (U.S. Fire Administration, 2004). Next to deaths caused by motor vehicle accidents, fires are the leading cause of death among young children (Stickle & Blechman, 2002). Not all these fires, of course, were set with criminal intent or would qualify as arson.

Most fires set by youth go undetected, unreported, or unsolved (Zipper & Wilcox, 2005). It is generally acknowledged, for example, that only a small proportion of fires set by juveniles is reported, probably less than 10 percent (Adler et al., 1994). Zipper and Wilcox (2005) report that, of the 1,241 Massachusetts juveniles referred for counseling services because of arson, only 11 percent of the blazes these youths started were reported. No one reported these incidents, apparently because witnesses or caretakers did not consider the behavior dangerous because no loss of life or significant destruction of property occurred. In these situations, many people worry that charging juveniles with arson will give them a criminal record that will hamper their future careers. Another study of youth from the third to the eighth grades in 15 school districts in Oregon found that 32 percent of the students reported setting fires outside their homes, and 29 percent said they had started fires in their own residences (Zipper & Wilcox, 2005).

Developmental Stages of Firesetting

Arson is the term that specifically defines the setting of fires under certain conditions as a crime. **Firesetting** is the term commonly used in the literature on child psychopathology for essentially the same behavior. It is intentional and willful behavior with an understanding of the potential consequences of that behavior. Child firesetters have attracted considerable interest among researchers in psychology.

Gaynor (1996) outlines three developmental phases related to fire: (1) fire interest, (2) fireplay, and (3) firesetting. Fascination and experimentation with fire appears to be a common feature of normal child development. Kafrey (1980) discovered that fascination with fire appears to be nearly universal in children between 5 and 7 years old. Furthermore, this fascination with fire begins early, with one in five children setting fires before the age of 3. As the child gets older, fireplay (experimentation) normally takes place between the ages of 5 and 9. In this stage, the child experiments with how a fire starts and what it can do. Children during this phase are especially vulnerable to the hazards of fire because of their more limited ability to understand the consequences and their lack of effective strategies for extinguishing the fire once it gets out of control (Lambie, McCardle, & Coleman, 2002). By age 10, most children have learned the dangers of fire and its consequences; if they continue to set fires at this point, they have reached the firesetting phase. These youths most often demonstrate an intention to use fires to destroy, as a form of excitement, or as a communicative device to draw attention to themselves and their problems.

The children who *continue* to set fires tend to demonstrate poor social skills, inadequate social competence, and impulsiveness compared with their peers (Kolko, 2002; Kolko & Kazdin, 1989). In a national sample of nearly five thousand 12- to 17-year-olds, Chen, Arria and Anthony (2003) were able to conclude that children rejected by peers were more likely to set fires than those who were not rejected. In fact, in this study, a combination of aggression and peer rejection was significantly related to firesetting.

In general, persistent firesetters are more likely to demonstrate attention deficit hyperactivity disorders and poor impulse control (Forehand et al., 1991), and many are considered to have "conduct problems" by their teachers. Lambie et al. (2002) report a similar finding. From their clinical experiences, they found that firesetting is but one part of a more comprehensive set of behavior problems, the motives of which occur for a variety of reasons and typically include impulse control problems and misdirected anger and boredom. There is also some evidence that children who are consistently cruel to animals and other children also tend to engage in consistent firesetting behavior (Slavkin, 2001). Lambie et al. (2002) also point out that adolescent firesetters frequently commit a variety of other crimes, including rape and other sex offenses.

This range of criminal offending has been noted by other researchers as well. It seems that a very large majority of firesetters known to the juvenile justice system have committed many other serious juvenile acts besides arson

(Ritvo, Shanok, & Lewis, 1983; Stickle & Blechman, 2002). Stickle and Blechman (2002) found that "firesetting juvenile offenders exhibit a pattern of developmentally advanced, serious antisocial behavior consistent with an early starter or life-course-persistent trajectory" (p. 190), a finding also reported by other researchers (Becker, Stuewig, Herrera, & McCloskey, 2004; Forehand et al., 1991). As might be expected, research has revealed a large portion of the persistent firesetters are boys, probably at a ratio of 9 to 1 to girls (Zipper & Wilcox, 2005).

Nearly all children who set fires beyond the normal fascination and experimental stages tend to have poor relationships with their parents and also appear to be victims of physical abuse (Jackson, Glass, & Hope, 1987). Kolko, Kazdin, and Meyer (1985) in their comprehensive review suggest that firesetting may be closely associated with parental ineffectiveness and faulty or nonexistent supervision. In a retrospective study by Saunders and Awad (1991), the records of 13 adolescent girls referred to the Toronto Family Court Clinic for setting fires were examined. The authors noted,

> Reading through the 13 charts was a depressing experience even for those of us who have worked for years with families who have many problems and serious difficulties meeting their children's basic needs. These parents had a history of marital problems, separation, violence against the spouse and the children, criminal behaviour, drug and/or alcohol abuse, and inability to take care of the children. (Saunders & Awad, 1991, p. 403)

Children who continue to light fires well into adulthood tend to be less intellectually able, less assertive, have limited interpersonal skills, have less schooling, are more likely to be underemployed or unemployed, and are more prone toward depression and feelings of helplessness (Murphy & Clare, 1996). In general, research findings continually find that as a group, arsonists are inadequate socially and interpersonally, although the exact nature of the inadequacy varies among individuals (Jackson, Glass, & Hope, 1987). Research also indicates that firesetting is used by this group as a communicative vehicle in response to conflict and stress (Day & Berney, 2001). Some researchers (e.g., Vandersail & Wiener, 1970) have found that firefighters lit fires to impress peers. Day and Berney also note that firesetting is a very common behavioral pattern for the mentally disabled. In this case, however, we must question the degree to which the behavior could be considered intentional. Interestingly, the prevalence rate of firesetting appears to be significantly higher in children referred to a clinic for psychological problems (Kolko & Kazdin, 1989; Lambie et al., 2002).

Research suggests that firesetters (adolescent or adult) usually come from a disadvantaged group who have little or no effective means for influencing their environment and who find themselves in highly undesirable situations (Jackson, Glass, & Hope, 1987). The most consistent research finding on the psychology of adult repetitive arsonists is that they, as a group, experience and perceive little control over their environment or personal lives. Consequently, the arsonist experiences worthlessness and social ineffectiveness. Some suggest setting fires may provide conditions whereby the person experiences control or, at least, some influence over the environment.

Persistent and Repetitive Firesetting

Theoretically, repetitive firesetting may be motivated by the arsonist's attempt to take control of his or her life and gain some social recognition. For example, the firesetting seems to be precipitated by events that exacerbate the arsonist's feelings of low self-esteem, sadness, and depression (Bumpass, Fagelman, & Birx, 1983). In addition, following a firesetting, many arsonists stay at the scene of the fire, often sound the alarm, and even help fight the fire. In some cases they take heroic action to save lives. The recognition they receive for these actions probably enhances their self-esteem and instills a sense of control in their lives. Jackson, Glass, and Hope (1987) note that most acts of firesetting by repetitive arsonists progress from small fires to large fires, and the arsonists also become increasingly involved in fighting the fire. Furthermore, repetitive arsonists set fires alone and in secret, with virtually no one aware of their actions until they are caught. If they are caught, their history of firesetting presents an additional opportunity for them to gain attention and recognition from others.

Thus, firesetting may be just one component in the constellation of maladaptive behaviors displayed by these individuals. Firesetting may be among these behaviors because of previous experiences with fire. Ritvo, Shanok, and Lewis (1983) found that a surprisingly large number of firesetters had been burned and maltreated with fire as children. They describe how one frequent firesetter during his early childhood had his feet severely burned by his father as a punishment for lighting fires. Another boy had been beaten on his buttocks with a hot spatula by his father. Still another had his hands held over a lighted stove burner by his mother until burned for lighting fires. Ritvo et al. (1983, p. 266) speculate that these punishments may have "conveyed the message that the use of fire was an acceptable mode of retaliation."

In this section we have concentrated on the repetitive or serial arsonists who set fires primarily for psychological and social gain. This focus is not to imply that a majority of arson fires are set by these individuals. Obviously, arson is committed for a variety of reasons by a variety of offenders, although much of it is probably committed for monetary gain, such as insurance.

Motives of Arsonists

There appears to be a wide variety of motives for arson. In an effort to systematize the reasons, Boudreau and his associates (Boudreau, Kwan, Faragher, & Denault, 1977) listed six primary motives for arson:

- *Revenge, Spite, or Jealousy:* Arsonists in this category include jilted lovers, feuding neighbors, disenchanted employees, and people who want to get back at someone whom they believe cheated or abused them. Alcohol and/or drugs are often associated with this motive.

- *Vandalism or Malicious Mischief:* Fires set to challenge authority or to relieve boredom are by far the most common of those set by juveniles.

- *Crime Concealment or Diversionary Tactics:* At least 7 percent to 9 percent of convicted arsonists are believed to be trying to obliterate evidence of burglaries, larcenies, and murders (Inciardi, 1970; Robbins & Robbins, 1964). The offender in this category expects that the fire will destroy any evidence that a crime was committed. Usually the fire is set near the object or incident the offender wishes to conceal. In some cases, the firesetter may try to cover his or her suicide for insurance purposes. Some arsonists try to destroy records that may link them to embezzlement or other occupational crime. Arson has also been used to divert attention while the offender burglarizes another building or residence.

- *Profit, Insurance Fraud:* This is the category most likely to attract professional or semiprofessional arsonists, who generally escape detection. Consequently, there are few hard data and few statistics to support this motive. However, since the profits gained from arson of this type are so large and the probability of detection so small, actual incidence is believed to be much higher than reported statistically. The property may be residential property, businesses, or modes of transportation (vehicles, boats, planes). According to Douglas, Burgess, Burgess, and Ressler (1992), this type of arson usually has two offenders: the primary offender who is the dominant personality in the offense, and the secondary offender who is the "torch for hire." The torch for hire is usually male, 25 to 40 years of age, and unemployed. The torch is likely to have a prior arrest record for a variety of offenses, including burglary, assault, and public intoxication.

- *Intimidation, Extortion, Terrorism, Sabotage:* This category refers to fires set for the purpose of frightening or deterring. Examples are fires set by striking workers or employees to intimidate management or by extortionists to show that they mean business. Another example is the destruction of abortion clinics, presumably set by antiabortionists wishing to intimidate. Members of the radical environmental activist group ELF claimed responsibility in the 1990s for the burnings of highly expensive homes built on land that the group argued should not have been developed. By most accounts, arsons in this category are extremely rare. Douglas et al. (1992) refer to these as extremist-motivated arsonists who are committed to further a social, political, or religious cause.

- *Pyromania and Other Psychological Motives:* **Pyromania** is a psychiatric term for an "irresistible urge" or passion to set fires along with an intense fascination with flames. Before setting the fire, the individual is said to experience a buildup of tension; once the fire is underway, he or she experiences intense pleasure or release (DSM-IV, 1994). Although the firesetting urge is believed to be uncontrollable, the individual often provides many clues about his or her intention before setting the fire. Pyromania is believed to be a motive in only a small percentage of all arsons, but we will discuss it shortly in more detail to illustrate how some crimes lend themselves well to psychoanalytical interpretation.

Douglas et al. (1992) suggest an additional category that is close to the pyromaniac classification: excitement-motivated (E-M) arson. Excitement-motivated arsonists set fires because they crave stimulation that is satisfied by firesetting and by watching all the excitement that accompanies the fighting of the fire. The offender often selects a location that offers a good vantage point from which to safely observe the firefighting and investigation. Sometimes he mingles with the crowd watching the fire, primarily to hear comments and feel the excitement of the crowd. This E-M arsonist is usually a juvenile or young adult, usually unemployed and living with his or her parents. Generally, the E-M arsonist is socially inadequate and has poor interpersonal skills.

Juvenile Motives

In a comprehensive study of 1,016 juveniles and adults arrested for arson and fire-related crimes, Icove and Estepp (1987) discovered that vandalism was the most frequently identified motive, accounting for 49 percent of the arsons in the sample. Research (e.g., Robbins & Robbins, 1964) has consistently shown that most fires set by juveniles appear to be motivated by the wish to get back at authority or gain status or prompted by a dare or a need for excitement. Therefore, it is not surprising that the Icove-Estepp investigation revealed that the vast majority (96%) of the vandalism fires were set by juveniles, who often set the fire within a one-mile radius of their homes. Moreover, they are generally accompanied by other juveniles. About one-half of these juvenile firesetters remained at the scene. About two-thirds of the fires set by juveniles are for thrills and the excitement involved, although these fires are most often set by juveniles working alone.

Female Arsonists

Harmon, Rosner, and Wiederlight (1985) studied the psychological and demographic characteristics of 27 women arsonists that were evaluated in the Forensic Psychiatric Clinics for the Criminal and Supreme Courts of New York between 1980 and 1983. Although the sample is small and restricted to a specific geographic area, the findings are still of interest because we have so little data on female arsonists. The researchers found these women were somewhat older than male arsonists (midthirties), African American, and with a history of alcohol and drug abuse. Generally, the group was uneducated, unmarried, and relying on public assistance for support. Most often, their motivation was revenge, a consistent finding also reported by Icove and Estepp for female arsonists. In their revenge, the women tended to act impulsively, responding to a perceived wrong committed against them or a perceived threat to their persons. In their haste, they used whatever flammable material was handy to set the fire. Generally, they set fires to places they lived in—apartments or common, public spaces of their buildings.

Pyromania

According to the DSM-IV, pyromania is "the presence of multiple episodes of deliberate and purposeful firesetting" (p. 614). Moreover, it is characterized by high levels of tension or emotional arousal before the act, and there is relief or reduction of this tension when setting fires, or when observing or participating in their aftermath. Pyromaniacs are believed to be regular spectators at fires in their neighborhoods and communities. They are also believed to set off false alarms and to show unusual interest in firefighting paraphernalia.

The term *pyromania* was coined in the early nineteenth century to refer to a form of "insanity" identified by the impulse to set fires without apparent motive (Schmideberg, 1953). Stadolnik (2000) believes the term originated in France in the 1833 writings of a man named Marc, who argued that firesetters were suffering from a specific mental illness he called "monomanie incendiaire." According to Stadolnik, firesetting was referred to in the literature of the nineteenth century as "pyromania of Marc." In the mid-1800s, clinicians suggested that there was a relationship between firesetting and sexual disturbances, and psychoanalytic and psychiatric literature in particular continued to promote that link throughout the twentieth century. For instance, Gold (1962, p. 416) contended that the roots of arson are "deep within the personality and have some relationship to sexual disturbance and urinary malfunction." Abrahamsen (1960, p. 129) wrote, "Firesetting is a substitute for a sexual thrill, and the devastating and destructive powers of fire reflect the intensity of the pyromaniac's sexual desires, as well as his sadism."

Orthodox psychoanalytic thinking draws a connection between pleasurable urination (urethral eroticism) and firesetting. Fenichel (1945, p. 371) concluded, "Regularly deep-seated relationship to urethral eroticism is to be found. . . . In the same way that there are coprophilic perversions based on urethral eroticism, perversions may also be developed based on the derivative of urethral eroticism, pleasure in fire." This theory is based in part on the presumption that many firesetters are or have been enuretic (bedwetters) (Halleck, 1967). The theory does not suggest that enuretic people are likely to be firesetters, only that firesetters have more than their share of bedwetting behavior. Whether this relationship actually exists is still very unclear from the available research.

The relationship between sexual arousal and firesetting is plausible, since, through the process of classical conditioning, virtually any object or event can become associated with sexual arousal and gratification. The fact that some arsonists have fetishes or records of previous arrests for sexual offenses (Mac-Donald, 1977) lends some support to this possibility. Individuals who are sexually aroused by fire may, in general, be highly conditionable introverts. We may also expect them to be sexually, socially, and vocationally inadequate (as noted by Levin, 1976). Firesetting could be a way of feeling significant and resolving conflicts.

While some firesetters may obtain sexual arousal and gratification from fire, there is very little evidence that many do. In an extensive analysis of 68 convicted arsonists imprisoned in Florida, South Carolina, and North Carolina, sexual "abnormality" was no more in evidence than it was in a comparable group of controls (nonarsonist offenders) (Wolford, 1972). Nor is there much evidence for the diagnostic label "pyromaniac." Koson and Dvoskin (1982) were unable to find any arsonists in their sample that met the DSM-III criteria of pyromania. More specifically, even though 38 percent of the sample were repetitive arsonists, none qualified as exhibiting a recurrent failure to resist impulses to set fires compounded by an intense fascination with firesetting and seeing the fires burn. Doley (2003) was unable to document the evidence of pyromania in her investigations of Australia's arson population.

In their investigation of 1,016 offenders of arson and fire-related crimes in the Prince George's County area of Maryland, Icove and Estepp (1987) reported only two offenders who may have qualified as pyromaniacs. In Canada, Bradford (1982) found only one individual out of 34 repetitive arsonists who could even remotely qualify as a pyromaniac, and Hill and colleagues (Hill et al., 1982), in another Canadian sample of 38 arsonists, found none. Rice and Harris (1991) identified only six out of their sample of 243 male firesetters who reported having sexual arousal in the presence of fire. Quinsey, Chaplin, and Upfold (1989) report no differences between normal subjects and firesetters' sexual arousal to fire-related stimuli. Yesavage and associates (Yesavage et al., 1983) found no indications that 50 French arsonists were attracted to fire for sexual reasons. Similar findings have been reported for child firesetters (Kuhnley, Hendren, & Quinlan, 1982; Stewart & Culver, 1982).

BOMBINGS

In 1995, bombing incidents in the United States decreased 18.5 percent to 2,577 from the 3,163 reported in 1994 (Federal Bureau of Investigation, 1996). Bombs killed 193 people in 1995 and injured 744, a dramatic increase from the 31 fatalities and 308 injured in 1994. This increase is largely due to the tragic bombing incident that killed 168 people and injured 518 in Oklahoma City. In addition, each year there are a substantial number of hoaxes, involving threats of bombing and bogus bomb devices, usually involving businesses. About one-third of these incidences are preceded by a threatening note, letter, or telephone call.

TABLE 15–4   Total Number of Bombing Incidents by Motive

| | 1997 | | | |
MOTIVE	EXPLOSIVES NUMBER	EXPLOSIVES DAMAGE ($)	INCENDIARY NUMBER	INCENDIARY DAMAGE ($)
Extortion	1	0	0	0
Homicide	10	270,100	3	55,000
Insurance fraud	1	50,000	3	60,000
Labor	4	0	0	0
Protest	4	3,000	7	797,550
Revenge	137	203,690	166	989,245
Robbery/burglary	12	29,500	2	1,000
Suicide	8	1,000	0	0
Unreported/undetermined	760	1,516,960	269	3,024,820
Vandalism	748	186,112	82	2,130,771
Total	1,685	2,260,362	532	7,058,386

Data are derived from current National Repository data provided by the Bureau of Alcohol, Tobacco and Firearms AEXIS 2000 and the Federal Bureau of Investigation's Bomb Data Center systems.

Motives

In over half of all bombings, the motives were unknown. In bombings where the motives were identified, the most frequent was mischief or vandalism (nearly 50%). In about 25 percent of all incidents, revenge or intimidation was the primary motive. (See Table 15–4.)

Many of the motives for bombing are believed to resemble those for arson. However, it would appear that some bombers are more intent on destruction and injury than arsonists are, and they do not wish to cover up the cause of the destruction. Moreover, the bombing generally requires more technical knowledge than arson, and it is more dangerous. The planning, construction, safe transportation, placing, and activating of an explosive device require more skill than dropping a match onto gasoline-soaked rags under a stairwell.

The apparent motives for bombings change with the times. Between the years 1968 and 1971, nearly half of the bombings in the United States were a result of "social protest" (Moll, 1974), while in 1975 over a third of the bombings were due to "personal animosity," and another third to "malicious destruction" (U.S. Department of Justice, 1976). In 1975, only 10 percent of the bombings were related to social protest. From 1980 to 1983, there was a steady decline of bombings in this country; the incidence leveled for a couple of years, followed by a dramatic increase since 1987.

While there is certainly no single bomber-type personality, MacDonald (1977) contends that there is a personality pattern that is drawn to bombing that demonstrates most of the characteristics of the "compulsive firesetter"; he calls it the "compulsive bomber." Compulsive implies that the individual is drawn to the activity again and again, the behavior seemingly out of the individual's control.

MacDonald reports that the compulsive bombers he has known exhibited a fascination with bombs from childhood. In addition, he found them keenly interested in discussing explosive devices and various techniques of detonating. Large segments of their life appear devoted to the study, development, and experience of bombing. More important, they derive excitement from their actions and are aroused by only one aspect of the explosion: the power, the fire, or the noise. One bomber confessed, "I want to become more than what I am" (MacDonald, 1977, p. 40).

In line with the psychoanalytic tradition, however, MacDonald links sexual gratification with bombing, claiming that one in six compulsive bombers obtains sexual pleasure from his or her explosions. This is apparently based on his observation that sexual deviation is prominent in many bombers.

Two of the more dramatic and best-known bombers were George Metesky, a 56-year-old, known as the Mad Bomber of New York, and Theodore Kaczynski, a 55-year-old mathematical genius known as the Unabomber. Metesky planted 32 different pipe bombs between 1940 and 1956, all supposedly designed to draw attention to the alleged unfair labor practices of a major utility company. Metesky was working for United Electric (now known as Consolidated Edison, or Con Ed) in 1931 when a gush of hot gas from a boiler knocked him down. At the time, he got up and walked away without apparent injury, but he later claimed illness and inability to work as a result of the accident and he expected compensation. When the company repeatedly denied his requests, Metesky undertook an intense campaign designed to bring attention to Con Ed's "dastardly deeds." He planted bombs in locations that would receive heavy press coverage (Macy's Department Store, the New York Public Library, Grand Central Station), but he maintained he did not intend to harm anyone. Fortunately, no one was killed during his bombing missions, but some 22 people were injured. Although his first bombing attempt failed, he subsequently became more sophisticated, technically competent, and successful.

Metesky at one point wrote a letter to the editor of a New York newspaper:

> Have you noticed the bombs in your city, if you are worried, I am sorry, and also if anyone is injured. But it cannot be helped, for justice will be served, I am not well and for this I will make the Con Edison sorry. Yes, they will regret their dastardly deeds. I will bring them before the bar of justice, public opinion will condemn them, for beware, I will place more units under theater seats in the near future. F. P. (MacDonald, 1977, p. 47)

The phrase "dastardly deeds" eventually spelled Metesky's downfall. Investigators searching the files of Con Ed for evidence of disgruntled employees uncovered it in the file folder of Metesky, who had used it in a letter to the company many years before.

Brussel (1978), the consulting psychiatrist in the Mad Bomber case, wrote a detailed account of the events surrounding the search for the bomber and of the arrest, when over a half-dozen law enforcement agents closed in on Metesky's home. He greeted them cordially and immediately guessed their purpose. He smiled frequently and appeared to be in a state of high self-satisfaction at capture. Throughout the trial Metesky beamed and seemed to be enjoying the excitement he had created and the attention he was gaining. In 1957, the court found him insane (Brussel contends he was suffering from "paranoia"), and he was committed to Matteawan State Hospital. Metesky was released in 1973.

Although he was considered insane, he displayed a lifelong pattern of drawing attention to his plight and the perceived injustice done to him. Metesky's behavior probably was his way of coping with his feelings of helplessness. Possibly another principal reason for his bombings was to add excitement to his life or to become famous as the Mad Bomber. Overall, it appears that Metesky was successful in creating some significance for himself.

The search for the Unabomber—Theodore Kaczynski—was one of the longest, most difficult, and most frustrating cases in the history of the FBI. The search took over 17 years until he was apprehended in 1996. In 1993, a UNABOM Task Force (UTF) was established in the search for Kaczynski, with 50 FBI agents assigned full time to the unit. The UTF investigated more than 2,400 suspects, and accumulated 3,600 volumes of information, 175 computer bases, 82 million records, 12,000 event records, 8,182 items of evidence, 22,000 pages of evidentiary documents, and 9,000 evidence photographs.

The Unabomber caused the deaths of three innocent victims and 23 serious injuries by mailing 16 explosive devices to carefully selected target persons. The first few bombings were directed at individuals at universities and airlines—thus the "un" and the "a" in the FBI's code name. His victims included the chief lobbyist for the California Forestry Association, an Engineering professor at University of California–Berkeley, a geneticist at University of California–San Francisco, a computer science professor at Yale, the assistant to psychology professor James McConnell, and the president of United Airlines.

The Unabomber continually changed and improved both his bombs and his tactics, indicating a strong intelligence, and he maintained his cover for a long time. Investigators were continually impressed by the combination of intellect, malice, and showmanship during the 17 years. The primary motive of Kaczynski was his desire to have society return to the era before electric power and aircraft. He also believed that mail bombs, mostly sent to universities and airlines, could lead to a massive uprising against technology.

Kaczynski grew up in the Chicago suburb of Evergreen Park, graduated from Harvard University at the age of 20, majoring in mathematics and physics. He went on to earn a Ph.D. in mathematics from the University of Michigan, and appeared headed for a brilliant career in academics. Instead, he became a recluse who shunned family and friends and lived in a remote, isolated cabin in Montana.

The Unabomber's downfall resulted when his brother, David Kaczynski, recognized his brother's work—a 35,000-word personal and political manifesto—published in the *New York Times* and the *Washington Post*. The piece was published in the *Times* and *Post* after the Unabomber promised he would stop mailing bombs if his statement was published in full. Although his lawyers wanted to use the insanity defense on his behalf before his trial, Kaczynski strongly rejected the defense. On January 22, 1998, Kaczynski pleaded guilty and agreed to a life sentence in prison without possibility of parole. He is currently serving his sentence.

Summary and Conclusions

The crimes discussed in the chapter are all either violent or, in most cases, have the potential of doing great physical harm to victims. Even if violence does not occur, however, the crimes typically put the victims in fear. Thus, there is great psychological impact on the victim.

We began with a discussion of robbery, its categories and its motives. Although financial gain or material gain is the primary reason for robbery, the secondary motive of controlling and instilling fear in a victim does occur, particularly in some street robberies. Bank robberies, in contrast to many depictions in the entertainment media, are rarely carried out by professionals or well planned. The typical bank robbery is the work of an amateur who undoubtedly sees this as a way of getting quick cash. Commercial robberies are usually carried out against convenience stores or fast-food restaurants. These establishments are seen as more accessible than banks, but they produce smaller return. Nevertheless, they are considered easier targets, generally late at night, when few workers and customers are on the premises. Street robberies are rarely planned; the robber sees the opportunity with a likely target and takes it. Interestingly, the latest data show strong-arm robberies were slightly more frequent than robberies carried out with firearms or knives. Victims also are more likely to be physically harmed during a strong-arm robbery, both because they are more likely to resist and because the perpetrator has less confidence in his ability to control the victim. Professional robbers are a separate group that can conduct any of the above types of robbery but are most likely to be involved in street robbery.

Wright and Decker (1997) and Wright, Brookman, and Bennett (2006) interviewed robbers who had committed many robberies over a number of years but, in many cases (60%) had never been convicted. In that sense they were professional robbers. Like the other robber categories, they seemed primarily motivated by a desire for money, drugs, or material goods; however, some did enjoy the psychological effect of control over their victims. Although most of the robberies were unplanned, it is likely that these robbers relied on their cognitive scripts to carry out their crimes. In other words, they had played out the robberies over and over in their minds, considering what tactics to use under what situation.

We gave some attention to cybercrime—or computer crime—which is becoming increasingly problematic and which challenges the resources of the law enforcement community. In addition to economically motivated cybercrime, we also discussed cyberstalking and cyberbullying. Both allow the perpetrator to harass the victim while remaining anonymous, and both qualify as crimes of intimidation. To date we have very little research knowledge about the prevalence of the offenses or the psychological attributes of the offenders.

The most well-known crime of intimidation, stalking, has received increasing public attention since it was first reported as a problem—or first given a name—in the 1980s. It is estimated that one of every 12 women and one of every 45 men has been a victim of stalking. The perpetrator's motive is almost invariably to control, intimidate, and frighten the victim. Restraining orders, sought by about half of the victims who report the crime to police, unfortunately have had little success, since they are ignored by most stalkers. However, some do respond to the restraining order and some do cease stalking when confronted by law enforcement. We reviewed the major stalking study by Tjades and Toennes (1997) that provides information about the prevalence of stalking and its effect on victims. Many women who are stalked had previously experienced violence at the hands of their stalkers, and future violence is a continuing possibility. Although stalking typically stops within a two-year-period, in some cases the victim's best option is to move out of the area.

We also reviewed and provided illustrations of the four major categories of stalking: simple obsession, love obsession, erotomania, and vengeance. The first is the most common, but also the one most likely to be accompanied by physical harm to the victim. As a group, stalkers are not typically mentally disordered. The exception is the erotomania stalkers, who tends to be delusional and plagued with a variety of mental disorders.

Hostage taking is a major crime of intimidation that places its victim in great fear, even though no physical violence may result. Strategies for law enforcement negotiating with hostage takers were reviewed as were suggestions for hostages in these terrifying situations. Remaining calm, not challenging the hostage taker, and not bringing attention to oneself (in the case of multiple hostages) were among these suggestions. The Stockholm Syndrome—in which the hostage identifies with and becomes emotionally close to the hostage taker—is extremely rare. There is no research evidence that this is a strong phenomenon.

The chapter ended with discussions of arson and bombing. Although some forms of arson are clearly economically motivated, the focus of the arson section was persistent firesetting, particularly by children. Considerable psychological research has studied this behavior. Although most children are fascinated by fire, particularly between the ages of 5 and 7, in a small but very problematic minority this fascination is accompanied first by experimental firesetting and gradually by continuing and persistent firesetting behavior. Persistent firesetters are usually identified by age 10. They typically have extremely dysfunctional family backgrounds, often lacking parental supervision and plagued by physical abuse and alcohol and other drug problems. Persistent adult arsonists often began their firesetting behavior as children. We reviewed categories of these arsonists and emphasized that very few fall under the term "pyromaniac," indicating a serious mental disorder characterized by abnormal fascination with fire.

Bombings invariably cause extensive physical harm, often death, to individuals, unless the bomb is set to go off in an empty building or, of course, is successfully disarmed by bomb squads. Motives for bombings are often not known, but research indicates that—when the motives were known—about one-half were for the purpose of mischief or vandalism, not to harm or kill. Social protest bombings are relatively infrequent (e.g., about 10%), although they can reach higher percentages during some time periods (e.g., 1968–1971). Personal animosity against victims is another motive for bombing, with some studies finding one-third of bombings associated with that motive. Little research has been directed at individual bombers, although much anecdotal data information has been provided about high-profile bombers, such as Theodore Kaczynski, the UnaBomber, or George Metesky, the "Mad Bomber." There is, however, no indication of a single bomber personality.

KEY CONCEPTS

Robbery	Strong-arm robbery
Cognitive scripts	Street culture
Cybercrime	Cyberstalking
Cyberbullying	Stalking
Simple obsession stalking	Love obsession stalking
Erotomania stalking	Vengeance stalking
Instrumental hostage taking	Expressive hostage taking
Barricade situation	Stockholm syndrome
Survivors	Succumbers
London syndrome	Firesetting
Arson	Pyromania

REVIEW QUESTIONS

1. In what important way is the street culture and the concept of cognitive scripts related to opportunity crime?
2. Define cyberstalking.
3. What is the difference between the Stockholm syndrome and the London syndrome?
4. What is the major difference between firesetting and arson?
5. Does the research literature support pyromania? Explain.
6. Describe the difference between survivors and succumbers.

7. Describe the difference between instrumental hostage taking and expressive hostage taking.
8. Describe the psychological motives of arson.
9. What are the psychological characteristics of (a) repetitive firesetters and (b) bombers, as identified in the research.
10. What is meant by strong-arm robbery?

CHAPTER 16

SUBSTANCE ABUSE, ALCOHOL, AND CRIME

CHAPTER OBJECTIVES

- Summarize the effects of the psychoactive drugs that have been most connected to crime and delinquency.
- Caution about and emphasize the many individual differences in reactions to drugs and alcohol.
- Define and explain drug tolerance and dependence.
- Examine closely the extent of juvenile substance and alcohol use.
- Note the illegal drugs most commonly used by American culture.
- Explain and discuss "club drugs."
- Focus on the effects and extent of marijuana use, because this is the most popular illicit drug today.
- Sketch the relationship between alcohol abuse and crime and delinquency.
- Explain the tripartite conceptual model and experimental substance use.

Over the past 30 years, the United States has been waging a "drug war" against individuals who transport, sell, and use a wide variety of illegal substances. While other periods in history have also seen a focus on drugs, it was in the 1980s that the government began to adopt conservative policies in response to perceived epidemics in the trafficking and use of cocaine, crack cocaine, heroin, and marijuana, among others (Walker, 2001). Billions of dollars have been expended on both reducing the supply of drugs and punishing convicted individuals with long prison sentences. According to

Walker (2001), the federal government spent $17.1 billion in drug enforcement alone in 1999. Although federal and some state law enforcement priorities shifted after September 11, 2001, illicit drugs continue to be a prominent target.

Many members of the public believe the above approaches are justified. For example, in a poll of one thousand individuals randomly selected across the continental United States (Strasser, 1989), two-thirds of the respondents felt that the sale and usage of drugs was the key cause of crime. In this chapter we review the evidence in support of or against this public perception. Others believe the drug war has been in many ways a colossal failure, neither making significant headway in interdiction nor adequately addressing the widespread problems associated with substance abuse. According to the National Council on Crime and Delinquency (NCCD), substance abuse should be considered *"primarily* [emphasis added] as a health-related problem that should reside in the public health domain" (Rosenbaum, 1989, p. 17). Increasingly in recent years, we have heard more such calls for addressing the illegal use of drugs as at least as much a health problem as a crime problem.

Each year, it is estimated that more than sixteen thousand Americans die due to an overdose or misuse of illegal drugs, and at least five-hundred thousand drug-related emergencies occur in emergency departments throughout the United States (Federal Bureau of Investigation, 1999a). Many of the fatalities and serious reactions involved youth. For example, the availability of higher-purity, lower-cost drugs has led to an increase in widespread experimental drug use among middle school and high school students. We begin the chapter, then, with a discussion of juvenile drug use.

JUVENILE DRUG USE

Juvenile illicit drug use is widely regarded as one of today's most important social concerns (Ramirez et al., 2004). Although recent surveys (e.g., Johnston et al., 2006; Substance Abuse and Mental Health Administration, 2005) indicate an overall decline or leveling off in the use of drugs and alcohol nationwide, a significant proportion of youth continues to be exposed to the deleterious effects of substance abuse. In 2004, 19.1 million Americans, or 7.9 percent of the population aged 12 or older, were current illicit drug users (used the drug within the past month) (Substance Abuse and Mental Health Administration, 2005). Among all youths ages 12 to 17, 10.6 percent were illicit drug users in 2004. Marijuana was, by far, the most commonly used drug among this age group (Substance Abuse and Mental Health Administration, 2005).

Drug use in early adolescence is associated with serious health problems, deviant and antisocial behavior, high risk behaviors, and poor academic performance. High-level chronic juvenile offenders are far more likely to use drugs and alcohol excessively compared with other juveniles (Wiesner, Kim, & Capaldi, 2005).

Extent of Juvenile Drug Use

A special report from the U.S. Department of Justice (Federal Bureau of Investigation, 2005) reveals that juvenile arrests for drug abuse violations—involving all drugs—increased 22.9 percent from 1994 to 2003. However, the data also reveal that in 1994, persons under 18 accounted for 11.8 percent of the number of arrests for drug abuse. Ten years later the juvenile proportion of arrests for drug abuse violations remained virtually identical at 11.6 percent, demonstrating that while the number of juvenile arrests for drug abuse increased, the percentage of juvenile arrests to the *total* arrests was virtually unchanged. However, the patterns of the type of drug used has changed. For example, although the number of juvenile arrests for cocaine has dropped during the past 10 years, the arrests for synthetic narcotics has increased dramatically (see **Table 16–1**).

The FBI Special Report defines "drug abuse" as including the sale/manufacturing or possession of the illegal drug. In this regard, the report finds that most of the arrests of juveniles for the period studied (ranging from 73.8% in 1994 to 83.7% in 2003) were for possession of drugs rather than the sale or manufacturing of illegal substances (see **Table 16–2**).

When an individual is arrested for a drug abuse violation in the United States, the arresting agency reports to the Department of Justice the type of drug. The types fall under one of four categories: (1) opium or cocaine and their derivatives (e.g., morphine, heroine, codeine), (2) marijuana, (3) synthetic narcotics, and (4) dangerous nonnarcotic drugs, such as Demerol and methadone. Between 1994 and 2003, the number of arrests of juveniles for violations involving opium or cocaine declined, while arrests involving marijuana increased.

Marijuana remains the drug associated with the highest percentage of juveniles arrested for drug abuse (see **Figure 16–2**). For example, male juveniles arrested for the sale/manufacturing and possession of marijuana combined increased from 55.1 percent of the arrests of male juveniles in 1994 to 74 percent in 2003. We review more up-to-date statistics shortly when we focus on

TABLE 16–1   Percent Change in the Number of Estimated Drug Arrests of Juveniles by Drug Type and Arrestee's Sex 2-, 5-, and 10-year Comparisons

	2003/1994		2003/1999		2003/2002	
	MALE	FEMALE	MALE	FEMALE	MALE	FEMALE
All drug types	15.4	79.2	−0.2	22.6	5.1	10.2
Opium or cocaine	−54.8	−10.7	−30.5	−8.5	−7.0	1.5
Marijuana	54.9	97.7	2.1	16.8	7.4	10.7
Synthetic narcotics	133.6	293.6	64.9	141.3	6.7	14.7
Dangerous nonnarcotics	23.0	127.9	47.4	86.3	6.3	14.4

Source: Federal Bureau of Investigation, 2005.

TABLE 16–2   Estimated Number of Drug Arrests of Juveniles by Sale/Manufacturing and Possession by Drug Type, 2003

DRUG TYPE	NUMBER
Total	195,468
Sale/Manufacturing	**31,895**
Opium or cocaine	11,385
Marijuana	15,178
Synthetic narcotics	1,513
Dangerous nonnarcotics	3,820
Possession	**163,573**
Opium or cocaine	14,408
Marijuana	127,524
Synthetic narcotics	4,166
Dangerous nonnarcotics	17,474

Source: Federal Bureau of Investigation, 2005, p. 349.

marijuana. Arrests of juveniles for violations involving synthetic narcotics and dangerous nonnarcotics consistently accounted for the lowest percentage of juveniles arrested for drug abuse violations during the 10-year period. Furthermore, these arrests show a downward trend. The percentage of arrests of both male and female juveniles for violations involving opium or cocaine also shows decline during the 10-year period. Arrests of male juveniles for violations involving opium or cocaine fell from 34.2 percent of the arrests of male juveniles for drugs in 1994 to 13.4 percent in 2003.

In 1994, 60.6 percent of juveniles arrested for drug abuse violations were white. By 2003, however, that number had increased to 74.9 percent. Male juveniles were more frequently arrested for drug abuse violations than female juveniles at an average ratio of 6 to 1. The data for the 10 years covered in the FBI Special Report showed that of the number of arrests in 1994 for drug abuse violations involving juveniles under age 10, 83 percent were males and 17 percent were females. A decade later, the percentage of arrests for drug abuse violations of males under age 10 dropped to 78.9 percent, and the percentage of arrests of females increased to 21.1 percent, indicating that there may be a growing trend for female juveniles to be arrested at a younger age for drug abuse violations than male juveniles.

Who Is Selling to Juveniles?

In a recent survey, one in nine high school students reported *selling* drugs during the past year, and most of them said they sold the drugs in school (Steinman, 2005). About 10 percent of the juveniles who bought marijuana said they purchased it at school (Substance Abuse and Mental Health Administration, 2005). Those students most likely to sell drugs on a *regular* basis are also more likely to engage in a variety of delinquent acts, including violence, heavy mar-

FIGURE 16–1 Percent Distribution of the Estimated Number of Drug Arrests of Juveniles by Drug Type, 1994–2003

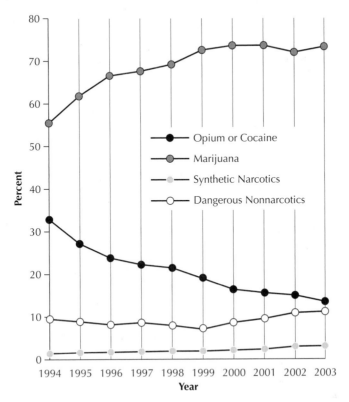

Source: Federal Bureau of Investigation, 2005, p. 350.

ijuana use, and other risk behaviors. These youths are often hired by older deal-ers, especially in cities and metropolitan areas. Moreover, regular juvenile sell-ers generally do not have a strong relationship with family and prefer to associate with other deviant peers who use and sell drugs. Many are members of gangs. However, for the purposes of explaining delinquency, students who *occasionally* sell drugs to friends and relatives should not be placed in the same category as the more routine seller who distributes a variety of substances. Oc-casional, friend-based sellers rarely are detected by the authorities and do not usually become involved in serious delinquency.

Gender Differences in Juvenile Drug Use

Most research on drug and alcohol abuse and dependence has concentrated on males. The few studies that have focused on gender differences in alcohol and drug use among adolescents have consistently shown that males consume alco-hol and drugs of various kinds more frequently and in higher quantities than females and are prone to experience more drug- and alcohol-related problems (Fothergill & Ensminger, 2006; Webb, Bray, Getz, & Adams, 2002). In addition, there is increasing evidence that males and females experience different substance abuse trajectories and consequences (Fothergill & Ensminger, 2006). Girls who show little commitment to school and academic achievement are at increased risk for later substance abuse problems (Fothergill & Ensminger, 2006).

SIX CONSISTENT RESEARCH FINDINGS ON ILLICIT DRUG ABUSE

The relationship between drugs and crime may be viewed from two perspectives: (1) the use, sale, manufacture, distribution, and possession of illegal drugs, all of which are themselves crimes, and (2) the pharmacological effects certain drugs have on a user's behavior in promoting criminal actions. Research directed at these two perspectives in recent years has reached the following six conclusions, each of which are discussed in some detail below:

1. More individuals are incarcerated or held in jails and prisons for drug offenses than for any other offense, and this has contributed to burgeoning jail and prison populations.
2. Arrestees frequently test positive for illicit drug use.
3. Arrestees and incarcerated offenders were often under the influence of illicit drugs when they committed their offenses.
4. Some offenders commit property crime to support their drug habit.
5. Drug trafficking often engenders violent crime.
6. The drug-crime relationship is difficult to identify and measure.

The first consistent finding has major implications for jail and prison crowding: More individuals are incarcerated or held in jails and prisons for drug offenses than for any other offense. (**Jails** are operated by local [or sometimes state] governments to hold persons temporarily detained, awaiting trial, or sentenced to confinement for a misdemeanor, usually for less than one year. **Prisons** are operated by state and federal governments to hold persons sentenced under state and federal laws to terms of more than one year.)

According to the 2002 National Survey on Drug Use and Health, 19.5 million (8.3%) of Americans aged 12 and older are current illicit drug users (Department of Health and Human Services, 2003). Current drug use means use of an illicit drug during the month prior to the survey. In 2004, 1.2 million people were arrested for drug abuse violations in the United States (Federal Bureau of Investigation, 2005). Another 439,648 were arrested for liquor law offenses. From October 1, 1999 to September 30, 2000, of the 76,952 defendants in U.S. district courts, 27,274 (35.4%) had committed a drug offense (Office of National Drug Control Policy, 2003d). A vast majority of these drug offenders (93.8%) had committed a trafficking offense. Most (91.2%) of these offenders were convicted, and most were incarcerated (91.7%). In state courts, 195,133 people were convicted of drug trafficking in 1998, and another 119,443 were convicted of drug possession (Bureau of Justice Statistics, 2006).

Approximately, in any given year, two-thirds of the inmates in state and county jails had committed a drug offense or used drugs regularly (Wilson, 2000). A quarter of those jail inmates had a current charge or conviction for drug law violations. About 15 percent had a charge or conviction for drug possession and 9 percent for drug trafficking. About two-thirds of federal prisoners were also held for drug offenses during the same year (Beck, 2000; Mumola, 1999). Eighty-five percent of those federal prisoners incarcerated for a drug offense were involved in trafficking at the time of their arrest, and only 5 percent were incarcerated because of possession of an illicit drug.

As noted, with growing recognition that substance abuse is a serious health problem that requires intervention and treatment, many communities have established drug courts. Initiated in Miami, Florida, in 1989, they are designed to be a first step in diverting nonviolent offenders with drug problems into treatment and other community-based programs. Offenders who go through the drug court model often are expected to undergo long-term treatment and counseling, sanctions, incentives, and frequent court appearances. If they successfully complete their program, they not only avoid jail or prison but also, in many jurisdictions, a criminal record. In 2003, there were 1,424 drug courts in existence or being planned in the United States (Office of National Drug Control Policy, 2003d). Recidivism among drug court participants ranges between 5 percent and 28 percent and is less than 4 percent for drug court *graduates* (Office of National Drug Control Policy, 2003d).

The *second* consistent finding from the research is that arrestees frequently test positive for illicit drug use. In 1999, the Arrestees Drug Abuse Monitoring (ADAM) Program collected data from more than thirty thousand adult male arrestees in 34 geographical locations (called sites), and more than ten thousand adult female arrestees in 32 sites. In addition, data were collected from more than 2,500 juvenile male detainees in 9 sites, and more than 400 female juvenile detainees in 6 sites. The ADAM utilizes both urinalysis and self-report data to identify the level of recent drug use by the arrestees and detainees.

The ADAM program continually finds that the level of drug use of arrestees is substantial. In 1999, for instance, every site reported that at least 50 percent of adult male arrestees tested positive for at least one drug (Arrestees Drug Abuse Monitoring Program, 2000). Overall, the median rate for use of any drug for adult male arrestees was 64 percent, and for adult female arrestees the median rate was 67 percent. These figures were basically the same in 1998, with about two-thirds of the adult arrestees and more than half of the juvenile detainees testing positive for at least one drug (Arrestees Drug Abuse Monitoring, 1999). Marijuana was the drug most frequently detected in male arrestees, followed by cocaine. Among adult female arrestees, cocaine was the drug most commonly detected, followed by marijuana and methamphetamine. Multiple drug (polydrug) use was also common, with more than one-quarter of the adult male arrestees testing positive for two or more drugs. Marijuana continues to be a very popular drug among all arrestees, particularly among young males, ages 15 to 20. In fact marijuana was the most commonly used drug for both juvenile and female detainees, with cocaine and methamphetamine substantially

TABLE 16–3   Overall Average of Positive Test Results for Various Illicit Drugs in Detained Arrestees in the United States and England, 1999

DRUG TYPE	Overall Average IN UNITED STATES	Overall Average IN ENGLAND
Marijuana	46.9%	40.6%
Opiates	8.4	17.9
Cocaine	40.7	8.7
Amphetamines	0.5	5.3
Benzodiazepines	9.0	8.2
Methadone	2.8	6.3
Multiple Drugs	27.2	21.7

Source: International Arrestees Drug Abuse Monitoring System, 2000.

less frequently detected. Among adult males marijuana was the drug most frequently detected, followed by cocaine. Among females cocaine was the drug most frequently detected, followed by methamphetamine. Among juvenile arrestees, marijuana was far and away the most frequently detected drug. **Table 16–3** shows types of illicit drugs that persons in the United States and England tested positive for at the time of their arrest. As you can see, marijuana was the drug most often found in arrestees in both countries. Cocaine was a close second in the United States, but opiates were a very distant second in England.

The *third* consistent finding of illicit drug research findings in recent years is that arrestees and incarcerated offenders were often under the influence of illicit drugs when they committed their offenses. **Table 16–4** shows that about one-quarter of federal (prison) inmates and over one-third of state prison inmates admitted they had been using drugs at the time of the offense.

Furthermore, certain professional criminal groups often prefer one drug over another. Professional pickpockets, shoplifters, and burglars, for example—when they use drugs—have a distinct preference for those that steady their

TABLE 16–4   1997 State and Federal Prison Inmate Drug Use at Time of Offense (in Percentages)

CURRENT OFFENSE	DRUGS		ALCOHOL		EITHER DRUGS OR ALCOHOL	
	Fed.	State	Fed.	State	Fed.	State
All offenses	22.4%	32.6%	20.4%	37.2%	34.0%	52.5%
Violent offenses	24.5	29.0	24.5	41.7	39.8	51.9
Property offenses	10.8	36.6	15.6	34.5	22.6	53.2
Drug offenses	25.0	41.9	19.8	27.4	34.6	52.4
Public order offenses	15.6	23.1	20.6	43.2	30.2	56.2

Source: Office of National Drug Control Policy, 1999c, p. 2.

nerves and provide relief from the pressures of their occupation (Inciardi, 1981). Professional pickpockets often consider opiates instrumental in furthering their careers. To some extent, this has a cyclical effect, since their material gain from their crimes is used to obtain the drugs.

In reference to the *fourth* point—that some offenders commit property crime to support their drug habit—19 percent of state prisoners and 16 percent of federal prisoners said they committed their current offenses to obtain money for drugs in 1997 (Bureau of Justice Statistics, 2000b). Table 16.4 suggests that over one-third of all property offenses were committed by state prison inmates to support their habit. These figures are actually quite low compared with public perceptions that stealing to support a drug habit is widespread.

The *fifth* finding of recent research is that drug trafficking often engenders violent crime. There is considerable evidence that violence accompanies drug distribution in the course of territorial disputes between rival organizations and gangs, or in conflicts between the buyer and the seller (Roth, 1996; Walker, 2001). Places where drug deals occur bring together valuable drugs, big money, weapons, and people accustomed to violence. This volatile mix creates a high potential for violence.

The *sixth* and final point is that the drug-crime relationship is difficult to identify and measure. The relationship between drugs and crimes is complicated by a fourfold interaction: (1) the pharmacological effects of the drug, which refer to the chemical impact of the drug on the body; (2) the psychological characteristics of the individual using the drug; (3) the psychosocial conditions under which the drug is taken; and (4) the interactions a particular drug has with other drugs consumed simultaneously. Discussion of pharmacological effects includes features of the nervous system, such as the amount of neurotransmitter substances within neurons, and body weight, blood composition, and other neurophysiological features that significantly influence the chemical effects of the drug. Psychological variables include the mood of the person at the time the drug is consumed, previous experience with the drug, and the person's expectancies about the drug's effects. Psychosocial variables include the social atmosphere under which the drug is taken. The people who are present and their expectations, moods, and behavior all may influence an individual's reactions to a drug. The interaction factor must be considered in any discussion of drug effects because most illegal drugs are taken in combinations, especially with alcohol. For example, it is not unusual to find teenagers and young adults consuming a variety of club drugs in combination with alcohol; more experienced users sometimes combine cocaine powder or crack with heroin (called a "speedball"). More than two-thirds of the arrestees in 1999 who tested positive for opiates also tested positive for another drug (National Drug Control Policy, 2001).

In order to understand the effects of any drug, the pharmacological, psychological, psychosocial, and interacting variables all must be taken into account. Considering the fact that crime is complex to begin with, deciphering the drug-crime connection becomes very difficult, and the conclusions are necessarily that much more elusive and tentative. The relationship between drugs and crime is further complicated by the cultural, subcultural, and ethnographic aspects of drug consumption. The attitudes and perceptions of different age groups and cultures about specific drugs are often in a state of flux. Cultural preferences shift and change depending on drug availability, law enforcement priorities, and changes in cultural attitudes. In addition, demographic studies have shown that drug popularity and epidemics go through four distinct stages: incubation, expansion, plateau, and decline (Golub & Johnson, 1997). During the *incubation* stage, users experiment with the new and emerging drug, learn how to use it, and develop techniques for its use. During the *expansion* stage, prices drop, it becomes easy to use, its availability increases, and word gets around about the drug, all of which contribute to its popularity. During the *plateau* stage, there is a relatively high and constant use of the drug. But during the *decline* stage, the drug is shunned—usually by a new generation of youth—and a new drug emerges in popularity.

The Tripartite Conceptual Model

A helpful way of understanding the drug–crime relationship is the **tripartite conceptual model** proposed by Paul Goldstein (1985). Goldstein identifies three main types of drug-related crime: (1) *psychopharmacologically* driven crime, (2) *systemic* crime, and (3) *economically compulsive* crime. Goldstein's psychopharmacological component of the model presupposes that some individuals, as a result of short-term or long-term ingestion of specific drugs or chemical substances, become excitable, and/or irrational and demonstrate violent behavior. In other words, the assumption in this component is that some drugs *cause* some people (even usually nonviolent ones) to become violent and engage in a variety of criminal behaviors. The prevailing view about psychopharmacological violence, however, is that it is rare and attributable mostly to alcohol rather than illicit drugs (MacCoun, Kilmer, & Reuter, 2003).

The *systemic* component of the model hypothesizes that crime arises out of the system of drug trafficking and distribution. Examples of this component include disputes over territory between rival drug dealers and threats, assaults, and murders committed within and by drug dealing organizations. Essentially, it refers to the violence inherent in the enterprise of drug trafficking and distribution, and is similar to the fifth observation of research noted previously.

Economically compulsive crime refers to criminal behavior that supports an expensive drug addiction. Robbery committed by drug users to support a costly drug habit is an example. Compulsive drug seeking and use is presumably an overwhelming drive, even in the face of negative health and social consequences (MacCoun et al., 2003). The economically compulsive component is similar to the fourth observation discussed earlier in this section. As each of the major drug categories are examined in the following sections, the pharmacologically driven aspect as a cause for violence and criminal activity will be, by far, the most difficult to support.

Before entering into this discussion, it is important to stress that we do not in this text give more than passing attention to public policy with respect to drugs. As noted at the beginning of the chapter, there is considerable disagreement over the extent to which the government should continue on its present course of being harsh on drug offenders. The events of September 11, 2001, have shifted priorities to some extent to a war on terrorism. Nevertheless, drug enforcement and harsh punishments continue, and the individuals who are most often affected are members of racial and economic minority groups. Although this book focuses on the individual behavior of drug users, readers also should be aware of the controversy surrounding public policy on this matter.

MAJOR CATEGORIES OF DRUGS

Four major categories of **psychoactive drugs** will be covered in the chapter: (1) hallucinogens or psychedelics, (2) stimulants, (3) opiate narcotics, and (4) sedative-hypnotics or depressants. A psychoactive drug is a chemical substance that influences a person's mood, perception, mode of thinking, and behavior. To keep the chapter within manageable limits, however, we will focus only on specific drugs within each category that represent a serious risk to public safety or that are most closely associated with criminal activity, such as the illegal manufacturing, selling, and distributing of a controlled substance. A **controlled substance** is any psychoactive drug or chemical substance whose availability is restricted, as designated by state or federal law.

The *Controlled Substances Act* (CSA), Title II of the *Comprehensive Drug Abuse Prevention and Control Act of 1970*, places all substances of potential abuse into one of five schedules. This placement is based on the substance's medical use, potential for abuse, and dependence potential (see **Table 16–5**).

TABLE 16–5 Formal Scheduling as Outlined by the Controlled Substances Act

SCHEDULE	POTENTIAL FOR ABUSE	ACCEPTED MEDICAL USE IN U.S.	PHYSICAL DEPENDENCE	PSYCHOLOGICAL DEPENDENCE	EXAMPLES
I	High	No	High	High	Heroin, LSD, marijuana
II	High	Yes	High	High	PCP, cocaine, morphine, methamphetamine
III	Medium	Yes	Moderate	High	Codeine, steroids, barbiturates
IV	Low	Yes	Low	Low	Darvon, Talwin, Valium, Xanax
V	Low	Yes	Low	Low	Cough medicines with codeine

Source: Drug Enforcement Administration, 2005.

The purpose of the act is to control the distribution, classification, sale, and use of psychoactive drugs that have the potential for abuse. Although the term "potential for abuse" is not specifically defined in the CSA, scheduling classifications are based on available evidence that the drugs can create a hazard to health or jeopardize the safety of other individuals, or that there is a significant diversion of the drug from legitimate drug channels. Proceedings to add, delete, or change the schedule of a drug or other substance may be initiated by the Drug Enforcement Administration (DEA), the Department of Health and Human Services (HHS), or by petition from any interested party (Drug Enforcement Administration, 2000).

The **hallucinogens** or **psychedelics,** which include LSD (lysergic acid diethylamide), mescaline, psilocybin, phencyclidine, ketamine, marijuana, and hashish, will be our first category. So called because they sometimes generate hallucinations, the hallucinogens are chemicals that lead to a change in consciousness involving an alteration of reality. In some respects they replace the present world with an alternative one, although persons using them can generally attend to their altered state and to reality simultaneously. Marijuana, classified as a hallucinogen, is certainly a mild one for a majority who use it. Because of its widespread use and the public's tendency to mistakenly associate it with crime and bizarre behavior, it will be the main drug covered under the hallucinogens category. We will also include phencyclidine (PCP), a powerful drug that has been linked to crime during the past two decades.

Next we discuss the **stimulants,** so called because they appear to stimulate central nervous system functions. They include amphetamines, clinical antidepressants, cocaine, MDMA (Ecstasy), caffeine, and nicotine. Again because of an alleged relationship with crime, the amphetamines, MDMA, and cocaine will be highlighted.

The third group includes the **opiate narcotics,** which generally have sedative (sleep-inducing) and analgesic (pain-relieving) effects. Heroin—a drug whose use appears to be growing at alarming rates in many communities—is featured in this section. The heroin addict appears frequently in crime statistics, since it is believed that he or she often turns to crime—particularly property crime—to finance this expensive habit.

Finally, alcohol and the "club drugs" will represent the **sedative-hypnotic compounds** that depress central nervous system functions. In most instances, the sedative-hypnotics are all capable of sedating the nervous system and reducing anxiety and tension. Examples include alcohol and the benzodiazepines.

Tolerance and Dependence

Before proceeding we must distinguish two terms that are consistently used in the drug literature: **tolerance** and **dependence.** Drug tolerance is the "state of progressively decreased responsiveness to a drug" (Julien, 1975, p. 29). Tolerance is indicated if the individual requires a larger dose of the drug to reach the same effects he or she has previously experienced. In other words, the person has become psychologically and physiologically used to, or habituated to, the drug.

Dependence may be physical or psychological, or both. In simple terms, physical dependence refers to the physiological distress and physical pain a person suffers if he or she goes without the drug for any length of time. Psychological dependence is difficult to distinguish from physical dependence, but it is characterized by an overwhelming desire to use the drug for a favorable effect. The person is convinced that he or she needs the drug to maintain an optimal sense of well-being. The degree of psychological dependence varies widely from person to person and drug to drug. In its extreme form, the person's life is permeated with thoughts of procuring and using the drug, and he or she may resort to crime to obtain it. In common parlance, the person who is extremely psychologically and/or physically dependent is an addict.

Secondary psychological dependence may also develop. While primary dependence is associated with the reward of the drug experience (positive reinforcement), secondary dependence refers to expectancies about aversive withdrawal or the painful effects that will accompany absence of the drug. Thus, to avoid the anticipated pain and discomfort associated with withdrawal, the individual continues to take the drug (negative reinforcement).

The data reported in this chapter concerning illicit drug use and abuse were primarily gathered from the *National Household Survey on Drug Abuse* (NHSDA) (sponsored by the Substance Abuse and Mental Health Services Administration), the *2005 National Survey on Drug Abuse and Health* (the updated version of the NDSDA, also sponsored by the Substance Abuse and Mental Health Services Administration), the Office of National Drug Control Policy (sponsored by the Office of the President), the National Drug Intelligence Center (NDIC), the Bureau of Justice Statistics (BJS), the University of Michigan's 2005 *Monitoring the Future Study*, the FBI, the Drug Enforcement Administration (DEA), and the National Institute on Drug Abuse. Most of these organizations and agencies maintain up-to-date Web sites on the Internet. **Table 16–6** provides an illustration of data obtained from self-report surveys.

TABLE 16–6   Percent of Students Reporting Drug Use, 1999–2003

	1999	2001	2003
Lifetime marijuana	47.2%	42.4%	40.2%
Current marijuana	26.7	23.9	22.4
Lifetime cocaine	9.5	9.4	8.7
Current cocaine	4.0	4.2	4.1
Lifetime inhalant	14.6	14.7	12.1
Current inhalant	4.2	4.7	3.9
Lifetime heroin	2.4	3.1	3.3
Lifetime metham.	9.1	9.8	7.6
Lifetime MDMA	na	na	11.1

Source: Substance Abuse and Mental Health Administration, 2006.

THE HALLUCINOGENS

Marijuana is the most popular illegal drug used in the United States (Substance Abuse and Mental Health Administration, 2005), although there are surveys showing a *slight* decline in use over the past 5 years (Johnstone et al., 2006). In 2004, there were 14.6 million current users in the United States (Substance Abuse and Mental Health Administration, 2005). Forty percent of the U.S. population ages 12 and older have reported trying marijuana at least once. Approximately 3.2 million Americans use marijuana on a daily or almost daily basis (Office of National Drug Control Policy, 2005).

Marijuana is also one of the most popular illegal drugs used by juveniles (Department of Health and Human Services, 2003; Federal Bureau of Investigation, 2005), third only to alcohol and tobacco in terms of prevalence of use (Windle & Wiesner, 2004). Almost all youth who report any substance use report using marijuana (McClelland, Teplin, & Abram, 2004). According to the 2005 *Monitoring the Future Study,* 16.5 percent of eighth graders, 34.1 percent of tenth graders, and 44.8 percent of the twelfth graders reported lifetime use of marijuana. In that same national study, 6.6 percent of eighth graders, 15.2 percent of tenth graders, and 19.8 percent of twelfth graders said they used marijuana in the previous month (see **Table 16–7**). Another survey found that 50.7 percent of college students indicated that they had used marijuana at least once during their lifetimes (National Institute on Drug Abuse and University of Michigan, 2005). (See also **Table 16–8**.) In those surveys, a substantial majority of the middle-school, high-school, and college students all indicated that marijuana is "fairly easy" or "very easy" to obtain. In 2005, for example, 85.6 percent of twelfth graders said it was "fairly easy" or "very easy" to get marijuana (Johnston et al., 2006). Perhaps even more startling, 41.1 percent of eighth graders said marijuana was relatively easy to get in 2005.

Of all the arrests made in 2004, 39 percent were for marijuana possession, and another 5 percent were for marijuana sale, production, or trafficking (Office of National Drug Control Policy, 2005). Although marijuana is usually not considered a "hard" and dangerous drug, it is illegal and can lead to conviction and incarceration, and its heavy use has been linked to a range of poor health outcomes similar to those of heavy cigarette smoking (Windel & Wiesner, 2004). Incarceration for possession, however, is rare, especially for a first offense.

TABLE 16–7   Percent of Students Reporting Marijuana Use, 2004–2005

	8th Grade		10th Grade		12th Grade	
	2004	2005	2004	2005	2004	2005
Past month	6.4%	6.6%	15.9%	15.2%	19.9%	19.8%
Past year	11.8	12.2	27.5	26.6	34.3	33.6
Lifetime	16.3	16.5	35.1	34.1	45.7	44.8

Source: Office of National Drug Control Policy, 2006a.

TABLE 16–8   Percent of College Students/Young Adults Using Marijuana, 2003–2004

	College Students		Young Adults	
	2003	2004	2003	2004
Past month	19.3%	18.9%	17.3%	16.5%
Past year	33.7	33.3	29.0	29.2
Lifetime	50.7	49.1	57.2	57.4

Source: Office of National Drug Control Policy, 2006a.

Marijuana, which apparently originated in Asia, is among the oldest and most frequently used intoxicants. The earliest reference to marijuana was found in a book on pharmacy written by the Chinese emperor Shen Nung in 2737 B.C. (Ray, 1972). It was called the "Liberator of Sin" and was recommended for such ailments as "female weakness," constipation, and absentmindedness. The word marijuana is commonly believed to have derived from "Mary Jane," Mexican slang for cheap tobacco, or from the Portuguese word *mariguano,* meaning intoxicant. Street names for the drug include pot, grass, reefer, weed, Mary Jane, and Acapulco gold.

How Is Marijuana Prepared?

The drug is prepared from the plant *cannabis,* an annual that is cultivated or grows freely as a weed in both tropical and temperate climates. There are at least three species of cannabis—sativa, indica, and ruderalis—each differing in psychoactive potency. The psychoactive (intoxicating) properties of the plant reside principally in the chemical Delta-9 tetrahydrocannabinol (THC), found mainly in its resin. Thus, the concentration and quality of THC within parts of the plant determine the potency or psychoactive power of the drug.

THC content varies from one preparation to another, partly due to the quality of the plant itself, but also due to its environment. The strain of the plant, the climate, and the soil conditions all affect THC content. For example, the resin is believed to retard the dehydration of the flowering elements and thus is produced in greater quantities in hot, tropical climates than in temperate zones. Consequently, cannabis grown in the tropics (Mexico, Columbia, Jamaica, and North Africa) presumably has greater psychoactive potential than American-grown hemp. More recent information suggests, however, that THC potency has become more a feature of the species of the cannabis plant than of geographic area or climatic conditions. Although marijuana produced in Mexico remains the most widely available in the United States, high-potency marijuana also enters the U.S. drug market from Canada (usually grown indoors). Domestically grown marijuana, either grown outdoors or indoors, also represents a substantial proportion of the U.S. drug market.

The THC content for Mexican commercial-grade marijuana ranges from 4 percent to 6 percent, whereas the higher-grade sinsemilla THC content ranges from 15 percent to 22 percent (Office of National Drug Control Policy, 2003e). *Sinsemilla* is the Spanish word for "without seed." The on-the-street cost for commercial-grade Mexican marijuana usually ranges from $100 to $200 per ounce, and high-potency sinsemilla marijuana may sell up to $1,200 an ounce (Office of National Drug Control Policy, 2003e).

The cannabis extracts used most commonly in the United States are marijuana and hashish. Marijuana is usually prepared by cutting the stem beneath the lowest branches, air drying, and stripping seeds, bracts, flowers, leaves, and small stems from the plant. There is evidence that the unpollinated female cannabis plant contains more THC than the male. Hashish, the Arabic word for "dry grass," is produced by scraping or in some other way extracting the resin secreted by the flowers. Therefore, hashish, which is usually sold in this country in small cubes, cakes, or even cookielike shapes, has more THC content than marijuana. During the 1990s the THC content of hashish averaged around 6 percent. Hashish or hash oil is produced by repeated extractions of cannabis plant materials, a process that results in a dark, viscous liquid with a THC content as high as 20 percent (Abadinsky, 1993) but usually averaging around 15 percent (Drug Enforcement Administration, 2000). One or two drops of hash oil on a cigarette provide the same psychoactive effects as a joint. When exposed to air over a period of time, marijuana appears to lose its psychoactive potency, since THC is converted to cannabinol and other inactive compounds (Mechoulam, 1970). Cannabis extracts with higher levels of resin deteriorate more rapidly than those with lower levels.

In the United States, marijuana and hashish are usually smoked, most often in hand-rolled cigarettes called "joints," or in hollowed-out commercial cigars called "blunts." It is still popular to lace the joint or blunt with other drugs, such as phencyclidine (PCP) or crack. A common practice in other countries is to consume cannabis as "tea," or mixed with other beverages or food.

The psychological effects of cannabis are so subjective and depend on such a wide range of variables that any generalizations must be accompanied by the warning that there are numerous exceptions. Reactions to cannabis, like all psychoactive drugs, depend on the complex interactions of both pharmacological and extrapharmacological factors. As we noted, these include the mood of the user, the user's expectations about the drug, the social context in which it is used, and the user's past experiences with the drug. The strong influence of these extrapharmacological factors together with the widespread variation in THC content in any sample of cannabis make it exceedingly difficult to obtain comparable research data. Essentially, the effects of cannabis are unique to each individual. Except for increases in heart rate, increases in peripheral blood flow, and reddening of the membranes around the eyes, there are few consistent physiological changes reported for all persons.

Addiction to THC does occur, but only at doses and continued use far above what is now used recreationally. Furthermore, the person who uses marijuana must learn to use the drug to reach a euphoric "stoned" or "high" state. Ray (1983) reports that a three-stage learning process is involved. First, users must inhale the smoke deeply and hold it in their lungs for approximately twenty seconds. Then they must learn to identify and control the effects. Finally, they must learn to label the effects as pleasant.

Cannabis and Crime

Numerous research projects directed at the effects of cannabis were launched during the 1950s, 1960s, and early 1970s. Many of these studies had methodological shortcomings and did not control for parity of dosage levels, means of administering the drug, and THC content in the drug itself. Psychological factors associated with the subjects were not considered carefully enough, and experimental settings and instructions were haphazard. At first, some of the research suggested a relationship between cannabis use and criminal behavior. However, with more sophisticated statistical analyses that controlled demographic and criminal background variables, the earlier results were found to be spurious (National Commission on Marihuana and Drug Abuse, 1972). To date no investigation has established a causal link between the use of cannabis and criminal activity (Walker, 2001). Of course this assertion excludes the illegal acts of selling, possessing, or using the drug.

Both independent research and investigations conducted by government-sponsored commissions strongly indicate that marijuana does not directly contribute to criminal behavior. After an extensive review of available literature, the National Commission on Marihuana and Drug Abuse (1972, p. 470) came to this conclusion: "There is no systematic empirical evidence, at least that is drawn from the American experience, to support the thesis that the use of marijuana either inevitably or generally causes, leads to or precipitates criminal, violent, aggressive, or delinquent behavior of sexual or nonsexual nature." The Commission Report (p. 470) adds, "If anything, the effects observed suggest that marijuana may be more likely to neutralize criminal behavior and to militate against the commission of aggressive acts."

One of the predominant effects of THC is relaxation and a marked decrease in physical activity (Tinklenberg & Stillman, 1970). THC induces muscular weakness and inability to sustain physical effort, so that the user wishes nothing more strenuous than to stay relatively motionless. As Tinklenberg and Stillman (1970, p. 341) note, "'being stoned' summarizes these sensations of demobilizing lethargy." It is difficult to imagine "stoned" users engaging in assaultive or violent activity. If anything, THC should reduce the likelihood of criminal activity, particularly aggressive conduct, as the Commission suggested. There is some evidence to support this conclusion.

Tinklenberg and Woodrow (1974) found that drug users who use mainly marijuana seem less inclined toward violence and aggression than their counterparts who prefer other drugs, such as alcohol or amphetamines. After examining drug usage among lower-class minority youth, Blumer and his associates (Blumer, Sutter, Ahmed, & Smith, 1967) made the same observation. In fact, they found that marijuana users deliberately shunned aggression and violence; in order to maintain one's status in the group, it was important to remain "cool" and nonaggressive, regardless of provocation.

Although the empirical evidence so far indicates that cannabis does not, as a rule, stimulate aggressive behavior or other criminal actions, whenever we deal with human behavior there will be exceptions. Individuals familiar with the effects of cannabis have heard of occasional negative experiences produced by THC. Although the phenomenon is rare, some people do report feelings of panic, hypersensitivity, feelings of being out of contact with their surroundings, and bizarre behavior. Some individuals have experienced rapid, disorganized intrusions of irrelevant thoughts, which prompted them to feel they were losing control of their mind. Under these conditions, it is plausible that one would interpret the actions of others as threatening. It is also possible that these panicked individuals might attack those surrounding them.

However, those who investigate cannabis effects usually agree that people who act violently under the influence of the drug were probably *predisposed* to act that way, with or without the drug (National Commission, 1972). The evidence indicates that violent marijuana users were violent prior to using cannabis. In other words they learned the behavioral pattern independently of cannabis. In addition, they have come to expect that the drug will "bring out" aggression or violence in them.

Summary

In summary, there is no solid evidence to indicate that cannabis contributes to or encourages violent or property crime, in spite of waning beliefs that this relationship exists. In fact there is evidence to suggest that cannabis users are less criminally or violently prone under the influence of the drug than users of other drugs, such as alcohol and amphetamines. There are also no supportive data that cannabis is habit forming to the point where the user must get a "fix" and will burglarize or rob to obtain funds to purchase the drug. Marijuana trafficking and distribution are also not fraught with the extensive systematic violence that accompanies other drugs of abuse. For most people the primary negative effect of marijuana use is diminished psychomotor performance, thereby putting the public safety at risk when someone intoxicated with marijuana drives a motor vehicle, boat, or operates machinery.

Marijuana certainly promotes relaxation and interferes with judgment, and probably makes people more daring and more prone to risk taking. It also alters the experience of reality and often improves mood. The drug is clearly used extensively as a recreation enhancer. As noted earlier nearly 50 percent of individuals arrested for a variety of offenses had been using marijuana just prior to or at the time of their offense, and it is also very popular among delinquents. Most likely, arrestees and detainees used the drug to improve their sense of well-being, frequently in combination with other drugs. And the drug is classified as a Schedule I drug by the DEA. Although it is illegal to produce, possess, sell, or consume marijuana, there is little evidence that the drug propels nonviolent people to become violent or antisocial, or to engage in some kind of serious criminal behavior.

Phencyclidine (PCP)

PCP may be classified as a central nervous system depressant, anesthetic, tranquilizer, or hallucinogen. It has many effects, but most pronounced is its barbiturate-like downer effect, perceptual distortions and hallucinations, and its amphetamine-like upper effects, such as excitation and hyperactivity. An overdosed person, for example, may show signs of moving from upper to downer effects while having hallucinations.

PCP was first synthesized in 1957, but due to its psychotic and hallucinogenic reactions, it was taken off the market for human consumption in 1965 and limited to veterinary medicine as an animal immobilizing agent. Because of its serious and numerous side effects, it is no longer used even in veterinary medicine. Between 1973 and 1979 its popularity increased, but then declined briefly between 1979 and 1981. Since 1982, however, it has showed a resurgence in popularity (Crider, 1986). Most users are male, African American, and between the ages of 20 and 29 (Crider, 1986). The behavior of some individuals under the influence of PCP is highly unpredictable and may lead to life-threatening situations. Under the spell of PCP psychosis, delusions of superhuman strength, persecution, and grandiosity are not uncommon. In general, PCPs are associated with a number of serious risks, and many experts believe it is one of the most dangerous illicit drugs on the streets. On occasion, individuals under the influence of PCP may use weapons to defend themselves and to commit other acts of violence.

There is wide variation in degree of purity and dosage forms of PCP manufactured in clandestine laboratories. It comes in capsules, tablets, liquids, or powders. It may be administered orally, by inhalation (snorted or smoked), and at times by intravenous injection. If it is smoked, PCP is often applied to leafy material such as mint, parsley, oregano, or marijuana. Users usually combine PCP with other drugs, particularly marijuana and alcohol. It can cause death, although the majority of fatal doses were combined with alcohol (Brunet, Reiffenstein, Williams, & Wong, 1985–1986). Because of its adverse and negative effects, the reasons for its popularity remain obscure. In addition, the popularity of PCP moves in cycles. In some years it is extremely popular, followed by limited use for a few years. The drug is marketed under a number of other names, including Angel Dust, Supergrass, Killer Weed, Embalming Fluid, and Rocket Fuel, because of its range of bizarre and volatile effects (Drug Enforcement Administration, 2005).

PCP and Crime

The available evidence clearly indicates that PCP users tend to be multiple illicit drug users (polydrug users). To what extent PCP propels a person toward a life of crime is largely unknown, but it does *not* seem likely that the PCP user regularly engages in crime to support his or her habit. PCPs are inexpensive, easily available, and only marginally addictive after chronic use. PCP users are generally polydrug users who have demonstrated a variety of types of antisocial conduct prior to PCP usage. Polydrug usage is more likely to be one symptom within a complicated matrix of other symptoms found in certain individuals habitually "going against" their environment. Currently phencyclidine is classified as a Schedule I drug of abuse by the DEA.

THE STIMULANTS

Amphetamines

Amphetamines and cocaine are classified as central nervous system stimulants and have highly similar effects. Amphetamines are part of a group of synthetic drugs known collectively as amines. Cocaine (coke, snow, candy) is a chemical extracted from the coca plant (Erythroxylon coca), an extremely hardy plant native to Peru. The amines in particular produce effects in the sympathetic nervous system, a subdivision of the autonomic nervous system, which arouse the person to actions that might include fighting or fleeing from a frightening situation. Amphetamines are traditionally classified into three major categories: (1) amphetamine (Benzedrine), (2) dextroamphetamine (Dexedrine), and (3) methamphetamine (Methedrine or Desoxyn). Of the three, Benzedrine is the least potent. All may be taken orally, inhaled, or injected, and all act directly on the central nervous system, particularly the reticular activating system.

Methamphetamine

In this section methamphetamine is the focus of the amphetamine group because it is the drug most preferred by drug users, and carries the most health risks. It is a Schedule II stimulant because it has a high potential for abuse and is available only through a prescription that cannot be refilled (National Institute on Drug Abuse, 2002). Methamphetamine has traditionally been the drug of preference when the user injects the substance directly into the bloodstream. More recently, though, the preferred method of consumption is by smoking, especially the crystallized form of methamphetamine known as "ice" (Maxwell, 2004). "Ice," also known as "shard," "shabu," "tweak," "crystal," "super ice," "LA glass," or "crystal meth," is methamphetamine that has been washed in solvent such as alcohol to remove the impurities. Evaporation of the solvent produces crystals that resemble glass shards or ice shavings. Some users prefer snorting the powder form of the drug. Snorting the drug affects the user in about five minutes, whereas the effects take a bit longer if smoked. If the user orally ingests the drug, the drug takes effect in about 20 minutes. The illegal form of the drug is manufactured in clandestine laboratories (meth labs or super labs). Methamphetamine is relatively easy to produce, and the ingredients can be purchased at local drug stores (Office of National Drug Control Policy, 2003b). Currently methamphetamine is the primary drug of abuse in rural America (Maxwell, 2004).

Methamphetamine produces an increase in alertness and a decrease in appetite. The effects may last as long as 12 hours. In high doses, the drug can cause violent behavior, anxiety, insomnia, and symptoms of paranoid behavior, including delusions, hallucinations, and mood swings. Some chronic users develop sores on their bodies from scratching "crank bugs," bugs that, under the user's delusional state, are believed to be crawling under the skin.

A form of methamphetamine that has appeared recently in the United States is methcathionone, known on the streets as "cat." It was classified as a Schedule I drug in 1993. The drug is usually snorted, although it can be taken orally by mixing it with some drink or injected intravenously. Its psychoactive effects are identical to those of methamphetamine.

Methylphenidate, a stimulant known as Ritalin, has a high potential for abuse and produces many of the same effects as methamphetamine. Many children who were diagnosed with attention deficit hyperactivity disorder take Ritalin to stabilize their behavior. Thus, Ritalin is considered easily accessible to children and adolescents who can obtain the drug from classmates or friends who have a prescription for it.

The amphetamines are synthetic compounds, and, unlike cannabis or cocaine, can be easily produced by self-appointed chemists for large-scale illegal distribution. The manufacture of methamphetamine, for example, requires precursor drugs (drugs that are necessary in the manufacture of another) such as ephedrine or pseudoephedrine, which are widely available in Mexico and are believed to be smuggled into the United States in large quantities (Feucht & Kyle, 1996). Over-the-counter cold medicines containing ephedrine or pseudoephedrine and other materials can also be "cooked" to make methamphetamine (Office of National Drug Control Policy, 1999b). Therefore, it is exceedingly difficult to estimate the quantity of amphetamines consumed each year in the Unites States. The Comprehensive Methamphetamine Act of 1996 was passed, among other things, to control the sale of ephedrine and pseudoephedrine.

TABLE 16–9   Percent of Students Reporting Methamphetamine Use, 2004–2005

	8th Grade		10th Grade		12th Grade	
	2004	2005	2004	2005	2004	2005
Past month	0.6%	0.7%	1.3%	1.1%	1.4%	0.9%
Past year	1.5	1.8	3.0	2.9	3.4	2.9
Lifetime	2.5	3.1	5.3	4.1	6.2	4.5

Source: Office of National Drug Control Policy, 2006b.

TABLE 16–10   Percent of College Students/Young Adults Using Methamphetamine, 2003–2004

	College Students		Young Adults	
	2003	2004	2003	2004
Past month	0.6%	0.2%	0.7%	0.6%
Past year	2.6	2.9	2.7	2.8
Lifetime	5.8	5.2	8.9	9.0

Source: Office of National Drug Control Policy, 2006b.

According to the 2004 National Survey on Drug Use and Health, approximately 11.7 million Americans ages 12 and older reported trying methamphetamine at least once during their lifetime (Substance Abuse and Mental Health Services Administration, 2005). The 2004–2005 data reported by the *2005 Monitoring the Future Study* indicates that crystal methamphetamine continues to be popular among high school seniors, although it has dropped since 2001 (Office of National Drug Control Policy, 2006b). The reported lifetime use of methamphetamine by high school seniors dropped from 12.8 percent in 2001 to 6.2 percent in 2005 (Office of National Drug Control Policy, 2006b). Available research indicates that the majority of methamphetamine users are male, white, and over age 26 (Office of National Drug Control Policy, 1999b). See **Tables 16–9** and **16–10**.)

Yaba, the Thai name for a tablet form of methamphetamine mixed with caffeine, is being used with some frequency in regions of California and is becoming popular in the rave scene as a club drug (Office of National Drug Control Policy, 2003b). These tablets are popular and produced in Southeast and East Asia.

Cocaine and Its Derivatives

Cocaine is the second most commonly used illicit drug (following marijuana in the United States (Drug Enforcement Administration, 2005)). Approximately 1.5 million Americans could be classified as dependent on or abusing cocaine (National Institute on Drug Abuse, 2004). Adults 18 to 25 years old have a higher rate of cocaine use than any other age group. Males are more likely to use the drug than females.

In general, there has been little change in the use of crack or powder cocaine between the years 2001 and 2005 among adolescents (Johnston et al., 2006). Perceived risk and disapproval of the drug among this age group has also been steady over the years. Nevertheless its use is still significant. In 2005, 5.1 percent of twelfth graders, 3.5 percent of tenth graders, and 2.2 percent of eighth graders had used cocaine over the previous 12 months (Office of National Drug Control Policy, 2006c) (see **Tables 16–11** and **16–12**). Additional data indicate that 1.9 percent of twelfth graders, 1.7 percent of tenth graders, and 1.4 percent

TABLE 16–11   Percent of Students Reporting Cocaine Use, 2004–2005

	8th Grade		10th Grade		12th Grade	
	2004	2005	2004	2005	2004	2005
Past month	0.9%	1.0%	1.7%	1.5%	2.3%	2.3%
Past year	2.0	2.2	3.7	3.5	5.3	5.1
Lifetime	3.4	3.7	5.4	5.2	8.1	8.0

Source: Office of National Drug Control Policy, 2006c.

of eighth graders used crack cocaine during the course of the year. According to the Drug Abuse Warning Network (DAWN) (Office of Applied Studies, 2004), cocaine was involved in one of every five of the drug-related visits to emergency departments of hospitals and clinics in 2003. In addition, the two drugs most consistently prevalent among detained juveniles in recent years have been marijuana and cocaine (McClelland, Teplin, & Abram, 2004).

In the United States and Canada, cocaine is usually administered nasally (sniffing), intravenously, or by inhaling (smoking). Cocaine taken orally is poorly absorbed because it is hydrolyzed (neutralized) by gastrointestinal secretions. Smoking cocaine was first tried in America around 1914, but the high temperature (198 degrees C) required to burn the chemical resulted in the destruction of most of its psychoactive properties (Inaba & Cohen, 1993). As a consequence, cocaine smoking (in the form of "crack") did not become popular in the United States until the mid-1970s. Cocaine reached considerable popularity and extensive use during 1980s and 1990s. Crack is produced in such a way that the cocaine ingredient can be smoked without destroying its potency. There is no safe way to use cocaine. Any route of administration can lead to toxic amounts, leading to acute cardiovascular or cerebrovascular emergencies that could lead to sudden death (National Institute of Drug Abuse, 2004).

In 2001, the wholesale price for powder cocaine ranged from $10,000 to $36,000 per kilogram, $400 to $1,800 per ounce, and $20 to $200 per gram (Office of National Drug Control Policy, 2003f). Prices for crack cocaine ranged from $2 to $40 per rock, with prices usually between $10 and $20 depending on the size of the rock (Office of National Drug Control Policy, 2006c). Slang names

TABLE 16–12   Percent of College Students/Young Adults Using Cocaine, 2003–2004

	College Students		Young Adults	
	2003	2004	2003	2004
Past month	1.9%	2.4%	2.4%	2.2%
Past year	5.4	6.6	6.6	7.1
Lifetime	9.2	9.5	14.7	15.2

Source: Office of National Drug Control Policy, 2006c.

for powder cocaine include candy sugar, pariba, aspirin, mojo, icing, happy dust, oyster stew, and double bubble.

Cocaine has traditionally been much more expensive than the amphetamines, partly because it is a natural organic substance and cannot be produced synthetically. It has to be grown under certain unusual conditions. The coca plant from which it is extracted thrives at elevations of two to eight thousand feet with heavy rainfall (one hundred inches per year). It is an evergreen shrub, growing to about three feet tall, and generally found on the eastern slopes of the Andes. It has long been used by Peruvians living in or near the Andes. Mountain natives chew coca leaves almost continuously and commonly keep them tucked in their cheek (Ray, 1972). Coca leaves are also used for tea. There are at least two hundred strains of coca plants, but the vast majority contain little if any cocaine. However, with the increasing appetite of North Americans for cocaine, South American growers and entrepreneurs have not only developed vast new areas for the cultivation of coca but also new, more vigorous strains of the plant (Inciardi, 1986).

Interestingly, it was believed that Coca-Cola contained cocaine as an active ingredient until 1903, when caffeine was substituted (Kleber, 1988). This assertion is vigorously denied by representatives of the company who insist there is no evidence for it. However, around the turn of the century, cocaine *was* used as an important stimulant in some "soft" drinks (such as Kos-Kola, Wiseola, and Care-Cola). It was also used in cigarettes and cigars, various tonics, foods, sprays, and ointments (including hemorrhoid salves) (Smart, 1986). The famous drink "Vin Mariani," so popular among the wealthy at the time, was a combination of vintage French wine and cocaine. However, cocaine began to fall into disfavor when people became concerned about its dangerous and undesirable effects. By 1910, cocaine had become the most hated and feared drug in North America (Kleber, 1988). The Harrison Narcotics Act of 1914 in the United States, and the Propriety and Patents Medicines Act of 1908 in Canada, sharply curtailed or terminated its usage, and the popularity of cocaine correspondingly declined until the 1960s.

Psychological Effects

In small doses, both amphetamines and cocaine increase wakefulness, alertness, and vigilance, improve concentration, and produce a feeling of clear thinking. There is generally an elevation of mood, mild euphoria, increased sociability, and a belief that one can do just about anything. The duration of the stimulant's euphoric effects depends on the route of administration. The faster the absorption into the bloodstream, such as inhaling cocaine vapor into the lungs rather than snorting the powder form, the more rapid and intense the psychoactive effects. Cocaine vapor is usually produced by igniting the powder form of cocaine. In large doses, the effects may be irritability, hypersensitivity, delirium, panic aggression, hallucinations, and psychosis. Hallucinations sometimes include "coke bugs" that appear to be crawling all over the body. Injected at chronically high doses, these drugs may precipitate "toxic psychosis," a syndrome with many of the psychotic features of paranoid schizophrenia. With the metabolization and elimination of the drug, the psychotic episode usually dissipates. Cocaine, like any psychoactive drug, will engender different experiences for different individuals. Some people under the influence will exhibit violent, erratic, paranoid, or even suicidal behavior; others will display peaceful, friendly, sociable behavior.

Adverse Physical Effects

Frequent cocaine use may have some strong adverse effects, depending on how it is administered. Regularly snorting cocaine can lead to a loss of sense of smell, nosebleeds, problems with swallowing, hoarseness, and inflammation of the nasal septum (National Institute on Drug Abuse, 1999). Orally consuming cocaine can cause severe bowel gangrene because of reduced blood flow to the gastrointestinal system. Injecting cocaine can generate some serious allergic reactions, and sometimes results in death. Cocaine is usually processed with a variety of volatile solvents, such as gasoline, benzene, and kerosene, and traces of these toxic substances often remain in the powder form of cocaine.

Cocaine often has a dramatic effect on the cardiovascular system, such as disturbances in heart rhythm and heart attacks. It can adversely affect the respiratory systems, resulting in chest pain or respiratory failure. And it can cause strokes, seizures, blurred vision, nausea, fever, muscle spasms, and coma. Cocaine users who frequently inject the drug are at risk for bacterial infections and other infectious diseases. Sharing needles and using unsterilized drug paraphernalia also puts users at considerable risk for HIV, hepatitis, and a variety of other viruses.

There is a potentially very dangerous drug interaction between cocaine and alcohol that should be noted. When the user ingests cocaine and alcohol at once or closely together, the drugs are converted by the body to cocethylene. Cocethylene is substantially more toxic than either drug alone, and available evidence indicates that the mixture of cocaine and alcohol is the most common two-drug combination that results in drug-related death (National Institute on Drug Abuse, 1999).

Partly because of these many serious adverse effects, there has been a downward trend in cocaine use in recent years (National Institute on Drug Abuse, 2000). In 1997, an estimated 1.5 million Americans (0.7% of the entire population) age 12 and older were chronic cocaine users, a significant drop from 1985 when there were 5.7 million chronic users (3% of the population) (National Institute on Drug Abuse, 1999).

Stimulants, Cocaine, and Crime

As pointed out, heavy users of amphetamines typically prefer to inject methamphetamine directly into the bloodstream, cranking up with several hundred milligrams at one time. During these speed "runs" the user may engage in aggressive or violent behavior (Hofmann, 1975; National Commission on Marihuana and Drug Abuse, 1973; Tinklenberg & Stillman, 1970). However, it appears that people who behave violently under the effects of amphetamines are very often predisposed to behave violently long before they ingested amphetamines. In other words there is little evidence to conclude that amphetamines cause people to behave violently, but they do increase the likelihood that an already prone person will behave violently. As the data in the tables at the beginning of the chapter reveal, very few arrestees test positive for amphetamine use at the time of their arrest.

Research by the Arrestees Drug Abuse Monitoring program consistently reveals, however, that persons arrested frequently test positive for cocaine. **Tables 16–1** and **16–4** (on pages 523 and 528) suggest, for example, that cocaine-based drugs, including crack, are second only to marijuana in drug abuse in the United States. Both amphetamines and cocaine are considered Schedule II drugs by the DEA. In small doses these drugs increase alertness and concentration. In large doses, they generally produce negative psychological effects. But, to date, virtually no study has shown that stimulants or cocaine facilitate either property crime or violent crime. In an exhaustive review of the literature, the Panel on the Understanding and Control of Violent Behavior concluded, "There is no evidence to support the claim that snorting or injecting cocaine stimulates violent behavior." Morgan and Zimmer (1997) also conclude that there is very little convincing evidence that cocaine, either in crack or powder form, causes a nonviolent person to suddenly become violent or dangerous to others. Nor is there any evidence to support the assumption that cocaine, especially crack, causes women to abuse their children. It is more likely the lifestyle of the parent, rather than simply the pharmacologically driven aspect of the drug, that leads to child abuse (Morgan & Zimmer, 1997).

Powder cocaine, however, can be strongly addictive, and the dependence onset can be rapid and severe. It is also expensive, and acquisition of the drug must be accomplished through organized distribution and selling. In other words, powder cocaine is one of the drugs of abuse that encourages systematic violence on a wide scale. In addition, some cocaine abusers may have a difficult time controlling their habit and may rapidly build a tolerance to the drug, requiring larger and larger amounts of the costly drug. Some cocaine users may be forced to engage in shoplifting, theft, drug dealing, and prostitution to support their habit. **Table 16–3** shows percentages of detained adult arrestees testing positive for various drugs. The table suggests that in the U.S. cocaine is the hard drug most commonly used by offenders during the commission of a crime.

Crack Cocaine

The most common method of cocaine smoking in the United States is freebasing. Freebase is prepared by dissolving cocaine hydrochloride in water, and then adding a strong base such as ammonia or baking soda to the solution (Weiss &

Mirin, 1987). This cocaine freebase is generally dissolved in ether to extract the cocaine, and then the ether is removed by drying the solution. Other methods may be used that bypass the ether method by heating the mixture. The drying process produces crystalline, smokable pellets or nuggets. The result is a product ranging from 37 percent to 96 percent purity (Weiss & Mirin, 1987).

During the 1980s, a purified, high-potency form of freebase cocaine—known as crack—exploded in popularity. It was, according to Howard Abadinsky (1993), the drug abuser's answer to fast food. The drug is called "crack" because it makes a crackling sound when smoked (Abadinsky, 1993; Gold, 1984). Crack is several times more pure than ordinary street cocaine, and crack smoking generates a very rapid, intense state of euphoria, which peaks in about five minutes. The psychological and physical effects of crack are as powerful as any intravenously injected cocaine. However, the euphoria is short-lived, ending in about 10 to 20 minutes after inhalation, and is followed by depression, irritability, and often an intense craving for more. It is also extremely dangerous to the user and may result in a rapid and irregular heartbeat, respiratory failure, seizures, or a cerebral hemorrhage. Although most users limit themselves to one or two hits, some users seek multiple hits. Crack smokers, in order to stay high, often find a place where crack can be safely smoked, such as a crack house, because the smoke and smell are difficult to hide.

During the 1980s crack cocaine generated much concern to local officials across the United States because of its popularity, illegal drug trafficking, and health hazards to adolescents and young adults. At one point some experts regarded crack as the most addictive drug currently available on the street (Weiss & Mirin, 1987). This assumption has been seriously questioned by many research scientists in recent years (Morgan & Zimmer, 1997). Furthermore, it was thought that the craving for the drug might become so severe for some individuals that the user would lie, steal, or commit acts of violence in order to obtain more of the drug (Rosecan, Spitz, & Gross, 1987). Its popularity probably resided in the instantaneous psychological effects it provides, its inexpensiveness, and its wide availability throughout most major U.S. cities. The drug also provided tremendous profitability for the sellers. For a while, about one-third of all arrests made by the New York City Narcotics Division involved cocaine, and over half of them involved crack (Cohn, 1986). Because it was so inexpensive and available, it became a very popular drug for the young—including preteenagers.

Beginning in the early 1990s, the use of crack cocaine began to decline (Golub & Johnson, 1997). The reasons for the decline are multiple, but the most prominent appear to be its health risks and the changes in attitude among the new generation concerning its use. The youth today consider crack users "dumb" and "crackhead" a dirty word (Golub & Johnson, 1997). In some cities, many youths abuse crackheads or avoid them altogether. Overall, it appears that the primary users of crack cocaine who began using the drug during the 1980s continue to be the heavy users of the drug today. However, the more recent generation of youth called "Generation X" tend to avoid using the drug.

Crack and Crime

The relationship between crack and crime remains obscure. One thing that does emerge from the research literature is that crack users, especially persistent users, are often polydrug users. Surveys indicate that virtually all crack users have been frequent users of other drugs, and most also had an extensive history of prior drug use, drug selling, and nondrug criminality (Golub & Johnson, 1997). While it is difficult at this point in our knowledge to determine which comes first, drug use or involvement in crime, the evidence does suggest that persistent offenders have engaged in a variety of illegal activities and troublesome conduct throughout their lifetimes, probably before extensive drug abuse. One thing appears clear, though: Crack use by itself does not appear to cause violent behavior in normally nonviolent people (Golub & Johnson, 1997; Morgan & Zimmer, 1997).

The association between the crack cocaine black market and systemic violence, on the other hand, is a different matter. The production, distribution, and selling of powder and crack cocaine has been associated with violence for some time, although the amount of violence fluctuates with the illicit market economy.

Ecstasy (MDMA)

MDMA or "ecstasy" is a synthetic drug (completely manufactured rather than grown or occurring naturally) that is considered a stimulant, but it also has some strong psychedelic properties similar to methamphetamine and mescaline. MDMA is an abbreviation for 3-4 methylenedioxy-methamphetamine. It is sometimes confused with a similar compound 3, 4-methylenedioxyamphetamine, abbreviated MDA. The effects and pharmacological actions of MDA are similar but not identical to MDMA (Maxwell, 2004). Both MDMA and MDA are classified as Schedule I drugs. Other drugs confused with ecstasy include para-methoxyamphetamine (PMA) and p-methylthioamphetamine (MTA). These are substances packaged as ecstasy with the similar psychoactive properties and associated with several deaths, especially in Europe (Maxwell, 2004).

The use of ecstasy (also known as Adam, E, X, eccie) increased sharply among teenagers during the late 1990s, reaching its peak in 2001. Since that time there has been a steady moderate decease in popularity, but its popularity still remains high. In 2005, about 1.7 percent of eighth graders, 2.6 percent of tenth graders, and 3 percent of twelfth graders indicated they used the drug at least once during the year (Office of National Drug Control Policy, 2006d) (see **Table 16–13**). Sixteen percent of eighth graders and 40 percent of the twelfth graders said it was "fairly easy" or "very easy" to obtain in 2005 (Johnston, O'Malley, Bachman, & Schulenberg, 2006).

MDMA was first manufactured by a German company in 1912 to be used as a possible appetite depressant. The drug acquired some popularity in the 1990s as the "rave culture" swept over Europe's youth. MDMA is often referred to as a club drug because it is commonly used at all-night dance parties known

TABLE 16–13   Percent of Students Reporting MDMA Use, 2004–2005

	8th Grade		10th Grade		12th Grade	
	2004	2005	2004	2005	2004	2005
Past month	0.8%	0.6%	0.8%	1.0%	1.2%	1.0%
Past year	1.7	1.7	2.4	2.6	4.0	3.0
Lifetime	2.8	2.8	4.3	4.0	7.5	5.4

Source: Office of National Drug Control Policy, 2006g.

as "raves." Being under the drug's effects is often referred to as "rolling" because of the up-and-down rolling of emotions it engenders. In this sense the drug produces a unique sense of well-being, affection, and love (Strote, Lee, & Wechsler, 2002). It is normally taken in tablet, capsule, or powder form. Depending on the dosage, the drug's effects usually last between four and six hours.

The common psychological effects of MDMA include confusion, depression, anxiety, sleeplessness, drug cravings, and paranoia (Office of National Drug Control Policy, 2000a). Its adverse physical side effects include muscle tension, involuntary clenching of the teeth, nausea, blurred vision, faintness, tremors, sweating, and chills. Baby pacifiers are often used by ecstasy users to prevent danger to or excessive grinding of the teeth. Inhalation of Vicks VapoRub is also sometimes used to enhance the drug's psychedelic effects. MDMA may also predispose users to participate in high-risk behavior (Moreland, 2000).

The drug's stimulation properties provide an "energy rush" that encourages users to stay physically active for long periods of time, such as dancing all night at rave parties. Although the drug is considered safer than many other illicit drugs, there are physical risks. At very high doses, MDMA can cause the body temperature to rise as high as 110 degrees, leading to muscle breakdown and kidney or cardiovascular failure (National Institute on Drug Abuse, 2000). Also all-night raves and extensive dancing in crowded and overheated rooms pose the danger of producing not only high body temperatures but also dangerous levels of dehydration. Other adverse side effects of MDMA include hearing and liver damage, strokes, and long-term brain injury (National Institute of Health, 1999).

The majority of MDMA found in the United States comes from clandestine laboratories in Western Europe (primarily Netherlands and Belgium). MDMA is usually consumed in tablet form and takes effect within 30 to 45 minutes. It is estimated that 2 million tablets are smuggled into the United States every week (Drug Enforcement Administration, 2005).

Stimulants and Crime

The relationship between stimulants and crime and delinquency has many facets. One thing that emerges clearly from the research literature is that heavy stimulants users, especially those who heavily use crack cocaine, are often polydrug users (National Institute on Drug Abuse, 2004). Furthermore, persistent offenders tend to be polydrug users. Although it is difficult at this point in our knowledge to determine which comes first, drug use or involvement in delinquency or crime, the evidence strongly suggests that persistent offenders have engaged in a variety of illegal activities and troublesome conduct throughout their lifetimes, most probably beginning before the onset of drug or alcohol abuse.

NARCOTIC DRUGS

The word **narcotics** usually prompts intense negative reactions and very often is quickly associated with crime. Like the word *dope,* it is widely misused to denote all illegal drugs. In this chapter, narcotic drugs refer only to the derivatives of or products pharmacologically similar to the products of the opium or poppy plant, *Papaver sominferum.*

The opium plant, an annual, grows to about three to five feet in height. Today most opium is grown in Afghanistan, which produces approximately 75 percent of the world's opium and opium-based narcotics (Bureau of International Narcotics and Law Enforcement Affairs, 2000). However, the opium poppies that are of most concern to the United States are grown principally in Columbia and Mexico. Although these two countries together cultivate less than 6 percent of the world's total opium, most of the heroin found in the United States is from Columbian or Mexican suppliers. In fact, Mexico serves as the transit and distribution center for most of the drugs moving into this country.

Narcotic drugs can be divided into three major categories on the basis of the kind of preparation they require: (1) **natural narcotics,** which include the grown opium; (2) **semisynthetic narcotics,** which include the chemically prepared heroin; and (3) **synthetic narcotics,** which are wholly prepared chemically and include methadone, meperidine, and phenazocine. All are narcotics because they produce similar effects: relief of pain, relaxation, peacefulness, and sleep (*narco,* of Greek origin, means "to sleep"). The narcotics are highly addictive for some individuals; they develop a relentless and strong craving for the drug. Many heavy narcotic users, however, lead successful, productive lives, without significant interference in their daily routine. There is no single type of opium user.

Heroin

The most heavily used illegal *narcotic* in this country is heroin. During the 1970s, it was estimated that there were 400,000 to 600,000 heroin addicts in any given year. During the 1990s, it is estimated that there were 229,000 "casual" users and 500,000 "heavy" users per year (Epstein & Gfroerer, 1997). Data from the 2004 National Survey on Drug Use and Health indicate that 1.4 percent of Americans (3.1 Million), ages 12 and older, had used heroin at least once in their lifetime, and approximately 186,000 Americans who said they had used heroin within the month preceding the survey (Office of National Drug Control Policy, 2006e). (See **Tables 16–14** and **16–15** for self-reported student use.) It is a safe bet, however, that any self-report survey underestimates the actual drug use by the respondents. However, more complete estimates conclude that there are 980,000 heroin addicts and 1.2 million casual users in the United States (Bureau of International Narcotics and Law Enforcement Affairs, 2000).

Many cocaine users use heroin to cushion the "crash" that often follows the "rush" of using crack. The 1998 Drug Abuse Warning Network (DAWN), which collects data on drug-related hospital emergency departments, reported that 14 percent of all drug-related emergencies involved heroin.

Heroin continues to be widely available in almost all areas of the country, although its purity varies considerably from region to region. Most of the heroin seized in 1999 east of the Mississippi River was of Columbian origin, whereas most of the drugs seized west of the Mississippi were of Mexican origin (Bureau of International Narcotics and Law Enforcement Affairs, 2000). High-quality heroin from Afghanistan continues to move in large quantities into Europe, Russia, and other countries of the former Soviet Union. In recent years, a considerable and increasing amount of heroin is being produced in Southwest and Southeast Asia (Office of National Drug Control Policy, 2006e).

The heroin "bag" may be a glassine bag, capsules or "pills," or balloons. When heroin is sold by the "bag," its price does not always vary according to its purity. For example, the time of day it is sold or the geographic area may strongly influence the price due to the risks of detection perceived by the seller. Usually, heroin looks like a white, crystalline material and is characterized by the bitter taste of alkaloid. Its appearance is largely dictated by its diluents, which in most cases make up 95 percent to 98 percent of its total weight. In some instances, heroin will have a dark brown appearance due to the impurities left from the manufacturing process or the presence of additives.

Despite the popularity of cocaine, heroin still reigns as the illicit or hard drug of choice in much of the world. Mexican "black tar" heroin has hit the streets in recent years. It is a dark brown substance that has the appearance of black tar and is sticky like roofing tar or, in some instances, hard like coal. The color and consistency of black tar heroin is due to the crude processing methods used to manufacture the drug. High-quality Mexican black tar heroin sells for $600 to $800 per gram, and ranges in purity from 20 percent to 80 percent.

TABLE 16–14 Percent of Students Reporting Lifetime Heroin Use, 2001–2005

	2001	2003	2005
9th grade	3.2%	3.5%	2.8%
10th grade	3.3	2.9	2.5
11th grade	2.8	3.0	1.8
12th grade	3.0	2.9	2.0
Total	3.1	3.3	2.4

Source: Office of National Drug Control Policy, 2006e.

TABLE 16–15   College Students/Young Adults Reporting Heroin Use, 2003–2004

	College Students		Young Adults	
	2003	2004	2003	2004
Past month	<.05%	0.1%	0.1%	0.1%
Past year	0.2	0.4	0.4	0.3
Lifetime	1.0	0.9	1.9	1.9

Source: Office of National Drug Control Policy, 2006e.

In many areas, heroin users combine heroin with cocaine powder (HCl) or with crack, and then inject the mixture. As mentioned earlier, this practice is known as "speedballing." In some regions, particularly in the West, users often mix heroin and methamphetamine and then inject. Heroin is rarely taken orally, because the absorption rate is slow and incomplete. It may be administered intramuscularly, subcutaneously ("skin popping"), or intravenously ("mainlining"), or it may be inhaled ("snorted"). Heroin inhalers usually choose to use heroin and crack simultaneously.

In the past, experienced heroin users strongly preferred mainlining because of the sensational thrill, splash, rush, or kick it provided. Injection is probably the most practical and efficient way to administer low-purity heroin. Injection works fast. Intravenous injection provides the most intense and rapid feeling of euphoria, working within seven to eight seconds after injection. Intramuscular injection is slower, taking about five to eight minutes for peak effect. However, in recent years, the dramatic increase in heroin purity has changed the preferred method of administration. The high purity of Columbian heroin available in much of the eastern United States allows the user to snort or sniff the substance like cocaine. In New York, for example, cocaine and heroin are often alternately inhaled, a practice called "criss-crossing." The quality of heroin today also allows it to be smoked. Sniffing or smoking cocaine is often preferred over injections now that the fear of contracting AIDS or hepatitis from infected needles is so widespread. When heroin is snorted or smoked, peak effects are usually experienced within ten to fifteen minutes.

The effects of heroin depend on the quantity taken, the method of administration, the interval between administrations, the tolerance and dependence of the user, the setting, and the user's expectations. Effects usually wear off in five to eight hours, depending on the user's tolerance. In 1999, heroin-related deaths were rising due to the decreasing price and to the potency of the drug, resulting from significant increases in the purity of Columbian heroin.

Like all the narcotics, heroin is a central nervous system depressant. For many users it promotes mental clouding, dreamlike states, light sleep punctuated by vivid dreams, and a general feeling of "sublime contentment." The body may become permeated with a feeling of warmth, and the extremities may feel heavy. There is little inclination toward physical activity; the user prefers to sit motionless and in a fog.

Heroin and Crime

No other drug group is as closely associated with crime as the narcotics, particularly heroin. The image of the desperate "junkie" looking for a fix is widespread. Furthermore, because of the adverse effects of the drug, it is assumed that the heroin user is bizarre, unpredictable, and therefore dangerous. However, high doses of narcotics produce sleep rather than the psychotic or paranoid panic states sometimes produced by high doses of amphetamines. Therefore, narcotics users rarely become violent or dangerous. Research strongly indicates that addicts do not, as a general rule, participate in violent crimes such as assault, rape, or homicide (Canadian Government's Commission of Inquiry, 1971; National Commission on Marihuana and Drug Abuse, 1973; National Institute on Drug Abuse, 1978; Tinklenberg & Stillman, 1970).

Research evidence does suggest a relationship between heroin addiction and money-producing crime. A study in Miami of 573 narcotics users found that they were responsible for almost 6,000 robberies, 6,700 burglaries, 900 stolen vehicles, 25,000 instances of shoplifting, and 46,000 other events of larceny and fraud (Inciardi, 1986). Self-report surveys find that heroin users report financing their habits largely through "acquisitive crime" (Jarvis & Parker, 1989; Mott, 1986). Parker and Newcombe (1987) studied crime patterns and heroin use in the English community of Wirral, located in northwest England. They found that many heroin users were from the poor sections of the community and were young. The researchers were also able to divide their sample into three groups: (1) the largest group, consisting of young offenders who were not known to be using heroin but were highly criminally active; (2) heroin users who engaged in considerable acquisitive crime, but were involved in this type of crime prior to their heroin addiction; and (3) heroin users who started engaging in acquisitive crime after developing their habit in order to support the habit. The Parker-Newcombe investigation suggests that some heroin addicts do support their habit through crime.

Ball, Shaffer, and Nurco (1983) found that heroin addicts committed more money-producing crime when they were addicted compared with times when they were not. Still, it may be misleading to examine the heroin-crime relationship in isolation without considering the possible interactions between polydrug use and crime, or to conclude that heroin addiction causes crime. All we can say with some confidence at this point is that those who use heroin also seem to be deeply involved in money-producing crime. Heroin users, however, may not be driven to crime by the needs of their addiction. Heroin users, particularly polydrug users, may represent a segment of society that runs counter to society's rules and expectations in multiple ways, drug use and larceny among them. It may well be that most heroin-addicted criminals were involved in crime before they became addicted. Research by Faupel (1991) does support this hypothesis. However, studies also suggest that, although many heroin users have criminal records prior to their addiction, their criminal activity increases substantially during periods of heavy drug consumption (Faupel, 1991). Furthermore, polydrug users tend to switch from drug to drug, depending on what is available and inexpensive at the time, and do not seem physiologically desperate for any one particular drug. They simply substitute one drug for the other. Overall, the relationship between heroin use and criminal behavior is a complex one and varies throughout the addict's career.

Fentanyl

Fentanyl, first synthesized in Belgium in the late 1950s (under the trade name of Sublimaze), is highly similar to heroin in its biological and psychological effects. Fentanyl is a synthetic opiate about 50 times more potent than heroin. It is normally produced as a powder, and, on the market, it is often mixed with heroin and to a lesser extent with cocaine. It may be administered by intravenous injection, smoked, or snorted, but intravenous injection is currently the preferred method. According to the National Drug Intelligence Center (2006), the drug has been linked to hundreds of fatal and nonfatal doses across the United States during 2005 and 2006. An intravenous dose of fentanyl hydrochloride for pain relief is about 45 micrograms, depending on the weight of the user, but careless use can lead to an overdose and possible death.

Other Narcotic Drugs

Other drugs that are often classified as narcotics include thebaine, codeine, morphine, hydromorphone, oxycodone, and hydrocodone. Thebaine is chemically similar to both morphine and codeine, but generally produces a high rather than depressant effects. It is considered a Schedule II drug. Hydromorphone (Dilaudid) is a powerful analgesic that is sold in tablet or injectable forms as a painkiller, and may substitute for heroin or morphine. Oxycodone is similar to codeine but more powerful. It is often marketed in combination with aspirin (Percodan) or acetaminophen (Percocet) for the relief of pain. Hydrocodone is an orally active analgesic slightly less powerful than morphine.

Although oxycodone products have been illicit abuse for the 30 years, the oxycodone derivative OxyContin, has been used frequently in recent years.

OxyContin

OxyContin (oxycodone) is a narcotic that has the properties of a powerful analgesic for pain control. It is a drug that is growing in popularity with young people (Johnston et al., 2006). OxyContin is classified as an opioid analgesic that is available through prescription. The drug is chemically classified as an opiate agonist because it provides pain relief by acting on opioid receptors in the spinal cord and brain. It was approved in 1995 by the Food and Drug Administration for use as an analgesic in persons with moderate to severe pain requiring several days of relief or more (Cicero, Inciardi, & Muñoz, 2005). The drug is synthesized from thebaine, a minor constituent of opium. OxyContin comes

TABLE 16–16   DEA OxyContin Investigations/Arrests, 2000–2003

	2001	2002	2003
Investigations	172	140	71
Arrests	202	179	141

Source: Office of National Drug Control Policy, 2006f.

generally in tablet form, but some abusers crush the tablets and sniff the powder or dissolve the tablets in water for injection.

It usually comes in the form of a time-release tablet and acts for 12 hours, making it the longest lasting oxycodone on the market. The pharmacological effects of OxyContin are highly similar to heroin, and consequently tend to be attractive to the same abuser population (National Drug Intelligence Center, 2001).

OxyContin abuse is by far the most prevalent and widespread abuse of all the opioids and prescription drugs in the United States, and it shows no signs of declining at this time (Cicero et al., 2005). The abuse of drug is found almost exclusively by white persons (91%), especially those living in rural and suburban areas (Cicero et al., 2005). Interestingly, studies have discovered an overall increase across the country in the abuse of prescription drugs in general (Cicero et al., 2005). This is believed to be because prescription drugs are relatively easy to obtain compared with other illicit drugs, especially in rural areas.

In 2004, 5.5 percent of twelfth graders, 3.2 percent of tenth graders, and 1.8 percent of eighth graders reported using OxyContin at least once during the year. It is also being used by significant number of college students as well.

OxyContin and Crime

OxyContin abuse has led to an significant increase in the number of pharmacy robberies, thefts, fraudulent prescriptions, and health care fraud incidents during the early 2000s (National Drug Intelligence Center, 2001), but in recent years the numbers have decreased significantly (see **Table 16–16**). It also obtained through what is called "doctor shopping" and improper prescription practices by physicians. Doctor shopping refers to individuals visit numerous doctors, sometimes in several states, to acquire large amounts of the drug to use or sell to others.

THE CLUB DRUGS: SEDATIVE HYPNOTIC COMPOUNDS

Rohypnol, gamma-hydroxybutryrate (GHB), ecstasy (MDMA), ketamine, and methamphetamine have been considered the "club drugs" in recent years (Maxwell, 2004). They are called "club drugs" because they are most often consumed at teenage and young adult nightclubs, raves, or parties. Although club drugs have attracted considerable national attention, they comprise a relatively small proportion of the drug problem in the United States. Since we covered ecstasy and methamphetamine earlier in the chapter, we shall concentrate on the three sedative hypnotics in this section: ketamine, rohypnol and GHB.

Ketamine

Ketamine, also called "K," "Special K," "Super Acid," "LA Coke," or "cat valium," is a dissociative anesthetic with analgesic and amnestic properties. It was developed in 1962 to replace PCP in veterinary medicine. The drug was first manufactured in the United States in 1960s as Ketalar (Copeland & Dillon, 2005). Use of ketamine as a surgical anesthetic gained significant popularity on the battlefields of Vietnam (Copeland & Dillon, 2005). Much of the ketamine sold on the street in the United States is probably intended for veterinary clinics or is imported from overseas. When sold illicitly it is often converted from a liquid to a powder—similar in appearance to cocaine and heroin—or tablets. Reports have found that ketamine is increasingly being used in social rather than medical and scientific settings in many parts of the world, especially the United Kingdom and Australia (Copland & Dillon, 2005). It is often considered a "club drug" or "dance drug" because it is used at "raves" or dance parties, a popular scene for teenagers. Ketamine is also frequently used as a key component in fake MDMA (ecstasy) tablets.

Its chemical structure is similar to PCP but is much less potent and produces less confusion, irrationality, and violent behavior than PCP (Drug Enforcement Administration, 2005). As drug of abuse, ketamine can be administered orally, snorted, or injected. It sometimes is sprinkled on marijuana and smoked. High doses produce analgesia, amnesia, and coma.

Users report sensations ranging from a pleasant feeling of floating or being separated from their bodies (National Institute on Drug Abuse, 2005). It carries slang names such as jet, super acid, cat Valium, and honey oil. Approximately 50 percent of ketamine users have had a bad experience with the drug called the "K-hole" (Copeland & Dillon, 2005).

Ketamine is odorless and tasteless, so it can be added to beverages or food without being detected. Ketamine, along with GHB, is considered a "date rape" drug because it can be given to unsuspecting victims, inducing amnesia and a helpless physical state. Under these conditions, sexual assault can be carried out with the victim being unable to remember the incident.

According to the 2005 Monitoring the Future Survey, 1.6 percent of twelfth graders, 1 percent of tenth graders, and 0.6 percent of eighth graders reported using the drug during 2005 (Johnston et al., 2006) (see **Table 16–17**).

Gamma Hydroxbutyrate (GHB)

GHB (also known as "liquid ecstasy," "scoop," "liquid X," "grievous bodily harm" or "Georgia home boy") is a powerful and fast-acting drug most often taken by young users as a pleasure enhancer that produces a rapid state of intoxication.

TABLE 16–17   Percent of Students Reporting Past Year GHB/Ketamine Use, 2004–2005

	8th Grade		10th Grade		12th Grade	
	2004	2005	2004	2005	2004	2005
GHB	0.7%	0.5%	0.8%	0.8%	2.0%	1.1%
Ketamine	0.9	0.6	1.3	1.0	1.9	1.6

Source: Office of National Drug Control Policy, 2006g.

It is usually consumed orally, either as a grainy white- or sandy-colored powder that is often dissolved in alcohol, or as a liquid sold in small bottles. GHB is produced primarily in clandestine laboratories, and consequently there is no guarantee of quality or purity, making its psychoactive effects unpredictable. The drug can be easily produced by combining gammabutyrolactone (GBL) with either potassium hydroxide or sodium hydroxide in a container. Recipes or kits for making GHB are sold over the Internet. GHB is also marketed as an antidepressant that suppresses feelings of depression and anxiety, and is promoted and sold on the Internet as such. Prior to 1990, the drug was freely available in health food stores across the United States. However, in 1990 the Federal Drug Administration (FDA) banned GHB and does not approve the drug for any use at the present time. However, a pharmaceutical formulation of the drug is currently being developed for the treatment of cataplexy, a serious and debilitating disease.

Psychoactive effects of GHB begin to take effect within 15 to 30 minutes after consumption, and, depending on purity and dosage, may last as long as 6 hours. It is often used in conjunction with other drugs, especially alcohol. GHB has many severe and unpredictable side effects, such as nausea, drowsiness, vomiting, delusions, depression, vertigo (dizziness), hallucinations, seizures, respiratory distress, loss of consciousness, slowed heart rate, lowered blood pressure, amnesia, and coma (Office of National Drug Control Policy, 1999a). It also interferes with circulation, motor coordination, and balance, and, at higher doses (two to four grams), it produces considerable problems in motor and speech control. At these high doses, GHB usually produces a very deep sleep, resembling a coma. The drug also produces anterograde amnesia, a condition in which events that occurred during the time the drug was in effect are forgotten. In addition, the drug has increasingly been involved in poisonings, overdoses, and fatalities (National Institute on Drug Abuse, 1999).

GHB is tasteless and odorless, and mixes easily with alcohol or any nonalcoholic drink. Because it can be mixed with food and drinks without detection, and because of its ability to sedate and intoxicate unsuspecting victims, GHB has been connected to crime in recent years. It is sometimes used in the commission of sexual assault, and it often plays a role in "date rape." It is also used in some instances to pave the way for robbing heavily sedated or unconscious victims.

Because of its increasing use in sexual assaults, the Date-Rape Drug Prohibition Act of 2000 (also known as the Hillary J. Farias and Samantha Reid Date Drug Prohibition Act of 2000) was enacted in January 2000, specifically to target GHB. Congress found that the abuse of illicit gamma hydroxybutyrate acid was an imminent hazard to public safety, and moved to amend the federal *Controlled Substances Act* to include the drug as an illegal substance. The act also established a special unit of the Drug Enforcement Administration to assess the abuse of and trafficking in GHB, Rohypnol, ketamine, other controlled substances, and other so-called "designer drugs" whose use has been associated with sexual assault.

Rohypnol

The Drug Induced Rape Prevention and Punishment Act of 1996 was enacted into federal law specifically in response to the use of Rohypnol (generic name flunitrazepam), another club drug that can be used to sexually assault incapacitated individuals. It can mentally and physically incapacitate the victim. The law makes it a crime to give someone a controlled substance without his or her knowledge and with the intent to commit a crime. The law further imposes a penalty of up to 20 years for the distribution and importation of one gram or more of Rohypnol. Simple possession is punishable by up to three years in prison and a fine.

Since 1999, Rohypnol tablets have been manufactured to turn blue in a drink to increase visibility and thus more visually detectable to potential victims (Office of National Drug Control Policy, 2003a). However, the noncolored tablets continue to be on the market. Furthermore, persons who intend to commit a sexual assault may try to serve blue tropical drinks and punches so that the blue dye can be hidden.

Slang names for Rohypnol include date-rape drug, circles, roofies, Mexican valium, roach-2, forget-me drug, forget pill, or wolfies. Rohypnol is popular among youth because of its low costs, which is usually less than $5 to $10 per tablet (Office of National Drug Control Policy, 2003a). Rohypnol can be ground into a powder and snorted. Similar to GHB, Rohypnol is tasteless and odorless, and can be dissolved in liquids, but not as easily as GHB, and is also sometimes used by bodybuilders for its alleged anabolic effects. It can be taken orally,

Table 16–18   Percent of Students Reporting Rohypnol Use, 2004–2005

	8th Grade		10th Grade		12th Grade	
	2004	2005	2004	2005	2004	2005
Past month	0.2%	0.2%	0.3%	0.2%	n/a	n/a
Past year	0.6	0.7	0.7	0.5	1.6	1.2
Lifetime	1.0	1.1	1.2	1.0	n/a	n/a

Source: Office of National Drug Control Policy, 2006g.

snorted, or injected. It is often combined with alcohol or used as a remedy for the depression that often follows a stimulant high. The effects of Rohypnol usually begin in about 15 minutes after administration, and may last for more than 12 hours. In addition, the drug is detectable in urine for up to 72 hours after ingestion (Office of National Drug Control Policy, 2003).

Lower doses of Rohypnol can cause muscle relaxation. In higher doses, it can cause loss of muscle control, loss of consciousness, and, when combined with alcohol, anterograde amnesia. When combined with alcohol, as is often done, it can be deadly. Chemically, the drug is similar to Valium but ten times more powerful. Rohypnol is legally manufactured in over 80 countries as a prescribed sedative for the short-term treatment of severe sleep disorders, especially in Europe, but it is neither manufactured nor approved for sale in the United States.

The benzodiazepines include chlordiazepoxide (Librium), diszepam (Valium), oxazepam (Serax), and chlorazepate dipotassium (Tranxene), all of which are marketed legally and prescribed as antianxiety tranquilizers, or to treat muscle spasms or convulsions. The most common side effects are confusion, drowsiness, and loss of coordination. **Table 16–3** (on page 528) points out that 9 percent of arrestees in the United States and 8.2 percent of arrestees in England tested positive for benzodiazepines at the time of their arrest.

ALCOHOL

Despite the public concern over heroin, opium, marijuana, cocaine (especially crack), and the amphetamines, the number one drug of abuse has been, and continues to be, alcohol (ethanol, ethyl alcohol, grain alcohol). All 50 states have a legal drinking age of 21. However, most underage persons obtain and drink alcohol illegally. According to the Substance Abuse and Mental Health Administration (2005), 121 million Americans, aged 12 or older, were current drinkers of alcohol in 2004, representing 50 percent of the population (see **Table 16–19**). About 55 million (22.8%) participated in binge drinking, defined as five or more drinks on at least one occasion in the 30 days prior to the survey (Substance Abuse and Mental Health Administration, 2005). And 16.7 million (6.9%)

TABLE 16–19 Self-Reported Alcohol Use as a Function of Age

AGE	Alcohol Use	
	EVER	CURRENT
12 or older	82%	52%
12–17	41	21
18–25	84	61
26–34	90	63
35 or older	87	53

Source: Greenfeld, 1998, p. 8.

were considered heavy drinkers as defined as binge drinking on five or more days in the past month. Most of the binge and heavy drinkers were young adults between the ages of 18 to 25. Overall, alcohol is preferred by teenagers over other drugs by a significant margin.

About 10.8 million youths, aged 12 to 20, reported drinking alcohol a month prior to the survey, representing (28.7% of this age group) (Substance Abuse and Mental Health Administration, 2005). Approximately 19.6 percent of this age group were binge drinkers, and 6.3 percent were classified as heavy drinkers. In another study involving 930 high school students, Arata, Stafford, and Tims (2003) found that two-fifths of males and one-fifth of females reported frequent binge drinking. Other studies of gender differences in alcohol use among adolescents have consistently reported that males consume alcohol more frequently and in higher quantities than females and are susceptible to more alcohol-related problems (Webb, Bray, Getz, and Adams, 2002).

According to DAWN (Office of Applied Studies, 2004), 23 percent of all drug-related emergency department visits involved the effects of alcohol in persons under age 21 in 2003. Nearly one-third of the alcohol-related visits were because the youth—especially those between the ages of 12 and 17—had combined alcohol with other drugs. Marijuana (49%) and cocaine (22%) were the drugs most frequently found in combination with alcohol. Methamphetamine (8%) was also found with some frequency in these visits. There were no gender differences in alcohol-related visits to emergency departments in 2003.

Alcohol is responsible for more deaths and violence (it is the third major cause of death) than all other drugs combined. According to the National Highway Traffic Safety Administration (2005), approximately 25 percent of drivers aged 16 to 20 who were involved in fatal motor vehicle crashes in 2003 had been drinking alcohol.

The usual way to determine if an individual is intoxicated is by measuring his or her blood-alcohol concentration, abbreviated BAC. A BAC of .10 percent means there are 100 milligrams of alcohol per 100 milliliters of blood. For example, a 165-pound man would reach a BAC of .10% if he drank about five drinks within one hour on an empty stomach. (A drink is defined as one-and-a-half ounces of liquor, a 12-ounce beer, or a five-ounce glass of wine.) In most states, a driver is considered intoxicated if his or her BAC is .10 percent, and in some states the cutoff is .08 percent (e.g., California, Florida, Vermont) (see **Table 16–20** for data on BAC and fatal accidents).

Psychological Effects

The social, psychological, and psychobiological effects of excessive alcohol use can be just as destructive to the individual, his or her family, and society in general, as addictive substance abuse. Similar to the heroin addict, the alcoholic can develop a strong psychological and physical dependence on the drug. Society's attitudes toward alcohol are dramatically different from its attitudes toward other drugs of abuse, however. In virtually every part of the United States, it is

TABLE 16–20   Blood Alcohol Concentrations (BAC) of Drivers Involved in Fatal Accidents

BLOOD ALCOHOL CONCENTRATION	PERCENT OF FATAL ACCIDENTS
0	58.6%
0.26–0.29	4.7
0.26–0.30	1.9
0.26–0.31	2.4
0.26–0.32	17.2
0.26–0.33	9.1
0.26–0.34	3.5
0.30	2.6

Source: Greenfeld, 1998, p. 15.

legal and socially acceptable for adults to consume the drug. In public, drinking behavior is generally unregulated unless it involves heavy intoxication and correspondingly unacceptable conduct (e.g., disturbing the peace or operating a motor vehicle). In private, one can get as drunk as one wishes, a privilege not granted with respect to other drugs.

The psychoactive effects of alcohol are extremely complex. Miczek and his colleagues (1994) write that the effects of alcohol depend on "a host of interacting pharmacologic, endocrinologic, neurobiologic, genetic, situational, environmental, social, and cultural determinants" (p. 382). Consequently, we can provide only a cursory review of this complicated topic here. At low doses (e.g., two or four ounces of whiskey) alcohol seems to act as a stimulant on the central nervous system. Initially, it appears to affect the inhibitory chemical process of nervous system transmission, producing feelings of euphoria, good cheer, and social and physical warmth. In moderate and high quantities, however, alcohol begins to depress the excitatory processes of the central nervous system, as well as its inhibitory processes. Consequently, the individual's neuromuscular coordination and visual acuity are reduced, and he or she perceives pain and fatigue. The ability to concentrate is also impaired. Very often self-confidence increases, and the person becomes more daring, sometimes foolishly so. It is believed that alcohol at moderate levels begins to "numb" the higher brain centers which process cognitive information, especially judgment and abstract thought. It should be emphasized at this point that the levels of intoxication are not necessarily dependent on the amount of alcohol ingested; as for other psychoactive drugs, the effects depend on a myriad of interacting variables.

Alcohol, Crime, and Delinquency

The belief that alcohol is a major cause of crime appears to be deeply embedded in American society. Surveys, for example, suggest that over 50 percent of the population is convinced that alcohol is a major factor in crimes of violence

(Critchlow, 1986). This pervasive belief appears to be based on the premise that alcohol instigates aggressive conduct in some individuals, or somehow diminishes the checks and balances of nonaggressive, nonviolent behavior.

Roizen (1997), summarizing the research on alcohol and violence, found that up to 86 percent of homicide offenders had been drinking at the time of the offense. Roizen further discovered that 60 percent of sexual offenders, 37 percent of assault offenders, 57 percent of males in marital violence, and 13 percent of child abusers had also been drinking at the time of the crime. **Table 16–21** identifies the percentage of adult offenders who admitted to drinking at the time of their offense (in 1996). Outside of public order crimes, a higher percentage of offenders reported drinking at the time of violent offenses than during the other offense categories. About seven out of 10 alcohol-involved incidents of violence occurred in a residence, and most of the incidents (about two-thirds) are simple assaults. In addition, two-thirds of victims who suffered violence by an intimate reported that alcohol had been a factor. Ninety percent of alcohol-involved incidents of violence occur off campus (Greenfeld, 1998).

Many studies of adolescents have also concluded that alcohol use and violent behavior are linked (Swahn & Donovan, 2004). Several studies also indicate that alcohol use is more common among violent delinquents compared with nonviolent delinquents (Saner & Ellickson, 1996; Huizinga & Jakob-Chien, 1998). Dawkins (1997), on the basis of data collected on 312 youthful offenders at a public juvenile facility, reports that alcohol use is more strongly and consistently related to both violent and nonviolent offenses than is marijuana or other drugs. One study found that even after antecedent peer and family risk factors were adjusted for, young people who abused alcohol were much more likely to engage in violent offenses than those who did not misuse alcohol (Ferguson, Lynskey, & Horwood, 1996). According to Webb et al. (2002), alcohol use and serious delinquency are strongly associated, yet the direction of causality is unclear. Does alcohol cause violence, or do violent adolescents drink alcohol?

Furthermore, numerous other factors must be taken into account. For example, cultural differences may play a significant role in the alcohol-aggression relationship. Cognitive factors, such as a person's expectations or cognitions,

TABLE 16–21   Percent of Offenders Drinking at the Time of the Offense, 1996

Offense	Adults on Probation	Convicted Offenders in Local Jails	Convicted Offenders in State Prisons	Convicted Offenders in Federal Prisons
All offenses	39.9%	39.5%	32.3%	11.0%
Violent offenses	40.7	40.6	37.5	20.4
Property offenses	18.5	32.8	31.8	8.1
Drug offenses	16.3	28.8	18.0	8.2
Public order offenses	75.1	56.0	43.0	13.1

Source: Greenfeld, 1998, p. 21.

also influence how he or she responds to alcohol. Alcohol serves as a cue for acting intoxicated and doing things one normally would not do. In other words, a person may act the way he or she believes alcohol makes one act. It should further be emphasized that not all adolescents who drink heavily engage in violence and aggression. Many adolescents use alcohol experimentally, sometimes frequently, and may binge drink, without engaging in antisocial, violent, or delinquent behavior.

In summary, the evidence is quite clear that approximately one-third of all offenders who commit violent crime were drinking at the time of offense, and many were highly intoxicated. In their careful review of the research literature, Reiss and Roth (1993, p. 185) conclude, "In studies of prison inmates, those classified as 'heavy' or 'problem' drinkers had accumulated more previous arrests for violent crime, and reported higher average frequencies of assaults than did other inmates." And the National Institute on Alcohol Abuse and Alcoholism (1990, p. 92) asserts, "In both animals and human studies, alcohol more than any other drug, has been linked with a high incidence of violence and aggression." However, the link does not automatically mean that alcohol causes violence. It is most likely that under the influence of alcohol, individuals prone to be aggressive, violent, and antisocial are more likely to be more aggressive, violent, and antisocial. Alcohol may *facilitate* their aggressive tendencies. The available evidence does not allow cogent conclusions that alcohol makes normally nonviolent people act violently.

Does Substance or Alcohol Abuse Lead Directly to Violence?

There is little evidence that alcohol or drug use *cause* violence in adolescent offenders (White et al., 1990). Research indicates that aggressive and violent behavior in childhood generally *precedes* the initiation into drug and alcohol abuse, at least in boys. Aggressive behavior in the early school grades and poor school achievement are two of the best predictors of substance abuse later in adolescence and adulthood (Fothergill & Ensminger, 2006). On the other hand, serious male delinquents (including the most violent offenders) by far show the highest rates of consumption of alcohol, marijuana, and other drugs. Girls who are considered shy in early grades are more likely to have high levels of educational attainment and are at low risk for substance or alcohol abuse in adolescence or adulthood (Fothergill & Ensminger, 2006).

Many developmental psychologists contend that substance abuse often takes place in an orderly sequence, starting with tobacco use, followed by marijuana, and then hard drug use as a last step (Kandel, Yamaguichi, & Chen, 1992; White et al., 1990). This gives some credence to those who consider marijuana a "gateway drug" and urge zero tolerance, even for its possession in small amounts. However, before any adolescent becomes dependent on alcohol, tobacco, or any illicit substance, they pass through a stage of **experimental substance use** (abbreviated **ESU**) (Petraitis, Flay & Miller, 1995). An unknown number of youth experiment but do not continue with regular use. Events and variables that determine who experiments with substances and alcohol during adolescence and who continues are multiple, including the availability of drugs, family history, peer pressures, social attitudes concerning drug use, the social and economic context, and individual differences in biopsychological/psychological makeup. In addition, drug use and experimentation are strongly correlated with cognitions (attitudes and beliefs) about drugs. Adolescent substance and alcohol abuse is not a passive, one-dimensional process caused exclusively by social influence but is strongly influenced by subjective choice made by the youth (Getz & Bray, 2005). For example, rates of drug use are much higher in populations that do not perceive great risk of harm than in populations that do perceive great risk of harm. Thus, explanations for the sustained heavy use of marijuana in adolescents partly center around the belief that there is very little harm in the use of the drug. Due to the enormous complexity involved in ESU, many theories have been proposed to explain the phenomenon. However, very few of them have ever been empirically tested or provided cogent explanations for why some youth experiment with drugs, and others do not.

Inhalants

The term **inhalant** refers to a thousand or more different household and commercial products that can be abused by sniffing or "huffing" (inhaling though the mouth) for an intoxicating effect. They are found in organic solvents and volatile substances commonly found in adhesives, lighter fluids, cleaning solutions, paint products, and even "White-out." The effects of inhalants are usually highly similar to alcohol intoxication, including slurred speech, loss of motor coordination, distortion in perceptions, headache, vomiting, or nausea. Wheezing may be apparent, and in some instances a glue sniffer may experience a rash around the nose and mouth. At this writing 37 states have placed restrictions on the sale of one or more of these products to minors. Some states have introduced fines, incarceration, or mandatory treatment for the sale, distribution, use, and/or possession of inhalable substances.

Studies have estimated that between 5 percent and 15 percent of young people in the United States have tried inhalants (U.S. Department of Justice, 1998), but they are not considered "gateway drugs" that lead to chronic abuse of more powerful illicit drugs. The real danger of inhalants is their potential side effects. Chronic use of inhalants can produce kidney abnormalities, liver damage, and in rare cases heart failure or fatal breathing difficulties may occur.

 Summary and Conclusions

This chapter reviewed the relationship between crime and a number of drugs commonly associated with criminal behavior. Four major drug categories were identified: (1) the hallucinogens, (2) the stimulants, (3) the opiate narcotics, and (4) the sedative-hypnotics. Rather than discuss most of the drugs in each category, we considered only those commonly believed to be connected with criminal conduct. Moreover, we did not examine the crimes of drug distribution or possession. We are mainly concerned with whether the substance itself facilitates or instigates illegal action, especially violence, and what damage the drug does to the user. In other words, are persons under the influence of marijuana more violent than they are normally? And how does marijuana affect the health of users? Or, to what extent does alcohol directly contribute to loss of control or reduce self-regulatory mechanisms?

Because juvenile drug use is considered a major social problem, we discussed its prevalence and some of the characteristics of juvenile substance abusers early in the chapter. In addition, throughout the chapter, we distinguished between juvenile and adult drug use when data and research findings were available. Marijuana is the drug for which most juveniles are arrested, but there is troubling use and abuse by juveniles of prescription drugs, inhalants, and "club drugs" as well. There has been a 10-year decline in arrests relating to cocaine, opium, and synthetic narcotics, however. Girls are less likely than boys to have drug and alcohol problems, and their experiences with drugs differ. However, their arrest rates for drug-related behaviors is increasing, though it is still far lower than the male rate. Persistent drug use in juveniles is associated with poor academic performance, high-risk behaviors, serious health problems, and delinquency.

Cannabis, which includes marijuana and hashish, is a relatively mild hallucinogen with few psychological or physiological side effects. No significant relationship between cannabis use and crime has been consistently reported in the research literature. If anything, marijuana seems to reduce the likelihood of violence, since its psychoactive ingredient, THC, induces muscle weakness and promotes feelings of lethargy.

Amphetamines and cocaine (especially crack) represented the stimulant group. Most illegal users do not participate in crime other than the possession or sale of these drugs. Similar to marijuana, amphetamines are plentiful and inexpensive. However, there are some documented cases in which heavy users of amphetamines entered psychological states that presumably predisposed them to violence and paranoia. In addition, several studies have found correlations between violent offenders and a history of amphetamine abuse. As in all correlations, however, it is difficult to determine what contributes to what. Chronic amphetamine use has potential strong dangerous side effects if used improperly, or used in combination with other drugs of abuse. Cocaine, a natural drug that grows only in certain parts of the world, has traditionally been quite expensive. In recent years, the drug has become widely available and its cost less prohibitive. There is no strong evidence that cocaine generally renders one more violent, more out of control, or more likely to engage in property crimes, however.

We discussed heroin as the representative of the opiate narcotics. Like most other narcotics, heroin appears to be highly addictive, particularly in the sense that it creates a strong psychological dependency. Narcotics in general are so addictive and so expensive that substantial funds are needed to support a user's habit. Thus, some researchers have found a moderate correlation between narcotics and various income-generating crimes. On the other hand, others have noted that most addicts turned to drugs after they had developed criminal patterns.

Of all the drugs reviewed, alcohol—representing the sedative-hypnotic group—shows the strongest relationship with violent offenses, such as rape, homicide, and assault. At intermediate and high levels, alcohol appears to impair or disrupt the brain operations responsible for self-control. Alcohol may also impair information processing, thereby leading a person to misjudge social cues and encouraging overreactions to a perceived threat. However, it is likely that violent behavior associated with alcohol use is a joint function of pharmacological effects, cognitive expectancies, and situational influences. If the individual expects that alcohol will make him or her act aggressively, and if the social environment provides appropriate cues, aggression or violent behavior will be facilitated. The National Institute on Alcohol Abuse and Alcoholism (1997, p. 4) concluded in its extensive review of the relevant research literature that "alcohol apparently may increase the risk of violent behavior only for certain individuals or subpopulations and only under some situations and social/cultural influences." Furthermore, the National Institute noted, "intoxication alone does not cause violence" (p. 2). However, the relationship between alcohol consumption and violence is a strong one in Western civilization. The Panel on the Understanding and Control of Violent Behavior concludes, "For at least the past several decades, alcohol drinking—by the perpetrator of a crime, the victim, or both—has immediately preceded at least half of all violent events, including murders, in the sample studied by researchers" (Roth, 1996, p. 3). While the relationship between alcohol and violence clearly exists, the nature of that relationship is largely unknown. Does alcohol cause violence, or are violent people drawn to alcohol? No drug *directly causes* violence simply through its pharmacological action (Morgan & Zimmer, 1997).

In conclusion, the relationships between crime and all the drugs discussed in this chapter are complex, involving interactions among numerous pharmacological, social, and psychological variables. Research is beginning to ease some data out of the complexity, but additional studies employing well-designed methodology are greatly needed to understand the many possible influences of psychoactive drugs on human behavior, particularly criminal behavior.

At this point in our knowledge, substance abuse appears to be more of a health problem to those who use drugs more than a "crime problem." On the other hand, we cannot ignore the fact that there is a drug-crime connection, as the tripartite conceptual model proposed by Goldstein (1985) indicates. Goldstein conceived of drug-related crimes as being either psychopharmacologically driven, systemic, or economically compulsive. Those who advocate radical changes in government policy—such as decriminalization or legalization of certain drugs—argue that crimes characterized by the systemic and economically compulsive components would likely decrease. This conclusion reflects the continuing controversy over the "right" public policy to adopt with respect to drugs. Although this chapter has not focused on the residual effects of the nation's war on drugs—such as its effect on public health, minority groups, prison populations, and individual civil liberties—these effects also cannot be ignored.

Relating to the psychopharmacologically driven category proposed by Goldstein, we stress that, from the psychological perspective, it is unlikely that drugs "cause" people to engage in criminal activity. On the other hand, some drugs clearly allow some people to disengage from their usual constraints against antisocial conduct, including violence. Individuals who are chronic, persistent criminals often are polydrug users, but again it is unlikely that the drugs they ingest directly cause them to engage in criminal activity. It is more likely they were criminally prone prior to and independent of polydrug use.

KEY CONCEPTS

Substance abuse	Jails
Prisons	Tripartite model
Psychoactive drugs	Controlled substance
Hallucinogens	Psychedelics
Stimulants	Opiate narcotics
Sedative-hypnotic compounds	Tolerance
Dependence	Narcotics
Natural narcotics	Semisynthetic narcotics
Synthetic narcotics	Experimental substance abuse
ESU	Inhalant

REVIEW QUESTIONS

1. What are the four main categories of drugs discussed in this chapter? List their main effects, and provide one example of a drug from each category.
2. Describe and explain briefly Goldstein's tripartite conceptual model for understanding the drug/crime relationship.
3. Briefly list the common psychological effects of any three of the following: cocaine, MDMA, heroin, alcohol, metamphetamine.
4. Describe Rohynpnol and gamma hydroxybutyrate (GHB). What are they used for? What are some of the effects? How might they be involved in crime?
5. Of all the substances (drugs and alcohol) discussed in the chapter, which substance is most closely connected to crime? Why do you think this is?
6. Summarize and discuss the six main conclusions researchers have reached in recent years regarding the relationship between drugs and crime. When relevant, provide illustrations from the various categories of drugs.
7. Define and describe the three types of narcotics (based on their manufacture).
8. What are the differences between tolerance and dependence?
9. What is meant by the term "experimental substance use"?

CHAPTER 17

PREVENTION, INTERVENTION, AND TREATMENT: JUVENILE OFFENDERS

CHAPTER OBJECTIVES

- Describe the characteristics of successful prevention and intervention programs with juveniles.
- Present a brief overview of juvenile justice.
- Describe the types of prevention and intervention programs.
- Detail current strategies for building resilience in youth who face multiple risks.
- Review the prevention strategies often used in working with children and youth.
- Evaluate the treatment procedures for working with juvenile offenders.
- Examine the treatment approaches for working with juveniles with psychopathic features.
- Review treatment programs for juvenile sex offenders.

As we have seen throughout this text, juveniles are involved in a significant amount of antisocial behavior. For the great majority of juveniles, even those who manage to earn a "delinquent" label, this behavior is a normal part of the developmental process and will not be long lasting. We are most concerned, though, about the juvenile who engages in serious, persistent offending or the juvenile who commits a very small number—even one—of extremely serious crimes. The topics discussed in this chapter are relevant to these juveniles.

We devote a chapter to this age group both because it is the subject of extensive psychological research and because treatment is more likely to succeed with juveniles than with adults. In addition, because a significant number of persistent adult offenders began their criminal careers as juveniles, discussing juveniles before the adult offenders that are the subject of the following chapter is a logical thing to do.

TREATMENT AND REHABILITATION STRATEGIES

The number of prevention, intervention, and treatment programs that have been tried with delinquents and children at risk over the past three decades is overwhelming. Unfortunately, few programs designed to reduce delinquent or predelinquent behavior have been effective or shown lasting effects (Tarolla, Wagner, Rabinowitz, & Tubman, 2002; Zigler, Taussig & Black, 1992). Many have never been evaluated scientifically, based on sound research principles. Serious forms of antisocial behavior in school-aged children and adolescents have been particularly resistant to change (Borduin et al., 1995; Shaw, Gilliom, Ingoldsby, & Nagin, 2003). Serious juvenile offenders are especially prone to have low motivation for altering their antisocial behaviors and to display a lack of trust, noncompliance, and high levels of anger and impulsiveness (Tarolla et al., 2002). Although programs aimed at their conduct abound, most do not have significant positive effects. "By the time children reach these programs, often after referral by court personnel, they are already entrenched in a long history of antisocial interaction with parents, schools, and community that is not easily reversed" (Zigler et al., 1992, p. 997).

Although these conclusions are discouraging, it is noteworthy that positive changes have been occurring. Some programs are emerging as highly successful in eliminating antisocial behavior and reducing delinquent behavior, even in children with serious behavior problems and even in institutionalized delinquents. Others show considerable promise. Before discussing those programs, though, we identify what exactly is meant by a successful program.

CHARACTERISTICS OF SUCCESSFUL PROGRAMS

Effective prevention and treatment programs share common features. Zigler et al. (1992) concluded in their review that delinquency can be prevented by *early* childhood intervention programs that promote competence (social, interpersonal, and academic) in children across multiple systems in which they are embedded (family, school, peers, and community). By contrast, crisis-oriented programs emphasizing counseling or social casework chiefly to deal with a presenting problem have been ineffective, largely because they focus on a single setting or competency and often are applied too late. Successful and promising prevention and treatment programs have the following characteristics.

They Begin Early

Seriously antisocial children can be identified when they are as young as four or five years old on the basis of their aggressive, disruptive, and noncompliant behaviors across home and preschool or school settings. In fact, Terrie Moffitt (1993a; Moffitt et al., 1996) presents convincing evidence that the life-course-persistent (LCP) delinquent manifests discernible indicators of antisocial behavior as early as age three. Thus some researchers (e.g., Guerra et al., 1995) recommend that prevention preferably begin no later in life than the first grade and definitely before age 8. Because seriously antisocial children are likely to progress in a spiral of escalating and more severe antisocial and violent behaviors over time, early intervention is critical if it is to be effective (Conduct Problems Prevention Research Group, 2004). In addition, there appears to be a mysterious jump in antisocial behavior between the first and second grade for many children, and, therefore, prevention programs enacted later than the first grade will probably need to be more intensive. Guerra et al. (1995) have observed that aggressive and antisocial behavior begin to develop even earlier in children living in the most economically deprived urban neighborhoods, an observation that appears to hold for both boys and girls (Tolan & Thomas, 1995). In addition, as we learned earlier in the book, there is considerable evidence to suggest that the earlier the signs of antisocial behavior, the more serious or violent the antisocial or criminal behavior will be in later life (Tolan & Thomas, 1995).

Early antisocial indicators often forecast a life of crime. As noted by Rolf Loeber (1990, p. 6), "there is considerable continuity among disruptive and antisocial behavior over time, even though they may manifest themselves differently at different ages." Loeber further finds that as children and adolescents progress toward more serious delinquent behavior, they tend to move toward diversification, rather than moving from one specific deviant behavior to another. Thus, it is clear that without early intervention many children who are at risk for delinquency are more likely to engage in increasing levels of serious, chronic offending as they grow older.

They Follow Developmental Principles

Prevention programs that are effective are soundly based on child developmental principles obtained from well-designed research (Dodge, 2001). As noted in chapter 2, different developmental pathways can lead to serious violence and delinquency, and the age of onset of these behaviors can vary considerably. In designing programs to prevent violence and chronic antisocial behavior, it is critical to understand the factors that place youths on a developmental trajectory of serious delinquency. Further, it is equally important to understand how these factors interact with the social environment. As persons move through life, they enter and exit a series of developmental stages (Dahlberg & Power, 2001). Interestingly, data from the Rochester project (Thornberry,

Huizinga, & Loeber, 1995) indicate that protective factors must be *constantly present* at transition from early to late adolescence and not simply in place at a single point in childhood or adolescence (Conduct Problems Prevention Research Group, 2004). "Although the negative impact of early risk factors may be buffered by the provision of protective support services during the grade school years, the risk factors themselves may continue to influence developmental trajectories during adolescence" (Conduct Problems Prevention Research Group, 2004, p. 193). This point is especially relevant when the child or adolescent continues to live in a dangerous social, physical, and emotional environment.

In an extensive review, Tremblay, LeMarquand, and Vitaro (1999) examined 50 prevention programs and discovered that 20 of them had been evaluated under carefully designed test conditions. Those programs that were most effective were based on sound child developmental research (Dodge, 2001). Linking the appropriate prevention program with the developmental stage of the youth is paramount for significant, long-term success in delinquency prevention.

They Focus on Multiple Settings and Systems

Successful intervention programs must not only begin as early as possible, but also must be skillfully directed at as many causes and negative influences as possible. Targeting multiple potential risk or protective factors rather than one or two in isolation greatly increases the likelihood of positive adjustment and the significant reduction of antisocial and violent behavior (Tedeschi & Kilmer, 2005). Programs that have shown long-term success have utilized multipronged approaches concentrating on treating children through their broad social environment, including improving relationships with family and peers and helping them to develop better academic skills for school success. In addition, effective intervention programs include prenatal and perinatal medical care and intensive health education for pregnant women and mothers with young children (Coordinating Council on Juvenile Justice and Delinquency Prevention, 1996) These services reduce the delinquency risk factors of head and neurological injuries, exposure to toxins, maternal substance abuse, nutritional deficiencies, and perinatal difficulties. For example, recent research (Dietrich et al., 2001; Needleman et al., 2002) has discovered a strong relationship between high levels of lead in the bones of children and violence and delinquency in adolescence.

There is little doubt that living conditions in poorest inner city neighborhoods are extremely harsh and that—for many children—the daily onslaught of violence, substance abuse, child abuse, and hopelessness are highly disruptive to normal development, even if they experience these conditions only indirectly. For the child who is directly exposed to an adverse family life and inadequate living arrangements with little opportunity to develop even the rudiments of social, interpersonal, and academic skills for dealing effectively with his or her environment, the damage may be almost irreparable. Clearly, the longer a child is exposed to an adverse environment, the more difficult it will be to modify his or her life course away from crime and delinquency.

They Acknowledge and Respect Cultural Backgrounds

Although some urban neighborhoods contain numerous risk factors, these same neighborhoods also may be rich in values and traditions that, if acknowledged, would qualify as crucial protective factors. For example, various ethnic and racial groups place great value on the extended family, a particular style of music, or certain holiday traditions and celebrations. Even ways of communicating often vary among groups; some stress the importance of eye contact, for example, while others consider it disrespectful. These cultural markers can affect the development of antisocial behavior, sometimes promoting it but often suppressing it. Effective programs, then, are sensitive to a family's cultural background and heritage.

Even poverty may affect individuals differently on the basis of their ethnicity and the *meaning* of poverty within a given cultural context (Guerra et al., 1995). For example, whereas one group may regard being poor as matter of fact and to be expected—albeit something to be overcome—another group may view it as a sign of oppression by another dominant group in a society. In some cultural groups, stealing brings shame upon one's family; in others, stealing may be the norm, as long as the target of the theft is limited to those outside the group. This is not to suggest that individual members of these groups will necessarily act in accordance with the group's values and expectations. Effective treatment providers are constantly aware of the cultural background of the juveniles they deal with, as well as the caveat that they cannot assume that the culture will inevitably regulate the juveniles' behavior.

They Focus on the Family First

Research has continually shown that the most successful interventions concentrate first on improving parenting and the family system in general, followed by improving peer relations and academic skills. It is clear that certain family relationships and parenting practices strongly promote serious and violent delinquency. These family characteristics seem to be linked to delinquency regardless of ethnic or socioeconomic status (Gorman-Smith, Tolan, Huesmann, & Zelli, 1996). The family characteristics most closely connected to serious delinquency are poor parental monitoring and supervision of the child's activities, poor and inconsistent discipline, and a lack of family closeness or cohesion. According to Dishion and Andrews (1995), studies have consistently revealed that negative, coercive exchanges between parents and children are predictive of child antisocial behavior (e.g., Patterson, 1986), delinquent behavior (e.g., Bank & Patterson, 1992), and adolescent substance abuse (e.g., Dishion & Loeber, 1985). Research also indicates that emotional closeness and family cohesion, where the child receives emotional support, adequate communication, and love are essential in the prevention of antisocial behavior and delinquency (Gorman-Smith et al., 1996).

Peer systems are critically important, and research has shown that negative peer associations are significant predictors of both substance abuse and delinquency (O'Donnell et al., 1995). Thus far, though, intervention programs have been *unsuccessful* in utilizing peer groups as effective change agents in modifying these antisocial behaviors. Interventions that are peer focused can actually have unintended negative effects if they require increased contact with antisocial peers (Vitaro & Tremblay, 1994). Similarly, Dishion and Andrews (1995) found that placing high-risk teens into groups together encouraged escalations in tobacco use and problem behaviors in school. Dishion and Andrews further discovered that bringing high-risk peers together may have actually served to increase contact with deviant peers and in the long run, exacerbated their antisocial involvement. They recommended that intervention programs that use antisocial peers as change agents be discouraged unless very carefully designed. Likewise, research indicates that group homes for delinquents may increase delinquent behavior (Chamberlain, 1996). The assumption is that antisocial peers tend to model and encourage other antisocial peers.

In summary, effective prevention and treatment programs begin early, are based on child development principles, deal with multiple systems, recognize the cultural influences interacting on the child, and focus on the family and parental skills. When working directly with the developing antisocial child, the effective program focuses on improving positive social and prosocial skills, enhancing academic and learning skills, and promoting self-esteem and confidence.

Before discussing illustrations of prevention and treatment, we must review briefly the origin and organization of the juvenile justice system, which is typically responsible for assigning juveniles to treatment and which also may be involved even at the earlier stages, when children are at risk of committing delinquent acts. For our purposes we are interested in those components of juvenile justice most likely to come into contact with persistent offenders.

A Brief History of Juvenile Justice

For slightly over 100 years, juveniles and adults have been processed through courts and through correctional facilities in a separate fashion. Juvenile courts have traditionally been informal and rehabilitation oriented, at least in spirit; detention and correctional facilities, though sometimes very secure, have offered more education, recreation, and treatment opportunities for juveniles than similar facilities have offered adult offenders. Juveniles often have been treated in community settings—including group homes, their own homes, or halfway houses—as well as in camps or wilderness programs. Since the 1980s and 1990s, however, an increasing number of juveniles charged with criminal offenses are being transferred to adult criminal courts. To help us understand why this might be happening, it will be instructive to take a brief look at the changes that have occurred, both in the juvenile justice system itself and in society.

Juvenile justice was officially ushered into the United States on the last day of the 1899 session of the Illinois legislature, when that body passed the seminal **Juvenile Court Act.** This comprehensive child welfare law defined a delinquent as a child under the age of 16 who violated a state law or any village or city ordinance. It also established this country's first juvenile court and regulated juvenile institutions within the state. The philosophy underlying the law was that juvenile offenders should not be given the same punitive treatment as adults, but rather be given individual attention for their own protection, as well as that of society (Chute, 1949). In addition, the law included provisions for dealing with dependent and neglected children.

Although other states had adopted various procedures and regulations relevant to their wayward and neglected youth, the Illinois Act was the first comprehensive attempt at codification. It rapidly became the model for juvenile justice, and by 1911, 22 states had adopted similar measures. By 1925, all but two states had established juvenile courts (Tappan, 1949). Today they exist in some form in every state, either separately or as part of a family court system.

Most programs directed at preventing or treating juvenile delinquency in the early twentieth century were created and managed by psychiatrists, psychologists, or social workers. Not surprisingly, they called for individual counseling and psychotherapy for youthful offenders, usually by a social caseworker or a clinical practitioner. Illinois was also a pioneer in this area, since the first clinic established to provide psychiatric diagnoses to juvenile courts, the Juvenile Psychopathic Institute, opened its doors in Chicago in 1909. Shortly thereafter the Judge Harvey H. Baker Child Guidance Clinic was established in Boston (Chute, 1949).

In 1930, however, a monumental project was undertaken—again in Chicago—by sociologists proposing a different approach to the prevention of juvenile offenses. Called the Chicago Area Project, it paved the way for a reassessment of existing treatment and prevention programs for delinquents. It also represented the first systematic challenge by sociologists to the domination of psychologists and psychiatrists in both private and public juvenile programs (Schlossman & Sedlak, 1983).

The project, which lasted 30 years, has been amply described, lauded, and criticized in the sociological and criminal justice literature. Essentially it immersed researchers, practitioners, and volunteers into communities with higher than average rates of delinquency. They obtained oral histories and accounts of juvenile activities, organized recreational programs, offered "curbstone counseling," and mediated with police and juvenile courts on behalf of community youth. The project deemphasized the individualized casework approach and drew attention to the role of the community as an agent of informal social control to prevent delinquency. Furthermore, at about the same time as the project was undertaken, many adults had become aware of appalling conditions and treatment in some of the institutions that were receiving juveniles. Therefore preventing delinquency as well as dealing with children in their own communities became a paramount goal.

Approximately 20 years ago, Lloyd Ohlin (1983) traced three major shifts in federal policy regarding youth offending, beginning in the 1960s. He attributed the first shift to the Chicago Area Project and others like it. In the early 1960s, Ohlin noted, federal policy makers drew on community organization strategies to foster community responsibility for juvenile misbehavior and funded a variety of social programs toward that end. The programs in general were not successful, however, partly due to naiveté and partly due to the massive social changes in society that were occurring during the 1960s. "We are much more aware today that juvenile justice depends on the successful operation of a broad formal and informal network of social relationships that guide youth development" (Ohlin, 1983, p. 464). Ohlin noted that "the growing gap between expectation and achievable results fostered disillusionment, alienation, social unrest, and ultimately, abandonment of the programs themselves" (1983, p. 464). He also suggested, however, that we can learn valuable lessons from the failure of those early community programs.

The second shift in social policy was spearheaded by a series of presidential commissions studying the broad problems of crime and violence. In 1967 the first of these commissions, the President's Commission on Law Enforcement and Administration of Justice, set the tone. Its primary task was to recommend ways to identify and control delinquents and status offenders. The commission recommended six major strategies: (1) decriminalization of status offenses (such as running away from home); (2) diversion of youth from court procedures into public and private treatment programs; (3) extension of due process rights to juveniles in the same spirit as they had been extended to adult offenders; (4) deinstitutionalization, whereby those delinquents who did go through the court process would be cared for in group homes or small treatment centers instead of the traditional large institutions, reform schools, or training schools; (5) diversification of services; and (6) decentralization of control of juvenile proceedings and care. The spirit of the commission's recommendations was reflected in the landmark federal law, the **Juvenile Justice and Delinquency Prevention Act (JJDPA),** passed in 1974. At the same time, Congress created the **Office of Juvenile Justice and Delinquency Prevention,** a federal agency that conducts and sponsors research on juvenile issues, provides grants to states to study and implement changes in their juvenile justice systems, and generally serves as a watchdog over a wide range of practices affecting juveniles across the country.

As Ohlin (1983) noted, the mid-1970s also saw the beginning of a nationwide shift toward a law-and-order commitment. Apparently in response to a rapidly growing fear of crime and serious juvenile delinquency, the public began to demand quicker punishments and mandatory sentencing procedures, first for adults and eventually for juveniles. Ohlin noted that this new focus reflected in part a strong conservative reaction to the liberal policies advocated by the National Crime Commissions of the 1960s.

This law and order approach continued through the 1980s and 1990s, and it was often accompanied by broad legislative reform. For example, although all states have long had mechanisms for transferring some juveniles to criminal courts, in the 1990s the possibility of a transfer for a juvenile increased dramatically. Over the five-year period of 1992 to 1997, 45 states expanded laws making it possible to try juveniles in criminal courts (Snyder, Sickmund, & Poe-Yamagata, 2000). Most of these not only lowered the age at which youths may be tried as adult offenders for serious violent offenses like rape or murder, but also expanded the range of crimes for which juveniles could be tried as adults. Furthermore, by the end of 1997, 28 states excluded juveniles of certain ages charged with certain offenses from juvenile court jurisdiction. Pennsylvania, for example, enacted a law excluding juveniles 15 or older from juvenile court if they are charged with a specified violent crime, allegedly committed with a deadly weapon, or have previously been adjudicated for the same crime.

Researchers are still exploring the results of these statutory changes. Although the percentage of cases transferred to criminal courts by judges (judicial waiver) has remained small and stable (approximately 1% to 1.6%) (National Center for Juvenile Justice, 2003; Stahl et al., 1999), it is believed that prosecutors and state legislatures have widened the pool of juveniles whose cases are heard in criminal courts. The numbers and types of cases waived vary widely by jurisdiction, however, as documented in a recent study (Snyder, Sickmund, & Poe-Yamagata, 2000). Nevertheless, some common variables seem to be at work in transfer decisions. For example, Snyder et al. found that the use of weapons, injury to the victim, the juvenile's age, and the juvenile's prior history of offending all affected the transfer decision.

Transferring youth to criminal courts often has unintended consequences. According to a study involving data from Pennsylvania (Myers, 2000), juveniles tried in criminal courts received harsher sentences than their juvenile court counterparts, a fact that would not necessarily disturb those who advocate transfer. However, transferred juveniles also were more likely to reoffend while awaiting trial, because—like adults—they were released on bail while waiting further proceedings. Had they not been transferred, many of these youths would have been detained pending their delinquency hearing and/or adjudicated more quickly. Additionally, those juveniles who were transferred, convicted, and incarcerated were released while they were in their late teens or early twenties, often without having received adequate rehabilitative services. As Myers and others have argued, the juvenile system—imperfect though it may be—still offers better treatment than is provided during these short stays in jails and prisons.

Juvenile Courts

Despite increases in transfer provisions, the great majority of youths charged with crime nationwide—over 90 percent—are processed in the juvenile courts. (See **Figures 17–1** and **17–2** for illustrations of the juvenile justice process.) Nevertheless, in keeping with the trend to get tougher on offenders, even these juveniles have been given the message that they will be held accountable for their crimes.

Juvenile courts are part of the civil court system and differ significantly from criminal courts in both terminology and procedure. For example, prosecutors in juvenile courts file petitions of delinquency rather than criminal complaints; judges conduct hearings, not trials; if found to have committed the act, the juvenile becomes a delinquent, not an offender. In general, juvenile court proceedings are not open to the public. However, juveniles are still protected by many due process safeguards associated with criminal trials, such as written notice of charges, legal representation, the right to confront and cross-examine witnesses, and protection against self-incrimination. It should be noted, however, that a study of delinquency hearings in six jurisdictions (Feld, 1988) found that fewer than one-half of juveniles were represented by attorneys at their delinquency hearings. More recent studies indicate that rates of representation are increasing, but the actual figures vary widely by jurisdiction. Juveniles are not constitutionally entitled to a trial by jury, but a state may provide its juveniles with a jury trial if it so wishes. When juveniles are tried in criminal courts, the trial by jury is guaranteed, although like adults they are entitled to waive the jury and opt for a bench trial instead. A bench trial is where the presiding judge makes the decision as to the offender's guilt or innocence.

If a juvenile is adjudicated delinquent, a wide range of rehabilitation options is available, both in the community and in public and private residential facilities. As for adults, the most common sanction for juveniles is probation or supervision in the community. To the extent possible, the juvenile system tries to provide rehabilitative programs to the juvenile while he or she remains at home or, alternately, in a group or foster home setting. Secure, residential treatment facilities—the equivalent of adult jails or prisons—are usually considered the last alternative, when other placements have failed. Juveniles who have committed serious crimes, however, may be placed immediately in a secure, residential

FIGURE 17–1 A Simplified View of Caseflow through the Juvenile Justice System

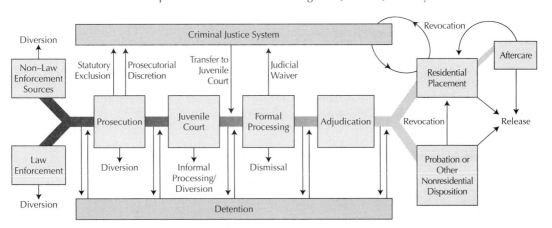

Note: Procedures vary among jurisdictions.

FIGURE 17–2   Case Processing Overview for Juveniles, 1999

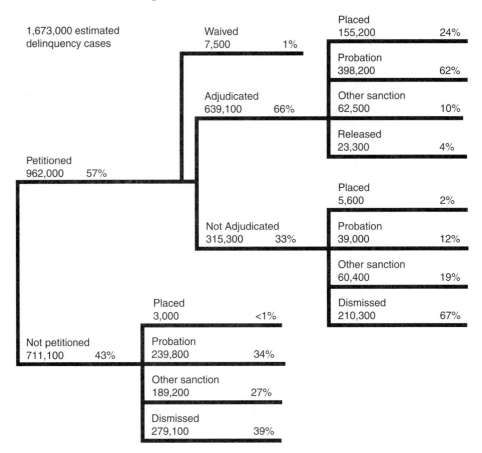

Note: Cases are categorized by their most severe or restrictive sanction. Category data may not add up to totals because of rounding.

Source: National Center for Juvenile Justice, 2003, p. 38.

setting. We turn now to a discussion of the varieties of programs that may be used with at-risk juveniles or already adjudicated juveniles, both in community settings and in institutional placements.

CLASSIFICATION OF PREVENTION AND INTERVENTION PROGRAMS

As mentioned at the beginning of the chapter, many prevention, intervention, and treatment programs have been tried with children and adolescents over the past 30 years, but few have been submitted to rigorous evaluation. For those that have been evaluated, most have failed if we use future offending or long-term lasting positive outcomes as criteria. That is to say, the programs were not effective at reducing antisocial behavior. Because of the very large number of programs, we will only cover those that are well known or that have been notably successful or promising.

In order to provide some structure to this array of programs, we will organize the remainder of chapter into three main sections: (1) primary prevention (also called universal prevention in the literature); (2) selective prevention (also called secondary prevention); and (3) treatment or intervention (also called tertiary prevention). (See **Figure 17–3**.) These three categories are similar to the public health model of prevention originally proposed by Gordon (1983), and elaborated upon further by Guerra, Tolan, and Hammond (1994) and Mulvey, Arthur, and Reppucci (1993). Although this classification provides structure for the purpose of discussing programs, there is often overlap between these convenient divisions because many programs target a mixture of populations. For example, Project Headstart—which was originally designed to provide a "catch-up" educational program for economically disadvantaged families and was considered a primary prevention program—has evolved into a broader program that helps a wider socioeconomic spectrum. Furthermore, because some of the children in Headstart may qualify as seriously "at risk" children, for them the program could be considered a selective program.

Primary (or **universal**) **prevention** is designed to prevent delinquent behavior before *any signs* of the behavioral pattern emerge. Primary prevention programs are most often implemented early in the developmental sequence of children, preferably before the ages of seven or eight. Typically, they are conducted in the school or preschool setting, and focus on large groups of children, *regardless of possible differences in risk for delinquency.* In most instances, primary prevention programs target all children within a particular geographic area or setting (e.g., a school or school grade) without any further selection criteria (Offord et al., 1998). Many of these programs require the promulgation of far-reaching policies and procedures, which often involve legislative authorization and funding. Examples include widespread programs to enhance prenatal care, maternal and infant care and nutrition, and family management programs for preschool children (Committee on Preventive Psychiatry, 1999). Another excellent example of this approach is the development of resilience or protective factors in young children before school entry or soon after entry. We discuss this far-reaching but powerful approach in more detail shortly.

Selective prevention consists of working with *specific* children and adolescents who are at *high risk* and who display some *early signs of antisocial behavior* but have not yet been classified or adjudicated delinquent by the court. The basic assumption in selective prevention is that early detection and early intervention will prevent the youngster from graduating into more serious, habitual offending. A good example of this type of prevention is the Perry Preschool Project started in 1962. The project was an organized educational program directed at the cognitive and social development of young children considered at *high risk* for delinquency and school failure (Berrueta-Clement, Schweinhart, Barnett, & Weikart, 1987). Another well-known example of this prevention strategy is juvenile diversion, which diverts first-time offenders from formal court processing but places them in short-term programs that presumably will discourage them from reoffending. An advantage of selective prevention programs is that they focus on those youth who should benefit most from the services. That is, the effort is more concentrated on those at risk rather than on an entire group of children, many of whom may show no risk factors at all.

The third approach (**tertiary**) is generally referred to as **treatment** (or intervention) in the delinquency literature. We prefer to use the term treatment, because it can be argued that primary and selective prevention are also forms of intervention. Furthermore although there is some overlap between selective prevention and treatment—in the sense that juveniles in selective prevention programs also often receive treatment—we reserve "treatment" to apply to those programs designed to reduce serious, habitual delinquent or antisocial behavior by adjudicated delinquents. Usually those fully involved delinquents or highly antisocial children have been referred for psychological care in the community or have been placed in residential correctional facilities, training schools, or rehabilitation centers.

PRIMARY PREVENTION

In the past, prevention and treatment programs tried to focus on reducing or eliminating *risk* factors that children and adolescents face during their formative years. In recent years, however, a discernible shift has taken place that emphasizes the development and enhancement of *protective* factors. While both

FIGURE 17–3   Prevention Strategies

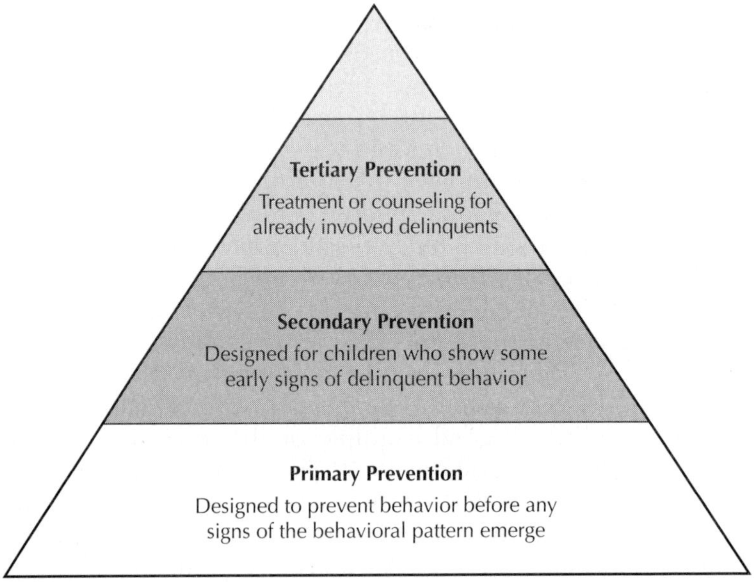

Tertiary Prevention
Treatment or counseling for already involved delinquents

Secondary Prevention
Designed for children who show some early signs of delinquent behavior

Primary Prevention
Designed to prevent behavior before any signs of the behavioral pattern emerge

approaches are important, in this chapter we focus on protective factors through the development of resilience. We contend that the development of resilience is an extremely effective method for primary and selective prevention of delinquency in children and adolescents and has enormous potential as an effective treatment strategy. Consequently, we begin the primary prevention section by describing how resilience can come into play across all three classifications of prevention and treatment.

The Enhancement and Development of Resilience

With increasing awareness of the *protective* factors that promote resilience in children and adolescence, theorists, researchers, and policy makers are now attempting to apply this knowledge toward the prevention of antisocial behavior, particularly in children considered at moderate to high risk. Prevention and treatment programs that are designed to foster and maintain resilience in youth are also known as *strength-based* programs. It should be emphasized that resilience is made up of ordinary rather than extraordinary processes, and that the *average* child can be taught to become resilient (Smith, 2006). Prevention programs that promote cognitive and social competencies in the child or adolescent, improve childrearing practices in the family, and foster the development and maintenance of effective social support systems are most likely to be effective in the long run.

Strategies for developing resilience include the enhancement of a child's strengths and interests, as well as the reduction of risk or stressors, and the facilitation of protective processes. Overall, the rallying cry for many programs focusing on enhancing resilience has become, "Every child has talents, strengths, and interests that offer the child potential for a bright future" (Damon, 2004, p. 13). These attitudes reflect a major transformation in conceptualizing the prevention of antisocial behavior and other childhood problems over the past few decades.

Children who are at risk of engaging in serious antisocial behavior have been exposed to aversive events. These can include dire economic situations, abuse (physical or emotional), rejection by peers, trauma such as the sudden loss of a parent or sibling, alone or in combination. There is no single means of maintaining equilibrium following highly aversive events, but rather there are multiple pathways to resilience (Bonanno, 2004), as there are multiple pathways on the road to delinquency. For example, McKnight and Loper (2002) found that the most prominent resilience factors in adolescent girls at risk for delinquency were an academic motivation and a desire to go to college, absence of substance abuse, feeling loved and wanted, belief that teachers treat students fairly, parents trusting adolescent children, and religiosity.

Waaktaar, Christie, Borge, and Torgerson (2004) conducted a study to explore how resilience or protective factors could be used to help at risk youths. The youth averaged 12.3 years of age, and a little over one-third were girls. They represented a medley of cultural and ethnic backgrounds, including the West

Indies, Far East, Central Asia, the Arab world, and northeast Africa. All the participants had experienced serious and/or multiple life stresses, and—at the time of the study—they were not receiving "satisfactory help" through "psychiatric" intervention.

The researchers targeted four resilience factors for therapeutic intervention: positive peer relations, self-efficacy, creativity, and coherence. Positive peer relations were defined as prosocial interactions, peer acceptance, and support. Self-efficacy is the belief that one can achieve desired goals through one's own actions (Bandura, 1989, 1997). Hundreds of studies have supported the observation that self-efficacy leads to a range of positive outcomes, and it is regarded as central to resilience (Lightsey, 2006). Creativity in this context refers to individual talent to create an artistic or other communicative product, such as a song, dance, film, play, poem, or short story. This approach requires that children be encouraged to express themselves and their experiences symbolically. Coherence refers to the ways in which people evaluate themselves and their circumstances both cognitively and emotionally. It involves "helping young people to find a coherent meaning to their past, present, and future life through positive thinking, accepting the reality of their bad experiences, avoiding self-blame for uncontrollable circumstances and finding adaptive paths forward" (Waaktaar et al., 2004, p. 173). The researchers discovered that child therapy that focuses on these four concepts has the potential to enhance resilience significantly.

An excellent illustration of a culturally sensitive program developed for resilience development is Project SELF, a school curriculum designed to promote self-esteem, self-efficacy, and improved problem-solving skills in inner-city fourth-grade black children through a culturally based curriculum (Hampson et al., 1998). The researchers write, "Using a pre/post evaluation design with a control group, we demonstrated that students who received the program exhibited greater improved knowledge of the curriculum, elevated self-esteem, a greater sense of self-efficacy, and improved long-term consequential thinking skills as compared to controls" (Hampson et al., 1998, p. 24). What really made the difference, the researchers concluded, was the program's focus on "the students' own ancestral history, biology, beliefs and values, choices and potential" throughout the curriculum (Hampson et al., 1998, p. 27). In order to improve resilience, the researchers reasoned, children must touch base with their cultural or ethnic identity.

SELECTIVE PREVENTION

Selective (or secondary) prevention is directed at children and adolescents who are believed to be "at risk" of engaging in delinquency on the basis of any number of risk factors (e.g., low self-concept, highly dysfunctional family situation, conduct disorder). In a comprehensive review of the research literature, Tremblay and Craig (1995) concluded that selective prevention programs with at-risk youths tend to be successful mainly when the intervention aims at more than one risk factor (e.g., children's disruptive behavior, aggressive behavior, and parenting), lasts for relatively long periods of time (at least one year), and is implemented before adolescence. The time must be quality time and the more intensive the intervention the better. Like much of the research reviewed thus far, the successful programs identified by Tremblay and Craig were especially effective when implemented during the preschool or the early elementary school years.

In light of the above, selective prevention programs increasingly are provided primarily to those children identified as showing *early* signs of developing serious and persistent antisocial behavior. It is clear that high-risk children can be identified with reasonable accuracy in early life, at least by the beginning of elementary school (Dodge & Pettit, 2003; Hill, Lochman, Coie, & Greenberg, 2004; Lochman & Conduct Problems Prevention Research Group, 1995). As noted by Dodge and Pettit (2003), the effectiveness of early screening has major consequences for public policy. Schools can play a more active role than they have in the past in identifying young children who could benefit from a prevention program. In addition, selective prevention programs can be more focused, more efficient, and more intensive than universal prevention programs (Hill et al., 2004). It should also be mentioned that prevention with young children offers far more hope than prevention with adolescents who may be already down the path of persistent antisocial behavior. However, prevention methods must span from childhood to adolescence because new risk factors emerge at each new developmental stage (Dodge & Pettit, 2003). That is to say that the child must be followed through his or her developmental years. According to the Carnegie Council on Adolescent Development (1995), approximately 25 percent of American youth ages 10 to 17 are *highly* vulnerable to the negative consequences of multiple high-risk behaviors, such as substance abuse, school failure, and delinquency. About 7 million youth are particularly vulnerable to delinquency, gang activity, violence, criminal activities, and violence (see Smith, 2006). An additional 7 million adolescents are at moderate risk for dropping out of school, for either bullying or being bullied in school, and/or committing suicide (Carnegie Council of Adolescent Development, 1995). We do not know, of course, how many of these children would have been identified as high risk in their preschool years.

The Fast-Track Experiment

The **Fast-Track Project** is a multisite, multicomponent prevention program for young children at high risk for long-term antisocial behavior (Conduct Problems Prevention Research Group, 1999). It is based on developmental pathway theory (e.g., Moffitt, 1993a) and is longitudinal in design. Fast Track is a two-pronged project. Participants in the program include both high-risk children (selective or secondary prevention) and all the children in school grades one to five (primary or universal prevention) within a particular school. The children in the high-risk group began to show persistent and serious antisocial behavior in early childhood (before first grade), as reported by parents and teachers.

The Fast Track Project is guided by developmental theory that posits that multiple influences interact in the development of antisocial behavior (Conduct Problems Prevention Research Group, 2004).

The program is divided into two major phases: the elementary-school (grades 1 to 5) and adolescent periods (grades 6 to 10). The elementary-school phase addresses six areas of risk and protective factors: parenting, child social problem solving and emotional coping skills, peer relations, classroom atmosphere and curriculum, academic achievement with a focus on reading, and home-school relations (Conduct Problems Prevention Research Group, 2004). The families of the children were invited to participate in weekly parent/child groups, plus home visits, tutoring, and school follow-up. The adolescent phase focuses on four areas associated with successful adolescent adjustment: peer affiliation and peer influence, academic orientation and achievement, social cognition and identity development, and parent and family relationships (Conduct Problems Prevention Research Group, 2004). The protective role of parental supervision and monitoring was also emphasized.

Children in the program were compared with a group of high-risk children (the control group) who did not participate in the program. Early results indicated that the participating children, relative to the children in the control condition, progressed significantly in their acquisition of most of the skills deemed to be critical protective factors (Conduct Problems Prevention Research Group, 1999). The high-risk experimental group children, compared with the control high-risk children, exhibited improvements in their social, emotional, and academic skills, especially their reading skills. Their peer relationships also improved significantly. The results were equally effective for both boys and girls. Parents who participated in the program displayed more warmth, appropriate and consistent discipline, self-efficacy, and positive school involvement. Evaluations of the program's effectiveness were taken at end of first and third grades.

The primary prevention effects of Fast Track were equally impressive. Classrooms that participated in the program were found to have lower peer-rated aggression and lower peer-related hyperactive-disruptive behaviors than were those classrooms that did not participate in the program (the control groups). Ratings by research observers in the classrooms indicated that prevention classrooms had better classroom atmosphere, students were better able to express their feelings appropriately (self-regulation), and the classroom as a whole was better able to stay focused and on task.

Fast Track provides an example of how a carefully articulated developmental model that accounts for the change and accumulation of risk factors and protective factors throughout the development period starting with children at school entry and continuing through adolescence in high school can be effective (Conduct Problems Prevention Research Group, 2004). However, designers of Fast Track faced many challenges and discovered how difficult it is to overcome the effects of dangerous, crime-ridden neighborhoods and the influences of impoverished families in which parental psychopathology and substance abuse are too familiar.

TREATMENT APPROACHES

Researchers have identified over 230 different treatment programs that are currently being used for children who engage in serious antisocial behavior (Kazdin, 1994). The effectiveness of most of these approaches has yet to be evaluated or empirically investigated. The small amount of research that has been conducted strongly indicates that treatment programs that concentrate on changing thought processes (cognitive and academic actors) and self-regulation hold considerable promise if the treatment programs also include the family, school, peers, and community).

A very wide range of treatment methods have been tried with juvenile delinquents. In a common scenario, the juvenile court refers a persistent delinquent youth to an outpatient mental health clinic for counseling and psychotherapy. The traditional approach relies on a one-on-one strategy of providing psychotherapy to an individual. Most commonly, the relationship with the therapist is the primary medium through which change is achieved (Kazdin, 1987). Presumably, the treatment provides a corrective experience by providing insight and exploring new ways of behaving (Kazdin, 1987). In some instances, the delinquent youth may receive individual counseling from a member of the juvenile court staff (Borduin, 1994). Delinquent youth who require a more restrictive setting are usually placed in a residential facility where group therapy is more common than individual counseling.

It is important to realize, though, that research has continually demonstrated that individual-based psychotherapy has not been shown to be effective when used in isolation (Committee on Preventive Psychiatry, 1999; Tarolla, Wagner, Rabinowitz, & Tubman, 2002). In other words, simply applying any form of psychotherapy to a child or adolescent already on a developmental path leading to serious delinquency without involving the social environment is, in most cases, a waste of time, money, and energy. Letourneau and Miner (2005) make the observation that "the developmental literature suggests that treatments that focus primarily on changing the individual characteristics (e.g., cognitions and behaviors) of youthful offenders, without also targeting relevant factors with caregivers (e.g., monitoring), peers (e.g., improving ties with prosocial peers), and school (e.g., increasing and improving caregiver-teacher communications) might be of limited usefulness" (p. 306).

Restrictive interventions for serious juvenile offenders, such as residential treatment and incarceration, have also not been effective and are extremely expensive (Henggeler, 1996). Moreover, any prevention or treatment program that focuses on only one risk factor is unlikely to lead to long-lasting change in delinquency because multiple other forces act to support antisocial development (Dodge & Pettit, 2003). According to Henggeler (1996, p. 139), "Restrictive out-of-home placements neither address the known determinants of serious antisocial behavior not alter the natural ecology to which the youth will eventually return. Indeed, data show that incarceration may not even serve a community protection function."

There are some additional points to note before proceeding. The characteristics of treatment programs may be different for those juveniles who receive treatment while confined in an institution compared with those who receive treatment in a noninstitutional setting. Not only is the setting different, but also the participants may differ in terms of offending history and the seriousness of the offending. For example, those offenders who are in an institution are likely to be considered dangerous or a high risk to reoffend. There are likely to be gender and age differences also.

Furthermore, it is difficult to make conclusions about wide range effectiveness of intervention programs under the auspices of juvenile corrections because there are so many different treatment programs with different polices, procedures, staff training, and outcome measures. For example, Krisberg and Howell (1998) remarked that in juvenile corrections "there are training schools, detention centers, camps, ranches, wagon trains, environmental institutes, group homes, boot camps, residential programs for emotionally disturbed youths, chemical dependency programs, correctional sailing shills, and independent living arrangements" (p. 347). Juvenile corrections also involve a wide range with respect to size, locations, and security levels.

Traditional treatment programs for the life-course-offender (LCPs) or serious delinquent offenders have had little success historically, whether provided in community or residential settings (Borduin, 1994). Treatment programs that have worked on mild or adolescent-limited offenders have been unsuccessful when applied to LCPs or serious delinquency. In most instances, as soon as youths leave the therapeutic milieu and return to their natural social environment, the chronic antisocial behavior reemerges. In fact, the poor track record with LCPs has prompted some professionals and policy makers to resist providing rehabilitative or treatment services to the serious offender (Borduin, 1994).

However, an examination of these failures reveals that rehabilitation and treatment services have often been too simplistic, individually based, or narrowly focused. As noted, many programs have failed to include or even recognize the many influences (family, peers, school, community) that unwittingly promote and contribute to antisocial behavior. Not only must effective treatment approaches be multisystemic and address the multidimensional causes of juvenile offending, but they must also be intensive and long-lasting if they are going to impact on juvenile offenders who have already become deeply entrenched into their antisocial behavioral patterns. The behaviors of hard-core juvenile offenders are often severe, pervasive, and well learned. While treatment for them is by no means hopeless, LCP delinquents require innovation and extreme patience for the many frustrating setbacks that will certainly occur over the long haul. Later in the chapter, we discuss one community-based treatment program that has shown considerable success in working with already involved delinquents.

With the above cautions in mind, we discuss below some of the treatment approaches that have been used with delinquents. We begin with treatments tried in residential settings then proceed to those based in the community.

Traditional Residential Treatment

The traditional form of **residential treatment** is the juvenile "training school" or "rehabilitation center," where youths are incarcerated for extended periods of time and often until they reach adulthood. These institutional settings are typically physically secure and may represent the "last stop" for youths with whom less restrictive community settings have been tried. On the other hand, a juvenile found to have committed a one-time heinous crime—such as a murder or a rape—may also be placed in such a setting. As a group, youths in residential treatment have high rates of substance abuse, emotional disturbance, and low academic achievement.

The evaluation research on institutional treatment is not encouraging. Studies have even demonstrated that incarcerated juvenile offenders who receive residential treatment have higher rates of criminal involvement after release than their counterparts who received intensive family and community-based treatment (Tarolla, Wagner, Rabinowitz, & Tubman, 2002).

Lipsey and Wilson (1998) examined the effectiveness of two-hundred treatment programs for serious juvenile offenders. The analysis included 83 studies of the effects of treatment with *institutionalized* offenders, 74 of which involved juveniles in the custody of juvenile justice institutions, and 9 that involved residential institutions administered by mental health or private agencies. The analysis also included 117 treatment programs for *noninstitutionalized* juveniles, most of who were on probation or parole. Although the results were mixed and confusing, with no one particular treatment program showing superiority, the average program for both institutionalized and noninstitutionalized offenders produced a 12 percent reduction in subsequent reoffense rates. The most effective programs (e.g., teaching family home, interpersonal skills development, and other broad-based interventions) were able to produce a 40 percent reduction rate, a very promising result, while some other traditional programs (e.g., Wilderness/Challenge, vocational programs, milieu therapy) were largely ineffective by most measures. The most effective programs included key components, such as focusing on social skills training, parent management, and family support.

Treatment of Juvenile Sex Offenders

While juvenile sexual offenders (JSOs) may also be treated in community settings, we focus here on the serious offenders who are most likely to be held in restrictive institutional settings. Nevertheless, it is important to keep in mind that juvenile sexual offenders—like adult sexual offenders—are often viewed as a homogeneous class of individuals. Research shows, however, that they vary widely in the frequency and type of sexual activity they engage in, and they differ in personal attributes, such as age, background, personality, race, religion, beliefs, attitudes, and social skills.

The foundation of treatment for JSOs is grounded on the premise that their deviant sexual behaviors are associated with distorted thought patterns that serve to deny, justify, minimize, and rationalize their actions (Eastman, 2004). Research reveals that sexually aggressive male juveniles subscribe to attitudes and ideology that encourage males to be dominant, controlling, and powerful, whereas females are expected to be submissive, permissive, and compliant. Such a cognitive orientation seems to have a particularly strong dishinhibitory effect on sexually aggressive juveniles, prompting them to interpret ambiguous behaviors of girls or women as come-ons, to believe that they are not really offended by coercive sexual behavior, and to perceive victims as desiring and deriving gratification from being sexually assaulted (Lipton, McDonel, & McFall, 1987).

Malamuth has discovered that sexually aggressive males have information-processing deficits in their ability to separate seductive from friendly behavior, or hostile from assertive behavior (Malamuth & Brown, 1994; Murphy, Coleman, & Haynes, 1986). For example, sexually aggressive males are significantly less accurate in reading a female's cues in first date interactions. This cognitive deficit is especially apparent when the female's communication is direct, clear, and strong. If she protests too much, it means—to the sexually aggressive male—that she really means the opposite. This information-processing deficiency may be the result of the lack of opportunity during early childhood to develop social and interpersonal skills for detecting correct cues from others. To the sexually aggressive male, she is game-playing and attempting to be seductive by using assertiveness or aggression. Consequently, treatment approaches to JSOs have traditionally included treatment of denial, past victimization, attitudes and values, social skills, and arousal patterns (Kahn & Lafond, 1988; Sciarra, 1999). In addition, these treatment programs have been modeled after treatment programs designed for adult sex offenders. However, few studies have examined whether these same programs are effective in the treatment of JSOs until recently.

Currently, there is considerable ongoing research evaluating treatment programs for juveniles (Veneziano & Veneziano, 2002). These programs designed to for JSOs are different from those that target adult sexual offenders. This is primarily because contemporary research suggests that juveniles are far more changeable than adults, are more influenced by the social environment, and appear to be at lower risk for sexual recidivism (Veneziano & Veneziano, 2002).

Before we get into some of the ongoing research on treatment effectiveness, one important point needs to be emphasized. Sexual behavior is culturally normed, and consideration must be made between culture and sexual offenses in juveniles. Well-trained clinicians must recognize that the traditional psychological assessment and treatment methods were developed from predominately Euro-American contexts and may be limited in their application to racial and culturally diverse populations. Hall (1997) has warned that psychologists and other mental health professionals may become culturally obsolete if they do not take into considerable cultural differences when providing treatment, and this is especially true when treating JSOs. Effective treatment must also include a change in contextual factors (e.g., alcohol and drug abuse, family abuse, peer rejection and bullying, support systems and resources after release, or posttreatment). Failure to do so will ultimately lead to re-offending within a relatively short period of time.

In 1988, a task force, known as the National Adolescent Perpetrator Network (1988), was commissioned to study JSOs and propose treatment strategies and goals. The group identified several characteristics of JSOs that treatment plans should focus on. They include having the offender accept responsibility for their antisocial sexual actions, challenging cognitive distortions and rationalizations that support or trigger their offending behavior, developing empathy for the victim, enhancing the management of emotions, teaching social and interpersonal skills (including dating skills), instilling a positive self-identity, and improving self-esteem (Eastman, 2004). In spite of these recommendations, the number of studies examining the effectiveness of treatment in reaching these goals remains small (Sciarra, 1999).

Eastman (2004) points out that a majority of studies concentrate on the recidivism rates of JSOs rather than on the goals outlined earlier. The outcome measure of recidivism, she notes, is used in different ways by different researchers in different contexts. Some studies define recidivism as the arrest of a juvenile offender after completion of treatment, while others define the term as the rearrest and conviction of a juvenile offender after the completion of treatment. "The scarcity of empirical treatment efficacy," Eastman (2004) writes concerning the treatment of JSOs, "has left professionals in the field making decisions on treatment and program effectiveness based on a small number studies using outcome measures that professionals in the field have not uniformly defined or that are subject to debate about whether their use is ethical" (p. 475). Still, regardless of how we define recidivism, studies of youth released from correctional and private facilities find that one-half to nearly three-quarters of these youths reoffend after release (Dalhberg & Potter, 2001; Feld, 1998). Therefore, recidivism does provide a powerful baseline measure of the effectiveness of various treatment programs.

Children and Adolescents with Psychopathic Features

As we note in the next chapter, the treatment and rehabilitation of adult criminal psychopaths has been shrouded with pessimism and discouragement. While there are exceptions, very few treatment approaches have been successful. Unfortunately, little is known about the effectiveness of prevention and treatment methods for child and adolescent psychopathy (Farrington, 2005a, p. 494) or, as many researchers and clinicians prefer to say, children and adolescent with psychopathic tendencies or characteristics. Recall from our discussion of psychopathy in chapter 6 that this is an extremely controversial area, with many preferring not to place such a negative label on juveniles.

Logically, it makes sense to hypothesize that children and adolescents with psychopathic features would respond more positively than psychopathic adults to prevention and treatment strategies because of their malleability. Consequently, researchers have begun to evaluate the effectiveness of (a) treatment programs designed specifically for juveniles with psychopathic characteristics and (b) programs for youthful offenders that include those with psychopathic characteristics.

Studies have underscored the observations that children and adolescents with psychopathic features show distinct sets of emotional and cognitive deficits that lead to their violent and antisocial behavior. According to Salekin and Frick (2005), knowledge about these areas may be important for designing more individualized interventions for youths with psychopathic traits. For example, laboratory studies have revealed that children with conduct problems and high levels of callous-unemotional (CU) traits exhibit tendencies to respond better to reward-driven interventions and respond poorly to punishment-driven or fear-induced forms of intervention (Hawes & Dadds, 2005). These findings imply that children displaying high-reward drive and low fearful inhibitions should, compared with conduct-problem children *without* CU traits, respond well to parents who use reward-based strategies for changing behavior (e.g., praise, rewards, reinforcement tokens), but remain insensitive to other parental disciplinary practices (e.g., time-outs, forms of verbal or behavioral punishments). "The assessment of CU traits in addition to other established risk factors," Hawes and Dadds (2005) conclude, "may allow such children to be targeted with more individualized intervention" (p. 740).

Juveniles with psychopathic characteristics did not fare well in an outpatient *substance abuse* treatment program, however (O'Neill, Lidz, & Heilbrun, 2003). In this study youths with higher scores on the PCL:YV were more likely to be rearrested and demonstrated higher attrition from the program, lower quality of participation, and more frequent use of alcohol and drugs while in the treatment program. The treatment program was based on a cognitive-behavioral model, whereby the adolescents would set goals and learn coping skills. They had daily group therapy sessions and twice-weekly one-hour sessions of individual therapy. While youths who scored low on the PCL:YV did benefit from the program, those with high scores did not. The reasons for the failure in this program are unknown.

On a more promising note, Salekin, Rogers, and Machin (2001) in their survey of over five hundred child clinical psychologists discovered that many of these clinicians reported that they were moderately to significantly successful in treating children and adolescents with psychopathic features. The treatment duration for these psychopathic youth averaged about 12 months. "After nearly 1 year of treatment these youths reportedly made marked improvement on such criteria as violence and recidivism" (Salekin et al., 2001, p. 192). The clinicians estimated that approximately 42 percent of the boys and 45 percent of the girls made moderate-to-marked improvement in reducing their psychopathic symptomatology overall. "These findings are important," Salekin et al. conclude, "and indicate that psychopathy, at least in youth, may be less recalcitrant to treatment than previously thought" (p. 192).

Salekin (2002) also published a comprehensive review of 42 studies specifically directed at treating psychopathy. Despite some methodological shortcomings with many of the studies (e.g., small sample size, diverse definitions of psychopathy), cognitive-behavioral, psychodynamic, and eclectic interventions were shown to be effective. The most notable benefits included a reduction in psychopathic characteristics, such as a decrease in lying, an increase in remorse or empathy, and improved relations with others. Salekin specifically noted that one intensive action-oriented program was highly successful (88%) with youngsters showing psychopathic tendencies. Ingram, Gerard, Quay, and Levison (1970) devised a program specifically designed to address psychopathic behaviors in youth. The program was based on the sensation-seeking model that kept the 20 young participants interested in treatment throughout the sessions. The program was able to decrease institutional aggressive behavior and improved overall adjustment in the community. Those psychotherapies that proved most effective tended to be more intensive and often combined with other programs, such as group psychotherapy, pharmacotherapy, or the involvement of family members. "These results indicate, at least preliminarily," Salekin writes, "that for complex problems such as psychopathy, more elaborate and intensive intervention programs involving individual psychotherapy, treatment of family members, and input from groups (other patients/inmates) are beneficial and may enhance their overall effectiveness" (p. 105). The key for success with psychopaths may be the scope, type, intensity, and duration of the treatment, as well as the training of the staff applying the intervention. Salekin points out that those intervention programs that were less successful were characterized by little input by trained mental health professionals and extremely little one-to-one patient-psychologist contact. He further stated that early intervention is particularly important in working with children exhibiting psychopathic traits. Salekin concludes that the therapeutic pessimism that surrounds the treatment of psychopathy and undermines motivation to search for effective modes of intervention for the disorder is unwarranted.

Treatment of Juveniles Who Kill

Although some juveniles who kill may have psychopathic traits, clearly not all do. Very little research is available by which to document the percentages, however. Most of the treatment information of juvenile murderers is from clinical case reports of a few cases referred for treatment (Heide, 2003). Juveniles who commit homicide—if not transferred to criminal courts—generally are placed in a juvenile facility where they rarely receive treatment tailored to the needs of the offender. In addition, the likelihood of juvenile murderers receiving intensive psychological treatment and intervention deceases as they enter adolescence (Heide, 2003; Myers, 1992). Older adolescent murders are often placed in adult prisons. Mental health care in juvenile facilities is typically minimal because of financial constraints and limited awareness of the psychological needs of this population (Heide, 2003). Psychiatric hospitalization, although commonly used for young children who kill, is rarely done for adolescent murders (Heide, 2003).

Overall, young killers appear to make a satisfactory adjustment in a correctional facility and in the community after release from custody (Heide, 2003). This is especially true for those youths who have killed family members as an isolated act of violence (Hillbrand, Alexandre, Young, & Spitz, 1999). On the other hand, hard-core, persistent, violent delinquents who killed in the course of committing other crimes do not make a good adjustment and often continue offending on release.

While there have been very few treatment programs that target juveniles who have murdered, the capital offender program at the Giddings State Home and School in Texas is a program specifically designed for juveniles who have been convicted of murder. In 1999 the program was expanded to include *some* youths who have committed other serious violent offenses. The program is intended to help these juveniles understand what makes them act violently and criminally, and help them identify ways to cope with the feelings that trigger dangerous behavior. Among other things, youths are required to reenact their crimes while role-playing as both the perpetrator and the victim. The Texas Youth Commission (2005) reported that this specialized treatment program reduced the recidivism (rearrest) of capital offenders by 46 percent during the five-year period 1999 to 2003. The Texas Youth Commission also evaluated the personality and behavioral changes while in the program and after release. According to the commission, they became significantly less hostile and aggressive, assumed more responsibility, and developed more empathy for their victims during program involvement (Heide, 2003).

Nontraditional Residential Treatment

Nontraditional forms of residential treatment include less restrictive physical settings, such as wilderness camps or juvenile boot camps. These settings typically may include youths who have committed serious crimes, but the offenses are more likely to have been nonviolent ones. Still, a highly aggressive youth may still be sent to one of these nontraditional settings.

Boot Camps

In the 1980s, many states developed a system of "shock incarceration"—commonly called **boot camps**—for adult offenders. Initially based on a military model, shock incarceration was intended to provide an intensively structured, short-term alternative to prison. In 1983 Georgia and Oklahoma tried boot camp–style, short-term alternatives to regulation institutional commitment for adults. By the end of the 1980s, the "model" boot-camp programs included military-style discipline, a rehabilitative component (such as substance-abused treatment), and community follow-up or "aftershock." Although there continues to be serious questions raised about the success of the boot-camp model, shock incarceration seems destined to remain an intermediate sanction for some adult offenders (MacKenzie & Herbert, 1995).

Boot camps were not immediately adopted in the juvenile justice system, primarily because there were questions about their appropriateness. Faced with increased overcrowding in juvenile facilities, however, juvenile justice policy makers began to consider the possibility of the boot camp alternative for less serious juvenile offenders who were believed to need more structure than the typical community probation experience and less structure than the institution. The first juvenile boot camp was established in 1985 in Orleans Parish, Louisiana (Tyler, Darville, & Stalnaker, 2001). In the early 1990s, the Office of Juvenile Justice and Delinquency Prevention (OJJDP) funded demonstration projects at three sites to develop a model boot-camp program for male juveniles, aged 13 to 18.

The ambitious goals of the boot-camp programs, as reported by Bourque et al. (1996), were as follows:

- Serve as a cost-effective alternative to institutionalization.
- Promote discipline through physical conditioning and teamwork.
- Instill moral values and a work ethic.
- Promote literacy and increase academic achievement.
- Reduce drug and alcohol abuse.
- Encourage participants to become productive, law-abiding citizens.
- Ensure that offenders are held accountable for their actions.

The boot camp experience included a 90-day residential program that was heavily focused on military drills, discipline, and physical conditioning. The regime included uniforms, military jargon, and an exhausting daily routine from 5:30 or 6:00 A.M. until 9:00 or 10:00 P.M. To a lesser extent, rehabilitation activities such as remedial education, life-skills education and counseling, and substance abuse education were included.

The boys in the programs had committed a wide range of offenses, including property, drug, and other felonies, but excluding violent offenses. In all three sites, the programs demonstrated short-term success during the residential phase. In all three sites, at least 80 percent of the boys graduated from boot camp. The boys improved in educational performance, physical fitness, and behavior, and the staff noted their improvements in respect for authority, self-discipline, teamwork, and physical appearance. The youths themselves rated their experience positively, noting that they believed they had significantly changed the direction of their lives.

However, the aftercare components of the program were discouraging, and began to raise important questions about the effectiveness of boot camps for juvenile offenders. A variety of aftercare services were made available, depending on the site. These included specially created aftercare centers, mainstreaming into local boys clubs, academic instruction, drug counseling, and support services. In a one-year follow up, all three sites reported high rates of noncompliance, absenteeism, and new arrests. "No site graduated more than 50 percent of its aftercare participants, and terminations were most commonly caused by new arrests in two sites" (Bourque et al., 1996).

In assessing what went wrong, Bourque and his colleagues suggest, among other things, that a more appropriate balance between militaristic and rehabilitative elements is needed. Although discipline can be an important motivating tool, they posit, the educational, psychological, and emotional needs of the youths must be better addressed. They also suggested fine-tuning the selection of youths, in particular noting that the youths with prior incarceration were less likely to survive the aftercare component. Additionally two programs seem to include too many serious offenders, whereas a third was overrestrictive, selecting youths who could have done just as well or better in another probation alternative.

Despite these shortcomings, the growth of juvenile boot camps in many states has continued unabated (Tyler, Darville, & Stalnaker, 2001). In Texas alone, the Board of Texas Juvenile Probation, in 1998, approved 18 proposals to construct juvenile boot camp facilities across the state. Although there are three identifiable style of boot camps that have evolved over the years (the military drilling style, the rehabilitative approach, and the educational/vocational model), a majority of the current juvenile boot camps still concentrate on the military drill which focuses on strict discipline as their central theme (Tyler et al., 2001). It appears that the military style is popular with the public and politicians because it projects the image of getting tough with juvenile crime. However, documented instances of extreme abuse have led to the closure of juvenile boot camps in Arizona, Georgia, and Maryland (Bottcher & Ezell, 2005). In 2000, Maryland disbanded its juvenile boot camps and fired top juvenile justice officials after publicity surrounding allegations of physical and emotional abuse of juveniles. One news story recounted split lips and bloody noses inflicted by staff who slammed the teens to the ground (Nelson, 2003). Florida disbanded its camps after a boy died from staff beatings.

Today's juvenile boot camps vary in cost, staff-to-inmate ratios, size, and style. However, the overall evaluation of juvenile boot camps is that, with very rare exceptions, their ability to reduce recidivism is extremely disappointing. It should not be surprising to anyone that a short-term residential program that is so discipline oriented is unlikely to produce positive long-term results. The research literature has continually reported that juvenile boot camps are ineffective in reducing recidivism (MacKenzie et al., 2001), even when intensive aftercare is provided (Bottcher & Ezell, 2005). In addition, juvenile boot camps are far more costly (at least 10 times more) than juvenile probation, including supervised intensive probation (Tyler et al., 2001). In their incisive review of the overall effectiveness of juvenile boot camps, Tyler and his associates (2001) assert, "The overall conclusion we must draw from this study is that juvenile boot camps are unlikely to be effective both in terms of costs and recidivism unless they incorporate a program to give a delinquent the skills, the motivation, and the resources to avoid the environment and lifestyle that contributed to the delinquency in the first place" (p. 456).

Wilderness and Adventure Programs

Wilderness and adventure programs are different from boot camps and seem to offer more hope as an effective strategy for *some* youth. A wide range of camps, ranches, and outdoor programs—mostly privately operated—are offered to juvenile offenders. Among the most well known are those supported by the Eckerd Foundation, a private organization based in Florida. Associated Marine Industries (AMI) is another such enterprise.

Wilderness and adventure programs accept both juveniles who are at risk of committing criminal acts and who are already adjudicated delinquent (thus they operate as both selective and tertiary prevention programs). In these programs at-risk juveniles are usually status offenders who are runaways or otherwise considered incorrigible and difficult to manage by their parents or guardians. The offenses of the adjudicated delinquents range from drug offenses to violent crime. Some programs accept juvenile sex offenders, but many do not. Wilderness camps are often considered the "last chance" for juveniles before being sent to a secure juvenile facility.

Descriptions of these programs suggest that, although they do not subscribe to a common model, they do have some thing in common. For example, they deemphasize traditional classroom education and emphasize the progressive development of physical skills that are believed to improve self-efficacy. Self-efficacy, as mentioned earlier in the chapter, is the belief that one is competent, resilient, and can succeed in challenges. The programs also attempt to develop a positive peer culture, wherein youth support one another's prosocial behavior and confront one another when antisocial behavior is displayed. They are far more likely than boot camps to include therapeutic components, such as drama therapy, development of communication and problem-solving skills, or individual counseling. However, it is unknown to what extent psychologists or trained clinicians provide treatment services.

Wilderness and adventure programs, compared with boot camps, have received some favorable research support, but, unfortunately, the studies are generally methodologically flawed and almost never use a control group for comparison purposes (Brown, Borduin, & Henggeler, 2001). Consequently, and unfortunately, their overall effectiveness is largely unknown.

Community Treatment: MST with Serious Offenders

Scott Henggeler and his colleagues have designed a treatment approach—**multisystemic therapy**—for serious juvenile offenders which is responsive to many of the social systems influencing the child's delinquent behavior (Henggeler & Borduin, 1990; Henggeler, Melton, & Smith, 1992; Scherer et al., 1994). The focus of MST is the family, and a major ingredient of the treatment is that the family must be actively involved in the program. The program addresses the cognitive and systemic (i.e., family, peer, and school) factors that are associated as risk factors to antisocial behavior (Schaeffer & Borduin, 2005). Together, counselors and family collaborate to develop pertinent treatment goals, as well as appropriate plans to meet these goals (Henggeler, 1996). Barriers and impediments to the plan, such as uncooperative family members, teachers, and school administrators, are worked with directly and actively. MST is an action-based treatment program in that it tries to get the involved family members to take "action" (behaviorally do something) rather than just talking.

MST is an intensive time-limited form of intervention where trained therapists have daily contact with the adolescent and his or her family for approximately 60 hours over four months. The caseload of the therapist is small, averaging four to six families per counselor. MST therapists identify both strengths and problems areas within the individual, the family, and the other social systems, such as peers, school, social service agencies, and parents' workplace. Basically, MST focuses on the strengths of the family. The program tries to identify family strengths and provide the parent(s) with the resources needed for effective parenting and for developing a better functioning and cohesive family unit. For example, the therapists might work with the parents on improving communication and problem-solving skills, being less susceptible to manipulation by the child, enhancing their consistency in administering discipline and rewards, helping them find ways to reduce stress, and reducing parental drug and alcohol abuse.

MST therapists also work with the targeted youth to remediate deficits in interpersonal skills that hinder acceptance by prosocial peers. Youth and therapist may work on modifying thought processes and coping mechanisms that may interfere with the family, peer, school, and neighborhood microsystems. Other MST strategies include decreasing the teenager's antisocial peer contacts and increasing affiliation with prosocial peers and activities. Another strategy is developing strategies to monitor and promote the youth's school performance. For example, the therapist would work toward opening and maintaining effective communication lines between parents, teachers, and administrators.

One of the first studies concerning the effectiveness MST was conducted with a population of youths from Simpsonville, South Carolina, who had at least three nonviolent arrests or one violent arrest and who were living with at least one parent. The participants in the study averaged 3.5 arrests and had spent an average of 9.5 weeks in lockup in a correctional facility. Their average age was 15.2 years. The results showed that those youths receiving MST were less likely to be arrested and reduced incarceration by 64 percent during a 59-week follow-up, compared with a control group of youths who received usual services (court-ordered curfew and/or referral to a community agency). They were also reportedly less aggressive with peers compared with the control group. The lower rearrest rates held for at least 2.5 years after treatment (Henggeler et al., 1993).This is a relatively long follow-up compared with most intervention studies and demonstrates that the program has considerable promise.

In another study, Borduin et al. (1995) examined the long-term effects of MST compared with individual therapy on the prevention of criminal behavior and violent offending among 176 juvenile offenders at high risk of committing more serious crimes. A four-year follow-up of rearrest data revealed that MST was more effective than individual therapy in preventing future criminal behavior, including violent behavior. The MST program reduced rearrests for violent and other serious crime by 63 percent over the four-year follow-up.

In a more recent follow-up of the Borduin et al. (1995) study, Shaeffer and Borduin (2005) followed the original 176 participants for nearly 14 years. The data showed that MST participants had significantly lower recidivism rates at follow-up than did those participants who received individual therapy (50% vs. 81%, respectively). Recidivism, depending on the study, refers to rearrest, reconviction, or incarceration after an initial juvenile arrest, conviction, or incarceration. Furthermore, MST offenders, compared with individually treated offenders, had 54 percent fewer arrests and 57 percent fewer days of confinement in adult correctional facilities.

 ## SUMMARY AND CONCLUSIONS

Prevention, intervention, and treatment programs for juvenile offenders give us reason to hope. In an era when much of the public fears crime and is skeptical about the prospect of reforming offenders, research results on some approaches to treating even serious juvenile offenders are promising. We began the chapter with a review of characteristics that programs with good results have in common. Not surprisingly, they begin early in a child's life, they are conscious of key principles of child and adolescent development, they focus on multiple settings in a child's life (e.g., the child, family, school), they acknowledge and respect cultural backgrounds, and they focus on the family first, with a goal of improving parental skills. With regard to the last characteristic, it is easy to give up on some families that seem highly dysfunctional. However, in many situations, the family is what is familiar to the child. If not sensitive to this, some therapists may overlook or diminish the love and sense of belonging that exists.

We provided a brief review of the history of juvenile justice. Slightly over one hundred years old, the juvenile courts exist as an alternative to criminal processing. They are informal and rehabilitative and ideally designed to give a child or adolescent a second chance. Juveniles courts, nevertheless, have high caseloads, may be more punitive than rehabilitative, and undoubtedly confine some juveniles to institutions where they are unlikely to receive the care and treatment they need. This has been a weakness of juvenile courts historically, despite the fact that a separate system for juveniles seems intuitively the wise approach. As we have seen, however, in recent years there has been a trend to transferring large number of juveniles to adult criminal courts, which are more structured but less likely to provide them with meaningful rehabilitative options.

Prevention and intervention programs in juvenile justice were classified according to a tripartite model: primary or universal prevention, secondary or selective prevention, and treatment or intervention (also called tertiary prevention). We provided illustrations of each category, focusing most on treatment programs. Primary prevention programs are intended for all children in a given group, whether or not they are "at risk" of engaging in delinquency. Prenatal services, tactics to encourage resilience, school nutrition programs, and Project D.A.R.E. are examples of such programs. Although research on such programs is positive, because of their universal nature it is difficult to conduct adequate follow-up studies to determine whether children do engage in delinquent behavior. Secondary programs are aimed at "at-risk" children: those with demographic or individual features suggesting that they are likely to engage in delinquency. We discussed the Fast Track Project as a prime illustration of this secondary approach.

The focus on treatment, or tertiary prevention, highlighted a variety of programs that have yielded favorable research results, both in institutional settings and in the community. Research on institutional treatment is discouraging at best. The rehabilitation approaches tried have often been simplistic and narrowly focused; alternatively they have not been submitted to empirical research, so we cannot know whether they were effective. Adolescents who have received either traditional or nontraditional (e.g., wilderness camps; boot camps) institutional treatment fare less well than those receiving intensive community treatment. Within the institutions, however, some programs may be more promising than others.

Juvenile sex offender treatment is a case in point. Treatment programs for JSOs (as well as for adults) focus on the distorted thought processes, or cognitions, characteristic of most offenders. Put another way, they often interpret the behavior of the victim as a come-on or as deriving gratification from sexual assault. Treatment approaches to juvenile sex offenders not only emphasize the fault in these interpretations and help develop victim empathy, but also develop social skills and the management of emotions in the offender. Other factors in the juvenile's life (e.g., peer rejection, family abuse) also must be considered. Treatment of juvenile sex offenders is not a simplistic enterprise, but current research suggests reason for optimism.

Juveniles who kill make up an extremely small but intriguing proportion of all juvenile offenders. We should note that, with the trend to transfer juveniles to criminal court, many of these individuals—particularly those 15 and above—will not be treated in juvenile facilities. Overall, for those who are, there appears to be a satisfactory adjustment both in the juvenile facility and in the community after release. However, this is far more likely for juveniles who killed parents, intimates, or close acquaintances in a one-time incident than it is for those who are hard core and persistent and kill in the process of committing other crimes.

Juveniles with psychopathic characteristics—whether or not they killed—are receiving considerable attention in psychological research. In contrast to the pessimistic conclusions about adult psychopaths, conclusions about juveniles suggest that their behavior can be changed. Randall Salekin and his associates (2006) have conducted meta-analyses of many treatment programs for these juveniles and have concluded that intensive, cognitive-based treatment can result in a development of empathy, less lying, and in general a decrease in psychopathic characteristics.

We ended the chapter with coverage of nontraditional forms of treatment, including boot camp and wilderness camp experiences and the community-based multisystemic therapy (MST). Despite widespread public support and support from some quarters in criminal justice, the military-based boot camp approach has little likelihood of therapeutic success. Even those camps that emphasize education or rehabilitation rather than a militaristic regimen do not produce good results. Boot camps are typically not intended for serious and persistent juvenile offenders, however. Wilderness camps, another nontraditional alternative, often include youths who were found to have committed sex offenses. Although these camps may promote positive characteristics, such as improvement in self-esteem, they do not seem to have a major impact on recidivism rates. Research on wilderness camps is notoriously weak methodologically, however. If there is success, it has not been demonstrated to the point where it meets rigid research criteria.

A far more promising approach is multisystemic therapy, the community-based, intensive therapy approach for serious offenders outlined by Henggeler and his associates (1992). A fundamental premise of MST is that youths—even those who committed violent crimes—are better served in their own homes, away from the influences of institutional life. MST offers intensive treatment that focuses on all of the juvenile's social systems: the family, the school, the neighborhood, and the peer group, to the extent that these are relevant. MST therapists—social workers and counselors—have very small caseloads and are able to focus extensively on developing resources to support the existing family unit.

Although community-based programs like MST are promising, even for some violent juveniles, it would be naïve to believe that all serious juvenile offenders can be treated in the community. Unless we do away with the juvenile justice system and place all juveniles in the custody of "adult" corrections, there will always be a need to hold some in secure residential settings. The challenge, therefore, is to develop effective treatment programs for the small group of adolescents who cannot benefit from less restrictive community alternatives.

KEY CONCEPTS

Juvenile Court Act	Fast-Track Project
Juvenile Justice and Delinquency	Boot camps
Prevention Act	Multisystemic therapy
Juvenile courts	OJJDP
Universe prevention	Office of Juvenile Justice and Delin-
Tertiary programs	quency Prevention

JJDPA

Primary prevention

Selective prevention

Treatment

Restrictive intervention

Wilderness and adventure programs

MST

REVIEW QUESTIONS

1. Describe the Juvenile Court Act and why it was originally enacted.
2. Define and identify the major difference between universal prevention and selective prevention. Give two examples of each.
3. Describe the effectiveness of treatment of juvenile sex offenders.
4. What is meant by restrictive interventions?
5. Are boot camps and wilderness and adventures programs successful in treating juveniles? Explain.
6. Describe the Fast-Track Project.
7. Carefully describe multisystemic therapy. On what group of juvenile offenders has it been most successful?
8. What is meant by the term "resilience"? Why is so important in prevention and intervention programs?

CHAPTER 18

CORRECTIONAL PSYCHOLOGY

CHAPTER OBJECTIVES

- Overview of correctional psychology.
- Briefly sketch what correctional psychologists do.
- Describe the correctional system at the state and federal levels.
- Review the rationales for the punishment of offenders.
- Summarize the classification systems used in corrections today.
- Provide the research on the psychological effects of imprisonment.
- Discuss treatment of special categories of offenders.

A s we have seen throughout this text, people who commit crime do so for a wide range of reasons and display a very broad range of behaviors. Even when we concentrate on the persistent, serious offender—as we have tended to do here—there is wide variability and no "typical" criminal. Persistent offenders engage in various crimes in a variety of ways for a variety of reasons, and they come from divergent social, psychological, neurological, and biological backgrounds. Correctional psychology, the subfield of psychology that is the topic of this chapter, must be highly attuned to these many nuances of criminal behavior. Correctional psychologists consult with the correctional system, provide direct services to persons convicted of crime, and conduct research on psychological issues relevant to prisons, jails, and community corrections.

Many persistent offenders tend to be polydrug users, using whatever combinations of drugs are on the market at an affordable price. Their crime may or may not be related to their drug use, but once incarcerated they would benefit from substance abuse treatment. Persistent offenders also do not typically specialize in any one type of offending, but tend to demonstrate a wide variety of antisocial behaviors, ranging from theft to aggravated assault. In fact, the frequency, seriousness, and variety of offending are highly correlated (Farrington, 1987). Moreover, the frequency of offending seems to decline with age, especially around age 40, but the reasons for this decline are unknown. The natural aging process, the need to compete with younger and more agile offenders, pressure from family and friends, or perhaps simply a desire to change one's ways all may help explain this desistance.

An increasingly recognized exception to all of the above general statements is the persistent white-collar offender, an individual who does not fit neatly into many of the above characteristics. White-collar offenders—whether they be individual occupational offenders or corporate offenders—probably do not have the educational or family backgrounds associated with the typical persistent offender. Furthermore, we may also speculate that their offending may begin later in life rather than in the typical teen or early adult years—but it may be that earlier antisocial behavior was not brought to the attention of public officials. Because researchers rarely investigate background or personality variables in these offenders, we have little information at our disposal. Furthermore, white-collar offenders are rarely mentioned in the psychological literature on corrections. The focus is predominantly on violent offenders, substance abusers, sex offenders, and mentally disordered inmates.

Although there are some good indications that persistent offenders have nervous systems that require high amounts of stimulation, there is little reason to believe that these neurological propensities cannot be overcome by learning and cognitive factors, as well as by the influences of the social environment. Human beings are not simply driven by animal instincts, genetic programming, chromosomal anomalies, or primitive biological urges or proclivities from their evolutionary past. They are also thinking, active agents with dreams, goals, and unique perceptions and versions of the world. These versions and goals influence their ongoing behavior, including behavior that violates criminal law. Cognitive processes and constructs can override biology in human action and conduct. Nor is there convincing evidence that any sizable portion of criminal behavior is propelled by some mental disease, biological abnormality, or addiction. As we learned in chapter 7, serious mental disorder can rob some individuals of the mental state needed to hold them responsible for their crimes. However, most mentally disordered individuals are not criminal, and most criminals are not mentally ill. Furthermore, empirical research does not support the frequent media portrayals that "addictions"—for example, sexual addiction, alcohol addiction, kleptomania—compel individuals to commit crime.

Human beings are highly adaptable and changeable. Thus, the focus of this chapter is on the work of correctional psychologists in understanding and changing criminal behavior patterns. In addition, correctional psychologists try to help inmates adapt to living in a jail or prison environment.

CAREERS IN CORRECTIONAL PSYCHOLOGY

The three main services provided by correctional psychologists are (1) assessment, diagnosis, and classification; (2) treatment or intervention; and (3) research, planning, and evaluation. Several studies have provided information from correctional psychologists themselves on the work they do in each of these three areas. In one of the earlier projects, Clements (1987) found that a majority of correctional psychologists working in or consulting with prison systems were located in assessment or reception centers that operated centrally or regionally to screen and classify newly received offenders. Some psychologists also provided treatment services at these centers. Other correctional psychologists treated inmates diagnosed as having mental disorders or adjustment problems within the correctional facility itself. Clements (1987) also found that psychologists made up about half of the professionally trained mental health staff in prisons and outnumbered psychiatrists by at least five to one.

In a nationwide survey of 120 American correctional psychologists, Bartol, Griffin, and Clark (1993) discovered that the *direct* services most commonly provided by psychologists working full time in the correctional setting were counseling (14.1% of their time) and psychological assessment (12.9%). A great percentage of their time was also spent at various administrative duties (14.3%) or consulting with correctional staff (9.1%). (See **Figure 18–1**.) Most of the correctional psychologists worked in state institutions or federal facilities (64.2% and 6.2%, respectively). The remainder worked in private, county, or municipal correctional institutions, such as jails and detention centers. The survey revealed that psychologists who work in the federal correctional system were paid a median salary of $60,500, compared with a $50,000 median salary for correctional psychologists working in state systems. A majority of the correctional psychologists (around 80%) thought that employment opportunities for psychologists in corrections would be excellent or very good in the future.

In a more extensive and updated study, Boothby and Clements (2000) surveyed 830 psychologists working in 48 state prisons and the Federal Bureau of Prisons. Most of the respondents (59%) held doctorate degrees, and most of the remainder held master's degrees as their highest degree (37%). Those respondents working in the Federal Bureau of Prisons all had doctorate degrees, mostly in clinical psychology. Sixty-two percent of the respondents were males, and 38% were females. Doctoral-level psychologists working in the Federal Bureau of Prisons averaged $61,800, whereas doctoral-level psychologists working in the state systems averaged $53,400. According to the Boothby-Clements survey, correctional psychologists spent most of their time on administrative tasks (30%), followed by direct treatment of inmates (26%) and psychological assessment (18%). Very little time was devoted to research (6%).

FIGURE 18–1   Percentage Distribution of What Correctional Psychologists Do

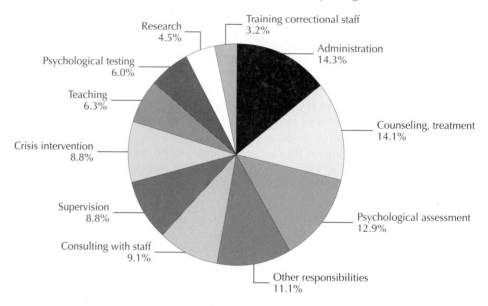

Source: Bartol, Griffin, and Clark (1993).

Boothby and Clements found that the direct treatment provided inmates was mostly one-on-one, with cognitive and behavioral therapies (88% and 69%, respectively) most preferred by the correctional psychologists. When the respondents were asked what emotional problems they most frequently treated, they reported that depression was by far the most common. Anger was a distant second, followed by psychotic symptoms, anxiety, and adjustment problems. In contrast to the more sanguine appraisals of the future of correctional psychology reported in the Bartol et al. (1993) survey, Boothby and Clements noted that many of their respondents were somewhat pessimistic about the future. They "expressed concern that the number of available jobs will gradually decrease, despite the growing need for psychological services in corrections. Those with doctorate degrees feared their positions would be lost to master's level professions, whereas those with master's degrees expressed concern about losing their jobs to social workers" (p. 726).

Nevertheless, other factors militate against this pessimistic appraisal, particularly in the federal system. The Federal Bureau of Prisons (BOP) offers internships and many career opportunities for psychologists with doctoral degrees. In the BOP, psychologists work independently, not under the supervision of psychiatrists, which occurs in many state facilities. They are involved in a wide variety of tasks, including training staff, conducting forensic evaluations for federal courts, conducting research, and of course providing direct services to prisoners, such as substance abuse treatment, crisis intervention, suicide prevention, and general mental health care. Psychologists working in state and local facilities are less likely to be employed full time—although many are— and perform similar tasks as those listed above. Finally it is important not to overlook the opportunities for psychologists consulting with community correctional agencies, such as departments of probation and parole. Community-based treatment has become more common in recent years and offers increased opportunities for psychologists (Heilbrun & Griffin, 1999).

Finally, because diagnosis, classification, and treatment are increasingly guided by evaluation research, the need for psychologists specializing in research is expected to become even greater. We will review many of the functions mentioned above in the remainder of this chapter. Before we do, however, it is important that we have some familiarity with the correctional system as a whole.

THE CORRECTIONAL SYSTEM

In the United States, detained, accused, and convicted persons—when incarcerated—are housed in three types of facilities: jails, community-based facilities, and prisons. As described briefly in the previous chapter, **jails** are operated by local (or sometimes state) governments to hold persons temporarily detained, awaiting trial, or sentenced to confinement for a misdemeanor, usually for less than one year. Therefore, jails house a mixture of persons at various stages of criminal justice processing. Nationwide about 50 percent to 60 percent of the jail population at any given time has not been convicted, but rather is awaiting trial.

Community-based corrections facilities are operated by public or private organizations (under governmental contract). They hold persons for less than 24 hours of each day to allow them limited opportunity to work, attend school, or make other community contacts. Group homes, substance abuse treatment centers, and halfway houses are examples of these facilities. Overall, community-based facilities of this sort house about 4 percent of all those *confined* in the correctional system. It is not, though, secure confinement. In addition, about two-thirds of all persons under correctional supervision remain in the community, such as on probation or parole (Bureau of Justice Statistics, 2002), without confinement. This is an important distinction to make, because psychologists often work with offenders who are allowed to remain in the community.

Prisons are operated by state and federal governments to hold persons sentenced under state and federal laws after being convicted of felonies, to terms of more than one year. Prisons are often classified according to three levels of security: maximum, medium, and minimum. In recent years, a new category—the ultramax prison—has appeared on the scene. In addition to these security classifications among facilities, there are parallel classifications *within* a facility.

Special units within prisons or within prison systems hold special categories of offenders, such as the mentally ill, chronically violent, or those with serious physical illnesses. Maximum or close-security prisons are typically surrounded by a double fence or wall (usually 18 to 25 feet high) guarded by armed correctional officers in observation towers. Medium security prisons typically are enclosed within double fences topped with razor wire and also typically have armed guards in towers or patrolling perimeters. Virtually all have video surveillance and various forms of electronic monitoring, with a control center capable of the remote closing off of sections of the facility, sometimes including individual cells, in the event of an emergency. Minimum security prisons usually do not have armed guards—though some may be—and may or may not have fences surrounding the buildings, but video surveillance is still a possibility. In the United States (as of 2000), states operated 1,375 correctional facilities and the Federal Bureau of Prisons operated 96 facilities.

Women comprise 6 percent to 10 percent of all persons incarcerated, and consequently the great majority of jails and prisons are male facilities. There are few *jails* specifically designed for women: On the whole, women in jail are kept in a separate unit within a predominantly male facility, but there are exceptions. The large New York City jail on Rikers Island, for example, has a separate building for women that is independent of the accommodations for male detainees. The massive Sybil Brand Institute in California is another example. Most states have no more than one or a few women's *prisons,* which means that women are more likely than men to be imprisoned in areas that are far from their homes. Women's prisons are also rarely classified according to maximum, medium, and minimum security levels. Thus, the one woman's prison is likely to be more rather than less secure, meaning that many women are kept in higher security levels than they actually need (Owen, 2000).

It is important to note that in at least six states the concepts of jail and prison are combined. In these jurisdictions, the state controls the entire correctional system, so no distinction is made between locally controlled jails and state controlled prisons. Thus, the same facility may house detainees, sentenced misdemeanants, and sentenced felons—although the detainees and convicted offenders are usually held in separate units of the facility. Additionally, in these "mixed system" states, there is typically one or more facilities set aside for special offender populations, such as highly dangerous offenders or the mentally disordered.

At the beginning of the twenty-first century, over 2 million individuals were held in jails and prisons in the United States, representing approximately one in 32 adults (Bureau of Justice Statistics, 2002). Approximately 4 million adults were under correctional supervision in the community, such as on probation or parole. Incarceration rates for women have increased more rapidly than those for men, although women continue to represent less than 10 percent of the incarcerated population. Black males are significantly overrepresented. Black males, between the ages 20 and 39, made up nearly 25 percent of the entire inmate population in all state and federal facilities (Harrison & Beck, 2006).

In 2005, the **Federal Bureau of Prisons (BOP)** had 184,484 inmates under custody in 96 facilities, which includes penitentiaries, federal correctional institutions, federal prison camps, and federal medical centers (Harrison & Beck, 2006). The BOP also has some inmates in contract facilities, mostly community corrections centers or detention facilities, which are operated by non-BOP staff. In fact, federal detainees are often kept in local jails because of the dearth of federal detention centers across the country. Interestingly, federal detention centers associated with the military came to public attention following the terrorist events of September 11, 2001, when the government began to hold persons either suspected of having information about or directly involved in these events. In spring 2006 the U.S. Supreme Court ruled that these detainees are entitled to some due process protections, including the right to consult with attorneys and to have the legality of their detentions reviewed by nonmilitary courts.

Over the years, there has been a steady increase in prison and jail populations in the United States, and a similar pattern in Canada (Bonta, Wallace-Capretta, & Rooney, 2000). As noted, the inmate population for women is increasing at a rate higher than for men, and has more than doubled since 1990 (Beck, 2000). Since 1990, the number of female prisoners has increased 108 percent, compared with a male increase of 77 percent (Bureau of Justice Statistics, 2001b). These increases in prison and jail populations probably reflect a judicial and societal change in attitude about what should be done about offenders, rather than any dramatic increase in crime rates, because crime rates during that same period have either stabilized or gone down.

Nearly 64 percent of all adult inmates have experienced prior incarceration—either in juvenile facilities, adult institutions, or both. About two-thirds of women confined in state prisons had a history of prior conviction, and three-fourths of men serving time in state prisons had a prior conviction record (Greenfeld, 1999). After release from prison, about 12 percent are likely to be back in prison within one year. After three years, about 24 percent of the parolees return to prison. However, more than half of all prison returns are for technical violations of parole, such as failure to notify a parole officer before leaving the state or failure to attend mandated treatment sessions. The remainder is for convictions of a new crime. When former inmates reach age 30, there is a high probability that they will not return to prison. The reasons are multiple, but one viable explanation is that the justice system, in effect, physically "wears down" offenders. In other words, they are tired of repeatedly being arrested, appearing in court, and having to adjust to incarceration. A more optimistic appraisal is that they have aged out of crime and have found alternatives to a criminal lifestyle. Recall that we earlier noted that the frequency of offending for persistent offenders typically decreases after age 40.

Tables 18–1 and **18–2** list the types of offenses for which inmates in state and federal prisons have been convicted. Notice that nearly 60 percent of the inmates serving time in U.S. federal prisons in 1998 were incarcerated for drug offenses.

TABLE 18–1   State Prison Population (624,900) by Offense Type, 2002

MOST SERIOUS OFFENSE	1995	2002
Total	100%	100%
Violent	47	51
Property	23	20
Drug	22	21
Public-Order	9	7

Source: Bureau of Justice Statistics, 2006.

TABLE 18–2   Number of Sentenced Inmates in U.S. Federal Prisons by Most Serious Offense, 1998

TYPE OF OFFENSE	NUMBER OF INMATES	PERCENTAGE OF TOTAL
Total	108,925	100.0%
Violent offenses	**12,656**	**11.6**
Homicide	1,344	1.2
Robbery	8,773	8.0
Other violent	2,539	2.3
Property offenses	**8,773**	**7.9**
Burglary	249	0.1
Fraud	6,465	5.9
Other property	1,913	1.8
Drug offenses	**63,011**	**57.9**
Public order offenses	**22,273**	**20.5**
Immigration	7,430	6.8
Weapons	8,742	8.0
Other public order	6,101	5.6
Other/unspecified	2,358	2.2

Source: Beck, 2000, p. 12.

SOCIETAL RATIONALE FOR PUNISHMENT OF OFFENDERS

Four fundamental considerations are usually in operation when offenders are sentenced: (1) protection of others, frequently called **incapacitation,** (2) **rehabilitation,** (3) **retribution,** and (4) **deterrence.** It is important to keep in mind that these goals can be achieved both by imprisonment and by community sanctions. In fact, some correctional scholars argue that imprisonment should be reserved only for serious, violent offenders or for repeat nonviolent offenders whose criminal activities do not desist (e.g., Newman, 1995).

Incapacitation is the most straightforward justification for punishing individuals, and it is most commonly applied to incarceration. Nevertheless, even persons living in their own homes can be incapacitated to some extent, as by means of house arrest or electronic monitoring. If the criminal is believed dangerous to society, on the basis of the crimes he or she has committed, it is obvious that society must be protected from future injury. However, if we rely heavily on incapacitation to remove the offender from the streets, we are in danger of increasing the inmate population dramatically and far beyond the present capacity of correctional facilities. Research has consistently documented that a small percentage—around 6 percent to 10 percent—of the criminal population commits an inordinate amount of the crime—perhaps more than 50 percent of the total (Walker, 2001; Wolfgang, 1972). For example, Peterson, Braiker, and Polich (1981) reported that the average prisoner committed about three serious crimes per year of street time, while the most frequent offender (about 8% of the inmate population) committed over 60 serious crimes per year of street time. Incapacitation directed at this small percent—a strategy called **selective incapacitation**—might be a more effective means of reducing crime. This was the principle behind the "three-strikes" laws that were passed in many states in the 1980s and remain in the statutes today. Unfortunately, these laws do not necessarily identify the most dangerous chronic offender and are often considered to be very poor policy by criminal justice scholars (Walker, 2001).

Rehabilitation as a justification for confinement often prompts heated debate. Rehabilitation is essentially restoring the person to a useful life, either through education, training, treatment (e.g., psychotherapy, behavior modification), or a combination of these. During the 1970s and 1980s, rehabilitation lost favor with much of society, including courts and criminal justice practitioners. Contributing to this disenchantment was a provocative article by R. M. Martinson (1974), arguing that the concept of rehabilitation, especially in the form of treatment methods then in operation, was ineffective. The concept of rehabilitation has yet to regain a comfortable foothold within the correctional system, but the 1990s saw a resurgence of interest, as we will discuss later in the chapter (e.g., Gaes, Flanagan, Motiuk, & Stewart, 1999).

Retribution as a goal of sanctioning refers to the belief that individuals should be held accountable for the harms they do to society and should be punished proportionally to those harms. If we break society's laws, it is only right and just that we be punished. The retributive philosophy is not identical to the concept of revenge, which suggests a more emotional response to a person's criminal behavior. Retribution implies *just* punishment that is not excessive or disproportionate to the crime committed.

Deterrence reflects society's assumption that some form of punishment—defined as aversive consequences for one's behavior—is an effective method of behavior control. In correctional literature, two forms of deterrence, general and specific, are discussed (Andeneas, 1968). **General deterrence** serves as a threat system to society as a whole. Thus, when an individual is sentenced (e.g., to a long prison term), the rest of society is given a message: "If you choose to violate this rule, this is what will happen." The threat and fear of similar punishment should act as a potent deterrent. **Specific** (sometimes called special) **deterrence** applies the threat directly to the person being sentenced. The punishment given should deter him or her from future violations.

Theoretical discussions on the effectiveness of punishment as a deterrent often revolve around the aforementioned dichotomy. The long-debated question surrounding the relationship between deterrence and criminal conduct has never been satisfactorily answered. It is usually assumed that direct application of aversive stimuli is more effective than the observation or knowledge of punishing consequences. In other words, many shoplifters are not deterred from a first offense by signs that warn them of possible prosecution, or by reading or hearing about other offenders (general deterrence). However, the embarrassment of actually having one's name published in the local newspaper and the pain of paying a fine or spending time in confinement is much more likely to prevent future violations.

It is reasonable to assume, however, that general deterrence or the threat of punishment does prevent a significant number of people from violating the law. However, as we have discussed throughout the book, many crimes occur when individuals are disengaged from their normal constructs or normal inhibitions. Furthermore, crime often brings rewards—monetary gain, status, physiological arousal, a way out of an unbearable situation—that are greater than the threats of possible punishment.

In addition, the general deterrence associated with the legal system may not be as powerful as the threat of punishment established through socialization and moral development. It is reasonable to assume that a very large segment of the population will not engage in serious criminal activity, even if there is no police officer at the elbow. For most people, fear of social, parental, or self-disapproval operate as sufficient deterrents to persistent offending. In keeping with our theme of the complexity of human behavior, it is probable that some combination of the aforementioned internal and external checks are operating for the majority of people who do not engage in serious crime.

In sum, society punishes criminal offenders under a variety of rationales, not all of which are persuasive from a psychological perspective. Given their choice, most correctional psychologists would probably maintain that rehabilitation is the most justified, because efforts are made to restore the individual to a point whereby he or she can again be a contributing member of society. As we will see shortly, rehabilitation can be a frustrating endeavor, although it is one well worth pursuing. In the following sections, we review some of the specific tasks performed by correctional psychologists, including those associated with the rehabilitative goal of corrections. We also focus on psychological adjustment to prison, specifically on the conditions within prison settings that may contribute to the decline of an inmate's mental health.

CLASSIFICATION AND PREDICTION

Classification, whether in jails and prisons or in community settings, is done for two purposes: custody and treatment. Correctional administrators want to know how closely an inmate or a person on parole should be supervised, as well as what services and programs should be offered. Classification for custody is not necessarily related to the crime for which a person was convicted, but it may be. For example, a person with no history of violent behavior in a prison setting, convicted of murdering his spouse, may not require a high security facility. On the other hand, a person convicted of sexual abuse of children may require placement in protective custody, to keep him safe from possible victimization at the hands of other prisoners. Likewise, a sex offender in the community may require more frequent and close monitoring than a parolee convicted of burglary who has served some prison time.

In sum, then, classification serves a number of important functions within the correctional system. First, it helps corrections officials make decisions about inmate placement in order to provide a safe environment for all inmates and staff. Specifically, classification helps correctional staff to differentiate low-risk offenders from high-risk ones, thereby insuring institutional security. This is the classification for the custody purpose already discussed. Second, it provides information for treatment, intervention, and rehabilitation—the treatment purpose mentioned earlier. Third, classification helps in making predictions about recidivism and other risks to society. For example, classification helps parole boards in their release decisions and enables probation and parole officers to assign different levels of supervision according to risk (Bonta & Cormier, 1999).

From a psychological perspective, the process of classification also simplifies and summarizes, enhances prediction, and reminds us that crime and delinquency are behaviorally and psychologically heterogeneous with multiple causes. The psychologist who works with the correctional system is often very closely involved with the classification of offenders.

If we do not intend to treat all offenders alike and do not intend to behave haphazardly toward them, some form of classification for treatment is necessary (Sechrest, 1987). Clements (1996), stated the same idea somewhat differently: "Somewhere between the extremes of 'all offenders are alike' and 'each offender is unique' lies a system (or systems) of categorization along pertinent dimensions that will prove to be of value in reaching correctional goals. Classification systems aggregate individuals into subgroups that share common symptoms, etiology, behavioral attributes, or other relevant characteristics" (p. 123).

Clements (1996) reviewed two decades of research on offender classification. He noted at the outset of his review that a variety of interrelated themes have occurred in the research. It is worthwhile to state these themes, because they provide an excellent illustration of what the classification process involves. The themes appearing in the research include the following: "risk assessment; the specification of offender typologies leading to differential treatment; process factors that facilitate or impede accurate classification and appropriate assignments; validity and extension studies of various approaches; the use of an offender classification database as a management and planning tool; the development of instruments and systems for both institutional and community correctional settings; assessment of specific offender needs; comparative studies of different approaches to classification assessment; and basic psychometric reports on various factor structures in offender profiles, particularly those based on the MMPI" (p. 121). After highlighting promising trends in these themes, Clements concluded that there was no one "right" classification system, nor was there one assessment instrument that could be integrated across all purposes. In the following section, we focus on a few of the more prominent methods of classification available in the correctional literature.

Classification Systems

One of the earliest classification systems was that proposed by Edward Megargee (Megargee & Bohn, 1977, 1979), based on the MMPI. Offenders are identified as one of 10 types, each type correlated with a specific behavioral and adjustment profile. Although Megargee's approach is widely recognized for its historical significance, this trait-based classification scheme has its limitations. Clements (1996) notes that it has held up "reasonably well" (p. 132), despite questions raised about the reproducibility of its 10 inmate types, its extensions to new correctional settings, and questions of its stability/reliability over time. However, as Clements (1996) implies, perhaps even more valuable is Megargee's list of seven criteria for a good classification system (e.g., sufficient completeness so that most offenders can be classified; provision of clear operational definitions).

Other early classification systems that we do not discuss here have included Quay's Adult Internal Management System (AIMS) (Quay, 1984), Warren's Interpersonal Maturity Level (I-level) (Warren, 1983), and the Jesness (1971) Inventory Classification System. In 1994, Patricia Van Voorhis published a text that remains the only contemporary scholarly book devoted exclusively to psychological classification in corrections. In that book she analyzed the field of correctional classification and also provided a comprehensive research report on five systems (Clements, 1996).

Although a good many schemes or systems of classification have been proposed over the years, corrections research in Canada has led the way in recent development of reliable and valid measures that are based on risk and/or needs appraisal. Examples include the Level of Service Inventory—Revised (LSI-R) (Andrews & Bonta, 1995), the Violence Risk Appraisal Guide (VRAG) (Harris, Rice, & Quinsey, 1993; Quinsey, Harris, Rice & Cormier, 1998), the HCR-20 (Webster, Douglas, Eaves, & Hart, 1997), the Self-Appraisal Questionnaire (Loza, Dhaliwal, Kroner, & Loza-Fanous, 2000), and, of course, the Psychopathy Checklist—Revised (PCL-R) (Hare, 1991) discussed in chapter 6. The HCR-20, described briefly in chapter 8, consists of 10 historical items (H variables), five clinical items (C variables), and five risk management items (R variables), hence the acronym HCR-20 (Grann, Belfrage, & Tengström, 2000). All of these scales and risk assessment instruments listed earlier have strengths and weaknesses, all show considerable promise, and very active research programs are focused on each.

Most recently David Simourd (1997; Simourd & Van De Ven, 1999) has advocated a reexamination of the Criminal Sentiments Scale—Modified (CSS-M) as a viable assessment instrument to measure attitudes, values, and beliefs of offenders. This is based on Simourd's contention that criminal attitudes have been identified as a crucial factor in the theoretical understanding and treatment of criminal behavior.

One of the key concepts emerging from the Canadian research is the concept of **dynamic risk factors** (Andrews & Bonta, 1998; Andrews, Bonta, & Hoge, 1990). Dynamic risk factors are the ones that *change* over time and situation. For example, attitudes, values, and beliefs have considerable potential for change, in contrast to the **static risk factors** (or historical factors) of biological parents, gender, birth order, race/ethnic background, and general background variables. Changing attitudes, beliefs, and values is a much more realistic goal in corrections than simply identifying which static predictors are associated with crime behavior. "Dynamic risk factors are characteristics that can change, and when changed, result in a corresponding increase or decrease in recidivism risk" (Hanson & Harris, 2000, p. 7). Dynamic risk factors can be subdivided into *stable* dynamic factors and *acute* dynamic factors (Hanson & Harris, 2000). Stable dynamic factors, although they are changeable, usually change slowly, sometimes taking months or even years to modify. An example is self-esteem. Acute dynamic factors, on the other hand, change rapidly (days, hours, or minutes), and include such things as alcohol or drug intoxication or mood swings. Hanson and Harris (2000), for example, found that acute dynamic factors, such as anger and subjective distress, were better predictors of recidivism for sex offenders (rapists and pedophiles) than were the more stable dynamic factors.

Offenders may have a variety of needs, but not all needs are related to criminal behavior (Bonta, Wallace-Capretta, & Rooney, 2000). To be effective, treatment or rehabilitation programs must target those needs that will change criminal behavior. Dynamic risk factors that are associated with ongoing criminal behavior are often called **criminogenic needs,** whereas other dynamic factors (e.g., self-esteem, fears) associated with noncriminal behavior are called *noncriminogenic needs*. The concept of criminogenic needs is becoming firmly established in Canadian corrections (Bonta & Cormier, 1999), and is slowly becoming established in U.S. corrections. Therefore, the more effective treatments and rehabilitation strategies in corrections—if a reduction in recidivism is the goal—should be focused on addressing criminogenic needs.

PSYCHOLOGICAL EFFECTS OF IMPRISONMENT

Clinical case studies on the effects of prison life have often concluded that, for many individuals, imprisonment can be brutal, demeaning, and generally devastating. These studies often describe a variety of psychological symptoms believed to be caused directly by imprisonment, including psychosis, severe depression, inhibiting anxiety, and social withdrawal. However, research (e.g., Adams, 1992; Toch & Adams, with Grant, 1989; Toch & Adams, 1989; Zamble & Porporino, 1988) raises serious questions about the extent of serious psychological deterioration that is *caused* by imprisonment. Nevertheless, whether individuals displayed symptoms after imprisonment or came in with these symptoms, it appears that a significant number of incarcerated individuals need mental health attention. It is estimated, for example, that 19 percent of the U.S. correctional population suffers from a variety of serious mental disorders (Ashford, Sales, & Reid, 2001). While this figure relates to both jail and prison populations, most of the research focuses on prisons, probably because prison stays are longer than jail stays. However, jail detainees and inmates are often more in psychological crisis than prison inmates.

Zamble and Porporino (1988) examined the coping strategies and adjustment characteristics of inmates in Canadian penitentiaries. They found that emotional disruption and adjustment were clearly problems for most inmates during the beginning of their sentences, particularly signs of serious to moderate depression. This deleterious reaction came as no surprise, as prison produces a dramatic disruption in customary behavior, compounded by restrictions, deprivations, and constraints. However, these initial reactions soon dissipated for most inmates, and no *lasting* emotional disturbance was discernible as the inmate became adjusted to his surroundings and prison routine. Toch and Adams (with Grant, 1989) report a similar pattern in their study of American prisoners. The Toch-Adams data suggest that inmates with serious emotional problems also tend to be disruptive in prison.

Inmate reactions to prison life appear to follow a curvilinear pattern, with stress indicators increasing at the beginning of the term, then dropping, and then rising again as the end of their term approaches (Bukstel & Kilmann, 1980). Sometimes referred to as the "short-timer's syndrome," many inmates exhibit signs of distress, sleeplessness, restlessness, and anxiety, probably in anticipation of the new coping strategies required for the outside.

Zamble and Porporino write, "We conclude that prisons do not produce permanent harm to the psychological well-being of inmates" (1988, p. 149). On the other hand, they did not find positive effects either. "Our data show very little positive behavioral change in prison, just as earlier we could see little evidence for generalized negative effects" (p. 151). Interestingly, Toch and Adams suggest that prison experiences actually temper or even improve inmate misbehavior, most particularly in the young inmate under age 25. "Young inmates, who are presumably more rambunctious and less mature than older inmates, appear to derive some benefit from this forced environment . . . it is encouraging to find that prison inmates who are initially most resistant to restrictions on their personal liberty demonstrate increasing levels of conformity over time" (pp. 19–20). Why this happens remains largely a mystery, but Toch and Adams (with Grant, 1989) suggest that the maturation process facilitated by *humane* prison environments plays a crucial role. The researchers contend that inmate behavior is likely to improve when inmates learn the association between behavior and its positive or negative consequences within the institution, and when they have psychological support, the opportunity to participate in conventional activities, form attachment bonds, and build relationships.

In summary, a vast majority of inmates do not demonstrate *long-lasting* psychological impairment or problems as a result of imprisonment. Nevertheless, a significant number of offenders do need help, if only in crisis situations. In addition, many observers note that the prison environment of today is more violent and impersonal than the prisons of the past (e.g., Haney & Zimbardo, 1998; Johnson, 1996), leading to the conclusion that in many places a humane prison may well be an oxymoron. In addition to a violent environment, other factors may exacerbate the stress felt by prisoners, specifically crowding and isolation.

Psychological Effects of Crowding

Prison crowding has become an increasingly important topic as the prison population reaches critical numbers. Prison crowding has probably always been a concern, but the sheer number of offenders being currently processed through the system is without precedent. Nationwide, as noted at the beginning of the chapter, the incarcerated population has reached beyond 2 million, a figure that represents a tripling of the incarceration rate since 1980 (Bureau of Justice Statistics, 2001a). Virtually every state in the U.S. faces a crowding problem in one or more of its correctional facilities.

Prison and jail overcrowding does seem related to a higher incidence of physical illness, socially disruptive behavior, and emotional distress (Bukstel & Kilmann, 1980). Some researchers also have suggested that disruptive behavior in correctional facilities increases directly as the available space decreases (Megargee, 1976; Nacci, Teitelbaum, & Prather, 1977). Indeed, the violence level in U.S. prisons has increased concurrently with the crowding problem (Tonry & Petersilia, 1999).

In a 15-year project on prison crowding, Paulus (1988) concluded that increasing the number of residents in correctional housing units significantly increased the negative psychological (e.g., tension, anxiety, depression) and physical reactions (e.g., headaches, high blood pressure, cardiovascular problems) in inmates. The critical factor appears to be the number of residents sharing a space and not simply the amount of space available. For example, providing some privacy and limiting the visual and physical access of other inmates, such as providing cubicles in open dormitories (for inmates in medium or minimum security), reduces the negative impact of living there.

Paulus also found that socioeconomic level, education level, and prior prison or jail confinements were related to inmate reactions to crowded conditions. Specifically, the higher the socioeconomic and education level, the more difficult the adjustment to prison, and the lower the tolerance for crowded conditions. Presumably, many members of the lower socioeconomic class are used to living under crowded conditions and therefore are more tolerant of invasions of privacy and other factors involved in crowded environments. On the other hand, DeRosia (1995) found that inmates from more advantaged socioeconomic backgrounds had, overall, far more personal resources for adjusting to prison life, including crowded conditions, so the research on this is not consistent. Surprisingly, Paulus found that prior confinement interfered with adjustment to crowded conditions. Prisoners who had some history of prior imprisonment exhibited more problems in adjustments than those without prior time. A reason suggested by Paulus is that individuals with extensive prison histories are likely to have spent part of their time in single cells or under less-crowded conditions. This may have made them particularly sensitive to crowded conditions, such as living in a dormitory setting or being double celled. Paulus also found that men and women, and blacks and whites, react similarly to variations in social density.

Paulus hypothesizes that crowding has its primary impact through its influence on social interaction. For one thing, crowding reduces one's sense of control over the social environment, and with that many people, things become unpredictable and uncertain. Second, crowded situations interfere with one's goals (such as carrying out desired activities), restrict freedom and privacy, and expose one to a variety of undesired intrusions. And third, crowded situations produce much more activity, noise, interactions, smells, violations of personal space, and generally excessive stimulation.

In summary, the available research does indicate that crowding is related to negative psychological and physical problems in confinement. However, individuals react differently to crowded conditions, some demonstrating much better adjustment than others. There are many other variables that have to be considered also, such as the type of institution, the institution's orientation, the level of violence, opportunities to move about and to participate in work programs, the type of social milieu, the degree of crowding, and the phase an individual is at in his or her sentence.

Psychological Effects of Isolation

Prison inmates may be physically isolated or segregated from the general population for a variety of reasons and under a wide range of conditions. For purposes of discussion we can identify the following main categories: (1) **isolation** or **segregation** as a form of punishment, (2) isolation or segregation for an inmate's own protection, and (3) administrative segregation, done for management purposes. For example, administrative segregation might occur while corrections officials are investigating an incident, such as a fight in the prison yard. Most recently, administrative segregation has taken on a new meaning, with the placement of large groups of inmate in high security—ultramax—facilities.

Segregation as a form of punishment—sometimes called solitary confinement, disciplinary segregation, or punitive isolation—is a temporary condition that is subject to some legal restrictions. For example, depending on the anticipated length of the segregation and loss of "good time" credits, prisoners who are alleged to violate prison rules may be offered a hearing and an opportunity to contest the charges (Palmer & Palmer, 1999). Although this form of segregation may be quite lengthy for some prisoners, it is rarely subjected to empirical psychological research.

Protective custody is a term reserved for isolation that is for the protection of the inmate, either from himself or herself, or from the other inmates. As noted earlier in the chapter, there is no question that many prisons in the United States are violent institutions. It has been estimated that about 25,000 nonsexual assaults and close to 300,000 sexual assaults occur each year in the nation's prisons and jails (Clear & Cole, 2000). Some prisoners voluntarily seek protection from violent others, while others are placed in protective custody—even over their objections—because prison officials believe it is in their best interest. Nevertheless protection or close supervison do not guarantee that a prisoner is safe. In a highly publicized incident in 2003, a former priest who was convicted of child molestation and believed to be responsible for other abuses over many years, was strangled to death in his prison cell by another inmate.

Prisoners also may be in protective custody because correctional staff are fearful of possible suicide. This is particularly a problem in jails, which have a higher suicide rate than prisons (Lester & Danto, 1993). Suicide is the leading cause of death in jails across the nation, although in some urban jail facilities, AIDS-related deaths outnumber suicide (Ashford, Sales, & Reid, 2001). On the other hand, suicide is the third leading cause of death in *prisons*, behind natural causes and AIDS. Suicide is usually committed by young, unmarried white males during the early stages of confinement. The most common method is by hanging. A history of mental disorder and previous attempts at suicide are also significantly linked to suicide in both jails and prisons (Ivanoff & Hayes, 2001). Under protective-suicide conditions, the level of social and perceptual-sensory isolation may be even more extreme than other forms of segregation, because many materials and items must be removed from the cell so that the inmate cannot use the objects to accomplish the suicide. Placement in segregated housing or single cells is especially related to suicide in prisons (Hayes, 1995).

Whether or not they are suicide risks, mentally disordered inmates also may be placed in "observation cells" for short periods of time. These are special cells that may or may not be housed in a mental health unit in the facility. They are typically stripped of all but the barest necessities—such as metal slab with mattress for sleeping—and again are used on a temporary basis until an individual can be stabilized or transferred to a more appropriate setting.

Systematic knowledge of the psychological effects of isolation comes primarily from the psychological laboratory, using volunteers who allow themselves to be socially isolated, sometimes with sensory restrictions such as a blindfold or earphones, for varying periods of time. The research so far demonstrates that individuals respond differently to such isolation; some show great tolerance and often welcome the quiet solitude from the hustle and bustle of daily living. Others experience stress and anxiety, even after relatively short periods of isolation. In general, however, the research shows that most individuals are able to tolerate and even adjust to isolation, if the isolation is short in duration, such as a few days, or even longer if the individual knows there is a reasonable time limit on the segregation.

In the past the conditions of disciplinary segregation in particular were often deplorable. Offenders were held in cells without adequate ventilation, heat, clothing, light, sanitary, and bathroom facilities for long periods of time.

Since no published research has examined the effects of such adverse conditions, it is difficult to determine what the psychological effects might be. Fortunately, the courts—as well as professional correctional standards—eventually called for minimum humane conditions that must be met during isolation, but it would be naïve to believe that abuses in this form of segregation have completely disappeared.

One form of isolation, however, is being extensively criticized in the psychological literature (e.g., Haney & Zimbardo, 1998). This is the administrative segregation popularly known as the "**supermax**" or "**ultramax**" prison. These prisons—or sometimes units within a prison—came on the scene in the 1990s and have now been established in many states, as well as the federal government. They are extremely high security facilities intended for use with the most recalcitrant offenders—or those hardest to manage in a "regular" prison setting. Although procedures vary, in the typical supermax facility prisoners are kept in their cells for as long as 23 hours a day, allowed out for exercise for one hour. They do not communicate with each other, and their communication with corrections officers or staff is the minimal necessary to obtain food, medical, legal, or other services. Prisoners are assigned to these facilities for lengthy time periods; some have been confined since the facilities first opened. Such severe isolation has led critics to question the extent to which these individuals can retain their mental health. Indeed, at least one court has already ruled that the conditions in these high security units are cruel and unusual punishment when used with inmates who are mentally disordered (*Madrid v. Gomez,* 1995).

TREATMENT STRATEGIES

In the 1970s, rehabilitation as a goal of corrections experienced a crisis of faith. A typical comment is one made by R. J. Carlson (1976) that rehabilitation by means of psychological treatment "is out of fashion today. It is not dead yet, but the literature is littered with death warrants" (p. 32). Carlson's comment came on the heels of a broader indictment of rehabilitation that had been advanced two years earlier by Robert Martinson (1974). Martinson reviewed 231 studies of prison rehabilitative programs and concluded, "With few and isolated exceptions, the rehabilitative efforts that have been reported so far have had no appreciable effect on recidivism" (p. 25). Martinson had looked at studies on a variety of rehabilitative approaches, not all of which were associated with psychological treatment (e.g., job training programs, education). Although Martinson did not himself conclude that "nothing works," his publication was widely interpreted to have come to that conclusion.

Martinson's article, together with an increasing trend toward punishment in the criminal justice system, had a powerful effect on corrections. There was an immediate shift away from rehabilitation and toward other models of corrections, such as strict punishment with minimal efforts to rehabilitate. Later, the dust settled somewhat, and administrators became more reluctant to discard rehabilitative programs in their entirety. However, pessimism toward rehabilitation continued throughout the 1980s.

In the 1990s rehabilitation experienced a rebirth, although many of its supporters argued that it never really died. The preferred term was that it was "reaffirmed" as an important goal of corrections (Cullen & Applegate, 1997). As Tonry and Petersilia (1999, p. 8) observed, "The pessimism associated with the 'nothing works' findings wrongly attributed to Martinson's famous 1974 article . . . appears to have passed, and there are grounds for cautious optimism about the positive effects, under some conditions, of some cognitive-skills, drug-treatment, vocational training, educational, and other programs in adult prisons."

Treatment programs in jails and prisons are often handicapped by inadequate facilities, staff, programs, and financial support, however. Furthermore, particularly in prisons where the length of incarceration is longer, two systems are at work—the formal system dictated by authorities and the informal system run by inmates. In the latter, two processes may be identified: criminalization and prisonization. In **criminalization,** inmates exchange, share, and support one another's construct systems, beliefs, attitudes, and feelings. The system creates a "deviant" culture in which inmates form subgroups and develop friendships, loyalty, and commitment. **Prisonization** is the process whereby inmates learn the specific rules, general culture, and expectation of the prison community. With these two learning processes at work, which are often in conflict with society, it seems that the longer the time inmates spend in prison, the more likely they will crystallize their thinking and become "better criminals." These aspects of prison life, as well as the numerous day-to-day practices and experiences that are characteristic of incarceration—lockdowns, violence, physical altercations—make it a challenge to offer meaningful treatment in the prison setting.

For the remainder of this section, we review some of the general treatment modalities in use in corrections and review the research on treatment efforts with two specific offenders, psychopaths and sex offenders.

Psychotherapy

The terms psychotherapy, therapy, counseling, and treatment are used interchangeably by clinicians. Broadly, they refer to a set of procedures or techniques used to help individuals or groups alter their maladaptive behavior, develop adaptive behavior, or both. The behavior must be considered maladaptive by the individual, however. In other words, the person must want to change. It has long been a principle that change cannot be forced, but even this principle is being questioned today. For example, a growing body of literature is suggesting that change can be coerced, in the sense that some individuals must first be "forced" into treatment settings, and then will gradually come to accept that the treatment is in their best interest (Farabee, 2002).

Psychotherapy can be divided into six very broad and overlapping areas: psychoanalytic, behavioral, humanistic-existential, interpersonal, group, and cognitive therapy. Each approach is designed to change a person's way of thinking about the world to some extent. Most psychotherapies try to change cognitive constructs about ourselves, others, or both. Skinnerian behaviorism is probably least inclined to worry about cognitive constructs, since it focuses heavily on overt behavior to the exclusion of the mediational processes. Lately, most behaviorists have shifted to a more cognitive-behavioral approach. Within corrections, this is the approach that is associated with the most effective treatment (Gaes et al., 1999). In the following pages, we discuss first behavior therapy, then shift to the cognitive-behavioral, which is the focus of much of the available treatment in corrections today.

Behavior Therapy

Behavior therapy was developed from learning-conditioning principles derived from well-controlled, precise laboratory environments or small-scale, well-designed demonstration projects. The social and physical environments are crucial considerations in the planning of any behavior therapy program. Before the treatment program can be effectively implemented, the target behaviors and the environmental events that accompany them must be accurately described and carefully evaluated as to how, when, and where they occur for a particular individual. This information is typically gathered through direct observation of the individual within situations where he or she typically exhibits the target behavior, and through interviews with the individual and acquaintances. In the planning stage, these initial data concerning the target behavior (such as frequency) provide baseline or pretreatment information that is useful for later determinations of how effective the treatment plan has been. Once the target behaviors and the conditions under which they occur are determined, the next step usually involves establishing a twofold plan: (1) The associative or reinforcement bond between the target behavior and the environmental event must be weakened; (2) more desirable behavior must be instituted through reinforcement. When the plan has been implemented, comparing treatment data with baseline data helps to determine whether it is working. If the original treatment plan does not work, the conditions will be reassessed and a modified plan will be introduced.

Behavior therapy (also called behavior modification) seems to have a number of advantages. It has been shown to be highly effective in changing and developing specific behaviors under controlled, experimental conditions. Its apparent simplicity and the ease with which it can be applied by paraprofessionals with minimal training are also appealing. Furthermore, it is economical, because it does not require a legion of high-level, expensive professionals, and it can be immediately beneficial for controlling unmanageable behavior within the institution. Finally, because it quantifies observable behaviors, it lends itself very well to evaluation and research.

However, behavior therapy has a number of problems. While it seems to offer a simple, straightforward method of alleviating pressing behavior problems, it actually requires sophistication on the part of the therapist, stringent environmental control, and a high degree of cooperation and commitment from those even remotely involved in the program. Transferring behavior techniques from the controlled psychological laboratory to the correctional institution, where there are bound to be numerous constraints, is an extremely difficult task. Another flaw is behavior therapy's lack of demonstrated generalizability to the natural environment outside the prison, where powerful, significant models and reference groups often dilute the short-term effectiveness of many behavior therapy approaches. Finally, and perhaps most important, behavior therapy in the correctional setting raises many questions about the rights of inmates, especially if there is any indication that they are being coerced to participate or are being deprived of basic physical needs.

Behavior therapy, well applied and with the inmate's willing participation, may be useful for controlling institutional behavior and can promote the acquisition of specific social and academic skills. Furthermore, when combined with social cognitive therapy, it is beginning to demonstrate its effectiveness in inhibiting or even reducing criminal behavior in the natural environment, such as with sex offenders.

Cognitive Therapy

Criminal behavior is not simply the result of imitating others in the social environment, or even the result of external reinforcement. Research in cognitive psychology goes one step further. "If actions were determined solely by external rewards and punishments, people would behave like weathervanes, constantly shifting in different directions to conform to the momentary influence impinging on them. They would act corruptly with unprincipled individuals and honorably with righteous ones, and liberally with libertarians and dogmatically with authoritarians" (Bandura, 1977, p. 128). Instead, most human behavior is motivated and regulated in large part by personally adopted beliefs, values, and expectations.

During the past three decades, cognitive theories have come to dominate the research on learning, memory, personality, motivation, and social psychology (Aronson, Wilson, & Akert, 2005; Mahoney & Lyddon, 1988). The growth of **cognition** has also been very strong in the areas of counseling and psychotherapy. A person's behavior is the result of both external events, such as rewards and reinforcements, and internal events, such as how we think about things and perceive our world. Cognitive treatment, although the strategies differ in form and substance from one another, focuses on cognitive processes that mediate or influence behavior and emotions. Cognitive behavior therapies (CBT) rely on changing individual behavioral patterns by changing the person's thoughts, beliefs, and attitudes. CBT emerged during the past 30 years as a result of dissatisfaction with the theoretical and empirical bases of strictly behavior therapy approach. CBT has become the preferred treatment approach for dealing with certain groups of offenders, including sex offenders, violent offenders, and a variety of persistent property offenders. Bonta and Cormier

(1999) rightfully note that, "The research on the cognitive-behavioural treatment of offenders has led to wide acceptance of this approach as the preferred method for treating offenders. More traditional counseling techniques (e.g., client-centered, psychodynamic) are slowly losing favour among clinicians working with offenders" (p. 239).

One of the forerunners of the cognitive approaches was **reality therapy,** a form of self-control therapy developed by the psychiatrist William Glasser (1965) and still commonly used in corrections today. The basic principles for the approach were developed at the Ventura (California) School for Girls, whose residents were seriously delinquent adolescent girls. The popularity of reality therapy stems partly from its straightforward approach and easy-to-understand procedures. Because of its apparent simplicity, paraprofessionals and frontline correctional staff can easily be trained to offer personal and group therapy to inmates. Reality therapy is based on the perspective that offenders must face reality—no matter what happened to them in the past—and take full responsibility for their behavior now. In essence, the focus is to teach offenders responsible behavior. A major contribution of reality therapy has been to focus attention on the irresponsible nature of crime and delinquency, rather than viewing them as the result of some psychological sickness or disorder.

Other important forerunners of commonly used cognitive treatment approaches are George Kelly's (1955) *personal construct therapy,* Albert Ellis's (1962) rational-emotive therapy, and Aron T. Beck's (1970) *cognitive therapy.* All of these early approaches have undergone extensive revision since their initial formulation, and have splintered into many different therapeutic perspectives.

In the 1980s, **constructivist therapy** emerged as a viable, rapidly growing approach across a wide area of cognitive therapies. "The basic assertion of constructivism is that each individual creates his or her own representational model of the world. This experiential scaffolding . . . in turn becomes a framework from which the individual orders and assigns meaning to new experience" (Mahoney & Lyddon, 1988, p. 200). The basic idea of the constructivist approach is that individuals do not formulate static templates through which ongoing experience is filtered, but rather develop more dynamic constructs that are always subject to change as a result of new experiences. Thus, "the constructivist does not view cognitive structures as static, storage entities but rather as systems of transformation" (Mahoney & Lyddon, 1988, p. 203).

From a constructivist perspective, developing human beings are active information processors, who explore and adapt to the environment, and who continually organize information about the world and themselves into increasingly complex views (Greenberg, 1988). On the other hand, repetitively violent and antisocial individuals may be those who are essentially trapped in an isolated, socially closed-off, and self-constructive cognitive system that relies on simple, straightforward aggressive solutions to survival. Moreover, they continually fall out of mainstream society, which results in their already isolated cognitive systems becoming more narrow, restrictive, and deviant. Instead of becoming more complex and integrative, the world versions of the repetitive offender may stagnate or deteriorate. Many repetitive offenders may become so caught up in their personal versions of the world that they refuse to allow alternative views to pierce their cognitive armor. Yochelson and Samenow (1976), for example, contend that there are 52 basic errors in thinking practiced by the hard-core criminals that must be corrected before there is any hope of change. It would seem that cognitive therapies offer the best hope for changing the thinking and belief systems of the repetitive offender.

How successful has CBT been in corrections? Most research concludes that it has been reasonably successful or shows considerable promise in reducing recidivism in violent offenders (Serin & Preston, 2001), juvenile sex offenders (Becker & Johnson, 2001), adult sex offenders (Rice, Harris, & Quinsey, 2001), criminally insane persons (NGRI patients) (Salekin & Rogers, 2001), and serious repetitive offenders (Gacono et al., 2001). However, before sweeping conclusions on the effectiveness of CBT can be made, we still need considerable well-done research using a wide variety of offenders within different contexts. One of the major shortcomings of the current research is the overreliance on self-report measures to determine treatment gain (Serin & Preston, 2001). Although self-report information is important because it may reflect an offender's self-perception, it is also fraught with many serious problems, especially when administered under duress within a correctional environment. In short, self-report answers can be faked or distorted by respondents. For example, respondents can provide answers they believe authorities want to hear. In addition, official recidivism measures as indices of treatment effectiveness may be too insensitive to what really happens after release from a correctional facility. For example, it might be more meaningful to gather information from parole officers concerning the offender's adaptation to life after release or other more subtle adjustment measures rather than relying strictly on official post-release arrests and conviction records.

Serin and Preston (2001) assert that treatment effectiveness will be increased when it is tailored to the specific needs of the individual offender. Recall the discussion earlier in the chapter about dynamic risk factors and criminogenic needs. Identifying these for any offender is clearly an illustration of tailoring treatment. Becker and Johnson (2001) recommend using multimodal treatment approaches (impulse control techniques, empathy training, anger management) that are firmly based on cognitive-behavioral techniques.

We also need to have a better understanding of the relationships among the vast array of swirling systems that affect delinquent and criminal behavior before we can have highly effective treatment or prevention programs. "Human action is . . . regulated by multilevel systems of control" (Bandura, 1989, p. 1181). One such approach is a social systems theory. A social systems approach facilitates a synthesis of what we know across the various disciplines and perspectives, whether we are discussing social class, neighborhood, community, culture, family, siblings, or the individual (Bartol, 1988). Social systems theory assumes that while it is helpful to study personality variables, family, the neighborhood, and the culture in isolation, it is far more effective to study these variables in relationship to one another. In order to change criminal behavior over long periods of time, we need to study not only the offenders themselves but also their families, peers, schools, neighborhoods, communities, and cultures, all in relationship to one another. The offender affects the other systems and the systems affect the offender in complex, poorly understood ways. Treatment and preventive approaches that are fully able to appreciate this dynamic interplay are far more likely to be successful than those that only concentrate on one aspect of an individual's life.

Treatment of Psychopaths

The treatment and rehabilitation of criminal psychopaths has been shrouded with pessimism and discouragement. Hare (1996, p. 41) asserts: "There is no known treatment for psychopathy." A long line of research documents that *adult* psychopaths are not responsive to treatment, whether in prisons, psychiatric treatment centers, or in the community (e.g., Hare, Clark, Grann, & Thornton, 2000). Some commentary has indicated that psychotherapy or intervention with psychopaths is basically a waste of time. Gacono et al., (2001) concluded from their review that "simply stated, at this time there is no empirical evidence to suggest that psychopathy is treatable" (p. 111). O'Neill, Lidz, and Heilbrun (2003) remarked that "to date, there is no treatment for psychopathy that has been established as effective" (p. 300). In fact, some forms of treatment (e.g., milieu therapy) have been linked to higher rates of violent recidivism in psychopaths (Rice, Harris, & Cormier, 1992). Several studies indicate that psychopaths are either completely non-responsive to treatment or play the treatment game well, pretending to cooperate but in actuality "conning" the treatment provider (Hare, 1996; Rice, Harris, & Cormier, 1992; Porter et al., 2000). Farrington (2005a) states that "it seems to be generally believed that psychopaths are difficult to treat because (a) they are an extreme, qualitatively distinct category; (b) psychopathy is extremely persistent throughout life; (c) psychopathy has biological causes which cannot be changed by psychosocial interventions; and (d) the lying, conning, and manipulativeness of psychopaths make them treatment resistant" (pp. 494–495).

Indeed, based on the research examining the effectiveness of various treatment programs, there does not appear to be any effective treatment program for adult psychopaths in the criminal justice system today. Hare (1996, p. 41) admonishes, though: "This does not necessarily mean that the egocentric and callous attitudes and behaviors of psychopaths are immutable, only that there are no methodologically sound treatments or 'resocialization' programs that have been shown to work with psychopaths." Other researchers take a decidedly different perspective and believe that untreatability statements concerning the psychopath are unwarranted (Salekin, 2002; Skeem, Monahan, & Mulvey, 2002; Skeem et al., 2003; Wong, 2000). There is some evidence that psychopaths who receive larger "doses" of treatment are less likely to demonstrate subsequent violent behavior than those who receive less treatment (Skeem et al., 2003). It should be mentioned that a vast majority of the research has focused on recidivism rates of male psychopathic offenders, and very little is known about the recidivism rates of female psychopathic offenders.

It is usually difficult to properly evaluate the effectiveness of programs designed to treat psychopaths because of their ability to manipulate the system. For example, many psychopaths volunteer for various prison treatment programs, show "remarkable improvement," and present themselves as model prisoners. They are skillful at convincing therapists, counselors, and parole boards that they have changed for the better. Upon release, however, there is a high probability that they will reoffend. In fact, there is some evidence to suggest that psychopaths who participate in therapy are more likely to engage in violent crime following the treatment than those psychopaths who did not receive treatment. Rice, Harris, and Cormier (1992) investigated the effectiveness of an intensive therapeutic community program offered in a maximum security facility. The study was retrospective in that the researchers examined records and files 10 years after the program was completed. The results showed that psychopaths who participated in the therapeutic community exhibited higher rates of violent recidivism than did the psychopaths who did not. The results were the reverse for nonpsychopaths. Nonpsychopaths who received treatment were less likely to reoffend than nonpsychopaths who did not receive treatment.

Some critics of this study have remarked that the therapeutic community referred to was highly atypical of treatment programs in correctional facilities and has limited generalizability. Furthermore, the researchers themselves cautioned that the psychopaths used in the study were an especially serious group of offenders. Eighty-five percent had a history of violent crimes. Whether less serious psychopathic offenders will show similar results is unknown. The researchers conclude, "The combined results suggest that a therapeutic community is not the treatment of choice for psychopaths, particularly those with extensive criminal histories" (Rice, Harris, & Cormier, 1992, p. 408). Hare (1996) suggests that group therapy and insight-oriented treatment programs—both of which were features of the program reviewed above—may help the psychopath develop better ways of manipulating and deceiving others.

Treatment of Sex Offenders

Sex offenders are often highly resistant to changing their deviant behavior patterns. Although a wide variety of treatment programs have been tried, very few have been successful in eradicating sexual offending. A 1994 survey of therapeutic services for sex offenders revealed that there were 710 adult and 684 juvenile treatment programs (Longo, Bird, Stevenson, & Fiske, 1995), compared with 297 adult and 346 juvenile treatment programs in 1985 (Knopp, Rosenberg, & Stevenson, 1986). Despite the increase in treatment programs, the success ratio remains disappointingly low. After careful review of the research and clinical literature, Furby, Weinrott, and Blackshaw (1989, p. 27) concluded, "There is as yet no evidence that clinical treatment reduces rates of sex reoffenses in general and no appropriate data for assessing whether it may be differentially effective for different types of offenders." The Furby review included all variants of therapeutic approaches. Likewise, Rice, Harris, and Quinsey (2001, p. 302) write, "The effectiveness of sex-offender treatment has yet to be demonstrated. . . .

Thus the treatment outcome literature is profoundly unhelpful in giving clues about what might be effective with particular kinds of sex offenders." Nevertheless, Rice et al. note that all is not hopeless. They urge clinicians to adopt individualized treatment approaches that take into account an offender's motivation. Specific interventions designed to reduce recidivism should then be undertaken. An essential component of the treatment, they point out, is ongoing supervision.

Prentky, Knight, and Lee (1997) conclude that sex offender therapy can be categorized into four broad approaches. One approach is **evocative therapy,** a treatment that focuses on (1) helping offenders to understand the causes and motivations of their sexual behavior and (2) increasing their empathy for the victims of the sexual assault. Evocative therapy may include individual, group, couples/marital, and family counseling. A second approach is **psychoeducational counseling,** which utilizes a group or class setting to remedy deficits in social and interpersonal skills. Psychoeducational strategies include anger management, the principles of relapse prevention, and other topics such as human sexuality, dating, and myths about sexuality and relationships. A third approach is **drug treatment.** This approach concentrates on "reducing sexual arousability and the frequency of deviant sexual fantasies through the use of antiandrogen and antidepressant medication" (Prentky et al., 1997, p. 13). The fourth approach is **cognitive behavior therapy,** which focuses on changing beliefs, fantasies, attitudes, and rationalizations that justify and perpetuate sexually violent behavior. Prentky et al. (1997) suggest that the most effective approach probably resides in using some combination of the four, although which specific combination remains unclear. They agree, however, that cognitive-behavioral approaches (complemented on occasion with some medication) continue to offer the most effective technique in the temporary cessation of deviant sexual behavior in motivated individuals. Cognitive-behavior therapy argues that maladaptive sexual behaviors are learned according to the same rules as normal sexual behavior, by means of classical and/or instrumental conditioning, modeling, reinforcement, generalization, and punishment. They are, therefore, modifiable. Cognitive-behavioral therapy, compared to traditional verbal, insight-oriented therapy, has demonstrated short-term effectiveness in eliminating exhibitionism and fetishism (Kilmann et al., 1982), some forms of pedophilia (Hall, 1995; Marshall & Barbaree, 1988), and sexual aggression and arousal (Quinsey & Marshall, 1983).

The major problem, however, is not with getting the motivated offender to stop his deviant sexual pattern, but with preventing his relapse across time and situations. It is analogous to dieting. Most diet regimens do work in getting the motivated individual to lose weight. However, they offer little help in preventing people from eventually relapsing into old eating habits. This is why ongoing therapeutic supervision of sex offenders is critical.

A treatment approach showing some promise in the treatment of sex offenders is called **relapse prevention (RP).** "RP is a self-control program designed to teach individuals who are trying to change their behavior how to anticipate and cope with the problem of relapse" (George & Marlatt, 1989, p. 2).

The program emphasizes self-management; clients are considered responsible not for the cause but for the solution of the problem. And as the name implies, the program concentrates on preventing a *relapse* of deviant sexual behavior. Therefore, RP distinguishes treatment from maintenance. As stated earlier, behavior therapy is effective in cessation of the behavior, but RP is specifically designed to be effective in helping the individual *maintain* the "cure." Distinctions are made between the terms *relapse* and *lapse*. "Relapse is a violation of a self-imposed rule or set of rules governing the rate or pattern of a selected target behavior" (George & Marlatt, 1989, p. 6). A *lapse* on the other hand, refers to "a single instance of violating the rule" (p. 6). "With sex offenders, the term relapse will refer to any occurrence of a sexual offense, thus connoting full-scale reestablishment of the problematic behavior. The term lapse will refer to any occurrence of willful and elaborate fantasizing about sexual offending or any return to sources of stimulation associated with the sexual offense pattern, but short of performance of the offense behavior" (p. 6).

RP, as a system of maintenance-oriented principles and interventions, has two central objectives: It teaches individuals (1) to cope effectively with "high-risk situations" (HRSs) and (2) to identify and respond to early warning signals of urges and "apparently irrelevant decisions" (AIDs). An HRS is any situation that poses a threat to the individual's sense of control over his behavior and consequently increases the probability of lapse or relapse. Examples of HRSs that may predispose an individual toward relapse include negative emotional states, such as anger and depression, interpersonal conflict, and various social pressures (George & Marlatt, 1989). Research by Pithers and associates (Pithers et al., 1988; Pithers, Beal, Armstrong, & Petty, 1989) has found that rapists often experience anger and use alcohol or other drugs before engaging in sexual aggression. Pedophiles, on the other hand, often experience anxiety or depression before seeking a child. A feeling of low self-esteem is experienced by both groups. These precursors reflect the beginning stages of an HRS. In other words, they psychologically predispose the individual toward a relapse.

Relapse seems to follow a sequence of events, all representing HRSs (George & Marlatt, 1989, Pithers, Marques, Gibat, & Marlatt, 1983). First, an urge, fleeting thought, or dream about committing an offense occurs. This is followed by elaborations of fantasies about committing the offense. Then, the aroused individual engages in masturbation coupled with fantasies and/or pornography related to the imagined sexual activity. The individual then plans how he is going to commit the act. Finally, the individual engages in the act. RP provides a framework within which a variety of behavioral, cognitive, educational, and skill-training techniques are used to train sex offenders to recognize and interrupt these chains of events (Marshall & Barbaree, 1988).

If the individual does not know how to cope with these HRSs, there is a high probability that he may lapse or relapse. On the other hand, if he learns how to cope, and he successfully manages to get through the HRS without violating his newly adopted rules, perceived control strengthens and the probability of relapse declines. The individual experiences a sense of mastery and self-efficacy and is better prepared for the next bout with an HRS.

The second component in RP intervention is AIDs—apparently irrelevant decisions. What at first glance seems to be an innocuous decision, unrelated to an HRS, may well be the first step toward relapse. For example, a pedophile's decision to take walks by parks and schoolyards at times when they are predictably crowded with children might be an early warning sign. It is important, therefore, that the individual learn to recognize and interrupt these apparently irrelevant decisions.

Critical to RP treatment intervention is the motivation of the offender. Without motivation, the program will not work. Remember, RP is aimed primarily at *maintaining* a cessation of the deviant behavior, not cessation itself. Therefore, a behavior therapy program or other conventional treatment intervention that stops the behavior must precede RP. The treatment phase normally takes a relatively short period of time. Another important point outlined by George and Marlatt (1989) is that incarceration without treatment will not prevent reoffending. They offer three reasons for this. First, externally imposed, forced control does little to encourage an offender to seek help in changing his ways. Second, the offender can still maintain attachment to his offense pattern through fantasy. Third, it is conceivable that an offender could continue to actually engage in some semblance of his offense patterns even during confinement.

A volunteer outpatient treatment program for child molesters described by Marshall and Barbaree (1988) illustrates very well some of the procedures used to stop the behavior. The program uses a variety of behavior techniques. First, clinicians utilize aversive conditioning by linking electric shock to an offender's deviant visual and verbal images. Second, they reduce the attraction of deviant fantasies during masturbation through satiation therapy. Satiation therapy attempts to reduce the sex drive by having the patient masturbate at a frequency that will substantially reduce urges and cravings. Third, they eliminate the occurrence of deviant thoughts elicited by children or by daydreams during their day-to-day living pattern through smelling salts. That is, each patient carries smelling salts, and each time a deviant thought occurs, the patient is instructed to place the salts close to his nose and to inhale deeply. Through aversive conditioning, deviant thoughts are soon strongly associated with the experience of unpleasant smelling salts. Currently, there is no evidence that this aversive therapy has a negative impact on "normal" sexual thoughts and behavior.

The program also enhances the social competence of the child molester by training him in the skills of conversation with adult partners as well as reducing the anxiety in the presence of adult partners. The treatment also addresses training in assertiveness, and counsels the patient in financial management, use of leisure time, and alcohol or drug use. So far, Marshall and Barbaree have been able to do a three-and-one-half year follow-up on 117 patients, some of whom received the treatment described and some who did not. While 32 percent of the nontreatment group has reoffended, only 14 percent of the treated group has reoffended. In another RP project, Pithers et al. (1988) found a 10 percent relapse rate for rapists, and a 3 percent relapse rate for pedophiles during a short follow-up (less than one year).

RP is a relatively recent development and its long-term success has yet to be established. However, it does have substantial promise for the elimination of deviant behavior in offenders motivated to change. And as noted by Prentky et al. (1997, p. 14), "Continuity of treatment is considered a critical factor in managing sex offenders. Maintenance is forever, and Relapse Prevention never ends. Community-based clinical management must be supportive, vigilant, and informed by current wisdom about maximally effective maintenance."

SUMMARY AND CONCLUSIONS

As the twentieth century closed, and into the early years of the twenty-first, prison and jail populations across the United States reached record high levels, even while the crime rate was showing signs of stabilizing. The United States consistently maintains its reputation of being the democratic country with the highest rate of incarceration. Although high numbers of individuals are serving time for violent offenses, nonviolent offenders—for example, those convicted of drug crimes, burglaries, auto thefts, and other felonies—comprise a substantial percentage of the incarcerated population. In some facilities, nonviolent offenders surpass the 50 percent mark. Young black males continue to be incarcerated in numbers disproportionate to their representation in the population. We also noted in this chapter that, while women continue to make up less than 10 percent of all incarcerated individuals, their incarceration rates are increasing more rapidly than those of men.

Although we have focused on imprisoned populations in this chapter, it is important to keep in mind that approximately two-thirds of all persons under correctional supervision in the United States are supervised in community settings, such as on probation or parole. Many psychologists working in corrections offer services to these individuals. For example, probationers and parolees are often required to participate in substance abuse treatment, sex offender treatment, and psychotherapy as a condition of remaining in the community. In addition, psychologists may be asked to conduct presentencing evaluations to determine whether a particular individual would be amenable to treatment. Thus, before deciding whether to send a convicted sex offender to prison or allow him to remain in the community, a judge may request an evaluation of the likelihood he will reoffend as well as the likelihood that he would benefit from sex offender treatment.

Although psychologists are not the only mental health professionals working in or consulting with corrections, we have emphasized that there are multiple opportunities for psychologists wishing to work in this arena. The tasks we focused upon in this chapter included the classification, assessment, and treatment of inmates, but others exist as well. For example, psychologists also may be involved in conducting research, providing hostage negotiation training, offering counseling services to staff, designing programs for families of inmates, and the screening and selection of corrections officers.

Classification in corrections is done both to determine the appropriate custody level for a prisoner and to determine what services (e.g., educational, health, psychological) are warranted. Psychologists have been at the forefront of developing classification schemes since Edward Megargee proposed a system based on the MMPI (Megargee, 1977). Although the Megargee approach continues to be used in some prison systems, increasingly more attention is given to classification systems proposed by Canadian psychologists, including the Level of Service Inventory—Revised (LSI-R) developed by Andrews and Bonta (1995).

Psychological treatment is provided to inmates both to meet their mental health needs and in recognition that rehabilitation is a goal worth pursuing. The growing numbers of individuals with mental health problems in jails and prisons was a topic of concern to correctional officials throughout the 1990s and continues into the twenty-first century. In addition, inmates who are generally stable may need crisis intervention services at various points in their incarceration. Most psychological research on treatment deals with the programs intended to aid in rehabilitation. As we noted in the chapter, rehabilitation was dealt a blow in the 1970s and 1980s, when pessimistic reviews questioned the efficacy of many rehabilitation programs. Today, it is recognized that some approaches clearly have merit for some offenders, and rehabilitation has experienced a re-affirmation, although not universally. Of the psychologically oriented approaches, those based on cognitive behavioral principles have received the most positive evaluations. In essence, prisoners are encouraged to "rethink" their assumptions and to find effective ways of managing their lives.

After reviewing key aspects of both behavior and cognitive therapies, we focused upon the treatment of two categories of offenders, the psychopath and the sex offender. In both cases, the research literature can be very discouraging because it often concludes that treatment was minimally effective, if at all. Nevertheless, optimistic reports have been provided for the treatment of both psychopaths and sex offenders, so it is important not to lose sight of these findings.

Some aspects of jail and prison life pose major challenges to psychologists working in corrections. From a psychological perspective, overcrowded facilities and isolation for long periods of time are extremely problematic. We have been especially critical of the ultra-max facilities that place difficult to manage prisoners in high-security isolation for years at a time. Critics have argued that they are expensive, overused, and conducive to rapid mental deterioration of the prisoners housed within them. However, the facilities as well as the inmates themselves are unique, and we must be cautious in making generalizations. Likewise, all prisons and jails vary widely in the extent to which they are violent, run-down, crowded, and program-oriented as opposed to custody-oriented. Furthermore, inmates vary widely in the degree to which they can adjust to control, threats of violence, isolation from the outside world, isolation from other inmates, boredom, and lack of autonomy.

As we noted at the beginning of this chapter, human beings are highly adaptable and changeable, particularly if they desire to change. The psychologist involved in rehabilitation efforts in jail and prison settings, as well as in the community, provides offenders with necessary skills to achieve this change. Although there are numerous challenges to accomplishing this goal, psychologists and other mental health professionals have made significant strides, particularly when cognitive behavioral treatment can be provided.

KEY CONCEPTS

Jails	Community-based corrections
Prisons	Federal Bureau of Prisons
BOP	Incapacitation
Rehabilitation	Retribution
Deterrence	Selective incapacitation
General deterrence	Specific deterrence
Dynamic risk factors	Static risk factors
Criminogenic needs	Isolation
Segregation	Protective custody
Supermax	Ultramax
Criminalization	Prisonization
Cognitive therapy	Reality therapy
Constructivist therapy	Evocative therapy
Psychoeducational counseling	Drug treatment
Cognitive behavior therapy	Relapse prevention
RP	

REVIEW QUESTIONS

1. Briefly describe the major roles of correctional psychologists working within or in consultation with prisons.
2. What are the four rationales for imprisonment of offenders? Briefly describe each one.
3. What is the purpose of classification? Identify and describe any three classification instruments used in corrections.
4. Define the following terms: criminogenic needs, relapse prevention, prisonization, evocative therapy, criminalization.
5. List and describe briefly any five features of prison life that pose challenges to the psychologist providing treatment to prisoners.
6. Discuss the significance of Robert Martinson's article, "What Works?" including reactions to the article and the efforts to challenge its apparent assumptions.
7. From a psychological perspective, discuss the effects of (a) crowding and (b) isolation on incarcerated individuals.
8. Define protective custody, supermax, disciplinary segregation, and administrative segregation.
9. Identify the major differences between dynamic risk factors and static risk factors, and why they are important in corrections.

GLOSSARY

adjudicative competence   The ability to participate in a variety of court proceedings. See also, **incompetent to stand trial.**

admitters   Refers to those sex offenders who are willing to take responsibility for their actions.

adolescent-limited (AL) offender   An individual who usually demonstrates delinquent or antisocial behavior only during his or her teen years and then stops offending during his or her young adult years.

advantageous comparison   An offender's process of convincing himself that his values and ways of life are superior to those of his victims; used to explain the cognitive restructuring that occurs in terrorism.

aggression, hostile (expressive)   Aggressive behavior characterized by the intent to cause the target discomfort or pain.

aggression, instrumental   Aggressive behavior characterized by the intent to gain material or financial rewards from the target.

aggressive driving   Reckless behavior while driving that indicates anger, hostility, or frustration as a result of a recent incident or series of incidents in the driver's life. The aggressive driving may be prompted by minor, irritating actions of another motorist but these actions are not the root cause of the reckless behavior. Should be distinguished from **road rage.**

aggressive (sadistic) pedophile   An adult drawn to children for both sexual and aggressive (violent) purposes.

ambiversion   Scoring in the average range on the extraversion-introversion scale developed by Hans J. Eysenck.

amnesia   Complete or partial (**limited**) memory loss of an incident, series of incidents, or some aspects of life's experiences.

anger rape   A rape situation, identified by Groth, in which an offender uses more force than necessary for compliance and engages in a variety of sexual acts that are particularly degrading or humiliating to the victim.

anger retaliation rapist   A classification of rapists proposed by the Massachusetts Research Center to identify those individuals who are more motivated to humiliate the victim than to gain sexual gratification. See also **displaced anger rapist.**

antisocial behavior   Clinical term reserved for serious habitual behavior, especially that involving direct harm to others.

antisocial personality disorder (APD or ASP)   A disorder characterized by a history of continuous behavior in which the rights of others are violated.

arson   Any willful or malicious burning or attempt to burn, with or without intent to defraud, a dwelling house, public building, motor vehicle, aircraft, or personal property of another.

assault   The intentional inflicting of bodily injury on another person, or the attempt to inflict such injury.

assault, aggravated   Inflicting, or attempting to inflict, bodily injury on another person, with the intent to inflict serious injury.

assault, simple   The unlawful, intentional inflicting of less than serious bodily injury without a deadly or dangerous weapon, or the attempt to inflict such bodily injury, again without a deadly or dangerous weapon.

attention deficit hyperactivity disorder (ADHD)   Traditionally considered a chronic neuro-biological condition characterized by developmentally poor attention, impulsivity, and hyper-activity. More contemporary perspectives see the behavioral pattern as a deficiency in interpersonal skills.

authoritarian style   The approach to parenting that sets a very rigid structure on the family set-ting and allows little decision making by the child.

authoritative style   The approach to parenting that sets firm rules yet encourages the devel-opment of autonomy in the child.

authority homicide   In the context of workplace violence, the killing of a supervisor or other person in authority by an employee.

autoeroticism   A term coined by Havelock Ellis that refers to the self-arousal and self-gratification of sexual arousal.

availability heuristic   The cognitive shortcuts that people use to make quick inferences about their world. It is the information that is most readily available to us mentally, and is usually based extensively on the most recent material we gain from the news or entertainment media.

avoidance learning   A process whereby, if a person responds in time to a warning signal, he or she avoids painful or aversive stimuli.

barricade situation   In hostage-taking scenarios, a situation in which an individual has forti-fied him or herself in a building or residence and threatens violence, typically to the hostages.

battered woman syndrome   A cluster of behavioral and psychological characteristics believed common to women who have been abused in relationships.

behaviorism   A perspective that focuses on observable, measurable behavior and argues that the social environment and learning are the key determinants of human behavior.

biopsychologists   Psychologists who study the biological aspects of behavior to determine which genetic and neurophysiological variables play a part. They generally see human behavior as the result of a complex interaction between the individual's physiological and social environment.

bioterrorism   The category of terrorism that involves the use of bacteria, viruses, germs, and other agents.

boot camps   Military-style, short term facilities for juvenile delinquents; most focus on instill-ing discipline rather than education or treatment.

boosters   Professional shoplifters.

Brawner Rule   A standard for evaluating the insanity defense that recognizes that the defendant suffers from a condition that substantially (1) affects mental or emotional processes or (2) im-pairs behavior controls. This rule expands on the ALI Rule.

burglary   The unlawful entry of a structure, with or without force, with intent to commit a felony or theft.

carjacking   The completed or attempted theft in which a motor vehicle is taken by force or threat of force.

caveat paragraph A section of the ALI/Brawner Rule that excludes abnormality manifested only by repeated criminal or antisocial conduct. It was specifically designed to disallow the insanity defense for psychopaths.

child delinquents Children between the ages of seven and 12 who have committed or are accused of committing a criminal act

classical (Pavlovian) conditioning The process of learning to respond to a formerly neutral stimulus that has been paired with another stimulus that already elicits a response. Also called **Pavlovian conditioning.**

classic mass murder A situation in which an individual enters a public place or barricades himself or herself inside a public building, such as a fast-food restaurant, and randomly kills patrons and other individuals.

classification In corrections, the process of placing offenders into categories for the purposes of custody and treatment.

clearance rate The proportion of reported crimes that have been "solved" through the arrest and turning over for prosecution of at least one person. Crimes also may be cleared through exceptional means.

coercion theory The belief the punitive and coercive tactics employed by parents will increase the likelihood of later aggressive behavior and family violence.

cognitions The internal processes that enable humans to imagine, to gain knowledge, to reason, and to evaluate. The attitudes, beliefs, values, and thoughts that a person holds about the environment, relationships, and him or herself.

cognitive behavior therapy An approach to therapy that focuses on changing beliefs, fantasies, attitudes, and rationalizations that justify and perpetuate antisocial or other problematic behavior. It is often used in the treatment of sex offenders.

cognitive learning The formation and development of mental concepts, schemas, theories, attitudes, beliefs, and other mental versions of the world.

cognitive-neoassociation model A revised theory of the frustration-aggression hypothesis proposed by Leonard Berkowitz.

cognitive processes Internal mental processes that enable humans to imagine, gain knowledge, reason, and evaluate information.

cognitive restructuring A psychological process that allows one to justify committing reprehensible actions; typically involves **moral justification, euphemistic language,** and **advantageous comparison.**

cognitive scripts Mental images of how one feels he or she should act in a variety of situations.

cognitive scripts model Rowell Huesmann's theory that social behavior in general and aggressive behavior in particular are controlled largely by cognitive scripts learned and memorized through daily experiences.

community-based corrections The term for a wide variety of options that allow convicted offenders to be supervised in the community rather than incarcerated. It includes probation and parole and their variants, such as halfway houses and intensive supervision programs.

compensatory rapist An offender who rapes in response to an intense sexual arousal initiated by stimuli in the environment, often quite specific stimuli (e.g., dark-haired women). His main motive is to prove his sexual prowess.

competency to stand trial The legal requirement that a defendant is able to understand the proceedings and to help the attorney in preparing a defense. See also **incompetency to stand trial.**

compulsion   An action a person feels compelled (driven) by internal thoughts to take, even though it may be irrational.

compulsive gambling   A psychiatric syndrome characterized by anxiety and an insatiable, unconscious desire to lose what was gained in previous gambling.

concordance   A term used in genetics to represent the degree to which related pairs of subjects both show a particular behavior or condition. It is usually expressed in percentages.

conduct disorder   A diagnostic label used to identify children who demonstrate habitual misbehavior.

conformity perspective   The theoretical position that humans are born basically good and generally try to do the right and just thing.

constructivist therapy   Psychotherapy based on the view that the therapist must begin and work with each person's unique version of the world.

contagion effect   A tendency for some people to model or copy a behavior or activity portrayed by the news or entertainment media.

controlled substance   Any psychoactive drug or chemical substance whose availability is restricted, as designated by state or federal law.

copycat effect   See **contagion effect.**

corporate crime   Any criminal offense committed by officers or employees in which the corporation benefits.

correlation   A mathematical index that reflects the nature of the relationship between two variables.

crimes against the public order   See **public order offenses**

crimes of obedience   Illegal acts that are committed under the order of someone in authority.

criminal homicide   A term that encompasses both murder and nonnegligent homicide.

criminalization   The process whereby inmates exchange, share, and support one another's beliefs, attitudes, and feelings, which in the long run promotes criminal activity.

criminal profiling   See **profiling.**

criminal psychopath   A primary psychopath who engages in repetitive antisocial or criminal behavior.

criminogenic needs   Those dynamic risk factors that are empirically found related to criminal behavior.

criminology   The multidisciplinary study of crime.

criminology, psychiatric   The branch of criminology that focuses on individual aspects of behavior, particularly internal forces and unconscious drives. Also called **forensic psychiatry.**

criminology, psychological   The branch of criminology that examines the individual behavior and especially the mental processes involved in criminal behavior.

criminology, sociological   The branch of criminology that examines the demographic, group, and societal variables related to crime.

cyberbullying   Sending or posting harmful or cruel text or images using the Internet or other digital communication devices. Primarily a problem with school-aged children and adolescents.

cybercrime   Any illegal act that involves a computer system. Also called **computer crime.**

cyberstalking   Threatening behavior or unwanted advances directed at another using the Internet or other forms of online communications.

cycle of violence   The continuation of violence which may occur across generations among individuals who have experienced and witnessed violence in their families. Also pertains to the violence experienced by women in domestic violence situations.

dangerousness   The characteristic of individuals which render them serious threats to their own wellbeing or the safety of others. See also, **risk assessment.**

dark figure   The number of crimes that go unreported in official crime data reports.

date rape   A sexual assault that occurs within the context of a dating relationship.

dehumanize   To engage in actions that obscure the identity of the victim, such as excessive facial battery, or to see and treat victims like objects rather than human beings.

deindividuation   A process by which individuals feel they cannot be identified, primarily because they are disguised or are subsumed within a group.

deniers   Refers to those sex offenders who are unwilling to take responsibility for their actions.

delusional (paranoid) disorder   Mental disorder characterized by a system of false beliefs.

delusions   False beliefs about the world

dependence   In substance abuse, a condition that may be physical, psychological, or both, whereby a person develops an intense craving for (and feels he or she cannot live without) a drug.

dependent variable   The variable that is measured to see how it is changed by manipulations of the independent variable.

deterrence   One of the four goals or purposes of sentencing; it refers to the use of punishment to dissuade individuals from committing crime in the future. **General deterrence** refers to the overall symbolic impact punishment has on the population as a whole. **Specific (or special) deterrence** is based on the actual experience of punishment, which presumably will deter the punished individual from engaging in future transgressions.

developmental approach   Examines the changes and influences (risk factors) across a person's lifetime that contribute to the formation of antisocial and criminal behavior or, alternately, that protect individuals with many risk factors in their lives

developmental disability   A status that is attributable to a cognitive or physical impairment.

developmental pathways   In the study of criminal behavior, these are the various tracks individuals follow that lead to antisocial behavior. Researchers began by identifying two pathways but have now found evidence of more.

Diagnostic and Statistical Manual of Mental Disorders (DSM)   The official guidebook or manual, published by the American Psychiatric Association, used to define and diagnose specific mental disorders. Now in its fourth revised edition (DSM-IV-R).

difference in degrees   The perspective of human nature that argues that humans are intimately tied to their animal ancestry in important and significant ways and differ only in the extent to which they have developed through the evolutionary process. For example, this perspective might argue that human violence is a result of innate, biological needs to obtain sufficient food supplies, territory, or mates.

differential association-reinforcement (DAR) theory   A theory of deviance developed by Ronald Akers that combines Skinner's behaviorism and Sutherland's differential association theory. The theory states that people learn deviant behavior through the reinforcements they receive from the social environment.

differential association theory   Formulated by Edwin Sutherland, a theory of crime that states that criminal behavior is primarily due to obtaining values or messages from others, including but not limited to those who engage in crime. The critical factors include with whom a person associates, how early, for how long, how frequently, and how personally meaningful the associations are.

discriminative stimuli   According to Akers, social signals or gestures transmitted by subcultural or peer groups to indicate whether certain kinds of behavior will be rewarded or punished within a particular social context.

disease attribution   A position that contends that sexual assault is due to a mental disorder.

disorganized crime scene   Demonstrates that the offender committed the crime without premeditation or planning. In other words, the crime scene indicators suggest the individual acted on impulse or in rage, or under extreme excitement.

displaced aggression rapist   The rapist whose attack is violent and aggressive, displaying minimum or total absence of sexual feeling. Also called **anger-retaliation rapist.**

displaced aggression theory   The theory that some aggression is directed at the target as a replacement for the individual who is the real source of the provocation.

displacement of responsibility   A concept that allows an individual to deny responsibility for an action because he or she was told to perform it by someone higher in authority; also referred to as **obedience to authority** or **strong respect for authority.** See also **crimes of obedience.**

dispositions   In personality theory, a term that signifies internal or personality determinants of human behavior. Dispositional theorists look to inner conflicts, beliefs, drives, personal needs, traits, or attitudes to explain behavior. See also **traits.**

dissociated state   A state of mind during which the person feels detached from self and surroundings.

dissociative identity disorder   A psychiatric syndrome characterized by the existence within an individual of two or more distinct personalities, any of which may be dominant at any given moment. Formerly called **multiple personality disorder (MPD).**

dizygotic twins   Twins who developed from two fertilized eggs and are no more *genetically* alike than non twins. Also called **fraternal twins.**

drug attribution   With respect to sex offending, the contention that alcohol and psychoactive drugs can cause one to momentarily lose control of one's sexual urges.

drug treatment   An approach to therapy that concentrates on reducing the targeted behavior through the use of medication.

DSM   See **Diagnostic and Statistical Manual.**

Durham Rule   A legal standard of insanity that holds that an accused is not criminally responsible if his or her unlawful act was the product of mental disease or defect. Also known as the **Product Rule.**

duty to protect   Requirement from the *Tarasoff* case that clinicians must take steps to protect possible victims from serious bodily harm as a result of threats made by the clinicians' clients. The duty to protect does not require that the clinician contact the potential victim.

duty to warn   Requirement from the *Tarasoff* case that clinicians must actively warn potential victims of threats of serious bodily harm made by their clients.

dynamic risk factors   Things about a person's developmental history that change over time, such as attitudes, opinions, and knowledge.

dyssocial psychopath   Individual with psychopathic characteristics who is antisocial because of social learning and does not possess the features of the primary psychopath.

ectomorphic   A body type characterized by thinness and fragility in structure.

eldercide   The killing of an older person, usually over 60.

emotional paradox   The research observation that psychopaths seem to be able to talk about emotional cues but lack the ability to use them effectively in the real world.

endomorphic   A body type characterized by roundness and fatty tissue.

enmeshed style   A parental style in which the parent takes extraordinary control of the child's life including imposing rigid rules and seeing even trivial, minor behaviors as problematic. Typically results in harsh punishment but inconsistent discipline. Opposite of **lax style.**

equivocal death analysis   See **reconstructive psychological evaluation (RPE).**

erotomania stalking   In this form of stalking, the stalker usually has serious mental disorders and is considered delusional. Public figures are typically the targets.

euphemistic language   Words used to make something appear more innocuous or less negative than it actually is.

evocative therapy   An approach to sex offender therapy that focuses on (1) helping offenders to understand the causes and motivations of their sexual behavior and (2) increasing their empathy for the victims of the sexual assault.

evolutionary psychology   The study of the evolution of behavior using the principles of natural selection.

excitation transfer theory   Theory explaining how physiological arousal can generalize from one situation to another; based on the assumption that physiological arousal, however produced, dissipates slowly over time.

executive functions   Higher order mental abilities involved in goal-directed behavior. They include organizing behavior, memory, inhibition processes, and planning strategies.

exhibitionism   The deliberate exposure of the genitals to another person to achieve sexual gratification. Also called **indecent exposure.**

expectancy theory   A theory of motivation that takes into account both the expectancy of achieving a particular goal and the value placed on it.

experimental substance use (ESU)   Experimentation—typically by adolescents—with various psychoactive substances before dependency or addiction to drugs occurs.

exploitative pedophile   An adult who seeks children almost exclusively for sexual gratification.

exploitative rapist   See **impulsive rapist.**

expressive aggression   Aggression in which a person's primary aim is to hurt or do injury to another. Also called **hostile aggression,** it is the opposite of **instrumental aggression.**

expressive burglars   Burglars who take considerable pride in developing ingenious techniques and skills for successful burglary.

expressive hostage taking   Hostage-taking situation in which the offender's primary goal is to gain some control over his or her life.

expressive sexual aggression   A rape situation in which the offender's primary goal is to gain some control over his life.

extinction   The decline and eventual disappearance of a conditioned or learned response when it is no longer reinforced.

extrafamilial child molester   An sex abuser whose victims are outside the immediate or extended family.

extraversion   In Eysenck's theory, a personality dimension that represents needs for stimulation.

Factor 1   A behavioral dimension, identified through factor analysis, representing the interpersonal and emotional aspects of psychopathy.

Factor 2   A behavioral dimension representing the socially deviant lifestyle characteristics of psychopaths.

factor analysis   A statistical procedure by which underlying patterns, factors, or dimensions are identified among a series of scale items.

false positive   A prediction that someone will do a certain thing when he or she does not.

false negative   A prediction that someone will not do a certain thing when he or she does.

family mass murder   A situation in which at least three family members are killed (usually by another family member).

Fast-Track Project   A theoretically-based, multisite, multicomponent prevention program for young children believed to be at high risk for long-term antisocial behavior.

Federal Bureau of Prisons (BOP)   Oversees all federal penitentiaries, correctional institutions, prison camps, and medical centers in the United States other than those operated by the military.

fence   An individual who accepts stolen goods and resells them.

fetishism   Sexual attraction to inanimate objects.

filicide   Killing of one's child older than 1 year.

fire setting   The term used in the literature on child psychopathology for an abnormal fascination with fire accompanied by successful or unsuccessful attempts to start harmful fires.

fixated pedophile   See **immature pedophile.**

forcible rape   The carnal knowledge of a female, forcibly and against her will. It includes rape by force, assault to rape, and attempted rape. Although victims may be both female and male, the UCR definition limits this to female victims.

forensic psychiatry   See **criminology, psychiatric.**

forensic psychology   The production and application of psychological knowledge to the civil and criminal justice systems.

fraternal twins   See **dizygotic twins.**

fratricide   The killing of one's brother.

frustration   An aversive internal state of arousal that occurs when one is prevented from responding in a way that previously produced rewards (or that one believes would produce rewards).

frustration-aggression hypothesis   The theory that frustration leads to aggressive behavior. The theory has been revised several times, with most substantial changes coming from the work of Leonard Berkowitz.

fundamental attribution error   A tendency to underestimate the importance of situational determinates and to overestimate the importance of personality or dispositional factors in identifying the causes of human behavior.

general deterrence   See **deterrence.**

geographic profiling   A type of profiling that focuses on the location of the crime and how it relates to the residence and/or base of operations of the offender. The fundamental assumption of geographic profiling is that serial offenders prefer to commit their crimes near their own residences.

good burglar   Refers to the burglar who demonstrates technical skill and overall competence in burglarizing.

Guilty but Mentally Ill (GBMI)   A verdict alternative in some states that allows defendants to be found guilty while seemingly affording them treatment for mental disorders.

habit strength   A construct that refers to the strong tendency to repeat a habitual behavior that has been frequently reinforced in the past.

habituation   Getting used to or adapting to a stimulus.

hallucinations   Things or events that a mental disordered person, but no others, see or perceive. Characteristic of schizophrenia.

hallucinogens   Those psychoactive drugs that sometimes generate hallucinations and lead to changes in perceptions of reality. Also called **psychedelics.**

Hate Crime Statistics Act   A 1990 federal statute that directs the FBI to collect data on all crimes motivated by hatred of or bias against victims based on their racial, ethnic, religious, or sexual orientation. Physical or mental disability bias was added in 1997.

hierarchy rule   In the UCR program, the rule that requires that only the most serious crime in a series be reported in the crime statistics.

hebephilia   The use of young adolescent girls or boys for sexual gratification by adults, usually males.

hemisphere asymmetry   An unusual or abnormal balance between the two hemispheres, both in language processing and in emotional states.

hostile attribution bias   The tendency to perceive hostile intent in others even when it is totally lacking.

hostile attribution model   A cognitive model of aggression developed by Kenneth Dodge and colleagues. See also **hostile attributional bias.**

human trafficking   The transportation and exploitation of individuals, usually for sex related purposes and high profits. Children and women from impoverished nations or parts of the U.S. are particularly vulnerable.

hydraulic model   A model of aggression that presumes aggressive energy accumulates in the individual and erupts in a display of violence. Also called **psychodynamic model.**

hyperactivity   A behavioral pattern demonstrated by both children and adults wherein there is considerable motor activity in an attempt to gain adequate amounts of cortical stimulation.

iatrogenic   A process whereby mental or physical disorders are unintentionally induced or developed in patients by physicians, clinicians, or psychotherapists.

identical twins   See **monozygotic twins.**

identity theft   The fraudulent use of another person's personal identification information—such as social security number, date of birth, or mother's maiden name—without that person's knowledge or permission.

imitational learning   See **observational learning.**

immature pedophile   A child sex abuser who demonstrates a long-standing, exclusive preference for children as both sexual and social companions. Also called **fixated pedophile.**

impulsive rapist   A rapist who demonstrates neither strong sexual nor aggressive features, but engages in spontaneous rape when the opportunity presents itself. The rape is usually carried out in the context of another crime, such as robbery or burglary. Also called **exploitative rapist.**

incapacitation   One of the four goals or purposes of punishment. Isolation of the individual from society so that he or she cannot commit more crime.

incompetent to stand trial (IST)   A judicial determination that a defendant lacks sufficient ability to understand the legal process against him or her and/or to assist a lawyer in the preparation of a defense. See also **adjudicative competence.**

independent variable   The measure whose effect is being studied, and, in most scientific investigations, that is manipulated by the experimenter in a controlled fashion.

index crimes (now commonly called Part I crimes)   The crimes that are of most concern, as defined by the FBI's Uniform Crime Reports, and are used to indicate the seriousness of the crime problem. The eight Part I crimes are murder and nonnegligent manslaughter, aggravated assault, robbery, forcible rape, burglary, larceny, theft, arson, and motor-vehicle theft.

individual offender   A person who consistently violates the law because of a series of frustrations and disappointments and/or as a matter of personal choice.

infanticide   Although this term literally means the killing of an infant, it has become synonymous with the killing of a child by a parent.

inhalants   Refers to a thousand or more different household and commercial products that can be abused by sniffing or "huffing" (inhaling though the mouth) for an intoxicating effect. They are found in organic solvents and volatile substances commonly found in adhesives, lighter fluids, cleaning solutions, and paint products.

Insanity Defense Reform Act of 1984   A law designed to make it more difficult for defendants using the insanity defense in the federal courts to be acquitted.

instrumental aggression   Aggression carried out for the primary purpose of gaining material goods or other rewards rather than for the purpose of harming the victim.

instrumental hostage taking   A hostage situation in which the primary goal of the offender is material or monetary gain.

instrumental learning   A form of learning in which a voluntary response is strengthened or diminished by its consequences. Also called **operant conditioning.**

instrumental sexual aggression   When the sexual offender uses just enough coercion to gain compliance from his victim.

interaction   An important concept in psychological criminology, it refers to the mutual influence of a multitude of internal and external factors on the behavior of the individual. See also **interactionism.**

interactionism   The perspective that argues that human behavior is determined or influenced by both internal (biological, psychological, cognitive) and external (social environmental) factors.

intimate partner violence   Crimes committed against persons by their current or former spouses, boyfriends, or girlfriends.

intrafamilial child molester   A child sex abuser whose victims are within the immediate or extended family.

invariance hypothesis   Proposed by Gottfredson and Hirschi, this hypothesis refers to the observation that crime seems to decline with age, no matter when in history and no matter what culture is being considered.

investigative psychology   The application of psychological research and concepts to the investigation of crime.

irrationality   A basic ingredient of the insanity standard. Refers to the legal assumption that a person cannot be held criminally responsible for his or her actions if it is determined he or she could not understand the consequences of his or her behavior.

irresistible impulse attribution   In sex offending, refers to a psychological state in which the normal restraints of self-control are substantially reduced or eliminated by an overwhelming sex drive.

isolation (or segregation)   In corrections, the separation of the inmate from the general jail or prison population. May be done for disciplinary, protective, or administrative reasons.

jail   A facility operated by a local government to hold persons temporarily detained, awaiting trial, or sentenced to confinement, after having been convicted of a misdemeanor.

just world hypothesis   A belief that one gets what one deserves in this world.

Juvenile Court Act   A statute passed by the Illinois legislature in 1899 that established a separate court for juveniles and marks the official beginning of juvenile justice in the United States.

juvenile courts   Specialized courts, separate from the criminal system, that deal with status offenses, delinquency cases, and other issues relating to juveniles, such as abuse or neglect. Also called family courts in many states

Juvenile Justice and Delinquency Prevention Act (JJDPA)   Landmark federal legislation passed in 1974 that attempted to address the needs of juveniles in the juvenile justice system as well as those considered at risk for delinquency.

kleptomania   The irresistible urge to steal unneeded objects. Whether there is such an urge is highly debatable.

language impairment   Broad term for a variety of problems in expressing or understanding language.

lax style   A parental style that does not respond sufficiently to problematic or antisocial behavior in children but rather allows it to occur without disciplinary action. Opposite of the **enmeshed style** and similar to the **permissive.**

learned helplessness   A learned passive and withdrawing response in the face of perceived hopelessness, as theorized by Martin Seligman (1975).

learning perspective   The theoretical position that humans are born basically neutral and behaviorally a blank slate. What they become as individuals depends on their learning experiences rather than innate predispositions.

life-course-persistent (LCP) offenders   A term by Terrie Moffitt to represent offenders who demonstrate a life-long pattern of antisocial behavior and who are resistant to treatment or rehabilitation.

limited amnesia   A pathological inability to remember a specific episode, or small number of episodes, from the recent past.

London syndrome   A behavioral pattern observed during a hostage situation at the Iranian Embassy in London. Refers to the explicit and consistent resistance and refusals by hostages to do what is expected by captors. This behavior often results in death or serious injury to the blatant resistors.

love obsession stalking   In this form of stalking, the stalker and victim are strangers or casual acquaintances. The stalker seeks a love relationship with the object of his or her obsession.

major depressive disorder   General label for symptoms that include an extremely depressed state, general slowing down of mental and physical activity, and feelings of self-worthlessness.

markers   A term used for the neurological indicators of a particular phenomenon, such as psychopathy.

mass murder   Murdering three or more persons at a single location with no cooling-off period between murders.

matricide   The killing of one's mother.

MDMA   Abbreviation for a drug called "ecstasy," which is a synthetic drug that is considered a stimulant with strong psychedelic effects.

mental disorder   See **mental illness.**

mental illness   Term used for a variety of psychiatric diagnoses that indicate that the individual has problems in living; also referred to as **mental disorder.**

mentally disordered sex offender (MDSO)   A classification established by some state legislatures to identify those mentally disordered individuals prone toward repetitive sexual attacks on children, women, or both. See also **sexually violent predator.**

mental retardation.   A developmental disability indicating that a person's cognitive skills are below normal in the general population.

mesomorphic   A muscular and well-developed body type. Some research has indicated that this body type is more likely to be involved in violent crime.

minor physical anomalies (MPAs)   Small, nearly undetectable physical abnormalities which some researchers believe may be associated with birth and neurological defects.

mixed crime scene   Indicates that the nature of the crime demonstrates both organized and disorganized behavioral patterns.

M'Naghten Rule   An insanity standard based on the conclusion that if a defendant has a defect of reason, or a disease of the mind, so as not to know the nature and quality of his or her actions, then he or she cannot be held criminally responsible. Also called **the right and wrong test.**

modeling   See **observational learning.**

models   Individuals or groups of individuals in the environment whose behavior is observed and imitated.

modus operandi (MO)   The actions and procedures an offender uses to commit a crime successfully.

Monitoring the Future (MTF)   A self-report survey administered to high school students nationwide focusing on drug use and abuse.

monozygotic twins   Twins who developed from one fertilized egg and share the same genes. Also called **identical twins.**

moral disengagement   The process of freeing oneself from one's own moral standards in order to act against those standards. The unacceptable conduct is usually undertaken under orders from someone higher in authority or under high social pressure.

moral justification   The process of convincing oneself that one's actions are worthy and have an ultimate moral and good purpose.

multiassaultive family   A nuclear family (traditional or nontraditional) characterized by multiple incidents of violence involving more than one perpetrator.

multiple personality disorder (MPD)   See **dissociative identity disorder.**

multisystemic therapy (MST)   A treatment approach for serious juvenile offenders that focuses on the family while being responsive to the many other contexts surrounding the family, such as the peer group, the neighborhood, and the school.

Munchausen syndrome by proxy (MSBP)   An unusual form of child abuse in which the parent (usually the mother), or parents, consistently bring a child for medical attention with symptoms falsified or directly induced by the parent or parents.

murder   The felonious killing of one human being by another with malice aforethought. See also **criminal homicide.**

narcotics   Psychoactive drugs that produce sleep and are derivatives of the poppy plant. Often divided into three categories depending on the amount of preparation needed: **natural, synthetic,** or **semisynthetic.** Examples are opium, heroin, and methadone, respectively.

National Crime Victimization Survey (NCVS)   A government-sponsored survey of victims of crime, intended to collect data from the victim's perspective on crimes both reported and not reported to police.

National Incident Based Reporting System (NIBRS)   The FBI's system of collecting *detailed* data from law enforcement agencies on known crimes and arrests. See also, **Uniform Crime Reporting.**

natural narcotics   Psychoactive substances classified as narcotics that require no chemical preparation.

negative reinforcement   See **reinforcement, negative**

negligent manslaughter   The unlawful killing of another through reckless or negligent behavior, without intention to kill.

neonaticide   The killing of a newborn, usually under 48 hours.

neuroticism   A dimension of personality that—according to Hans J. Eysenck—is characterized by a chronic level of emotional instability and proneness to psychological distress.

neurotransmitters   Biochemicals directly involved in the transmission of neural impulses and without which communication would not be possible. **Serotonin** is one example.

nonconformist perspective   The theoretical perspective that humans will naturally try to get away with anything they can, including illegal conduct, unless social controls are imposed.

nonindex crimes (Part II crimes)   Crimes not considered as serious as Part I crimes by the FBI and on which only arrest data are gathered for UCR purposes. Examples include simple assault, fraud, embezzlement, and vandalism.

nonnegligent manslaughter   The killing of a human being without premeditation but with the intention to kill in the "heat of the moment," such as under high emotional states of anger or passion.

nonshared environments   An important concept in twin studies, the refers to the living experiences that are different for each twin, such as being raised by different parents.

not guilty by reason of insanity (NGRI)   A legal determination that a defendant was so mentally disordered at the time of the crime that he or she cannot be held criminally responsible for his or her actions.

observational learning (modeling)   The process by which individuals learn patterns of behavior by observing another person performing the action.

occupational crime   (1) Any one of a variety of offenses committed by an individual through opportunity created by his or her occupation; see also, the four categories of **individual, organizational, professional,** and **state-authority** occupational crime. (2) The second category of **white-collar crime** (along with corporate) that refers to crimes committed by individuals for their own benefit.

Office of Juvenile Justice and Delinquency Prevention (OJJDP)   The federal agency charged with overseeing juvenile justice on the national level, providing grants for juvenile research and programs, and taking a leadership role in setting policies nationwide relative to juveniles.

operant conditioning   See **instrumental learning.**

opiate narcotics   Psychoactive drugs that have sedative (sleep-inducing) and analgesic (pain-relieving) effects.

organized crime scene   Indicates planning and premeditation on the part of the offender. In other words, the crime scene shows signs that the offender maintained control of himself or herself and of the victim, if it is a crime against a person.

overcontrolled personality   A person who has well-established inhibitions against aggressive behavior and rigidly adheres to them, even in the face of provocation.

paranoid disorders   See **delusional disorders**

paraphilia   The clinical term for a condition exhibited in fantasies, urges, or behaviors involving nonhuman objects, suffering or humiliation of oneself or one's partner, or children or other nonconsenting persons.

parental monitoring   Supervision by parents of their children's activities. Poor parental monitoring is a strong risk factor for delinquency.

parental practices   Methods employed by parents to meet some specific goal they would like to have their children achieve.

parental styles   Non-goal directed behaviors displayed by parents in their teaching methods.

Parricide   The killing of a parent.

Part 1 crime   See **index crimes.**

Part 2 crime   See **nonindex crimes.**

partialism   An exaggerated sexual interest in some part of the human anatomy not usually associated with sexual arousal, such as an ankle or elbow.

Patricide.   The killing of one's father.

passive-aggressive behavior   Hostile behavior that does not directly inflict physical harm, such as refusing to speak to someone against whom one holds a grudge.

Pavlovian conditioning   See **classical conditioning.**

pedophile   The clinical term for an adult who uses children for sexual gratification and companionship.

pedophilia   The use of children by adults for sexual gratification and companionship.

permissive style   a relaxed parenting style characterized by few demands, controls, or limits.

personation   See **signature.**

pervasive anger type   A rapist characterized by anger directed toward virtually everyone he knows.

plasticity   The characteristic of the brain that allows both its structure and its function to be profoundly responsive to experiences, particularly during early life.

positive reinforcement   See **reinforcement, positive.**

postpartum blues   The common mood swings, crying spells, irritability, and anxiety that occur in 50% to 80% of women after giving birth.

postpartum depression   More severe than postpartum blues, this affects 7 percent to 17 percent of childbearing women. Symptoms may include depression, loss of appetite, loss of interest in the newborn and in life activities. May represent a recurring mood swing across the woman's life cycle.

postpartum psychosis   A rare but severe mental disorder believed to be linked to childbirth; symptoms are similar to those of serious bipolar depression.

posttraumatic stress disorder (PTSD)   A cluster of behavioral patterns that result from a psychologically distressing event outside the usual range of human experience.

power rape   A rape situation, identified by Groth, in which the assailant seeks to establish power and control over his victim. Thus, the amount of force and threats used depends on the degree of submission shown by the victim.

primary prevention   An intervention program designed to prevent behavior or disorders before any signs of the behavioral pattern develops. Also called **universal prevention.**

primary psychopath   Robert Hare's classification of the "true" psychopath. That is, the individual who demonstrates those behavioral features that represent psychopathy—in contrast to **secondary psychopaths,** who commit antisocial acts because of severe emotional problems or inner conflicts, and **dyssocial psychopaths,** who are antisocial because of social learning.

prisonization   The process by which inmates adopt and internalize the prisoner subculture within a particular correctional facility.

prisons   Correctional facilities operated by state and federal governments to hold persons convicted of felonies and sentenced generally to terms of more than one year.

proactive aggression   In children, insensitive actions such as bullying, name-calling, and coercive actions.

product tampering homicide   A rare death or deaths occurring as the result of one or more individuals tampering with a product, usually for revenge or economic gain.

profiling   The process of identifying personality traits, behavioral tendencies, and demographic variables of an offender based on characteristics of the crime. See also **psychological profiling.**

prostitution   Offering or agreeing to engage in, or engaging in, a sex act with another in exchange for a fee.

protective custody   A form of isolation in which the inmate is separated from others for his or her own safety.

psychedelics   The category of psychoactive drugs that produce elevated mood, hallucinations, and altered states of consciousness. Also called **hallucinogens.**

psychiatric criminology   See **criminology, psychiatric**

psychoactive drugs   Drugs that exert their primary effect on the brain, thus altering mood or behavior.

psychodynamic model   The theoretical perspective that argues that human behavior can be best explained through the use of psychological forces and pressures. See also **hydraulic model.**

psychoeducational counseling   An approach to therapy that utilizes a group or class setting to remedy deficits in social and interpersonal skills.

psychological autopsy   Postmortem analysis often reserved for cases in which suicide occurred or is suspected or alleged. The psychological autopsy is frequently done to determine the reasons and precipitating factors for the death.

psychological criminology   See **criminology, psychological**

psychological profiling   The psychological description of a person or persons, whether or not suspected or involved in criminal activity.

psychometric approach   The perspective that human characteristics, attributes, and traits can be measured and quantified.

psychometric intelligence (PI)   A more contemporary designation of intelligence as measured by intelligence or IQ tests. However, the term is not yet widely used in comparison to "IQ."

psychopath   An individual who demonstrates a distinct behavioral pattern that differs from the general population in its level of sensitivity, empathy, compassion, and guilt. See also **primary psychopath.**

Psychopathic Factor I   Of the two behavioral dimensions of psychopathy, this reflects the interpersonal and emotional components, such as callousness and manipulation of others.

Psychopathic Factor II   Of the two behavioral dimensions of psychopathy, this reflects a socially deviant life style, such as impulsiveness, excessive need for stimulation, and lack of realistic goals.

Psychopathy Checklist (PCL)   and Psychopathy Checklist-Revised (PCL-R). Developed by Robert Hare, currently the best known instrument for the measurement of criminal psychopathy. Additional versions include the **Psychopathy Checklist—Screening Version,** the **P-Scan: Research Version,** and the **Psychopathy Checklist, Youth Version (PCL:YV).**

psychophysiology   The study of the dynamic interactions between behavior and the autonomic nervous system.

psychosis   A severe form of mental disorder characterized by hallucinations, delusions, and other indications of loss of contact with reality.

psychotechnology   Methods of permanently altering brain tissue through surgical, electrical (direct current), or chemical means.

psychoticism   A personality dimension, proposed by Eysenck, characterized by cold cruelty, social insensitivity, unemotionality, high risk taking, troublesome behavior, and a dislike of others.

public order offenses   Nonviolent offenses that disrupt the peace and tranquility of a community (e.g., public inebriation, disturbing the peace, vagrancy).

punishment   An event by which a person receives a noxious, painful, or aversive stimulus, usually as a consequence of behavior.

pyromania   A psychiatric term for an irresistible urge to set fires along with an intense fascination (usually sexual) with fire. The existence of this behavioral phenomenon has been brought into serious question by the available research.

racial profiling   Police-initiated action that relies on the race, ethnicity, or national origin rather than the behavior of an individual or on other information that leads the police to suspect him or her of criminal activity.

radical environmental groups   Environmental activists who have used terrorist tactics to draw attention to dangers to the environment.

rape by fraud   The act of having sexual relations with a supposedly consenting adult female under fraudulent conditions, such as when a physician or psychotherapist has sexual intercourse with a patient under the guise of "effective treatment."

rape myths   A variety of mistaken beliefs about the crime of rape and its victims held by many men and women.

rational reconstruction   A mental process whereby an individual engages in a reinterpretation of past behavior through which he or she recasts activities in a manner consistent with "what should have been" rather than "what was." The term in this book was used specifically for explaining research on burglary.

reactive aggression   In children, hot-blooded aggressive acts, such as temper tantrums and emotionally driven vengeful hostility.

reality therapy   Treatment based on the view that the patient must face reality and take full responsibility for his or her behavior.

recidivism   A return to criminal activity (usually measured by arrest) after being convicted of a criminal offense.

reconstructive psychological evaluation (RPE)   Reconstruction of the personality profile and cognitive features (especially intentions) of deceased individuals.

reductionism   A research approach that argues that in order to understand highly complex events or phenomenon, one must start examining the simplest parts first.

regressed pedophile   A male who had fairly normal relationships with adults but later reverted to children for sexual and social companionship because of feelings of inadequacy.

rehabilitation   One of the four goals or purposes of sentencing, it is any attempt to bring about change in behavior patterns or attitudes.

reinforcement   Anything that increases the probability of responding.

reinforcement, negative   The reward received for avoiding a painful or aversive condition, or stimuli.

reinforcement, positive   The acquisition of something desired as a result of one's behavior.

relapse prevention (RP)   A method of treatment primarily designed to prevent a relapse of an undesired behavioral pattern.

relative deprivation   A concept developed by Gresham Sykes for explaining economic crime. It refers to the perceived discrepancy between what an individual has and what he or she would like to have. It is a condition that is especially prominent when people of wealth and people of poverty live in close proximity.

repeat burglary   Refers to the observation that some burglars burglarize the same place repeatedly.

residential treatment   Juvenile training school or rehabilitation center where youths are incarcerated for extended periods of time. Usually considered the "last stop" for youths.

restrictive interventions   Secure institutional treatment of juveniles found to have committed serious offenses.

retribution   One of the four purposes of sentencing, it is the principle that individuals should be held accountable for offending against society and should be given appropriate sanctions, proportional to their crime.

right and wrong test   See **M'Naghten Rule.**

right-wing terrorists   Extremist groups that adhere to an anti-government or racist ideology and often engage in a variety of hate crimes and violence.

risk assessment   The enterprise in which clinicians offer probabilities that a given individual will engage in violent or otherwise antisocial behavior based on known factors relating to the individual.

ritualized aggression   The symbolic display of aggressive intentions or strength without actual physical combat or conflict.

road rage   Anger at another motorist expressed in highly reckless driving and, in some cases, attempts to harm the other motorist. To be distinguished from **aggressive driving,** in which the actions of the motorist are not the direct cause of the reckless behavior.

robbery   The taking or attempt to take anything of value from the care, custody or control of another by force or the threat of force.

Rohypnol   Sometimes referred to as a date-rape drug, it is a powerful depressant commonly abused by young adults and adolescents.

rumination   The focused attention on one's own thoughts and feelings that, if excessive, can lead to aggression against others.

sadistic pedophile   See **aggressive pedophile**

sadistic rape   A rape situation, identified by Groth, in which the offender experiences sexual arousal and excitement as a result of the victim's torment, distress, helplessness, and suffering. The assault usually involves bondage and torture, and the rapist directs considerable abuse and injury on various areas of the victim's body.

sadistic rapist   See **sexually aggressive rapist**

schizophrenia   Mental disorder characterized by severe breakdowns in thought patterns, emotions, and perceptions.

secondary prevention   An intervention program designed for individuals who demonstrate early signs or indicators of behavioral problems or antisocial behavior; also called **selective prevention.**

secondary psychopath   Individual with psychopathic characteristics, but who commits antisocial acts because of severe emotional problems or inner conflicts. Distinct from **primary psychopath.**

sedative-hypnotic compounds   Psychoactive drugs that depress central nervous system functioning, generally reducing anxiety and tension.

selective incapacitation   The imprisonment for longer terms of offenders who are believed to pose the greatest threat to society.

selective prevention   See **secondary prevention.**

self-regulation   The ability to control one's behavior in accordance with internal cognitive standards.

self-regulatory mechanisms   The personal characteristics that help one to control one's behavior, usually attained through social learning.

self-serving bias   A tendency to attribute positive things that happen to us to our abilities and personalities, and to attribute negative events to some cause outside ourselves or beyond our control.

semantic aphasia   A characteristic found in psychopaths whereby the words they speak are devoid of emotional sincerity.

semisynthetic narcotics   See **narcotics.**

serial murder   Incidents in which an individual (or individuals) kill a number of individuals (usually a minimum of three) over time.

serotonin   A chemical by which nerve cells communicate with one another. Low levels of this chemical may be related to aggressive behavior.

sexual aggressive rapist   A rapist who demonstrates both sexual and aggressive features in his attack. In order for him to experience sexual arousal, it must be associated with violence and pain, which excite him. Also called **sadistic rapist.**

Sexually Violent Predator Act   A law that allows a states to place restrictive conditions on sex offenders believed to represent heightened danger to the public. Some statutes allow civil commitment of sexually violent predators after they have completed their prison sentences.

sexual sadism   A deviation characterized by torture and/or killing and mutilation of other persons in order to achieve sexual gratification.

shaken baby syndrome (SBS)   A form of child abuse in which an adult (usually male) shakes a baby so hard that it causes significant brain damage or death.

shared environment   An important concept in twin studies, this refers to the prenatal and life experiences that are common to both twins, such as being raised by the same biological parents.

siblicide   The killing of one's brother or sister; **sororicide** is the killing of one's sister; **fratricide** is the killing of one's brother.

signature   Any behavior that goes beyond what is necessary to commit the crime. Also called **personation.**

simple obsession stalking   The form in which the stalker seeks power and control after a failed relationship with the victim; often associated with past domestic violence.

simulation   Research conducted in a laboratory setting that is designed to mimic as closely as possible the "real world."

situationism   A theoretical perspective that argues that environmental stimuli control behavior.

snitches   Amateur shoplifters

social class   Socioeconomic status typically based predominantly on one's family income. Also referred to as socioeconomic status.

social control theory   A theory proposed by Travis Hirschi that contends that crime and delinquency occur when an individual's ties to the conventional order or normative standards are weak or largely nonexistent.

social learning theory   A theory of human behavior based on learning from watching others in the social environment. This leads to an individual's development of his or her own perceptions, thoughts, expectancies, competencies, and values.

socialized offender   A person who violates the law consistently because of learning the behavioral patterns from his or her social environment.

sociological criminology   See **criminology, sociological.**

sociopath   A person who is repetitively in conflict with the law, apparently with very limited capacity to learn from past experience. Distinct from Hare's concept of primary psychopath.

somatotyping   William H. Sheldon's theory relating physique to delinquency; based on delineating three basic body builds: endomorphic, ectomorphic, and mesomorphic.

sororicide   See **sibicide.**

specific (or special) deterrence   See **deterrence.**

spree murder   The killing of three or more individuals without any cooling-off period, usually at two or more locations.

staging   The intentional alteration of a crime scene prior to the arrival of the police.

stalking   Conduct directed at a specific person that involves repeated physical or visual proximity, nonconsensual communication, or verbal, written, or implied threats sufficient to cause fear in a reasonable person.

static risk factors   Things about a person's developmental history that normally do not change, such as biological parents, gender, birth order, birth date, and ethnic background. Also called historical factors.

status offenses   A class of illegal behavior that only persons with certain characteristics or status can commit. Used almost exclusively to refer to the behavior of juveniles. Examples include running away from home, violating curfew, buying alcohol, or skipping school.

statutory rape   Rape for which the age of the victim is the crucial distinction, on the premise that a victim below a certain age (usually sixteen) cannot validly consent to sexual intercourse with an adult.

stimulants   A broad drug classification that refers to those psychoactive drugs that "stimulate" the central nervous system and elevate mood.

stimulus   A person, event, or situation that elicits behavior.

Stockholm syndrome   A term coined after a hostage situation in Sweden in 1973, it refers to the phenomenon of hostages becoming attracted to their captors. In the original incident, an escaped convict held four bank employees in Stockholm in the bank vault for 131 hours. One of the bank employees eventually married her hostage taker.

strain theory   A prominent sociological explanation for crime based on Robert Merton's theory that crime and delinquency occur when there is a perceived discrepancy between the materialistic values and goals cherished and held in high esteem by a society and the availability of the legitimate means for reaching these goals.

street culture   A variety of conduct norms, particularly in urban areas, that are conducive to robbery and other street crimes. Examples of these norms are disdain for conventional living, a hedonistic pursuit of sensory stimulation, and lack of future orientation.

strong-arm robbery   A robbery in which the main weapon used is one's own body rather than guns, knives, or other weapons.

substance abuse   A pattern of drug use characterized by recurrent negative or adverse consequences as a result of repeated ingestion of the drug.

succumbers   In hostage-taking situations, refers to those hostages who, after release, have considerable difficulty dealing with the aftereffects of the incident.

supermax prisons   See **ultramax prisons**

survivors   In hostage-taking situations, refers to those hostages who are able to return to a meaningful existence with little evidence of long-term depression, nightmares, or serious stress-induced illness.

synthetic narcotics   See **narcotics.**

temperament   A natural mood disposition determined largely by genetic and biological influences

territoriality   The tendency to attack violators of one's personal space.

terrorism   The unlawful use of force or violence against persons or property to intimidate or coerce a government, the civilian population, or any segment thereof, in furtherance of political or social objectives.

tertiary prevention   Intervention strategy designed to reduce or eliminate behavioral problems or antisocial behavior that is fully developed in individuals. Treatment or counseling of convicted offenders is an example of tertiary prevention.

theory   An integrated set of principles that describes, predicts, and explains some phenomena and that guides research.

theory of moral disengagement   Proposed by Bandura, it supposes that we must disengage our own moral values before committing a criminal act.

tolerance   In substance use, the condition in which only increasing dosages of the drug produce the desired effect.

traits   Relatively stable and enduring tendencies to behave in a particular way across time and place. Traits are believed by some psychologists to be the basic building blocks of personality.

treatment   In juvenile justice, a term reserved for psychologically-based programs designed to reduce serious, persistent, delinquent or antisocial behavior.

tripartite conceptual model   Identifies three major types of illicit drug crimes. Proposed by Paul Goldstein.

true negative   The correct prediction that someone will not do a certain act.

true positive   The correct prediction that someone will do a certain act (e.g., commit another violent crime).

ultramax prisons   Extremely high security prisons, or units within a prison, in which prisoners are held in isolation, often for 23 hours a day and for extended periods of time.

uncontrollable attribution   See **irresistible impulse attribution.**

undercontrolled personality   A person who has few inhibitions against aggressive behavior and frequently engages in violence when frustrated or provoked.

undoing   A behavioral pattern found at the crime scene whereby the offender tries to psychologically "undo" the murder.

Uniform Crime Reporting (UCR)   The FBI's system of gathering data from law enforcement agencies on the crimes that come to their attention and on arrests. See also, **NIBRS.**

variable   Any entity that can be measured.

vengeance stalkers   These stalkers do not seek a relationship with their victims but rather are trying to elicit a response or change of behavior from the victim.

victim attribution   The tendency to blame the victim; may be especially prevalent in cases of sexual assault.

victimological perspective   A proposal that suggests we can gain substantial amounts of knowledge on offender characteristics by also studying the nature and possibly the behavior of the victims selected by offenders.

victimology   The scientific study of the causes, circumstances, individual characteristics, and social contexts associated with crime victims.

volitional prong   The part of the insanity defense that requires acceptance of the possibility that a defendant could not control his or her behavior to conform to the requirements of the law. The volitional prong is not recognized in federal law or the law of many states.

voyeurism   The tendency to gain sexual excitement and gratification from observing unsuspecting others naked, undressing, or engaging in sexual activity.

weapons effect   Suggestion that the mere presence of a weapon leads a witness or victim to concentrate on the weapon itself rather than other features of the crime.

white-collar crime   A broad term, coined in 1939 by Edwin Sutherland, that refers to illegal acts committed by those of high social status in the process of their employment. Contemporary definitions often divide it into corporate crime and individual or occupational crime.

wilderness and adventure programs   Rehabilitative approaches for adjudicated delinquents (and preventive approaches for some youngsters at risk) that focus on skills-building and the development of self-esteem.

workplace aggression   A term for the conduct, usually on the part of employees, that qualifies as emotional harm or minor physical harm to other employees. Distinct from workplace violence.

workplace violence   The aggressive actions, including deaths, that occur at the workplace, not necessarily caused by those who work within the organization.

CASES CITED

......................................▶

Baxstrom v. Herold, 383 U.S. 107 (1966).

Carter v. United States, 252 F.2d 608 (D.C. Cir. 1957).

Dixon v. Attorney General of the Commonwealth of Pennsylvania, 325 F.Supp. 966 (M.D. Pa. 1971).

Durham v. United States, 214 F.2d 862 (D.C. Cir. 1954).

Dusky v. United States, 363 U.S. 402 (1960).

Foucha v. Louisiana, 51 Cr.L. 2084 (1992).

Jackson v. Indiana, 406 U.S. 715 (1972).

Kansas v. Crane, 521 U.S.346 (2002).

Kansas v. Hendricks, 117 S.Ct. 2072 (1997).

Madrid v. Gomez, 889 F. Supp. 1149 (N.D. Cal. 1995).

Miller v. State, 318 N.W.2d 673 (S.D. 1983).

M'Naghten, 10 Clark & Fin. 200, 210, 8 Eng.Rep 718, 722 (1843).

Roper v. Simmons, 543 U.S. 551 (2005).

Sell v. United States, 539 U.S. 166 (2003).

State v. Bianchi, No. 79-10116 (Wash. Super. Ct., October 19, 1979).

State v. Campanaro, Nos. 632-79, 1309–79, 1317–79, 514–80, & 707–80 (Superior Court of New Jersey Crim. Div., Union County, 1980).

State v. Felde, 422 So.2d 370 (La. 1982).

State v. Lafferty, 192 Conn. 571, 472 A.2d 1275 (1984).

State v. Milligan, No. 77-CR-11-2908 (Franklin Co., Ohio, December 4, 1978).

State v. Rodrigues, 679 P.2d 615 (Hawaii 1984).

Tarasoff v. Regents of the University of California, 529 F.2d 553 (Cal. 1974). vac., reheard en banc, & aff'd 131 Cal.Rptr. 1, 551 P.2d 334 (1976).

Thompson v. Oklahoma, 108 S.Ct. 2687 (1989).

United States v. Brawner, 471 F.2d 969 (D.C. Cir. 1972).

United States v. Davis, 772 F.2d 1339 (7th Cir. 1985), cert. denied, 106 S.Ct. 603 (1985).

United States v. Gillis, 773 F.2d 549 (4th Cir. 1985).

United States v. Gould, 741 F.2d 45 (4th Cir. 1984).

United States v. Krutschewski, 509 F.Supp. 1186 (D. Mass. 1981).

United States v. Lewellyn, 723 F.2d 615 (8th Cir. 1985).

United States v. Weston, 134 F. Supp. 2d 115 (D.D.C. 2001).

Vitek v. Jones, 445 United States 480 (1980).

Wilkins v. Maryland State Police, Civil Action No. CEB-93-483 (D.Md. 1993).

REFERENCES

Abadinsky, H. (1993). *Drug abuse* (2nd ed.). Chicago: Nelson-Hall.

Abel, G. G., Barlow, D. H., Blanchard, E. B., & Guild, D. (1977). The components of rapists' sexual arousal. *Archives of General Psychiatry, 34,* 895–903.

Abel, G. G., Becker, J. V., Blanchard, E. B., & Djenderedjian, A. (1978). Differentiating sexual aggressives with penile measures. *Criminal Justice and Behavior, 5,* 315–332.

Abel, G. G., Becker, J. V., Murphy, W. D., & Flanagan, B. (1981). Identifying dangerous child molesters. In R. B. Stuart (Ed.), *Violent behavior: Social learning approaches to prediction, management and treatment.* New York: Brunner/Mazel.

Abel, G. G., Mittelman, M., Becker, J. V., Rathner, J., & Rouleau, J. (1988). Predicting child molesters' response to treatment. R. A. Prentky & V. L. Quinsey (Eds.), *Human sexual aggression: Current perspectives.* New York: New York Academy of Sciences.

Abrahamsen, D. (1952). *Who are the guilty?* Westport, CT: Greenwood Press.

Abrahamsen, D. (1960). *The psychology of crime.* New York: Columbia University Press.

Achenbach, T. M., & Edelbrock, C. (1983). *Manual for the child behavior checklist and revised child behavior profile.* Burlington, VT: University of Vermont.

Acoca, L., & Austin, J. (1996). *The hidden crisis: The women offenders sentencing study and alternative sentencing recommendations project.* San Francisco, CA: National Council on Crime and Delinquency.

Acoca, L., & Dedel, K. (1998). *No place to hide: Understanding and meeting the needs of girls in the California juvenile justice system.* San Francisco, CA: National Council on Crime and Delinquency.

Adams, D. (1992). Biology does not make men more aggressive than women. In K. Bjorkquist & P. Niemela (Eds.), *Of mice and women: Aspects of female aggression.* San Diego, CA: Academic Press.

Adamson, L. A., & Thompson, R. A. (1998). Coping with interparental verbal conflict by children exposed to spouse abuse from nonviolent homes. *Journal of Family Violence, 13,* 213–232.

Adler, F. (1975). *Sisters in crime.* New York: McGraw-Hill.

Adler, J. (2002, February 25). The "thrill" of theft: It's not just movies stars. *Newsweek,* p. 52.

Adler, R., Nunn, R., Northam, E., Lebnan, V., & Ross, R. (1994). Secondary prevention of childhood firesetting. *Journal of the American Academy of Child and Adolescent Psychiatry, 33,* 1194–1202.

Akers, R. L. (1977). *Deviant behavior: A social learning approach* (2nd ed.). Belmont, CA: Wadsworth.

Akers, R. L. (1985). *Deviant behavior: A social learning approach* (3rd ed.). Belmont, CA: Wadsworth.

Akers, R. L., & Cochran, J. K. (1985). Adolescent marijuana use: A test of three theories of deviant behavior. *Deviant Behavior, 6,* 323–346.

Akers, R. L., & Lee, G. (1996). A longitudinal test of social learning theory: Adolescent smoking. *Journal of Drug Issues, 26,* 317–343.

Albanese, J. S. (1995). *White-collar crime in America.* Englewood Cliffs, NJ: Prentice Hall.

Alexander, M. A. (1999). Sexual offender treatment efficacy revised. *Sexual Abuse: A Journal of Research and Treatment, 11,* 101–116.

Alison, L., Bennett, C., Ormerod, D., & Mokros, A. (2002). The personality paradox in offender profiling: A theoretical review of the processes involved in deriving background characteristics from crime scene actions. *Psychology, Public Policy, and Law, 8,* 115–135.

Alison, L. J., & Canter, D. V. (1999). Professional, legal and ethical issues in offender profiling. In D. V. Canter & L. J. Alison (Eds.), *Profiling in policy and practice.* Aldershot, England: Ashgate.

Alison, L. J., Smith, M. D., & Morgan, K. (2003). Interpretating the accuracy of offender profiles. *Psychology, Crime & Law, 9,* 185–195.

Allen, M., Emmers, T., Gebhardt, L., & Giery, M. A. (2001). Exposure to pornography and acceptance of rape myths. *Journal of Communication, 45,* 5–53.

Allen, N. B., Lewinsohn, P. M., & Seeley, J. R. (1998). Prenatal and perinatal influences on risk for psychopathology in childhood and adolescence. *Development and Psychopathology, 10,* 513–529.

American Bar Association. (1979). *Juvenile justice standards project.* Chicago, IL: Author.

American Psychiatric Association (APA). (1994). *Diagnostic and statistical manual of mental disorders* (DSM-IV). Washington, DC: Author.

American Psychiatric Association (APA). (2000). *Diagnostice and statistical manual of mental disorders—revised* (DSM-IV-R). Washington, DC: Author.

American Psychological Association. (2003a). *Violence and the family: Report of the APA Presidential Task Force on Violence and the Family—executive summary.* APA Online. Available: www.apa.org/pi/pii/viol&fam.html.

American Psychological Association. (2003b). Is youth violence just another fact of life? *APA Online: Public Interest Initiatives.* Available: www.apa.org.

Amir, M. (1971). *Patterns in forcible rape.* Chicago, IL: University of Chicago Press.

Amsel, A. (1958). The role of frustrative nonreward in noncontinuous reward situations. *Psychological Bulletin, 55,* 102–119.

Andenaes, J. (1968). Does punishment deter crime? *The Criminal Law Quarterly, 11,* 76–93.

Andershed, H., Kerr, M., Stattin, H., & Levander, S. (2002). Psychopathic traits in non-referred youths: A new assessment tool. In E. Blauuw & L. Sheridan (Eds.), *Psychopaths: Current international perspectives.* The Hague, Netherlands: Elsevier.

Anderson, C. A. (1987). Temperature and aggression: Effects on quarterly, yearly, and city rates of violent and nonviolent crime. *Journal of Personality and Social Psychology, 52,* 1161–1173.

Anderson, C. A. (1989). Temperature and aggression: Ubiquitous effects of heat on occurrence of human violence. *Psychological Bulletin, 106,* 74–96.

Anderson, C. A. (2004). An update on the effects of playing violent video games. *Journal of Adolescence, 27,* 113–122.

Anderson, C. A., & Anderson, D. C. (1984). Ambient temperature and violent crime: Tests of the linear and curvilinear hypothesis. *Journal of Personality and Social Psychology, 46,* 91–97.

Anderson, C. A., & Bushman, B. J. (2001). Effects of violent games on aggressive behavior, aggressive cognition, aggressive effect, physiological asrousal, and prosocial behavior: A meta-analytic review of the scientific literature. *Psychological Science, 12,* 353–359.

Anderson, C. A., & Bushman, B. J. (2002). Human aggression. *Annual Review of Psychology, 53,* 27–51.

Anderson, C. A., Bushman, B. J., & Groom, R. W. (1997). Hot years and serious and deadly assault: Empirical tests of the heat hypothesis. *Journal of Peronality and Social Psychology, 73,* 1213–1223.

Anderson, C. A., & Dill, K. E. (2000). Video games and aggressive thoughts, feelings, and behavior in the laboratory and in life. *Journal of Personality and Social Psychology, 78,* 772–790.

Andreasen, N. C. (2001). *Brave new brain: Conquering mental illness in the era of the genome.* New York: Oxford University Press.

Andreasen, N. C., & Carpenter, W. T. (1993). Diagnosis and classification of schizophrenia. *Schizophrenia Bulletin, 19,* 199–214.

Andrew, J. M. (1978). Laterality on the tapping test among legal offenders. *Journal of Clinical Psychology, 7,* 149–150.

Andrews, D. A., & Bonta, J. (1994). *The psychology of criminal conduct.* Cincinnati, OH: Anderson.

Andrews, D. A., & Bonta, J. (1995). *The Level of Service Inventory—Revised.* Toronto, ON: Multi-Health Systems.

Andrews, D. A., & Bonta, J. (1998). *The psychology of criminal conduct* (2nd ed). Cincinnati, OH: Anderson.

Andrews, D. A., Bonta, J., & Hoge, R. D. (1990). Classification for effective rehabilitation: Rediscovering psychology. *Criminal Justice and Behavior, 17,* 19–52.

Anfuso, D. (1994). Deflecting workplace violence. *Personnel Journal, 73,* 66–77.

Appelbaum, P. S., Jick, R. Z., Grisso, T., Givelbar, D., Silver, E., & Steadman, H. J. (1993). Use of posttraumatic stress. *Psychiatry, 150,* 229–234.

Appelbaum, P. S., Robbins, P. C., & Monahan, J. (2000). Violence and delusions: Data from the MacArthur Violence Risk Assessment Study. *American Journal of Psychiatry, 157,* 566–572.

Araji, S. (1997). *Sexually aggressive children: Coming to understand them.* Thousand Oaks, CA: Sage.

Arata, C. M., Stafford, J., & Tims, M. S. (2003). High school drinking and its consequences. *Adolescence, 38,* 567–579.

Archer, J. (2004). Sex differences in aggression in real-world settings: A meta-analytic review. *Review of General Psychology, 8,* 291–322.

Arkow, P. (1998). The correlations between cruelty to animals and child abuse and the implications for veterinary medicine. In R. Lockwood & F. R. Ascione (Eds.), *Cruelty to animals and interpersonal violence: Readings in research and application.* West Lafayette, IN: Purdue University Press.

Aronson, E., Wilson, T. D., & Akert, R. M. (2005). *Social psychology* (5th ed.). Upper Saddle River, NJ: Prentice Hall.

Arrestees Drug Abuse Monitoring Program. (1999, April). *1998 annual report on marijuana use among arrestees.* Washington, DC: National Institute of Justice.

Arseneault, L., Tremblay, R. E., Boulerice, B., & Saucier, J-F. (2002). Obstetrical complications and violent delinquency: Testing two developmental pathways. *Child Development, 73,* 496–508.

Arseneault, L., Tremblay, R. G., Boulerice, B. Séguin, J. R., & Saucier, J. F. (2000). Minor physical anomalies and family adversity as risk factors for violent delinquency in adolescence. *American Journal of Psychiatry, 157,* 917–923.

Asbridge, M., Smart, R. G., & Mann, R. E. (2006). Can we prevent road rage? *Trauma, Violence, & Abuse, 7,* 109–121.

Ascione, R. R. (1997). *Animal welfare and domestic violence.* Logan, UT: Utah State University.

Ashford, J. B., Sales, B. D., & Reid, W. H. (2001). Introduction. In J. B. Ashford, B. D. Sales, & W. H. Reid (Eds.), *Treating adult and juvenile offenders with special needs.* Washington, DC: American Psychological Association.

Associated Press. (2006, May 17). Miami flagged for worst road rage. *Times Union,* p. A7.

Au Coin, K. (2003a). Family violence against older adults. In Canadian Centre for Justice Statistics (Ed.), *Family violence in Canada: A statistical profile 2003.* Ottawa: Canadian Centre for Justice Statistics.

Au Coin, K. (2003b). Violence and abuse against children and youth by family members. In Canadian Centre for Justice Statistics (Ed.), *Family violence in Canada: A statistical profile 2003.* Ottawa: Canadian Centre for Justice Statistics.

Augustine Fellowship. (1986). *Sex and love addicts anonymous.* Boston: Author.

Ault, R., & Reese, J. T. (1980). A psychological assessment of criminal profiling. *FBI Law Enforcement Bulletin, 49,* 22–25.

Avery-Clark, C. A., & Laws, D. R. (1984). Differential erection response patterns of sexual child abusers to stimuli describing activities with children. *Behavior Therapy, 15,* 71–83.

Babcock, J. C., Waltz, J., Jacobson, N. S., & Gottman, J. M. (1993). Power and violence: The relation between communication patterns, power discrepancies, and domestic violence. *Journal of Consulting and Clinical Psychology, 61,* 40–50.

Bagwell, C. L. (2004). Friendships, peer networks, and antisocial behavior. In J. B. Kupersmidt & K. A. Dodge (Eds.), *Children's peer relations: From development to intervention.* Washington, DC: American Psychological Association.

Ball, J. C., Shaffer, J. W., & Nurco, D. N. (1983). The day-to-day criminality of heroin addicts in Baltimore—a study in the continuity of offense rates. *Drug and Alcohol Dependence, 12,* 119–142.

Bamfield J. (1994). Electronic article surveillance: Management learning in curbing theft. In M. Gill (Ed.), *Crime at work: Studies in security and crime prevention.* Leiscester, Eng.: Perpetuity Press.

Bancroft, H. (1976). Behavioral treatments of sexual deviations. In N. H. Leitenberg (Ed.), *Handbook of behavioral modifications and behavioral therapy.* Englewood Cliffs, NJ: Prentice Hall.

Bandura, A. (1973a). *Aggression: A social learning analysis.* Englewood Cliffs, NJ: Prentice Hall.

Bandura, A. (1973b). Social learning theory of aggression. In J. F. Knutson (Ed.), *The control of aggression.* Chicago, IL: Aldine.

Bandura, A. (1977). *Social learning theory.* Englewood Cliffs, NJ: Prentice Hall.

Bandura, A. (1978). The self-system in reciprocal determinism. *American Psychologist, 33,* 344–358.

Bandura, A. (1983). Psychological mechanisms of aggression. In R. G. Geen & E. I. Donnerstein (Eds.), *Aggression: Theoretical and empirical reviews* (Vol. 1). New York: Academic Press.

Bandura, A. (1986). *Social foundations in thought and action: A social cognitive theory.* Englewood Cliffs, NJ: Prentice Hall.

Bandura, A. (1989). Human agency in social cognitive theory. *American Psychologist, 44,* 1175–1184.

Bandura, A. (1990). Selective activation and disengagement of moral control. *Journal of Social Issues, 46,* 27–46.

Bandura, A. (1991). Social cognitive theory or moral thought and action. In M. W. Kurtines & J. L. Gewirtz (Eds.), *Handbook of moral behavior and development: Vol. I. Theory.* Hillsdale, NJ: Erlbaum.

Bandura, A. (1997). *Self-efficacy: The exercise of control.* New York: Freeman.

Bandura, A. (1999). Moral disengagement in the perpetration of inhmanities. *Personality and Social Psychology Review, 3,* 193–209.

Bandura, A. (2004). The role of selective moral disengagement in terrorism and counterterrorism. In F. M. Moghaddam & A. J. Marsella (Eds.), *Understanding terrorism: Psychosocial roots, consequences, and interventions.* Washington, DC: American Psychological Association.

Bandura, A., Barbaranelli, C., Caprara, G. V., & Pastorelli, C. (1996). Mechanisms of moral disengagement in the exercise of moral agency. *Journal of Personality and Social Psychology, 71,* 364–374.

Bandura, A., Caprara, G. V., Barbaranelli, C., Pastorelli, C., & Regalia, C. (2001). Sociocognitive self-regulatory mechanisms governing transgressive behavior. *Journal of Personality and Social Psychology, 80,* 125–135.

Bandura, A., Ross, D., & Ross, S. (1963). Vicarious reinforcement and imitative learning. *Journal of Abnormal and Social Psychology, 67,* 601–607.

Bandura, A., & Walters, R. H. (1959). *Adolescent aggression.* New York: Ronald Press.

Bank, L., & Patterson, G. R. (1992). The use of structural equation modeling in combining data from different types of assessment. In J. C. Rosen & P. McReynolds (Eds.), *Recent advances in psychological assessment. Vol. 8.* New York: Plenum Press.

Bardone, A. M., Moffitt, T. E., & Caspi, A. (1996). Adult mental health and social outcomes of adolescent girls with depression and conduct disorder. *Development and Psychopathology, 8,* 811–829.

Barker, M. (2000). The criminal range of small-town burglars. In D. Canter & L. Alison (Eds.), *Profiling property crimes.* Dartmouth, Eng.: Ashgate.

Baron, R. A. (1977). *Human aggression.* New York: Plenum.

Baron, R. A. (1983). The control of human aggression: An optimistic perspective. *Journal of Social and Clinical Psychology, 1,* 97–119.

Baron, R. A., & Bell, P. A. (1975). Aggression and heat: Mediating effects of prior provocation and exposure to an aggressive model. *Journal of Personality and Social Psychology, 31,* 825–832.

Baron, R. A., & Byrne, D. (1977). *Social psychology* (2nd ed.). Boston, MA: Allyn and Bacon.

Baron, R. A., & Lawton, S. F. (1972). Environmental influences on aggression: The facilitation of modeling effects by high ambient temperatures. *Psychonomic Science, 26,* 80–83.

Baron, R. A., & Ransberger, V. M. (1978). Ambient temperature and the occurrence of collective violence: The "long, hot summer" revisited. *Journal of Personality and Social Psychology, 36,* 361–366.

Bartholow, B. D., Sestir, M. A., & Davis, E. B. (2005). Correlates and consequences of exposure to video game violence: Hostile personality, empathy, and aggressive behavior. *Personality and Social Psychology Bulletin, 31,* 1573–1586.

Bartol, C. R. (1988). Understanding delinquency: Causal loops and social systems. *Criminal Justice and Behavior, 15,* 394–401.

Bartol, C. R., & Bartol, A. M. (1998). *Delinquency and justice: A psychosocial approach* (2nd ed.). Upper Saddle River, NJ: Prentice Hall.

Bartol, C. R., & Bartol, A.M. (2004a). *Psychology and law: Theory, research, and application* (3rd ed.). Belmont, CA: Wadsworth/Thomson.

Bartol, C. R., & Bartol, A. M. (2004b). *Introduction to forensic psychology.* Thousand Oaks, CA: Sage.

Bartol, C. R., Griffin, R., & Clark, M. (1993, July). *Nationwide survey of American correctional psychologists.* Unpublished manuscript.

Bates, J. E., Pettit, G. S., Dodge, K. A., & Ridge, B. (1998). Interaction of temperamental resistance to control and restrictive parenting in the development of externalizing behavior. *Developmental Psychology, 34,* 982–995.

Battelle Law and Justice Center Report. (1977). *Forcible rape: An analysis of the legal issue.* Washington, DC: National Institute of Law Enforcement and Criminal Justice.

Baum, K. (2006, April). *Identity theft, 2004.* Washington, DC: U.S. Department of Justice, Bureau of Justice Statistics.

Baumer, T. L., & Rosenbaum, D. P. (1984). *Combating retail theft: Programs and strategies.* Boston, MA: Butterworth.

Baumrind, D. (1991). Parenting styles and adolescent development. In J. Brooks-Gunn, R. Lerner, & A. C. Petersen (Eds.), *The encyclopedia of adolescence.* New York: Garland.

Bear, M. F., Connors, B. W., & Paradiso, M. A. (1996). *Neuroscience: Exploring the brain.* Baltimore, MD: Williams & Wilkins.

Beatty, D. (2001). Stalking. In G. Coleman, M. Gaboury, M. Murray, & A. Seymour (Eds.), *1999 National Victim Assistance Academy.* Washington, DC: U.S. Department of Justice.

Beck, A. J. (2000, August). *Prisoners in 1999.* Washington, DC: Bureau of Justice Statistics.

Becker, J. V., Hall, S. R., & Stinson, J. D. (2001). Female sexual offenders: Clinical, legal and policy issues. *Journal of Forensic Psychology Practice, 1,* 29–50.

Becker, J. V., & Johnson, B. R. (2001). Treating juvenile sex offenders. In J. B. Ashford, B. D. Sales, & W. H. Reid (Eds.), *Treating adult and juvenile offenders with special needs.* Washington, DC: American Psychological Association.

Becker, K. D., Stuewig, J., Herrera, V. M., & McCloskey, L. A. (2004). A study of firesetting and animal cruelty in children: Family influences and adolescent outcomes. *Journal of the American Academy of Child and Adolescent Psychiatry, 43,* 905–913.

Bell, P. A., & Baron, R. A. (1977). Aggression and ambient temperature: The inhibiting and facilitating effects of hot and cold environments. *Bulletin of the Psychonomic Society, 6,* 240–242.

Bennett, D. S., Bedersky, M., & Lewis, M. (2002). Children's intellectual and emotional-behavioral adjustment at 4 years as a function of cocaine exposure, maternal characteristics, and environmental risk. *Developmental Psychology, 38,* 648–658.

Bennett, T., & Wright, R. (1984). *Burglars on burglary: Prevention and the offender.* Brookfield, VT: Gower.

Bereczkei, T. (2000). Evolutionary psychology: A new perspective in the behavioral sciences. *European Psychologist, 5,* 175–190.

Berkowitz, L. (1962). *Aggression: A social-psychological analysis.* New York: McGraw-Hill.

Berkowitz, L. (1969). The frustration-aggression hypothesis revisited. In L. Berkowitz (Ed.), *Roots of aggression.* New York: Atherton Press.

Berkowitz, L. (1970). The contagion of violence: An S-R mediational analysis of some effects of observed aggression. In W. J. Arnold & M. M. Page (Eds.), *Nebraska symposium on motivation.* Lincoln, NE: University of Nebraska Press.

Berkowitz, L. (1973). Words and symbols as stimuli to aggressive responses. In J. F. Knutson (Ed.), *The control of aggression.* Chicago, IL: Aldine.

Berkowitz, L. (1983). The experience of anger as a parallel process in the display of impulsive, "angry" aggression. In R. G. Geen & E. I. Donnerstein (Eds.), *Aggression: Theoretical and empirical reviews* (Vol. 1). New York: Academic Press.

Berkowitz, L. (1989). Frustration-aggression hypothesis: Examination and reformulation. *Psychological Bulletin, 106,* 59–73.

Berkowitz, L. (1994). Guns and youth. In L. E. Eron, J. H. Gentry, & P. Schlegel (Eds.), *Reason to hope: A psychosocial perspective on violence and youth.* Washington, DC: American Psychological Association.

Berkowitz, L., & LePage, A. (1967). Weapons as aggression-eliciting stimuli. *Journal of Personality and Social Psychology, 7,* 202–207.

Berlyne, D. E. (1960). *Conflict, arousal, and curiosity.* New York: McGraw-Hill.

Bernard, F. (1975). An inquiry among a group of pedophiles. *Journal of Sex Research, 11,* 242–255.

Bernstein, A., Newman, J. P., Wallace, J. F., & Luh, K. E. (2000). Left hemisphere activation and deficient response modulation in psychopaths. *Psychological Science, 11,* 414–418.

Berrueta-Clement, J. R., Schweinhart, L. J., Barnett, W. S., & Weikart. D. P. (1987). The effects of early educational intervention in adolescence and early adulthood. In J. D. Burhcard & S. N. Burchard (Eds.), *Prevention of delinquent behavior.* Newbury Park, CA: Sage.

Binder, A. (1988). Juvenile delinquency. *Annual Review of Psychology, 39,* 253–282.

Björkqvist, K., Lagerspetz, M. J., & Kaukianinen, A. (1992). Do girls manipulate and boys fight? Developmental trends in regard to direct and indirect aggression. *Aggressive Behavior, 18,* 117–127.

Black, H. C. (1990). *Black's law dictionary.* St. Paul, MN: West Publishing.

Black, M. S., & Pettway, C. (2001, December). *Profile of ODRC offenders assessed at the sex offender risk reduction center.* Columbus, OH: Ohio Office of Policy, Bureau of Research.

Blackburn, N., Weiss, J., & Lamberti, J. (1960). The sudden murderer. *Archives of General Psychiatry, 2,* 670–678.

Blackburn, R. (1968). Personality in relation to extreme aggression in psychiatric offenders. *British Journal of Psychiatry, 114,* 821–828.

Blackburn, R. (1993). *The psychology of criminal conduct: Theory, research and practice.* Chichester, Eng.: Wiley.

Blackburn, R. (1998). Criminality and the interpersonal circle in mentally disordered offenders. *Criminal Justice and Behavior, 25,* 155–176.

Blair, C. D., & Lanyon, R. I. (1981). Exhibitionism: An etiology and treatment. *Psychological Bulletin, 89,* 439–463.

Blair, R. J. R., Peschardt, K. S., Budhani, S., Mitchell, D. G. V., & Pine, D. S. (2006). The development of psychopathy. *Journal of Child Psychology and Psychiatry, 47,* 262–275.

Blanchard, R. Watson, M. S., Choy, A., Dickey, R., Klassen, P., Kuban, M., & Ferren, D. J. (1999). Pedophiles: Mental retardation, maternal age, and sexual orientation. *Archives of Sexual Behavior, 28,* 111–127.

Blitstein, J. L., Murray, D. M., Lytle, L. A., Birnbaum, A. S., & Perry, C. L. (2005). Predictors of violent behavior in an early adolescent cohort: Similarities and differences across genders. *Health Education and Behavior, 32,* 175–194.

Block, R. (1977). *Violent crime.* Lexington: MA: Lexington Books.

Blonigen, D. M., Carlson, S. R., Krueger, R. F., & Patrick, C. J. (2003). A twin study of self-reported psychopathic traits. *Personality and Individual Differences, 35,* 179–197.

Blonigen, D. M., Hicks, B. M., Krueger, R. F., Patrick, C. J., & Iacono, W. G. (2005). Psychopathic personality traits: Heritability and genetic overlap with internalizing and externalizing psychopathology. *Psychological Medicine, 35,* 637–648.

Blumenthal, D. R. (1999). *The banality of good and evil: Moral lessons form the Shoah and Jewish tradition.* Washington, DC: Georgetown University Press.

Blumer, D. (1976). Epilepsy and violence. In D. J. Madden & J. R. Lion (Eds.), *Rage, hate, assault, and other forms of violence.* New York: Spectrum Publishing.

Blumer, D., & Migeon, C. (1973). *Treatment of impulsive behavior disorders in males with medroxyprogesterone acetate.* Paper presented at the Annual Meeting of the American Psychiatric Association, Washington, DC

Blumer, H., Sutter, A., Ahmed, S., & Smith, R. (1967). *ADD center final report: The world of youthful drug use.* Berkeley, CA: University of California Press.

Boehnert, C. E. (1989). Characteristics of successful and unsuccessful insanity pleas. *Law and Human Behavior, 13,* 31–39.

Bolen, R. M., & Scannapieco, M. (1999). Prevalence of child sexual abuse: A corrective met-analysis. *Social Service Review, 73,* 281–313.

Bonanno, G. A. (2004). Loss, trauma, and human resilience: Have we underestimated the human capacity to thrive after extremely aversive events? *American Psychologist, 59,* 20–28.

Bongers, I. L., Koot, H. M., van der Ende, J., & Verhulst, F. C. (2003). The normative development of child and adolescent problem behavior. *Journal of Abnormal Psychology, 112,* 179–192.

Bonnie, R. J., & Grisso, T. (2000). Adjudicative competence and youthful offenders. In T. Grisso & R. G. Schwartz (Eds.), *Youth on trial.* Chicago: University of Chicago Press.

Bonta, J., & Cormier, R. B. (1999). Corrections research in Canada: Impressive progress and promising prospects. *Canadian Journal of Criminology, 41,* 235–245.

Bonta, J., Law, M., & Hanson, K. (1998). The prediction of criminal and violent recidivism among mentally disordered offenders: A meta-analysis. *Psychological Bulletin, 123,* 123–142.

Bonta, J., Wallace-Capretta, S., & Rooney, J. (2000). A quasi-experimental evaluation of an intensive rehabilitation supervision program. *Criminal Justice and Behavior, 27,* 312–329.

Boothby, J. L., & Clements, C. B. (2000). A national survey of correctional psychologists. *Criminal Justice and Behavior, 27,* 716–732.

Borduin, C. M. (1994). Innovative models of treatment and service delivery in the juvenile justice system. *Journal of Clinical Child Psychiatry, 23,* 19–21.

Borduin, C. M., Mann, B. J., Cone, L. T., Henggeler, S. W., Fucci, B. R., Blaske, D. M., & Williams, R. (1995). Multisystemic treatment of serious juvenile offenders: Long-term prevention of criminality and violence. *Journal of Consulting and Clinical Psychology, 63,* 569–578.

Borum, R. (1996). Improving the clinical practice of violence risk assessment. *American Psychologist, 51,* 945–956.

Borum, R., & Strentz, T. (1993, April). The borderline personality: Negotiation strategies. *FBI Law Enforcement Bulletin,* 6–10.

Bottcher, J., & Ezell, M. E. (2005). Examining the effectiveness of boot camps: A randomized experiment with a long-term follow up. *Journal of Research in Crime and Delinquency, 42,* 309–332.

Boudreau, J., Kwan, Q., Faragher, W., & Denault, G. (1977). *Arson and arson investigation.* Washington, DC: USGPO.

Bowker, L. H. (1983). *Beating wife-battering.* Lexington, MA: Lexington Books.

Boykin, A. W. (1986). The triple quandary and the schooling of Afro-American children. In U. Neisser (Ed.), *The school achievement of minority children.* Hillsdale, NJ: Erlbaum.

Boykin, A. W. (1994). Harvesting talent and culture: African-American children and educational reform. In R. Rossi (Ed.), *Schools and students at risk.* New York: Teachers College Press.

Bracey, D. H. (1982). Concurrent and consecutive abuse: The juvenile prostitute. In B. R. Price and N. Sokoloff (Eds.), *The criminal justice system and women.* New York: Clark Boardman.

Bradford, J. M. W. (1982). Arson: A clinical study. *Canadian Journal of Psychiatry, 27,* 188–193.

Bourque, B. B., Cronin, R. C., Felker, D. B., Pearson, F. R., Han, M., & Hill, S. M. (1996). *Boot camps for juvenile offenders: An implementation evaluation of three demonstration programs.* Research in Brief. Washington, DC: National Institute of Justice.

Braga, A. A., & Kennedy, D. M. (2001). The illicit acquisition of firearms by youth and juveniles. *Journal of Criminal Justice, 29,* 397–388.

Braithwaite, J. (1981). The myth of class and criminality reconsidered. *American Sociological Review, 46,* 36–57.

Brandt, J. R., Kennedy, W. A., Patrick, C. J., & Curtain, J. J. (1997). Assessment of psychopathy in a population of incarcerated adolescent offenders. *Psychological Assessment, 9,* 429–435.

Brantley, A. G., & Kosky, R. H., Jr. (2005, January). Serial murder in the Netherlands: A look at motivation, behavior, and characteristics. *FBI Law Enforcement Bulletin,* 26–32.

Brennan, P. A., Grekin, E. R., & Mednick, S. A. (1999). Maternal smoking during preganancy and adult male criminal outcomes. *Archives of General Psychiatry, 56,* 215–219.

Brennan, P. A., Hall, J., Bor, W., Najman, J. M., & Williams, G. (2003). Integrating biological and social processes in relation to early-onset persistent aggression in boys and girls. *Developmental Psychology, 39,* 309–323.

Brennan, P. A., Mednick, S. A., & Hodgins, S. (2000). Major mental disorders and criminal violence in a Danish birth cohort. *Archives of General Psychiatry, 53,* 1033–1039.

Brennan, P. A., Mednick, S. A., & Kandel, E. (1993). Congenital determinants of violent and property offending. In D. J. Pepler & K. H. Rubin (Eds.), *The development and treatment of childhood aggression.* Hillsdale, NJ: Erlbaum.

Brent, D. A. (1989). The psychological autopsy: Methodological issues for the study of adolescent suicide. *Suicide and Life Threatening Behavior, 19,* 43–57.

Brier, N. (1989). The relationship between learning disability and delinquency: A review and reappraisal. *Journal of Learning Disabilities, 22,* 546–553.

Briere, J. (1988). The long-term clinical correlates of childhood sexual victimization. In R. A. Prentky & V. L. Quinsey (Eds.), *Human sexual aggression: Current perspectives.* New York: New York Academy of Sciences.

Briere, J., Malamuth, N., & Ceniti, J. (1981). *Self-assessed rape proclivity: Attitudinal and sexual correlates.* Paper presented at APA Meeting, Los Angeles, CA.

Brodsky, S. L. (1973). *Psychologists in the criminal justice system.* Urbana, IL: University of Illinois Press.

Brodsky, S. L. (1977). Criminal and dangerous behavior. In D. Rimm & J. Somervill (Eds.), *Abnormal psychology.* New York: Academic Press.

Broidy, L. M., Nagin, D. S., Tremblay, R. E., Bates, J. E., Brame, B., Dodge, K. A., Fergusson, D., Horwood, J. L., Loeber, R., Laird, R., Lynam, D. R., Moffitt, T. E., Pettit, G. S., & Vitaro, F. (2003). Developmental trajectories of childhood disruptive behaviors and adolescent delinquency: A six-site, cross-national study. *Developmental Psychology, 39,* 222–245.

Brookman, F., & Nolan, J. (2006). The dark figure of infanticide in England and Wales: Complexes of diagnosis. *Journal of Interpersonal Violence, 21,* 869–889.

Brown, B. B., & Harris, P. B. (1989). Residential burglary victimization: Reactions to the invasion of a primary territory. *Journal of Environmental Psychology, 9,* 119–132.

Brown, J. S., & Farber, I. E. (1951). Emotions conceptualized as intervening variables—with suggestions toward a theory of frustration. *Psychological Bulletin, 48,* 465–495.

Brown, T. L., Borduin, C. M., & Henggeler, S. W. (2001). Treating juvenile offenders in community settings. In J. B. Ashford, B. D. Sales, & W. H. Reid (Eds.), *Treating adult and juvenile offenders with special needs.* Washington, DC: American Psychological Association.

Browne, A. (1987). *When battered women kill.* New York: Free Press.

Browne, A., & Finkelhor, D. (1986). Impact of child sexual abuse: A review of the research. *Psychological Bulletin, 99,* 66–77.

Browning, K., & Loeber, R.. (1999, February). Highlights of findings from the Pittsburgh Youth Study. *OJJDP Fact Sheet.* Washington, DC: U.S. Department of Justice, Office of Juvenile Justice and Delinquency Prevention.

Brownlie, E. B., Beitchman, J. J., Escobar, M., Young, A., Atkinson, L., Johnson, C., Wilson, B., & Douglas, L. (2004). Early language impairment and young adult delinquent and aggressive behavior. *Journal of Abnormal Child Psychology, 32,* 453–467.

Brunet, B. L., Reiffenstein, R. J., Williams, T., & Wong, L. (1985–1986). Toxicity of phencyclidine and ethanol in combination. *Alcohol and Drug Research, 6,* 341–349.

Brussel, J. A. (1978). *Casebook of a crime psychiatrist.* New York: Bernard Geis Associates.

Bryant, J., & Zillmann, D. (Eds.). (2002). *Media effects: Advances in theory and research* (2nd ed.). Mahwah, NJ: Erlbaum.

Buckle, A., & Farrington, D. P. (1994). Measuring shoplifting by systematic observation: A replication study. *Psychology, Crime & Law, 1,* 133–141.

Buckner, J. C., Mezzacappa, E., & Beardslee, W. R. (2003). Characteristics of resilient youths living in poverty: The role of self-regulatory processes. *Development and Psychopathology, 15,* 139–162.

Bukstel, L. H., & Kilmann, P. R. (1980). Psychological effects of imprisonment on confined individuals. *Psychological Bulletin, 88,* 469–493.

Bullock, H. A. (1955). Urban homicide in theory and fact. *Journal of Criminal Law, Criminology and Police Science, 45,* 565–575.

Bumby, K. M., & Bumby, N. H. (1997). Adolescent female sexual offenders. In J. R. Cellini & B. Schwartz (Eds.), *The sex offender: New insights, treatment innovations and legal developments* (Vol. 2). Kingston, NJ: Civil Research Institute.

Bumpass, E. R., Fagelman, F. D., & Birx, R. J. (1983). Intervention with children who set fires. *American Journal of Psychotherapy, 37,* 328–345.

Bureau of International Narcotics and Law Enforcement Affairs. (2000, March). *International narcotics control strategy report, 1999.* Washington, DC: U.S. Department of State. Available: www.state.gov/www/global/narcotics

Bureau of Justice Assistance. (2000, April). *Emerging judicial strategies for the mentally ill in the criminal caseload: Mental health courts.* Washington, DC: U.S. Department of Justice.

Bureau of Justice Statistics. (1999, July). *Mental health and treatment of inmates and prisoners.* Washington, DC: Author.

Bureau of Justice Statistics. (2000a, June). *An estimated 312,000 handgun sales blocked during the 1994–1998 Brady interim period.* Washington, DC: Author. Available: www.ojp.usdoj.gov/bjs/pub/press/phc98.pr

Bureau of Justice Statistics. (2000b, June). *Drugs and crime facts: Drug use and crime.* Washington, DC: Author. Available: www.ojp.usdoj.gov/bjs/dcf/duc.htm.

Bureau of Justice Statistics. (2001a, January). *Homicide trends in the United States: Infanticide.* Washington, DC: Author. Available: www.ojp.usdoi.gov/bjs/homicide/children.htm.

Bureau of Justice Statistics (2001b). *Prisoners in 2000.* Washington, DC: U.S. Department of Justice.

Bureau of Justice Statistics. (2002, April). *Hispanic vicitms of violent crime, 1993–2000.* Washington, DC: Author.

Bureau of Justice Statistics. (2003a). *Capital punishment statistics.* Washington, DC: Author.

Bureau of Justice Statistics. (2003b). *Victim characteristics.* Washington, DC: Author.

Bureau of Justice Statistics. (2003c, July). *Prisoners in 2002.* Washington, DC: Author.

Bureau of Justice Statistics. (2005, November 20). *School violence rate stable: Lowest level in a decade.* Washington, DC: U.S. Department of Justice, Author.

Bureau of Justice Statistics. (2006, June). Prison statistics: Summary findings. Washington, DC: U.S. Department of Justice, Author.

Bureau of Labor Statistics. (1999). *National census of fatal occupational injuries, 1998.* Washington, DC: U.S. Department of Labor.

Bureau of Labor Statistics. (2004). *Census of Fatal Occupational Injuries.* Washington, DC: U.S. Department of Labor.

Burgess, R. L., & Akers, R. L. (1966). A differential association-reinforcement theory of criminal behavior. *Social Problems, 14,* 128–147.

Bushman, B. J., & Anderson, C. A. (2001). Is it time to pull the plug on the hostile versus instrumental aggression dichotomy. *Psychological Review, 108,* 273–279.

Bushman, B. J., Bonacci, A. M., Pederson, W. C., Vasquez, E. A., & Miller, N. (2005). Chewing on it can chew you up: Effects of rumination on triggered displaced aggression. *Journal of Personality and Social Psychology, 88,* 969–983.

Bushman, B. J., Wang, M. C., & Anderson, C. A. (2005a). Is the curve relating temperature to aggression linear or curvilinear? Assaults and temperature in Minneapolis reexamined. *Journal of Personality and Social Psychology, 89,* 62–66.

Bushman, B. J., Wang, M. C., & Anderson, C. A. (2005b). Is the curve relating temperature to aggression linear or curvilinear? A response to Bell (2005) and to Cohn and Rotton (2005). *Journal of Personality and Social Psychology, 89,* 74–77.

Buss, A. H. (1971). Aggression pays. In J. L. Singer (Ed.), *The control of aggression and violence.* New York: Academic Press.

Buss, D. M., & Shackelford, T. K. (1997). Human aggression in evolutionary psychological perspective. *Clinical Psychology Review, 17,* 605–619.

Butler, R. A. (1954). Curiosity in monkeys. *Scientific American* (reprint #426). San Francisco, CA: W. H. Freeman.

Buzawa, E. S., & Buzawa, C. G. (1996). *Domestic violence: The criminal justice response* (2nd ed.). Thousand Oaks, CA: Sage.

Cacioppo, J. T., Berntson, G. G., Sheridan, J. F., & McClintock, M. K. (2000). Multilevel integrative analyses of human behavior: Social neuroscience and the complementing nature of social and biological approaches. *Psychological Bulletin, 6,* 829–843.

Cairns, R. B., Cairns, B. D., Neckerman, H. J., Ferguson, L. L., & Gariépy, J. L. (1989). Growth and aggression: I. Childhood to early adolescence. *Developmental Psychology, 25,* 320–330.

Cairns, R. B., Cairns, B. D., Neckerman, H. J., Gest, S. D., & Gariépy, J. L. (1988). Social networks and aggressive behavior: Peer support or peer rejection. *Developmental Psychology, 24,* 815–826.

Cale, E. M. (2006). A quantitative review of the relations between the "Big 3" higher order personality dimensions and antisocial behavior. *Journal of Research in Personality, 40,* 250–284.

Calhoun, J. B. (1961). Phenomena associated with population density. *Proceedings of the National Academy of Sciences, 47,* 428–429.

Calhoun, J. B. (1962). Population density and social pathology. *Scientific American, 206,* 139–148.

California Division of Occupational Safety and Health. (1995). *Guidelines for workplace security.* San Francisco: California Department of Industrial Relations.

Callahan, L. A., Steadman, H. J., McGreevy, M. A., & Robbins, P. C. (1991). The volume and characteristics of insanity defense pleas: An eight-state study. *Bulletin of Psychiatry and the Law, 19,* 331–338.

Cameron, M. O. (1964). *The booster and the snitch.* New York: Free Press.

Campbell, A. (1993). *Men, women, and aggression.* New York: Basic Books.

Campbell, A. (2006). Sex differences in direct aggression: What are the psychological mediators. *Aggression and Violent Behavior, 22,* 237–264.

Campbell, A., Muncer, S., & Coyle, E. (1992). Social representation of aggression as an explanation of gender differences: A preliminary study. *Aggressive Behavior, 18,* 95–108.

Campbell, B. J. (1996). *Validity and use of evidence concerning battering and its effects in criminal trials.* Washington, DC: U.S. Department of Justice, Violence Against Women Office.

Campbell, M. A., Porter, S., & Santor, D. (2004). Psychopathic traits in adolescent offenders: An evaluation of criminal history, clinical, and psychosocial correlates. *Behavioral Sciences & the Law, 22,* 23–47.

Canadian Government's Commission of Inquiry. (1971). *The non-medical use of drugs: Interim report.* London: Penguin Books.

Canter, D., & Alison, L. (2000). Profiling property crimes. In D. Canter & L. Alison (Eds.), *Profiling property crimes.* Burlington, VT: Ashgate.

Cantor, J. M., Blanchard, R., Robichaud, L. K., & Christensen, B. K. (2005). Quantitative reanalysis of aggregate date on IQ in sexual offenders. *Psychological Bulletin, 131,* 555–568.

Capaldi, D. M., Dishion, T. J., Stoolmiller, M., & Yoerger, K. (2001). Aggression toward female partners by at-risk young men: The contribution of male adolescent friendships. *Developmental Psychology, 37,* 61–73.

Carlson, B. E. (1991). Outcomes of physical abuse and observation of marital violence among adolescents in placement. *Journal of Interpersonal Violence, 6,* 526–534.

Carlson, M., Marcus-Newhall, A., & Miller, N. (1990). Effects of situational aggression cues: A quantitative review. *Journal of Personality and Social Psychology, 58,* 622–633.

Carlson, R. J. (1976). *The dilemmas of corrections.* Lexington, MA: Lexington Books.

Carnegie Council on Adolescent Development. (1995). *Great transitions: Preparing American Youth for a new century.* New York: Carnegie Corporation of New York.

Carnes, P. (1983). *Out of the shadows: Understanding sexual addiction.* Minneapolis, MN: Compcare Publications.

Carraher, T. N., Carraher, D., & Schliemann, A. D. (1985). Mathematics in the streets and schools. *British Journal of Developmental Psychology, 3,* 21–29.

Carter, D. L., & Katz, A. J. (1996). *Computer crime: An emerging challenge for law enforcement.* Washington, DC: U.S. Department of Justice. Available: www.fbi.gov/leb/dec961.txt.

Casey-Cannon, S., Hayward, C., & Gowen, K. (2001). Middle-school girls' reports of peer victimization: Concerns, consequences, and implications. *Professional School Counseling, 5,* 138–148.

Caspi, A., Wright, B. R. E., Moffitt, T. E., & Silva, P. A. (1998). Early failure in the labor market: Childhood and adolescent predictors of unemployment in the transition to adulthood. *American Sociological Review, 63,* 424–451.

Catalano, S. M. (2005). *Crime victimization, 2004.* Washington, DC: U.S. Department of Justice, National Crime Victimization Survey.

Cavior, N., & Howard, L. R. (1973). Facial attractiveness and juvenile delinquency among black offenders and white offenders. *Journal of Abnormal Child Psychology, 1,* 202–213.

Cellini, H. R. (1995). Assessment and treatment of the adolescent sexual offender. In B. Schwartz & H. R. Cellini (Eds.), *The sex offender: Corrections, treatment and legal practice* (Vol. 1). Kingston, NJ: Civil Research Institute.

Center, D. B., Jackson, N., & Kemp, D. (2005). A test of Eysenck's antisocial behavior hypothesis employing 11–15-year-old students dichotomous for PEN and L. *Personality and Individual Differences, 38,* 393–402.

Chaiken, J. M. (1998a, April). Learning more from national data collection programs. *National Conference on Sex Offender Registries.* Sacramento, CA: SEARCH group. Available: www.ojp.usdoj.gov/bjs/pub/.

Chaiken, J. M. (1998b, April). Foreword. *National Conference on Sex Offender Registries.* Sacramento, CA: SEARCH group. Available: www.ojp.usdoj.gov/bjs/pub/.

Chaiken, J. M. (1999, February). *Foreword. American Indians and Crime.* Washington, DC: U.S. Department of Justice.

Chalkley, A. J., & Powell, G. E. (1983). The clinical description of forty-eight cases of clinical fetishism. *British Journal of Psychiatry, 142,* 292–295.

Chamberlain, P. (1996). Treatment foster care for adolescents with conduct disorders and delinquency. In P. S. Jensen & D. Hibbs (Eds.), *Psychological treatment with research with children and adolescents.* Rockville, MD: National Institute of Mental Health.

Chamlin, M. B., & Cochran, J. R. (2005). Ascribed economic inequality and homicide among modern societies: Toward the development of a cross-national theory. *Homicide Studies, 9,* 3–29.

Chappell, D. (1977a). *Forcible rape: A national survey of the response by police (LEAA).* Washington, DC: USGPO.

Chappell, D. (1977b). *Forcible rape: A national survey of the response by prosecutors (LEAA).* Washington, DC: USGPO.

Chapple, C. L. (2003). Examining intergenerational violence: Violent role modeling or weak parental controls? *Violence and Victims, 18,* 143–159.

Chen, Y-H., Arria, A., & Anthony, J. C. (2003). Firesetting in adolescents and being aggressive, shy, and rejected by peers: New epidemiologic evidence from a national sample survey. *Journal of the American Academy of Psychiatry and Law, 31,* 44–52.

Chesney-Lind, M., & Shelden, R. (1998). *Girls, delinquency, and juvenile justice* (2nd ed.). Belmont, CA: West/Wadsworth.

Chesno, F. A., & Kilmann, P. R. (1975). Effects of stimulation intensity on sociopathic avoidance learning. *Journal of Abnormal Psychology, 84,* 144–150.

Child Abuse Prevention Center. (1998). *Shaken baby syndrome fatalities in the United States.* Ogden, UT: Author.

Chimbos, P. D. (1973). A study of breaking and entering offenses in "Northern City," Ontario. *Canadian Journal of Criminology and Corrections, 15,* 316–325.

Chorover, S. L. (1980). Violence: A localizable problem? In E. S. Valenstein (Ed.), *The psychosurgery debate.* San Francisco, CA: W. H. Freeman.

Christiansen, K. O. (1977). A review of studies of criminality among twins. In S. Mednick & K. O. Christiansen (Eds.), *Biosocial bases of criminal behavior.* New York: Gardiner Press.

Christie, M. M., Marshall, W. L., & Lanthier. R. D. (1979). *A descriptive study of incarcerated rapists and pedophiles.* Ottawa, ON: Report to the Solicitor General of Canada.

Chung, I-J, Hill, K. G., Hawkins, J. D., Gilchrist, L. D., & Nagin, D. S. (2002). Childhood predictors of offense trajectories. *Journal of Research in Crime and Delinquency, 39,* 60–90.

Churgin, M. M. (1983). The transfer of inmates of mental health facilities: Developments in the law. In J. Monahan & H. J. Steadman (Eds.), *Mentally disordered offenders.* New York: Plenum.

Chute, C. L. (1949). Fifty years of the juvenile court. In M. Bell (Ed.), *Current approaches to delinquency.* New York: National Probation and Parole Association.

Cicero, T. J., Inciardi, J. A., & Muñoz, A. (2005). Trends in abuse of OxyContin® and other opioid analgesics in the United States: 2002–2004. *The Journal of Pain, 6,* 662–672.

Cillessen, A. H. N., & Mayeux, L. (2004). Sociometric status and peer group behavior: Previous findings and current directions. In J. B. Kupersmidt & K. A. Dodge (Eds.), *Children's peer relations: From development to intervention.* Washington, DC: American Psychological Association.

Cirincione, C., & Jacobs, C. (1999). Identifying insanity acquittals: Is it easier? *Law and Human Behavior, 23,* 487–497.

Claridge, G. (1973). Final remarks. In G. Claridge, S. Canter, & W. I. Hume (Eds.), *Personality differences and biological variations.* Oxford, Eng.: Pergamon Press.

Clark, J. P., & Hollinger, R. C. (1983). *Theft by employees in work organizations.* Washington, DC: USGPO.

Clark, K. B. (1971). The pathos of power: A psychological perspective. *American Psychologist, 26,* 1047–1057.

Clear, T. R., & Cole, G. F. (2000). *American corrections* (5th ed.). Belmont, CA: West/Wadsworth.

Cleckley, H. (1976). *The mask of sanity* (5th ed.). St. Louis, MO: Mosby.

Clements, C. B. (1987). Psychologists in adult correctional institutions: Getting off the treadmill. In E. K. Morris & C. J. Braukmann (Eds.), *Behavioral approaches to crime and delinquency.* New York: Plenum.

Clements, C. B. (1996). Offender classification: Two decades of progress. *Criminal Justice and Behavior, 23,* 121–143.

Clinard, M. B., & Quinney, E. R. (1980). *Criminal behavior systems: A typology.* New York: Holt, Rinehart & Winston.

Cochrane, R. E., Grisso, T., & Frederick, R. I. (2001). The relationship between criminal charges, diagnoses, and psychological opinions among federal defendants. *Behavioral Science & the Law, 19,* 565–582.

Cocozza, J. J., & Steadman, H. J. (1976). The failure of psychiatric prediction of dangerousness: Clear and convincing evidence. *Rutgers Law Review, 29,* 1084–1101.

Cohen, F. (1998). *The mentally disordered inmate and the law.* Kingston, NJ: Civic Research Institute.

Cohen, F. (2000). *The mentally disordered inmate and the law: 2000–2001 supplement.* Kingston, NJ: Civic Research Institute.

Cohen, M., Seghorn, T., & Calmas, W. (1969). Sociometric study of the sex offender. *Journal of Abnormal Psychology, 74,* 249–255.

Cohen, M. L., Garafalo, R., Boucher, R., & Seghorn, T. (1971). The psychology of rapists. *Seminars in Psychiatry, 3,* 307–327.

Cohen, N. J., Menna, R., Vallance, D. D., Barwick, M., Im, N., & Horodezky, N. B. (1998). Language, social cognitive processing, and behavioral characteristics of psychiatrically disturbed children with previously identified and suspected language impairments. *Journal of Child Psychology and Psychiatry, 39,* 853–864.

Cohen, P., Cohen, J., & Brook, J. (1993). An epidemiological study of disorders in late childhood and adolescence—II. Persistent disorders. *Journal of Child Psychology and Psychiatry, 34,* 869–877.

Cohn, E. G., & Rotton, J. (1997). Assault as a function of time and temperature: A moderator-variable time-series analysis. *Journal of Personality and Social Psychology, 72,* 1322–1334.

Cohn, V. (1986). Crack use. *NIDA Notes, 1,* 6.

Coie, J. D. (2004). The impact of negative social experience on the development of antisocial behavior. In J. B. Kupersmidt & K. A. Dodge (Eds.), *Children's peer relations: From development to intervention.* Washington, DC: American Psychological Association.

Coie, J. D., Belding, M., & Underwood, M. (1988). Aggression and peer rejection in childhood. In B. Lahey & A. Kazdin (Eds.), *Advances in clinical child psychology* (Vol. 2). New York: Plenum.

Coie, J. D., Dodge, K., & Kupersmith, J. (1990). Peer group behavior and social status. In S. R. Asher & J. D. Coie (Eds.), *Peer rejection in childhood.* Cambridge, Eng.: Cambridge University Press.

Coie, J. D., & Miller-Johnson, S. (2001). Peer factors and interventions. In R. Loeber & D. P. Farrington (Eds.), *Child delinquents: Development, intervention, and service needs.* Thousand Oaks, CA: Sage.

Coleman, C. (2000, September 8). As thievery by insiders overtakes shoplifting, retailers crack down. *Wall Street Journal,* 1, p. A6.

Coleman, J. C. (1976). *Abnormal psychology and modern life* (5th ed.). Glenview, IL: Scott, Foresman.

Coleman, J. W. (1998). *The criminal elite* (4th ed.). New York: St. Martin's Press.

Coles, E., Freitas, T., & Tweed, R. (1996). Assessment of understanding by people manifesting mental retardation: A preliminary report. *Perceptual and Motor Skills, 83,* 187–192.

Colwell, M. J., Pettit, G. S., Meece, D., Bates, J. E., & Dodge, K. A. (2001). Cumulative risk and continuity in nonparental care from infancy to early adolescence. *Merrill-Palmer Quarterly, 47,* 207–234.

Comer, R. J. (1992). *Abnormal psychology.* New York: W. H. Freeman.

Comer, R. J. (2004). *Abnormal psychology* (5th ed.). New York: Worth.

Committee on Preventive Psychiatry. (1999). Violent behavior in children and youth: Preventive intervention from a psychiatric perspective. *Journal of the American Academy of Child and Adolescent Psychiatry, 38,* 235–241.

Community Research Associates. (1998). *Female juvenile offenders: A status of the states report.* Washington, DC: U.S. Department of Justice.

Conduct Problems Prevention Research Group. (2004). The fast track experiment: Translating the developmental model into a prevention design. In J. B. Kupersmidt & K. A. Dodge (Eds.), *Children's peer relations: From development to intervention.* Washington, DC: American Psychological Association.

Conklin, J. E. (1977). *"Illegal but not criminal."* Englewood Cliffs, NJ: Prentice Hall.

Connell, D. (1996, November). *Driver aggression.* Washington, DC: Automobile Association Group Public Policy Road Safety Unit.

Cook, P. J., & Ludwig, J. (1997). Guns in America: National survey on private ownership and use of firearms. *NIJ Research in Brief.* Washington, DC: National Institute of Justice.

Cook, S. E. (2000). Forced prostitution. In N. H. Rafter (Ed.), *Encyclopedia of women and crime.* Phoenix: Oryx Press.

Cooke, D. J., & Michie, C. (1997). An item response theory analysis of the Hare Psychopathy Checklist-Revised. *Psychological Assessment, 9,* 3–14.

Cooke, D. J., & Michie, C. (2001). Refining the construct psychopathy: Toward a hierarchical model. *Psychological Assessment, 13,* 171–188.

Cooke, D. J., Michie, C., Hart, S. D., & Clark, D. A. (2004). Reconstructing psychopathy: Clarifying the significance of antisocial and socially deviant behavior in the diagnosis of psychopathic personality disorder. *Journal of Personality Disorders, 18,* 337–357.

Cooke, D. J., Michie, C., Hart, S. D., & Hare, R. D. (1999). Evaluation of the screening version of the Hare Psychopathy Checklist—Revised (PCL:SV): An item response theory analysis. *Psychological Assessment, 11,* 3–13.

Coordinating Council on Juvenile Justice and Delinquency Prevention. (1996). *Combating violence and delinquency: The national juvenile justice action plan.* Washington, DC: USGPO.

Copeland, J., & Dillon, P. (2005). The health and psycho-social consequences of ketamine use. *International Journal of Drug Policy, 16,* 122–131.

Copes, H., & Cherbonneau, M. (2006). The key to auto theft. *British Journal of Criminology, 46,* 1–18.

Corrado, R. R., Vincent, G. M., Hart, S. D., & Cohen, I. M. (2004). Predictive validity of the Psychopathy Checklist: Youth Version for general and violent recidivism. *Behavioral Sciences & the Law, 22,* 5–22.

Cortes, J. B., & Gatti, F. M. (1972). *Delinquency and crime: A biopsychosocial approach.* New York: Seminar Press.

Coscina, D. V. (1997). The biopsychology of impulsivity: Focus on brain serotonin. In C. D. Webster & M. A. Jackson (Eds.), *Impulsivity: Theory, assessment, and treatment.* New York: Guilford Press.

Côté, S., Zoccolillo, M., Tremblay, R. E., Nagin, D., & Vitaro, F. (2001). Predicting girls' conduct disorder in adolescent from childhood trajectories of disruptive behaviors. *Journal of the American Academy of Child and Adolescent Psychiatry, 40,* 678–684.

Cowan, P. A., & Cowan, C. P. (2004). From family relationships to peer rejection to antisocial behavior in middle childhood. In J. B. Kupersmidt & K. A. Dodge (Eds.), *Children's peer relations: From development to intervention.* Washington, DC: American Psychological Association.

Cowley, G. (1993, July 26). The not-young and the restless. *Newsweek,* pp. 48–49.

Cox, D., Cox, A. D., & Moschis, G. P. (1990). When consumer behavior goes bad: An investigation of adolescent shoplifting. *Journal of Consumer Research, 17,* 149–159.

Cressey, D. R. (1953). *A study in the social psychology of embezzlement: Other people's money.* Glencoe, IL: Free Press.

Crick, N. R. (1995). Relational aggression: The role of intent attributions, feelings of distress, and provocation type. *Development and Psychopathology, 7,* 313–322.

Crick, N. R., & Grotpeter, J. K. (1995). Relational aggression, gender, and social-psychological adjustment. *Child Development, 66,* 710–722.

Crick, N. R., & Zahn-Waxler, C. (2003). The development of psychopathology in females and males: Current progress and future challenges. *Development and Psychopathology, 15,* 719–742.

Crider, R. (1986). Phencyclidine: Changing abuse patterns. In D. H. Clovet (Ed.), *Phencyclidine: An update.* Rockville, MD: National Institute of Drug Abuse.

Critchley, M. (1951). *The trial of Neville George Clevely Heath.* London: William Hodge.

Critchlow, B. (1986). The powers of John Barleycorn: Beliefs about the effects of alcohol on social behavior. *American Psychologist, 41,* 751–764.

Critchton, R. (1959). *The great imposter.* New York: Random House.

Critical Incident Response Group. (2001). *Workplace violence: Issues in response.* FBI Critical Incident Response Group, National Center for the Analysis of Violent Crime, Quantico, VA.

Crocker, A. G., & Hodgins, S. (1997). The criminality of noninstitutionalized mentally retarded person: Evidence from a birth cohort followed to age 30. *Criminal Justice and Behavior, 24,* 432–454.

Cromwell, P. F., Olson, J. F., & Avary, D. W. (1991). *Breaking and entering: An ethnographic analysis of burglary.* Newbury Park, CA: Sage.

Crowe, R. R. (1974). An adoptive study of antisocial personality. *Archives of General Psychiatry, 31,* 785–791.

Cruise, K. R., Colwell, L. H., Lyons, P. M., & Baker, M. D. (2003). Prototypical analysis of adolescent psychopathy: Investigating the juvenile justice perspective. *Behavioral Sciences & the Law, 21,* 829–846.

Cruise, K. R., & Rogers, R. (1998). An analysis of competency to stand trial: An integration of case law and clinical knowledge. *Behavioral Sciences & the Law, 16,* 35–50.

Culberton, F. M., Feral, C. H., & Gabby, S. (1989). Pattern analysis of Wechlser Intelligence Scale for Children-Revised profiles of delinquent boys. *Journal of Clinical Psychology, 45,* 651–660.

Cullen, F. T., & Applegate, B. K. (1997). *Offender rehabilitation.* Brookfield, VT: Ashgate Publishing.

Cunnien, A. J. (1985). Pathological gambling as an insanity defense. *Behavioral Sciences & the Law, 3,* 85–101.

Dabbs, J. M., Jr., Carr, T. S., Frady, R. L., & Riad, J. K (1995). Testosterone, crime, and misbehavior among 692 male prison inmates. *Personality and Individual Differences, 18,* 627–633.

Dabbs, J. M. Jr., Riad, J. K., & Chance, S. E. (2001). Testosterone and ruthless homicide. *Personality and Individual Differences, 31,* 599–603.

Dåderman, A. M., & Kristiansson, M. (2003). Degree of psychopathy: Implications for treatment in male juvenile delinquents. *International Journal of Law and Psychiatry, 26,* 310–315.

Dahlberg, L. L., & Potter, L. B. (2001). Youth violence: Developmental pathways and prevention challenges. *American Journal of Preventive Medicine, 20* (1s), 3–14.

Dalgaard, O. S., & Kringlen, E. (1976). A Norwegian twin study of criminality. *British Journal of Criminology, 16,* 213–233.

Damon, W. (2004). What is positive youth development? *Annals, AAPSS, 591,* 13–24.

Daniels, D. N., & Gilula, M. F. (1970). Violence and the struggle for existence. In D. Daniels, M. Gilula, & F. Ochberg (Eds.), *Violence and the struggle for existence.* Boston, MA: Little, Brown.

Darling, N., & Steinberg, L. (1993). Parenting style as context: An integrative model. *Psychological Bulletin, 113,* 487–496.

David, P. R. (1974). *The world of the burglar.* Albuquerque, NM: University of New Mexico Press.

Davies, M. (2002). Male sexual assault victims: A selected review of the literature and implications for support services. *Aggression and Violent Behavior, 7,* 203–214.

Davis, M. G., Lundman, R. J., & Martinez, R. (1991). Private corporate justice: Store police, shoplifters, and civil recovery. *Social Problems, 38,* 395–411.

Dawkins, M. P. (1997). Drug use and violent crime among adolescents. *Adolescence, 32,* 395–405.

Dawson, J. M., & Langan, P. A. (1994). *Murder in families.* Washington, DC: Bureau of Justice Statistics.

Day, K., & Berney, T. (2001). Treatment and care for offenders with mental retardation. In Ashford, J. B., Sales, B. D., & Reid, W. H. (Eds.), *Treating adult and juvenile offenders with special needs.* Washington, DC: American Psychological Association.

Day, R., & Wong, S. (1996). Anomalous perceptual asymmetries for negative emotional stimuli in the psychopath. *Journal of Abnormal Psychology, 105,* 648–652.

De Boer, S. F., & Koolhaas, J. M. (2005). 5-HT1A and 5HT1B receptor agonists and aggression: A pharmacological challenge of the serotonin deficiency hypothesis. *European Journal of Pharmacology, 526,* 125–139.

Decker, S. H., Pennel, S., & Caldwell, A. (1997). *Illegal firearms: Access and use by arrestees.* Washington, DC: U.S. Department of Justice, National Institute of Justice.

Decker, S. H., Wright, R., Redfern, A., & Smith, D. (1993). A woman's place is in the home: Females and residential burglary. *Justice Quarterly, 10,* 143–163.

Deem, D., & Murray, M. (2000). Financial crime. In G. Coleman, M. Gaboury, M. Murray, & A. Seymour (Eds.), *1999 National Victim Assistance Academy.* Washington, DC: U.S. Department of Justice.

Delgado-Escueta, A., Mattson, R., & King, L. (1981). The nature of aggression during epileptic seizures. *New England Journal of Medicine, 305,* 711–716.

D'Emilio, J., & Freedman, E. B. (1988). *Intimate matters: A history of sexuality in America.* New York: Harper & Row.

Department of Health and Human Services. (2003, September). *Overview of findings from the 2002 national survey on drug use and health.* Rockville, MD: Substance Abuse and Mental Health Services, Office of Applied Studies.

DeRosia, V. R. (1995). *Living inside prison walls: Adjustment behavior.* Westport, CT: Praeger.

Developments in the Law. (1974). Civil commitment of the mentally ill. *Harvard Law Review, 87,* 1190–1406.

Diener, E. (1980). Deindividuation: The absence of self-awareness and self-regulation in group members. In P. Paulus (Ed.), *The psychology of group influence.* Hillsdale, NJ: Erlbaum.

Dietrich, K. N., Ris, M. D., Succop, P. A., Berger, O. G., & Bornschein, R. L. (2001). Early exposure to lead and juvenile delinquency. *Neurotoxicology and Teratology, 23*, 511–518.

Dietz, T. L. (1998). An examination of violence and gender role portrayals in video games: Implications for gender socialization and aggressive behavior. *Sex Roles, 38*, 425–442.

Dill, K. E., Anderson, C. A., Anderson, K. B., & Deuser, W. E. (1997). Effects of aggressive personality on social expectations and social perceptions. *Journal of Research in Personality, 31*, 272–292.

Dill, K. E., & Dill, J. C. (1998). Video game violence: A review of the empirical literature. *Aggression and Violent Behavior, 3*, 407–428.

DiLonardo, R. L. (1996). Defining and measuring the economic benefit of electronic article surveillance. *Security Journal, 7*, 3–9.

Dion, K. (1972). Physical attractiveness and evaluations of children's transgressions. *Journal of Personality and Social Psychology, 24*, 207–213.

Dion, K., Berscheid, E., & Walster, E. (1972). What is beautiful is good. *Journal of Personality and Social Psychology, 24*, 285–290.

Diserens, C. M. (1925). Psychological objectivism. *Psychological Review, 32*, 121–152.

Dishion, T. J., & Andrews, D. W. (1995). Preventing escalation in problem behaviors with high-risk young adolescents: Immediate and 1-year outcomes. *Journal of Consulting and Clinical Psychology, 63*, 538–548.

Dishion, T. J., & Loeber, R. (1985). Male adolescent marijuana and alcohol use: The role of parents and peers revisited. *American Journal of Drug and Alcohol Abuse, 11*, 11–25.

Ditton, P. M. (1999). *Mental health and treatment of inmates and probationers: Special report.* Washington: U.S. Department of Justice, Bureau of Justice Statistics.

Ditzler, T. F. (2004). Malevolent minds: The teleology of terrorism. In F. M. Moghaddam & A. J. Marsella (Eds.), *Understanding terrorism: Psychosocial roots, consequences, and interventions.* Washington, DC: American Psychological Association.

Dix, G. E. (1980). Clinical evaluation of the "dangerous" if "normal" criminal defendants. *Virginia Law Review, 66*, 523–581.

Dobson, V., & Sales, B. (2000). The science of infanticide and mental illness. *Psychology, Public Policy, and Law, 6*, 1098–1112.

Dodge, K. A. (1986). A social information processing model of social competence in children. In M. Perlmutter (Ed.), *The Minnesota symposium on child psychology.* Hillsdale, NJ: Erlbaum.

Dodge, K. A. (1991). The structure and function of reactive and proactive aggression. In D. J. Pepler & K. H. Rubin (Eds.), *The development and treatment of childhood aggression.* Hillsdale, NJ: Erlbaum.

Dodge, K. A. (1993a). The future of research on the treatment of conduct disorder. *Development and Psychopathology, 5*, 311–319.

Dodge, K. A. (2001). The science of youth violence prevention: Progressing from developmental epidemiology to efficacy to effectiveness in public policy. *American Journal of Preventive Medicine, 20* (1S), 63–70.

Dodge, K. A. (2003). Do social information-processing patterns mediate aggressive behavior? In B. B. Lahey, T. E. Moffitt, & A. Caspi (Eds). *Causes of conduct disorder and juvenile delinquency.* New York: Guilford Press.

Dodge, K. A., Bates, J. E., & Pettit, G. S. (1990). Mechanisms in the cycle of violence. *Science, 250*, 1678–1683.

Dodge, K. A., & Coie, J. D. (1987). Social information processing factors in reactive and proactive aggression in children's peer groups. *Journal of Personality and Social Psychology, 53*, 1146–1158.

Dodge, K. A., Laird, R., Lochman, Zelli, A., & Conduct Problems Prevention Research Group. (2002). Mulit-dimensional latent construct analysis of children's social information-processing patterns: Correlations with aggressive behavior problems. *Psychological Assessment, 14,* 60–73.

Dodge, K. A., Lochman, J. E., Harnish, J. D., Bates, J. E., & Pettit, G. S. (1997). Reactive and proactive aggression in school children and psychiatrically impaired chronically assaultive youth. *Journal of Abnormal Psychology, 106,* 37–51.

Dodge, K. A., & Pettit, G. S. (2003). A biopsychological model of the development of chronic conduct problems in adolescence. *Developmental Psychology, 39,* 349–371.

Doerner, W. G. (1988). The impact of medical resources on criminally induced lethality: A further examination. *Criminology, 26,* 171–179.

Doerner, W. G., & Speir, J. C. (1986). Stitch and sew: The impact of medical resources upon criminally induced lethality. *Criminology, 24,* 319–330.

Doley, R. (2003). Pyromania: Fact or Fiction? *British Journal of Criminology, 43,* 797–807.

Dollard, J., Doob, L. W., Miller, N. E., Mowrer, O. H., & Sears, R. R. (1939). *Frustration and aggression.* New Haven, CT: Yale University Press.

Donnerstein, E. (1983). Erotica and human aggression. In R. G. Geen & E. I. Donnerstein (Eds.), *Aggression: Theoretical and empirical reviews* (Vol. 2). New York: Academic Press.

d'Orban, P. T., & O'Connor, A. (1989). Women who kill their parents. *British Journal of Psychiatry, 154,* 27–33.

Doren, D. M. (2005). *Evaluating sex offenders.* Thousand Oaks, CA: Sage.

Douglas, J. E., Burgess, A. W., Burgess, A. G., & Ressler, R. K. (1992). *Crime classification manual.* New York: Lexington Books.

Douglas, J. E., & Munn, C. (1992a). The detection of staging and personation at the crime scene. In J. E. Douglas, A. W. Burgess, A. G. Burgess, & R. K. Ressler (Eds.), *Crime classification manual.* New York: Lexington Books.

Douglas, J. E., & Munn, C. (1992b). Modus operandi and the signature aspects of violent crime. In J. E. Douglas, A. W. Burgess, A. G. Burgess, & R. K. Ressler (Eds.), *Crime classification manual.* New York: Lexington Books.

Douglas, J. E., & Munn, C. (1992c, February). Violent crime scene analysis. *FBI Law Enforcement Bulletin,* 1–10.

Douglas, J. E., Ressler, R. K., Burgess, A. W., & Hartman. C. R. (1986). Criminal profiling from crime scene analysis. *Behavioral Sciences & the Law, 4,* 401–421.

Douglas, V. I. (2004). Cognitive deficits in children with attention deficit hyperactivity disorder: A long-term follow up. *Canadian Psychology, 46,* 23–31.

Driver, E. D. (1961). Interaction and criminal homicide in India. *Social Forces, 40,* 153–158.

Drug Enforcement Administration. (2000). *Drugs of abuse.* Washington, DC: U.S. Department of Justice. Available: www.usdoj.gov/dea/concern/abuse.

Drug Enforcement Administration. (2005). *Drugs of abuse, 2005 edition.* Washington, DC: U.S. Department of Justice.

DSM-II. (1968). *Diagnostic and statistical manual of mental disorders* (2nd ed.). Washington, DC: American Psychiatric Association.

DSM-III. (1980). *Diagnostic and statistical manual of mental disorders* (3rd ed.). Washington, DC: American Psychiatric Association.

DSM-III-R. (1987). *Diagnostic and statistical manual of mental disorders* (Rev. ed.). Washington, DC: American Psychiatric Association.

DSM-IV. (1994). *Diagnostic and statistical manual of mental disorders* (4th ed.). Washington, DC: American Psychiatric Association.

Duhaime, A., Christian, C. W., Rorke, L. B., & Zimmerman, R. A. (1998). Nonaccidental head injury in infants: The "shaken-baby syndrome." *New England Journal of Medicine, 338,* 1822–1829.

Dull, R. T., & Giacopassi, D. J. (1987). Demographic correlates of sexual and dating attitudes: A study of date rape. *Criminal Justice and Behavior, 14,* 175–193.

Dunn, C. S. (1976). *The patterns and distribution of assault incident characteristics among social areas.* Albany, NY: Criminal Justice Research Center, Analytic Report 14.

Durand, V. M., & Barlow, D. H. (2000). *Abnormal psychology: An introduction.* Belmont, CA: Wadsworth.

Durose, M. R., Harlow, C. W., Langan, P. A., Motivans, M., Rantala, R. R., & Smith, E. L. (2005, June). *Family violence statistics: Including statistics on strangers and acquaintances.* Washington, DC: U.S. Department of Justice, Bureau of Justice Statistics.

Dvorak, J. A. (2000, December 21). *Kansas launches racial profiling study. Kansas City Star,* pp. 1, 11.

Easterbrook, J. A. (1959). The effect of emotion on cue utilization and the organization of behavior. *Psychological Review, 66,* 183–201.

Eastman, B. J. (2004). Assessing the efficacy of treatment for adolescent sex offenders: A crossover longitudinal study. *Prison Journal, 84,* 472–485.

Eaton, J., & Polk, K. (1961). *Measuring delinquency.* Pittsburgh, PA: University of Pittsburgh Press.

Ebert, B. W. (1987). Guide to conducting a psychological autopsy. *Professional Psychology: Research and Practice, 18,* 52–56.

Eccles, J., & Robinson, D. N. (1984). *The wonder of being human: Our brain and our mind.* New York: Free Press.

Eck, J. (2000) Preventing crime at places. In L. W. Sherman, D. Gottfresson, D. MacKenzie, J. Eck, P. Reuter, & S. Bushway (Eds.), *Preventing crime: What works, what doesn't, what's promising.* A Report to the United State Congress. Available: www.ncjrs.org/works.

Eddy, J. M. (2003). *Conduct disorders: The latest assessment and treatment strategies.* Kansas City, MO: Compact Clinicals.

Edens, J. F., Petrila, J., & Buffington-Vollum, J. K. (2001). Psychopathy and the death penalty: Can the Psychopathy Checklist-Revised identify offenders who represent "a continuing threat to society?" *Journal of Psychiatry and Law, 29,* 433–481.

Edens, J. F., Skeem, J. L., Cruise, K. R., & Cauffman, E. (2001). Assessment of "juvenile psychopathy" and its association with violence: A critical review. *Behavioral Sciences & the Law, 19,* 53–80.

Edleson, J. L. (1999). Children's witnessing of adult domestic violence. *Journal of Interpersonal Violence, 14,* 839–870.

Edwards, S. (1983). Sexuality, sexual offenses, and conception of victims in the criminal justice process. *Victimology: An International Journal, 8,* 113–128.

Efran, M. G., & Cheyne, J. A. (1974). Affective concomitants of the invasion of shared space: Behavioral, physiological, and verbal indicators. *Journal of Personality and Social Psychology, 29,* 219–226.

Eisenhower, M. S. (Chairman). (1969). *Commission statement on violence in television entertainment programs.* Washington, DC: USGPO.

Elliott, D. S. (1989). Criminal justice procedures in family violence crimes. In L. Ohlin & M. Tonry (Eds.), *Family violence* (Vol. 11). Chicago, IL: University of Chicago Press.

Elliott, D. S., Ageton, S. S., & Huizinga, D. (1980). *The national youth survey.* Boulder, CO: Behavioral Research Institute.

Elliott, D. S., Dunford, T. W., & Huizinga, D. (1987). The identification and prediction of career offenders utilizing self-reported and official data. In J. D. Burchard & S. N. Burchard (Eds.), *Prevention of delinquent behavior.* Newbury Park, CA: Sage.

Elliott, D. S., & Menard, S. (1996). Delinquent friends and delinquent behavior: Temporal and developmental patterns. In J. D. Hawkins (Ed.), *Delinquency and crime: Current theories.* New York: Cambridge University Press.

Ellis, C. A., & Lord, J. (2001). Homicide. In G. Coleman, M. Gaboury, M. Murray, & A. Seymour (Eds.), *1999 National Victim Assistance Academy.* Washington, DC: U.S. Department of Justice.

Ellis, L. (1998). Why some sexual assaults are not committed by men: A biosocial analysis. In P. Anderson & C. Struckman-Johnson (Eds.), *Sexually aggressive women.* New York: Guilford Press.

Else-Quest, N. M., Hyde, J. S., Goldsmith, H. H., & Van Hulle, C. A. (2006). Gender differences in temperament: A meta-analysis. *Psychological Bulletin, 132,* 33–72.

Emery, R. E., & Laumann-Billings, L. (1998). An overview of the nature, causes, and consequences of abusive family relationships. *American Psychologist, 53,* 121–135.

Epstein, J. F., & Gfroerer, J. C. (1997, August). *Heroin abuse in the United States.* Rockville, MD: Substance Abuse and Mental Health Services Administration.

Erhardt, D., & Hinshaw, S. P. (1994). Initial sociometric impressions of attention-deficit hyperactivity disorder and comparison boys: Predictions from social behaviors and from nonbehavioral variables. *Journal of Consulting and Clinical Psychology, 62,* 833–842.

Eron, L. D., & Huesmann, L. P. (1984). The relation of prosocial behavior to the development of aggression and psychopathology. *Aggressive Behavior, 10,* 201–211.

Eron, L. D., & Slaby, R. G. (1994). Introduction. In L. D. Eron, J. H. Gentry, & P. Schlegel (Eds.), *Reason to hope: A psychosocial perspective on violence and youth.* Washington, DC: American Psychological Association.

Eskridge, C. W. (1983). Prediction of burglary: A research note. *Journal of Criminal Justice, 11,* 67–75.

Esquirol, E. (1838). *Des maladies mentales.* Paris: Bailliére.

Evans, D. (1970). Exhibitionism. In C. G. Costello (Ed.), *Symptoms of psychopathology: A handbook.* New York: Wiley.

Evans, G. W. (2004). The environment of childhood poverty. *American Psychologist, 59,* 77–92.

Ewing, C. P. (1990). Psychological self-defense: A proposed justification for battered women who kill. *Law and Human Behavior, 14,* 579–594.

Eysenck, H. J. (1964). *Crime and personality.* London: Routledge & Kegan Paul.

Eysenck, H. J. (1967). *The biological basis of personality.* Springfield, IL: Charles C Thomas.

Eysenck, H. J. (1971). *Readings in extraversion-introversion. Vol. 2. Fields of application.* New York: Wiley-Interscience.

Eysenck, H. J. (1973). *The inequality of man.* San Diego, CA: EDITS Publishers.

Eysenck, H. J. (1977). *Crime and personality* (2nd ed.). London: Routledge & Kegan Paul.

Eysenck, H. J. (1981). *A model for personality.* New York: Springer.

Eysenck, H. J. (1983). Personality, conditioning, and antisocial behavior. In W. S. Laufer & J. M. Day (Eds.), *Personality theory, moral development, and criminal behavior.* Lexington, MA: Lexington Books.

Eysenck, H. J. (1996). Personality and crime: Where do we stand? *Psychology, Crime & Law, 2,* 143–152.

Eysenck, H. J., & Gudjonsson, G. H. (1989). *The causes and cures of criminality.* New York: Plenum.

Eysenck, H. J., & Rachman, S. (1965). *The causes and cures of neurosis.* San Diego, CA: Robert R. Knapp.

Fagan, J. (1989). Cessation of family violence. In L. Ohlin & M. Tonry (Eds.), *Family violence* (Vol. 11). Chicago, IL: University of Chicago Press.

Falkenbach, D. M. Poythress. N. G., & Heide, K. M. (2003). Psychoapthic fetres in a juvenile diversion population: Reliability and predictive validity of two self-report measures. *Behavioral Sciences and the Law, 21,* 787–805.

Fantuzzo, J. W., Boruch, R., Abdullahi, B., Atkins, M., & Marcus, S. (1997). Domestic violence and children: Prevalence and risk in five major U.S. cities. *Journal of American Academy of Child and Adolescent Psychiatry, 36,* 116–122.

Fantuzzo, J. W., DePaola, L. M., Lambert, L., Martino, T., Anderson, G., & Sutton, S. (1991). Effects of interparental violence on the psychological adjustment and competencies of young children. *Journal of Consulting and Clinical Psychology, 59,* 258–265.

Farabee, D. (Ed.). (2002). Making people change: The effectiveness of coerced psychological treatment. Special Issue. *Criminal Justice and Behavior, 29,* 3–109.

Farrell, G., Phillips, C., & Pease, K. (1995). Like taking candy, why does repeat victimization occur? *British Journal of Criminology, 35,* 384–399.

Farrington, D. P. (1987). Predicting individual crime rates. In D. M. Gottfredson & M. Tonry (Eds.), *Prediction and classification* (Vol. 10). Chicago, IL: University of Chicago Press.

Farrington, D. P. (1991). Childhood aggression and adult violence: Early precursors and later life outcomes. In D. J. Pepler & K. H. Rubin (Eds.), *The development and treatment of childhood aggression.* Hillsdale, NJ: Erlbaum.

Farrington, D. P. (1995). Crime and physical health: Illnesses, injuries, accidents, and offending in the Cambridge study. *Criminal Behaviour and Mental Health, 5,* 278.

Farrington, D. P. (2005a). The importance of child and adolescent psychopathy. *Journal of Abnormal Child Psychology, 33,* 489–497.

Farrington, D. P. (2005b). Family background and psychopathy. In C. J. Patrick (Ed.), *Handbook of psychopathy.* New York: Guilford.

Farrington, D. P., Bowen, S., Buckle, A., Burns-Howell, T., Burrows, J., & Speed, M. (1993). An experiment on the prevention of shoplifting. In R. V. Clarke (Ed.), *Crime prevention studies* (Vol. 1). Monsey, NY: Criminal Justice Press.

Farrington, D. P., & Burrows, J. N. (1993). Did shoplifting really decrease? *British Journal of Criminology, 33,* 57–59.

Faupel, C. E. (1991). *Shooting dope: Career patterns of hard-core heroin users.* Gainesville, FL: University of Florida Press.

Federal Bureau of Investigation. (1985, August). Crime scene and profile characteristics of organized and disorganized murders. *FBI Law Enforcement Bulletin, 54,* 18–25.

Federal Bureau of Investigation. (1992). *Killed in the line of duty: A study of selected felonious killings of law enforcement officers.* Washington, DC: U.S. Department of Justice.

Federal Bureau of Investigation. (1996). *Terrorism in the United States, 1995.* Washington, DC: USGPO.

Federal Bureau of Investigation. (1997). *Uniform Crime Reports—1996.* Washington, DC: USGPO.

Federal Bureau of Investigation. (2002). *Uniform Crime Reports—2001.* Washington, DC: U.S. Department of Justice.

Federal Bureau of Investigation. (2003). *Uniform Crime Reports—2002.* Washington, DC: U.S. Department of Justice.

Federal Bureau of Investigation. (2005). Crime in the United States 2004: Uniform Crime Reports. Washington, DC: U.S. Department of Justice.

Federal Interagency Forum on Child and Family Statistics. (2005). *America's children: Key national indicators of well-being 2005.* Washington, DC: Author.

Fehrenbach, P. A., & Monasterky, C. (1988). Characteristics of females sexual offenders. *American Journal of Orthopsychiatry, 58,* 148–151.

Fehrenbach, P. A., Smith, W., Monastersky, C., & Deisher, R. W. (1986). Adolescent sexual offenders: Offender and offense characteristics. *American Journal of Orthopsychiatry, 56,* 225–233.

Feinberg, G. (1984). Profile for the elderly shoplifter. In E. S. Newman, D. J. Newman, & M. L. Gewirtz (Eds.), *Elderly criminals.* Cambridge, MA: Oelgeschlager, Gunn & Hain.

Feld, B. C. (1988). In re Gault revised: A cross-state comparison of the right to counsel in juvenile court. *Crime and Delinquency, 34,* 393–424.

Feld, B. C. (1998). Juvenile and criminal justice systems' responses to youth violence. In M. Tonry & M. H. Moore (Eds.), *Youth violence. Crime and Justice: A review of research.* (Vol. 24). Chicago: University of Chicago Press.

Feldman, M. P. (1977). *Criminal behavior: A psychological analysis.* London: Wiley.

Felthous, A. R. (2001). Introduction to this issue: The clinician's duty to warn or protect. *Behavioral Sciences & the Law, 19,* 321–324.

Fenichel, O. (1945). *The psychoanalytic theory of neurosis.* New York: W. W. Norton.

Ferguson, D. M., Lynskey, M. T., & Horwood, L. J. (1996). Alcohol misuse and juvenile offending in adolescence. *Addiction, 91,* 483–494.

Feshbach, S. (1964). The function of aggression and the regulation of aggressive drive. *Psychological Review, 71,* 257–272.

Festinger, L., Pepitone, A., & Newcomb, T. (1952). Some consequences of de-individuation in a group. *Journal of Abnormal and Social Psychology, 47,* 382–389.

Feucht, T. W., & Kyle, G. M. (1996, November). Methamphetamine use among adult arrestees: Findings of the DUF program. *NIJ Research in Brief.* Washington, DC: U.S. Department of Justice.

Field, S. (1992). The effect of temperature on crime. *British Journal of Criminology, 32,* 340–351.

Fields, G. (2006, September 26). Police are changing how they confront the mentally ill. *The Wall Street Jorunal,* pp. A1, A11.

Finckenauer, J. O., & Schrock, J. (2000). Human trafficking: A growing criminal market in the U.S. Washington, DC: National Institute of Justice, International Center. Available: www.ojp.usdoj.gov/nij/international/ht.html.

Finkelhor, D. (1979). *Sexually victimized children.* New York: Free Press.

Finkelhor, D., & Araji, S. (1986). Explanations of pedophilia: A four factor model. *The Journal of Sex Research, 22,* 145–161.

Finkelhor, D., & Dziuba-Leatherman, J. (1994). Children as victims of violence: A national survey. *Pediatrics, 94,* 413–420.

Finkelhor, D., & Lewis, I. A. (1988). An epidemiologic approach to the study of child molestation. In R. A. Prentky & V. L. Quinsey (Eds.), *Human sexual aggression: Current perspectives.* New York: New York Academy of Sciences.

Finkelhor, D., Ormrod, R., Turner, H., & Hamby, S. L. (2005). The victimization of children and youth: A comprehensive, national survey. *Child Maltreatment, 10,* 5–25.

Firestone, P., Bradford, J. M., Greenberg, D. M., & Larose, M. R. (1998). Homicidal sex offenders: Psychological, phallometric, and diagnostic features. *Journal of the American Academy of Psychology and Law, 26,* 537–552.

Fishbein, D. (2001). *Biobehavioral perspectives in criminology.* Belmont, CA: Wadsworth/Thomson Learning.

Fiske, D. E., & Maddi, S. R. (1961). *Functions of varied experience.* Homewood, IL: Dorsey.

Fitzgerald, L. F. (2003). Sexual harassment and social justice: Reflections and distance yet to go. *American Psychologist, 11,* 915–924

Fitzhugh, K. B. (1973). Some neuropsychological features of delinquent subjects. *Perceptual and Motor Skills, 36,* 494.

Flannery, D. J., Williams, L. L., & Vazsonyi, A. T. (1999). Who are they with and what are they doing? Delinquent behavior, substance abuse, and early adolescence' after-school time. *American Journal of Orthopsychiatry, 69,* 247–253.

Flor-Henry, P. (1973). Psychiatric syndromes considered as manifestations of lateralized temporal-limbic dysfunction. In L. V. Latiner & K. E. Livingston (Eds.), *Surgical approaches in psychiatry.* Lancaster, Eng.: Medical and Technical Publishing.

Flor-Henry, P., & Yeudall, L. T. (1973). Lateralized cerebral dysfunction in depression and in aggressive criminal psychopathy. *International Research Communications, 7,* 31.

Flynn, E. E. (1983). Crime as a major social issue. *American Behavioral Scientist, 27,* 7–42.

Forbes, G. B., Adams-Curtis, L. E., & White, K. B. (2004). First- and second-generation measures of sexism, rape myths and related beliefs, and hostility toward women. *Violence Against Women, 10,* 236–261.

Forehand, R., Wierson, M., Frame, C. L., Kemptom, T., & Armistead, L. (1991). Juvenile firesetting: A unique syndrome or an advanced level of antisocial behavior? *Behavioral Research and Therapy, 29,* 125–128.

Forrstrom-Cohen, B., & Rosenbaum, A. (1985). The effects of parental marital violence on young adults: An exploratory investigation. *Journal of Marriage and Family, 47,* 467–472.

Forth, A. E., & Burke, H. C. (1998). Psychopathy in adolescence: Assessment, violence, and developmental precursors. In D. J. Cooke, A. E. Forth, & R. D. Hare (Eds.), *Psychopathy: Theory, research and implications for society.* Boston: Kluwer Academic.

Forth, A. E., Kosson, D. S., & Hare, R. D. (2003). *Psychopathy Checklist-Youth Version: Technical manual.* Toronto: Multi-Health Systems.

Fothergill, K. E., & Ensminger, M. E. (2006). Childhood and adolescent antecedents of drug and alcohol problems: A longitudinal study. *Drug and Alcohol Dependence, 82,* 61–76.

Fox, R. G. (1971). The XYY offender: A modern myth? *Journal of Criminal Law, Criminology, and Police Science, 62,* 59–73.

Franke, D. (1975). *The torture doctor.* New York: Avon.

Frederick, R. I. (2000). Mixed group validation: A method to address the limitations of criterion group validation in research on malingering detection. *Behavioral Science & the Law, 18,* 693–718.

Freedman, J. L. (1975). *Crowding and behavior.* San Francisco, CA: W. H. Freeman.

Freedman, J. L., Levy, A., Buchanan, R. W., & Price, J. (1972). Crowding and human aggressiveness. *Journal of Experimental Social Psychology, 8,* 528–548.

Freedman, J. L., Sears, D. O., & Carlsmith, J. J. (1978). *Social psychology* (3rd ed.). Englewood Cliffs, NJ: Prentice Hall.

French, J. D. (1957). The reticular formation. *Scientific American, 196,* 54–60.

Frick, P. J. (1998). Callous-unemotional traits and conduct problems: Applying the two-factor model of psychopathy to children. In D. J. Cooke, A. E. Forth, & R. D. Hare (Eds.), *Psychopathy: Theory, research and implications for society.* Boston: Kluwer Academic.

Frick, P. J., Bodin, S. D., & Barry, C. T. (2000). Psychopathic traits and conduct problems in community and clinic-referred samples of children: Further development of the psychopathy screening device. *Psychological Assessment, 12,* 382–393.

Frick, P. J., & Hare, R. D. (2001). *The Antisocial Process Screening Device.* Toronto: Multi-Health Systems.

Frick, P. J., & Morris, A. S. (2004). Temperament and developmental pathways to conduct problems. *Journal of Clinical Child and Adolescent Psychology, 33,* 54–68.

Frick, P. J., O'Brien, B. S., Wootton, J., & McBurnett, K. (1994). Psychopathy and conduct problems in children. *Journal of Abnormal Psychology, 103,* 700–707.

Frieze, I. H., & Browne, A. (1989). Violence in marriage. In L. Ohlin & M. Tonry (Eds.), *Family violence* (Vol. 11). Chicago, IL: University of Chicago Press.

Frintner, M., & Rubinson, L. (1993). Acquaintance rape: The influence of alcohol, fraternity membership and sports team membership. *Journal of Sex Education and Therapy, 19,* 272–284.

Frisbie, L. V. (1965). Treated sex offenders who reverted to sexually deviant behavior. *Federal Probation, 29,* 52–57.

Fung, M. T., Raine, A., Loeber, R., Lynam, D. R., Steinhauser, S. R., Venables, P. H., & Stouthamer-Loeber, M. (2005). Reduced electrodermal activity in pychopathy-prone adolescents. *Journal of Abnormal Psychology, 114,* 187–196.

Funk, J. B., Baldacci, H. B., Pasold, T., & Baumgarnder, J. (2004). Violence exposure to real-life, video games, television, movies, and the internet: is there desensitization? *Journal of Adolescence, 27,* 23–39.

Funk, J. B., & Buchman, D. D. (1996). Playing violent video and computer games and the adolescent self-concept. *Journal of Communications,* Spring, 84–89.

Furby, L., Weinrott, M. R., & Blackshaw, L. (1989). Sex offender recidivism: A review. *Psychological Bulletin, 105,* 3–30.

Fuselier, G. D. (1999, July). Placing the Stockholm syndrome in perspective. *FBI Law Enforcement Bulletin,* 9–12.

Fuselier, G. D., & Noesner, G. W. (1990, July). Confronting the terrorist hostage taker. *FBI Law Enforcement Bulletin,* 6–11.

Gabrielli, W. F., & Mednick, S. A. (1983). Genetic correlates of criminal behavior. *American Behavioral Scientist, 27,* 59–74.

Gacono, C. B., Nieberding, R. J., Owen, A., Rubel, J., & Bodholdt, R. (2001). Treating conduct disorder, antisocial, and psychopathic personalities. In J. B. Ashford, B. D. Sales, & W. H. Reid (Eds.), *Treating adult and juvenile offenders with special needs.* Washington, DC: American Psychological Association.

Gaes, G. G., Flanagan, T. J., Motiuk, L. L., & Stewart, L. (1999). Adult correctional treatment. In M. Tonry & J. Petersilia, (Eds.), *Prisons: Crime and justice. Review of the research* (Vol. 26). Chicago: University of Chicago Press.

Galovski, T. E., & Blanchard, E. B. (2002). The effectiveness of a brief psychological intervention on court-referred and self-referred aggressive drivers. *Behavior and Research Therapy, 40,* 1385–1402.

Galovski, T. E., & Blanchard, E. B. (2004). Road rage: A domain for psychological intervention. *Aggression and Violent Behavior, 9,* 105–127.

Ganley, A. L., & Schechter, S. (1996). *Domestic violence: A national curriculum for children's protective services.* San Francisco, CA: Family Violence Prevention Fund.

Garbarino, J. (1989). The incidence and prevalence of child maltreatment. In L. Ohlin & M. Tonry (Eds.), *Family violence* (Vol. 11). Chicago, IL: University of Chicago Press.

Garbarino, J., & Asp, C. E. (1981). *Successful schools and competent students.* Lexington, MA: Lexington Books.

Gardner, T. J. (1985). *Crime law: Principles and cases.* St. Paul, MN: West Publishing.

Garofalo, J. (1977). *Public opinion about crime: The attitudes of victims and nonvictims in selected cities.* Washington, DC: USGPO.

Garside, R. B. & Klimes-Dougan, B. (2002). Socialization of discrete negative emotions: Gender differences and links with psychological distress. *Sex Roles: A Journal of Research, 14,* 115–129.

Gaynor, J. (1996). Firesetting. In M. Lewis (Ed.), *Child and adolescent psychiatry: A comprehensive textbook.* Baltimore, MD: Williams & Wilkins.

Gebhard, P. H., Gagnon, J. H., Pomeroy, W. B., & Christenson, C. V. (1965). *Sex offenders.* New York: Harper & Row.

Geis, G. (1988). From Deuteronomy to deniability: A historical perlustration on white-collar crime. *Justice Quarterly, 5,* 7–32.

Geis, G. (1997). Preface. In G. Green, *Occupational crime* (2nd ed.). Chicago, IL: Nelson-Hall.

Gelinas, D. J. (1993, October 3). *Recognizing and treating dissociative processes trauma survivors.* Professional workshop sponsored by Vermont Trauma Institute, Burlington, VT.

Gelles, R. J. (1982). Domestic criminal violence. In M. E. Wolfgang & N. A. Weiner (Eds.), *Criminal violence.* Beverly Hills, CA: Sage.

Gelles, R. J. (1997). *Intimate violence in families.* Thousand Oaks, CA: Sage.

Gelles, R. J., & Straus, M. A. (1979). Determinants of violence in the family: Toward a theoretical integration. In W. R. Burr, F. I. Nye, & I. L. Reiss (Eds.), *Contemporary theories about the family*. New York: Free Press.

Gendreau, P., Little, T., & Goggin, C. (1996). A meta-analysis of the predictors of adult offender recidivism: What works! *Criminology, 34,* 575–607.

Gendreau, P., & Ross, P. (1983). Correctional treatment. *Juvenile and Family Court Journal,* Winter, 31–39.

Gentile, D. A., Lynch, P. J., Linder, J. R., & Walsh, D. A. (2004). The effects of violent video game habits on adolescent hostility, aggressive behaviors, and school performance. *Journal of Adolescence, 27,* 5–22.

Gentile, D. A., & Walsh, D. A. (2002). A normative study of family media habits. *Journal of Applied Developmental Psychology, 23,* 157–178.

George, W. H., & Marlatt, G. A. (1989). Introduction. In D. R. Laws (Ed.), *Relapse prevention with sex offenders*. New York: Guilford Press.

Gerbner, G., Gross, L., Morgan, M., & Signorielli, N. (1981). Health and medicine on television. *The New England Journal of Medicine, 305,* 901–904.

Getz, J. G., & Bray, J. H. (2005). Predicting heavy alcohol use among adolescents. *American Journal of Orthopsychiatry, 75,* 102–116.

Gibbens, T. C. (1957). Female offenders. *British Journal of Delinquency, 8,* 23–25.

Gibbens, T. C. (1981). Female crime in England and Wales. In F. Adler (Ed.), *The incidence of female criminality in the contemporary world*. New York: New York University Press.

Gibbons, D. C. (1977). *Society, crime and criminal careers* (3rd ed.). Englewood Cliffs, NJ: Prentice Hall.

Gibbons, D. C. (1988). Some critical observation on criminal types and criminal careers. *Criminal Justice and Behavior, 15,* 8–23.

Giddan, J. J., Milling, L., & Campbell, N. B. (1996). Unrecognized language and speech deficits in preadolescent psychiatric patients. *American Journal of Orthopsychiatry, 66,* 85–92.

Glasser, W. D. (1965). *Reality therapy*. New York: Harper & Row.

Glueck, S., & Glueck, E. (1950). *Unraveling juvenile delinquency*. New York: Harper & Row.

Glueck, S., & Glueck, E. (1956). *Physique and delinquency*. New York: Harper & Row.

Goetting, A. (1993). Patterns of homicide among children. In A. V. Wilson (Ed.), *Homicide: The victim/offender connection*. Cincinnati, OH: Anderson.

Gold, L. H. (1962). Psychiatric profile of the firesetter. *Journal of Forensic Sciences, 7,* 404–417.

Gold, M. S. (1984*). 800-cocaine*. New York: Bantam.

Golding, S. L., Skeem, J. L., Roesch, R., & Zapf, P. A. (1999). The assessment of criminal responsibility: Current controversies. In I. B. Weiner & A. K. Hess (Eds.), *Handbook of forensic psychology* (2nd ed.). New York: Wiley.

Goldman, M. J. (1991). Kleptomania: Making sense of the nonsensical. *American Journal of Psychiatry, 148,* 986–995.

Goldstein, J. H. (1975). *Aggression and crimes of violence*. New York: Oxford University Press.

Goldstein, M. (1974). Brain research and violent behavior. *Archives of Neurology, 30,* 1–34.

Goldstein, M. J. (1977). A behavioral scientist looks at obscenity. In B. D. Sales (Ed.), *The criminal justice system* (Vol. 1). New York: Plenum.

Goldstein, N. E., Arnold, D. H., Rosenberg, J. L., Stowe, R. M., & Ortiz, C. (2001). Contagion of aggression in day care classrooms as a function of peer and toddler responses. *Journal of Educational Psychology, 93,* 708–719.

Goldstein, P. J. (1985). The drugs-violence nexus: A tri-partite conceptual framework. *Journal of Drug Issues, 15,* 493–506.

Golub, A. L., & Johnson, B. D. (1997, July). *Crack's decline: Some surprises across U.S. cities.* NIJ Research in Brief. Washington, DC: U.S. Department of Justice.

Gordon, R. (1983). An operational definition of prevention. *Public Health Reports, 98,* 107–109.

Gorenstein, E. E. (1982). Frontal lobe functions in psychopaths. *Journal of Abnormal Psychology, 91,* 368–379.

Gorman-Smith, D., & Loeber, R. (2005). Are developmental pathways in disruptive behaviors the same for girls and boys? *Journal of Child and Family Studies, 14,* 15–27.

Gosselin, C., & Wilson, G. (1984). Fetishism, sadomasochism and related behaviours. In K. Howells (Ed.), *The psychology of sexual diversity.* London: Basil Blackwell.

Gottman, J. M. (2001). Crime, hostility, wife battering, and the heart: On the Meehan et al. (2001) failure to replicate the Gottman et al. (1995) typology. *Journal of Family Psychology, 15,* 409–414.

Gove, W. R., & Crutchfield, R. D. (1982). The family and delinquency. *Sociological Quarterly, 23,* 301–319.

Grann, M., Belfrage, H., & Tengström, A. (2000). Actuarial assessment of risk for violence: Predictive validity of the VRAG and the historical part of the HCR-20. *Criminal Justice and Behavior, 27,* 97–114.

Grant, V. (1977). *The menacing stranger.* New York: Dover.

Green, G. S. (1997). *Occupational crime* (2nd ed.). Chicago, IL: Nelson-Hall.

Greenberg, L. S. (1988). Constructive cognition: Cognitive therapy coming of age. *Counseling Psychologist, 16,* 235–238.

Greendlinger, V., & Byrne, D. (1987). Coercive sexual fantasies of college men as predictors of self-reported likelihood to rape and overt sexual aggression. *Journal of Sex Research, 23,* 1–11.

Greenfeld, L. A. (1996, March). *Child victimization: Violent offenders and their victims.* Washington, DC: U.S. Department of Justice, Bureau of Justice Statistics.

Greenfeld, L. A. (1997, February). *Sex offenses and offenders: An analysis of data on rape and sexual assault.* Washington, DC: U.S. Department of Justice, Bureau of Justice Statistics.

Greenfeld, L. A. (1998, April). *Alcohol and crime: An analysis of national data on the prevalence of alcohol involvement in crime.* Washington, DC: U.S. Department of Justice.

Greenfeld, L. A. (1999, December). *Women offenders.* Washington, DC: U.S. Department of Justice.

Greenfeld, L. A., & Smith, S. K. (1999, February). *American Indians and crime.* Washington, DC: U.S. Department of Justice.

Greenwald, H. (1958). *The call girl.* New York: Ballantine Books.

Gregorie, T. (2000). Workplace violence. In G. Coleman, M. Gaboury, M. Murray, & A. Seymour (Eds.), *1999 National Victim Assistance Academy.* Washington, DC: U.S. Department of Justice.

Gretton, H. M., McBrdie, M., Hare, R. D., O'Shaughnessy, R., & Kumka, G. (2001). Psychopathy and recidivism in adolescent sex offenders. *Criminal Justice and Behavior, 28,* 427–449.

Griffith, W., & Veitch, R. (1971). Hot and crowded: Influences of population density and temperature on interpersonal affective behavior. *Journal of Personality and Social Psychology, 17,* 92–98.

Grisso, T. (1986). *Evaluating competencies: Forensic assessments and instruments.* New York: Plenum.

Groth, A. N. (1978). Patterns of sexual assault against children and adolescents. In A. W. Burgess, A. N. Groth, L. L. Holmstrom, & S. M. Sgroi (Eds.), *Sexual assault of children and adolescents.* Lexington, MA: Lexington Books.

Groth, A. N. (1979). *Men who rape: The psychology of the offender.* New York: Plenum.

Groth, A. N., & Burgess, A. W. (1977). Motivational intent in the sexual assault of children. *Criminal Justice and Behavior, 4,* 253–271.

Groth, A. N., Hobson, W. F., & Gary, T. S. (1982). The child molester: Clinical observation. *Journal of Social Work and Human Sexuality, 1,* 129–144.

Guerette, R. T. (2002). Geographical profiling. In D. Levinson (Ed.), *Encyclopedia of crime and punishment.* Thousand Oaks, CA: Sage.

Guerra, N. G., Huesmann, L. R., Tolan, P. H., Van Acker, R., & Eron, L. D. (1995). Stressful events and individual beliefs as correlates of economic disadvantage and aggression among urban children. *Journal of Consulting and Clinical Psychology, 63*, 518–528.

Guerra, N., Tolan, P. H., & Hammond, W. R. (1994). Prevention and treatment of adolescent violence. In L. R. Eron, J. H., Gentry, & P. Schlegel (Eds.), *Reason to hope: A psychological perspective on violence and youth.* Washington, DC: American Psychological Association.

Guze, S. B. (1976). *Criminality and psychiatric disorders.* New York: Oxford University Press.

Haft, M. G. (1976). Hustling for rights. In L. Crites (Ed.), *The female offender.* Lexington, MA: Lexington Books.

Häkkänen, H. & Laajasalo, T. (2006). Homicide crime scene behaviors in a Finnish sample of mentally ill offenders. *Homicide Studies, 10*, 33–54.

Hall, C. S., & Lindzey, G. (1970). *Theories of personality* (2nd ed.). New York: Wiley.

Hall, C. L. (1997). Cultural malpractice: The growing obsolescence of psychology with the changing U.S. population. *American Psychologist, 52*, 642–651.

Hall, D. M. (1998). The victims of stalking. In J. R. Meloy (Ed.), *The psychology of stalking: Clinical and forensic perspectives.* San Diego, CA: Academic Press.

Hall, G. C. N. (1995). Sexual offender recidivism revisited: A meta-analysis of recent treatment studies. *Journal of Consulting and Clinical Psychology, 63*, 802–809.

Hall, G. C. N., Proctor, W. C., & Nelson, G. M. (1988). Validity of physiological measures of pedophilic sexual arousal in a sexual offender population. *Journal of Consulting and Clinical Psychology, 56*, 118–122.

Halleck, S. L. (1967). *Psychiatry and the dilemmas of crime.* New York: Harper & Row.

Hallett, B. (2004). Dishonest crimes, dishonest language: An argument about terrorism. In F. M. Moghaddam & A. J. Marsella (Eds.), *Understanding terrorism: Psychosocial roots, consequences, and interventions.* Washington, DC: American Psychological Association.

Hämäläinen, T., & Haapasalo, J. (1996). Retrospective reports of childhood abuse and neglect among violent and property offenders. *Psychology, Crime & Law, 3*, 1–13.

Hammond, W. R., & Yung, B. (1994). African Americans. In L. D. Eron, J. H. Gentry, & P. Schlegel (Eds.), *Reason to hope: A psychosocial perspective on violence and youth.* Washington, DC: American Psychological Association.

Hampson, J. E., Rahman, M. A., Brown, B., Taylor, M. E., & Donaldson, C. J. (1998). Project SELF: Beyond resilience. *Urban Education, 33*, 6–33.

Haney, C., & Zimbardo, P. (1998). The past the future of U.S. prison policy: Twenty-five years after the Stanford prison experiment. *American Psychologist, 53*, 709–727.

Haney, C. W. (1983). The good, the bad, and the lawful: An essay on psychological injustice. In W. S. Laufer & J. M. Day (Eds.), *Personality theory, moral development, and criminal behavior.* Lexington, MA: Lexington Books.

Hanson, R. K. (2001). *Age and sexual recidivism: A comparison of rapists and child molesters.* Ottawa, Ontario: Solicitor General Canada.

Hanson, R. K., & Harris, A. J. R. (2000). Where should we intervene? Dynamic predictors of sexual offense recidivism. *Criminal Justice and Behavior, 27*, 6–35.

Harbin, H. T., & Madden, D. J. (1979). Battered parents: A new syndrome. *American Journal of Psychiatry, 136*, 1288–1291.

Hare, R. D. (1965a). A conflict and learning theory analysis of psychopathic behavior. *Journal of Research in Crime and Delinquency, 2*, 12–19.

Hare, R. D. (1965b). Acquisition and generalization of a conditioned-fear response in psychopathic and nonpsychopathic criminals. *Journal of Psychology, 59*, 367–370.

Hare, R. D. (1968). Psychopathy, autonomic functioning, and the orienting response. *Journal of Abnormal Psychology, 73*, 1–24.

Hare, R. D. (1970). *Psychopathy: Theory and research.* New York: Wiley.

Hare, R. D. (1976). Anxiety, stress and psychopathy. In G. Shean (Ed.), *Dimensions in abnormal psychology.* Chicago, IL: Rand McNally.

Hare, R. D. (1980). A research scale for the assessment of psychopathy in criminal populations. *Personality and Individual Differences, 1,* 111–119.

Hare, R. D. (1984). Performance of psychopaths on cognitive tasks related to frontal lobe function. *Journal of Abnormal Psychology, 93,* 133–140.

Hare, R. D. (1986). Criminal psychopaths. In J. C. Yuille (Ed.), *Selection and training: The role of psychology.* Boston, MA: Martinus Nijhoff.

Hare, R. D. (1991). *The Hare psychopathy checklist-revised.* Toronto, ON: Multi-Health Systems.

Hare, R. D. (1993). *Without conscience: The disturbing world of the psychopaths among us.* New York: Pocket Books.

Hare, R. D. (1996). Psychopathy: A clinical construct whose time has come. *Criminal Justice and Behavior, 23,* 25–54.

Hare, R. D. (1998). Emotional processing in psychopaths. In D. J. Cooke, R. D. Hare, & A. Forth (Eds.), *Psychopathy: Theory, research, and implications for society.* The Netherlands: Kluwer Academic Publishers.

Hare, R. D. (2003). *The Hare Psychopathy Checklist—Revised* (2nd ed.). Toronto: Multi-Health Systems.

Hare, R. D., Clark, D., Grann, M., & Thornton, D. (2000). Psychopathy and the predictive validity of the PCL-R: An international perspective. *Behavioral Sciences & the Law, 18,* 623–645.

Hare, R. D., & Connolly, J. F. (1987). Perceptual asymmetries and information processing in psychopaths. In S. A. Mednick, T. E. Moffitt, & S. A. Stack (Eds.), *The causes of crime: New biological approaches.* Cambridge, Eng.: Cambridge University Press.

Hare, R. D., & Craigen, D. (1974). Psychopathy and physiological activity in a mixed-motive game. *Psychophysiology, 11,* 197–206.

Hare, R. D., Forth, A. E., & Stachan, K. E. (1992). Psychopathy and crime across the life span. In R. D. Peters, R. J. McMahon, & V. L. Quinsey (Eds.), *Aggression and violence throughout the life span.* Newbury Park, CA: Sage.

Hare, R. D., & McPherson, L. M. (1984). Violent and aggressive behavior by criminal psychopaths. *International Journal of Law and Psychiatry, 7,* 35–50.

Hare, R. D., & Quinn, M. (1971). Psychopathy and autonomic conditioning. *Journal of Abnormal Psychology, 77,* 223–239.

Harmon, R. B., Rosner, R., & Wiederlight, M. (1985). Women and arson: A demographic study. *Journal of Forensic Sciences, 10,* 467–477.

Harpur, T. J., Hakstian, A., & Hare, R. D. (1988). Factor structure of the Psychopathy Checklist. *Journal of Consulting and Clinical Psychology, 56,* 741–747.

Harries, K. D. (1980). *Crime and the environment.* Springfield, IL: Charles C Thomas.

Harris, D. A. (1999, June). *Driving while Black: Racial profiling on our nation's highways.* New York: American Civil Liberties Union. Available: www.aclu.org/profiling/report/index.html.

Harris, G. T., Rice, M. E., & Quinsey, V. L. (1993). Violent recidivism of mentally disordered offenders: The development of a statistical prediction instrument. *Criminal Justice and Behavior, 20,* 315–335.

Harrison, P. M., & Beck, A. J. (2006a). Prison and jail inmates at midyear 2005. Washington, DC: U.S. Department of Justice, Bureau of Justice Statistics.

Harrison, P. M., & Beck, A. J. (2006b, May). *Prison and jail inmates at midyear 2005.* Bureau of Justice Statistics Bulletin (NJ 213133). Washington, DC: U.S. Department of Justice.

Hart, C. H., Nelson, A. A., Robinson, C. C., Olsen, S. F., & McNeilly-Choque, M. K. (1998). Overt and relational aggression in Russian nursery-school-age children: Parenting style and marital linkages. *Developmental Psychology, 34,* 687–697.

Hart, S. D., Cox, D. N., & Hare, R. D. (1995). *The Hare Psychopathy Checklist: Screening Version.* Toronto, ON: Multi-Health Systems.

Hart, S. D., & Dempster, R. J. (1997). Impulsivity and psychopathy. In C. D. Webster & M. A. Jackson (Eds.), *Impulsivity: Theory, assessment and treatment.* New York: Guilford.

Hart, S. D., & Hare, R. D. (1997). Psychopathy: Assessment and association with criminal conduct. In D. M. Stoff, J. P. Maser, & J. Breiling (Eds.), *Handbook of antisocial behavior.* New York: Wiley.

Hart, S. D., Hare, R. D., & Forth, A. E. (1993). Psychopathy as a risk marker for violence: Development and validation of a screening version of the Revised Psychopathy Checklist. In J. Monahan & H. Steadman (Eds.), *Violence and mental disorder: Development in risk assessment.* Chicago, IL: University of Chicago Press.

Hartl, E. M., Monnelly, E. P., & Elderkin, R. D. (1982). *Physique and delinquent behavior.* New York: Academic Press.

Hawes, D. J., & Dadds, M. R. (2005). The treatment of conduct problems in children with callous-unemotional traits. *Journal of Consulting and Clinical Psychology, 73,* 737–741.

Hawke, C. C. (1950). Castration and sex crimes. *American Journal of Mental Deficiency, 55,* 220–226.

Hawkins, D. L., Pepler, D. J., & Craig, W. M. (2001). Naturalistic observations of peer interventions in bullying. *Social Development, 10,* 512–527.

Hayes, L. M. (1995). Prison suicide: An overview and guide to prevention. *Prison Journal, 75,* 431–456.

Hazelwood, R. R., & Burgess, A. W. (1987, September). An introduction to the serial rapist. *FBI Law Enforcement Bulletin, 16*–24.

Heaven, P. C. L., Newbury, K., & Wilson, V. (2004). The Eysenck psychoticism dimension and delinquent behaviours among non-criminals: Changes across the lifespan? *Personality and Individual Differences, 36,* 1817–1825.

Hebb, D. O. (1955). Drives and the C.N.S. (Conceptual Nervous System). *Psychological Review, 62,* 243–254.

Heckel, R. V., & Shumaker, D. M. (2001). *Children who murder: A psychological perspective.* Westport, CT: Praeger.

Heide, K. (1993). Adolescent parricide offenders: Synthesis, illustration and future directions. In A. V. Wilson (Ed.), *Homicide—the victim/offender connection.* Cincinnati, OH: Anderson.

Heide, K. M. (2003). Youth homicide: A review of the literature and blueprint for action. *International Journal of Offender Therapy and Comparative Criminology, 47,* 6–36.

Heilbrun, K., & Griffin, R. (1999). Forensic treatment: A review of programs and research. In R. Roesch, S. D. Hart, & J. R. P. Ogle (Eds.), *Psychology and law: The state of the discipline.* New York: Kluwer Academic/Plenum.

Heilbrun, K., Marczyk, G. R., & Dematteo, D. (2002). *Forensic mental health assessment: A casebook.* New York: Kluwer Academic.

Hemphill, J. F., & Hare, R. D. (2004). Some misconceptsions about the Hare PCL-R and risk assessment: A reply to Gendreau, Goggin, and Smith. *Criminal Justice and Behavior, 31,* 203–243.

Hemphill, J. F., Hare, R. D., & Wong, S. (1998). Psychopathy and recidivism: A review. *Legal and Criminological Psychology, 3,* 139–170.

Henderson, M. (1983). An empirical classification of non-violent offenders using the MMPI. *Personality and Individual Differences, 4,* 671–677.

Henggeler, S. W. (1996). Treatment of violent juvenile offenders—we have the knowledge. *Journal of Family Psychology, 10,* 137–141.

Henggeler, S. W., & Borduin, C. M. (1990). *Family therapy and beyond: A multisystemic approach to treating the behavior problems of children and adolescents.* Pacific Grove, CA: Brooks/Cole.

Henggeler, S. W., Melton, G. B., & Smith, L. A. (1992). Family preservation using multisystemic therapy—an effective alternative to incarcerating serious juvenile offenders. *Journal of Consulting and Clinical Psychology, 60,* 953–961.

Henggeler, S. W., Melton, G. B., Smith, L. A., Schoenwald, S. K., & Hanley, J. (1993). Family preservation using multisystemic therapy: Long-term follow-up to a clinical trial with serious juvenile offenders. *Journal of Child and Family Studies, 2,* 283–293.

Henker, B., & Whalen, C. K. (1989). Hyperactivity and attention deficits. *American Psychologist, 44,* 216–244.

Henn, F. A., Herjanic, M., & Vanderpearl, R. H. (1976a). Forensic psychiatry: Profiles of two types of sex offenders. *American Journal of Psychiatry, 133,* 694–696.

Henn, F. A., Herjanic, M., & Vanderpearl, R. H. (1976b). Forensic psychiatry: Diagnosis of criminal responsibility. *The Journal of Nervous and Mental Disease, 162,* 423–429.

Henry, B., Caspi, A., Moffitt, T. E., & Silva, P. A. (1996). Temperament and familial predictors of violent and nonviolent criminal conviction: Age 3 to age 18. *Developmental Psychology, 32,* 614–623.

Hepburn, J., & Voss, H. L. (1970). Patterns of criminal homicide: A comparison of Chicago and Philadelphia. *Criminology, 8,* 19–45.

Hepburn, L. M., & Hemenway, D. (2004). Firearm availability and homicide: A review of the literature. *Aggression and Violent Behavior, 9,* 417–429.

Hepworth, W., & Towler, A. (2004). The effects of individual differences and charismatic leadership on workplace aggression. *Journal of Occupational Health Psychology, 9,* 176–185.

Herpertz, S. C., & Sass, H. (2000). Emotional deficiency and psychopathy. *Behavioral Sciences & the Law, 18,* 567–580.

Herzberg, J. L., & Fenwick, P. B. C. (1988). The aetiology of aggression in temporal lobe epilepsy. *British Journal of Psychiatry, 153,* 50–55.

Hetherington, E. M., & Parke, R. D. (1975). *Child psychology: A contemporary viewpoint.* New York: McGraw-Hill.

Hickey, E. (1991). *Serial killers and their victims.* Pacific Grove, CA: Brooks/Cole.

Hickey, E. W. (1997). *Serial murderers and their victims.* Belmont, CA: Wadsworth.

Higley, J., Mehlman, P., Taub, M., Higley, B., Surmi, S., Linnoila, M., & Vickers, J. (1992). Cerebrospinal fluid monoamine and adrenal correlates of aggression free-ranging rhesus monkeys. *Archives of General Psychiatry, 49,* 436–441.

Hill, H. M., Soriano, F. I., Chen, S. A., & LaFromboise, T. D. (1994). Sociocultural factors in the etiology and prevention of violence among ethnic minority youth. In L. D. Eron, J. H. Gentry, & P. Schlegel (Eds.), *Reason to hope: A psychosocial perspective on violence and youth.* Washington, DC: American Psychological Association.

Hill, L. G., Lochman, J. E., Coie, J. D., & Geenberg, M. T. (2004). Effectiveness of early screening for externalizing problems: Issues of screening accuracy and utility. *Journal of Consulting and Clinical Psychology, 72,* 809–820.

Hill, P. (1960). *Portrait of a sadist.* New York: Avon.

Hill, R. W., Langevin, R., Paitich, D., Handy, L., Russon, A., & Wilkinson, L. (1982). Is arson an aggressive act or a property offense? *Canadian Journal of Psychiatry, 27,* 648–654.

Hillbrand, M., Alexandre, J. W., Young, J. L., & Spitz, R. T. (1999). Parricide: Characteristics of offenders and victims, legal factors, and treatment issues. *Aggression and Violent Behavior, 4,* 179–190.

Hindelang, M. J. (1974). Decisions of shoplifting victims to invoke the criminal justice process. *Social Process, 21,* 580–593.

Hindelang, M. J., Dunn, C. S., Sutton, L. P., & Aumick, A. (1976). *Sourcebook of criminal justice statistics, 1975.* Washington, DC: USGPO.

Hinshaw, S. P. (1992). Externalizing behavior problems and academic underachievement in childhood and adolescence: Causal relationships and underlying mechanisms. *Psychological Bulletin, 111,* 127–155.

Hirschi, T., & Hindelang, M. J. (1977). Intelligence and delinquency. *American Sociological Review, 42,* 571–587.

Hockenbury, D. H., & Hockenbury, S. E. (2004). *Discovering psychology* (3rd edition). New York: Worth.

Hochstedler, E. (Ed.). (1984). *Corporations as criminals.* Beverly Hills, CA: Sage.

Hoffman, B. (1993). *"Holy terror": The implications of terrorism motivated by a religious imperative* (RAND Research Paper P-7834). Santa Monica, CA: RAND.

Hoffman, J. J., Hall, R. W., & Bartsch, T. W. (1987). On the relative importance of "psychopathic" personality and alcoholism measures of frontal lobe dysfunction. *Journal of Abnormal Psychology, 96,* 158–160.

Hoffman, K. L., & Kiecolt, K. J., & Edwards, J. N. (2005). Physical violence between siblings: A theoretical and empirical analysis. *Journal of Family Issues, 26,* 1103–1130.

Hofmann, F. G. (1975). *A handbook on drug and alcohol abuse: The biomedical aspects.* New York: Oxford University Press.

Hoge, S. K., Poythress, N., Bonnie, R., Eisenberg, M., Monahan, J., Feucht-Haviar, T., & Oberlander, L. (1996). Mentally ill and non-mentally ill defendants' abilities to understand information relevant to adjudication: A preliminary study. *Bulletin of the American Academy of Psychiatry and the Law, 24,* 187–197.

Hoge, S. K., Poythress, N., Bonnie, R., Monahan, J., Eisenberg, M., & Feucht-Haviar, T. (1997). The MacArthur adjudicative competence study: Diagnosis, psychopathology, and competence-related abilities. *Behavioral Sciences & the Law, 15,* 329–345.

Hollinger, R. (1986). Acts against the workplace: Social bonding and employee deviance. *Deviant Behavior, 7,* 53–75.

Hollister-Wagner, G. H., Foshee, V. A., & Jackson, C. (2001). Adolescent aggression: Models of resilience. *Journal of Applied Social Psychology, 31,* 445–466.

Holmes, C. T. (1989). Grade level retention effects: A meta-analysis of research studies. In L. A. Shepard & M. L. Smith (Eds.), *Flunking grades: Research and policies on retention.* Philadelphia: Falmer Press.

Holmes, R. M. (1991). *Sex crimes.* Newbury Park, CA: Sage.

Holmes, R. M., & DeBurger, J. (1988). *Serial murder.* Newbury Park, CA: Sage.

Holmes, R. M., & Holmes, S. T. (1998). *Serial murder* (2nd ed.). Thousand Oaks, CA: Sage.

Holmes, S. T., Hickey, E., & Holmes, R. M. (1991). Female serial murderesses: Constructing differentiating typologies. *Journal of Contemporary Criminal Justice, 7,* 245–256.

Holt, S. E., Meloy, J. R., & Stack, S. (1999). Sadism and psychopath in violent and sexual violent offenders. *Journal of the American Academy of Psychiatry and Law, 27,* 23–32.

Holtzworth-Monroe, A., & Stuart, G. L. (1994). Typologies of male batterers: Three subtypes and the differences among them. *Psychological Bulletin, 116,* 476–497.

Home Office. (1986). *Criminal statistics: England and Wales 1985.* London: HMSO.

Horning, D. N. M. (1970). Blue-collar theft: Conceptions of property, attitudes toward pilfering, and work group norms in a modern industrial plant. In E. O. Smigel & H. L. Ross (Eds.), *Crimes against bureaucracy.* New York: Van Nostrand Reinhold.

Hornung, C. A., McCullough, B. C., & Sugimoto, T. (1981). Status relationships in marriage: Risk factors in spouse abuse. *Journal of Marriage and the Family, 43,* 675–692.

Hotaling, G. T., & Straus, M. A. (1989). Intrafamily violence, and crime and violence outside the family. In L. Ohlin & M. Tonry (Eds.), *Family violence* (Vol. 11). Chicago, IL: University of Chicago Press.

Howes, C., & Olenick, M. (1986). Family and child care influences on toddlers' compliance. *Child Development, 57,* 202–216.

Hubbard, J. A., Dodge, K. A., Cillessen, A. H. N., Coie, J. D., & Schwartz, D. (2001). The dyadic nature of social information processing in boys' reactive and proactive aggression. *Journal of Personality and Social Psychology, 80,* 268–280.

Hudson, M. I. (1986). Elder maltreatment: Current research. In K. A. Pillemer & R. S. Wolf (Eds.), *Elder abuse: Conflict in the family.* Dover, MA: Auburn House.

Huesmann, L. R. (1988). An information processing model for the development of aggression. *Aggressive Behavior, 14,* 13–24.

Huesmann, L. R. (1997). Observational learning of violent behavior: Social and biosocial processes. In A. Raine, P. A. Brennan, D. P. Farrington, & S. A. Mednick (Eds.), *Biosocial bases of violence.* New York: Plenum.

Huesmann, L. R. (1998). The role of social information processing and cognitive schema in the acquistion and maintenance of habitual aggressive behavior. In R. G. Geen & E. Donnerstein (Eds.), *Human aggression: Theories, research, and implications for social policy.* San Diego, CA: Academic Press.

Huesmann, L. R., Moise-Titus, J., Podolski, C., & Eron, L. D. (2003). Longitudinal relations between children's exposure to TV violence and their aggressive and violent behavior in young adulthood: 1977–1992. *Developmental Psychology, 39,* 201–221.

Hughes, H. M. (1988). Psychological and behavioral correlates of family violence in child witnesses and victims. *American Journal of Orthopsychiatry, 58,* 77–90.

Hughes, H. M., & Barad, S. J. (1983). Psychological functioning of children in a battered women's shelter: A preliminary investigation. *American Journal of Orthopsychiatry, 53,* 525–531.

Hughes, H. M., Parkinson, D., & Vargo, M. (1989). Witnessing spouse abuse and experiencing physical abuse: A "double whammy"? *Journal of Family Violence, 4,* 197–209.

Huizinga, D., & Jakob-Chien, C. (1998). The contemporaneous co-occurrence of serious and violent juvenile offending and other problem behaviors. In R. Loeber & D. P. Farrington (Eds.), *Serious & violent juvenile offenders: Risk factors and successful interventions.* Thousand Oaks, CA: Sage.

Hunter, J. A., & Becker, J. V. (1999). Motivators of adolescent sex offenders and treatment perspectives. In J. Shaw (Ed.), *Sexual aggression.* Washington, DC: American Psychiatric Press.

Hunter, J. A., Figueredo, A. J., Malamuth, N. M., & Becker, J. V. (2003). Juvenile sex offenders: Toward the development of a typology. *Sexual Abuse: A Journal of Research and Treatment, 15,* 27–48.

Hutchings, B., & Mednick, S. A. (1975). Registered criminality in the adoptive and biological parents of registered male criminal adoptees. In R. R. Fieve, D. Rosenthal, & H. Brill (Eds.), *Genetic research in psychiatry.* Baltimore, MD: Johns Hopkins University Press.

Icove, D. J., & Estepp, M. H. (1987, April). Motive-based offender profiles of arson and fire-related crime. *FBI Law Enforcement Bulletin,* 17–23.

Inaba, D. S., & Cohen, W. E. (1993). *Uppers, downers, all arounders: Physical and mental effects of psychoactive drugs* (2nd ed.). Ashland, OR: CNS Productions.

Inciardi, J. A. (1970). The adult firesetter, a typology. *Criminology, 3,* 145–155.

Inciardi, J. A. (1980). Women, heroin, and property crime. In S. K. Datesman & F. R. Scarpitti (Eds.), *Women, crime and justice.* New York: Oxford University Press.

Inciardi, J. A. (1981). Crime and alternative patterns of substance abuse. In S. E. Gardner (Ed.), *Drug and alcohol abuse.* Rockville, MD: National Institute on Drug Abuse.

Inciardi, J. A. (1986). *The war on drugs: Heroin, cocaine, crime and public policy.* Palo Alto, CA: Mayfield Publishing.

Informant, The. (2003). Newsletter of National White Collar Crime Center (August issue). Richmond, VA: National White Collar Crime Center.

Ingram, G. L., Gerard, R. E., Quay, H. C., & Levison, R. B. (1970). An experimental program for the psychopathic delinquent: Looking in the "correctional wastebasket." *Journal of Research in Crime and Delinquency, 7,* 24–30.

Insight Canada Research. (1998). *Prevalence of problem and pathological gambling in Ontario using the South Oaks Gambling Screen.* Ottawa, ON: Canadian Foundation on Compulsive Gambling. Available: www.cfcg.on.ca.

International Arrestees Drug Abuse Monitoring Program. (2000). *Comparing drug use rates of detained arrestees in the United States and England.* Washington, DC: U.S. Department of Justice.

Ishikawa, S. S., & Raine, A. (2004). Prefrontal deficits and antisocial behavior: A causal model. In B. B. Lahey, T. E. Moffitt, & A. Caspi (Eds.), *Causes of conduct disorder and juvenile delinquency.* New York: Guilford.

Ishikawa, S. S., Raine, A., Lencz, T., Bihrle, S., & Lacasse, L. (2001). Autonomic stress reactivity and executive fucntions in successful and unsuccessful criminal psychopaths from the community. *Journal of Abnormal Psychology, 110,* 423–432.

Ivanoff, A., & Hayes, L. M. (2001). Preventing, managing, and treating suicidal actions in high-risk offenders. In J. B. Ashford, B. D. Sales, & W. H. Reid (Eds.), *Treating adult and juvenile offenders with special needs.* Washington, DC: American Psychological Association.

Jackson, H. F., Glass, C., & Hope, S. (1987). A functional analysis of recidivistic arson. *British Journal of Clinical Psychology, 26,* 175–185.

Jacobs, B. A., Topalli, V., & Wright, R. (2003). Carjacking, streetlife and offender motivation. *British Journal of Criminology, 43,* 673–688.

Jacobs, G. D., & Snyder, D. (1996). Frontal brain asymmetry predicts affective style in men. *Behavioral Neuroscience, 110,* 3–6.

Jacobs, P. A., Brunton, M., Melville, H. M., Brittain, R. P., & McClemont, W. F. (1965). Aggressive behavior, mental subnormality and the XYY male. *Nature, 208,* 1351–1352.

Jaffee, S. R., Caspi, A., Moffitt, T. E., Dodge, K. A., Rutter, M., Taylor, A., & Tully, L. A. (2005). Nature X nurture: Genetic vulnerabilities interact with physical maltreatment to promote conduct problems. *Development and Psychopathology, 17,* 67–84.

James, J. (1976). Motivations for entrance into prostitution. In L. Crites (Ed.), *The female offender.* Lexington, MA: Lexington Books.

James, J. (1978). The prostitute as victim. In J. R. Chapman & M. Gates (Eds.), *The victimization of women.* Beverly Hills, CA: Sage.

Jamison, R. N. (1980). Psychoticism, deviancy, and perception of risk in normal children. *Personality and Individual Differences, 1,* 87–91.

Janus, E. S. (2000). Sexual predator commitment laws: Lessons for law and the behavioral sciences. *Behavioral Sciences and the Law, 18,* 5–21.

Janus, E. S., & Walbek, N. H. (2000). Sex offender commitments in Minnesota: A descriptive study of second generation commitments. *Behavioral Sciences & the Law, 18,* 343–374.

Jarvik, L. F., Klodin, V., & Matsuyama, S. S. (1973). Human aggression and the extra Y chromosome. *American Psychologist, 28,* 674–682.

Jarvis, G., & Parker, H. (1989). Young heroin users and crime. *British Journal of Criminology, 29,* 175–185.

Jeffrey, C. R. (1965). Criminal behavior and learning theory. *Journal of Criminal Law, Criminology and Police Science, 56,* 294–300.

Jenkins, P. (1988). Serial murder in England 1940–1985. *Journal of Criminal Justice, 16,* 1–15.

Jenkins, P. (1993). Chance or choice: The selection of serial murder victims. In A. V. Wilson (Ed.), *Homicide: The victim/offender connection.* Cincinnati, OH: Anderson.

Jenson, B. (1996 May). *Cyberstalking: Crime, enforcement and personal responsibility in the on-line world.* Available: www. law.ucla.edu/Classes/Archive.S96/340/cyberlaw.htm.

Jesness, C. (1971). Jesness Inventory Classification System. *Criminal Justice and Behavior, 15*, 78–91.

Johns, J. H., & Quay, H. C. (1962). The effect of social reward on verbal conditioning in psychopathic military offenders. *Journal of Consulting Psychology, 26*, 217–220.

Johnson, R. (1996). *Hard time: Understanding and reforming the prison* (2nd ed.). Belmont, CA: Wadsworth.

Johnston, L. D., O'Malley, P. M., & Bachman, J. G., & Schulenberg, J. E. (2006). *Monitoring the future national results on adolescent drug use: Overview of key findings, 2005*. Bethesda, MD: National Institute on Drug Abuse.

Joint, M. (1995, March). *Road rage*. Washington, DC: Automobile Association Group Public Policy Road Safety Unit.

Jolin, A. (1994). On the backs of working prostitutes: Feminist theory and prostitution policy. *Crime and Delinquency, 40*, 69–83.

Jones, C., & Aronson, E. (1973). Attribution of fault to a rape victim as a function of respectability of the victim. *Journal of Personality and Social Psychology, 26*, 415–419.

Jones, J. G., Butler, H. L., Hamilton, B., Perdue, J. D., Stern, H. P., & Woody, R. C. (1986). Munchausen syndrome by proxy. *Child Abuse and Neglect, 10*, 33–40.

Jones, J. W., & Bogat, G. A. (1978). Air pollution and human aggression. *Psychological Reports, 43*, 721–722.

Julien, R. M. (1975). *A primer of drug action*. San Francisco, CA: W. H. Freeman.

Julien, R. M. (1992). *A primer of drug action* (6th ed.). New York: W. H. Freeman.

Junger, M., West, R., & Timman, R. (2001). Crime and risk behavior in traffice: An example of cross-situational consistency. *Journal of Resarch in Crime and Delinquency, 38*, 439–459.

Kafrey, D. (1980). Playing with matches: Children and fire. In D. Canter (Ed.), *Fires and human behaviour*. Chichester, Eng.: Wiley.

Kahn, T. J., & LaFond, M. A. (1988). Treatment of the adolescent sex offender. *Child and Adolescent Social Work, 5*, 135–148.

Kandel, D., Yamaguchi, K., & Chen, K. (1992). Stages of drug involvement from adolescence to adulthood: Further evidence for the gateway theory. *Journal of Studies on Alcohol, 53*, 447–457.

Kandel, E., Mednick, S. A., Kirkegaard-Sorenson, L., Hutchings, B., Knop, J., Rosenberg, R., & Schulsinger, F. (1988). IQ as a protective factor for subjects at high risk for antisocial behavior. *Journal of Consulting and Clinical Psychology, 56*, 224–226.

Kanin, E. J. (1984). Date rape: Unofficial criminals and victims. *Victimology, 9*, 95–108.

Kaplan, M. S. & Green, A. (1995). Incarcerated female sexual offenders: A comparison of sexual histories with eleven female nonsexual offenders. *Sexual Abuse, 7*, 287–300.

Karmen, A. (1996). *Crime victims: An introduction to victimology* (3rd ed.). Belmont, CA: Wadsworth.

Karmen, A. (2001). *Crime victims* (4th ed.). Belmont, CA: Wadsworth/Thomson Learning.

Katz, J. (1988). *Seduction of crime: Moral and sensual attractions in doing evil*. New York: Basic Books.

Kazdin, A. E. (1989). Developmental psychopathology: Current research, issues, and directions. *American Psychologist, 44*, 180–187.

Kazdin, A. E. (1994). Psychotherapy for children and adolescents. In A. E. Bergrin & S. LO. Garfield (Eds.), *Handbook of psychotherapy and behavior change* (4th ed.). New York: Wiley.

Kelleher, M. D. (1997). *Profiling the lethal employee: Case studies of violence in the workplace*. Westport, CT: Praeger.

Kelley, T. M., Kennedy, D. B., & Homant, R. J. (2003). Evaluation of an individualized treatment program for adolescent shoplifters. *Adolescence, 38*, 725–733.

Kelman, H. C., & Hamilton, V. L. (1989). *Crimes of obedience: Toward a social psychology of authority and responsibility*. New Haven, CT: Yale University Press.

Kempe, C. H., Silverman, F. N., Steele, B. B., Droegemueller, W., & Silver, H. K. (1962). The battered-child syndrome. *Journal of the American Medical Association, 181*, 17–24.

Kemp, D. E., & Center, D. B. (2003). An investigation of Eysenck's antisocial behavior hypothesis in general education students and students with behavior disorders. *Personality and Individual Differences, 35*, 1359–1371.

Kendall, P. C., & Hammen, C. (1995). *Abnormal psychology.* Boston: Houghton Mifflin.

Kenrick, D. T., & MacFarland, S. W. (1986). Ambient temperature and horn honking. *Environment and Behavior, 18*, 179–191.

Kiehl, K. A. (2006). A cognitive neuroscience perspective on psychopathy: Evidence for paralimbic system dysfunction. *Psychiatry Research, 142*, 107–128.

Kiehl, K. A., Smith, A. M., Hare, R. D., Mendrek, A., Forster, B. B., Brink, J. et al. (2001). Limbic abnormalities in affective processing by criminal psychopaths as revealed by functional magnetic resonance imaging. *Biological Psychiatry, 50*, 677–684.

Kilgore, K., Snyder, J., & Lentz, C. (2000). The contribution of parental discipline, parental monitoring, and school risk to early-onset conduct problems in African American boys and girls. *Developmental Psychology, 36*, 835–845.

Kilmann, P. R., Sabalis, R. F., Gearing, M. L., Bukstel, L. H., & Scovern, A. W. (1982). The treatment of sexual paraphilias: A review of the outcome research. *Journal of Sex Research, 18*, 193–252.

Kilpatrick, D. G., Best, C. L., Saunders, B. E., & Veronen, L. J. (1988). Rape in marriage and in dating relationships: How bad is it for mental health? In R. A. Prentky & V. L. Quinsey (Eds.), *Human sexual aggression: Current perspectives.* New York: New York Academy of Sciences.

Kilpatrick, D. G., Whalley, A., & Edmunds, C. (2000). Sexual assault. In A. Seymour, M. Murray, J. Sigmon, M. Hook, C. Edmunds, M. Gaboury, & G. Coleman (Eds.), *2000 National Victim Assistance Academy.* Washington, DC: U.S. Department of Justice.

Kilpatrick, D. G., Whalley, A., & Edmunds, C. (2002). Sexual assault. In A. Seymour, M. Murray, J. Sigmon, M. Hook, C. Edmunds, M. Gaboury, & G. Coleman (Eds.), *2002 National Victim Assistance Academy.* Washington, DC: U.S. Department of Justice.

Kinports, K. (2002). Sex offenses. In K. L. Hall (Ed.), *The Oxford companion to American law.* New York: Oxford University Press.

Kirmeyer, S. L. (1978). Urban density and pathology—a review of research. *Environment and Behavior, 10*, 247–269.

Klassen, D., & O'Connor, W. (1988). Crime, inpatient admissions, and violence among male mental patients. *International Journal of Law and Psychiatry, 11*, 305–312.

Klassen, D., & O'Connor, W. (1990). Assessing the risk of violence in released mental patients: A cross-validation study. *Psychological Assessment: A Journal of Consulting and Clinical Psychology, 1*, 75–81.

Klaus, P. (1999, March). *Carjackings in the United States, 1992–1996.* Washington, DC: U.S. Department of Justice, Bureau of Justice Statistics.

Klaus, P. (2000, January). *Crimes against persons age 65 or older, 1992–97* (NCJ 176352). Washington, DC: U.S. Department of Justice, Bureau of Justice Statistics.

Klaus, P. (2004, July). *Carjacking, 1993–2002.* Washington, DC: U.S. Department of Justice, National Crime Victimization Survey.

Kleber, H. D. (1988). Epidemic cocaine abuse: America's present, Britain's future. *British Journal of Addiction, 83*, 1359–1371.

Klemke, L. W. (1992). *The sociology of shoplifting: Boosters and snitches today.* Westport, CT: Praeger.

Klinteberg, B., Magnusson, D., & Schalling, D. (1989). Hyperactive behavior in childhood and adult impulsivity: A longitudinal study of male subjects. *Personality and Individual Differences, 10*, 43–50.

Knight, R. A. (1988). A taxonomic analysis of child molesters. In R. A. Prentky & V. L. Quinsey (Eds.), *Human sexual aggression: Current perspectives.* New York: New York Academy of Science.

Knight, R. A. (1989). An assessment of the concurrent validity of a child molester typology. *Journal of Interpersonal Violence, 4*, 131–150.

Knight, R. A., Carter, D. L., & Prentky, R. A. (1989). A system for the classification of child molesters: Reliability and application. *Journal of Interpersonal Violence, 4,* 3–23.

Knight, R. A., & Prentky, R. A. (1987). The developmental antecedents and adult adaptations of rapist subtypes. *Criminal Justice and Behavior, 14,* 403–426.

Knight, R. A., & Prentky, R. A. (1990). Classifying sexual offenders: The development and corroboration of taxonomic models. In W. L. Marshall, D. R. Laws, & H. E. Barbaree (Eds.), *The handbook of sexual assault: Issues, theories, and treatment of the offender.* New York: Plenum.

Knight, R. A., & Prentky, R. A. (1993). Exploring characteristics for classifying juvenile sex offenders. In H. E. Barbaree, W. L. Marshall, & S. M. Hudson (Eds.), *The juvenile sex offender.* New York: Guilford.

Knight, R. A., Rosenberg, R., & Schneider, B. A. (1985). Classification of sexual offenders: Perspectives, methods, and validation. In A. W. Burgess (Ed.), *Rape and sexual assault.* New York: Garland.

Knight, R. A., Warren, J. I., Reboussin, R., & Soley, B. J. (1998). Predicting rapist type from crime-scene variables. *Criminal Justice and Behavior, 25,* 46–80.

Knopp, F. H., Rosenberg, J., & Stevenson, W. (1986). *Report on nationwide survey of juvenile and adult sex-offender treatment programs and providers.* Syracuse, NY: Safer Society Press.

Kochanska, G., Friesenborg, A. E., Lange, L. A., & Martel, M. M. (2004). Parents' personality and infants' temperament as contributors to their emerging relationship. *Journal of Personality and Social Psychology, 86,* 744–759.

Kocsis, R. N., Cooksey, R. W., & Irwin, H. J. (2002). Psychological profiling of offender characteristics from crime behaviors in serial rape offenses. *International Journal of Offender Therapy and Comparative Criminology, 46,* 144–169.

Koivisto, H., & Haapasalo, J. (1996). Childhood maltreatment and adulthood in psychopathy in light of file-based assessments among mental state examinees. *Studies on Crime and Crime Prevention, 5,* 91–104.

Kokko, K., & Pulkkinen, L. (2005). Stability of aggressive behavior from childhood to middle age in women and men. *Aggressive Behavior, 31,* 485–497.

Kolko, D. (Ed.). (2002). *Handbook on Firesetting in children and youth.* Boston, MA: Academic Press.

Kolko, D. J., & Kazdin, A. E. (1989). The children's firesetting interview with psychiatrically referred and nonreferred children. *Journal of Abnormal Child Psychology, 17,* 609–624.

Konečni, V. J. (1975). The mediation of aggressive behavior: Arousal levels vs. anger and cognitive labeling. *Journal of Personality and Social Psychology, 32,* 706–712.

Korman, A. (1974). *The psychology of motivation.* Englewood Cliffs, NJ: Prentice Hall.

Kornhauser, R. R. (1978). *Social sources of delinquency.* Chicago, IL: University of Chicago Press.

Koson, D. F., & Dvoskin, J. (1982). Arson: A diagnostic study. *Bulletin of the American Academy of Psychiatry and the Law, 10,* 39–49.

Koss, M. P., & Dinero, T. E. (1988). Predictors of sexual aggression among a national sample of male college students. In R. A. Prentky and V. L. Quinsey (Eds.), *Human sexual aggression: Current perspectives.* New York: New York Academy of Sciences.

Koss, M. P., Gidycz, C. A., & Wisniewski, N. (1987). The scope of rape: Incidence and prevalence of sexual aggression and victimization in a national sample of higher education students. *Journal of Consulting and Clinical Psychology, 55,* 162–170.

Kosson, D. S. (1998). Divided visual attention to psychopathic and nonpsychopathic offenders. *Personality and Individual Differences, 24,* 373–391.

Kosson, D. S., Cyterski, T. D., Steverwald, B. L., Neuman, C. S., Walker-Matthes, S. (2002). The reliability and validity of the Psychopathy Checklist Youth Version (PCL:YV) in nonincarcerated adolescent males. *Psychological Assessment, 14,* 97–109.

Kosson, D. S., Smith, S. S., & Newman, J. P. (1990). Evaluating the construct validity of psychopathy in black and white male inmates: Three preliminary studies. *Journal of Abnormal Psychology, 99,* 250–259.

Kosson, D. S., Suchy, Y., Mayer, A. R., & Libby, J. (2002). Facial affect recogntion in criminal psychopaths. *Emotion, 2,* 398–411.

Kovacs, M. (1996). Presentation and course of major depressive disorder during childhood and later years of the life span. *Journal of the American Academy of Child and Adolescent Psychiatry, 35,* 705–715.

Kozol, H. L., Boucher, R. L., & Garofalo, P. F. (1972). The diagnosis and treatment of dangerousness. *Crime and Delinquency, 8,* 371–392.

Krahé, B. (2005). Predictors of women's aggressive driving behavior. *Aggressive Behavior, 31,* 537–546.

Krahé, B. & Möller, I. (2004). Playing violent electronic games, hostile attributional style, and aggression-related norms in German adolescents. *Journal of Adolescence, 27,* 53–69.

Kramer, R. C. (1984). Corporate criminality: The development of an idea. In E. Hochstedler (Ed.), *Corporations as criminals.* Beverly Hills, CA: Sage.

Krasnovsky, T., & Lane, R. (1998). Shoplifting: A review of the literature. *Aggression and Violence Behavior, 3,* 219–235.

Kratzer, L., & Hodgins, S. (1999). A typology of offenders: A test of Moffitt's theory among males and females from childhood to age 30. *Criminal Behavior and Mental Health, 9,* 57–73.

Krisberg, B. (1992). Youth crime and its prevention: A research agenda. In I. M. Schwartz (Ed.), *Juvenile justice and public policy.* New York: Lexington Books.

Krisberg, B. (1995). The legacy of juvenile corrections. *Corrections Today, 57,* 122–126.

Krisberg, B., & Howell, J. C. (1998). The impact of the juvenile justice system and prospects for graduated sanctions in a comprehensive strategy. In R. Loeber & D. P. Farrington (Eds.), *Serious & violent juvenile offenders: Risk factors and successful interventions.* Thousand Oaks, CA: Sage.

Krisberg, B., & Schwartz, I. (1983). Rethinking juvenile justice. *Crime and Delinquency, 29,* 333–364.

Krohn, M. D., Akers, R. L., Radosevich, M. J., & Lanza-Kaduce, L. (1982). Norm qualities and adolescent drinking and drug behavior: The effects of norm quality and reference group on using and abusing alcohol and marijuana. *Journal of Drug Issues, 4,* 343–360.

Kruesi, M. J. P. (1979). Cruelty to animals and CSF 5HIAA. *Psychiatry Research, 28,* 115–116.

Kruesi, M. J. P., & Jacobsen, T. (1997). Serotonin and human violence: Do environmental mediators exist? In A. Raine, P. A. Brennan, D. P. Farrington, S. A. Mednick (Eds.), *Biological bases of violence.* New York: Plenum.

Kruesi, M. J. P., Rapoport, J., Hamburger, S., Hibbs, E., Potter, W., Levane, M., & Brown, G. (1990). Cerebrospinal fluid monoamine metabolites, aggression, and impulsivity in disruptive behavior disorders of children and adolescents. *Archives of General Psychiatry, 47,* 419–426.

Kuhnley, E. J., Hendren, R. L., & Quinlan, D. M. (1982). *Journal of the American Academy of Child Psychiatry, 21,* 560–563.

Kulka, R. A., Schlenger, W. E., Fairbank, J. A., Jordan, B. K., Hough, R. L., Marmar, C. R., & Weiss, D. S. (1991). Assessment of post-traumatic stress disorder in the community: Prospects and pitfalls from recent studies of Vietnam veterans. *Psychological Assessment: A Journal of Consulting and Clinical Psychology, 4,* 547–560.

Kurtzberg, R. L., Mandell, W., Lewin, M., Lipton, D. S., & Shuster, M. (1978). Plastic surgery on offenders. In N. Johnson & L. Savitz (Eds.), *Justice and corrections.* New York: Wiley.

Labato, A. (2000). Criminal weapon use in Brazil: A psychological analysis. In D. Canter & L. Alison (Eds.), *Profiling property crimes.* Dartmouth, UK: Ashgate.

LaFon, D. S. (2002). The psychological autopsy. In B. E. Turvey (Ed.), *Criminal profiling: An introduction to behavioral evidence analysis.* San Diego, CA: Academic Press.

La Fond, J. Q. (2003). Outpatient commitment's next frontier: Sexual predators. *Psychology, Public Policy, and Law, 9,* 159–182.

Lahey, B. B., Loeber, R., Hart, E. L., Frick, P. J., Applegate, B., Zhang, Q., Green, S. M., & Russo, M. (1995). Four-year longitudinal study of conduct disorder in boys: Patterns and predictors of persistence. *Journal of Abnormal Psychology, 104,* 83–93.

Lahey, B. B., & Waldman, I. D. (2003). A developmental propensity model of the origins of conduct problems during childhood and adolescence. In B. B. Lahey, T. E. Moffitt, and A. Caspi (Eds.), *Causes of conduct disorder and juvenile delinquency.* New York: Guilford.

Laird, R. D., Jordan, K., Dodge, K. A., Pettit, G. S. & Bates, J. E. (2001). Peer rejection in childhood, involvement with antisocial peers in early adolescence, and the development of externalizing problems. *Development and Psychopathology, 13,* 337–354.

Laird, R. D., Pettit, G. S., Bates, J. E., & Dodge, K. A. (2003). Parents' monitoring—relevant knowledge and adolescents' delinquent behavior: Evidence of correlated developmental changes and reciprocal influences. *Child Development, 74,* 752–768.

Laird, R. D., Pettit, G. S., Dodge, K. A., & Bates, J. E. (2005). Peer relationship antecedents of delinquent behavior in late adolescence: Is there evidence of demographic group differences in developmental processes. *Development and Psychopathology, 17,* 127–144.

Lamb, H. R., Weinberger, L. E., & Gross, B. H. (2004). Mentally ill persons in the criminal justice system: Some perspectives. *Psychiatric Quarterly, 75,* 107–126.

Lambie, I., McCardle, S., & Coleman, R. (2002). Where there's smoke there's fire: Firesetting behaviour in children and adolescents. *New Zealand Journal of Psychology, 31,* 73–79.

Lamontagne, Y., Boyer, R., Hetu, C., & Lacerte-Lamontagne, C. (2000). Anxiety, significant losses, depression, and irrational beliefs in first-offence shoplifters. *Canadian Journal of Psychiatry, 45,* 63–66.

Lance, D. (1988, April). Product tampering. *FBI Law Enforcement Bulletin,* 20–23.

Landy, D., & Aronson, E. (1969). The influence of the character of the criminal and his victim on the decisions of simulated jurors. *Journal of Experimental Social Psychology, 5,* 141–152.

Lang, S., af Klinteberg, B., & Alm, P-O. (2002). Adult psychopathy and violent behavior in males with early neglect and abuse. *Acta Psychiatrica Scandinavica, 106,* 93–100.

Langan, P. A., Schmitt, E. L., & Durose, M. R. (2003, November). *Recidivism of sex offenders released from prison in 1994.* Washington, DC: U.S. Department of Justice, Bureau of Justice Statistics.

Langer, E. J., & Miransky, J. (1983). Burglary (non) prevention. In E. J. Langer (Ed.), *The psychology of control.* Beverly Hills, CA: Sage.

Langevin, R. (1983). *Sexual strands.* Hillsdale, NJ: Erlbaum.

Langlois, J. H., Kalakanis, L., Rubenstein, A. J., Larson, A., Hallam, M., & Smoot, M. (2000). Maxims or myths of beauty? A meta-analytic and theoretical review. *Psychological Bulletin, 126,* 390–423.

Lansford, J. E., Dodge, K. A., Pettit, G. S., Bates, J. E., Crozier, I., & Kaplow, J. (2002). Long-term effects of early child physical maltreatment on psychological, behavioral, and academic problems in adolescence: A 12-year propsective study. *Archives of Pediatrics and Adolescent Medicine, 156,* 824–830.

Lanyon, R. I. (1986). Theory and treatment in child molestation. *Journal of Consulting and Clinical Psychology, 54,* 176–182.

Laws, D. R., & Marshall, W. L. (1990). A conditioning theory of the etiology and maintenance of deviant sexual preference and behavior. In W. L. Marshall, D. R. Laws, and H. E. Barabaree (Eds.), *Handbook of sexual assault.* New York: Plenum.

Leach, E. (1973). Don't say "boo" to a goose. In A. Montagu (Ed.), *Man and aggression* (2nd ed.). London: Oxford University Press.

Lee, M., Zimbardo, P. G., & Bertholf, M. (1977, November). Shy murderers. *Psychology Today,* 68–70, 148.

Lee, M. Y. (2002). Asian battered women: Assessment and treatment. In A. R. Roberts (Ed.), *Handbook of domestic violence intervention strategies: Policies, programs, and legal remedies.* New York: Oxford University Press.

Legras, A. M. (1932). *Psychese en Criminaliteit bij Twellingen.* Utrecht, Neth.: Keminken ZOON N. V.

Le Maire, L. (1956). Danish experiences regarding the castration of sexual offenders. *Journal of Criminal Law and Criminology, 47,* 294–310.

Lemon, N. K. D. (1994, December). *Domestic violence & stalking: A comment on the Model Anti-Stalking Code proposed by the National Institute of Justice.* Duluth, MN: Battered Women's Justice Project.

Lerner, M. J. (1970). The desire for justice and reactions to victims. In J. Macaulay & L. Berkowitz (Eds.), *Altruism and helping behavior.* New York: Academic Press.

Lerner, M. J. (1980). *The belief in a just world: A fundamental delusion.* New York: Plenum.

Lesch, K. P., & Merschdorf, U. (2000). Impulsivity, aggression, and serotonin: A molecular psychobiological perspective. *Behavioral Sciences & the Law, 18,* 581–604.

Lester, D., & Danto, B. L. (1993). *Suicide behind bars: Prediction and prevention.* Philadelphia, PA: Charles Press.

Letkemann, P. (1973). *Crime as work.* Englewood Cliffs, NJ: Prentice Hall.

Letourneau, E. J., & Miner, M. H. (2005). Juvenile sex offenders: A case against the legal and clinical status quo. *Sexual Abuse: A Journal of Research and Treatment, 17,* 293–312.

Levant, R. F. (2002). Psychology responds to terrorism. *Professional Psychology: Research and Practice, 33,* 507–509.

Levant, R. F., Barbanel, L., & DeLeon, P. H. (2004). Psychology's response to terrorism. In F. M. Moghaddam & A. J. Marsella (Eds.), *Understanding terrorism: Psychosocial roots, consequences, and interventions.* Washington, DC: American Psychological Association.

Leve, L. D., & Chamberlain, P. (2004). Female juvenile offenders: Defining an early-onset pathway for delinquency. *Journal of Child and Family Studies, 13,* 439–452.

Levin, B. (1976). Psychological characteristics of firesetters. *Fire Journal, 70,* 36–41.

Levine, S. A., & Jackson, C. J. (2004). Eysenck's theory of crime revisited: Factors or primary scales? *Journal of Legal and Criminological Psychology, 9,* 135–152.

Lewin, T. (2001, January 1). New state laws tackle familiar national issues. *New York Times.* Available: www.nytimes.com/2001/01/01/politics/01laws.html.

Lewis, C. F., Baranoski, M. V., Buchanan, J. A., & Benedek, E. P. (1998). Factors associated with weapon use in maternal filicide. *Journal of Forensic Sciences, 43,* 613–618.

Lewis, D. O., Lovely, R., Yeager, C., Ferguson, G., Friedman, M., Sloane, G., Friedman, H., & Pincus, J. H. (1988). Intrinsic and environmental characteristics of juvenile murderers. *Journal of the American Academy of Child and Adolescent Psychiatry, 27,* 582–587.

Lewis, D. O., Moy, E., Jackson, L. D., Aarsonson, R., Restifo, N., Serra, S., & Simos, A. (1985). Biopsychological characteristics of children who later murder: A prospective study. *American Journal of Psychiatry, 142,* 1161–1167.

Li, Q. (2006). Cyberbullying in schools: A research on gender differences. *School Psychology International, 27,* 157–170.

Lickliter, R., & Honeycutt, H. (2003). Developmental dynamics: Toward a biologically plausible evolutionary psychology. *Psychological Bulletin, 129,* 819–835.

Light, R. J. (1973). Abused and neglected children in America: A study of alternative policies. *Harvard Educational Review, 43,* 556–598.

Lightsey, O. R., Jr. (2006). Resilience, meaning, and well-being. *Counseling Psychologist, 34,* 96–107.

Lilienfeld, S. O., Gershon, J., Duke, M., Marion, L., & de Waal, F. B. M. (1999). A preliminary investigation of the construct of psychopathic personality (psychopathy) in chimpanzees (*Pan troglodytes*). *Journal of Comparative Psychology, 113,* 365–375.

Linedecker, C., & Burt, W. (1990). *Nurses who kill.* New York: Pinnacle Books.

Lingren, H. G. (2001). *Dating violence and acquaintance assault.* Nebraska Cooperative Extension. University of Nebraska: Lincoln

Lipsey, M. W., & Wilson, D. B. (1998). Effective interventions with serious juvenile offenders: A synthesis of research. In R. Loeber & D. P. Farrington (Eds.), *Serious and violent juvenile offenders: Risk factors and successful intervention.* Thousand Oaks, CA: Sage.

Lipton, D. N., McDonel, E. C., & McFall, R. M. (1987). Heterosocial perception in rapists. *Journal of Consulting and Clinical Psychology, 55,* 17–21.

Litwack, T. R., & Schlesinger, L. B. (1999). Dangerous risk assessments: Research, legal, and clinical considerations. In A. K. Hess & I. B. Weiner (Eds.), *The handbook of forensic psychology* (2nd ed.). New York: Wiley.

Liu, J., Raine, A., Venables, P. H., & Mednick, S. A. (2004). Malnutrition at age 3 years and exernalizing behavior at ages 8, 11, and 17 years. *American Journal of Psychiatry, 161,* 2005–2013.

Lizotte, A., & Sheppard, D. (2001, July). *Gun use by male juveniles: Research and prevention.* Washington, DC: U.S. Department of Justice, office of Juvenile Justice and Delinquency Prevention.

Loeber, R. (1990). Development and risk factors of juvenile antisocial behavior and delinquency. *Clinical Psychology Review, 10,* 1–41.

Loeber, R., Farrington, D. P., & Petechuk, D. (2003, May). Child delinquency: Early intervention and prevention. *Child Delinquency Bulletin Series.* Washington, DC: U.S. Department of Justice, Office of Juvenile Justice and Delinquency Prevention.

Loeber, R., Farrington, D. P., Stouthamer-Loeber, M., & Van Kammen, W. B. (1998). *Antisocial behavior and mental health problems: Explanatory factors in childhood and adolescence.* Mahmah, NJ: Lawrence Erlbaum.

Loeber, R., Lahey, B. B., & Thomas, C. (1991). The diagnostic conundrum of oppositional defiant disorder and conduct disorder. *Journal of Abnormal Psychology, 100,* 379–390.

Loeber, R., & Stouthamer-Loeber, M. (1986). Family factors as correlates and predictors of juvenile conduct problems and delinquency. In N. Morris & M. Tonry (Eds.), *Crime and justice: An annual review of research* (Vol. 7). Chicago, IL: University of Chicago Press.

Loeber, R., & Stouthamer-Loeber, M. (1998). Development of juvenile aggression and violence: Some common misconceptions and controversies. *American Psychologist, 53,* 242–259.

Loehlin, J. C. (1992). *Genes and environment in personality development.* Newbury Park, CA: Sage.

Lombardo, V. S., & Lombardo, E. F. (1991). The link between learning disabilities and juvenile delinquency: Fact or fiction? *International Journal of Biosocial and Medical Research, 13,* 112–117.

Longo, R. F., Bird, S., Stevenson, W. F., & Fiske, J. A. (1995). *1994 nationwide survey of treatment programs and models.* Brandon, VT: Safer Society Program and Press.

Lonsway, K. A., & Fitzgerald, L. F. (1994). Rape myths: In review. *Psychology of Woman Quarterly, 18,* 133–164.

Lorber, M. F. (2004). Psychophysiology of aggression, psychopathy, and conduct problems: A meta-analysis. *Psychological Bulletin, 130,* 531–552.

Lorenz, A. R., & Newman, J. P. (2002). Deficient response modulation and emotion processing in low-anxious caucasian psychopathic offenders: Results from a lexical decision task. *Emotion, 2,* 91–104.

Lorenz, K. (1966). *On aggression.* New York: Harcourt Brace Jovanovich.

Lottes, I. L. (1988). Sexual socialization and attitudes toward rape. In A. W. Burgess (Ed.), *Rape and sexual assault II.* New York: Garland Publishing.

Loukas, A., Zucker, R. A., Fitzgerald, H. F., & Krull, J. L. (2003). Developmental trajectories of descriptive behavior problems among sons of alcoholics: Effects of parent psychopathology, family conflict, and child undercontrol. *Journal of Abnormal Psychology, 112,* 119–131.

Loza, W., Dhaliwal, G., Kroner, D. G., & Loza-Fanous, A. (2000). Reliability, construct, and concurrent validity of the Self-Appraisal Questionnaire. *Criminal Justice and Behavior, 27,* 356–374.

Lubenow, G. C. (1983, June 27). When kids kill their parents. *Newsweek, 35–36.*

Lumley, V. A., McNeil, C. B., Herschell, A. D., & Bahl, A. B. (2002). An examination of gender differences among young children with disruptive behavior disorders. *Child Study Journal, 32,* 89–100.

Luxenburg, J. (2000). Prostitution. In N. H. Rafter (Ed.), *Encyclopedia of women and crime.* Phoenix: Oryx Press.

Lykken, D. T. (1955). *A study of anxiety in the sociopathic personality* (Doctoral dissertation, University of Minnesota). Ann Arbor, MI: University Microfilms, No. 55–944.

Lykken, D. T. (1957). A study of anxiety in the sociopathic personality. *Journal of Abnormal and Social Psychology, 55,* 6–10.

Lykken, D. T. (1978). The psychopath and the lie detector. *Psychophysiology, 15,* 137–142.

Lykken, D. T., & Venables, P. H. (1971). Direct measurement of skin conductance: A proposal for standardization. *Psychophysiology, 8,* 856–872.

Lynam, D. R. (1998). Early identification of the fledgling psychopath: Locating the psychopathic child in the current nomenclature. *Journal of Abnormal Psychology, 107,* 566–575.

Lynam, D., Moffitt, T., & Stouthamer-Loeber, M. (1993). Explaining the relation between IQ and delinquency: Class, race, test motivation, school failure, or self control? *Journal of Abnormal Psychology, 102,* 187–196.

Maccoby, E. E. (1986). Social groupings in childhood. In D. Olweus, J. Block, & M. Radke-Yarrow (Eds.), *Development of antisocial and prosocial behavior: Research, theories, and issues.* New York: Academic Press.

MacCoun, R., Kilmer, B., & Reuter, P. (2003, July). *Research on drugs-crime linkages: The next generation. NIJ Special Report: Toward a drug and crime research agenda for the 21st century.* Washington, DC: National Institute of Justice.

MacDonald, J. M. (1977). *Bombers and firesetters.* Springfield, IL: C. C Thomas.

MacKenzie, D. L., & Hebert, E. (Eds.). (1995). *Correctional boot camps: A tough intermediate sanction.* Washington, DC: National Institute of Justice.

Mahoney, M. J., & Lyddon, W. J. (1988). Recent developments in cognitive approaches to counseling and psychotherapy. *Counseling Psychologist, 16,* 190–234.

Maker, A. H., Kemmelmeier, M., & Peterson, C. (1998). Long-term psychological consequences in women witnessing parental physical conflict and experiencing abuse in childhood. *Journal of Interpersonal Violence, 13,* 574–589.

Malamuth, N. M. (1981). Rape proclivity among males. *Journal of Social Issues, 37,* 138–157.

Malamuth, N. M. (1989). The attraction to sexual aggression scale: Part one. *Journal of Sex Research, 26,* 26–49.

Malamuth, N. M., & Check, J. V. P. (1981). The effects of violent-sexual movies: A field experiment. *Journal of Research in Personality, 15,* 436–446.

Malamuth, N. M., Check, J. V. P., & Briere, J. (1986). Sexual arousal in response to aggression: Ideological, aggressive, and sexual correlates. *Journal of Personality and Social Psychology, 50,* 330–340.

Malamuth, N. M., Haber, S., & Feshbach, S. (1980). Testing hypothesis regarding rape: Exposure to sexual violence, sex differences, and the "normality" of rape. *Journal of Research in Personality, 14,* 121–137.

Malamuth, N. M., Heim, M., & Feshbach, S. (1980). The sexual responsiveness of college students to rape depictions: Inhibitory and disinhibitory effects. *Journal of Personality and Social Psychology, 38,* 399–408.

Mann, C. R. (1993). Maternal filicide of preschoolers. In A. V. Wilson (Ed.), *Homicide: The victim/offender connection.* Cincinnati, OH: Anderson.

Mann, J., Arango, V., & Underwood, M. (1990). Serotonin and suicidal behavior. *Annals of the New York Academy of Sciences, 600,* 476–485.

Marques, J. K., & Nelson, C. (1989). Elements of high-risk situations for sex offenders. In D. R. Laws (Ed.), *Relapse prevention with sex offenders.* New York: Guilford.

Marsella, A. J. (2004). Reflections on international terrorism: Issues, concepts, and directions. In F. M. Moghaddam & A. J. Marsella (Eds.), *Understanding terrorism: Psychosocial roots, consequences, and interventions.* Washington, DC: American Psychological Association.

Marshall, C. E., Benton, D., & Brazier, J. M. (2000). Elder abuse: Using clinical tools to identify clues of mistreatment. *Geriatrics, 55,* 42–53.

Marshall, L. A., & Cooke, D. J. (1999). The childhood experiences of psychopaths: A retrospective study of familial and societal factors. *Journal of Personality Disorders, 13,* 211–225.

Marshall, W. L. (1988). The use of sexually explicit stimuli by rapists, child molesters, and nonoffenders. *Journal of Sex Research, 25,* 267–288.

Marshall, W. L., & Barbaree, H. E. (1988). An outpatient treatment program for child molesters. In R. A. Prentky and V. L. Quinsey (Eds.), *Human sexual aggression: Current perspectives.* New York: New York Academy of Sciences.

Marshall, W. L., Barbaree, H. E., & Fernandez, M. (1995). Some aspects of social competence in sexual offenders. *Sexual Abuse, 7,* 113–127.

Marshall, W. L., & Christie, M. M. (1981). Pedophilia and aggression. *Criminal Justice and Behavior, 8,* 145–158.

Marshall, W. L., & Mazzucco, A. (1995). Self-esteem and parental attachments in child molesters. *Sexual Abuse, 7,* 229–285.

Martinez, R., Jr. (2002). *Latino homicide: Immigration, violence, and community.* New York: Routledge.

Martinson, R. M. (1974). What works—questions and answers about prison reform. *Public Interest, 35,* 22–54.

Maslow, A. H. (1954). *Motivation and personality.* New York: Harper.

Matheny, A. P. (1989). Children's behavioral inhibition over age and across situations: Genetic similarity for a trait during change. *Journal of Personality, 57,* 215–235.

Mathews, J. K., Hunter, J. A., & Vuz, I. (1997). Juvenile female sexual offenders: Clinical characteristics and treatment issues. *Sexual Abuse: A Journal of Research and Treatment, 9,* 187–199.

Maxwell, C. D., Robinson, A. L., & Post, L. A. (2003). The nature and predictors or sexual victimization and offending among adolescents. *Journal of Youth and Adolescence, 32,* 465–478.

Maxwell, J. C. (2004). *Patterns of club drug use in the U.S., 2004.* Austin, TX: The Center for Excellence in Drug Epidemiology, The Gulf Coast Addition Technology Transfer Center, University of Texas.

Mayes, L. C. (1999). Developing brain and in utero cocaine exposure: Effects on neural ontogeny. *Development and Psychopathology, 11,* 685–714.

Mazerolle, P., Brame, R., Paternoster, R., Piquero, A., & Dean, C. (2000). Onset age, persistence, and offending versatiltiy: Comparisons across gender. *Criminology, 38,* 1143–1172.

Mazulis, A. H., Hyde, J. S., & Clark, R. (2004). Father involvement moderates the effect of maternal depression during a child's infancy on child behavior problems in kindergarten. *Journal of Family Psychology, 18,* 575–588.

McCabe, K. M., Hough, R., Wood, P. A., & Yeh, M. (2001). Childhood and adolescent onset conduct disorder: A test of the developmental taxonomy. *Journal of Abnormal Child Psychology, 29,* 305–316.

McCabe, K. M., Rodgers, C., Yeh, M., & Hough, R. (2004). Gender differences in childhood onset conduct disorder. *Development and Psychopathology, 16,* 179–192.

McCaghy, C. H. (1967). Child molesters: A study of their careers as deviants. In M. Clinard & R. Quinney (Eds.), *Criminal behavior systems: A typology.* New York: Holt, Rinehart & Winston.

McCaghy, C. H. (1980). *Crime in American society.* New York: Macmillan.

McCandless, B. R., Persons, W. S., & Roberts, A. (1972). Perceived opportunity, delinquency, race and body build among delinquent youth. *Journal of Consulting and Clinical Psychology, 38,* 281–287.

McCarthy, J. (2003, November 29). Police link 2 shootings on stretch of highway. *Boston Globe,* pp. 1, 13.

McClearn, G. E., & DeFries, J. C. (1973). *Introduction to behavioral genetics.* San Francisco, CA: W. H. Freeman.

McClelland, G. M., Teplin, L. A., & Abram, K. M. (2004, June). Detection and prevalence of substance abuse among juvenile detainees. *Juvenile Justice Bulletin.* Washington, DC: Office of Justice Programs, Office of Juvenile Justice and Delinquency Prevention.

McClosky, L. A., Figueredo, A. J., & Koss, M. P. (1995). The effects of systemic family violence on children's mental health. *Child Development, 66,* 1239–1261.

McCord, D. (1987). Syndromes, profiles and other mental exotica: A new approach to the admissibility of nontraditional psychological evidence in criminal cases. *Oregon Law Review, 66,* 19–108.

McCord, W., McCord, J., & Zola, I. K. (1959). *Origins of crime: A new evaluation of the Cambridge-Somerville Youth Study.* New York: Columbia University Press.

McElroy, S. L., Pope, H. G., Hudson, J. I., Keck, P. E., & White, K. L. (1991). Kleptomania: A report of 20 cases. *American Journal of Psychiatry, 148,* 652–657.

McGinley, H., & Paswark, R. A. (1989). National survey of the frequency and success of the insanity plea and alternate pleas. *Journal of Psychiatry and Law, 17,* 205–221.

McKee, G. R., & Shea, S. J. (1998). Maternal filicide: A cross-national comparison. *Journal of Clinical Psychology, 54,* 679–687.

McKnight, L. R., & Loper, A. B. (2002). The effect of risk and resilience factors on the prediction of delinquency in adolescent girls. *School Psychology International, 23,* 186–198.

McShane, D. A., & Plas, J. M. (1984a). Response to a critique of the McShane & Plas review of American Indian performance on the Wecshler Intelligence Scales. *School Psychology Review, 13,* 83–88.

McShane, D. A., & Plas, J. M. (1984b). The cognitive functioning of American Indian children: Moving from the WISC to the WISC-R. *School Psychology Review, 13,* 61–73.

Meadows, S. (2006, July 17). Murder on their minds. *Newsweek,* pp. 28–29.

Mechoulam, R. (1970). Marihuana chemistry. *Science, 168,* 1159–1166.

Mednick, S. A., Gabrielli, W. F., & Hutchings, B. (1984). Genetic influences in criminal convictions: Evidence from an adoption cohort. *Science, 234,* 891–894.

Mednick, S. A., Gabrielli, W. F., & Hutchings, B. (1987). Genetic factors in the etiology of criminal behavior. In S. A. Mednick, T. E. Moffitt, & S. A. Stack (Eds.), *The causes of crime: New biological approaches.* Cambridge, Eng.: Cambridge University Press.

Mednick, S. A., & Kandel, E. (1988). Genetic and perinatal factors in violence. In S. A. Mednick & T. Moffitt (Eds.), *Biological contributions to crime causation.* Dordrecht, North Holland: Martinus Nijhoff.

Megargee, E. I. (1966). Undercontrolled and overcontrolled personality types in extreme antisocial aggression. *Psychological Monographs, 80,* No. 3.

Megargee, E. I. (1976). Population density and disruptive behavior in prison settings. In A. K. Cohen, F. G. Cole, & R. G. Bailey (Eds.), *Prison violence.* Lexington, MA: Lexington Books.

Megargee, E. I. (1982). Psychological determinants and correlates of criminal violence. In M. E. Wolfgang & N. A. Weinder (Eds.), *Criminal violence.* Beverly Hills, CA: Sage.

Megargee, E. I., & Bohn, M. J. (1977). Empirically determined characteristics of the ten types. *Criminal Justice and Behavior, 4,* 149–210.

Megargee, E. I., & Bohn, M. J. (1979). *Classifying criminal offenders.* Newbury Park, CA: Sage.

Meloy, J. R. (1998). The psychology of stalking. In J. R. Meloy (Ed.), *The psychology of stalking: Clinical and forensic perspectives.* San Diego, CA: Academic Press.

Melton, G. B., Petrila, J., Poythress, N. G., & Slobogin, C. (1997). *Psychological evaluations for the courts: A handbook for mental health professionals and lawyers* (2nd ed.). New York: Guilford.

Mercy, J., & Salzman, L. (1989). Fatal violence among spouses in the United States, 1986–1987. *American Journal of Public Health, 79,* 595–599.

Merry, S., & Hansent, L. (2000). Intruders, pilferers, raiders, and invaders: The interpersonal dimension of burglary. In D. Canter & L. Alison (Eds.), *Profiling property crimes.* Dartmouth, Eng.: Ashgate.

Messner, S., & Rosenfeld, R. (1994). *Crime and the American dream.* Belmont, CA: Wadsworth.

Meyer, T. P. (1972). The effects of sexually arousing and violent films on aggressive behavior. *Journal of Sex Research, 8,* 324–333.

Miczek, K. A., DeBold, J. F., Haney, M., Tidey, J., Vivian, J., & Weerts, E. M. (1994). Alcohol, drugs of abuse, aggression, and violence. In A. J. Reiss & J. A. Roth (Eds.), *Understanding and preventing violence. Vol. 3. Social influences.* Washington, DC: National Academy Press.

Middlebrook, P. M. (1974). *Social psychology and modern life.* New York: Knopf.

Milgram, S. (1963). Behavioral study of obedience. *Journal of Abnormal and Social Psychology, 67,* 371–378.

Milgram, S. (1974). *Obedience to authority.* New York: Harper & Row.

Milgram, S. (1977). *The individual in a social world.* Reading, MA: Addison-Wesley.

Miller, J. L. (1991). Prostitution in contemporary American society. In E. Graverholtz & M. A. Koralewski (Eds.), *Sexual coercion: A sourcebook on its nature, causes, and prevention.* Lexington, MA: Lexington Books.

Miller, M., Hennenway, D., & Solop, D. (2002). Road rage in Arizona: Armed and dangerous. *Accident Analysis and Prevention, 34,* 807–814.

Miller, N., Pedersen, W. C., Earleywine, M., & Pollack, V. E. (2003). A theoretical model of triggered displaced aggression. *Personality and Social Psychology Review, 7,* 75–97.

Miller, R. D. (2003). Hospitalization of criminal defendants for evaluation of competence to stand trial or for restoration of competence: Clinical and legal issues. *Behavioral Sciences & the Law, 21,* 369–391.

Miller-Johnson, S., Coie, J. D., Maumary-Gremaud, A., Bierman, K., & the Conduct Problems Prevention Research Group. (2002). Peer rejection and aggression and early starter models of conduct disorder. *Journal of Abnormal Child Psychology, 30,* 217–230.

Miner, M. H., Day, D. M., & Nafpaktitis, M. K. (1989). Assessment of coping skills: Development of situational competency test. In D. R. Laws (Ed.), *Relapse prevention with sex offenders.* New York: Guilford.

Miron, M. S., & Goldstein. A. P. (1978). *Hostage.* Kalamazoo, MI: Behaviordelia.

Mischel, W. (1976). *Introduction to personality* (2nd ed.). New York: Holt, Rinehart & Winston.

Mizell, L. (1995). *Aggressive driving.* Washington, DC: AAA Foundation for Traffic Safety.

Moffitt, T. E. (1990a). The neuropsychology of juvenile delinquency: A critical review. In M. Tonry & N. Morris (Eds.), *Crime and justice: A review of research.* Chicago, IL: University of Chicago Press.

Moffitt, T. E. (1990b). Juvenile delinquency and attention deficit disorder: Boys' developmental trajectories from age 13 to age 15. *Child Development, 61,* 893–910.

Moffitt, T. E. (1993a). Adolescence-limited and life-course-persistent antisocial behavior: A developmental taxonomy. *Psychological Review, 100,* 674–701.

Moffitt, T. E. (1993b). The neuropsychology of conduct disorder. *Development and Psychopathology, 5,* 135–151.

Moffitt, T. E. (2003). Life-course-persistent and adolescent-limited antisocial behavior: A 10-year research review and research agenda. In B. B. Lahey, T. E. Moffitt, and A. Caspi (Eds.), *Causes of conduct disorder and juvenile delinquency.* New York: Guilford.

Moffitt, T. E. (2005). The new look of behavioral genetics in developmental psychopathology: Gene-environment interplay in antisocial behaviors. *Psychological Bulletin, 131,* 533–534.

Moffitt, T. E., & Caspi, A. (2001). Childhood predictors differentiate life-course persistent and adolescence-limited antisocial pathways among males and females. *Development and Psychopathology, 13,* 355–375.

Moffitt, T. E., Caspi, A., Dickson, N., Silva, P., & Stanton, W. (1996). Childhood-onset versus adolescent-onset antisocial conduct problems in males: Natural history from ages 3 to 18. *Development and Psychopathology, 8,* 399–424.

Moffitt, T. E., Caspi, A., Fawcett, P., Brammer, G. L., Raleigh, M., Yuwiler, A., & Silva, P. (1997). Whole blood serotonin and family background relate to male violence. In A. Raine, P. A. Brennan, D. P. Farrington, S. A. Mednick (Eds.), *Biological bases of violence.* New York: Plenum.

Moffitt, T. E., Caspi, A., Harrington, H., & Milne, B. J. (2002). Males on the life-course-persistent and adolescence-limited antisocial pathways: Follow-up at age 26 years. *Development and Psychopathology, 14,* 179–207.

Moffitt, T. E., Lynam, D. R., & Silva, P. A. (1994). Neuropsychological tests predicting persistent male delinquency. *Criminology, 33,* 111–139.

Moffitt, T. E., & Silva, P. A. (1988). Self-reported delinquency, neuropsychological deficit, and history of attention deficit disorder. *Journal of Abnormal Child Psychology, 16,* 553–569.

Moghaddam, F. M., & Marsella, A. J. (2004a). Preface. In F. M. Moghaddam & A. J. Marsella (Eds.), *Understanding terrorism: Psychosocial roots, consequences, and interventions.* Washington, DC: American Psychological Association.

Moghaddam, F. M., & Marsella, A. J. (2004b). Introduction. In F. M. Moghaddam & A. J. Marsella (Eds.), *Understanding terrorism: Psychosocial roots, consequences, and interventions.* Washington, DC: American Psychological Association.

Mohr, J. W., Turner, R. E., & Jerry, N. B. (1964). *Pedophilia and exhibitionism.* Toronto, ON: University of Toronto Press.

Moll, K. D. (1974). *Arson, vandalism and violence: Law enforcement problems affecting fire departments (LEAA).* Washington, DC: USGPO.

Monahan, J. (1976). The prevention of crime. In J. Monahan (Ed.), *Community mental health and the criminal justice system.* New York: Pergamon Press.

Monahan, J. (1981). *Predicting violent behavior.* Beverly Hills, CA: Sage.

Monahan, J. (1984). The prediction of violent behavior: Toward a second generation of theory and policy. *American Journal of Psychiatry, 141,* 10–15.

Monahan, J. (1988). Risk assessment of violence among the mentally disordered: Generating useful knowledge. *International Journal of Law and Psychiatry, 11,* 249–257.

Monahan, J. (1992). Mental disorder and violent behavior: Perceptions and evidence. *American Psychologist, 47,* 511–521.

Monahan, J. (1996). *Mental illness and violent crime.* NIJ Research Preview. Washington, DC: National Institute of Justice.

Monahan, J., & Geis, G. (1976). Controlling "dangerous" people. *Annals of the American Academy of Political and Social Science, 423,* 142–151.

Monahan, J., & Walker, L. (1990). *Social science and law: Cases and materials* (2nd ed.). Westbury, NY: Foundation Press.

Monahan, J., & Walker, L. (1994). *Social science and law: Cases and materials* (3rd ed.). Waterbury, NY: Foundation Press.

Monahan, T. P. (1957). Family status and the delinquent child: A reappraisal and some new findings. *Social Forces, 35,* 250–258.

Montagu, A. (1973). *Man and aggression* (2nd ed.). London: Oxford University Press.

Montagu, A. (1976). *The nature of human aggression.* New York: Oxford University Press.

Moore, R. H. (1984). Shoplifting in middle America: Patterns and motivational correlates. *International Journal of Offender Therapy and Comparative Criminology, 28,* 53–64.

Moreland, J. (2000). Toxicity of drug abuse—amphetamine designer drugs (ectasy): Mental effects and consequences of a single dose. *Tox Letters,* 147–152.

Morgan, A. B., & Lilienfeld, S. O. (2000). A meta-analytic review of the relation between antisocial behavior and neuropsychological measures of executive function. *Clinical Psychology Review, 20,* 113–146.

Morgan, J. P., & Zimmer, L. (1997). The social pharmacology of smokeable cocaine: Not all it's cracked up to be. In C. Reinarman & H. G. Levine (Eds.), *Crack in America: Demon drugs and social justice.* Berkeley, CA: University of California Press.

Morris, N. (1982). *Madness and the criminal law.* Chicago, IL: University of Chicago Press.

Morris, N., & Miller, M. (1985). Prediction of dangerousness. In M. Tonry & N. Morris (Eds.), *Crime and justice: An annual review of research.* Chicago, IL: University of Chicago Press.

Morse, S. J. (1978). Behavior, morals, and science: An analysis of mental health law. *Southern California Law Review, 51,* 527–654.

Morse, S. J. (1985). Excusing the crazy: The insanity defense reconsidered. *Southern California Law Review, 58,* 777–836.

Morse, S. J. (1986). Why amnesia and the law is not a useful topic. *Behavioral Sciences & the Law, 4,* 99–102.

Mott, J. (1986). Opoid use and burglary. *British Journal of Addiction, 81,* 671–677.

Mounts, N. S. (2002). Parental management of adolescent peer relationships in context: The role of parenting style. *Journal of Family Psychology, 16,* 58–69.

Moyer, K. E. (1976). *The psychobiology of aggression.* New York: Harper & Row.

Mueller, C. W. (1983). Environmental stressors and aggressive behavior. In R. G. Geen & E. I. Donnerstein (Eds.), *Aggression: Theoretical and empirical reviews* (Vol. 2). New York: Academic Press.

Mulder, R. T., Wells, J. E., Joyce, P. R., & Bushnell, J. A. (1994). Antisocial women. *Journal of Personality Disorders, 8,* 279–287.

Müller, J. L., Sommer, M., Wagner, V., Lange, K., Taschler, H., Röder, C. H. et al. (2003). Abnormalities in emotion processing within cortical and subcortical regions in criminal psychopaths: Evidence from a functional magnetic resonance imaging study using pictures with emotional content. *Biological Psychiatry, 54,* 152–162.

Mulvey, E. P., Arthur, M. W., & Reppucci, N. D. (1993). The prevention and treatment of juvenile delinquency: A review of the research. *Clinical Psychology Review, 13,* 133–167.

Mumley, D. L., Tillbrook, C. E., & Grisso, T. (2003). Five year research update (1996–2000): Evaluations for competence to stand trial (adjudicative competence). *Behavioral Sciences & the Law, 21,* 329–350.

Mumola, C. J. (1999). *Substance abuse and treatment, state and federal prisoners.* Washington, DC: Bureau of Justice Statistics.

Murphy, G. H., & Clare, C. H. (1996). Analysis of motivation in people with mild learning disabilities (mental handicap) who set fires. *Psychology, Crime, & Law, 2,* 153–164.

Murray, J. B. (1997). Munchausen syndrome/Munchausen syndrome by proxy. *The Journal of Psychology, 131,* 343–350.

Murrie, D. C., & Cornell, D. G., Kaplan, S., McConville, D., & Levy-Elkon, A. (2004). Psychopathy scores and violence among juvenile offenders: A multi-measure study. *Behavioral Sciences & the Law, 22,* 49–67.

Myers, D. G. (1996). *Social psychology* (5th ed.). New York: McGraw-Hill.

Myers, D. L. (2000). *Excluding violent youths from juvenile court: The effectiveness of legislative waiver*. Unpublished dissertation. University of Maryland, Department of Criminology and Criminal Justice. Available. www.preventingcrime.org.

Myers, W. C. (1992). What treatments do we have for children and adolescents who have killed. *Bulletin of the American Academy of Psychiatry and Law, 20*, 47–58.

Myers, W. C., & Blashfield, R. (1997). Psychopathology and personality in juvenile sexual homicide offenders. *Journal of the American Academy of Psychiatry and Law, 25*, 497–508.

Myers, W. C., & Mutch, P. J. (1992). Language disorders in disruptive behaviour disordered homicidal youth. *Journal of Forensic Sciences, 37*, 919–922.

Myers, W. C., & Scott, K. (1998). Psychotic and conduct disorder symptoms in juvenile murderers. *Homicide Studies, 2*, 160–175.

Myers, W. C., Scott, K., Burgess, A. W., & Burgess, A. G. (1995). Psychopathology, biopsychosocial factors, crime characteristics, and classification of 25 homicidal youths. *Journal of the American Academy of Child and Adolescent Psychiatry, 34*, 1483–1489.

Nacci, P. L., Teitelbaum, H. E., & Prather, J. (1977). Population density and inmate misconduct rates in the federal prison system. *Federal Probation, 41*, 26–31.

Nachshon, I. (1983). Hemisphere dysfunction in psychopathy and behavior disorders. In M. Myslobodsky (Ed.), *Hemisyndromes: Psychobiology, neurology, psychiatry*. New York: Academic Press.

Nachshon, I., & Denno, D. (1987). Violent behavior and cerebral hemisphere function. In S. A. Mednick, T. E. Moffitt, & S. A. Stack (Eds.), *The causes of crime: New biological approaches*. Cambridge, Eng.: Cambridge University Press.

Nagin, D. S., & Land, K. C. (1993). Age, criminal careers, and population heterogeneity: Specification and estimation of a nonparametric mixed Poisson model. *Criminology, 31*, 163–189.

Nash, J. R. (1975). *Bloodletters and badmen: Book 3*. New York: Warner Books.

National Adolescent Perpetrator Network. (1988). Preliminary report from the National Task Force on Juvenile Sexual Offending. *Juvenile and Family Court Journal, 38*, 1–67.

National Cable Television Association. (1998). *National Television Violence Study* (Vol. 3). Thousand Oaks, CA: Sage.

National Center for Education Statistics. (2005). *Executive summary: Indicators of school crime and safety, 2003.* Available: www.nces.ed.gov/pubs2004/crime03.

National Center for Juvenile Justice. (2003, July). *Juvenile court statistics 1999*. Washington, DC: U.S. Department of Justice, Office of Juvenile Justice and Delinquency Prevention.

National Center for Victims of Crime. (2000). *Cyberstalking*. Available: www.ncvc/special/cyber_stk.htm.

National Institute of Health. (1999, June). *NIDA news release: Long-term brain injury from use of "ecstasy."* Rockville, MD: National Institute of Drug Abuse. Available: www.nida.nih.gov/MedAdv/99/NR-614b.html.

National Center on Elder Abuse. (1994). *Findings from a national study of domestic elder abuse reports conducted by the National Center on Elder Abuse*. Washington, DC: Department of Health and Human Services.

National Center on Elder Abuse. (1998). *The national elder abuse incidence study 1996: Final report*. Washington, DC: U.S. Department of Health and Human Services.

National Center on Elder Abuse. (1999). *Types of elder abuse in domestic settings*. Washington, DC: Author.

National Commission on Marihuana and Drug Abuse. (1972). *Marihuana: A signal of misunderstanding*. (Appendix, Vol. 1). Washington, DC: USGPO.

National Commission on Marihuana and Drug Abuse. (1973). *Drug use in America: Problem in perspective* (2nd report). Washington, DC: USGPO.

National Drug Intelligence Center. (2001, January). *OxyContin diversion and abuse.* Washington, DC: Author.

National Drug Intelligence Center. (2006, June 5). *Fentanyl: Situation Report.* Washington, DC: U.S. Department of Justice.

National Highway Traffic Safety Administration. (2005, March). *Alcohol involvement in fatal motor vehicle traffic crashes, 2003.* Springfield, VA: Author.

National Information Support and Referral Service (1998). Available: www.ojp.usdoij.gov/nisrs.

National Institute on Alcohol Abuse and Alcoholism. (1990). *Alcohol and health: Neuroscience.* Rockville, MD: USGPO.

National Institute on Alcohol Abuse and Alcoholism. (1997, October). Alcohol, violence, and aggression. *Alcohol Alert.* Rockville, MD: USGPO.

National Institute on Drug Abuse. (1978). Drug abuse and crime. In L. D. Savitz & N. Johnson (Eds.), *Crime in society.* New York: Wiley.

National Institute on Drug Abuse. (1999, May). *Cocaine: Abuse and addiction.* Rockville, MD: USGPO. Available: www.nida.nih.gov/researchreports/cocaine/cocaine.html.

National Institute on Drug Abuse. (2000, June). *Epidemiologic trends in drug abuse.* Rockville, MD: USGPO. Available: www.nida.gov/CEWG/AdvancedRep/6_20ADV/0600adv.html.

National Institute on Drug Abuse. (2002). *Methamphetamine: Abuse and Addiction.* Rockville, MD: U.S. Department of Health and Human Services.

National Institute on Drug Abuse. (2004, November). *Cocaine: Abuse and addiction.* Rockville, MD: U.S. Department of Health and Human Services.

National Institute on Drug Abuse. (2005). *Hallucinogens and dissociative drugs.* Rockville, MD: U.S. Department of Health and Human Services.

National Institute on Drug Abuse and University of Michigan. (2005, December). *Monitoring the Future National survey results on drug use, 1975–2003. Volume II: College students & Adults ages 19–45.* Washington, DC: National Institute on Drug Abuse.

Naudts, K., & Hodgins, S. (2005, December 29). Neurobiological correlates of violent behavior among persons with schizophrenia. *Schizophrenia Bulletin,* 1–11.

Nebylitsyn, V. D., & Gray, J. A. (1972). *Biological bases of individual behavior.* New York: Academic Press.

Nee, C., & Taylor, M. (1988). Residential burglary in the Republic of Ireland: A situational perspective. *Howard Journal,* 27, 105–116.

Needleman, H. L., McFarland, C., Ness, R. B., Fienberg, S. E., & Tobin, M. J. (2002). Bone lead levels in adjudicated delinquents: A case control study. *Neurotoxicology and Teratology, 24,* 711–717.

Neighbors, C., Vietor, N. A., & Knee, C. R. (2002). A motivational model of driving anger and aggression. *Personality and Social Psychology Bulletin, 28,* 324–335.

Neisser, U., et al. (1996). Intelligence: Knowns and unknowns. *American Psychologist, 51,* 77–101.

Nelson, C. A., & Bloom, F. E. (1997). Child development and neuroscience. *Child Development, 68,* 970–987.

Nelson, D. R., Hammen, C., Brennan, P. A., & Ullman, J. B. (2003). The impact of maternal depression in adolescent adjustment: The role of expressed emotion. *Journal of Consulting and Clinical Psychology, 71,* 935–944.

Nelson, D. W. (2003). *On adolescent crime: Trend to end fad justice.* Baltimore, MD: Annie E. Casey Foundation Newsletter.

Nelson, S., & Amir, M. (1975). The hitchhike victim of rape: A research report. In I. Drapkin & E. Viano (Eds.), *Victimology: A new focus* (Vol. 5). Lexington, MA: Lexington Books.

Nettler, G. (1984). *Explaining crime* (3rd ed.). New York: McGraw-Hill.

Neugebauer, R., Hoek, H. W., & Susser, E. (1999). Prenatal exposure to wartime famine and development of antisocial personality disorder in early adulthood. *Journal of the American Medical Association, 4,* 479–481.

Neuman, J.H., & Baron, R. A. (1998). Workplace violence and workplace aggression: Evidence concerning specific forms, potential causes, and preferred targets. *Journal of Management, 24,* 391–419.

Newcomb, A. F., Bukowksi, W. M., & Pattee, L. (1993). Children's peer relations: A meta-analytic review of popular, rejected, neglected, controversial and average sociometric status. *Psychological Bulletin, 113,* 99–128.

Newman, G. (1995). *Just and painful: A case for the corporal punishment of criminals,* (2nd ed.) Monsey, NY: Criminal Justice Press.

Newman, J. P. (1987). Reaction to punishment in extroverts and psychopaths: Implications for the impulsive behavior of disinhibited individuals. *Journal of Research in Personality, 21,* 464–480.

Newman, J. P., & Kosson, D. S. (1986). Passive avoidance learning in psychopathic and nonpsychopathic offenders. *Journal of Abnormal Psychology, 95,* 252–256.

Newman, J. P., Patterson, C. M., Howland, E. W., & Nichols, S. L. (1990). Passive avoidance in psychopaths: The effects of reward. *Personality and Individual Differences, 11,* 1101–1114.

Newman, J. P., Patterson, C. M., & Kosson, D. S. (1987). Response preservation in psychopaths. *Journal of Abnormal Psychology, 96,* 145–148.

Newman, J. P., Schmitt, W. A., & Voss, W. D. (1997). The impact of motivationally neutral cues on psychopathic individuals: Assessing the generality of the response modulation hypothesis. *Journal of Abnormal Psychology, 106,* 563–575.

Nicholson, R. A., & Kugler, K. E. (1991). Competent and incompetent criminal defendants: A quantitative review of comparative research. *Psychological Bulletin, 109,* 355–370.

Nicholson, R. A., & Norwood, S. (2000). The quality of forensic psychological assessments, reports, and testimony: Acknowledging the gap between promise and practice. *Law and Human Behavior, 24,* 9–44.

Nielsen, A. L., Martinez, Jr., R., & Rosenfeld, R. (2005). Firearm use, injury, and lethality in assaultive violence: An examination of ethnic differences. *Homicide Studies, 9,* 83–108.

Nietzel, M. T. (1979). *Crime and its modification: A social learning perspective.* New York: Pergamon.

Nigg, J. T., & Huang-Pollock, C. L. (2003). An early-onset model of the role of executive functions and intelligence in conduct disorder/delinquency. In B. B. Lahey, T. E. Moffitt, and A. Caspi (Eds.), *Causes of conduct disorder and juvenile delinquency.* New York: Guilford.

Nisbett, R. E. (2005). Heredity, environment, and race differences in IQ. *Psychology, Public Policy, and Law, 11,* 302–310.

Noesner, G. W., & Dolan, J. T. (1992, August). First responder negotiation training. *FBI Law Enforcement Bulletin,* 1–4.

Obeidallah, D. A., & Earls, F. J. (1999). *Adolescent girls: The role of depression in the development of delinquency.* Washington, DC: National Institute of Justice.

O'Donnell, J., Hawkins, J. D., & Abbott, R. D. (1995). Predicting serious delinquency and substance abuse among aggressive boys. *Journal of Consulting and Clinical Psychology, 63,* 529–537.

Office of Applied Studies. (2004). *Drug abuse warning network, 2003.* Rockville, MD: U.S. Department of Health and Human Services.

Office of National Drug Control Policy. (1999a, November). *Gamma Hydroxybutyrate (GHB).* Washington, DC: Executive Office of the President. Available: www.whitehousedrugpolicy.gov.

Office of National Drug Control Policy. (1999b, May). *Methamphetamine.* Washington, DC: Executive Office of the President. Available: www.whitehousedrugpolicy.gov.

Office of National Drug Control Policy. (1999c, April). *Drug data summary.* Available: www.whitehousedrugpolicy.gov.

Office of National Drug Control Policy. (2003b, November). *Methamphetamine.* Washington, DC: Author.

Office of National Drug Control Policy. (2003d, November). *Drug data summary.* Washington, DC: Author.

Office of National Drug Control Policy. (2003e, October). *Marijuana.* Washington, DC: Author.

Office of National Drug Control Policy. (2003f, November). *Cocaine.* Washington, DC: Author.

Office of National Drug Control Policy, (2003g, June). *Heroin.* Washington, DC: Author.

Office of National Drug Control Policy. (2005, November). *Marijuana.* Washington, DC: Author.

Office of National Drug Control Policy. (2006a, July). *Marijuana.* Washington, DC: Author.

Office of National Drug Control Policy. (2006b, July). *Methamphetamine.* Washington, DC: Author.

Office of National Drug Control Policy. (2006c, June). *Cocaine.* Washington, DC: Author.

Office of National Drug Control Policy. (2006d, June). *MDMA.* Washington, DC: Author.

Office of National Drug Control Policy. (2006e, May). *Heroin.* Washington, DC: Author.

Office of National Drug Control Policy. (2006f, July). *OxyContin.* Washington, DC: Author.

Office of National Drug Control Policy. (2006g, July). *Club drugs.* Washington, DC: Author.

Offord, D. R., Boyle, M. C., & Racine, Y. A. (1991). The epidemiology of antisocial behavior in childhood and adolescence. In D. J. Pepler & K. H. Rubin (Eds.), *The development and treatment of childhood aggression.* Hillsdale, NJ: Erlbaum.

Offord, D. R., Chmura Kraemeer, H., Kazdin, A. E., Jensen, P. S., & Harrington, R. (1998). Lowering the burden of suffering from child psychiatric disorder: Trade-offs among clinical, targeted, and universal interventions. *Journal of the American Academy of Child & Adolescent Psychiatry, 37,* 686–694.

Ogloff, J. R., & Wong, S. (1990) Electrodermal and cardiovascular evidence of a coping response in psychopaths. *Criminal Justice and Behavior, 17,* 231–245.

Ohlin, L. E. (1983). The future of juvenile justice policy and research. *Crime and Delinquency, 29,* 463–472.

Ohlin, L. E., & Tonry, M. (1989). Family violence in perspective. In L. Ohlin & M. Tonry (Eds.), *Family violence* (Vol. 11). Chicago, IL: University of Chicago Press.

Olson, S. L., Sameroff, A. J., Kerr, D. C. R., Lopez, N. L., & Wellman, H. M. (2005). Developmental foundations of externalizing problems in young children: The role of effortful control. *Development and Psychopathology, 17,* 25–45.

Ondrovik, J., & Hamilton, D. (1991). Credibility of victims diagnosed as multiple personality: A case study. *American Journal of Forensic Psychology, 9,* 13–17.

O'Neill, M. L., Lidz, V., & Heilbrun, K. (2003). Adolescents with psychopathic characteristics in a substance abusing cohort: Treatment process and outcomes. *Law and Human Behavior, 27,* 299–313.

Orne, M. T., Dinges, D. F., & Orne, E. C. (1984). On the differential diagnosis of multiple personality in the forensic context. *International Journal of Clinical and Experimental Hypnosis, 32,* 118–169.

Orris, J. B. (1969). Visual monitoring performance in three subgroups of male delinquents. *Journal of Abnormal Psychology, 74,* 227–229.

O'Toole, M. E. (2000). *The school shooter: A threat assessment perspective.* Quantico, VA: Critical Incident Response Group, National Center for the Analysis of Violent Crime.

Owen, B. (2000). Prison security. In N. H. Rafter (Ed.), *The encyclopedia of women and crime.* Phoenix: Oryx Press.

Pagani, L., Larocque, D., Vitaro, F., & Tremblay, R. E. (2003). Verbal and physical abuse toward mothers: The role of family configuration, environment, and coping strategies. *Journal of Youth and Adolescence, 32,* 215–222.

Pagelow, M. D. (1989). The incidence and prevalence of criminal abuse of other family members. In L. Ohlin & M. Tonry (Eds.), *Family violence* (Vol. 11). Chicago, IL: University of Chicago Press.

Palmer, J. W., & Palmer, S. E. (1999). *Constitutional rights of prisoners* (6th ed.). Cincinnati, OH: Anderson Publishing.

Parker, H., & Newcombe, R. (1987). Heroin use and acquisitive crime in an English community. *British Journal of Sociology, 38,* 331–350.

Parker, J. G., & Asher, S. R. (1987). Peer relations and later personal adjustment: Are low-accepted children at risk? *Psychological Bulletin, 102,* 357–389.

Patrick, C. J., Bradley, M. M., & Lang, P. J. (1993). Emotion in the criminal psychopath: Start reflex modulation. *Journal of Abnormal Psychology, 102,* 82–92.

Patrick, C. J., Zempolich, K.A., & Levenston, G. K. (1997). Emotionality and violent behavior in psychopaths: A biosocial analysis. In A. Raine, P. A. Brennan, D. P. Farrington, & S. A. Mednick (Eds.), *Biosocial bases of violence.* New York: Plenum.

Patterson, G. R. (1982). *Coercive family processes.* Eugene, OR: Castalia Press.

Patterson, G. R. (1986). Performance models for antisocial boys. *American Psychologist, 41,* 432–444.

Patterson, G. R., & Yoerger, K. (2002). A developmental model for early- and late-onset delinquency. In J. B. Reid, G. R. Patterson & J. J. Snyder (Eds.), *Antisocial behavior in children and adults: A developmental analysis and the Oregon model for intervention.* Washington, DC: American Psychological Association.

Paulus, P. B. (1988). *Prison crowding: A psychological perspective.* New York: Springer-Verlag.

Paull, D. (1993). *Fitness to stand trial.* Springfield, IL: C. C Thomas.

Pearl, P. T. (1995). Identifying and responding to Munchausen syndrome by proxy. *Early Child Development and Care, 106,* 177–185.

Penfield, W. (1975). *The mystery of the mind.* Princeton, NJ: Princeton University Press.

Penrod, S. (1983). *Social psychology.* Englewood Cliffs, NJ: Prentice Hall.

Pepler, D. J., & Slaby, R. G. (1994). Theoretical and development perspectives on youth and violence. In L. D. Eron, J. H. Gentry, & P. Schlegel (Eds.), *Reason to hope: A psychosocial perspective on violence and youth.* Washington, DC: American Psychological Association.

Perkins, C. (2003, September). *Weapon use and violent crime.* Washington, DC: U.S. Department of Justice, Bureau of Justice Statistics.

Peters, S. D., Wyatt, G. E., & Finkelhor, D. (1986). Prevalence. In D. Finkelhor (Ed.), *Sourcebook on child sexual abuse.* Beverly Hills, CA: Sage.

Peterson, M. A., Braiker, H. B., & Polich, S. M. (1981). *Who commits crimes?* Cambridge, MA: Oelgeschlager, Gunn & Hain.

Petraitis, J., Flay, B. R., & Miller, T. Q. (1995). Reviewing theories of adolescent substance abuse: Organizing pieces in the puzzle. *Psychological Bulletin, 117,* 67–86.

Petras, H., Schaeffer, C. M., Ialongo, N., Hubbard, S., Muthén., Lambert, S. F., Poduska, J., & Kellam, S. (2004). When the course of aggressive behavior in childhood does not predict antisocial behavior outcomes in adolescence and young adulthood: An examination of potential explanatory variables. *Development and Psychopathology, 16,* 919–941.

Pettit, G. S., Laird, R. D., Bates, J. E., & Dodge, K. A. (1997). Patterns of after-school care in middle childhood: Risk factors and developmental outcomes. *Merrill-Palmer Quarterly, 43,* 515–538.

Pihl, R. O., & Peterson, J. B. (1993). Alcohol, serotonin, and aggression. *Alcohol, Health & Research World, 17,* 113–116.

Pillemer, K., & Finkelhor, D. (1988). The prevalence of elder abuse: A random sample survey. *Gerontologist, 28,* 51–57.

Pillemer, K., & Suitor, J. J. (1988). Elder abuse. In V. B. van Hasselt, R. L. Morrison, A. S. Morrison, A. S. Bellak, & M. Hersen (Eds.), *Handbook of family violence.* New York: Plenum.

Pillmann, F., Rohde, A., Ullrich, S., Draba, S., Sannemueller, U., & Marnerous, A. (1999). Violence, criminal behavior, and the EEG: Significance of left hemispheric focal abnormalities. *Journal of Neuropsychiatry & Clinical Neurosciences, 11,* 454–457.

Pincus, J. H. (1980). Can violence be a manifestation of epilepsy? *Neurology, 30,* 304–306.

Pine, D. S., Shaffer, D., Schonfeld, I. S., & Davies, M. (1997). Minor physical anomalies: Modifiers of environmental risks for psychiatric impairment? *Journal of the American Academy of Child and Adolescent Psychiatry, 36,* 395–404.

Pinizzotto, A. J. (1984). Forensic psychology: Criminal personality profiling. *Journal of Police Science and Administration, 12,* 32–40.

Pinizzotto, A. J., & Finkel, N. J. (1990). Criminal personality profiling: An outcome and process study. *Law and Human Behavior, 14,* 215–234.

Pithers, W. D., Beal, L. S., Armstrong, J., & Petty, J. (1989). Identification of risk factors through clinical interviews and analysis of records. In D. R. Laws (Ed.), *Relapse prevention with sex offenders.* New York: Guilford.

Pithers, W. D., Kashima, K. M., Cumming, G. F., Beal, L. S., & Buell, M. M. (1988). Relapse prevention of sexual aggression. In R. A. Prentky & V. L. Quinsey (Eds.), *Human sexual aggression: Current perspectives.* New York: New York Academy of Sciences.

Pithers, W. D., Marques, J. K., Gibat, C. C., & Marlatt, G. A. (1983). Relapse prevention with sexual aggressives. In J. G. Greer & I. R. Stuart (Eds.), *The sexual aggressor: Current perspectives on treatment.* New York: Van Nostrand Reinhold.

Pleck, E. (1989). Criminal approaches to family violence, 1640–1980. In L. Ohlin & M. Tonry (Eds.), *Family violence* (Vol. 11). Chicago, IL: University of Chicago Press.

Plomin, R. (1986). *Development, genetics, and psychology.* Hillsdale, NJ: Erlbaum.

Plummer, D. L., & Graziano, W. G. (1987). Impact of grade retention on the social development of elementary school children. *Developmental Psychology, 23,* 267–275.

Podnieks, E., Pillemer, K., & Nicolson, J. P., (1990). *National survey on abuse of the elderly in Canada: Final report.* Toronto, ON: Ryerson Polytechnic Institute.

Pope, C. E. (1977a). *Crime-specific analysis: An empirical examination of burglary offender characteristics (LEAA).* Washington, DC: USGPO.

Pope, C. E. (1977b). *Crime-specific analysis: The characteristics of burglary incidents (LEAA).* Washington, DC: USGPO.

Pope, C. E. (1977c). *Crime-specific analysis: An empirical examination of burglary offense and offense characteristics (LEAA).* Washington, DC: USGPO.

Popova, N., Voitenko, N., Kulikov, A., & Augustinovich, D. (1991). Evidence for the involvement of central serotonin in mechanism of domestication of silver foxes. *Psychopharmacology: Biochemistry and Behavior, 40,* 751–756.

Porter, S., Birt, A. R., & Boer, D. P. (2001). Investigation of the criminal and conditional release histories of Canadian federal offenders as a function of psychopathy and age. *Law and Human Behavior, 25,* 647–661.

Porter, S., Fairweather, D., Drugge, J., Herve, H., Birt, A. R., & Boer, D. (2000). Profiles of psychopathy in incarcerated sexual offenders. *Criminal Justice and Behavior, 27,* 216–233.

Porter, S., Woodworth, M., Earle, J., Drugge, J., and Boer, D. (2003). Characteristics of sexual homicides committed by psychopathic and nonpsychopathic offenders. *Law and Human Behavior, 27,* 459–470.

Posner, J. K., & Vandell, D. L. (1999). After-school activities and the development of low-income urban children: A longitudinal study. *Developmental Psychology, 35,* 868–879.

Postmes, T., & Spears, R. (1998). Deindividuation and antinormative behavior: A meta-analysis. *Psychological Bulletin, 123,* 238–259.

Potoczniak, M. J., Mourot, J. E., Crosbie-Burnett, M., & Potoczniak, D. J. (2003). Legal and psychological perspectives on same-sex domestic violence: A mutlisystematic approach. *Journal of Family Violence, 17,* 252–259.

Poulin, F., & Boivin, M. (2000). Reactive and proactive aggression: Evidence of a two-factor model. *Psychological Assessment, 12,* 115–122.

Power, R. (2000, Spring). 2000 CSI/FBI computer crime and security survey. *Computer Security: Issues & Trends, 6* (1).

Poythress, N. G., Otto, R. K., Darkes, J., & Starr, L. (1993). APA's expert panel in the Congressional review of the USS Iowa incident. *American Psychologist, 48,* 8–15.

Prentice-Dunn, S., & Rogers, R. (1983). Deindividuation in aggression. In R. G. Geen & E. I. Donnerstein (Eds.), *Aggression: Theoretical and empirical reviews* (Vol. 2). New York: Academic Press.

Prentky, R. A., Harris, B., Frizzell, K., & Righthand, S. (2000). An actuarial procedure of assessing risk in juvenile sex offenders. *Sexual Abuse: A Journal of Research and Treatment, 12,* 71–93.

Prentky, R. A., & Knight, R. A. (1986). Impulsivity in the life style and criminal behavior of sexual offenders. *Criminal Justice and Behavior, 13,* 141–164.

Prentky, R. A., Knight, R. A., & Lee, A. F. S. (1997). *Child sexual molestation: Research issues.* NIJ Research Report. Rockville, MD: National Criminal Justice Reference Service. Available: www.ncjrs.org/txtfiles/163390.txt.

President's Commission on Law Enforcement and Administration of Justice. (1967). *The challenge of crime in free society.* Washington, DC: USGPO.

Price, W. H., & Whatmore, P. B. (1967). Behaviour disorders and patterns of crime among XYY males identified at a maximum security hospital. *British Medical Journal, 1,* 533–536.

PRIDE Surveys. (2003). *2002–2003 PRIDE surveys national summary, grades 6 through 12.* Bowling Green, KY: Author.

Prinstein, M. J., Boergers, J., & Vernberg, E. M. (2001). Overt and relational aggression in adolescents: Social-psychological adjustment of aggressors and victims. *Journal of Clinical Child Psychology, 30,* 479–491.

Prinstein, M. J., & La Greca, A. M. (2004). Childhood peer rejection and aggression predictors of adolescent girls' externalizing and health risk behaviors: A 6-year longitudinal study. *Journal of Consulting and Clinical Psychology, 72,* 103–112.

Putnam, C.T., & Kirkpatrick, J. T. (2005, May). Juvenile firesetting: A research overview. *Juvenile Justice Bulletin* (NCJ 207606). Washington, DC: U.S. Department of Justice, Office of Juvenile Justice and Delinquency Prevention.

Puzzanchera, C. M., Stahl, A. L., Finnegan, T. A., Tierney, N., & Snyder, H. N. (2004, December). *Juvenile court statistics 2000.* Washington, DC: Office of Juvenile Justice and Delinquency Prevention, National Center for Juvenile Justice.

Quay, H. C. (1964). Dimensions of personality in delinquent boys as inferred from the factor analysis of case history data. *Child Development, 35,* 479–484.

Quay, H. C. (1965). Psychopathic personality: Pathological stimulation-seeking. *American Journal of Psychiatry, 122,* 180–183.

Quay, H. C. (1984). *Managing adult inmates: Classification for housing and program assignment.* College Park, MD: American Correctional Association.

Quay, H. C. (1987). Intelligence. In H. C. Quay (Ed.), *Handbook of juvenile delinquency.* New York: Wiley.

Queen's Bench Foundation. (1978). The rapist and his crime. In L. D. Savitz & N. Johnson (Eds.), *Crime in society.* New York: Wiley.

Quinsey, V. L., Chaplin, T. C., & Upfold, D. (1989). Arsonists and sexual arousal to firesetting: Correlation unsupported. *Journal of Behaviour Therapy and Experimental Psychiatry, 20,* 203–209.

Quinsey, V. L., & Marshall, W. L. (1983). Procedures for reducing inappropriate sexual arousal: An evaluation review. In J. G. Greer & I. R. Stuart (Eds.), *The sexual aggressor.* New York: Van Nostrand Reinhold.

Quinsey, V. L., Rice, M. E., & Harris, G. T. (1995). Actuarial prediction of sexual recidivism. *Journal of Interpersonal Violence, 10,* 85–105.

Quinsey, V. L., Skilling, T. A., Lalumière, & Craig, W. M. (2004). *Juvenile delinqueny: Understanding the origins of individual differences.* Washington, DC: American Psychological Association.

Rabkin, J. G. (1979). Criminal behavior of discharged mental patients: A critical appraisal of the research. *Psychological Bulletin, 86,* 1–27.

Rachman, S. J. (1966). Sexual fetishism: An experimental analogue. *Psychological Record, 16,* 293–296.

Rafter, N. H. (1992). Criminal anthropology in the United States. *Criminology, 30,* 525–546.

Raine, A. (1993). *The psychopathology of crime: Criminal behavior as a clinical disorder.* San Diego, CA: Academic Press.

Raine, A. (2002). Biosocial studies of antisocial and violent behavior in children and adults: A review. *Journal of Abnormal Child Psychology, 30,* 311–326.

Raine, A., Brennan, P., & Mednick, S. A. (1997). Interaction between birth complications and early maternal rejection in predisposing individuals to adult violence: Specificity to serious, early-onset violence. *American Journal of Psychiatry, 134,* 1265–1271.

Raine, A., Venables, P. H., & Williams, M. (1995). High autonomic arousal and electrodermal orienting at age 15 years as protective factors against criminal behavior at age 29 years. *American Journal of Psychiatry, 152,* 1595–1600.

Raine, A., Venables, P. H., & Williams, M. (1996). Better autonomic arousal and faster electrodermal half-recovery time at age 15 years as possible protective factors against crime at age 29 years. *Developmental Psychology, 32,* 624–630.

Ramirez, D., McDevitt, J., & Farrell, A. (2000, November). *A resource guide on racial profiling data collection systems: Promising practices and lessons learned.* Boston, MA: Northeastern University Press. Available: www.usdoj.gov.

Ramirez, J. M. (2003). Hormones and aggression in childhood and adolescence. *Aggression and Violent Behavior, 8,* 621–644.

Ramirez, J. R., Crano, W. D., Quist, R., Burgoon, M., Alvaro, E. M., & Grandpre, J. (2004). Acculturation, familism, parental monitoring, and knowledge as predictors of marijuana and inhalant use in adolescents. *Psychology of Addictive Behavior, 18,* 3–11.

Rantala, R. R. (2004, March). *Cybercrime against businesses.* Washington, DC: U.S. Department of Justice, Bureau of Justice Statistics.

Rapaport, K., & Burkhart, B. R. (1984). Personality and attitudinal characteristics of sexually coercive college males. *Journal of Abnormal Psychology, 93,* 216–221.

Räsänen, P., Tiihonen, J., Isohanni, M. Rantakallio, P., Lehtonen, J., & Moring, J. (1998). Schizophrenia, alcohol abuse, and violent behavior: A 26-year follow-up study of an unselected birth cohort. *Schizophrenia Bulletin, 24,* 432–441.

Rasche, C. (1993). Given reason for violence in intimate relationships. In A. Wilson (Ed.), *Homicide.* Cincinnati, OH: Anderson.

Raskin, D. C., & Hare, R. D. (1978). Psychopathy and detection of deception in a prison population. *Psychophysiology, 15,* 126–136.

Ray, O. (1972). *Drugs, society and human behavior.* St. Louis, MO: C. V. Mosby.

Ray, O. (1983). *Drugs, society and human behavior* (3rd ed.). St. Louis, MO: C. V. Mosby.

Reid, J. B. (1993). Prevention of conduct disorder before and after school entry: Relating interventions to developmental findings. *Development and Psychopathology, 5,* 243–262.

Reidel, M. (2003). Homicide in Los Angeles County: A study of Latino victimization. In D. F. Hawkins (Ed.), *Violent crime: Assessing race and ethnic differences.* Cambridge, Eng.: Cambridge University Press.

Reifman, A. S., Larrick, R. P., & Fein, S. (1991). Temper and temperature on the diamond: The heat-aggression relationship in major league baseball. *Personality and Social Psychology Bulletin, 17,* 580–585.

Reiman, J. (1995). *The rich get richer and the poor get prison* (4th ed.). Needham Heights, MA: Allyn & Bacon.

Reiss, A. J., & Roth, J. A. (Eds.) (1993). *Understanding and preventing violence.* Washington, DC: National Academy Press.

Reiss, J. (1977). "Voluntary" castration of mentally disordered sex offenders. *Criminal Law Bulletin, 13,* 30–48.

Reitzel, L. R. (2003, January). Sexual offender update: Juvenile sexual offender recidivism and treatment effectiveness. *Correctional Psychologist, 35*(1), 3–4.

Rengert, G., & Wasilchick, J. (1985). *Suburban burglary: A time and place for everything.* Springfield, IL: Charles C Thomas.

Rennison, C. M. (2002, April). *Hispanic victims of violent crime, 1993–2000* (NCJ 191208). Washington, DC: U.S. Department of Justice, Bureau of Justice Statistics.

Rennison, C. M. (2003, February). *Intimate partner violence, 1993–2001* (NCJ 197838). Washington, DC: U.S. Department of Justice, Bureau of Justice Statistics.

Rennison, C. M., & Rand, M. R. (2003, August). *Criminal victimization, 2002.* Washington, DC: U.S. Department of Justice, Bureau of Justice Statistics.

Rennison, C. M., & Welchans, S. (2000, May). *Intimate partner violence.* Washington, DC: U.S. Department of Justice.

Resnick, P. J. (1969). Child murder by parents. *American Journal of Psychiatry, 126,* 325–334.

Resnick, P. J. (1970). Murder of the newborn: A psychiatric review of neonaticide. *American Journal of Psychiatry, 126,* 1414–1420.

Revitch, E., & Schlesinger, L. B. (1988). Clinical reflections on sexual aggression. In R. A. Prentky & V. L. Quinsey (Eds.), *Human sexual aggression: Current perspectives.* New York: New York Academy of Sciences.

Revitch, E., & Weiss, R. G. (1962). The pedophiliac offender. *Diseases of the Nervous System, 23,* 73–78.

Rhee, S. H., & Waldman, I. D. (2002). Genetic and environmental influences on antisocial behavior: A meta-analysis of twin and adoption studies. *Psychological Bulletin, 128,* 490–529.

Rhoads, J. M., & Borjes, E. D. (1981). The incidence of exhibitionism in Guatemala and U.S. *British Journal of Psychiatry, 139,* 242–244.

Rice, M. E. (1997). Violent offender research and implications for the criminal justice system. *American Psychologist, 52,* 414–423.

Rice, M. E., & Harris, G. T. (1991). Firesetters admitted to a maximum security psychiatric institution. *Journal of Interpersonal Violence, 6,* 461–475.

Rice, M. E., & Harris, G. T. (2002). Men who molest their sexually immature daughters: Is a special explanation required? *Journal of Abnormal Psychology, 111,* 329–339.

Rice, M. E., Harris, G. T., & Cormier, C. A. (1992). An evaluation of a maximum security therapeutic community for psychopaths and other mentally disordered offenders. *Law and Human Behavior, 16,* 399–412.

Rice, M. E., Harris, G. T., & Quinsey, V. L. (2001). Research on the treatment of adult sex offenders. In J. B. Ashford, B. D. Sales, & W. H. Reid (Eds.), *Treating adult and juvenile offenders with special needs.* Washington, DC: American Psychological Association.

Richard, A. (1999, November). *International trafficking in women to the United States: A contemporary manifestation of slavery and organized crime.* Washington, DC: Center for the Study of Intelligence.

Richards, H., Casey, J., & Lucente, S. (2003). Psychopathy and treatment response to incarcerated female substance abusers. *Criminal Justice and Behavior, 30,* 251–276.

Righthand, S., & Welch, C. (2001, March). *Juveniles who have sexually offended: A review of the professional literature.* Washington, DC: Office of Juvenile Justice and Delinquency Prevention.

Riley, S. (1998). Competency to stand trial adjudication: A comparison of female and male defendants. *Journal of the American Academy of Psychiatry and the Law, 26,* 223–240.

Ringel, C. (1997, November). *Criminal victimization in 1996: Changes 1995–1996 with trends 1993–1996.* Washington, DC: U.S. Department of Justice.

Ritvo, E., Shanok, S. S., & Lewis, D. O. (1983). Firesetting and nonfiresetting delinquents. *Child Psychiatry and Human Development, 13,* 259–267.

Robbins, E., & Robbins, L. (1964). Arson with special reference to pyromania. *New York State Journal of Medicine, 2,* 795–798.

Roberts, A. R. (2002). Preface. In A. R. Roberts (Ed.), *Handbook of domestic violence intervention strategies: Policies, programs, and legal remedies.* New York: Oxford University Press.

Robins, L. N. (1966). *Deviant children grow up.* Baltimore, MD: Williams & Wilkins.

Robins, L. N., & Regier, D. A. (1991). *Psychiatric disorders in America: The epidemiologic catchment area study.* New York: Free Press.

Roche, P. Q. (1958). *The criminal mind: A study of communication between criminal law and psychiatry.* New York: Grove Press.

Roche, T. (2006, July 7). Andrea Yates: More to the story. *Time.* Available: www.time.com/time/nation/article/0,8599,218445,00html.

Rodman, H., & Grams, P. (1967). *Juvenile delinquency and the family: A review and discussion.* Task Force Report: Juvenile delinquency and youth crime. Washington, DC: USGPO.

Roesch, R., Zapf, P. A., Golding, S. L., & Skeem, J. L. (1999). Defining and assessing competency to stand trial. In A. K. Hess & I. B. Weiner (Eds.), *The handbook of forensic psychology* (2nd ed.). New York: Wiley.

Rogers, R. (1997). *Clinical assessment of malingering and deception* (2nd ed.). New York: Guilford.

Rogers, R. W., & Ketcher, C. M. (1979). Effects of anonymity and arousal on aggression. *Journal of Psychology, 102,* 13–19.

Roizen, J. (1997). Epidemiological issues in alcohol-related violence. In M. Galanter (Ed.), *Recent developments in alcoholism* (Vol. 13). New York: Plenum.

Rooth, G. (1973). Exhibitionism outside Europe and America. *Archives of Sexual Behavior, 2,* 351–363.

Rooth, G. (1974). Exhibitionists around the world. *Human Behavior, 3,* 61.

Rose, A. J., Swenson, L. P., & Waller, E. M. (2004). Overt and relational aggression and perceived popularity: Developmental differences in concurrent and prospective relations. *Developmental Psychology, 40,* 378–387.

Rosecan, J. S., Spitz, H. I., & Gross, B. (1987). Contemporary issues in the treatment of cocaine abuse. In H. I. Spitz & J. S. Rosecan (Eds.), *Cocaine abuse: New directions in treatment and research.* New York: Brunner/Mazel.

Rosenbaum, D. P., Lurigio, A. J., & Davis, R. C. (1998). *The prevention of crime: Social and situational strategies.* Belmont, CA: West/Wadsworth.

Rosenbaum, M. (1989). *Just saw what? An alternative view on solving America's drug problem.* San Francisco: National Council of Crime and Delinquency.

Rosenfeld, B., & Ritchie, K. (1998). Competence to stand trial: Clinician reliability and the role of offense severity. *Journal of Forensic Sciences, 43,* 151–157.

Rosenthal, D. (1970). *Genetic theory and abnormal behavior.* New York: McGraw-Hill.

Rosenthal, D. (1971). *Genetics of psychopathology.* New York: McGraw-Hill.

Rosenthal, D. (1975). Heredity in criminality. *Criminal Justice and Behavior, 2,* 3–21.

Rosenzweig, M. R., Leiman, A. L., & Breedlove, S. M. (1999). *Biological psychology: An introduction to behavioral, cognitive, and clinical neuroscience.* Sunderland, MA: Sinauer Associates.

Rosoff, S. M., Pontell, H. N., & Tillman, R. (1998). *Profit without honor: White-collar crime and the looting of America.* Upper Saddle River, NJ: Prentice Hall.

Ross, M. P., & Bachar, K. J. (2002). Rape. In D. Levinson (Ed.), *Encyclopedia of crime and punishment* (Vol. 3). Thousand Oaks, CA: Sage.

Rossmo, D. K. (1997). Geographic profiling. In J. L. Jackson & D. A. Bekerain (Eds.), *Offender profiling: Theory, research, and practice*. Chichester, Eng.: Wiley.

Roth, J. A. (1996). *Psychoactive substances and violence*. Washington, DC: U.S. Department of Justice. Available: www.ncjrs.org/txtfile/psycho.txt.

Rotton, J. (1983). Affective and cognitive consequences of malodorous pollution. *Basic and Applied Psychology, 4*, 171–191.

Rotton, J., & Frey, J. (1985). Air pollution, weather, and violent crimes: Concomitant time-series analysis of archival data. *Journal of Personality and Social Psychology, 49*, 1207–1220.

Rowe, D. C., & Gulley, B. (1992). Sibling effects on substance abuse and delinquency. *Criminology, 35*, 217–233.

Rowe, D. C., Rodgers, D. C., & Meseck-Bushey, S. (1992). Sibling delinquency and the family environment: Shared and unshared influences. *Child Development, 63*, 57–67.

Ruback, R. B., & Carr, T. S. (1984). Crowding in a women's prison: Attitudinal and behavioral effects. *Journal of Applied Social Psychology, 14*, 57–68.

Rubin, B. (1972). Predictions of dangerousness in mentally ill criminals. *Archives of General Psychiatry, 27*, 397–407.

Rubin, K. H., Bukowski, W., & Parker, J. G. (1998). Peer interactions, relationships, and groups. In W. Damon (Series Ed.) & N. Eisenberg (Vol. Ed.), *Handbook of child psychology: Vol. 3. Social, emotional, and personality development* (5th ed.). New York: Wiley.

Rubin, K. H., Burgess, K. B., Dwyer, K. M., & Hastings, P. d. (2003). Predicting preschoolers' externalizing behaviors from toddler temperament, conflict, and maternal negativity. *Developmental Psychology, 39*, 164–176.

Rubinsky, E. W., & Brandt, J. (1986). Amnesia and criminal law: A clinical overview. *Behavioral Sciences & the Law, 4*, 27–46.

Rubinstein, M., Yeager, C. A., Goodstein, C., & Lewis, D. O. (1993). Sexually assaultive male juveniles: A follow-up. *American Journal of Psychiatry, 150*, 262–265.

Ruchkin, V. (2002). Family impact on violent youth. In R. R. Corrado, R. Roesch, S. D. Hart, & J. K. Gierowski (Eds.), *Multi-problem violent youth: A foundation for comparative research on needs, interventions, and outcomes*. Amsterdam: IOS Press.

Russell, D. (1973). Emotional aspects of shoplifting. *Psychiatric Annals, 3*, 77–86.

Russell, D. E. H. (1975). *The politics of rape: The victim's perspective*. New York: Stein & Day.

Russell, D. E. H. (1983). The prevalence and incidence of forcible rape and attempted rape of females. *Victimology: An International Journal, 7*, 81–93.

Russell, D. E. H. (1984). *Sexual exploitation*. Beverly Hills, CA: Sage.

Russell, D. E. H., & Finkelhor, D. (1984). The gender gap among perpetrators of child sexual abuse. In D. E. H. Russell (Ed.), *Sexual exploitation*. Beverly Hills, CA: Sage.

Russell, D. E. H., & Howell, N. (1983). The prevalence of rape in the United States revisited. *Signs: Journal of Women in Culture and Society, 8*, 688–695.

Rutter, M. (2005). Commentary: What is the meaning and utility of the psychopathy concept? *Journal of Abnormal Child Psychology, 33*, 499–503.

Rutter, M. (1997). Individual differences and levels of antisocial behavior. In A. Raine & P. A. Brennan (Eds.), *Biological bases of violence*. New York: Plenum.

Rutter, M., & Giller, H. (1984). *Juvenile delinquency: Trends and perspectives*. New York: Guilford Press.

Rutter, M., Giller, H., & Hagell, A. (1998). *Antisocial behavior by young people*. Cambridge, Eng.: Cambridge University Press.

Ryan, G., Miyoshi, T. J., Metzner, J. L., Krugman, R. D., & Fryer, G. E. (1996). Trends in a national sample of sexually abusive youths. *Journal of the American Academy of Child and Adolescent Psychiatry, 33*, 17–25.

Salekin, R. T. (2002). Psychopathy and therapeutic pessimism: Clinical lore or clinical reality? *Clinical Psychology Review, 22*, 79–112.

Salekin, R. T., Brannen, D. N., Zalot, A. A., Leistico, A-M, & Neumann, C. S. (2006). Factor structure of psychopathy in youth: Testing the applicability of the new four-factor model. *Criminal Justice and Behavior, 33,* 135–157.

Salekin, R. T., & Frick, P. J. (2005). Psychopathy in children and adolescents: The need for a developmental perspective. *Journal of Abnormal Child Psychology, 33,* 403–409.

Salekin, R. T., Leistico, A-M. R., Trobst, K. K., Schrum, C. L., & Lochman, J. E. (2005). Adolescent psychopathy and personality theory—the interpersonal circumplex: Expanding evidence of a nomological net. *Journal of Abnormal Child Psychology, 33,* 445–460.

Salekin, R. T., & Rogers, R. (2001). Treating patients found not guilty by reason of insanity. In J. B. Ashford, B. D. Sales, & W. H. Reid (Eds.), *Treating adult and juvenile offenders with special needs.* Washington, DC: American Psychological Association.

Salekin, R. T., Rogers, R., & Machin, D. (2001). Psychopathy in youth: Pursuing diagnostic clarity. *Journal of Youth and Adolescence, 30,* 173–195.

Salekin, R. T., Rogers, R., & Sewell, K. W. (1997). Construct validity of psychopathy in a female offender sample: A multitrait-multimethod evaluation. *Journal of Abnormal Psychology, 106,* 576–585.

Salekin, R. T., Rogers, R., Ustad, K. L., & Sewell, K. W. (1998). Psychopathy and recidivism among female inmates. *Law and Human Behavior, 22,* 109–128.

Salekin, R. T., Ziegler, T. A., Larrea, M. A., Anthony, V. L., & Bennett, A. D. (2003). Predicting psychopathy with two Millon Adolescent psychopathy scales. The importance of egocentric and callous traits. *Journal of Personality Assessment, 80,* 154–163.

Saltaris, C. (2002). Psychopathy in juvenile offenders: Can temperament and attachment be considered as robust developmental precursors? *Clinical Psychology Review, 22,* 729–752.

Sameroff, A. J., Peck, S. C., & Eccles, J. S. (2004). Changing ecological determinants of conduct problems form early adolescence to early childhood. *Development and Psychopathology, 16,* 873–896.

Sampson, R. J., & Laub, J. H. (1997). Unraveling the social context of physique and delinquency: A new, long-term look at the Gluecks' classic study. In A. Raine, P. A. Brennan, D. P. Farrington, & S. A. Mednick (Eds.), *Biosocial bases of violence.* New York: Plenum.

Sampson, R. J., & Lauritsen, J. L. (1994). Violent victimization and offending: Individual, situational and community-level risk factors. In A. T. Reiss Jr. & J. Roth (Eds.), *Understanding and preventing violence: Social Influences* (Vol. 3). Washington, DC: National Academy Press.

Sampson, R. J., & Wilson, W. J. (1993). Toward a theory of race, crime, and urban inequality. In J. Hagan & R. Peterson (Eds.), *Crime and inequality.* Stanford, CA: Stanford University Press.

Saner, H., & Ellickson, P. (1996). Concurrent risk factors for adolescent violence. *Journal of Adolescent Health, 19,* 94–103.

Santiago, G. B. (2002). Latina battered women: Barriers to service delivery and cultural considerations. In A. R. Roberts (Ed.), *Handbook of domestic violence intervention strategies: Policies, programs, and legal remedies.* New York: Oxford University Press.

Sarasalo, E., Bergman, B., & Toth, J. (1996). Personality traits and psychiatric and somatic morbidity among kleptomaniacs. *Acta Psychiatrica Scandinavica, 94,* 358–364.

Sarasalo, E., Bergman, B., & Toth, J. (1997). Kleptomania-like behaviour and psychosocial characteristics among shoplifters. *Legal and Criminological Psychology, 2,* 1–10.

Sarbin, T. R. (1979). The myth of the criminal type. In T. R. Sarbin (Ed.), *Challenges to the criminal justice system: The perspective of community psychology.* New York: Human Services Press.

Satterfield, J. H., Swanson, J., Schell, A., & Lee, F. (1994). Prediction of antisocial behavior in attention-deficit hyperactivity disorder boys from aggression/defiance scores. *Journal of the American Academy of Child and Adolescent Psychiatry, 33,* 185–191.

Saulnier, K., & Perlman, D. (1981). The actor-observer bias is alive and well in prison: A sequel to Wells. *Personality and Social Psychology, 7,* 559–564.

Saunders, D. G., & Azar, S. T. (1989). Treatment programs for family violence. In L. Ohlin & M. Tonry (Eds.), *Family violence* (Vol. 11). Chicago, IL: University of Chicago Press.

Saunders, E. B., & Awad, G. A. (1991). Adolescent female firesetters. *Canadian Journal of Psychiatry, 36,* 401–404.

Scaret, D., & Wilgosh, L. (1989). Learning disabilities and juvenile delinquency: A causal relationship? *International Journal for the Advancement of Counselling, 12,* 113–123.

Scarr, S. (1998). American child care today. *American Psychologist, 53,* 95–108.

Schaeffer, C. M., & Borduin, C. M. (2005). Long-term follow-up to a randomized clinical trial of multisystemic therapy with serious and violent juvenile offenders. *Journal of Consulting and Clinical Psychology, 73,* 445–453.

Schauer, E. J., & Wheaton, E. M. (2006). Sex trafficking into the United States: A literature review. *Criminal Justice Review, 31,* 146–169.

Schachter, S. (1971). *Emotion, obesity and crime.* New York: Academic Press.

Schachter, S., & Latane, B. (1964). Crime, cognition, and the autonomic nervous system. In M. R. Jones (Ed.), *Nebraska symposium on motivation.* Lincoln, NE: University of Nebraska Press.

Schacter, D. L. (1986). On the relation between genuine and simulated amnesia. *Behavioral Sciences & the Law, 4,* 47–64.

Schaeffer, C. M., & Borduin, C. M. (2005). Long-term follow-up to a randomized clinical trial of multisystemic therapy with serious and violent juvenile offenders. *Journal of Consulting and Clinical Psychology, 73,* 445–453.

Schlosser, E. (2001). *Fast food nation: The dark side of the all-American meal.* Boston: Houghton Mifflin.

Schlossman, S., & Sedlak, M. (1983). The Chicago area project revisited. *Crime and Delinquency, 29,* 398–462.

Schmideberg, M. (1953). Pathological firesetters. *Journal of Criminal Law, Criminology and Police Science, 44,* 30–39.

Schrager, L., & Short, J. (1978). Toward a sociology of organizational crime. *Social Problems, 25,* 407–419.

Schuller, R. A., & Vidmar, V. (1992). Battered woman syndrome evidence in the courtroom: A review of the literature. *Law and Human Behavior, 16,* 272–292.

Schulsinger, F. (1972). Psychopathy: Heredity and environment. *International Journal of Mental Health, 1,* 190–206.

Schultz, L. G. (1975). *Rape victimology.* Springfield, IL: Charles C Thomas.

Schuster, M. A., Stein, B. D., Jaycox, L. H., Collins, R. L., Marshall, G. N., & Elliott, M. N. (2001). A national survey of stress reactions after the September 11, 2001, terrorist attacks. *New England Journal of Medicine, 345,* 1507–1512.

Schwartz, J. P., Hage, S. M., Bush, I., & Burns, L. K. (2006). Unhealthy parenting and potential mediators as contributing factors to future intimate violence: A review of the literature. *Trauma, Violence, & Abuse, 7,* 206–221.

Schwartz, I. M. (1989). *(In) Justice for juveniles: Rethinking the best interests of the child.* Lexington, MA: Lexington Books.

Sciarra, D. (1999). Assessment and treatment of adolescent sex offenders: A review from a cross-cultural perspective. *Journal of Offender Rehabilitation, 28,* 103–118.

Scientific American. (1999). *The Scientific American book of the brain.* New York: Author.

Scully, D., & Marolla, J. (1984). Convicted rapists' vocabulary of motive: Excuses and justifications. *Social Problems, 31,* 530–544.

Scully, D., & Marolla, J. (1985). Rape and vocabularies of motive: Alternative perspectives. In A. W. Burgess (Ed.), *Rape and sexual assault*. New York: Garland Publishing.

Seagrave, D., & Grisso, T. (2002). Adolescent development and measurement of juvenile psychopathy. *Law and Human Behavior, 26*, 219–239.

Sears, R., Maccoby, E., & Levin, H. (1957). *Patterns of child rearing*. Evanston, IL: Row, Peterson.

Sechrest, L. (1987). Classification for treatment. In D. M. Gottfredson & M. Tonry (Eds.), *Prediction and classification: Criminal justice decision making* (Vol. 9). Chicago, IL: University of Chicago Press.

Séguin, J. R., Nagin, D., Asaad, J-M., & Tremblay, R. E. (2004). Cognitive-neuropsychological function in chronic physical aggression and hyperactivity. *Journal of Abnormal Psychology, 113*, 603–613.

Seligman, M. E. (1975). *Helplessness: On depression, development, and death*. San Francisco, CA: W. H. Freeman.

Selkin, J. (1987). *Psychological autopsy in the courtroom*. Denver, CO: Author.

Selkin, J. (1994). Psychological autopsy: Scientific psychohistory or clinical intuition? *American Psychologist, 49*, 74–75.

Sellbom, M., & Verona, E. (in press). Neuropsychological correlates of psychopathic traits in a non-incarcerated sample. *Journal of Research in Personality*.

Sellin, T. (1970). A sociological approach. In M. E. Wolfgang, L. Savitz, & N. Johnson (Eds.), *The sociology of crime and delinquency* (2nd ed.). New York: Wiley.

Serin, R. C., & Amos, N. L. (1995). The role of psychopathy in the assessment of dangerousness. *International Journal of Law & Psychiatry, 18*, 231–238.

Serin, R. C., Peters, R. D., & Barbaree, H. E. (1990). Predictors of psychopathy and release outcome in a criminal population. *Psychological Assessment, 2*, 419–422.

Serin, R. C., & Preston, D. L. (2001). Managing and treating violent offenders. In J. B. Ashford, B. D. Sales, & W. H. Reid (Eds.), *Treating adult and juvenile offenders with special needs*. Washington, DC: American Psychological Association.

Seto, M. C., & Barbaree, H. E. (1999). Psychopathy, treatment behavior, and sex offender recidivism. *Journal of Interpersonal Violence, 14*, 1235–1248.

Seto, M. C., Maric, A., & Barbaree, H. E. (2001). The role of pornography in the etiology of sexual aggression. *Aggression and Violent Behavior, 6*, 35–53.

Seymour, A. (2000). Campus crime and victimization. In G. Coleman, M. Gaboury, M. Murray, & A. Seymour (Eds.), *1999 National Victim Assistance Academy*. Washington, DC: U.S. Department of Justice.

Seymour, A. (2001). Victimization of the elderly. In G. Coleman, M. Gaboury, M. Murray, & A. Seymour (Eds.), *1999 National Victim Assistance Academy*. Washington, DC: U.S. Department of Justice.

Shain, R., & Phillips, J. (1991). The stigma of mental illness: Labeling and stereotyping in the news. In L. Wilkins & P. Patterson (Eds.), *Risky business: Communicating issues of science, risk, and public policy*. Westport, CT: Greenwood Press.

Shaw, D. S., Gilliom, M., Ingoldsby, E. M., & Nagin, D. S. (2003). Trajectories leading to school-age conduct problems. *Developmental Psychology, 39*, 189–200.

Shaw, D. S., Owens, E. B., Giovannelli, J., & Winslow, E. B. (2001). Infant and toddler pathways leading to early externalizing disorders. *Journal of the American Academy of Child and Adolescent Psychiatry, 40*, 36–43.

Sheldon, W. H., Hartl, E. M., & McDermott, E. (1949). *Varieties of delinquent youth: An introduction to constitutional psychiatry*. New York: Harper.

Sheldon, W. H., & Stevens, S. S. (1942). *The varieties of temperament*. New York: Harper.

Sherman, L. W., & Berk, R. A. (1984). The specific deterrent effects of arrest for domestic assault. *American Sociological Review, 49*, 261–272.

Shields, J. (1962). *Monozygotic twins brought up apart and together.* Oxford, UK: Oxford University Press.

Shneidman, E. S. (1994). The psychological autopsy. *American Psychologist, 49,* 75–76.

Short, J. F. (1968). *Gang delinquency and delinquency subcultures.* New York: Harper & Row.

Short, J. F., & Nye, I. (1957). Reported behavior as a criterion of deviant behavior. *Social Problems, 5,* 207–213.

Shover, N. (1972). Structures and careers in burglary. *Journal of Criminal Law, Criminology and Police Science, 63,* 540–548.

Showers, J. (1999). *Never never never shake a baby: The challenges of shaken baby syndrome.* Alexandria, VA: National Association of Children's Hospitals and Related Institutions.

Sickmund, M. (2004, June). *Juveniles in corrections.* (NCJ 202885). Washington, DC: U.S. Department of Justice, Office of Juvenile Justice and Delinquency Prevention.

Siegel, A., & Kohn, L. (1959). Permissiveness, permission, and aggression: The effect of adult presence or absence on aggression in children's play. *Child Development, 30,* 131–141.

Siegel, J. M., Sorenson, S. B., Golding, J. M., Burnam, M. A., & Stein, J. A. (1987). The prevalence of childhood sexual assault: The Los Angeles Epidemiological Catchment Area Project. *American Journal of Epidemiology, 126,* 1141–1153.

Sieh, E. W. (1987). Garment workers: Perceptions of inequity and employee theft. *British Journal of Criminology, 27,* 174–190.

Sigall, H., & Ostrove, N. (1978). Physical attractiveness and jury decisions. In N. Johnson & L. Savitz (Eds.), *Justice and corrections.* New York: Wiley.

Silberman, E. K., & Weingartner, H. (1996). Hemispheric lateralization of functions related to emotion. *Brain and Cognition, 5,* 322–353.

Silverman, R. A., & Mukhergee, S. K. (1987). Intimate homicide: An analysis of violent social relationships. *Behavioral Sciences & the Law, 5,* 37–47.

Silvern, L., Karyl, J., Waelde, L., Hodges, W. F., Starek, J., Heidt, E., Min, K. (1995). Retrospective reports of parental partner abuse: Relationships to depression, trauma symptoms and self-esteem among college students. *Journal of Family Violence, 10,* 177–202.

Silverthorn, P., & Frick, P. J. (1999). Developmental pathways to antisocial behavior: The delayed-onset pathway in girls. *Development and Psychopathology, 11,* 101–126.

Simon, R. J. (1983). The defense of insanity. *Journal of Psychiatry and Law, 11,* 183–201.

Simon, R. J., & Aaronson, D. E. (1988). *The insanity defense.* New York: Praeger.

Simon, R. J., & Cockerham, W. (1977). Civil commitment, burden of proof, and dangerous acts: A comparison of the perspectives of judges and psychiatrists. *Journal of Psychiatry and Law, 5,* 571–594.

Simonelli, C. J., Mullis, T., & Rohde, C. (2005). Scale of negative family interactions: A measure of parental and sibling aggression. *Journal of Interpersonal Violence, 20,* 792–803.

Simons, R. L., Lin, K. H., & Gordon, L. C. (1998). Socialization in the family of origin and male dating violence: A propsective study. *Journal of Marriage and the Family, 60,* 467–478.

Simourd, D. J. (1997). The Criminal Sentiments Scale—Modified and Pride in Delinquency scale: Psychometric properties and construct validity of two measures of criminal attitudes. *Criminal Justice and Behavior, 24,* 52–70.

Simourd, D. J., & Hoge, R. D. (2000). Criminal psychopathy: A risk-and-need perspective. *Criminal Justice and Behavior, 27,* 256–272.

Simourd, D. J., & Van De Ven, J. (1999). Assessment of criminal attitudes: Criterion-related validity of the Criminal Sentiments Scale-Modified and Pride in Delinquency scale. *Criminal Justice and Behavior, 26,* 90–106.

Sipe, R., Jensen, E. L., & Everett, R. S. (1988). Adolescent sexual offenders grown up: Recidivism in young adulthood. *Criminal Justice and Behavior, 25,* 109–124.

Skeem, J. L., & Cauffman, E. (2003). Views of the downward extension: Comparing the youth version of the Psychopathy Checklist with the Youth Psychopathic Traits Inventory. *Behavioral Sciences & the Law, 21,* 737–770.

Skeem, J. L., Edens, J. F., & Colwell, L. H. (2003, April). Are there racial differences in levels of psychopathy? A meta-analysis. *Paper presented at the 3rd annual conference of the International Association of Forensic Mental Health Services,* Miami, FL.

Skeem, J. L., Edens, J. F., Sanford, G. M., & Colwell, L. H. (in press). Psychopathic personality and racial/ethnic differences reconsidered: A reply to Lynn (2002). *Personality and Individual Differences.*

Skeem, J. L., Emke-Francis, P., & Louden, J. L. (2006). Probation, mental health, and mandated treatment: A national survey. *Criminal Justice and Behavior, 33,* 158–184.

Skeem, J. L., & Golding, S. (1998). Community examiners' evaluations of competence to stand trial: Common problems and suggestions for improvements. *Professional Psychology: Research and Practice, 29,* 357–367.

Skeem, J. L., Monahan, J., & Mulvey, E. P. (2002). Psychopathy, treatment involvement, and subsequent violence among civil psychiatric patients. *Law and Human Behavior, 26,* 577–603.

Skeem, J. L., Poythress, N., Edens, J., Lilienfeld, S., & Cale, E. (2003). Psychopathic personality or personalities? Exploring potential variants of psychopathy and their implications for risk assessment. *Aggression and Violent Behavior, 8,* 513–546.

Skilling, T. A., Quinsey, V. L., & Craig, W. M. (2001). Evidence of a tax on underlying serious antisocial behavior in boys. *Criminal Justice and Behavior, 28,* 450–470.

Skinner, B. F. (1964). Behaviorism at fifty. In T. W. Wann (Ed.), *Behaviorism and phenomenology.* Chicago, IL: University of Chicago Press.

Skogan, W. G. (1977). Dimensions of the dark figure of unreported crime. *Crime and Delinquency, 23,* 41–50.

Skrzpek, G. J. (1969). The effects of perceptual isolation and arousal on anxiety, complexity preference, and novelty preference in psychopathic and neurotic delinquents. *Journal of Abnormal Psychology, 74,* 321–329.

Slavkin, M. L. (2001). Enuresis, firesetting, and cruelty to animals: Does the ego triad show predictive validity? *Adolescence, 36,* 461–467.

Slobogin, C. (1985). The guilty but mentally ill verdict: An idea whose time should not have come. *George Washington Law Review, 53,* 494–580.

Slobogin, C. (1999). The admissibility of behavioral science information in criminal trials: From primitivism to *Daubert* to voice. *Psychology, Public Policy, and Law, 5,* 100–119.

Slovenko, R. (1989). The multiple personality: A challenge to legal concepts. *The Journal of Psychiatry and Law, 17,* 681–719.

Smallbone, S. W., & Wortley, R. K. (2004). Criminal diversity and paraphilic interests among adult males convicted of offenses against children. *International Journal of Offender Therapy and Comparative Criminology, 48,* 175–188.

Smart, C. (1976). *Women, crime, and criminology: A feminist critique.* London: Routledge & Kegan Paul.

Smart, R. G. (1986). Cocaine use and problems in North America. *British Journal of Criminology, 28,* 109–128.

Smart, R. G., Asbridge, M., Mann, R. E., & Adlaf, E. M. (2003). Psychiatric distress among road rage victims and perpetrators. *Canadian Journal of Psychiatry, 48,* 681–688.

Smigel, E. O. (1970). Public attitudes toward stealing as related to the size of the victim organization. In E. O. Smigel & H. L. Ross (Eds.), *Crimes against bureaucracy.* New York: Van Nostrand Reinhold.

Smith, D. (2002, June). Helping mentally ill offenders. *Monitor on Psychology, 33,* 64.

Smith, E. J. (2006). The strength-based counseling model. *The Counseling Psychologist, 34,* 13–79.

Smith, G. A., & Hall, J. A. (1982). Evaluating Michigan's guilty but mentally ill verdict: An empirical study. *Michigan Journal of Law Reform, 16,* 75–112.

Smith, S., & Hudson, R. (1995). A quick screening test of competency to stand trial for defendants with mental retardation. *Psychological Reports, 78,* 234.

Smith, S. S., & Newman, J. P. (1990). Alcohol and drug abuse-dependence disorder in psychopathic and nonpsychopathic criminal offenders. *Journal of Abnormal Psychology, 99,* 430–439.

Smithey, M. (1998). Infant homicide: Victim-offender relationship and causes of death. *Journal of Family Violence, 13,* 285–287.

Smithey, M. (2002). Infanticide. In D. Levinson (Ed.), *Encyclopedia of crime and punishment* (Vol. 2). Thousand Oaks, CA: Sage.

Snyder, H. N. (2000a). *Juvenile arrests 1999.* Washington, DC: Office of Juvenile Justice and Delinquency Prevention.

Snyder, H. N. (2000b). *Sexual assault of young children as reported to law enforcement: Victim, incident, and offender characteristics.* Washington, DC: U.S. Department of Justice, Bureau of Justice Statistics.

Snyder, H. N. (2001). Epidemiology of official offending. In R. Loeber & D. P. Farrington (Eds.), *Child delinquents: Development, intervention, and service needs.* Thousand Oaks, CA: Sage.

Snyder, H. N. (2002, November). *Juvenile arrests 2000.* Washington, DC: U.S. Department of Justice, Office of Juvenile Justice and Delinquency Prevention.

Snyder, H. N., Espiritu, R. C., Huizinga, D., Loeber, R., & Petechuk, D. (2003, March). Prevalence and development of child delinquency. *Child Delinquency Bulletin Series* (NCJ193411). Washington, DC: U.S. Department of Justice, Office of Juvenile Justice and Delinquency Prevention.

Snyder, H. N., Sickmund, M., & Poe-Yamagata, E. (2000). *Juvenile transfer to criminal court in the 1990s: Lessons learned from four studies.* Washington, DC: Office of Juvenile Justice and Delinquency Prevention.

Snyder, J., & Patterson, G. (1987). Family interaction and delinquent behavior. In H. C. Quay (Ed.), *Handbook of juvenile delinquency.* New York: Wiley.

Snyder, J., Reid, J., & Patterson, G. (2003). A social learning model of child and adolescent antisocial behavior. In B. B. Lahey, T. E. Moffitt, & A. Caspi (Eds.), *Causes of conduct disorder and juvenile delinquency.* New York: Guilford.

Sorenson, S. B., Stein, J. A., Siegel, J. M., Golding, J. M., & Burnam, M. A. (1987). The prevalence of adult sexual assault: The Los Angeles Epidemiological Catchment Area Project. *American Journal of Epidemiology, 126,* 1154–1164.

Southerland, M. D., Collins, P. A., & Scarborough, K. E. (1997). *Workplace violence.* Cincinnati, OH: Anderson.

Spaccarelli, S., Coatsworth, J. D., & Bowden, B. S. (1995). Exposure to serious family violence among incarcerated boys: Its association with violent offending and potential mediating variables. *Violence and Victims, 10,* 163–182.

Spallone, P. (1998). The new biology of violence: New geneticisms for old? *Body and Society, 4,* 47–65.

Sperry, R. (1983). *Science and moral priority.* New York: Columbia University Press.

Stadolnik, R. F. (2000). *Drawn to the flame: Assessment and treatment of juvenile firesetting behavior.* Sarasota, FL: Professional Resources Press.

Stagg, V., Wills, G. D., & Howell, M. (1989). Psychopathology in early childhood witnesses of family violence. *Topics in Early Childhood Special Education, 9,* 73–87.

Stahl, A., Sickmund, M., Finnegan, T., Synder, H., Poole, R., & Tierney, N. (1999). *Juvenile court statistics 1996.* Washington, DC: U.S. Department of Justice.

Staller, J. A. (2006). Diagnostic profiles in outpatient child psychiatry. *American Journal of Orthopsychiatry, 76,* 98–102.

Stanger, C., Achenbach, T. M., & Verhulst, F. C. (1997). Accelerated longitudinal comparisons of aggressive versus delinquent syndromes. *Development and Psychopathology, 9,* 43–58.

Stanley, B., Molcho, A., Stanley, M., Winchel, R., Gamerroff, M. J., Parsons, B., & Mann, J. J. (2000). Assocation of aggressive behavior with altered sertonergic function in patients who are not suicidal. *American Journal of Psychiatry, 157,* 609–614.

Stark, E. (2002). Preparing for expert testimony in domestic violence cases. In A. R. Roberts (Ed.), *Handbook of domestic violence intervention strategies: Policies, programs, and legal remedies.* New York: Oxford University Press.

Stattin, H., & Klackenberg-Larsson, I. (1993). Early language and intelligence development and their relationship to future criminal behavior. *Journal of Abnormal Psychology, 102,* 369–378.

Stattin, H., & Magnusson, D. (1991). Stability and change in criminal behaviour up to age 30. *The British Journal of Criminology, 31,* 327–346.

Staub, E. (2001). Genocide and mass killing: Their roots and prevention. In D. J. Christie, R. V. Wagner, & D. D. Winter (Eds.), *Peace, conflict, and violence: Peace psychology for the 21st century.* Upper Saddle River, NJ: Prentice Hall.

Staub, E. (2004). Understanding and responding to group violence: Genocide, mass killing, and terrorism. In F. M. Moghaddam & A. J. Marsella (Eds.), *Understanding terrorism: Psychosocial roots, consequences, and interventions.* Washington, DC: American Psychological Association.

Steadman, H. J. (1976). Predicting dangerousness. In D. J. Madden & J. R. Lion (Eds.), *Rage, hate, assault, and other forms of violence.* New York: Spectrum Publishers.

Steadman, H. J. (1979). *Beating a rap? Defendants found incompetent to stand trial.* Chicago, IL: University of Chicago Press.

Steadman, H. J., & Cocozza, J. J. (1974). *Careers of the criminally insane.* Lexington, MA: Lexington Books.

Steadman, H. J., Fabisiak, S., Dvoskin, J., & Holobean, E. (1987). A survey of mental disability among state prison inmates. *Hospital and Community Psychiatry, 38,* 1086–1090.

Steadman, H. J., McGreevy, M. A., Morrissey, J. P., Callahan, L. A., Robbins, P. C., & Cirincione, C. (1993). *Before and after Hinckley: Evaluating insanity defense reform.* New York: Guilford Press.

Steadman, H. J., Mulvey, E. P., Monahan, J., Robbins, P. C., Appelbaum, P. S., Grisso, T., Roth, L. H., & Silver, E. (1998). Violence by people discharged from acute psychiatric inpatient facilities and by others in the same neighborhoods. *Archives of General Psychiatry, 55,* 393–401.

Steffan, J. S., & Morgan, R. D. (2005, February). Meeting the needs of mentally ill offenders: Inmate service utilization. *Corrections Today,* pp. 38–43.

Steinman, K. J. (2005). Drug selling among high school students: Related risk behaviors and psychosocial characteristics. *Journal of Adolescent Health, 36,* 71–79.

Steinmetz, S. K. (1981). A cross-cultural comparison of sibling violence. *International Journal of Family Psychiatry, 2,* 337–351.

Stern, K. R. (2001, May). A treatment study of children with attention deficit hyperactivity disorder. *OJJDP Fact Sheet.* Washington, DC: U.S. Department of Justice, Office of Juvenile Justice and Delinquency Prevention.

Sternberg, R. J. (2003). A duplex theory of hate: Development and application of terrorism, massacres, and genocide. *Review of General Psychology, 7,* 299–328.

Stewart, M. A., & Culver, K. W. (1982). Children who set fires: The clinical picture and a follow-up. *British Journal of Psychiatry, 140,* 357–363.

Stickle, T., & Blechman, E. (2002). Aggression and fire: Antisocial behavior in firesetting and non-firesetting juvenile offenders. *Journal of Psychopathology and Behavioral Assessment, 24,* 177–193.

Stone, A. (1975). *Mental health law: A system in transition.* Washington, DC: USGPO.

Stone, M. H. (1998). Sadistic personality in murders. In T. Millon, E. Simonsen, M. Burket-Smith, & R. Davis (Eds.), *Psychopathy: Antisocial, criminal, and violent behavior.* New York: Guilford.

Strasser, F. (1989, August 7). One nation, under siege. *National Law Journal,* S2–S3, S15.

Straus, M. (1991). Discipline and deviance: Physical punishment of children and violence and other crime in adulthood. *Social Problems, 38,* 133–154.

Straus, M. A., & Gelles, R. J. (1990). *Physical violence in American families.* New Brunswick, NJ: Transaction Publishers.

Strentz, T. (1987, November). A hostage psychological survival guide. *FBI Law Enforcement Bulletin,* pp. 1–7.

Strote, J., Lee, J. E., & Wechsler, H. (2002). Increasing MDMA use among college students: Results of a national survey. *Journal of Adolescent Health, 30,* 64–72.

Substance Abuse and Mental Health Administration. (2005, September). *2004 National Survey on Drug Abuse and Mental Health.* Rockville, MD: U.S. Department of Health and Human Services, Author.

Substance Abuse and Mental Health Administration. (2006, March). State estimates of substance use from the 2003–2004 national surveys on drug use and health. Rockville, MD: U.S. Department of Health and Human Services, Author.

Surette, R. (1999). *Media, crime, and criminal justice,* 2nd ed. Belmont, CA: West/Wadsworth.

Sutherland, E. H. (1947). *Principles of criminology,* 4th ed. Philadelphia: Lippincott.

Sutherland, E. H. (1949). *White-collar crime.* New York: Holt, Rinehart & Winston.

Sutherland, E. H. (1983). *White-collar crime: The uncut version.* New Haven, CT: Yale University Press.

Sutherland, E. H., & Cressey, D. R. (1974). *Criminology* (9th ed.). Philadelphia: Lippincott.

Sutherland, E. H., & Cressey, D. R. (1978). *Criminology* (10th ed.). Philadelphia: Lippincott.

Sutherland, E. H., Cressey, D. R., & Luckenbill, D. F. (1992). *Principles of criminology,* (11th ed). Dix Hills, NY: General Hall.

Sutker, P. B., & Allain, A. N. (1983). Behavior and personality assessment in men labeled adaptive sociopaths. *Journal of Behavioral Assessment, 5,* 65–79.

Sutker, P. B., Uddo-Crane, M., & Allain, A. N. (1991). Clinical and research assessment of posttraumatic stress disorder: A conceptual overview. Psychological Assessment: *A Journal of Consulting and Clinical Psychology, 3,* 520–530.

Sutton, S. K., Vitale, J. E., & Newman, J. P. (2002). Emotion among women with psychopathy during picture perception. *Journal of Abnormal Psychology, 111,* 610–619.

Svalastoga, K. (1956). Homicide and social contact in Denmark. *American Journal of Sociology, 62,* 37–41.

Swahn, M. H., & Donovan, J. E. (2004). Correlates and predictors of violent behavior among adolescent drinkers. *Journal of Adolescent Health, 34,* 480–492.

Sykes, G. M. (1956). *Crime and society.* New York: Random House.

Tappan, P. W. (1947). Who is the criminal? *American Sociological Review, 12,* 100–110.

Tappan, P. W. (1949). *Juvenile delinquency.* New York: McGraw-Hill.

Tarolla, S. M., Wagner, E. F., Rabinowitz, J., & Tubman, J. G. (2002). Understanding and treating juvenile offenders: A review of current knowledge and future directions. *Aggression and Violent Behavior, 7,* 125–143.

Taylor, D. M., & Louis, W. (2004). Terrorism and the quest for identity. In F. M. Moghaddam & A. J. Marsella (Eds.), *Understanding terrorism: Psychosocial roots, consequences, and interventions.* Washington, DC: American Psychological Association.

Taylor, J., Iacono, W. G., & McGue, M. (2000). Evidence for a genetic etiology of early-onset delinquency. *Journal of Abnormal Psychology, 109,* 634–643.

Taylor, M., & Nee, C. (1988). The role of cues in simulated residential burglary. *British Journal of Criminology, 28,* 396–401.

Tedeschi, R. G., & Kilmer, R. P. (2005). Assessing strengths, resilience, and growth to guide clinical interventions. *Professional Psychology: Research and Practice, 36,* 230–237.

Tengström, A., Hodgins, S., Grann, M., Långström, N., & Kullgren, G. (2004). Schizophrenia and criminal offending: The role of psychopathy and substance use disorders. *Criminal Justice and Behavior, 31,* 367–391.

Teplin, L. (1984). Criminalizing mental disorder. *American Psychologist, 39,* 794–803.

Teplin, L. (1990). The prevalence of severe mental disorder among male urban jail detainees: Comparisons with the epidemiologic catchment area program. *American Journal of Public Health, 80,* 663–669.

Teplin, L. (2000, October). Psychiatric disorders in youthful offenders. *National Institute of Justice Journal,* 30–32.

Terrorism Research Center. (1997). *The basics: Combating terrorism.* Alexandria, VA: Author.

Terry, K. J., & Tallon, J. (2004). *Child sexual abuse.* New York: John Jay College Research Team, John Jay College of Criminal Justice.

Texas Youth Commission (2005, January 12). *Agency treatment effectiveness 2004.* Austin: Author.

Thompson, K. M. (1990). Refacing inmates: A critical appraisal of plastic surgery programs in prison. *Criminal Justice and Behavior, 17,* 448–466.

Thompson, R. A., & Nelson, C. A. (2001). Developmental science and the media: Early brain development. *American Psychologist, 56,* 5–15.

Thorley, G. (1984). Review of follow-up and follow-back studies of childhood hyperactivity. *Psychological Bulletin, 96,* 116–132.

Thornberry, T. P., Huizinga, D., & Loeber, R. (1995). The prevention of serious delinquency and violence: Implication from the program of research on the causes and correlates of delinquency. In J. C. Howell, B. Krisberg, J. D. Hawkins, & J. Wilson (Eds.), *Sourcebook on serious violent and chronic juvenile offenders.* Thousand Oaks, CA: Sage.

Thornberry, T. P., & Jacoby, J. E. (1979). *The criminally insane: A community follow-up of mentally ill offenders.* Chicago, IL: University of Chicago Press.

Thornberry, T. P., Krohn, M., Lizotte, A. J., & Chard-Wierschem, D. (1993). The role of juvenile gangs in facilitating delinquent behavior. *Journal of Research in Crime and Delinquency, 30,* 55–87.

Tingle, D., Barnard, G. W., Robbins, L., Newman, G., & Hutchinson, D. (1986). Childhood and adolescent characteristics of pedophiles and rapists. *International Journal of Law and Psychiatry, 9,* 103–116.

Tinklenberg, J. R., & Stillman, R. C. (1970). Drug use and violence. In D. Daniels, M. Gilula, & F. Ochberg (Eds.), *Violence and the struggle for existence.* Boston, MA: Little, Brown.

Tinklenberg, J. R., & Woodrow, K. M. (1974). Drug use among youthful assaultive and sexual offenders. In S. H. Frazier (Ed.), *Aggression.* Baltimore, MD: Williams & Wilkins.

Tittle, C. R. (1980). *Sanctions and social deviance: The question of deterrence.* New York: Praeger.

Tittle, C. R. (1983). Social class and criminal behavior: A critique of the theoretical foundation. *Social Forces, 62,* 334–358.

Tittle, C. R., & Villemez, W. J. (1977). Social class and criminality. *Social Forces, 56,* 474–502.

Tjaden, P. (1997, November). *The crime of stalking: How big is the problem?* NIJ Research Preview. Washington, DC: U.S. Department of Justice.

Tjaden, P., & Thoennes, N. (1997). *Stalking in America: Findings from the national violence against women survey.* Denver, CO: Center for Policy Research.

Tjaden, P., & Thoennes, N. (1998). *Stalking in America: Findings from the national violence against women survey.* Washington, DC: U.S. Department of Justice.

Toch, H. (1969). *Violent men: An inquiry into the psychology of violence.* Chicago, IL: Aldine.

Toch, H. (1977). *Police, prisons, and the problems of violence.* National Institute of Mental Health. Washington, DC: USGPO.

Toch, H., & Adams, K. (1989). *The disturbed violent offender.* New Haven, CT: Yale University Press.

Toch, H., & Adams, K., with Grant, J. D. (1989). *Coping: Maladaptation in prisons.* New Brunswick, NJ: Transaction Publishers.

Tolan, P. H., Gorman-Smith, D., & Henry, D. B. (2003). On developmental ecology of urban males' youth violence. *Developmental Psychology, 39,* 274–279.

Tolan, P. H., & Thomas, P. (1995). The implications of age of onset for delinquency II: Longitudinal data. *Journal of Abnormal Child Psychology, 23,* 157–169.

Tomarken, A. J., Davidson, R. J., Wheeler, R. E., & Doss, R. C. (1992). Individual differences in anterior brain asymmetry and fundamental dimensions of emotion. *Journal of Personality and Social Psychology, 62,* 676–687.

Tonry, M., & Petersilia, J. (1999). (Eds.) *Prisons. Crime and justice. A review of the research* (Vol. 26). Chicago: University of Chicago Press.

Tran, H., & Weinraub, M. (2006). Child care effects in context. Quality, stability, and multiplicity in nonmaternal child care arrangements during the first 15 months of life. *Developmental Psychology, 42,* 566–582.

Trasler, G. (1987). Some cautions for the biological approach to crime causation. In S. A. Mednick, E. Moffitt, & S. A. Stack (Eds.), *The causes of crime: New biological approach.* Cambridge, Eng.: Cambridge University Press.

Tremblay, R. E., & Craig, W. (1995). Developmental crime prevention. In M. Tonry & D. P. Farrington (Eds.), *Building a safer society: Strategic approaches to crime prevention.* Chicago: University of Chicago Press.

Tremblay, R. W., LeMarquand, D., & Vitaro, F. (1999). The prevention of oppositional defiant disorder and conduct disorder. In H. C. Quay & A. F. Hogan (Eds.), *Handbook of disruptive behavior disorders.* New York: Kluwer Academic/Plenum Publishers.

Tsang, J. (2002). Moral rationalizaiton and the integration of situational factors and psychological processes in immoral behavior. *Review of General Psychology, 6,* 25–50.

Tucker, D. M. (1981). Lateral brain function, emotion and conceptualization. *Psychological Bulletin, 89,* 19–46.

Tupin, J. P., Mahar, D., & Smith, D. (1973). Two types of violent offenders with psychosocial descriptors. *Diseases of the Nervous System, 34,* 356–363.

Turrell, S. C. (2000). A descriptive analysis of same-sex relationship violence for a diverse sample. *Journal of Family Violence, 15,* 281–293.

Turvey, B. (2002). *Criminal profiling: An introduction to behavioral evidence analysis* (2nd ed.). San Diego, CA: Academic Press.

Tuvblad, C., Eley, T. C., & Lichtenstein, P. (2005). The development of antisocial behaviour from childhood to adolescence: A longitudinal twin study. *European Child and Adolescent Psychiatry, 14,* 216–225.

Tyler, J., Darville, R., & Stalnaker, K. (2001). Juvenile boot camps: A descriptive analysis of program diversity and effectiveness, *Social Science Journal, 38,* 445–460.

Ullman, A., & Straus, M. A. (2003). Violence by children against mothers in relation to violence between parents and corporal by parents. *Journal of Comparative Family Studies, 34,* 41–64.

Ullman, S. E., & Knight, R. A. (1993). The efficacy of women's resistance strategies in rape situations. *Psychology of Women Quarterly, 17,* 23–38.

Underwood, R. C., & Patch, P. C. (1999). Siblicide: A descriptive analysis of sibling homicide. *Homicide Studies, 3,* 333–348.

U.S. Bureau of the Census. (2001). *2000 census of population and housing.* Washington, DC: USGPO.

U.S. Bureau of the Census. (2002). *Who's minding the kids? Child care arrangements.* Washington, DC: USGPO.

U.S. Conference of Majors. (1998). *A status report on hunger and homelessness in America's cities: 1998.* Washington, DC: Author.

U.S. Department of Health and Human Services. (2003, April 1). *Child abuse prevention: An overview* .Washington, DC: Author.

U.S. Department of Justice. (1976). *Bomb summary—1975.* Washington, DC: USGPO.

U.S. Department of Justice. (1988). *Report to the nation on crime and justice: The data* (2nd ed.). Washington, DC: USGPO.

U.S. Department of Justice. (1989). *Criminal victimization in the United States, 1987.* Washington, DC: USGPO.

U.S. Department of Justice. (1998). *Inhalants.* Washington, DC: Author.

U.S. Department of Justice. (1999). *Cyberstalking: A new challenge for law enforcement and industry.* Washington, DC: Author. Available: www.usdoj.gov/criminal/cybercrime/cyberstalking .htm.

U.S. Department of Justice. (2000a). *Terrorism in the United States–1998.* Washington, DC: Author.

U.S. Department of Justice. (2000b). *The structure of family violence: An analysis of selected incidents.* Washington, DC: Author.

U.S. Fire Administration. (2004). *Arson and juveniles: Responding to the violence.* Washington, DC: Federal Emergency Management Agency, National Fire Data Center.

University of Iowa Injury Prevention Research Center. (2001). *Workplace violence: A report to the nation.* Iowa City: Author.

Valenstein, E. S. (1973). *Brain control.* New York: Wiley.

van Beijsterveldt, C. E. M., Bartels, M., Hudziak, J. J., & Boomsma, D. I. (2003). Causes of stability of aggression from early childhood to adolescence: A longitudinal genetic analysis in Dutch twins. *Behavior Genetics, 33,* 591–605.

Van Dam, C., Janssens, J. M. A. M., & De Bruyn, E. E. J. (2006). PEN, Big Five, juvenile delinquency and criminal recidivism. *Personality and Individual Differences, 39,* 7–19.

Vandell, D. L., & Posner, J. K. (1999). Conceptualization and measurement of children's after-school environments. In S. L. Freidman & T. D. Wachs (Eds.), *Measuring environment across the lifespan: Emerging methods and concepts.* Washington, DC: American Psychological Association.

Vandersall, T. A., & Wiener, J. M. (1970). Children who set fires. *Archives of General Psychology, 22,* 63–71.

van Lier, P. A. C., Vuijk, P., & Crijen, A. M. (2005). Understanding mechanisms of change in the development of antisocial behavior: The impact of a universal intervention. *Journal of Abnormal Psychology, 33,* 521–533.

van Wijik, A., van Horn, J., Bullens, R., Bijleveld, C., & Doreleijers, T. (2005). Juvenile sex offenders: A group on its own? *International Journal of Offender Therapy and Comparative Criminology, 49,* 25–36.

Veneziano, C., & Veneziano, L. (2002). Adolescent sex offenders: A review of the literature. *Trauma, Violence, & Abuse, 3,* 247–260.

Verlinden, S., Hersen, M., & Thomas, J. (2000). Risk factors in school shootings. *Clinical Psychology Review, 20,* 3–56.

Verona, E., Joiner, T. E., Johnson, F., & Bender, T. W. (2006). Gender specific gene-environment interactions on laboratory-assessed aggression. *Biological Psychology, 71,* 33–41.

Vetter, H. J., & Silverman, I. J. (1978). *The nature of crime.* Philadelphia, PA: W. B. Saunders.

Viding, E., Blair, R. J. R., Moffitt, T. E., & Plomin, R. (2005). Evidence for substantial genetic risk for psychopathy in 7-year-olds. *Journal of Child Psychology and Psychiatry, 46,* 592–597.

Vien, A., & Beech, A. R. (2006). Psychopathy: Theory, measurement, and treatment. *Trauma, Violence, & Abuse, 7,* 155–174.

Vincent, K. R. (1991). Black/white IQ difference? *Journal of Clinical Psychology, 47,* 266–270.

Virrkunen, M., & Linnoila, M. (1993). Brain serotonin, Type II alcoholism and impulsive violence. *Journal of Studies on Alcohol* (Supplement), *11,* 163–169.

Vitacco, M. J., Neumann, C. S., & Jackson, R. L. (2005). Testing a four-factor model of psychopathy and its association with ethnicity, gender, intelligence, and violence. *Journal of Consulting and Clinical Psychology, 73,* 466–476.

Vitale, J. E., Newman, J. P., Serin, R. C., & Bolt, D. M. (2005). Hostile attributions in incarcerated adult male offenders: An exploration of diverse pathways. *Aggressive Behavior, 31,* 99–115.

Vitale, J. E., Smith, S. S., Brinkley, C. A., & Newman, J. P. (2002). The reliability and validity of the Psychopathy Checklist-Revised in a sample of female offenders. *Criminal Justice and Behavior, 29,* 202–231.

Vitaro, F., & Brendgen, M. (2005). Proactive and reactive aggression: A developmental perspective. In R. E. Tremblay, W. W. Hartrup, & J. Archer (Eds.), *The developmental origins of aggression.* New York: Guilford Press.

Vitaro, F., Brendgen, M., & Barker, E. D. (2006). Subtypes of aggressive behaviors: A developmental perspective. *International Journal of Behavioral Development, 30,* 12–19.

Vitaro, F., & Tremblay, R. P. (1994). Impact of a prevention program on aggressive children's friendships and social adjustment. *Journal of Abnormal Child Psychology, 22,* 457–476.

Vold, G. B. (1958). *Theoretical criminology.* New York: Oxford University Press.

Waaktaar, T., Christie, H. J., Borge, A. I. H., & Torgerson, S. (2004). How can young people's resilience be enhanced? Experiences from a clinical intervention project. *Clinical Child Psychology and Psychiatry, 9,* 167–183.

Wadsworth, M. E. J. (1979). *Roots of delinquency: Infancy, adolescence and crime.* Oxford, UK: Martin Robinson.

Wagner, R. V., & Long, K. R. (2004). Terrorism from a peace psychology prspective. In F. M. Moghaddam & A. J. Marsella (Eds.), *Understanding terrorism: Psychosocial roots, consequences, and interventions.* Washington, DC: American Psychological Association.

Waite, D., Keller, A., McGarvey, E. L., Wieckowski, E., Pinkerton, R., & Brown, G. L. (2005). Juvenile sex offender re-arrest rates for sexual, violent nonsexual, and property crimes. *Sexual Abuse: A Journal of Research and Treatment, 17,* 313–331.

Wakefield, J. C. (1992). Disorder as harmful dysfunction: A conceptual critique of DSM-III-R's definition of mental disorder. *Psychological Review, 99,* 232–247.

Wakschlag, L. S., & Hans, S. L. (2002). Maternal smoking during pregnancy and conduct problems in high-risk youth: A developmental framework. *Development and Psychopathology, 14,* 351–369.

Walker, J. S., & Gudjonsson, G. H. (2006). The Maudsley Violence Questionnaire: Relationship to personality and self-reported offending. *Personality and Individual Differences, 40,* 795–806.

Walker, K. L., & Chestnut, D. (2003). The role of ethnocultural variables in response to terrorism. *Cultural Diversity and Ethnic Minority Psychology, 9,* 251–262.

Walker, L. E. (1979). *The battered woman.* New York: Harper Colophon Books.

Walker, S. (2001). *Sense and nonsense about crime and drugs* (5th ed.). Belmont, CA: Wadsworth/Thomson Learning.

Wallace, H. (1996). *Family violence: Legal, medical, and social perspectives.* Boston: Allyn & Bacon.

Wallace, H., & Seymour, A. (2001). Domestic violence. In G. Coleman, M. Gaboury, M. Murray, & A. Seymour (Eds.), *1999 National Victim Assistance Academy.* Washington, DC: U.S. Department of Justice.

Waller, M. A. (2001). Resilience in ecosystemic context: Evolution of the concept. *American Journal of Orthopsychiatry, 71,* 290–297.

Wallerstein, J. S., & Wyle, J. (1947). *Our law-abiding law breakers.* Probation, 25, 107–112.

Walsh, A. (2005). African Americans and serial killing in the media. *Homicide Studies, 9,* 271–291.

Walsh, D. (1980). *Break-ins: Burglary from private houses.* London: Constable.

Walster, E. (1966). Assignment of responsibility for an accident. *Journal of Personality and Social Psychology, 3,* 73–79.

Walters, G. C., & Grusec, J. E. (1977). *Punishment.* San Francisco, CA: W. H. Freeman.

Walters, G. D. (2003). Predicting institutional adjustment and recidivism with the Psychopathy Checklist factor scores: A meta-analysis. *Law and Human Behavior, 27,* 541–558.

Ward, T., & Hudson, S. M. (2000). Sexual offenders' implicit planning: A conceptual model. *Sexual Abuse: A Journal of Research and Treatment, 12,* 189–202.

Warren, J. I., Rosenfeld, B., Fitch, W. L., & Hawk, G. (1997). Forensic mental health clinical evaluation: An analysis of interstate and intersystemic differences. *Law and Human Behavior, 21,* 377–390.

Warren, M. Q. (1983). Application of interpersonal maturity theory of offender population. In W. S. Laufer & J. M. Day (Eds.), *Personality theory, moral development, and criminal behavior.* Lexington, MA: Lexington Books.

Wasserman, G. A., & Seracini, A. M. (2001). Family risk factors and interventions. In R. Loeber & D. P. Farrington (Eds.), *Child delinquents: Development, intervention, and service needs.* Thousand Oaks, CA: Sage.

Watson, R. I. (1973). Investigation into deindividuation using a cross-cultural survey technique. *Journal of Personality and Social Psychology, 25,* 342–345.

Webb, J. A., Bray, J. H., Getz, J. G., & Adams, G. (2002). Gender, perceived parental monitoring, and behavioral adjustment: Influences on adolescent alcohol use. *American Journal of Orthopsychiatry, 72,* 392–400.

Webster, C. D., Douglas, K. S., Eaves, D., & Hart, S. D. (1997). Assessing risk to violence to others. In C. D. Webster & M. A. Jackson (Eds.), *Impulsivity: Theory, assessment and treatment.* New York: Guilford.

Webster, C. D., Harris, G. T., Rice, M. E., Cormier, C., & Quinsey, V. L. (1994). *The violence prediction scheme: Assessing dangerousness in high-risk men.* Toronto, ON: University of Toronto Press.

Webster, C. D., & Menzies, R. J. (1993). Supervision in the deinstitutionalized community. In S. Hodgins (Ed.), *Mental disorder and crime.* Newbury Park, CA: Sage.

Weiler, B. L., & Widom, C. S. (1996). Psychopathy and violent behavior in abused and neglected young adults. *Criminal Behavior and Mental Health, 6,* 253–271.

Weis, J. G. (1989). Family violence methodology and design. In L. Ohlin & M. Tonry (Eds.), *Family violence* (Vol. 11). Chicago, IL: University of Chicago Press.

Weis, J. G., & Sederstrom, J. (1981). *The prevention of serious delinquency. What to do?* Washington, DC: U.S. Department of Justice.

Weiss, J., Lamberti, J., & Blackburn, N. (1960). The sudden murderers. *Archives of General Psychiatry, 2,* 670–678.

Weiss, R. D., & Mirin, S. M. (1987). *Cocaine.* Washington, DC: American Psychiatric Press.

Welte, J. W., & Abel, E. L. (1989). Homicide: Drinking by the victim. *Journal of Studies on Alcohol, 50,* 197–201.

Wenk, E. A., Robison, J. O., & Smith, G. W. (1972). Can violence be predicted? *Crime and Delinquency, 18,* 393–402.

Wessler, S., & Moss, M. (2001, October). *Hate crimes on campus: The problem and efforts to confront it.* Washington, DC: U.S. Department of Justice, Office of Justice Programs.

West, D. J., & Farrington, D. P. (1973). *Who becomes delinquent?* London: Heinemann Educational.

Wettstein, R. M. (1984). The prediction of violent behavior and the duty to protect third parties. *Behavioral Sciences & the Law, 2,* 291–316.

Wheatman, S. R., & Shaffer, D. R. (2001). On finding for defendants who plead insanity: The crucial impact of dispositional instructions and opportunity to deliberate. *Law and Human Behavior, 25,* 167–183.

Wheeler, R. W., Davidson, R. J., & Tomarken, A. J. (1993). Frontal brain asymmetry and emotional reactivity: A biological substrate of affective style. *Psychophysiology, 30,* 82–89.

Whitcomb, D. (2001). Child victimization. In G. Coleman, M. Gaboury, M. Murray, & A. Seymour (Eds.), *1999 National Victim Assistance Academy.* Washington, DC: U.S. Department of Justice.

White, J. L., Moffitt, T. E., Earls, F., Robins, L., & Silva, P. A. (1990). How early can we tell? Predictors of childhood conduct disorder and delinquency. *Criminology, 28,* 507–533.

White, J. L., Moffitt, T. E., & Silva, P. A. (1989). A prospective replication of the protective effects of IQ in subjects at high risk for juvenile delinquency. *Journal of Consulting and Clinical Psychology, 57,* 719–724.

Whitehill, M., DeMyer-Gapin, S., & Scott, T. G. (1976). Stimulation seeking in antisocial preadolescent children. *Journal of Abnormal Psychology, 85,* 101–104.

Wicker, T. (1976). *Time to die.* New York: Ballatine.

Widiger, T. A., Frances, A. J., Pincus, H. A., Davis, W. W., & First, M. B. (1991). Toward an empirical classification of the DSM-IV. *Journal of Abnormal Psychology, 100,* 280–288.

Widom, C. S. (1978). A methodology for studying non-institutionalized psychopaths. In R. D. Hare & D. Schalling (Eds.), *Psychopathic behavior: Approaches to research.* Chichester, UK: Wiley.

Widom, C. S. (1992, September). *The cycle of violence.* Research in Brief. Washington, DC: U.S. Department of Justice.

Widom, C. S. (2000, January). Childhood victimization: Early adversity, later psychopathology. *National Institute of Justice Journal,* 3–9.

Widom, C. S., & Newman, J. P. (1985). Characteristics of noninstituionalized psychopaths. In J. Gunn & D. Farrington (Eds.), *Current research in forensic psychiatry and psychology* (Vol. 2). New York: Wiley.

Wiesen, A. E. (1965). *Differential reinforcing effects of onset and offset of stimulation on the operant behavior of normals, neurotics, and psychopaths.* Doctoral dissertation, University of Florida. Ann Arbor, MI: University Microfilms, No. 65–9625.

Wiesner, M., Kim, H. K., & Capaldi, D. M. (2005). Developmental trajectories of offending: Validation and prediction to young adult alcohol use, drug use, and depressive symptoms. *Development and Psychopathology, 17,* 251–270.

Wiesner, M., & Windle, M. (2004). Assessing covariates of adolescent delinquency trajectories: A latent growth mixture modeling approach. *Journal of Youth and Adolescence, 33,* 431–432.

Wilczynski, A. (1991). Images of women who kill their infants: The mad and the bad. *Women & Criminal Justice, 2,* 71–88.

Wilczynski, A. (1997). Mad or bad? Child-killers, gender, and the courts. *British Journal of Criminology, 37,* 419–436.

Williams, F. P., & McShane, M. D. (2004). *Criminological theory* (4th ed.). Upper Saddle River, NJ: Prentice Hall.

Williams, J. E., & Holmes, K. A. (1981). *The second assault: Rape and public attitudes.* Westport, CT: Greenwood Press.

Williams, W., & Miller, K. S. (1981). The processing and disposition of incompetent mentally ill offenders. *Law and Human Behavior, 5,* 245–261.

Williamson, S., Hare, R. D., & Wong, S. (1987). Violence: Criminal psychopaths and their victims. *Canadian Journal of Behavioral Science, 19,* 454–462.

Wilson, D. J. (2000). *Drug use, testing, and treatment in jails.* Washington, DC: Bureau of Justice Statistics.

Wilson, J. Q., & Herrnstein, R. J. (1985). *Crime and human nature.* New York: Simon & Schuster.

Wincze, J. P. (1977). Sexual deviance and dysfunction. In D. Rimm & J. Somervill (Eds.), *Abnormal psychology.* New York: Academic Press.

Windle, M., & Wiesner, M. (2004). Trajectories of marijuana use from adolescence to young adulthood: Predictors and outcomes. *Development and Psychopathology, 16,* 1007–1027.

Wolf, R. S. (1992). Victimization of the elderly: Elder abuse and neglect. *Reviews in Clinical Gerontology, 2,* 269–276.

Wolfe, D. A. (1985). Child-abusive parents: An empirical review and analysis. *Psychological Bulletin, 97,* 462–582.

Wolfe, D. A., Jaffe, P. G., Wilson, S. K., & Zak, L. (1985). Children of battered women: The relation of child behavior to family violence and maternal stress. *Journal of Consulting and Clinical Psychology, 53,* 657–665.

Wolfgang, M. E. (1958). *Patterns in criminal homicide.* Philadelphia, PA: University of Pennsylvania Press.

Wolfgang, M. E. (1961). A sociological analysis of criminal homicide. *Federal Probation, 25,* 48–55.

Wolfgang, M. E. (1972). Cesare Lombroso (1835–1909). In H. Mannheim (Ed.), *Pioneers in criminality.* Montclair, NJ: Patterson Smith.

Wolfgang, M. E., & Ferracuti, F. (1967). *The subculture of violence.* London: Tavistock.

Wolford, M. R. (1972). Some attitudinal, psychological and sociological characteristics of incarcerated arsonists. *Fire and Arson Investigator, 16,* 8–13.

Wong, M., & Singer, K. (1973). Abnormal homicide in Hong Kong. *British Journal of Psychiatry, 123,* 37–46.

Wong, M. T. H., Lumsden, J., Fenton, G. W., & Fenwick P. B. C. (1994). Epilepsy and violence in mentally abnormal offenders in a maximum security mental hospital. *Journal of Epilepsy, 7,* 253–258.

Wong, S. (2000). Psychopathic offenders. In S. Hodgins & R. Muller-Isberner (Eds.), *Violence, crime and mentally disordered offenders: Concepts and methods for effective treatment and prevention.* New York: Wiley.

Wood, J. J., Cowan, P. A., & Baker, B. L. (2002). Behavior problems and peer rejection in preschool boys and girls. *Journal of Genetic Psychology, 163,* 72–89.

Woodworth, M. & Porter, S. (2001). Historical foundations and current applications of criminal profiling in violent crime investigations. *Expert Evidence, 7,* 241–264.

Woodworth, M. & Porter, S. (2002). In cold blood: Characteristics of criminal homicides as a function of psychopathy. *Journal of Abnormal Psychology, 111,* 436–445.

Worling, J. R. (1995). Adolescent sibling incest offenders: Differences in family and individual functioning when compared to adolescent nonsibling sex offenders. *Child Abuse & Neglect, 19,* 633–643.

Wright, J. C., Huston, A. C., Vandewater, E. A., Bickman, D. S., Scantlin, R. M., Kotler, J. A., Caplovitz, A. G., Lee, J. H., Hofferth, S., & Finkelstein, J. (2001). American children's use of electronic media in 1997: A national survey. *Applied Developmental Psychology, 22,* 31–47.

Wright, J. D., & Rossi, P. H. (1994). *Armed and considered dangerous: A survey of felons and their firearms.* New York: Aldine De Gruyter.

Wright, R., Brookman, F., & Bennett, T. (2006). The foreground dynamics of street robbery in Britain. *British Journal of Criminology, 46,* 1–15.

Wright, R. T., & Decker, S. (1997). *Armed robbers in action: Stickup and street culture.* Boston, MA: Northeastern University Press.

Xie, H., Farmer, T. W., & Cairns, B. D. (2003). Different forms of aggression among inner-city African-American Children: Gender, configurations, and school social networks. *Journal of School Psychology, 41,* 355–375.

Yang, Y., Raine, A., Lencz, T., Bihrle, S., LaCasse, L., & Colletti, P. (2005). Volume reduction in prefrontal gray matter in unsuccessful criminal psychopaths. *Biological Psychiatry, 57,* 1103–1108.

Yates, E. (1986). The influence of psychosocial factors on nonsensical shoplifting. *International Journal of Offender Therapy and Comparative Criminology, 30,* 203–211.

Yegidis, B. L. (1986). Date rape and other forced sexual encounters among college students. *Journal of Sex Education and Therapy, 12,* 51–54.

Yesavage, J. A., Benezech, M., Ceccaldi, P., Bourgeois, M., & Addad, M. (1983). Arson in mentally ill and criminal populations. *Journal of Clinical Psychiatry, 44,* 128–130.

Yochelson, S., & Samenow, S. E. (1976). *The criminal personality* (Vol. 1). New York: Jason Aronson.

Yu, J., Evans, P. C., & Perfetti, L. (2004). Road aggression among drinking drivers: Alcohol and non-alcohol effects on aggressive driving and road rage. *Journal of Criminal Justice, 32,* 421–430.

Zamble, E., & Porporino, F. G. (1988). *Coping, behavior, and adaptation in prison inmates.* New York: Springer-Verlag.

Zawitz, M. W., & Strom, K. J. (2000, October). *Firearm injury and death from crime, 1993–1997.* Washington, DC: U.S. Department of Justice.

Zebrowitz, L. A., Andreoletti, C., Collins, M. A., Lee, S. Y., & Blumenthal, J. (1998). Bright, bad, babyfaced boys: Appearance stereotypes do not always yield self-fulfilling prophecy effects. *Journal of Personality and Social Psychology, 75,* 1300–1320.

Zebrowitz, L. A., Collins, M. A., & Dutta, R. (1998). The relationship between appearance and personality across the lifespan. *Personality and Social Psychology Bulletin, 24,* 736–749.

Zigler, E., Taussig, C., & Black, K. (1992). Early childhood intervention: A promising prevention for juvenile delinquency. *American Psychologist, 47,* 997–1006.

Zillmann, D. (1971). Excitation transfer in communication-mediated aggressive behavior. *Journal of Experimental Social Psychology, 7,* 419–434.

Zillmann, D. (1979). *Hostility and aggression.* Hillsdale, NJ: Erlbaum.

Zillmann, D. (1983). Arousal and aggression. In R. G. Geen & E. I. Donnerstein (Eds.), *Aggression: Theoretical and empirical reviews* (Vol. 1). New York: Academic Press.

Zillmann, D. (1988). Cognitive-excitation interdependencies in aggressive behavior. *Aggressive Behavior, 14,* 51–64.

Zillmann, D., Baron, R., & Tamborini, R. (1981). Social costs of smoking: Effects of tobacco smoke on hostile behavior. *Journal of Applied Social Psychology, 11,* 548–561.

Zimbardo, P. G. (1970). The human choice. Individuation, reason, and order versus deindividuation, impulse, and chaos. In W. J. Arnold & D. Levine (Eds.), *Nebraska symposium on motivation 1969.* Lincoln, NE: University of Nebraska Press.

Zimbardo, P. G. (1973). The psychological power and pathology of imprisonment. In E. Aronson and R. Helmreich (Eds.), *Social psychology.* New York: Van Nostrand.

Zipper, P., & Wilcox, D. K. (2005, April). The importance of early intervention. *FBI Law Enforcement Bulletin, 74,* 3–9.

Zoccoulillo, M. (1993). Gender and the development of conduct disorder. *Development and Psychopathology, 5,* 65–78.

Zorza, J. (1991). Woman battering: A major cause of homelessness. *Clearinghouse Review, 25* (4).

Zucker, R. A., Fitzgerald, H. E., Refior, S. K., Puttler, L. I., Pallas, D. M., & Ellis, D. A. (2000). The clinical and social ecology of childhood for children of alcoholics: Description of a study and implications for a differentiated social policy. In H. E. Fitzgerald, B. M. Lester, & B. S. Zuckerman (Eds.), *Children of addiction: Research, health, and public policy issues* (pp. 109–141). New York: RoutledgeFalmer.

AUTHOR INDEX

Aaronson, D. E., 246, 247
Abadinsky, H., 536, 547
Abel, G. G., 413, 414, 424, 437
Abrahamsen, D., 9, 512
Abram, K. M., 534, 543
Achenbach, T. M., 163, 323
Acoca, L., 60
Adams-Curtis, L. E., 415
Adams, D., 59
Adams, G., 560
Adams, K., 613, 614
Adamson, L. A., 324
Adlaf, E. M., 154
Adler, F., 480, 481
Adler, J., 465
Adler, R., 506
Ageton, S. S., 290
Ahmed, S., 538
Akers, R. L., 116, 120, 125, 126, 127
Akert, R. M., 621
Albanese, J. S., 475
Alexander, M. A., 438
Alexandre, J. W., 592
Alison, L., 130, 331, 336, 338
Allain, A. N., 211, 249
Allen, M., 417
Allen, N. B., 87
Alm, P.-O., 222
American Bar Association, 30
American Psychiatric Association (APA), 28, 57, 188, 195, 422
American Psychological Association, 175, 301
Amir, M., 396, 399
Amos, N. L., 200
Amsel, A., 128
Andeneas, J., 609
Andershed, H., 206
Anderson, C. A., 13, 145, 152, 159, 168, 169, 170, 172, 175
Anderson, D. C., 169
Anderson, K. B., 159
Andreasen, N. C., 181, 231
Andreoletti, C., 94
Andrew, J. M., 210
Andrews, D. A., 274, 612, 613, 630
Andrews, D. W., 572, 573
Appelbaum, P. S., 249, 250, 251, 261
Applegate, B., 619
Araji, S., 389, 421, 438

Arango, V., 177
Arat, C. M., 560
Archer, J., 165
Ardrey, R., 147
Arkow, P., 306
Armstrong, J., 398, 627
Aronson, E., 34, 621
Arrestees Drug Abuse Monitoring Program, 527
Arseneault, L., 86, 95
Arthur, M. W., 579
Asbridge, M., 153, 154
Ascione, R. R., 306
Asher, S. R., 40
Ashford, J. B., 54, 265, 614, 617
Asp, C. E., 54
Au Coin, K., 310, 318
Augustine Fellowship, 402
Ault, R., 334
Aumick, A., 395
Austin, J., 60
Avary, D. W., 453
Avery-Clark, C. A., 414
Awad, G. A., 508
Azar, S. T., 326

Babcock, J. C., 316
Bachman, G. G., 467
Bachman, J. G., 548
Bagwell, C. L., 40, 43
Bahl, A. B., 165
Baker, B. L., 165
Baker, M. D., 204
Baldacci, H. B., 173
Ball, J. C., 553
Bamfield J., 471
Bancroft, H., 441
Bandura, A., 121, 123, 125, 130, 134, 137, 138, 145, 148, 156, 157, 369, 370, 376, 377, 378, 379, 385, 386, 476, 582, 621, 623
Bank, L., 572
Barad, S. J., 324
Baranoski, M. V., 312
Barbanel, L., 371
Barbaranelli, C., 138
Barbaree, H. E., 200, 414, 416, 429, 437, 626, 627, 628
Bard, L. A., 438
Bardone, A. M., 58
Barker, E. D., 165

Barker, M., 457
Barlow, D. H., 234, 413
Barnett, W. S., 579
Baron, R., 169
Baron, R. A., 135, 141, 142, 168, 355, 356
Barry, C. T., 203
Bartels, M., 79
Bartholow, B. D., 175
Bartol, A. M., 6, 8, 19, 31, 314, 325, 334, 422
Bartol, C. R., 6, 8, 19, 31, 314, 325, 334, 422, 603,
    604, 623
Bartsch, T. W., 211
Bates, J. E., 40, 44, 49, 84, 160
Battelle Law and Justice Center Report, 400
Baum, K., 464, 465
Baumer, T. L., 467
Baumgarnder, J., 173
Baumrind, D., 47, 69
Beal, L. S., 398, 627
Bear, M. F., 176
Beatty, D., 499
Beck, A. J., 287, 527, 607, 608
Beck, A. T., 622
Becker, J. V., 389, 400, 413, 424, 427, 436, 438, 623
Becker, K. D., 508
Beech, A. R., 207
Belding, M., 62
Belfrage, H., 612
Bell, P. A., 168
Bendersky, M., 50
Benedek, E. P., 312
Bennett, C., 130, 338
Bennett, D. S., 50
Bennett, T., 455, 489, 493, 517
Benton, D., 317, 318
Bereczkei, T., 4
Bergman, B., 470
Berk, R. A., 326
Berkowitz, L., 128, 148, 149, 150, 151, 164, 168,
    184, 295, 373, 378
Berlyne, D. E., 213, 282
Bernard, F., 424
Berney, T., 178, 443, 508
Bernstein, A., 210
Berntson, G. G., 74
Berrueta-Clement, J. R., 579
Berscheid, E., 93
Bertholf, M., 375
Best, C. L., 393, 399
Binder, A., 54
Bird, S., 625
Birnbaum, A. S.
Birt, A. R., 196
Birx, R. J., 509
Björkqvist, K., 166
Black, H. C., 285
Black, K., 569
Black, M. S., 401
Blackburn, N., 375
Blackburn, R., 78, 160, 161, 236, 237, 262, 374

Blackshaw, L., 396, 625
Blair, C. D., 442
Blair, R. J. R., 194, 205, 207
Blanchard, E. B., 153, 154, 413, 429
Blanchard, R., 422
Blashfield, R., 299
Blechman, E., 506, 508
Blitstein, J. L., 49
Block, R., 293, 295
Blonigen, D. M., 207
Blumenthal, D. R., 134
Blumer, D., 178, 183
Blumer, H., 538
Bodin, S. D., 203
Boehnert, C. E., 242
Boer, D., 196
Boergers, J., 166
Bogat, G. A., 169
Bohn, M. J., 612
Boivin, M., 164
Bolen, R. N., 424
Bolt, D. M., 160, 161
Bonanno, G. A., 581
Bongers, I. L., 176
Bonnie, R., 237
Bonta, J., 274, 607, 611, 612, 613, 621, 630
Boomsma, D. I., 79
Boothby, J. L., 603
Borduin, C. M., 569, 585, 586, 595, 596, 597
Borge, A. I. H., 581
Borjes, E. D., 441
Borum, R., 270, 275, 501
Bottcher, J., 594
Boucher, R., 271, 272, 405, 406
Boudreau, J., 509
Boulerice, B., 86
Bourque, B. B., 593, 594
Bowden, B. S., 24
Bowker, L. H., 326
Boyer, R., 471
Boykin, A. W., 53
Boyle, M. C., 57
Bracey, D. H., 482
Bradford, J. M., 513
Bradley, M. M., 220
Braga, A. A., 294
Braiker, H. B., 609
Braithwaite, J., 290
Brandt, J., 205, 255, 256
Brantley, A. G., 344, 346
Bray, J. H., 560, 564
Brazier, J. M., 317, 318
Breedlove, S. M., 176
Brendgen, M., 165
Brennan, P. A., 50, 64, 66, 83, 86, 87, 95, 96, 260
Brent, D. A., 335
Brier, N., 55
Briere, J., 414, 415, 426
Brinkley, C. A., 201
Brodsky, S. L., 260

Broidy, L. M., 60
Brook, J., 58
Brookman, F., 310, 489, 493, 517
Brown, B. B., 461
Brown, J. S., 128
Brown, T. L., 595
Browne, A., 31, 313, 315, 324, 426
Browning, K., 50
Brownlie, E. B., 51
Brunet, B. L., 539
Brussel, J. A., 516
Bryant, J., 125
Buchanan, J. A., 312
Buchanan, R. W., 167
Buchman, D. D., 172
Buckle, A., 466
Buffington-Vollum, J. K., 202, 203
Bukowski, W., 40
Bukstel, L. H., 614, 615
Bullock, H. A., 290
Bumby, K. M., 436
Bumby, N. H., 436
Bumpass, E. R., 509
Bureau of International Narcotics and Law En-
    forcement Affairs, 550, 551
Bureau of Justice Assistance, 266
Bureau of Justice Statistics, 287, 290, 293, 311, 353,
    526, 529, 605, 606, 607, 615
Bureau of Labor Statistics, 355
Burgess, A. G., 300, 336, 351, 359, 510
Burgess, A. W., 300, 333, 334, 336, 337, 343, 351,
    359, 360, 434, 446, 510
Burgess, K. B., 84
Burgess, R. L., 120, 125
Burke, H. C., 195, 205, 222
Burkhart, B. R., 396
Burnam, M. A., 390
Burns, L. K., 322
Burrows, J., 466, 467
Burt, M. R., 346
Bush, I., 322
Bushman, B. J., 145, 152, 153, 159, 168, 169
Bushnell, J. A., 201
Buss, A. H., 144
Buss, D. M., 4
Butler, R. A., 283
Buzawa, C. G., 326
Buzawa, E. S., 326
Byrne, D., 135, 414

Cacioppo, J. T., 74, 110
Cairns, B. D., 165
Cairns, R. B., 166
Caldwell, A., 294
Cale, E., 96, 108
Calhoun, J. B., 166
Callahan, L. A., 241, 242, 248
Calmas, W., 405, 430
Calpaldi, 68
Cameron, M. O., 467, 468, 470

Campbell, A., 59, 165, 380
Campbell, B. J., 300
Campbell, M. A., 205
Campbell, N. B., 51
Canadian Government's Commission of Inquiry,
    553
Canter, D., 331, 336, 338
Canter, S., 76
Cantor, J. M., 428
Capaldi, D. M., 62, 522
Caprara, G. V., 138
Carlsmith, J. J., 503
Carlson, B. E., 324
Carlson, M., 150
Carlson, R. J., 618
Carlson, S. R., 207
Carnegie Council on Adolescent Development, 583
Carnes, P., 402
Carpenter, W. T., 231
Carr, T. S., 177
Carraher, D., 53
Carraher, T. N., 53
Carter, D. L., 432, 496
Casey-Cannon, S., 166
Casey, J., 200
Caspi, A., 58, 62, 63, 64, 84
Catalano, S. M., 452
Cauffman, E., 203, 205
Cavior, N., 93
Cellini, H. R., 400, 435
Ceniti, J., 415
Center, D. B., 108, 109
Chaiken, J. M., 288, 390, 391, 395
Chalkley, A. J., 445
Chamberlain, P., 573
Chamlin, M. B., 290
Chance, S. E., 177
Chaplin, T. C., 513
Chappell, D., 396, 397, 399
Chapple, C. L., 322
Chard-Wierschem, D., 43
Check, J. V. P., 414, 416, 417
Chen, K., 563
Cherbonneau, M., 462
Chesney-Lind, M., 40, 60, 482
Chesno, F. A., 215
Chestnut, D., 371
Cheyne, J. A., 148
Child Abuse Prevention Center, 309
Chimbos, P. D., 457
Chorover, S. L., 179
Christenson, C. V., 429
Christian, C. W., 309
Christiansen, K. O., 77, 78
Christie, H. J., 581
Christie, M. M., 425
Chung, I.-J., 68
Churgin, M. M., 267
Chute, C. L., 574
Cicero, T. J., 554, 555

Cillessen, A. H. N., 41
Cirincione, C., 242, 248
Clare, C. H., 508
Claridge, G., 77
Clark, D., 198, 199, 624
Clark, J. P., 477, 478, 479
Clark, K. B., 180
Clark, M., 603, 604
Clark, R., 50
Clear, T. R., 617
Cleckley, H., 190, 197, 221
Clements, C. B., 603, 611, 612
Clinard, M. B., 472, 474
Coatsworth, J. D., 324
Cochran, J. K., 128
Cochrane, R., 242, 290
Cockerham, W., 269
Cocozza, J. J., 271, 272
Cohen, F., 248, 267, 277
Cohen, I. M., 205
Cohen, J., 58
Cohen, M., 405, 430
Cohen, M. L., 405
Cohen, N. J., 51
Cohen, P., 58
Cohen, W. E., 543
Cohn, E. G., 168
Cohn, V., 547
Coie, J. D., 40, 41, 42, 43, 50, 62, 159, 160, 164, 583
Cole, G. F., 617
Coleman, C., 465
Coleman, J. C., 440, 481
Coleman, J. W., 475
Coleman, R., 506, 507
Coles, E., 240
Collins, M. A., 94
Collins, P. A., 357, 358
Colwell, L. H., 201, 202, 204
Colwell, M. J., 45
Comer, R. J., 178, 180, 183, 230, 249, 254
Committee on Preventive Psychiatry, 579, 585
Community Research Associates, 60
Conduct Problems Prevention Research Group, 570, 571, 583
Conklin, J. E., 476, 477
Connell, D., 155
Connolly, J. F., 209
Connors, B. W., 176
Cook, P. J., 293, 294
Cook, S. E., 484
Cooke, D. J., 199
Cooksey, R. W., 334
Coordinating Council on Juvenile Justice and Delinquency Prevention, 571
Copeland, J., 556
Copes, H., 462
Cormier, C. A., 612
Cormier, R. B., 611, 613, 621, 624, 625
Corrado, R. R., 205

Cortes, J. B., 91
Coscina, D. V., 176
Côté, S., 64, 68
Cowan, C. P., 40
Cowan, P. A., 40, 165
Cowley, G., 55
Cox, A. D., 466
Cox, D., 466
Cox, D. N., 197
Coyle, E., 380
Craig, W. M., 4, 165, 205, 582
Craigen, D., 219
Cressey, D. R., 125, 126, 477
Cretton, H. M., 196
Crick, N. R., 42, 166
Crider, R., 539
Crijen, A. M., 62
Critchlow, B., 562
Critchton, R., 189
Critical Incident Response Group, 355, 357, 358, 359
Crocker, A. G., 54
Cromwell, P. F., 453, 454, 455, 456, 458, 459
Crosbie-Burnett, M., 314
Crowe, R. R., 80
Cruise, K. R., 203, 204, 237, 238
Crutchfield, R. D., 46
Culberton, F. M., 54
Cullen, F., 619
Culver, K. W., 513
Cunnien, A. J., 251
Curtain, J. J., 205

Dabbs, J. M., Jr., 177
Dadds, M. R., 590
Daderman, A. M., 205
Dahlberg, L. L., 61, 570, 589
Dalgaard, O. S., 78
Damon, W., 581
Daniels, D. N., 146
Danto, B. L., 617
Darkes, J., 340
Darling, N., 48
Darville, R., 593, 594
David, P. R., 459
Davidson, R. J., 209
Davies, M., 95
Davis, E. B., 175
Davis, M. G., 466
Davis, R. C., 410
Dawson, J. M., 319
Day, D. M., 425
Day, K., 178, 229, 443, 508
Day, R., 210
De Boer, S. F., 176
De Bruyn, E. E. J., 109
DeBurger, J., 345, 360
Decker, S., 294, 457, 458, 493, 495, 517
Dedel, K., 60

Deem, D., 464
DeFries, J. C., 77
Deisher, R. W., 319
DeLeon, P. H., 371
Delgado-Escueta, A., 183
D'Emilio, J., 481
Dempster, R. J., 193, 196, 199
DeMyer-Gapin, S., 212
Denault, G., 509
Denno, D., 210
Department of Health and Human Services, 526, 534
DeRosia, D. R., 615
Deuser, W. E., 159
Developments in the Law, 268
Dhaliwal, G., 612
Diener, E., 381, 383
Dietrich, K. N., 86, 571
Dietz, T. L., 172
Dill, K. E., 159, 175
Dillon, P., 556
DiLonardo, R. L., 471
Dinero, T. E., 413
Dinges, D. F., 253
Dion, K., 93
Diserens, C. M., 116
Dishion, T., 68, 572, 573
Ditton, P. M., 264, 265
Ditzler, T. F., 367
Dix, G. E., 271
Djenderedjian, A., 413
Dobson, V., 234, 312
Dodge, K. A., 38, 40, 44, 45, 49, 62, 78, 79, 84, 85, 125, 159, 160, 164, 222, 570, 571, 583, 585
Doerner, W. G., 284
Dolan, J. T., 502
Doley, R., 513
Dollard, J., 149
Donnerstein, E., 416
Donovan, J. E., 562
d'Orban, P. T., 301, 320
Doren, D. M., 276
Doss, R. C., 209
Douglas, J. E., 331, 332, 333, 334, 336, 337, 343, 351, 352, 359, 360, 510, 511
Douglas, K. S., 275, 612
Douglas, V., 56
Driver, E. D., 290
Drug Enforcement Administration, 531, 532, 536, 539, 542, 549, 556
DSM-IV, 230, 233, 251, 252, 421, 445, 511
Duhaime, A., 309
Dull, R. T., 396
Dunford, T. W., 31
Dunn, C. S., 284, 395
Durand, V. M., 234
Durose, M. R., 319, 393, 400, 401, 437
Dutta, R., 94
Dvorak, J. A., 342

Dvoskin, J., 266, 513
Dwyer, K. M., 84
Dziuba-Leatherman, J., 423

Earleywine, M., 152
Earls, F. J., 233
Easterbrook, J. A., 458
Eastman, B. J., 588, 589
Eaton, J., 46
Eaves, D., 275, 612
Ebert, B. W., 335
Eccles, J., 4, 45
Eck, J., 471, 491
Eddy, J. M., 58
Edelbrock, C., 323
Edens, J., 201, 202, 203, 204
Edleson, J. L., 323, 324
Edmunds, C., 398, 399
Edwards, J. N., 319
Edwards, S., 401, 407
Efran, M. G., 148
Eisenhower, M. S., 175
Elderkin, R. D., 91
Eley, T. C., 79
Ellickson, P., 562
Elliott, D. S., 31, 43, 290, 326
Ellis, A., 622
Ellis, C. A., 309
Ellis, L., 424
Else-Quest, N. M., 84
Emery, R. E., 310
Emke-Francis, P., 260
Emmers, T., 417
Ensminger, M. E., 526, 563
Epstein, J. F., 550
Erhardt, D., 42
Eron, L., 125, 160, 161, 172
Eskridge, C. W., 457
Estepp, M. H., 511, 513
Evans, D., 441, 442
Evans, G. W., 39, 153
Everett, R. S., 438
Ewing, C. P., 313
Eysenck, H. J., 77, 96, 97, 99, 101, 104, 105, 106, 107, 108, 214
Eysenck, S. B. G., 96
Ezell, M. E., 594

Fabisiak, S., 266
Fagan, J., 326, 327
Fagelman, F. D., 509
Falkenbach, D. M., 205
Fantuzzo, J. W., 323, 324
Farabee, D., 619
Faragher, W., 509
Farber, I. E., 128
Farmer, T. W., 165
Farrell, A., 242, 336, 341
Farrell, G., 459

Farrington, D. P., 27, 38, 45, 62, 92, 206, 222, 299, 466, 471, 589, 602, 624
Faupel, C. E., 553
Federal Bureau of Investigation, 11, 12, 13, 14, 15, 18, 19, 20, 31, 32, 196, 281, 286, 287, 288, 289, 290, 291, 292, 293, 296, 297, 298, 299, 301, 302, 303, 313, 319, 320, 333, 334, 363, 392, 395, 396, 436, 451, 452, 453, 461, 462, 480, 489, 490, 491, 492, 506, 513, 514, 522, 523, 524, 525, 526, 534
Federal Interagency Forum on Child and Family Statistics, 85
Fehrenbach, P. A., 319, 436
Fein, S., 168
Feinberg, G., 468
Feld, B. C., 577, 589
Feldman, M. P., 441
Felthous, A. R., 269
Fenichel, O., 512
Fenton, G. W., 183
Fenwick, P. B. C., 183
Feral, C. H., 54
Ferguson, D. M., 562
Fernandez, M., 429
Ferracuti, F., 157
Feshbach, S., 144, 416
Festinger, L., 134, 135
Feucht, T. W., 541
Field, S., 170, 171
Fields, G., 264
Figueredo, A. J., 324, 400, 436
Finckenauer, J. O., 484, 485
Finkel, N. J., 336, 337, 338
Finkelhor, D., 304, 305, 318, 421, 423, 426, 427, 438
Firestone, P., 196
Fishbein, D., 207, 217
Fiske, D. E., 213
Fiske, J. A., 625
Fitch, W. L., 242
Fitzgerald, H. F., 50
Fitzgerald, L. F., 398, 415
Fitzhugh, K. B., 210
Flanagan, B., 424
Flanagan, T. J., 609
Flannery, D. J., 44
Flay, B. R., 563
Flor-Henry, P., 210
Flynn, E. E., 46
Forbes, G. B., 415
Forehand, R., 507, 508
Forrstrom-Cohen, B., 323
Forth, A. E., 195, 197, 198, 203, 205, 206, 222
Foshee, V. A., 49
Fothergill, K. E., 526, 563
Fox, R. G., 182
Frady, R. L., 177
Frederick, R. I., 242, 255
Freedman, E. B., 481
Freedman, J. L., 167, 503
Freitas, T., 240
French, J. D., 99

Frey, J., 169
Frick, P. J., 64, 203, 205, 206, 207, 590
Friesenborg, A. E., 83
Frieze, I. H., 315, 316, 324
Frintner, M., 393
Frisbie, L. V., 437
Frizzell, K., 436
Funk, J. B., 172, 173
Furby, L., 396, 625
Fuselier, G. D., 501, 502, 504

Gabby, S., 54
Gabrielli, W. F., 82
Gacono, C. B., 187, 200, 236, 237, 623, 624
Gaes, G. G., 609, 620
Gagnon, J. H., 429
Galovski, T. E., 153, 154
Garafalo, R., 405, 406
Garbarino, J., 54, 322
Garcia, M. M., 50
Gardner, T. J., 285
Garofalo, J., 489
Garofalo, P. F., 271, 272
Garside, R. B., 166
Gary, T. S., 425, 426, 438
Gatti, F. M., 91
Gaynor, J., 507
Gebhard, P. H., 429
Gebhardt, L., 417
Geis, G., 228, 472, 476
Gelinas, D. J., 254
Gelles, R. J., 304, 319, 320, 323, 325
Gendreau, P., 274
Gentile, D. A., 171, 172
George, W. H., 414, 626, 627, 628
Gerard, R. E., 591
Gerbner, G., 228
Getz, J. G., 560, 564
Gfroerer, J. C., 550
Giacopassi, D. J., 396
Gibat, C. C., 627
Gibbens, T. C., 467, 483
Gibbons, D. C., 126, 130
Giddan, J. J., 51
Gidycz, C. A., 396
Giery, M. A., 417
Giller, H., 92, 176
Gilliom, M., 68, 569
Gilula, M. F., 146
Giovannelli, J., 84
Glass, C., 508, 509
Glasser, W. D., 622
Glueck, E., 46, 91, 111, 130
Glueck, S., 46, 91, 111, 130
Goetting, A., 299
Goggin, C., 274
Gold, M. S., 512
Golding, S. L., 238, 240, 241, 243
Goldman, M. J., 470, 471
Goldsmith, H. H., 84

Goldstein. A. P., 501
Goldstein, M., 183
Goldstein, M. J., 412
Goldstein, N. E., 44
Goldstein, P. J., 530, 566
Golub, A. L., 530, 547, 548
Goodstein, C., 438
Gordon, L. C., 322, 579
Gorenstein, E. E., 211
Gorman-Smith, D., 65, 572, 573
Gosselin, C., 445
Gottfredson, D. C., 354
Gottfredson, G. D., 354
Gottfredson, N. C., 354
Gottman, J. M., 218, 316
Gove, W. R., 46
Gowen, K., 166
Grams, P., 46
Grann, M., 196, 198, 612, 624
Grant, J. D., 613, 614
Grant, V., 194
Gray, J. A., 110
Graziano, W. G., 45
Green, A., 427
Green, G., 472, 473, 475
Greenberg, L. S., 622
Greenberg, M. T., 583
Greendlinger, V., 414
Greenfeld, L. A., 288, 299, 399, 559, 561, 562, 607
Greenwald, H., 483
Gregorie, T., 356
Grekin, E. R., 87
Gretton, H. M., 200
Griffin, R., 603, 604, 605
Griffith, W., 167
Grisso, T., 203, 204, 205, 206, 221, 237, 238, 240
Groom, R. W., 169
Gross, B., 547
Gross, B. H., 265
Gross, L., 228
Groth, A. N., 411, 412, 414, 417, 425, 426, 427, 434, 438
Grotpeter, J. K., 166
Grusec, J. E., 125
Gudjonsson, G. H., 96, 97, 109
Guerette, R. T., 335, 340
Guerra, N. G., 39, 570, 572, 579
Guild, D., 413
Gulley, B., 50
Guy, L. S., 204
Guze, S. B., 236

Haapasalo, J., 222, 322
Haber, S., 416
Haft, M. G., 481
Hage, S. M., 322
Hagell, A., 176
Häkkänen, H., 261
Hakstian, A., 198
Hall, C. L., 588

Hall, C. S., 89
Hall, D. M., 498
Hall, G. C. N., 425, 626
Hall, J. A., 248
Hall, R. W., 211
Hall, S. R., 427, 436
Halleck, S. L., 512
Hallett, B., 364
Hämäläinen, T., 322
Hamby, S. L., 305
Hamilton, D., 254
Hamilton, V. L., 131, 134
Hammond, W. R., 38, 39, 579
Hampson, J. E., 582
Haney, C., 131, 134, 615, 618
Hans, S. L., 87
Hansent, L., 460, 461
Hanson, K., 274
Hanson, R. K., 427, 428, 437, 613
Harbin, H. T., 319
Hare, R. D., 188, 191, 192, 193, 194, 195, 196, 197, 198, 199, 200, 201, 206, 209, 211, 218, 219, 220, 612, 624, 625
Harmon, R. B., 511
Harpur, T. J., 196, 197, 198
Harries, K. D., 167
Harrington, H., 62, 63
Harris, A. J. R., 613
Harris, B., 436
Harris, D. A., 341, 342
Harris, G. T., 200, 422, 441, 443, 513, 612, 623, 624, 625
Harris, P. B., 461
Harrison, P. M., 287, 607
Hart, C. H., 46, 47
Hart, S. D., 195, 196, 197, 199, 201, 205, 275, 612
Hartl, E. M., 89, 91
Hartman, C. R., 333, 334, 337, 343, 360
Hastings, P. D., 84
Hawes, D. J., 590
Hawk, G., 242
Hawke, C. C., 178
Hawkins, D. L., 165
Hayes, L. M., 617
Hayward, C., 166
Hazelwood, R. R., 446
Heaven, P. C. L., 108
Hebb, D. O., 162, 213
Hebert, E., 593
Heckel, R. V., 300
Heide, K. M., 205, 299, 320, 591, 592
Heilbrun, K., 276, 590, 605, 624
Heim, M., 416
Hemenway, D., 295
Hemphill, J. F., 200
Henderson, M., 375
Hendren, R. L., 513
Henggeler, S. W., 585, 595, 596, 599
Henker, B., 56
Henn, F. A., 236, 260, 427

Hennenway, D., 154
Henry, B., 84
Hepburn, J., 290, 293, 295, 296
Hepburn, L. M., 295
Hepworth, W., 355
Herjanic, M., 236, 260, 427
Herpertz, S. C., 210, 218
Herrera, V. M., 508
Herrnstein, R. J., 59, 92
Herschell, A. D., 165
Hersen, M., 353, 354
Herzberg, J. L., 183
Hetherington, E. M., 77
Hickey, E., 345, 347
Higley, J., 176
Hill, H. M., 38, 39
Hill, L. G., 583
Hill, P., 190
Hill, R. W., 513
Hillbrand, M., 592
Hindelang, M. J., 51, 52, 395, 465
Hinshaw, S. P., 42, 45
Hirschi, T., 51, 52
Hobson, W. F., 425, 426, 438
Hochstedler, E., 476
Hockenbury, D. H., 208
Hockenbury, S. E., 208
Hodgins, S., 54, 64, 260, 261
Hoek, H. W., 86
Hoffman, B., 367
Hoffman, J. J., 211
Hoffman, K. L., 319
Hofmann, F. G., 546
Hoge, R. D., 195, 197, 613
Hoge, S. K., 238
Hollinger, R., 21, 478, 479
Hollister-Wagner, G. H., 49
Holmes, C. T., 45
Holmes, K. A., 399
Holmes, R. M., 332, 345, 349
Holmes, S. T., 332, 345, 346, 349, 360
Holobean, E., 266
Holt, S. E., 196
Holtzworth-Monroe, A., 315
Homant, R. J., 466
Home Office, 301
Honeycutt, H., 175
Hope, S., 508, 509
Horning, D. N. M., 472
Hornung, C. A., 316
Horwood, L. J., 562
Hotaling, G. T., 315, 316, 321, 325
Hough, R., 58, 65
Howard, L. R., 93
Howell, J. C., 586
Howell, M., 324
Howell, N., 396
Howes, C., 44
Howland, E. W., 215
Hubbard, J. A., 158, 160, 164

Hudson, M. I., 317
Hudson, R., 240
Hudson, S. M., 495
Hudziak, J. J., 79
Huesmann, L. R., 125, 156, 158, 159, 161, 172, 174, 175, 185, 572
Hughes, H. M., 324
Huizinga, D., 31, 290, 562, 571
Hunter, J. A., 400, 436, 438
Huston, A., 125
Hutchings, B., 81, 82
Hyde, J. S., 50, 84

Iacono, W. G., 80
Icove, D. J., 511, 513
Inaba, D. S., 543
Inciardi, J. A., 482, 510, 529, 544, 554
Indermaur, 153
The Informant, 474, 478, 495
Ingoldsby, E. M., 68, 569
Ingram, G. L., 591
International Arrestees Drug Abuse Monitoring Program, 528
Irwin, H. J., 334
Ishikawa, S. S., 87, 192, 211
Ivanoff, A., 617

Jackson, C., 49
Jackson, C. J., 109
Jackson, H. F., 508, 509
Jackson, N., 108
Jackson, R. L., 199
Jacobs, C., 242
Jacobs, B. A., 181, 463
Jacobsen, T., 177
Jacobs, G. D., 209
Jacobson, N. S., 316
Jacoby, J. E., 272
Jaffee, S. R., 62, 79
Jaffe, P. G., 324
Jakob-Chien, C., 562
James, J., 480, 481, 482, 483, 484
Janssens, J. M. A. M., 109
Janus, E. S., 277, 278
Jarvik, L. F., 182
Jarvis, G., 553
Jeffrey, C. R., 120
Jenkins, P., 343, 344, 346, 347, 348
Jensen, E. L., 438
Jenson, B., 500
Jerry, N. B., 442
Jesness, C., 612
Johns, J. H., 194
Johnson, B. D., 530, 547, 548
Johnson, B. R., 389, 424, 623
Johnson, R., 136, 502, 615
Johnstone, L. D., 467, 534, 556
Johnston, L. D., 522, 548, 554
Joiner, T. E., 173
Joint, M., 153, 155

Jolin, A., 481
Jones, C., 34
Jones, J. G., 308
Jones, J. W., 169
Joyce, P. R., 201
Judice, S., 56
Julien, R. M., 532
Junger, M., 153, 154

Kafrey, D., 507
Kahn, E., 588
Kandel, E., 54, 95, 96, 563
Kanin, E. J., 399, 403
Kaplan, M. S., 427
Karmen, A., 299, 394
Katz, A. J., 496
Katz, J., 494
Kaukianinen, A., 166
Kazdin, A. E., 61, 507, 583
Kelleher, M. D., 358, 359
Kelley, T. M., 466
Kelly, G. A., 622
Kelman, H. C., 131, 134
Kemmelmeier, M., 324
Kemp, D., 108, 109
Kempe, C. H., 303
Kennedy, D. B., 466
Kennedy, D. M., 294
Kennedy, W. A., 205
Kenrick, D. T., 169
Kerr, M., 206
Ketcher, C. M., 151
Kiecolt, K. J., 319
Kiehl, K. A., 210, 212
Kilgore, K., 50
Kilmann, P. R., 215, 614, 615, 626
Kilmer, B., 530
Kilmer, R. P., 571
Kilpatrick, D. G., 393, 398, 399
Kim, H. K., 62, 522
King, L., 183
Kinports, K., 398
Kirkpatrick, J. T., 506
Kirmeyer, S. L., 167
Klackenberg-Larson, I., 51
Klassen, D., 260
Klaus, P., 317, 318, 463
Kleber, H. D., 544
Klemke, L. W., 467, 469, 470
Klimes-Dougan, B., 166
af Klinteberg, B., 55
Klodin, V., 182
Knee, C. R., 153
Knight, R. A., 329, 335, 339, 389, 405, 406, 407,
   408, 409, 410, 426, 427, 429, 430, 431, 432, 433,
   434, 626
Knopp, F. H., 625
Kochanska, G., 83
Kocsis, R. N., 334
Kohlmeier, L. M.

Kohn, L., 157
Koivisto, H., 222
Kokko, K., 142
Kolko, D., 507
Konecni, V. J., 169
Koolhaas, J. M., 176
Korman, A., 215
Kornhauser, R. R., 127
Kosky, R. H.,Jr., 344, 346
Koson, D. F., 513
Koss, M. P., 324, 396, 413
Kosson, D. S., 197, 202, 206, 209, 211, 215
Kovacs, M., 233
Kozol, H. L, 271, 272
Krahé, B., 153, 173
Kramer, R. C., 475
Krasnovsky, T., 465, 467
Kratzer, L., 64
Kringlen, E., 78
Krisberg, B., 29, 31, 585
Kristiansson, M., 205
Krohn, M., 43, 128
Kroner, D. G., 612
Krueger, R. F., 207
Kruesi, M. J. P., 177
Krull, J. L., 50
Kugler, K. E., 238, 240
Kuhnley, E. J., 513
Kulka, R. A., 249
Kupersmith, J., 62
Kurtzberg, R. L., 93
Kwan, Q., 509
Kyle, G. M., 541

La Fon, D. S., 340
La Greca, A. M., 42
Laajasalo, T., 261
Labato, A., 99
Lacerte-Lamontagne, C., 471
LaFond, J. Q., 277, 588
Lagerspetz, M. J., 166
Lahey, B. B., 58, 84, 163, 290
Laird, R., 40, 44, 49
Lalumière, 4
Lamberti, J., 375
Lamb, H. R., 265
Lambie, I., 506, 507, 508
Lamontagne, Y., 471
Lance, D., 351
Land, K. C., 68
Landy, D., 34
Lane, R., 465, 467
Lang, A. R., 220, 222
Langan, P. A., 319, 393, 400, 401, 437
Lange, J., 77
Lange, L. A., 83
Langer, E. J., 453
Langevin, R., 425
Langlois, J. H., 92, 93
Lansford, J. E., 79

Lanthier, R. D., 425
Lanyon, R. I., 402, 425, 442
Lanza-Kaduce, L., 128
Larrick, R. P., 168
Latane, B., 218
Laub, J. H., 92
Laumann-Billings, L., 310
Lauritsen, J. L., 39
Law, M., 274
Laws, D. R., 414
Lawton, S. F., 168
Le Bon, G., 134, 380
Le Maire, L., 178
Leach, E., 148
Lee, A. F. S., 427, 429, 626
Lee, F., 57
Lee, G., 128
Lee, J. E., 549
Lee, M., 375
Lee, M. Y., 301
Legras, A. M., 77
Leiman, A. L., 176
LeMarquand, D., 571
Lemon, N. K. D., 497
Lentz, C., 50
LePage, A., 150, 295
Lerner, M. J., 34, 404
Lesch, K. P., 176
Lester, D., 617
Letkemann, P., 492
Letourneau, E. J., 585
Levander, S., 206
Levant, R. F., 371
Leve, L. D., 65
Levenston, G. K., 222
Levin, B., 157, 513
Levine, S. A., 109
Levison, R. B., 591
Levy, A., 167
Lewinsohn, P. M., 87
Lewin, T., 342
Lewis, C. F., 312
Lewis, D. O., 300, 438, 508, 509
Lewis, I. A., 304, 423
Lewis, M., 50
Lichtenstein, P., 79
Lickliter, R., 175
Lidz, V., 590, 624
Lightsey, O. R. Jr., 582
Lilienfeld, S. O., 89, 198, 207, 210, 211
Linder, J. R., 172
Lindzey, G., 89
Linedecker, C., 346
Lingren, H. G., 393
Lin, K. H., 322
Linnoila, M., 177
Lipsey, M. W., 587
Lipton, D. N., 413, 588
Li, Q., 496
Little, T., 274

Litwack, T. R., 269
Liu, J., 89
Lizotte, A., 43, 294
Lochman, J. E., 583
Loeber, R., 27, 50, 56, 65, 68, 162, 163, 165, 166, 176, 299, 321, 570, 571, 572
Loehlin, J. C., 76
Lombardo, E. F., 55
Lombardo, V. S., 55
Long, K. R., 369, 371, 372
Longo, R. F., 625
Lonsway, K. A., 415
Loper, A. B., 581
Lorber, M. F., 218
Lorenz, A. R., 209, 210
Lorenz, K., 147
Lottes, I. L., 403
Louden, J. L., 260
Louis, W., 369
Loukas, A., 50, 51
Loza-Fanous, A., 612
Loza, W., 612
Lubenow, G. C., 320
Lucente, S., 200
Luckenbill, D. F., 125
Ludwig, J., 293, 294
Luh, K. E., 210
Lumley, V. A., 165
Lumsden, J., 183
Lundman, R. J., 466
Lurigio, A. J., 410
Luxenburg, J., 481, 482
Lyddon, W. J., 621, 622
Lykken, D. T., 216, 217, 219, 220
Lynam, D., 54, 176, 205, 222
Lynch, P. J., 172
Lynskey, M. T., 562
Lyons, P. M., 204

Maccoby, E., 59, 157
MacCoun, R., 530
MacDonald, J. M., 513, 514, 515
MacFarland, S. W., 169
Machin, D., 590
MacKenzie, D. L., 593, 594
Madden, D. J., 319
Maddi, S. R., 213
Magnusson, D., 55, 67
Mahar, D., 375
Mahoney, M. J., 621, 622
Maker, A. H., 324
Malamuth, N., 400, 414, 415, 416, 417, 588
Mann, C. R., 312
Mann, J., 177
Mann, R. E., 153, 154
Marcus-Newhall, A., 150
Maric, A., 416
Marlatt, G. A., 414, 626, 627, 628
Marolla, J., 400, 401, 403, 404
Marques, J. K., 398, 627

Marsella, A. J., 364, 366, 367, 368, 369, 371
Marshall, C. E., 317, 318
Marshall, W. L., 414, 425, 429, 437, 438, 626, 627, 628
Martel, M. M., 83
Martinez, R., 287, 290, 293, 294, 466
Martinson, R. M., 609, 618
Maslow, A. H., 129
Matheny, A. P., 76
Mathews, J. K., 436
Matsuyama, S. S., 182
Mattson, R., 183
Maxwell, C. D., 400, 540, 541, 548, 555
Mayes, L. C., 87
Mayeux, L., 41
Mazerolle, P., 64
Mazulis, A. H., 50
Mazzucco, A., 429
McBurnett, K., 56, 206
McCabe, K. M., 58, 65
McCaghy, C. H., 425, 428, 429, 461
McCandless, B. R., 91
McCardle, S., 506, 507
McCarthy, J., 296
McClearn, G. E., 77
McClelland, G. M., 534, 543
McClintock, M. K., 74
McCloskey, L. A., 324, 508
McCord, D., 251, 252
McCord, J., 130
McCord, W., 130
McCullough, B. C., 316
McDermott, E., 89
McDevitt, J., 336, 341, 342
McDonel, E. C., 413, 588
McElroy, S. L., 471
McFall, R. M., 413, 588
McGinley, H., 241, 248
McGreevy, M. A., 241, 242, 248
McGue, M., 80
McKee, G. R., 312
McKnight, L. R., 581
McNeil, C. B., 165
McPherson, L. M., 209
McShane, D. A., 53
McShane, M. D., 120, 126
Meadows, S., 353, 354
Mechoulam, R., 536
Mednick, S. A., 81, 82, 83, 86, 87, 89, 95, 96, 260
Megargee, E. I., 315, 321, 325, 374, 612, 615, 630
Meloy, J. R., 196, 498, 500
Melton, G. B., 236, 595
Menard, S., 43
Menzies, R. J., 274
Mercy, J., 301
Merry, S., 460, 461
Merschdorf, U., 176
Meseck-Bushey, S., 50
Meyer, E. C., 508
Meyer, T. P., 416

Michie, C., 199
Miczek, K. A., 561
Middlebrook, P. M., 504
Migeon, C., 178
Milgram, S., 132, 133, 134, 379
Miller-Johnson, S., 40, 41, 42, 50, 160
Miller, J. L., 479, 480
Miller, K. S., 240
Miller, M., 154, 269
Miller, N., 150, 152, 239
Miller, T. Q., 563
Milling, L., 51
Milne, B. J., 62, 63
Miner, M. H., 425, 585
Miransky, J., 453
Mirin, S. M., 547
Miron, M. S., 501
Mischel, W., 130
Mizell, L., 153, 154
Moffitt, T. E., 38, 54, 56, 57, 58, 61, 62, 63, 64, 74, 79, 85, 88, 176, 207, 570, 583, 584
Moghaddam, F. M., 364, 369
Mohr, J. W., 442
Moise-Titus, J., 125, 172
Mokros, A., 130, 338
Möller, I., 173
Moll, K. D., 514
Monahan, J., 46, 228, 249, 250, 260, 261, 262, 271, 272, 278, 624
Monastersky, C., 319, 436
Monnelly, E. P., 91
Montagu, A., 141, 148
Moore, R. H., 467, 468
Moreland, J., 549
Morgan, A. B., 89, 207, 210, 211
Morgan, J. P., 546, 547, 548, 566
Morgan, K., 338
Morgan, M., 228
Morgan, R. D., 265
Morris, A. S., 207
Morris, D., 147, 269
Morris, N., 277, 278
Morse, S. J., 229, 244, 248
Moschis, G. P., 466
Moss, M., 19
Motiuk, L. L., 609
Mott, J., 553
Mounts, N. S., 40, 46, 47
Mourot, J. E., 314
Mueller, C. W., 167
Mukhergee, S. K., 301
Mulder, R. T., 201
Müller, J. L., 212
Mullis, T., 319
Mulvey, E. P., 579, 624
Mumley, D. L., 237, 240
Mumola, C. J., 527
Muncer, S., 380
Munn, C., 331, 332
Muñoz, A., 554

Murphy, G. H., 508
Murphy, W. D., 424
Murray, J. B., 308
Murray, M., 464
Murrie, D. C., 205
Mutch, P.J., 300
Myers, D. G., 172
Myers, D. L., 576
Myers, W. C., 299, 300, 348, 349, 591

Nacci, P. L., 615
Nachshon, I., 210
Nafpaktitis, M. K., 425
Nagin, D., 68, 569
Nash, J. R., 431
National Adolescent Perpetrator Network, 589
National Cable Television Association, 172
National Center for Education Statistics, 352, 353
National Center for Juvenile Justice, 26, 29, 30, 33, 576, 578
National Center for Victims of Crime, 500
National Center on Child Abuse and Neglect, 427
National Center on Elder Abuse, 317, 318
National Commission on Marihuana and Drug Abuse, 537, 538, 546, 553
National Drug Intelligence Center, 554, 555
National Highway Traffic Safety Administration, 560
National Information Support and Referral Service, 309
National Institute of Health, 549
National Institute on Alcohol Abuse and Alcoholism, 563, 566
National Institute on Drug Abuse, 534, 540, 542, 543, 545, 549, 550, 553, 557
Naudts, K., 260, 261
Nebylitsyn, V. D., 110
Nee, C., 454
Needleman, H. L., 86, 571
Neighbors, C., 153
Neisser, U., 52, 53, 54
Nelson, C., 398
Nelson, C. A., 88
Nelson, D. R., 50
Nelson, D. W., 594
Nelson, G. M., 425
Nelson, S., 396
Nettler, G., 21
Neugebauer, R., 86
Neuman, J., 355, 356
Neumann, C. S., 199
Newbury, K., 108
Newcomb, A. F., 40, 135
Newcombe, R., 553
Newman, G., 608
Newman, J. P., 160, 161, 195, 201, 202, 209, 210, 211, 215, 221
Nicholson, R. A., 237, 238, 240
Nichols, S. L., 215
Nicolson, J. P., 318
Nielsen, A. L., 290, 293, 294

Nietzel, M. T., 120
Nisbett, R. E., 53
Noesner, G. W., 501, 502
Nolan, J., 310
Norwood, S., 237, 238
Nurco, D. N., 553
Nye, I., 21

Obiedallah, D. A., 233
O'Brien, B. S., 206
O'Connor, A., 301, 320
O'Connor, W., 260
O'Donnell, J., 573
Office of Applied Studies, 543, 560
Office of National Drug Control Policy, 526, 527, 528, 529, 534, 535, 536, 541, 542, 543, 548, 549, 551, 552, 555, 557, 558, 559
Offord, D. R., 57, 579
Ogloff, J. R., 218
Ohlin, L. E., 25, 575
Olenick, M., 44
Olson, J. F., 453
Olson, S. L., 84
O'Malley, P. M., 467, 548
Ondrovik, J., 254
O'Neill, M. L., 590, 624
Ormerod, D., 130, 338
Ormrod, R., 305
Orne, E. C., 253
Orne, M. T., 253, 254
Orris, J. B., 213
Osgood, W. D., 467
Ostrove, N., 93
Otto, R. K., 340
Owen, B., 606
Owens, E. B., 84

Pagani, L. S., 320, 321
Pagelow, M. D., 317, 318, 320
Palmer, J. W., 616
Palmer, S. E., 616
Paradiso, M. A., 176
Parke, R. D., 77
Parker, H., 553
Parker, J. G., 40
Parkinson, D., 324
Pasold, T., 173
Pastorelli, C., 138
Paswark, R. A., 241, 248
Patch, P. C., 319, 320
Patrick, C. J., 205, 207, 220, 222
Pattee, L., 40
Patterson, C. M., 211, 215
Patterson, G., 45, 48, 49, 66, 67, 69, 322, 572
Paull, D., 255
Paulus, P. B., 615
Payne, A. A., 354
Pearl, P. T., 308
Pease, K., 459
Peck, S. C., 45

Pedersen, W. C., 152
Penfield, W., 4
Pennel, S., 294
Penrod, S., 134, 150
Pepitone, A., 135
Pepler, D. J., 59
Perfetti, L., 153
Perkins, C., 354
Persons, W. S., 91
Petechuk, D., 27, 299
Petersilia, J., 615, 619
Peterson, C., 324
Peterson, J. B., 177
Peterson, M. A., 609
Peters, R. D., 200
Peters, S. D., 423
Petraitis, J., 563
Petras, H., 45
Petrila, J., 202, 203
Pettit, G. S., 40, 44, 45, 49, 78, 79, 84, 85, 125, 160, 222, 583, 585
Pettway, C., 401
Petty, J., 398, 627
Pfiffner, L. J., 56
Phillips, C., 459
Phillips, J., 228
Pihl, R. O., 177
Pillemer, K., 318
Pillmann, F., 210
Pincus, J. H., 183
Pine, D. S., 95
Pinizzotto, A. J., 336, 337, 338
Pithers, W. D., 398, 627, 628
Plas, J. M., 53
Pleck, E., 303, 304
Plomin, R., 76, 207
Plummer, D. L., 45
Podnieks, E., 318
Podolski, C., 125, 172
Poe-Yamagata, E., 576
Polich, S. M., 609
Polk, K., 46
Pollack, V. E., 152
Pomeroy, W., 429
Pontell, H. N., 475
Pope, C. E., 454, 457, 458
Porporino, F. G., 613, 614
Porter, S., 195, 196, 200, 205, 338, 624
Posner, J. K., 44
Post, L. A., 400
Postmes, T., 135, 136
Potoczniak, D. J., 314
Potoczniak, M. J., 314
Potter, L. B., 61, 589
Poulin, F., 164
Powell, G. E., 445
Power, R., 570
Poythress, N. G., 203, 340
Prather, J., 615
Prentice-Dunn, S., 383

Prentky, R. A., 329, 405, 406, 407, 408, 427, 429, 432, 436, 626, 629
President's Commission on Law Enforcement and Administration of Justice, 115
Preston, D. L., 160, 376, 378, 623
Price, J., 167
Price, W. H., 182
PRIDE Surveys, 294
Prinstein, M. J., 166
Proctor, W. C., 425
Pulkkinen, L., 142
Putnam, C.T., 506
Puzzanchera, C., 28, 299

Quay, H. C., 54, 194, 212, 591
Queen's Bench Foundation, 444
Quinlan, D. M., 513
Quinney, E. R., 472, 474
Quinn, M., 219
Quinsey, V. L., 4, 200, 205, 441, 443, 513, 612, 623, 624, 626

Rabinowitz, J., 569, 585, 587
Rabkin, J. G., 260, 263
Rachman, S., 99, 445
Racine, Y. A., 57
Radosevich, M. J., 128
Rafter, N. H., 5
Raine, A., 74, 78, 79, 82, 83, 86, 87, 88, 89, 94, 95, 211, 215, 220
Ramirez, D., 336, 340, 342
Ramirez, J. M., 177
Ramirez, J. R., 522
Rand, M. R., 24, 25
Ransberger, V. M., 168
Rantala, R. R., 496
Rapaport, K., 396
Räsänen, P., 87, 261
Rasche, C., 315
Raskin, D. C., 219
Rathouz, P. J., 56
Ray, O., 535, 537, 544
Reboussin, R., 335, 339, 408
Redfern, A., 457
Reese, J. T., 334
Regier, D. A., 266
Reid, J., 45, 56, 66
Reid, W. H., 54, 57, 265, 614, 617
Reiffenstein, R. J., 539
Reifman, A. S., 168
Reiman, J., 476
Reiss, A. J., 310, 563
Reiss, J., 178
Reitzel, L. R., 438
Rengert, G., 459
Rennison, C. M., 24, 25, 288, 313
Reppucci, N. D., 579
Resnick, P. J., 310, 311
Ressler, R. K., 333, 334, 336, 337, 343, 351, 359, 360, 510

Reuter, P., 530
Revitch, E., 390, 428
Rhee, S. H., 75, 76, 79, 80, 110
Rhoads, J. M., 441
Riad, J. K., 177
Rice, M. E., 200, 274, 422, 441, 443, 513, 612, 623, 624, 625
Richard, A., 485
Richards, H., 200
Ridge, B., 84
Righthand, S., 161, 329, 389, 436
Ringel, C., 395
Ritchie, K., 240
Ritvo, E., 508, 509
Robbins, E., 510, 511
Robbins, L., 510, 511
Robbins, P. C., 241, 242, 261
Roberts, A., 91, 153, 300, 301, 313
Robins, L., 201, 266
Robinson, A. L., 400
Robinson, D. N., 4
Robison, J. O., 271, 272
Roche, P. Q., 9
Roche, T., 227
Rodgers, C., 65
Rodgers, D. C., 50
Rodman, H., 46
Roesch, R., 238, 240, 241, 243
Rogers, R., 201, 202, 237, 238, 255, 383, 590, 623
Rogers, R. W., 151
Rohde, C., 99, 319
Roizen, J., 562
Rooney, J., 607, 613
Rooth, G., 441
Rorke, L. B., 309
Rose, A. J., 41
Rosecan, J. S., 547
Rosenbaum, A., 323
Rosenbaum, D. P., 410, 467
Rosenbaum, M., 522
Rosenberg, J., 625
Rosenberg, R., 389, 426, 427, 430, 431
Rosenfeld, B., 240, 242
Rosenfeld, R., 3, 290, 293, 294
Rosenthal, D., 77, 78
Rosenzweig, M. R., 176
Rosner, R., 511
Rosoff, S. M., 475
Ross, D., 125
Rossi, P. H., 294
Ross, M. P., 398
Rossmo, D. K., 335, 339
Ross, S., 125
Roth, J. A., 529, 563, 566
Rotton, J., 168, 169
Rowe, D. C., 50
Rubin, B., 271, 272
Rubin, K. H., 84
Rubinsky, E. W., 255, 256
Rubinson, L., 393

Rubinstein, M., 438
Russell, D., 395, 396, 412, 423, 424, 427, 468, 470
Rutter, M., 64, 92, 176, 203

Salekin, R. T., 199, 200, 201, 202, 205, 590, 591, 599, 623, 624
Sales, B., 54, 234, 265, 312, 614, 617
Saltaris, C., 196
Salzman, L., 301
Samenow, S. E., 623
Sameroff, A. J., 45
Sampson, R. J., 38, 39, 92
Saner, H., 562
Sanford, G. M., 202
Santa Clara Criminal Justice Pilot Program, 457
Santiago, G. B., 301
Santor, D., 205
Sarasalo, E., 470
Sarbin, T. R., 34
Sass, H., 210, 218
Satterfield, J. H., 57
Saucier, J. -F., 86
Saunders, B. E., 393, 399
Saunders, D. G., 326
Saunders, E. B., 508
Scannapieco, M., 424
Scarborough, K. E., 357, 358
Scaret, D., 55
Scarr, S., 44
Schachter, S., 218, 255, 504
Schaeffer, C. M., 596, 597
Schalling, D., 55
Schauer, E. J., 484
Schell, A., 57
Scherer, D. G., 595
Schlesinger, L. B., 269, 390
Schliemann, A. D., 53
Schlosser, E., 491, 492
Schlossman, S., 574
Schmideberg, M., 512
Schmitt, E. L., 393, 400, 401, 437
Schmitt, W. A., 195
Schneider, B. A., 389, 426, 427, 430, 431
Schonfeld, I. S., 95
Schrager, L., 476
Schrock, J., 484, 485
Schulenberg, J. E., 548
Schuller, R. A., 313
Schulsinger, F., 80
Schultz, L. G., 425
Schuster, M. A., 371
Schwartz, I. M., 40
Schwartz, J. P., 322
Schweinhart, L. J., 579
Sciarra, D., 588, 589
Scientific American, 208
Scott, K., 300
Scott, T. G., 212
Scully, D., 400, 401, 403, 404
Seagrave, D., 203, 204, 205, 206, 212

Sears, D. O., 503
Sears, R., 157
Sechrest, L., 611
Sederstrom, J., 31
Sedlak, M., 574
Seeley, J. R., 87
Seghorn, T., 405, 406, 430
Séguin, J. R., 176
Seligman, M. E., 376
Selkin, J.335, 340
Sellbom, M., 210
Sellin, T., 33
Seracini, A. M., 38
Serin, R. C., 160, 161, 200, 376, 378, 623
Sestir, M. A., 175
Seto, M. C., 416, 417
Sewell, K. W., 201, 202
Seymour, A., 299, 301, 317
Shaffer, D., 95
Shaffer, D. R., 242
Shaffer, J. W., 553
Shain, R., 228
Shanok, S. S., 508, 509
Shaw, D. S., 68, 84, 469
Shea, S. J., 312
Shelden, R., 40, 482
Sheldon, W. H., 89, 111
Sheppard, D., 294
Sheridan, J. F., 74
Sherman, L. W., 326
Shields, J., 76
Short, J. F., 21, 157, 476
Shover, N., 457, 459
Showers, J., 309
Sickmund, M., 26, 576
Siegel, A., 157
Siegel, J. M., 390
Sieh, E. W., 479
Sigall, H., 93
Signorielli, N., 228
Silberman, E. K., 482
Silva, P. A., 56, 62, 64, 85, 176
Silverman, I. J., 458
Silverman, R. A., 301
Silvern, L., 323
Silverthorn, P., 64
Simonelli, C. J., 319
Simon, R. J., 243, 246, 247, 269
Simons, R. L., 322
Simourd, D. J., 195, 197, 612
Sipe, R., 438
Skeem, J. L., 201, 202, 203, 205, 238, 240, 243, 260, 624
Skilling, T. A., 4, 205
Skinner, B. F., 118
Skogan, W. G., 15
Skrzpek, G. J., 212
Slaby, R. G., 59, 160
Slavkin, M. L., 507
Slobogin, C., 248

Slovenko, R., 252, 254
Smallbone, S. W., 389
Smart, C., 467
Smart, R. G., 153, 154, 544
Smigel, E. O., 479
Smith, D., 264, 375, 457
Smith, E. J., 581, 583
Smithey, M., 309, 310
Smith, G. A., 248
Smith, G. W., 271, 272
Smith, L. A., 595
Smith, M. D., 338
Smith, R., 538
Smith, S., 221, 240
Smith, S. K., 288
Smith, S. S., 201, 202
Smith, W., 319
Snyder, D., 209
Snyder, H. N., 16, 17, 27, 30, 31, 32, 33, 59, 60, 299, 424, 576
Snyder, J., 45, 48, 49, 50, 66, 67, 68, 69
Soley, B. J., 335, 339, 408
Solop, D., 154
Sorenson, S. B., 390
Southerland, M. D., 357, 358
Spaccarelli, S., 324
Spallone, P., 149
Spears, R., 135, 136
Speir, J. C., 284
Sperry, R., 4
Spitz, H. I., 547
Spitz, R. T., 592
Stachan, K. E., 198
Stack, S., 196
Stadolnik, R. F., 512
Stafford, J., 560
Stagg, V., 324
Stahl, A., 576
Staller, J. A., 55
Stalnaker, K., 593, 594
Stanger, C., 163
Stanley, B., 176
Stark, E., 314
Starr, L., 340
Stattin, H., 51, 67, 206
Staub, E., 368, 369, 370, 379
Steadman, H. J., 240, 241, 242, 246, 248, 262, 266, 270, 271, 272, 275
Steffan, J. S., 265
Steinberg, L., 48
Steinman, K. J., 524
Steinmetz, S. K., 319
Sternberg, R. J., 364
Stern, K. R., 55, 56
Stevenson, W., 625
Stevens, S. S., 89, 111
Steward, M. A., 513
Stewart, L., 609
Stickle, T., 506, 508
Stillman, R. C., 537, 546, 553

Stinson, J. D., 427, 436
Stone, A., 270
Stoolmiller, M., 68
Stouthamer-Loeber, M., 45, 54, 68, 162, 163, 165, 166, 176, 321
Strasser, F., 522
Straus, M., 315, 316, 320, 321, 323, 325
Strentz, T., 501, 504
Strom, K. J., 293, 295
Strote, J., 549
Stuart, G. L., 315
Stuewig, J., 508
Substance Abuse and Mental Health Services Administration, 522, 524, 533, 534, 542, 550, 560
Sugimoto, T., 316
Suitor, J. J., 318
Surette, R., 227
Susser, E., 86
Sutherland, E. H., 125, 126, 471, 472
Sutker, P. B., 211, 249
Sutter, A., 538
Sutton, L. P., 395
Sutton, S. K., 201
Svalastoga, K., 290
Swahn, M. H., 562
Swanson, J., 57
Swenson, L. P., 41
Sykes, G. M., 450, 451
Symons, D., 401

Tallon, J., 423
Tamborini, R., 169
Tappan, P. W., 33, 472, 574
Tarolla, S. M., 569, 585, 587
Taussig, C., 569
Taylor, D. M., 369
Taylor, J., 80
Taylor, M., 454
Tedeschi, R. G., 571
Teitelbaum, H. E., 615
Tengström, A., 222, 261, 612
Teplin, L., 233, 260, 263, 266, 534, 543
Terrorism Research Center, 367
Terry, K. J., 423
Texas Youth Commission, 592
Thoennes, N., 398, 497, 518
Thomas, C., 163
Thomas, J., 353, 354
Thomas, P., 570
Thompson, K. M., 94
Thompson, R. A., 88, 324
Thorley, G., 55
Thornberry, T. P., 43, 272, 570
Thornton, D., 196, 198, 624
Tillbrook, C. E., 237, 240
Tillman, R., 475
Timman, R., 153, 154
Tims, M. S., 560
Tingle, D., 400
Tinklenberg, J. R., 537, 546, 553

Tittle, C. R., 21, 290
Tjaden, P., 25, 398, 497, 518
Toch, H., 372, 377, 613, 614
Tolan, P. H., 570, 572, 579
Tomarken, A. J., 209
Tonry, M., 25, 615, 619
Topalli, V., 463
Torgerson, S., 581
Toth, J., 470
Towler, A., 355
Tran, H., 44
Trasler, G., 110
Tremblay, R., 86, 571, 573, 582
Tsang, J., 132, 134, 138
Tubman, J. G., 569, 585, 587
Tucker, D. M., 209
Tupin, J. P., 375
Turner, H., 305
Turner, R. E., 442
Turrell, S. C., 314
Turvey, B., 336
Tuvblad, C., 79, 80
Tweed, R., 240
Tyler, J., 593, 594

Uddo-Crane, M., 249
Ullman, A., 320
Ullman, J. B., 50
Ullman, S. E., 410
Underwood, M., 62, 177
Underwood, R. C., 319, 320
University of Iowa Injury Prevention Research Center, 357, 358
University of Michigan, 533, 534
Upfold, D., 513
U.S. Bureau of the Census, 44, 45
U.S. Department of Health and Human Services, 305, 306
U.S. Department of Justice, 11, 30, 292, 298, 302, 307, 308, 364, 365, 399, 489, 496, 499, 500, 514, 564
U.S. Fire Administration, 506
Ustad, K. L., 201

Valenstein, E. S., 180, 183
van Beijsterveldt, C. E. M., 79
Van Dam, C., 109
Van De Ven, J., 612
Van Hulle, C. A., 84
Van Kammen, W. B., 45
van Lier, P. A. C., 62
Van Voorhis, P., 612
van Wijk, A., 435
Vanderpearl, R. H., 236, 260, 427
Vandersall, T. A., 508
Vargo, M., 324
Vazsonyi, A. T., 44
Veitch, R., 167
Venables, P. H., 83, 89, 216
Veneziano, C., 436, 588

Veneziano, L., 436, 588
Verhulst, F. C., 163
Verlinden, S., 353, 354
Vernberg, E. M., 166
Verona, E., 176, 210
Veronen, L. J., 393, 399
Vetter, H. J., 458
Viding, E., 207
Vidmar, V., 313
Vien, A., 207
Vietor, N. A., 153
Villemez, W. J., 290
Vincent, G. M., 205
Vincent, K. R., 53
Virkkunen, M., 177, 425
Vitacco, M. J., 199
Vitale, J. E., 160, 161, 201, 202
Vitaro, F., 165, 571, 573
Vold, G. B., 126
Voss, H. L., 293, 295, 296
Voss, W. D., 196
Vuijk, P., 62
Vuz, I., 436

Waaktaar, T., 581, 582
Wadsworth, M. E. J., 91
Wagner, E. F., 569, 585, 587
Wagner, R. V., 369, 371, 372
Waite, D., 438
Wakefield, J. C., 230
Wakschlag, L. S., 87
Walbek, N. H., 277, 278
Waldman, I. D., 75, 76, 79, 80, 84, 110, 290
Walker, J. S., 109
Walker, K. L., 371
Walker, L., 249, 250, 313
Walker, S., 521, 522, 529, 537, 609
Wallace-Capretta, S., 607, 613
Wallace, H., 301, 319
Wallace, J. F., 210
Waller, E. M., 41
Wallerstein, J. S., 20
Walsh, A., 348
Walsh, D., 460
Walsh, D. A., 171, 172
Walster, E., 34, 93
Walters, G. C., 125
Walters, G. D., 199
Walters, R. H., 130
Waltz, J., 316
Wang, M. C., 168, 169
Ward, T., 495
Warren, J., 08, 240, 242, 335, 339, 612
Wasilchick, J., 459
Wasserman, G. A., 38
Watson, J. B., 116
Webb, J. A., 560, 562
Webster, C. D., 274, 275, 612
Wechsler, H., 549
Weikart. D. P., 579

Weiler, B. L., 222
Weinberger, L. E., 265
Weinraub, M., 44
Weinrott, M. R., 396, 625
Weis, J. G., 31, 304, 316, 325
Weiss, J., 375
Weiss, R. D., 546
Weiss, R. G., 428
Welchans, S., 25
Welch, C., 161, 329, 389, 436
Wells, J. E., 201
Wenk, E. A., 271, 272
Wessler, S., 19
West, D. J., 92
West, R., 153, 154
Wettstein, R. M., 272
Whalen, C. K., 56
Whalley, A., 398, 399
Wheatman, S. R., 242
Wheaton, E. M., 484
Wheeler, R. E., 209
Whitcomb, D., 306, 307
White, K. B., 415
Whitehill, M., 212
White, J. L., 54, 564
Wicker, T., 502
Widiger, T. A., 234
Widom, C. S., 211, 222, 309
Wiederlight, M., 511
Wiener, J. M., 508
Wiesen, A. E., 212
Wiesner, M., 60, 62, 68, 522, 534
Wilcox, D. K., 506
Wilczynski, A., 311
Wilgosh, L., 55
Williams, F. P., 120, 126
Williams, J. E., 399
Williams, L. L., 44
Williams, M., 83
Williamson, S., 196
Williams, T., 539
Williams, W., 250
Wills, G. D., 324
Wilson, D. B., 587
Wilson, D. J., 527
Wilson, G., 445
Wilson, J. Q., 59, 92
Wilson, S. K., 324
Wilson, T. D., 621
Wilson, V., 108
Wilson, W. J., 38
Wincze, J. P., 440
Windel, M., 60, 68, 5344
Winslow, E. B., 84
Wisniewski, N., 396
Wolfe, D. A., 304, 324
Wolfgang, M. E., 157, 287, 289, 290, 293, 295, 296, 609
Wolford, M. R., 513
Wolf, R. S., 318

Wong, L., 539
Wong, M. T. H., 183, 290
Wong, S., 196, 200, 210, 218
Wood, J. J., 165
Wood, P. A., 58
Woodrow, K. M., 537
Woodworth, M., 196, 338
Wootton, J., 206
Worling, J. R., 436
Wortley, R. K., 389
Wright, B. R. E., 62
Wright, J. C., 175
Wright, J. D., 294
Wright, R., 455, 457, 463, 489, 493, 494, 517
Wright, R. T., 493, 495, 517
Wyatt, G. E., 423
Wyle, J., 20

Xie, H., 165

Yamaguchi, K., 563
Yates, E., 471
Yeager, C., 438
Yegidis, B. L., 396
Yeh, M., 58, 65
Yesavage, J. A., 513

Yeudall, L. T., 210
Yochelson, S., 623
Yoerger, K., 66, 67, 68
Young, J. L., 592
Yu, J., 153
Yung, B., 38, 39

Zahn-Waxler, C., 166
Zak, L., 324
Zamble, E., 613, 614
Zapf, P. A., 238, 240, 241, 243
Zawitz, M. W., 293, 295
Zebrowitz, L. A., 94
Zelli, A., 572
Zempolich, K. A., 222
Zigler, E., 569
Zillmann, D., 125, 148, 152, 162, 169, 373, 378, 416
Zimbardo, P. G., 134, 135, 136, 375, 381, 382, 615, 618
Zimmer, L., 546, 547, 566
Zimmerman, R. A., 309
Zipper, P., 506
Zoccoulillo, M., 58
Zola, I. K., 130
Zorza, J., 25
Zucker, R. A., 50

SUBJECT INDEX

ADHD (attention deficit hyperactivity disorder),
     55–56
   and criminal behavior, 56-57
   and peer rejection, 42
Adler, Alfred, 9
Adolescent-limited (AL) offenders, 62
Aggravated assault, 12
Aggression, 141–143, 183–185
   classifications, 143–144, 144t
   covert, 162–163, 164t
   definition, 145
   developmental aspects of, 163
   emotional ingredients of, 163–164
   gender differences in, 165–166
   hostile (expressive) and instrumental aggression,
     144–145
   overt, 162, 164t
   passive-aggressive behaviors, 143, 163
   reactive/proactive forms of, 164–165
   ritualized, 147
   simplicity of, 161–162
   See also Cognitive models of aggression; Envi-
     ronmental factors and aggression; Social
     learning factors in aggression/violence
Aggression (biology of), 175–176
   biological control through surgery/drugs,
     177–179
   brain centers and violence control, 179–181
   epilepsy and, 183
   heredity and XYY chromosome, 181–183
   hormones and neurotransmitters, 176–177
Aggression/theoretical perspectives, 146
   cognitive-neoassociation model, 151–152
   displaced aggression theory, 152–155
   ethological viewpoints, 147–149
   excitation transfer theory, 152
   frustration-aggression hypothesis, 149–151
   psychoanalytic/psychodynamic, 146–147
Aggressive driving vs. road rage, 153–155
Akers, Ronald, differential-association-reinforce-
     ment (DAR) theory, 125–128
Alcohol, 566
   crime and delinquency, 561–563
   measurement of intoxication, 560
   psychological effects, 560–561
   usage, 559–560
Amnesia, 255–256
Antiandrogen drugs, 178

Antisocial behavior, 28, 35
   vs. criminal behavior, 33
Antisocial personality disorder (APD), 28, 188
   and alcoholism, 236
   criticism of, 234–235, 236
   distinction from psychopath, 187, 189
   essential features, 235
   and gender, 235–236
   prevalence, 195
Arrestees Drug Abuse Monitoring Program
     (ADAM), 22, 23
Arson, 518
   definition, 506
   incidence/prevalence, 506
Arsonists
   gender differences, 511–512
   motives, 509–511
   motives (juvenile), 511
   See also Firesetting; Pyromania
Assault, 286
   aggravated, 286
   demographics of, 298–299
   and homicide, 284
   See also Family violence; Homicide
Authoritarian parental style, 47
Authoritative parental style, 47
Autoeroticism, 332
Availability heuristic, 283

Bandura/imitational model of social learning,
     123–125
Battered woman syndrome, 250, 313–314
Battering, 301
Baxstrom v. Herold (1966), 271–272
Behavior predictors, 273–274
Behavior therapy (behavior modification), 620–621
Behaviorism, 116, 138–139
   as method of science, 117–118
   as perspective of human nature, 118
   Skinner's theory, 116–121
   variables, 117
Berkowitz, Leonard, frustration and criminality
     studies, 128–129
Biological factors in criminal behavior origins,
     73–74, 110–112
   birth complications, 86
   brain development, 87–88
   environmental risk factors, 85–86

Biological factors in criminal behavior origins (*cont.*)
  genetic influences on antisocial/aggressive behavior, 74–75
  interaction of hereditary and environmental factors, 74, 96
  neuropsychological factors, 88–89
  nicotine/alcohol/drug exposure, 86–87, 220–221
  psychophysiological factors, 82–83
  See also Adoption studies; Eysenck's theory/personality and crime; Neurophysiological concepts; Physique and crime; Temperament; Twin studies
Biological factors/psychopathy, 206–207, 223–224
  arousal hypothesis, 215
  autonomic functioning, 220–221
  avoidance learning experiments, 217–220
  emotional processing problems and amygdala dysfunction, 211–212
  frontal neuropsychological studies, 210–211
  genetic aspects, 207, 221
  hemisphere asymmetry/deficiency, 208–210
  neurophysiological markers, 207
  Quay's hypothesis, 212
  stimulation seeking, 212–213
Biological/neurobiological theories of crime, 3
  See also Neurophysiological concepts
Biophyschologists, 74
Bombings, 513, 519
  motives, 514–517
  statistics, 514t
  See also "Mad Bomber" of New York; Unabomber
"Boosters," 467
Brain centers/violence control, 179
  executive functions, 211
  permanent brain alterations, 179–180
  research methods, 179
  See also Neurophysiological concepts
Brawner Rule, 245
  and caveat paragraph, 245
Burglar
  "expressive burglar," 460
  "good burglar," 459–460
Burglars, 453–454
  accomplices, 457
  and alcohol/other drugs, 458
  cognitive processes, 455–456
  geographic scope, 457
  methods/patterns by gender, 457–458
Burglary, 452
  characteristics of, 452–453
  cues and selected targets, 454–455
  motives, 459–460
  property disposition, 458–459
  psychological impact (on victim/s), 460–461
  repeat, 459
  See also Property crimes
Bush, George H., 18
Byrd, James, Jr., 20

Carjacking, 463–464
Castration, 178
"Cat," 541
Child abuse
  incidence/prevalence/demographics, 305–306
  infanticide, 309–313
  missing/abducted/runaway/thrownaway children, 307–308
  Munchausen syndrome by proxy, 308–309
  shaken baby syndrome (SBS), 309
  types, 306t
Child molestation, 421, 446
  incidence/prevalence, 423–424
  intrafamilial/extrafamilial, 422
  psychological effects on child victims, 426
  sexual contact types, 425–426
  situational and victimization characteristics, 424–425
  terminology, 422t
  See also Pedophilia; Pedophilia causes (theories of)
Child molester, 421–422, 446
  age, 427–428
  attitudes toward victims, 428
  characteristics, 426–427
  cognitive functions, 428–429
  comparison with rapist, 429t
  gender, 427
  interpersonal and social skills, 429–430
  occupational/socioeconomic status, 429
  recidivism, 437–438
  See also Pedophile
Child Pornography Prevention Act, 392
"Child sex tourism" offense, 392
Clearance rate, 14
Clerkley, Hervey, 190–191
"Club" drugs. *See* Sedative-hypnotic compounds
Cocaine, 565
  cost, 544
  crack, 546–547
  crack and crime, 548
  and crime, 545–546
  other uses for, 544
  physical effects (adverse), 545
  psychological effects, 544–545
  usage, 542–544, 543t
  See also Stimulants
Coercion developmental theory, 66
  developmental trajectories, 66–67
  gender differences, 67–68
Cognitions, 6
Cognitive models of aggression, 158–159
  cognitive scripts model, 159
  hostile attribution bias, 159–161
Cognitive-neoassociation model, 151–152
Cognitive processes, 116
Cognitive restructuring (as justification for terror), 369
  advantageous comparison, 370
  euphemistic language, 370
  moral justification, 369–370

Cognitive scripts, 455, 495
Cognitive therapy, 621–624
   constructivist therapy influences on, 622
   efficacy of, 623
   reality therapy foundation, 622
Columbine High School shooting, 173, 175
Competency to stand trial issues, 237–240, 257
   "adjudicative competence," 237
   forensic assessments, 237–240
   incompetence to stand trial (IST) vs. insanity, 238
Compulsive gambling, 251–252
Conduct disorder, 28, 57–58
Conformity perspective, 3
Copycat effect/contagion effect, 174–175
Corporate crime. *See* Occupational crime
Correctional psychology, 601–603, 629
   careers in, 603–605
   employers and earnings, 603–604
   services provided by, 603, 604f
   See also Correctional system
Correctional system, 605
   community-based corrections facilities, 605
   Federal Bureau of Prisons (BOP), 607, 608t
   jails, 605
   prison population, 607–608
   prisons, 605–607, 606t
   See also Psychological effects of imprisonment; Punishment considerations; Treatment strategies
Correctional system classification, 610–612, 629–630
   dynamic and static risk factors, 613
   early classification systems, 612
Crime
   complexity of causes, 2
   definition, 1
   reactions to, 2
   "victimless," 450
   See also Measurement of crime; Theories of crime
Crime rate, 12
Crime reporting. *See* National Incident-Based Reporting System (NIBRS); Uniform Crime Reporting (UCR) Program (FBI)
Crime scene investigative methods, 331–334
   autoeroticism, 332
   MO determination, 331
   organized/disorganized/mixed crime scene, 333–334, 333t–334t
   personation/signature, 332
   staging, 332
   "undoing," 332–333
Crime statistics. *See* Measurement of crime
Crimes against the public, 450
Crimes of obedience, 131–134
Criminal
   legal process of becoming, 34
   vs. convicted person, 35
   See also Criminal behavior

Criminal behavior
   as complex and poorly understood phenomenon, 2
   conditionability of, 105–108
   definition, 1, 10, 35
   vs. antisocial behavior, 33
   See also Biological factors in criminal behavior origins; Frustration-induced criminality; Learning factors in criminal behavior; Situational factors in criminal behavior
Criminal conviction, requirements for, 1
Criminal intent, 1
Criminal profiling, 7–8, 335, 360
   effectiveness of, 337–339
   history of, 336
   media depictions of, 338
   vs. psychological autopsy, 336
Criminal psychopath, 189, 195
   examples, 190
   measurement tools, 197–198
   offending patterns, 195–196
   prevalence, 195
Criminal responsibility, 240–241, 256
   insanity standards, 243–246
   standards, 247t
   success of insanity defense, 241–242
   use of insanity defense, 242
   See also Defense strategies/uncommon psychiatric diagnoses
Criminology, 10t
   definition, 5
   interdisciplinary nature of, 2
   psychiatric criminology, 8–10
   psychological criminology, 6–8
   sociological criminology, 5–6
Crowd violence
   and deindividuation, 381
   and deindividuation experiments, 381–383
   historical interest in, 380–381
Cybercrime, 163, 495–497, 518
   cyberstalking, 496, 499–500
   types, 496t
Cycle of violence, 321–322

Dangerous Child Abuser Index, 414
Dangerousness, 267–268
DBRS (Dangerous Behavior Rating Scheme), 274
Defense strategies/uncommon psychiatric diagnoses, 248–256, 257
   amnesia, 255–256
   battered woman syndrome, 250
   compulsive gambling, 251–252
   dissociative identity disorder, 252–255
   posttraumatic stress disorder (PTSD), 248–251
Dehumanization, 450
   by terrorists, 450
   in violent crimes, 379
Deindividuation, 134–137
Deindividuation experiments, 381–383

Delinquency
  legal definitions, 26–27
  psychological definitions, 28
  social definitions, 27–28
  See also Developmental theories of delinquency;
    Juvenile delinquency
Delusional disorders, 232–233
Demara, Ferdinand Waldo, Jr., 189–190
Depo-Provera, 178
Depressive disorders, 233
Developmental disability, 229
Developmental pathway, 37, 68–69
  gender differences, 59–60, 70
  LCP (life-course-persistent) offender research,
    222–223
  research, 70–71
  risk factors, 38, 58t, 69
  See also Developmental theories of delinquency;
    Parental and family risk factors; Psychologi-
    cal risk factors; Social risk factors
Developmental theories of delinquency, 60–61, 68, 70
  coercion developmental theory, 66–68
  Moffitt's theory, 61–64
"Difference-in-degree" perspective, 148
difference-in-kind perspective, 4
Differential association-reinforcement (DAR) the-
  ory, 125–128
Differential association theory (Edwin H. Suther-
    land), 4, 125–126
Disengagement practices/dealing with our own an-
    tisocial conduct, 385–386
Disengagement practices developing motivation for
    terrorism
  dehumanization, 370–371
  deindividuation, 371
  displacement of responsibility, 370
Displaced aggression theory, 152–153
  road rage, 153–155
Dispositions/traits, 7
Dissociative identity disorder, 252–255
  iatrogenic question, 254
Domestic violence. *See* Family violence
Drugs
  /alcohol abuse and violence connections,
    563–564, 566–567
  categories, 532
  "controlled substance," 531–532, 531t
  drug abuse and crime correlations, 526–530
  ESU (experimental substance use), 563
  "gateway" drugs, 564
  inhalants, 564
  psychoactive, 531
  tolerance and dependence, 532–533, 533f
  war on, 521
  See also Alcohol; Hallucinogens; Juvenile drug
    use; Opiate narcotics; Stimulants; Tripartite
    conceptual model/drug-related crime
DSM (Diagnostic and Statistical Manual of Mental
    Disorders), 229–231
Durham Rule, 245–246

Eccles, Sir John, difference-in-kind perspective, 4
Economic crimes (violent), 488
  See also Arson; Robbery
Eldercide, 318
Elderly abused, 317–319
  types, 317f
ELF (Earth Liberation Front), 265–366
Enmeshed parental style, 48–49
Environmental factors and aggression
  ambient temperature, 168–171
  contagion effect, 174–175
  media violence, 171–174
  population density, 166–167
Epilepsy, and violence, 183
Equivocal death analysis, 335
Ethology, 147
  viewpoints on aggression, 147–149
Evolutionary psychology perspective, 4
  and aggression, 148–149
Excitation transfer theory, 152
Exhibitionism, 440–441
  offender characteristics, 442–443
  situational characteristics, 441–442
Expectancy theory, 123
Eysenck's theory/personality and crime, 96, 104t
  ambiversion, 97
  "conditioned conscience," 106–108
  evidence for, 108–109
  extraversion, 97, 98–102, 103f, 104
  focus on interaction, 74, 96
  genetic predispositions toward antisocial/crimi-
    nal conduct, 96
  importance of, 109–110
  measurement of, 97–98, 98f
  neuroticism, 97, 101–104
  psychoticism, 97, 104
  temperament factors, 97

Family mass murders, 343
Family violence, 300, 328
  child-to-parent, 320–321
  cycle of violence, 321–322
  definitions, 301
  effects on children, 322–324
  ethnic/minority differences, 301–302
  history of study of, 303–305
  multiassaultive families, 321
  prevalence, 301
  reduction strategies and procedures, 326–327
  sibling-to-sibling, 319–320
  theories and systematic studies of, 324–325
  victims, 302–303
  See also Child abuse; Elderly abused; Intimate
    partner abuse
Fast-Track Project, 583–584
Fence, 458
Firesetting, 507–509
  motives, 511
Fish, Albert, 431
Forcible rape, 12

Forensic psychology, 6
Fraud, 464–465
Freud, Sigmund, 9
  on violence, 146–147
Frustration-aggression hypothesis, 149–150
  cognitive-neoassociation model, 151–152
  weapons effect, 150–151
Frustration-induced criminality, 128, 130
  frustration-induced riots, 129–130
  socialized and individual offender, 128
Fundamental attribution error, 131

Gacy, John Wayne, Jr., 431–432
Gangs, influences on rejected youth, 42–43
GBMI (Guilty but Mentally Ill) defense, 247–248
Gender differences, of psychopaths, 201–202
Groth classification model (child molesters), 434
  sex force offenders, 435
  sex pressure offenders, 434–435
Groth typology, 411–412
  anger rape, 411
  power rape, 411
  sadistic rape, 411–412

Habituation, 214
Hallucinogens/psychedelics, 532, 534–540
  marijuana and crime, 537–539
  marijuana preparation, 535–537
  marijuana usage, 534–535, 534t, 535t, 565
  PCP, 539
  PCP and crime, 540
Hate crimes
  bias crime statutes, 19
  definition, 19
  Hate Crime Statistics Act and amendments,
    18–19
  motivations, 20, 20f
  statistics on, 18
  victims, 19–20
HCR-20 (Historical/Clinical/Risk Management)
  scale, 275
Heath, Neville, 190
Hebephilia, 422
Hemisphere asymmetry, 209
Heroin, 550–552, 565
  and crime, 553–554
Hierarchy rule (UCR system), 15
Hinkley, John, 241
Hirschi, Travis, social control theory, 3–4
Holmes, Sherlock, 336
Homicide, 328
  and assault, 284
  criminal homicide (murder and nonnegligent
    manslaughter), 284–285, 286
  disproportionate attention (reasons for),
    282–283
  infanticide, 309–313
  juvenile murder, 299–300
  media fascination with, 281
  sniper attacks, 296–298
  statistics, 281–282
  temporal factors, 295
  victim precipitation, 296
  See also Family violence; Multiple murder;
    Weapons (use in violence)
Homicide demographics, 286
  age, 289–290
  gender, 288t, 289, 292t
  race/ethnic origin, 286–288, 288t
  socioeconomic class, 290
  victim–offender relationship, 290–293, 291f
Hostage-taking offenses, 488, 500–501, 518
  barricade situation, 502
  categories of, 501–502
  guidelines for victims, 504–505
  instrumental and expressive, 501
  strategies/negotiation guidelines, 502–503, 502t
  See also London syndrome; Stockholm syn-
    drome
Huberty, James, 269
Human biology. *See* Aggression (biology of)
Human nature, 5t
  differences-in-degrees and difference-in-kind
    perspectives, 4
  theories about, 3–4
Human trafficking, 484–485
Hydraulic model, 146–147

Identity theft, 464–465, 465t
Imprisonment. *See* Psychological effects of impris-
    onment; Punishment considerations
Impulsivity, 372–374
  and habit strength, 373
Index crimes, 12
Insanity defense. *See* Criminal responsibility
Insanity Defense Reform Act (1984), 246–247
  "volitional prong" test removal, 247
Intelligence and delinquency, 51–53, 55
  IQ and adult offenders, 54–55
  IQ and ethnicity, 53–54
  psychometric approach/psychometric intelli-
    gence (PI), 52
Intervention, need to begin early, 71
Intimate partner abuse, 313
  and alcohol, 316
  battered woman syndrome, 313–314
  psychological and demographic characteristics
    of abusers, 314–316
  same-sex domestic violence (SSDV), 314
Intimate partner violence, 25
Intimidation (crimes of), 488
  cyberbullying, 496
  See also Arson; Bombings; Hostage-taking of-
    fenses; Stalking
Investigative psychology, 331
  See also Crime scene investigative methods; Pro-
    filing

Jacob Wetterling Act (1994), 391
Jung, Carl, 9

"Just world" hypothesis, 34
Juvenile delinquency, 26
  "child delinquent," 27
  juvenile offending scope/type, 28–33, 32t, 33t
  See also Delinquency
Juvenile drug use, 522, 565
  extent of, 523–524, 523t, 524t
  gender differences in use, 525–526
  source of, 524–525
Juvenile justice overview, 573–578, 597
  Chicago Area Project, 574
  Juvenile Court Act, 574
  juvenile courts, 576–578, 577f, 578f
  policy shifts, 575–576
Juvenile murder, 299
  demographics of, 300
Juvenile prevention programs (classification of),
    578–579, 598
  primary (universal) prevention, 579
  selective prevention, 579–580, 582–584
Juvenile prevention/treatment programs, 597
  cultural sensitivity, 572
  family focus, 572–573
  foundation on developmental principles,
    570–571
  multiple settings/systems focus, 571–572
  starting at early antisocial indicators, 570
  strategies, 569
  successful characteristics, 568–569
Juvenile psychopathy, 203, 224
  ethical considerations, 204–205
  identification, 203–204
  measures, 2–6
  traits in juvenile delinquents, 205–206
  treatment approaches, 589–591
  See also Firesetting
Juvenile sex offenders, 435–436, 447
  female offenders, 436–437
  recidivism, 438
  treatment approaches, 587–589m598
Juvenile treatment approaches, 585
  children with psychopathic features, 589–591,
    598–599
  community treatment (MST/multi-systemic
    therapy), 595–597
  juvenile murderers, 591–592, 598
  of juvenile sex offenders, 587–589
  restrictive interventions, 585–586
  traditional residential treatment, 587
  See also Nontraditional residential treatment for
    juveniles

Kleptomania, 470–471

Language impairment, 51
Larceny-theft, 461–464, 462f
  carjacking, 463–464
  "garbage-can," 461
  motor vehicle theft, 461–462

Law and Order, 227
Lax parental style, 49
LCP (life-course-persistent) offender research,
    222–223
Learning factors in criminal behavior, 114–115
  crime as "adaptation," 115
  learning perspective, 118
  operant learning and crime, 120–121
  situational instigators and regulators,
    130–138
  See also Behaviorism; Frustration-induced
    criminality; Social learning theory
Learning theories, 105
  classical/Pavlovian conditioning, 105
  cognitive learning, 121
  Eysenck's perspective on conditioned con-
    science, 106–108
  instrumental/operant conditioning, 105–106,
    118
  social learning, 4, 106, 121–128
Lechter, Hannibal, 190
Left-hemisphere activation hypothesis, 209
Life-course-persistent (LCP) offenders, 61
London syndrome, 505

MacArthur Research Network, 262–263, 275
"Mad Bomber" of New York, 515–516
Manslaughter
  negligent, 285
  nonnegligent, 284, 285
Manson, Charles, 190
Marijuana, 537–539
Markers, for psychopathology, 207
Mass murderers, 350, 360–361
Mass murders, 343
  classic, 350–351
  family mass murders, 343
  product tampering, 351–352
McVeigh, Timothy, 365
MDMA (Ecstasy), 548–549
MDSO (mentally disordered sex offender),
    276–278
Measurement of crime, 10–11
  self-report studies, 20–23
  victimization surveys, 23–25
  See also Self-report (SR) studies; Uniform Crime
    Reporting (UCR) Program (FBI); Victimiza-
    tion surveys
Media
  depiction of criminal profiling, 338–339
  focus on homicide, 281
  and masturbatory conditioning, 414–415
  and violence, 171–174
Megan's Law (1996), 391
Mental disorder
  categories associated with crimes, 230–231
  "crazy behavior," 229
  and criminal justice system, 259–260
  definition, 228, 256

and violence, 260–262
and violence (research), 263–264
See also Antisocial personality disorder (APD);
Delusional disorders; Depressive disorders;
DSM; Postpartum depression; Psychological
risk factors; Risk assessment instruments;
Schizophrenic disorders
Mental disorder (individuals with)
dangerousness, 267, 278
diagnoses of inmates, 266–267
duty to warn/protect, 269
incarceration statistics, 264–266, 265t
interactions with police, 263–264
MDSO (mentally disordered sex offender),
276–278
risk assessment, 268–273, 273t, 279
Mental illness
definition, 228, 256
and media portrayals of crimes, 227–228
vs. "evil," 227
Mental retardation. *See* Developmental disability
Merton, Robert K., strain theory, 3
Methamphetamine, 540–542
usage, 541t, 542, 542t
Milgram, Stanley, experiments in obedience to authority, 132–134
Minnesota Domestic Violence Experiment, 326
M'Naghten Rule, 244–245
MO (Modus operandi), 331
Moffitt's developmental theory, 61–65, 65t
adolescent-limited (AL) offenders, 62
gender differences, 64–65
life-course-persistent (LCP) offenders, 61
Monitoring the Future Study (MFS), 22–23
"Moon Maniac," 431–432
Motor vehicle theft, 461–462
MSBP (Munchausen syndrome by proxy),
308–309
MST (multi-systemic therapy) treatment approach
for juvenile offenders, 595–597, 599
MTC:CM3 (Massachusetts Treatment Center:Child
Molester), 432–434, 433f
MTC (Massachusetts Treatment Center) classification system of rapists, 405–411
compensatory rapists, 406–407
displaced aggression rapists, 405–406
impulsive/exploitative, 408
MTC:R3 subtype classification, 408–411, 409f
sexually aggressive/sadistic rapist, 407–408
Multiple murder, 330–331
case examples, 342–343
See also Family mass murders; Investigative psychology; Mass murders; Product tampering;
School violence; Serial murders; Spree murders; Workplace violence
Multiple personality disorder (MPD). *See* Dissociative identity disorder
Murder, 12, 284–285
See also Multiple murder

Narabayashi, Hirataro, 180
National Crime Survey (NCS). *See* National Crime
Victimization Survey (NCVS)
National Crime Victimization Survey (NCVS),
23–25
demographic differences in victimization rates,
24
focus, 24
history of, 23
relationship patterns and victimization, 25
National Household Survey on Drug Abuse
(NHSDA), 22
National Incident-Based Reporting System
(NIBRS), 16–18
additional categories (not in UCR), 18
benefits of, 17–18
Group A offenses, 16–17, 18t
Group B offenses, 16
Neurophysiological concepts, 207–208, 208t
amygdala dysfunction, 211–212
autonomic nervous system research,
217–221
central nervous system (CNS) differences,
208
cerebral cortex stimulation, 213–216, 213f
frontal neuropsychological studies, 210–211
hemisphere asymmetry and deficiency,
208–210
neurotransmitters, 178–179
peripheral nervous system (PNS) research,
216–217
NGRI (not guilty by reason of insanity). *See* Criminal responsibility
Nonconformist perspective, 3–4
Nonindex crimes, 12
Nonnegligent manslaughter, 12
Nontraditional residential treatment for juveniles,
592, 599
boot camps, 592–595
wilderness and adventure programs, 595

Occupational crime, 472–473, 486
blue-collar crime, 472
corporate crime, 472, 475–476
individual occupational crime, 477–479
justifications/neutralizations, 476–477
prevalence of, 474–475
typology, 473–474, 473t
"white collar" crime, 472
Oklahoma City bombing, 365
Operant conditioning, 119
Opiate narcotics, 532, 550, 554, 565
fentanyl (Sublimaze), 554
heroin, 550–552
heroin and crime, 553–554
OxyContin, 554–555

Pam Lyncher Act (1996), 391–392
Paranoid disorders. *See* Delusional disorders

Paraphilia, 422
Parental and family risk factors
  enmeshed/lax parental styles, 48–49
  parental monitoring, 49–50
  parental practices, 46–47
  parental psychopathology, 50–51
  parental styles, 47–48, 48t
  sibling influence, 50
  single-parent households, 45–46
Part I crimes (violent and property), 12, 13t
  clearance rate of, 14, 15t
  distribution, 14, 14f
  murder (violent), 12
  requirements, 12
Part II crimes, 12, 13t
Partialism, 444
Passive-aggressive behaviors, 143
PCL. *See* Psychopathy Checklist (PCL) and variations
PCP (Phencyclidine), 539–540
Pedophilia, 421
  See also Child molestation
Pedophilia causes (theories of), 438–439, 440t
  blockage theories, 440
  disinhibition theories, 440
  emotional congruence theories, 439
  sexual arousal theories, 439
Pedophile, 421–422
  See also Child molester
Pedophile characteristics, 430
  aggressive/sadistic pedophile, 431–432
  exploitative pedophile, 431
  fixated (immature) pedophile, 430
  regressed pedophile, 430–431
  See also Groth classification model (child moles-
    ters); MTC:CM3 (Massachusetts Treatment
    Center:Child Molester)
"Peeping Toms," 444
Peer relations
  as a social risk factor, 40–41
  gang influences on rejected youth,
    42–43
  gender and peer rejection, 42
  predisposition for peer rejection,
    41–42
  reasons for peer rejection, 41
  temptation talk, 43
Permissive parental style, 47
Personation/signature, 332
Phillips, Dr. George Baxter, 336
Physique and crime
  attractiveness, 92–94
  minor physical anomalies (MPAs), 94–96
  research, 91–92
  somatotyping, 89, 90f, 91
Plasticity (of brain), 88
Pornography
  definition, 416
  and rape, 415–418, 419
Postpartum depression, 233–234

Posttraumatic stress disorder (PTSD), 248–251
Poverty, as a social risk factor, 38–40
Prevention, need to begin early, 71, 570
Primary prevention for juveniles, 579
  resilience (development of), 581–582
  strategies, 580–581, 580f
Product tampering, 351–352
Profiling
  equivocal death analysis/psychological autopsy,
    335
  geographical, 335, 339–340
  psychological, 334
  racial, 336, 340–342
  and sexual offenders, 389
  See also Criminal profiling
Property crimes, 449–450, 485
  reasons for, 451–452
  statistics, 451, 451t
  See also Burglary; Fraud; Identity theft; Larceny-
    theft; Occupational crime; Shoplifting
Prostitutes
  backgrounds and early negative sexual experi-
    ences, 481–482
  drug use assumptions, 482
  motives, 482–484
Prostitution, 479–482, 486
  decriminalization arguments, 480
  definition, 480
  estimates of, 481
  sex trafficking, 484–485, 487
Psychiatric criminology, 8–9
Psychiatrists/forensic psychiatrists, 8
  psychoanalytic tradition in, 9–10
Psychoanalytical/psychodynamic theories, 9,
    146–147
  contemporary trends in, 10
Psychological autopsy, 335, 340
Psychological criminology, 6–8
  cognitions, 7
  developmental approach, 7, 37
  dispositions/traits, 7
  See also Criminal profiling; Developmental path-
    way; Investigative psychology
Psychological effects of imprisonment, 613–615,
    630–631
  effects of crowding, 615–616
  effects of isolation for protective custody,
    616–617
  effects of isolation/segregation as punishment,
    616
  effects of isolation ("supermax"/"ultramax"),
    618
Psychological responses to terrorism, 371–372
Psychological risk factors
  ADHD, 55–57
  cognitive and language deficiencies, 51
  conduct disorder, 57–58
  intelligence and delinquency, 51–55
  See also Risk assessment instruments
  See also Correctional psychology

Psychology/forensic psychologists, 8–9
  biopsychologists, 74
  duty to warn/protect, 269
  psychopathology research, 187
Psychometric approach/psychometric intelligence
  (PI), 52
Psychopath
  behaviors, 190–191, 191t
  charm/verbal fluency, 191
  core factors/factor analysis, 198–200
  definition, 188, 223
  developmental factors, 221–223
  distinction from antisocial personality disorder,
    187
  dyssocial, 188
  egocentricity, 192–193
  emotional paradox, 210
  example, 189–190
  female, 201–202
  impulsivity, 193–194
  lack of remorse, 194
  mental disorders, 192
  neuropsychological need for thrills, 194
  primary, 188, 189
  racial/ethnic differences, 202–203
  recidivism, 200–201
  secondary, 188
  semantic aphasia, 194
  sexual, 276
  "successful" vs. "unsuccessful," 192
  treatment of, 624–625
  See also Biological factors/psychopathy; Crimi-
    nal psychopath; Juvenile psychopathy
Psychopathy Checklist (PCL) and variations,
  197–198
Psychophysiological factors, 82–83
Psychosocial contexts of crimes, terrorism,
  368–369
Psychotechnology, 180–181
Psychotherapy, 619–620, 630
Public order crimes, 449–450
  See also Prostitution
Punishment, 119
  extinction, 119–120
  relationship to characteristics of victim, 34
Punishment considerations
  deterrence (general and specific/special),
    609–610
  incapacitation, 608–609
  rehabilitation, 608, 609
  retribution, 608, 609
  societal rationale, 608–610
Pyromania, 510, 512–513

Quay's hypothesis, 212

Rape, 392
  attitudes toward, 413–415
  causes of, 412–413, 418
  classification of rape patterns, 405–412, 418

classification of resistance strategies,
  410–411
date (acquaintance) rape, 393–394
forcible rape, 392
impact on victims, 397–399
incidence and prevalence, 395–397, 418
"index," 414
myths, 415
offense classifications, 394–395
and pornography, 415–418
rape by fraud, 393
and Rohypnol, 558–559
statutory rape, 392–393
See also Groth typology; MTC (Massachusetts
  Treatment Center) classification system
  of rapists
Rape offender characteristics, 399–400
  admitters, 403
  age, 400
  assumptions about, 401–403, 403t
  comparison with pedophile, 429t
  demographics, 401
  derniers, 403–404
  drug attribution, 402
  immaturity hypothesis, 412–413
  mental illness/disease attribution, 402
  offending history, 400
  self-reported reasons for rape, 404–405
  "uncontrollable"/"irresistible" impulse attribu-
    tion, 401–402
  victim attribution, 402–403
  See also Groth typology; MTC
Rational reconstruction, 456
Recidivism, among psychopaths, 200–201
Reconstructive psychological evaluation, 335
Reductionism, 118
Reinforcement, 119
Relative deprivation, 451–452
Risk assessment instruments, 274–276
Road rage, 153–155
Robbers, 517
  motives/cultural influences, 493–495
  professional, 492–493
Robbery, 12, 488–489, 517
  bank robbery, 490–491
  commercial robbery, 491–492
  statistics, 489–490, 490t
  street robbery, 492
  "strong-arm," 489
Rotter, Julian/expectancy theory, 123
RP (relapse prevention) treatment for sex
  offenders, 626–627
  AIDS (apparently irrelevant decisions),
    628
  effectiveness, 629
  HRSs (high-risk situations) coping skills,
    627
  motivation to participate, 628
  objectives, 627
Rumination, 153

SBS (shaken baby syndrome), 309
Schizophrenic disorders, 231
  catatonic, 232
  disorganized, 231
  paranoid, 232
  residual, 232
  schizphreniform disorder, 232
  undifferentiated, 232
School violence, 361
  common characteristics of school shooters,
    353–354
  common characteristics of schools with less vio-
    lence, 354–355
  myths about, 353
  shootings, 174–175
  statistics, 353, 354f
SCR (skin conductance response), 216–217
Secondary prevention for juveniles, 579,
    582–583
  Fast-Track Project, 583–584
Sedative-hypnotic compounds, 532
  "club" drugs, 555–556
  GHB (gamma hydroxbutyrate), 556–558,
    557t
  Rohypnol, 558–559, 558t
Self-report (SR) studies, 20–22
  drug abuse self-report surveys, 22–23
Self-serving biases, 131
Semantic aphasia, 194
September 11, 2001, 363–364
  impact of, 383–384
Serial murderers, 196
  female, 345–346
  hedonistic type, 349
  juveniles, 348–349
  mission-oriented type, 349
  power/control type, 350
  typologies, 349–350
  visionary killers, 349
Serial murders, 343, 360
  characteristics, 345
  ethnic/racial characteristics, 348
  geographical perspective, 347–348
  statistics/detection, 344
  victimological perspective, 346–347
Sex offender/s
  ages of, 389
  causes, 389
  expressive sexual aggression, 390
  instrumental sexual aggression, 390
  legislation, 390–392
  and masturbatory conditioning, 414–415
  MDSO (mentally disordered sex offender),
    276
  multiple profiles, 389
  sexual predator, 277
  sexually violent predator, 276, 277
  See also Juvenile sex offenders; Pedophile char-
    acteristics; Rape offender characteristics

Sex offender/s (treatment of), 448, 625–629
  cognitive behavior therapy, 626
  drug treatment, 626
  evocative therapy, 626
  psychoeducational counseling, 626
  relapse prevention (RP), 626–729
  resistance to change, 625
Sex offenses, *See also* Child molestation; Exhibi-
    tionism; Rape; Victims of sex offenses;
    Voyeurism and fetishism
Sexual behavior, and cultural norms, 388
Shepard, Matthew, 20
Shoplifters, 466–468
  boosters/snitches, 467
  motives, 468
  types, 469–470
  See also Kleptomania
Shoplifting, 465–466, 485
  methods, 468–469
Signature/personation, 331
Situational factors in criminal behavior, 130–131,
    139–140
  authority as instigator, 131–134
  deindividuation, 134–137
  fundamental attribution error, 131
  moral disengagement, 137–138
  self-serving biases, 131
  situationalism, 118
  victimology, 131
Skinner, B. F./Skinnerian perspective,
    116–117
  extinction (vs. punishment), 119–120
  operant learning, 118–119
  reinforcement, 119
  as situationalist, 118
Sniper attacks, 296–298
"Snitches," 467
Social control theory (Travis Hirschi), 3–4
Social learning factors in aggression/violence,
    155–156
  modeling, 156
  models (types of), 156–157
  observing modeling, 157–158
Social learning theory, 4, 106, 121–123
  differential association-reinforcement (DAR)
    theory, 125–128
  expectancy theory, 123
  observational learning/modeling, 123–125
Social risk factors, 38
  after-school care, 44–45
  peer rejection/antisocial peers, 40–43
  poverty, 38–40
  preschool experiences, 43–44
  school failure, 45
Sociological criminology, 5–6
  focus on uneven power distribution in society, 6
Somatotyping, 89, 90f, 91
Speck, Richard, 182
Sperry, Roger, difference-in-kind perspective, 4

Spouse abuse. *See* Intimate partner abuse
Spree murders, 343
Stalking, 497, 518
  categories of, 498–500
  cyberstalking, 499–500
  erotomania stalking, 499
  love obsession stalking, 499
  obsession stalking, 498–499
  statutes, 497
  survey of victims, 497–498
  vengeance stalking, 499
Status offenses, 26, 29–31
  and gender, 29–30, 30f
Stimulants, 532
  amphetamines, 540, 565
  and crime, 545–546, 548, 549–550
  Ecstasy (MDMA), 548–549
  methamphetamine, 540–542
  See also Cocaine
Stimulus, 116
  discriminative, 127
Stockholm syndrome, 503–504
Strain theory (Robert K. Merton), 3
Strict liability offenses, 1
Sutherland, Edwin H./differential association theory, 4, 125–126
SVPA (Sexually Violent Predator Act), 277

Tait, Robert Peter, 182
Tarasoff case, 269
Tegen, Howard, 336
Temperament, 83–84
  aspects of, 84–85
"Temptation talk," 43
Terrorism
  cognitive perspective on motives/justifications,
    369–370, 384
  definitions, 364–365
  disengagement practices developing motivation
    for, 370–371
  domestic, 365
  examples, 363, 365
  group classifications, 365–367
  psychosocial context of, 368–369
  and terrorist activities (statistics on), 18
  terrorist typology, 367–368
  See also Psychological responses to
    terrorism
Terrorist groups, 384
  bioterrorism, 366
  chemical, 367
  nuclear, 367
  radical environmental groups, 365–366
  right-wing, 365
  special interest extremists, 366
Terrorist typology, 367–368
  culturally motivated terrorist, 367–368
  psychologically motivated terrorists, 367
  rationally motivated terrorists, 367

Texas Tower killings, 268
Theories of crime, underlying perspectives about
  human nature, 3–5
Theory, definition, 146
Treatment strategies, 618–619
  criminalization, 619
  prisonization, 619
  psychotherapy, 619–620
  See also Behavior therapy; Cognitive therapy;
    Psychopath (treatment of); Sex offender/s
    (treatments of)
Tripartite conceptual model/drug-related crime,
  530–531
Twin studies, 75
  concordance, 76–78, 77t
  recent research, 78–80
  shared/nonshared environments, 75–76

Unabomber, 365, 515–516
"Undoing," 332–333
Uniform Crime Reporting (UCR) Program (FBI),
  11
  hierarchy rule, 15
  Part I and Part II crimes, 12
  pre-2004 data collection ("index crime"), 12
  problems, 15–16

VAWA-2(Violence Against Women Act (1994), 300,
  392
Victimization surveys, 23–25
Victimology, 131
  victimological perspective, 346–347
Victims of burglary, psychological impact on,
  460–461
Victims of sex offenses
  effects of pedophilia on children, 426
  psychological damage to, 390
  psychological effects of rape, 397–398
  rape survivor (terminology issue), 397
  situational and victimization characteristics of
    rape, 398–400
  trauma of date rape, 394
Video games, 172–173
Violence, 141–143
  battering, 301
  definition, 146
  depiction of and aggression toward women,
    417
  and epilepsy, 183
  and heredity, 181–183
  overt aggression in children, 163
  theoretical frameworks for, 115
  See also Aggression; Brain centers/violence
    control; Crowd violence; Media violence;
    Social learning factors in aggression/
    violence; Violent crime (general)/psycho-
    logical factors in
Violent Crime Control and Law Enforcement Act
  (1994), 390–391

Violent crime (general)/psychological factors in, 372
  cognitive self-regulatory mechanisms, 376–378, 385
  dehumanizing to downplay internal standards, 379
  displacement of responsibility, 379
  gender differences in, 380
  impulsivity, 372–374
  learned helplessness, 376
  overcontrolled/undercontrolled personalities, 374–376
Violent economic crimes, 488
  See also Arson; Robbery
Voyeurism and fetishism, 444–446
VRAG (Violence Risk Assessment Guide), 274–275

Watson, John B., 116
Weapons effect, 150–151

Weapons (use in violence), 293–294, 293t, 295
  juvenile weapons possession, 294
"White-collar crime," 471–472
  See also Occupational crime
Whitman, Charles, 268
Workplace violence, 355, 361
  examples/classification of offenders, 356–358
  problematic behaviors of coworkers, 359t
  statistics, 355–356, 355t
  vs. workplace aggression, 355
  workplace offenders (profiles of), 358–359

XYY chromosomal syndrome, 181–183

Yaba, 542
Yates, Andrea, 226–227, 233–234, 242

Zimbardo's experiments on deindividuation, 381–383